Microsoft®*Press*

Programming
Microsoft®
Visual
Basic® 6.0

D1361587

Francesco Balena

PUBLISHED BY
Microsoft Press
A Division of Microsoft Corporation
One Microsoft Way
Redmond, Washington 98052-6399

Library of Congress Cataloging-in-Publication Data
Balena, Francesco, 1960–
    Programming Microsoft Visual Basic 6.0 / Francesco Balena.
       p.   cm.
    Includes index.
    ISBN 0-7356-0558-0
    1. Microsoft Visual BASIC. 2. BASIC (Computer program language)
I. Title.
QA76.73.B3B345   1999
005.26'8--dc21
                                     99-20381
                                       CIP

Printed and bound in the United States of America.

12 13 14 15   QWT   7 6 5 4 3

Distributed in Canada by H.B. Fenn and Company Ltd.

A CIP catalogue record for this book is available from the British Library.

Microsoft Press books are available through booksellers and distributors worldwide. For further information about international editions, contact your local Microsoft Corporation office or contact Microsoft Press International directly at fax (425) 936-7329. Visit our Web site at www.microsoft.com/mspress. Send comments to *mspinput@microsoft.com.*

Acquisitions Editor: Eric Stroo
Project Editor: Kathleen Atkins
Manuscript Editors: Kathleen Atkins, Sally Stickney
Technical Editor: Marzena Makuta

Part No. 097-0008261

Contents

Contents

Contents

Contents

Contents

x

Part III Database Programming

Contents

Contents

Contents

Foreword

I was excited to hear that Francesco was writing this book.

Certainly, there's no shortage of books on Visual Basic. At our magazine, *Visual Basic Programmer's Journal*, we see stacks of development books sent to us every week. Reading another Visual Basic book is about as exciting as seeing yet another grid control.

But what Francesco is doing is important for several reasons. First, anything he writes is going to be good. We know that because he is one of our most respected magazine authors, and he's a popular speaker at our VBITS conferences from San Francisco to Stockholm. Beyond that, he brings a pragmatic real-world view to everything he writes. He's an actual Visual Basic developer and has a unique eye for tips, tricks, and techniques that make his readers more productive in their work.

Finally, the project itself, how he's defined his book, fills an important gap. His book is a truly comprehensive look at Visual Basic from a professional developer's perspective. I don't know of anything quite like it.

There are three general types of books for developers. The first are the ones rushed out to grab sales when the product initially ships. These are of value but have inherent problems. They are by nature hurried and are based on working with beta releases, whose feature sets may or may not exactly match the final release. Also, as Visual Basic gets more complex, those early book authors simply lack the time to learn the tool in depth. Next come the "build a complete data warehouse in 7 days" books, aimed at exploiting less skilled wannabe developers by making unrealistic promises. Then there are the massive, vertical tomes that probe one subject in depth. These are generally more valuable. But if your work is broad, you end up collecting a dozen of these and never read them all.

What Francesco is doing is fundamentally different. He has spent over a year and a half, from the early beta to the latest updates, learning Visual Basic and using it for professional development. He's sharing that hard-won knowledge in a book that's almost encyclopedic in scope. As a developer, you know that the product is getting deeper and much more complex with every release. Mastering it takes much more work than before.

Francesco's book can help you get to work faster, perhaps helping you learn a few things you wouldn't have discovered on your own. The book is not a rehashing of the language manuals, as so many of the larger books are, but an extensive compiling of coding techniques that are the results of Francesco's own work. Tutorials span HTML, Dynamic HTML, scripting, and ASP programming—topics sorely missing from Visual Basic's documentation.

This is an ambitious project I'm confident any Visual Basic developer, from intermediate to experienced, can benefit from.

Sincerely,
James E. Fawcette
President
Fawcette Technical Publications
Producers of VBPJ, VBITS, JavaPro, Enterprise Development, The Development Exchange family of Web sites, and other information services for developers.

Acknowledgments

Several people have helped me make this book, and it's such a joy to have an opportunity to publicly thank them all.

I'd like to especially mention four of my best friends, who dedicated some of their evenings and nights to reviewing the manuscript while I was writing it. Marco Losavio is a great Visual Basic programmer and was precious help in refining all the chapters about VBA, classes, and controls. Luigi Intonti has that special intuition that makes a developer a great developer and used it to help me enrich the book with some tricky techniques and tips. Giuseppe Dimauro, simply the finest C++ programmer I have ever met on this side of the Atlantic Ocean, revealed to me many intriguing details about Windows architecture. Finally, the sections about database and Internet programming wouldn't have been complete and accurate without the support of Francesco Albano, who has amazed me by always having the correct answers to all my questions about Jet, SQL Server, and Windows DNA architecture. Marco, Luigi, Giuseppe, and Francesco are well-known Italian technical writers, and I hope you'll read some of their works in English on my *www.vb2themax.com* Web site.

The book also contains many traces of my conversations with two other renowned Italian authors. Giovanni Librando has shared with me his knowledge of ADO and COM, while Dino Esposito has given me much good advice and made many suggestions. Also, I'm very grateful to Matt Curland, who on several occasions helped me understand what happens behind the Visual Basic scenes.

When writing a technical book, acquiring knowledge is only half the story. The other half consists in putting this knowledge in a form that other people can easily understand, especially when you're writing in a language that isn't your own mother tongue. In recent years, many people have devoted time teaching me how to write better English. They include the editors at the *Visual Basic Programmer's Journal* magazine, especially Lee Thé and Patrick Meader. I also want to thank editor-in-chief Jeff Hadfield for permission to mention a couple of interesting tips that originally appeared in the magazine's Tech Tips supplement, and of course, publisher Jim Fawcette for the opportunity to write for VBPJ in the first place.

Acknowledgments

I was so excited to write this book with Microsoft Press, and I was even happier when I finally met the people I had worked with for these nine months. Kathleen Atkins, Marzena Makuta, and Sally Stickney are among the best editors an author can hope to work with. In spite of all the text they had to revert from italics to roman, and vice versa, they often found the time to explain to me all the subtle dos and don'ts of the editing black art. And big thanks to Eric Stroo, the one who started it all and gave me the chance to write the book that I always wanted to write.

Finally, I am grateful to Dave Sanborn, Keith Jarrett, Pat Metheny, and Jan Garbarek, a few of the many great musicians who provided the soundtrack for this book. Their music kept me company for many nights and helped even more than the one thousand cups of espresso coffee I drank during these months.

I still haven't mentioned the two people who have helped me more than anyone else. It's not a coincidence that they are also the ones I love most.

Thank you, Andrea, for always strolling in my room and insisting on playing on my knees with those weird widgets called mouse and keyboard. In the end, I had to give up my Windows NT Server system for your experiments with Paint and WordArt, but in return you continuously reminded me of how exciting being the dad of a lively two-year-old baby is.

Thank you, Adriana, for convincing me to write this book and for helping me be in the right humor and find the concentration to be at my best to write it. Living together is more and more like a fascinating, never-ending journey. What else can I say? You're simply the best wife I could dream of.

This book is dedicated to you both.

Introduction

In its six versions, Visual Basic has evolved from the simplest programming language for Microsoft Windows to an exceedingly complex development environment, capable of delivering virtually anything from tiny utilities to huge n-tier client/server applications. For this reason, the job of writing a book that encompasses all the language's features has become a daunting task, and I was actually intimidated when I began to write this book. I would have preferred to write several books on specific topics, or at least this is what I thought at first.

It took me some months of hard work, but in the end I managed to put everything I wanted to write about in one big tome. I believe that from the reader's point of view this is much better than having to deal with a collection of books or one thick volume written by several authors. One big book by one author ensures a uniform approach to problems and no redundancy. Nevertheless, *Programming Microsoft Visual Basic 6.0* has been such a large undertaking that I like to think of it as many books in one. The following list will help you to understand what you'll find in it.

A survey of the new Visual Basic 6 features   Visual Basic 6 includes many new features, especially in the database and Internet areas. Among these are ADO, DHTML applications, and WebClasses, just to mention the outstanding ones. I have explored these new features and shown you how you can take advantage of them to create the next generation of your applications. But at the same time, I've noted some of their rough edges, so you won't be lost when you find that something doesn't work as expected. This is one of the advantages of a book that isn't rushed to the market as soon as the product is released.

A demystifying tutorial on object-oriented programming   You've been able to build classes using Visual Basic since version 4, yet a relatively small number of developers actively use objects in their applications. This isn't surprising, after all, since most of the available OOP code examples are "toy classes" that deal with dogs, fleas, and other animals. This hardly stimulates the imagination of programmers who must deal with invoices, products, customers, and orders. You won't find the source code for a complete object-oriented invoicing application in this book, but you'll surely learn a lot about *practical* uses of classes in Chapters 6, 7, and 9 or by browsing the 100 classes on the companion CD, some of which can be immediately reused in your applications. And in Chapters 16 through 20, you'll see how you can leverage your OOP skills to create ActiveX controls, local and remote ActiveX components, and exotic variations such as components for ADO, RDS, and ASP.

An in-depth reference to Visual Basic and the VBA language   I didn't want to write a book that simply rehashes the language manuals and the on-line help. If you want to know the syntax of Visual Basic's keywords, don't buy a book: Just press F1 and see what appears on the screen. I've organized the material in Chapters 2 through 5 so that each property, method, and event is introduced only when it becomes logical to do so. Even more important, you'll see all these features in action, with a lot of source code for you to study.

A closer look at ADO technology   Database programming is important for most Visual Basic developers, and ADO has much to offer in this field. That's why I devoted 4 out of 20 chapters—that is, Chapters 8, 13, 14, and 15—to it, covering the basics to more advanced topics, such as optimistic batch updates, asynchronous operations, hierarchical Recordsets, and some of the ADO 2.1 new features. Moreover, Chapter 18 covers data-aware components and OLE DB Simple Providers. And Chapter 19 includes a section about Remote Data Services, which shows how you can create thin clients that access a remote database through the Internet.

A painless introduction to Internet programming   Visual Basic 6 can create great Internet applications, but it requires that you already know the basics of HTML, Dynamic HTML, VBScript, and Active Server Pages development. For this reason, Chapters 19 and 20 include tutorials that cover all these arguments, plus an introduction to Microsoft Internet Information Server 4 and a guide to creating ASP components. Armed with this knowledge, you'll find using the new Internet-related features a breeze.

A transition guide for Visual Basic 5 developers   Each time a new version of the language is released, programmers are eager to know what has changed from the previous one. It's not just a matter of curiosity: Programmers need to determine how long it will take to port existing applications to the new version. And, of course, they need to ensure that the new features don't have a negative impact on the existing code. Throughout the book, each description of a new Visual Basic feature has been marked with a *NEW* icon so that developers can spot the new features quickly.

A digest of advanced programming techniques   To some developers, doing advanced programming means writing a lot of API calls, possibly with some obscure and tricky techniques that only a few experts can understand. The truth is that you can solve several thorny programming problems with nothing but the power of Visual Basic, as I'll demonstrate throughout the book. But if you like API programming, you can refer to the Appendix to learn how to access the Registry, exploit the hidden features of Visual Basic controls, and master advanced techniques such as subclassing. You'll even find a ready-to-use DLL for safe subclassing inside the environment, together with its source code.

Just a few other notes about the five-part structure of the book.

Part I, "The Basics," is about general programming. Chapter 1 is an introduction to the environment for those who have never worked with Visual Basic. Chapters 2 through 5 focus on forms, intrinsic controls, and the VBA language, and contain a lot of reusable, optimized routines. Chapters 6 and 7 cover all the object-oriented features that will be exploited in the rest of the book. Chapter 8 introduces the new Visual Basic 6 database features, including Visual Database Tools and the DataEnvironment designer, and it defines a few concepts that are made use of in Part II, but that will be completely developed only in Part III.

Part II, "The User Interface," takes a closer look at forms and ActiveX controls. Chapter 9 builds on the object-oriented nature of forms to create reusable user interface modules, parameterized forms, and generic MDI containers that can be reused as is in many applications. It also shows how you can exploit the dynamic control creation feature to create data-driven forms. Chapters 10 and 11 describe all the Windows common controls that come with Visual Basic, including the newer ImageCombo, MonthView, DateTimePicker, and CoolBar controls. Chapter 12 covers a few of the other controls that are provided in the package, such as the MaskEdBox and SSTab controls.

Part III, "Database Programming," continues where Chapter 8 left off. Chapter 13 explores the ADO 2 object model, with a detailed description of all the properties, methods, and events. It also covers the DDL and security extensions provided with ADO 2.1. Chapter 14 illustrates how you can apply ADO in real-world programs and covers more advanced topics such as hierarchical Recordsets and stored procedures. Chapter 15 is about additional tools and controls that you can use for easily creating database applications, such as the DataGrid control, the Hierarchical FlexGrid control, and the DataReport designer.

Part IV, "ActiveX Programming," covers the ActiveX components that you can create in Visual Basic. Chapter 16 describes ActiveX code components, from the basics to advanced topics such as COM callbacks, multithreading, satellite DLLs, and DCOM security. Chapter 17 is about ActiveX controls and guides you through the creation of useful controls of increasing difficulty. It also covers major new Visual Basic 6 features in this area, such as windowless controls, and some advanced techniques for the best performances. Chapter 18 illustrates the new types of ActiveX components that you can create with Visual Basic 6, such as data source and data consumer components and OLE DB Simple Providers.

Part V, "Internet Programming," consists of just two long chapters. Chapter 19 is about client programming: It includes tutorials on HTML, Dynamic HTML, and VBScript, followed by an in-depth description of the DHTMLPage designer. This chapter also contains a detailed coverage of Remote Data Services, including the exciting capabilities offered by components that you can instantiate on a remote Web server. Chapter 20 is about programming for Internet Information Server 4: It begins with a tutorial on the ASP object model, continues with the creation of components for Active Server Pages, and ends with an in-depth description of the new Visual Basic 6 WebClasses. The step-by-step descriptions guide you through the creation of a complete ASP application that lets remote users place their orders using a database of products.

The Appendix is about API programming. The first part of the Appendix shows how you can augment the capabilities of standard controls, retrieve important system configuration values, control the keyboard and the mouse, and access the Registry. The second part explains how to get the best from advanced techniques, such as callback and window subclassing.

On the companion CD, you'll find the complete source code for all the samples described or mentioned in the text. I'm talking about 150 projects and about 2 megabytes of well-commented source code, so you have something to keep you busy for a while. You'll also find a library of more than 170 routines, ready to be reused in your applications.

Have fun.

F.B.

Part I
The Basics

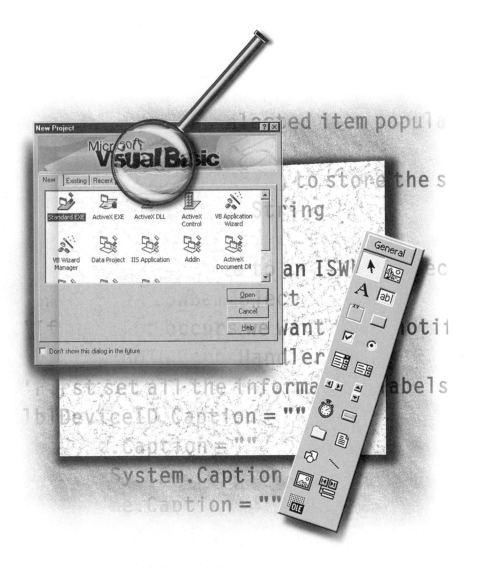

Chapter 1

First Steps with Microsoft Visual Basic 6

This chapter introduces you to the Visual Basic environment and guides you through the creation of your first Visual Basic program. It also presents a number of important concepts that are crucial to Visual Basic programming, such as the event-driven programming model. If you aren't new to Visual Basic, you can probably skip over this chapter without any problem. Interspersed in the main text, however, you might find a few interesting tips for making the best use of the environment as well as a couple of introductions to features of Visual Basic that are new in version 6, so I suggest that you give this chapter a quick look, regardless of your Visual Basic experience.

THE INTEGRATED DEVELOPMENT ENVIRONMENT

Much of the popularity of Visual Basic comes from its Integrated Development Environment, or IDE for short. In theory, you can edit your Visual Basic programs using any editor, including the aged Notepad, but I never met a programmer insane enough to do that. In fact, the IDE gives you everything you need to create great applications, to write code for them, to test and fine-tune them, and, finally, to produce executable files. These files are independent of the environment and therefore can be delivered to customers for execution on their machines, even if they haven't installed Visual Basic.

Running the IDE

You can choose from several ways to launch the Visual Basic IDE, as is true for any Windows executable:

■   You can run the Visual Basic 6 environment from the Start Menu; the exact path to the menu command depends on whether you have installed Visual Basic as part of the Microsoft Visual Studio suite.

■   You can create a shortcut to the IDE on your desktop and run it by simply double-clicking on it.

■   When Visual Basic is installed, it registers the .vbp, .frm, .bas, and a few other extensions with the operating system. Therefore, you can run the environment by double-clicking on any Visual Basic file.

■   If you have installed Microsoft Active Desktop, you can create a shortcut to the Visual Basic IDE on the system taskbar. This is probably the fastest way to run the IDE: it's similar to a desktop shortcut, but you don't have to minimize other windows to uncover it.

Don't underestimate the convenience of running the Visual Basic IDE in the fastest way possible. When you develop COM components or add-ins, you might need to follow the commonplace practice of opening multiple instances of the environment at the same time. You might need to repeat this operation several times during your working day.

Selecting the Project Type

The first time you run the Visual Basic IDE, you're asked to select the type of project you want to create, as you can see in Figure 1-1. In this chapter, as well as in many chapters in the first part of this book, we're going to create Standard EXE projects only, so you can click on the Open button—or just press the Enter key—to start working with a regular project that, once compiled, will deliver a stand-alone EXE application. You can also decide to tick the "Don't show this dialog in future" check box if you want to avoid this operation the next time you launch the IDE.

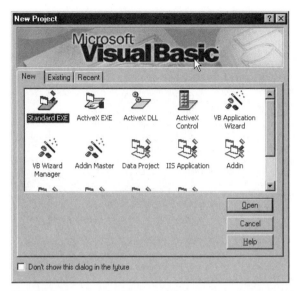

Figure 1-1. *The New Project dialog box that appears when you launch the Visual Basic 6 environment.*

IDE Windows

If you have worked with Visual Basic 5, the Visual Basic 6 IDE will look very familiar to you, as you can see in Figure 1-2 on the following page. In fact, the only indication that you're not interacting with Visual Basic 5 is a couple of new top-level menus—Query and Diagram—and two new icons on the standard toolbar. When you begin to explore the IDE's menus, you might find a few other commands (in the Edit, View, Project, and Tools menus) that were missing in Visual Basic 5. But overall changes are minimal, and if you're familiar with the Visual Basic 5 environment you can start working with Visual Basic 6 right away.

On the other hand, if you have worked only with versions of Visual Basic earlier than 5, you're going to be surprised by the many changes in the working environment. For one thing, the IDE is now an MDI (Multiple Document Interface) application, and you can reduce it and its dependent window with a single operation. You can restore the SDI (Single Document Interface) working mode, if you prefer, by choosing Options from the Tools menu, clicking the Advanced tab, and ticking the SDI Development Environment check box.

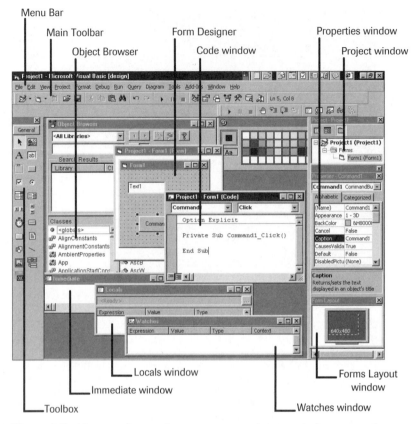

Menu Bar

Main Toolbar

Object Browser

Form Designer

Code window

Properties window

Project window

Figure 1-2. *The Visual Basic 6 environment with most windows opened.*

Locals window

Immediate window

Toolbox

Forms Layout window

Watches window

Finally, if this is your first exposure to Visual Basic, you'll surely be confused by the many menu commands, toolbars, and windows that the IDE hosts. Let's quickly review the purpose of each item. You can display any of the windows using an appropriate command in the View menu. Many of them can also be opened using a keyboard shortcut, as described in the following paragraphs, or by clicking on an icon in the main toolbar.

■   The Project window gives you an overview of all the modules that are contained in your application. You can display such modules grouped by their types or in alphabetical order by clicking on the rightmost icon on the Project window's toolbar. You can then view the code in each module or the object associated with each module (for example, a form) by clicking the first or the second icon, respectively. You can quickly display the Project window or put it in front of other windows by pressing the Ctrl+R key combination or by clicking on the Project Explorer icon on the standard toolbar.

■ You use the Form Designer window to design your application's user interface. Any application can contain multiple forms, and you can open a number of form designers at the same time. Moreover, both Visual Basic 5 and 6 support additional designers, such as the UserControl and UserDocument designers.

■ The Toolbox window includes a set of objects that you can place on a form or on another designer. Visual Basic comes with a fixed set of controls—the so-called *intrinsic controls*—but you can add other Microsoft ActiveX controls to this window. To avoid filling this window with too many controls, you can create multiple *tabs* on it: just right-click on the window, select the Add Tab command, and at a prompt assign a name to the new tab. Then you can place additional ActiveX controls on this new tab or drag one or more controls from the General tab. Similarly, you can delete or rename any tab by right-clicking on it and selecting the Delete Tab or Rename Tab commands, respectively. You can't delete or rename the General tab, though.

■ You use the Code window to write code that determines the behavior of your forms and other objects in your application. You can keep a number of code windows visible at one time, each one displaying the code related to a form or, more generally, to a module in your application. You can't open two code windows for the same module; however, you can split a code window into two distinct and independent portions by dragging the small gray rectangle located immediately above the vertical scrollbar.

TIP You can quickly show the code window associated with a form or another designer by pressing the F7 function key while the focus is on the designer. Similarly, if you have opened the code window related to a designer, press the Shift-F7 key combination to display the associated designer.

■ The Properties window lists all the properties of the object that's currently selected and gives you the opportunity to modify them. For instance, you can change the foreground and background colors of the form or the control that's currently selected. You can list properties in alphabetical order or group them in categories, and you can find a short description of the currently selected property near the bottom of this window. When you select an object, its properties are automatically displayed in the Properties window. If the window isn't visible, you can quickly display it by pressing the F4 key or by clicking on the Toolbox icon on the toolbar.

■ The Color Palette window is handy for quickly assigning a color to an object, such as the control that's currently selected on a form designer. You can select the foreground color of an object by left-clicking on the desired color, and if you click on an empty item in the bottom row of cells you can also define a custom color. Finally, you can select the background color of an object if you click on the larger square located near the upper left corner of the Color Palette window.

■ The Form Layout window shows how a given form will be displayed when the program runs. You can drag a form to the place on the screen where you want it to appear during execution, and you can also compare the relative sizes and positions of two or more forms. By right-clicking on this window, you can show its *resolution guides,* which enable you to check how your forms display at screen resolutions different from the current one.

■ The Immediate window lets you enter a Visual Basic command or expression and see its result using the *Print* command (which can also be shortened to *?*). In *break mode*—that is, when you have temporarily suspended a running program—you can use these commands to display the current value of a variable or an expression. You can also write diagnostic messages from your application's code to this window using the *Debug.Print* statement. Because the Immediate window isn't visible when the application is compiled and executed outside the environment, such diagnostic statements aren't included in the executable file. You can quickly open the Immediate window by pressing the Ctrl+G key combination.

Tip No menu command or toolbar icon lets you delete the current contents of the Immediate window. The quickest way to do it is by pressing the Ctrl+A key combination to select the Immediate window's entire contents, after which you press the Delete key to delete it or simply begin typing to replace the contents with whatever you want to type in instead.

■ The Object Browser is one of the most important tools available to the Visual Basic developer. It lets you explore external libraries so that you can learn about the objects they expose and their properties, methods, and events. The Object Browser also helps you quickly locate and jump to any procedure in any module of your application. You can open the Object Browser by pressing the F2 key or by clicking its icon on the standard toolbar.

■ The Locals window is active only when a program is executing. It lists the values of all the variables that are local to a module or to a procedure. If the variable is an object itself (a form or a control, for example) a plus (+) sign appears to the left of the variable name, which means that you can expand it and look at its properties.

■ The Watches window has a dual purpose: it lets you continuously monitor the value of a variable or an expression in your program—including a global variable, which is outside the capabilities of the Locals window—and it also gives you the ability to stop the execution of a program when a given expression becomes True or whenever it changes its value. You can add one or more watch expressions using the Add Watch command from the Debug menu, or you can select the Add Watch command from the pop-up menu that appears when you right-click the Watches window itself.

■ The Call Stack window (not visible in Figure 1-2) appears only when you break the execution of a running program and press Ctrl+L. It shows all the procedures that are waiting for the current procedure to complete. It's a useful debugging tool in that it lets you understand the execution path that led to the current situation. Note that this is a modal window, so you must close it to resume regular execution.

■ The Data View window is new to Visual Basic. (See Figure 1-3 on the following page.) In a nutshell, the Data View window offers an integrated tool to administer your databases and to explore their structures and the attributes of their tables and fields. The Data View window is particularly versatile when connecting to a Microsoft SQL Server or Oracle database because you can also add and delete its tables, views, and fields and edit stored procedures. Regardless of the database you're using, you can often drag tables and fields from the Data View window onto other windows in the IDE. You display this window using the Data View command from the View menu or by clicking on its icon on the standard toolbar.

Most of the windows I've just described can be *docked*: in other words, they can stick to the external frame of the main window of the IDE and are always on top of all other windows. By default, the majority of IDE windows are docked, although only the Toolbox, Project, Properties, and Form Layout windows are visible when the environment is launched. You can switch the *Docked* attribute on and off for a single window by right-clicking in it and then selecting the Dockable menu command. Alternatively, you can modify the *Docked* attribute individually for all the windows in the IDE by choosing Options from the Tools menu and then clicking the Docking tab. Just tick the check box associated with any window you want to be docked.

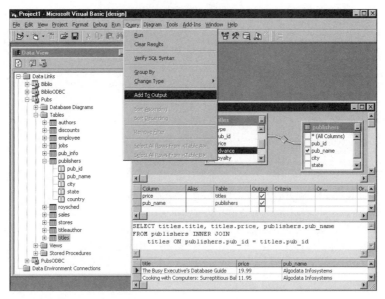

Figure 1-3. *The Data View window lets you interactively create a new View object in an SQL Server database.*

Menus

It's unnecessary to describe in detail the purpose of each menu command at this point in the book because most of the commands are related to advanced features of Visual Basic. But I think that an overview of all the top-level menus is useful, in that it gives you an idea of where to look for a given function when you need it.

- The File menu includes the commands to load and save a Visual Basic project or a group of projects (Visual Basic 6 can open multiple projects in the environment), to save the current module, to print the entire project or selected portions of it, and to build the executable file.

- The Edit menu lets you perform the typical editing commands, including Cut, Copy, Paste, Find, Replace, Undo, and Redo. It also includes commands that act on database tables, but they are active only when you're viewing the structure of a database or a database diagram. This menu also includes a bunch of commands related to Microsoft IntelliSense, a feature of the Visual Basic IDE that lets you automatically complete commands, list the syntax of functions and expected arguments, and so forth.

- The View menu is the primary means of displaying any of the environment's windows described previously. It also includes some database-related commands that are enabled only if you have activated a tool for data-base maintenance.

■ The Project menu lets you add modules to the current project, including forms, standard (BAS) modules, class modules, UserControl modules, and so on. It also lets you add *designer* modules, which are the key to many new Visual Basic 6 features. The last three commands in this menu are particularly useful because they give you access to the References, the Components, and the Project Properties dialog boxes, respectively.

■ The Format menu is used to align and resize one or more controls on a form or on a designer of any type. You can also center a control on its form and increase or decrease the distance among a group of controls. When you're satisfied with the appearance of your form, you should se-lect the Lock Controls option so that you can't accidentally move or resize the controls using the mouse.

■ The Debug menu contains the commands that you usually issue when you're testing an application within the IDE. You can execute your code step-by-step, display the value of a variable or an expression, and set one or more *breakpoints* in code. Breakpoints are special points in the code that, when reached during the program's execution, cause the Visual Basic environment to interrupt execution, thus entering break mode. You can also create *conditional breakpoints,* which are expressions that are moni-tored as each statement is executed. When the value of a conditional breakpoint changes or when the condition you specified becomes True, the program enters break mode and you can debug it easily.

■ The Run menu is probably the simplest of the group. It contains the com-mands to start the execution of the application being developed, to stop it and enter break mode, and to definitively end it.

■ The Query menu is new to the Visual Basic environment. It's available only in Visual Basic Enterprise and Professional Editions and only when you're interactively creating an SQL query using the Microsoft Query Builder utility, which you can see in Figure 1-3.

■ The Diagram menu, shown in Figure 1-4 on the following page, is also new to Visual Basic. As with the Query menu, the Diagram menu is avail-able only in the Enterprise and Professional Editions and only when you're interacting with SQL Server or Oracle databases to create or edit a data-base diagram.

Figure 1-4. *The Diagram menu becomes active only when you're building a query or editing an SQL Server View object.*

- The Tools menu contains several miscellaneous commands, the most important of which is the Options command. This command allows you to access a dialog box that lets you customize the IDE.

- The Add-In menu lists a collection of commands related to external modules that integrate into the environment. Visual Basic 6 itself comes with a number of such external add-ins, and you can also write your own.

- The Window menu is the typical menu that you find in most MDI applications; it lets you arrange and tile your windows.

- The Help menu is also standard for Microsoft Windows applications. Visual Basic 6 doesn't use standard HLP files any longer, and its help subsystem requires that you install Microsoft Developer Network (MSDN) to access its documentation.

Toolbars

Visual Basic comes with a standard toolbar that includes many common commands, such as those for loading and saving the project, running the program, and opening the most frequently used windows. Three more toolbars, Debug, Edit, and Form Editor, are visible only after you right-click on the standard toolbar and select one toolbar at a time from the submenu that appears. You can also make these toolbars visible by selecting the Toolbars option from the View menu.

All the toolbars can be docked in the upper portion of the main IDE window, or they can freely float in the environment, as you can see in Figure 1-5. You can quickly dock a floating toolbar by double-clicking on its title bar, and you can make a docked toolbar float by double-clicking on its left-most vertical stripes. If you want

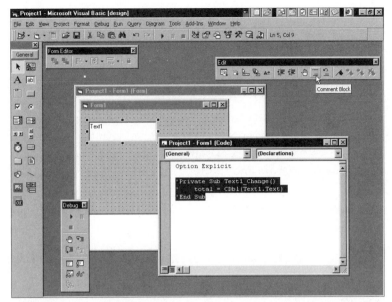

Figure 1-5. *Visual Basic 6 comes with four toolbars, which can float or be docked.*

to know what a particular toolbar icon represents, place the mouse cursor over it and a yellow ToolTip showing a short explanation will appear after about a second.

The Debug toolbar hosts most of the commands that are found in the Debug menu. The Edit toolbar is useful when you're editing code and setting breakpoints and bookmarks. The Form Editor toolbar includes most of the commands in the Format menu and is useful only when you're arranging controls on a form's surface.

Making these additional toolbars visible or not is largely a matter of personal taste. I usually prefer not to waste valuable desktop space with toolbars other than the standard one. If you work with a higher screen resolution, this might not be an issue for you.

TIP The Edit toolbar is unusual because it contains two commands that aren't available through menu commands—the Comment Block and Uncomment Block commands, which are useful when you're testing an application. (See Figure 1-5 for an example of a routine that has been commented using the Comment Block command.) For this reason, you might want to make the Edit toolbar visible.

You can customize the appearance of all the Visual Basic toolbars and even create new ones, as you can see in Figure 1-6 on the following page. The procedure for creating a new toolbar is simple:

1. Right-click on any toolbar, and select the Customize menu command; this brings up the Customize dialog box.

2. Click the New button, and type a name for the new custom toolbar (for example, *Custom Toolbar*). The name of the new toolbar appears in the

list of toolbars, and its check box is ticked. The empty toolbar appears on the screen. You're now ready to add commands to it.

3. Click the Commands tab, and then click a menu name in the leftmost list box. Click on an item in the list box on the right, and drag it over the custom toolbar to the spot where you want to insert it.

4. Right-click on the icon you have just added, and select a command from the pop-up menu that appears. The commands in this menu let you replace the icon with a different one, associate it with a caption, make it the beginning of a group, and so on.

5. Repeat steps 3 and 4 for all the commands you want to add to the custom toolbar, and then click on the Close button to make your additions permanent.

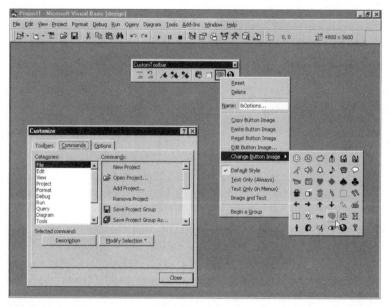

Figure 1-6. *Creating a custom toolbar.*

Here are a few commands that you should consider for inclusion in a custom toolbar because they're frequently used but don't have any associated hot keys:

- The References and Properties commands from the Project menu
- The Comment Block and Uncomment Block commands from the Edit toolbar (not displayed on the menu)
- All the Bookmark submenu commands from the Edit menu
- The Options command from the Tools menu

The Toolbox

The Toolbox window is probably the first window you'll become familiar with because it lets you visually create the user interface for your applications. More specifically, the Toolbox contains the icons of all the intrinsic controls—that is, all the controls that are included in the Visual Basic runtime.

If you have already programmed with a previous version of Visual Basic, you surely know the characteristics of all the controls that are present in the Toolbox. If you haven't, refer to Figure 1-7 while you read the following condensed descriptions.

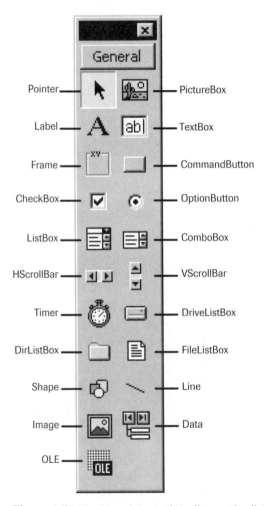

Figure 1-7. *The Visual Basic 6 Toolbox with all the intrinsic controls.*

■ The Pointer isn't a control; click this icon when you want to select controls already on the form rather than create new ones.

■ The PictureBox control is used to display images in any of the following formats: BMP, DIB (bitmap), ICO (icon), CUR (cursor), WMF (metafile), EMF (enhanced metafile), GIF, and JPEG.

■ The Label control serves to display static text or text that shouldn't be edited by the user; it's often used to label other controls, such as TextBox controls.

■ The TextBox control is a field that contains a string of characters that can be edited by the user. It can be single-line (for entering simple values) or multiline (for memos and longer notes). This is probably the most widely used control of any Windows application and is also one of the richest controls in terms of properties and events.

■ The Frame control is typically used as a container for other controls. You rarely write code that reacts to events raised by this control.

■ The CommandButton control is present in almost every form, often in the guise of the OK and Cancel buttons. You usually write code in the *Click* event procedure of this control.

■ The CheckBox control is used when the user has to make a yes/no, true/false selection.

■ OptionButton controls are always used in groups, and you can select only one control in the group at a time. When the user selects a control in the group, all other controls in the group are automatically deselected. OptionButton controls are useful for offering to the user a number of mutually exclusive selections. If you want to create two or more groups of OptionButton controls on a form, you must place each group inside another container control (most often a Frame control). Otherwise, Visual Basic can't understand which control belongs to which group.

■ The ListBox control contains a number of items, and the user can select one or more of them (depending on the value of the control's *MultiSelect* property).

■ The ComboBox control is a combination of a TextBox and a ListBox control, with the difference that the list portion is visible only if the user clicks on the down arrow to the right of the edit area. ComboBox controls don't support multiple selections.

■ The HScrollBar and VScrollBar controls let you create stand-alone scroll bars. These controls are used infrequently because the majority of other controls display their own scroll bars if necessary. Stand-alone scroll bars are sometimes used as sliders, but in this case you'd better use other, more eye-catching controls, such as the Slider control, which is covered in Chapter 10.

- The Timer control is peculiar in that it isn't visible at run time. Its only purpose is to regularly raise an event in its parent form. By writing code in the corresponding event procedure, you can perform a task in the background—for instance, updating a clock or checking the status of a peripheral device.

- The DriveListBox, DirListBox, and FileListBox controls are often used together to create file-oriented dialog boxes. DriveListBox is a ComboBox-like control filled automatically with the names of all the drives in the system. DirListBox is a variant of the ListBox control; it shows all the subdirectories of a given directory. FileListBox is another special ListBox control; this control fills automatically with names of the files in a specified directory. While these three controls offer a lot of functionality, in a sense they have been superseded by the Common Dialog control, which displays a more modern user interface (to be covered in Chapter 12). If you want to write applications that closely conform to the Windows 9x look, you should avoid using these controls.

- The Shape and Line controls are mostly cosmetic controls that never raise any events and are used only to display lines, rectangles, circles, and ovals on forms or on other designers.

- The Image control is similar to the PictureBox control, but it can't act as a container for other controls and has other limitations as well. Nevertheless, you should use an Image control in place of a PictureBox control whenever possible because Image controls consume fewer system resources.

- The Data control is the key to *data binding,* a Visual Basic feature that lets you connect one or more controls on a form to fields in a database table. The Data control works with Jet databases even though you can also use attached tables to connect to data stored in databases stored in other formats. But it can't work with ActiveX Data Objects (ADO) sources and is therefore not suitable for exploiting the most interesting database-oriented Visual Basic 6 features.

- The OLE control can host windows belonging to external programs, such as a spreadsheet window generated by Microsoft Excel. In other words, you can make a window provided by another program appear as if it belongs to your Visual Basic application.

From this short description, you can see that not all the intrinsic controls are equally important. Some controls, such as the TextBox, Label, and CommandButton controls, are used in virtually every Visual Basic application, while other controls, such as the DriveListBox, DirListBox, and FileListBox controls, have been replaced, in practice, by newer controls. Similarly, you shouldn't use the Data control in any application that uses the ADO data sources.

YOUR VERY FIRST VISUAL BASIC PROGRAM

Visual Basic lets you build a complete and functional Windows application by dropping a bunch of controls on a form and writing some code that executes when something happens to those controls or to the form itself. For instance, you can write code that executes when a form loads or unloads or when the user resizes it. Likewise, you can write code that executes when the user clicks on a control or types while the control has the input focus.

This programming paradigm is also known as *event-driven programming* because your application is made up of several event procedures executed in an order that's dependent on what happens at run time. The order of execution can't, in general, be foreseen when the program is under construction. This programming model contrasts with the procedural approach, which was dominant in the old days.

This section offers a quick review of the event-driven model and uses a sample application as a context for introducing Visual Basic's intrinsic controls, with their properties, methods, and events. This sample application, a very simple one, queries the user for the lengths of the two sides of a rectangle, evaluates its perimeter and area, and displays the results to the user. Like all lengthy code examples and programs illustrated in this book, this application is included on the companion CD.

Adding Controls to a Form

We're ready to get practical. Launch the Visual Basic IDE, and select a Standard EXE project. You should have a blank form near the center of the work area. More accurately, you have a *form designer,* which you use to define the appearance of the main window of your application. You can also create other forms, if you need them, and you can create other objects as well, using different designers (the UserControl and UserDocument designers, for example). Other chapters of this book are devoted to such designers.

One of the greatest strengths of the Visual Basic language is that programmers can design an application and then test it without leaving the environment. But you should be aware that designing and testing a program are two completely different tasks. At *design time,* you create your forms and other visible objects, set their properties, and write code in their event procedures. Conversely, at *run time* you monitor the effects of your programming efforts: What you see on your screen is, more or less, what your end users will see. At run time, you can't invoke the form designer, and you have only a limited ability to modify the code you have written at design time. For instance, you can modify existing statements and add new ones, but you can't add new procedures, forms, or controls. On the other hand, at run time you can use some diagnostic tools that aren't available at design time because they would make no sense in that context (for example, the Locals, the Watches, and the Call Stack windows).

To create one or more controls on a form's surface, you select the control type that you want from the Toolbox window, click on the form, and drag the mouse cursor until the control has the size and shape you want. (Not all controls are resizable. Some, such as the Timer control, will allow you to drag but will return to their original size and shape when you release the mouse button.) Alternatively, you can place a control on the form's surface by double-clicking its icon in the Toolbox: this action creates a control in the center of the form. Regardless of the method you follow, you can then move and resize the control on the form using the mouse.

> **TIP**   If you need to create multiple controls of the same type, you can follow this three-step procedure: First, click on the control's icon on the Toolbox window while you keep the Ctrl key pressed. Next, draw multiple controls by clicking the left button on the form's surface and then dragging the cursor. Finally, when you're finished creating controls, press the Escape key or click the Pointer icon in the upper left corner of the Toolbox.

To complete our Rectangle sample application, we need four TextBox controls—two for entering the rectangle's width and height and two for showing the resulting perimeter and area, as shown in Figure 1-8 on the following page. Even if they aren't strictly required from an operational point of view, we also need four Label controls for clarifying the purpose of each TextBox control. Finally we add a CommandButton control named *Evaluate* that starts the computation and shows the results.

Place these controls on the form, and then move and resize them as depicted in Figure 1-8. Don't worry too much if the controls aren't perfectly aligned because you can later move and resize them using the mouse or using the commands in the Format menu.

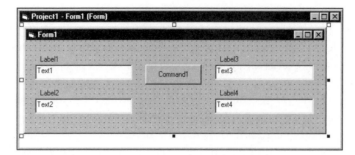

Figure 1-8. *The Rectangle Demo form at design time, soon after the placement of its controls.*

Setting Properties of Controls

Each control is characterized by a set of properties that define its behavior and appearance. For instance, Label controls expose a *Caption* property that corresponds to the character string displayed on the control itself, and a *BorderStyle* property that affects the appearance of a border around the label. The TextBox control's most important property is *Text*, which corresponds to the string of characters that appears within the control itself and that can be edited by the user.

In all cases, you can modify one or more properties of a control by selecting the control in the form designer and then pressing F4 to show the Properties window. You can scroll through the contents of the Properties window until the property you're interested in becomes visible. You can then select it and enter a new value.

Using this procedure, you can modify the *Caption* property of all four Label controls to *&Width*, *&Height*, *&Perimeter*, and *&Area*, respectively. You will note that the ampersand character doesn't appear on the control and that its effect is to underline the character that follows it. This operation actually creates a *hot key* and associates it with the control. When a control is associated with a hot key, the user can quickly move the focus to the control by pressing an Alt+*x* key combination, as you normally do within most Windows applications. Notice that only controls exposing a *Caption* property can be associated with a hot key. Such controls include the Label, Frame, CommandButton, OptionButton, and CheckBox.

> **TIP**   There is one handy but undocumented technique for quickly selecting a given property of a control. You just have to select the control on the form and press the Ctrl+Shift+*x* key, where *x* is the first letter in the property's name. For instance, select a Label control, and then press Ctrl+Shift+C to display the Properties window and select the *Caption* property in one operation. Pressing the Ctrl+Shift+C key again moves the focus to the next property whose name begins with the C character, and so on in a cyclic fashion.

Notice that once you have selected the *Caption* property for the first Label control, it stays selected when you then click on other controls. You can take advantage of this mechanism to change the *Caption* property of the CommandButton control to *&Evaluate* and the *Caption* property of the Form itself to *Rectangle Demo,* without having to select the *Caption* item in the Properties window each time. Note that ampersand characters within a form's caption don't have any special meaning.

As an exercise, let's change the font attributes used for the controls, which you do through the *Font* property. While you can perform this action on a control-by-control basis, it's much easier to select the group of controls that you want to affect and then modify their properties in a single operation. To select multiple controls, you can click on each one of them while you press either the Shift or the Ctrl key, or you can drag an imaginary rectangle around them. (This technique is also called *lassoing* the controls.)

> **TIP**　A quick way to select all the controls on a form is to click anywhere on the form and press the Ctrl+A key combination. After selecting all controls, you can deselect a few of them by clicking on them while pressing the Shift or Ctrl key. Note that this shortcut doesn't select controls that are contained in other controls.

When you select a group of controls and then press the F4 key, the Properties window displays only the properties that are common to all the selected controls. The only properties that are exposed by any control are *Left*, *Top*, *Width*, and *Height*. If you select a group of controls that display a string of characters, such as the TextBox, Label, and CommandButton controls in our Rectangle example, the *Font* property is also available and can therefore be selected. When you double-click on the *Font* item in the Properties window, a Font dialog box appears. Let's select a Tahoma font and set its size to 11 points.

> **TIP**　If you want to copy a number of properties from one control to one or more other controls, you can select the control you want to copy from, press Shift and select the other controls, press F4 to show the Properties window, and triple-click the name of the property you want to copy. Note that you must click the name of the property on the left, not the value cell on the right. The values of the properties on which you triple-click are copied from the source controls to all the other selected controls. This technique doesn't work with all the items in the Properties window.

Finally we must clear the *Text* property of each of the four TextBox controls so that the end user will find them empty when the program begins its execution. Oddly, when you select two or more TextBox controls, the *Text* property doesn't appear in the Properties window. Therefore, you must set the *Text* property to an empty string for each individual TextBox control on the form. To be honest, I don't know why this property is an exception to the rule stated earlier. The result of all these operations is shown in Figure 1-9 on the following page.

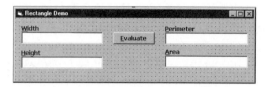

Figure 1-9. *The Rectangle Demo form at design time, after setting the controls' properties.*

TIP   When a control is created from the Toolbox, its *Font* property reflects the font of the parent form. For this reason, you can often avoid individual font settings by changing the form's *Font* property before placing any controls on the form itself.

Naming Controls

One property that every control has and that's very important to Visual Basic programmers is the *Name* property. This is the string of characters that identifies the control in code. This property can't be an empty string, and you can't have two or more controls on a form with the same name. The special nature of this property is indirectly confirmed by the fact that it appears as (Name) in the Properties window, where the initial parenthesis serves to move it to the beginning of the property list.

When you create a control, Visual Basic assigns it a default name. For example, the first TextBox control that you place on the form is named *Text1*, the second one is named *Text2*, and so forth. Similarly, the first Label control is named *Label1*, and the first CommandButton control is named *Command1*. This default naming scheme frees you from having to invent a new, unique name each time you create a control. Notice that the *Caption* property of Label and CommandButton controls, as well as the *Text* property of TextBox controls, initially reflect the control's *Name* property, but the two properties are independent of each other. In fact, you have just modified the *Caption* and *Text* properties of the controls in the Rectangle Demo form without affecting their *Name* properties.

Because the *Name* property identifies the control in code, it's a good habit to modify it so that it conveys the meaning of the control itself. This is as important as selecting meaningful names for your variables. In a sense, most controls on a form are special variables whose contents are entered directly by the user.

Microsoft suggests that you always use the same three-letter prefix for all the controls of a given class. The control classes and their recommended prefixes are shown in Table 1-1.

Control Class	Prefix	Control Class	Prefix
CommandButton	cmd	Data	dat
TextBox	txt	HScrollBar	hsb
Label	lbl	VScrollBar	vsb
PictureBox	pic	DriveListBox	drv
OptionButton	opt	DirListBox	dir
CheckBox	chk	FileListBox	fil
ComboBox	cbo	Line	lin
ListBox	lst	Shape	shp
Timer	tmr	OLE	ole
Frame	fra	Form	frm

Table 1-1. *Standard three-letter prefixes for forms and all intrinsic controls.*

For instance, you should prefix the name of a TextBox control with txt, the name of a Label control with lbl, and the name of a CommandButton control with cmd. Forms should also follow this convention, and the name of a form should be prefixed with the *frm* string. This convention makes a lot of sense because it lets you deduce both the control's type and meaning from its name. This book sticks to this naming convention, especially for more complex examples when code readability is at stake.

In our example, we will rename the Text1 through Text4 controls as txtWidth, txtHeight, txtPerimeter, and txtArea respectively. The Command1 control will be renamed cmdEvaluate, and the four Label1 through Label4 controls will be renamed lblWidth, lblHeight, lblPerimeter, and lblArea, respectively. However, please note that Label controls are seldom referred to in code, so in most cases you can leave their names unmodified without affecting the code's readability.

Moving and Resizing Controls

You probably won't be able to place your controls on the form in the right position on your first attempt. Most likely, you will try several layouts until you are satisfied with the overall appearance of the form. Fortunately, the IDE offers you many ways to modify the position and size of your controls without much effort.

- Select one or more controls, and move them as a single entity using the mouse.

- Move one or more controls with arrow keys while you press the Ctrl key. The steps along the x- and y-axes are determined by the Grid Units settings.

You can view and modify these settings using the General tab of the Options dialog box from the Tools menu.

- Resize the selected control(s) by using the arrow keys while you press the Shift key. You can also resize a control by dragging one of the blue handles surrounding it when it is selected. Like the move operation, the resize step depends on the Grid Units settings.

- Center a control or a group of controls on the form, either horizontally or vertically, using the Center In Form submenu of the Format menu.

- Align a group of controls with respect to another control using the commands in the Align submenu of the Format menu. The control used as a reference in the aligning process is the one that was selected last (that is, the one with blue handles around it).

- Resize a group of controls by selecting them and invoking a command in the Make Same Size submenu of the Format menu. All selected controls will be resized to reflect the size of the control that was selected last.

- You can align or resize a group of controls by selecting them, pressing F4 to display the Properties window, and then manually modifying the *Left*, *Top*, *Width*, or *Height* properties. This procedure is useful when you know the absolute position or size of the controls.

TIP   A ComboBox control is peculiar in that its height is determined by the system and depends on its *Font* property. Therefore, if you have ComboBox and single-line TextBox controls on the same form, you should use either one of the last two techniques that I just described to resize the TextBox controls to reflect the height of the ComboBox control(s) placed on the form. This will give your form a consistent look.

Setting the Tab Order

Windows standards dictate that the user can press the Tab key to visit all the fields in a window in the logical order. Such a sequence is known as the *Tab order* sequence. In Visual Basic, you set the correct Tab order sequence by assigning a proper value to the *TabIndex* property for all the controls that can receive the input focus, starting with 0 for the control that should receive the input focus when the form appears and assigning increasing values for all the others. In our Rectangle sample application, this means assigning 0 to the txtWidth control's *TabIndex* property, 1 to the txtHeight control's *TabIndex* property, and so on.

But wait, there's more to know about the Tab order setting. Even if Label controls never get the focus themselves, they expose a *TabIndex* property. Why?

As I mentioned previously, TextBox controls—or more to the point, controls that don't expose a *Caption* property—can't be directly associated with a hot key.

This means that you can't use an Alt+*x* key combination to activate them. In our Rectangle example, we overcome this limitation by placing Label controls above each individual TextBox control. Unfortunately, placing a Label control near another control doesn't automatically provide it with hot key capabilities. To have a Label control lend its hot key to another control on the form, you must assign the Label's *TabIndex* property a value that is 1 less than the value of the other control's *TabIndex* property.

In our Rectangle sample application, this means assigning the TabIndex property as follows: 0 to lblWidth, 1 to txtWidth, 2 to lblHeight, 3 to txtHeight, 4 to cmdEvaluate, 5 to lblPerimeter, 6 to txtPerimeter, 7 to lblArea, and 8 to txtArea.

It's immediately apparent that when you have forms with tens or even hundreds of controls, correctly setting the *TabIndex* property for each one of them is a nuisance. For this reason, a number of third-party commercial or shareware vendors have developed special add-ins that permit you to solve this task in a visual manner, for example by clicking on each control, or in a semiautomatic manner by analyzing the relative position of all controls on the form. While these add-ins are real lifesavers, here's a trick well known among Visual Basic programmers that solves the problem with relatively little effort:

1. Select the *last* control in your planned Tab order.

2. Press the Ctrl+Shift+T key combination to activate the Properties window. For most controls, this combination selects the *TabIndex* properties; for others, you might need to press it more than once.

3. Press the 0 key, thus assigning a 0 to the *TabIndex* property of the selected control.

4. Click on the next to last control in the Tab order, and press the 0 key again; this assigns a 0 to the *TabIndex* property of the current control and 1 to the *TabIndex* property of the last control. This occurs because Visual Basic prevents you from using the same *TabIndex* value for two or more controls on the same form.

5. Repeat step 4, working backward in the Tab order sequence and pressing the 0 key after selecting each control. When you reach the first control in the sequence, the *TabIndex* property for all the controls on the form will be set correctly.

TIP   Visual Basic 5 and 6 also come with an add-in that permits you to arrange the *TabIndex* property for all the controls on the current form. This add-in is provided in source code format, in the TabOrder.vbp project located in the Samples\CompTool\AddIns subdirectory. To use this add-in, you must compile and install it manually. This tool lets you save a lot of time when arranging the Tab order for forms with many controls.

Now that we have completed our project, we'll save it. Choose Save Project from the File menu, or click the floppy disk icon. Visual Basic will ask you for the name of the form file, and again for the name of the project file; type *Rectangle* for both. You'll see that you now have two new files, Rectangle.frm and Rectangle.vbp.

Adding Code

Up to this point, you have created and refined the user interface of your program and created an application that in principle can be run. (Press F5 and run it to convince yourself that it indeed works.) But you don't have a useful application yet. To turn your pretty but useless program into your first working application, you need to add some code. More precisely, you have to add some code in the *Click* event of the cmdEvaluate control. This event fires when the user clicks on the Evaluate button or presses its associated hot key (the Alt+E key combination, in this case).

To write code within the *Click* event, you just select the cmdEvaluate control and then press the F7 key, or right-click on it and then invoke the View Code command from the pop-up menu. Or you simply double-click on the control using the left mouse button. In all cases, the code editor window appears, with the flashing cursor located between the following two lines of code:

```
Private Sub cmdEvaluate_Click()

End Sub
```

Visual Basic has prepared the template of the *Click* event procedure for you, and you have to add one or more lines of code between the *Sub* and *End Sub* statements. In this simple program, you need to extract the values stored in the txtWidth and txtHeight controls, use them to compute the rectangle's perimeter and area, and assign the results to the txtPerimeter and txtArea controls respectively:

```
Private Sub cmdEvaluate_Click()
    ' Declare two floating point variables.
    Dim reWidth As Double, reHeight As Double
    ' Extract values from input TextBox controls.
    reWidth = CDbl(txtWidth.Text)
    reHeight = CDbl(txtHeight.Text)
    ' Evaluate results and assign to output text boxes.
    txtPerimeter.Text = CStr((reWidth + reHeight) * 2)
    txtArea.Text = CStr(reWidth * reHeight)
End Sub
```

TIP Many developers, especially those with prior experience in the QuickBasic language, are accustomed to extracting numeric values from character strings using the *Val* function. The *CDbl* or *CSng* conversion functions are better choices in most cases, however, because they're *locale-aware* and correctly interpret the number in those countries where the decimal separator is the comma instead of the period. Even more important, the *CDbl* or *CSng* functions conveniently skip over separator characters and currency symbols (as in $1,234), whereas the *Val* function doesn't.

Note that you should always use the *Dim* statement to declare the variables you are going to use so that you can specify for them the most suitable data type. If you don't do that, Visual Basic will default them to the Variant data type. While this would be OK for this sample program, for most occasions you can make better and faster applications if you use variables of a more specific type. Moreover, you should add an *Option Explicit* statement at the very beginning of the code module so that Visual Basic will automatically trap any attempt to use a variable that isn't declared anywhere in the program code. By this single action, you'll avoid a lot of problems later in the development phase.

Running and Debugging the Program

You're finally ready to run this sample program. You can start its execution in several ways: By invoking the Start command from the Run menu, by clicking the corresponding icon on the toolbar, or by pressing the F5 key. In all cases, you'll see the form designer disappear and be replaced (but not necessarily in the same position on the screen) by the real form. You can enter any value in the leftmost TextBox controls and then click on the Evaluate button (or press the Alt+E key combination) to see the calculated perimeter and area in the rightmost controls. When you're finished, end the program by closing its main (and only) form.

CAUTION You can also stop any Visual Basic program running in the environment by invoking the End command from the Run menu, but in general this isn't a good approach because it prevents a few form-related events—namely the *QueryUnload* and the *Unload* events—from firing. In some cases, these event procedures contain the so-called *clean-up code,* for example, statements that close a database or delete a temporary file. If you abruptly stop the execution of a program, you're actually preventing the execution of this code. As a general rule, use the End command only if strictly necessary.

This program is so simple that you hardly need to test and debug it. Of course, this wouldn't be true for any real-world application. Virtually all programs need to be tested and debugged, which is probably the most delicate (and often tedious) part of a programmer's job. Visual Basic can't save you from this nuisance, but at least it offers so many tools that you can often complete it very quickly.

To see some Visual Basic debugging tools in action, place a breakpoint on the first line of the *Click* event procedure while the program is in design mode. You can set a breakpoint by moving the text cursor to the appropriate line and then invoking the Toggle Breakpoint command from the Debug menu or pressing the F9 shortcut key. You can also set and delete breakpoints by left-clicking on the gray vertical strip that runs near the left border of the code editor window. In all cases, the line on which the breakpoint is set will be highlighted in red.

After setting the breakpoint at the beginning of the *Click* event procedure, press F5 to run the program once again, enter some values in the Width and Height fields, and then click on the Evaluate button. You'll see the Visual Basic environment enter break mode, and you are free to perform several actions that let you better understand what's actually going on:

- Press F8 to execute the program one statement at a time. The Visual Basic instruction that's going to be executed next—that is, the current statement —is highlighted in yellow.

- Show the value of an expression by highlighting it in the code window and then pressing F9 (or selecting the Quick Watch command from the Debug menu). You can also add the selected expression to the list of values displayed in the Watch window, as you can see in Figure 1-10.

- An alternative way to show the value of a variable or a property is to move the mouse cursor over it in the code window; after a couple of seconds, a yellow *data tip* containing the corresponding value appears.

- Evaluate any expression by clicking on the Immediate window and typing *?* or *Print* followed by the expression. This is necessary when you need to evaluate the value of an expression that doesn't appear in the code window.

- You can view the values of all the local variables (but not expressions) by selecting the Locals command from the View menu. This command is particularly useful when you need to monitor the value of many local variables and you don't want to set up a watching expression for each one.

- You can affect the execution flow by placing the text cursor on the statement that you want to execute next and then selecting the Set Next Statement command from the Debug menu. Or you can press the Ctrl+F9 key combination. You need this technique to skip over a piece of code that you don't want to execute or to reexecute a given block of lines without restarting the program.

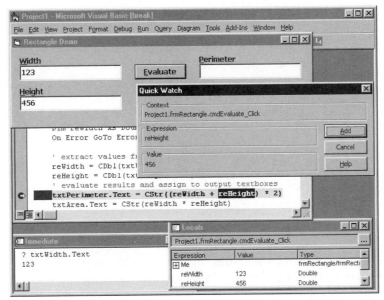

Figure 1-10. *The Rectangle Demo program in break mode, with several debug tools activated.*

Refining the Sample Program

Our first Visual Basic project, Rectangle.vbp, is just a sample program, but this is no excuse not to refine it and turn it into a complete and robust, albeit trivial, application.

The first type of refinement is very simple. Because the txtPerimeter and txtArea controls are used to show the results of the computation, it doesn't make sense to make their contents editable by the user. You can make them read-only fields by setting their *Locked* property to True. (A suggestion: select the two controls, press F4, and modify the property just once.) Some programmers prefer to use Label controls to display result values on a form, but using read-only TextBox controls has an advantage: The end user can copy their contents to the clipboard and paste those contents into another application.

A second refinement is geared toward increasing the application's consistency and usability. Let's suppose that your user uses the Rectangle program to determine the perimeter and area of a rectangle, takes note of the results, and then enters a new width or a new height (or both). Unfortunately, an instant before your user clicks on the Evaluate button the phone rings, engaging the user in a long conversation. When he or she hangs up, the form shows a plausible, though incorrect, result. How can you be sure that those values won't be mistaken for good ones? The solution is simple, indeed: as soon as the user modifies either the txtWidth or the txtHeight TextBox controls, the result fields must be cleared. In Visual Basic, you can accomplish this task by trapping each source control's *Change* event and writing a couple of statements in the corresponding event procedure. Since *Change* is the default event for TextBox controls—just as the *Click* event is for CommandButtons controls—you only have to double-click the txtWidth and txtHeight controls on the form designer to have Visual Basic create the template for the corresponding event procedures. This is the code that you have to add to the procedures:

```
Private Sub txtWidth_Change()
    txtPerimeter.Text = ""
    txtArea.Text = ""
End Sub

Private Sub txtHeight_Change()
    txtPerimeter.Text = ""
    txtArea.Text = ""
End Sub
```

Note that you don't have to retype the statements in the *txtHeight*'s *Change* event procedure: just double-click the control to create the *Sub … End Sub* template, and then copy and paste the code from the *txtWidth_Click* procedure. When you're finished, press F5 to run the program to check that it now behaves as expected.

The purpose of the next refinement that I am proposing is to increase the program's robustness. To see what I mean, run the Rectangle project and press the Evaluate button without entering width or height values: the program raises a Type Mismatch error when trying to extract a numeric value from the txtWidth control. If this were a real-world, compiled application, such an *untrapped* error would cause the application to end abruptly, which is, of course, unacceptable. All errors should be trapped and dealt with in a convenient way. For example, you should show the user where the problem is and how to fix it. The easiest way to achieve this is by setting up an error handler in the *cmdEvaluate_Click* procedure, as follows. (The lines you would add are in boldface.)

```
Private Sub cmdEvaluate_Click()
    ' Declare two floating point variables.
    Dim reWidth As Double, reHeight As Double
    On Error GoTo WrongValues

    ' Extract values from input textbox controls.
    reWidth = CDbl(txtWidth.Text)
    reHeight = CDbl(txtHeight.Text)
    Ensure that they are positive values.
    If reWidth <= 0 Or reHeight <= 0 Then GoTo WrongValues
    ' Evaluate results and assign to output text boxes.
    txtPerimeter.Text = CStr((reWidth + reHeight) * 2)
    txtArea.Text = CStr(reWidth * reHeight)
    Exit Sub
WrongValues:
    MsgBox "Please enter valid Width and Height values", vbExclamation
End Sub
```

Note that we have to add an *Exit Sub* statement to prevent the *MsgBox* statement from being erroneously executed during the normal execution flow. To see how the *On Error* statement works, set a breakpoint on the first line of this procedure, run the application, and press the F8 key to see what happens when either of the TextBox controls contains an empty or invalid string.

Ready, Compile, Run!

Visual Basic is a very productive programming language because it allows you to build and test your applications in a controlled environment, without first producing a compiled executable program. This is possible because Visual Basic converts your source code into *p-code* and then interprets it. P-code is a sort of intermediate language, which, because it's not executed directly by the CPU, is slower than real natively compiled code. On the other hand, the conversion from source code to p-code takes only a fraction of the time needed to deliver a compiled application. This is a great productivity bonus unknown to many other languages. Another benefit of p-code is that you can execute it step-by-step while the program is running in the environment, investigate the values of the variables, and—to some extent—even modify the code itself. This is a capability that many other languages don't have or have acquired only recently; for example, the latest version of Microsoft Visual C++ has it. By comparison, Visual Basic has always offered this feature, which undoubtedly contributed to making it a successful language.

At some time during the program development, you might want to create an executable (EXE) program. There are several reasons to do this: compiled programs are often (much) faster than interpreted ones, users don't need to install Visual Basic to run your application, and you usually don't want to let other people peek at your source code. Visual Basic makes the compilation process a breeze: when you're sure that your application is completed, you just have to run the Make *projectname* command from the File menu.

It takes a few seconds to create the Rectangle.exe file. This executable file is independent of the Visual Basic environment and can be executed in the same way as any other Windows application—for example, from the Run command of the Start menu. But this doesn't mean that you can pass this EXE file to another user and expect that it works. All Visual Basic programs, in fact, depend on a number of ancillary files—most notably the MSVBVM60.DLL file, a part of the Visual Basic runtime—and won't execute accurately unless all such files are correctly installed on the target system.

For this reason, you should never assume that a Visual Basic program will execute on every Windows system because it's working on your computer or on other computers in your office. (If your business is software development, it's highly probable that the Visual Basic environment is installed on all the computers around you.)

Instead, prepare a standard installation using the Package and Deployment Wizard, and try running your application on a clean system. If you develop software professionally, you should always have such a clean system at hand, if possible with just the operating system installed. If you're an independent developer, you probably won't be inclined to buy a complete system just to test your software. I found a very simple and relatively inexpensive solution to this dilemma: I use one computer with removable hard disks, so I can easily test my applications under different system configurations. And since a clean system requires only hundreds of megabytes of disk space, I can recycle all of my old hard disks that aren't large enough for any other use.

Before I conclude this chapter, you should be aware of one more detail. The compilation process doesn't necessarily mean that you aren't using p-code. In the Visual Basic jargon, *compiling* merely means *creating an executable file*. In fact, you can compile to p-code, even if this sounds like an oxymoron to a developer coming from another language. (See Figure 1-11.) In this case, Visual Basic creates an EXE file that embeds the same p-code that was used inside the development environment. That's why you can often hear Visual Basic developers talking about *p-code* and *native-code* compilations to better specify which type of compilation they're referring to.

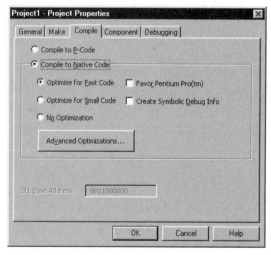

Figure 1-11. *You can opt to compile to p-code or native code in the Compile tab of the Project Properties dialog.*

In general, such p-code–compiled programs run at the same speed as interpreted programs within the IDE, so you're missing one of the biggest benefits of the compilation process. But here are a few reasons why you might decide to create a p-code executable:

■ P-code–compiled executables are often smaller than programs compiled to native code. This point can be important if you're going to distribute your application over the Internet or when you're creating ActiveX controls that are embedded in an HTML page.

■ P-code compilation is often faster than native code compilation, so you might prefer to stick to p-code when you compile the program in the test phase. (A few types of applications can't be tested within the IDE, most notably multithreaded components.)

■ If your application spends most of its time accessing databases or redrawing windows, compilation to native code doesn't significantly improve its performance because the time spent executing Visual Basic code is only a fraction of the total execution time.

We've come to the end of this *tour de force* in the Visual Basic IDE. In this chapter, I've illustrated the basics of Visual Basic development, and I hope I've given you a taste of how productive this language can be. Now you're ready to move to the next chapters, where you can learn more about forms and controls and about how to make the best of their properties, methods, and events.

Chapter 2

Introduction to Forms

Forms are the first Microsoft Visual Basic objects you get acquainted with. Although you can write useful programs with only rudimentary user interfaces—command-line driven utilities, for example—most Visual Basic applications include one or more forms, and so you need to be familiar with their properties and features.

Despite their different natures, forms and controls have one important thing in common: All of them are Visual Basic *objects*, and as such they expose properties, react to methods, and raise events. In this sense, Visual Basic is said to be an *object-based* programming language because the developer's job consists of reading and modifying objects' properties, calling their methods, and responding to their events. Moreover, Visual Basic can be considered a *visual* programming environment in that the appearance of such objects can be defined by means of interactive tools at design time and without writing any code.

Forms and controls expose dozens of properties, and when you explore them in the Object Browser you might legitimately wonder how you can learn the meaning of all of them. It takes some time until you realize that there are a few recurring patterns and that most of the properties are shared among forms and among most types of controls. In the end, properties that are peculiar to form objects or to a given class of controls are relatively few.

This consideration led me to structure this and the following chapter in a somewhat unusual way. Most language manuals introduce forms first, describe each intrinsic control class and illustrate its features, passing from one control to the next, and so on. In my opinion, this approach forces you to study each particular object as if it were a separate case. Such fragmentation of information makes it difficult to get the big picture, and in the end it makes for a steeper leaning curve. Worse, this mnemonic effort doesn't help much in understanding how things actually work behind the scenes.

For example, why do some controls expose a *TabIndex* property but not a *TabStop* property? Why do some controls support the *hWnd* property, while others do not?

After some thinking, I decided to depart from the typical control-by-control description and focus instead on the many properties, methods, and events that forms and most intrinsic controls have in common. The features and peculiarities of forms are covered only later in this chapter, and Chapter 3 is entirely devoted to Visual Basic's intrinsic controls. This means that you won't see complete programming examples until the second half of this chapter, even though I use some shorter pieces of code that explain how a property can be used or how you usually react to the events that are shared by most types of controls. After all, when you're working in the Visual Basic environment, the complete list of all the properties, methods, and events supported by each object is always just one keystroke away: Just press F2 to display the Object Browser or F1 to get more complete and descriptive help. You don't want to read the same information here, do you?

I have another reason for explaining common properties in one section. In its six versions, Visual Basic has undergone many important changes: Each version has added new features and, consequently, forms and controls have acquired more and more new properties, methods, and events. Backward compatibility has always been a primary goal in Microsoft's plans, however, and old features are still supported. In fact, you can often load a Visual Basic 3 project in the Visual Basic 6 environment and run it without changing a single line of code. (The most notable exceptions are code that refers to external libraries and controls that access databases.) Backward compatibility has its drawbacks, though, the first of which is the ever-growing list of properties, methods, and events. For example, there are duplicated sets of properties that have to do with drag-and-drop, and there are two distinct ways to set font attributes. The result is that most beginning programmers are confused, and more seasoned developers tend to continue to use the old (and often inefficient) features because they don't want to learn a new syntax. I hope that the following descriptions of common properties, methods, and events can contribute to making things clearer to both kinds of readers.

COMMON PROPERTIES

At first glance, it might seem that Visual Basic 6 supports countless properties for various objects. Fortunately, there's a set of properties many objects of different classes share. In this section, we'll examine these common properties.

The *Left, Top, Width,* and *Height* Properties

All visible objects—forms and controls—expose these properties, which affect the object's position and size. These values are always relative to the object's container— that is, the screen for a form and the parent form for a control. A control can also be contained in another control, which is said to be its *container:* In this case, *Top* and *Left* properties are relative to such a container control. By default, these properties are measured in *twips,* a unit that lets you create resolution-independent user interfaces, but you can switch to another unit, for example, pixels or inches, by setting the container's *ScaleMode* property. But you can't change the unit used for forms because they have no container: *Left*, *Top*, *Width*, and *Height* properties for forms are always measured in twips. For more information about the twip measurement unit, see the section "The *ScaleMode* Property" later in this chapter.

While you can enter numeric values for these properties right in the Properties window at design time, you often set them in a visual manner by moving and resizing the control on its parent form. Keep in mind that Visual Basic also offers many interactive commands in the Format menu that let you resize, align, and space multiple controls in one operation. You can also access and modify these properties through code to move or resize objects at run time:

```
' Double a form's width, and move it to the
' upper left corner of the screen.
Form1.Width = Form1.Width * 2
Form1.Left = 0
Form1.Top = 0
```

Note that while all controls—even invisible ones—expose these four properties at design time in the Properties window, controls that are inherently invisible—Timer controls, for example—don't support these properties at run time, and you can't therefore read or modify them through code.

> **CAUTION**   Controls don't necessarily have to support all four properties in a uniform manner. For example, ComboBox controls' *Height* property can be read but not written to, both at design time and run time. As far as I know, this is the only example of a property that appears in the Properties window but can't be modified at design time. This happens because the height of a ComboBox control depends on the control's Font attributes. Remember this exception when writing code that modifies the *Height* property for all the controls in a form.

The *ForeColor* and *BackColor* Properties

Most visible objects expose *ForeColor* and *BackColor* properties, which affect the color of the text and the color of the background, respectively. The colors of a few controls— scroll bars, for example—are dictated by Microsoft Windows, however, and you won't find *ForeColor* and *BackColor* entries in the Properties window. In other cases, the effect of these properties depends on other properties: for example, setting the *BackColor* property of a Label control has no effect if you set the *BackStyle* property of that Label to 0-Transparent. CommandButton controls are peculiar in that they expose a *BackColor* property but not a *ForeColor* property, and the background color is active only if you also set the *Style* property to 1-Graphical. (Because the default value for the *Style* property is 0-Standard, it might take you a while until you understand why the *BackColor* property doesn't affect the background color in the usual manner.)

When you're setting one of these two properties in the Properties window, you can select either a standard Windows color or a custom color using the System tab in the first case and the Palette tab in the second, as you can see in Figure 2-1. My first suggestion is always use a standard color value unless you have a very good reason to use a custom color. System colors display well on any Windows machine, are likely to conform to your customers' tastes, and contribute to making your application look well integrated in the system. My second suggestion is if you want to use custom colors, develop a consistent color scheme and use it throughout your application. I also have a third suggestion: Never mix standard and custom colors on the same form, and don't use a standard color for the *ForeColor* property and a custom color for the *BackColor* property of the same control (or vice versa), because the user might change the system palette in a way that makes the control completely unreadable.

You can choose from several ways to assign a color in code. Visual Basic provides a set of symbolic constants that correspond to all the colors that appear in the System tab in the Properties window at design time:

```
' Make Label1 appear in a selected state.
Label1.ForeColor = vbHighlightText
Label1.BackColor = vbHighlight
```

All the symbolic constants are shown in Table 2-1, but you can also browse them in the Object Browser window, after clicking the SystemColorConstants item in the leftmost list box. (If you don't see it, first select <All libraries> or VBRUN in the top ComboBox control). Note that all the values of these constants are negative.

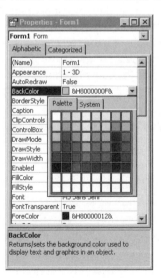

Figure 2-1. *Two different ways to set the* ForeColor *and* BackColor *properties at design time.*

Constant	*Hex Value*	*Description*
vb3DDKShadow	&H80000015	Darkest shadow
vb3Dface	&H8000000F	Dark shadow color for 3-D display elements
vb3Dhighlight	&H80000014	Highlight color for 3-D display elements
vb3Dlight	&H80000016	Second lightest of the 3-D colors after vb3Dhighlight
vb3Dshadow	&H80000010	Color of automatic window shadows
vbActiveBorder	&H8000000A	Active window border color
vbActiveTitleBar	&H80000002	Active window caption color
vbActiveTitleBarText	&H80000009	Text color in active caption, size box, scroll bar arrow box
vbApplicationWorkspace	&H8000000C	Background color of multiple-document interface (MDI) applications
vbButtonFace	&H8000000F	Face shading on command buttons
vbButtonShadow	&H80000010	Edge shading on command buttons
vbButtonText	&H80000012	Text color on push buttons
vbDesktop	&H80000001	Desktop color
vbGrayText	&H80000011	Grayed (disabled) text
vbHighlight	&H8000000D	Background color of items selected in a control
vbHighlightText	&H8000000E	Text color of items selected in a control
vbInactiveBorder	&H8000000B	Inactive window border color
vbInactiveCaptionText	&H80000013	Color of text in an inactive caption
vbInactiveTitleBar	&H80000003	Inactive window caption color
vbInactiveTitleBarText	&H80000013	Text color in inactive window caption, size box, scroll bar arrow box
vbInfoBackground	&H80000018	Background color of ToolTips
vbInfoText	&H80000017	Color of text in ToolTips
vbMenuBar	&H80000004	Menu background color

Table 2-1. *Visual Basic constants for system colors.*   *(continued)*

Table 2-1. *continued*

Constant	Hex Value	Description
vbMenuText	&H80000007	Text color in menus
vbScrollBars	&H80000000	Scroll bar gray area color
vbTitleBarText	&H80000009	Text color in active caption, size box, scroll bar arrow box
vbWindowBackground	&H80000005	Window background color
vbWindowFrame	&H80000006	Window frame color
vbWindowText	&H80000008	Text color in windows

When you're assigning a custom color, you can use one of the symbolic constants that Visual Basic defines for the most common colors (*vbBlack, vbBlue, vbCyan, vbGreen, vbMagenta, vbRed, vbWhite,* and *vbYellow*), or you can use a numeric decimal or hexadecimal constant:

```
' These statements are equivalent.
Text1.BackColor = vbCyan
Text1.BackColor = 16776960
Text1.BackColor = &HFFFF00
```

You can also use an *RGB* function to build a color value composed of its red, green, and blue components. Finally, to ease the porting of existing QuickBasic applications, Visual Basic supports the *QBColor* function:

```
' These statements are equivalent to the ones above.
Text1.BackColor = RGB(0, 255, 255)    ' red, green, blue values
Text1.BackColor = QBColor(11)
```

The *Font* Property

Forms and those controls that can display strings of characters expose the *Font* property. At design time, you set font attributes using a common dialog box, which you can see in Figure 2-2. Dealing with fonts at run time, however, is less simple because you must account for the fact that Font is a compound object, and you must assign its properties separately. Font objects expose the *Name, Size, Bold, Italic, Underline,* and *Strikethrough* properties.

```
Text1.Font.Name = "Tahoma"
Text1.Font.Size = 12
Text1.Font.Bold = True
Text1.Font.Underline = True
```

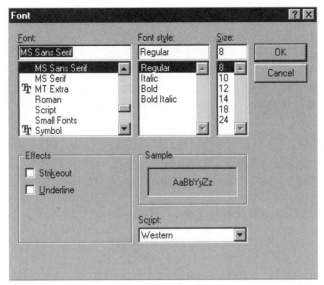

Figure 2-2. *At design time the Font dialog box lets you modify all font attributes at once and preview the result.*

TIP   You can use the *Set* command to assign whole Font objects to controls (thus avoiding having to set individual font attributes for each control), as you can see in the following code fragment:

```
' Assign to Text2 the same font as used by Text1.
Set Text2.Font = Text1.Font
```

It should be made clear, however, that the preceding code actually assigns the *same* Font objects to both controls. This means that if you later change Text1's font attributes, the appearance of Text2 will also be affected. This behavior is perfectly consistent with the Font object's nature, even though the reasons for it will become clear only later in Chapter 6. You can take advantage of this approach—for example, if all the controls in your form always use the same font—but you should absolutely avoid it when the controls in question are supposed to have independent font attributes.

Visual Basic 6 still supports old-style Font properties such as *FontName*, *FontSize*, *FontBold*, *FontItalic*, *FontUnderline*, and *FontStrikethru*, but you can modify them only through code because they don't appear in the Properties window at design time. You can use the syntax that you like most because the two forms are perfectly interchangeable. In this book, however, I mostly follow the newer object-oriented syntax.

The *Font.Size* property (or the equivalent *FontSize* property) is peculiar because in general you can't be sure that Visual Basic is able to create a font of that particular size, especially if you aren't working with a TrueType font. The short code snippet on the next page proves this.

```
Text1.Font.Name = "Courier"
Text1.Font.Size = 22
Print Text1.Font.Size   ' Prints 19.5
```

Note that no error is raised if you specify a font size that isn't actually available.

> **CAUTION**   In general, Visual Basic doesn't raise errors when you try to assign invalid font names. In this case, the effect is somewhat unpredictable. For example, try the following code:
>
> ```
> ' Warning: you may get different results on your system.
> Print Font.Name        ' Displays "Ms Sans Serif"
> Font.Name = "xyz"
> Print Font.Name        ' Displays "Arial"
> ```

The *Caption* and *Text* Properties

The *Caption* property is a string of characters that appears inside a control (or in the title bar of a form) and that the user can't directly modify. Conversely, the *Text* property corresponds to the "contents" of a control and is usually editable by the end user. No intrinsic control exposes both a *Caption* and a *Text* property, so in practice a look at the Properties window can resolve your doubts as to what you're working with. Label, CommandButton, CheckBox, OptionButton, Data, and Frame controls expose the *Caption* property, whereas TextBox, ListBox, and ComboBox controls expose the *Text* property.

The *Caption* property is special in that it can include an ampersand (&) character to associate a hot key with the control. The *Text* property, when present, is always the default property for the control, which means that it can be omitted in code:

```
' These statements are equivalent.
Text2.Text = Text1.Text
Text2 = Text1
```

> **NOTE**   Specifying or omitting the name of the default property in code is mostly a matter of personal taste. I always try to specify the name of all the properties referenced in code because doing so tends to make the code more readable. However, if you have long lines of code, specifying all the default properties can sometimes make the code *less* readable and can force you to horizontally scroll through the code window. This consideration has been followed in this book: Most of the time, I specify the default property, but don't be surprised if I sometimes omit it, especially in longer listings.
>
> While we are on this topic, note that many programmers mistakenly believe that using default properties can make their code run faster. This is a leftover notion from Visual Basic 3 days, but it hasn't been true since Visual Basic 4 changed the internal implementation of controls.

In general, if a control exposes the *Text* property it also supports the *SelText*, *SelStart*, and *SelLength* properties, which return information about the portion of text that's currently selected in the control.

The *Parent* and *Container* Properties

The *Parent* property is a run time–only property (that is, you don't see it in the Properties window), which returns a reference to the form that hosts the control. The *Container* property is also a run time–only property, which returns a reference to the container of the control. These two properties are correlated, in that they return the same object—the parent form—when a control is placed directly on the form surface.

While you can't move a control from one form to another using the *Parent* property (which is read-only), you can move a control to another container by assigning a different value to its *Container* property (which is a read-write property). Because you're assigning objects and not plain values, you must use the *Set* keyword:

```
' Move Text1 into the Picture1 container.
Set Text1.Container = Picture1
' Move it back on the form's surface.
Set Text1.Container = Form1
```

The *Enabled* and *Visible* Properties

By default, all controls and forms are both visible and enabled at run time. For a number of reasons, however, you might want to hide them or show them in a disabled state. For example, you might use a hidden DriveListBox control simply to enumerate all the drives in the system. In this case, you set the *Visible* property of the DriveListBox control to False in the Properties window at design time. More frequently, however, you change these properties at run time:

```
' Enable or disable the Text1 control when
' the user clicks on the Check1 CheckBox control.
Private Sub Check1_Click()
    Text1.Enabled = (Check1.Value = vbChecked)
End Sub
```

Disabled controls don't react to user's actions, but otherwise they're fully functional and can be manipulated through code. Invisible controls are automatically disabled, so you never need to set both these properties to False. All mouse events for disabled or invisible controls are passed to the underlying container or to the form itself.

If an object works as a container for other objects—for instance, a Form is a container for its controls and a Frame control can be a container for a group of

OptionButton controls—setting its *Visible* or *Enabled* properties indirectly affects the state of its contained objects. This feature can often be exploited to reduce the amount of code you write to enable or disable a group of related controls.

> **TIP**   Most controls change their appearance when they're disabled. Generally speaking, this is a useful practice because the user can understand at first glance which controls he or she can act on. If you have a good reason to disable a control but still display it in an active state, you can place the control inside a container (a Frame or a PictureBox, for example) and then set the container's *Enabled* property to False. Visual Basic will disable all contained controls, but they will continue to appear in an enabled state. This trick works better if you also set the container's *BorderStyle* property to 0-None.

Some programmers set the *Enabled* properties to False for TextBox or ComboBox controls that must work in a read-only mode. This is reminiscent of the way things worked under Visual Basic 3 and previous versions. But these controls now expose a *Locked* property that, if True, makes the controls completely functional, except that users can't modify their *Text* property. This means that users can scroll through their content but can't accidentally modify it.

The *hWnd* Property

The *hWnd* property doesn't appear in the Properties window because its value is available only at run time. Moreover, it's a read-only property, and therefore you can't assign a value to it. The *hWnd* property returns the 32-bit integer value that Windows uses internally to identify a control. This value is absolutely meaningless in standard Visual Basic programming and only becomes useful if you invoke Windows API routines (which I'll cover in Appendix A). Even if you're not going to use this property in your code, it's good for you to know that not all controls support it and it's important to understand why.

Visual Basic controls—both intrinsic controls and external Microsoft ActiveX controls—can be grouped in two categories: *standard* controls and *windowless* (or *lightweight*) controls. To grasp the difference between the two groups, let's compare the PictureBox control (a standard control) and the Image control (a windowless control). Even though they appear similar at a first glance, behind the scenes they are completely different.

When you place a standard control on the form, Visual Basic asks the operating system to create an instance of that control's class, and in return Windows passes back to Visual Basic the internal *handle* to that control, which the language then exposes to the programmer through the *hWnd* property. All subsequent operations that Visual Basic performs on that control—resizing, font setting, and so on—are actually delegated to Windows. When the application raises an event (such as resizing),

Visual Basic runtime calls an internal Windows API function and passes it the handle so that Windows knows which control is to be affected.

Lightweight controls such as Image controls, on the other hand, don't correspond to any Windows object and are entirely managed by Visual Basic itself. In a sense, Visual Basic just simulates the existence of that control: It keeps track of all the lightweight controls and redraws them each time the form is refreshed. For this reason, lightweight controls don't expose an *hWnd* property because there aren't any Windows handles associated with them. Windows doesn't even know a control is there.

From a practical point of view, the distinction between standard and lightweight controls is that the former consume system resources and memory while the latter don't. For this reason, you should always try to replace standard controls with lightweight controls. For example, use an Image control instead of a PictureBox control unless you really need some of PictureBox's specific features. To give you an idea of what this means in practice, a form with 100 PictureBox controls loads *10 times slower* than a form with 100 Image controls.

To understand whether a control is lightweight, see whether it supports the *hWnd* property. If it does, it surely is a standard control. A trip to the Object Browser reveals that the TextBox, CommandButton, OptionButton, CheckBox, Frame, ComboBox, and OLE controls, as well as both scroll bar controls and the ListBox control and all its variations, are standard controls. The Label, Shape, Line, Image, and Timer controls don't expose the *hWnd* property and should be therefore considered lightweight controls. But note that a missing *hWnd* property in an external ActiveX control doesn't necessarily mean that the control is windowless because the control's creator might decide not to expose the window's handle to the outside. For more information about standard and windowless controls, see the description of the *ZOrder* method later in this chapter.

The *TabStop* and *TabIndex* Properties

If a control is able to receive the input focus, it exposes the *TabStop* property. Most intrinsic controls support this property, including TextBox, OptionButton, CheckBox, CommandButton, OLE, ComboBox, both types of scroll bars, the ListBox control, and all its variations. In general, intrinsic lightweight controls don't support this property because they can never receive the input focus. The default value for this property is True, but you can set it to False either at design time or run time.

If a control supports the *TabStop* property, it also supports the *TabIndex* property, which affects the Tab order sequence—that is, the sequence in which the controls are visited when the user presses the Tab key repeatedly. (See the section "Setting the Tab Order" in Chapter 1.) The *TabIndex* property is also supported by Label and Frame controls, but since these two controls don't support the *TabStop* property, the resulting effect is that when the user clicks on a Label or a Frame control (or presses the hot key specified in the Label or Frame *Caption* property), the input focus goes to the control that follows in the Tab order sequence. You can exploit this feature to use Label and Frame controls to provide hot keys to other controls:

```
' Let the user press the Alt+N hot key
' to move the input focus on the Text1 control.
Label1.Caption = "&Name"
Text1.TabIndex = Label1.TabIndex + 1
```

The *MousePointer* and *MouseIcon* Properties

These properties affect the shape of the mouse cursor when it hovers over a control. Windows permits a very flexible mouse cursor management in that each form and each control can display a different cursor, and you can also set an application-wide mouse cursor using the Screen global object. Nevertheless, the rules that affect the actual cursor used aren't straightforward:

■   If the *Screen.MousePointer* property is set to a value different from 0-vbDefault, the mouse cursor reflects this value and no other properties are considered. But when the mouse floats over a different application (or the desktop), the cursor appearance depends on *that* application's current state, not yours.

■   If *Screen.MousePointer* is 0 and the mouse cursor is over a control, Visual Basic checks that control's *MousePointer* property; if this value is different from 0-vbDefault, the mouse cursor is set to this value.

■   If *Screen.MousePointer* is 0 and the mouse is over a form's surface or it's over a control whose *MousePointer* property is 0, Visual Basic uses the value stored in the form's *MousePointer* property.

If you want to show an hourglass cursor, wherever the user moves the mouse, use this code:

```
' A lengthy routine
Screen.MousePointer = vbHourglass
...
' Do your stuff here
...
' but remember to restore default pointer.
Screen.MousePointer = vbDefault
```

Here's another example:

```
' Show a crosshair cursor when the mouse is over the Picture1
' control and an hourglass elsewhere on the parent form.
Picture1.MousePointer = vbCrosshair
MousePointer = vbHourglass
```

The *MouseIcon* property is used to display a custom, user-defined mouse cursor. In this case, you must set the *MousePointer* to the special value 99-vbCustom and then assign an icon to the *MouseIcon* property:

```
' Display a red Stop sign mouse cursor. The actual path may differ,
' depending on the main directory where you installed Visual Basic.
MousePointer = vbCustom
MouseIcon = LoadPicture("d:\vb6\graphics\icons\computer\msgbox01.ico")
```

You don't need to load a custom mouse cursor at run time using the *LoadPicture* command. For example, you can assign it to the *MouseIcon* property at design time in the Properties window, as you can see in Figure 2-3, and activate it only when needed by setting the *MousePointer* property to 99-vbCustom. If you need to alternate among multiple cursors for the same control but don't want to distribute additional files, you can load additional ICO files in hidden Image controls and switch among them at run time.

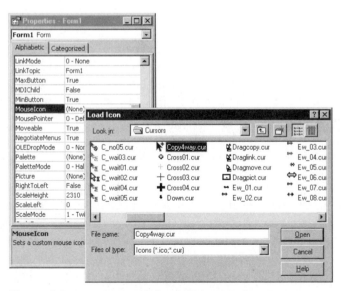

Figure 2-3. *Visual Basic 6 comes with a lot of ready-to-go custom cursors, icons, and bitmaps in the \GRAPHICS subdirectory.*

The *Tag* Property

All controls support the *Tag* property, without exception. This is true even for ActiveX controls, including any third-party controls. How can I be so certain that all controls support this property? The reason is that the property is provided by Visual Basic itself, not by the control. *Tag* isn't the only property provided by Visual Basic to any control: *Index, Visible, TabStop, TabIndex, ToolTipText, HelpContextID,* and *WhatsThisHelpID* properties all belong to the same category. These properties are collectively known as *extender properties.* Note that a few extender properties are available only under certain conditions. For example, *TabStop* is present only if the control can actually receive the focus. The *Tag* property is distinctive because it's guaranteed to be always available, and you can reference it in code without any risk of raising a run-time error.

The *Tag* property has no particular meaning to Visual Basic: It's simply a container for any data related to the control that you want to store. For example, you might use it to store the initial value displayed in a control so that you can easily restore it if the user wants to undo his or her changes.

Other Properties

The *Value* property is common to several intrinsic controls, namely CheckBox, OptionButton, CommandButton, and scroll bar controls, as well as to many external ActiveX controls. The meaning of this property varies from control to control, but in all cases it's a numerical or Boolean property.

The *Index* property is the key to building *control arrays,* a nifty Visual Basic feature that helps you create more versatile programs. (I explain control arrays more fully in Chapter 3.) If you don't want to create a control array, just leave this property blank in the Properties window at design time. Note that this property is read-only at run time for controls that belong to a control array. Note that Visual Basic raises an error if you reference the *Index* property of a control that doesn't belong to a control array.

Most intrinsic controls support the *Appearance* property, which can be assigned at design time only and is read-only at run time. By default, Visual Basic creates controls with a three-dimensional aspect, unless you modify the value of this property to 0-Flat. You might decide to do so for visual consistency with older programs. For all your new applications, you should simply forget about the *Appearance* property and leave it at its default value (1-3D).

You can have Visual Basic automatically attach a control to the border of its parent window by setting its *Align* property to a non-Null value. Only two intrinsic controls support this property—PictureBox and Data controls—but several external ActiveX controls can be aligned in this way. Possible values for this property are 0-None, 1-Align Top, 2-Align Bottom, 3-Align Left, and 4-Align Right.

The *BorderStyle* property is supported by a few intrinsic controls, namely the TextBox, Label, Frame, PictureBox, Image, and OLE controls. You can set this property to 0-None to suppress a border around the controller to 1-Fixed Single to draw it. Forms also support this property, but they allow different settings (as you'll see later in this chapter).

ToolTips are those tiny, usually yellow windows that appear in most Windows applications when you move the mouse over a control or an icon and keep the mouse pointer still for a second or two. (Figure 2-4 shows you helpful advice from a ToolTip.) Until Visual Basic 4, developers had to create special routines or buy third-party tools to add this functionality to their programs. In Visual Basic 5 and 6, you only have to assign a string to the *ToolTipText* property of the control. Unfortunately, form objects don't support this property. Note that you have no control over the position or size of ToolTip windows and can modify their foreground and background color only on a systemwide basis. (Open the Control Panel window, double-click on the Display icon, and then move to the Appearance tab of the Display Properties dialog box where you can change the font and the background color of your ToolTips.)

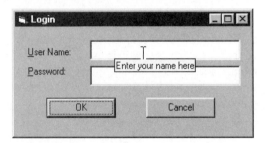

Figure 2-4. *A tiny ToolTip tells you to enter your name.*

The *DragMode* and *DragIcon* properties (as well as the *Drag* method) were used to drag controls on the form, but they have been superseded by the *OLExxxx* methods and properties. The old properties are still included for backward compatibility, but you shouldn't use them if you want to make your application conform to Windows 95 standards. OLE Drag and Drop properties, methods, and events are described in the "Using Drag-and-Drop" section of Chapter 9.

You use *LinkMode*, *LinkTopic*, *LinkItem*, and *LinkTimeout* properties (as well as *LinkPoke*, *LinkExecute*, *LinkRequest*, and *LinkSend* methods) to enable a control or form to communicate through DDE (Dynamic Data Exchange) protocol with other controls or forms, possibly in another application. Before the advent of OLE and COM, Dynamic Data Exchange was the preferred way for two Windows programs to communicate. These days, you shouldn't use this technique because these properties have been maintained only for backward compatibility with applications written in previous versions of Visual Basic. I won't cover DDE in this book.

COMMON METHODS

Just as there are many properties that most objects share, they also have many methods in common. In this section, we examine these methods.

The *Move* Method

If a control supports *Left*, *Top*, *Width*, and *Height* properties, it also supports the *Move* method, through which you can change some or all four properties in a single operation. The following example changes three properties: *Left*, *Top*, and *Width*.

```
' Double a form's width, and move it to the upper left corner of the screen.
' Syntax is: Move Left, Top, Width, Height.
Form1.Move 0, 0, Form1.Width * 2
```

Note that all arguments but the first one are optional, but you can't omit any of them in the middle of the command. For example, you can't pass the *Height* argument if you omit the *Width* argument. As I mentioned in the description of individual properties, you should be aware that the *Height* property is read-only for the ComboBox control.

> **TIP**   The *Move* method should always be preferred to individual property assignment for at least two reasons: This operation is two to three times faster than four distinct assignments, and if you're modifying the *Width* and *Height* properties of a form, each individual property assignments would fire a separate *Resize* event, thus adding a lot of overhead to your code.

The *Refresh* Method

The *Refresh* method causes the control to be redrawn. You normally don't need to explicitly call this method because Visual Basic automatically refreshes the control's appearance when it has a chance (usually when no user code is running and Visual Basic is in an idle state). But you can explicitly invoke this method when you modify a control's property and you want the user interface to be immediately updated:

```
For n = 1000 To 1 Step -1
    Label1.Caption = CStr(i)
    Label1.Refresh          ' Update the label immediately.
Next
```

> **CAUTION**   You can also refresh a form using the *DoEvents* command because it yields the control to Visual Basic, and the Visual Basic form engine exploits this opportunity to update the user interface. But you should be aware that

DoEvents performs additional processing as well—for example, it checks whether any button has been clicked and if so it executes its *Click* procedure. Therefore, the two techniques aren't always equivalent. In general, using the *Refresh* method on the only control that has been modified delivers better performance than executing a *DoEvents* command. It also avoids reentrancy problems that can occur, for example, when the user clicks again on the same button before the previous *Click* procedure has completed its processing. If you want to update all the controls on a form but you don't want the end user to interact with the program, just execute the *Refresh* method of the parent form.

The *SetFocus* Method

The *SetFocus* method moves the input focus on the specified control. You need to call this method only if you want to modify the default Tab order sequence that you implicitly create at design time by setting the *TabIndex* property of the controls on the form, as we saw in Chapter 1. The control whose *TabIndex* property is set to 0 receives the focus when the form loads.

A potential problem with the *SetFocus* method is that it fails and raises a runtime error if the control is currently disabled or invisible. For this reason, avoid using this method in the *Form_Load* event (when all controls aren't yet visible) and you should either ensure that the control is ready to receive the focus or protect the method with an *On Error* statement. Here's the code for the former approach:

```
' Move the focus to Text1.
If Text1.Visible And Text1.Enabled Then
    Text1.SetFocus
End If
```

And here's the code for the other possible approach, using the *On Error* statement:

```
' Move the focus to Text1.
On Error Resume Next
Text1.SetFocus
```

> **TIP** The *SetFocus* method is often used in the *Form_Load* event procedure to programmatically set which control on the form should receive the focus when the form initially appears. Because you can't use *SetFocus* on invisible controls, you're forced to make the form visible first:
>
> ```
> Private Sub Form_Load()
>     Show              ' Make the form visible.
>     Text1.SetFocus
> End Sub
> ```

Here's another possible solution:

```
Private Sub Form_Load()
    Text1.TabIndex = 0
End Sub
```

Note that if *Text1* isn't able to receive the input focus (for example, its *TabStop* property is set to False), Visual Basic automatically moves the focus on the next control in the Tab order sequence, without raising any error. The drawback of this second approach is that it affects the Tab order of all other controls on the form.

The *ZOrder* Method

The *ZOrder* method affects the visibility of the control with respect to other overlapping controls. You just execute this method without any argument if you want to position the control in front of other controls; or you can pass 1 as an argument to move the control behind other controls:

```
' Move a control behind any other control on the form.
Text1.ZOrder 1
Text1.ZOrder        ' Move it in front.
```

Note that you can set the relative z-order of controls at design time using the commands in the Order submenu of the Format menu, and you can also use the Ctrl+J key combination to bring the selected control to the front or the Ctrl+K key combination to move it behind other controls.

The actual behavior of the *ZOrder* method depends on whether the control is standard or lightweight. In fact, lightweight controls can never appear in front of standard controls. In other words, the two types of controls—standard and lightweight—are located on distinct z-order layers, with the layer of standard controls in front of the layer of lightweight controls. This means that the *ZOrder* method can change the relative z-order of a control only within the layer it belongs to. For example, you can't place a Label (lightweight) control in front of a TextBox (standard) control. However, if the standard control can behave like a container control—a PictureBox or a Frame control, for example—you can make a lightweight control appear in front of the standard control if you place the lightweight control inside that container control, as you can see in Figure 2-5.

The *ZOrder* method also applies to forms. You can send a form behind all other forms in the same Visual Basic application, or you can bring it in front of them. You can't use this method, however, to control the relative position of your forms with respect to windows belonging to other applications.

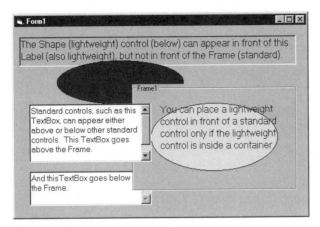

Figure 2-5. *Relative z-order of controls.*

COMMON EVENTS

In addition to common properties and methods, Visual Basic 6 forms and controls support common events. In this section, we'll describe these events in some detail.

The *Click* and *DblClick* Events

A *Click* event occurs when the user left-clicks on a control, whereas the *DblClick* event occurs—you guessed it—when he or she double-clicks on the control using the left mouse button. But don't be fooled by this apparent simplicity because the *Click* event can occur under different circumstances as well. For example, whenever a CheckBox or an OptionButton control's *Value* property changes through code, Visual Basic fires a *Click* event, exactly as if the user had clicked on it. This behavior is useful because it lets you deal with the two different cases in a uniform way. ListBox and ComboBox controls also fire *Click* events whenever their *ListIndex* properties change.

Click and *DblClick* events don't pass arguments to the program, and therefore you can't count on these events to tell you where the mouse cursor is. To get this information, you must trap the *MouseDown* event instead, about which I'll say more later in this chapter. Also notice that when you double-click on a control, it receives both the *Click* and the *DblClick* events. This makes it difficult to distinguish single clicks from double-clicks because when Visual Basic calls your *Click* event procedure you don't know whether it will later call the *DblClick* procedure. At any rate, you should avoid assigning different functions to click and double-click actions on the same control because it tends to confuse the user.

> **TIP**   While you shouldn't assign separate effects to click and double-click actions on the same control, here's a simple method to work around the problem of finding out what the user actually did:

```
' A module-level variable
Dim isClick As Boolean

Private Sub Form_Click()
    Dim t As Single
    isClick = True
    ' Wait for the second click for half a second.
    t = Timer
    Do
        DoEvents
        ' If the DblClick procedure canceled this event,
        ' bail out.
        If Not isClick Then Exit Sub
        ' The next test accounts for clicks just before midnight.
    Loop Until Timer > t + .5 Or Timer < t
    ' Do your single-click processing here.
    ...
End Sub

Private Sub Form_DblClick()
    ' Cancel any pending click.
    isClick = False
    ' Do your double-click processing here.
    ...
End Sub
```

The *Change* Event

The *Change* event is the simplest event offered by Visual Basic: Whenever the contents of a control change, Visual Basic fires a *Change* event. Unfortunately, this simple scheme hasn't been consistently followed in the Visual Basic architecture. As I explained in the previous section, when you click on CheckBox and OptionButton controls, they fire a *Click* event (rather than a *Change* event). Fortunately, this inconsistency isn't a serious one.

TextBox and ComboBox controls raise a *Change* event when the user types something in the editable area of the control. (But be careful, the ComboBox control raises a *Click* event when the user *selects* an item from the list portion rather than types in a box.) Both scroll bar controls raise the *Change* event when the user clicks on either arrows or moves the scroll boxes. The *Change* event is also supported by the PictureBox, DriveListBox, and DirListBox controls.

The *Change* event also fires when the contents of the control are changed through code. This behavior often leads to some inefficiencies in the program. For instance, many programmers initialize the *Text* properties of all TextBox controls in the form's *Load* event, thus firing many *Change* events that tend to slow down the loading process.

The *GotFocus* and *LostFocus* Events

These events are conceptually very simple: *GotFocus* fires when a control receives the input focus, and *LostFocus* fires when the input focus leaves it and passes to another control. At first glance, these events seem ideal for implementing a sort of validation mechanism—that is, a piece of code that checks the contents of a field and notifies the user if the input value isn't correct as soon as he or she moves the focus to another control. In practice, the sequence of these events is subject to several factors, including the presence of *MsgBox* and *DoEvents* statements. Fortunately, Visual Basic 6 has introduced the new *Validate* event, which elegantly solves the problem of field validation. (See the "The *CausesValidation* Property and the *Validate* Event" section in Chapter 3 for more details.)

Finally, note that forms support both *GotFocus* and *LostFocus* events, but these events are raised only when the form doesn't contain any control that can receive the input focus, either because all of the controls are invisible or the *TabStop* property for each of them is set to False.

The *KeyPress*, *KeyDown*, and *KeyUp* Events

These events fire whenever the end user presses a key while a control has the input focus. The exact sequence is as follows: *KeyDown* (the users presses the key), *KeyPress* (Visual Basic translates the key into an ANSI numeric code), and *KeyUp* (the user releases the key). Only keys that correspond to control keys (Ctrl+*x*, BackSpace, Enter, and Escape) and printable characters activate the *KeyPress* event. For all other keys—including arrow keys, function keys, Alt+*x* key combinations, and so on—this event doesn't fire and only the *KeyDown* and *KeyUp* events are raised.

The *KeyPress* event is the simplest of the three. It's passed the ANSI code of the key that has been pressed by the user, so you often need to convert it to a string using the *Chr$()* function:

```
Private Text1_KeyPress(KeyAscii As Integer)
    MsgBox "User pressed " & Chr$(KeyAscii)
End Sub
```

If you modify the *KeyAscii* parameter, your changes affect how the program interprets the key. You can also "eat" a key by setting this parameter to 0, as shown in the code on the following page.

```
Private Sub Text1_KeyPress(KeyAscii As Integer)
    ' Convert all keys to uppercase, and reject blanks.
    KeyAscii = Asc(UCase$(Chr$(KeyAscii)
    If KeyAscii = Asc(" ") Then KeyAscii = 0
End Sub
```

The *KeyDown* and *KeyUp* events receive two parameters, *KeyCode* and *Shift*. The former is the code of the pressed key, the latter is an Integer value that reports the state of the Ctrl, Shift, and Alt keys; because this value is bit-coded, you have to use the AND operator to extract the relevant information:

```
Private Sub Text1_KeyDown(KeyCode As Integer, Shift As Integer)
    If Shift And vbShiftMask Then
        ' Shift key pressed
    End If
    If Shift And vbCtrlMask Then
        ' Ctrl key pressed
    End If
    If Shift And vbAltMask Then
        ' Alt key pressed
    End If
    ' ...
End Sub
```

The *KeyCode* parameter tells which physical key has been pressed, and it's therefore different from the *KeyAscii* parameter received by the *KeyPress* event. You usually test this value using a symbolic constant, as in the following code:

```
Private Sub Text1_KeyDown(KeyCode As Integer, Shift As Integer)
    ' If user presses Ctrl+F2, replace the contents
    ' of the control with the current date.
    If KeyCode = vbKeyF2 And Shift = vbCtrlMask Then
        Text1.Text = Date$
    End If
End Sub
```

In contrast to what you can do with the *KeyPress* event, you can't alter the program's behavior if you assign a different value to the *KeyCode* parameter.

You should note that *KeyPress*, *KeyDown*, and *KeyUp* events might pose special problems during the debugging phase. In fact, if you place a breakpoint inside a *KeyDown* event procedure, the target control will never receive a notification that a key has been pressed and the *KeyPress* and *KeyUp* events will never fire. Similarly, if you enter break mode when Visual Basic is executing the *KeyPress* event procedure, the target control will receive the key but the *KeyUp* event will never fire.

TIP While you can't edit the *KeyCode* parameter and let the modified value affect the program, here's a trick that, in most cases, lets you discard an unwanted key in TextBox controls:

```
Private Sub Text1_KeyDown(KeyCode As Integer, Shift As Integer)
    If KeyCode = vbKeyDelete Then
        ' Make the control read-only; this actually
        ' discards the key.
        Text1.Locked = True
    End If
End Sub

Private Sub Text1_KeyUp(KeyCode As Integer, Shift As Integer)
    ' Restore normal operation.
    Text1.Locked = False
End Sub
```

The *KeyDown*, *KeyPress*, and *KeyUp* events are received only by the control that has the input focus when the key is pressed. This circumstance, however, makes it difficult to create *form-level key handlers,* that is, code routines that monitor keys pressed in any control on the form. For example, suppose that you want to offer your users the ability to clear the current field by pressing the F7 key. You don't want to write the same piece of code in the *KeyDown* event procedure for each and every control on your form, and fortunately you don't have to. In fact, you only have to set the form's *KeyPreview* property to True (either at design time or at run time, in the *Form_Load* procedure, for example) and then write this code:

```
Private Sub Form_KeyDown(KeyCode As Integer, Shift As Integer)
    If KeyCode = vbKeyF7 Then
        ' An error handler is necessary because we can't be sure
        ' that the active control actually supports the Text
        ' property.
        On Error Resume Next
        ActiveControl.Text = ""
    End If
End Sub
```

If the form's *KeyPreview* property is set to True, the Form object receives all keyboard-related events before they're sent to the control that currently has the input focus. Use the form's *ActiveControl* property if you need to act on the control with the input focus, as in the previous code snippet.

The *MouseDown, MouseUp,* and *MouseMove* Events

These events fire when the mouse is clicked, released, or moved on a control, respectively. All of them receive the same set of parameters: the state of mouse buttons, the state of Shift/Ctrl/Alt keys, and the *x*- and *y*-coordinates of the mouse cursor. The coordinates are always relative to the upper left corner of the control or the form. Following Figure 2-6 is a code sample that displays the status and position of the mouse on a Label control and creates a log in the Immediate window. You can see the results of running this code in Figure 2-6.

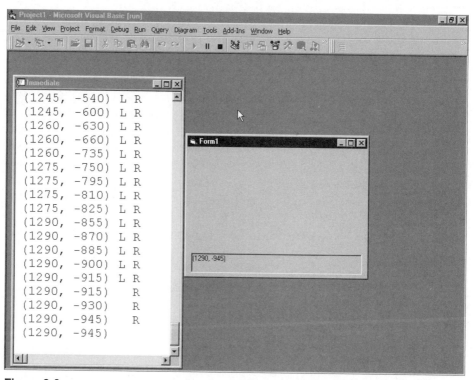

Figure 2-6. *Monitor mouse state using the* MouseDown, MouseMove, *and* MouseUp *events. Note the negative* y *value when the cursor is outside the form's client area.*

```
Private Sub Form_MouseDown(Button As Integer, _
    Shift As Integer, X As Single, Y As Single)
    ShowMouseState Button, Shift, X, Y
End Sub

Private Sub Form_MouseMove(Button As Integer, _
    Shift As Integer, X As Single, Y As Single)
    ShowMouseState Button, Shift, X, Y
End Sub
```

```
Private Sub Form_MouseUp(Button As Integer, _
    Shift As Integer, X As Single, Y As Single)
    ShowMouseState Button, Shift, X, Y
End Sub

Private Sub ShowMouseState (Button As Integer, _
    Shift As Integer, X As Single, Y As Single)
    Dim descr As String
    descr = Space$(20)
    If Button And vbLeftButton Then Mid$(descr, 1, 1) = "L"
    If Button And vbRightButton Then Mid$(descr, 3, 1) = "R"
    If Button And vbMiddleButton Then Mid$(descr, 2, 1) = "M"
    If Shift And vbShiftMask Then Mid$(descr, 5, 5) = "Shift"
    If Shift And vbCtrlMask Then Mid$(descr, 11, 4) = "Ctrl"
    If Shift And vbAltMask Then Mid$(descr, 16, 3) = "Alt"
    descr = "(" & X & ", " & Y & ") " & descr
    Label1.Caption = descr
    Debug.Print descr
End Sub
```

While writing code for mouse events, you should be aware of a few implementation details as well as some pitfalls in using these events. Keep in mind the following points:

■   The *x* and *y* values are relative to the *client area* of the form or the control, not to its external border; for a form object, the coordinates (0,0) correspond to the pixel in the upper left corner below the title bar or the menu bar (if there is one). When you move the mouse cursor outside the form area, the values of coordinates might become negative or exceed the height and width of the client area.

■   When you press a mouse button over a form or a control and then move the mouse outside its client area while keeping the button pressed, the original control continues to receive mouse events. In this case, the mouse is said to be *captured* by the control: the capture state terminates only when you release the mouse button. All the *MouseMove* and *MouseUp* events fired in the meantime might receive negative values for the *x* and *y* parameters or values that exceed the object's width or height, respectively.

■   *MouseDown* and *MouseUp* events are raised any time the user presses or releases a button. For example, if the user presses the left button and then the right button (without releasing the left button), the control receives two *MouseDown* events and eventually two *MouseUp* events.

- The *Button* parameter passed to *MouseDown* and *MouseUp* events reports which button has just been pressed and released, respectively. Conversely, the *MouseMove* event receives the current state of all (two or three) mouse buttons.

- When the user releases the only button being pressed, Visual Basic fires a *MouseUp* event and then a *MouseMove* event, even if the mouse hasn't moved. This detail is what makes the previous code example work correctly after a button release: The current status is updated by the extra *MouseMove* event, not by the *MouseUp* event, as you probably expected. Note, however, that this additional *MouseMove* event doesn't fire when you press two buttons and then release only one of them.

It's interesting to see how *MouseDown*, *MouseUp*, and *MouseMove* events relate to *Click* and *DblClick* events:

- A *Click* event occurs after a *MouseDown ... MouseUp* sequence and before the extra *MouseMove* event.

- When the user double-clicks on a control, the complete event sequence is as follows: *MouseDown*, *MouseUp*, *Click*, *MouseMove*, *DblClick*, *MouseUp*, *MouseMove*. Note that the second *MouseDown* event isn't generated.

- If the control is clicked and then the mouse is moved outside its client area, the *Click* event is never raised. However, if you double-click a control and then you move the mouse outside its client area, the complete event sequence occurs. This behavior reflects how controls work under Windows and shouldn't be considered a bug.

THE FORM OBJECT

After this long introductory description of properties, methods, and events that are common to most Visual Basic objects, it's time to see the particular features of all of them individually. The most important visible object is undoubtedly the Form object because you can't display any control without a parent Form. Conversely, you can write some moderately useful applications using only forms that have no controls on them. In this section, I'll show a number of examples that are centered on forms' singular features.

You create a new form at design time using the Add Form command from the Project menu or by clicking on the corresponding icon on the standard toolbar. You can create forms from scratch, or you can take advantage of the many form templates provided by Visual Basic 6. If you don't see the dialog box shown in Figure 2-7, invoke the Options command from the Tools menu, click the Environment tab, and select the topmost check box on the right.

Feel free to create new form templates when you need them. A form template doesn't necessarily have to be a complex form with many controls on it. Even an empty form with a group of properties carefully set can save you some precious time. For example, see the Dialog Form template provided by Visual Basic. To produce your custom form templates, you just have to create a form, add any necessary controls and code, and then save it in the \Template\Forms directory. (The complete path of Visual Basic's template directory can be read and modified in the Environment tab of the Options dialog box.)

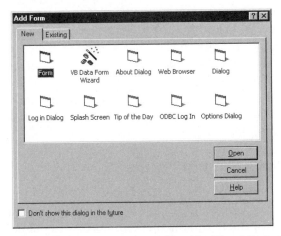

Figure 2-7. *Form templates offered by Visual Basic 6.*

Basic Form Properties

After creating a form and resizing it to meet your requirements, you'll probably want to set a few key properties. *BorderStyle* is one of the properties that largely affects the form's behavior. Its default value is 2-Sizable, which creates a resizable window. To create a nonresizable form, you should set it to 1-Fixed Single or 3-Fixed Dialog: the only difference between the two settings is that the latter can't show Minimize and Maximize buttons. If you're creating a floating, toolboxlike form, you should use the values 4-Fixed Toolwindow or 5-Sizable Toolwindow. Theoretically, you can also use the value 0-None to exclude any type of border and caption, but you'll rarely find a use for such borderless forms.

Next you must decide what should appear on the title bar. Apart from assigning a suitable string to the form's *Caption* property, you should also decide whether you want the form to support a system menu and a Close button (*ControlBox* property, default is True) and a Minimize and a Maximize button (*MinButton* and

MaxButton property, respectively). Selecting the right values for these properties is important because you can't change them at run time through code. If you want the form to start in maximized state, you can set the *WindowState* property to 2-Maximized.

> **TIP** To create a captionless resizable window, you must set the *ControlBox*, *MinButton*, and *MaxButton* properties to False and the *Caption* property to an empty string. If you assign a non-empty string to the *Caption* property at run time, Visual Basic creates the form's title bar on the fly. Assigning it an empty string at run time makes the title bar disappear again. You can't move a captionless form using the mouse as you normally do with other types of windows.

Visual Basic 5 added three important form properties, which are also present in Visual Basic 6. You can have the form appear in the center of the screen by setting its *StartupPosition* property to the value 2-Center Screen. And you can make your window unmovable by setting the *Moveable* property to False. You can set these properties only at design time. The third new property is *ShowInTaskbar*; if you set this property to False, the form isn't shown in the Windows taskbar. Captionless forms appear in the taskbar as "blank" forms, so you might want to set the *ShowInTaskbar* property to False for such forms.

Fine-Tuning the Performance of Forms

A few form properties noticeably affect performance. First and foremost, the *AutoRedraw* property dictates whether the form is backed up by a persistent bitmap so that when it's covered by another form and then uncovered, Visual Basic can quickly restore its contents from the internal bitmap. *AutoRedraw*'s default value is False: setting it to True speeds up refresh operations but also causes a lot of memory to be allocated for the persistent bitmap. To give you an idea of what this means in practice, for a system with 1024-by-768 screen resolution and 256 colors, a persistent bitmap for a resizable form takes 768 KB. On an 800-by-600 pixel, true-color system, the persistent bitmap takes 1406 KB. If you have more forms running at the same time, you can clearly see that you shouldn't set the *AutoRedraw* property to True, at least not for all the forms. *AutoRedraw* affects performance in another way: Each time you perform a graphic method (including printing text and drawing figures), Visual Basic creates the output on the hidden persistent bitmap and then copies the bitmap as a whole on the visible area of the form. Needless to say, this is slower than creating the output directly on the form's surface.

> **TIP** If *AutoRedraw* is set to True, Visual Basic creates a persistent bitmap as large as the largest possible size for the form, which means the entire screen for resizable windows. Therefore, you can limit the memory overhead caused by the persistent bitmap if you create smaller forms and set their *BorderStyle* property to 1-Fixed Single or 3-Fixed Dialog.

The *ClipControls* property also affects performance. If you execute many graphic methods—such as Line, Circle, Point, and Print—you should set this property to False because all your graphic methods are going to execute about twice as fast. When you set this property to False, Visual Basic doesn't have to create a *clipping region*. However, if your graphic methods do overlap controls on the form, you're going to experience the unpleasant effect shown in Figure 2-8, so be very careful. (Compare this figure with Figure 2-9, which shows the same application with the more appropriate setting of True for the *ClipControls* property.) If you don't execute graphic methods, you might leave it set to True (the default value) because it won't slow down the application.

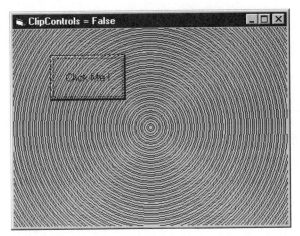

Figure 2-8. *Nasty effects of the* ClipControls *setting when graphic methods overlap existing controls.*

Figure 2-9. *Running the application shown in Figure 2-8 with the more appropriate setting for the* ClipControls *property.*

The *HasDC* property is new to Visual Basic 6. The default value for this property is True, which causes Visual Basic to create a permanent device context for this form, and this device context exists as long as the form itself is loaded in memory. (A *device context* is a structure used by Windows for drawing on a window's surface.) If you set this property to False, Visual Basic creates a device context for the form only when strictly needed and discards it as soon as it's not useful anymore. This setting reduces the application's requirements in terms of system resources and can therefore improve its performance on less powerful machines. On the other hand, it adds a little overhead whenever Visual Basic creates and destroys the temporary device context. This happens when Visual Basic fires an event in the program's code.

> **CAUTION**   You can set the *HasDC* property to False and still run any existing Visual Basic application without any problem. If, however, you use advanced graphic techniques that bypass Visual Basic and write directly onto the form's device context, you shouldn't cache the form's *hDC* property in a module-level or a global variable, because Visual Basic can destroy and re-create the form's device context between events. Instead, query the *hDC* property at the beginning of each event procedure.

A Form's Life Cycle

To understand how Form objects really work, the best approach is having a look at the sequence of events that they raise. This sequence is shown in the illustration on the facing page. I'll describe each event in turn.

The *Initialize* event

The first event in the life of any form is the *Initialize* event. This event fires as soon as you reference the form's name in your code, even before Visual Basic creates the actual window and the controls on its surface. You usually write code in this event to correctly initialize the form's variables:

```
Public CustomerName As String
Public NewCustomer As Boolean

Private Sub Form_Initialize()
    CustomerName = ""        ' This isn't really needed.
    NewCustomer = True       ' This is necessary.
End Sub
```

When a form is initialized, all its module-level variables (*CustomerName* and *NewCustomer*, in the preceding example) are assigned their default values. So it isn't strictly necessary to assign a value to a variable if the value is 0 or an empty string. In the code above, for example, there's no need for the assignment to the *CustomerName* variable, but you might want to leave it there for better readability.

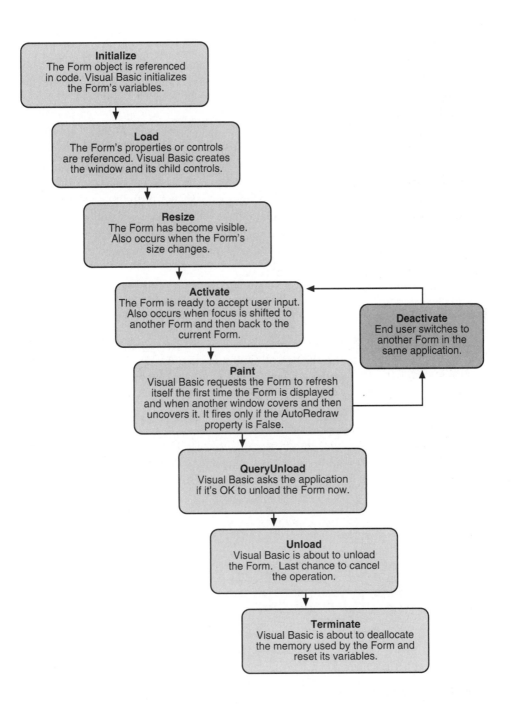

The *Load* event

What happens after the *Initialize* event depends on how you referenced the form in your code. If you referenced only one of its public variables (or, more correctly, its *Public* properties), as in the following line of code,

```
frmCustomer.CustomerName = "John Smith"
```

nothing else happens and execution flow goes back to the caller. Your code is now able to set the *CustomerName* variable/property to the new value because in the meantime Visual Basic has created a new instance of the *frmCustomer* object. On the other hand, if your code had referenced a form's own property or a control on the form itself, Visual Basic can't complete the operation until it actually creates the window and its child controls. When this step is completed, a *Load* event is fired:

```
Private Sub Form_Load()
    ' You can initialize child controls.
    txtName.Text = CustomerName
    If NewCustomer Then chkNewCustomer.Value = vbChecked
End Sub
```

At this point, the form isn't visible yet. This implies that if you execute graphic commands in this event procedure—including a Print command, which is considered a graphic command in Visual Basic—you won't see anything. Likewise, while you can freely read and modify most controls' properties, you should avoid any operation that can't be performed on invisible controls. For example, you can't invoke a *SetFocus* method to move the focus on a particular control.

Loading a form doesn't necessarily mean that the form is going to become visible. A form becomes visible only if you invoke its *Show* method or if the form is the application's startup form. You can decide to load a form and keep it hidden until you set some of its properties, as follows:

```
' The Load method is optional: Visual Basic loads the form
' when you reference the form or one of its controls.
Load frmCustomer
' Directly assign a control's property.
' (Not recommended, but this is just an example.)
frmCustomer.txtNotes.Text = gloCustomerNotes
frmCustomer.Show
```

Directly referencing a form's control from outside the form itself, as the previous code example does, is considered a bad programming technique. I will show you how to correctly initialize control properties in Chapter 9.

The *Resize* event

One instant before the form becomes visible, Visual Basic fires a *Resize* event. You usually take advantage of this event to rearrange the controls on the form so that they fit the available space in a nice layout. For example, you might want the txtCustomer control to extend to the right border and the multiline txtNotes control to extend to both the right and the bottom border:

```
Private Sub Form_Resize()
    txtCustomer.Width = ScaleWidth - txtCustomer.Left
    txtNotes.Width = ScaleWidth - txtNotes.Left
    txtNotes.Height = ScaleHeight - txtNotes.Top
End Sub
```

The *Resize* event also fires when the user resizes the form manually and when you programmatically alter the form's size.

The *Activate* event

Soon after the first *Resize* event comes the *Activate* event. This event also fires whenever the form becomes the active form in the current application but not if it loses and then regains the focus because the user switched to another application. The *Activate* event is most useful when you need to update the form's contents with data that might have been modified in another form. When the focus returns to the current form, you refresh its fields:

```
Private Sub Form_Activate()
    ' Refresh displayed information from global variables.
    txtTotalOrders.Text = gloTotalOrders
    ...
End Sub
```

The *Paint* event

Another event might fire before the form becomes fully functional—the *Paint* event. This event doesn't fire if you set the form's *AutoRedraw* property to True. In a *Paint* event procedure, you're expected to redraw the form's contents using graphic methods, such as *Print, Line, Circle, Point, Cls*, and so on. Here's an example that draws a colorful circular target:

```
Private Sub Form_Paint()
    Dim r As Single, initR As Single
    Dim x As Single, y As Single, qbc As Integer

    ' Start with a clean surface.
    Cls
    ' The center of all circles
    x = ScaleWidth / 2: y = ScaleHeight / 2
    ' Initial radius is the lower of the two values.
    If x < y Then initR = x Else initR = y
    FillStyle = vbFSSolid            ' Circles are filled.
    ' Draw circles, from the outside in.
```

(continued)

```
        For r = initR To 1 Step -(initR / 16)
            ' Use a different color for each circle.
            FillColor = QBColor(qbc)
            qbc = qbc + 1
            Circle (x, y), r
        Next
        ' Restore regular filling style.
        FillStyle = vbFSTransparent
End Sub
```

The *Paint* event procedure is executed whenever the form needs to be re-freshed—for example, when the user closes or moves away a window that partially or totally covered the form. The *Paint* event also fires when the user resizes the form and uncovers new areas. But it does *not* fire if the user shrinks the form. To complete the example above, you may want to manually force a *Paint* event from within the *Resize* event so that concentric circles are always in the center of the form:

```
Private Sub Form_Resize()
    Refresh
End Sub
```

> **CAUTION**   You might be tempted to force a *Paint* event by manually calling the *Form_Paint* procedure. Don't do that! The correct and most efficient way to repaint a window is to execute its *Refresh* method and let Visual Basic decide the most appropriate moment to do that. Moreover, if you replace the *Refresh* method with a direct call to the *Form_Paint* procedure, in some cases the result is that the *Paint* event procedure is executed twice!

After the very first *Paint* event—or immediately after the *Activate* event, if the *AutoRedraw* property is set to True—the form is finally ready to accept user input. If the form doesn't contain any controls or if none of its controls can receive the input focus, the form itself receives a *GotFocus* event. You will rarely write code in a form's *GotFocus* event, though, because you can always use the *Activate* event instead.

The *Deactivate* event

As I mentioned previously, when you switch to another form in your application, the form receives a *Deactivate* event and another *Activate* event when it regains the input focus. The same sequence occurs if you temporarily make a form invisible by setting its *Visible* property to False or by invoking its *Hide* method.

The *QueryUnload* event

When the form is about to be unloaded, the form object receives a *QueryUnload* event. You can learn why a form is unloading by examining the *UnloadMode* parameter. I have created this code skeleton, which I reuse in my applications as necessary:

```
Private Sub Form_QueryUnload(Cancel As Integer, _
    UnloadMode As Integer)
    Select Case UnloadMode
        Case vbFormControlMenu    ' = 0
            ' Form is being closed by user.
        Case vbFormCode           ' = 1
            ' Form is being closed by code.
        Case vbAppWindows         ' = 2
            ' The current Windows session is ending.
        Case vbAppTaskManager     ' = 3
            ' Task Manager is closing this application.
        Case vbFormMDIForm        ' = 4
            ' MDI parent is closing this form.
        Case vbFormOwner          ' = 5
            ' The owner form is closing.
    End Select
End Sub
```

You can refuse to unload by setting the *Cancel* parameter to True, as in the following code:

```
Private Sub Form_QueryUnload(Cancel As Integer, _
    UnloadMode As Integer)
    ' Don't let the user close this form.
    Select Case UnloadMode
        Case vbFormControlMenu, vbAppTaskManager
            Cancel = True
    End Select
End Sub
```

The *Unload* event

If you don't cancel the unload operation, Visual Basic eventually raises the *Unload* event and gives you a last chance to prevent the closure of the form. In most cases, you take this opportunity to alert the user that data needs to be saved:

```
' This is a module-level variable.
Dim Saved As Boolean

Private Sub Form_Unload(Cancel As Integer)
    If Not Saved Then
        MsgBox "Please save data first!"
        Cancel = True
    End If
End Sub
```

Unless you canceled the request, Visual Basic destroys all the controls and then unloads the form and releases all the Windows resources allocated at load time when the *Unload* event procedure exits. Depending on how you invoked the form, it might also fire the form's *Terminate* event, which is where you put your clean-up code, close your files, and so on. The reasons why this event might fire (or not) are explained in Chapter 9.

> **CAUTION**   When the *Terminate* event is fired, the form object is already gone, so you shouldn't reference it or its controls in code. If you accidentally do that, no error is raised. Instead, Visual Basic creates another, new instance of the form object, which silently remains hidden in memory, unnecessarily consuming a lot of system resources.

The Controls Collection

Forms expose a special property, the Controls collection, which contains all the controls that are currently loaded on the form itself. This collection lets you streamline the code in your form modules often and is the key to some programming techniques that would be otherwise impossible. For example, see how simple it is to clear all the TextBox and ComboBox controls in the form with just four lines of code:

```
On Error Resume Next
For i = 0 To Controls.Count - 1
    Controls(i).Text = ""
Next
```

Error handling is necessary here because you must account for all the controls on the form that don't support the *Text* property. For example, the Controls collection also includes all the menu items on a form, and menu items don't have a *Text* property. So, you must account for these cases when you iterate over the collection. Here's an alternative way to loop on all the controls in the collection using the generic Control object and a *For Each...Next* statement:

```
Dim ctrl As Control
On Error Resume Next
For Each ctrl In Controls
    ctrl.Text = ""
Next
```

Both preceding code snippets work with any number of controls on the form, and they also work if you cut and paste them in another form module. The beauty of the Controls collection is that it makes it possible to create such generic routines, which couldn't be written in any other way. Later in this book, you'll see many other programming techniques based on the Controls collection.

The Screen Object

Visual Basic forms live on your computer screen. Even if you plan to use only a portion of the screen estate for your application, you need in many cases to learn more about what's around you. To this end, Visual Basic provides you with a Screen object, a global object that corresponds to the visible desktop.

A form's *Left*, *Top*, *Width*, and *Height* properties are expressed in *twips*. Twips are measurement units that can be used for both screen and printer devices. On the printer, 1 inch corresponds to 1,440 twips; on the screen, it depends on the monitor's size and the video card's current resolution. You can find the current size of the screen, in twips, through the *Width* and *Height* properties of the Screen object. You can then use the values of these properties; for example, you can move the current form to the bottom right corner of your monitor using this line of code:

```
Move Screen.Width - Width, Screen.Height - Height
```

Although you can't have the Screen object's properties returned in a unit other than twips, you can easily convert these values into pixels using the Screen object's *TwipsPerPixelX* and *TwipsPerPixelY* properties:

```
' Evaluate the screen width and height in pixels.
scrWidth = Screen.Width / Screen.TwipsPerPixelX
scrHeight = Screen.Height / Screen.TwipsPerPixelY

' Shrink the current form of 10 pixels along the
' x-axis and 20 pixels along the y-axis.
Move Left, Top, Width - 10 * Screen.TwipPerPixelX, _
    Height - 20 * Screen.TwipsPerPixelY
```

The Screen object also lets you enumerate all the character fonts that are available for the screen through its *Font* and *FontCount* properties:

```
' Load the names of all the screen's fonts in a list box.
Dim i As Integer
For i = 0 To Screen.FontCount - 1
    lstFonts.AddItem Screen.Fonts(i)
Next
```

The only two properties of the Screen object that can be written to are *Mouse-Pointer* and *MouseIcon*. (I described these properties earlier in this chapter.) You can modify the mouse pointer using the following statement:

```
Screen.MousePointer = vbHourglass
```

A value assigned to this property actually affects only the current application: If you move the mouse cursor to the desktop or over a window belonging to another application, the original mouse cursor is restored. In this sense, therefore, you aren't actually dealing with a screen property. This concept also applies to the remaining Screen properties, *ActiveForm* and *ActiveControl*. *ActiveForm* is a read-only property that returns a reference to the active form in the current application; *ActiveControl* returns a reference to the control that has the input focus on the active form. You often use these properties together:

```
' If the current form is frmCustomer, clear the control that has
' the focus.
' On Error is necessary because you can't be sure that it supports
' the Text property, or even that there actually *is* an active
' control.
On Error Resume Next
If Screen.ActiveForm.Name = "frmCustomer" Then
    Screen.ActiveControl.Text = ""
End If
```

A form can be the active form without even having the input focus. If you have switched to another application, the Screen object continues to return a reference to the last form that was current in your application as the active form. Always keep in mind that the Screen object can't see beyond the current application's boundaries. As far as it's concerned, the current application is the only application running on the system. This is a sort of axiom in Win32 programming: No application should know anything about, or affect in any way, other applications running on the system.

Printing Text

In most Visual Basic applications, you don't display text directly on a form's surface. Instead, you usually make use of Label controls or print your messages inside PictureBox controls. But understanding how you can display text in a form can help you in many situations because it reveals how Visual Basic deals with text in general. Moreover, anything I say here about a form's graphic commands and properties also applies to PictureBox controls.

The most important graphic method for showing text is the *Print* method. This command has been part of the Basic language since its early incarnations and has survived for all these years without any relevant modification, until it found its way into Visual Basic. Because old MS-DOS programs written in Basic heavily relied on this command for all their user interfaces, it was essential for Visual Basic to support it. Since modern Visual Basic programming doesn't rely on this command anymore, however, I'll cover only its basic features.

> **NOTE**   Don't look for the *Print* method in the Object Browser because you won't find it. The hybrid nature of this command and its contorted syntax—just think of the many separators you can use in a *Print* statement, including commas, semicolons, and *Tab()* functions—prevented Microsoft engineers from including it there. Instead, the *Print* method is directly implemented in the language at run time, at the expense of a more coherent and complete object-oriented implementation of the language as a whole.

You often use the *Print* method for a quick-and-dirty output on the form's client area. For example, you can show the form's current size and position with this simple code:

```
Private Sub Form_Resize()
    Cls                    ' Resets the printing position to (0,0)
    Print "Left = " & Left & vbTab & "Top = " & Top
    Print "Width = " & Width & vbTab & "Height = " & Height
End Sub
```

> **TIP** You can use semicolons instead of the & operator and commas instead of the vbTab constant. But if you purposely stick to a standard syntax and stay clear of special features of the *Print* method, you can easily recycle your arguments and pass them to your custom methods or assign them to the *Caption* property of a Label. This can save you some time later, when you want to turn a quick-and-dirty prototype into a regular application.

The output from the *Print* method is affected by the current values of the *Font* and *ForeColor* properties, which I described earlier in this chapter. By default, the *BackColor* property doesn't affect the *Print* command because the text is usually printed as if it had a transparent background. Most of the time, this situation doesn't cause any problems because you often print over a clean form's surface, and it accounts for better performance because only the text's pixels must be transferred, not the background color. But if you want to print a message and at the same time you want to erase a previous message in the same position, you can do it by setting the *FontTransparent* property to False. Otherwise, you'll end up with one message on top of another, making both unreadable.

Normally, each Print command resets the *x*-coordinate of the current graphic position to 0 and advances the *y*-coordinate so that the next string is displayed immediately below the previous one. You can learn where the next Print command will display its output by querying the form's *CurrentX* and *CurrentY* properties. Under normal conditions, the point (0,0) represents the upper left corner in the client area (that is, the portion of the form inside its border and below its title bar). The *x*-coordinates increase from left to right, and the *y*-coordinates increase when you go from top to bottom. You can assign a new value to these properties to print anywhere on your form:

```
' Show a message centered on the form (more or less).
CurrentX = ScaleWidth / 2
CurrentY = ScaleHeight / 2
Print "I'm here!"
```

This code, however, doesn't really center the message on the form because only the initial printing point is centered while the rest of the string runs toward the right border. To precisely center a message on a screen, you must first determine how wide and tall it is, which you do using the form's *TextHeight* and *TextWidth* methods:

```
msg = "I'm here, in the center of the form."
CurrentX = (ScaleWidth - TextWidth(msg)) / 2
CurrentY = (ScaleHeight - TextHeight(msg)) / 2
Print msg
```

You often use the *TextWidth* and *TextHeight* methods to see whether a message can fit within a given area. This strategy is especially useful when you print to a form because the *Print* method doesn't support automatic wrapping for longer lines. To see how you can remedy this deficiency, add the following code to a blank form and then run the program and resize the form at will. Figure 2-10 illustrates how form resizing works.

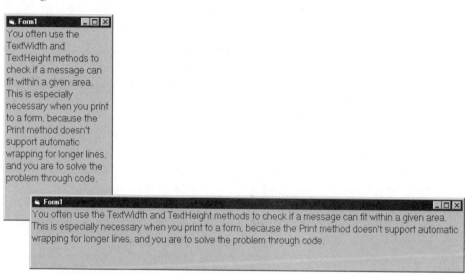

Figure 2-10. *Automatic wrapping for longer lines of text.*

```
' A routine that formats Print output
Private Sub Form_Paint()
    Dim msg As String, pos As Long, spacePos As Long
    msg = "You often use the TextWidth and TextHeight methods" _
        & " to check if a message can fit within a given area. " _
        & vbCrLf & " This is especially necessary when you" _
        & " print to a form, because the Print method doesn't" _
        & " support automatic wrapping for long lines, and you" _
        & " need to solve the problem through code."

    Cls
    Do While pos < Len(msg)
        pos = pos + 1
```

```
        If Mid$(msg, pos, 2) = vbCrLf Then
            ' A CR-LF pair, print the string so far and reset variables.
            Print Left$(msg, pos - 1)
            msg = LTrim$(Mid$(msg, pos + 2))
            pos = 0: spacePos = 0
        ElseIf Mid$(msg, pos, 1) = " " Then
            ' A space, remember its position for later.
            spacePos = pos
        End If

        ' Check the message width so far.
        If TextWidth(Left$(msg, pos)) > ScaleWidth Then
            ' The message is too long, so let's split it.
            ' If we just parsed a space, split it there.
            If spacePos Then pos = spacePos
            ' Print the message up to the split point.
            Print Left$(msg, pos - 1)
            ' Discard printed characters, and reset variables.
            msg = LTrim$(Mid$(msg, pos))
            pos = 0: spacePos = 0
        End If
    Loop
    ' Print residual characters, if any.
    If Len(msg) Then Print msg
End Sub

Private Sub Form_Resize()
    Refresh
End Sub
```

The preceding code works with any font you're using. As an exercise, you can build a general routine that accepts any string and any form reference so that you can easily reuse it in your applications.

Another problem that you might need to solve is how to determine the most appropriate font size for a message so that it fits in a given area. Because you can't be sure which sizes are supported by the current font, you usually find the best font size using a *For...Next* loop. The following simple program creates a digital clock, which you can enlarge and shrink as you like. The actual clock update is performed by a hidden Timer control:

```
Private Sub Form_Resize()
    Dim msg As String, size As Integer
    msg = Time$
    For size = 200 To 8 Step -2
        Font.Size = size
        If TextWidth(msg) <= ScaleWidth And _
```

(continued)

```
                    TextHeight(msg) <= ScaleHeight Then
                        ' We've found a font size that is OK.
                        Exit For
                    End If
            Next
            ' Enable the timer.
            Timer1.Enabled = True
            Timer1.Interval = 1000
    End Sub

    Private Sub Timer1_Timer()
        ' Just print the current time using current font settings.
        Cls
        Print Time$
    End Sub
```

Graphic Methods

Visual Basic supplies developers with several graphic methods. You can draw individual points and lines as well as more complex geometric shapes, such as rectangles, circles, and ellipses. You have complete control over line color, width, and style, and you can even fill your shapes with a solid color or a pattern.

Undoubtedly, the simplest graphic method to use is *Cls*. It clears the form's surface, fills it with the background color defined by the *BackColor* property, and then moves the current graphic position to the (0,0) coordinates. If you assign a new value to the *BackColor* property, Visual Basic clears the background on its own so that you never need to issue a *Cls* method yourself after you change the form's background color.

Drawing points

A more useful method is *PSet*, which modifies the color of a single pixel on the form surface. In its basic syntax, you simply need to specify the x and y coordinates. A third, optional argument lets you specify the color of the pixel, if different from the *ForeColor* value:

```
ForeColor = vbRed
PSet (0, 0)                  ' A red pixel
PSet (10, 0), vbCyan         ' A cyan pixel to its right
```

Like many other graphic methods, *PSet* supports relative positioning using the *Step* keyword; when you use this keyword, the two values within brackets are treated as offsets from the current graphic point (the position on screen that *CurrentX* and *CurrentY* currently point to). The point you draw with the *PSet* method becomes the current graphic position:

```
' Set a starting position.
CurrentX = 1000: CurrentY = 500
```

```
' Draw 10 points aligned horizontally.
For i = 1 To 10
    PSet Step (8, 0)
Next
```

The output from the *PSet* method is also affected by another form's property, *DrawWidth*. You can set this property to a value greater than 1 (the default) to draw larger points. Note that while all graphic measures are expressed in twips, this value is in pixels. When you use a value greater than 1, the coordinates passed to the *PSet* method are considered to be the center of the thicker point (which is actually a small circle). Try these few lines of code for a colorful effect:

```
For i = 1 To 1000
    ' Set a random point width.
    DrawWidth = Rnd * 10 + 1
    ' Draw a point at random coordinates and with random color.
    PSet (Rnd * ScaleWidth, Rnd * ScaleHeight), _
        RGB(Rnd * 255, Rnd * 255, Rnd * 255)
Next
' Be polite: restore the default value.
DrawWidth = 1
```

The *PSet* method's counterpart is the *Point* method, which returns the RGB color value of a given pixel. To see this method in action, create a form with a Label1 control on it, draw some graphics on it (the previous code snippet would be perfect), and add the following routine:

```
Private Sub Form_MouseMove (Button As Integer, _
    Shift As Integer, X As Single, Y As Single)
    Label1.Caption = "(" & X & "," & Y & ") = " _
        & Hex$(Point(X, Y))
End Sub
```

Run the program, and move the mouse cursor over the colored spots to display their coordinates and color values.

Drawing lines and rectangles

The next graphic method that you might use in your Visual Basic application is the *Line* method. It's a powerful command, and its syntax variants let you draw straight lines, empty rectangles, and rectangles filled with solid colors. To draw a straight line, you need only to provide the coordinates of starting and ending points, plus an optional color value. (If you omit a color value, the current *ForeColor* value is used):

```
' Draw a thick diagonal red "X" across the form.
' The Line method is affected by the current DrawWidth setting.
DrawWidth = 5
Line (0, 0) - (ScaleWidth, ScaleHeight), vbRed
Line (ScaleWidth, 0) - (0, ScaleHeight), vbRed
```

Like the *PSet* method, the *Line* method supports the *Step* keyword to specify relative positioning. The *Step* keyword can be placed in front of either pair of coordinates, so you can freely mix absolute and relative positioning. If you omit the first argument, the line is drawn from the current graphic position:

```
' Draw a triangle.
Line (1000, 2000)- Step (1000, 0)   ' Horizontal line
Line -Step (0, 1000)                ' Vertical line
Line -(1000, 2000)                  ' Close the triangle.
```

The output of the *Line* method is affected by another form's property, *DrawStyle*. The default value for this property is 0 (*vbSolid*), but you can also draw dotted lines in a variety of styles, as you can see in Figure 2-11. Table 2-2 summarizes these styles.

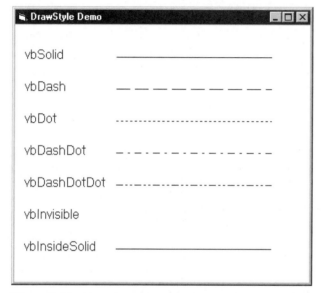

Figure 2-11. *The effects of various settings of the* DrawStyle *property.*

Constant	Value	Description
vbSolid	0	Solid (default value)
vbDash	1	Dashed line
vbDot	2	Dotted line
vbDashDot	3	Line with alternating dashes and dots
vbDashDotDot	4	Line with alternating dashes and double dots
vbInvisible	5	Invisible line
vbInsideSolid	6	Inside solid

Table 2-2. *Constants for the* DrawStyle *property.*

Note that the *DrawStyle* property affects the graphic output only if *DrawWidth* is set to 1 pixel; in all other cases, the *DrawStyle* property is ignored and the line is always drawn in solid mode. Adding *B* as a fourth argument to the *Line* method allows you to draw rectangles; in this case, the two points are the coordinates of any two opposite corners:

```
' A blue rectangle, 2000 twips wide and 1000 twips tall
Line (500, 500)- Step (2000, 1000), vbBlue, B
```

Rectangles drawn in this way are affected by the current settings of the *DrawWidth* and *FillStyle* properties.

Finally, you can draw filled rectangles using the *BF* argument. The capability of creating empty and filled rectangles lets you create interesting effects. For example, you can draw your own 3-D yellow notes floating on your forms using three lines of code:

```
' A gray rectangle provides the shadow.
Line (500, 500)-Step(2000, 1000), RGB(64, 64, 64), BF
' A white rectangle provides the canvas.
Line (450, 450)-Step(2000, 1000), vbYellow, BF
' Complete it with a black border.
Line (450, 450)-Step(2000, 1000), vbBlack, B
```

Even if you can paint filled rectangles using the *BF* argument, Visual Basic offers more advanced filling capabilities. You can activate a solid filling style by setting the *FillStyle* property, the results of which you can see in Figure 2-12. Interestingly, Visual Basic offers a separate color property for the color to be used to fill regions, *FillColor*, which allows you to draw a rectangle's contour with one color and paint its interior with another color in a single operation. Here's how you can take advantage of this feature to recode the previous example with just two *Line* methods:

```
Line (500, 500)-Step(2000, 1000), RGB(64, 64, 64), BF
FillStyle = vbFSSolid     ' We want a filled rectangle.
FillColor = vbYellow      ' This is the paint color.
Line (450, 450)-Step(2000, 1000), vbBlack, B
```

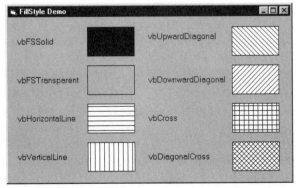

Figure 2-12. *The eight styles offered by the* FillStyle *property.*

The *FillStyle* property can be assigned one of several values, as you can see in Table 2-3.

Constant	Value	Description
vbFSSolid	0	Solid filling
vbFSTransparent	1	Transparent (default value)
vbHorizontalLine	2	Horizontal lines
vbVerticalLine	3	Vertical lines
vbUpwardDiagonal	4	Upward diagonal lines
vbDownwardDiagonal	5	Downward diagonal lines
vbCross	6	Vertical and horizontal crossing lines
vbDiagonalCross	7	Diagonal crossing lines

Table 2-3. *Constants for the* FillStyle *property.*

Drawing circles, ellipses, and arcs

The last graphic method offered by Visual Basic is *Circle*, which is also the most complex of the group in that it enables you to draw circles, ellipses, arcs, and even pie slices. Drawing circles is the simplest action you can do with this method because you merely have to specify the circle's center and its radius:

```
' A circle with a radius of 1000 twips, near the
' upper left corner of the form
Circle (1200, 1200), 1000
```

The *Circle* method is affected by the current values of the *DrawWidth*, *DrawStyle*, *FillStyle*, and *FillColor* properties, which means that you can draw circles with thicker borders and fill them with a pattern. The circle's border is usually drawn using the current *ForeColor* value, but you can override it by passing a fourth argument:

```
' A circle with a 3-pixel wide green border
' filled with yellow solid color
DrawWidth = 3
FillStyle = vbFSSolid
FillColor = vbYellow
Circle (1200, 1200), 1000, vbGreen
```

The preceding example draws a perfect circle on any monitor and at any screen resolution because Visual Basic automatically accounts for the different pixel density along the *x*- and *y*-axes. To draw an ellipse, you must skip two more optional arguments (which I'll explain later) and append an *aspect ratio* to the end of the command. The aspect ratio is the number you get when you divide the *y*-radius by the *x*-radius of the ellipse. To complicate matters, however, the value that you pass as the third argument of the method is always the larger of the two radii. So if you want to draw an ellipse inside a rectangular area, you must take additional precautions. This reusable routine lets you draw an ellipse using a simplified syntax:

```
Sub Ellipse(X As Single, Y As Single, RadiusX As Single, _
    RadiusY As Single)
    Dim ratio As Single, radius As Single
    ratio = RadiusY / RadiusX
    If ratio < 1 Then
        radius = RadiusX
    Else
        radius = RadiusY
    End If
    Circle (X, Y), radius, , , , ratio
End Sub
```

The *Circle* method also allows you to draw both circle and ellipse arcs, using two arguments, *start* and *end*. (These are the arguments we skipped a moment ago.) The values of these arguments are the starting and ending angles formed by imaginary lines that connect that arc's extreme points with the center of the figure. Such angles are measured in radians, in a counterclockwise direction. For example, you can draw one quadrant of a perfect circle in this way:

```
Const PI = 3.14159265358979
Circle (ScaleWidth / 2, ScaleHeight / 2), 1500, vbBlack, 0, PI / 2
```

Of course, you can add a *ratio* argument if you want to draw an ellipse arc. The *Circle* method can even draw pie slices, that is, arcs that are connected by a radius to the center of the circle or the ellipse. To draw such figures, you must specify a negative value for the *start* and *end* arguments. Figure 2-13 on the following page, which shows a pie chart with an "exploded" portion, was drawn using the following code:

```
' Draw a pie with an "exploded" portion.
' NOTE that you can't specify a Null "negative" value
'       but you can express it as -(PI * 2).
Const PI = 3.14159265358979
FillStyle = vbFSSolid
FillColor = vbBlue
Circle (ScaleWidth / 2 + 200, ScaleHeight / 2 - 200), _
    1500, vbBlack, -(PI * 2), -(PI / 2)
FillColor = vbCyan
Circle (ScaleWidth / 2, ScaleHeight / 2), _
    1500, vbBlack, -(PI / 2), -(PI * 2)
```

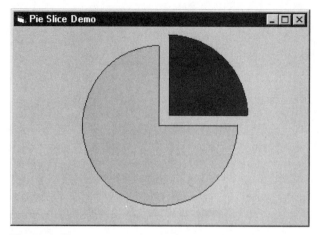

Figure 2-13. *Drawing pie charts.*

The *DrawMode* Property

As if all the properties and methods you've seen so far weren't enough, you must take into account yet another property of a Form, *DrawMode*, when you're writing graphic-intensive applications. This property specifies how the figures you're drawing interact with the pixels that are already on the form's surface. By default, all the pixels in your lines, circles, and arcs simply replace whatever is on the form, but this isn't necessarily what you want all the time. In fact, the *DrawMode* property lets you vary the effects that you get when you blend the pixels coming from the figure being drawn with those already on the form's surface. (Table 2-4 shows you the values that achieve various effects.)

Constant	*Value*	*Description*	*Bit-op (S=Screen, P=Pen)*
vbBlackness	1	The screen color is set to all 0s. (The pen color isn't actually used.)	S = 0
vbNotMergePen	2	The OR operator is applied to the pen color and the screen color, and then the result is inverted (by applying the NOT operator).	S = Not (S Or P)
vbMaskNotPen	3	The pen color is inverted (using the NOT operator), and then the AND operator is applied to the result and the screen color.	S = S And Not P
vbNotCopyPen	4	The pen color is inverted.	S = Not P

Table 2-4. *Constants for the* DrawMode *property.*   *(continued)*

Constant	Value	Description	Bit-op (S=Screen, P=Pen)
vbMaskPenNot	5	The screen color is inverted (using the NOT operator), and then the AND operator is applied to the result and the pen color.	S = Not S And P
vbInvert	6	Invert the screen color. (The pen color isn't actually used.)	S = Not S
vbXorPen	7	The XOR operator is applied to the pen color and the screen color.	S = S Xor P
vbNotMaskPen	8	The AND operator is applied to the pen color and the screen color, and then the result is inverted (using the NOT operator).	S = Not (S And P)
vbMaskPen	9	The AND operator is applied to the pen color and the color on the screen.	S = S And P
vbNotXorPen	10	The XOR operator is applied to the pen color and the screen color, and then the result is inverted (using the NOT operator).	S = Not (S Xor P)
vbNop	11	No operation (actually turns off drawing).	S = S
vbMergeNotPen	12	The pen color is inverted (by using the NOT operator), and then the OR operator is applied to the result and the screen color.	S = S Or Not P
vbCopyPen	13	Draw a pixel in the color specified by the *ForeColor* property (default).	S = P
vbMergePenNot	14	The screen color is inverted (using the NOT operator), and then the OR operator is applied to the result and the pen color.	S = Not S Or P
vbMergePen	15	The OR operator is applied to the pen color and the screen color.	S = S Or P
vbWhiteness	16	The screen color is set to all 1s. (The pen color isn't actually used.)	S = −1

To understand what each drawing mode really does, you should remember that colors are ultimately represented simply by bits, so the operation of combining the pen color and the color already on the form's surface is nothing but a bit-wise operation on 0s and 1s. If you look at Table 2-4 from this perspective, the contents of the rightmost column make more sense, and you can use it to anticipate the results of your graphic commands. For example, if you draw a yellow point (correspond-ing to hex value &HFFFF) over a cyan background color (&HFFFF00), you can expect the following results:

vbCopyPen	Yellow (Screen color is ignored.)
vbXorPen	Magenta (&HFF00FF)
vbMergePen	White (&HFFFFFF)
vbMaskPen	Green (&H00FF00)
vbNotMaskPen	Magenta (&HFF00FF)

Different draw modes can deliver the same result, especially if you're working with solid colors. (See the *vbXorPen* and *vbNotMaskPen* examples above.) I can almost hear you asking, "Should we really worry about all these modes?" The answer is no and yes. No, you don't usually need to worry about them if you're writing applica-tions with trivial or no graphic output. Yes, you should at least know what Visual Basic has to offer you when it's time to do some advanced pixel manipulation.

One of the most useful things that you can do with the *DrawMode* property is *rubber banding,* the ability to draw and resize new shapes using the mouse without disturbing the underlying graphic. You use rubber banding techniques—without even knowing it—whenever you draw a shape in Microsoft Paint or any Windows paint program. Have you ever wondered what really happens when you drag one of the rectangle's corners using the mouse? Is Microsoft Paint actually erasing the rectangle and redrawing it in another position? How can you implement the same feature in your Visual Basic applications? The answer is much simpler than you might think and is based on the *DrawMode* property.

The trick is that if you apply the XOR operator twice to a value on the screen and the same pen value, after the second XOR command the original color on the screen is restored. (If you are familiar with bit-wise operations, this shouldn't surprise you; if you aren't, experiment with them until you are convinced that I am telling the truth.) Therefore, all you have to do is set *DrawMode* to the 7-vbXorPen value; then draw the rectangle (or line, circle, arc, and so on) once to show it and a second time to erase it. When the user eventually releases the mouse cursor, you set the *DrawMode* property to 13-vbCopyPen and draw the final rectangle on the form's surface. The following program lets you experiment with rubber banding: You can draw empty rectangles (with random line width and color) by dragging the left button and filled rectangles by dragging the right mouse button.

```
' Form-level variables
Dim X1 As Single, X2 As Single
Dim Y1 As Single, Y2 As Single
' True if we are dragging a rectangle
Dim dragging As Boolean
```

```
Private Sub Form_Load()
    ' Rubber-banding works particularly well on a black background.
    BackColor = vbBlack
End Sub

Private Sub Form_MouseDown(Button As Integer, Shift As Integer, _
    X As Single, Y As Single)
    If Button And 3 Then
        dragging = True
        ' Remember starting coordinates.
        X1 = X: Y1 = Y: X2 = X: Y2 = Y
        ' Select a random color and width.
        ForeColor = RGB(Rnd * 255, Rnd * 255, Rnd * 255)
        DrawWidth = Rnd * 3 + 1
        ' Draw the very first rectangle in Xor mode.
        DrawMode = vbXorPen
        Line (X1, Y1)-(X2, Y2), , B
        If Button = 2 Then
            ' Filled rectangles
            FillStyle = vbFSSolid
            FillColor = ForeColor
        End If
    End If
End Sub

Private Sub Form_MouseMove(Button As Integer, Shift As Integer, _
    X As Single, Y As Single)
    If dragging Then
        ' Delete old rectangle (repeat the same command in Xor mode).
        Line (X1, Y1)-(X2, Y2), , B
        ' Redraw to new coordinates.
        X2 = X: Y2 = Y
        Line (X1, Y1)-(X2, Y2), , B
    End If
End Sub

Private Sub Form_MouseUp(Button As Integer, Shift As Integer, _
    X As Single, Y As Single)
    If dragging Then
        dragging = False
        ' Draw the definitive rectangle.
        DrawMode = vbCopyPen
        Line (X1, Y1)-(X, Y), , B
        FillStyle = vbFSTransparent
    End If
End Sub
```

The *ScaleMode* Property

While the twip is the default unit of measurement for Visual Basic when placing and resizing objects on screen, it isn't the only one available. In fact, forms and some other controls that can work as containers—most notably, PictureBox controls—expose a *ScaleMode* property that can be set either at design time or run time with one of the values displayed in Table 2-5.

Constant	Value	Description
vbUser	0	User-defined scale mode
vbTwips	1	Twips (1440 twips per logical inch; 567 twips per logical centimeter)
vbPoints	2	Points (72 points per logical inch)
vbPixels	3	Pixels
vbCharacters	4	Characters (horizontal = 120 twips per unit; vertical = 240 twips per unit)
vbInches	5	Inches
vbMillimeters	6	Millimeters
vbCentimeters	7	Centimeters
vbHimetric	8	Himetric (1000 units = 1 centimeter)

Table 2-5. *Constants for the* ScaleMode *property.*

The form object exposes two methods that let you easily convert between different units of measurement; you use the *ScaleX* method for horizontal measurements and the *ScaleY* method for vertical measurements. Their syntax is identical: You pass the value to be converted (the source value), a constant from among those in Table 2-5 that specifies the unit used for the source value (the *fromscale* argument), and another constant that specifies which unit you want to convert it to (the *toscale* argument). If you omit the *fromscale* argument, vbHimetric is assumed; if you omit the *toscale* argument, the current value of the *ScaleMode* property is assumed:

```
' How many twips per pixel along the x-axis?
Print ScaleX(1, vbPixels, vbTwips)

' Draw a 50x80 pixel rectangle in the upper left corner
' of the form, regardless of the current ScaleMode.
Line (0, 0)-(ScaleX(50, vbPixels), ScaleY(80, vbPixels)), _
    vbBlack, B
```

NOTE The *ScaleX* and *ScaleY* methods offer the same functionality as the Screen object's *TwipsPerPixelX* and *TwipsPerPixelY* properties, work for other measurement units, and don't require that you write the actual conversion code. The only time you should continue to use the Screen's properties is when you are writing code in a BAS module (for example, a generic function or procedure) and you don't have any form reference at hand.

The *ScaleMode* property is closely related to four other properties. *ScaleLeft* and *ScaleTop* correspond to the *(x,y)* values of the upper left pixel in the client area of the form and are usually both set to 0. *ScaleWidth* and *ScaleHeight* correspond to the coordinates of the pixel in the bottom right corner in the client area. If you set a different *ScaleMode*, these two properties immediately reflect the new setting. For example, if you set *ScaleMode* to 3-vbPixels, you can then query *ScaleWidth* and *ScaleHeight* to learn the size of the client area in pixels. Keep in mind that, even if the current *ScaleMode* is 1-vbTwips, the *ScaleWidth* and *ScaleHeight* properties return values that differ from the form's *Width* and *Height* properties, respectively, because the latter ones account for the window's borders and title bar, which are outside the client area. If you know the relationship among these quantities, you can derive some useful information about your form:

```
' Run this code from inside a form module.
' Ensure that ScaleWidth and ScaleHeight return twips.
' (Next line is useless if you are using default settings.)
ScaleMode = vbTwips
' Evaluate the border's width in pixels.
BorderWidth = (Width - ScaleWidth) / Screen.TwipsPerPixelX / 2

' Evaluate the caption's height in pixels.
' (Assumes that the form has no menu bar)
CaptionHeight = (Height - ScaleHeight) / _
    Screen.TwipsPerPixelY - BorderWidth * 2
```

You can assign the *ScaleMode* property any value that fits your requirements, but the values that are most frequently used are vbTwips and vbPixels. The latter is useful if you want to retrieve the coordinates of child controls in pixels, which is often necessary if you're performing some advanced graphic command that involves Windows API calls.

The vbUser setting is unique in that you don't usually assign it to the *ScaleMode* property. Instead, you define a custom coordinate system by setting *ScaleLeft*, *ScaleTop*, *ScaleWidth*, and *ScaleHeight* properties. When you do it, the *ScaleMode* property is automatically set to 0-vbUser by Visual Basic. You might need to create a custom coordinate system to simplify the code in an application and have Visual Basic perform all the needed conversions on your behalf. The following program plots a function on a form, using a custom coordinate system. (See the results in Figure 2-14 on the following page.)

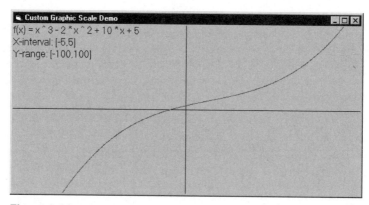

Figure 2-14. *Plotting a third-degree polynomial function using a custom coordinate system.*

```
' The portion of X-Y plane to be plotted
Const XMIN = -5, XMAX = 5, YMIN = -100, YMAX = 100
Const XSTEP = 0.01

Private Sub Form_Resize()
    ' Set a custom graphic coordinate system so that
    ' the visible viewport corresponds to constants above.
    ScaleLeft = XMIN
    ScaleTop = YMAX
    ScaleWidth = XMAX - XMIN
    ScaleHeight = -(YMAX - YMIN)
    ' Force a Paint event.
    Refresh
End Sub

Private Sub Form_Paint()
    Dim x As Single, y As Single
    ' Start with a blank canvas.
    Cls
    ForeColor = vbBlack
    ' Explain what is being displayed.
    CurrentX = ScaleLeft
    CurrentY = ScaleTop
    Print "f(x) = x ^ 3 - 2 * x ^ 2 + 10 * x + 5"
    CurrentX = ScaleLeft
    Print "X-interval: [" & XMIN & "," & XMAX & "]"
    CurrentX = ScaleLeft
    Print "Y-range: [" & YMIN & "," & YMAX & "]"
    ' Draw x- and y-axes.
    Line (XMIN, 0)-(XMAX, 0)
    Line (0, YMIN)-(0, YMAX)
```

```
        ' Plot the math function.
        ForeColor = vbRed
        For x = XMIN To XMAX Step XSTEP
            y = x ^ 3 - 2 * x ^ 2 + 10 * x + 5
            PSet (x, y)
        Next
    End Sub
```

You should pay attention to several notable things about the preceding code:

- The *ScaleHeight* property is negative, which is perfectly legal; in fact, when showing a *y*-axis, you'll often have to set up negative values for this property because by default *y*-coordinates increase their value going from top to bottom, while you usually need exactly the opposite.

- You can resize the form at will, and it will always display the same portion of the *x-y* plane, distorting it if necessary.

- Once you have set a custom system in the *Resize* event procedure, you can reason in terms of *x-y* coordinates in your own coordinate system, which greatly simplifies the plotting code.

- The *Cls* graphic method resets the *CurrentX* and *CurrentY* coordinates to (0,0), which in this case corresponds to the center of the screen, so you have to manually set *CurrentX* and *CurrentY* properties to print in the upper left corner.

- The *Print* method always resets the *CurrentX* property to 0, so you have to set it each time you print a line of text.

Palette Support

First, some theory. Most video cards are theoretically able to display 16 million distinct colors. (I say theoretically because we humans can't distinguish most colors from those nearest in the continuum.) Only relatively few *true-color* video cards are capable, however, of actually showing that many colors in a given instant on the screen, especially at higher screen definitions. (For the sake of simplicity, I omit a description of *hi-color* cards capable of 65,536 simultaneously displayed colors.) In all other cases, Windows has to resort to *palettes*.

A palette is a subset of 256 colors among those theoretically supported by the video card. If a video card works in the palette mode, it devotes 1 byte to each pixel on the screen (instead of the 3 bytes that would be necessary to hold 16 million different color values), thus saving a lot of memory and accelerating most graphic operations. Each of the possible 256 values points to another table, where the video card can find the actual RGB value for each color. Each pixel can have a well-defined color, but there can be no more than 256 distinct colors on the screen at a given moment.

Windows reserves for itself 16 colors and leaves the remaining ones available for use by applications. When the foreground application has to display an image, it uses the available palette entries and tries to match the colors in the image. If the image embeds more distinct colors than the number of available colors, the application has to find a decent compromise—for example, by using the same palette entry for two similar colors. In practice, this isn't a big issue, at least compared with what follows. A more serious problem with palettes, in fact, is that when an application has to display multiple images at the same time, it must arbitrate among different sets of colors. Which one has precedence? What happens to the other images?

Until Visual Basic 5, the solution available to Visual Basic developers wasn't actually a solution. Visual Basic 4 and previous versions simply gave the precedence to the image that was first in z-order—in other words, the form or the control that had the focus. All the other images on the screen were displayed using a palette that in most cases didn't fit their set of colors, and the results were often obscene. Starting with Visual Basic 5, we finally have a choice.

The key to this new capability is the form's *PaletteMode* property, which can be assigned—both at design time and run time—three different values: 0-vbPaletteModeHalftone, 1-vbPaletteModeUseZOrder, and 2-vbPaletteModeCustom. The *Halftone* palette is a special fixed palette that contains an assortment of "average" colors; it should provide a reasonable rendering for many images and, above all, should allow multiple images with different palettes to peacefully coexist on the form. (This is the default mode for Visual Basic 5 and 6 forms). The *ZOrder* mode is the only setting available to previous versions of the language. The Form or PictureBox that has the focus affects the palette used by the video card; it will be shown in the best way possible, but all others probably won't be shown to advantage. The third setting, *Custom* mode, lets you set up a custom palette. To do so, you assign a bitmap—at design time or at run time, using the *LoadPicture* function—to the *Palette* property. In this case, the palette associated with the image you provide becomes the palette used by the form.

This concludes the description of all the properties, methods, and events supported by the Form object. Much of this knowledge will be useful in the next chapter too, where I describe the features of all the intrinsic Visual Basic controls.

Chapter 3

Intrinsic Controls

In Microsoft Visual Basic jargon, *intrinsic controls* (or *built-in* controls) are those controls visible in the Toolbox window when you launch the environment. This important group includes controls, such as Label, TFextbox, and CommandButton controls, that are used in nearly every application. As you know, Visual Basic can be extended using additional Microsoft ActiveX Controls (formerly known as OCX controls, or OLE custom controls) either provided in the Visual Basic package or available as commercial, shareware, or even freeware third-party products. Even if such external controls are often more powerful than built-in controls, intrinsic controls have a few advantages that you should always take into account:

- Support for intrinsic controls is included in the MSVBVM60.DLL, the runtime file that's distributed with every Visual Basic application. This means that if a program exclusively uses intrinsic controls, you don't need to distribute any additional OCX files, which greatly simplifies the installation process and reduces disk requirements.

- In general, Visual Basic can create and display intrinsic controls faster than it can external ActiveX controls because the code for their management is already in the Visual Basic runtime module and doesn't have to be loaded when a form references an intrinsic control for the first time. Also, applications based on intrinsic controls usually perform faster on machines with less memory; no extra memory is needed by additional OCX modules.

- Because programs based exclusively on intrinsic controls require fewer ancillary files, they can be downloaded faster through the Internet. Moreover, if end users previously installed any other Visual Basic application, Visual Basic runtime files are already installed on the target machine, which reduces download times to the minimum.

For all these reasons, it's important to learn how to make the best of intrinsic controls. In this chapter, I focus on their most important properties, methods, and events, and I also show how to address some common programming issues using intrinsic controls exclusively.

TextBox Controls

TextBox controls offer a natural way for users to enter a value in your program. For this reason, they tend to be the most frequently used controls in the majority of Windows applications. TextBox controls, which have a great many properties and events, are also among the most complex intrinsic controls. In this section, I guide you through the most useful properties of TextBox controls and show how to solve some of the problems that you're likely to encounter.

After you place a TextBox control on a form, you must set a few basic properties. The first thing I do as soon as I create a new TextBox control is clear its *Text* property. If this is a multiline field, I also set the *MultiLine* property to True.

You can set the *Alignment* property of TextBox controls to left align, right align, or center the contents of the control. Right-aligned TextBox controls are especially useful when you're displaying numeric values. But you should be aware of the following quirk: while this property always works correctly when the *Multiline* property is set to True, it works with single-line controls only under Microsoft Windows 98, Microsoft Windows NT 4 with Service Pack 3, or later versions. Under previous versions of Windows 9*x* or Windows NT, no error is raised but single-line TextBox controls ignore the *Alignment* property and always align their contents to the left.

You can prevent the user from changing the contents of a TextBox control by setting its *Locked* property to True. You usually do this if the control contains the result of a calculation or displays a field taken from a database opened in read-only mode. In most cases, you can achieve the same result using a Label control with a border and white background, but a locked TextBox control also permits your users to copy the value to the Clipboard and scroll through it if it's too large for the field's width.

If you're dealing with a numeric field, you probably want to set a limit on the number of characters that the user can enter in the field. You can do it very easily using the *MaxLength* property. A 0 value (the default) means that you can enter any number of characters; any positive value *N* enforces a limit to the length of the field's contents to be *N* characters long.

If you're creating password fields, you should set the *PasswordChar* property to a character string, typically an asterisk. In this case, your program can read and modify the contents of this TextBox control as usual, but users see only a row of asterisks.

CAUTION Password-protected TextBox controls effectively disable the Ctrl+X and Ctrl+C keyboard shortcuts, so malicious users can't steal a password entered by another user. If, however, your application includes an Edit menu with all the usual clipboard commands, it's up to you to disable the Copy and Cut commands when the focus is on a password-protected field.

You can set other properties for a better appearance of the control—the *Font* property, for example. In addition, you can set the *ToolTipText* property to help users understand what the TextBox control is for. You can also make borderless TextBox controls by setting their *BorderStyle* property to 0-None, but controls like these don't appear frequently in Windows applications. In general, you can't do much else with a TextBox control at design time. The most interesting things can be done only through code.

Run-Time Properties

The *Text* property is the one you'll reference most often in code, and conveniently it's the default property for the TextBox control. Three other frequently used properties are these:

■ The *SelStart* property sets or returns the position of the blinking *caret* (the insertion point where the text you type appears). Note that the blinking cursor inside TextBox and other controls is named *caret*, to distinguish it from the *cursor* (which is implicitly the mouse cursor). When the caret is at the beginning of the contents of the TextBox control, *SelStart* returns 0; when it's at the end of the string typed by the user, *SelStart* returns the value *Len(Text)*. You can modify the *SelStart* property to programmatically move the caret.

■ The *SelLength* property returns the number of characters in the portion of text that has been highlighted by the user, or it returns 0 if there's no highlighted text. You can assign a nonzero value to this property to programmatically select text from code. Interestingly, you can assign to this property a value larger than the current text's length without raising a runtime error.

■ The *SelText* property sets or returns the portion of the text that's currently selected, or it returns an empty string if no text is highlighted. Use it to directly retrieve the highlighted text without having to query *Text*, *SelStart*, and *SelLength* properties. What's even more interesting is that you can assign a new value to this property, thus replacing the current selection with your own. If no text is currently selected, your string is simply inserted at the current caret position.

TIP When you want to append text to a TextBox control, you should use the following code (instead of using the concatenation operator) to reduce flickering and improve performance:

```
Text1.SelStart = Len(Text1.Text)
Text1.SelText = StringToBeAdded
```

One of the typical operations you could find yourself performing with these properties is selecting the entire contents of a TextBox control. You often do it when the caret enters the field so that the user can quickly override the existing value with a new one, or start editing it by pressing any arrow key:

```
Private Sub Text1_GotFocus()
    Text1.SelStart = 0
    ' A very high value always does the trick.
    Text1.SelLength = 9999
End Sub
```

Always set the *SelStart* property first and then the *SelLength* or *SelText* properties. When you assign a new value to the *SelStart* property, the other two are automatically reset to 0 and an empty string respectively, thus overriding your previous settings.

Trapping Keyboard Activity

TextBox controls support *KeyDown*, *KeyPress*, and *KeyUp* standard events, which Chapter 2 covered. One thing that you will often do is prevent the user from entering invalid keys. A typical example of where this safeguard is needed is a numeric field, for which you need to filter out all nondigit keys:

```
Private Sub Text1_KeyPress(KeyAscii As Integer)
    Select Case KeyAscii
        Case Is < 32           ' Control keys are OK.
        Case 48 To 57          ' This is a digit.
        Case Else              ' Reject any other key.
            KeyAscii = 0
    End Select
End Sub
```

You should never reject keys whose ANSI code is less than 32, a group that includes important keys such as Backspace, Escape, Tab, and Enter. Also note that a few control keys will make your TextBox beep if it doesn't know what to do with them—for example, a single-line TextBox control doesn't know what to do with an Enter key.

CAUTION Don't assume that the *KeyPress* event will trap all control keys under all conditions. For example, the *KeyPress* event can process the Enter key only if there's no CommandButton control on the form whose *Default* property is set to True. If the form has a default push button, the effect of pressing the Enter key is clicking on that button. Similarly, no Escape key goes through this event if there's a Cancel button on the form. Finally, the Tab control key is trapped by a *KeyPress* event only if there isn't any other control on the form whose *TabStop* property is True.

You can use the *KeyDown* event procedure to allow users to increase and decrease the current value using Up and Down arrow keys, as you see here:

```
Private Sub Text1_KeyDown(KeyCode As Integer, Shift As Integer)
    Select Case KeyCode
        Case vbKeyUp
            Text1.Text = CDbl(Text1.Text) + 1
        Case vbKeyDown
            Text1.Text = CDbl(Text1.Text) - 1
    End Select
End Sub
```

NOTE There's a bug in the implementation of TextBox ready-only controls. When the *Locked* property is set to True, the Ctrl+C key combination doesn't correctly copy the selected text to the Clipboard, and you must manually implement this capability by writing code in the *KeyPress* event procedure.

Validation Routines for Numbers

Although trapping invalid keys in the *KeyPress* or *KeyDown* event procedures seems a great idea at first, when you throw your application to inexperienced users you soon realize that there are many ways for them to enter invalid data. Depending on what you do with this data, your application can come to an abrupt end with a run-time error or—much worse—it can appear to work correctly while it delivers bogus results. What you really need is a bullet-proof method to trap invalid values.

Before I offer you a decent solution to the problem, let me explain why you can't rely solely on trapping invalid keys for your validation chores. What if the user pastes an invalid value from the clipboard? Well, you might say, let's trap the Ctrl+V and Shift+Ins key combinations to prevent the user from doing that! Unfortunately, Visual Basic's TextBox controls offer a default edit menu that lets users perform any clipboard operation by simply right-clicking on them. Fortunately, there's a way around this problem: Instead of trapping a key *before* it gets to the TextBox control, you trap its effect in the *Change* event and reject it if it doesn't pass your test. But this makes the structure of the code a little more complex than you might anticipate:

```
' Form-level variables
Dim saveText As String
Dim saveSelStart As Long
```

(continued)

```
Private Sub Text1_GotFocus()
    ' Save values when the control gets the focus.
    saveText = Text1.Text
    saveSelStart = Text1.SelStart
End Sub

Private Sub Text1_Change()
    ' Avoid nested calls.
    Static nestedCall As Boolean
    If nestedCall Then Exit Sub

    ' Test the control's value here.
    If IsNumeric(Text1.Text) Then
        ' If value is OK, save values.
        saveText = Text1.Text
        saveSelStart = Text1.SelStart
    Else
        ' Prepare to handle a nested call.
        nestedCall = True
        Text1.Text = saveText
        nestedCall = False
        Text1.SelStart = saveSelStart
    End If
End Sub

Private Sub Text1_KeyUp(KeyCode As Integer, Shift As Integer)
    saveSelStart = Text1.SelStart
End Sub
Private Sub Text1_MouseDown(Button As Integer, _
    Shift As Integer, X As Single, Y As Single)
    saveSelStart = Text1.SelStart
End Sub
Private Sub Text1_MouseMove(Button As Integer, _
    Shift As Integer, X As Single, Y As Single)
    saveSelStart = Text1.SelStart
End Sub
```

If the control's value doesn't pass your tests in the *Change* event procedure, you must restore its previous valid value; this action recursively fires a *Change* event, and you must prepare yourself to neutralize this nested call. You might wonder why you also need to trap the *KeyUp*, *MouseDown*, and *MouseMove* events: The reason is that you always need to keep track of the last valid position for the insertion point because the end user could move it using arrow keys or the mouse.

The preceding code snippet uses the *IsNumeric* function to trap invalid data. You should be aware that this function isn't robust enough for most real-world applications. For example, the *IsNumeric* function incorrectly considers these strings as valid numbers:

```
123,,,123
345-
$1234      ' What if it isn't a currency field?
2.4E10     ' What if I don't want to support scientific notation?
```

To cope with this issue, I have prepared an alternative function, which you can modify for your particular purposes. (For instance, you can add support for a currency symbol or the comma as the decimal separator.) Note that this function always returns True when it's passed a null string, so you might need to perform additional tests if the user isn't allowed to leave the field blank:

```
Function CheckNumeric(text As String, DecValue As Boolean) As Boolean
    Dim i As Integer
    For i = 1 To Len(text)
        Select Case Mid$(text, i, 1)
            Case "0" To "9"
            Case "-", "+"
                ' Minus/plus signs are only allowed as leading chars.
                If i > 1 Then Exit Function
            Case "."
                ' Exit if decimal values not allowed.
                If Not DecValue Then Exit Function
                ' Only one decimal separator is allowed.
                If InStr(text, ".") < i Then Exit Function
            Case Else
                ' Reject all other characters.
                Exit Function
        End Select
    Next
    CheckNumeric = True
End Function
```

If your TextBox controls are expected to contain other types of data, you might be tempted to reuse the same validation framework I showed you previously—including all the code in the *GotFocus, Change, KeyUp, MouseDown,* and *MouseMove* event procedures—and replace only the call to *IsNumeric* with a call to your custom validation routine. Things aren't as simple as they appear at first, however. Say that you have a date field: Can you use the *IsDate* function to validate it from within the *Change* event? The answer is, of course, no. In fact, as you enter the first digit of your date value, *IsDate* returns False and the routine therefore prevents you from entering the remaining characters, and so preventing you from entering *any* value.

This example explains why a *key-level* validation isn't always the best answer to your validation needs. For this reason, most Visual Basic programmers prefer to rely on *field-level* validation and test the values only when the user moves the input focus to another field in the form. I explain field-level validation in the next section.

The *CausesValidation* Property and the *Validate* Event

Visual Basic 6 has finally come up with a solution for most of the validation issues that have afflicted Visual Basic developers for years. As you'll see in a moment, the Visual Basic 6 approach is simple and clean; it really astonishes me that it took six language versions to deliver such a lifesaver. The keys to the new validation features are the *Validate* event and the *CausesValidation* property. They work together as follows: When the input focus leaves a control, Visual Basic checks the *Causes-Validation* property of the control that is about to receive the focus. If this property is True, Visual Basic fires the *Validate* event in the control that's about to lose the focus, thus giving the programmer a chance to validate its contents and, if necessary, cancel the focus shift.

Let's try a practical example. Imagine that you have five controls on a form: a required field (a TextBox control, txtRequired, that can't contain an empty string), a numeric field, txtNumeric, that expects a value in the range 1 through 1000, and three push buttons: OK, Cancel, and Help. (See Figure 3-1.) You don't want to perform validation if the user presses the Cancel or Help buttons, so you set their *Causes-Validation* properties to False. The default value for this property is True, so you don't have to modify it for the other controls. Run the sample program on the companion CD, type something in the required TextBox, and then move to the second field. Because the second field's *CausesValidation* property is True, Visual Basic fires a *Validate* event in the first TextBox control:

```
Private Sub txtRequired_Validate(Cancel As Boolean)
    ' Check that field is not empty.
    If txtRequired.Text = "" Then
        MsgBox "Please enter something here", vbExclamation
        Cancel = True
    End If
End Sub
```

If the *Cancel* parameter is set to True, Visual Basic cancels the user's action and takes the input focus back on the txtRequired control: No other *GotFocus* and *Lost-Focus* events are generated. On the other hand, if you typed something in the required field, the focus will now be on the second field (the numeric text box). Try clicking on the Help or Cancel buttons: No *Validate* event will fire this time because you set the *CausesValidation* property for each of these controls to False. Instead, click on the OK button to execute the *Validate* event of the numeric field, where you can check it for invalid characters and valid range.

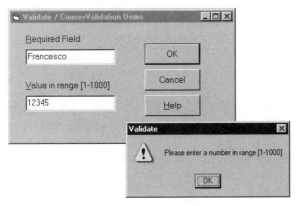

Figure 3-1. *A demonstration program that lets you experiment with the new Visual Basic* Validate *features.*

```
Private Sub txtNumeric_Validate(Cancel As Boolean)
    If Not IsNumeric(txtNumeric.Text) Then
        Cancel = True
    ElseIf CDbl(txtNumeric.Text) < 1 Or CDbl(txtNumeric.Text) > 1000 Then
        Cancel = True
    End If
    If Cancel Then
        MsgBox "Please enter a number in range [1-1000]", vbExclamation
    End If
End Sub
```

In some circumstances, you might want to programmatically validate the control that has the focus without waiting for the user to move the input focus. You can do it with the form's *ValidateControls* method, which forces the *Validate* event of the control that has the input focus. Typically, you do it when the user closes the form:

```
Private Sub Form_QueryUnload(Cancel As Integer, UnloadMode As Integer)
    ' You can't close this form without validating the current field.
    If UnloadMode = vbFormControlMenu Then
        On Error Resume Next
        ValidateControls
        If Err = 380 Then
            ' The current field failed validation.
            Cancel = True
        End If
    End If
End Sub
```

Checking the *UnloadMode* parameter is important; otherwise, your application will mistakenly execute a *ValidateControls* method when the user clicks on the Cancel button. Note that *ValidateControls* returns an error 380 if Cancel was set in the *Validate* event procedure of the control that had the focus.

> **CAUTION**   Visual Basic 6's validation scheme has two flaws, though. If your form has a CommandButton whose *Default* property is set to True, pressing the Enter key while the input focus is on another control results in a click on the CommandButton control but doesn't fire a *Validate* event, even if the *CausesValidation* property of the CommandButton control is set to True. The only way to solve this problem is to invoke the *ValidateControls* method from within the default CommandButton control's *Click* event procedure.
>
> The second flaw is that the *Validate* event doesn't fire when you're moving the focus from a control whose *CausesValidation* property is False, even if the control that receives the focus has its *CausesValidation* property set to True.

The new Visual Basic 6 validation mechanism is simple and can be implemented with little effort. But it isn't the magic answer to all your validation needs. In fact, this technique can only enforce *field-level* validation; it does nothing for *record-level* validation. In other words, it ensures that one particular field is correct, not that all fields in the form contain valid data. To see what I mean, run the demonstration program, enter a string in the first field, and press Alt+F4 to close the form. Your code won't raise an error, even if the second field doesn't contain a valid number! Fortunately, it doesn't take much to create a generic routine that forces each control on the form to validate itself:

```
Private Sub Form_QueryUnload(Cancel As Integer, UnloadMode As Integer)
    ' You can't close this form without validating all the fields on it.
    If UnloadMode = vbFormControlMenu Then
        On Error Resume Next
        Dim ctrl As Control
        ' Give the focus to each control on the form, and then
        ' validate it.
        For Each ctrl In Controls
            Err.Clear
            ctrl.SetFocus
            If Err = 0 Then
                ' Don't validate controls that can't receive input focus.
                ValidateControls
                If Err = 380 Then
                    ' Validation failed, refuse to close.
                    Cancel = True: Exit Sub
                End If
            End If
        Next
    End If
End Sub
```

The *CausesValidation* property and the *Validate* event are shared by all the intrinsic controls that are able to get the focus as well as by most external ActiveX controls, even those not specifically written for Visual Basic. This is possible because they are *extender features,* provided by the Visual Basic runtime to all the controls placed on a form's surface.

> **TIP** One Visual Basic operator has great potential when it comes time to validate complex strings but is neglected by most Visual Basic developers. Let's say you have a product code that consists of two uppercase characters followed by exactly three digits. You might think that you need some complex string functions to validate such a string until you try the *Like* operator, as follows:
>
> ```
> If "AX123" Like "[A-Z][A-Z]###" Then Print "OK"
> ```
>
> See Chapter 5 for more information about the *Like* operator.

Auto-Tabbing Fields

Users aren't usually delighted to spend all their time at the keyboard. Your job as a programmer is to make their jobs easier, and so you should strive to streamline their everyday work as much as possible. One way to apply this concept is to provide them with *auto-tabbing* fields, which are fields that automatically advance users to the next field in the Tab order as soon as they enter a valid value. Most often, auto-tabbing fields are those TextBox controls whose *MaxLength* property has been assigned a non-null value. Implementing such an auto-tabbing field in Visual Basic is straightforward:

```
Private Sub Text1_Change()
    If Len(Text1.Text) = Text1.MaxLength Then SendKeys "{Tab}"
End Sub
```

The trick, as you see, is to have your program provide the Tab key on behalf of your user. In some cases, this simple approach doesn't work—for example, when you paste a long string into the field. You might want to write code that works around this and other shortcomings. Auto-tabbing is a nice feature but not vital to the application, so whether you write a workaround or not isn't a real problem in most cases.

Formatting Text

Many business applications let you enter data in one format and then display it in another. For example, numeric values can be formatted with thousand separators and a fixed number of decimal digits. Currency values might have a $ symbol (or whatever your national currency symbol is) automatically inserted. Phone numbers can be formatted with dashes to split into groups of digits. Credit-card numbers can be made more readable with embedded spaces. Dates can be shown in *long-date* format ("September 10, 1999"). And so on.

The *LostFocus* event is an ideal occasion to format the contents of a TextBox control as soon as the input focus leaves it. In most cases, you can perform all your formatting chores using the *Format* function. For example, you can add thousand separators to a numeric value in the txtNumber control using this code:

```
Private Sub txtNumber_LostFocus()
    On Error Resume Next
    txtNumber.Text = Format(CDbl(txtNumber.Text), _
        "#,###,###,##0.#####")
End Sub
```

When the field regains the focus, you'll want to get rid of those thousand separators. You can do it easily using the *CDbl* function:

```
Private Sub txtNumber_GotFocus()
    ' On Error is necessary to account for empty fields.
    On Error Resume Next
    txtNumber.Text = CDbl(txtNumber.Text)
End Sub
```

In some cases, however, formatting and unformatting a value isn't that simple. For example, you can format a Currency value to add parentheses around negative numbers, but there's no built-in Visual Basic function able to return a string formatted in that way to its original condition. Fear not, because nothing prevents you from creating your own formatting and unformatting routines. I have built two general-purpose routines for you to consider.

The *FilterString* routine filters out all unwanted characters in a string:

```
Function FilterString(Text As String, validChars As String) As String
    Dim i As Long, result As String
    For i = 1 To Len(Text)
        If InStr(validChars, Mid$(Text, i, 1)) Then
            result = result & Mid$(Text, i, 1)
        End If
    Next
    FilterString = result
End Function
```

FilterNumber builds on *FilterString* to strip down all formatting characters in a number and can also trim trailing decimal zeros:

```
Function FilterNumber(Text As String, TrimZeros As Boolean) As String
    Dim decSep As String, i As Long, result As String
    ' Retrieve the decimal separator symbol.
    decSep = Format$(0.1, ".")
    ' Use FilterString for most of the work.
    result = FilterString(Text, decSep & "-0123456789")
    ' Do the following only if there is a decimal part and the
    ' user requested that nonsignificant digits be trimmed.
    If TrimZeros And InStr(Text, decSep) > 0 Then
        For i = Len(result) To 1 Step -1
```

```
            Select Case Mid$(result, i, 1)
                Case decSep
                    result = Left$(result, i - 1)
                    Exit For
                Case "0"
                    result = Left$(result, i - 1)
                Case Else
                    Exit For
            End Select
        Next
    End If
    FilterNumber = result
End Function
```

The feature I like most in *FilterNumber* is that it's *locale-independent*. It works equally well on both sides of the Atlantic ocean (and on other continents, as well.) Instead of hard-coding the decimal separator character in the code, the routine determines it on the fly, using the Visual Basic for Applications (VBA) *Format* function. Start thinking internationally now, and you won't have a nervous breakdown when you have to localize your applications in German, French, and Japanese.

TIP The *Format* function lets you retrieve many locale-dependent characters and separators.

```
Format$(0.1, ".")                            ' Decimal separator
Format$(1, ",")                              ' Thousand separator
Mid$(Format(#1/1/99#, "short date"), 2, 1)   ' Date separator
```

You can also determine whether the system uses dates in "mm/dd/yy" (U.S.) format or "dd/mm/yy" (European) format, using this code:

```
If Left$(Format$("12/31/1999", "short date"), 2) = 12 Then
    ' mm/dd/yy format
Else
    ' dd/mm/yyyy format
End If
```

There's no direct way to determine the currency symbol, but you can derive it by analyzing the result of this function:

```
Format$(0, "currency")                       ' Returns "$0.00" in US
```

It isn't difficult to write a routine that internally uses the information I've just given you to extract the currency symbol as well as its default position (before or after the number) and the default number of decimal digits in currency values. Remember, in some countries the currency symbol is actually a string of two or more characters.

To illustrate these concepts in action, I've built a simple demonstration program that shows how you can format numbers, currency values, dates, phone numbers, and credit-card numbers when exiting a field, and how you can remove that formatting from the result when the input focus reenters the TextBox control. Figure 3-2 shows the formatted results.

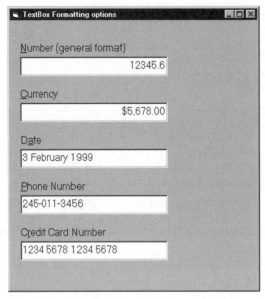

Figure 3-2. *Formatting and unformatting the contents of TextBox controls makes for more professional-looking applications.*

```
Private Sub txtNumber_GotFocus()
    ' Filter out nondigit chars and trailing zeros.
    On Error Resume Next
    txtNumber.Text = FilterNumber(txtNumber.Text, True)
End Sub
Private Sub txtNumber_LostFocus()
    ' Format as a number, grouping thousand digits.
    On Error Resume Next
    txtNumber.Text = Format(CDbl(txtNumber.Text), _
        "#,###,###,##0.######")
End Sub

Private Sub txtCurrency_GotFocus()
    ' Filter out nondigit chars and trailing zeros.
    ' Restore standard text color.
    On Error Resume Next
```

```
        txtCurrency.Text = FilterNumber(txtCurrency.Text, True)
        txtCurrency.ForeColor = vbWindowText
End Sub
Private Sub txtCurrency_LostFocus()
    On Error Resume Next
    ' Show negative values as red text.
    If CDbl(txtCurrency.Text) < 0 Then txtCurrency.ForeColor = vbRed
    ' Format currency, but don't use parentheses for negative numbers.
    ' (FormatCurrency is a new VB6 string function.)
    txtCurrency.Text = FormatCurrency(txtCurrency.Text, , , vbFalse)
End Sub

Private Sub txtDate_GotFocus()
    ' Prepare to edit in short-date format.
    On Error Resume Next
    txtDate.Text = Format$(CDate(txtDate.Text), "short date")
End Sub
Private Sub txtDate_LostFocus()
    ' Convert to long-date format upon exit.
    On Error Resume Next
    txtDate.Text = Format$(CDate(txtDate.Text), "d MMMM yyyy")
End Sub

Private Sub txtPhone_GotFocus()
    ' Trim embedded dashes.
    txtPhone.Text = FilterString(txtPhone.Text, "0123456789")
End Sub
Private Sub txtPhone_LostFocus()
    ' Add dashes if necessary.
    txtPhone.Text = FormatPhoneNumber(txtPhone.Text)
End Sub

Private Sub txtCreditCard_GotFocus()
    ' Trim embedded spaces.
    txtCreditCard.Text = FilterNumber(txtCreditCard.Text, True)
End Sub
Private Sub txtCreditCard_LostFocus()
    ' Add spaces if necessary.
    txtCreditCard.Text = FormatCreditCard(txtCreditCard.Text)
End Sub
```

Instead of inserting the code that formats phone numbers and credit-card numbers right in the *LostFocus* event procedures, I built two distinct routines, which can be more easily reused in other applications, as shown in the code on the following page.

```
Function FormatPhoneNumber(Text As String) As String
    Dim tmp As String
    If Text <> "" Then
        ' First get rid of all embedded dashes, if any.
        tmp = FilterString(Text, "0123456789")
        ' Then reinsert them in the correct position.
        If Len(tmp) <= 7 Then
            FormatPhoneNumber = Format$(tmp, "!@@@-@@@@")
        Else
            FormatPhoneNumber = Format$(tmp, "!@@@-@@@-@@@@")
        End If
    End If
End Function

Function FormatCreditCard(Text As String) As String
    Dim tmp As String
    If Text <> "" Then
        ' First get rid of all embedded spaces, if any.
        tmp = FilterNumber(Text, False)
        ' Then reinsert them in the correct position.
        FormatCreditCard = Format$(tmp, "!@@@@ @@@@ @@@@ @@@@")
    End If
End Function
```

Unfortunately, there isn't any way to create locale-independent routines that can format any phone number anywhere in the world. But by grouping all your formatting routines in one module, you can considerably speed up your work if and when it's time to convert your code for another locale. Chapter 5 covers the *Format* function in greater detail.

Multiline TextBox Controls

You create multiline TextBox controls by setting the *MultiLine* property to True and the *ScrollBars* property to 2-Vertical or 3-Both. A vertical scroll bar causes the contents of the control to automatically wrap when a line is too long for the control's width, so this setting is most useful when you're creating memo fields or simple word processor–like programs. If you have both a vertical and a horizontal scroll bar, the TextBox control behaves more like a programmer's editor, and longer lines simply extend beyond the right border. I've never found a decent use for the other settings of the *ScrollBars* property (0-None and 1-Horizontal) in a multiline TextBox control. Visual Basic ignores the *ScrollBars* property if *MultiLine* is False.

Both these properties are read-only at run time, which means that you can't alternate between a regular and a multiline text box, or between a word processor–

like multiline field (*ScrollBars* = 2-Vertical) and an editorlike field (*ScrollBars* = 3-Both). To tell the whole truth, Visual Basic's support for multiline TextBox controls leaves much to be desired. You can do very little with such controls at run time, except to retrieve and set their *Text* properties. When you read the contents of a multiline TextBox control, it's up to you to determine where each line of text starts and ends. You do this with a loop that searches for carriage return (CR) and line feed (LF) pairs, or even more easily using the new *Split* string function:

```
' Print the lines of text in Text1, labeling them with their line numbers.
Dim lines() As String, i As Integer
lines() = Split(Text1.Text, vbCrLf)
For i = 0 To UBound(lines)
    Print (i + 1) & ": " & lines(i)
Next
```

The support offered by Visual Basic for multiline TextBox controls ends here. The language doesn't offer any means for learning such vital information as at which point each line of text wraps, which are the first visible line and the first visible column, which line and column the caret is on, and so on. Moreover, you have no means of programmatically scrolling through a multiline text box. The solutions to these problems require Microsoft Windows API programming, which I'll explain in the Appendix. In my opinion, however, Visual Basic should offer these features as built-in properties and methods.

You should account for two minor issues when including one or more multiline TextBox controls on your forms. When you enter code in a word processor or an editor, you expect that the Enter key will add a newline character (more precisely, a CR-LF character pair) and that the Tab key will insert a tab character and move the caret accordingly. Visual Basic supports these keys, but because both of them have special meaning to Windows the support is limited: The Enter key adds a CR-LF pair only if there isn't a default push button on the form, and the Tab key inserts a tab character only if there aren't other controls on the form whose *TabStop* property is set to True. In many circumstances, these requirements can't be met, and some of your users will find your user interface annoying. If you can't avoid this problem, at least add a reminder to your users that they can add new lines using the Ctrl+Enter key combination and insert tab characters using the Ctrl+Tab key combination. Another possible approach is to set the *TabStop* property to False for all the controls in the form in the multiline TextBox's *GotFocus* event and to restore the original values in the *LostFocus* event procedure.

LABEL AND FRAME CONTROLS

Label and Frame controls have a few features in common, so it makes sense to explain them together. First they're mostly "decorative" controls that contribute to the user interface but are seldom used as programmable objects. In other words, you often place them on the form and arrange their properties as your user interface needs dictate, but you rarely write code to serve their events, generally, or manipulate their properties at run time.

Label Controls

Most people use Label controls to provide a descriptive caption and possibly an associated hot key for other controls, such as TextBox, ListBox, and ComboBox, that don't expose the *Caption* property. In most cases, you just place a Label control where you need it, set its *Caption* property to a suitable string (embedding an ampersand character in front of the hot key you want to assign), and you're done. *Caption* is the default property for Label controls. Be careful to set the Label's *TabIndex* property so that it's 1 minus the *TabIndex* property of the companion control.

Other useful properties are *BorderStyle* (if you want the Label control to appear inside a 3D border) and *Alignment* (if you want to align the caption to the right or center it on the control). In most cases, the alignment depends on how the Label control relates to its companion control: for example, if the Label control is placed to the left of its companion field, you might want to set its *Alignment* property to 1-Right Justify. The value 2-Center is especially useful for stand-alone Label controls. (See Figure 3-3.)

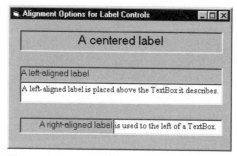

Figure 3-3. *Different settings for the* Alignment *property of Label controls.*

TIP You can insert a literal & character in a Label control's *Caption* property by doubling it. For example, to see Research & Development you have to type *&Research && Development*. Note that if you have multiple but isolated &s, the one that selects the hot key is the last one and all others are ignored. This tip applies to all the controls that expose a *Caption* property. (The & has no special meaning in forms' Caption properties, however.)

If the caption string is a long one, you might want to set the Label's *WordWrap* property to True so that it will extend for multiple lines instead of being truncated by the right border of the control. Alternatively, you might decide to set the *AutoSize* property to True and let the control automatically resize itself to accommodate longer caption strings.

You sometimes need to modify the default value of a Label's *BackStyle* property. Label controls usually cover what's already on the form's surface (other lightweight controls, output from graphic methods, and so on) because their background is considered to be opaque. If you want to show a character string somewhere on the form but at the same time you don't want to obscure underlying objects, set the *BackStyle* property to 0-Transparent.

If you're using the Label control to display data read from elsewhere—for example, a database field or a text file—you should set its *UseMnemonics* property to False. In this case, & characters have no special meaning to the control, and so you indirectly turn off the control's hot key capability. I mention this property because in older versions of Visual Basic, you had to manually double each & character to make the ampersand appear in text. I don't think all developers are aware that you can now treat ampersands like regular characters.

As I said before, you don't usually write code in Label control event procedures. This control exposes only a subset of the events supported by other controls. For example, because Label controls can never get the input focus, they don't support *GotFocus*, *LostFocus*, or any keyboard-related events. In practice, you can take advantage only of their mouse events: *Click*, *DblClick*, *MouseDown*, *MouseMove*, and *MouseUp*. If you're using a Label control to display data read from a database, you might sometimes find it useful to write code in its *Change* event. A Label control doesn't expose a specific event that tells programmers when users press its hot keys.

You can do some interesting tricks with Label controls. For example, you can use them to provide rectangular hot spots for images loaded onto the form. To see what I mean, have a look at Figure 3-4 on the following page. To create that context-sensitive ToolTip, I loaded the image on the form using the form's *Picture* property and then I placed a Label control over the Microsoft BackOffice logo, setting its *Caption* property to an empty string and the *BackStyle* property to 0-Transparent. These properties make the Label invisible, but it correctly shows its ToolTip when necessary. And because it still receives all mouse events, you can use its *Click* event to react to users' actions.

Figure 3-4. *Create hot spots the easy way with invisible Label controls.*

Frame Controls

Frame controls are similar to Label controls in that they can serve as captions for those controls that don't have their own. Moreover, Frame controls can also (and often do) behave as containers and host other controls. In most cases, you only need to drop a Frame control on a form and set its *Caption* property. If you want to create a borderless frame, you can set its *BorderStyle* property to 0-None.

Controls that are contained in the Frame control are said to be *child controls*. Moving a control at design time *over* a Frame control—or over any other container, for that matter—doesn't automatically make that control a child of the Frame control. After you create a Frame control, you can create a child control by selecting the child control's icon in the Toolbox and drawing a new instance *inside* the Frame's border. Alternatively, to make an existing control a child of a Frame control, you must select the control, press Ctrl+X to cut it to the Clipboard, select the Frame control, and press Ctrl+V to paste the control inside the Frame. If you don't follow this procedure and you simply move the control over the Frame, the two controls remain completely independent of each other, even if the other control appears in front of the Frame control.

Frame controls, like all container controls, have two interesting features. If you move a Frame control, all the child controls go with it. If you make a container control disabled or invisible, all its child controls also become disabled or invisible. You can exploit these features to quickly change the state of a group of related controls.

COMMANDBUTTON, CHECKBOX, AND OPTIONBUTTON CONTROLS

When compared to TextBox controls, these controls are really simple. Not only do they expose relatively few properties, they also support a limited number of events, and you don't usually write much code to manage them.

CommandButton Controls

Using CommandButton controls is trivial. In most cases, you just draw the control on the form's surface, set its *Caption* property to a suitable string (adding an & character to associate a hot key with the control if you so choose), and you're finished, at least with user-interface issues. To make the button functional, you write code in its *Click* event procedure, as in this fragment:

```
Private Sub Command1_Click()
    ' Save data, then unload the current form.
    Call SaveDataToDisk
    Unload Me
End Sub
```

You can use two other properties at design time to modify the behavior of a CommandButton control. You can set the *Default* property to True if it's the default push button for the form (the button that receives a click when the user presses the Enter key—usually the OK or Save button). Similarly, you can set the *Cancel* property to True if you want to associate the button with the Escape key.

The only relevant CommandButton's run-time property is *Value*, which sets or returns the state of the control (True if pressed, False otherwise). *Value* is also the default property for this type of control. In most cases, you don't need to query this property because if you're inside a button's *Click* event you can be sure that the button is being activated. The *Value* property is useful only for programmatically clicking a button:

```
' This fires the button's Click event.
Command1.Value = True
```

The CommandButton control supports the usual set of keyboard and mouse events (*KeyDown, KeyPress, KeyUp, MouseDown, MouseMove, MouseUp*, but not the *DblClick* event) and also the *GotFocus* and *LostFocus* events, but you'll rarely have to write code in the corresponding event procedures.

CheckBox Controls

CheckBox controls are useful when you want to offer your users a yes or no, true or false choice. Anytime you click on this control, it toggles between the yes state and the no state. This control can also be *grayed* when the state of the CheckBox is unavailable, but you must manage that state through code.

When you place a CheckBox control on a form, all you have to do, usually, is set its *Caption* property to a descriptive string. You might sometimes want to move the little check box to the right of its caption, which you do by setting the *Alignment* property to 1-Right Justify, but in most cases the default setting is OK. If you want to display the control in a checked state, you set its *Value* property to 1-Checked right in the Properties window, and you set a grayed state with 2-Grayed.

The only important event for CheckBox controls is the *Click* event, which fires when either the user or the code changes the state of the control. In many cases, you don't need to write code to handle this event. Instead, you just query the control's *Value* property when your code needs to process user choices. You usually write code in a CheckBox control's *Click* event when it affects the state of other controls. For example, if the user clears a check box, you might need to disable one or more controls on the form and reenable them when the user clicks on the check box again. This is how you usually do it (here I grouped all the relevant controls in one frame named Frame1):

```
Private Sub Check1_Click()
    Frame1.Enabled = (Check1.Value = vbChecked)
End Sub
```

Note that *Value* is the default property for CheckBox controls, so you can omit it in code. I suggest that you not do that, however, because it would reduce the readability of your code.

OptionButton Controls

OptionButton controls are also known as *radio buttons* because of their shape. You always use OptionButton controls in a group of two or more because their purpose is to offer a number of mutually exclusive choices. Anytime you click on a button in the group, it switches to a selected state and all the other controls in the group become unselected.

Preliminary operations for an OptionButton control are similar to those already described for CheckBox controls. You set an OptionButton control's *Caption* property to a meaningful string, and if you want you can change its *Alignment* property to make the control right aligned. If the control is the one in its group that's in the selected state, you also set its *Value* property to True. (The OptionButton's *Value* property is a Boolean value because only two states are possible.) *Value* is the default property for this control.

At run time, you typically query the control's *Value* property to learn which button in its group has been selected. Let's say you have three OptionButton controls, named *optWeekly*, *optMonthly*, and *optYearly*. You can test which one has been selected by the user as follows:

```
If optWeekly.Value Then
    ' User prefers weekly frequency.
ElseIf optMonthly.Value Then
    ' User prefers monthly frequency.
ElseIf optYearly.Value Then
    ' User prefers yearly frequency.
End If
```

Strictly speaking, you can avoid the test for the last OptionButton control in its group because all choices are supposed to be mutually exclusive. But the approach I just showed you increases the code's readability.

A group of OptionButton controls is often hosted in a Frame control. This is necessary when there are other groups of OptionButton controls on the form. As far as Visual Basic is concerned, *all* the OptionButton controls on a form's surface belong to the same group of mutually exclusive selections, even if the controls are placed at the opposite corners of the window. The only way to tell Visual Basic which controls belong to which group is by gathering them inside a Frame control. Actually, you can group your controls within any control that can work as a container—PictureBox, for example—but Frame controls are often the most reasonable choice.

Going Graphical

CheckBox, OptionButton, and CommandButton controls have been with Visual Basic since version 1, and their basic set of properties have remained unchanged for years. Visual Basic 5, however, introduced a new, interesting graphic mode, which transforms these old-fashioned controls into more modern user-interface gadgets that are more likely to catch your users' attention, as you can see in Figure 3-5 on the following page. Since the properties involved are exactly the same for all three controls, I'll describe them together.

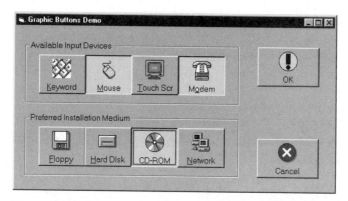

Figure 3-5. *CheckBox, OptionButton, and CommandButton controls come with a graphic flavor.*

If you want to create a graphical control, you begin by setting its *Style* property to 1-Graphical; the appearance of the control changes, and a border is drawn around it. (This is more evident with CheckBox and OptionButton controls.) Then you choose a suitable image by clicking on the *Picture* property and navigating through your collection of icons and bitmaps. (You have a collection of icons and bitmaps, don't you?) In most cases, this is all you need to do to create graphical buttons. If you care about the details, you can select a second icon for the down state and assign it to the *DownPicture* property. You can also select a different icon for the disabled state and assign it to the *DisabledPicture* property. You can set these properties at run time, even though this is strictly necessary only when you create the user interface dynamically (for instance, a user-defined toolbar with his or her favorite commands):

```
Command1.Picture = LoadPicture("c:\vb6\myicon.ico")
```

You might need to consider two additional properties when you're assigning images. The *MaskColor* property defines which color in the bitmap is to be considered the transparent color. Any pixels in the loaded picture that match this color won't be transferred; in their place, the regular button background color will be used. (The default value for this property is &HC0C0C0, light gray. The *MaskColor* property is active only if you also set the *UseMaskColor* to True, however—otherwise, it's ignored. These properties are useful only for bitmaps because icons (ICO files) and metafiles (WMF and EMF files) already include information about transparency. Note that you should always assign an RGB color to the *MaskColor* property (as opposed to a system color) because system colors depend on the end user's settings, and your button might not appear on other systems as it appears on yours.

Apart from the graphical look, CheckBox, OptionButton, and CommandButton controls using the Style=1-Graphical setting behave exactly like their textual counterparts. If you have a series of graphical radio buttons, only one of them stays down when pressed. When you press a graphical CheckBox control once, it goes into the down state, which is really the checked state. You press the button again to make it go in the up, or the clear, state. It's that simple.

LISTBOX AND COMBOBOX CONTROLS

ListBox and ComboBox controls share many properties, methods, and events. ListBox controls are somewhat more powerful, so let's start with them. Explaining ComboBox controls afterward will be a walk in the park.

ListBox Controls

Once you have dropped a ListBox control on a form's surface, you might need to assign a few properties. For example, you set the *Sorted* attribute to True to create ListBox controls that automatically sort their items in alphabetical order. By acting on the *Columns* property, you create a different type of list box, with several columns and a horizontal scroll bar, as you can see in Figure 3-6, instead of the default list box with a single column and a vertical scroll bar along its right border. You can make assignments for both these properties only at design time, and you can't change the style of the ListBox control while the program is running.

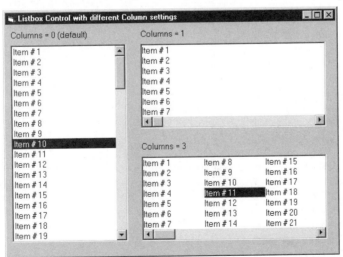

Figure 3-6. *Effects of different settings for the* Column *property.*

The *IntegralHeight* property is seldom modified, but it deserves some explanation because it indirectly gets in the way during regular programming. By default, Visual Basic automatically adjusts the height of ListBox controls so that they display entire rows; no item is shown only partially. The exact height assigned to the control depends on several factors, including current font attributes. This behavior is usually OK, and you normally don't have to worry about this issue. But if you want to resize the control to align it with other controls on the form or with the form's border, this feature might prevent you from doing such an adjustment. In this case, you should set the *IntegralHeight* property to False in the Properties window: Visual Basic won't enforce a particular height and you're free to resize the control as you prefer. Unfortunately, you can't modify this property at run time.

If you know at design time which items must appear in the ListBox control, you can save some code and enter the items right in the Properties window, in the List property mini-editor, as you can see in Figure 3-7. But if you're going to enter more than four or five items, you'd probably better add them via code at run time.

Figure 3-7. *Entering items at design time. (Press Ctrl+Enter to move to the next line.)*

Both ListBox and ComboBox controls expose the *AddItem* method, which lets you add items when the program is executing. You usually use this method in the *Form_Load* event procedure:

```
Private Sub Form_Load()
    List1.AddItem "First"
    List1.AddItem "Second"
    List1.AddItem "Third"
End Sub
```

In real-world applications, you rarely load individual items in this way. Most often your data is already stored in an array or in a database, and you have to scan the source of your data with a *For...Next* loop, as in the following code:

```
' MyData is an array of strings.
For i = LBound(MyData) To UBound(MyData)
    List1.AddItem MyData(i)
Next
```

> **TIP** If you want to load many items in a list box but don't want to create an array, you can resort to Visual Basic's *Choose* function, as follows:
>
> ```
> For i = 1 To 5
>     List1.AddItem Choose(i, "America", "Europe", "Asia", _
>         "Africa", "Australia")"
> Next
> ```
>
> Some special cases don't even require you to list individual items:
>
> ```
> ' The names of the months (locale-aware)
> For i = 1 To 12
>     List1.AddItem MonthName(i)
> Next
> ' The names of the days of the week (locale-aware)
> For i = 1 To 7
>     List1.AddItem WeekDayName(i)
> Next
> ```
>
> *MonthName* and *WeekDayName* are new Visual Basic string functions, described in Chapter 5.

If you want to load dozens or hundreds of items, a better approach is to store them in a text file and have your program read the file when the form loads. This way you can later change the contents of your ListBox controls without recompiling the source code:

```
Private Sub Form_Load()
    Dim item As String
    On Error Goto Error_Handler
    Open "listbox.dat" For Input As #1
    Do Until EOF(1)
        Line Input #1, item
        List1.AddItem item
    Loop
    Close #1
    Exit Sub
Error_Handler:
    MsgBox "Unable to load Listbox data"
End Sub
```

Sometimes you need to add an item in a given position, which you do by passing a second argument to the *AddItem* method. (Note that indexes are zero-based.)

```
' Add at the very beginning of the list.
List1.AddItem "Zero", 0
```

This argument has precedence over the *Sorted* attribute, so you can actually insert some items out of order even in sorted ListBox controls. Removing items is easy with the *RemoveItem* or *Clear* methods:

```
' Remove the first item in the list.
List1.RemoveItem 0
' Quickly remove all items (no need for a For…Next loop).
List1.Clear
```

The most obvious operation to be performed at run time on a filled ListBox control is to determine which item has been selected by the user. The *ListIndex* property returns the index of the selected item (zero-based), while the *Text* property returns the actual string stored in the ListBox. The *ListIndex* property returns –1 if the user hasn't selected any element yet, so you should test for this condition first:

```
If List1.ListIndex = -1 Then
    MsgBox "No items selected"
Else
    MsgBox "User selected " & List1.Text & " (#" & List1.ListIndex & ")"
End If
```

You can also assign a value to the *ListIndex* property to programmatically select an item, or set it to –1 to deselect all items:

```
' Select the third item in the list.
List1.ListIndex = 2
```

The *ListCount* property returns the number of items in the control. You can use it with the *List* property to enumerate them:

```
For i = 0 To List1.ListCount - 1
    Print "Item #" & i & " = " & List1.List(i)
Next
```

Reacting to user actions

If your form doesn't immediately react to a user's selections on the ListBox control, you don't have to write any code to handle its events. But this is true only for trivial Visual Basic applications. In most cases, you'll have to respond to the *Click* event, which occurs whenever a new element has been selected (with the mouse, with the keyboard, or programmatically):

```
Private Sub List1_Click()
    Debug.Print "User selected item #" & List1.ListIndex
Next
```

The logic behind your user interface might require that you monitor the *DblClick* event as well. As a general rule, double-clicking on a ListBox control's item should have the same effect as selecting the item and then clicking on a push button (often the default push button on the form). Take, for example, the mutually exclusive ListBox controls shown in Figure 3-8, a type of user interface that you see in many Windows applications. Implementing this structure in Visual Basic is straightforward:

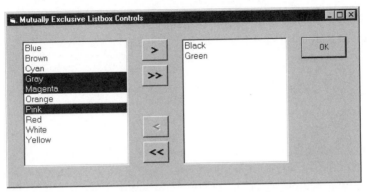

Figure 3-8. *A pair of mutually exclusive ListBox controls. You can move items around using the buttons in the middle or by double-clicking them.*

```
Private Sub cmdMove_Click()
    ' Move one item from left to right.
    If lstLeft.ListIndex >= 0 Then
        lstRight.AddItem lstLeft.Text
        lstLeft.RemoveItem lstLeft.ListIndex
    End If
End Sub


Private Sub cmdMoveAll_Click()
    ' Move all items from left to right.
    Do While lstLeft.ListCount
        lstRight.AddItem lstLeft.List(0)
        lstLeft.RemoveItem 0
    Loop
End Sub


Private Sub cmdBack_Click()
    ' Move one item from right to left.
    If lstRight.ListIndex >= 0 Then
        lstLeft.AddItem lstRight.Text
        lstRight.RemoveItem lstRight.ListIndex
    End If
End Sub
```

(continued)

```
Private Sub cmdBackAll_Click()
    ' Move all items from right to left.
    Do While lstRight.ListCount
        lstLeft.AddItem lstRight.List(0)
        lstRight.RemoveItem 0
    Loop
End Sub

Private Sub lstLeft_DblClick()
    ' Simulate a click on the Move button.
    cmdMove.Value = True
End Sub

Private Sub lstRight_DblClick()
    ' Simulate a click on the Back button.
    cmdBack.Value = True
End Sub
```

The *Scroll* event comes in handy when you need to synchronize a ListBox control with another control, often another list box; in such cases, you usually want to scroll the two controls together, so you need to know when either one is scrolled. The *Scroll* event is often used in conjunction with the *TopIndex* property, which sets or returns the index of the first visible item in the list area. Using the *Scroll* event together with the *TopIndex* property, you can achieve really interesting visual effects, such as the one displayed in Figure 3-9. The trick is that the leftmost ListBox control is partially covered by the other control. Its companion scroll bar is never seen by users, who are led to believe that they're acting on a single control. For the best effect, you need to write code that keeps the two controls always in sync, and you achieve that by trapping *Click*, *MouseDown*, *MouseMove*, and *Scroll* events. The following code synchronizes two lists, *lstN* and *lstSquare*:

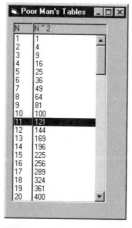

Figure 3-9. *You don't need a grid control to simulate a simple table; two partially overlapping ListBox controls will suffice.*

```
Private Sub lstN_Click()
    ' Synchronize list boxes.
    lstSquare.TopIndex = lstN.TopIndex
    lstSquare.ListIndex = lstN.ListIndex
End Sub
Private Sub lstSquare_Click()
    ' Synchronize list boxes.
    lstN.TopIndex = lstSquare.TopIndex
    lstN.ListIndex = lstSquare.ListIndex
End Sub

Private Sub lstN_MouseDown(Button As Integer, Shift As Integer, _
    X As Single, Y As Single)
    Call lstN_Click
End Sub
Private Sub lstSquare_MouseDown(Button As Integer, _
    Shift As Integer, X As Single, Y As Single)
    Call lstSquare_Click
End Sub

Private Sub lstN_MouseMove(Button As Integer, Shift As Integer, _
    X As Single, Y As Single)
    Call lstN_Click
End Sub
Private Sub lstSquare_MouseMove(Button As Integer, _
    Shift As Integer, X As Single, Y As Single)
    Call lstSquare_Click
End Sub

Private Sub lstN_Scroll()
    lstSquare.TopIndex = lstN.TopIndex
End Sub
Private Sub lstSquare_Scroll()
    lstN.TopIndex = lstSquare.TopIndex
End Sub
```

The *ItemData* property

The information you place in a ListBox control is rarely independent from the rest of the application. For example, the customer's name that you see on screen is often related to a corresponding CustomerID number, a product name is associated with its description, and so on. The problem is that once you load a value into the ListBox control you somehow disrupt such relationships; the code in event procedures sees only *ListIndex* and *List* properties. How can you retrieve the CustomerID value that was originally associated with the name that the user has just clicked on? The answer to this question is provided by the *ItemData* property, which lets you associate a 32-bit integer value with each item loaded in the ListBox control, as in the code on the following page.

```
' Add an item to the end of the list.
lstCust.AddItem CustomerName
' Remember the matching CustomerID.
lstCust.ItemData(lstCust.ListCount - 1) = CustomerId
```

Note that you must pass an index to the *ItemData* property: Because the item you have just added is now the last one in the ListBox control, its index is *ListCount–1*. Unfortunately, this simple approach doesn't work with sorted ListBox controls, which can place new items anywhere in the list. In this case, you use the *NewIndex* property to find out where an item has been inserted:

```
' Add an item to the end of the list.
lstCust.AddItem CustomerName
' Remember the matching ID. (This also works with Sorted list boxes.)
lstCust.ItemData(lstCust.NewIndex) = CustomerId
```

In real-world applications, associating a 32-bit integer value with an item in a ListBox control is often inadequate, and you usually need to store more complex information. In this case, you use the *ItemData* value as an index into another structure, for example, an array of strings or an array of records. Let's say you have a list of product names and descriptions:

```
Type ProductUDT
    Name As String
    Description As String
    Price As Currency
End Type
Dim Products() As ProductUDT, i As Long

Private Sub Form_Load()
    ' Load product list from database into Products.
    ' ... (code omitted)
    ' Load product names into a sorted ListBox.
    For i = LBound(Products) To UBound(Products)
        lstProducts.AddItem Products(i).Name
        ' Remember where this product comes from.
        lstProducts.ItemData(lstProducts.NewIndex) = i
    Next
End Sub

Private Sub lstProducts_Click()
    ' Show the description and price of the item
    ' currently selected, using two companion labels.
    i = lstProducts.ItemData(lstProducts.ListIndex)
    lblDescription.Caption = Products(i).Description
    lblPrice.Caption = Products(i).Price
End Sub
```

Multiple-selection ListBox controls

The ListBox control is even more flexible than I've shown so far because it lets users select multiple items at the same time. To enable this feature, you assign the *MultiSelect* property the values 1-Simple or 2-Extended. In the former case, you can select and deselect individual items only by using the Spacebar or the mouse. In extended selection, you can also use the Shift key to select ranges of items. Most popular Windows programs use extended selection exclusively, so you shouldn't use the value 1-Simple unless you have a good reason to do so. The *MultiSelect* property can't be changed when the program is running, so this is a design-time decision.

Working with a multiple selection ListBox control isn't different from interacting with a regular ListBox in the sense that you still use the *ListIndex*, *ListCount*, *List*, and *ItemData* properties. In this case, the most important piece of information is held in the *SelCount* and *Selected* properties. The *SelCount* property simply returns the number of items that are currently selected. You usually test it within a *Click* event:

```
Private Sub lstProducts_Click()
    ' The OK button should be enabled only if the
    ' user has selected at least one product.
    cmdOK.Enabled = (lstProducts.SelCount > 0)
End Sub
```

You retrieve the items that are currently selected using the *Selected* property. For example, this routine prints all selected items:

```
' Print a list of selected products.
Dim i As Long
For i = 0 To lstProducts.ListCount - 1
    If lstProducts.Selected(i) Then Print lstProducts.List(i)
Next
```

The *Select* property can be written to, which is sometimes necessary to clear the current selection:

```
For i = 0 To lstProducts.ListCount - 1
    lstProducts.Selected(i) = False
Next
```

Visual Basic 5 introduced a new variant of multiple selection ListBox controls, which let users select items by flagging a check box, as you see in Figure 3-10 on the following page. To enable this capability, you set the ListBox control's *Style* property to 1-Checkbox at design time. (You can't change it at run time.) ListBox controls with check boxes are always multiselect, and the actual value of the *MultiSelect* property is ignored. These ListBox controls let the user select and deselect one item at a time, so it's often convenient to provide the user with two buttons—Select All and Clear All (and sometimes Invert Selection too).

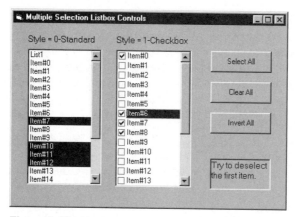

Figure 3-10. *Two variants for multiple selection ListBox controls.*

Apart from their appearance, there's nothing special about ListBox controls set as Style = 1-Checkbox, in that you can set and query the selected state of items through the *Selected* property. However, selecting and deselecting multiple items through code doesn't happen as quickly as you might believe. For example, this is the code for handling the *Click* event of the Select All button:

```
Private Sub cmdSelectAll_Click()
    Dim i As Long, saveIndex As Long, saveTop As Long
    ' Save current state.
    saveIndex = List2.ListIndex
    saveTop = List2.TopIndex
    ' Make the list box invisible to avoid flickering.
    List2.Visible = False
    ' Change the select state for all items.
    For i = 0 To List2.ListCount - 1
        List2.Selected(i) = True
    Next
    ' Restore original state, and make the list box visible again.
    List2.TopIndex = saveTop
    List2.ListIndex = saveIndex
    List2.Visible = True
End Sub
```

The code for the Clear All and Invert All buttons is similar, except for the statement inside the *For…Next* loop. This approach is necessary because writing to the *Selected* property also affects the *ListIndex* property and causes a lot of flickering. Saving the current state in two temporary variables solves the former problem, while making the control temporarily invisible solves the latter.

Interestingly, making the control invisible doesn't actually hide it, not immediately at least. If you operate on a control and want to avoid flickering or other disturbing visual effects, make it invisible, do your stuff, and then make it visible again before the procedure ends. If the procedure doesn't include any *DoEvents* or *Refresh* statement, the screen isn't updated and the user will never notice that the control has been made temporarily invisible. To see how the code would work without resorting to this technique, add a *DoEvents* or a *Refresh* statement to the preceding code, immediately before the *For...Next* loop.

ListBox controls with Style = 1-Checkbox offer an additional event, *ItemCheck*, that fires when the user selects or deselects the check box. You can use this event to refuse to select or deselect a given item:

```
Private Sub List2_ItemCheck(Item As Integer)
    ' Refuse to deselect the first item.
    If Item = 0 And List2.Selected(0) = False Then
        List2.Selected(0) = True
        MsgBox "You can't deselect the first item", vbExclamation
    End If
End Sub
```

ComboBox Controls

ComboBox controls are very similar to ListBox controls, so much of what I have explained so far applies to them as well. More precisely, you can create ComboBox controls that automatically sort their items using the *Sorted* property, you can add items at design time using the *List* item in the Properties window, and you can set a Combo-Box control's *IntegralHeight* property as your user interface dictates. Most run-time methods are common to both kinds of controls too, including *AddItem*, *RemoveItem*, and *Clear*, as are the *ListCount*, *ListIndex*, *List*, *ItemData*, *TopIndex*, and *NewIndex* properties and the *Click*, *DblClick*, and *Scroll* events. ComboBox controls don't support multiple columns and multiple selections, so you don't have to deal with the *Column*, *MultiSelect*, *Select*, and *SelCount* properties and the *ItemCheck* event.

The ComboBox control is a sort of mixture between a ListBox and a TextBox control in that it also includes several properties and events that are more typical of the latter, such as the *SelStart*, *SelLength*, *SelText*, and *Locked* properties and the *KeyDown*, *KeyPress*, and *KeyUp* events. I've already explained many things that you can do with these properties and won't repeat myself here. Suffice it to say that you can apply to ComboBox controls most of the techniques that are valid for TextBox controls, including automatic formatting and deformatting of data in *GotFocus* and *LostFocus* event procedures and validation in *Validate* event procedures.

The most characteristic ComboBox control property is *Style*, which lets you pick one among the three styles available, as you can see in Figure 3-11 on the following page. When you set Style = 0-DropDown Combo, what you get is the classic combo; you can enter a value in the edit area or select one from the drop-down list. The setting *Style* = 1-Simple Combo is similar, but the list area is always visible so that in this case you really have a compounded TextBox plus ListBox control. By default, Visual Basic creates a control that's only tall enough to show the edit area, and you must resize it to make the list portion visible. Finally, *Style* = 2-Dropdown List suppresses the edit area and gives you only a drop-down list to choose from.

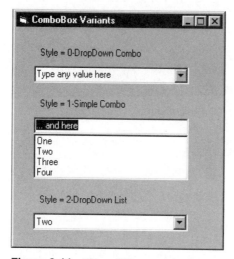

Figure 3-11. *Three different styles for ComboBox controls. The drop-down list variant doesn't allow direct editing of the contents.*

When you have a ComboBox control with *Style* = 0-Dropdown Combo or 2-Dropdown List, you can learn when the user is opening the list portion by trapping the *DropDown* event. For example, you can fill the list area just one instant before the user sees it (a sort of just-in-time data loading):

```
Private Sub Combo1_DropDown()
    Dim i As Integer
    ' Do it only once.
    If Combo1.ListCount = 0 Then
        For i = 1 To 100
            Combo3.AddItem "Item #" & i
        Next
    End If
End Sub
```

The ComboBox control supports the *Click* and *DblClick* events, but they relate only to the list portion of the control. More precisely, you get a *Click* event when the user selects an item from the list, and you get a *DblClick* event only when an item in the list is double-clicked. The latter can occur only when *Style* = 1-Simple Combo, though, and you'll never get this event for other types of ComboBox controls.

NOTE For reasons that, honestly, are beyond my imagination, *MouseDown*, *MouseUp*, and *MouseMove* events aren't supported by the ComboBox intrinsic controls. Don't ask me why. Ask Microsoft.

ComboBox controls with *Style* = 1-Simple Combo possess an intriguing feature, called *extended matching*. As you type a string, Visual Basic scrolls the list portion so that the first visible item in the list area matches the characters in the edit area.

Drop-down list controls pose special problems in programming. For example, they never raise *Change* and keyboard-related events. Moreover, you can't reference all the properties that are related to activity in the edit area, such as *SelStart*, *SelLength*, and *SelText*. (You get error 380—"Invalid property value.") The *Text* property can be read and can also be written to, provided that the value you assign is among the items in the list. (Visual Basic performs a case-insensitive search.) If you try to assign a string that isn't in the list, you get a run-time error (383—"*Text* property is read-only"), which isn't really appropriate because the *Text* property can sometimes be assigned).

PICTUREBOX AND IMAGE CONTROLS

Both PictureBox and Image controls let you display an image, so let's compare them and see when it makes sense to choose one or the other.

The PictureBox Control

PictureBox controls are among the most powerful and complex items in the Visual Basic Toolbox window. In a sense, these controls are more similar to forms than to other controls. For example, PictureBox controls support all the properties related to graphic output, including *AutoRedraw*, *ClipControls*, *HasDC*, *FontTransparent*, *CurrentX*, *CurrentY*, and all the *Drawxxxx*, *Fillxxxx*, and *Scalexxxx* properties. PictureBox controls also support all graphic methods, such as *Cls*, *PSet*, *Point*, *Line*, and *Circle* and conversion methods, such as *ScaleX*, *ScaleY*, *TextWidth*, and *TextHeight*. In other words, all the techniques that I described for forms can also be used for PictureBox controls (and therefore won't be covered again in this section).

Loading images

Once you place a PictureBox on a form, you might want to load an image in it, which you do by setting the *Picture* property in the Properties window. You can load images in many different graphic formats, including bitmaps (BMP), device independent bitmaps (DIB), metafiles (WMF), enhanced metafiles (EMF), GIF and JPEG compressed files, and icons (ICO and CUR). You can decide whether a control should display a border, resetting the *BorderStyle* to 0-None if necessary. Another property that comes handy in this phase is *AutoSize*: Set it to True and let the control automatically resize itself to fit the assigned image.

You might want to set the *Align* property of a PictureBox control to something other than the 0-None value. By doing that, you attach the control to one of the four form borders and have Visual Basic automatically move and resize the PictureBox control when the form is resized. PictureBox controls expose a *Resize* event, so you can trap it if you need to move and resize its child controls too.

You can do more interesting things at run time. To begin with, you can programmatically load any image in the control using the *LoadPicture* function:

```
Picture1.Picture = LoadPicture("c:\windows\setup.bmp")
```

and you can clear the current image using either one of the following statements:

```
' These are equivalent.
Picture1.Picture = LoadPicture("")
Set Picture1.Picture = Nothing
```

The *LoadPicture* function has been extended in Visual Basic 6 to support icon files containing multiple icons. The new syntax is the following:

```
LoadPicture(filename, [size], [colordepth], [x], [y])
```

where values in square brackets are optional. If *filename* is an icon file, you can select a particular icon using the *size* or *colordepth* arguments. Valid sizes are 0-vbLPSmall, 1-vbLPLarge (system icons whose sizes depend on the video driver), 2-vbLPSmallShell, 3-vbLPLargeShell (shell icons whose dimensions are affected by the *Caption Button* property as set in the Appearance tab in the screen's Properties dialog box), and 4-vbLPCustom (size is determined by *x* and *y*). Valid color depths are 0-vbLPDefault (the icon in the file that best matches current screen settings), 1-vbLPMonochrome, 2-vbLPVGAColor (16 colors), and 3-vbLPColor (256 colors).

You can copy an image from one PictureBox control to another by assigning the target control's *Picture* property:

```
Picture2.Picture = Picture1.Picture
```

The *PaintPicture* method

PictureBox controls are equipped with a very powerful method that enables the programmer to perform a wide variety of graphic effects, including zooming, scrolling, panning, tiling, flipping, and many fading effects: This is the *PaintPicture* method. (This method is also exposed by form objects, but it's most often used with PictureBox controls.) In a nutshell, this method performs a pixel-by-pixel copy from a source control to a destination control. The complete syntax of this method is complex and rather confusing:

```
DestPictBox.PaintPicture SrcPictBox.Picture, destX, destY, [destWidth], _
    [destHeight], [srcX], [srcY2], [srcWidth], [srcHeight], [Opcode])
```

The only required arguments are the source PictureBox control's *Picture* property and the coordinates inside the destination control where the image must be copied. The *destX* / *destY* arguments are expressed in the *ScaleMode* of the destination control; by varying them, you can make the image appear exactly where you want. For example, if the source PictureBox control contains a bitmap 3000 twips wide and 2000 twips tall, you can center this image on the destination control with this command:

```
picDest.PaintPicture picSource.Picture, (picDest.ScaleWidth - 3000) / 2, _
    (picDest.ScaleHeight - 2000) / 2
```

TIP In general, Visual Basic doesn't provide a way to determine the size of a bitmap loaded into a PictureBox control. But you can derive this information if you set the control's *AutoSize* property to True and then read the control's *ScaleWidth* and *ScaleHeight* properties. If you don't want to resize a visible control just to learn the dimensions of a bitmap, you can load it into an invisible control, or you can use this trick, based on the fact that the *Picture* property returns an StdPicture object, which in turn exposes the *Height* and *Width* properties:

```
' StdPicture's Width and Height properties are expressed in
' Himetric units.
With Picture1
    width = CInt(.ScaleX(.Picture.Width, vbHimetric, vbPixels))
    height = CInt(.ScaleY(.Picture.Height, vbHimetric, _
        vbPixels))
End With
```

By the way, in all subsequent code examples I assume that the source PictureBox control's *ScaleWidth* and *ScaleHeight* properties match the actual bitmap's size. By default, the *PaintPicture* method copies the entire source bitmap. But you can copy just a portion of it, passing a value for *srcWidth* and *srcHeight*:

```
' Copy the upper left portion of the source image.
picDest.PaintPicture picSource.Picture, 0, 0, , , , , _
    picSource.ScaleWidth / 2, picSource.ScaleHeight / 2
```

If you're copying just a portion of the source image, you probably want to pass a specific value for the *srcX* and *srcY* values as well, which correspond to the coordinates of the top-left corner of the area that will be copied from the source control:

```
' Copy the bottom-right portion of the source image
' in the corresponding corner in the destination.
wi = picSource.ScaleWidth / 2
he = picSource.ScaleHeight / 2
picDest.PaintPicture picSource.Picture, wi, he, , , wi, he, wi, he
```

You can use this method to tile a target PictureBox control (or form) with multiple copies of an image stored in another control:

```
' Start with the leftmost column.
x = 0
Do While x < picDest.ScaleWidth
    y = 0
    ' For each column, start at the top and work downward.
    Do While y < picDest.ScaleHeight
        picDest.PaintPicture picSource.Picture, x, y, , , 0, 0
```

(continued)

```
       ' Next row
       y = y + picSource.ScaleHeight
   Loop
   ' Next column
   x = x + picSource.ScaleWidth
Loop
```

Another great feature of the *PaintPicture* method lets you resize the image while you transfer it, and you can even specify different zoom-in and zoom-out factors for the *x*- and *y*-axes independently. You just have to pass a value to the *destWidth* and *destHeight* arguments: If these values are greater than the source image's corresponding dimensions, you achieve a zoom-in effect, and if they are less you get a zoom-out effect. For example, see how you can double the size of the original image:

```
picDest.PaintPicture picSource.Picture, 0, 0, _
    picSource.ScaleWidth * 2, picSource.ScaleHeight * 2
```

As a special case of the syntax of the *PaintPicture* method, the source image can even be flipped along its *x*-axis, *y*-axis, or both by passing negative values for these arguments:

```
' Flip horizontally.
picDest.PaintPicture picSource.Picture, _
    picSource.ScaleWidth, 0, -picSource.ScaleWidth
' Flip vertically.
picDest.PaintPicture picSource.Picture, 0, _
    picSource.ScaleHeight, , -picSource.ScaleHeight
' Flip the image on both axes.
picDest.PaintPicture picSource.Picture, picSource.ScaleWidth, _
    picSource.ScaleHeight, -picSource.ScaleWidth, -picSource.ScaleHeight
```

As you might expect, you can combine all these effects together, magnifying, reducing, or flipping just a portion of the source image, and have the result appear in any point of the destination PictureBox control (or form). I have prepared a demonstration program (see Figure 3-12 on the following page) that recaps what I have explained so far and also includes the complete source code for many interesting dissolve and tiling effects. You should find no problem in reusing all those routines in your own applications.

As if all these capabilities weren't enough, we haven't covered the last argument of the *PaintPicture* method yet. The *opcode* argument lets you specify which kind of Boolean operation must be performed on pixel bits as they're transferred from the source image to the destination. The values you can pass to this argument are the same that you assign to the *DrawMode* property. The default value is 13-vbCopyPen, which simply copies the source pixels in the destination control. By playing with the other settings, you can achieve many interesting graphical effects, including simple animations. For more information about the *DrawMode* property, see Chapter 2.

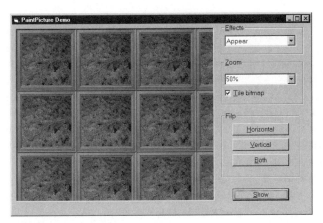

Figure 3-12. *The PaintPicture demonstration program shows several graphic effects.*

The Image Control

Image controls are far less complex than PictureBox controls. They don't support graphical methods or the *AutoRedraw* and the *ClipControls* properties, and they can't work as containers, just to hint at their biggest limitations. Nevertheless, you should always strive to use Image controls instead of PictureBox controls because they load faster and consume less memory and system resources. Remember that Image controls are windowless objects that are actually managed by Visual Basic without creating a Windows object. (For an explanation of lightweight windowless controls, see Chapter 2.) Image controls can load bitmaps and JPEG and GIF images.

When you're working with an Image control, you typically load a bitmap into its *Picture* property either at design time or at run time using the *LoadPicture* function. Image controls don't expose the *AutoSize* property because by default they resize to display the contained image (as it happens with PictureBox controls set at *AutoSize* = True). On the other hand, Image controls support a *Stretch* property that, if True, resizes the image (distorting it if necessary) to fit the control. In a sense, the *Stretch* property somewhat remedies the lack of the *PaintPicture* method for this control. In fact, you can zoom in to or reduce an image by loading it in an Image control and then setting its *Stretch* property to True to change its width and height:

```
' Load a bitmap.
Image1.Stretch = False
Image1.Picture = LoadPicture("c:\windows\setup.bmp")
' Reduce it by a factor of two.
Image1.Stretch = True
Image1.Move 0, 0, Image1.Width / 2, Image1.Width / 2
```

Image controls support all the usual mouse events. For this reason, many Visual Basic developers have used Image controls to simulate graphical buttons and toolbars. Now that Visual Basic natively supports these controls, you'd probably better use Image controls only for what they were originally intended.

SCROLLBAR CONTROLS

The HScrollBar and the VScrollBar controls are perfectly identical, apart from their different orientation. After you place an instance of such a control on a form, you have to worry about only a few properties: *Min* and *Max* represent the valid range of values, *SmallChange* is the variation in value you get when clicking on the scroll bar's arrows, and *LargeChange* is the variation you get when you click on either side of the scroll bar indicator. The default initial value for those two properties is 1, but you'll probably have to change *LargeChange* to a higher value. For example, if you have a scroll bar that lets you browse a portion of text, *SmallChange* should be 1 (you scroll one line at a time) and *LargeChange* should be set to match the number of visible text lines in the window.

The most important run-time property is *Value*, which always returns the relative position of the indicator on the scroll bar. By default, the *Min* value corresponds to the leftmost or upper end of the control:

```
' Move the indicator near the top (or left) arrow.
VScroll1.Value = VScroll1.Min
' Move the indicator near the bottom (or right) arrow.
VScroll1.Value = VScroll1.Max
```

While this setting is almost always OK for horizontal scroll bars, you might sometimes need to reverse the behavior of vertical scroll bars so that the zero is near the bottom of your form. This arrangement is often desirable if you want to use a vertical scroll bar as a sort of slider. You obtain this behavior by simply inverting the values in the *Min* and *Max* properties. (In other words, it's perfectly legal for *Min* to be greater than *Max*.)

There are two key events for scrollbar controls: the *Change* event fires when you click on the scroll bar arrows or when you drag the indicator; the *Scroll* event fires while you drag the indicator. The reason for these two distinct possibilities is mostly historical. First versions of Visual Basic supported only the *Change* event, and when developers realized that it wasn't possible to have continuous feedback when users dragged the indicator, Microsoft engineers added a new event instead of extending the *Change* event. In this way, old applications could be recompiled without unexpected changes in their behavior. At any rate, this means that you must often trap two distinct events:

```
' Show the current scroll bar's value.
Private VScroll1_Change()
    Label1.Caption = VScroll1.Value
End Sub
Private VScroll1_Scroll()
    Label1.Caption = VScroll1.Value
End Sub
```

The example shown in Figure 3-13 uses three VScrollBar controls as sliders to control the individual RGB (red, green, blue) components of a color. The three scroll bars have their *Min* property set to 255 and their *Max* property set to 0, while their *SmallChange* is 1 and *LargeChange* is 16. This example is also a moderately useful program in itself because you can select a color and then copy its numeric value to the clipboard and paste it in your application's code as a decimal value, a hexadecimal value, or an RGB function.

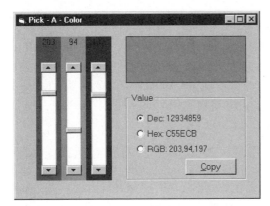

Figure 3-13. *Use scrollbar controls to visually create colors.*

Scrollbar controls can receive the input focus, and in fact they support both the *TabIndex* and *TabStop* properties. If you don't want the user to accidentally move the input focus on a scrollbar control when he or she presses the Tab key, you must explicitly set its *TabStop* property to False. When a scrollbar control has the focus, you can move the indicator using the Left, Right, Up, Down, PgUp, PgDn, Home, and End keys. For example, you can take advantage of this behavior to create a read-only TextBox control with a numeric value that can be edited only through a tiny companion scroll bar. This scroll bar appears to the user as a sort of spin button, as you can see in Figure 3-14 on the next page. To make the trick work, you need to write just a few lines of code:

```
Private Sub Text1_GotFocus()
    ' Pass the focus to the scroll bar.
    VScroll1.SetFocus
End Sub
```

(continued)

```
Private Sub VScroll1_Change()
    ' Scroll bar controls the text box value.
    Text1.Text = VScroll1.Value
End Sub
```

Figure 3-14. *You don't need external ActiveX controls to create functional spin buttons.*

Scrollbar controls are even more useful for building scrolling forms, like the one displayed in Figure 3-15 on page 136. To be certain, scrolling forms aren't the most ergonomic type of user interface you can offer to your customers: If you have that many fields in a form, you should consider using a Tab control, child forms, or some other custom interface. Sometimes, however, you badly need scrollable forms, and in this situation you are on your own because Visual Basic forms don't support scrolling.

Fortunately, it doesn't take long to convert a regular form into a scrollable one. You need a couple of scrollbar controls, plus a PictureBox control that you use as the container for all the controls on the form, and a filler control—a CommandButton, for example—that you place in the bottom-right corner of the form when it displays the two scroll bars. The secret to creating scrollable forms is that you don't move all the child controls one by one. Instead, you place all the controls in the PictureBox control (named *picCanvas* in the following code), and you move it when the user acts on the scroll bar:

```
Sub MoveCanvas()
    picCanvas.Move -HScroll1.Value, -VScroll1.Value
End Sub
```

In other words, to uncover the portion of the form near the right border, you assign a negative value to the PictureBox's *Left* property, and to display the portion near the form's bottom border you set its *Top* property to a negative value. It's really that simple. You do this by calling the *MoveCanvas* procedure from within the scroll bars' *Change* and *Scroll* events. Of course, it's critical that you write code in the *Form_Resize* event, which makes a scroll bar appear and disappear as the form is resized, and that you assign consistent values to *Max* properties of the scrollbar controls:

```
' size of scrollbars in twips
Const SB_WIDTH = 300    ' width of vertical scrollbars
Const SB_HEIGHT = 300   ' height of horizontal scrollbars
```

```
Private Sub Form_Resize()
    ' Resize the scroll bars along the form.
    HScroll1.Move 0, ScaleHeight - SB_HEIGHT, ScaleWidth - SB_WIDTH
    VScroll1.Move ScaleWidth - SB_WIDTH, 0, SB_WIDTH, _
        ScaleHeight - SB_HEIGHT
    cmdFiller.Move ScaleWidth - SB_WIDTH, ScaleHeight - SB_HEIGHT, _
        SB_WIDTH, SB_HEIGHT

    ' Put these controls on top.
    HScroll1.ZOrder
    VScroll1.ZOrder
    cmdFiller.ZOrder
    picCanvas.BorderStyle = 0

    ' A click on the arrow moves one pixel.
    HScroll1.SmallChange = ScaleX(1, vbPixels, vbTwips)
    VScroll1.SmallChange = ScaleY(1, vbPixels, vbTwips)
    ' A click on the scroll bar moves 16 pixels.
    HScroll1.LargeChange = HScroll1.SmallChange * 16
    VScroll1.LargeChange = VScroll1.SmallChange * 16

    ' If the form is larger than the picCanvas picture box,
    ' we don't need to show the corresponding scroll bar.
    If ScaleWidth < picCanvas.Width + SB_WIDTH Then
        HScroll1.Visible = True
        HScroll1.Max = picCanvas.Width + SB_WIDTH - ScaleWidth
    Else
        HScroll1.Value = 0
        HScroll1.Visible = False
    End If
    If ScaleHeight < picCanvas.Height + SB_HEIGHT Then
        VScroll1.Visible = True
        VScroll1.Max = picCanvas.Height + SB_HEIGHT - ScaleHeight
    Else
        VScroll1.Value = 0
        VScroll1.Visible = False
    End If
    ' Make the filler control visible only if necessary.
    cmdFiller.Visible = (HScroll1.Visible Or VScroll1.Visible)
    MoveCanvas
End Sub
```

Working with scrollable forms at design time isn't comfortable. I suggest that you work with a maximized form and with the PictureBox control sized as large as possible. When you're finished with the form interface, resize the PictureBox control to the smallest area that contains all the controls, and then reset the form's *WindowState* property to 0-Normal.

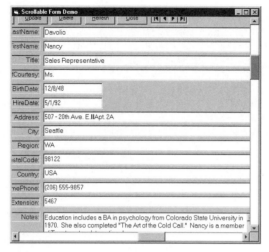

Figure 3-15. *Scrollable forms.*

DRIVELISTBOX, DIRLISTBOX, AND FILELISTBOX CONTROLS

In a nutshell, the DriveListBox control is a combobox-like control that's automatically filled with your drive's letters and volume labels. The DirListBox is a special list box that displays a directory tree. The FileListBox control is a special-purpose ListBox control that displays all the files in a given directory, optionally filtering them based on their names, extensions, and attributes.

These controls often work together on the same form; when the user selects a drive in a DriveListBox, the DirListBox control is updated to show the directory tree on that drive. When the user selects a path in the DirListBox control, the FileListBox control is filled with the list of files in that directory. These actions don't happen automatically, however—you must write code to get the job done.

After you place a DriveListBox and a DirListBox control on a form's surface, you usually don't have to set any of their properties; in fact, these controls don't expose any special property, not in the Properties window at least. The FileListBox control, on the other hand, exposes one property that you can set at design time—the *Pattern* property. This property indicates which files are to be shown in the list area: Its default value is *.* (all files), but you can enter whatever specification you need, and you can also enter multiple specifications using the semicolon as a separator. You can also set this property at run time, as in the following line of code:

```
File1.Pattern = "*.txt;*.doc;*.rtf"
```

After these preliminary steps, you're ready to set in motion the chain of events. When the user selects a new drive in the DriveListBox control, it fires a *Change* event and returns the drive letter (and volume label) in its *Drive* property. You trap this event and set the DirListBox control's *Path* property to point to the root directory of the selected drive:

```
Private Sub Drive1_Change()
    ' The Drive property also returns the volume label, so trim it.
    Dir1.Path = Left$(Drive1.Drive, 1) & ":\"
End Sub
```

When the user double-clicks on a directory name, the DirListBox control raises a *Change* event; you trap this event to set the FileListBox's *Path* property accordingly:

```
Private Sub Dir1_Change()
    File1.Path = Dir1.Path
End Sub
```

Finally, when the user clicks on a file in the FileListBox control, a *Click* event is fired (as if it were a regular ListBox control), and you can query its *Filename* property to learn which file has been selected. Note how you build the complete path:

```
Filename = File1.Path
If Right$(Filename, 1) <> "\" Then Filename = Filename & "\"
Filename = Filename & File1.Filename
```

The demonstration program shown in Figure 3-16 builds on these controls to provide a functional Image Preview utility. It also supports dynamic resizing of the controls when the form they're on is resized.

The DirListBox and FileListBox controls support most of the properties typical of the control they derive from—the ListBox control—including the *ListCount* and the *ListIndex* properties and the *Scroll* event. The FileListBox control supports multiple selection; hence you can set its *MultiSelect* property in the Properties window and query the *SelCount* and *Selected* properties at run time.

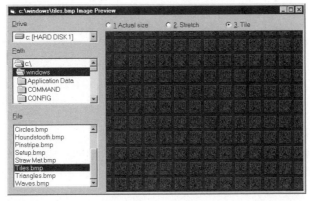

Figure 3-16. *A minimal but completely functional Image Preview utility that also supports bitmap tiling.*

The FileListBox control also exposes a few custom Boolean properties, *Normal*, *Archive*, *Hidden*, *ReadOnly*, and *System*, which permit you to decide whether files with these attributes should be listed. (By default, the control doesn't display hidden and system files.) This control also supports a couple of custom events, *PathChange* and *PatternChange*, that fire when the corresponding property is changed through code. In most cases, you don't have to worry about them, and I won't provide examples of their usage.

The problem with the DriveListBox, DirListBox and FileListBox controls is that they're somewhat outdated and aren't used by most commercial applications any longer. Moreover, these controls are known to work incorrectly when listing files on network servers and sometimes even on local disk drives, especially when long file and directory names are used. For this reason, I discourage you from using them and suggest instead that you use the Common Dialog controls for your FileOpen and FileSave dialog boxes. But if you need to ask the user for the name of a directory rather than a file, you're out of luck because—while Windows does include such a system dialog box, named BrowseForFolders dialog—Visual Basic still doesn't offer a way to display it (unless you do some advanced API programming). Fortunately, Visual Basic 6 comes with a new control—the ImageCombo control—that lets you simulate the appearance of the DriveListBox control. It also offers you a powerful library—the FileSystemObject library—that completely frees you from using these three controls, if only as hidden controls that you use just for quickly retrieving information on the file system. For more information about the FileSystemObject library and the ImageCombo control, see Chapters 5 and 10, respectively. Command dialogs are covered in Chapter 12.

OTHER CONTROLS

We still have to briefly discuss a few other controls in the Toolbox.

The Timer Control

A Timer control is invisible at run time, and its purpose is to send a periodic pulse to the current application. You can trap this pulse by writing code in the Timer's *Timer* event procedure and take advantage of it to execute a task in the background or to monitor a user's actions. This control exposes only two meaningful properties: *Interval* and *Enabled*. *Interval* stands for the number of milliseconds between subsequent pulses (*Timer* events), while *Enabled* lets you activate or deactivate events. When you place the Timer control on a form, its *Interval* is 0, which means no events. Therefore, remember to set this property to a suitable value in the Properties window or in the *Form_Load* event procedure:

```
Private Sub Form_Load()
    Timer1.Interval = 500    ' Fire two Timer events per second.
End Sub
```

Timer controls let you write interesting programs with just a few lines of code. The typical (and abused) example is a digital clock. Just to make things a bit more compelling, I added flashing colons:

```
Private Sub Timer1_Timer()
    Dim strTime As String
    strTime = Time$
    If Mid$(lblClock.Caption, 3, 1) = ":" Then
        Mid$(strTime, 3, 1)= " "
        Mid$(strTime, 6, 1) = " "
    End If
    lblClock.Caption = strTime
End Sub
```

CAUTION You must be careful not to write a lot of code in the *Timer* event procedure because this code will be executed at every pulse and therefore can easily degrade your application's performance. Just as important, never execute a *DoEvents* statement inside a *Timer* event procedure because you might cause the procedure to be reentered, especially if the *Interval* property is set to a small value and there's a lot of code inside the procedure.

Timer controls are often useful for updating status information on a regular basis. For example, you might want to display on a status bar a short description of the control that currently has the input focus. You can achieve that by writing some code in the *GotFocus* event for all the controls on the form, but when you have dozens of controls this will require a lot of code (and time). Instead, at design time load a short description for each control in its *Tag* property, and then place a Timer control on the form with an *Interval* setting of 500. This isn't a time-critical task, so you can use an even larger value. Finally add two lines of code to the control's *Timer* event:

```
Private Sub Timer1_Timer()
    On Error Resume Next
    lblStatusBar.Caption = ActiveControl.Tag
End Sub
```

The Line Control

The Line control is a decorative control whose only purpose is let you draw one or more straight lines at design time, instead of displaying them using a *Line* graphical method at run time. This control exposes a few properties whose meaning should sound familiar to you by now: *BorderColor* (the color of the line), *BorderStyle* (the same as a form's *DrawStyle* property), *BorderWidth* (the same as a form's *DrawWidth* property), and *DrawMode*. While the Line control is handy, remember that using a *Line* method at run time is usually better in terms of performance.

The Shape Control

In a sense, the Shape control is an extension of the Line control. It can display six basic shapes: Rectangle, Square, Oval, Circle, Rounded Rectangle, and Rounded Square. It supports all the Line control's properties and a few more: *BorderStyle* (0-Transparent, 1-Solid), *FillColor*, and *FillStyle* (the same as a form's properties with the same names). The same performance considerations I pointed out for the Line control apply to the Shape control.

The OLE Control

When OLE first made its appearance, the concept of Object Linking and Embedding seemed to most developers nothing short of magic. The ability to embed a Microsoft Word Document or a Microsoft Excel worksheet (see Figure 3-17) within another Windows application seemed an exciting one, and Microsoft promptly released the OLE control—then called the OLE Container control—to help Visual Basic support this capability.

In the long run, however, the *Embedding* term in OLE has lost much of its appeal and importance, and nowadays programmers are more concerned and thrilled about Automation, a subset of OLE that lets them control other Windows applications from the outside, manipulating their object hierarchies through OLE. For this reason, I won't describe the OLE control: It's a rather complex object, and a thorough description of its many properties, methods, and events (and quirks) would take too much space.

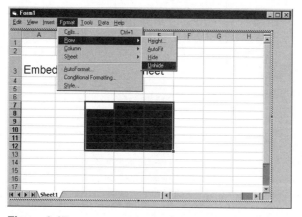

Figure 3-17. *Your Visual Basic application can host an Excel worksheet—and its menus too.*

MENUS

Menus are intrinsic controls, and as such they deserve a place in this chapter. On the other hand, menus behave differently from other controls. For example, you don't drop menu items on a form from the Toolbox; rather, you design them in the Menu Editor window, as you can see in Figure 3-18 on the following page. You invoke this tool from the Menu Editor button on the standard toolbar or by pressing the Ctrl+E shortcut key. There's also a Menu Editor command in the Tools menu, but you probably won't use it often.

Basically, each menu item has a *Caption* property (possibly with an embedded & character to create an access key) and a *Name*. Each item also exposes three Boolean properties, *Enabled*, *Visible*, and *Checked*, which you can set both at design time and at run time. At design time, you can assign the menu item a shortcut key so that your end users don't have to go through the menu system each time they want to execute a frequent command. (Do you *really* like pulling down the Edit menu any time you need to clear some text or copy it to the Clipboard?) The assigned shortcut key can't be queried at run time, much less modified. Menu items support a few other properties, but I won't describe them until Chapter 9.

Building a menu is a simple, albeit more tedious, job: You enter the item's *Caption* and *Name*, set other properties (or accept the default values for those properties), and press Enter to move to the next item. When you want to create a submenu, you press the Right Arrow button (or the Alt+R hot key). When you want to return to work on top-level menus—those items that appear in the menu bar when the application runs—you click the Left Arrow button (or press Alt+L). You can move items up and down in the hierarchy by clicking the corresponding buttons or the hot keys Alt+U and Alt+B, respectively.

You can create up to five levels of submenus (six including the menu bar), which are too many even for the most patient user. If you find yourself working with more than three menu levels, think about trashing your specifications and redesigning your application from the ground up.

You can insert a separator bar using the hypen (-) character for the *Caption* property. But even these separator items must be assigned a unique value for the *Name* property, which is a real nuisance. If you forget to enter a menu item's *Name*, the Menu Editor complains when you decide to close it. The convention used in this book is that all menu names begin with the three letters *mnu*.

Figure 3-18. *The Menu Editor window.*

One of the most annoying defects of the Menu Editor tool is that it doesn't permit you to reuse the menus you have already written in other applications. It would be great if you could open another instance of the Visual Basic IDE, copy one or more menu items to the clipboard, and then paste those menu items in the application under development. You can do that with controls and with pieces of code, but not with menus! The best thing you can do in Visual Basic is load the FRM file using an editor such as Notepad, find the portion in the file that corresponds to the menu you're interested in, load the FRM file you're developing (still in Notepad), and paste the code there. This isn't the easiest operation, and it's also moderately dangerous: If you paste the menu definition in the wrong place, you could make your FRM form completely unreadable. Therefore, always remember to make backup copies of your forms before trying this operation.

Better news is that you *can* add a finished menu to a form in your application with just a few mouse clicks. All you have to do is activate the Add-In Manager from the Add-Ins menu, choose the *VB 6 Template Manager*, and tick the Loaded/Unloaded check box. After you do that, you'll find three new commands in the Tools menu: Add Code Snippet, Add Menu, and Add Control Set. Visual Basic 6 comes with a few menu templates, as you can see in Figure 3-19, that you might find useful as a starting point for building your own templates. To create your menu templates, you only have to create a form with the complete menu and all the related code and then store this form in the \Templates\Menus directory. (The complete path, typically c:\Program Files\Microsoft Visual Studio\VB98\Template, can be found in the Environment tab of the Options dialog box on the Tools menu. The Template Manager was already available with Visual Basic 5, but it had to be installed manually and relatively few programmers were aware of its existence.

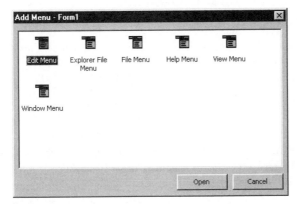

Figure 3-19. *The Template Manager in action.*

Accessing Menus at Run Time

Menu controls expose only one event, *Click*. As you expect, this event fires when the user clicks on the menu:

```
Private Sub mnuFileExit_Click()
    Unload Me
End Sub
```

You can manipulate menu items at run time through their *Checked*, *Visible*, and *Enabled* properties. For example, you can easily implement a menu item that acts as a switch and displays or hides a status bar:

```
Private Sub mnuViewStatus_Click()
    ' First, add or remove the check sign.
    mnuViewStatus.Checked = Not mnuViewStatus.Checked
    ' Then make the status bar visible or not.
    staStatusBar.Visible = mnuViewStatus.Checked
End Sub
```

While menu items can be responsible for their own *Checked* status, you usually set their *Visible* and *Enabled* properties in another region of the code. You make a menu item invisible or disabled when you want to make the corresponding command unavailable to the user. You can choose from two different strategies to achieve this goal: You can set the menu properties as soon as something happens that affects that menu command, or you can set them one instant before the menu is dropped down. Let me explain these strategies with two examples.

Let's say that the Save command from the File menu should look disabled if your application has loaded a read-only file. In this case, the most obvious place in code to set the menu *Enabled* property to False is in the procedure that loads the file, as shown in the code on the following page.

```
Private Sub LoadDataFile(filename As String)
    ' Load the file in the program.
    ' ... (code omitted)...
    ' Enable or disable the menu enabled state according to the file's
    ' read-only attribute (no need for an If...Else block).
    mnuFileSave.Enabled = (GetAttr(filename) And vbReadOnly)
End Sub
```

This solution makes sense because the menu state doesn't change often. By comparison, the state of most of the commands in a typical Edit menu (Copy, Cut, Clear, Undo, and so on) depends on whether any text is currently selected in the active control. In this case, changing the menu state any time a condition changes (because the user selects or deselects text in the active control, for example) is a waste of time, and it also requires a lot of code. Therefore, it's preferable to set the state of those menu commands in the parent menu's *Click* event just before displaying the menu:

```
Private Sub mnuEdit_Click()
    ' The user has clicked on the Edit menu,
    ' but the menu hasn't dropped down yet.
    On Error Resume Next
    ' Error handling is necessary because we don't know if
    ' the Active control actually supports these properties.
    mnuEditCopy.Enabled = (ActiveControl.SelText <> "")
    mnuEditCut.Enabled = (ActiveControl.SelText <> "")
    mnuEditClear.Enabled = (ActiveControl.SelText <> "")
End Sub
```

Pop-Up Menus

Visual Basic also supports pop-up menus, those context-sensitive menus that most commercial applications show when you right-click on an user interface object. In Visual Basic, you can display a pop-up menu by calling the form's *PopupMenu* method, typically from within the *MouseDown* event procedure of the object:

```
Private Sub List1_MouseDown(Button As Integer, Shift As Integer, _
    X As Single, Y As Single)
    If Button And vbRightButton Then
        ' User right-clicked the list box.
        PopupMenu mnuListPopup
    End If
End Sub
```

The argument you pass to the *PopupMenu* method is the name of a menu that you have defined using the Menu Editor. This might be either a submenu that you can reach using the regular menu structure or a submenu that's intended to work only as a pop-up menu. In the latter case, you should create it as a top-level menu in the Menu Editor and then set its *Visible* attribute to False. If your program includes many pop-up menus, you might find it convenient to add one invisible top-level entry and then add all the pop-up menus below it. (In this case, you don't need to make each individual item invisible.) The complete syntax of the *PopupMenu* method is quite complex:

```
PopupMenu Menu, [Flags], [X], [Y], [DefaultMenu]
```

By default, pop-up menus appear left aligned on the mouse cursor, and even if you use a right-click to invoke the menu you can select a command only with the left button. You can change these defaults using the *Flags* argument. The following constants control the alignment: 0-vbPopupMenuLeftAlign (default), 4-vbPopupMenu-CenterAlign, and 8-vbPopupMenuRightAlign. The following constants determine which buttons are active during menu operations: 0-vbPopupMenuLeftButton (default) and 2-vbPopupMenuRightButton. For example, I always use the latter because I find it natural to select a command with the right button since it's already pressed when the menu appears:

```
PopupMenu mnuListPopup, vbPopupMenuRightButton
```

The *x* and *y* arguments, if specified, make the menu appear in a particular position on the form, rather than at mouse coordinates. The last optional argument is the name of the menu that's the default item for the pop-up menu. This item will be displayed in boldface. This argument has only a visual effect; If you want to offer a default menu item, you must write code in the *MouseDown* event procedure to trap double-clicks with the right button.

> **TIP** You can take advantage of the *x* and *y* arguments in a *PopupMenu* method to make your program more Windows compliant, and show your pop-up menus over the control that has the focus when the user presses the Application key (the key beside the Windows key on the right side of a typical extended keyboard, such as the Microsoft Natural Keyboard). But remember that Visual Basic doesn't define any key-code constant for this key. Here's how you must proceed:

```
Private Sub List1_KeyDown(KeyCode As Integer, Shift As Integer)
    If KeyCode = 93 Then
        ' The system pop-up menu key has been pressed.
        ' Show a pop-up menu near the list box's center.
        PopupMenu mnuListPopup, , List1.Left + _
            List1.Width / 2, List1.Top + List1.Height / 2
    End If
End Sub
```

Visual Basic's implementation of pop-up menus has a serious flaw. All Visual Basic TextBox controls react to right-clicks by showing the standard Edit pop-up menu (with the usual commands, such as Undo, Copy, Cut, and so on). The problem is that if you invoke a *PopupMenu* method from within the TextBox control's *MouseDown* event, your custom pop-up menu will be displayed only after the standard one, which is obviously undesirable. You can solve it only by resorting to the unorthodox and undocumented technique shown on the following page.

```
Private Sub Text1_MouseDown(Button As Integer, _
    Shift As Integer, X As Single, Y As Single)
    If Button And vbRightButton Then
        Text1.Enabled = False
        PopupMenu mnuMyPopup
        Text1.Enabled = True
    End If
End Sub
```

This technique appeared for the first time in a Tech Tips supplement of the *Visual Basic Programmer's Journal*. VBPJ publishes two such supplements each year, in February and August, and they're always packed with useful tricks for Visual Basic developers of any level of expertise. You can download past issues from their *http://www.dex.com* Web site.

Control Arrays

So far, we've dealt with individual controls, each one with a distinctive name and a distinct set of properties and events. In addition to these, Visual Basic embodies the concept of *control arrays*, in which multiple controls share the same set of event procedures even though each individual element in the array can have different values for its properties. A control array can be created only at design time, and at the very minimum at least one control must belong to it. You create a control array following one of these three methods:

- You create a control and then assign a numeric, non-negative value to its *Index* property; you have thus created a control array with just one element.

- You create two controls of the same class and assign them an identical *Name* property. Visual Basic shows a dialog box warning you that there's already a control with that name and asks whether you want to create a control array. Click on the Yes button.

- You select a control on the form, press Ctrl+C to copy it to the clipboard, and then press Ctrl+V to paste a new instance of the control, which has the same *Name* property as the original one. Visual Basic shows the warning mentioned in the previous bullet.

Control arrays are one of the most interesting features of the Visual Basic environment, and they add a lot of flexibility to your programs:

- Controls that belong to the same control array share the same set of event procedures; this often dramatically reduces the amount of code you have to write to respond to a user's actions.

■ You can dynamically add new elements to a control array at run time; in other words, you can effectively create new controls that didn't exist at design time.

■ Elements of control arrays consume fewer resources than regular controls and tend to produce smaller executables. Besides, Visual Basic forms can host up to 256 different control *names,* but a control array counts as one against this number. In other words, control arrays let you effectively overcome this limit.

The importance of using control arrays as a means of dynamically creating new controls at run time is somewhat reduced in Visual Basic 6, which has introduced a new and more powerful capability. Read about dynamic control creation in Chapter 9.

Don't let the term *array* lead you to think *control array* is related to *VBA arrays*; they're completely different objects. Control arrays can only be one-dimensional. They don't need to be dimensioned: Each control you add automatically extends the array. The *Index* property identifies the position of each control in the control array it belongs to, but it's possible for a control array to have holes in the index sequence. The lowest possible value for the *Index* property is 0. You reference a control belonging to a control array as you would reference a standard array item:

```
Text1(0).Text = ""
```

Sharing Event Procedures

Event procedures related to items in a control array are easily recognizable because they have an extra *Index* parameter, which precedes all other parameters. This extra parameter receives the index of the element that's raising the event, as you can see in this example:

```
Private Sub Text1_KeyPress(Index As Integer, KeyAscii As Integer)
    MsgBox "A key has been pressed on Text1(" & Index & ") control"
End Sub
```

The fact that multiple controls can share the same set of event procedures is often in itself a good reason to create a control array. For example, say that you want to change the background color of each of your TextBox controls to yellow when it receives the input focus and restore its background color to white when the user clicks on another field:

```
Private Sub Text1_GotFocus(Index As Integer)
    Text1(Index).BackColor = vbYellow
End Sub
Private Sub Text1_LostFocus(Index As Integer)
    Text1(Index).BackColor = vbWhite
End Sub
```

Control arrays are especially useful with groups of OptionButton controls because you can remember which element in the group has been activated by adding one line of code to their shared *Click* event. This saves code when the program needs to determine which button is the active one:

```
' A module-level variable
Dim optFrequencyIndex As Integer

Private Sub optFrequency_Click(Index As Integer)
    ' Remember the last button selected.
    optFrequencyIndex = Index
End Sub
```

Creating Controls at Run Time

Once you have created a control array at design time, even with just one item, it's straightforward to create new items at run time using the *Load* command:

```
' Suppose you created Text(0) at design time.
Load Text1(1)
' Move the new control where you need it, and resize it.
Text1(1).Move 1200, 2000, 800, 350
' Set other properties as required.
Text1(1).MaxLength = 10
...
' Finally make it visible.
Text1(1).Visible = True
```

The *Load* command creates the new control with exactly the same set of properties that the first item of the array—*Text1(0)* in the preceding example—had at design time, including the position on the form. The only exception to this rule is that the *Visible* property for a control created in this way is always False because Visual Basic correctly expects that you want to move the new control to a different position before making it visible. Once you have dynamically added a control, it belongs to the control array and can be treated exactly like those controls created at design time.

You can remove controls from a control array using the *Unload* command, as in the following line of code:

```
Unload Text1(1)
```

You can unload only controls that were added dynamically at run time; if you use the *Unload* command on an item of the array that had been created at design time, an error occurs. If you unload an item and then reload an item with the same index, you're actually creating a brand-new instance, which inherits its properties, size, and position from the first element in the array, as I explained previously.

Iterating on the Items of a Control Array

Control arrays often let you save many lines of code because you can execute the same statement, or group of statements, for every control in the array without having to duplicate the code for each distinct control. For example, you can clear the contents of all the items in an array of TextBox controls as follows:

```
For i = txtFields.LBound To txtFields.UBound
    txtFields(i).Text = ""
Next
```

Here you're using the *LBound* and *UBound* methods exposed by the *control array object,* which is an intermediate object used by Visual Basic to gather all the controls in the array. In general, you shouldn't use this approach to iterate over all the items in the array because if the array has holes in the Index sequence an error will be raised. A better way to loop over all the items of a control array is using the *For Each* statement:

```
Dim txt As TextBox
For Each txt In txtFields
    txt.Text = ""
Next
```

A third method exposed by the control array object, *Count*, returns the number of elements it contains. It can be useful on several occasions (for example, when removing all the controls that were added dynamically at run time):

```
' This code assumes that txtField(0) is the only control that was
' created at design time (you can't unload it at run time).
Do While txtFields.Count > 1
    Unload txtFields(txtFields.UBound)
Loop
```

Arrays of Menu Items

Control arrays are especially useful with menus because arrays offer a solution to the proliferation of menu *Click* events and, above all, permit you to create new menus at run time. An array of menu controls is conceptually similar to a regular control array, only you set the *Index* property to a numeric (non-negative) value in the Menu Editor instead of in the Properties window.

There are some limitations, though: All the items in an array of menu controls must be adjacent and must belong to the same menu level, and their *Index* properties must be in ascending order (even though holes in the sequence are allowed). This set of requirements severely hinders your ability to create new menu items at run time. In fact, you can create new menu items in well-defined positions of your menu hierarchy—namely, where you put a menu item with a nonzero *Index* value—but you can't create new submenus or new top-level menus.

Now that you have a thorough understanding of how Visual Basic's forms and controls work, you're ready to dive into the subtleties of the Visual Basic for Applications (VBA) language. The next chapter is devoted to the many data types you can use in your programs. In Chapter 5, I illustrate the many VBA functions and commands.

Chapter 4

Variables and Procedures

Microsoft Visual Basic doesn't merely offer you a visual environment for creating your application's user interface in almost no time. It also includes a powerful programming language, Visual Basic for Applications (VBA), that lets you manipulate controls, files, databases, objects exposed by other applications, and so on. This chapter and the next one focus on many aspects of the VBA language, including a few underdocumented features and several ways to improve performance. As usual, I assume that you're familiar with the basics of programming, so I won't spend too much time explaining what a variable is, the difference between integer and floating point types, and so on. This assumption lets me focus on the more interesting topics and the new features that have been introduced in Visual Basic 6.

SCOPE AND LIFETIME OF VARIABLES

Not all variables are born equal. Certain variables live for the entire life of the application, and others are created and destroyed a thousand times every second. A variable could be visible only from within a procedure or a module or could be in existence only during well-defined time windows over the lifetime of the application. To better define these concepts, I need to introduce two formal definitions.

- The *scope* (or *visibility*) of a variable is the portion of code from which that variable can be accessed. For example, a variable declared with the Public attribute in a BAS module is visible—and can therefore be read from and written to—from anywhere in the application, whereas if the variable is declared Private, it's visible only from within that BAS module.

- The *lifetime* of a variable is the time period during which that variable stays alive and uses memory. The lifetime of the Public variable described in the previous paragraph coincides with the application's life, but in general this isn't always the case. For instance, a local dynamic variable in a procedure is created each time Visual Basic executes that procedure and is destroyed when the procedure exits.

Global Variables

In Visual Basic jargon, global variables are those variables declared using the *Public* keyword in BAS modules. Conceptually, these variables are the simplest of the group because they survive for the life of the application and their scope is the entire application. (In other words, they can be read and modified from anywhere in the current program.) The following code snippet shows the declaration of a global variable:

```
' In a BAS module
Public InvoiceCount as Long     ' This is a global variable.
```

Visual Basic 6 still supports the *Global* keyword for backward compatibility with Visual Basic 3 and previous versions, but Microsoft doesn't encourage its use.

In general, it's a bad programming practice to use too many global variables. If possible, you should limit yourself to using module-level or local variables because they allow easier code reuse. If your modules and individual routines rely on global variables to communicate with each other, you can't reuse such code without also copying the definitions of the involved global variables. In practice, however, it's often impossible to build a nontrivial application without using global variables, so my suggestion is this: Use them sparingly and choose for them names that make their scope evident (for example, using a *g_* or *glo* prefix). Even more important, add clear comments stating which global variables are used or modified in each procedure:

```
' NOTE: this procedure depends on the following global variables:
'     g_InvoiceCount  : number of invoices (read and modified)
'     g_UserName      : name of current user (read only)
Sub CreateNewInvoice()
   ...
End Sub
```

An alternative approach, which I often find useful, is to define a special *GlobalUDT* structure that gathers all the global variables of the application and to declare one single global variable of type *GlobalUDT* in one BAS module:

```
' In a BAS module
Public Type GlobalUDT
    InvoiceCount As Long
    UserName As String
    ....
End Type
Public glo As GlobalUDT
```

You can access these global variables using a very clear, unambiguous syntax:

```
' From anywhere in the application
glo.InvoiceCount = glo.InvoiceCount + 1
```

This technique has a number of advantages. First, the scope of the variable is evident by its name. Then if you don't remember the name of your variable, you can just type the three characters *glo*, and then type the dot and let Microsoft IntelliSense show you the list of all the components. In most cases, you just need to type a few characters and let Visual Basic complete the name for you. It's a tremendous time saver. The third advantage is that you can easily save all your global variables to a data file:

```
' The same routine can save and load global data in GLO.
Sub SaveLoadGlobalData(filename As String, Save As Boolean)
    Dim filenum As Integer, isOpen As Boolean
    On Error Goto Error_Handler
    filenum = FreeFile
    Open filename For Binary As filenum
    isOpen = True
    If Save Then
        Put #filenum, , glo
    Else
        Get #filenum, , glo
    End If
Error_Handler:
    If isOpen Then Close #filenum
End Sub
```

The beauty of this approach is that you can add and remove global variables—actually, components of the *GlobalUDT* structure—without modifying the *SaveLoadGlobalData* routine. (Of course, you can't correctly reload data stored with a different version of *GlobalUDT*.)

Module-Level Variables

If you declare a variable using a *Private* or a *Dim* statement in the declaration section of a module—a standard BAS module, a form module, a class module, and so on—you're creating a private module-level variable. Such variables are visible only from within the module they belong to and can't be accessed from the outside. In general, these variables are useful for sharing data among procedures in the same module:

```
' In the declarative section of any module
Private LoginTime As Date      ' A private module-level variable
Dim LoginPassword As String    ' Another private module-level variable
```

You can also use the Public attribute for module-level variables, for all module types except BAS modules. (Public variables in BAS modules are global variables.) In this case, you're creating a strange beast: a Public module-level variable that can be accessed by all procedures in the module to share data and that also can be accessed from outside the module. In this case, however, it's more appropriate to describe such a variable as a *property*:

```
' In the declarative section of Form1 module
Public CustomerName As String          ' A Public property
```

You can access a module property as a regular variable from inside the module and as a custom property from the outside:

```
' From outside Form1 module...
Form1.CustomerName = "John Smith"
```

The lifetime of a module-level variable coincides with the lifetime of the module itself. Private variables in standard BAS modules live for the entire life of the application, even if they can be accessed only while Visual Basic is executing code in that module. Variables in form and class modules exist only when that module is loaded in memory. In other words, while a form is active (but not necessarily visible to the user) all its variables take some memory, and this memory is released only when the form is completely unloaded from memory. The next time the form is re-created, Visual Basic reallocates memory for all variables and resets them to their default values (0 for numeric values, "" for strings, Nothing for object variables).

Dynamic Local Variables

Dynamic local variables are defined within a procedure; their scope is the procedure itself, and their lifetime coincides with that of the procedure:

```
Sub PrintInvoice()
    Dim text As String       ' This is a dynamic local variable.
    ...
End Sub
```

Each time the procedure is executed, a local dynamic variable is re-created and initialized to its default value (0, an empty string, or Nothing). When the procedure is exited, the memory on the stack allocated by Visual Basic for the variable is released. Local variables make it possible to reuse code at the procedure level. If a procedure references only its parameters and its local variables (it relies on neither global nor module-level variables), it can be cut from one application and pasted into another without any dependency problem.

Static Local Variables

Static local variables are a hybrid because they have the scope of local variables and the lifetime of module-level variables. Their value is preserved between calls to the procedure they belong to until their module is unloaded (or until the application ends, as is the case for procedures inside standard BAS modules). These variables are declared inside a procedure using the *Static* keyword:

```
Sub PrintInvoice()
    Static InProgress As Boolean   ' This is a Static local variable.
    ...
End Sub
```

Alternatively, you can declare the entire procedure to be Static, in which case all variables declared inside it are considered to be Static:

```
Static Sub PrintInvoice()
    Dim InProgress As Boolean      ' This is a Static local variable.
    ...
End Sub
```

Static local variables are similar to private module-level variables, to the extent that you can move a *Static* declaration from inside a procedure to the declaration section of the module (you only need to convert *Static* to *Dim*, because *Static* isn't allowed outside procedures), and the procedure will continue to work as before. In general, you can't always do the opposite: Changing a module-level variable into a Static procedure-level variable works if that variable is referenced only inside that procedure. In a sense, a Static local variable is a module-level variable that doesn't need to be shared with other procedures. By keeping the variable declaration inside the procedure boundaries, you can reuse the procedure's code more easily.

Static variables are often useful in preventing the procedure from being accidentally reentered. This is frequently necessary for event procedures, as when, for example, you don't want to process user clicks of the same button until the previous click has been served, as shown in the code on the following page.

```
Private Sub cmdSearch_Click()
    Static InProgress As Boolean
    ' Exit if there is a call in progress.
    If InProgress Then MsgBox "Sorry, try again later": Exit Sub
    InProgress = True
    ' Do your search here.
    ...
    ' Then reenable calls before exiting.
    InProgress = False
End Sub
```

OVERVIEW OF NATIVE DATA TYPES

Visual Basic for Applications supports several native data types, including integer and floating point numbers, strings, date and time values, and so on. You can store data in a variable of the proper type, or you can use the Variant data type—the default type in VBA—which is a sort of jolly data type that's able to host any type of data.

The Integer Data Type

Integer variables can hold integer values (whole numbers) included in the range from −32,768 through 32,767. These variables are also known as 16-bit integers because each value of this type takes 2 bytes of memory.

Integer variables were probably the most used type of variables, at least until Visual Basic made its debut on 32-bit Microsoft Windows platforms. For all practical purposes, in a 32-bit environment you can use a Long value instead of an Integer value without a performance hit, at the same time reducing the probability of an overflow error when the value of your variable outgrows the valid range of Integers. One of the few occasions when Integers should be preferred to Longs is when you create very large arrays. In all other cases, I suggest you use Long values, unless you have good reasons not to do so (as when you're calling an external program or a DLL that expects an Integer).

> **NOTE** You can indirectly specify that an undeclared variable is of type Integer by appending a % symbol to its name. However, this feature is supported by Visual Basic 6 only for compatibility with older Visual Basic and QuickBasic programs. All new applications should exclusively use variables declared in an explicit way. The same suggestion of course applies to other data types, including Long (&), Single(!), Double(#), Currency(@), and String($).

All the integer constants in your code are implicitly of type Integer, unless their value is outside the range for this data type, in which case they are stored as Long.

The Long Data Type

Long variables can hold integer values in the range from −2,147,483,648 through 2,147,483,647 and are also known as 32-bit integers because each value takes 4 bytes of memory. As I mentioned previously, you're encouraged to use Longs in your applications as the preferred data type for integer values. Long variables are as fast as Integer variables, and in most cases they prevent the program from breaking when dealing with numbers larger than expected. One example is when you have to process strings longer than 32,767 characters: In this case, you must use a Long index instead of an Integer variable. Watch out for this quirk when you convert code written for older Visual Basic versions.

As I explained previously, you are strongly advised not to declare Long variables with a trailing *&* character in their names. However, it's common practice to append an *&* symbol to those constants that would be stored as Integer but that you want the compiler to explicitly interpret as Long. Sometimes the difference can be important:

```
Result = value And &HFFFF     ' here &HFFFF means -1
Result = value And &HFFFF&    ' here &HFFFF& means 65535
```

If you don't want to concentrate on such microscopic details, just declare an explicit constant:

```
Const LOWWORD_MASK As Long = &HFFFF&
```

> **CAUTION** For historical reasons, Visual Basic lets you enforce a particular data type as the default data type using the Def*type* directive, so you might be tempted to use the *DefLng A-Z* directive at the beginning of each module to ensure that all undeclared variables are Long. My advice is: *don't do that!* Using Def*type* directives instead of carefully declaring all your variables is a dangerous practice. Moreover, Def*type* directives impair code reusability in that you can't safely cut and paste code from one module to another without also copying the directive.

The Boolean Data Type

Boolean variables are nothing but Integers that can hold only values 0 and −1, which stand for False and True, respectively. When you use a Boolean, you are actually wasting 15 out of 16 bits in the variable, because this information could be easily held in one single bit. That said, I suggest you use Boolean instead of Integer variables whenever it makes sense to do so because this increases the readability of your code. On a few occasions, I have also experienced a slight improvement in performance, but usually it's negligible and shouldn't be a decisive factor.

The Byte Data Type

Byte variables can hold an integer numeric value in the range 0 through 255. They take only one byte (8 bits) each and are therefore the smallest data type allowed by Visual Basic. Visual Basic 4 introduced the Byte data type to ease the porting of 16-bit applications to Windows 95 and Microsoft Windows NT. Specifically, while Visual Basic 4 for the 32-bit platform and later versions are source-code compatible with Visual Basic 3 and Visual Basic 4 for the 16-bit platform applications, they store their strings in Unicode instead of ANSI format. This difference raised a problem with strings passed to API functions because Visual Basic 3 programmers used to store binary data in strings for passing it to the operating system, but the Unicode-to-ANSI automatic conversion performed by Visual Basic makes it impossible to port this code to 32-bit without any significant change.

To make a long story short, the Byte data type was added to Visual Basic primarily to solve this problem. Apart from this advanced use, you should use Byte values only when you're dealing with arrays holding binary data. For individual values, an Integer or a Long variable is usually a better choice.

The Single Data Type

Single variables can hold decimal values in the range from −3.402823E38 through −1.401298E-45 for negative values and 1.401298E-45 through 3.402823E38 for positive values. They take 4 bytes and are the simplest (and least precise) of the floating point data types allowed by Visual Basic.

Contrary to what many programmers believe, Single variables aren't faster than Double variables, at least on the majority of Windows machines. The reason is that on most systems, all floating point operations are performed by the math coprocessor, and the time spent doing the calculations is independent of the original format of the number. This means that in most cases you should go with Double values because they offer a better precision, a wider range, fewer overflow problems, and no performance hit.

The Single data type is a good choice when you're dealing with large arrays of floating point values, and you can be satisfied with its precision and valid range. Another good occasion to use the Single data type is when you're doing intensive graphical work on your forms and in PictureBox controls. In fact, all the properties and methods that deal with coordinates—including *CurrentX/Y*, *Line*, *Circle*, *ScaleWidth*, *ScaleHeight*, and so on—use values of type Single. So you might save Visual Basic some conversion work if you store your coordinate pairs in Single variables.

The Double Data Type

Double variables can hold a floating point value in the range −1.79769313486232E308 through −4.94065645841247E-324 for negative values and 4.9406564581247E-324 through 1.79769313486232E308 for positive values. They take 8 bytes and in most cases are the preferable choice when you're dealing with decimal values. A few built-in Visual Basic functions return Double values. For example, the *Val* function always returns a Double value, even if the string argument doesn't include a decimal point. For this reason, you might want to store the result from such functions in a Double variable, which saves Visual Basic an additional conversion at run time.

The String Data Type

All 32-bit flavors of Visual Basic—Visual Basic 4 for 32-bit platforms, 5, and 6—store strings of characters in Unicode format, while all previous versions used the ANSI format. The difference is that Unicode uses two bytes for each character, so theoretically a Unicode character can assume as many as 65,536 different values. This makes Unicode strings ideal for writing code that displays its messages in non-Latin alphabets, such as Chinese, Japanese, and Hebraic. If you don't localize your software in these alphabets, you'll probably look at Unicode strings mainly as a way to waste memory in your program, especially if you use many long strings. Note that Windows NT and some portions of Windows 95/98 use Unicode strings.

Visual Basic manages two different types of strings: conventional variable-length strings and fixed-length strings. You declare them in different ways:

```
Dim VarLenStr As String
Dim FixedLenStr As String * 40
```

The first, obvious difference is that in any given moment a variable-length string takes only the memory that it needs for its characters (actually, it takes 10 additional bytes for holding other information about the string, including its length), whereas a fixed-length string always takes a fixed amount of memory (80 bytes, in the preceding example).

If you are a performance-savvy programmer, you should remember that conventional strings are *usually* faster than fixed-length string. This happens because all VBA native string functions can deal only with variable-length strings. In a sense, a fixed-length string is something that VBA isn't even aware of: When you pass a fixed-length string to a VBA function, the compiler generates hidden statements that convert that argument into a temporary variable-length string.

But even with all this overhead, fixed-length strings aren't always going to make your programs slower. For one, Visual Basic excels at allocating and releasing memory for fixed-length strings, so if your program spends a lot of time assigning new values to variables or creates large string arrays, fixed-length strings might prove even faster than conventional ones. Just to give you an example, on a 233-KHz system Visual Basic 6 takes about 9 seconds to load 100,000 30-character strings into a conventional string array, and 0.4 seconds to remove them. Both operations are completed almost instantaneously if performed on an array of fixed-length strings.

String constants are enclosed within quotes, and you can embed quotes within the string by doubling them:

```
Print "<My Name Is ""Tarzan"">"     ' displays  <My Name Is "Tarzan">
```

Visual Basic additionally defines a number of intrinsic string constants, such as *vbTab* (the Tab character) or *vbCrLf* (the carriage return-line feed pair). Using these constants usually improves the readability of your code as well as its performance because you don't have to use a *Chr* function to create the strings.

The Currency Data Type

Currency variables can hold decimal values in a fixed-point format, in the range from −922,337,203,685,477.5808 through 922,337,203,685,477.5807. They differ from floating-point variables, such as Single and Double, in that they always include four decimal digits. You can think of a currency value as a big integer that's 8 bytes long and whose value is automatically scaled by a factor of 10,000 when it's assigned to the variable and when it's read back and displayed to the user.

Using a fixed-point value has its advantages over floating-point variables. For one, Currency values suffer less from the rounding problems that you often experience using Double values. When you're adding or subtracting values, however, Currency variables don't offer a performance advantage, and multiplying and dividing Currency values is about five times slower than doing the same for Double values. Keep this in mind if your application does a lot of math.

The Date Data Type

Date variables can hold any date between January 1, 100, through December 31, 9999, as well as any time value. They take 8 bytes, exactly like Double variables. This isn't a casual resemblance because internally these date/time values are stored as floating-point numbers, in which the integer part stores the date information and the decimal part stores the time information. (For example, 0.5 means 12 A.M., 0.75 means 6 P.M., and so on.) Once you know how Date variables store their values, you can perform many meaningful math operations on them. For example, you can truncate date or time information using the *Int* function, as follows:

```
MyVar = Now                   ' MyVar is a Date variable.
DateVar = Int(MyVar)          ' Extract date information.
TimeVar = MyVar - Int(MyVar)  ' Extract time information.
```

You can also add and subtract dates, as you would do with numbers:

```
MyVar = MyVar + 7            ' Advance one week.
MyVar = MyVar - 365          ' Go back one (nonleap) year.
```

VBA provides many functions for dealing with date and time information in more advanced ways, which I'll cover in Chapter 5. You can also define a Date constant using the format *#mm/dd/yyyy#*, with or without a time portion:

```
MyVar = #9/5/1996 12.20 am#
```

The Object Data Type

Visual Basic uses object variables to store reference objects. Note that here we are talking about storing a *reference* to an object, not storing an *object*. The difference is subtle but important, and I'll talk about it at length in Chapter 6. There are several types of object variables, but they can be grouped in two broad categories: *generic* object variables and *specific* object variables. Here are a few examples:

```
' Examples of generic object variables
Dim frm As Form            ' A reference to any form
Dim midfrm As MDIForm      ' A reference to any MDI form
Dim ctrl As Control        ' A reference to any control
Dim obj As Object          ' A reference to any object
' Examples of specific object variables
Dim inv As frmInvoice      ' A reference to a specific type of form
Dim txtSalary As TextBox   ' A reference to a specific type of control
Dim cust As CCustomer      ' A reference to an object defined by a
                           ' class module in the current project
Dim wrk As Excel.Worksheet ' A reference to an external object
```

The most evident difference when dealing with object variables (as opposed to regular variables) is that you assign object references to them using the *Set* keyword, as in the following code:

```
Set frm = Form1
Set txtSalary = Text1
```

After the assignment, you can use the object variable to access the original object's properties and methods:

```
frm.Caption = "Welcome to Visual Basic 6"
txtSalary.Text = Format(99000, "currency")
```

> **CAUTION** One of the most common errors that programmers make when dealing with object variables is omitting the *Set* command during assignments. What happens if you omit this keyword depends on the object involved. If it doesn't support a default property, Visual Basic raises a compile-time error ("Invalid use

of property"); otherwise, the assignment succeeds, but the result won't be the one you expect:

```
frm = Form1            ' A missing Set raises a compiler error.
txtSalary = Text1      ' A missing Set assigns Text1's Text property
                       ' to txtSalary's Text property.
```

Object variables can also be cleared so that they don't point to any particular object anymore. You do this by assigning them the special Nothing value:

```
Set txtSalary = Nothing
```

The Variant Data Type

Variant variables were introduced in Visual Basic 3, but their internal format changed in version 4, where their capabilities were greatly enhanced. The Variant format is defined by OLE, and so it's highly unlikely that it will be modified again in the future. Variant variables can hold any type of data described so far, and then some. Variables of this type take 16 bytes, in this format:

Bytes 0 and 1	2 through 7	8 through 15
VarType	Unused	Value

Bytes 0 and 1 hold an integer value that states which type of data is stored in bytes 8 through 15. Bytes 2 through 7 are unused (with only one exception, the Decimal subtype), and in most cases not all the bytes in the second half of the variable are used. For example, if a Variant holds an Integer value, the first two bytes contain the value 2-vbInteger, bytes 8 and 9 hold the actual 16-bit value, and all other bytes are unused.

A Variant variable holds a value in its original format and doesn't enforce a metaformat that encompasses all the data types supported by Visual Basic. For example, when Visual Basic adds numbers held in two Variant variables, it checks their type and uses the most efficient math routine possible. And so, if you're adding two Variants that hold one Integer and one Long, Visual Basic promotes the Integer to Long and then invokes the routine for addition between Longs.

> **CAUTION** Automatic data coercion is always dangerous because you might not get the results that you expect. For example, if you use the + operator on two Variants that hold numeric values, Visual Basic interprets the + as the addition operator. If both values are strings, Visual Basic interprets the + as the append operator. When one data type is a string and the other is a number, Visual Basic tries to convert the string to a number so that an addition can be performed; if this isn't possible, a "Type Mismatch" error is raised. If you want to be sure to

execute an append operation regardless of the data types involved, use the & operator. Finally note that you can't store fixed-length strings in Variant variables.

Variant is the default data type for Visual Basic. In other words, if you use a variable without declaring its type, as in the following line of code:

```
Dim MyVariable
```

this will be a Variant variable, unless this line is preceded by a *Def*type directive that sets a different default data type. Likewise, if you use a variable without first declaring it (and you don't use a *Def*type directive), Visual Basic creates a Variant variable.

> **NOTE** If I could give only one suggestion to novice Visual Basic programmers, it would be this: *Always* add an *Option Explicit* directive at the beginning of every module in your programs. Even better, enable the Require Variable Declaration option in the General tab of the Options dialog box from the Tools menu so that Visual Basic automatically adds this directive whenever you create a new module. I can't overestimate the importance of having Visual Basic check for you that you haven't accidentally misspelled a variable's name. Be aware that some template projects create modules that lack the *Option Explicit* directive.

The type of data actually stored in a Variant variable depends on the last assignment to it. You can test the type of the current contents of such a Variable using the *VarType* function:

```
Dim v As Variant
v = True
Print VarType(v)      ' Prints "11", that is vbBoolean
```

Variant variables can also host special values that don't correspond to any data values described so far. The *Empty* value is the state of a Variant variable when nothing has been assigned to it yet. You can test this special value using the *IsEmpty* function, or you can test the *VarType* function for the value 0-vbEmpty:

```
Dim v As Variant
Print IsEmpty(v)      ' Prints "True" (uninitialized variant).
v = "any value"       ' The variant isn't empty anymore.
v = Empty             ' Restore the Empty state using the Empty constant.
```

The Null value is useful in database programming to mark fields that don't contain a value. You can explicitly assign the Null value to a Variant using the Null constant, test for a Null value using the *IsNull* function, or compare the return value of the *VarType* function with the value 1-vbNull:

```
v = Null              ' Stores a Null value
Print IsNull(v)       ' Prints "True"
```

Variant variables can also contain an Error value. This is useful, for example, if you want a routine to return a meaningful value if it succeeds or an error value if it doesn't. In this case, you declare a function that returns a Variant value: if no error occurs, you return the result. Otherwise, you use the *CVErr* function to create a Variant of subtype Error:

```
Function Reciprocal(n As Double) As Variant
    If n <> 0 Then
        Reciprocal = 1 / n
    Else
        Reciprocal = CVErr(11)    ' Division By Zero error code
    End If
End Function
```

You can test the Error subtype using the *IsError* function or by comparing the return value of *VarType* with the value 10-vbError. Error codes must be in the range 0 through 65535. To convert the error code into an integer, you can use the *CLng* function. Here's the typical client code for a function that could return an error code in a Variant:

```
Dim res As Variant
res = Reciprocal(CDbl(Text1.Text))
If IsError(res) Then
    MsgBox "Error #" & CLng(res)
Else
    MsgBox "Result is " & res
End If
```

I'm reporting this style of error trapping exclusively for the sake of completeness. My advice, in fact, is that you should never use this approach for error management; rather, you should rely on the Err object, which is able to convey more information about errors.

Variant variables can also host object values. You must assign object values using the *Set* keyword; otherwise, the results are unpredictable, as this short code snippet demonstrates:

```
Dim v As Variant
Set v = Text1        ' A correct object assignment that uses Set
v.Text = "abcde"     ' This works, because V points to Text1.
v = Text1            ' Wrong object assignment, Set is omitted.
                     ' Actually, it assigns the value of default property
                     ' and is equivalent to v = Text1.Text
Print v              ' Displays "abcde"
v.Text = "12345"     ' Error 424: Object Required
```

You can test whether a Variant holds an object using the *IsObject* function. Don't use *VarType* to test whether a Variant variable holds an object reference. In fact, if the object supports a default property, the *VarType* function returns the type of that property, not the *vbObject* constant.

Starting with Visual Basic 6, Variant variables can also hold *user-defined type* (UDT) structures, and the *VarType* function can return the new value 36-vbUserDefinedType. But this capability is available only if the *Type* statement that defines the UDT structure appears with the Public scope attribute in a Public class module. You can't assign UDT structures to Variant variables within Standard EXE projects because they can't expose Public class modules.

You can use other functions to test the type of the value stored in a Variant variable. The *IsNumeric* function returns True if the value can be successfully converted to a number using the *CDbl* function, even if the native format is different. (The Variant variable holds a string, for example.) The *IsDate* function checks whether the value can be successfully converted to a date using the *CDate* function. Finally, the *TypeName* function is similar to *VarType* but returns the current data type as a readable string:

```
v = 123.45: Print TypeName(v)        ' Displays "Double"
Set v = Text1: Print TypeName(v)     ' Displays "TextBox"
```

One last point: Variant variables can also hold arrays. For more information, read the section about arrays later in this chapter.

The Decimal Data Type

Decimal is a floating-point data type with a higher precision than Double, but it has a smaller range. In fact, you can store values in the range plus or minus 79,228,162,514,264,337,593,543,950,335 with no decimal point, or plus or minus 7.9228162514264337593543950335 with 28 places to the right of the decimal point. The smallest nonzero number is plus or minus 0.0000000000000000000000000001. Decimal is a singular case among the data types supported by Visual Basic in that you can't explicitly declare a variable using *As Decimal*. Instead, you assign a value to a Variant variable using the *CDec* conversion function, for example:

```
Dim v As Variant
v = CDec(Text1.Text)
```

Once you have assigned a Decimal value to a Variant, you can perform all the usual math operations. You don't need to ensure that both operands are of Decimal type because Visual Basic will do the necessary conversions for you. Decimal is an exception among Variant subtypes in that it exploits all the bytes in the Variant structure, that is, all 14 bytes that follow the subtype identifier. If you apply the *VarType* function to a Variant containing a Decimal value, you get the return value of *14-vbDecimal*.

AGGREGATE DATA TYPES

The native data types we have examined so far have been simple. While useful in their own right, they can also serve as building blocks to form aggregate data types. In this section, we examine this concept more closely.

User-Defined Types

A user-defined type (UDT) is a compound data structure that holds several variables of simpler data types. Before you can use a UDT variable, you must first define its structure, using a *Type* directive in the declaration section of a module:

```
Private Type EmployeeUDT
    Name As String
    DepartmentID As Long
    Salary As Currency
End Type
```

UDTs can be declared as Private or Public. Under Visual Basic 5 or previous versions, only UDTs declared in BAS modules can be Public. In Visual Basic 6, all modules except forms can include Public UDT definitions, provided that the project type isn't Standard EXE and that the class isn't Private. For more information, see Chapter 16.

Once you have defined a Type structure, you can create variables of that type as you would do with any Visual Basic native type. You can then access its individual items using the dot syntax:

```
Dim Emp As EmployeeUDT
Emp.Name = "Roscoe Powell"
Emp.DepartmentID = 123
```

UDTs can contain both conventional and fixed-length strings. In the former case, the structure in memory holds just a pointer to the actual data, whereas in the latter case the strings' characters are stored in the same block as the other items of the UDT structure. This is reflected by the *LenB* function, which you can use on any UDT variable to learn the number of actual bytes used:

```
Print LenB(Emp)    ' Prints 16: 4 for Name, regardless of its length +
                   ' 4 for DepartmentID (Long) + 8 for Salary (Currency)
```

Type structures can also contain substructures, for example:

```
Private Type LocationUDT
    Address As String
    City As String
    Zip As String
    State As String * 2
```

```
End Type
Private Type EmployeeUDT
    Name As String
    DepartmentID As Long
    Salary As Currency
    Location As LocationUDT
End Type
```

When you access such nested structures, you can resort to the *With...End With* clause to produce more readable code:

```
With Emp
    Print .Name
    Print .Salary
    With .Location
        Print .Address
        Print .City & "  " & .Zip & "  " & .State
    End With
End Type
```

When you're working with a complex UDT, assigning a value to all its individual components is often a nuisance. Fortunately, since VBA supports functions that return UDTs, you can write support procedures that considerably simplify the job:

```
Emp = InitEmployee("Roscoe Powell", 123, 80000)
...
Function InitEmployee(Name As String, DepartmentID As Long, _
    Salary As Currency) As EmployeeUDT
    InitEmployee.Name = Name
    InitEmployee.DepartmentID = DepartmentID
    InitEmployee.Salary = Salary
End Function
```

Visual Basic lets you copy one UDT to another UDT with the same structure using a regular assignment, as in the following code:

```
Dim emp1 As EmployeeUDT, emp2 As EmployeeUDT
...
emp2 = emp1
```

Arrays

Arrays are ordered sets of homogeneous items. Visual Basic supports arrays made up of elementary data types. You can build one-dimensional arrays, two-dimensional arrays, and so on, up to 60 dimensions. (I never met a programmer who bumped into this limit in a real application, though.)

Static and dynamic arrays

Basically, you can create either *static* or *dynamic* arrays. Static arrays must include a fixed number of items, and this number must be known at compile time so that the compiler can set aside the necessary amount of memory. You create a static array using a *Dim* statement with a constant argument:

```
' This is a static array.
Dim Names(100) As String
```

Visual Basic starts indexing the array with 0. Therefore, the preceding array actually holds 101 items.

Most programs don't use static arrays because programmers rarely know at compile time how many items you need and also because static arrays can't be resized during execution. Both these issues are solved by dynamic arrays. You declare and create dynamic arrays in two distinct steps. In general, you *declare* the array to account for its visibility (for example, at the beginning of a module if you want to make it visible by all the procedures of the module) using a *Dim* command with an empty pair of brackets. Then you *create* the array when you actually need it, using a *ReDim* statement:

```
' An array defined in a BAS module (with Private scope)
Dim Customers() As String
...
Sub Main()
    ' Here you create the array.
    ReDim Customer(1000) As String
End Sub
```

If you're creating an array that's local to a procedure, you can do everything with a single *ReDim* statement:

```
Sub PrintReport()
    ' This array is visible only to the procedure.
    ReDim Customers(1000) As String
    ' ...
End Sub
```

If you don't specify the lower index of an array, Visual Basic assumes it to be 0, unless an *Option Base 1* statement is placed at the beginning of the module. My suggestion is this: Never use an Option Base statement because it makes code reuse more difficult. (You can't cut and paste routines without worrying about the current Option Base.) If you want to explicitly use a lower index different from 0, use this syntax instead:

```
ReDim Customers(1 To 1000) As String
```

Dynamic arrays can be re-created at will, each time with a different number of items. When you re-create a dynamic array, its contents are reset to 0 (or to an empty string) and you lose the data it contains. If you want to resize an array without losing its contents, use the *ReDim Preserve* command:

```
ReDim Preserve Customers(2000) As String
```

When you're resizing an array, you can't change the number of its dimensions nor the type of the values it contains. Moreover, when you're using *ReDim Preserve* on a multidimensional array, you can resize only its last dimension:

```
ReDim Cells(1 To 100, 10) As Integer
...
ReDim Preserve Cells(1 To 100, 20) As Integer    ' This works.
ReDim Preserve Cells(1 To 200, 20) As Integer    ' This doesn't.
```

Finally, you can destroy an array using the *Erase* statement. If the array is dynamic, Visual Basic releases the memory allocated for its elements (and you can't read or write them any longer); if the array is static, its elements are set to 0 or to empty strings.

You can use the *LBound* and *UBound* functions to retrieve the lower and upper indices. If the array has two or more dimensions, you need to pass a second argument to these functions to specify the dimension you need:

```
Print LBound(Cells, 1)    ' Displays 1, lower index of 1st dimension
Print LBound(Cells)       ' Same as above
Print UBound(Cells, 2)    ' Displays 20, upper index of 2nd dimension
' Evaluate total number of elements.
NumEls = (UBound(Cells) - LBound(Cells) + 1) * _
    (UBound(Cells, 2) - LBound(Cells, 2) + 1)
```

Arrays within UDTs

UDT structures can include both static and dynamic arrays. Here's a sample structure that contains both types:

```
Type MyUDT
    StaticArr(100) As Long
    DynamicArr() As Long
End Type
...
Dim udt As MyUDT
' You must DIMension the dynamic array before using it.
ReDim udt.DynamicArr(100) As Long
' You don't have to do that with static arrays.
udt.StaticArr(1) = 1234
```

The memory needed by a static array is allocated within the UDT structure; for example, the *StaticArr* array in the preceding code snippet takes exactly 400 bytes. Conversely, a dynamic array in a UDT takes only 4 bytes, which form a pointer to the memory area where the actual data is stored. Dynamic arrays are advantageous when each individual UDT variable might host a different number of array items. As with all dynamic arrays, if you don't dimension a dynamic array within a UDT before accessing its items, you get an error 9—"Subscript out of range."

Arrays and variants

Visual Basic lets you store arrays in Variant variables and then access the array items using the Variant variable as if it were an array:

```
ReDim Names(100) As String, var As Variant
' Initialize the Names array (omitted).
var = Names()          ' Copy the array into the Variant.
Print var(1)           ' Access array items through the Variant.
```

You can even create an array of Variant elements on the fly using the *Array* function and store it in a Variant variable:

```
' Arrays returned by the Array() function are zero-based.
Factorials = Array(1, 1, 2, 6, 24, 120, 720, 5040, 40320, 362880, 3628800)
```

Likewise, you can pass an array to a procedure that expects a *Variant* parameter and then access the elements of the array through that parameter:

```
' A polymorphic function that sums the values in any array
Function ArraySum(arr As Variant) As Variant
    Dim i As Long, result As Variant
    For i = LBound(arr) To UBound(arr)
        result = result + arr(i)
    Next
    ArraySum = result
End Function
```

The most interesting feature of the preceding routine is that it works correctly with *any* type of numeric one-dimensional array. It even works with String arrays, but in that case you get the concatenation of all items, not their sum. This procedure is extremely powerful and reduces the amount of code you have to write to deal with different kinds of arrays. But you should be aware that accessing array items through a *Variant* parameter noticeably slows down the execution. If you need the best performance, write specific routines that process specific types of arrays.

You can also pass a multidimensional array to a routine that expects a *Variant* parameter. In this case, you can still access the array elements through the Variants, but if you don't know at compile time how many dimensions the array has, your routine has to determine that number before proceeding. You can get this value using a trial-and-error approach:

```
' This routine returns the number of dimensions of the array
' passed as an argument, or 0 if it isn't an array.
Function NumberOfDims(arr As Variant) As Integer
    Dim dummy as Long
    On Error Resume Next
    Do
        dummy = UBound(arr, NumberOfDims + 1)
        If Err Then Exit Do
        NumberOfDims = NumberOfDims + 1
    Loop
End Function
```

> **TIP** It's perfectly legal to use the function name inside a function's code as if it were a local variable, as the previous code snippet does. Often this technique lets you save a local variable and a final assignment before exiting the routine, which indirectly makes your code run slightly faster.

Here's a modified *ArraySum* routine that uses *NumberOfDims* and works with both one- and two-dimensional arrays:

```
Function ArraySum2(arr As Variant) As Variant
    Dim i As Long, j As Long, result As Variant
    ' First check whether we can really work with this array.
    Select Case NumberOfDims(arr)
        Case 1        ' One-dimensional array
            For i = LBound(arr) To UBound(arr)
                result = result + arr(i)
            Next
        Case 2        ' Two-dimensional array
            For i = LBound(arr) To UBound(arr)
                For j = LBound(arr, 2) To UBound(arr, 2)
                    result = result + arr(i, j)
                Next
            Next
        Case Else    ' Not an array, or too many dimensions
            Err.Raise 1001, , "Not an array or more than two dimensions"
    End Select
    ArraySum2 = result
End Function
```

Often, if a Variant contains an array, you don't know the basic type of that array in advance. The *VarType* function returns the sum of the *vbArray* constant (decimal 8192), plus the *VarType* of the data included in the array. This lets you test that the array passed to a routine is of a given type:

```
If VarType(arr) = (vbArray + vbInteger) Then
    ' Array of integers
```

(continued)

```
ElseIf VarType(arr) = (vbArray + vbLong) Then
    ' Array of Longs
ElseIf VarType(arr) And vbArray Then
    ' An array of another type (just tests a bit)
End If
```

You can also test whether a Variant holds an array using the *IsArray* function. When a Variant variable holds an array, the *TypeName* function appends a pair of empty parentheses to its result:

```
Print TypeName(arr)      ' Displays "Integer()"
```

As I've explained, you can either assign an array to a Variant variable or you can pass an array as a Variant parameter of a procedure. While the two operations look very similar, they're substantially different. To execute an assignment, Visual Basic makes a physical copy of the array. As a result, the Variant variable doesn't point to the original data but to the copy; from this point on, all the manipulations you do through the Variant variable don't affect the original array. Conversely, if you call a procedure and pass an array as a Variant parameter, no data is physically copied and the Variant simply works as an *alias* of the array. You can reorder array items or modify their values, and your changes are immediately reflected in the original array.

Assigning and returning arrays

Visual Basic 6 adds two important features to arrays. First, you can perform assignments between arrays. Second, you can write procedures that return arrays. You can assign arrays only of the same type and only if the target is a dynamic array. (The latter condition is necessary because Visual Basic might need to resize the target array.)

```
ReDim a(10, 10) As Integer
Dim b() As Integer
' Fill the a array with data  (omitted).
b() = a()        ' This works!
```

It's no surprise that native assignment commands are always faster than the corresponding *For...Next* loops that copy one item at a time. The actual increment in speed heavily depends on the data type of the arrays and can vary from 20 percent to 10 times faster. A native assignment between arrays also works if the source array is held in a Variant. Under Visual Basic 4 and 5, you could store an array in a Variant, but you couldn't do the opposite—that is, retrieve an array stored in a Variant variable and store it back in an array of a specific type. This flaw has been fixed in Visual Basic 6:

```
Dim v As Variant, s(100) As String, t() As String
' Fill the s() array   (omitted).
v = s()          ' Assign to a Variant.
t() = v          ' Assign from a Variant to a dynamic string array.
```

You often use the capacity to assign arrays to build functions that return arrays. Notice that pair of brackets at the end of the first line in the following procedure:

```
Function InitArray(first As Long, Last As Long) As Long()
    ReDim result(first To Last) As Long
    Dim i As Long
    For i = first To Last
        result(i) = i
    Next
    InitArray = result
End Function
```

The new capability of returning arrays lets you write highly versatile array routines. Visual Basic 6 itself includes a few new string functions—namely *Join*, *Split*, and *Filter*—that rely on it. (You'll find more about these new string functions in Chapter 5). Here are two examples of what you can do with this intriguing feature:

```
' Returns a portion of a Long array
' Note: fails if FIRST or LAST are not valid
Function SubArray(arr() As Long, first As Long, last As Long, _
    newFirstIndex As Long) As Long()
    Dim i As Long
    ReDim result(newFirstIndex To last - first + newFirstIndex) As Long
    For i = first To last
        result(newFirstIndex + i - first) = arr(i)
    Next
    SubArray = result
End Function


' Returns an array with all the selected items in a ListBox
Function SelectedListItems(lst As ListBox) As String()
    Dim i As Long, j As Long
    ReDim result(0 To lst.SelCount) As String
    For i = 0 To lst.ListCount - 1
        If lst.Selected(i) Then
            j = j + 1
            result(j) = lst.List(i)
        End If
    Next
    SelectedListItems = result
End Function
```

Byte arrays

Byte arrays are somewhat special because Visual Basic lets you directly assign strings to them. In this case, Visual Basic performs a direct memory copy of the contents of the string. Because all Visual Basic 5 and 6 strings are Unicode strings (two bytes per character), the target array is redimensioned to account for the actual string length in bytes (which you can determine using the *LenB* function). If the string contains only characters whose code is in the range 0 through 255 (the case if you work with Latin alphabets), every other byte in the array will be 0:

```
Dim b() As Byte, Text As String
Text = "123"
b() = Text       ' Now b() contains six items: 49 0 50 0 51 0
```

It's also possible to perform the opposite operation:

```
Text = b()
```

This special treatment reserved for Byte arrays is meant to ease the conversion from old Visual Basic 3 applications that use strings to hold binary data, as I explained in "The Byte Data Type" section, earlier in this chapter. You can exploit this feature to create blindingly fast string routines when you have to process each individual character in a string. For example, see how quickly you can count all the spaces in a string:

```
' NOTE: this function might not work with non-Latin alphabets.
Function CountSpaces(Text As String) As Long
    Dim b() As Byte, i As Long
    b() = Text
    For i = 0 To UBound(b) Step 2
        ' Consider only even-numbered items.
        ' Save time and code using the function name as a local variable.
        If b(i) = 32 Then CountSpaces = CountSpaces + 1
    Next
End Function
```

The preceding routine is about three times faster than a regular routine, which uses *Asc* and *Mid$* functions to process all the characters in the argument, and even faster if you turn on the Remove Array Bounds Check compiler optimization. The only drawback of this technique is that it isn't Unicode-friendly because it considers only the least significant byte in each 2-byte character. If you plan to convert your application to some language that relies on Unicode—Japanese, for example—you should stay clear of this optimization technique.

Inserting and deleting items

Some of the most common operations you perform on arrays are inserting and deleting items, shifting all the remaining elements toward higher indices to make room or toward lower indices to fill the "hole" a deletion has left. You usually do this with a *For...Next* loop, and you can even write generic array procedures that work with any type of array (with the usual restrictions about arrays of UDTs and fixed-length strings that can't be passed to a Variant parameter):

```
Sub InsertArrayItem(arr As Variant, index As Long, newValue As Variant)
    Dim i As Long
    For i = UBound(arr) - 1 To index Step -1
        arr(i + 1) = arr(i)
    Next
    arr(index) = newValue
End Sub

Sub DeleteArrayItem(arr As Variant, index As Long)
    Dim i As Long
    For i = index To UBound(arr) - 1
        arr(i) = arr(i + 1)
    Next
    ' VB will convert this to 0 or to an empty string.
    arr(UBound(arr)) = Empty
End Sub
```

If your application works intensively with arrays, you might find that an approach based on *For...Next* loops is too slow. In some cases, you can considerably speed up these operations by using the *RtlMoveMemory* API function, which many Visual Basic programmers know under its popular alias name, *CopyMemory*.[1] This function lets you move a block of bytes from one memory address to another memory address and works correctly even if the two areas partially overlap. Here's the code that inserts a new item in an array of Longs:

```
Private Declare Sub CopyMemory Lib "kernel32" Alias "RtlMoveMemory" _
    (dest As Any, source As Any, ByVal numBytes As Long)

Sub InsertArrayItemLong(arr() As Long, index As Long, newValue As Long)
    ' We let VB evaluate the size of each item using LenB().
    If index < UBound(arr) Then
        CopyMemory arr(index + 1), arr(index), _
            (UBound(arr) - index) * LenB(arr(index))
    End If
    arr(index) = newValue
End Sub

Sub DeleteArrayItemLong(arr() As Long, index As Long)
    If index < UBound(arr) Then
```

(continued)

---

1. You won't find a reference to the *CopyMemory* API function in the Windows API or in Visual Basic's API Viewer. This term was first introduced by Bruce McKinney in the first edition of his *Hardcore Visual Basic* (Microsoft Press, 1995) as an alias for the *hmemcopy* API function when working with 16-bit platforms and for *RtlMoveMemory* when working with 32-bit platforms. The *CopyMemory* name describes so closely what those functions do that it rapidly became widely used by Visual Basic programmers, who, in most cases, didn't even know where the term originated. This short note should help refresh everyone's memory and give Bruce his due.

```
            CopyMemory arr(index), arr(index + 1), _
                (UBound(arr) - index) * LenB(arr(index))
        End If
        arr(index) = Empty
End Sub
```

> **CAUTION**   The prerequisite for using the *CopyMemory* API function is that data must be stored in contiguous memory locations, so you absolutely can't use it to insert or remove elements in String and Object arrays, nor in arrays of UDTs that contain conventional strings, object references, or dynamic arrays. (Fixed-length strings and static arrays in UDTs are OK, though.)

Note that while you can't use the preceding routines for arrays other than Long arrays, the statements in the procedure body can be recycled for another data type without any change, thanks to the use of the *LenB* function. Therefore, you can derive new array functions that work for other data types by simply modifying the procedure's name and its parameter list. For example, you can create a new function that deletes an item in a Double array by editing just the first line of code (shown in boldface):

```
Sub DeleteArrayItemDouble(arr() As Double, index As Long)
    ' All the other statements here are the same as in DeleteArrayItemLong
    ' ...
End Sub
```

Sorting

Sorting is an operation that you often perform on arrays. As you probably know, there are dozens of different sort algorithms, each one with its strengths and weaknesses. I found that the *Shell Sort* algorithm works well in most cases, and I've prepared a generic routine that sorts any one-dimensional array of a data type compatible with the Variant type, either in ascending or descending order:

```
Sub ShellSortAny(arr As Variant, numEls As Long, descending As Boolean)
    Dim index As Long, index2 As Long, firstItem As Long
    Dim distance As Long, value As Variant
    ' Exit if it is not an array.
    If VarType(arr) < vbArray Then Exit Sub
    firstItem = LBound(arr)
    ' Find the best value for distance.
    Do
        distance = distance * 3 + 1
    Loop Until distance > numEls
    ' Sort the array.
    Do
        distance = distance \ 3
        For index = distance + firstItem To numEls + firstItem - 1
            value = arr(index)
            index2 = index
```

```
        Do While (arr(index2 - distance) > value) Xor descending
            arr(index2) = arr(index2 - distance)
            index2 = index2 - distance
            If index2 - distance < firstItem Then Exit Do
        Loop
        arr(index2) = value
    Next
  Loop Until distance = 1
End Sub
```

Arrays of arrays

While you can create two-dimensional arrays in Visual Basic, their structure isn't really flexible for at least two reasons: All rows in the array must have the same number of elements, and you can use *ReDim Preserve* to change the number of columns but you can't add new rows. The first point is especially important because it often leads you to declare an array that's far too large for your needs, thus allocating a lot of memory that in most cases remains largely unused. You can solve both problems using a structure known as *an array of arrays*.

The technique is conceptually simple: Since you can store an array in a Variant variable, you can build an array of Variants, where each item holds an array. Each subarray—a row of this pseudo-array—can hold a different number of elements, and you don't need to use more memory than is strictly necessary.

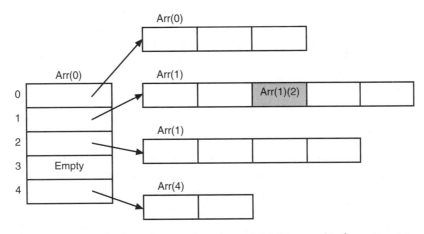

Here's an example, based on an imaginary PIM (Personal Information Manager) program. In this program, you need to keep track of a list of appointments for each day of the year. The simplest solution would be to use an array in which each row corresponds to a day in the year and each column to a possible appointment. (For the sake of simplicity, let's assume that each appointment's data can be held in a string.)

```
ReDim apps(1 To 366, 1 To MAX_APPOINTMENTS) As String
```

Of course, you now have the problem of setting a reasonable value for the MAX_APPOINTMENTS symbolic constant. It should be high enough to account for all possible appointments in a day but not too high because you might be wasting a lot of memory without any real reason. Let's see how the array of arrays technique can help us save memory without posing any artificial limit to your application:

```
' A module-level variable
Dim apps(1 To 366) As Variant

' Add an appointment for a given day.
Sub AddNewAppointment(day As Integer, description As String)
    Dim arr As Variant
    If IsEmpty(apps(day)) Then
        ' This is the first appointment for this day.
        apps(day) = Array(description)
    Else
        ' Add the appointment to those already scheduled.
        arr = apps(day)
        ReDim Preserve arr(0 To UBound(arr) + 1) As Variant
        arr(UBound(arr)) = description
        apps(day) = arr
    End If
End Sub

' Extract all the appointments for a given day.
Sub ListAppointments(day As Integer, lst As ListBox)
    Dim i As Long
    For i = 0 To UBound(apps(1))
        lst.AddItem apps(1)(i)
    Next
End Sub
```

In this example, I kept the code as simple as possible and used an array of Variant arrays. You could save even more memory if each row of this array were built using an array of a more specific data type (String, in this case). Note the special syntax used to address an item in an array of arrays:

```
' Change the description for the Nth appointment.
apps(day)(n) = newDescription
```

Nothing keeps you from extending this concept further, introducing an array of arrays of arrays, and so on. If you're dealing with arrays in which each row can vary considerably in length, this approach is going to save you a lot of memory and, in most cases, improve your overall performance too. A key feature of an array of arrays is that you can process entire rows of your pseudo-array as if they were single entities. For example, you can swap them, replace them, add and delete them, and so on.

```
' Move the January 1st appointments to January 2nd.
apps(2) = apps(1)
apps(1) = Empty
```

Finally, an important advantage of this technique is that you can add new rows without losing the current contents of the array. (Remember that you can use *ReDim Preserve* on regular arrays only to modify the number of columns, not the number of rows.)

```
' Extend the appointment book for another nonleap year.
ReDim Preserve apps(1 to UBound(apps) + 365) As Variant
```

Collections

Collections are objects exposed by the VBA library. They can be used in Visual Basic applications to store groups of related data. In this sense, Collections are similar to arrays, but the similarities stop here because of these substantial differences:

- Collection objects don't need to be predimensioned for a given number of elements; you can add items to a Collection, and it will grow as needed.

- You can insert items in the middle of a Collection without worrying about making room for the new element; likewise, you can delete items without having to shift all other items to fill the hole. In both cases, the Collection object takes care of all these chores automatically.

- You can store nonhomogeneous data in a Collection, whereas arrays can host only data of the type set at compile time (with the exception of Variant arrays). In general, you can store in a Collection any value that you could store in a Variant variable (that is, everything except fixed-length strings and possibly UDTs).

- A Collection offers a way to associate a key with each item so that later you can quickly retrieve that item even if you don't know where it's stored in the Collection. You can also read items by their numerical index in the collection, as you would do with regular arrays.

- In contrast to the situation for arrays, once you have added an item to a Collection you can read the item but not modify it. The only way to modify a value in a Collection is to delete the old value and add the new one.

With all these advantages, you might wonder why collections haven't supplanted arrays in the hearts of Visual Basic developers. The main reason is that Collections are slow, or at least they're noticeably slower than arrays. To give you an idea, filling an array of 10,000 Long elements is about 100 times faster than filling a Collection of the same size. Take this into account when you're deciding which data structure best solves your problem.

The first thing you must do before using a Collection is create it. Like all objects, a Collection should be declared and then created, as in the following code:

```
Dim EmployeeNames As Collection
Set EmployeeNames = New Collection
```

Or you can declare an auto-instancing collection with one single line of code:

```
Dim EmployeeNames As New Collection
```

You can add items to a Collection object by using its *Add* method; this method expects the value you're adding and a string key that will be associated with that value:

```
EmployeeNames.Add "John Smith", "Marketing"
```

where *value* can be virtually anything that can be stored in a Variant. The *Add* method usually appends the new value to the collection, but you can decide where exactly you want to store it using either the *before* argument or the *after* argument:

```
' Insert this value before the first item in the collection.
EmployeeNames.Add "Anne Lipton", "Sales"
' Insert this new value after the element added previously.
EmployeeNames.Add value2, "Robert Douglas", ,"Sales"
```

Unless you have a good reason to store the new value somewhere other than at the end of the Collection, I suggest that you not use the *before* or *after* arguments because they slow down the *Add* method. The string key is optional. If you specify it and there's another item with the same key, the *Add* method will raise an error 457—"This key is already associated with an element of this collection." (Keys are compared in a case-insensitive way.)

Once you have added one or more values, you can retrieve them using the *Item* method; this method is the default member of the Collection class, so you can omit it if you want. Items can be read using their numeric indices (as you do with arrays) or their string keys:

```
' All the following statements print "Anne Lipton".
Print EmployeeNames.Item("Sales")
Print EmployeeNames.Item(1)
Print EmployeeNames("Sales")
Print EmployeeNames(1)
```

> **TIP** If you want to write faster programs, always access a Collection's items using their string keys rather than their numeric indices. As counterintuitive as it may appear, using string keys is almost always faster than using numeric

indices, especially if the Collection has thousands of elements and the one you're interested in isn't near the beginning of it.

If you pass a numeric index that's either negative or greater than the number of items currently in the collection, you get an error code 9—"Subscript out of range" (exactly as if you were acting on a standard array); if you pass a nonexistent string key, you get error code 5—"Invalid procedure call or argument." Curiously, the Collection object doesn't offer a native method to test whether an item actually exists. The only way to learn whether an element is already in a Collection is by setting up an error handler and testing for the existence of that element. Here's a function that does the trick, and you can reuse it with any Collection:

```
Function ItemExists(col As Collection, Key As String) As Boolean
    Dim dummy As Variant
    On Error Resume Next
    dummy = col.Item(Key)
    ItemExists = (Err <> 5)
End Function
```

The *Count* method returns the number of items in the collection:

```
' Retrieve the last item in the EmployeeNames collection.
' Note that collections are one-based.
Print EmployeeNames.Item(EmployeeNames.Count)
```

You can remove items from a Collection object using the *Remove* method; this method accepts either a numeric index or a string key:

```
' Remove the Marketing Boss.
EmployeeNames.Remove "Marketing"
```

If the key doesn't exist, the Collection object raises an error 5—"Invalid procedure call or argument." Collections don't offer a native way to remove all the items in a single operation, so you're forced to write a loop. Here's a general function that does it for you:

```
Sub RemoveAllItems(col As Collection)
    Do While col.Count
        col.Remove 1
    Loop
End Sub
```

TIP A faster way to remove all the items in a Collection is to destroy the Collection object itself by setting it to Nothing or to another fresh, new instance:

```
' Both these lines destroy the current contents
' of the Collection.
Set EmployeeNames = Nothing
Set EmployeeNames = New Collection
```

This approach works only if there isn't any other object variable pointing to the Collection object, however. If you aren't sure of this, the only safe way to remove all items is the loop I showed you previously.

Finally, as I mentioned before, Collections don't allow you to modify the value of an item. If you want to change the value of an item, you must first delete it and then add a new item. Here's generic routine that uses this technique:

```
' INDEX can be either a numeric or a string value.
Sub ReplaceItem(col As Collection, index As Variant, newValue As Variant)
    ' First remove that item (exits with error if it doesn't exist).
    col.Remove index
    ' Then add it again.
    If VarType(index) = vbString Then
        ' Add a new item with the same string key.
        col.Add newValue, index
    Else
        ' Add a new item in the same position (without any key).
        col.Add newValue, , index
    End If
End Sub
```

Iterating on Collection objects

Since you can address items using their numeric indices, you can loop on all the elements of a Collection object using a regular *For...Next* loop:

```
' Load the contents of a Collection into a ListBox control.
Dim i As Long
For i = 1 To EmployeeNames.Count
    List1.AddItem EmployeeNames(i)
Next
```

While this code works, Collection objects offer another, better way to perform the same task, based on the *For Each...Next* loop:

```
Dim var As Variant
For Each var in EmployeeNames
    List1.AddItem var
Next
```

Notice that the loop's controlling variable (*var*, in this example) must be of type Variant so that it can host any value that had been added to the Collection. The only exception to this rule is when you're sure that the Collection contains only a given class of objects (forms, controls, or user-defined objects), in which case you can use a controlling variable of that specific type:

```
' If the Customers collection includes only references
' to individual Customer objects
```

```
Dim cust As Customer
For Each cust In Customers
    List1.AddItem cust.Name
Next
```

Using a controlling variable of a specific object type usually offers better performance than a generic Variant or Object variable. Iterating on the elements of a collection using a *For Each...Next* loop is generally faster than a regular *For...Next* loop because the latter forces you to refer to individual elements using their numeric indices, which is a relatively slow operation.

Working with Collection objects

Collections are very flexible structures and are useful in many cases for solving simple but recurring programming jobs. The very nature of Collection objects suggests that you use them whenever you need to associate a key with a value for a faster retrieval. The following routine builds on the fact that Collections accept only unique keys to filter out all duplicated entries in an array of any Variant-compatible type:

```
' Filter out all duplicate entries in any Variant-compatible array.
' On entry, NUMELS should be set to the number of items to be examined.
' On exit, NUMELS holds the number of nonduplicate items.
Sub FilterDuplicates(arr As Variant, numEls As Long)
    Dim col As New Collection, i As Long, j As Long
    On Error Resume Next
    j = LBound(arr) - 1
    For i = LBound(arr) To numEls
        ' Add a dummy zero value, but use the array's value as the key.
        col.Add 0, CStr(arr(i))
        If Err = 0 Then
            j = j + 1
            If i <> j Then arr(j) = arr(i)
        Else
            Err.Clear
        End If
    Next
    ' Clear all remaining items.
    For i = j + 1 To numEls: arr(i) = Empty: Next
    numEls = j
End Sub
```

In some cases, you might feel limited by the fact that Collection objects can't hold UDT values, so you don't know what to do when you need to store multiple values associated with the same key. One solution is to use objects instead of UDTs, but employing this technique is often overkill because you rarely want to add a class module to your project just to store multiple values in a Collection. A much better solution is to build arrays on the fly and store them as items in the Collection. A practical example is shown on the following page.

```
' Store Employees data in a Collection.
Dim Employees As New Collection
' Each item is made up of (Name, Dept, Salary).
Employees.Add Array("John", "Marketing", 80000), "John"
Employees.Add Array("Anne", "Sales", 75000), "Anne"
Employees.Add Array("Robert", "Administration", 70000), "Robert"
...

' List all employees' names.
Dim var As Variant
For Each var in Employees
    Print var(0)        ' Item 0 is the employee's name.
Next
' Where does Anne work?
Print Employees("Anne")(1)
' How much does Robert earn?
Print Employees("Robert")(2)
```

Of course, you can make these compound structures as complex as you need
to. For example, each Employees element might hold a Collection of other pieces
of information, such as how many hours each employee has worked for a given
customer:

```
Dim Employees As New Collection, Customers As Collection
' Each item is made up of (Name, Dept, Salary, Customers).
Set Customers = New Collection
Customers.Add 10, "Tech Eight, Inc"
Customers.Add 22, "HT Computers"
Employees.Add Array("John", "Marketing", 80000, Customers), "John"
' Start with a fresh collection each time.
Set Customers = New Collection
Customers.Add 9, "Tech Eight, Inc"
Customers.Add 44, "Motors Unlimited"
Employees.Add Array("Anne", "Sales", 75000, Customers), "Anne"
' etc.  ....
```

This complex structure lets you quickly and elegantly solve a number of problems and answer a few interesting questions:

```
' Is John working with customer "HT Computers"?
Dim hours As Long, var As Variant
On Error Resume Next
hours = Employees("John")(3)("HT Computers")
' HOURS holds zero if the above statement failed.

' How many hours has Anne worked for external customers?
hours = 0
For Each var In Employees("Anne")(3)
    hours = hours + var
Next
```

```
' How many hours have been devoted to customer "Tech Eight, Inc"?
On Error Resume Next
hours = 0
For Each var In Employees
    hours = hours + var(3)("Tech Eight, Inc")
Next
```

As you can see, collections are highly flexible data structures. I suggest that you explore their capabilities in depth, and I'd bet that you'll find yourselves using them more often than you anticipated.

Dictionary Objects

Dictionary objects are new to the Visual Basic language. Technically speaking, however, they don't belong to Visual Basic as Collections do, nor do they belong to the VBA language. Rather, they're exposed by an external library, the Microsoft Scripting Library. In fact, to use these objects you must add a reference to the SCRRUN.DLL library (which appears under the name Microsoft Scripting Runtime, as you can see in Figure 4-1). Once you do that, you can press F2 to invoke the Object Browser and explore Dictionary's methods and properties.

Dictionary objects are very similar to Collection objects. Actually, they were originally created to provide VBScript programmers with a Collection-like object. The Dictionary object isn't exclusive to Visual Basic 6; the Scripting Library can be

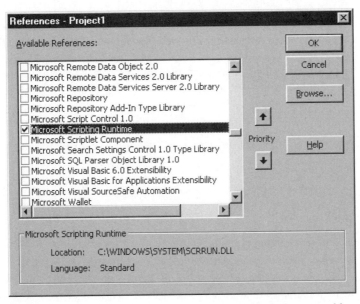

Figure 4-1. *Add a reference to the Microsoft Scripting Runtime library in the References dialog box in order to use the Dictionary object.*

freely downloaded from *http://www.microsoft.com/scripting* and used with any Automation-compliant programming language, including Visual Basic 5. Visual Basic 6 installs this library as part of its setup procedure, so you don't have to download and register it separately.

You'll see in a moment how closely akin Dictionary objects are to Collection objects, so it's easy to illustrate their features by comparing these two. You create a Dictionary object as you do any object, for example using an auto-instancing variable:

```
Dim dict As New Scripting.Dictionary
```

In all cases, note that the *Scripting* prefix is optional, but I suggest you use it in case your References dialog box includes other external libraries that happen to expose a Dictionary object. Using the complete *libraryname.classname* syntax when declaring object variables is an intelligent way to avoid bugs in the future.

> **CAUTION**   The VBScript-oriented nature of Dictionary objects has somewhat resisted the migration to Visual Basic. All the examples in the Visual Basic 6 manuals are taken as is from VBScript documentation and therefore use a *CreateObject* function to create the Dictionary. (VBScript doesn't support the *New* operator.) Besides, all examples store references to Dictionary objects in Variant variables. (VBScript doesn't support specific object variables.)
>
> ```
> ' This is what VB6 docs report.
> Dim dict          ' Variant is VB's default data type.
> Set dict = CreateObject("Scripting.Library")
> ```
>
> While this code works, you should absolutely avoid it for two reasons: *CreateObject* is about twice as slow as *New*, and above all, using a generic Variant variable instead of a more specific variable of type Dictionary adds overhead any time you access the object's properties and methods because you are actually doing late binding instead of early binding. My informal benchmarks show that a specific variable speeds up the code to 30 times faster, and it also delivers more robust applications because all syntactical errors are trapped by the compiler.

You add an item to a Dictionary object using its *Add* method, as you do with Collection objects. But the order of the two arguments is reversed (first the key and then the item's value), and you can't omit the key or specify the *before* or *after* arguments:

```
dict.Add "key", value
```

If the Dictionary object contains a value associated with the same string key, an error 457 is raised (the same as that raised by Collection objects). Dictionary objects support the *Item* member, but there are important differences from Collection objects in the way the *Item* member is implemented. For Dictionary objects, *Item* is a read-write property, not a method, and you can reference an element only by using a key (which can be a string or a number), but not through its numeric index in the Dictionary. In other words, you can reference an item only by its key, not by its position:

```
Print dict("key")              ' Print the current value,
dict("key") = newValue         ' and then modify it.
Print dict(1)                  ' Displays an empty string because
                               ' there's no item with this key.
```

There's also a third important difference: If the key isn't found in the Dictionary, no error is raised. If your code was trying to read that item, the Dictionary returns an Empty value; if it was assigning a value, another item is added to the Dictionary. In other words, you can add new items without using the *Add* method:

```
Print dict("key2")             ' Returns Empty.
dict(key2) = "new value"       ' Adds a new element, and
                               ' no error is raised.
```

In this respect, Dictionary objects are more akin to PERL associative arrays than to Visual Basic's Collection objects. Like Collections, Dictionaries support the *Count* property, but you can't use it to set up *For...Next* loops.

You can remove Dictionary items using the *Remove* method:

```
dict.Remove "key"              ' Numeric indices aren't supported.
```

If the key isn't found in the Dictionary, an error 32811 is raised. (The corresponding message isn't very helpful about the real cause: "Method 'Remove' of object 'IDictionary' failed"). As is *not* the case for Collections, you can remove all items in a Dictionary object in one shot by using the *RemoveAll* method:

```
dict.RemoveAll                 ' No need for a loop.
```

Dictionary objects are also more flexible than Collection objects in that you can modify the key associated with an element by using the *Key* property:

```
dict.Key("key") = "new key"
```

The *Key* property is write-only, but this isn't a real limitation: It wouldn't make any sense to *read* the value of a key, since you can reference it only by using the current key value. Dictionary objects expose an *Exists* method that lets you test whether an element actually exists. You need this method because otherwise you couldn't discern between nonexistent and Empty values:

```
If dict.Exists("John") Then Print "Item ""John"" exists"
```

Dictionary objects also expose two methods, *Items* and *Keys*, which quickly retrieve all values and keys into an array in one single operation:

```
Dim itemValues() As Variant, itemKeys() As Variant, i As Long
itemValues = dict.Items     ' Retrieve all values.
itemKeys = dict.Keys        ' Retrieve all keys.
' Put keys and values into a single list.
For i = 0 To UBound(itemValues)
    List1.AddItem itemKeys(i) & " = " & itemValues(i)
Next
```

The *Items* and *Keys* methods are also the only ways to access the elements of a Dictionary object because you can't use either the *For...Next* loop (because numeric indices are actually interpreted as keys) or the *For Each...Next* loop. If you don't want to explicitly load items and keys into Variant arrays, however, you can take the following shortcut, based on the fact that Variant arrays do support enumeration through the *For Each...Next* loop:

```
Dim key As Variant
For Each key In dict.Keys
    List1.AddItem key & " = " & dict(key)
Next
```

Interestingly, *Keys* is also the default method for the Dictionary object, so you can omit it in the preceding code snippet and you end up with a code syntax that makes it appear as if the Dictionary object supported enumeration through the *For Each...Next* loop:

```
For Each key In dict
    List1.AddItem key & " = " & dict(key)
Next
```

The last property of the Dictionary object is the *CompareMode* property, which states how a Dictionary object compares keys. It can be assigned three values: 0-BinaryCompare (case-sensitive comparisons, the default setting), 1-TextCompare (case-insensitive comparisons), and 2-DatabaseCompare (not supported under Visual Basic). You can assign this property only when the Dictionary object is empty.

Dictionary vs. Collection objects

After this overview, it should be clear that Dictionary objects are more flexible than Collection objects. Their only missing feature is the ability to address items by their numeric indices (which, on the other hand, is one of the slowest operations you can perform on Collection objects). Unless you need this capability, the choice seems clear: Use Dictionary objects whenever you need their flexibility. But remember that you will need to distribute another ancillary file with your application.

Microsoft hasn't revealed how Collection and Dictionary objects are implemented internally, but it seems to me that the Dictionary object is based on a more efficient algorithm than the Collection object. My informal benchmarks show that creating a 10,000-item Dictionary is about 7 times faster than adding the same number of items to an empty Collection object. Reading these items back is about 3 to 4 times faster. This gap decreases when you create larger structures (only 2.5 times faster with 100,000 items), but in general a Dictionary object can be considered faster than a Collection object. The actual speed difference might depend on how keys are distributed, available memory, and other factors. I suggest that you do some benchmarks with your own actual data before opting for one solution or another.

PROCEDURES

Visual Basic modules are made of a declaration section—in which you declare types, constants, and variables used in the module—plus a collection of procedures. These can be of type Sub or Function, depending on whether they return a value to the caller. They can also be Property procedures, but we won't discuss those until Chapter 6. Each procedure has a unique name, a scope, a list of expected arguments, and—if it's a function—a return value.

Scope

The scope of a procedure can be Private, Public, or Friend. A Private procedure can be invoked only from within the module in which it's defined. A Public procedure can be invoked from outside the module. If the module is itself Public (a module whose *Instancing* property isn't 1-Private, contained in a project whose type isn't Standard EXE), the procedure can be called from outside the current program through COM. Since Public is the default scope attribute for procedures, you can always omit it:

```
' Public function that provides access to a control on a form.
Function GetTotal() As Currency
    GetTotal = CCur(txtTotal.Text)
End Function
```

If the scope isn't Public, you must specify it explicitly:

```
' All event procedures are Private.
Private Sub Form_Load()
    txtTotal.Text = ""
End Sub
```

The scope of a Friend procedure is halfway between Private and Public: Such a procedure can be called from anywhere in the current project, but not from outside it. This difference becomes important only if you're within a project of a type other than Standard EXE, one that therefore exposes its classes to other applications in the form of COM components. I'll talk about COM components in depth in Chapter 16, but here we need to anticipate some key concepts.

To understand how a Friend procedure can be useful, imagine the following scenario: You have a Public class module that shows a dialog box and asks the user for his or her name and password. It also exposes a *GetPassword* function so that another module in the project can validate the password and enable or disable specific functions for that particular user. Should you declare this function as Private? No, because it could be invoked from another module. Should the function be Public? No, because that would enable a malicious programmer to query your class module from outside the project and steal users' passwords. (For the sake of simplicity, let's assume that getting a reference to your class isn't a problem.) In this case, the best choice is to make the function a Friend.

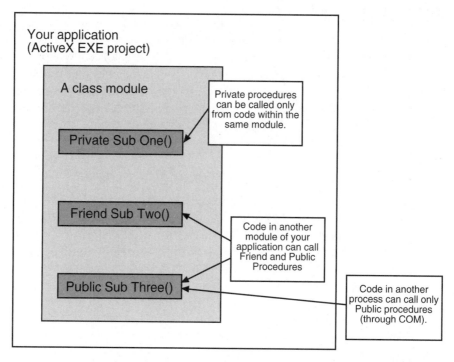

Your application
(ActiveX EXE project)

A class module

Private Sub One()

Private procedures
can be called only
from code within the
same module.

Friend Sub Two()

Public Sub Three()

Code in another
module of your
application can call
Friend and Public
Procedures

Code in another
process can call only
Public procedures
(through COM).

If you're within a Standard EXE project, or within a Private class in any type of project, Friend and Public attributes are equivalent because the procedure can't be called from the outside anyway.

Parameter Lists and Return Values

Both Sub and Function procedures can accept arguments. Functions also return a value. Setting a reasonable list of expected parameters and a return value is the key to making your procedure more useful. You can pass a procedure any simple data type supported by Visual Basic, including Integer, Boolean, Long, Byte, Single, Double, Currency, Date, String, and Variant. You can also declare your parameter an Object, a Collection, a class defined in your program, or external to it (for example, a Dictionary object). Finally you can pass an array of any of the previously mentioned types. The same is true for the return type too, which can be of any simple type supported by Visual Basic, including arrays—a new Visual Basic 6 feature.

You should be aware that an *argument* is the value passed to a procedure, whereas a *parameter* is the value received by it. Both words refer to the same actual value, and the most appropriate term depends on the direction from which you're looking at the value: the caller code sees arguments, and the called procedure sees parameters. In this section, the words *argument* and *parameter* are used somewhat interchangeably except where ambiguity would arise.

Passing by value or by reference

An argument can be passed by value (using the *ByVal* keyword) or by reference (using the *ByRef* keyword or by omitting any qualifier). Arguments passed by reference can be modified by the called procedure, and the modified value can be read back by the caller. Conversely, changes to arguments passed by value are never propagated back to the caller. The rule you should stick to is *always pass by reference those arguments that must be modified by the procedure, and pass by value all the others*. This approach minimizes the risk of accidentally modifying the value of a variable passed to the method. Let me explain this concept with an example:

```
' Z is incorrectly declared ByRef.
Sub DrawPoint(ByVal X As Long, ByVal Y As Long, Z As Long)
    ' Keep arguments positive.
    If X < 0 Then X = 0
    If Y < 0 Then Y = 0
    If Z < 0 Then Z = 0        ' Probable cause of bugs !!!
    ' ...
End Sub
```

This procedure modifies its parameters to make them fit their valid range; if a parameter is passed using *ByRef*, as Z is in the previous example, these changes are propagated to the calling code. This type of bug can be undetected for some time, especially if in most cases you call the procedure using constants or expressions. The fact that your code works in these situations can convince you that the procedure is correct and lull you into a false sense of security:

```
' This works. (Argument is a constant.)
DrawPoint 10, 20, 40
' This works too. (Argument is an expression.)
DrawPoint x * 2, y * 2, z * 2
' This works but modifies Z if it's negative.
DrawPoint x, y, z
```

Declaring a parameter using *ByVal* offers another benefit: you can call the procedure passing a variable or an expression of any type and let Visual Basic do the data type conversion for you. Conversely, if a parameter is declared *ByRef* and you pass a variable, their types must match:

```
' Assuming that x,y,z aren't Long variables
' (for example, they are either Single or Double)
DrawPoint x, y, 100    ' This works, Visual Basic does the conversion.
DrawPoint x, y, z      ' This doesn't. (ByRef argument type mismatch.)
```

There is one exception to the above rule, though: If a procedure exposes a *ByRef* Variant parameter, you can pass really anything to it. You can exploit this feature to write procedures that aren't specific to a particular data type, as you can see in the code on the next page.

```
' Swap values of any type.
Sub Swap(first As Variant, second As Variant)
    Dim temp As Variant
    temp = first: first = second: second = temp
End Sub
```

There's another, subtler reason for using the *ByVal* keyword whenever possible. When a procedure can access the same memory location by means of two or more different names—for instance, a global variable or a module-level variable that's also passed as an argument—that variable is said to be *aliased* within that procedure. The problem with aliased variables is that they prevent the Visual Basic compiler from generating optimized code that holds variables' values inside CPU registers when it would otherwise be possible to do so. When all variables are passed to procedures and methods by value, it isn't possible for the routine to modify a global value through one of its parameters, and the compiler can produce better code. If you're sure that all the procedures in your program adhere to this restriction, the native compiler can safely optimize your code. To inform Visual Basic that there aren't any aliased variables in your program, open the Project-Properties dialog box, switch to the Compile tab, click on the Advanced Optimizations button, and tick the Assume No Aliasing check box in the dialog box that appears, as you can see in Figure 4-2.

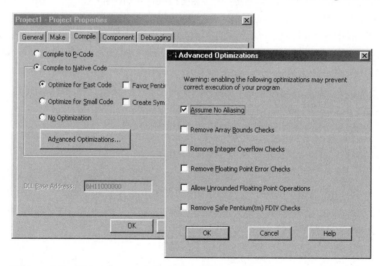

Figure 4-2. *The Advanced Optimizations dialog box.*

Passing user-defined types

You might have noticed that I didn't mention UDT structures among the data types that can be passed to a procedure or returned from a function. In fact, you can't always pass such structures as an argument to a procedure. Consider these cases:

■ If a UDT structure is declared as Private to a module, it can be passed and returned only by Private procedures inside that module.

■ If the UDT structure is defined as Public in a standard BAS module, it can be used as an argument for Private and Friend procedures defined in any type of module in the current project. It can also be used as an argument in Public procedures defined in any BAS module of the application, but not in other types of modules (including forms).

■ If you want to write a Public procedure that accepts a UDT argument in a module other than a BAS module, you must place a Public Type definition in a Public class module—that is, a module whose *Instancing* property is different from 1-Private. (You can't therefore place the declaration in form modules, because they are always Private.) Since you must define the UDT structure in a Public class, you can do that only within project types other than Standard EXE projects.

You can't even declare a Public UDT structure in a class module that isn't Public itself. This prevents you from declaring a Public UDT in a Standard EXE project in any modules except standard BAS modules.

> **CAUTION** If you're creating a Microsoft ActiveX EXE project, you should be aware that you can exchange UDT values across processes only if you have DCOM98 (on Windows 9x systems) or Service Pack 4 (on Windows NT 4.0 systems). If you don't, when Visual Basic tries to pass a UDT value to another process an error 458 is raised ("Variable uses an Automation Type not supported in Visual Basic"). You need these operating system updates on both your own and your users' machines.
>
> Note that this isn't an issue when working with an ActiveX DLL project because it shares the same address space as its caller, so UDTs can be passed without the intervention of COM.

Passing Private types

There are restrictions when passing Private objects to a procedure, where a *private object* is defined in your application but not visible outside it. Private objects are those defined by classes whose *Instancing* property is set to 1-Private, or objects exposed by the Visual Basic library, including forms, controls, and objects such as App, Clipboard, Screen, and Printer. In general, you can neither include such private objects among the arguments of a procedure nor use them as the return value of a function if the procedure can be called from another application through COM. This restriction makes perfect sense. COM arbitrates the exchange of information between the application that provides the object and the programs that use it. COM is able to deal with all the basic data types supported by Visual Basic and with all the Public objects defined by any program in the Windows environment. On the other hand, COM is unable to pass information in a format that is defined within a program, such as a Private class, as you can see in the code snippet on the next page.

```
' Visual Basic won't compile the following lines
' if this procedure is located in a Public class.
Public Sub ClearField(frm As Form)
...
End Sub
```

This restriction isn't enforced if the method is declared as Private or Friend because such a method can't be invoked from another application through COM and can be called only by another module of the current application. In this case, there's no point in limiting the data types that can be passed to the method, and in fact the Visual Basic compiler doesn't complain if a Private data type appears among the arguments or if it is the return value of a method.

```
' This is compiled without problems, even within a Public class.
Friend Sub ClearField(frm As Form)
...
End Sub
```

> **NOTE** There's an easy workaround for the limitation on passing Private objects to a procedure, though. Just declare the argument or the return value using As Object or As Variant: in this case, the compiler can't know which object will be actually passed at run time and won't flag the line as an error. While this technique works, you should at least be aware that Microsoft strongly discourages it and has publicly stated that it might not work in future versions of the language. Forewarned is forearmed.

The *Optional* keyword

Visual Basic 4 introduced the ability to include optional parameters in the parameter list of procedures and methods. Optional parameters must always come after regular (required) parameters. Visual Basic 4 supports only optional parameters of Variant type and permits testing for whether a parameter is actually passed by means of the *IsMissing* function:

```
' A public method of a form.
Sub PrintData1(text As String, Optional color As Variant)
    If IsMissing(color) Then color = vbWhite
    ForeColor = color
    Print text
End Sub
```

Be very careful when you use the *IsMissing* function because if you assign a value to a missing parameter, this function returns False from that point on. Study this code excerpt, and see why it doesn't work as expected:

```
Sub PrintData2(text As String, Optional color As Variant)
    Dim saveColor As Long
    If IsMissing(color) Then
        Form1.FontTransparent = False
```

```
            color = vbWhite
      End If
      Form1.ForeColor = color
      Form1.Print text
      If IsMissing(color) Then
            ' Next statement will be never executed!
            Form1.FontTransparent = False
      End If
End Sub
```

Visual Basic 5 has added the ability to use optional arguments of any type—not just Variant—and to set their default values right in the parameter list. The *PrintData1* routine can be rewritten more concisely under Visual Basic 5 and 6 as follows:

```
Sub PrintData3(text As String, Optional color As Long = vbWhite)
      Form1.ForeColor = color
      Form1.Print text
End Sub
```

> **CAUTION**   If an optional argument is of a type other than Variant, the *IsMissing* function always returns False. This behavior can cause many subtle errors, as in the following code:

```
Sub PrintData4(text As String, Optional color As Long)
      If IsMissing(color) Then
            ' The next line will never be executed!
            Form1.FontTransparent = False
      End If
      ' ...
End Sub
```

When a non-Variant optional parameter isn't initialized to a specific default value in the parameter list, the procedure receives a zero value, an empty string, or Nothing, depending on the type of the parameter. The only data types that can't be used with the Optional keyword are UDT structures.

Optional arguments are very handy for writing flexible procedures, but contrary to what some programmers believe, they don't produce more efficient code. The (wrong) assumption is: Since the calling code doesn't have to push the missing values on the stack, fewer CPU statements are executed and the program runs faster. Unfortunately, this isn't true. When an optional argument is omitted, Visual Basic actually pushes a special "missing" value on the stack. So there's no real speed advantage in omitting an optional argument.

The "missing" magic value used by Visual Basic compiler is Error value &H80020004. The *IsMissing* function does nothing but test the Variant and return True if it contains this value. Incidentally, this explains why the *IsMissing* function always returns False with any data type different from Variant: Only a Variant variable can hold an Error value. You can't directly create this special value because the *CVErr* function accepts only values in the range 0 through 65,535. But you can use the following trick:

```
' Always call this function without any argument.
Function MissingValue(Optional DontPassThis As Variant) As Variant
    MissingValue = DontPassThis
End Function
```

Named arguments

While Optional arguments are a great addition to the VBA language, they surely tend to reduce the readability of your code. Take this statement as an example:

```
Err.Raise 999, , , "Value out range"
```

It appears as if the programmer is raising a custom error; unfortunately, there are too many commas, and the *Value out of range* string falls in the *HelpFile* field. How many developers can spot this kind of error just by browsing their source code? Fortunately, you can reduce this adverse effect of optional parameters by using named arguments when calling the procedure. Here's how you can correctly rewrite the previous statement:

```
Err.Raise Number:=999, Description:="Value out of range"
```

Named arguments let you alter the order in which arguments appear in the line that invokes the procedure, but they don't allow you to omit an argument that isn't optional. All the procedures that you create in Visual Basic automatically support named arguments. For instance, if you have the following routine:

```
Sub Init(Optional Name As String, Optional DeptID As Integer, _
    Optional Salary As Currency)
    ' ...
End Sub
```

you can call it as follows:

```
Init Name:="Roscoe Powell", Salary:=80000
```

The *ParamArray* keyword

You can implement a routine that accepts any number of arguments using the *ParamArray* keyword:

```
Function Sum(ParamArray args() As Variant) As Double
    Dim i As Integer
    ' All ParamArrays are zero-based.
    For i = 0 To UBound(args)
        Sum = Sum + args(i)
    Next
End Function
```

You call the *Sum* function as follows:

```
Print Sum(10, 30, 20)  ' Displays "60"
```

A few simple rules dictate how the *ParamArray* keyword should be used:

- There can be only one *ParamArray* keyword, and it must be at the end of the parameter list.

- The array declared by the *ParamArray* keyword can only be of the Variant type.

- No *Optional* parameter can precede the *ParamArray* keyword.

The *ParamArray* keyword can be an invaluable aid in creating truly generic functions. For instance, you can build a function that returns the maximum of any number of values:

```
Function Max(first As Variant, ParamArray args() As Variant) As Variant
    Dim i As Integer
    Max = first
    For i = 0 To UBound(args)
        If args(i) > Max Then Max = args(i)
    Next
End Function
```

Note that there's one required argument in the previous procedure because it doesn't make sense to evaluate the maximum of 0 values. Even though it isn't documented, you can use the *IsMissing* function on the *args()* parameter. Thus, you have two ways to exit the function if no optional values were passed to the routine:

```
' The documented way
If LBound(args) > UBound(args) Then Exit Function
' The undocumented way is more concise and readable
If IsMissing(args) Then Exit Function
```

The *ParamArray* keyword can be coupled with the ability to return arrays. For example, while the *Array* function lets you build Variant arrays on the fly, VBA doesn't offer a similar function for building other types of arrays. Here's how you can remedy this problem:

```
Function ArrayLong(ParamArray args() As Variant) As Long()
    Dim numEls As Long, i As Long
    numEls = UBound(args) - LBound(args) + 1
    If numEls <= 0 Then Err.Raise 5      ' Invalid procedure call
    ReDim result(0 To numEls - 1) As Long
    For i = 0 To numEls - 1
        result(i) = args(i)
    Next
    ArrayLong = result
End Function
```

One last note about the *ParamArray* keyword: If you want to get the best performances, stay clear of it. It forces you to use Variant parameters, which are the slowest data type supported by Visual Basic. If you need to use optional arguments, use non-Variant Optional parameters, which are much faster.

Error Handling

Error handling is an important feature of the Visual Basic language and is closely related to the structure of your procedures. Visual Basic offers three statements that give you control over what happens when an error occurs during the execution of your code:

- The *On Error Resume Next* statement tells Visual Basic to ignore any error. When an error actually occurs, Visual Basic proceeds with executing the next statement. You can test the error code using the *Err* function, or you can ignore it completely.

- The *On Error Goto <label>* statement tells Visual Basic that any error will cause a jump to the named label, which must be located in the same procedure in which this statement appears. You can use the same label name in different procedures because a label's scope is the procedure, not the module.

- The *On Error Goto 0* statement tells Visual Basic to cancel the effect of any active *On Error Resume Next* or *On Error Goto <label>* statement. When an error occurs, Visual Basic behaves as if error trapping is disabled.

Selecting one form of error trapping or another depends on your programming style and the requirements of the specific routine, so no rule can be provided that's valid in every case. All the *On Error* statements clear the current error code.

The *On Error Goto <label>* statement

When you're dealing with files, the *On Error Goto <label>* statement is often a better choice because in this case there are so many things that can go wrong, and you don't want to test the *Err* code after every statement. The same concept applies to intensive math routines that are subject to multiple errors, such as division by 0, overflow, and illegal arguments in function calls. In most cases, when an error occurs in these routines, the best you can do is exit right away and report the error to the calling code.

On the other hand, there are many cases when the "error" isn't a fatal error. Suppose that you want your user to insert a given disk in drive A, but you want to give him or her another chance if the disk isn't the one you were expecting instead of aborting the whole procedure when the user inserts a wrong disk. Here's a reusable procedure that lets you check whether a drive contains a disk with a given label and prompts the user to insert a disk if the drive is empty:

```
Function CheckDisk(ByVal Drive As String, VolumeLabel As String)_
    As Boolean
    Dim saveDir As String, answer As Integer
    On Error GoTo Error_Handler
    Drive = Left$(Drive, 1)
    ' Save the current drive for restoring later.
    saveDir = CurDir$
    ' Next statement is likely to fire an error.
    ' Check the drive specified in the parameter.
    ChDrive Drive
    ' Return True if the label matches, False otherwise.
    CheckDisk = (StrComp(Dir$(Drive & ":\*.*", vbVolume), _
        VolumeLabel, vbTextCompare) = 0)
    ' Restore the original current drive.
    ChDrive saveDir
    Exit Function
Error_Handler:
    ' If error is Device Unavailable or Disk Not Ready, and it's a disk,
    ' give the user the chance to insert the diskette in the drive.
    If (Err = 68 Or Err = 71) And InStr(1, "AB", Drive, _
        vbTextCompare) Then
        answer = MsgBox("Please enter a diskette in drive " & Drive, _
            vbExclamation + vbRetryCancel)
        ' Retry the ChDir statement, or exit returning False.
        If answer = vbRetry Then Resume
    Else
        ' In all other cases, return the error to the calling program.
        Err.Raise Err.Number, Err.Source, Err.Description
    End If
End Function
```

You can exit from an error routine in at least five ways:

- You can execute a *Resume* statement to retry the line of code that caused the error.

- You can execute a *Resume Next* statement to resume execution in the procedure body at the line immediately after the one that caused the error.

- You can execute a *Resume <line>* statement to resume execution at a given line in the procedure body; *<line>* can be a line number or label name.

- You can report the error to the calling routine by executing an *Err.Raise* method.

- You can exit the procedure by executing an *Exit Sub* or *Exit Function* statement or by letting the execution flow into the *End Sub* or *End Function* directive. In both cases, the calling procedure receives a zero error code.

The *On Error Resume Next* statement

The *On Error Resume Next* statement is most useful when you don't expect many errors or when you don't need to trap all of them. In some cases, you can use this approach when the exception can be safely ignored, as in the following example:

```
' Hide all controls in Form1.
Dim ctrl As Control
' Not all controls support the Visible property (Timers don't).
On Error Resume Next
For Each ctrl In Form1.Controls
    Ctrl.Visible = False
Next
```

If you want to test an error condition, you must do it immediately after each statement that could cause an error. Or you can test the *Err* function at the end of a group of statements. In fact, if any statement raises an error, Visual Basic doesn't reset the *Err* value until the programmer does it explicitly with an *Err.Clear* method.

If an error occurs while there's an active *On Error Resume Next* statement, the execution continues with the next statement in the procedure, *whichever the next statement is*. This feature permits you to test attributes of controls and objects in ways that would be impossible otherwise:

```
' Hide all visible controls on Form1, and then restore
' their visibility.
Dim ctrl As Control, visibleControls As New Collection
On Error Resume Next
For Each ctrl In Form1.Controls
    If ctrl.Visible = False Then
        ' This control doesn't support the Visible property
        ' or it is already hidden: in either case, don't do anything.
    Else
        ' Remember that this is a visible control, and then hide it.
        visibleControls.Add ctrl
        ctrl.Visible = False
    End If
Next
' Do whatever you need to do (omitted), and
' then correctly restore the original controls' Visible property.
For Each ctrl In visibleControls
    ctrl.Visible = True
Next
```

This unorthodox way to use *On Error Resume Next* is a powerful weapon in the hands of expert Visual Basic programmers, but it tends to obscure the logic behind your code. My suggestion is to resort to this technique only if it's impossible or impractical to follow other approaches, and—above all—to add exhaustive comments to your code so that it's clear exactly what you're doing and why.

When a procedure that contains an *On Error Resume Next* statement exits, the calling code sees the code of the last error that occurred inside the procedure. Compare this behavior with procedures containing an *On Error Goto <label>* statement, which always clears the error code when the control returns to the calling code.

Unhandled errors

So far, we've seen what happens when an error fires in a procedure that is protected with an *On Error Resume Next* or *On Error Goto* <line> statement. When either one of these statements is currently active (when it hasn't been cancelled by a subsequent *On Error Goto 0* statement), the procedure is said to have an *active error handler*. However, not all procedures are so well written, and in many cases you must consider exactly what happens when Visual Basic fires an error that you aren't prepared to deal with. (These are also known as *unanticipated errors.*)

■ If the procedure has been called by another procedure, Visual Basic immediately terminates the current procedure and reports the error to the calling procedure, at the line that called the now-terminated procedure. If the calling procedure has an active error handler, it deals with the error locally (as if the error actually occurred there); otherwise, it exits immediately and reports the error to the procedure that called it, and so on until Visual Basic finds a pending procedure on the procedure stack that has an active error handler.

■ If no procedure on the procedure stack has an active error handler, Visual Basic has no code to notify of the error, so it immediately stops the program with an error. If you are within the IDE, you can now spot the original statement that produced the error so that you can modify the code right away and restart the program. If the error occurred in a compiled EXE program, the application terminates with a fatal error.

■ It's important to remember that all event procedures—such as *Form_Load* or *Command1_Click*—aren't generally called by code in your application; instead, they're called by the Visual Basic runtime file. So if an error occurs in those event procedures, there's no code to which to delegate the error and the application always terminates with a fatal error. Keep this in mind when distributing your *On Error* statements, and never omit them in event procedures unless you're 100 percent sure that they can never raise an error.

> **NOTE** Any error that occurs while processing the code in an error handler is treated by Visual Basic as an unanticipated error and is subject to all the rules you've seen so far. This explains why you can execute an *Err.Raise* method within an error handling routine and be sure that the error will be passed to the calling procedure.

Here's an example that summarizes what I have said so far. Just add a *Command1* button to a form, and then enter the following code:

```
Private Sub Command1_Click()
    ' Comment next line to see what happens when an event
    ' procedure isn't protected against unanticipated errors.
    On Error GoTo Error_Handler
    Print EvalExpression(1)
    Print EvalExpression(0)
    Print EvalExpression(-1)
    Exit Sub
Error_Handler:
    Print "Result unavailable"
    Resume Next
End Sub

Function EvalExpression(n As Double) As Double
    On Error GoTo Error_Handler
    EvalExpression = 1 + SquareRootReciprocal(n)
    Exit Function
Error_Handler:
    If Err = 11 Then
        ' If Division by zero, return -1 (no need to Resume).
        EvalExpression = -1
    Else
        ' Notify the caller that an error occurred.
        Err.Raise Err.Number, Err.Source, Err.Description
    End If
End Function

Function SquareRootReciprocal(n As Double) As Double
    ' This might cause a Division By Zero error (Err = 11) or
    ' an Invalid Procedure Call or Argument (Err = 5).
    SquareRootReciprocal = 1 / Sqr(n)
End Function
```

Run the program, and click on the button. You should see this output:

```
2
-1
Result Unavailable
```

Then comment out the *On Error* statement in the *Command1_Click* procedure to watch what happens when an event procedure isn't completely protected by an error handler.

> **CAUTION**   Not all run-time errors are trappable. The most notable exception is error 28—"Out of stack space." When this error occurs, the application always comes to a fatal end. But since all 32-bit Visual Basic applications have about 1 MB of available stack space, the probability that you incur this error is quite

small. When this happens, odds are that you are performing some wild recursion: In other words, you're caught in a sequence of procedures that call themselves in an endless loop. This is a typical logic programming error that should usually be fixed before you compile the program, so I don't consider the inability to trap the "Out of stack space" error at run time a serious problem.

The Err object

Visual Basic automatically associates several useful pieces of information with any error that it fires, and it gives you the ability to do the same when you raise a custom error. This capability is provided through the Err object, which exposes six properties and two methods. The most important property is *Number*, the numeric error code. This is the default property for this object, so you can use either *Err* or *Err.Number* in your code, which permits backward compatibility to be maintained with older versions of Visual Basic, and even QuickBasic.

The *Source* property is automatically filled with a string that states where the error occurred. If an error occurs in a standard or form module, Visual Basic sets this property to the name of the project (for example, *Project1*); if an error occurs in a class module, Visual Basic sets this property to the complete name of the class (for example, *Project1.Class1*). You can test this property to understand whether the error is internal or external to your application, and you can modify it before you notify the calling code of the error.

The *Description* property is also automatically filled with a string that describes the error that just occurred (for example, "Division by Zero"). In most cases, this string is more descriptive than the mere error code number. You can modify it in code before notifying the caller about the error. The *HelpFile* and *HelpContext* properties are filled by Visual Basic with information about which page in a help file contains an additional description of the error, how to handle it, and so on. Each native Visual Basic error corresponds to a page in Visual Basic's own help file. If you write libraries for other developers, you should devise a custom error numbering scheme and associate each custom error code with a page in a help file that you provide to your customers. This is rarely needed with business applications. Finally, the *LastDllError* is a read-only property that is set by Visual Basic when an error occurs during the processing of an API routine and isn't useful in any other case.

The *Raise* method raises an error and optionally assigns a value to all the properties seen above. Its syntax is the following:

```
Err.Raise Number, [Source], [Description], [HelpFile], [HelpContext])
```

All arguments are optional except the first one. For more readable code, use named arguments, as in this line:

```
Err.Raise Number:=1001, Description:="Customer Not Found"
```

The *Clear* method resets all the properties in one operation.

Visual Basic's Err object is compatible with the COM mechanism of notifying error codes and information among different processes. The importance of this feature will become apparent in Chapter 16.

Error handling inside the Visual Basic IDE

So far, I've described what happens when an error occurs in a compiled application. When the code is executed inside the IDE, however, Visual Basic behaves in a slightly different way in an attempt to simplify your debugging chores. More precisely, the IDE can behave differently according to the settings found in the General tab of the Options dialog box from the Tools menu, which you can see in Figure 4-3. Here are the possibilities:

- Break On All Errors: All errors stop execution as soon as they occur; this setting enables the programmer to see exactly which errors are raised before they're reported to the calling code.

- Break In Class Module: All errors in class modules stop execution as soon as they occur and before they're returned to the calling code. Class modules might need this special treatment because the calling code could be located in another process if the class is Public. This is the default setting for handling errors in the IDE.

- Break On Unhandled Errors: Errors stop execution only if they aren't handled anywhere in the program. This setting exactly mimics what happens in a compiled application, but during the test phase it might hide what really goes on inside your code. For this reason, you should choose this mode only if you know for sure that all errors are processed correctly. If you set this mode in an application that works like a COM component and provides classes to the outside, no error will ever be trapped in the application's code because such applications always have a caller to transmit the error to.

The settings in the Options dialog box shown in Figure 4-3 are the default settings for the Visual Basic environment and are persistent throughout your sessions. If you want to change the error-handling mode of the current environment without affecting the general setting, right-click inside the code window and select one of the commands in the Toggle submenu, shown in Figure 4-4. This approach is usually faster and lets you work with multiple instances of the IDE, each one with a different error-handling mode.

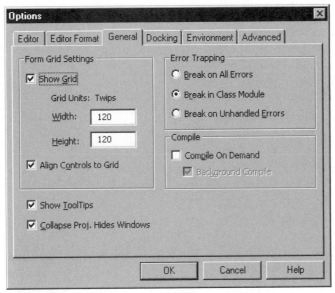

Figure 4-3. *The General tab in the Options dialog box.*

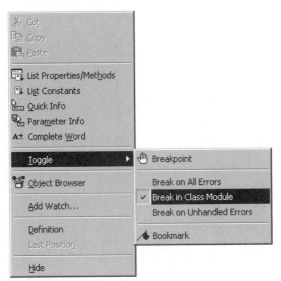

Figure 4-4. *The Toggle pop-up menu in the Code Editor.*

You've finally reached the end of this chapter devoted to Visual Basic data types, and you're now aware of a few subtleties that aren't clearly documented in the language manuals. Now you're ready to inspect the many functions that VBA gives you to process these data types.

Chapter 5

The Visual Basic for Applications and Visual Basic Libraries

Broadly speaking, Microsoft Visual Basic can be considered the sum of the Visual Basic for Applications library, plus a group of objects exposed by the Visual Basic library and the Visual Basic runtime. In this chapter, I focus on the VBA language, with an overview of its functions and commands, and some advanced or less obvious techniques that you can apply to it. You can browse most of the objects covered in this chapter by using the Object Browser utility and selecting the VBA library. In the last part of the chapter, I introduce a few important system objects, such as App and Clipboard, which are located in the VB library.

Control Flow

All programming languages must provide one or more ways to execute some statements out of the sequence in which they appear in the program listing. Apart from calls to Sub and Function procedures, you can gather all the basic control flow statements in two groups: *branch* statements and *loop* statements.

Branch Statements

The main branch statement is the *If...Else...Else If...End If* block. Visual Basic supports several flavors of this statement, including single-line and multiline versions:

```
' Single line version, without Else clause
If x > 0 Then y = x
' Single line version, with Else clause
If x > 0 Then y = x Else y = 0
' Single line, but with multiple statements separated by colons
If x > 0 Then y = x: x = 0 Else y = 0

' Multiline version of the above code (more readable)
If x > 0 Then
    y = x
    x = 0
Else
    y = 0
End If

' An example of If..ElseIf..Else block
If x > 0 Then
    y = x
ElseIf x < 0 Then
    y = x * x
Else                ' X is surely 0, no need to actually test it.
    x = -1
End If
```

You should be aware that any nonzero value after the *If* keyword is considered to be True and therefore fires the execution of the *Then* block:

```
' The following lines are equivalent.
If value <> 0 Then Print "Non Zero"
If value Then Print "Non Zero"
```

Even if this latter notation lets you save some typing, you shouldn't believe that it also makes your program faster, at least not necessarily. Benchmarks show that if the variable being tested is of type Boolean, Integer, or Long, this shortened notation doesn't make your program run faster. With other numeric types, however, you can expect some modest speed increment, about 20 percent or less. If you feel comfortable with this technique, go ahead and use it, but be aware that in many cases the speed improvement isn't worth the decreased readability.

Many advanced optimization techniques become possible when you combine multiple conditions using AND and OR operators. The following examples show how you can often write more concise and efficient code by rewriting a Boolean expression:

```
' If two numbers are both zero, you can apply the OR operator
' to their bits and you still have zero.
If x = 0 And y = 0 Then ...
If (x Or y) = 0 Then ...

' If either value is <>0, you can apply the OR operator
' to their bits and you surely have a nonzero value.
If x <> 0 Or y <> 0 Then ...
If (x Or y) Then ...

' If two integer numbers have opposite signs, applying the XOR
' operator to them yields a result that has the sign
'  bit set. (In other words, it is a negative value.)
If (x < 0 And y >= 0) Or (x >= 0 And y < 0) Then ...
If (x Xor y) < 0 Then ...
```

It's easy to get carried away when you're working with Boolean operators and inadvertently introduce subtle bugs into your code. For example, you might believe that the following two lines of code are equivalent, but they aren't. (To understand why, just think how numbers are represented in binary.)

```
' Not equivalent: just try with x=3 and y=4, whose binary
' representations are 0011 and 0100 respectively.
If x <> 0 And y <> 0 Then ...
If (x And y) Then ...
' Anyway, you can partially optimize the first line as follows:
If (x <> 0) And y Then ...
```

Another frequent source of ambiguity is the NOT operator, which toggles all the bits in a number. In Visual Basic, this operator returns False only if its argument is True (−1), so you should never use it with anything except the Boolean result of a comparison or with a Boolean variable:

```
If Not (x = y) Then ...   ' The same as x<>y
If Not x Then ...         ' The same as x<>-1, don't use instead of x=0
```

For more information, see the section "Boolean and Bit-Wise Operators" later in this chapter.

One detail that surprises many programmers coming to Visual Basic from other languages is that the *If* statement doesn't support the so-called *short-circuit evaluation*. In other words, Visual Basic always evaluates the whole expression in the *If* clause, even if it has enough information to determine that it is False or True, as in the following code:

```
' If x<=0, it makes no sense to evaluate Sqr(y)>x
' because the entire expression is guaranteed to be False.
If x > 0 And Sqr(y) < z Then z = 0

' If x=0, it makes no sense to evaluate x*y>100.
' because the entire expression is guaranteed to be True.
If x = 0 Or x * y > 100 Then z = 0
```

Even though Visual Basic isn't smart enough to optimize the expression automatically, it doesn't mean that you can't do it manually. You can rewrite the first *If* statement above as follows:

```
If x > 0 Then If Sqr(y) < z Then z = 0
```

You can rewrite the second *If* statement above as follows:

```
If x = 0 Then
    z = 0
ElseIf x * y > 100 Then
    z = 0
End If
```

The *Select Case* statement is less versatile than the *If* block in that it can test only one expression against a list of values:

```
Select Case Mid$(Text, i, 1)
    Case "0" To "9"
        ' It's a digit.
    Case "A" To "Z", "a" To "z"
        ' It's a letter.
    Case ".", ",", " ", ";", ":", "?"
        ' It's a punctuation symbol or a space.
    Case Else
        ' It's something else.
End Select
```

The most effective optimization technique with the *Select Case* block is to move the most frequent cases toward the top of the block. For instance, in the previous example you might decide to test whether the character is a letter before testing whether it's a digit. This change will slightly speed up your code if you're scanning regular text that's expected to contain more words than numbers.

Surprisingly, the *Select Case* block has an interesting feature that's missing in the more flexible *If* statement—namely, the ability to perform short circuit evaluation, sort of. In fact, *Case* subexpressions are evaluated only until they return True, after which all the remaining expressions on the same line are skipped. For example, in the *Case* clause that tests for punctuation symbols in the preceding code snippet, if the character is a dot all the other tests on that line are never executed. You can exploit this interesting feature to rewrite (and optimize) some complex *If* statements composed of multiple Boolean subexpressions:

```
' This series of subexpressions connected by the AND operator:
If x > 0 And Sqr(y) > x And Log(x) < z Then z = 0
' can be rewritten as:
Select Case False
    Case x > 0, Sqr(y) > x, Log(x) < z
        ' Do nothing if any of the above meets the condition,
        ' that is, is False.
    Case Else
        ' This is executed only if all the above are True.
        z = 0
End Select

' This series of subexpressions connected by the OR operator:
If x = 0 Or y < x ^ 2 Or x * y = 100 Then z = 0
' can be rewritten as:
Select Case True
    Case x = 0, y < x ^ 2, x * y = 100
        ' This is executed as soon as one of the above is found
        ' to be True.
        z = 0
End Select
```

As it is for similarly unorthodox optimization techniques, my suggestion is to thoroughly comment your code, explaining what you're doing and always including the original *If* statement as a remark. This technique is highly effective for speeding up portions of your code, but you should never forget that optimization isn't all that important if you're going to forget what you did or if your code looks obscure to colleagues who have to maintain it.

Then comes the *GoTo* statement, deemed to be the main cause of tons of spaghetti code that plagues many applications. I must admit, however, that my attitude toward this four-letter keyword isn't so negative. In fact, I still prefer one single *GoTo* statement to a chain of *Exit Do* or *Exit For* statements for getting out of a series of nested loops. I suggest this: Use the *GoTo* statement as an exception to the regular flow of execution, and always use significant label names and meaningful remarks all over the code to explain what you're doing.

The *GoSub...Return* keyword pair is a little bit better than *GoTo* because it's more structured. In some cases, using *GoSub* to call a piece of code inside the current procedure is better than calling an external *Sub* or *Function*. You can neither pass arguments nor receive return values; but, on the other hand, the called code shares all the parameters and local variables with your current procedure, so in most cases you don't need to pass anything. You should be aware, however, that when you compile to native code, the *GoSub* keyword is about 6 to 7 times *slower* than a call to an external procedure in the same module, so always benchmark the two approaches if you're writing time-critical code.

Loop Statements

The most frequently used looping structure in Visual Basic is undoubtedly the *For...Next* loop:

```
For counter = startvalue To endvalue [Step increment]
    ' Statements to be executed in the loop...
Next
```

You need to specify the *Step* clause only if *increment* is not equal to 1. You can exit the loop using an *Exit For* statement, but unfortunately Visual Basic doesn't provide any sort of "Repeat" command that lets you skip the remaining part of the current iteration and restart the loop. The best you can do is use (nested) *If* statements or, if you don't want to make the logic too complex, use a plain *GoTo* keyword that points to the end of the loop. In fact, this is one of the few occasions when a single *GoTo* statement can make your code *more* readable and maintainable:

```
For counter = 1 To 100
    ' Do your stuff here ...
    ' if you want to skip over what follows, just GoTo NextLoop.
    If Err Then Goto NextLoop
    ' more code that you don't want to enclose within nested IF blocks
    ' ...
NextLoop:
Next
```

> **TIP**   Always use an Integer or Long variable as the controlling variable of a *For...Next* loop because they're faster than a Single or a Double controlling variable, by a factor of 10 or more. If you need to increment a floating-point quantity, the most efficient technique is explained in the next example.

> **CAUTION**   A compelling reason to stay clear of floating-point variables as controlling variables in *For...Next* loops is that, because of rounding errors, you can't be completely sure that a floating-point variable is incremented correctly when the increment is a fractional quantity, and you might end up with fewer or more iterations than expected:

```
Dim d As Single, count As Long
For d = 0 To 1 Step 0.1
    count = count + 1
Next
Print count              ' Displays "10" but should be "11"
```

When you want to be absolutely sure that a loop is executed a given number of times, use an integer controlling variable and explicitly increment the floating-point variable within the loop:

```
Dim d As Single, count As Long
' Scale start and end values by a factor of 10
' so that you can use integers to control the loop.
For count = 0 To 10
    ' Do what you want with the D variable, and then increment it
    ' to be ready for the next iteration of the loop.
    d = d + 0.1
Next
```

I covered the *For Each...Next* loop already in Chapter 4, and I won't repeat its description here. I just want to show you a neat trick that's based on this type of loop and the *Array* function. This technique permits you to execute a block of statements with different values for a controlling variable, which don't need to be in sequence:

```
' Test if Number can be divided by any of the first 10 prime numbers.
Dim var As Variant, NotPrime As Boolean
For Each var In Array(2, 3, 5, 7, 11, 13, 17, 19, 23, 29)
    If (Number Mod var) = 0 Then NotPrime = True: Exit For
Next
```

The values don't even have to be numeric:

```
' Test if SourceString contains the strings "one", "two", "three", etc.
Dim var2 As Variant, MatchFound As Boolean
For Each var2 In Array("one", "two", "three", "four", "five")
    If InStr(1, SourceString, var2, vbTextCompare) Then
        MatchFound = True: Exit For
    End If
Next
```

The *Do...Loop* structure is more flexible than the *For...Next* loop in that you can place the termination test either at the beginning or the end of the loop. (In the latter case, the loop is always executed at least once.) You can use either the *While* clause (repeat while the test condition is True) or the *Until* clause (repeat while the test condition is False). You can exit a *Do* loop at any moment by executing an *Exit Do* statement, but—as with *For...Next* loops—VBA doesn't offer a keyword that skips over the remaining statements in the loop and immediately restarts the loop.

```
' Example of a Do loop with test condition at the top.
' This loop is never executed if x <= 0.
Do While x > 0
    y = y + 1
    x = x \ 2
Loop

' Example of a Do loop with test condition at the bottom.
' This loop is always executed at least once, even if x <= 0.
Do
    y = y + 1
    x = x \ 2
Loop Until x <= 0

' Endless loop: requires an Exit Do statement to get out.
Do
    ...
Loop
```

The *While...Wend* loop is conceptually similar to the *Do While...Loop*. But you can test the condition only at the beginning of the loop, you don't have an *Until* clause, and you don't even have an *Exit While* command. For these reasons, most programmers prefer the more flexible *Do...Loop* structure, and in fact you won't see a single *While...Wend* loop in this entire book.

Other Functions

A few VBA functions are closely related to control flow, even if by themselves they don't alter the execution flow. The *IIf* function, for example, can often replace an *If...Else...End If* block, as in the following code:

```
' These lines are equivalent.
If x > 0 Then y = 10 Else y = 20
y = IIf(x > 0, 10, 20)
```

The *Choose* function lets you select a value in a group; you can use it to distinguish among three or more cases. So, instead of this code:

```
' The classic three-choices selection
If x > y Then
    Print "X greater than Y"
ElseIf x < y Then
    Print "X less than Y"
Else
    Print "X equals Y"
End If
```

you can use this shorter version:

```
' Shortened form, based on Sgn() and Choose() functions.
' Note how you keep the result of Sgn() in the range 1-3.
Print "X " & Choose(Sgn(x - y) + 2, "less than", "equals", _
    "greater than") & " Y"
```

The *Switch* function accepts a list of *(condition, value)* pairs and returns the first *value* that corresponds to a *condition* that evaluates as True. See, for example, how you can use this function to replace this *Select Case* block:

```
Select Case x
    Case Is <= 10: y = 1
    Case 11 To 100: y = 2
    Case 101 To 1000: y = 3
    Case Else: y = 4
End Select
```

Same effect in just one line.

```
' The last "True" expression replaces the "Else" clause.
y = Switch(x <= 10, 1, x <= 100, 2, x <= 1000, 3, True, 4)
```

You should remember two things when you're using this function: First, if none of the expressions returns a True value, the *Switch* function returns Null. Second, all the expressions are always evaluated, even though only one value is returned. For these reasons, you might get unexpected errors or undesired side effects. (For example, if one expression raises an overflow or division-by-zero error.)

> **CAUTION** While the *IIf*, *Choose*, and *Switch* functions are sometimes useful for reducing the amount of code you have to write, you should be aware that they're always slower than the *If* or *Select Case* structure that they're meant to replace. For this reason, you should never use them in time-critical loops.

WORKING WITH NUMBERS

Visual Basic offers a rich assortment of math operators and functions. Most of these operators are *polymorphic* in the sense that they work equally well with arguments of any type, including Integer, Long, Single, Double, Date, and Currency. Depending on the particular operator or function, the Visual Basic compiler can decide to convert the operands to a more suitable data type. However, this is the language's job, and you don't have to worry because everything is done automatically for you.

Math Operators

As you know, Visual Basic supports all four math operators. When combining two values of different types, Visual Basic automatically applies the *data coercion* and converts the simpler type to the more comprehensive one (for example, Integer to Long or Single to Double). Interestingly, the division operator (/) always converts both its operands to Double, which can cause some unexpected overhead. If you're dividing an Integer or Long number by another Integer or Long number and you aren't interested in the decimal part of the quotient, you should use the integer division operator (\), which executes faster:

```
Dim a As Long, b As Long, result As Long
result = a / b           ' Floating point division
result = a \ b           ' This is about 4 times faster.
```

Visual Basic also supports the exponentiation operator (^), which raises a number to an exponent. In this case, the result is always of type Double, even if you're raising an integer number to an integer exponent. In general, the ^ operator is relatively slow, and for small integer exponents you might decide to use a chain of multiplication operations instead:

```
Dim x As Double, result As Double
x = 1.2345
result = x ^ 3
result = x * x * x       ' This is about 20 times faster.
```

The MOD operator extracts the remainder of a division between integer values. It's often used to test whether a number is an exact multiple of another number. This operator is very efficient but has a limitation: It converts its operands to Long and therefore can't be used with arbitrarily large values. It also truncates any decimal part. Here's a function that works with any Double value:

```
Function FPMod(ByVal Number As Double, ByVal divisor As Double) As Double
    ' Note: this differs from MOD when Number is negative.
    FPMod = Number - Int(Number / divisor) * divisor
End Function
```

Several other functions are often useful when you're working with numbers:

- *Abs* returns the absolute value of its argument.

- *Sgn* returns −1, 0, or +1 if the argument is negative, zero, or positive, respectively.

- *Sqr* returns the square root of a number.

- *Exp* raises *e* (the base of natural logarithms) to the power passed in the argument.

- *Log* returns the natural logarithm of its argument. You can evaluate a decimal logarithm using the following function:

    ```
    Function Log10(Number As Double) As Double
        Log10 = Log(Number) / 2.30258509299405
    End Function
    ```

Comparison Operators

Visual Basic supports six comparison operators, which can be applied to both numeric and string operands:

```
=   <   <=   >   >=   <>
```

These operators are often used in *If* blocks, but you should keep in mind that they aren't conceptually different from any other math operators, in the sense that they accept two operands and deliver a result. Such a result can be False (0) or True (–1). You can sometimes exploit this fact to write more concise code, as in the following:

```
' The following lines are equivalent.
If x > y Then x = x - 1
x = x + (x > y)
```

> **CAUTION**   You should always be careful when using the = operator on Single and Double values because Visual Basic often introduces small rounding errors when operating on floating-point numbers. For example, look at this code:
>
> ```
> Dim d As Double, i As Integer
> For i = 1 To 10: d = d + 0.1: Next
> Print d, (d = 1)        ' Displays "1  False" !!!
> ```
>
> The preceding result seems absurd because the variable appears to contain the correct value, but the test (*d = 1*) returns False. You shouldn't rely on what Visual Basic shows you in a *Print* statement because it always rounds decimal numbers. In fact, the actual value of the *d* variable is slightly less than 1, the exact difference being 1.11022302462516E-16 (a number with 15 zeros after the decimal separator), but this is enough to make the equality test fail. Therefore, my recommendation is that you never use the = on floating-point numbers. Here's a better approach:
>
> ```
> ' "equal" up to 10th decimal digit
> Function AlmostEqual(x, y) As Boolean
>     AlmostEqual = (Abs(x - y) <= 0.0000000001)
> End Function
> ```

Boolean and Bit-Wise Operators

Visual Basic for Applications supports a few Boolean operators, which are especially useful for combining multiple Boolean subexpressions. The operators used most frequently are AND, OR, XOR, and NOT. For example, the following code uses Boolean operators to determine the signs of two variables:

```
If (x > 0) And (y > 0) Then
    ' Both X and Y are positive.
ElseIf (x = 0) Or (y = 0) Then
    ' Either X or Y (or both) are zero.
```

(continued)

```
ElseIf (x > 0) Xor (y > 0) Then
    ' Either X or Y (but not both of them) are positive.
ElseIf Not (x > 0) Then
    ' X is not positive.
End If
```

Remember that these operators are actually *bit-wise* operators, in that they act on each individual bit of their operands. In practice, this can make a difference if the operands aren't Boolean values (that is, they have a value different from −1 and 0). You can use the AND operator to test one or more bits of a number:

```
If (number And 1) Then Print "Bit 0 is set (number is an odd value)"
If (number And 6) = 6 Then Print "Both bits 1 and 2 are set"
If (number And 6) Then Print "Either bits 1 and 2, or both, are set"
```

You usually use the OR operator to set one or more bits:

```
number = number Or 4          ' Set bit 2.
number = number Or (8 + 1)    ' Set bits 3 and 0.
```

To reset one or more bits, you combine the AND and NOT operators:

```
Number = number And Not 4     ' Reset bit 2.
```

Finally you use the XOR operator to flip the state of one or more bits:

```
Number = number Xor 2         ' Flip the state of bit 1.
```

If you don't know at compile time which bit should be set, reset, or flipped, you can use the exponentiation operator, as in the following code:

```
Number = Number Or (2 ^ N)    ' Set Nth bit (N in range 0-30).
```

This approach has two defects: It raises an overflow error if $N = 31$, and it's highly inefficient because it relies on a floating-point operation. You can solve both problems with the following function:

```
Function Power2(ByVal exponent As Long) As Long
    Static result(0 To 31) As Long, i As Integer
    ' Evaluate all powers of 2 only once.
    If result(0) = 0 Then
        result(0) = 1
        For i = 1 To 30
            result(i) = result(i - 1) * 2
        Next
        result(31) = &H80000000         ' This is a special value.
    End If
    Power2 = result(exponent)
End Function
```

Rounding and Truncating

The *Int* function truncates a number to the integer value equal or lower than its argument. This is different from just saying "truncates the decimal part of a number." The difference becomes apparent if the argument is negative:

```
Print Int(1.2)        ' Displays "1"
Print Int(-1.2)       ' Displays "-2"
```

The function that actually truncates the decimal part of a number is *Fix*:

```
Print Fix(1.2)        ' Displays "1"
Print Fix(-1.2)       ' Displays "-1"
```

Visual Basic 6 introduces a new math function, *Round*, which lets you round a decimal number to the number of digits you want (or to the nearest integer, if the second argument is omitted):

```
Print Round(1.45)        ' Displays "1"
Print Round(1.55)        ' Displays "2"
Print Round(1.23456, 4)  ' Displays "1.2346"
```

Round has an undocumented quirk: When the fractional part is exactly 0.5, it rounds up if the integer portion is an odd number and rounds down if it's even:

```
Print Round(1.5), Round(2.5)    ' Both display "2".
```

This behavior is necessary so that you can avoid introducing errors when you're doing statistical evaluations, and it shouldn't be considered a bug.

When rounding, you sometimes need to determine the nearest integer higher or equal to the argument, but Visual Basic lacks such a function. You can remedy this problem with this short routine:

```
Function Ceiling(number As Double) As Long
    Ceiling = -Int(-number)
End Function
```

Converting Among Different Numeric Bases

VBA supports numeric constants in decimal, hexadecimal, and octal systems:

```
value = &H1234      ' The value 4660 as a hexadecimal constant
value = &O11064     ' The same value as octal constant
```

You can convert any hexadecimal or octal string into its decimal value using the *Val* function:

```
' If Text1 holds a hexadecimal value
value = Val("&H" & Text1.Text)
```

You do the opposite conversion—from decimal to hexadecimal or octal—using the *Hex* and *Oct* functions:

```
Text1.Text = Hex$(value)
```

Oddly, Visual Basic doesn't include a function that converts to and from binary numbers, which are by far more common than octal values. You can achieve these conversions using a pair of functions, which build on the *Power2* function seen in the section "Boolean and Bit-Wise Operators" earlier in this chapter:

```
' Convert from decimal to binary.
Function Bin(ByVal value As Long) As String
    Dim result As String, exponent As Integer
    ' This is faster than creating the string by appending chars.
    result = String$(32, "0")
    Do
        If value And Power2(exponent) Then
            ' We found a bit that is set, clear it.
            Mid$(result, 32 - exponent, 1) = "1"
            value = value Xor Power2(exponent)
        End If
        exponent = exponent + 1
    Loop While value
    Bin = Mid$(result, 33 - exponent)  ' Drop leading zeros.
End Function

' Convert from binary to decimal.
Function BinToDec(value As String) As Long
    Dim result As Long, i As Integer, exponent As Integer
    For i = Len(value) To 1 Step -1
        Select Case Asc(Mid$(value, i, 1))
            Case 48      ' "0", do nothing.
            Case 49      ' "1", add the corresponding power of 2.
                result = result + Power2(exponent)
            Case Else
                Err.Raise 5  ' Invalid procedure call or argument
        End Select
        exponent = exponent + 1
    Next
    BinToDec = result
End Function
```

Format Options for Numbers

All versions of the VBA language include the *Format* function, which is a powerful tool that meets most of your formatting requirements. Its syntax is rather complex:

```
result = Format(Expression, [Format], _
    [FirstDayOfWeek As VbDayOfWeek = vbSunday], _
    [FirstWeekOfYear As VbFirstWeekOfYear = vbFirstJan1])
```

Fortunately, the first two arguments are sufficient for all your tasks unless you're formatting dates, which I'll talk about later in this chapter. Right now I'll summarize the *Format* function's many capabilities when formatting numeric values, although I suggest that you have a look at Visual Basic documentation for more details.

When formatting numbers, the *Format* function supports both *named formats* and *custom formats*. Named formats include the following strings: *General Number* (no special formatting, use the scientific notation if needed), *Currency* (currency symbol, thousand separator and two decimal digits), *Fixed* (two decimal digits), *Standard* (thousand separator and two decimal digits), *Percent* (a percentage, with the % symbol appended), *Scientific* (scientific notation), *Yes/No, True/False, On/Off* (False or Off if 0, True or On otherwise). *Format* is a *locale-aware* function and automatically uses the currency symbol, the thousand separator, and the decimal separator that are appropriate to the current locale.

If a named format doesn't do the job, you can create your own custom format using a format string made up of special characters. (For a detailed list and the meaning of such formatting characters, see the Visual Basic documentation.)

```
' Decimal and thousand separators. (Format rounds its result.)
Print Format(1234.567, "#,##0.00")    ' "1,234.57"
' Percentage values
Print Format(0.234, "#.#%")           ' "23.4%"
' Scientific notation
Print Format(12345.67, "#.###E+")     ' "1.235E+4"
Print Format(12345.67, "#.###E-")     ' "1.235E4"
```

A great feature of the *Format* function is its ability to apply different format strings if the number is positive, negative, 0, or Null. You use the semicolon as the delimiter of the section in the custom format string. (You can specify one, two, three, or four different sections.)

```
' Two decimal digits for positive numbers, enclose negative numbers within
' a pair of parentheses, use a blank for zero, and "N/A" for Null values.
Print Format(number, "##,###.00;(##,###.00); ;N/A")
```

Visual Basic 6 has introduced three new formatting functions for numbers—namely *FormatNumber*, *FormatPercent*, and *FormatCurrency*—that have been borrowed from VBScript. (Three more functions—*FormatDate*, *MonthName*, and *WeekdayName*—are explained in the section "Working with Dates," later in this chapter.) These new functions duplicate the capabilities of the more powerful, all-in-one *Format* workhorse, but their syntax is more intuitive, as you can see in the code at the top of the following page.

```
result = FormatNumber(expr, [DecDigits], [InclLeadingDigit], _
    [UseParens], [GroupDigits] )
result = FormatPercent(expr, [DecDigits], [InclLeadingDigit], _
    [UseParens], [GroupDigits] )
result = FormatCurrency(expr, [DecDigits], [InclLeadingDigit], _
    [UseParens], [,GroupDigits] )
```

In all cases, *DecDigits* is the number of decimal digits you want (2 is the default); *InclLeadingDigit* tells whether numbers in the range [−1,1] are displayed with a leading 0; *UseParens* specifies whether negative numbers are enclosed in parentheses; *GroupDigits* tells whether a thousand separator should be used. The last three optional arguments can each be one of the following values: 0-vbFalse, −1-vbTrue, or −2-vbUseDefault (the default setting for the user's locale). If you omit a value, vbUseDefault is assumed by default.

Random Numbers

At times, you need to generate one or more random values. Among the types of software for which you need to do this, games come to mind, but this ability is also useful in business applications that include simulations. Visual Basic offers only one statement and one function for generating random values. You initialize the seed of the internal random number generators using the *Randomize* statement. You can pass it a number that will be used as a seed; otherwise, Visual Basic automatically uses the value returned by the *Timer* function:

```
Randomize 10
```

The *Rnd* function returns a random value each time you call it. The returned value is always less than 1 and greater than or equal to 0, so you need to scale the result to get a number in the range you want:

```
' Simple computerized dice
Randomize
For i = 1 To 10
    Print Int(Rnd * 6) + 1
Next
```

At times, you might want to repeat the same sequence of random numbers, especially when debugging your code. It might seem that you can obtain this behavior by calling the *Randomize* statement with the same seed, but this isn't so. Instead, as counterintuitive as it may seem, to repeat the same random sequence you call the *Rnd* function with a negative argument:

```
dummy = Rnd(-1)              ' Initialize the seed. (No Randomize is needed!)
For i = 1 To 10             ' This loop will always deliver the same
    Print Int(Rnd * 6) + 1  ' sequence of random numbers.
Next
```

You can also reread the random number that you have just generated by passing 0 as an argument to *Rnd*.

A common task when you're dealing with random numbers is the generation of a casual permutation of the numbers in a given range: for example, this might be useful for shuffling a deck of cards in a game. Here's a simple and efficient routine that returns an array of all Long numbers in the range of *first* and *last*, in random order:

```
Function RandomArray(first As Long, last As Long) As Long()
    Dim i As Long, j As Long, temp As Long
    ReDim result(first To last) As Long
    ' Initialize the array.
    For i = first To last: result(i) = i: Next
    ' Now shuffle it.
    For i = last To first Step -1
        ' Generate a random number in the proper range.
        j = Rnd * (last - first + 1) + first
        ' Swap the two items.
        temp = result(i): result(i) = result(j): result(j) = temp
    Next
    RandomArray = result
End Function
```

WORKING WITH STRINGS

Visual Basic for Applications includes many powerful string functions, and it's sometimes difficult at first glance to determine which one meets your requirements. In this section, I briefly describe all the string functions at your disposal, offer some tips for selecting the most suitable one in some typical situations, and also provide some useful string functions that you can reuse in your applications.

Basic String Operators and Functions

The basic string operator & performs a string concatenation. The result is a string consisting of all the characters of the first string followed by all the characters of the second string:

```
Print "ABCDE" & "1234"        ' Displays "ABCDE1234"
```

Many programmers with roots in QuickBasic still use the + operator for performing string concatenation. This is a dangerous practice that impacts code readability and might introduce unexpected behaviors when either operand isn't a string.

The next bunch of popular string functions, shown on the following page, includes *Left$, Right$,* and *Mid$*, which extract a substring from the beginning, the end, or the middle of the source string.

```
Text = "123456789"
Print Left$(text, 3)        ' Displays "123"
Print Right$(text, 2)       ' Displays "89"
Print Mid$(text, 3, 4)      ' Displays "3456"
```

> **TIP**   The VBA documentation consistently omits the trailing $ character in all string functions and invites you to use the new $-less functions. *Don't do it!* A $-less function returns a Variant that contains the string result, which means in most cases the Variant must be reconverted to a string before it can be reused in expressions or assigned to a String variable. This is a time-consuming process that gives you nothing in return. Informal benchmarks show that, for example, the *Left$* function is up to twice as fast as its $-less counterpart. A similar reasoning applies to other functions that exist in both forms, including *LCase, UCase, LTrim, RTrim, Trim, Chr, Format, Space,* and *String*.

Mid$ can also work as a command in that it lets you modify one or more characters inside a string:

```
Text = "123456789"
Mid$(Text, 3, 4) = "abcd"    ' Now Text = "12abcd789"
```

The *Len* function returns the current length of a string. It's often used to test whether a string contains any characters:

```
Print Len("12345")           ' Displays "5"
If Len(Text) = 0 Then ...    ' Faster than comparison with an empty string.
```

To discard unwanted trailing or leading blanks, you can use the *LTrim$, RTrim$,* and *Trim$* functions:

```
Text = "  abcde  "
Print LTrim$(Text)           ' Displays "abcde  "
Print RTrim$(Text)           ' Displays "  abcde"
Print Trim$(Text)            ' Displays "abcde"
```

These functions are especially useful with fixed-length strings that are filled with extra spaces to account for their expected length. You can trim those extra spaces using the *RTrim$* function:

```
Dim Text As String * 10
Text = "abcde"               ' Text now contains "abcde     ".
Print Trim$(Text)            ' Displays "abcde"
```

> **CAUTION**   When a fixed-length string is declared but hasn't been used yet, it contains Null characters, not spaces. This means that the *RTrim$* function can't trim such a string:
> ```
> Dim Text As String * 10
> Print Len(Trim$(Text))        ' Displays "10", no trimming has occurred.
> ```
> You can avoid this problem by simply assigning an empty string to all the fixed-length strings in your application soon after their declaration and before using them.

The *Asc* function returns the character code of the first letter in a string. Functionally, it's similar to extracting the first character using the *Left$* function, but *Asc* is considerably faster:

```
If Asc(Text) = 32 Then          ' Test whether the fist char is a space.
If Left$(Text, 1) = " " Then    ' Same effect, but 2 to 3 times slower
```

When you're using the *Asc* function, you should ensure that the string isn't empty because in that case the function raises an error. In a sense, *Chr$* is the opposite of *Asc* in that it transforms a numeric code into the corresponding character:

```
Print Chr$(65)                  ' Displays "A"
```

The *Space$* and *String$* functions are very similar. The former returns a string of spaces of the length you want, and the latter returns a string that consists of the character specified in the second parameter repeated as many times as you indicated in the first parameter:

```
Print Space$(5)                 ' Displays "     " (five spaces)
Print String$(5, " ")           ' Same effect
Print String$(5, 32)            ' Same effect, using the char code
Print String$(50, ".")          ' A row of 50 dots
```

Finally the *StrComp* function lets you compare strings in a case-insensitive fashion and returns –1, 0, or 1 if the first argument is less than, equal to, or greater than the second argument. The third argument specifies whether the comparison should be performed in a case-insensitive way:

```
Select Case StrComp(first, second, vbTextCompare)
    Case 0
        ' first = second    (e.g. "VISUAL BASIC" vs. "Visual Basic")
    Case -1
        ' first < second    (e.g. "C++" vs. "Visual Basic")
    Case 1
        ' first > second    (e.g. "Visual Basic" vs. "Delphi")
End Select
```

The *StrComp* function is sometimes convenient even for case-sensitive comparisons because you don't need two separate tests to decide whether a string is less than, equal to, or greater than another one.

Conversion Functions

The most frequently used functions for converting strings are *UCase$* and *LCase$*, which transform their arguments to uppercase and lowercase, respectively:

```
Text = "New York, USA"
Print UCase$(Text)              ' "NEW YORK, USA"
Print LCase$(Text)              ' "new york, usa"
```

The *StrConv* function encompasses the functionality of the first two and adds more capabilities. You can use it to convert to uppercase, lowercase, and propercase (where the first letter of each word is uppercase, and all the others are lowercase):

```
Print StrConv(Text, vbUpperCase)   ' "NEW YORK, USA"
Print StrConv(Text, vbLowerCase)   ' "new york, usa"
Print StrConv(Text, vbProperCase)  ' "New York, Usa"
```

(Valid word separators are spaces, Null characters, carriage returns, and line feeds.) The function can also perform ANSI-to-Unicode conversion and back, using the *vbUnicode* and *vbFromUnicode* symbolic constants. You'll rarely use these functions in your regular Visual Basic applications.

The *Val* function converts a string into its decimal representation. (See also the section "Converting Among Different Numeric Bases," earlier in this chapter). Visual Basic also includes functions that can convert from a string to a numeric value, such as *CInt*, *CLng*, *CSng*, *CDbl*, *CCur*, and *CDate*. The main difference between them and the *Val* function is that they're locale aware. For example, they correctly recognize the comma as the decimal separator in countries where this is the case and ignore any thousand separator characters. Conversely, the *Val* function recognizes only the decimal point and stops parsing its argument when it finds any invalid characters (including a currency symbol or a comma used for grouping thousand digits).

The *Str$* function converts a number into its string representation. The main difference between *Str$* and *CStr* is that the former adds a leading space if the argument is positive, whereas the latter does not.

Find and Replace Substrings

The *InStr* function searches for a substring in another string, either in case-sensitive or case-insensitive mode. You can't omit the starting index if you want to pass the argument that specifies which kind of search you want to perform:

```
Print InStr("abcde ABCDE", "ABC")     ' Displays "7" (case sensitive)
Print InStr(8, "abcde ABCDE", "ABC")  ' Displays "0" (start index > 1)
Print InStr(1, "abcde ABCDE", "ABC", vbTextCompare)
                                      ' Displays "1" (case insensitive)
```

The *InStr* function is very handy for building other powerful string functions that are missing in the VBA language. For example, this is a function that searches for the first occurrence of a character among those included in a search table. It's useful for extracting words that can be delimited by many different punctuation characters:

```
Function InstrTbl(source As String, searchTable As String, _
    Optional start As Long = 1, _
    Optional Compare As VbCompareMethod = vbBinaryCompare) As Long
    Dim i As Long
    For i = start To Len(source)
```

```
        If InStr(1, searchTable, Mid$(source, i, 1), Compare) Then
            InstrTbl = i
            Exit For
        End If
    Next
End Function
```

Visual Basic 6 lets you perform backward searches, using the new *InStrRev* function. Its syntax is similar to the original *InStr* function, but the order of its arguments is different:

```
found = InStrRev(Source, Search, [Start], [CompareMethod])
```

Here are a few examples. Note that if you omit the *start* argument, the search starts at the end of the string:

```
Print InStrRev("abcde ABCDE", "abc")       ' Displays "1" (case sensitive)
Print InStrRev("abcde ABCDE", "abc", ,vbTextCompare )
                                   ' Displays "7" (case insensitive)
Print InStrRev("abcde ABCDE", "ABC", 4, vbTextCompare )
                            ' Displays "1" (case insensitive, start<>0)
```

Visual Basic also includes a handy string operator, the *Like* operator, which is often a life saver when you're parsing a string and performing complex searches. The syntax of this operator is the following:

```
result = string Like pattern
```

where *string* is the string being parsed and *pattern* is a string made up of special characters that define the search condition. The most frequently used special characters are *?* (any single character), *** (zero or more characters), and *#* (any single digit). Here are a few examples:

```
' The Like operator is affected by the current Option Compare setting.
Option Compare Text               ' Enforce case-insensitive comparisons.
' Check that a string consists of "AB" followed by three digits.
If value Like "AB###" Then ...     ' e.g. "AB123" or "ab987"
' Check that a string starts with "ABC" and ends with "XYZ".
If value Like "ABC*XYZ" Then ...   ' e.g. "ABCDEFGHI-VWXYZ"
' Check that starts with "1", ends with "X", and includes 5 chars.
If value Like "1???X" Then ...     ' e.g. "1234X" or "1uvwx"
```

You can also specify which characters you want to include (or exclude) in the search by inserting a list enclosed in square brackets:

```
' One of the letters "A","B","C" followed by three digits
If value Like "[A-C]###" Then ...           ' e.g. "A123" or "c456"
' Three letters, the first one must be a vowel
If value Like "[AEIOU][A-Z][A-Z]" Then... ' e.g. "IVB" or "OOP"
```

(continued)

```
' At least three characters, the first one can't be a digit.
' Note: a leading "!" symbol excludes a range.
If value Like "[!0-9]??*" Then ...  ' e.g. "K12BC" or "ABHIL"
```

Visual Basic 6 introduces the new *Replace* function, which quickly finds and replaces substrings. The syntax of this function isn't straightforward because the function includes several optional arguments:

```
Text = Replace(Source, Find, Replace, [Start], [Count], [CompareMethod])
```

The simplest form searches substrings in case-sensitive mode and replaces all occurrences:

```
Print Replace("abc ABC abc", "ab", "123")          ' "123c ABC 123c"
```

By acting on the other arguments, you can start your search from a different position, limit the number of substitutions, and perform a case-insensitive search. Note that a value for *start* greater than 1 actually trims the source argument before starting the search:

```
Print Replace("abc ABC abc", "ab", "123", 5, 1)              ' "ABC 123c"
Print Replace("abc ABC abc", "ab", "123", 5, 1, vbTextCompare) ' "123C abc"
```

You can also use the *Replace* function in a somewhat unorthodox way to count the number of occurrences of a substring inside another string:

```
Function InstrCount(Source As String, Search As String) As Long
    ' You get the number of substrings by subtracting the length of the
    ' original string from the length of the string that you obtain by
    ' replacing the substring with another string that is one char longer.
    InstrCount = Len(Replace(Source, Search, Search & "*")) - Len(Source)
End Function
```

The new *StrReverse* function quickly reverses the order of characters in a string. This function is rarely useful in itself, but it adds value to other string-processing functions:

```
' Replace only the LAST occurrence of a substring.
Function ReplaceLast(Source As String, Search As String, _
    ReplaceStr As String) As String
        ReplaceLast = StrReverse(Replace(StrReverse(Source), _
            StrReverse(Search), StrReverse(ReplaceStr), , 1))
End Function
```

You can use the new *Split* function to find all the delimited items in a string. Its syntax is the following:

```
arr() = Split(Source, [Delimiter], [Limit], [CompareMethod])
```

where *delimiter* is the character used to delimit individual items. You can pass a positive value for the *limit* argument if you don't want more items than a given value, and you can pass the *vbTextCompare* value to the last argument to perform case-insensitive searches. Since the default delimiter character is the space, you can easily extract all the words in a sentence using this code:

```
Dim words() As String
words() = Split("Microsoft Visual Basic 6")
' words() is now a zero-based array with four elements.
```

The *Join* function is complementary to the *Split* function in that it accepts an array of strings and one delimiter character and rebuilds the original string:

```
' Continuing the preceding example ...
' The delimiter argument is optional here, because it defaults to " ".
Print Join(words, " ")        ' Displays "Microsoft Visual Basic 6"
```

Note that the delimiter argument in both the *Split* and *Join* functions can be longer than just one character.

Another welcome addition to the VBA language is the *Filter* function, which quickly scans an array searching for a substring and returns another array that contains only the items that include (or don't include) the searched substring. The syntax for the *Filter* function is the following:

```
arr() = Filter(Source(), Search, [Include], [CompareMethod])
```

If the *Include* argument is True or omitted, the result array contains all the items in *source* that contain the *search* substring; if it's False, the result array contains only the items that don't contain it. As usual, the *CompareMethod* argument specifies whether the search is case sensitive:

```
ReDim s(2) As String
s(0) = "First": s(1) = "Second": s(2) = "Third"
Dim res() As String
res = Filter(s, "i", True, vbTextCompare)
' Print the result array  ("First" and "Third").
For i = 0 To UBound(res): Print res(i): Next
```

If no items in the source array meet the search requirements, the *Filter* function delivers a special array that returns –1 when passed to the *UBound* function.

Format Options for Strings

You can also use the *Format* function to format strings. In this case, you can specify only a custom format (no named formats are available for string data) and you have a limited choice of special characters, but you can get a lot of flexibility anyway. You can specify two sections, one for non-empty string values and one for empty string values as shown on the following page.

```
' By default, placeholders are filled from right to left.
' "@" stands for a character or a space, "&" is a character or nothing.
Print Format("abcde", "@@@@@@@")                         ' "   abcde"
' You can exploit this feature to right align numbers in reports.
Print Format(Format(1234.567, "Currency"), "@@@@@@@@@@@") '   "   $1,234.57"
' "!" forces left to right fill of placeholders.
Print Format("abcde", "!@@@@@@@")                        ' "abcde   "
' ">" forces to uppercase, "<" forces to lowercase.
Print Format("abcde", ">& & & & &")                      ' "A B C D E"
' This is a good way to format phone numbers or credit-card numbers.
Print Format("6152127865", "&&&-&&&-&&&&")               ' "615-212-7865"
' Use a second section to format empty strings.
' "\" is the escape character.
Print Format("", "!@@@@@@@;\n\o\n\e")                     ' "none"
```

WORKING WITH DATES AND TIMES

Not only does Visual Basic let you store date and time information in the specific Date data type, it also provides a lot of date- and time-related functions. These functions are very important in all business applications and deserve an in-depth look.

Getting and Setting the Current Date and Time

Strictly speaking, *Date* and *Time* aren't functions: They're properties. In fact, you can use them to either retrieve the current date and time (as Date values) or assign new values to them to modify the system settings:

```
Print Date & " " & Time        ' Displays "8/14/98 8:35:48 P.M.".
' Set a new system date using any valid date format.
Date = "10/14/98"
Date = "October 14, 1998"
```

> **NOTE**   To help you compare the outcome of all date and time functions, all the examples in this section assume that they're executed at the date and time shown in the preceding code snippet: August 14, 1998, 8:35:48 P.M.

The outdated *Date$* and *Time$* properties can also be used for the same task. They're String properties, however, and therefore recognize only the *mm/dd/yy* or *mm/dd/yyyy* formats and the *hh:mm:ss* and *hh:mm* formats, respectively. For this reason, it's usually better to use the new *$*-less functions.

The *Now* function returns a Date value that contains the current date and time:

```
Print Now                      ' Displays "8/14/98 8:35:48 P.M.".
```

But the time-honored *Timer* function returns the number of seconds elapsed from midnight and is more accurate than *Now* because the *Timer* function includes fractional parts of seconds. (The actual accuracy depends on the system.) This function is often used for benchmarking a portion of code:

```
StartTime = Timer
' Insert the code to be benchmarked here.
Print Timer - StartTime
```

The preceding code suffers from some inaccuracy: The *StartTime* variable might be assigned when the system tick is about to expire, so your routine could appear to take longer than it actually does. Here's a slightly better approach:

```
StartTime = NextTimerTick
' Insert the code to be benchmarked here.
Print Timer - StartTime

' Wait for the current timer tick to elapse.
Function NextTimerTick() As Single
    Dim t As Single
    t = Timer
    Do: Loop While t = Timer
    NextTimerTick = Timer
End Function
```

If you're using the *Timer* function in production code, you should be aware that it's reset at midnight, so you always run the risk of introducing unlikely but potentially serious errors. Try to spot the bug in this routine, which adds a CPU-independent pause in your code:

```
' WARNING: this procedure has a bug.
Sub BuggedPause(seconds As Integer)
    Dim start As Single
    start = Timer
    Do: Loop Until Timer - start  >= seconds
End Sub
```

The bug manifests itself very rarely—for example, if the program asks for a 2-second pause at 11:59:59 P.M. Even if this probability is small, the effect of this minor bug is devastating and you'll have to press Ctrl+Alt+Del to kill your compiled application. Here's a way to work around this issue:

```
' The correct version of the procedure
Sub Pause(seconds As Integer)
    Const SECS_INDAY = 24! * 60 * 60    ' Seconds per day
    Dim start As Single
    start = Timer
    Do: Loop Until (Timer + SECS_INDAY - start) Mod SECS_INDAY >= seconds
End Sub
```

Building and Extracting Date and Time Values

There are many ways to assemble a Date value. For example, you can use a Date constant, such as the following:

```
StartDate = #8/15/1998 9:20:57 PM#
```

but more often you'll build a Date value using one of the many functions that VBA gives you. The *DateSerial* function builds a Date value from its year/month/day components; similarly, the *TimeSerial* function builds a Time value from its hour/minute/second components:

```
Print DateSerial(1998, 8, 14)          ' Displays "8/14/98"
Print TimeSerial(12, 20, 30)           ' Displays "12:20:30 P.M."
' Note that they don't raise errors with invalid arguments.
Print DateSerial(1998, 4, 31)          ' Displays "5/1/98"
```

The *DateSerial* function is also useful for determining indirectly whether a particular year is a leap year:

```
Function IsLeapYear(year As Integer) As Boolean
    ' Are February 29 and March 1 different dates?
    IsLeapYear = DateSerial(year, 2, 29) <> DateSerial(year, 3, 1)
End Function
```

The *DateValue* and *TimeValue* functions return the date or time portions of their argument, which can be a string or a Date expression:

```
' The date a week from now
Print DateValue(Now + 7)               ' Displays "8/21/98"
```

A bunch of VBA functions let you extract date and time information from a Date expression or variable. The *Day*, *Month*, and *Year* functions return date values, whereas the *Hour*, *Minute*, and *Second* functions return time values:

```
' Get information about today's date.
y = Year(Now): m = Month(Now): d = Day(Now)
' These functions also support any valid date format.
Print Year("8/15/1998 9:10:26 PM")     ' Displays "1998"
```

The *Weekday* function returns a number in the range 1 through 7, which corresponds to the day of the week of a given Date argument:

```
Print Weekday("8/14/98")               ' Displays "6" (= vbFriday)
```

The *Weekday* function returns 1 when the date is the first day of the week. This function is locale aware, which means that under different localizations of Microsoft Windows it could consider the first day of the week to be different from *vbSunday*. In most cases, this condition doesn't affect the structure of your code. But if you want to be sure that 1 means Sunday, 2 means Monday, and so on, you can force the function to return a consistent value under all Windows systems, as follows:

```
Print Weekday(Now, vbSunday)
```

Although using the optional second argument forces the function to return the correct value, it doesn't change the system localization. If you next call the *Weekday* function without the second argument, it will still consider the first day of the week to be what it was before.

Finally you can extract any date and time information from a Date value or expression using the *DatePart* function, for which the syntax is

```
Result = DatePart(Interval, Date, [FirstDayOfWeek], [FirstWeekOfYear])
```

You'll rarely need to resort to this function because you can do most of your calculations using the other functions I've shown you so far. In two cases, however, this function is really useful:

```
' The quarter we are in
Print DatePart("q", Now)          ' Displays "3"
' The week number we are in (# of weeks since Jan 1st)
Print DatePart("ww", Now)         ' Displays "33"
```

The first argument can be one of the String constants listed in Table 5.1. For more information about the two optional arguments, see the description of the *DateAdd* function in the next section.

Setting	*Description*
"yyyy"	Year
"q"	Quarter
"m"	Month
"y"	Day of the year (same as *d*)
"d"	Day
"w"	Weekday
"ww"	Week
"h"	Hour
"n"	Minute
"s"	Second

Table 5-1. *Possible values for the* interval *argument in* DatePart, DateAdd, *and* DateDiff *functions.*

Date Arithmetic

In most cases, you don't need any special functions to perform date arithmetic. All you need to know is that the integer part in a Date variable holds the date information, and the fractional part holds the time information:

```
' 2 days and 12 hours from now
Print Now + 2 + #12:00#          ' Displays "8/17/98 8:35:48 A.M."
```

For more sophisticated date math, you can use the *DateAdd* function, for which the syntax is the following:

```
NewDate = DateAdd(interval, number, date)
```

The *interval* is a string that indicates a date or time unit (see Table 5-1 on the previous page), *number* is the number of units you are adding, and *date* is the starting date. You can use this function to add and subtract date and time values:

```
' The date three months from now
Print DateAdd("m", 3, Now)               ' Displays "11/14/98 8:35:48 P.M."
' One year ago (automatically accounts for leap years)
Print DateAdd("yyyy", -1, Now)           ' Displays "8/14/97 8:35:48 P.M."
' The number of months since Jan 30, 1998
Print DateDiff("m", #1/30/1998#, Now)        ' Displays "7"
' The number of days since Jan 30, 1998 - you can use "d" or "y".
Print DateDiff("y", #1/30/1998#, Now)        ' Displays "196"
' The number of entire weeks since Jan 30, 1998
Print DateDiff("w", #1/30/1998#, Now)        ' Displays "28"
' The number of weekends before 21st century - value <0 means
' future dates.
' Note: use "ww" to return the number of Sundays in the date interval.
Print DateDiff("ww", #1/1/2000#, Now)        ' Displays "-72"
```

When you have two dates and you want to evaluate the difference between them—that is, the time elapsed between one date and the next—you should use the *DateDiff* function, for which the syntax is

```
Result = DateDiff(interval, startdate, enddate _
    [, FirstDayOfWeek[, FirstWeekOfYear]])
```

where *interval* has the meaning shown in Table 5-1, *FirstDayOfWeek* is an optional argument that you can use to specify which weekday should be considered as the first day of the week (you can use the constants *vbSunday*, *vbMonday*, and so on), and *FirstWeekOfYear* is another optional argument that lets you specify which week should be considered as the first week of the year. (See Table 5-2.)

Constant	*Value*	*Description*
vbUseSystem	0	Use the NLS API setting.
vbFirstJan1	1	The first week is the one that includes January 1. (This is the default value for this setting.)
vbFirstFourDays	2	The first week is the first one that has at least four days in the new year.
vbFirstFullWeek	3	This first week is the first one that's completely contained in the new year.

Table 5-2. *Possible values for the* FirstWeekOfYear *argument in the* DateDiff *function.*

Format Options for Date and Time Values

The most important and flexible function for formatting date and time values is the *Format* function. This function gives you seven different, named formats for date and time:

- *General Date* (date and time in general format; only the date if the fractional part is 0; only the time if the integer part is 0)

- *Long Date* (for example, *Friday, August 14, 1998,* but results vary depending on your locale)

- *Medium Date* (for example, *14-Aug-98)*

- *Short Date* (for example, *8/14/98)*

- *Long Time* (for example, *8:35:48)*

- *Medium Time* (for example, *8:35 A.M.)*

- *Short Time* (for example, *8:35* in a 24 hour format)

You also have a few special characters with which you can build your own custom date and time format strings, including one- and two-digit day and month numbers, complete or abbreviated month and weekday names, A.M./P.M. indicators, week and quarter numbers, and so on:

```
' mmm/ddd = abbreviated month/weekday,
' mmmm/dddd = complete month/weekday
Print Format(Now, "mmm dd, yyyy (dddd)")  ' "Aug 14, 1998 (Friday)"
' hh/mm/ss always use two digits, h/m/s use one or two digits
Print Format(Now, "hh:mm:ss")             ' "20:35:48"
Print Format(Now, "h:mm AMPM")            ' "8:35 P.M."
' y=day in the year, ww=week in the year, q=quarter in the year
' Note how a backslash can be used to specify literal characters.
Print Format(Now, "mm/dd/yy (\d\a\y=y \w\e\e\k=ww \q\u\a\r\t\e\r=q)")
                    ' Displays "08/14/98 (day=226 week=33 quarter=3)"
```

Visual Basic 6 has introduced the new *FormatDateTime* function. It's far less flexible than the standard *Format* function and permits only a subset of the *Format* function's named formats. The only advantage of the *FormatDateTime* function is that it's also supported under VBScript and so can contribute to the ease of porting pieces of code from Visual Basic and VBA to VBScript and vice versa. Its syntax is

```
result = FormatDateTime(Expression, [NamedFormat])
```

where *NamedFormat* can be one of the following intrinsic constants: 0-vbGeneralDate (the default), 1-vbLongDate, 2-vbShortDate, 3-vbLongTime, or 4-vbShortTime. Here are a few examples:

```
Print FormatDateTime(Now)                ' "8/14/98 8:35:48 P.M."
Print FormatDateTime(Now, vbLongDate)    ' "Saturday, August 15, 1998"
Print FormatDateTime(Now, vbShortTime)   ' "20:35"
```

Visual Basic 6 also includes two new functions related to date formatting. The *MonthName* function returns the complete or abbreviated name of a month, whereas the *WeekdayName* function returns the complete or abbreviated name of a weekday. Both are locale aware, so you can use them to list month and weekday names in the language the operating system has been configured for:

```
Print MonthName(2)              ' "February"
Print MonthName(2, True)        ' "Feb"
Print WeekdayName(1, True)      ' "Sun"
```

WORKING WITH FILES

Visual Basic has always included many powerful commands for dealing with text and binary files. While Visual Basic 6 hasn't extended the set of built-in functions, it has nonetheless indirectly extended the potential of the language by adding a new and interesting FileSystemObject object that makes it very easy to deal with files and directories. In this section, I provide an overview of all the VBA functions and statements related to files, with many useful tips so that you can get as much as you can from them and stay away from the most recurrent problems.

Handling Files

In general, you can't do many things to a file without opening it. Visual Basic lets you delete a file (using the *Kill* command), move or rename it (using the *Name ... As* command), and copy it elsewhere (using the *FileCopy* command):

```
' All file operations should be protected against errors.
' None of these functions works on open files.
On Error Resume Next
' Rename a file--note that you must specify the path in the target,
' otherwise the file will be moved to the current directory.
Name "c:\vb6\TempData.tmp" As "c:\vb6\TempData.$$$"
' Move the file to another directory, possibly on another drive.
Name "c:\vb6\TempData.$$$" As "d:\VS98\Temporary.Dat"
' Make a copy of a file--note that you can change the name during the copy
' and that you can omit the filename portion of the target file.
FileCopy "d:\VS98\Temporary.Dat", "d:\temporary.$$$"
' Delete one or more files--Kill also supports wildcards.
Kill "d:\temporary.*"
```

You can read and modify the attributes of a file using the *GetAttr* function and the *SetAttr* command, respectively. The *GetAttr* function returns a bit-coded value, so you need to test its individual bits using intrinsic constants provided by VBA. Here's a reusable function that builds a descriptive string with all the attributes of the file:

```
' This routine also works with open files
' and raises an error if the file doesn't exist.
Function GetAttrDescr(filename As String) As String
    Dim result As String, attr As Long
    attr = GetAttr(filename)
    ' GetAttr also works with directories.
    If attr And vbDirectory Then result = result & " Directory"
    If attr And vbReadOnly Then result = result & " ReadOnly"
    If attr And vbHidden Then result = result & " Hidden"
    If attr And vbSystem Then result = result & " System"
    If attr And vbArchive Then result = result & " Archive"
    ' Discard the first (extra) space.
    GetAttrDescr = Mid$(result, 2)
End Function
```

Similarly, you change the attributes of a file or a directory by passing the *SetAttr* command a combination of values, as in the following code:

```
' Mark a file as Archive and Read-only.
filename = "d:\VS98\Temporary.Dat"
SetAttr filename, vbArchive + vbReadOnly
' Change a file from hidden to visible, and vice versa.
SetAttr filename, GetAttr(filename) Xor vbHidden
```

You can't use the *SetAttr* function on open files, and of course you can't morph a file into a directory (or vice versa) by flipping the value of the *vbDirectory* bit. You can determine two more pieces of information about a file without opening it: its length in bytes and its date and time of creation, which you do with the *FileLen* and *FileDateTime* functions, respectively.

```
Print FileLen("d:\VS98\Temporary.Dat")          ' Returns a Long value
Print FileDateTime("d:\VS98\Temporary.Dat")     ' Returns a Date value
```

You can use the *FileLen* function against open files too, but in this case you'll retrieve the length that was current before the file was opened.

Handling Directories

You can learn the name of the current directory using the *CurDir$* function (or its $-less equivalent, *CurDir*). When this function is passed a drive letter, it returns the current directory on that particular path. In this example, I assume that Microsoft Visual Studio was installed on drive D and that Microsoft Windows NT resides on drive C, but you'll probably get different results on your system:

```
' Always use On Error--the current dir might be on a removed floppy disk.
On Error Resume Next
Print CurDir$                       ' Displays "D:\VisStudio\VB98"
' The current directory on drive C:
Print = CurDir$("c")                ' Displays "C:\WinNT\System"
```

You can change both current drive and directory using the *ChDrive* and *ChDir* commands, respectively. If you execute a *ChDir* command on a drive that's not current, you're actually changing the current directory on that drive only, so you must use both commands to ensure you're changing the system's current directory:

```
' Make "C:\Windows" the current directory.
On Error Resume Next
SaveCurDir = CurDir$
ChDrive "C:": ChDir "C:\Windows"
' Do whatever you need to do...
' ....
' and then restore the original current directory.
ChDrive SaveCurDir: ChDir SaveCurDir
```

You can also create and remove subdirectories using the *MkDir* and *RmDir* commands, respectively:

```
' Create a new folder in the current directory, and then make it current.
On Error Resume Next
MkDir "TempDir"
ChDir CurDir$ & "\TempDir"         ' (Assumes current dir is not the root)
' Do whatever you need to do...
' ....
' then restore the original directory and delete the temporary folder.
' You can't remove directories with files in them.
Kill "*.*"                          ' No need for absolute path.
ChDir ".."                          ' Move to the parent directory.
RmDir CurDir$ & "\TempDir"          ' Remove the temporary directory.
```

You can rename a directory using the *Name* command, but you can't move a directory elsewhere:

```
' Assumes that "TempDir" is a subdirectory of the current directory
Name "TempDir" As "TempXXX"
```

Iterating Over All Files in a Directory

The VBA's *Dir* function offers a primitive but effective way to iterate over all the files in a directory. You start by calling the *Dir* function with a *filespec* argument (which can include wildcards) and an optional argument that specifies the attributes of the files you're interested in. Then at each iteration, you call *Dir* without any argument until it returns an empty string. The following routine returns an array of filenames in a given directory and also demonstrates the correct way to set up the loop:

```
Function GetFiles(filespec As String, Optional Attributes As _
    VbFileAttribute) As String()
    Dim result() As String
    Dim filename As String, count As Long, path2 As String
    Const ALLOC_CHUNK = 50
    ReDim result(0 To ALLOC_CHUNK) As String
    filename = Dir$(filespec, Attributes)
    Do While Len(filename)
        count = count + 1
        If count > UBound(result) Then
            ' Resize the result array if necessary.
            ReDim Preserve result(0 To count + ALLOC_CHUNK) As String
        End If
        result(count) = filename
        ' Get ready for the next iteration.
        filename = Dir$
    Loop
    ' Trim the result array.
    ReDim Preserve result(0 To count) As String
    GetFiles = result
End Function
```

> **TIP** You can also use the *Dir$* function to indirectly test for the existence of a file or a directory, using the following functions:
>
> ```
> Function FileExists(filename As String) As Boolean
>     On Error Resume Next
>     FileExists = (Dir$(filename) <> "")
> End Function
> Function DirExists(path As String) As Boolean
>     On Error Resume Next
>     DirExists = (Dir$(path & "\nul") <> "")
> End Function
> ```

While the code in *FileExists* is rather straightforward, you might be puzzled by *DirExists*: where does that "\nul" string come from? The explanation dates back to MS-DOS days and its special filenames "*nul*", "*con*", and so on. These names actually refer to special devices (the null device, the console device, and so on) that appear in any directory you search, provided that the directory actually exists. This approach works with any directory, whereas using *Dir$("*.*")* would fail when you're testing the existence of empty directories.

The *GetFiles* routine can be used to load a bunch of filenames into a ComboBox control. This is particularly effective if you set the control's *Sorted* property to True:

```
Dim Files() As String, i As Long
' All files in C:\WINDOWS\SYSTEM directory, including system/hidden ones.
Files() = GetFiles("C:\windows\system\*.*", vbNormal + vbHidden _
    + vbSystem)
Print "Found " & UBound(Files) & " files."
For i = 1 To UBound(Files)
    Combo1.AddItem Files(i)
Next
```

If you include the *vbDirectory* bit in the *Attribute* argument, the *Dir$* function also returns the names of the directories in its results. You can use this feature to create a *GetDirectories* function that returns the names of all the subdirectories in a given path:

```
Function GetDirectories(path As String, Optional Attributes As _
    VbFileAttribute, Optional IncludePath As Boolean) As String()
    Dim result() As String
    Dim dirname As String, count As Long, path2 As String
    Const ALLOC_CHUNK = 50
    ReDim result(ALLOC_CHUNK) As String
    ' Build the path name + backslash.
    path2 = path
    If Right$(path2, 1) <> "\" Then path2 = path2 & "\"
    dirname = Dir$(path2 & "*.*", vbDirectory Or Attributes)
    Do While Len(dirname)
        If dirname = "." Or dirname = ".." Then
            ' Exclude the "." and ".." entries.
        ElseIf (GetAttr(path2 & dirname) And vbDirectory) = 0 Then
            ' This is a regular file.
        Else
            ' This is a directory.
            count = count + 1
            If count > UBound(result) Then
                ' Resize the result array if necessary.
                ReDim Preserve result(count + ALLOC_CHUNK) As String
            End If
            ' Include the path if requested.
            If IncludePath Then dirname = path2 & dirname
```

```
            result(count) = dirname
        End If
        dirname = Dir$
    Loop
    ' Trim the result array.
    ReDim Preserve result(count) As String
    GetDirectories = result
End Function
```

A common programming task is to process all files in a directory tree. Thanks to the routines I just listed and the ability to create recursive routines, this becomes (almost) child's play:

```
' Load the names of all executable files in a directory tree into a ListBox.
' Note: this is a recursive routine.
Sub ListExecutableFiles(ByVal path As String, lst As ListBox)
    Dim names() As String, i As Long, j As Integer
    ' Ensure that there is a trailing backslash.
    If Right(path, 1) <> "\" Then path = path & "\"
    ' Get the list of executable files.
    For j = 1 To 3
        ' At each iteration search for a different extension.
        names() = GetFiles(path & "*." & Choose(j, "exe", "bat", "com"))
        ' Load partial results in the ListBox lst.
        For i = 1 To UBound(names)
            lst.AddItem path & names(i)
        Next
    Next
    ' Get the list of subdirectories, including hidden ones,
    ' and call this routine recursively on all of them.
    names() = GetDirectories(path, vbHidden)
    For i = 1 To UBound(names)
        ListExecutableFiles path & names(i), lst
    Next
End Sub
```

Processing Text Files

Text files are the simplest type of files to process. You open them using the *Open* statement with the *For Input*, *For Output*, or *For Appending* clause, and then start reading data from them or writing data to them. To open a file—either text or a binary file—you need a file number, as in the following code:

```
' Error if file #1 is already open
Open "readme.txt" For Input As #1
```

Within an individual application, you're usually able to assign unique file numbers to the different routines that deal with files. However, this approach severely hinders code reusability, so I suggest that you use the *FreeFile* function and query Visual Basic about the first available file number:

```
Dim fnum As Integer
fnum = FreeFile()
Open "readme.txt" For Input As #fnum
```

After you open a text file for input, you usually read it one line of text at a time using the *Line Input* statement until the *EOF* (End-Of-File) function returns True. Any file routine must also take errors into account, both when it opens the file and when it reads its contents. But you can often do a better job if you use the *LOF* function to determine the length of the file and read all characters in one operation with the *Input$* function. Here's a reusable routine that uses this optimized approach:

```
Function ReadTextFileContents(filename As String) As String
    Dim fnum As Integer, isOpen As Boolean
    On Error GoTo Error_Handler
    ' Get the next free file number.
    fnum = FreeFile()
    Open filename For Input As #fnum
    ' If execution flow got here, the file has been open without error.
    isOpen = True
    ' Read the entire contents in one single operation.
    ReadTextFileContents = Input(LOF(fnum), fnum)
    ' Intentionally flow into the error handler to close the file.
Error_Handler:
    ' Raise the error (if any), but first close the file.
    If isOpen Then Close #fnum
    If Err Then Err.Raise Err.Number, , Err.Description
End Function

' Load a text file into a TextBox control.
Text1.Text = ReadTextFileContents("c:\bootlog.txt")
```

When you want to write data to a file, you open the file using the *For Output* clause if you want to replace the current contents or the *For Append* clause to simply append new data to the file. You usually send output to this output file with a series of *Print #* statements, but it's much faster if you gather your output in a string and print that instead. Here's a reusable function that does it all for you:

```
Sub WriteTextFileContents(Text As String, filename As String, _
    Optional AppendMode As Boolean)
    Dim fnum As Integer, isOpen As Boolean
    On Error GoTo Error_Handler
    ' Get the next free file number.
    fnum = FreeFile()
    If AppendMode Then
        Open filename For Append As #fnum
```

```
    Else
         Open filename For Output As #fnum
    End If
    ' If execution flow gets here, the file has been opened correctly.
    isOpen = True
    ' Print to the file in one single operation.
    Print #fnum, Text
    ' Intentionally flow into the error handler to close the file.
Error_Handler:
    ' Raise the error (if any), but first close the file.
    If isOpen Then Close #fnum
    If Err Then Err.Raise Err.Number, , Err.Description
End Sub
```

Even if Visual Basic 6 didn't add any function specifically intended to work with text files, its new *Split* function turns out to be extremely useful for text processing. Let's say that your text file contains items to be loaded into a ListBox or ComboBox control. You can't use the *ReadTextFileContents* routine that I showed you previously to load it directly in the control, but you can use it to make your code more concise:

```
Sub TextFileToListbox(lst As ListBox, filename As String)
    Dim items() As String, i As Long
    ' Read the file's contents, and split it into an array of strings.
    ' (Exit here if any error occurs.)
    items() = Split(ReadTextFileContents(filename), vbCrLf)
    ' Load all non-empty items into the ListBox.
    For i = LBound(items) To UBound(items)
        If Len(items(i)) > 0 Then lst.AddItem items(i)
    Next
End Sub
```

Processing Delimited Text Files

Delimited text files contain multiple fields in each line of text. Even if no serious programmer would ever use delimited text files as the primary means to store an application's data, these files nevertheless play an important role because they offer a great way to exchange data between different database formats. For example, delimited text files are often the only viable way to import and export data to mainframe databases. Here's the structure of a simple semicolon-delimited text file. (Note that it's customary for the first line of the file to hold the field's names.)

```
Name;Department;Salary
John Smith;Marketing;80000
Anne Lipton;Sales;75000
Robert Douglas;Administration;70000
```

Taken together, the *Split* and the *Join* functions are especially useful for importing and exporting delimited text files. For example, see how easy it is to import the contents of a semicolon-delimited data file into an array of arrays:

```
' The contents of a delimited text file as an array of strings arrays
' NOTE: requires the GetTextFileLines routine
Function ImportDelimitedFile(filename As String, _
    Optional delimiter As String = vbTab) As Variant()
    Dim lines() As String, i As Long
    ' Get all lines in the file.
    lines() = Split(ReadTextFileContents(filename), vbCrLf)
    ' To quickly delete all empty lines, load them with a special char.
    For i = 0 To UBound(lines)
        If Len(lines(i)) = 0 Then lines(i) = vbNullChar
    Next
    ' Then use the Filter function to delete these lines.
    lines() = Filter(lines(), vbNullChar, False)
    ' Create a string array out of each line of text
    ' and store it in a Variant element.
    ReDim values(0 To UBound(lines)) As Variant
    For i = 0 To UBound(lines)
        values(i) = Split(lines(i), delimiter)
    Next
    ImportDelimitedFile = values()
End Function

' An example of using the ImportDelimitedFile routine
Dim values() As Variant, i As Long
values() = ImportDelimitedFile("c:\datafile.txt", ";")
' Values(0)(n) is the name of the Nth field.
' Values(i)(n) is the value of the Nth field on the ith record.
' For example, see how you can increment employees' salaries by 20%.
For i = 1 to UBound(values)
    values(i)(2) = values(i)(2) * 1.2
Next
```

Using an array of arrays is a particularly good strategy because it makes it easy to add new records:

```
' Add a new record.
ReDim Preserve values(0 To UBound(values) + 1) As Variant
values(UBound(values)) = Split("Roscoe Powell;Sales;80000", ";")
```

or delete existing ones:

```
' Delete the Nth record
For i = n To UBound(values) - 1
    values(i) = values(i + 1)
Next
ReDim Preserve values(0 To UBound(values) - 1) As Variant
```

Writing an array of string arrays back to a delimited file is also a simple task, thanks to this reusable routine that builds on the *Join* function:

```
' Write the contents of an array of string arrays to a delimited
' text file.
' NOTE: requires the WriteTextFileContents routine
Sub ExportDelimitedFile(values() As Variant, filename As String, _
    Optional delimiter As String = vbTab)
    Dim i As Long
    ' Rebuild the individual lines of text of the file.
    ReDim lines(0 To UBound(values)) As String
    For i = 0 To UBound(values)
        lines(i) = Join(values(i), delimiter)
    Next
    ' Create CRLFs among records, and write them.
    WriteTextFileContents Join(lines, vbCrLf), filename
End Sub
```

```
' Write the modified data back to the delimited file.
ExportDelimitedFile values(), "C:\datafile.txt", ";"
```

All the routines described in this section rely on the assumption that the delimited text file is small enough to be held in memory. While this might sound like a serious limitation, in practice text files are mostly used to create small archives or to move small quantities of data between different database formats. If you find that you're having problems because of the size of the array, you need to read and write it in chunks using multiple *Line Input #* and *Print #* statements. In most cases, you can deal with files up to 1 or 2 megabytes in size (or even more, depending on how much RAM memory you have) without any problem.

Processing Binary Files

To open a binary file, you use the *Open* statement with the *For Random* or *For Binary* options. Let me first explain the latter mode, which is the simpler of the two. In *Binary* mode, you write to file using the *Put* statement and read data back with the *Get* statement. Visual Basic determines how many bytes are written or read by looking at the structure of the variable you pass as the last argument:

```
Dim numEls As Long, text As String
numEls = 12345: text = "A 16-char string"
' Binary files are automatically created if necessary.
Open "data.bin" For Binary As #1
Put #1, , numEls          ' Put writes 4 bytes.
Put #1, , text            ' Put writes 16 bytes (ANSI format).
```

When reading data back, you must repeat the same sequence of statements but it's up to you to correctly dimension variable length strings. You don't need to close and reopen a binary file because you can use the *Seek* statement to reposition the file pointer to a specific byte:

```
Seek #1, 1                  ' Back to the beginning (first byte is byte 1)
Get #1, , numEls            ' All Long values are 4 bytes.
text = Space$(16)           ' Prepare to read 16 bytes.
Get #1, , text              ' Do it.
```

Alternatively, you can move the file pointer right before writing or reading data using a second argument, as in this code:

```
Get #1, 1, numEls           ' Same as Seek + Get
```

> **CAUTION**   When you open a binary file, Visual Basic automatically creates it if it doesn't exist. Therefore, you can't use an *On Error* statement to determine whether the file exists already. In this case, use the *Dir$* function to ascertain that the file actually exists before opening it.

You can quickly write an entire array to disk and read it back in one single operation; but because you must correctly dimension the array before reading it, you'll also have to prefix the data with the number of actual elements, in most cases:

```
' Store a zero-based array of Double.
Put #1, 1, CLng(UBound(arr)) ' First store the UBound value.
Put #1, , arr()              ' Then store all items in one shot.
' read it back
Dim LastItem As Long
Get #1, 1, LastItem          ' Read the number of items.
ReDim arr2(0 To LastItem) As Double
Get #1, , arr2()             ' Read the array in memory in one operation.
Close #1
```

> **CAUTION**   If you read data back using a read sequence different from the original write sequence, you'll read wrong data into your variables. In some cases, this mistake might cause the Visual Basic environment to crash when trying to display the contents of those variables. For this reason, always double-check the order of write and read operations. When in doubt, save your work before running the code.

When you're reading from a binary file, you can't use the *EOF* function to find out when you're at the end of the data; instead, you should test the value returned by the *LOF* function (the length of the file in bytes) and use the *Seek* function to determine when you have read all the data in it:

```
Do While Seek(1) < LOF(1)
    ' Continue to read.
    ....
Loop
```

CAUTION When storing strings to disk—either to text or binary files—Visual Basic automatically converts them from Unicode to ANSI, which saves a noticeable amount of disk space and lets you exchange data with 16-bit Visual Basic applications. If you're writing Unicode-aware programs for the international market, however, this behavior gets in the way and can cause loss of data because the string you're reading back from a file won't necessarily match the one you had stored previously. To fix a problem, you have to move the string into a *Byte* array and save that instead:

```
Dim v As Variant, s As String, b() As Byte
s = "This is a string that you want to save in Unicode format"
b() = s: v = b()      ' You need this double step.
Put #1, , v           ' Write that to disk.

' Read it back.
Get #1, 1, v: s = v   ' No need for intermediary Byte array here.
```

Opening a binary file using the *For Random* clause differs from what I have illustrated so far in a number of important respects:

- Data is written to and read from file as if it were a record of fixed length. Such a record length can be specified when you open the file (using the *Len* clause in the *Open* statement), or it's evaluated during individual *Put* and *Get* statements. If the actual data passed to a *Put* statement is shorter than the expected record length, Visual Basic pads it with random characters (more precisely, the current contents of the internal file buffer). If it's longer, an error occurs.

- The argument for the *Seek* command, as well as the second argument for *Put* and *Get* statements, is meant to be the record number, not the absolute byte position in the binary file. The first record in a file is record 1.

- You don't have to worry about storing and retrieving variable-length data, including strings and arrays, because the *Put* and *Get* statements correctly deal with those cases. But I strongly advise that you stay clear of UDTs that contain conventional (non-fixed-length) strings and dynamic arrays so that the length of the record doesn't depend on its actual contents.

Strings stored to binary files opened with the *For Random* clause are prefixed by a 2-byte value that indicates the number of characters that follow. This means that you can't write a string that contains more than 32,767 characters, which is also the largest valid record size. To write a longer string, you should use the *For Binary* clause.

One final note: All the code examples seen so far assume that we're working in a single-user environment and don't account for issues such as the errors you get when opening a file already opened by another user, or the capability to lock all or a portion of a data file using the *Lock* statement (and later unlock it using the *Unlock* statement). For more information, see the Visual Basic documentation.

> **TIP** If you don't want to get involved with lots of additional evaluations when writing and reading data in a binary file, you can follow a shorter path using an intermediate Variant variable. If you store a value of any type (other than object) into a Variant variable and then write the variable to a binary file, Visual Basic writes the type of the variable (that is, the *VarType* return value) and then the data. If the variable holds a string or an array, Visual Basic also stores enough information to read exactly the necessary number of bytes, freeing you from additional read statements:

```
Dim v As Variant, s(100) As String, i As Long
' Fill the s() array with data... (omitted)
Open "c:\binary.dat" For Binary As #1
v = s()                 ' Store the array in a Variant variable,
Put #1, , v             ' and write that to disk.
v = Empty               ' Release memory.

' Read data back.
Dim v2 As Variant, s2() As String
Get #1, 1, v2           ' Read data in the Variant variable,
s2() = v2               ' and then move it to the real array.
v2 = Empty              ' Release memory.
Close #1
```

This approach also works with multidimensional arrays.

The FileSystemObject Hierarchy

Visual Basic 6 comes with a new library of file commands, which enables programmers to easily scan drives and directories, perform basic file operations (including copy, delete, move, and so on), and extract information not available through regular Visual Basic functions. But in my opinion, the best feature of the new commands is that you can do all that using a modern, coherent, object-oriented syntax, which makes your code much more readable. All this power is provided in the form of the external FileSystemObject hierarchy, embedded in the Microsoft Scripting Library, the library that also hosts the Dictionary object. (See Chapter 4 for instructions about installing and using this library.) The FileSystemObject hierarchy includes many complex objects (see Figure 5-1), and each object exposes many interesting properties and methods.

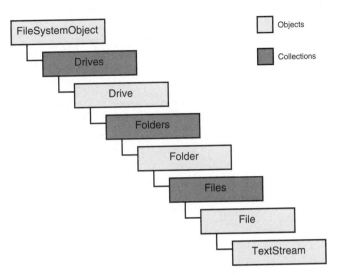

Figure 5-1. *The FileSystemObject hierarchy.*

The FileSystemObject root object

At the root of the hierarchy is the FileSystemObject object itself. It exposes many methods and only one property, *Drives,* which returns the collection of all the drives in the system. The FileSystemObject object (abbreviated as FSO in the following text and code) is the only creatable object in the hierarchy—that is, it's the only object that can be declared using the *New* keyword. All the other objects are dependent objects that derive from this one and are exposed in the form of methods or properties. See how easy it is to fill an array with the list of all the ready drives in the system and their capacities:

```
Dim fso As New Scripting.FileSystemObject, dr As Scripting.Drive
On Error Resume Next        ' Needed for not-ready drives
For Each dr In fso.Drives
    Print dr.DriveLetter & " [" & dr.TotalSize & "]"
Next
```

Table 5-3 on the following page summarizes the many methods exposed by the FSO object. A few of them are also available (often with different names and syntax) as methods of secondary Folder and File objects. Most of these methods add functionality to commands already present in Visual Basic. For example, you can delete non-empty folders (be *very* careful!) and copy and rename multiple files and directories with one single command. You can also easily extract portions of a filename without having to write special routines.

Syntax	Description
BuildPath (Path, Name)	Returns a complete filename, obtained by concatenating the path (relative or absolute) and name.
CopyFile Source, Destination, [Overwrite]	Copies one or more files: Source can include wildcards, and Destination is considered to be a directory if it ends with a backslash. It overwrites existing files unless you set Overwrite to False.
CopyFolder Source, Destination, [Overwrite]	Same as CopyFile, but copies entire folders with their contents (subfolders and files). If Destination doesn't correspond to an existing directory, it's created (but not if Source contains wildcards).
CreateFolder(Path) As Folder	Creates a new Folder object and returns it; raises an error if the folder already exists.
CreateTextFile(FileName, [Overwrite], [Unicode]) As TextStream	Creates a new TextFile object and returns it; set Overwrite = False to avoid overwriting an existing file; set Unicode = True to create a Unicode TextFile object.
DeleteFile FileSpec, [Force]	Deletes one or more files. FileSpec can include wildcards; set Force = True to force the deletion of read-only files.
DeleteFolder(FolderSpec, [Force])	Deletes one or more folders, together with their contents; set Force = True to force the deletion of read-only files.
DriveExists(DriveName)	Returns True if a given logical drive exists.
FileExists(FileName)	Returns True if a given file exists. (The path can be relative to the current directory.)
FolderExists(FolderName)	Returns True if a given folder exists. (The path can be relative to the current directory.)
GetAbsolutePathName(Path)	Converts a path relative to the current directory into an absolute path.
GetBaseName(Filename)	Extract the base filename (without its path and extension); it doesn't check whether the file and/or the path actually exist.
GetDrive(DriveName) As Drive	Returns the Drive object that corresponds to the letter or the UNC path passed as an argument. (It checks that the drive actually exists).
GetDriveName(Path)	Extracts the drive from a path.
GetExtensionName(FileName)	Extracts the extension string from a filename.
GetFile(FileName)	Returns the File object corresponding to the name passed as the argument. (Can be absolute or relative to the current directory.)

Table 5-3. *All the methods of the FileSystemObject object.*

(continued)

Syntax	Description
GetFileName(	Extract the filename (without its path but with its extension); it doesn't check whether the file and/or the path actually exist.
GetFolder(*FolderName) As Folder*	Returns the Folder object corresponding to the path passed as the argument. (Can be absolute or relative to the current directory.)
GetParentFolderName(*Path)*	Returns the name of the parent directory of the directory passed as the argument (or an empty string if the parent directory doesn't exist).
GetSpecialFolder(*SpecialFolder) As Folder*	Returns a Folder object that corresponds to one of the special Windows directories. *SpecialFolder* can be 0-WindowsFolder, 1-SystemFolder, 2-TemporaryFolder.
GetTempName()	Returns the name of a nonexistent file that can be used as a temporary file.
MoveFile(Source, *Destination)*	Same as *CopyFile*, but it deletes the source file. It can also move among different drives, if this function is supported by the operating system.
MoveFolder(Source, *Destination)*	Same as *MoveFile*, but works on directories instead.
OpenTextFile(FileName, *[IOMode], [Create],* *[Format])As TextStream*	Opens a text file and returns the corresponding TextStream object. *IOMode* can be one or a combination (use the OR operator) of the following constants: 1-ForReading, 2-ForWriting, 8-ForAppending; set Create to True if you want to create a new file; Format can be 0-TristateFalse (ANSI), –1-TristateTrue (Unicode) or –2-TristateUseDefault (determined by the system).

The Drive object

This object exposes only properties (no methods), all of which are summarized in Table 5-4 on the following page. All the properties are read-only, except the *VolumeName* property. This short code snippet determines the local drives that are ready and have at least 100 MB of free space on them:

```
Dim fso As New Scripting.FileSystemObject, dr As Scripting.Drive
For Each dr In fso.Drives
    If dr.IsReady Then
        If dr.DriveType = Fixed Or dr.DriveType = Removable Then
            ' 2 ^ 20 equals one megabyte.
            If dr.FreeSpace > 100 * 2 ^ 20 Then
                Print dr.Path & " [" & dr.VolumeName & "] = " _
```

(continued)

```
                        & dr.FreeSpace
                End If
            End If
        End If
    Next
```

Syntax	Description
AvailableSpace	The free space on the drive, in bytes; it usually coincides with the value returned by the *FreeSpace* property, unless the operating system supports disk quotas.
DriveLetter	The letter associated with the drive or an empty string for network drives not associated with a letter.
DriveType	A constant that indicates the type of the drive: 0-Unknown, 1-Removable, 2-Fixed, 3-Remote, 4-CDRom, 5-RamDisk.
FileSystem	A string that describes the file system in use: FAT, NTFS, CDFS.
FreeSpace	The free space on the drive. (See *AvailableSpace*.)
IsReady	True if the drive is ready, False otherwise.
Path	The path associated with the drive, without the backslash (for example, C:).
RootFolder	The Folder object that corresponds to the root directory.
SerialNumber	A Long number that corresponds to the serial disk number.
ShareName	The network shared name for the drive or an empty string if it isn't a network drive.
TotalSize	The total capacity of the drive, in bytes.
VolumeName	The disk label (can be read and written).

Table 5-4. *All the properties of the Drive object.*

The Folder object

The Folder object represents an individual subdirectory. You can obtain a reference to such an object in different ways: by using the *GetFolder* or *GetSpecialFolder* methods of the FileSystemObject object, through the *RootFolder* property of a Drive object, through the *ParentFolder* property of a File object or another Folder object, or by iterating over the *SubFolders* collection of another Folder object. The Folder object exposes a number of interesting properties (see Table 5-5), but only the *Attribute* and *Name* properties can be written to. The most intriguing properties are probably the *SubFolders* and *Files* collections, which let you iterate through subdirectories and files using an elegant and concise syntax:

```
' Print the names of all first-level directories on all drives
' together with their short 8.3 names.
Dim fso As New Scripting.FileSystemObject
Dim dr As Scripting.Drive, fld As Scripting.Folder
On Error Resume Next
For Each dr In fso.Drives
    If dr.IsReady Then
        Print dr.RootFolder.Path        ' The root folder.
        For Each fld In dr.RootFolder.SubFolders
            Print fld.Path & " [" & fld.ShortName & "]"
        Next
    End If
Next
```

Syntax	*Description*	*Applies To*
Attributes	The attributes of the file or the folder, as a combination of the following constants: 0- Normal, 1-ReadOnly, 2-Hidden, 4-System, 8-Volume, 16-Directory, 32-Archive, 64-Alias, 2048-Compressed. The attributes Volume, Directory, Alias, and Compressed can't be modified.	Folder and File
DateCreated	Creation date (a read-only Date value).	Folder and File
DateLastAccessed	The date of the last access (a read-only Date value).	Folder and File
DateLastModified	The date of the last modification (a read-only Date value).	Folder and File
Drive	The Drive object where the file or the folder is located.	Folder and File
Files	The collection of all the contained File objects.	Folder only
IsRootFolder	True if this is the root folder for its drive.	Folder only
Name	The name of the folder or the file. Assign a new value to rename the object.	Folder and File
ParentFolder	The parent Folder object.	Folder and File
Path	The path of the Folder or the File. (This is the default property.)	Folder and File
ShortName	The name of the object in 8.3 MS-DOS format.	Folder and File
ShortPath	The path of the object in 8.3 MS-DOS format.	Folder and File

Table 5-5. *All the properties of Folder and File objects.*   *(continued)*

Table 5-5. *continued*

·*Syntax*	*Description*	*Applies To*
Size	The size in bytes of a File object; the sum of the size of all contained files and sub-folders for a Folder object.	Folder and File
SubFolders	The collection of all the subfolders contained in this folder, including system and hidden ones.	Folder only
Type	A string description of the object. For example: *fso.GetFolder("C:\Recycled").Type* returns "Recycle Bin"; for File objects, this value depends on their extensions (for example, "Text Document" for a TXT extension).	Folder and File

The Folder object also exposes a few methods, summarized in Table 5-6. Note that you can often achieve similar results using appropriate methods of the main FSO object. You can also create a new Folder using the *Add* method applied to the *SubFolders* collection, as shown in the following recursive routine, which duplicates the directory structure of one drive onto another drive without also copying the contained files:

```
' Call this routine to initiate the copy process.
' NOTE: the destination folder is created if necessary.
Sub DuplicateDirTree(SourcePath As String, DestPath As String)
    Dim fso As New Scripting.FileSystemObject
    Dim sourceFld As Scripting.Folder, destFld As Scripting.Folder
    ' The source folder must exist.
    Set sourceFld = fso.GetFolder(SourcePath)
    ' The destination folder is created if necessary.
    If fso.FolderExists(DestPath) Then
        Set destFld = fso.GetFolder(DestPath)
    Else
        Set destFld = fso.CreateFolder(DestPath)
    End If
    ' Jump to the recursive routine to do the real job.
    DuplicateDirTreeSub sourceFld, destFld
End Sub

Private Sub DuplicateDirTreeSub(source As Folder, destination As Folder)
    Dim sourceFld As Scripting.Folder, destFld As Scripting.Folder
    For Each sourceFld In source.SubFolders
        ' Copy this subfolder into destination folder.
```

```
        Set destFld = destination.SubFolders.Add(sourceFld.Name)
        ' Then repeat the process recursively for all
        ' the subfolders of the folder just considered.
        DuplicateDirTreeSub sourceFld, destFld
    Next
End Sub
```

Syntax	Description	Applies To
Copy Destination, [OverWriteFiles]	Copy the current File or the Folder object to another path; this is similar to FSO's *CopyFolder* and *CopyFile* methods, which are also able to copy multiple objects in one operation.	Folder and File
CreateTextFile(FileName, [Overwrite], [Unicode]) As TextStream	Creates a text file in the current Folder and returns the corresponding TextStream object. See the corresponding FSO's method for an explanation of the individual arguments.	Folder only
Delete [Force]	Delete this File or this Folder object (with all its contained subfolders and files). Similar to FSO's *DeleteFile* and *DeleteFolder* methods.	Folder and File
Move DestinationPath	Move this File or Folder object to another path; similar to FSO's *MoveFile* and *MoveFolder* methods.	Folder and File
OpenAsTextStream([IOMode], [Format]) As TextStream	Open this File object as a text file and return the corresponding TextStream object.	File only

Table 5-6. *All the methods of Folder and File objects.*

The File object

The File object represents a single file on disk. You can obtain a reference to such an object in two ways: by using the *GetFile* method of the FSO object or by iterating over the *Files* collection of its parent Folder object. Despite their different natures, File and Folder objects have many properties and methods in common, so I won't repeat the descriptions that were given in Tables 5-5 and 5-6.

A limitation of the FSO hierarchy is that you have no direct way to filter filenames using wildcards, as you can do with the *Dir$* function. All you can do is iterate through the *Files* collection of a Folder object and test the file's name, extensions, or other attributes to see whether you are interested in it as shown on the following page.

```
' List all the DLL files in the C:\WINDOWS\SYSTEM directory.
Dim fso As New Scripting.FileSystemObject, fil As Scripting.File
For Each fil In fso.GetSpecialFolder(SystemFolder).Files
    If UCase$(fso.GetExtensionName(fil.Path)) = "DLL"  Then
        Print fil.Name
    End If
Next
```

The FileSystemObject hierarchy doesn't permit many operations on files. More specifically, while you can list their properties (including many properties that are beyond the current capabilities of native VBA file functions), you can open files only in text mode, as I explain in the next section.

The TextStream object

The TextStream object represents a file opened in text mode. You can obtain a reference to such an object in the following ways: by using the *CreateTextFile* or the *OpenTextFile* method of the FSO object, by using the *CreateTextFile* method of a Folder object, or by using the *OpenAsTextStream* method of a File object. The TextStream object exposes a number of methods and read-only properties, all of which are described in Table 5-7. The TextStream object does offer some new features in addition to regular VBA file commands—for example, the ability to keep track of the current line and column while reading from or writing to the text file. This feature is exploited in this reusable routine that scans all the TXT files in a directory for a search string and returns an array of results (actually, an array of arrays) with all the files that contain that search string as well as the line number and the column number to indicate the position of the string within the file:

```
' For each TXT file that contains the search string, the  function
' returns a Variant element that contains a 3-item array that holds
' the filename, the line number, and the column number.
' NOTE: all searches are case insensitive.
Function SearchTextFiles(path As String, search As String) As Variant()
    Dim fso As New Scripting.FileSystemObject
    Dim fil As Scripting.File, ts As Scripting.TextStream
    Dim pos As Long, count As Long
    ReDim result(50) As Variant

    ' Search for all the TXT files in the directory.
    For Each fil In fso.GetFolder(path).Files
        If UCase$(fso.GetExtensionName(fil.path)) = "TXT" Then
            ' Get the corresponding TextStream object.
            Set ts = fil.OpenAsTextStream(ForReading)
            ' Read its contents, search the string, close it.
            pos = InStr(1, ts.ReadAll, search, vbTextCompare)
            ts.Close

            If pos > 0 Then
```

```
            ' If the string has been found, reopen the file
            ' to determine string position in terms of (line,column).
            Set ts = fil.OpenAsTextStream(ForReading)
            ' Skip all preceding characters to get where
            ' the search string is.
            ts.Skip pos - 1
            ' Fill the result array, make room if necessary.
            count = count + 1
            If count > UBound(result) Then
                ReDim Preserve result(UBound(result) + 50) As Variant
            End If
            ' Each result item is a 3-element array.
            result(count) = Array(fil.path, ts.Line, ts.Column)
            ' Now we can close the TextStream.
            ts.Close
        End If
      End If
    Next

    ' Resize the result array to indicate number of matches.
    ReDim Preserve result(0 To count) As Variant
    SearchTextFiles = result
End Function

' An example that uses the above routine: search for a name in all
' the TXT files in E:\DOCS directory, show the results in
' the lstResults ListBox, in the format "filename [line, column]".
Dim v() As Variant, i As Long
v() = SearchTextFiles("E:\docs", "Francesco Balena")
For i = 1 To UBound(v)
    lstResults.AddItem v(i)(0) & " [" & v(i)(1) & "," & v(i)(2) & "]"
Next
```

Property or Method	Syntax	Description
Property	*AtEndOfLine*	True if the file pointer is at the end of the current line.
Property	*AtEndOfFile*	True if the file pointer is at the end of file (similar to VBA's *EOF* function).
Method	*Close*	Closes the file (similar to VBA's *Close* statement).
Property	*Column*	Current column number.
Property	*Line*	Current line number.

Table 5-7. *All the properties and methods of the TextStream object.*   *(continued)*

Table 5-7. *continued*

Property or Method	Syntax	Description
Method	*Read(Characters)*	Reads a specified number of characters and returns a string (similar to VBA's *Input$* function).
Method	*ReadAll()*	Reads the entire file into a string (similar to VBA's *Input$* function when used with the *LOF* function).
Method	*ReadLine()*	Reads the next line of text and returns a string (similar to VBA's *Line Input* statement).
Method	*Skip Characters*	Skips over a specified number of characters.
Method	*SkipLine*	Skips over a line of text.
Method	*Write Text*	Writes a string of characters, without a trailing Newline character (similar to the *Print#* command with a trailing semicolon).
Method	*WriteBlankLines Lines*	Writes the indicated number of blank lines (similar to one or more *Print#* commands without any argument).
Method	*WriteLine [Text]*	Writes a string of characters, with a trailing Newline character (similar to the *Print#* command without a trailing semicolon).

INTERACTING WITH WINDOWS

So far, we've concentrated on self-contained applications that haven't come in contact with the outside world. But on many occasions, you'll need your application to interact with its environment, including other applications that run in parallel with yours. This section introduces the topic and describes some techniques for managing such interactions.

The App Object

The App object is provided by the Visual Basic library and represents the application being executed. The App object exposes a lot of properties and methods, many of which are somewhat advanced and will be explained later in the book.

The *EXEName* and the *Path* properties return the name and the path of the executable file (if running as a stand-alone EXE file) or the project name (if running inside the environment). These properties are often used together—for example, to locate an INI file that's stored in the same directory as the executable and that has the same base name:

```
IniFile = App.Path & IIf(Right$(App.Path, 1) <> "\", "\", "") _
    & App.EXEName & ".INI"
Open IniFile For Input As #1
' and so on.
```

Another common use for the *App.Path* property is to set the current directory to match the directory of the application so that all its ancillary files can be found without your having to specify their complete path:

```
' Let the application's directory be the current directory.
On Error Resume Next
ChDrive App.Path: ChDir App.Path
```

> **CAUTION** The preceding snippet of code might fail under some conditions, in particular when the Visual Basic application is started from a remote network server. This happens because the *App.Path* property could return a UNC path (for example, *\\servername\dirname\...*) and the *ChDrive* command is unable to deal with such paths. For this reason, you should protect this code against unanticipated errors, and you should always provide your users with alternative ways to make the application point to its own directory (for example, by setting a key in the system Registry).

The *PrevInstance* property lets you determine whether there's another (compiled) instance of the application running in the system. This can be useful if you want to prevent the user from accidentally running two instances of your program:

```
Private Sub Form_Load()
    If App.PrevInstance Then
        ' Another instance of this application is running.
        Dim saveCaption As String
        saveCaption = Caption
        ' Modify this form's caption so that it isn't traced by
        ' the AppActivate command.
        Caption = Caption & Space$(5)
        On Error Resume Next
        AppActivate saveCaption
        ' Restore the Caption, in case AppActivate failed.
        Caption = saveCaption
        If Err = 0 Then Unload Me
    End If
End Sub
```

A couple of properties can be both read and modified at run time. The *TaskVisible* Boolean property determines whether the application is visible in the task list. The *Title* property is the string that identifies the application in the Windows task list. Its initial value is the string you enter at design time in the Make tab of the Project Properties dialog box.

Other properties of the App object return values that you entered at design time in the General and Make tabs of the Project Properties dialog box. (See Figure 5-2.) For example, the *HelpFile* property is the name of the associated help file, if you have any. The *UnattendedApp* and the *RetainedProject* properties report the state of the corresponding check boxes on the General tab of the dialog box (but their meaning will be made clear in Chapters 16 and 20, respectively). Taken together, the *Major*, *Minor*, and *Revision* properties return information about the version of the running executable. The *Comments*, *CompanyName*, *FileDescription*, *LegalCopyright*, *Legal-Trademarks*, and *ProductName* properties let you query at run time other values that have been entered in the Make tab of the Project Properties dialog box. They're useful mostly when you're creating informative About Box dialog boxes or splash screens.

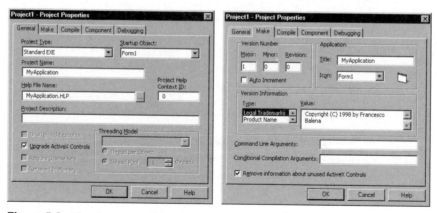

Figure 5-2. *The General and Make tabs of the Project Properties dialog box.*

The Clipboard Object

In the 32-bit world of Windows 9x and Windows NT, exchanging information with other applications through the system clipboard might seem a bit old-fashioned, but it is a fact that the clipboard remains one of the simplest and most effective ways for end users to quickly copy data among applications. Visual Basic lets you control the system clipboard using the Clipboard global object. Compared with other Visual Basic objects, this is a very simple one in that it exposes only six methods and no properties.

Copying and pasting text

To place a piece of text in the clipboard, you use the *SetText* method:

```
Clipboard.SetText Text, [Format]
```

where *format* can be 1-vbCFText (plain text, the default), &HBF01-vbCFRTF (text in RTF format), or &HBF00-vbCFLink (DDE conversation information). This argument is necessary because the clipboard can store pieces of information in multiple formats. For example, if you have a RichTextBox control (a Microsoft ActiveX control described in Chapter 12), you can store the selected text in either *vbCFText* or *vbCFRTF* format and let the user paste your text in whatever format fits the target control.

```
Clipboard.Clear
Clipboard.SetText RichTextBox1.SelText        ' vbCFText is the default.
Clipboard.SetText RichTextBox1.SelRTF, vbCFRTF
```

> **CAUTION** In some circumstances and with some external applications, placing text on the clipboard doesn't work correctly unless you first reset the Clipboard object using its *Clear* method, as shown in the preceding code snippet.

You retrieve the text currently in the clipboard using the *GetText* method. You can specify which format you want to retrieve using the following syntax:

```
' For a regular TextBox control
Text1.SelText = Clipboard.GetText()        ' You can omit vbCFText.
' For a RichTextBox control
RichTextBox1.SelRTF = Clipboard.GetText(vbCFRTF)
```

In general, you don't know whether the clipboard actually includes text in RTF format, so you should test its current contents using the *GetFormat* method, which takes a format as an argument and returns a Boolean value that indicates whether the clipboard format matches the format parameter:

```
If Clipboard.GetFormat(vbCFRTF) Then
    ' The Clipboard contains data in RTF format.
End If
```

The value of *format* can be 1-vbCFText (plain text), 2-vbCFBitmap (bitmap), 3-vbCFMetafile (metafile), 8-vbCFDIB (Device Independent Bitmap), 9-vbCFPalette (color palette), &HBF01-vbCFRTF (text in RTF format), or &HBF00-vbCFLink (DDE conversation information). This is the correct sequence for pasting text into a RichTextBox control:

```
If Clipboard.GetFormat(vbCFRTF) Then
    RichTextBox1.SelRTF = Clipboard.GetText(vbCFRTF)
ElseIf Clipboard.GetFormat(vbCFText) Then
    RichTextBox1.SelText = Clipboard.GetText()
End If
```

Copying and pasting images

When you work with PictureBox and Image controls, you can retrieve an image stored in the Clipboard using the *GetData* method, which also requires a format attribute (vbCFBitmap, vbCFMetafile, vbCFDIB, or vbCFPalette—although with Image controls, you can use only vbCFBitmap). The correct sequence is

```
Dim frmt As Variant
For Each frmt In Array(vbCFBitmap, vbCFMetafile, _
    vbCFDIB, vbCFPalette)
    If Clipboard.GetFormat(frmt) Then
        Set Picture1.Picture = Clipboard.GetData(frmt)
        Exit For
    End If
Next
```

You can copy the current contents of a PictureBox or an Image control to the clipboard using the *SetData* method:

```
Clipboard.SetData Picture1.Picture
' You can also load an image from disk onto the clipboard.
Clipboard.SetData LoadPicture("c:\myimage.bmp")
```

A generic Edit menu

In many Windows applications, all the clipboard commands are typically gathered in the Edit menu. The commands available to the user (and how your code processes them) depends on which control is the active control. Here you have two problems to solve: For a really user-friendly interface, you should disable all the menu items that don't apply to the active control and the current contents of the clipboard, and you must devise a cut-copy-paste strategy that works well in all situations.

When you have multiple controls on your forms, things become confusing quickly because you have to account for several potential problems. I have prepared a simple but complete demonstration program. (See Figure 5-3.) To let you easily reuse its code in your applications, all the references to controls are done through the form's *ActiveControl* property. Instead of testing the control type using a *TypeOf* or *TypeName* keyword, the code indirectly tests which properties are actually supported using the *On Error Resume Next* statement. (See the code in boldface in the following listing.) This approach lets you deal with any type of control, including third-party ActiveX controls, without having to modify the code when you add a new control to your Toolbox.

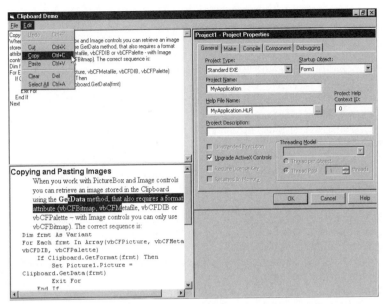

Figure 5-3. *The Clipbord.vbp demonstration project shows how you can create a generic Edit menu that works with TextBox, RTF TextBox, and PictureBox controls.*

```
' Items in Edit menu belong to a control array. These are their indices.
Const MNU_EDITCUT = 2, MNU_EDITCOPY = 3
Const MNU_EDITPASTE = 4, MNU_EDITCLEAR = 6, MNU_EDITSELECTALL = 7


' Enable/disable items in the Edit menu.
Private Sub mnuEdit_Click()
    Dim supSelText As Boolean, supPicture As Boolean
    ' Check which properties are supported by the active control.
    On Error Resume Next
    ' These expressions return False only if the property isn't supported.
    supSelText = Len(ActiveControl.SelText) Or True
    supPicture = (ActiveControl.Picture Is Nothing) Or True

    If supSelText Then
        mnuEditItem(MNU_EDITCUT).Enabled = Len(ActiveControl.SelText)
        mnuEditItem(MNU_EDITPASTE).Enabled = Clipboard.GetFormat(vbCFText)
        mnuEditItem(MNU_EDITCLEAR).Enabled = Len(ActiveControl.SelText)
        mnuEditItem(MNU_EDITSELECTALL).Enabled = Len(ActiveControl.Text)

    ElseIf supPicture Then
        mnuEditItem(MNU_EDITCUT).Enabled = Not (ActiveControl.Picture _
            Is Nothing)
        mnuEditItem(MNU_EDITPASTE).Enabled = Clipboard.GetFormat( _
            vbCFBitmap) Or Clipboard.GetFormat(vbCFMetafile)
```

(continued)

```
            mnuEditItem(MNU_EDITCLEAR).Enabled = _
                Not (ActiveControl.Picture Is Nothing)

        Else
            ' Neither a text- nor a picture-based control
            mnuEditItem(MNU_EDITCUT).Enabled = False
            mnuEditItem(MNU_EDITPASTE).Enabled = False
            mnuEditItem(MNU_EDITCLEAR).Enabled = False
            mnuEditItem(MNU_EDITSELECTALL).Enabled = False
        End If
        ' The Copy menu command always has the same state as the Cut command.
        mnuEditItem(MNU_EDITCOPY).Enabled = mnuEditItem(MNU_EDITCUT).Enabled
End Sub


' Actually perform copy-cut-paste commands.
Private Sub mnuEditItem_Click(Index As Integer)
    Dim supSelText As Boolean, supSelRTF As Boolean, supPicture As Boolean
    ' Check which properties are supported by the active control.
    On Error Resume Next
    supSelText = Len(ActiveControl.SelText) >= 0
    supSelRTF = Len(ActiveControl.SelRTF) >= 0
    supPicture = (ActiveControl.Picture Is Nothing) Or True
    Err.Clear
    Select Case Index
        Case MNU_EDITCUT
            If supSelRTF Then
                Clipboard.Clear
                Clipboard.SetText ActiveControl.SelRTF, vbCFRTF
                ActiveControl.SelRTF = ""
            ElseIf supSelText Then
                Clipboard.Clear
                Clipboard.SetText ActiveControl.SelText
                ActiveControl.SelText = ""
            Else
                Clipboard.SetData ActiveControl.Picture
                Set ActiveControl.Picture = Nothing
            End If

        Case MNU_EDITCOPY
            ' Similar to Cut, but the current selection isn't deleted.
            If supSelRTF Then
                Clipboard.Clear
                Clipboard.SetText ActiveControl.SelRTF, vbCFRTF
            ElseIf supSelText Then
                Clipboard.Clear
                Clipboard.SetText ActiveControl.SelText
```

```
        Else
            Clipboard.SetData ActiveControl.Picture
        End If

    Case MNU_EDITPASTE
        If supSelRTF And Clipboard.GetFormat(vbCFRTF) Then
            ' Paste RTF text if possible.
            ActiveControl.SelRTF = Clipboard.GetText(vbCFText)
        ElseIf supSelText Then
            ' Else, paste regular text.
            ActiveControl.SelText = Clipboard.GetText(vbCFText)
        ElseIf Clipboard.GetFormat(vbCFBitmap) Then
            ' First, try with bitmap data.
            Set ActiveControl.Picture = _
                Clipboard.GetData(vbCFBitmap)
        Else
            ' Else, try with metafile data.
            Set ActiveControl.Picture = _
                Clipboard.GetData(vbCFMetafile)
        End If

    Case MNU_EDITCLEAR
        If supSelText Then
            ActiveControl.SelText = ""
        Else
            Set ActiveControl.Picture = Nothing
        End If

    Case MNU_EDITSELECTALL
        If supSelText Then
            ActiveControl.SelStart = 0
            ActiveControl.SelLength = Len(ActiveControl.Text)
        End If
    End Select
End Sub
```

The Printer Object

Many applications need to deliver their results on paper. Visual Basic provides you with a Printer object that exposes a number of properties and methods to finely control the appearance of your printer documents.

The Visual Basic library also exposes a Printers collection, which lets you collect information about all the printers installed on your system. Each item of this collection is a Printer object, and all its properties are read-only. In other words, you can read the characteristics of all the installed printers, but you can't modify them directly. If you want to modify a characteristic of a printer, you must first assign the item from the collection that represents your chosen printer to the Printer object and then change its properties.

Retrieving information on installed printers

The Printer object exposes many properties that allow you to determine the characteristics of an available printer and its driver. For example, the *DeviceName* property returns the name of the printer as it appears in the Control Panel, and the *DriverName* returns the name of the driver used by that peripheral. It's simple to fill a ListBox or a ComboBox control with this information:

```
For i = 0 To Printers.Count - 1
    cboPrinters.AddItem Printers(i).DeviceName & " [" & _
        Printers(i).DriverName & "]"
Next
```

The *Port* property returns the port the printer is connected to (for example, LPT1:). The *ColorMode* property determines whether the printer can print in color. (It can be 1-vbPRCMMonochrome or 2-vbPRCMColor.) The *Orientation* property reflects the current orientation of the page. (It can be 1-vbPRORPortrait, 2-vbPROR-Landscape.) The *PrinterQuality* property returns the current resolution. (It can be 1-vbPRPQDraft, 2-vbPRPQLow, 3-vbPRPQMedium, or 4-vbPRPQHigh.)

Other properties include *PaperSize* (the size of the paper), *PaperBin* (the paper bin the paper is fed from), *Duplex* (the ability to print both sides of a sheet of paper), *Copies* (the number of copies to be printed), and *Zoom* (the zoom factor applied when printing). For more information about these properties, see the Visual Basic documentation. On the companion CD, you'll find a demonstration program (shown in Figure 5-4) that lets you enumerate all the printers in your system, browse their properties, and print a page on each of them.

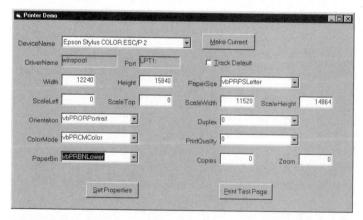

Figure 5-4. *Run this demonstration program to see the Printers collection and the Printer object in action.*

Working with the current printer

A modern application should give its users the ability to work with any printer among those installed on the system. In Visual Basic, you do this by assigning an element of the Printers collection that describes your chosen printer to the Printer object. For example, if you've filled a ComboBox control with the names of all installed printers, you can let users select one of them by clicking on a Make Current button:

```
Private Sub cmdMakeCurrent_Click()
    Set Printer = Printers(cboPrinters.ListIndex)
End Sub
```

In contrast to the restrictions you must observe for Printer objects stored in the Printers collection, whose properties are read-only, you can modify the properties of the Printer object. Theoretically, all the properties seen so far can be written to, with the only exceptions being *DeviceName*, *DriverName*, and *Port*. In practice, however, what happens when you assign a value to a property depends on the printer and the driver. For example, if the current printer is monochrome it doesn't make any sense to assign the 2-vbPRCMColor value to the *ColorMode* property. This assignment either can be ignored or it can raise an error, depending on the driver in use. In general, if a property isn't supported, it returns 0.

At times, you might need to understand which item in the Printers collection the Printer object corresponds to, for example, when you want to print temporarily using another printer and then restore the original printer. You can do this by comparing the *DeviceName* property of the Printer object with the value returned by each item in the Printers collection:

```
' Determine the index of the Printer object in the Printers collection.
For i = 0 To Printers.Count - 1
    If Printer.DeviceName = Printers(i).DeviceName Then
        PrinterIndex = i: Exit For
    End If
Next
' Prepare to output to the printer selected by the user.
Set Printer = Printers(cboPrinters.ListIndex)
' ...
' Restore the original printer.
Set Printer = Printers(PrinterIndex)
```

Another way to let users print to the printer of their choice is to set the Printer's *TrackDefault* property to True. When you do that, the Printer object automatically refers to the printer selected in the Control Panel.

Outputting data to the Printer object

Sending output to the Printer object is trivial because this object supports all the graphic methods that are exposed by the Form and the PictureBox objects, including *Print*, *PSet*, *Line*, *Circle*, and *PaintPicture*. You can also control the appearance of the output using standard properties such as the Font object and the individual *Fontxxxx* properties, the *CurrentX* and *CurrentY* properties, and the *ForeColor* property.

Three methods are peculiar to the Printer object. The *EndDoc* method informs the Printer object that all the data has been sent and that the actual printing operation can start. The *KillDoc* method terminates the current print job before sending anything to the printer device. Finally the *NewPage* method sends the current page to the printer (or the print spooler) and advances to the next page. It also resets the printing position at the upper left corner of the printable area in the page and increments the page number. The current page number can be retrieved using the *Page* property. Here's an example that prints a two-page document:

```
Printer.Print "Page One"
Printer.NewPage
Printer.Print "Page Two"
Printer.EndDoc
```

The Printer object also supports the standard properties *ScaleLeft*, *ScaleTop*, *ScaleWidth*, and *ScaleHeight*, which are expressed in the measurement unit indicated by the *ScaleMode* property (usually in twips). By default, the *ScaleLeft* and *ScaleTop* properties return 0 and refer to the upper left corner of the printable area. The *ScaleWidth* and *ScaleHeight* properties return the coordinates of the lower right corner of the printable area.

Running Other Applications

Visual Basic lets you run other Windows applications using the *Shell* command, which has this syntax:

```
TaskId = Shell(PathName, [WindowStyle])
```

PathName can include a command line. *WindowStyle* is one of the following constants: 0-vbHide (window is hidden and focus is passed to it), 1-vbNormalFocus (window has focus and is restored to its original size and position), 2-vbMinimizedFocus (window is displayed as an icon with focus—this is the default value), 3-vbMaximizedFocus (window is maximized and has the focus), 4-vbNormalNoFocus (window is restored but doesn't have the focus), or 6-vbMinimizedNoFocus (window is minimized and the focus doesn't leave the active window). See, for example, how you can run Notepad and load a file in it:

```
' No need to provide a path if Notepad.Exe is on the system path.
Shell "notepad c:\bootlog.txt", vbNormalFocus
```

The *Shell* function runs the external program asynchronously. This means that the control immediately returns to your Visual Basic application, which can therefore continue to execute its own code. In most cases, this behavior is OK because it takes advantage of the multitasking nature of Windows. But at times you might need to wait for a shelled program to complete (for example, if you need to process its results) or simply to check whether it's still running. Visual Basic doesn't give you a native function to obtain this information, but you can use a few Windows API calls to do the job. I've prepared a multipurpose function that checks whether the shelled program is still executing, waits for the optional timeout you specified (omit the argument to wait forever), and then returns True if the program is still running:

```
' API declarations
Private Declare Function WaitForSingleObject Lib "kernel32" _
    (ByVal hHandle As Long, ByVal dwMilliseconds As Long) As Long
Private Declare Function OpenProcess Lib "kernel32" (ByVal dwAccess As _
    Long, ByVal fInherit As Integer, ByVal hObject As Long) As Long
Private Declare Function CloseHandle Lib "kernel32" _
    (ByVal hObject As Long) As Long


' Wait for a number of milliseconds, and return the running status of a
' process. If argument is omitted, wait until the process terminates.
Function WaitForProcess(taskId As Long, Optional msecs As Long = -1) _
    As Boolean
    Dim procHandle As Long
    ' Get the process handle.
    procHandle = OpenProcess(&H100000, True, taskId)
    ' Check for its signaled status; return to caller.
    WaitForProcess = WaitForSingleObject(procHandle, msecs) <> -1
    ' Close the handle.
    CloseHandle procHandle
End Function
```

The argument passed to this routine is the return value of the *Shell* function:

```
' Run Notepad, and wait until it is closed.
WaitForProcess Shell("notepad c:\bootlog.txt", vbNormalFocus)
```

You have several ways to interact with a running program. In Chapter 16, I show how you can control an application through COM, but not all the external applications can be controlled in this way. And even if they could, sometimes the results aren't worth the additional effort. In less demanding situations, you can get the job done using a simpler approach based on the *AppActivate* and *SendKeys* commands. The *AppActivate* command moves the input focus to the application that matches its first argument:

```
AppActivate WindowTitle [,wait]
```

WindowTitle can be either a string or the return value of a *Shell* function; in the former case, Visual Basic compares the value with the titles of all the active windows in the system. If there isn't an exact match, Visual Basic repeats the search looking for a window whose title begins with the string passed as an argument. When you pass the *taskid* value returned by a *Shell* function, there's no second pass because *taskid* uniquely identifies a running process. If Visual Basic is unable to find the requested window, a run-time error occurs. *Wait* is an optional argument that indicates whether Visual Basic should wait until the current application has the input focus before passing it to the other program (*Wait* = True) or whether the command must execute immediately. (*Wait* = False, the default behavior.)

The *SendKeys* statement sends one or more keys to the application that currently has the input focus. This statement supports a rather complex syntax, which lets you specify control keys such as Ctrl, Alt, and Shift keys, arrow keys, function keys, and so on. (See the Visual Basic documentation for more information.) This code runs Notepad and then gives it the focus and pastes the current clipboard contents in its window:

```
TaskId = Shell("Notepad", vbMaximizedFocus)
AppActivate TaskId
SendKeys "^V"          ' ctrl-V
```

You now have all you need to run an external program, interact with it, and find out, if you want, when it completes its execution. I've prepared a demonstration program that does this and lets you experiment with a few different settings. (See Figure 5-5.) Its complete source code is on the companion CD.

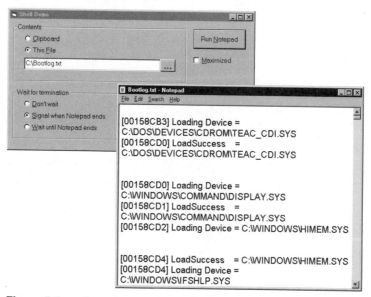

Figure 5-5. *A demonstration program that illustrates how to use* Shell, AppActivate, *and* SendKeys *statements.*

Showing Help

A successful Windows application should always provide a guide to novice users, typically in the form of a help file. Visual Basic supports two different ways to display such user information, both using the pages of HLP files.

Writing a help file

In both cases, you must first create a help file. To do this, you need a word processor capable of generating files in RTF format (such as Microsoft Word) and a help compiler. On the Visual Basic 6 CD-ROM, you can find the Microsoft Help Workshop, shown in Figure 5-6, which lets you assemble all the docs and bitmaps you have prepared and compile them into an HLP file.

Writing a help file is a complex matter, well beyond the scope of this book. You can get information about this topic from the documentation installed with the Microsoft Help Workshop. In my opinion, however, the most effective approach to this issue is to rely on third-party shareware or commercial programs, such as Blue Sky Software's RoboHelp or WexTech's Doc-to-Help, which make the building of a help file a simple and visual process.

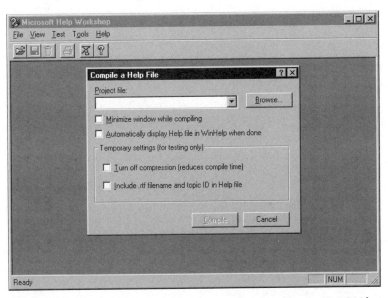

Figure 5-6. *The Help Workshop utility is on the Visual Basic CD-ROM but must be installed separately.*

Once you have generated an HLP file, you can reference it in your Visual Basic application. You do that either at design time by typing the file's name in the General tab of the Project Properties dialog box or at run time by assigning a value to the *App.HelpFile* property. The latter approach is necessary when you aren't sure about where the help file will be installed. For instance, you can set this path in a directory under the main folder of your application:

```
' If this file reference is incorrect, Visual Basic raises an error
' when you later try to access this file.
App.HelpFile = App.Path & "\Help\MyApplication.Hlp"
```

Standard Windows help

The first way to offer context-sensitive help is based on the F1 key. This type of help uses the *HelpContextID* property, which is supported by all Visual Basic visible objects, including forms, intrinsic controls, and external ActiveX controls. You can also enter an application-wide help context ID at design time, in the Project Properties dialog box. (The App object doesn't expose an equivalent property at run time, though.)

When the user presses F1, Visual Basic checks whether the *HelpContextID* property of the control that has the focus has a nonzero value: in this case, it displays the help page associated with that ID. Otherwise, Visual Basic checks whether the parent form has a nonzero *HelpContextID* property, and in that case displays the corresponding help page. If both the control's and the form's *HelpContextID* properties are 0, Visual Basic displays the page that corresponds to the project's help context ID.

What's This help

Visual Basic also supports an additional way of displaying help, the so-called What's This help. You can add support for this help mode by showing the What's This button at the upper right of a form, as you can see in Figure 5-7. When the user clicks on this button, the mouse cursor changes into an arrow and a question mark, and the user can then click on any control on the form to get a quick explanation of what that control is and does.

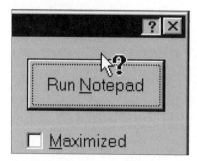

Figure 5-7. *A zoomed screenshot of the upper right corner of a form whose What's This button has just been clicked.*

To take advantage of this feature in your programs, you must set the form's *WhatsThisButton* property to True, which makes the What's This button appear on the form caption. This property is read-only at run time, so you can set it only at design time in the Properties window. Moreover, to get the What's This button to appear, you must either set the *BorderStyle* property to 1-Fixed Single or to 3-Fixed Dialog, or you must set the properties *MaxButton* and *MinButton* to False.

If you can't meet these requirements, you can't display the What's This button. But you can always provide users with a button or a menu command that enters this mode by executing the form's *WhatsThisMode* method:

```
Private Sub cmdWhatsThis_Click()
    ' Enter What's This mode and change mouse cursor shape.
    WhatsThisMode
End Sub
```

Each control on the form (but not the form itself) exposes the *WhatsThisHelpID* property. You assign this property the help context ID of the page that will be displayed when the user clicks on the control while in What's This mode.

Finally the form's *WhatsThisHelp* property must be set to True to activate the What's This help. If this property is set to False, Visual Basic reverts to the standard help mechanism based on the F1 key and the *HelpContextID* property. The *WhatsThisHelp* property can be set only at design time. At this point, you have three different ways to display a What's This? help topic:

■ The user clicks on the What's This button and then on a control; in this case, Visual Basic automatically displays the What's This help associated with the *WhatsThisHelpID* property of the clicked control.

■ The user clicks on a button or selects a menu item that programmatically enters the What's This help mode by means of the *WhatsThisMode* method (see the previous code snippet) and then clicks on a control. Again, Visual Basic displays the What's This help associated with the *WhatsThisHelpID* property of the clicked control.

■ You can programmatically invoke the What's This help associated with the *WhatsThisHelpID* property of a control by executing the control's *ShowWhatsThis* method. (All intrinsic and external controls support this method.)

Whatever approach you follow, don't forget that you have to prepare a help page for each control on each form of your application. It's legal to have multiple controls share the same help page, but this arrangement can be quite confusing to the user. Therefore, you typically associate a distinct page with each control.

In these first five chapters, I've shown you how to get the maximum out of the Visual Basic environment and the VBA language. By now, you have enough information to write nontrivial programs. The focus of this book, however, is on object-oriented programming, and in the next two chapters I hope to convince you how much you need OOP to build complex, real-world applications.

Chapter 6

Classes
and Objects

Since Microsoft Visual Basic 4 introduced the concept of class modules, a furious debate has raged among Visual Basic developers about the object-oriented nature of the language. Is Visual Basic a *real* object-oriented programming (OOP) language? Is it just an *object-based* language? Or is it somewhere between these two extremes?

For what it's worth, my position on the question is a compromise: Visual Basic definitively is *not* a true OOP language and it won't be one until it possesses some essential OOP features, such as inheritance. But this deficit shouldn't excuse your not learning in depth what classes and objects have to offer developers. This is what I'll show in this chapter and in the remainder of this book:

■ Class modules can immensely improve your productivity, help you solve many common and intricate programming problems, and even permit you to perform tasks that would be extremely difficult, if not impossible, otherwise.

■ Even if Visual Basic isn't a full-fledged object-oriented programming language, you can still use its classes to better organize your code into truly reusable modules and design your applications entirely using concepts derived from the Object-Oriented Design discipline. In this sense, the inclusion of a tool such as Visual Modeler in the Enterprise Edition is a clear sign of Microsoft's will to pursue this goal.

■   Most important, objects are the base on which almost every feature of Visual Basic is implemented. For example, without objects you can't do serious database programming, you can't deliver Internet applications, and you can't write components for COM, DCOM, or MTS. In short, you can do little or nothing without a firm grasp on what objects are and how you can take advantage of them.

If you're absolutely new to object-oriented programming, this could be the most difficult chapter of the entire book for you to grasp. To understand how objects can help you write better programs in less time, you must be ready for a conceptual leap, not unlike the leap that many programmers had to take when switching from pure procedural MS-DOS languages such as QuickBasic to newer and more sophisticated event-driven programming environments such as Visual Basic. But once you grasp the basic concepts of OOP, you'll probably agree that objects are the most exciting thing to happen to Visual Basic since its first version. When you dive into object-oriented programming, you'll soon find yourself devising new, concise, and elegant solutions to old problems, often in less time and with less code. But I don't want to sound intimidating. As a Visual Basic programmer, you've already learned to master many advanced programming techniques concerned with, for example, events, database programming, and user interface issues. OOP isn't more difficult, it's merely different. And it's certainly a lot of fun.

If you've ever read books or articles about OOP, you surely found dozens of different definitions for the term *object*. Most of the definitions are correct and confusing at the same time. The definition I like most is this one:

An object is an entity that embeds both data and the code that deals with it.

Let's see what this means in practice.

THE BASIC CONCEPTS

I have noticed that many programmers exposed for the first time to OOP tend to confuse classes and objects, so a very short explanation is in order. A *class* is a portion of the program (a source code file, in Visual Basic) that defines the properties, methods, and events—in a word, behavior—of one or more objects that will be created during execution. An *object* is an entity created at run time, which requires memory and possibly other system resources, and is then destroyed when it's no longer needed or when the application ends. In a sense, classes are design time–only entities, while objects are run time–only entities.

Your users will never *see* a class; rather, they'll probably see and interact with objects created from your classes, such as invoices, customer data, or circles on the screen. As a programmer, your point of view is reversed because the most concrete thing you'll have in front of you while you're writing the application is the class, in the form of a class module in the Visual Basic environment. Until you run the application, an object isn't more real than a variable declared with a *Dim* statement in a code listing. In my opinion, this dichotomy has prevented many Visual Basic programmers from embracing the OOP paradigm. We have been spoiled by the RAD (Rapid Application Development) orientation of our favorite tool and often think of objects as *visible* objects, such as forms, controls, and so on. While Visual Basic can also create such visible objects—including Microsoft ActiveX controls—you won't grasp the real power of object orientation until you realize that *almost everything* in your program can be an object, from concrete and visible entities such as invoices, products, customers, employees, and so on to more abstract ones such as the validation process or the relationship between two tables.

The Main Benefits of OOP

Before getting practical, I'd like to hint at what object-oriented programming has to offer you. I'll do that by listing the key features of OOPLs (object-oriented programming languages) and explaining some concepts. An understanding of these ideas will turn out to be very useful later in the chapter.

Encapsulation

Encapsulation is probably the feature that programmers appreciate most in object-oriented programming. In a nutshell, an object is the sole owner of its own data. All data is stored inside a memory area that can't be directly accessed by another portion of the application, and all assignment and retrieval operations are performed through methods and properties provided by the object itself. This simple concept has at least two far-reaching consequences:

- ■ You can check all the values assigned to object properties before they're actually stored in memory and immediately reject all invalid ones.

- ■ You're free to change the internal implementation of the data stored in an object without changing the way the rest of the program interacts with the object. This means that you can later modify and improve the internal workings of a class without changing a single line of code elsewhere in the application.

As with most OOP features, it's your responsibility to ensure that the class is well encapsulated. The fact that you're using a class doesn't guarantee that the goals of encapsulation are met. In this and the next chapter, I'll show you how some simple rules—and common sense—help you implement *robust* classes. A robust class is one that actively protects its internal data from tampering. If an object derived from a class holds valid data and all the operations you perform on that object transform the data only into other valid data (or raise an error if the operation isn't valid), you can be absolutely sure that the object will always be in a valid state and will never propagate a wrong value to the rest of the program. This is a simple but incredibly powerful concept that lets you considerably streamline the process of debugging your code.

The second goal that every programmer should pursue is *code reusability,* which you achieve by creating classes that are easily maintained and reused in other applications. This is a key factor in reducing the development time and cost. Classes offer much in this respect, but again they require your cooperation. When you start writing a new class, you should always ask yourself: Is there any chance that this class can be useful in other applications? How can I make this class as independent as possible from the particular software I'm developing right now? In most cases, this means adding a few additional properties or additional arguments to methods, but the effort often pays off nicely. Don't forget that you can always resort to default values for properties and optional arguments for methods, so in most cases these enhancements won't really make the code that uses the class more complex than it actually needs to be.

The concept of *self-containment* is also strictly related to code reuse and encapsulation. If you want to create a class module that's easily reusable, you absolutely must not allow that class to depend on any entity outside it, such as a global variable. This would break encapsulation (because code elsewhere in the application might change the value of the variable to some invalid data) and above all, it would prevent you from reusing the class elsewhere without also copying the global variable (and its parent BAS module). For the same reason, you should try to make the class independent of general-purpose routines located in another module. In most cases, I prefer to duplicate shorter routines in each class module, if this makes the class easily movable elsewhere.

Polymorphism

Informally, *Polymorphism* is the ability of different classes to expose similar (or identical) interfaces to the outside. The most evident kind of polymorphism in Visual Basic is forms and controls. TextBox and PictureBox controls are completely different objects, but they have some properties and methods in common, such as *Left, Back-Color,* and *Move.* This similarity simplifies your job as a programmer because you don't have to remember hundreds of different names and syntax formats. More important, it lets you manage a group of controls using a single variable (typed as Control, Variant, or Object) and create generic procedures that act on all the controls on a form and therefore noticeably reduce the amount of code you have to write.

Inheritance

Inheritance is the ability, offered by many OOP languages, to derive a new class (the *derived* or *inherited* class) from another class (the *base* class). The derived class automatically inherits the properties and methods of the base class. For example, you could define a generic *Shape* class with properties such as *Color* and *Position* and then use it as a base for more specific classes (for example, *Rectangle, Circle,* and so on) that inherit all those generic properties. You could then add specific members, such as *Width* and *Height* for the *Rectangle* class and *Radius* for the *Circle* class. It's interesting to note that, while polymorphism tends to reduce the amount of code necessary to use the class, inheritance reduces the code inside the class itself and therefore simplifies the job of the class creator. Unfortunately, Visual Basic doesn't support inheritance, at least not in its more mature form of implementation inheritance. In the next chapter, I show how you can simulate inheritance by manually writing code and explain when and why this can be useful.

Your First Class Module

Creating a class in Visual Basic is straightforward: just issue an Add Class Module command from the Project menu. A new code editor window appears on an empty listing. By default, the first class module is named *Class1*, so the very first thing you should do is change this into a more appropriate name. In this first example, I show how to encapsulate personal data related to a person, so I'm naming this first class CPerson.

> **NOTE** I admit it: I'm not a fanatic about naming conventions. Microsoft suggests that you use the *cls* prefix for class module names, but I don't comply simply because I feel it makes my code less readable. I often prefer to use the shorter *C* prefix for classes (and *I* for interfaces), and sometimes I use no prefix at all, especially when objects are grouped in hierarchies. Of course, this is a matter of personal preference, and I don't insist that my system is more rational than any other.

The first version of our class includes only a few properties. These properties are exposed as Public members of the class module itself, as you can see in this code and also in Figure 6-1 on the following page:

```
' In the declaration section of the CPerson class module
Public FirstName As String
Public LastName As String
```

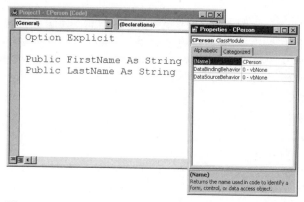

Figure 6-1. *Creating a class module, giving it a name in the Properties window, and adding some Public variables in the code editor window.*

This is a very simple class, but it's a good starting point for experimenting with some interesting concepts, without being distracted by details. Once you have created a class module, you can declare an object variable that refers to an instance of that class:

```
' In a form module
Private Sub cmdCreatePerson_Click()
    Dim pers As CPerson                                  ' Declare.
    Set pers = New CPerson                               ' Create.
    pers.FirstName = "John"                              ' Assign properties.
    pers.LastName = "Smith"
    Print pers.FirstName & " " & pers.LastName           ' Check that it works.
End Sub
```

The code's not very impressive, admittedly. But remember that here we're just laying down concepts whose real power will be apparent only when we apply them to more complex objects in real-world applications.

Auto-instancing object variables

Unlike regular variables, which can be used as soon they have been declared, an object variable must be explicitly assigned an object reference before you can invoke the object's properties and methods. In fact, when an object variable hasn't been assigned yet, it contains the special *Nothing* value: In other words, it doesn't contain any valid reference to an actual object. To see what this means, just try out this code:

```
Dim pers As CPerson             ' Declare the variable,
' Set pers = New CPerson        ' but comment out the creation step.
Print pers.FirstName            ' This raises an error 91 - "Object variable
                                ' or With block variable not set"
```

In most cases, this behavior is desirable because it doesn't make much sense to print a property of an object that doesn't exist. A way to avoid the error is to test the current contents of an object variable using the *Is Nothing* test:

```
' Use the variable only if it contains a valid object reference
If Not (pers Is Nothing) Then Print pers.FirstName
```

In other cases, however, you just want to create an object, *any* object, and then assign its properties. In these circumstances, you might find it useful to declare an *auto-instancing* object variable using the *As New* clause:

```
Dim pers As New CPerson        ' Auto-instancing variable
```

When at run time Visual Basic encounters a reference to an auto-instancing variable, it first determines whether it's pointing to an existing object and creates a brand new instance of the class if necessary. Auto-instancing variables have virtues and liabilities, plus a few quirks you should be aware of:

■ Auto-instancing variables obviously reduce the amount of code you need to write to be up and running with your classes. For this reason, they're often valuable during the prototyping phase.

■ Auto-instancing variables can't be tested against the Nothing value. In fact, as soon as you use one in the *Is Nothing* test, Visual Basic relentlessly creates a new instance and the test always returns False. In some cases, this could be the decisive factor in whether to stay clear of auto-instancing variables.

■ Auto-instancing variables tend to eliminate errors, but sometimes this is precisely what you don't need. In fact, during the development phase you *want* to see errors because they're the symptoms of other serious flaws in the code logic. Auto-instancing variables make the debugging step a little more obscure because you can never be sure when and why an object was created. This is probably the most persuasive reason *not* to use auto-instancing variables.

■ You can't declare an auto-instancing variable of a generic type, such as Object, Form, or MDIForm because Visual Basic must know in advance which kind of object should be created when it references that variable for the first time.

■ In some complex routines, you might declare a variable but never actually use it: this happens all the time with standard variables and with object variables too, but it creates a problem with regular (non-auto-instancing) object variables. In fact, if you create the object with a *Set* command at the beginning of a procedure, you might be creating an object—thus taking both time and memory—for no real purpose. On the other hand, if you delay the creation of an object until you actually need it, you could soon find yourself drowning in a sea of *Set* commands, each preceded by an *Is Nothing* test to avoid re-creating an object instanced previously. By comparison, auto-instancing variables are automatically created by Visual Basic only if and when they are referenced: In all other cases, no time or memory will be wasted without reason. This is probably the situation in which auto-instancing variables are most useful.

■ Finally, each time Visual Basic references an auto-instancing variable, it incurs a small performance hit because it has to check whether it's Nothing. This overhead is usually negligible, but in some time-critical routines it could affect the overall time.

In summary, auto-instancing variables often aren't the best choice, and in general I advise you not to use them. Most of the code shown in this chapter doesn't make use of auto-instancing variables, and you can often do without them in your own applications as well.

Property procedures

Let's go back to the CPerson class and see how the class can protect itself from invalid assignments, such as an empty string for its *FirstName* or *LastName* properties. To achieve this goal, you have to change the internal implementation of the class module because in its present form you have no means of trapping the assignment operation. What you have to do is transform those values into Private members and encapsulate them in pairs of Property procedures. This example shows the code for *Property Get* and *Let FirstName* procedures, and the code for *LastName* is similar.

```
' Private member variables
Private m_FirstName As String
Private m_LastName As String

' Note that all Property procedures are Public by default.
Property Get FirstName() As String
    ' Simply return the current value of the member variable.
    FirstName = m_FirstName
End Property

Property Let FirstName(ByVal newValue As String)
    ' Raise an error if an invalid assignment is attempted.
    If newValue = "" Then Err.Raise 5    ' Invalid procedure argument
    ' Else store in the Private member variable.
    m_FirstName = newValue
End Property
```

NOTE You can save some typing using the Add Procedure command from the Tools menu, which creates for you the templates for *Property Get* and *Let* procedures. But you should then edit the result because all properties created in this way are of type Variant.

Add this code and write your own procedures for handling the *LastName*; then run the program, and you'll see that everything works as before. What you have done, however, is make the class a bit more robust because it now refuses to assign invalid values to its properties. To see what I mean, just try this command:

```
pers.Name = ""        ' Raises error "Invalid procedure call or argument"
```

If you trace the program by pressing F8 to advance through individual statements, you'll understand what those two Property procedures actually do. Each time you assign a new value to a property, Visual Basic checks whether there's an associated *Property Let* procedure and passes it the new value. If your code can't validate the new value, it raises an error and throws the execution back to the caller. Otherwise, the execution proceeds by assigning the value to the private variable *m_FirstName*. I like to use the *m_* prefix to keep the property name and the corresponding private member variable in sync, but this is just another personal preference; feel free to use it or to create your own rules. When the caller code requests the value of the property, Visual Basic executes the corresponding *Property Get* procedure, which (in this case) simply returns the value of the Private variable. The type expected by the *Property Let* procedure must match the type of the value returned by the *Property Get* procedure. In fact, as far as Visual Basic is concerned, the type of the property *is* the returned type of the *Property Get* procedure. (This distinction will make more sense later, when I'm explaining Variant properties.)

It isn't always clear what *validating* a property value really means. Some properties can't be validated without your also considering what happens outside the class. For example, you can't easily validate a product name without accessing a database of products. To keep things simpler, add a new *BirthDate* property and validate it in a reasonable way:

```
Private m_BirthDate As Date

Property Get BirthDate() As Date
    BirthDate = m_BirthDate
End Property
Property Let BirthDate(ByVal newValue As Date)
    If newValue >= Now Then Err.Raise 1001, , "Future Birth Date !"
    m_BirthDate = newValue
End Property
```

Methods

A class module can also include Sub and Function procedures, which are collectively known as *methods* of the class. As in other types of modules, the only difference between a Function method and a Sub is that a Function method returns a value, whereas a Sub method doesn't. Since Visual Basic lets you invoke a function and discard its return value, I usually prefer to create Function methods that return a secondary value: This practice adds value to the procedure without getting in the way when the user of the class doesn't actually need the return value.

What methods could be useful in this simple CPerson class? When you start dealing with records for many people, you could easily find yourself printing their complete names over and over. So you might want to devise a way to print a full name quickly and simply. The *procedural way of thinking* that solves this simple task would suggest that you create a function in a global BAS module:

```
' In a BAS module
Function CompleteName(pers As CPerson) As String
    CompleteName = pers.FirstName & " " & pers.LastName
End Function
```

While this code works, it isn't the most elegant way to perform the task. In fact, the complete name concept is internal to the class, so you're missing an opportunity to make the class smarter and easier to use. Besides, you're also making it difficult to reuse the class itself because you now have scattered its intelligence all over your application. The best approach is to add a new method to the CPerson class itself:

```
' In the CPerson class
Function CompleteName() As String
    CompleteName = FirstName & " " & LastName
End Function
```

```
' In the form module, you can now execute the method.
Print pers.CompleteName          ' Prints "John Smith"
```

While you're within the class module, you don't need the dot syntax to refer to the properties of the current instance. On the other hand, if you're within the class and you refer to a Public name for a property (*FirstName*) instead of the corresponding Private member variable (*m_FirstName*), Visual Basic executes the *Property Get* procedure as if the property were referenced from outside the class. This is perfectly normal, and it's even desirable. In fact, you should always try to adhere to the following rule: Reference private member variables in a class only from the corresponding *Property Let/Get* procedures. If you later modify the internal implementation of the property, you'll have to modify only a small portion of the code in the class module. Sometimes you can't avoid substantial code modifications, but you should do your best to apply this rule as often as you can. Once you understand the mechanism, you can add much intelligence to your class, as in the following code:

```
Function ReverseName() As String
    ReverseName = LastName & ", " & FirstName
End Function
```

Remember that you're just adding code and that no additional memory will be used at run time to store the values of complete and reversed names.

The more intelligence you add to your class, the happier the programmer who uses this class (yourself, in most cases) will be. One of the great things about classes is that all the methods and properties you add to them are immediately visible in the Object Browser, together with their complete syntax. If you carefully select the names of your properties and methods, picking the right procedure for each different task becomes almost fun.

The *Class Initialize* event

As you start building classes, you'll soon notice how often you want to assign a well-defined value to a property at the time of the creation of the object itself, without having to specify it in the caller code. For example, if you're dealing with an Employee object you can reasonably expect that in most cases its *Citizenship* property is "American" (or whatever nationality applies where you live). Similarly, in most cases the *AddressFrom* property in a hypothetical Invoice object will probably match the address of the company you're working for. In all cases, you'd like for these default values to be assigned when you create an object, rather than your having to assign them manually in the code that uses the class.

Visual Basic offers a neat way to achieve this goal. In fact, all you have to do is write some statements in the *Class_Initialize* event of the class module. To have the editor create a template for this event procedure, you select the Class item in the leftmost combo box in the code editor. Visual Basic automatically selects the Initialize item from the rightmost combo box control and inserts the template into the code window. Here's a *Citizenship* property that defaults to "American":

```
' The Private member variable
Private m_Citizenship As String

Private Sub Class_Initialize()
    m_Citizenship = "American"
End Sub
' Code for Public Property Get/Let Citizenship procedure ... (omitted)
```

If you now run the program you have built so far and trace through it, you'll see that as soon as Visual Basic creates the object (the *Set* command in the form module), the *Class_Initialize* event fires. The object is returned to the caller with all the properties correctly initialized, and you don't have to assign them in an explicit way. The *Class_Initialize* event has a matching *Class_Terminate* event, which fires when the object instance is destroyed by Visual Basic. In this procedure, you usually close your open files and databases and execute your other cleanup tasks. I will describe the *Class_Terminate* event at the end of this chapter.

Debugging a class module

In most respects, debugging code inside a class module isn't different from debugging code in, say, a form module. But when you have multiple objects that interact with one another, you might easily get lost in the code. Which particular instance are you looking at in a given moment? What are its current properties? Of course, you can use all the usual debugging tools—including *Debug.Print* statements, data tips, Instant Watch, and so on. But the one that beats them all is the Locals window, which you can see in Figure 6-2. Just keep this window open and you'll know at every moment where you are, how your code affects the object properties, and so on. All in real time.

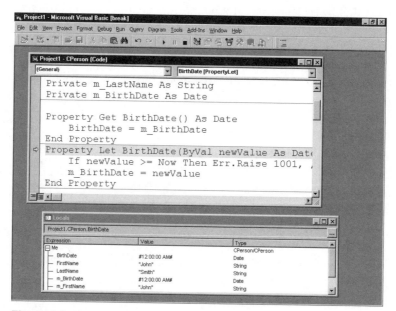

Figure 6-2. *The Locals window is a great debugging tool when you're working with multiple objects.*

The *Me* keyword

Sometimes a class must reference itself in code. This is useful, for instance, when an object must pass a reference to itself to another routine. This can be done using the *Me* keyword. In the following sample code, I have prepared a couple of general-purpose routines in a BAS module, which help keep track of when an object is created and destroyed:

```
' In a Standard BAS module
Sub TraceInitialize (obj As Object)
    Debug.Print "Created a " & TypeName(obj) _
        & " object at time " & Time$
End Sub
Sub TraceTerminate (obj As Object)
    Debug.Print "Destroyed a " & TypeName(obj) _
        & " object at time " & Time$
End Sub
```

Here's how you use these routines from within the CPerson class module:

```
Private Sub Class_Initialize()
    TraceInitialize Me
End Sub

Private Sub Class_Terminate()
    TraceTerminate Me
End Sub
```

The *Me* keyword has other uses as well, as you'll discover in this and the next chapter.

PROPERTIES, METHODS, AND EVENTS

It's time to see how you can put all the capabilities you've seen so far to good use. I'll continue to develop the original CPerson class as an example and expand it as I introduce new concepts.

Read-Only and Write-Only Properties

If you look at how Visual Basic defines its own objects (forms, controls, and so on), you'll notice that not all properties can be both read from and written to. For example, you can't modify the *MultiSelect* property of a ListBox control at run time, and you can't modify the height of a ComboBox control even at design time. Depending on the nature of your class, you might have many good reasons to limit the access to your properties, making them read-only or (less frequently) write-only.

Read-only properties
Say that you want to add an *Age* property to your CPerson class. It depends on the *BirthDate* property, so it should be a read-only property. In Visual Basic, you can make a property read-only by simply omitting its *Property Let* procedure:

```
Property Get Age() As Integer
    Age = Year(Now) - Year(BirthDate)
End Property
```

To prove that you now have a read-only property, try to execute this code:

```
pers.Age = 50
```

The Visual Basic compiler traps this logical error as soon as you try to run your program and won't compile the program until you correct or delete the statement.

Write-only properties

Occasionally, you might even want to create write-only properties. A typical example is a *Password* property exposed by an imaginary LoginDialog object. The property can be assigned to validate the login process but shouldn't be readable so as not to compromise the security of the application itself. In Visual Basic, such a write-only property can be easily implemented by writing a *Property Let* procedure while omitting the corresponding *Property Get* routine:

```
Private m_Password As String

Property Let Password(ByVal newValue As String)
    ' Validate the password, raise error if not valid.
    ' ...
    ' If all is OK, assign to Private member variable.
    m_Password = newValue
End Property
```

To be honest, I don't often find anything very useful for this particular Visual Basic feature to do, so I have reported it mostly for the sake of completeness. Write-only properties are often confusing and are perceived as unnatural by most developers. If need dictates a write-only property, I prefer to create a method that accepts the value as an argument (*SetPassword*, in this particular example).

Write-once/read-many properties

Write-once/read-many properties are a bit more interesting and useful than pure write-only properties. For example, the LoginDialog object described in the previous paragraph might expose a *UserName* property of this type. Once a user logs in, your code assigns his or her name to this property; the rest of the application can then read it but can't modify it. Here's another example: in an *Invoice* class, the *Number* property might be rendered as a write-once/read-many property because once you assign a number to an invoice, arbitrarily changing it might cause serious problems in your accounting system.

Visual Basic doesn't offer a native system to implement such write-once/read-many properties, but it's easy to do that with some additional lines of code. Let's say that you want to provide our CPerson class with an *ID* property that can be assigned only once but read as many times as you need. Here's a possible solution, based on a Static local variable:

```
Private m_ID As Long

Public Property Get ID() As Long
    ID = m_ID
End Property
Public Property Let ID(ByVal newValue As Long)
    Static InitDone As Boolean
    If InitDone Then Err.Raise 1002, , "Write-once property"
    InitDone = True
    m_ID = newValue
End Property
```

Here's an alternative solution, which spares you the additional Static variable but consumes some additional bytes in memory (16 bytes instead of 6):

```
Private m_ID As Variant

Public Property Get ID() As Long
    ID = m_ID
End Property
Public Property Let ID(ByVal newValue As Long)
    If Not IsEmpty(m_ID) Then Err.Raise 1002, , "Write-once property"
    m_ID = newValue
End Property
```

In both cases, the interface that the class exposes to the outside is the same. (*ID* is a Long property.) This is another example of how a good encapsulation scheme lets you vary the internal implementation of a class without affecting the code that uses it.

Read-only properties vs. methods

From the point of view of the client code (that is, the code that actually uses your class), a read-only property is similar to a function. In fact, in all cases a read-only property can be invoked only in expressions and can never appear to the left of an assignment symbol. So this raises a sort of semantic problem: When is it preferable to implement a read-only property and when is a function better? I can't offer rigid rules, just a few suggestions:

■ Most programmers expect properties to be quick shortcuts to values stored in the class. If the routine that you're building serves mostly to *return* a value stored inside the class or can be quickly and easily reevaluated, create a property because this is probably the way the client code will look at it anyway. If the routine serves mostly to *evaluate* a complex value, use a function.

- If you can find it useful to call the routine and discard its return value (in other words, it's more important what the routine does than what it returns), write a function. VBA lets you call a function as if it were a Sub, which isn't possible with a *Property Get* procedure.

- If you can imagine that in the future the value returned by the routine could be assigned to, use a *Property Get* procedure, and reserve for yourself the chance to add a *Property Let* routine when it's needed.

> **NOTE** What happens when you try to assign a value to a read-only property is slightly different from when you try to assign to a function. In the former case, you receive a plain error—"Can't assign to read-only property"—whereas in the latter, you get a more cryptic "Function call on left-hand side of assignment must return Variant or Object." The real meaning of this strange message will be clear when I cover object properties later in this chapter.

Let's take the *CompleteName* member of the CPerson class as an example. It has been implemented as a method, but most programmers would undoubtedly think of it as a read-only property. Moreover—and this is the really important point—nothing prevents you from morphing it into a read/write property:

```
Property Get CompleteName() As String
    CompleteName = FirstName & " " & LastName
End Property
Property Let CompleteName(ByVal newValue As String)
    Dim items() As String
    items() = Split(newValue)
    ' We expect exactly two items (no support for middle names).
    If UBound(items) <> 1 Then Err.Raise 5
    ' If no error, assign to the "real" properties.
    FirstName = items(0): LastName = items(1)
End Property
```

You have increased the usability of the class by letting the client code assign the *FirstName* and *LastName* properties in a more natural way, for example, directly from a field on the form:

```
pers.CompleteName = txtCompleteName.Text
```

And of course you can still assign individual *FirstName* and *LastName* properties without the risk of creating inconsistencies with the *CompleteName* property. This is another of those cute little things you can do with classes.

Properties with arguments

So far, I've illustrated *Property Get* procedures with no arguments and their matching *Property Let* procedures with just one argument, the value being assigned to the procedure. Visual Basic also lets you create Property procedures that accept any number of arguments, of any type. This concept is also used by Visual Basic for its own controls: for example, the *List* property of ListBox controls accepts a numerical index.

Let's see how this concept can be usefully applied to the CPerson sample class. Suppose you need a *Notes* property, but at the same time you don't want to limit yourself to just one item. The first solution that comes to mind is using an array of strings. Unfortunately, if you declare a Public array in a class module as follows:

```
Public Notes(1 To 10) As String        ' Not valid!
```

the compiler complains with the following message, "Constants, fixed-length strings, arrays, user-defined types, and Declare statements not allowed as Public member of object modules." But you can create a Private member array and expose it to the outside using a pair of Property procedures:

```
' A module-level variable
Private m_Notes(1 To 10) As String

Property Get Notes(Index As Integer) As String
    Notes = m_Notes (Index)
End Property
Property Let Notes(Index As Integer, ByVal newValue As String)
    ' Check for subscript out of range error.
    If Index < LBound(m_Notes) Or Index > UBound(m_Notes) Then Err.Raise 9
    m_Notes(Index) = newValue
End Property
```

> **CAUTION**   You might be tempted not to check the *Index* argument in the *Property Let* procedure in the preceding code, relying instead on the default behavior of Visual Basic that would raise an error anyway. Think about it again, and try to imagine what would happen if you later decide to optimize your code by setting the Remove Array Bounds Checks optimization for the compiler. (The answer is easy: Can you spell "G-P-F"?)

Now you can assign and retrieve up to 10 distinct notes for the same person, as in this code:

```
pers.Notes(1) = "Ask if it's OK to go fishing next Sunday"
Print pers.Notes(2) ' Displays "" (not initialized)
```

You can improve this mechanism by making *Index* an optional argument that defaults to the first item in the array, as in the following code:

```
Property Get Notes(Optional Index As Integer = 1) As String
    ' ... (omitted: no need to change code inside the procedure)
End Property
```

(continued)

```
Property Let Notes(Optional Index As Integer = 1, _
    ByVal newValue As String)
    ' ... (omitted : no need to change code inside the procedure)
End Property


' In the client code, you can omit the index for the default note.
pers.Notes = "Ask if it's OK to go fishing next Sunday"
' You can always display all notes with a simple For-Next loop.
For i = 1 To 10: Print pers.Notes(i): Next
```

You can also use optional Variant arguments and the *IsMissing* function, as you would do for regular procedures in a form or standard module. In practice, this is rarely required, but it's good to know that you can do it if you need to.

Properties as Public variables in a class

I have already described the convenience of using *Property Get* and *Let* procedures instead of plain Public variables in a class: You get more control, you can validate data assigned to the property, you can trace the execution flow, and so on. But here's one more interesting detail that you should be aware of. Even if you declare a Public variable, what Visual Basic actually does is create a hidden pair of Property procedures for you and calls them whenever you reference the property from outside the class:

```
' Inside the CPerson class
Public Height As Single   ' Height in inches


' Outside the class
pers.Height = 70.25       ' This calls a hidden Property Let procedure.
```

Apart from a slight performance hit—invoking a procedure is surely slower than accessing a variable—this Visual Basic behavior doesn't appear to be a detail worth mentioning. Unfortunately, this isn't the case. Let's suppose that you want to convert all your measurements into centimeters, so you prepare a simple procedure that does the job with its *ByRef* argument:

```
' In a standard BAS module
Sub ToCentimeters (value As Single)
    ' Value is received by reference, therefore it can be changed.
    value = value * 2.54
End Sub
```

You think you can legitimately expect an easy conversion for your objects' properties, as follows:

```
ToCentimeters pers.Height                     ' Doesn't work!
```

The reason the preceding approach fails should be clear, now that you know that Public variables are implemented as hidden procedures. In fact, when you pass the *pers.Height* value to the *ToCentimeters* procedure you're passing the result of an expression, not an actual memory address. Therefore, the routine has no address to which to deliver the new value, and the result of the conversion is lost.

> **CAUTION** Microsoft changed the way the Public variables in class modules are implemented. In Visual Basic 4, these variables weren't encapsulated in hidden property procedures; therefore, they could be modified if passed to a procedure through a *ByRef* argument. This implementation detail changed when Visual Basic 5 was released, and many Visual Basic 4 programmers had to re-work their code to comply with the new style by creating a temporary variable that actually receives the new value:
>
> ```
> ' The fix that VB4 developers had to apply when porting to VB5
> Dim temp As Single
> temp = pers.Height
> ToCentimeter temp
> pers.Height = temp
> ```
>
> This code is neither elegant nor efficient. Worse, since this technique isn't clearly documented, many programmers had to figure it out on their own. If you are about to port some Visual Basic 4 code to versions 5 or 6, don't be caught off guard.

Anyway, here's yet another untold episode of the story. What I have described so far is what happens when you reference the Public variable from *outside* the class. If you invoke the external procedure from inside the class module and pass it your variable, everything works as expected. In other words, you can write this code in the CPerson class:

```
' Inside the CPerson class
ToCentimeter Height                    ' It works!
```

and the *Height* property will be correctly updated. In this case, the value passed is the address of the variable, not the return value of a hidden procedure. This point is important if you want to move code from outside the class to inside the class (or vice versa) because you must be prepared to deal with subtle issues like this one.

> **CAUTION** One last note, just to add confusion to confusion: If you prefix the properties in your class module with the *Me* keyword, they're again seen as properties instead of variables and Visual Basic invokes the hidden procedure instead of using the variable address. Therefore, this code won't work even inside the class module:
>
> ```
> ToCentimeter Me.Height                 ' It doesn't work!
> ```

Advanced Uses of Methods

You already know a lot about methods. Here are, however, a few more interesting details that you should be aware of concerning how methods can be used within a class module.

Saving results for subsequent calls

Let's say that you have a function that returns a complex value—for example, the grand total of an invoice—and you don't want to reevaluate it each time the client code makes a request. On the other hand, you don't want to store it somewhere and run the risk that its value becomes obsolete because some other property of the invoice changes. This is similar to the decision that a database developer has to make: Is it better to create a *GrandTotal* field that contains the actual value (thus putting the consistency of the database at stake and also wasting some disk space) or to evaluate the total each time you need it (thus wasting CPU time each time you do it)?

Class modules offer a simple and viable alternative that applies equally well to all dependent values, be they implemented as functions or read-only properties. As an example, reconsider the *ReverseName* function in the CPerson class, and pretend that it takes a lot of processing time to evaluate its result. Here's how you can modify this function to keep the overhead to a minimum without modifying the interface that the class exposes to the outside. (Added statements are in boldface.)

```
' A private member variable
Private m_ReverseName As Variant

Property Let FirstName(ByVal newValue As String)
    ' Raise an error if an invalid assignment is attempted.
    If newValue = "" Then Err.Raise 5    ' Invalid procedure argument
    ' Else store in the Private member variable.
    m_FirstName = newValue
    m_ReverseName = Empty
End Property

Property Let LastName(ByVal newValue As String)
    ' Raise an error if an invalid assignment is attempted.
    If newValue = "" Then Err.Raise 5    ' Invalid procedure argument
    ' Else store in the Private member variable.
    m_LastName = newValue
    m_ReverseName = Empty
End Property

Function ReverseName() As String
    If IsEmpty(m_ReverseName) Then
        m_ReverseName = LastName & ", " & FirstName
    End If
    ReverseName = m_ReverseName
End Function
```

In other words, you store the return value in a Private Variant variable before returning to the client and reuse that value if possible in all subsequent calls. The trick works because each time either *FirstName* or *LastName* (the *independent* properties) are assigned a new value, the Private variable is cleared, which forces it to be reevaluated the next time the *ReverseName* function is invoked. Examine this simple client code and try to figure out how difficult it would have been to implement equivalent logic using other techniques:

```
' This line takes some microseconds the first time it is executed.
If pers.ReverseName <> "Smith, John" Then
    ' If this line is executed, it internally resets m_ReverseName.
    pers.FirstName = "Robert"
End If
' In all cases, the next statement will be as fast as possible.
Print pers.ReverseName
```

Of course, we might have also reevaluated the *m_ReverseName* value right in the *Property Let* procedures of *FirstName* and *LastName*, but that would undermine our main purpose, which is to avoid unnecessary overhead or postpone it as long as possible. In a real-world application, this difference might involve unnecessarily opening a database, reestablishing a remote connection, and so on, so it's apparent that the advantages of this technique shouldn't be underestimated.

Simulating class constructors

So far, I've explained that a class can be considered robust if it always contains valid data. The primary way to achieve this goal is to provide Property procedures and methods that permit the outside code to transform the internal data only from one valid state to another valid state. In this reasoning, however, is a dangerous omission: What happens if an object is used immediately after its creation? You can provide some useful initial and valid values in the *Class_Initialize* event procedure, but this doesn't ensure that all the properties are in a valid state:

```
Set pers = New CPerson
Print pers.CompleteName          ' Displays an empty string.
```

In more mature OOPLs such as C++, this issue is solved by the language's ability to define a *constructor method*. A constructor method is a special procedure defined in the class module and executed whenever a new instance is created. Because you define the syntax of the constructor method, you can force the client code to pass all the values that are needed to create the object in a robust state from its very beginning, or refuse to create the object at all if values are missing or invalid.

Alas, Visual Basic completely lacks constructor methods, and you can't prevent users of your class from using the object as soon as they create it. The best you can do is create a *pseudo-constructor* method that correctly initializes all the properties and let other programmers know that they can initialize the object in a more concise and robust way:

```
Friend Sub Init(FirstName As String, LastName As String)
    Me.FirstName = FirstName
    Me.LastName = LastName
End Sub
```

Your invitation should be gladly accepted because now the client code can initialize the object in fewer steps:

```
Set pers = New CPerson
pers.Init "John", "Smith"
```

Two issues are worth noting in the preceding code. First, the scope of the method is Friend: This doesn't make any difference in this particular case, but it will become important when and if the class becomes Public and accessible from the outside, as we'll see in Chapter 16. In Standard EXE projects, Friend and Public are synonymous; using the former doesn't hurt, and you'll save a lot of work if you later decide to transform the project into an ActiveX component.

The second noteworthy point is that arguments have the same names as the properties they refer to, which makes our pseudo-constructor easier to use for the programmer who already knows the meaning of each property. To avoid a name conflict, inside the procedure you refer to the real properties using the *Me* keyword. This is slightly less efficient but preserves the data encapsulation and ensures that any validation code will be properly executed when the constructor routine assigns a value to properties.

The concept of constructors can be refined by using optional arguments. The key properties of our CPerson class are undoubtedly *FirstName* and *LastName*, but in many cases the client code will also set *BirthDate* and *ID*. So why not take this opportunity to make life easier for the programmer who uses the class?

```
Friend Sub Init(FirstName As String, LastName As String, _
    Optional ID As Variant, Optional BirthDate As Variant)
    Me.FirstName = FirstName
    Me.LastName = LastName
    If Not IsMissing(ID) Then Me.ID = ID
    If Not IsMissing(BirthDate) Then Me.BirthDate = BirthDate
End Sub
```

In this case, you must adopt optional arguments of type Variant because it is essential that you use the *IsMissing* function and bypass the assignment of values that were never provided by the client:

```
pers.Init "John", "Smith", , "10 Sept 1960"
```

You can do one more thing to improve the class's usability and acceptance by other programmers. This point is really important because if you convince the user of your class to call the constructor you provide—and you must choose this "softer" approach, since you can't force them to—your code and the entire application will be more robust. The trick I'm suggesting is that you write a constructor function in a BAS module in your application:

```
Public Function New_CPerson(FirstName As String, LastName As String, _
    Optional ID As Variant, Optional BirthDate As Variant) As CPerson
    ' You don't even need a temporary local variable.
    Set New_CPerson = New CPerson
    New_CPerson.Init FirstName, LastName, ID, BirthDate
End Function
```

Procedures of this type are sometimes called *factory methods*. Now see how this can streamline the portion of the client code that creates an instance of the class:

```
Dim pers As CPerson
' Creation, initialization, and property validation in one step!
Set pers = New_CPerson("John", "Smith", , "10 Sept 1960")
```

> **TIP** You can reduce the typing and the guesswork when using these sort-of constructors if you gather them into a single BAS module and give this module a short name, such as *Class* or *Factory*. (You can't use *New*, sorry.) Then when you need to type the name of a constructor method, you just type *Class* and let Microsoft IntelliSense guide you through the list of constructor methods contained in that module. You can use this approach anytime you don't remember the name of a procedure in a module.

Creating all your objects by means of explicit constructors has other benefits as well. For example, you can easily add some trace statements in the *New_CPerson* routine that keeps track of how many objects were created, the initial values of properties, and so on. Don't underestimate this capability if you're writing complex applications that use many class modules and object instances.

Advanced Uses of Properties

I want to tell you more about properties that can make your classes even more useful and powerful.

Enumerated properties

Some properties are intended to return a well-defined subset of integer numbers. For example, you could implement a *MaritalStatus* property that can be assigned the values 1 (NotMarried), 2 (Married), 3 (Divorced), and 4 (Widowed). The best solution possible under Visual Basic 4 was to define a group of constants and consistently use them in the code both inside and outside the class. This practice, however, forced the developer to put the *CONST* directives in a separate BAS module, which broke the self-containment of the class.

Visual Basic 5 solved this issue by adding a new *Enum* keyword to the VBA language and thus the ability to create *enumerated values*. An *Enum* structure is nothing but a group of related constant values that automatically take distinct values:

```
' In the declaration section of the class
Enum MaritalStatusConstants
    NotMarried = 1
    Married
    Divorced
    Widowed
End Enum
```

You don't need to assign an explicit value to all the items in the *Enum* structure: for all the subsequent omitted values, Visual Basic just increments the preceding value. (So in the previous code, Married is assigned the value 2, Divorced is 3, and so on.) If you also omit the first value, Visual Basic starts at 0. But because 0 is the default value for any integer property when the class is created, I always prefer to stay clear of it so that I can later trap any value that hasn't been initialized properly.

After you define an *Enum* structure, you can create a Public property of the corresponding type:

```
Private m_MaritalStatus As MaritalStatusConstants

Property Get MaritalStatus() As MaritalStatusConstants
    MaritalStatus = m_MaritalStatus
End Property
Property Let MaritalStatus(ByVal newValue As MaritalStatusConstants)
    ' Refuse invalid assignments. (Assumes that 0 is always invalid.)
    If newValue <= 0 Or newValue > Widowed Then Err.Raise 5
    m_MaritalStatus = newValue
End Property
```

The benefit of using enumerated properties becomes apparent when you write code that uses them. In fact, thanks to IntelliSense, as soon as you press the equal sign key (or use any other math or Boolean operator, for that matter), the Visual Basic editor drops down a list of all the available constants, as you can see in Figure 6-3. Moreover, all the *Enum*s you define immediately appear in the Object Browser, so you can check the actual value of each individual item there.

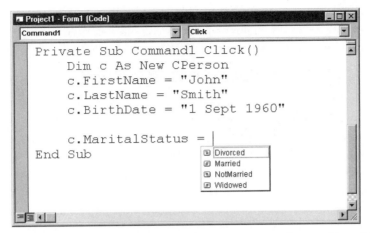

Figure 6-3. *Use IntelliSense to speed up your typing when working with* Enum
properties.

Here are a few details you must account for when dealing with *Enum*
values:

■ All variables and arguments are internally managed as Longs. As far as
Visual Basic is concerned, they *are* Longs and their symbolic names are
just a convenience for the programmer.

■ For the same reason, you can assign an enumerated variable or property
any valid 32-bit integer value without raising an error. If you want to
enforce a better validation, you must explicitly validate the input data in
all your *Property Let* procedures, as you do with any other property.

■ *Enum* structures aren't exclusively used with properties. In fact, you can
also create methods that accept enumerated values as one of their arguments or that return enumerated values.

■ *Enum* blocks can be Public or Private to a class, but it rarely makes sense
to create a Private *Enum* because it couldn't be used for any argument or
return value of a Public property or method. If the class is itself Public—
in an ActiveX EXE or DLL project, for example—programmers who use
the class can browse all the public *Enum*s in the class using a standard
Object Browser.

■ It isn't essential that the *Enum* block be physically located in the same
class module that uses it. For example, a class module can include an
Enum used by other classes. But if you're planning to make your class
Public (see previous point), it's important that all the *Enum*s that it uses

are defined in other Public classes. If you put them in a Private module or a standard BAS module, you'll get a compile error when you run the application, which you can see in Figure 6-4.

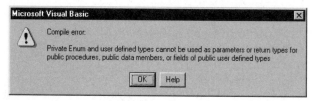

Figure 6-4. *You can't use* Enum *values in a Public class if the* Enum *block is located in a form module, in a Private class, or in a standard BAS module.*

■ Never forget that *Enums* are just shortcuts for creating constants. This means that all the enumerated constants defined within an *Enum* block should have unique names in their scope. (Because *Enums* are typically Public structures, their scope is often the entire application.)

The last point is especially important, and I strongly advise you to devise a method for generating unique names for all your enumerated constants. If you fail to do that, the compiler refuses to compile your application and raises the "Ambiguous name detected: <itemname>" error. The easy way to avoid this problem is to add to all the enumerated constants a unique 2- or 3-letter prefix, for example:

```
Enum SexConstants
    sxMale = 1
    sxFemale
End Enum
```

The other way to avoid trouble is to use the complete *enumname.constantname* syntax whenever you refer to an ambiguous *Enum* member, as in the following code:

```
pers.MaritalStatus = MaritalStatusConstants.Married
```

Enum values don't need to be in an increasing sequence. In fact, you can provide special values out of the expected order to signal some special conditions, as in the following code:

```
' In a hypothetical Order class
Enum OrderStatusConstants
    osShipping = 1
    osBackOrder
    osError = -9999    ' Tip: use negative values for such special cases.
End Enum
```

Another common example of enumerated properties whose values aren't in sequence are *bit-fielded* properties, as in this code:

```
Enum FileAttributeConstants
    Normal = 0                  ' Actually means "no bit set"
    ReadOnly = 1                ' Bit 0
    Hidden = 2                  ' Bit 1
    System = 4                  ' Bit 2
    Directory = 16             ' Bit 3
    Archive = 32               ' Bit 4
End Enum
```

While enumerated properties are very useful and permit you to store some descriptive information in just 4 bytes of memory, you shouldn't forget that sooner or later you'll have to extract and interpret this information and sometimes even show it to your users. For this reason, I often add to my classes a read-only property that returns the textual description of an enumerated property:

```
Property Get MaritalStatusDescr() As String
    Select Case m_MaritalStatus
        Case NotMarried: MaritalStatusDescr = "NotMarried"
        Case Married: MaritalStatusDescr = "Married"
        Case Divorced: MaritalStatusDescr = "Divorced"
        Case Widowed
            If Sex = Male Then      ' Be precise for your users.
                MaritalStatusDescr = "Widower"
            ElseIf Sex = Female Then
                MaritalStatusDescr = "Widow"
            End If
        Case Else
            Err.Raise 5                 ' Defensive programming!
    End Select
End Property
```

It seems a lot of work for such a little piece of information, but you'll be glad that you did it every time you have to show the information on screen or in a printed report. You might wonder why I added a *Case Else* block (shown in boldface). After all, the *m_MaritalStatus* variable can't be assigned a value outside its range because it's protected by the *Property Let MaritalStatus* procedure, right? But you should never forget that a class is often an evolving entity, and what's true today might change tomorrow. All the validation code that you use for testing the valid range of such properties might become obsolete without your even noticing it. For example, what happens if you later add a fifth *MaritalStatus* constant? Are you really going to hunt through your code for possible bugs each and every time you add a new enumerated value? Explicitly testing all the values in a *Select Case* block and rejecting those that fall through the *Case Else* clause is a form of defensive programming that you should always exercise if you don't want to spend more time debugging the code later.

Here's an easy trick that lets you safely add new constants without also modifying the validation code in the corresponding *Property Let* procedure. Instead of testing against the largest constant, just define it explicitly in the *Enum* structure:

```
Enum MaritalStatusConstants
    NotMarried = 1
    Married
    Divorced
    Widowed
    MARITALSTATUS_MAX = Widowed      ' Uppercase is easier to spot.
End Enum

Property Let MaritalStatus(ByVal newValue As MaritalStatusConstants)
    ' Refuse invalid assignments. (Assumes that 0 is always invalid.)
    If newValue <= 0 Or newValue > MARITALSTATUS_MAX Then Err.Raise 5
    m_MaritalStatus = newValue
End Property
```

When you then append constants to the *Enum* block, you need to make the MARITALSTATUS_MAX item point to the new highest value. If you add a comment, as in the preceding code, you can hardly miss it.

Properties that return objects

Visual Basic's own objects might expose properties that return object values. For example, forms and all visible controls expose a *Font* property, which in turn returns a Font object. You realize that this is a special case because you can append a dot to the property name and have IntelliSense tell you the names of the properties of the object:

```
Form1.Font.Bold = True
```

What Visual Basic does with its own objects can also be done with your custom classes. This adds a great number of possibilities to your object-oriented programs. For example, your CPerson class still lacks an *Address* property, so it's time to add it. In most cases, a single *Address* string doesn't suffice to point exactly to where a person lives, and you usually need several pieces of related information. Instead of adding multiple properties to the CPerson object, create a new CAddress class:

```
' The CAddress class module
Public Street As String
Public City As String
Public State As String
Public Zip As String
Public Country As String
Public Phone As String
Const Country_DEF = "USA"   ' A default for Country property
```

```
Private Sub Class_Initialize()
    Country = Country_DEF
End Sub
Friend Sub Init(Street As String, City As String, State As String, _
    Zip As String, Optional Country As Variant, Optional Phone As Variant)
    Me.Street = Street
    Me.City = City
    Me.State = State
    Me.Zip = Zip
    If Not IsMissing(Country) Then Me.Country = Country
    If Not IsMissing(Phone) Then Me.Phone = Phone
End Sub
Property Get CompleteAddress() As String
    CompleteAddress = Street & vbCrLf & City & ", " & State & " " & Zip _
        & IIf(Country <> Country_DEF, Country, "")
End Property
```

For the sake of simplicity, all properties have been declared Public items, so this class isn't particularly robust. In a real-world example, a lot of nice things could be done to make this class a great piece of code, such as checking that the *City*, *State*, and *Zip* properties are compatible with one another. (You probably need a lookup search against a database for this.) You could even automatically provide an area code for the *Phone* property. I gladly leave these enhancements as an exercise to readers. For now, let's focus on how you can exploit this new class together with CPerson. Adding a new *HomeAddress* property to our CPerson class requires just one line of code in the declaration section of the module:

```
' In the CPerson class module
Public HomeAddress As CAddress
```

Now you can create a CAddress object, initialize its properties, and then assign it to the *HomeAddress* property just created. Thanks to the *Init* pseudo-constructor, you can considerably reduce the amount of code that's actually needed in the client:

```
Dim addr As CAddress
Set addr = New CAddress
addr.Init "1234 North Rd", "Los Angeles", "CA", "92405"
Set pers.HomeAddress = addr
```

While this approach is perfectly functional and logically correct, it's somehow unnatural. The problem stems from having to explicitly create a CAddress object before assigning it to the *HomeAddress* property. Why not work directly with the *HomeAddress* property?

```
Set pers.HomeAddress = New CAddress
pers.HomeAddress.Init "1234 North Rd", "Los Angeles", "CA", "92405"
```

When you work with nested object properties, you'll like the *With...End With* clause:

```
With pers.HomeAddress
    .Street = "1234 North Rd"
    .City = "Los Angeles"
    ' etc.
End With
```

As I showed you previously, you can provide an independent constructor method in a standard BAS module (not shown here) and do without a separate *Set* statement:

```
Set pers.HomeAddress = New_CAddress("1234 North Rd", "Los Angeles", _
    "CA", "92405")
```

Property Set **procedures**

A minor problem that you have to face is the lack of control over what can be assigned to the *HomeAddress* property. How can you be sure that no program will compromise the robustness of your CPerson object by assigning an incomplete or invalid CAddress object to the *HomeAddress* property? And what if you need to make the *HomeAddress* property read-only?

As you see, these are the same issues that you faced when working with regular, nonobject properties, which you resolved thanks to *Property Get* and *Property Let* procedures. So it shouldn't surprise you to learn that you can do the same with object properties. The only difference is that you use a third type of property procedure, the *Property Set* procedure, instead of the *Property Let* procedure:

```
Dim m_HomeAddress As CAddress        ' A module-level private variable.

Property Get HomeAddress() As CAddress
    Set HomeAddress = m_HomeAddress
End Property
Property Set HomeAddress(ByVal newValue As CAddress)
    Set m_HomeAddress = newValue
End Property
```

Because you're dealing with object references, you must use the *Set* keyword in both procedures. A simple way to ensure that the CAddress object being assigned to the *HomeAddress* property is valid is to try out its *Init* method with all the required properties:

```
Property Set HomeAddress(ByVal newValue As CAddress)
    With newValue
        .Init .Street, .City, .State, .Zip
    End With
```

```
    ' Do the assignment only if the above didn't raise an error.
    Set m_HomeAddress = newValue
End Property
```

Unfortunately, protecting an object property from invalid assignments isn't as simple as it appears. If the innermost class—*CAddress* in this case—doesn't protect itself in a robust way, the outermost class can do little or nothing. To explain why, just trace this apparently innocent statement:

```
pers.HomeAddress.Street = ""   ' An invalid assignment raises no error.
```

At first, you might be surprised to see that execution doesn't flow through the *Property Set HomeAddress* procedure; instead, it goes through the *Property Get Home-Address* procedure, which seems nonsensical because we are *assigning* a value, not reading it. But if we look at the code from a compiler's standpoint, things are different. The language parser scans the line from left to right: it first finds a reference to a property exposed by the CPerson class (that is, *pers.HomeAddress*) and tries to resolve it to determine what it's pointing to. For this reason, it has to evaluate the corresponding *Property Get* procedure. The result is that you can't effectively use the *Property Get HomeAddress* procedure to protect the CPerson class module from invalid addresses: you must protect the CAddress dependent class itself. In a sense, this is only fair because each class should be responsible for itself.

Let's see how you can use the CAddress class to improve the CPerson class even further. You have already used it for the *HomeAddress* property, but there are other possible applications:

```
' In the declaration section of CPerson
Private m_WorkAddress As CAddress
Private m_VacationAddress As CAddress
' Corresponding Property Get/Set are omitted here....
```

It's apparent that you have achieved a lot of functionality with minimal effort. Not only have you dramatically reduced the amount of code in the CPerson class (you need only three pairs of *Property Get/Set* procedures), you also simplified its structure because you don't have a large number of similar properties with confusing names (*HomeAddressStreet*, *WorkAddressStreet*, and so on). But above all, you have the logic for the CAddress entity in one single place, and it has been automatically propagated elsewhere in the application, without your having to set up distinct validation rules for each distinct type of address property. Once you have assigned all the correct addresses, see how easy it is to display all of them:

```
On Error Resume Next
' The error handler skips unassigned (Nothing) properties.
Print "Home: " & pers.HomeAddress.CompleteAddress
Print "Work: " & pers.WorkAddress.CompleteAddress
Print "Vacation: " & pers.VacationAddress.CompleteAddress
```

Variant properties

Properties that return Variant values aren't different from other properties: You just need to declare a Public Variant member and you're done. But things are a bit more complex if the property can receive either a regular value or an object value. For example, say that you want to implement a *CurrentAddress* property, but you want to keep it more flexible and capable of storing either a CAddress object or a simpler string, as in this code:

```
' The client code can assign a regular string
pers.CurrentAddress = "Grand Plaza Hotel, Rome"
' or a reference to another CAddress object (requires Set).
Set pers.CurrentAddress = pers.VacationAddress
```

While this sort of flexibility adds a lot of power to your class, it also reduces its robustness because nothing keeps a programmer from adding a nonstring value or an object of a class other than CAddress. To be more in control of what is actually assigned to this property, you need to arbitrate all accesses to it through Property procedures. But in this case, you need *three* distinct Property procedures:

```
Private m_CurrentAddress As Variant

Property Get CurrentAddress() As Variant
    If IsObject(m_CurrentAddress) Then
        Set CurrentAddress = m_CurrentAddress    ' Return a CAddress object.
    Else
        CurrentAddress = m_CurrentAddress        ' Return a string.
    End If
End Property

Property Let CurrentAddress(ByVal newValue As Variant)
    m_CurrentAddress = newValue
End Property

Property Set CurrentAddress(ByVal newValue As Variant)
    Set m_CurrentAddress = newValue
End Property
```

The *Property Let* procedure is invoked when a regular value is assigned to the property, while the *Property Set* procedure comes into play when the client assigns an object with a *Set* command. Note how the *Property Get* procedure returns a value to the caller code: It has to test whether the private variable currently contains an object, and it must use a *Set* command if it does. The *Property Let* and *Set* pair lets you enforce a better validation scheme:

```
Property Let CurrentAddress(ByVal newValue As Variant)
    ' Check that it is a string value.
    If VarType(newValue) <> vbString Then Err.Raise 5
```

```
        m_CurrentAddress = newValue
End Property

Property Set CurrentAddress(ByVal newValue As Variant)
    ' Check that it is a CAddress object.
    If TypeName(newValue) <> "CAddress" Then Err.Raise 5
    Set m_CurrentAddress = newValue
End Property
```

Here's a technique that lets you save some code and slightly improve run-time performances. The trick is to declare the type of the object you're expecting right in the parameter list of the *Property Set* procedure, as in this code:

```
Property Set CurrentAddress(ByVal newValue As CAddress)
    Set m_CurrentAddress = newValue
End Property
```

You can't use this approach in all circumstances; for example, you can't use it when you're willing to accept two or more objects of different types. In that case, it's best to use an *As Object* parameter:

```
Property Set CurrentAddress(ByVal newValue As Object)
    If TypeName(newValue) <> "CAddress" And TypeName(newValue) <> _
        "COtherType" Then Err.Raise 5
    Set m_CurrentAddress = newValue
End Property
```

As far as Visual Basic is concerned, the *real* type is determined by the value declared in the *Property Get* procedure. In fact, that's the type reported in the Object Browser.

Properties in BAS modules

While this fact is undocumented in Visual Basic manuals, you can create Property procedures in standard BAS modules as well. This capability makes a few interesting techniques possible. You can use a pair of Property procedures to encapsulate a global variable and arbitrate all accesses to it. Let's say that you have a global *Percent* variable:

```
' In a standard BAS module
Public Percent As Integer
```

For really robust code, you want to be sure that all values assigned to it are in the proper 0 through 100 range, but you don't want to test all the assignment statements in your code. The solution is easy, as you'll see on the following page.

```
Dim m_Percent As Integer

Property Get Percent() As Integer
    Percent = m_Percent
End Property
Property Let Percent(newValue As Integer)
    If newValue < 0 Or newValue > 100 Then Err.Raise 5
    m_Percent = newValue
End Property
```

Other interesting variations of this technique are read-only and write-once/read-many global variables. You can also use this technique to work around the inability of Visual Basic to declare string constants that contain *Chr$* functions and concatenation operators:

```
' You can't do this with a CONST directive.
Property Get DoubleCrLf() As String
    DoubleCrLf = vbCrLf & vbCrLf
End Property
```

Finally, you can use Property procedures in BAS modules to trace what happens to the global variables in your code. Let's say that your code incorrectly assigns a wrong value to a global variable, and you want to understand when this happens. Just replace the variable with a pair of Property procedures, and add *Debug.Print* statements as required (or print values to a file, if you want). When you have fixed all the problems, delete the procedures and restore the original global variable. The best thing about all this is that you won't need to edit a single line of code in the rest of your application.

The *CallByName* Function

Visual Basic 6 includes a welcome addition to the VBA language, in the form of the *CallByName* function. This keyword lets you reference an object's method or property by passing its name in an argument. Its syntax is as follows:

```
result = CallByName(object, procname, calltype [,arguments..])
```

where *procname* is the name of the property or method, and *calltype* is one of the following constants: 1-vbMethod, 2-vbGet, 4-vbLet, 8-vbSet. You must pass any argument the method is expecting, and you should avoid retrieving a return value if you're invoking a Sub method or a *Property Let/Get* procedure. Here are a few examples:

```
Dim pers As New CPerson
' Assign a property.
CallByName pers, "FirstName", vbLet, "Robert"
' Read it back.
Print "Name is " & CallByName(pers, "FirstName", vbGet)
```

```
' Invoke a function method with one argument.
width = CallByName(Form1, "TextWidth", vbMethod, "ABC")
```

Here are a couple of noteworthy bits of information about this function, both of which affect its usefulness:

- While adding a lot of flexibility when dealing with an object, neither the *CallByName* function nor the VBA language as a whole is able to *retrieve* the list of the properties and methods exposed by an object. So in this sense the *CallByName* function is only a half-solution to the problem because you have to build the property names yourself. If you know these names in advance, you might invoke your properties and methods directly, using the familiar dot syntax.

- The *CallByName* function invokes the object's member using a late binding mechanism (see "The Binding Mechanism" later in this chapter), which is considerably slower than regular access through the dot syntax.

As a general rule, you should never use the *CallByName* function when you can reach the same result using the regular dot syntax. There are times, however, when this function permits you to write very concise and highly parameterized code. One interesting application is quickly setting a large number of properties for controls on a form. This might be useful when you give your users the ability to customize a form and you then need to restore the last configuration in the *Form_Load* event. I have prepared a couple of reusable procedures that do the job:

```
' Returns an array of "Name=Values" strings
' Supports only nonobject properties, without indices
Function GetProperties(obj As Object, ParamArray props() As Variant) _
    As String()
    Dim i As Integer, result() As String
    On Error Resume Next
    ' Prepare the result array.
    ReDim result(LBound(props) To UBound(props)) As String
    ' Retrieve all properties in turn.
    For i = LBound(props) To UBound(props)
        result(i) = vbNullChar
        ' If the call fails, this item is skipped.
        result(i) = props(i) & "=" & CallByName(obj, props(i), vbGet)
    Next
    ' Filter out invalid lines.
    GetProperties = Filter(result(), vbNullChar, False)
End Function

' Assign a group of properties in one operation.
' Expects an array in the format returned by GetProperties
```

(continued)

```
Sub SetProperties(obj As Object, props() As String)
    Dim i As Integer, temp() As String
    For i = LBound(props) To UBound(props)
        ' Get the Name-Value components.
        temp() = Split(props(i), "=")
        ' Assign the property.
        CallByName obj, temp(0), vbLet, temp(1)
    Next
End Sub
```

When you're using *GetProperties*, you have to provide a list of the properties you're interested in, but you don't need a list when you restore the properties with a call to *SetProperties*:

```
Dim saveprops() As String
saveprops() = GetProperties(txtEditor, "Text", "ForeColor", "BackColor")
...
SetProperties txtEditor, saveprops()
```

Attributes

You can't entirely define a class in the code window. In fact, you must specify a few important attributes in a different way. These attributes might concern the class module as a whole or its individual members (that is, its properties and methods).

Class module attributes

The attributes of the class module itself are conceptually simpler because you can edit them through the Properties window, as you might for any other source code module that can be hosted in the Visual Basic environment. But in contrast to what happens with form and standard modules, what you see in the Properties window when you press the F4 key depends on the type of the project. (See Figure 6-5.) There are six attributes: *Name*, *DataBindingBehavior*, *DataSourceBehavior*, *Instancing*, *MTSTransactionMode*, and *Persistable*. They will be covered in detail in subsequent chapters.

Figure 6-5. *Only a Public class module in an ActiveX DLL project exposes all possible class attributes in the Properties window.*

The default member of a class

Most Visual Basic controls and intrinsic objects expose a default property or method. For example, the TextBox control's default property is *Text*; the Error object's default property is *Number*; Collections have a default *Item* method; and so on. Such items are said to be *default members* because if you omit the member name in an expression, Visual Basic will implicitly assume you meant to refer to that particular member. You can implement the same mechanism even with your own classes by following this procedure:

1. Click in the code editor on the property or method definition, invoke the Procedure Attributes command from the Tools menu, and then select the name of the item in the topmost combo box if it isn't already displayed.

2. Alternatively, press F2 to open the Object Browser, select the class module name in the leftmost pane; in the rightmost pane, right-click the item that must become the default member, and then select the Properties command from the pop-up menu that appears, as you can see in Figure 6-6.

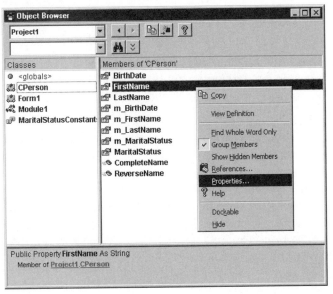

Figure 6-6. *Selecting the Properties menu command from the Object Browser.*

3. Once the item you're interested in is highlighted in the topmost Name combo box, click on the Advanced button to expand the Procedure Attributes dialog box. (See Figure 6-7 on the following page.)

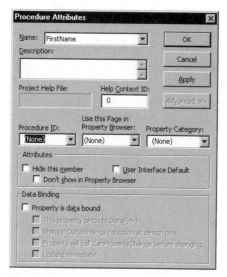

Figure 6-7. *The expanded view of the Procedure Attributes dialog box.*

4. In the Procedure ID combo box, select the (default) item; alternatively, you can just type *0* (zero) in the edit area of the combo box.

5. Click the OK button to make your decision permanent, and close the dialog box. In the Object Browser, you'll notice that a small, round indicator has appeared next to the member's name. This is the confirmation that it has become the default member of the class.

A class can't expose more than one default property or method. If you try to create a second default item, Visual Basic complains and asks you to confirm your decision. In general, it isn't a good idea to change the default member of a class because this amendment could break all the client code written previously.

While I certainly agree that providing a default property to a class module tends to make it more easily usable, I want to warn you against some potential problems that can arise from using this feature. Let's go back to our CPerson class and its *HomeAddress* and *WorkAddress* properties. As you know, you can assign one object property to another, as in this code:

```
Set pers.HomeAddress = New CAddress
Set pers.WorkAddress = New CAddress
pers.HomeAddress.Street = "2233 Ocean St."
...
Set pers.WorkAddress = pers.HomeAddress    ' This person works at home.
```

Since the preceding code uses the *Set* command, both properties are actually pointing to the same CAddress object. This is important because it implies that no additional memory has been allocated to store this duplicate data and also because you can then freely modify the address properties through any of the two CPerson properties without introducing any inconsistencies:

```
pers.HomeAddress.Street = "9876 American Ave"
Print pers.WorkAddress.Street    ' Correctly displays "9876 American Ave"
```

Now see what happens if you mistakenly omit the *Set* keyword in the original assignment:

```
pers.WorkAddress = pers.HomeAddress    ' Error 438 "Object doesn't support
                                       ' this property or method"
```

Don't be alarmed by this (admittedly cryptic) error message: You made a logic error in your code, and Visual Basic has spotted it for you at run time, which is a good thing. Alas, this helpful error disappears if the class exposes a default property. To see it for yourself, make *Street* the default item of the class, and then run this code:

```
Set pers.HomeAddress = New CAddress
Set pers.WorkAddress = New CAddress
pers.HomeAddress.Street = "2233 Ocean St."
pers.WorkAddress = pers.HomeAddress    ' No error! But has it worked?
```

Instead of rejoicing about the absence of an error message, see how the two properties are now related to each other:

```
'Change the Street property of one object.
pers.HomeAddress.Street = "9876 American Ave"
Print pers.WorkAddress.Street          ' Still displays "2233 Ocean St."
```

In other words, the two properties aren't pointing to the same object anymore. The assignment without the *Set* command has cheated the compiler into thinking that we were asking it to assign the values of the default *Street* property (which is a legal operation) and that we weren't interested in creating a new reference to the same object.

In short, by adding a default property you have deprived yourself of an important cue about the correctness of your code. My personal experience is that missing *Set* commands are subtle bugs that are rather difficult to exterminate. Keep this in mind when you're deciding to create default properties. And if you're determined to create them, always double-check your *Set* keywords in code.

> **CAUTION** You might notice that if the object property on the left side of the assignment is Nothing, Visual Basic correctly raises error 91 even if we omit the *Set* keyword. This doesn't happen, however, if the target property had been declared to be auto-instancing because in that case Visual Basic would create an object for you. This is just further proof that auto-instancing objects should always be looked at with suspicion.

A useful example

Now that I have warned you against using default properties, I want to show you a case in which they could turn out to be very useful. But first I need to introduce the concept of *sparse matrices*. A sparse matrix is a large, two-dimensional (or multidimensional) array that includes a relatively small number of nonzero items. A 1000-by-1000 array with just 500 nonzero items can be considered a great example of a sparse matrix. Sparse matrices have several common applications in math and algebra, but you can also find a use for them in business applications. For example, you might have a list of 1000 cities and a two-dimensional array that stores the distance between any two cities. Let's assume further that we use 0 (or some other special value) for the distance between cities that aren't directly connected. Large sparse arrays raise a serious memory overhead problem: a two-dimensional array of Single or Long values with 1000 rows and 1000 columns takes nearly 4 MB, so you can reasonably expect that it will noticeably slow your application on less powerful machines.

One simple solution to this problem is to store only the nonzero elements, together with their row and column indices. You need 8 additional bytes for each element to do this, but in the end you're going to save a lot of memory. For example, if only 10,000 items are nonzero (filling factor = 1:100), your sparse array will consume less than 120 KB—that is, about 33 times less than the original array—so this seems to be a promising approach. You might believe that implementing a sparse array in Visual Basic requires quite a bit of coding, so I bet you'll be surprised to learn how simple it is when you're using a class module:

```
' The complete source code of the CSparseArray class
Private m_Value As New Collection

Property Get Value(row As Long, col As Long) As Single
    ' Returns an item, or 0 if it doesn't exist.
    On Error Resume Next
    Value = m_Value(GetKey(row, col))
End Property

Property Let Value(row As Long, col As Long, newValue As Single)
    Dim key As String
    key = GetKey(row, col)
    ' First destroy the value if it's in the collection.
    On Error Resume Next
    m_Value.Remove key
    ' Then add the new value, but only if it's not 0.
    If newValue <> 0 Then m_Value.Add newValue, key
End Property


' A private function that builds the key for the private collection.
Private Function GetKey(row As Long, col As Long) As String
    GetKey = row & "," & col
End Function
```

Make sure that the *Value* property—the only public member of this class—is also its default property, which dramatically simplifies how the client uses the class. See how easy it is using your brand-new, resource-savvy data structure instead of a regular matrix:

```
Dim mat As New CSparseArray
' The rest of the application that uses the matrix isn't unchanged.
mat(1, 1) = 123              ' Actually using mat's Value property!
```

In other words, thanks to a default property you have been able to change the inner workings of this application (and, it's to be hoped, to optimize it too) *by changing only one line in the client code!* This should be a convincing argument in favor of default properties.

Actually, the CSparseArray class is even more powerful than it appears. In fact, while its original implementation uses Long values for the *row* and *col* arguments and a Single return value, you might decide to use Variant values for the two indices and for the return value. This first amendment permits you to create arrays that use strings as indices to data with no effort, as in this code:

```
' The distance between cities
Dim Distance As New CSparseArray
Distance("Los Angeles", "San Bernardino") = 60
```

Using a Variant return type doesn't waste more memory than before because the internal *m_Values* collection allocates a Variant for each value anyway.

Before concluding this section, let me hint at another special type of array, the so-called *symmetrical array*. In this type of two-dimensional array, *m(i,j)* always matches *m(j,i)*, so you can always save some memory by storing the value just once. The *Distance* matrix is a great example of a symmetrical array because the distance between two cities doesn't depend on the order of the cities themselves. When you're dealing with a regular Visual Basic array, it's up to you to remember that it's symmetrical and that you must therefore store the same value twice, which means more code, memory, and chances for errors. Fortunately, now that you have encapsulated everything in a class module, you just need to edit one private routine:

```
' Note that row and col are now Variants.
Private Function GetKey(row As Variant, col As Variant) As String
    ' Start with the lesser of the two--a case-insensitive comparison
    ' is needed because collections search their keys in this way.
    If StrComp(row, col, vbTextCompare) < 0 Then
        ' Using a nonprintable delimiter is preferable.
        GetKey = row & vbCr & col
    Else
        GetKey = col & vbCr & row
    End If
End Function
```

This is enough to make this client code work as expected:

```
Dim Distance As New CSparseMatrix
Distance("Los Angeles", "San Bernardino") = 60
Print Distance("San Bernardino", "Los Angeles")    ' Displays "60"
```

Other attributes

You might have noticed that the Procedure Attributes dialog box in Figure 6-7 on page 312 contains many more fields than I have explained so far. The majority of the corresponding attributes are somewhat advanced and won't be covered in this chapter, but there are three that are worth some additional explanation in this context.

Description   You can associate a textual description with any property and method defined in your class module. This description is then reported in the Object Browser and provides the users of your class with some information about how each member can be used. The description text is visible even when you compile the class into a COM component and another programmer browses its interface from outside the current process.

HelpContextID   You can provide a help file that contains a longer description for all the classes, properties, methods, events, controls, and so on exposed by your project. If you do so, you should also specify a distinct ID for each item in the project. When the item is selected in the rightmost pane of the Object Browser, a click on the ? icon automatically takes you to the corresponding help page. The name of the help file can be entered in the Project Properties dialog box.

Hide This Member   If you select this option, the property or method in the class module won't be visible in the Object Browser when the class is browsed from outside the project. This setting has no effect within the current project, and it makes sense to use it only in project types other than Standard EXE. Note that "hiding" an item doesn't mean that it's absolutely invisible to other programmers. In fact, even the simple Object Browser that comes with Visual Basic includes a Show Hidden Members menu command (which you can see in Figure 6-6 on page 311) that lets you discover undocumented features in other libraries (including VB and VBA's own libraries). The decision to hide a given item should be intended just as a suggestion to users of your class, meaning something like, "Don't use this item because it isn't supported and could disappear in future versions of the product."

> **CAUTION**   None of the class attributes—including those described in this section and others that I describe in forthcoming chapters—are stored in source code, so they aren't copied and pasted among different class modules when you copy the code of the procedure they're connected to. Even worse, they aren't

even preserved when you use cut-and-paste operations to rearrange the order of methods and properties inside the same class module. If you want to move code in your class modules without also losing all the attributes that are invisibly connected to it, you have to first copy the code where you want to place it and then delete it from its original location. This isn't an issue when you're just renaming a property or a method.

TIP Oddly, Visual Basic documentation doesn't mention that class modules also support their own *Description* and *HelpContextID* attributes and therefore doesn't explain how you can modify them. The trick is simple: Right-click on the class name in the leftmost pane of the Object Browser, and select the Properties command from the pop-up menu.

THE INNER LIFE OF OBJECTS

Now that you have a solid understanding of how a class module can be written and organized and how properties and methods work, it's time to learn something more about the intimate nature of objects in Visual Basic.

What an Object Variable Really Is

This could seem a rather silly question, but it isn't. The first answer that springs to mind is this: *An object variable is a memory area that holds the object's data*. This definition evidently derives from the resemblance of objects to UDT structures (which also hold aggregate data), but unfortunately it's completely wrong. The fact that these are two separate concepts becomes clear if you create two object variables that refer to the same object, as in:

```
Dim p1 As New CPerson, p2 As CPerson
p1.CompleteName = "John Smith"
Set p2 = p1
' Both variables now point to the same object.
Print p2.CompleteName          ' Displays "John Smith" as expected.
' Change the property using the first variable.
p1.CompleteName = "Robert Smith"
Print p2.CompleteName          ' 2nd variable gets the new value!
```

If objects and UDTs behaved in the same way, the last statement would have still returned the original value in *p2* (*"John Smith"*), but it happened that the assignment to *p1* in the second to last line also affected the other variable. The reason for this behavior is that an object variable is actually a pointer to the memory area where the object data is stored. This is an important concept that has a lot of interesting, and somewhat surprising, consequences, as you'll see in the list on the next page.

■   Each object variable always takes 4 bytes of memory because it is nothing but a pointer to a memory address, regardless of the size and complexity of the object it refers to.

■   Whenever you use the *Set* keyword to assign one object variable to another, you're actually assigning the 32-bit memory address. No data in the object is duplicated, and no additional memory is allocated, which makes object assignment a very fast operation.

■   When two or more object variables point to the same object instance, you can manipulate the object's properties using any of these variables because they all point to the same data area. The first object variable that receives a reference to the object isn't privileged in any way, nor does it have any special features that distinguish it from variables assigned later.

■   Object variables are therefore a great way to reduce resource consumption (because data is allocated only once) and prevent discrepancies among data. There's only one copy of the properties; once it's updated through one object variable, all other variables immediately "see" the new value. To get some perspective, consider the difficult problem many database developers face when they scatter their data among multiple tables. If the data is duplicated in more tables, they must carefully update all the tables when they need to modify the data. Failing to do so will corrupt a database.

■   Setting an object variable to Nothing—or letting it get out of scope and be automatically set to Nothing by Visual Basic—doesn't necessarily mean that you're destroying the object the variable is pointing to. In fact, if other variables are pointing to the same object, the memory area, with all its properties, isn't released.

The last point implicitly raises a question: When is an object actually released? It turns out that Visual Basic destroys an object when no object variables are pointing to it:

```
Sub TryMe()
    Dim p1 As CPerson, p2 As CPerson
    Set p1 = New CPerson              ' Creates object "A"
    p1.LastName = "Smith"
    Set p2 = p1                       ' Adds a 2nd reference to "A"
    Set p1 = New CPerson              ' Creates object "B", but doesn't
                                      ' release "A", pointed to by p2
    p1.LastName = p2.LastName         ' Copies a value, not an object ref
    Set p2 = Nothing                  ' Destroys the original "A" object
End Sub                               ' Destroys the second "B" object
```

As you see, keeping track of how many variables are pointing to a given object can easily become a daunting task. Fortunately, it's Visual Basic's problem, not yours. Visual Basic solves it using the so-called *reference counter,* which I'll talk about in the next section.

Under the Objective Hood

Figure 6-8 shows how a typical object is laid out in memory. The Visual Basic programmer sees just a few object variables: In this example, we have two variables, P1 and P2, which point to an instance of the CPerson class, and a third variable P3 that points to a distinct instance of the same class. Anytime Visual Basic creates a new instance of the class, it allocates a separate, well-defined area of memory (the *instance data* area). The structure and size of that area is fixed for any given class and depends on how many properties the class exposes, the types of properties, as well as other factors of no interest in this context. The structure of this area hasn't been documented by Microsoft, but fortunately you don't need to understand what data is stored there or how it's arranged.

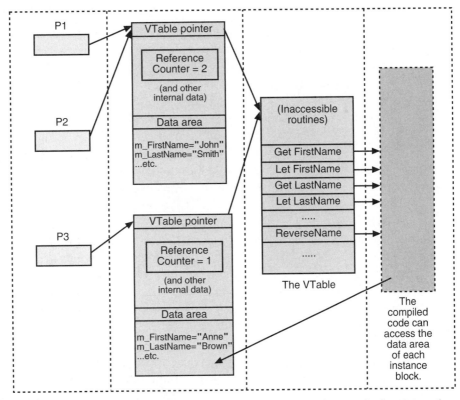

Figure 6-8. *The structure of objects is probably more complex than you had anticipated.*

One piece of information is especially important, however, for all OO developers: the *reference counter*. It's a four-byte memory location that always holds the number of object variables pointing to that particular instance data block. In this example, the John Smith object has a reference counter equal to 2, while the Anne Brown object has a reference counter equal to 1. It's impossible for this counter to contain a value less than 1 because it would mean that no variable is pointing to that specific object, and the object would be immediately destroyed. Anyway, keep in mind that, as far as programmers are concerned, the reference counter is an abstract entity because it can't be read or modified in any way (using orthodox programming techniques, at least). The only changes that you can legitimately make to the reference counter are indirectly increasing and decreasing it using *Set* commands:

```
Set p1 = New CPerson     ' Creates an object and sets
                         ' its reference counter to 1
Set p2 = p1              ' Increments the reference counter to 2
Set p1 = Nothing         ' Decrements the reference counter back to 1
Set p2 = Nothing         ' Decrements the reference counter to 0
                         ' and destroys the object
                         ' (Or you can let p2 go out of scope....)
```

At the end of the instance data block are the values of all the class module's variables, including all module-level variables and Static variables in procedures (but excluding dynamic local variables, which are allocated on the stack during each call). Of course, these values vary from instance to instance, even though their layout is the same for all instances of the class.

Another undocumented piece of information in the instance data block is very important: It contains the *VTable pointer*. This 32-bit memory location can be found at the top of the instance data block and is a pointer to another key memory area named *VTable*. All objects that belong to the same class point to the same *VTable*; hence the first 4 bytes in their instance data blocks always match. Of course, the first 4 bytes for objects instantiated by different classes differ.

The *VTable* is what actually characterizes the behavior of a class, but in itself it's a remarkably small structure. In fact, it's just a sort of *jump table,* a series of Long pointers to the actual compiled code. Each pointer corresponds to a function, a sub, or a Property procedure and points to the first byte of the compiled code generated for each procedure during the compilation process. Read/write properties have two distinct entries in the *VTable*, and Variant properties might have up to three entries if you also provided a *Property Set* procedure. Because it's impossible to know at compile time where the application can find a free block of memory to load the compiled code into, the address of each compiled routine is known only at run time. For this reason, the *VTable* structure is dynamically created at run time as well.

Object instantiation

The first time Visual Basic creates an object of a given class, its run-time module performs the following sequence of operations (here in a simplified form):

1. Allocates a block of memory for the compiled code generated from the class module and loads the code from disk.

2. Allocates a (smaller) block of memory for the *VTable* itself, and then fills it with the entry point addresses of each public routine in the class module.

3. Allocates a block for the particular object instance and sets its first 32-bit value to point to the *VTable*. At this point, it also fires the *Class_Initialize* event procedure so that the variable area can be correctly initialized.

4. Stores the address of the instance data area in the target object variable. At this point, the client code can do whatever it wants with the object.

This long sequence has to be performed only the very first time your code creates an object of a given class. For all subsequent objects of the same class, steps 1 and 2 are skipped because the *VTable* is already in place. And when you're simply assigning object variables (that is, *Set* commands without a *New* clause), step 3 is also skipped and the whole operation becomes just an assignment of a 32-bit value.

Object usage

Let's see now what happens when the client code invokes an object's method or property. Here we're examining only one of the many possible cases, which is when you're using an object from a class that resides in the same project. Since the compiler knows how the class is arranged, it also knows what the *VTable* of that class looks like. Of course, it isn't possible to know at compile time where the class's compiled code will be loaded, but at least its structure can be determined when the class is compiled. Therefore, the compiler can safely translate a reference to a property or a method into an offset in the *VTable*. Because the first seven items in the *VTable* are usually taken by other addresses (of no interest in this context), the first property procedure or method defined in the class has an offset equal to 28 (7 items * 4 bytes each). Let's say that in our class, this offset corresponds to the *Property Get FirstName* procedure. When the client code executes this statement:

```
Print p1.FirstName
```

here's what more or less happens behind the scenes:

1. Visual Basic retrieves the 32-bit value currently in the P1 variable so that it can access the instance data block that object variable points to.

2. At the beginning of the instance data block, Visual Basic finds the address of the *VTable*. Since the compiler knows that we asked to execute the

Property Get FirstName, it adds 28 to this value and finds the address of the beginning of the compiled routine we want to execute.

3. Finally the program calls the compiled code and passes it the contents of the original P1 object variable (the address of the instance data block). Because the compiled code knows the structure of the instance data block for that given class, it can access all private variables, such as *m_FirstName*, process them, and return a meaningful result to the caller.

It's a long trip just to retrieve a value, but this is how things work in the marvelous world of objects. Knowing all this won't help you write better code, at least not immediately. But I'm sure that you will badly need this information some time in the future.

> TIP   As a rule, allocating and releasing the instance data block for an object is a relatively slow operation. If your class module executes a lot of code in its *Class-_Initialize* event—for example, it has to retrieve data from a database, the Registry, or an INI file—this overhead can become critical. For this reason, try to keep an instance alive by assigning it to a global object variable and release it only when you're sure that you won't need that object anymore. (Or let Visual Basic automatically set the variable to Nothing when the application comes to a natural termination.) You might also provide a special method—for example, *Reset*—that reinitializes all private variables without having to create a new instance.

Object termination

When no more object variables point to a given instance data block, the object is destroyed. Just before releasing the memory, the Visual Basic runtime invokes the *Class_Terminate* event procedure in the class module—if the programmer created one. This is the routine in which you place your clean-up code.

Visual Basic never goes further than that, and for example, it doesn't release the *VTable* either even if there isn't any other object pointing to it. This is an important detail because it ensures that the next time another object of this class is created, the overhead will be minimal. There are just a couple of other things that you should know about the termination phase:

■   Visual Basic relies on a safety mechanism that prevents an object from being destroyed while its procedures are being executed. To see what I mean, think of the following scenario: You have a global object variable that holds the only reference to an object, and within a procedure in the class module you set the global variable to Nothing, thus destroying the only reference that keeps the object alive. If Visual Basic were really stupid, it would immediately terminate the procedure as soon as it performed the assignment. Instead, Visual Basic patiently waits for the procedure to end and only then destroys the object and invokes its *Class_Terminate* event procedure. I am mentioning this problem only for the sake of completeness because I absolutely don't mean to encourage you to resort to this inelegant programming technique. A class module should never reference a global variable because this would break its self-containment.

■ Once you're executing code in the *Class_Terminate* event procedure, Visual Basic has already started the object termination process and you can't do anything to prevent the object from being destroyed. For example, in a situation like the preceding one, you might believe that you could keep an object alive by assigning a new object reference to the global variable, hoping to reincrement the internal reference counter and prevent the object destruction. If you tried that, however, what actually would happen is that Visual Basic would first complete the destruction of the current object and then create a new instance that had nothing to do with the one you were in.

The binding mechanism

In the previous section, I've emphasized that the application invokes methods and properties using offset values in the *VTable* and little else. This makes all object references really efficient because the CPU has to perform only some additions and other elementary steps. The process of obtaining the offset in the *VTable* from the name of a property or method is known as *binding*. As you've seen, this process is usually performed by the compiler, which then delivers efficient code ready to be executed at run time. Unfortunately, not all object references are so efficient. Let's see how we can embarrass the compiler:

```
Dim obj As Object
If n > = 0.5 Then
    Set obj = New CPerson
Else
    Set obj = New CCustomer
End If
Print obj.CompleteName
```

As smart as it is, the Visual Basic compiler can't determine what the *obj* variable will actually contain at run time, and, in fact, its contents are entirely unpredictable. The problem is that even though the CPerson and CCustomer classes support the same *CompleteName* method, it hardly ever appears at the same offset in the *VTable*. So the compiler can't complete the binding process and can store in the executable code only the *name* of the method that must be invoked at run time. When execution finally hits that line, the Visual Basic runtime queries the *obj* variable, determines which object it contains, and finally calls its *CompleteName* method.

This is dramatically different from the situation we saw before, when we knew at compile time exactly which routine would be called. We have three different types of binding.

Early *VTable* Binding   The early binding process is completed at compile time. The compiler produces *VTable* offsets that are then efficiently used at run time to access the object's properties and methods. If the property or the method isn't supported, the compiler can trap the error right away, which means that early binding implicitly delivers more robust applications. Early binding is used whenever you use a variable of a well-defined type. You have an indirect confirmation that an object variable will use early binding when you append a dot to its name: The Visual Basic editor is able to give you a list of all the possible methods and properties. If the editor can do that, the compiler will later be able to complete the binding.

Late Binding   When you declare an object variable using an *As Object* or *As Variant* clause, the compiler can't deduce which type of object such a variable will contain and can therefore store only information about the property's or the method's name and arguments. The binding process is completed at run time and is performed any time the variable is referenced. As you might imagine, this takes a lot of time, and moreover there's no guarantee that the variable contains an object that supports the method you want. If the actual object doesn't support the method, a trappable run-time error will occur. If you have a generic *As Object* variable, appending a dot to its name in the code module doesn't invoke IntelliSense's drop-down list of properties and methods.

Early ID Binding   For the sake of completeness, I have to let you know about a third type of binding, whose behavior falls between that of the previous two. In the case of early ID binding, the compiler can't derive the actual offset in the *VTable*, but at least it can check that the property or method is there. If so, the compiler stores a special ID value in the executable code. At run time, Visual Basic uses this ID for a very quick look in the object's list of methods. This is slower than early *VTable* binding, but it's still much more efficient than late binding. It also ensures that no error occurs because we know with certainty that the method is supported. This type of binding is used for some external objects used by your application—for example, all ActiveX controls.

The easy rule is, therefore, that you should always strive to use early binding in your code. Apart from robustness considerations, late binding adds a performance penalty that in most cases you simply can't afford. Just to give you a broad idea, accessing a simple property using late binding is *about two hundred times slower* than with the most efficient early binding! When the called code is more complex, this gap tends to be reduced because early binding affects only the call time, not the execution of the code inside the method. Even so, you can hardly consider the difference in performance negligible.

Finally note that the way you declare an object variable affects whether Visual Basic uses early binding or late binding, but you have no control over which type of early binding Visual Basic uses. You can be sure, however, that it always uses the most convenient one. If the object is defined inside the current application, or its library exports the information about how its *VTable* is structured, Visual Basic uses the more efficient *VTable* binding; otherwise, it uses early ID binding.

Revisiting Object Keywords

Armed with all the intimate knowledge about objects that I've now given you, you should find it very simple to understand the real mechanism behind a few VBA keywords.

The *New* keyword

The *New* keyword (when used in a *Set* command) tells Visual Basic to create a brand-new instance of a given class. The keyword then returns the address of the instance data area just allocated.

The *Set* command

The *Set* command simply copies what it finds to the right of the equal sign into the object variable that appears to the left of it. This value can be, for example, the result of a *New* keyword, the contents of another variable that already exists, or the result of an expression that evaluates to an object. The only other tasks that the *Set* command performs are incrementing the reference counter of the corresponding instance data area and decrementing the reference counter of the object originally pointed to by the left-hand variable (if the variable didn't contain the Nothing value):

```
Set P1 = New CPerson        ' Creates an object, stores its address
Set P2 = P1                 ' Just copies addresses
Set P2 = New CPerson()      ' Lets P2 point to a new object, but also
                            ' decrements the reference counter
                            ' of the original object
```

The *Nothing* value

The *Nothing* keyword is the Visual Basic way of saying *Null* or *0* to an object variable. The statement

```
Set P1 = Nothing
```

isn't a special case in the *Set* scenario because it simply decreases the reference counter of the instance data block pointed to by P1 and then stores 0 in the P1 variable itself, thus disconnecting it from the object instance. If P1 was the only variable currently pointing to that instance, Visual Basic also releases the instance.

The *Is* operator

The *Is* operator is used by Visual Basic to check whether two object variables are pointing to the same instance data block. At a lower level, Visual Basic does nothing but compare the actual addresses contained in the two operands and return True if they match. The only possible variant is when you use the *Is Nothing* test, in which case Visual Basic compares the contents of a variable with the value 0. You need this special operator because the standard equal symbol, which has a completely different meaning, would fire the evaluation of the objects' default properties:

```
' This code assumes that P1 and P2 are CPerson variables, and that
' Name is the default property of the CPerson class.
If P1 Is P2 Then Print "P1 and P2 point to the same CPerson object"
If P1 = P2 Then Print "P1's Name and P2's Name are the same"
```

The *TypeOf ... Is* statement

You can test the type of an object variable using the *TypeOf...Is* statement:

```
If TypeOf P1 Is CPerson Then
    Print "P1 is of type CPerson"
ElseIf TypeOf P1 Is CEmployee Then
    Print "P1 is of type CEmployee"
End If
```

You should be aware of a couple of limitations. First, you can test only one class at a time, and you can't even directly test to see whether an object is *not* of a particular class. In this case, you need a workaround:

```
If TypeOf dict Is Scripting.Dictionary Then
    ' Do nothing in this case.
Else
    Print "DICT is NOT of a Dictionary object"
End If
```

Second, the preceding code works only if the Scripting library (or more in general, the referenced library) is currently included in the References dialog box. If it isn't, Visual Basic will refuse to compile this code. This is sometimes a nuisance when you want to write reusable routines.

> **TIP** You often use the *TypeOf ...Is* statement to avoid errors when assigning object variables, as in this code:
> ```
> ' OBJ holds a reference to a control.
> Dim lst As ListBox, cbo As ComboBox
> If TypeOf obj Is ListBox Then
>     Set lst = obj
> ElseIf TypeOf Obj Is ComboBox Then
>     Set cbo = obj
> End If
> ```

But here's a faster and more concise way:

```
Dim lst As ListBox, cbo As ComboBox
On Error Resume Next
Set lst = obj     ' The assignment that fails will leave
Set cbo = obj     ' the corresponding variable set to Nothing.
On Error Goto 0   ' Cancel error trapping.
```

The *TypeName* function

The *TypeName* function returns the name of an object's class in the form of a string. This means that you can find the type of an object in a more concise form, as follows:

```
Print "P1 is of type " & TypeName(P1)
```

In many situations, testing an object's type using the *TypeName* function is preferable to using the *TypeOf...Is* statement because it doesn't require that the object class be present in the current application or in the References dialog box.

ByVal and *ByRef* keywords

The fact the object variables are just pointers can puzzle many a programmer when object variables are passed to a procedure as *ByVal* arguments. The familiar rule—a procedure can alter a *ByVal* value without affecting the original value seen by the caller—is obviously void when the value is just a pointer. In this case, you're simply creating a copy of the pointer, not of the instance data area. Both the original and the new object reference are pointing to the same area, so the called procedure can freely read and modify all the properties of the object. If you want to prevent any modifications of the original object, you must pass the procedure a copy of the object. To do so, you must create a new object yourself, duplicate all the properties' values, and pass that new object instead. Visual Basic doesn't offer a shortcut for this.

That said, you need to understand that there's a subtle difference when you declare an object parameter using *ByRef* or *ByVal*, as this code snippet demonstrates:

```
Sub Reset(pers As CPerson)       ' ByRef can be omitted.
    Set pers = Nothing           ' This actually sets the original
End Sub                          ' variable to Nothing.

Sub Reset2(ByVal pers As CPerson)
    Set pers = Nothing           ' This code doesn't do anything.
End Sub
```

When you pass an object using *ByVal*, its internal reference counter is temporarily incremented and is decremented when the procedure exits. This doesn't happen if you pass the object by reference. For this reason, the *ByRef* keyword is slightly faster when used with objects.

The *Class_Terminate* Event

Visual Basic fires the *Class_Terminate* event one instant before releasing the data instance block and terminating the object's life. You usually write code for this event when you need to undo things that you did at initialization time or during the life of the instance. Typically in this event procedure, you close any open files and release Windows resources obtained through direct API calls. If you want to make the object's properties persist in a database for a future session, this is where you usually do it. All in all, however, you'll rarely write code for this event or at least you'll need it less frequently than code for the *Class_Initialize* event. For example, the CPerson class module doesn't actually require code in its *Class_Terminate* event procedure.

On the other hand, the mere fact that you can write some executable code and be sure that it will be executed when an object is destroyed opens up a world of possibilities that couldn't be exploited using any other, non-OOP technique. To show you what I mean, I've prepared three sample classes that are almost completely based on this simple concept. It's a great occasion to show how you can streamline several common programmer tasks using the power that objects give you.

> **CAUTION**   Visual Basic calls the *Class_Terminate* event procedure only when the object is released in an orderly manner—that is, when all references pointing to it are set to Nothing or go out of scope, or when the application comes to an end. This includes the case when the application ends because of a fatal error. The only case when Visual Basic does *not* invoke the *Class_Terminate* event is when you abruptly stop a program using the End command from the Run menu or the End button on the toolbar. This immediately stops all activity in your code, which means that no *Class_Terminate* event will ever be invoked. If you inserted critical code in the *Terminate* events—for example, code that releases Windows resources allocated via APIs—you'll experience problems. Sometimes these are *big* problems, including system crashes. By the same token, *never* terminate a program using an *End* statement in code: This has exactly the same effect, but it's going to create problems even after you compile the application and run it outside the environment.

Example 1: managing the mouse cursor

Programmers commonly change the shape of the mouse cursor, typically to an hourglass, to inform the user that some lengthy operation is going on. Of course, you also have to restore the cursor before exiting the current procedure; otherwise, the hourglass stays visible and the user never realizes that the wait is over. As simple as this task is, I've found that a good number of commercial applications fail to restore the original shape under certain circumstances. This is a clear symptom that the procedure has exited unexpectedly and therefore missed its opportunity to restore the original shape. How can classes and objects help you avoid the same error? Just have a look at this simple CMouse class module:

```
' The CMouse class - complete source code
Dim m_OldPointer As Variant

' Enforce a new mouse pointer.
Sub SetPointer(Optional NewPointer As MousePointerConstants = vbHourglass)
    ' Store the original pointer only once.
    If IsEmpty(m_OldPointer) Then m_OldPointer = Screen.MousePointer
    Screen.MousePointer = NewPointer
End Sub

' Restore the original pointer when the object goes out of scope.
Private Sub Class_Terminate()
    ' Only if SetPointer had been actually called
    If Not IsEmpty(m_OldPointer) Then Screen.MousePointer = m_OldPointer
End Sub
```

Not bad, eh? Just eight lines of code (not counting comments) to solve a recurring bug once and for all! See how easy it is to use the class in a real program:

```
Sub ALengthyProcedure()
    Dim m As New CMouse
    m.SetPointer vbHourglass          ' Or any other pointer shape
    ' ... slow code here ... (omitted)
End Sub
```

The trick works because as soon as the variable goes out of scope, the object is destroyed and Visual Basic fires its *Class_Terminate* event. The interesting point is that this sequence also occurs if the procedure is exited because of an error; even in that case, Visual Basic releases all the variables that are local to the procedure in an orderly fashion.

Example 2: opening and closing files

Another common programming task is opening a file to process it and then closing it before exiting the procedure. As we've seen in Chapter 5, all the procedures that deal with files have to protect themselves against unanticipated errors because if they were exited in an abrupt way they wouldn't correctly close the file. Once again, let's see how a class can help us to deliver more robust code with less effort:

```
' The CFile class--complete source code
Enum OpenModeConstants
    omInput
    omOutput
    omAppend
    omRandom
    omBinary
End Enum
Dim m_Filename As String, m_Handle As Integer
```

(continued)

329

```
Sub OpenFile(Filename As String, _
    Optional mode As OpenModeConstants = omRandom)
    Dim h As Integer
    ' Get the next available file handle.
    h = FreeFile()
    ' Open the file with desired access mode.
    Select Case mode
        Case omInput: Open Filename For Input As #h
        Case omOutput: Open Filename For Output As #h
        Case omAppend: Open Filename For Append As #h
        Case omBinary: Open Filename For Binary As #h
        Case Else     ' This is the default case.
            Open Filename For Random As #h
    End Select
    ' (Never reaches this point if an error has occurred.)
    m_Handle = h
    m_Filename = Filename
End Sub

' The filename (read-only property)
Property Get Filename() As String
    Filename = m_Filename
End Property

' The file handle (read-only property)
Property Get Handle() As Integer
    Handle = m_Handle
End Property

' Close the file, if still open.
Sub CloseFile()
    If m_Handle Then
        Close #m_Handle
        m_Handle = 0
    End If
End Sub

Private Sub Class_Terminate()
    ' Force a CloseFile operation when the object goes out of scope.
    CloseFile
End Sub
```

This class solves most of the problems that are usually related to file processing, including finding the next available file handle and closing the file before exiting the procedure:

```
' This routine assumes that the file always exists and can be opened.
' If it's not the case, it raises an error in the client code.
```

```
Sub LoadFileIntoTextBox(txt As TextBox, filename As String)
    Dim f As New CFile
    f.OpenFile filename, omInput
    txt.Text = Input$(LOF(f.Handle), f.Handle)
    ' No need to close it before exiting the procedure!
End Sub
```

Example 3: creating a log of your procedures

I'll conclude this chapter with a simple class that you'll probably find useful when debugging dozens of nested procedures that call one another over and over. In such cases, nothing can preserve your sanity more effectively than a log of the actual sequence of calls. Unfortunately, this is easier said than done because while it is trivial to add a *Debug.Print* command as the first executable statement of every procedure, trapping the instant when the procedure is exited is a complex matter—especially if the procedure has multiple exit points or isn't protected by an error handler. However, this thorny problem can be solved with a class that counts exactly eight lines of executable code:

```
' Class CTracer - complete source code.
Private m_procname As String, m_enterTime As Single

Sub Enter(procname As String)
    m_procname = procname: m_enterTime = Timer
    ' Print the log when the procedure is entered.
    Debug.Print "Enter " & m_procname
End Sub

Private Sub Class_Terminate()
    ' Print the log when the procedure is exited.
    Debug.Print "Exit " & m_procname & " - sec. " & (Timer - m_enterTime)
End Sub
```

Using the class is straightforward because you have to add only two statements on top of any procedure that you want to trace:

```
Sub AnyProcedure()
    Dim t As New Ctracer
    t.Enter "AnyProcedure"
    ' ... Here is the code that does the real thing ...(omitted).
End Sub
```

The CTracer class displays the total time spent within the procedure, so it also works as a simple profiler. It was so easy to add this feature that I couldn't resist the temptation.

This chapter introduced you to object-oriented programming in Visual Basic, but there are other things to know about classes and objects, such as events, polymorphism, and inheritance. I describe all these topics in the next chapter, along with several tips for building more robust Visual Basic applications.

Chapter 7

Events, Polymorphism, and Inheritance

In the previous chapter, we reviewed the basics of object-oriented programming and how you can put objects to good use to develop more concise and robust applications. In this chapter, we dive into more advanced topics than we touched upon in Chapter 6—such as polymorphism, secondary interfaces, events, inheritance, and object hierarchies—that extend the OOP potential even further. In a sense, the division of the treatment of classes and objects into two distinct chapters reflects the chronological development of object-oriented features: most of the basic features described in Chapter 6 appeared for the first time in Microsoft Visual Basic 4, while this chapter is mostly focused on improvements added in Visual Basic 5 and inherited without any substantial change in Visual Basic 6.

EVENTS

Until Visual Basic 4, the term *class events* could refer only to the internal *Class_Initialize* and *Class_Terminate* events that the Visual Basic runtime fires when an object is created and destroyed. In versions 5 and 6, however, classes are able to raise events to the outside, exactly as controls and forms can. This ability dramatically increases the potential of class modules, making it possible to integrate them more tightly in applications while continuing to consider them separate and reusable modules.

Events and Code Reusability

Before showing how a class module can expose events to the outside and how the client code can trap them, let me explain why events are so important for code reuse. The ability to create a piece of code that can be recycled *as is* in other projects is too tantalizing to leave any programmer indifferent to the possibility. To illustrate the concept, I'll describe an imaginary class module whose primary job is copying a series of files and optionally informing the caller about the progress of the operation (so that the caller code can display a progress bar or a message on the status bar for the user). Without events, we have two possible ways to implement this code, both of which are clearly unsatisfactory:

- You split the class module into several (related) methods. For instance, you create a *ParseFileSpec* method that receives the file specification (such as C:\Word*.doc) and returns a list of files, and you also create a *CopyFile* method that copies one file at a time. In this case, the client doesn't need a notification because it governs the entire process and calls each method in turn. Unfortunately, this means writing more code on the client side, which diminishes the class's usability. For more complex jobs, this approach is absolutely inappropriate.

- You create a more intelligent class module, which performs its chores internally but at the same time calls back the client when it needs to notify the client that something has occurred. This works better, but you need to solve a problem: How exactly does the class call back its client? Does it invoke a procedure with a given name? This would force you to include this procedure even if you aren't actually interested in a notification; otherwise, the compiler wouldn't run the code. A second, more serious problem is what happens if your application uses the same class in two or more distinct circumstances. Each instance of the class will clearly call back the same procedure, so the client code would have to figure out which instance has called it. And if the caller code is a class itself, that would break its self-containment. Again, we need a better approach. (Note: More advanced *callback techniques* are available to Visual Basic programmers, and I'll describe them in Chapter 16. They aren't as simple as depicted in this paragraph.)

Finally events made their appearance and offered the best solution so far to the dilemma:

■   You can create a class as described in the previous point, but when the time comes for a notification the class simply *raises* an event. The client code might not be listening to this specific event, but the class will continue with its copy operation and return from the method only when all files have been copied (unless of course you also provide clients with a mechanism to stop the process). This approach permits you to keep the structure of the client as simple as possible because it doesn't need to implement an event procedure for all the possible events raised by the class. This is similar to what happens when you place a TextBox control on a form and then decide to respond to just one or two of the many events that the control raises.

Syntax for Events

Implementing events in a class module and using them in a client module is a straightforward process, which consists of just a few logical, easy steps. Figure 7-1 shows how the implementation works. I'm using as an example the hypothetical CFileOp class, which copies multiple files, as I described previously.

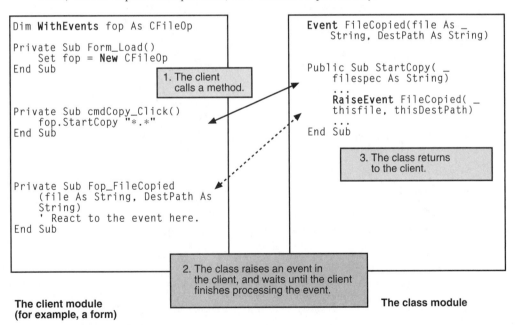

Figure 7-1. *Implementing events in a class module.*

Declaring an event

To expose an event to its clients, a class must include an *Event* statement in its declaration section. This statement serves to inform the outside world about the event's name as well as its arguments. For example, the CFileOp class might expose this event:

```
Event FileCopyComplete(File As String, DestPath As String)
```

There's nothing special about the syntax of arguments, and you can in fact declare arguments of any type supported by Visual Basic, including objects, collections, and *Enum* values.

Raising an event

When the time comes for the class to raise an event, it executes a *RaiseEvent* statement, which specifies both the event name and its actual arguments. Again, this isn't conceptually different from calling a procedure, and you'll also find that Microsoft IntelliSense can give you a hand in both selecting the event name and the values for its arguments. In the CFileOp class, you could therefore write something like this:

```
RaiseEvent FileCopyComplete "c:\bootlog.txt", "c:\backup"
```

This is all you need to do in the class module. Now let's see what the client code does.

Declaring the object in the client module

If you're writing code in a form or a class module and you want to receive events from an object, you must declare a reference to that object in the declaration section of the module, using the *WithEvents* keyword:

```
' You can use Public, Private, or Dim, as needed.
Dim WithEvents FOP As CFileOp
```

You should be aware of a few facts about the *WithEvents* clause:

- It can appear only in the declaration section of a module and can't be local to a procedure. It can be used in any type of module except for standard BAS modules.

- It can't be used with the *New* keyword; in other words, you can't create auto-instancing object variables if you also use *WithEvents*. Instead, you must declare and create the instance as a separate step, as in this code:

  ```
  Private Sub Form_Load()
      Set FOP = New CFileOp
  End Sub
  ```

- You can't declare an array of object variables in a *WithEvents* clause.

- *WithEvents* doesn't work with generic object variables.

Trapping the event

At this point, Visual Basic has all the information it needs to respond to events raised by the object. In fact, if you look at the list portion of the leftmost combo box at the top of the code editor window, you'll see that the variable you have declared using *WithEvents* appears in the list, together with all the controls already on the form. Select it and move to the rightmost combo box control to choose the event that interests you. (In this example, there's only one such event.) As it happens for events coming from controls, Visual Basic automatically creates the procedure template for you, and all you have to do is fill it with some meaningful code:

```
Private Sub Fop_FileCopyComplete(File As String, DestPath As String)
    MsgBox "File " & File & " has been copied to " & DestPath
End Sub
```

A First, Complete Sample Application

Now that all syntax details have been explained, it's time to complete the CFileOp class, which is able to copy one or multiple files and provide feedback to the caller. As you'll see shortly, this initial sample program provides us with the playground for more complex and interesting programming techniques based on events.

The CFileOp class module

Let's create a class module and name it CFileOp. This class exposes a few properties that allow the client to decide which files should be copied (*FileSpec*, *Path*, and *Attributes* properties) and a method that starts the actual copy process. As I indicated, the class also exposes a *FileCopyComplete* event:

```
' The CFileOp class module
Event FileCopyComplete(File As String, DestPath As String)
Private m_FileSpec As String
Private m_Filenames As Collection
Private m_Attributes As VbFileAttribute

Property Get FileSpec() As String
    FileSpec = m_FileSpec
End Property
Property Let FileSpec(ByVal newValue As String)
    ' Reset the internal Collection if a new file specification is given.
    If m_FileSpec <> newValue Then
        m_FileSpec = newValue
        Set m_Filenames = Nothing
    End If
End Property
```

(continued)

```
Property Get Path() As String
    Path = GetPath(m_FileSpec)
End Property
Property Let Path(ByVal newValue As String)
    ' Get current file specification, and then substitute just the path.
    FileSpec = MakeFilename(newValue, GetFileName(FileSpec))
End Property

Property Get Attributes() As VbFileAttribute
    Attributes = m_Attributes
End Property
Property Let Attributes(ByVal newValue As VbFileAttribute)
    ' Reset the internal Collection only if a new value is given.
    If m_Attributes <> newValue Then
        m_Attributes = newValue
        Set m_Filenames = Nothing
    End If
End Property

' Holds the list of all the files that match FileSpec,
' plus any other file added by the client code (read-only property)
Property Get Filenames() As Collection
    ' Build the file list "on demand", and only if necessary.
    If m_Filenames Is Nothing Then ParseFileSpec
    Set Filenames = m_Filenames
End Property

' Parses a file specification and attributes and adds
' the resulting filename to the internal m_Filenames Collection
Sub ParseFileSpec(Optional FileSpec As Variant, _
    Optional Attributes As VbFileAttribute)
    Dim file As String, Path As String
    ' Provide a default for arguments.
    If IsMissing(FileSpec) Then
        ' In this case, we need a file specification.
        If Me.FileSpec = "" Then Err.Raise 1001, , "FileSpec undefined"
        FileSpec = Me.FileSpec
        Attributes = Me.Attributes
    End If

    ' Create the internal Collection if necessary.
    If m_Filenames Is Nothing Then Set m_Filenames = New Collection
    Path = GetPath(FileSpec)
    file = Dir$(FileSpec, Attributes)
    Do While Len(file)
        m_Filenames.Add MakeFilename(Path, file)
        file = Dir$
    Loop
End Sub
```

```
Sub Copy(DestPath As String)
    Dim var As Variant, file As String, dest As String
    On Error Resume Next
    For Each var In Filenames
        file = var
        dest = MakeFilename(DestPath, GetFileName(file))
        FileCopy file, dest
        If Err = 0 Then
            RaiseEvent FileCopyComplete(file, DestPath)
        Else
            Err.Clear
        End If
    Next
End Sub


' Support routines that parse a filename. They are used internally
' but are also exposed as Public for convenience.
Sub SplitFilename(ByVal CompleteName As String, Path As String, _
    file As String, Optional Extension As Variant)
    Dim i As Integer
    ' Assume there isn't any embedded path.
    Path = "": file = CompleteName
    ' Backward search for a path delimiter
    For i = Len(file) To 1 Step -1
        If Mid$(file, i, 1) = "." And Not IsMissing(Extension) Then
            ' We have found an extension, and the caller asked for it.
            Extension = Mid$(file, i + 1)
            file = Left$(file, i - 1)
        ElseIf InStr(":\", Mid$(file, i, 1)) Then
            ' Paths don't have a trailing backslash.
            Path = Left$(file, i)
            If Right$(Path, 1) = "\" Then Path = Left$(Path, i - 1)
            file = Mid$(file, i + 1)
            Exit For
        End If
    Next
End Sub


Function GetPath(ByVal CompleteFileName As String) As String
    SplitFilename CompleteFileName, GetPath, ""
End Function


Function GetFileName(ByVal CompleteFileName As String) As String
    SplitFilename CompleteFileName, "", GetFileName
End Function
```

(continued)

```
Function MakeFilename(ByVal Path As String, ByVal FileName As String, _
    Optional Extension As String) As String
    Dim result As String
    If Path <> "" Then
        ' Path might include a trailing backslash.
        result = Path & IIf(Right$(Path, 1) <> "\", "\", "")
    End If
    result = result & FileName
    If Extension <> "" Then
        ' Extension might include a dot.
        result = result & IIf(Left$(Extension, 1) = ".", ".", "") _
            & Extension
    End If
    MakeFilename = result
End Function
```

The structure of the class should be self-evident, so I'll just explain a few minor details. When you assign a value to either the *FileSpec* or the *Attributes* property, the class resets an internal *m_Filenames* Collection variable. When eventually the *Filenames* Public property is referenced—from outside or inside the class module—the corresponding *Property Get* procedure checks whether the file list should be rebuilt, and if so, it invokes the *ParseFileSpec* method. This method could have been made Private to the class module, but keeping it Public adds some flexibility, as I'll show in the "Filtering Input Data" section, later in this chapter. At this point, everything is ready for the *Copy* method, which requires only the *DestPath* argument to learn where files are to be copied and which can raise a *FileCopyComplete* event back in the client code. All the other functions—*SplitFilename*, *GetPath*, *GetFilename*, and so on—are support routines used for parsing filenames and paths. They're also exposed as Public methods, however, because they can be useful to the client code as well.

The client form module

Add a form module to your project, and add a few controls, as depicted in Figure 7-2:

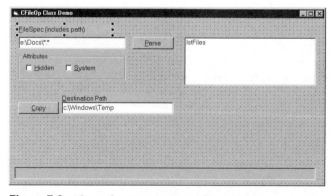

Figure 7-2. *The preliminary version of the CFileOp sample application at design time.*

Use the following code to help you decide what names to use for your controls. (Or you can just load the demonstration program from the companion CD). I've used self-explanatory names for controls, so you shouldn't have problems understanding the function of each one of them. This is the code in the form module:

```
' The client Form1 module
Dim WithEvents Fop As CFileOp

Private Sub Form_Load()
    ' WithEvents objects can't be auto-instancing.
    Set Fop = New CFileOp
End Sub

Private Sub cmdParse_Click()
    Dim file As Variant
    InitFOP
    lstFiles.Clear
    For Each file In Fop.Filenames
        lstFiles.AddItem file
    Next
    picStatus.Cls
    picStatus.Print "Found " & Fop.Filenames.count & " files.";
End Sub

Private Sub cmdCopy_Click()
    InitFOP
    Fop.Copy txtDestPath.Text
End Sub

' A useful routine shared by many procedures in the form
Private Sub InitFOP()
    Fop.FileSpec = txtFilespec
    Fop.Attributes = IIf(chkHidden, vbHidden, 0) + _
        IIf(chkSystem, vbSystem, 0)
End Sub

' Trapping events from CFileOp class
Private Sub Fop_FileCopyComplete(File As String, DestPath As String)
    picStatus.Cls
    picStatus.Print "Copied file " & File & " ==> " & DestPath;
End Sub
```

To get a taste of how events actually work, there's nothing that beats a trace session. Set some breakpoints, type some reasonable paths for the source and destination, click on the Parse or Copy button (be careful not to overwrite the files you need!), and press F8 to see the code come alive before your eyes.

Improving the Sample Application

In its simplicity, the CFileOp class module is a good piece of code that can be extensively improved with the addition of many new features. What's more important from our standpoint is that most of these additions demonstrate compelling new techniques you can implement with events.

Filtering input data

In its first version, the CFileOp class simply parses the value assigned to the *FileSpec* property and builds the list of the files to be copied, taking into account the value of the *Attributes* property. Unfortunately, the client code has no way to filter out particular files, for example, temporary or backup files or files with specific names. Thanks to the flexibility offered by events, however, you can add this capability in just a matter of seconds. You only have to add a new event declaration to the class:

```
' In the declaration section of the CFileOp class module
Event Parsing(file As String, Cancel As Boolean)
```

and add a few lines (shown here in boldface) inside the *ParseFileSpec* routine:

```
    ' ... inside the ParseFileSpec routine
    Dim Cancel As Boolean
    Do While Len(file)
        Cancel = False
        RaiseEvent Parsing(file, Cancel)
        If Not Cancel Then
            m_Filenames.Add MakeFilename(Path, file)
        End If
        file = Dir$
    Loop
```

Taking advantage of the new event in the client code is even easier. Let's say that you want to exclude temporary files from the copy process. All you have to do is trap the *Parsing* event and set its *Cancel* parameter to True when the class is about to copy a file you aren't interested in, as this code demonstrates:

```
' In the client form module
Private Sub Fop_Parsing(file As String, Cancel As Boolean)
    Dim ext As String
    ' GetExtension is a handy method exposed by CFileOp.
    ext = LCase$(Fop.GetExtension(file))
    If ext = "tmp" Or ext = "$$$" Or ext = "bak" Then Cancel = True
End Sub
```

HANDLING MULTIPLE FILE SPECIFICATIONS

This doesn't have to do with events, but I just want to demonstrate how a carefully designed structure of your class module can simplify your work when you want to extend its features. Because the class exposes the *ParseFileSpec* routine as a Public method, nothing prevents the client code from calling it directly—instead of indirectly through the *FileSpec* property—to add unrelated filenames, with or without wildcards:

```
' Prepare to copy EXE files, using the standard FileSpec property.
Fop.FileSpec = "C:\Windows\*.exe"
' But also copy all executable files from another directory.
Fop.ParseFileSpec "C:\Windows\System\*.Exe", vbHidden
Fop.ParseFileSpec "C:\Windows\System\*.Com", vbHidden
```

The great advantage of this approach is that the *CFileOp* class module will always raise a *Parsing* event in your client code, which has, therefore, an opportunity to filter out filenames, regardless of how they were added to the internal list. Another example of flexible design is offered by the ability to have the *ParseFileSpec* routine search for multiple file specifications. The routine doesn't directly depend on module-level variables, so you can easily add a few lines (shown here in boldface) to turn it into a powerful recursive routine:

```
' Create the internal Collection if necessary.
If m_Filenames Is Nothing Then Set m_Filenames = New Collection
' Support for semicolon delimited multiple file specifications
Dim MultiSpecs() As String, i As Integer
If InStr(FileSpec, ";") Then
    MultiSpecs = Split(FileSpec, ";")
    For i = LBound(MultiSpecs) To UBound(MultiSpecs)
        ' Recursive call to this routine
        ParseFileSpec MultiSpecs(i)
    Next
    Exit Sub
End If
Path = GetPath(FileSpec)
' And so on....
```

Because the *FileSpec* property internally uses the *ParseFileSpec* routine, it automatically inherits the ability to accept multiple semicolon-delimited file specifications. The class module provided on the companion CD is based on this technique.

Prenotification events

So far, you have seen that the *FileCopyComplete* event is raised immediately after the copy operation because it's intended to give the client code a clue that something has occurred inside the class module. A more flexible class would envision the capability for the client to intervene even *before* the operation takes place. In other words, what you need is a *WillCopyFile* event:

```
Enum ActionConstants
    foContinue = 1
    foSkip
    foAbort
End Enum
Event WillCopyFile(file As String, DestPath As String, _
    Action As ActionConstants)
```

I could have used a standard Boolean *Cancel* argument, but an enumerated value adds a lot of flexibility. You raise a *WillCopyFile* event in the *Copy* method, just before doing the actual copy. Here's the revised procedure, with added or modified statements showed in boldface:

```
Sub Copy(DestPath As String)
    Dim var As Variant, file As String, dest As String
    Dim Action As ActionConstants
    On Error Resume Next
    For Each var In Filenames
        file = var
        dest = MakeFilename(DestPath, GetFileName(file))
        Action = foContinue
        RaiseEvent WillCopyFile(file, dest, Action)
        If Action = foAbort Then Exit Sub
        If Action = foContinue Then
            FileCopy file, dest
            If Err = 0 Then
                RaiseEvent FileCopyComplete(file, GetPath(dest))
            Else
                Err.Clear
            End If
        End If
    Next
End Sub
```

To take advantage of this new event, the client form module has been enriched with a Confirm CheckBox control that, if selected, gives the user control over the copy process. Thanks to the *WillCopyFile* event, you can implement this new feature with just a handful of statements:

```
Private Sub Fop_WillCopyFile(File As String, DestPath As String, _
    Action As ActionConstants)
```

```
' Exit if user isn't interested in file-by-file confirmation.
If chkConfirm = vbUnchecked Then Exit Sub
Dim ok As Integer
ok = MsgBox("Copying file " & File & " to " & DestPath & vbCr _
    & "Click YES to proceed, NO to skip, CANCEL to abort", _
    vbYesNoCancel + vbInformation)
Select Case ok
    Case vbYes: Action = foContinue
    Case vbNo: Action = foSkip
    Case vbCancel: Action = foAbort
End Select
End Sub
```

You can use the mechanism of prenotification events to much greater effect than just as a means for allowing or preventing the completion of a given process. In fact, a significant point of these types of events is that most or all their arguments are passed by reference and can therefore be altered by the caller. This is similar to what you usually do with the *KeyAscii* argument passed to the *KeyPress* event procedure of a standard control. For example, you might decide that all BAK files should be copied to a different directory:

```
' Inside the WillCopyFile event procedure (in the client)...
If LCase$(Fop.GetExtension(file)) = "bak" Then
    DestPath = "C:\Backup"
End If
```

Notifying clients of error conditions

In most cases, the best means for a class to return an error to the client is by using the standard *Err.Raise* method. This allows the client to get a definitive confirmation that something went wrong and that appropriate steps must be taken. However, when a class communicates with its clients through events, you can explore a few alternatives to the *Err.Raise* method. For example, if the CFileOp class isn't able to copy a particular file, should the entire copy process be terminated? Needless to say, only the client code knows the answer, so the right thing to do is to ask it—by means of an event, of course:

```
Event Error(OpName As String, File As String, File2 As String, _
    ErrCode As Integer, ErrMessage As String, Action As ActionConstants)
```

You see that I've added a generic *OpName* argument so that the same *Error* event can be shared by all the methods in the class module. Adding support for this new event in the *Copy* method requires little effort:

```
' Inside the Copy method in the CFileOp class module...
FileCopy File, dest
If Err = 0 Then
```

(continued)

```
    RaiseEvent FileCopyComplete(File, DestPath)
Else
    Dim ErrCode As Integer, ErrMessage As String
    ErrCode = Err.Number: ErrMessage = Err.Description
    RaiseEvent Error("Copy", File, DestPath, ErrCode, _
        ErrMessage, Action)
    ' Report the error to the client if user aborted the process.
    If Action = foAbort Then
        ' You need to cancel error handling, otherwise the Err.Raise
        ' method won't return the control to the client.
        On Error GoTo 0
        Err.Raise ErrCode, , ErrMessage
    End If
Err.Clear
End If
```

The client now has the ability to trap errors and decide what to do with them. For example, an "Error 76 – Path not found" means that either the source or the destination isn't valid, so there isn't any point in continuing the operation:

```
Private Sub Fop_Error(OpName As String, File As String, File2 As String, _
    ErrCode As Integer, ErrMessage As String, Action As ActionConstants)
    If ErrCode = 76 Then
        MsgBox ErrMessage, vbCritical
        Action = foAbort
    End If
End Sub
```

This code doesn't test the *OpName* argument: This is an intentional omission because the same code can manage errors raised by all methods in the class. Also note that the class passes both *ErrCode* and *ErrMessage* by reference, and the client can, for example, modify them at will:

```
    ' Use a custom error scheme for this client.
    If OpName = "Copy" Then
        ErrCode = ErrCode + 1000: ErrMessage = "Unable to Copy"
    ElseIf OpName = "Move" Then
        ErrCode = ErrCode + 2000: ErrMessage = "Unable to Move"
    End If
    Action = foAbort
```

Notifying clients of progress

The task of notifying the user about the progress of a process is among the most common uses for events. In a sense, each prenotification and postnotification event can be considered a signal that the process is active, so it could seem that a separate *Progress* event is superfluous. But you can offer your clients better service if you also expose an event that clients can use to inform the user about the progress of a task, for example using a progress bar that shows the percentage of the job accomplished.

The trick is to raise this event only when the actual percentage changes so that you don't force the client to continuously update the user interface without any real reason to do so:

```
Event ProgressPercent(Percent As Integer)
```

After writing some classes that expose the *ProgressPercent* event, you realize that you can put most of the logic for this event in a generic procedure, which can be reused in all your class modules:

```
Private Sub CheckProgressPercent(Optional NewValue As Variant, _
    Optional MaxValue As Variant)
    Static Value As Variant, Limit As Variant
    Static LastPercent As Integer
    Dim CurrValue As Variant, CurrPercent As Integer
    If Not IsMissing(MaxValue) Then
        Limit = MaxValue
        If IsMissing(NewValue) Then Err.Raise 9998, , _
            "NewValue can't be omitted in the first call"
        Value = NewValue
    Else
        If IsEmpty(Limit) Then Err.Raise 9999, , "Not initialized!"
        Value = Value + IIf(IsMissing(NewValue), 1, NewValue)
    End If
    CurrPercent = (Value * 100) \ Limit
    If CurrPercent <> LastPercent Or Not IsMissing(MaxValue) Then
        LastPercent = CurrPercent
        RaiseEvent ProgressPercent(CurrPercent)
    End If
End Sub
```

The structure of the *CheckProgressPercent* routine is somewhat contorted because it has to account for many possible default values of its arguments. You can call it with two, one, or no arguments. You call it with two arguments when you want to reset its internal counters *Value* and *Limit*. You call it with just one argument when you simply want to increment *Value*. Finally, you call it with no arguments when you increment *Value* by 1 (a case so common that it deserves a courtesy treatment). This flexible scheme simplifies how the routine is invoked by the methods in the class, and in most cases you just need two statements to fire the *Progress* event at the right time:

```
' In the Copy method
On Error Resume Next
CheckProgressPercent 0, Filenames.Count       ' Reset internal counters.
For Each var In Filenames
    CheckProgressPercent                      ' Increment by 1.
    File = var
    ...
```

The *CheckProgressPercent* routine is optimized and raises a *ProgressPercent* event only when the percentage actually changes. This allows you to write code in the client without worrying about tracing the changes yourself:

```
Private Sub Fop_ProgressPercent(Percent As Integer)
    ShowProgress picStatus, Percent
End Sub

' A reusable routine that prints to a generic PictureBox
Private Sub ShowProgress(pic As PictureBox, Percent As Integer, _
    Optional Color As Long = vbBlue)
    pic.Cls
    pic.Line (0, 0)-(pic.ScaleWidth * Percent / 100, _
        pic.ScaleHeight), Color, BF
    pic.CurrentX = (pic.ScaleWidth - pic.TextWidth(CStr(Percent) _
        & " %")) / 2
    pic.CurrentY = (pic.ScaleHeight - pic.TextHeight("%")) / 2
    pic.Print CStr(Percent) & " %";
End Sub
```

The CFileOp class that you'll find on the companion CD includes many other improvements, such as the support for *Move* and *Delete* commands, and the inclusion of a *Parsing* event that lets the client filter out specific files during the parsing process. (See Figure 7-3.)

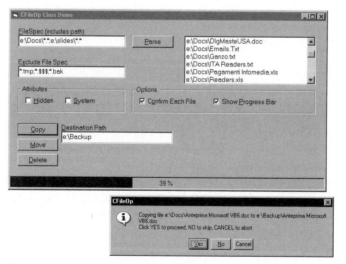

Figure 7-3. *This version of the CFileOp demonstration program supports multiple filespecs, wildcards, additional file commands, a progress bar with a percentage indicator, and full control of individual file operations.*

Multicasting

Now that I have shown you several ways to exploit events in your own classes in hopes of piquing your interest, I admit that I've reserved the best news for the grand finale (of this section about events, at least). In fact, what I've purposefully left out is that the event mechanism on which *WithEvents* is based is compatible with COM and with all the events raised by Visual Basic's own forms and controls.

This mechanism is also known as *event multicasting*. This term means that an object can raise events in all the client modules containing a *WithEvents* variable that points to that object. This might seem to be a negligible detail until you see how far-reaching its consequences are.

As you all know, a form module is always able to trap events from its own controls. Before multicasting, trapping controls' events in the parent form's module was the best thing a programmer could do. Well, it probably is *still* the best thing that you can do with events, but surely it isn't the only one. In fact, you can declare an explicit object variable, let it point to a particular control, and use it to trap that control's events. The multicasting mechanism ensures that the variable receives the event notification *wherever it is declared*! This means that you can move the variable to another module in the program (or to another form, or class, or actually anything but a standard BAS module) and still react to all the events raised by the control.

A class for validating TextBox controls

Let's see what this means to us, mere Visual Basic programmers. To show multicasting in action, you just need a very simple CTextBxN class module, whose only purpose is to reject any nondigit keys from a TextBox control:

```
Public WithEvents TextBox As TextBox

Private Sub TextBox_KeyPress(KeyAscii As Integer)
    Select Case KeyAscii
        Case 0 To 31                    ' Accept control chars.
        Case 48 To 57                   ' Accept digits.
        Case Else
            KeyAscii = 0                ' Reject anything else.
    End Select
End Sub
```

To test drive this class, create a form, place a TextBox control on it, and add this code:

```
Dim Amount As CTextBxN
Private Sub Form_Load()
    Set Amount = New CTextBxN
    Set Amount.TextBox = Text1
End Sub
```

Run the program, and try to type a nondigit key in Text1. After a few attempts, you'll realize that the CTextBxN class is trapping all the *KeyPress* events raised from Text1 and processing the validation code on behalf of the Form1 module. Seems interesting, eh? The real power of this technique becomes apparent when you have other numerical fields on your form, for example, a new Text2 control that holds a percentage value:

```
Dim Amount As CTextBxN, Percentage As CTextBxN
Private Sub Form_Load()
    Set Amount = New CTextBxN
    Set Amount.TextBox = Text1
    Set Percentage = New CTextBxN
    Set Percentage.TextBox = Text2
End Sub
```

Instead of creating distinct event procedures in the parent form module, each one validating the keys going to a distinct TextBox control, you've encapsulated the validation logic in the CTextBxN class once, and you're now reusing it over and over again. And you can do it for all the fields in Form1, as well as for any number of fields in any form of your application (not to mention all the future applications that you'll write from now on). This is *reusable* code!

Improving the CTextBxN class

The benefits of multicasting shouldn't make you forget that CTextBxN is a regular class module, which can be improved with properties and methods. Just as an example, let's add three new properties that make the class more useful: *IsDecimal* is a Boolean property that, if True, allows decimal values; *FormatMask* is a string used to format the number when the focus leaves the control; and *SelectOnEntry* is a Boolean property that states whether the current value should be highlighted when the control gets the focus. Here's the new version of the class:

```
Public WithEvents TextBox As TextBox
Public IsDecimal As Boolean
Public FormatMask As String
Public SelectOnEntry As Boolean

Private Sub TextBox_KeyPress(KeyAscii As Integer)
    Select Case KeyAscii
        Case 0 To 31                      ' Accept control chars.
        Case 48 To 57                     ' Accept digits.
        Case Asc(Format$(0.1, "."))       ' Accept the Decimal separator.
            If Not IsDecimal Then KeyAscii = 0
        Case Else
            KeyAscii = 0                  ' Reject anything else.
    End Select
End Sub
```

```
Private Sub TextBox_GotFocus()
    TextBox.Text = FilterNumber(TextBox.Text, True)
    If SelectOnEntry Then
        TextBox.SelStart = 0
        TextBox.SelLength = Len(TextBox.Text)
    End If
End Sub

Private Sub TextBox_LostFocus()
    If Len(FormatMask) Then
        TextBox.Text = Format$(TextBox.Text, FormatMask)
    End If
End Sub
' Code for FilterNumber is omitted. (See Chapter 3.)
```

Using the new properties is a pleasure. Just set them in the *Form_Load* procedure and then enjoy your smarter TextBox controls:

```
' In the Form_Load event procedure
Amount.FormatMask = "#,###,###"
Amount.SelectOnEntry = True
Percentage.FormatMask = "0.00"
Percentage.IsDecimal = True
Percentage.SelectOnEntry = True
```

Send custom events to the container

Because CTextBxN is a regular class module, it can even declare and raise its own custom events. This ability is really interesting: The class "steals" controls' events from the original form but then sends the form other events. This permits a degree of sophistication that couldn't be possible otherwise. To demonstrate this concept in action, I'll show you how to add to the class full support for validation against *Min* and *Max* properties. In a regular program, validation is performed in the *Validate* event on the parent form. (See Chapter 3.) But now you can trap that event and preprocess it against your new custom properties:

```
' In the CTextsBxN class module
Event ValidateError(Cancel As Boolean)
Public Min As Variant, Max As Variant

Private Sub TextBox_Validate(Cancel As Boolean)
    If Not IsEmpty(Min) Then
        If CDbl(TextBox.Text) < Min Then RaiseEvent ValidateError(Cancel)
    End If
    If Not IsEmpty(Max) Then
        If CDbl(TextBox.Text) > Max Then RaiseEvent ValidateError(Cancel)
    End If
End Sub
```

If the class detects a potential out-of-range error, it just raises a *ValidationError* in the original form, passing the *Cancel* argument by reference. In the client form module, you can therefore decide whether you actually want to abort the shift focus, exactly as you would do under normal circumstances:

```
' Now Percentage must be declared using WithEvents.
Dim WithEvents Percentage As CTextBxN
Private Sub Form_Load()
    ' ...
    Percentage.Min = 0
    Percentage.Max = 100
End Sub
' ...
Private Sub Percentage_ValidateError(Cancel As Boolean)
    MsgBox "Invalid Percentage Value", vbExclamation
    Cancel = True
End Sub
```

Alternatively, you could set *Cancel* to True in the class module and give the client code an opportunity to reset it to False. These are just details. The important point is that you're now in complete control of what happens inside the control, and you're doing that with a minimum amount of code on the form itself because most of the logic is encapsulated in the class module.

Trapping events from multiple controls

Now that you know how you can have a class module trap events from a control, you can extend the technique to multiple controls as well. For example, you can trap events from a TextBox control and a tiny ScrollBar control beside it to simulate those fancy spin buttons that are so trendy in many Windows applications. Or you can rework the scrollable form example in Chapter 3 and build a CScrollForm class module that traps events from a form and its two companion scroll bars. Instead of rehashing such simple tasks, I prefer to focus on something new and more interesting. In the following example, I'll show you how easily you can create *calculated fields* using multicasting. This example is a bit more complex, but I'm sure that in the end you'll be glad to have spent some time on it.

The CTextBoxCalc class module I built is able to trap the *Change* event from up to five distinct TextBox controls (the *independent* fields) and use this capability to update the contents of another Textbox on the form (the *dependent* field) without any intervention from the main program. To create a generic calculated field, I needed to devise a way for the client code to specify the expression that must be reevaluated each time one of the independent controls raises a *Change* event. To this end, the class exposes a *SetExpression* method that accepts an array of parameters. Each parameter can be a reference to a control, a number, or a string that represents one of the four math operators. Look, for example, at the following code:

```
' Example of client code that uses the CTextBoxCalc class
' txtTax and txtGrandTotal depend on txtAmount and txtPercent.
Dim Tax As New CTextBoxCalc, GrandTotal As New CTextBoxCalc
' Link the class to the control on which the result is to be displayed.
Set Tax.TextBox = txtTax
' Set the expression "Amount * Percent / 100".
Tax.SetExpression txtAmount, "*", txtPercent, "/", 100
' Create a GrandTotal calculated field, equal to "Amount + Tax".
Set GrandTotal.TextBox = txtGrandTotal
GrandTotal.SetExpression txtAmount, "+", txtTax
```

The intricacy of the CTextBoxCalc class derives mostly from the need to parse the arguments passed to the *SetExpression* method. I kept this intricacy to a minimum and renounced sophisticated features such as allowing different priorities among operators, bracketed subexpressions, and functions. This leaves the four math operators, which are evaluated in a strict left-to-right order. (For example, "2+3*4" evaluates to 20 instead of 14.) On the other hand, the complete class module has just 80 lines of code:

```
' The complete source code for CTextBoxCalc class
Public TextBox As TextBox
Public FormatMask As String
' We can trap events from max 5 TextBox controls.
Private WithEvents Text1 As TextBox
Private WithEvents Text2 As TextBox
Private WithEvents Text3 As TextBox
Private WithEvents Text4 As TextBox
Private WithEvents Text5 As TextBox
' Here we store the arguments passed to SetExpression.
Dim expression() As Variant

Sub SetExpression(ParamArray args() As Variant)
    Dim i As Integer, n As Integer
    ReDim expression(LBound(args) To UBound(args)) As Variant
    For i = LBound(args) To UBound(args)
        If IsObject(args(i)) Then
            ' Objects must be stored as such, using Set.
            Set expression(i) = args(i)
            If TypeName(args(i)) = "TextBox" Then
                n = n + 1
                If n = 1 Then Set Text1 = args(i)
                If n = 2 Then Set Text2 = args(i)
                If n = 3 Then Set Text3 = args(i)
                If n = 4 Then Set Text4 = args(i)
                If n = 5 Then Set Text5 = args(i)
            End If
        Else
```

(continued)

```
                          ' Store number and strings without the Set keyword.
                          expression(i) = args(i)
                  End If
          Next
  End Sub


  ' Here we actually evaluate the result.
  Sub EvalExpression()
      Dim i As Integer, opcode As Variant
      Dim value As Variant, operand As Variant
      On Error GoTo Error_Handler
      For i = LBound(expression) To UBound(expression)
          If Not IsObject(expression(i)) And VarType(expression(i)) _
              = vbString Then
                  opcode = expression(i)
          Else
              ' This works with numbers and Text (default) properties alike.
              operand = CDbl(expression(i))
              Select Case opcode
                  Case Empty: value = operand
                  Case "+": value = value + operand
                  Case "-": value = value - operand
                  Case "*": value = value * operand
                  Case "/": value = value / operand
              End Select
              opcode = Empty
          End If
      Next
      If Len(FormatMask) Then value = Format$(value, FormatMask)
      TextBox.Text = value
      Exit Sub
  Error_Handler:
      TextBox.Text = ""
  End Sub


  ' Here we trap events from the independent fields.
  Private Sub Text1_Change()
      EvalExpression
  End Sub
  ' ... Text2-Text5 Change procedures .... (omitted)
```

The class can trap events from a maximum of five TextBox independent controls, but the expression could refer to just one or two of them. This is OK: If a *WithEvents* variable isn't assigned and remains Nothing, it simply stays inert and never raises events in the class. It isn't useful but doesn't do any harm either.

To get an idea of the potential of this class, run the demonstration program on the companion CD and see how you can grow a spreadsheet-like form that accepts data in a couple of fields and automatically updates the other two fields. (See Figure 7-4 for an example of how that might work.) The same application demonstrates both the CTextBxN and the CTextBoxCalc classes.

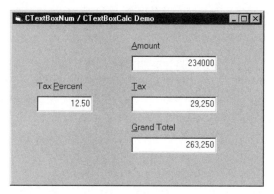

Figure 7-4. *You can create smart forms that contain live calculated fields by using reusable external class modules exclusively.*

The pitfalls of multicasting

Exploiting the event multicasting features in your application is among the best favors you can do yourself. Before you get too carried away, though, you should be aware that there are a few problems with this technique.

- The *WithEvents* keyword doesn't work with arrays of object variables. This makes it difficult to create extremely generic routines. For example, in the CTextBoxCalc class we had to set a limit of five external TextBox controls—the variables *Text1* through *Text5* in the class—because it wasn't possible to create an array of objects. This problem has a solution, but it isn't simple and you won't see it until the "Data-Driven Form" section in Chapter 9.

- You have absolutely no control over the order in which events are dispatched to *WithEvents* variables. In general, you should avoid having the same event served in two distinct places in your code—for example, a *KeyPress* event for a control trapped both in the form and in an external class. If you can't avoid it, at least ensure that your code will work in whatever order the events arrive. (This order is random, so one or two attempts won't be enough to prove the correctness of your approach.)

■   There's an undocumented bug in how Visual Basic implements the *With-Events* keyword: you can't use *WithEvents* with controls that belong to a control array:

```
Dim WithEvents TextBox As TextBox
Private Sub Form_Load()
    ' Raises a Type Mismatch run-time error.
    Set TextBox = Text1(0)
End Sub
```

This bug prevents you from dynamically creating a new control from a control array and then trapping its events using multicasting. Unfortunately, there isn't any known solution to this problem. Curiously, this bug doesn't manifest itself if the control you're assigning to a *WithEvents* variable is an ActiveX control authored in Visual Basic.

POLYMORPHISM

The term *polymorphism* describes the capability of different objects to expose a similar set of properties and methods. The most obvious and familiar examples of polymorphic objects are Visual Basic's own controls, most of which share property and method names. The advantage of polymorphism is evident when you think of the sort of generic routines that work on multiple objects and controls:

```
' Change the BackColor property for all the controls on the form.
Sub SetBackColor(frm As Form, NewColor As Long)
    Dim ctrl As Control
    On Error Resume Next                 ' Account for invisible controls.
    For Each ctrl In frm.Controls
        ctrl.BackColor = NewColor
    Next
End Sub
```

Leveraging Polymorphism

You can exploit the benefits of polymorphism to write better code in many ways. In this section, I examine the two that are most obvious: procedures with polymorphic arguments and classes with polymorphic methods.

Polymorphic procedures

A polymorphic procedure can do different things depending on which arguments you pass it. In previous chapters, I have often implicitly used this idea, for example, when writing routines that use a *Variant* argument to process arrays of different types. Let's see now how you can expand on this concept for writing more flexible classes. I'll illustrate a simple CRectangle class, which exposes a number of simple properties (*Left*, *Top*, *Width*, *Height*, *Color*, and *FillColor*) and a *Draw* method that displays it on a surface. Here's the source code of the class module:

```
' In a complete implementation, we would use property procedures.
Public Left As Single, Top As Single
Public Width As Single, Height As Single
Public Color As Long, FillColor As Long

Private Sub Class_Initialize()
    Color = vbBlack
    FillColor = -1                  ' -1 means "not filled"
End Sub


' A pseudoconstructor method
Friend Sub Init(Left As Single, Top As Single, Width As Single, Height As _
    Single, Optional Color As Variant, Optional FillColor As Variant)
    ' .... code omitted for brevity
End Sub


' Draw this shape on a form, a picture box, or the Printer object.
Sub Draw(pic As Object)
    If FillColor <> -1 Then
        pic.Line (Left, Top)-Step(Width, Height), FillColor, BF
    End If
    pic.Line (Left, Top)-Step(Width, Height), Color, B
End Sub
```

For the sake of brevity, all the properties are implemented as Public variables, but in a real implementation you would surely use Property procedures to enforce validation rules. The real focal point of this class, however, is the *Draw* method, which expects an Object argument. This means that we can display the rectangle on any object that supports the *Line* method:

```
Dim rect As New CRect
' Create a white rectangle with a red border.
rect.Init 1000, 500, 2000, 1500, vbRed, vbWhite
' Display it wherever you want.
If PreviewMode Then
    rect.Draw Picture1          ' A picture box
Else
    rect.Draw Printer           ' A printer
End If
```

This first form of polymorphism is interesting, though limited. In this particular case, in fact, we can't do much more than what we've done because forms, PictureBox controls, and the Printer are the only objects that support the *Line* method with its exotic syntax. The really important point is that the client application benefits from this capability to simplify its code.

Polymorphic classes

The real power of polymorphism becomes apparent when you create multiple class modules and select the names of their properties and methods in a way that ensures a complete or partial polymorphism among them. For example, you can create a CEllipse class that's completely polymorphic with the CRectangle class, even if the two classes are implemented differently:

```
' The CEllipse class
Public Left As Single, Top As Single
Public Width As Single, Height As Single
Public Color As Long, FillColor As Long

Private Sub Class_Initialize()
    Color = vbBlack
    FillColor = -1                  ' -1 means "not filled"
End Sub

' Draw this shape on a form, a picture box, or the Printer object.
Sub Draw(pic As Object)
    Dim aspect As Single, radius As Single
    Dim saveFillColor As Long, saveFillStyle As Long
    aspect = Height / Width
    radius = IIf(Width > Height, Width / 2, Height / 2)
    If FillColor <> -1 Then
        saveFillColor = pic.FillColor
        saveFillStyle = pic.FillStyle
        pic.FillColor = FillColor
        pic.FillStyle = vbSolid
        pic.Circle (Left + Width / 2, Top + Height / 2), radius, Color, _
            , , aspect
        pic.FillColor = saveFillColor
        pic.FillStyle = saveFillStyle
    Else
        pic.Circle (Left + Width / 2, Top + Height / 2), radius, Color, _
            , , aspect
    End If
End Sub
```

You can also create classes that are only partially polymorphic with respect to CRectangle. For example, a CLine class might support the *Draw* method and the *Color* property but use different names for its other members:

```
' The CLine class
Public X As Single, Y As Single
Public X2 As Single, Y2 As Single
Public Color As Long

Private Sub Class_Initialize()
    Color = vbBlack
End Sub

' Draw this shape on a form, a picture box, or the Printer object.
Sub Draw(pic As Object)
    pic.Line (X, Y)-(X2, Y2), Color
End Sub
```

Now you have three classes that are polymorphic with one another with respect to their *Draw* methods and their *Color* properties. This permits you to create a first version of a very primitive CAD-like application, named Shapes, shown in Figure 7-5. You can do this by using an array or a collection that holds all your shapes so that you can redraw all of them quite easily. To keep the client code as concise and descriptive as possible, you can also define a number of factory methods in a separate BAS module (not shown here because it's not terribly interesting for our purposes):

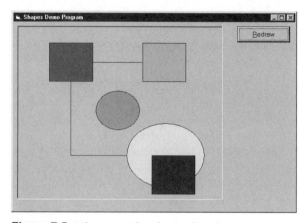

Figure 7-5. *Playing with polymorphic shapes.*

```
' This is a module-level variable.
Dim Figures As Collection

Private Sub Form_Load()
    CreateFigures
End Sub
Private Sub cmdRedraw_Click()
    RedrawFigures
End Sub
```

(continued)

```
' Create a set of figures.
Private Sub CreateFigures()
    Set Figures = New Collection
    Figures.Add New_CRectangle(1000, 500, 1400, 1200, , vbRed)
    Figures.Add New_CRectangle(4000, 500, 1400, 1200, , vbCyan)
    Figures.Add New_CEllipse(2500, 2000, 1400, 1200, , vbGreen)
    Figures.Add New_CEllipse(3500, 3000, 2500, 2000, , vbYellow)
    Figures.Add New_CRectangle(4300, 4000, 1400, 1200, , vbBlue)
    Figures.Add New_CLine(2400, 1100, 4000, 1100, vbBlue)
    Figures.Add New_CLine(1700, 1700, 1700, 4000, vbBlue)
    Figures.Add New_CLine(1700, 4000, 3500, 4000, vbBlue)
End Sub

' Redraw figures.
Sub RedrawFigures()
    Dim Shape As Object
    picView.Cls
    For Each Shape In Figures
        Shape.Draw picView
    Next
End Sub
```

While complete polymorphism is always preferable, you can still use a lot of interesting techniques when objects have just a few properties in common. For example, you can quickly turn the contents of the Figures collection into a series of wire-framed objects:

```
On Error Resume Next      ' CLine doesn't support the FillColor property.
For Each Shape In Figures
    Shape.FillColor = -1
Next
```

It's easy to add sophistication to this initial example. For example, you might add support for moving and zooming objects, using the *Move* and *Zoom* methods. Here's a possible implementation of these methods for the CRectangle class:

```
' In CRectangle class module...
' Move this object.
Sub Move(stepX As Single, stepY As Single)
    Left = Left + stepX
    Top = Top + stepY
End Sub

' Enlarge or shrink this object on its center.
Sub Zoom(ZoomFactor As Single)
    Left = Left + Width * (1 - ZoomFactor) / 2
```

```
    Top = Top + Height * (1 - ZoomFactor) / 2
    Width = Width * ZoomFactor
    Height = Height * ZoomFactor
End Sub
```

The implementation for the CEllipse class is identical to this code because it's perfectly polymorphic with CRectangle and therefore exposes *Left*, *Top*, *Width*, and *Height* properties. The CLine class supports both the *Move* and the *Zoom* method as well, even if their implementation is different. (See the code on the companion CD for more details.)

Figure 7-6 on the following page shows an improved Shapes sample program, which also permits you to move and zoom the objects on the playground. This is the code behind the buttons on the form:

```
Private Sub cmdMove_Click(Index As Integer)
    Dim shape As Object
    For Each shape In Figures
        Select Case Index
            Case 0: shape.Move 0, -100      ' Up
            Case 1: shape.Move 0, 100       ' Down
            Case 2: shape.Move -100, 0      ' Left
            Case 3: shape.Move 100, 0       ' Right
        End Select
    Next
    RedrawFigures
End Sub

Private Sub cmdZoom_Click(Index As Integer)
    Dim shape As Object
    For Each shape In Figures
        If Index = 0 Then
            shape.Zoom 1.1                  ' Enlarge
        Else
            shape.Zoom 0.9                  ' Reduce
        End If
    Next
    RedrawFigures
End Sub
```

If you want to appreciate what polymorphism can do for your programming habits, just think of the many lines of code you would have written to solve this simple programming task using any other means. And of course consider that you can apply these techniques to more complex business objects, including Documents, Invoices, Orders, Customers, Employees, Products, and so on.

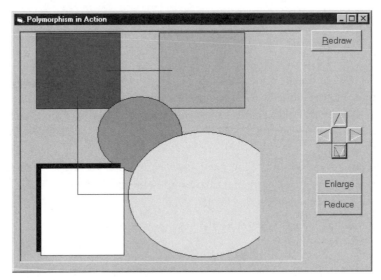

Figure 7-6. *More fun with polymorphic shapes.*

Polymorphism and late binding

I haven't yet talked about one aspect of polymorphism in the depth it deserves. The most important trait in common among all the polymorphic examples seen so far is that you have been able to write polymorphic code only because you use *generic* object variables. For example, the *pic* argument in the *Draw* method is declared with *As Object*, as is the *Shape* variable in all *Click* procedures in the preceding code. You might use Variant variables that hold an object reference, but the concept is the same: you are doing polymorphism through late binding.

As you'll recall from Chapter 6, late binding is a technique that has several defects, the most serious being a sloppy performance—it's even *hundreds* of times slower than early binding—and less robust code. Depending on the particular piece of code you're working on, these defects can easily nullify all the benefits you get from polymorphism. Fortunately, Visual Basic offers a solution to this problem—a great solution, I daresay. To understand how it works, you must be familiar with the concept of *interfaces*.

Working with Interfaces

When you start using polymorphism in your code, you realize that you're logically subdividing all the properties and methods exposed by your objects into distinct groups. For example, the CRectangle, CEllipse, and CLine classes expose a few members in common (*Draw*, *Move*, and *Zoom*). With real-world objects, which include dozens or even hundreds of properties and methods, creating groups of them isn't just a luxury, it's necessary. A group of related properties and methods is called an *interface*.

Under Visual Basic 4, any object could have only one interface, the *main* interface. Starting with version 5, Visual Basic's class modules can include one or more *secondary interfaces*. This is exactly what you need to better organize your object-oriented code. And you'll see that this innovation has many other beneficial implications.

Creating a secondary interface

In Visual Basic 5 and 6, the definition of a secondary interface requires that you create a separate class module. This module doesn't contain any executable code, just the definition of properties and methods. For this reason, it's often called an *abstract class*. As with any Visual Basic module, you need to give it a name. It's customary to distinguish interface names from class names by using a leading letter *I*.

Back to our mini-CAD example: Let's create an interface that gathers the *Draw*, *Move*, and *Zoom* methods—that is, the members in common to all the shapes we're dealing with. This will be the IShape interface. To add some spice, I am also adding the *Hidden* property:

```
' The IShape class module
Public Hidden As Boolean

Sub Draw(pic As Object)
    ' (Empty comment to prevent automatic deletion of this routine)
End Sub
Sub Move(stepX As Single, stepY As Single)
    '
End Sub
Sub Zoom(ZoomFactor As Single)
    '
End Sub
```

> **NOTE** You might need to add a comment inside all methods to prevent the editor from automatically deleting empty routines when the program is executed.

This class doesn't include any executable statements and only serves as a model for the IShape interface. What really matters are the names of properties and methods, their arguments, and the type of each one of them. For the same reason, you don't need to create pairs of Property procedures because a simple Public variable is usually enough. For only two cases do you need explicit Property procedures:

■ You want to specify that a property is read-only: in this case, you explicitly omit the *Property Let* or *Property Set* procedure.

■ You want to specify that a *Variant* property can never return an object: in this case, you include the *Property Get* and *Property Let* procedures but omit the *Property Set* procedure.

Interfaces never include *Event* declarations. Visual Basic takes only Public properties and methods into account when you're using a CLS module as an abstract class that defines a secondary interface.

Implementing the interface

The next step is letting Visual Basic know that the CRectangle, CEllipse, and CLine classes expose the IShape interface. You do this by adding an *Implements* keyword in the declaration section of each class module:

```
' In the CRectangle class module
Implements IShape
```

Declaring that a class exposes an interface is only half of the job because you now have to actually *implement* the interface. In other words, you must write the code that Visual Basic will execute when any member of the interface is invoked. The code editor does part of the job on your behalf by creating the code template for each individual routine. The mechanism is similar to the one available for events: In the leftmost combo box, you select the name of the interface (it appeared in the box as soon as you moved the caret away from the *Implements* statement) and select the name of a method or a property in the rightmost combo box, which you can see in Figure 7-7. Notice this important difference from events, though: When you implement an interface, you must create *all* the procedures listed in this combo box. If you don't do this, Visual Basic won't even run your application. For this reason, the fastest way to proceed is to select all the items in the rightmost combo box to create all the procedure templates, and then add code to them. Note that all names have been prefixed with IShape_, which solves any name conflict with the methods already in the module, and that all routines have been declared to be Private. This is what you want because if they were Public, they would appear in the main interface. Also note that the *Hidden* property has generated a pair of Property procedures.

Writing the actual code

To complete the implementation of the interface, you must write code inside the procedure templates. If you don't, the program will run but the object will never respond to the IShape interface.

Interfaces are said to be *contracts*: If you implement an interface, you implicitly agree to respond to all the properties and methods of that interface in a way that complies with the interface specifications. In this case, you're expected to react to the *Draw* method with code that displays the object, to the *Move* method with code that moves the object, and so on. If you fail to do so, you're breaking the interface contract and you're the only one to blame for this.

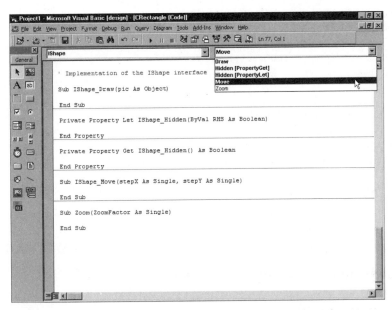

Figure 7-7. *Let the code editor create the procedure templates for you.*

Let's see how you can implement the IShape interface in your CRectangle class. In this case, you already have the code that displays, moves, and scales the object—namely, the *Draw*, *Move*, and *Zoom* methods in the main interface. One of the goals of secondary interfaces, however, is to get rid of redundant members in the main interface. In line with this, you should delete the *Draw*, *Move*, and *Zoom* methods from CRectangle's primary interface and move their code inside the IShape interface:

```
' A (private) variable to store the IShape_Hidden property
Private Hidden As Boolean

Private Sub IShape_Draw(pic As Object)
    If Hidden Then Exit Sub
    If FillColor >= 0 Then
        pic.Line (Left, Top)-Step(Width, Height), FillColor, BF
    End If
    pic.Line (Left, Top)-Step(Width, Height), Color, B
End Sub

Private Sub IShape_Move(stepX As Single, stepY As Single)
    Left = Left + stepX
    Top = Top + stepY
End Sub
```

(continued)

```
Private Sub IShape_Zoom(ZoomFactor As Single)
    Left = Left + Width * (1 - ZoomFactor) / 2
    Top = Top + Height * (1 - ZoomFactor) / 2
    Width = Width * ZoomFactor
    Height = Height * ZoomFactor
End Sub

Private Property Let IShape_Hidden(ByVal RHS As Boolean)
    Hidden = RHS
End Property
Private Property Get IShape_Hidden() As Boolean
    IShape_Hidden = Hidden
End Property
```

This completes the implementation of the IShape interface for the CRectangle class. I won't show here the code for CEllipse and CLine because it's substantially the same, and you'll probably prefer to browse it on the companion CD.

Accessing the secondary interface

Accessing the new interface is simple. All you have to do is declare a variable of the IShape class and assign the object to it:

```
' In the client code ...
Dim Shape As IShape      ' A variable that points to an interface
Set Shape = Figures(1) ' Get the first figure in the list.
Shape.Draw picView       ' Call the Draw method in the IShape interface.
```

The Set command in the previous code is somewhat surprising because you would expect that the assignment would fail with a Type Mismatch error. Instead, the code works because the compiler can ascertain that the Figures(1) object (a CRectangle object in this particular sample program) supports the IShape interface and that a valid pointer can be returned and safely stored in the *Shape* variable. It's as if Visual Basic queried the source CRectangle object, "Do you support the IShape interface?" If it does, the assignment can be completed, otherwise an error is raised. This operation is referred to as *QueryInterface*, or *QI* for short.

> **NOTE**   In Chapter 6, you learned that a class is always paired with a *VTable* structure, which holds the addresses of all its procedures. A class that implements a secondary interface comes with a secondary *VTable* structure, which of course points to the procedures of that secondary interface. When a *QI* command is attempted for a secondary interface, the value returned in the target variable is the address of a memory location inside the instance data area, which in turn holds the address of this secondary *VTable* structure. (See Figure 7-8.) This mechanism enables Visual Basic to deal with primary and secondary interfaces using the same low-level core routines.

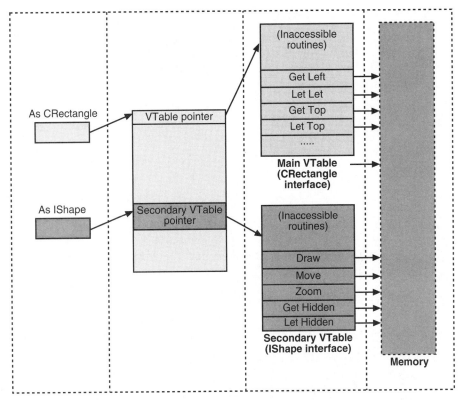

Figure 7-8. *Secondary interfaces and* VTable *structures. (Compare this with Figure 6-8.)*

QueryInterface is a symmetrical operation, and Visual Basic lets you do assignments in both directions:

```
Dim Shape As IShape, Rect As CRectangle
' You can create a CRectangle object on the fly.
Set Shape = New CRectangle
Set Rect = Shape                ' This works.
Rect.Init 100, 200, 400, 800    ' Rect points to primary interface.
Shape.Move 30, 60               ' Shape points to its IShape interface.
' Next statement proves that both variables point to the same instance.
Print Rect.Left, Rect.Top       ' Displays "130" and "260"
```

Refining the client code

If you implement the IShape interface in the CEllipse and CLine classes as well, you'll see that you can call code inside any of these three classes using the *Shape* variable. In other words, you're doing polymorphism using a variable of a specific type, hence, you can now use early binding.

When two or more classes share an interface, they're said to be *polymorphic with each other* with respect to that particular interface. This technique lets you speed up the Shapes program and make it more robust at the same time. What's really astonishing is that you can accomplish all this by replacing one single line in the original client code:

```
Sub RedrawFigures()
    Dim shape As IShape          ' Instead of "As Object"
    picView.Cls
    For Each shape In Figures
        shape.Draw picView
    Next
End Sub
```

The performance benefit you can get using this approach can vary greatly. This particular routine spends most of its time doing graphics, so the speed improvement might go unnoticed. Most of the time, however, you'll literally see the difference before your eyes.

Playing with VBA keywords

Before diving into another (I hope) fascinating OOP topic, let's see how a few VBA keywords behave when applied to object variables that point to a secondary interface.

The *Set* keyword   As you just saw, you can freely assign object variables to each other, even if they're of different types. The only condition is that the source object (the right side of the assignment) must implement the target class (the left side of the assignment) as a secondary interface. The opposite is also possible—that is, when the source class is an interface implemented by the target class. In both cases, remember that you're assigning a reference to the *same* object.

The *TypeName* function   This function returns the name of the original class of the object pointed to by the object variable, regardless of the type of argument. For example, consider this code:

```
Dim rect As New CRectangle, shape As IShape
Set shape = rect
Print TypeName(shape)     ' Displays "CRectangle", not "IShape"!
```

The *TypeOf...Is* statement   The *TypeOf...Is* statement tests whether an object supports a given interface. You can test for primary and secondary interfaces, as in this example:

```
Dim rect As New CRectangle, shape As IShape
Set shape = rect
' You can pass a variable and test a secondary interface.
If TypeOf rect Is IShape Then Print "OK"          ' Displays "OK"
' You can also pass a variable pointing to a secondary interface
' and test the primary interface (or a different secondary interface).
If TypeOf shape Is CRectangle Then Print "OK"     ' Displays "OK"
```

In Chapter 6, I suggested that you use *TypeName* instead of a *TypeOf...Is* statement. This is correct when you're dealing with primary interfaces exclusively, but when you're testing for a secondary interface you really need *TypeOf...Is*.

The *Is* keyword   In Chapter 6, I explained that the Is operator simply compares the contents of the involved object variables. This is true only when you're comparing variables that hold pointers to the primary interface: when you compare object variables of different types, Visual Basic is smart enough to understand whether they're pointing to the same instance data area, even if the values stored in the variables are different:

```
Set shape = rect
Print (rect Is shape)                 ' Displays "True".
```

Support functions to retrieve secondary interfaces

When you get more involved with secondary interfaces, you'll soon find yourself writing a lot of code just to retrieve the secondary interface of an object. This effort usually requires declaring a variable of the given type and executing a Set command. You might instead find it convenient to write a simple function in a BAS module that does it for you:

```
Function QI_IShape(shape As IShape) As IShape
    Set QI_IShape = shape
End Function
```

For example, see how you can invoke the *Move* method in the IShape interface of a CRectangle object:

```
QI_IShape(rect).Move 10, 20
```

In most cases, you don't need a temporary variable even when assigning multiple properties or multiple methods:

```
With QI_IShape(rect)
    .Move 10, 20
    .Zoom 1.2
End With
```

INHERITANCE

After encapsulation and polymorphism, inheritance is the third major characteristic of all mature object-oriented programming languages. In Chapter 6, I briefly described what inheritance is and how it could be useful to programmers. And I also told you that—unfortunately—inheritance isn't natively supported by Visual Basic. In this section, I explain what you can do to remedy this deficiency.

Back to the Shapes sample program. This time, you'll write a CSquare class module, which adds support for drawing squares. Because this class is so similar to CRectangle, this could actually be a one-minute job: Just copy the CRectangle code into the CSquare module, and edit it where appropriate. For example, because a square is nothing but a rectangle with width equal to height, you could make both the *Width* and *Height* properties point to the same private variable.

This solution is somewhat unsatisfactory, however, because we have duplicated the code in the CRectangle class. If we later discover that the CRectangle class includes a bug, we must remember to correct it in the CSquare module, as well as in all other classes that were derived from CRectangle in the meantime. If Visual Basic supported true inheritance, we could just declare that the CSquare class inherits all its properties and methods from CRectangle, and then we could focus only on the few differences. Alas, this isn't possible, at least with the current version of Visual Basic. (I am an irrepressibly optimistic guy...) On the other hand, the concept of inheritance is so alluring and promising that you might take a second look at it. As I'll show shortly, you can resort to a coding technique that lets you simulate inheritance at the expense of some manual coding.

Inheritance Through Delegation

The technique of simulating inheritance is called *delegation*. The concept is simple: because most of the logic needed in CSquare (the *derived* class) is embodied in CRectangle (the *base* class), the code in CSquare can simply ask a CRectangle object to do the work on its behalf.

Basic delegation techniques

So you do this trick by declaring a private CRectangle object inside the CSquare class and passing it all the calls that CSquare doesn't want to deal with directly. These calls include all methods and all read/write operations for properties. Here's a possible implementation of this technique:

```
' The CSquare Class
' This is the Private instance of the CRectangle class.
Private Rect As CRectangle

Private Sub Class_Initialize()
    ' Create the private variable for doing the delegation.
```

```
        Set Rect = New CRectangle
End Sub

' A simple pseudoconstructor for ease of use
Friend Sub Init(Left As Single, Top As Single, Width As Single, _
        Optional Color As Variant, Optional FillColor As Variant)
        ...
End Sub

' The delegation code
Property Get Left() As Single
        Left = Rect.Left
End Property
Property Let Left(ByVal newValue As Single)
        Rect.Left = newValue
End Property

Property Get Top() As Single
        Top = Rect.Top
End Property
Property Let Top(ByVal newValue As Single)
        Rect.Top = newValue
End Property

Property Get Width() As Single
        Width = Rect.Width
End Property
Property Let Width(ByVal newValue As Single)
        ' Squares are rectangles whose Width = Height.
        Rect.Width = newValue
        Rect.Height = newValue
End Property

Property Get Color() As Long
        Color = Rect.Color
End Property
Property Let Color(ByVal newValue As Long)
        Rect.Color = newValue
End Property

Property Get FillColor() As Long
        FillColor = Rect.FillColor
End Property
Property Let FillColor(ByVal newValue As Long)
        Rect.FillColor = newValue
End Property
```

Admittedly, it's a lot of code for such a simple task, but you shouldn't forget that we're playing with toy objects here. In a real program, the base class might include hundreds or thousands of lines of code. In that case, the relatively few lines needed for the delegation would be absolutely negligible.

Support for secondary interfaces

While our CSquare class is functional, it still doesn't know how to redraw itself. If the CRectangle class exposed the *Draw*, *Move*, and *Zoom* methods in its primary interface—as it did in the first version of the Shapes program—this would have been child's play. Unfortunately, we moved the *Draw* method from the CRectangle main interface to its IShape secondary interface. For this reason, in order to delegate this method we first need to get a reference to that interface:

```
' In the CSquare class
Private Sub IShape_Draw(pic As Object)
    Dim RectShape As IShape
    Set RectShape = Rect        ' Retrieve the IShape interface.
    RectShape.Draw pic          ' Now it works!
End Sub
```

Since you'll need a reference to Rect's IShape interface many times during the life of the CSquare class, you can speed up execution and reduce the amount of code by creating a module-level *RectShape* variable:

```
' CSquare also supports the IShape interface.
Implements IShape

' This is the private instance of the CRectangle class.
Private Rect As CRectangle
' This points the Rect's IShape interface.
Private RectShape As IShape

Private Sub Class_Initialize()
    ' Create the two variables for doing the delegation.
    Set Rect = New CRectangle
    Set RectShape = Rect
End Sub
' ... code for Left, Top, Width, Color, FillColor properties ...(omitted)

' The IShape interface
Private Sub IShape_Draw(pic As Object)
    RectShape.Draw pic
End Sub

Private Property Let IShape_Hidden(ByVal RHS As Boolean)
    RectShape.Hidden = RHS
End Property
```

```
Private Property Get IShape_Hidden() As Boolean
    IShape_Hidden = RectShape.Hidden
End Property

Private Sub IShape_Move(stepX As Single, stepY As Single)
    RectShape.Move stepX, stepY
End Sub

Private Sub IShape_Zoom(ZoomFactor As Single)
    RectShape.Zoom ZoomFactor
End Sub
```

Subclassing the base class

While inheritance through delegation could be easily disregarded as a hack by any serious OO programmer working with mature OOPLs, the fact that you're in complete control of what happens during execution has several advantages. For example, when the client invokes a method in your derived class, you have several choices:

- You simply delegate the call to the base class and return any results to the caller. This is the purest implementation of inheritance, and it's more or less what the compiler would do for you if Visual Basic were a true OOPL.

- You don't delegate the call and process it all inside the derived class. This is often necessary for methods that vary greatly between the two classes.

- You delegate the call but modify the values of the arguments passed to the base class. For example, the CSquare class doesn't expose the *Height* property, so the client will never see such an argument. It's up to the CSquare class to create a dummy value (equal to *Width*) and pass it where appropriate to the base class.

- You delegate the call and then intercept the return value and process it before returning to the caller.

In the last two cases, your code is sometimes said to be *subclassing* the base class. It uses the base class for what can be useful but also executes some pre- and postprocessing code that adds power to the derived class. Even if the concept is vaguely similar, don't confuse it with *control* or *Windows subclassing,* which is a completely different (and more advanced) programming technique that lets you modify the behavior of standard Windows controls. (This type of subclassing is described in the Appendix.)

Subclassing the VBA language

You might not be aware that VBA gives you the means to subclass itself. As you know, Visual Basic can be considered the sum of the Visual Basic library and the VBA language. These libraries are always present in the References dialog box and can't be removed as other external libraries can. Even if you can't remove them, however, as far as the Visual Basic parser is concerned, the names that you use in your own code have a higher priority than the names defined in external libraries, *including the VBA library!* To see what I mean, add this simple procedure in a standard BAS module:

```
' An IIf replacement that accepts just one argument
' If FalsePart is omitted and the expression is False, it returns Empty.
Function IIf(Expression As Boolean, TruePart As Variant, _
    Optional FalsePart As Variant) As Variant
    If Expression Then
        IIf = TruePart
    ElseIf Not IsMissing(FalsePart) Then
        IIf = FalsePart
    End If
End Function
```

You can call native VBA statements even if you're currently subclassing them, provided that you specify the name of the VBA library:

```
Function Hex(Value As Long, Optional Digits As Variant) As String
    If IsMissing(Digits) Then
        Hex = VBA.Hex(Value)
    Else
        Hex = Right$(String$(Digits, "0") & VBA.Hex(Value), Digits)
    End If
End Function
```

You should always try to keep the syntax of your new custom function compatible with that of the original VBA function so that you won't break any existing code.

One word of caution: This technique could give rise to problems, especially if you work on a team of programmers and not all of them are familiar with it. You can cope with this issue in part by always enforcing a compatible syntax, but this doesn't solve the problem when it falls to your colleagues to maintain or revise your code. For this reason, always consider the opportunity to define a new function with a different name and syntax so that your code isn't unnecessarily ambiguous.

Inheritance and Polymorphism

If you completely inherit a class module from another class—that is, you implement *all* the methods of the base class into the derived class—you end up with two modules that are very similar to one another, often to the point that you can use an *Object* variable to leverage their polymorphism and simplify your client code. On the other hand, you know that you don't need to resort to late binding (that is, *Object* variables) to get all the advantages of polymorphism because secondary interfaces always offer a much better alternative.

Implementing the base class as an interface

As an illustration of this concept, the CSquare class could implement the CRectangle interface:

```
' In the CSquare class module
Implements IShape
Implements CRectangle

' The primary and the IShape interface are identical... (omitted)....
' This is the secondary CRectangle interface.

Private Property Let CRectangle_Color(ByVal RHS As Long)
    Rect.Color = RHS
End Property
Private Property Get CRectangle_Color() As Long
    CRectangle_Color = Rect.Color
End Property

Private Property Let CRectangle_FillColor(ByVal RHS As Long)
    Rect.FillColor = RHS
End Property
Private Property Get CRectangle_FillColor() As Long
    CRectangle_FillColor = Rect.FillColor
End Property

' The rect's Height property is replaced by the Width property.
Private Property Let CRectangle_Height(ByVal RHS As Single)
    rect.Width = RHS
End Property
Private Property Get CRectangle_Height() As Single
    CRectangle_Height = rect.Width
End Property

Private Property Let CRectangle_Left(ByVal RHS As Single)
    Rect.Left = RHS
End Property
Private Property Get CRectangle_Left() As Single
    CRectangle_Left = Rect.Left
End Property

Private Property Let CRectangle_Top(ByVal RHS As Single)
    Rect.Top = RHS
End Property
```

(continued)

```
Private Property Get CRectangle_Top() As Single
    CRectangle_Top = Rect.Top
End Property

Private Property Let CRectangle_Width(ByVal RHS As Single)
    Rect.Width = RHS
End Property
Private Property Get CRectangle_Width() As Single
    CRectangle_Width = Rect.Width
End Property
```

In the CRectangle interface, you're using the same delegation technique that you saw before, so actually this isn't much of a shift in the organization of the class module. The benefits of this approach, however, are visible in the client application, which can now refer to either a CRectangle or a CSquare object using a single variable and through early binding:

```
Dim figures As New Collection
Dim rect As CRectangle, Top As Single

' Create a collection of rectangles and squares.
figures.Add New_CRectangle(1000, 2000, 1500, 1200)
figures.Add New_CSquare(1000, 2000, 1800)
figures.Add New_CRectangle(1000, 2000, 1500, 1500)
figures.Add New_CSquare(1000, 2000, 1100)

' Fill them, and stack them one over the other using early binding!
For Each rect In figures
    rect.FillColor = vbRed
    rect.Left = 0: rect.Top = Top
    Top = Top + rect.Height
Next
```

Add executable code to abstract classes

When I introduced abstract classes as a means of defining interfaces, I said that abstract classes never contain executable code, but only the definition of the interface. But the previous example shows that it's perfectly legal to use the same class module as an interface blueprint for an *Implements* statement and at the same time use the code inside it.

The CRectangle class is a rather complex application of this technique because it works as a regular class, as a base class from which you can inherit, and as an interface that you can implement in other classes. When you begin to be acquainted with objects, this approach will become natural.

The Benefits of Inheritance

Inheritance is a great OOP technique that lets programmers derive new classes with minimum effort. Simulation of true inheritance through delegation is the next best thing, and even if it takes some coding effort you should always consider it when you're creating several classes that are similar to one another because inheritance lets you reuse code and logic, enforce a better encapsulation, and ease code maintenance:

- The derived class doesn't need to know how the base class works internally. All that matters is the interface exposed by the base class. The derived class can consider the base class a sort of *black box,* which accepts inputs and returns results. If the base class is robust and well encapsulated, the inherited class can use it safely and will inherit its robustness as well.

- A consequence of the black box approach is that you can even "inherit" from classes for which you don't have the source code, for example, an object embedded in an external library.

- If you later modify the internal implementation of one or more routines in the base class—typically to fix a bug or improve performance—all the derived classes will inherit the improvements, without your having to edit their code. You need to modify code in derived classes only when you change the interface of the base class, add new properties and methods, or delete existing ones. This is a great concept if you're interested in the easy maintenance of your code.

- You don't need to perform validation in the derived class because it's performed in the base class. If an error occurs, it propagates through the derived class and eventually to the client code. The client code receives the error as if it were generated in the derived class, which means that inheritance doesn't affect how errors are managed and corrected in the client.

- All the actual data is stored inside the base class, not the inherited class. In other words, you aren't duplicating data, and the derived class needs an additional object reference only for doing the delegation.

- Calling the code in the base class imposes a slight performance penalty. But this overhead is usually minimal. I prepared a benchmark showing that on a 233-MHz machine, you can easily perform about 1.5 million delegation calls per second (in natively compiled code). This is less than one millionth of a second for each call. In most cases, this overhead will go unnoticed, especially in complex methods.

OBJECT HIERARCHIES

So far, I have shown you how you can store complex pieces of logic in a class and reuse these pieces elsewhere in your application and in your future projects with very little effort. But what you have seen so far are *individual* classes that solve particular programming problems. The real power of objects is striking when you use them to create larger cooperative structures, also known as *object hierarchies*.

Relationships Among Objects

If you want to aggregate multiple objects in larger structures, you need a way to establish relationships among them.

One-to-one relationships

In the world of OOP, establishing a relationship between two objects is as simple as providing the former object with an object property that points to the latter. For example, a typical CInvoice object might expose a *Customer* property (which points to a Customer object) and two properties, *SendFrom* and *ShipTo*, that can contain references to a CAddress object:

```
' In the CInvoice class module
Public Customer As CCustomer        ' In a real app, these would
Public SendFrom As CAddress         ' be implemented as pairs
Public ShipTo As CAddress           ' of property procedures.
```

This code *declares* that the class is able to support these relationships. You actually *create* the relationships at run time when you assign a non-Nothing reference to the properties:

```
Dim inv As New CInvoice, cust As CCustomer
inv.Number = GetNextInvoiceNumber()    ' A routine defined somewhere else
' For simplicity, let's not worry about how the CUST object is created.
Set cust = GetThisCustomer()           ' This returns a CCustomer object.
Set inv.Customer = cust                 ' This creates the relationship.
' You don't always need an explicit variable.
Set inv.SendFrom = GetFromAddress()    ' This returns a CAddress object,
Set inv.ShipTo = GetToAddress()        ' as does this one.
```

Once the relationship has been established, you can start playing with the infinite possibilities offered by VBA and write code that is extremely concise and elegant:

```
' In the CInvoice class module
Sub PrintHeader(obj As Object)
    ' Print the invoice on a form, PictureBox, or the Printer.
    obj.Print "Number " & Number
    obj.Print "Customer: " & Customer.Name
    obj.Print "Send From: " & SendFrom.CompleteAddress
    obj.Print "Ship To: " & ShipTo.CompleteAddress
End Sub
```

Being able to deal with data already logically grouped in subproperties noticeably improves the quality and style of your code. Because, in most cases, the *ShipTo* address coincides with the address of the customer, you can offer a reasonable default for that property. You only have to delete the Public *ShipTo* member in the declaration section and add the following code:

```
Private m_ShipTo As CAddress

Property Get ShipTo() As CAddress
    If m_ShipTo Is Nothing Then
        Set ShipTo = Customer.Address
    Else
        Set ShipTo = m_ShipTo
    End If
End Property
Property Let ShipTo(newValue As CAddress)
    Set m_ShipTo = newValue
End Property
```

Because you aren't touching the class's interface, the rest of the code—both inside and outside the class itself—continues to work without a glitch.

Once the relation is set, there's no way to accidentally invalidate it by tampering with the involved objects. In the CInvoice example, even if you explicitly set the *cust* variable to Nothing—or let it go out of scope, which has the same effect—Visual Basic won't destroy the CCustomer instance, and therefore the relationship between Invoice and Customer will continue to work as before. This isn't magic; it's simply a consequence of the rule that states that an object instance is released only when all the object variables that reference it are set to Nothing. In this case, the *Customer* property in the CInvoice class keeps that particular CCustomer instance alive until you set the *Customer* property to Nothing or the CInvoice object itself is destroyed. You don't need to explicitly set the *Customer* property to Nothing in the *Class_Terminate* event of the CInvoice class: When an object is released, Visual Basic neatly sets all its object properties to Nothing before proceeding with the actual deallocation. This operation decreases the reference counter of all the referenced objects, which in turn are destroyed if their reference counter goes to 0. In larger object hierarchies, it often happens that destroying an object causes a complex chain of cascading deallocation operations. Fortunately, you don't have to worry about it because it's Visual Basic's business, not yours.

One-to-many relationships

Things are a bit more complex when you create one-to-many relationships among objects. There are countless occasions when one-to-many relationships are necessary. For example, your CInvoice class might have to point to multiple product descriptions. Let's see how this problem can be solved efficiently.

For your object-oriented experiment, you need an auxiliary class, CInvoiceLine, which holds information about a product, ordered quantity, and unit price. What follows is a very simple implementation of it, with no validation at all. (Don't use this implementation in your real invoicing software, *please!*) The version on the companion CD also has a constructor, a *Description* property, and other features, but you need just three variables and a property procedure to get started:

```
' A workable CInvoiceLine class module
Public Qty As Long
Public Product As String
Public UnitPrice As Currency

Property Get Total() As Currency
    Total = Qty * UnitPrice
End Property
```

You can choose, basically, from two ways to implement such one-to-many relations: You can use an array of object references, or you can use a collection. The array solution is trivial:

```
' We can't expose arrays as Public members.
Private m_InvoiceLines(1 To 10) As CInvoiceLine

Property Get InvoiceLines(Index As Integer) As CInvoiceLine
    If Index < 1 Or Index > 10 Then Err.Raise 9    ' Subscript out of range
    Set InvoiceLines(Index) = m_InvoiceLines(Index)
End Property
Property Set InvoiceLines(Index As Integer, newValue As CInvoiceLine)
    If Index < 1 Or Index > 10 Then Err.Raise 9    ' Subscript out of range
    Set m_InvoiceLines(Index) = newValue
End Property


' In the client code
' (Assumes that we defined a constructor for the CInvoiceLine class)
Set inv.InvoiceLine(1) = New_CInvoiceLine(10, "Monitor ZX100", 225.25)
Set inv.InvoiceLine(2) = New_CInvoiceLine(14, "101-key Keyboard", 19.99)
' etc.
```

As easy as they are to implement, arrays of object references have a lot of problems, especially because it isn't clear how you can use them effectively when you don't know in advance how many child CInvoiceLine items you need. In fact, I suggest that you use them only if you're absolutely sure that the number of possible related objects is well defined in advance.

The collection solution is more promising because it doesn't pose any limit to the number of related objects, and also because it permits a more natural, OO-like syntax in the client code. Besides, you *can* declare a collection (unlike an array) as a Public member, so the code in the class module is even simpler:

```
' In the CInvoice class
Public InvoiceLines As New Collection

' In the client code (no need to keep track of line index)
inv.InvoiceLines.Add New_CInvoiceLine(10, "Monitors ZX100", 225.25)
inv.InvoiceLines.Add New_CInvoiceLine(14, "101-key Keyboards", 19.99)
```

Using a collection improves the code inside the CInvoice class in other ways as well. See how easily you can enumerate all the lines in an invoice:

```
Sub PrintBody(obj As Object)
    ' Print the invoice body on a form, PictureBox, or the Printer.
    Dim invline As CInvoiceLine, Total As Currency
    For Each invline In InvoiceLines
        obj.Print invline.Description
        Total = Total + invline.Total
    Next
    obj.Print "Grand Total = " & Total
End Sub
```

This solution has one major drawback, though. It leaves the CInvoice class completely at the mercy of the programmer who uses it. To see what I mean, just try out this bogus code:

```
inv.InvoiceLines.Add New CCustomer            ' No error!
```

This isn't surprising, of course: Collection objects store their values in Variants, so they accept anything you throw at them. This seemingly innocent detail undermines the robustness of the CInvoice class and completely undoes all our efforts. Must we tolerate it?

Collection Classes

The solution to the robustness problem comes in the form of *collection classes*. These are special classes that you write in plain Visual Basic code and that closely resemble native Collection objects. Since you are in control of their implementation, you can establish a particular syntax for their methods and check what's being added to the collection. As you'll see, they're so alike that you won't even need to retouch the client code.

Collection classes are an application of the concept of inheritance that I described earlier in this chapter. A collection class keeps a reference to a private collection variable and exposes to the outside a similar interface so that the client code believes it's interacting with a real Collection. To enhance the CInvoice example, you therefore need a special CInvoiceLines collection class. (It's customary for the name of a collection class to be the plural form of the name of the base class.) Now that you have mastered the secrets of inheritance, you should have no problem understanding how the code on the following page works.

```
' The private collection that holds the real data
Private m_InvoiceLines As New Collection

Sub Add(newItem As CInvoiceLine, Optional Key As Variant, _
    Optional Before As Variant, Optional After As Variant)
    m_InvoiceLines.Add newItem, Key
End Sub
Sub Remove(index As Variant)
    m_InvoiceLines.Remove index
End Sub
Function Item(index As Variant) As CInvoiceLine
    Set Item = m_InvoiceLines.Item(index)
End Function
Property Get Count() As Long
    Count = m_InvoiceLines.Count
End Property
```

You need to do two more things to make your CInvoiceLines collection class perfectly mimic a standard Collection: You must provide support for the default item and for enumeration.

Make *Item* the default member

Programmers are used to omitting the *Item* member's name in code when working with Collection objects. To support this feature in your collection class, you just have to make *Item* the default member of the class, which you do by issuing the Procedure Attributes command from the Tools menu, selecting *Item* in the uppermost combo box, expanding the dialog box, and typing *0* (zero) in the ProcID field. Or you can select *(default)* in the drop-down list. This procedure was explained in more detail in Chapter 6.

Add support for enumeration

No collection class could hope to win the hearts of hardcore Visual Basic developers if it didn't support the *For Each* statement. Visual Basic lets you add such support, though in a rather cryptic way. First add the following procedure to your class module:

```
Function NewEnum() As IUnknown
    Set NewEnum = m_InvoiceLines.[_NewEnum]
End Function
```

and then invoke the Procedure Attributes dialog box. Then select the *NewEnum* member, assign it a ProcID equal to −4, tick the Hide This Member check box, and close the dialog box.

NOTE Understanding how this weird technique works requires some intimate knowledge of OLE mechanisms, in particular the IEnumVariant interface. Without going into too many details, suffice it to say that when an object appears in a *For Each* statement, it has to expose an auxiliary *enumerator object.* OLE conventions dictate that the class must provide this enumerator object through a function whose ProcID is equal to −4. At run time, Visual Basic calls the corresponding procedure and uses the returned enumerator object to progress through the loop iteration.

Unfortunately, you can't manufacture an enumerator object using plain Visual Basic code, but you can borrow the enumerator object exposed by the private Collection object, which is exactly what the *NewEnum* function shown previously does. Collection objects expose their enumerators using a hidden method named _NewEnum (search for it in the Object Browser with the Show Hidden Members option enabled), which is an invalid name in VBA and must therefore be enclosed in a pair of square brackets. By the way, Dictionary objects don't expose any Public enumerator objects, and for this reason you can't use them as the basis of your collection classes.

Testing the collection class

You can now improve the CInvoice class by making it use your new CInvoiceLines class instead of the standard Collection object:

```
' In the declaration section of CInvoice
Public InvoiceLines As New CInvoiceLines
```

The mere fact that the CInvoiceLines class checks the type of object passed to its *Add* method is enough to morph the CInvoice class into a secure object. Interestingly, you don't strictly need any other changes in code, either inside or outside the class. Just press F5 to see it for yourself.

Improving the collection class

If collection classes were useful only to improve the robustness of your code, they would be worth the effort. But the real fun only begins here. Since you have complete control over what happens inside your class, you can decide to improve it with new methods or modify how existing ones react to their arguments. For example, you can have the *Item* method return Nothing if the element doesn't exist, instead of obnoxiously raising an error as regular collections do:

```
Function Item(index As Variant) As CInvoiceLine
    On Error Resume Next
    Set Item = m_InvoiceLines.Item(index)
End Function
```

Or you can add an explicit *Exists* function as shown on the following page.

```
Function Exists(index As Variant) As Boolean
    Dim dummy As CInvoiceLine
    On Error Resume Next
    Set dummy = m_InvoiceLines.Item(index)
    Exists = (Err = 0)
End Function
```

You can also supply a handy *Clear* method:

```
Sub Clear()
    Set m_InvoiceLines = New Collection
End Sub
```

All these custom members are completely generic, and you can often implement them in most of the collection classes you write. Methods and properties that are specific to the particular collection class are undoubtedly more interesting:

```
' Evaluate the total of all invoice lines.
Property Get Total() As Currency
    Dim result As Currency, invline As CInvoiceLine
    For Each invline In m_InvoiceLines
        result = result + invline.Total
    Next
    Total = result
End Property


' Print all invoice lines.
Sub PrintLines(obj As Object)
    Dim invline As CInvoiceLine
    For Each invline In m_InvoiceLines
        obj.Print invline.Description
    Next
End Sub
```

These new members simplify the structure of the code in the main class:

```
' In the CInvoice class
Sub PrintBody(obj As Object)
    InvoiceLines.PrintLines obj
    obj.Print "Grand Total = " & InvoiceLines.Total
End Sub
```

Of course, the total amount of code doesn't vary, but you have distributed it in a more logical way. Each object is responsible for what happens inside it. In real projects, this approach has many beneficial consequences in code testing, reuse, and maintenance.

Add real constructors to the game

Collection classes offer one additional benefit that object-oriented programmers can't live without: *real constructors*. I have already explained that the lack of constructor methods is a major defect in the otherwise decent support for encapsulation supplied by Visual Basic.

If you wrap a collection class around a base class—as CInvoiceLines and CInvoiceLine do, respectively—you can create a constructor by adding a method to the collection class that creates a new base object and adds it to the collection in one single step. In most cases, this double operation makes a lot of sense. For example, a CInvoiceLine object would have a very hard life outside a parent CInvoiceLines collection. (Have you ever seen a lone invoice line wandering around all by itself in the external world?) It turns out that such a constructor is just a variant of the *Add* method:

```
Function Create(Qty As Long, Product As String, UnitPrice As Currency) _
    As CInvoiceLine
    Dim newItem As New CInvoiceLine ' Auto-instancing is safe here.
    newItem.Init Qty, Product, UnitPrice
    m_InvoiceLines.Add newItem
    Set Create = newItem            ' Return the item just created.
End Function


' In the client code
inv.InvoiceLines.Create 10, "Monitor ZX100", 225.25
inv.InvoiceLines.Create 14, "101-key Keyboard", 19.99
```

A key difference between the *Add* and the *Create* methods is that the latter also returns the object just added to the collection, which is never strictly necessary with *Add* (because you already have a reference to it). This greatly simplifies how you write your client code. For example, say that the CInvoiceLine object supports two new properties, *Color* and *Notes*. Both are optional, and as such they shouldn't be included among the required arguments of the *Create* method. But you can still set them using a concise and efficient syntax, as follows:

```
With inv.InvoiceLines.Create(14, "101-key Keyboard", 19.99)
    .Color = "Blue"
    .Notes = "Special layout"
End With
```

Depending on the nature of the specific problem, you can build your collection classes with both the *Add* and *Create* methods, or you can just use one of the two. It's important, however, that if you leave the *Add* method in the collection, you add some form of validation to it. In most cases—but not always—you just need to let the class validate itself, as in this code:

```
Sub Add(newItem As CinvoiceLine)
    newItem.Init newItem.Qty, newItem.Product, newItem.UnitPrice
    ' Add to the collection only if no error was raised.
    m_InvoiceLines.Add newItem, Key
End Sub
```

If you have encapsulated an inner class into its parent collection class in such a robust way, it's impossible for any developer to accidentally or intentionally add an incoherent object to the system. The worst that they can do is create a disconnected CInvoiceLine object, but they won't be able to add it to your self-protected CInvoice object.

Full-Fledged Hierarchies

Once you know how to create efficient collection classes, there isn't much to stop you from building complex and incredibly powerful object hierarchies, such as those exposed by well-known models Microsoft Word, Microsoft Excel, DAO, RDO, ADO, and so on. You already have all the pieces in the right places and only need to take care of details. Let me show you a few recurring problems when building hierarchies and how you can fix them.

Class static data

When you build a complex hierarchy, you're often faced with the following problem: How can all the objects of a given class share a common variable? For example, it would be great if the CInvoice class were able to correctly set its *Number* property in its *Class_Initialize* event so that from that point on *Number* could be exposed as a read-only property. This would improve the formal correctness of the class because it would guarantee that there aren't two invoices with the same number. This problem would be quickly solved if it were possible to define *class static variables* in the class module, that is, variables that are shared among all the instances of the class itself. But this is beyond the current capabilities of the VBA language.

The easy and obvious solution to this problem is to use a global variable in a BAS module, but that would break the class's encapsulation because anyone could modify this variable. Any other similar approach—such as storing the value in a file, in a database, in the Registry, and so on—is subject to the same problem. Fortunately, the solution is really simple: Use a parent collection class to gather all the instances of the class that share the common value. Not only do you solve the specific problem, you can also provide a more robust constructor for the base class itself. In the CInvoice sample program, you can create a CInvoices collection class:

```
' The CInvoices Collection class
Private m_LastInvoiceNumber As Long
Private m_Invoices As New Collection

' The number used for the last invoice (read-only)
Public Property Get LastInvoiceNumber() As Long
    LastInvoiceNumber = m_LastInvoiceNumber
End Property
```

```
' Create a new CInvoice item, and add it to the private collection.
Function Create(InvDate As Date, Customer As CCustomer) As CInvoice
    Dim newItem As New CInvoice
    ' Don't increment the internal variable yet!
    newItem.Init m_LastInvoiceNumber + 1, InvDate, Customer
    ' Add to the internal collection, using the number as a key.
    m_Invoices.Add newItem, CStr(newItem.Number)
    ' Increment the internal variable now, if no error occurred.
    m_LastInvoiceNumber = m_LastInvoiceNumber + 1
    ' Return the new item to the caller.
    Set Create = newItem
End Function
' Other procedures in the CInvoices collection class ... (omitted)
```

Similarly, you can create a CCustomers collection class (not shown here) that creates and manages all the CCustomer objects in the application. Now your client code can create both CInvoice and CCustomer objects in a safe way:

```
' These variables are shared in the application.
Dim Invoices As New CInvoices
Dim Customers As New CCustomers

Dim inv As CInvoice, cust As CCustomer
' First create a customer.
Set cust = Customers.Create("Tech Eleven, Inc")
cust.Address.Init "234 East Road", "Chicago", "IL", "12345"
' Now create the invoice.
Set inv = Invoices.Create("12 Sept 1998", cust)
```

At this point, you can complete your artwork by creating a top-level class named CCompany, which exposes all the collections as properties:

```
' The CCompany class (the company that sends the invoices)
Public Name As String
Public Address As CAddress
Public Customers As New CCustomers
Public Invoices As New CInvoices
' The next two collections are not implemented on the companion CD.
Public Orders As New COrders
Public Products As New CProducts
```

You enjoy many advantages when you encapsulate classes in this way, a few of which aren't immediately apparent. Just to give you an idea of the potential of this approach, let's say that your boss asks you to add support for multiple companies. It won't be a walk in the park, but you can do it relatively effortlessly by creating a new CCompanies collection class. Since the CCompany object is well isolated from its surroundings, you can reuse entire modules without the risk of unexpected side effects.

Backpointers

When you deal with hierarchies, a dependent object frequently needs access to its parent; for example, to query one of its properties or to invoke its methods. The natural way to do that is to add a *backpointer* to the inner class. A backpointer is an explicit object reference to its parent object. This can be a Public property or a Private variable.

Let's see how this fits in our sample invoicing application. Say that when an invoice prints itself it should add a warning to the customer if there are any other invoices that must be paid and tell the customer the total sum due. To do this, the CInvoice class must scan its parent CInvoices collection and so needs a pointer to it. By convention, this backpointer is named *Parent* or *Collection*, but feel free to use whatever name you prefer. If you want to make this pointer Public, it's essential that it be a read-only property, at least from the outside of the project. (Otherwise, anyone could detach an invoice from the CInvoices collection.) You can achieve this by making the pointer's *Property Set* procedure with a Friend scope:

```
' In the CInvoice class
Public Paid As Boolean
Private m_Collection As CInvoices          ' The actual backpointer

Public Property Get Collection() As CInvoices
    Set Collection = m_Collection
End Property
Friend Property Set Collection(newValue As CInvoices)
    Set m_Collection = newValue
End Property
```

The parent CInvoices collection class is now responsible for correctly setting up this backpointer, which it does in the *Create* constructor method:

```
' Inside the CInvoices' Create method (rest of the code omitted)
newItem.Init m_LastInvoiceNumber + 1, InvDate, Customer
Set newItem.Collection = Me
```

Now the CInvoice class knows how to encourage recalcitrant customers to pay their bills, as you can see in Figure 7-9 and in the following code:

```
Sub PrintNotes(obj As Object)
    ' Print a note if customer has other unpaid invoices.
    Dim inv As CInvoice, Found As Long, Total As Currency
    For Each inv In Collection
        If inv Is Me Then
            ' Don't consider the current invoice!
        ElseIf (inv.Customer Is Customer) And inv.Paid = False Then
            Found = Found + 1
            Total = Total + inv.GrandTotal
```

```
        End If
    Next
    If Found Then
        obj.Print "WARNING: Other " & Found & _
            " invoices still waiting to be paid ($" & Total & ")"
    End If
End Sub
```

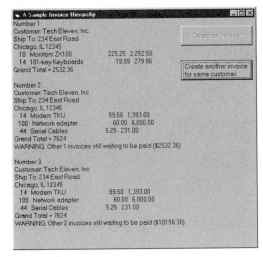

Figure 7-9. *Don't let the rudimentary user interface fool you: There are as many as eight classes working together to supply you with a skeleton for a robust invoicing application.*

Circular references

No description of object hierarchies would be complete without an acknowledgment of the circular reference problem. In short, you have a *circular reference* when two objects point to each other, either directly or indirectly (that is, through intermediate objects). The invoicing hierarchy didn't include a circular reference until you added the *Collection* backpointer to the CInvoice class. What makes circular references a problem is that the two involved objects will keep each other alive indefinitely. This isn't a surprise; it's just the same old rule that governs the lives of objects.

In this case, unless we take appropriate steps, the reference counter of the two objects will never decrease to 0, even if the main application has released all its references to them. This means that you have to forego a portion of memory until the application comes to an end and wait for Visual Basic to return all its memory to Windows. It isn't just a matter of wasted memory: In many sophisticated hierarchies, the robustness of the entire system often depends on the code inside the *Class_Terminate* event (for example, to store properties back in the database). When the application ends, Visual Basic correctly calls the *Class_Terminate* event in all objects that are still alive, but that might happen after the main application has already closed its own files. The likely result is a corrupted database.

Now that I have warned you about all the possible nasty consequences of circular references, let me scare you even more: Visual Basic doesn't offer any definitive solution to this problem. You have only two half-solutions, both of which are largely unsatisfactory: You avoid circular references in the first place, and you manually undo all circular references before your application destroys the object reference.

In the invoicing example, you can avoid backpointers if you let the inner CInvoice class access its parent collection using a global variable. But you know that this is forbidden behavior that would break class encapsulation and would compromise the application's robustness. The second solution—manually undoing all circular references—is often too difficult when dealing with complex hierarchies. Above all, it would force you to add tons of error-handling code, just to be sure that no object variable is automatically set to Nothing by Visual Basic before you have the opportunity to resolve all the existing circular references.

The only good news I can tell you is that this problem can be solved, but it requires some really advanced, low-level programming techniques based on the concept of *weak object pointers*. This technique is well beyond the scope of this book, and for this reason I won't show any code here. However, the bravest of you might have a look at the CInvoice class on the companion CD. I have bracketed these special advanced sections using *#If* directives, so you can easily see what happens using regular and weak object pointers. You probably need to review how objects are stored in memory and what an object variable really is (see Chapter 6), but the comments in the code should help you understand what the code actually does. Be sure to study this technique before using it in your own applications because when you play with objects at this low level, any mistake causes a GPF.

The Class Builder Add-In

Visual Basic 6 comes with a revamped version of the Class Builder Add-In. This is a major utility that lets you design the structure of a class hierarchy, create new classes and collection classes, and define their interfaces down to the attributes of each property, method, or event. (See Figure 7-10.) The new version adds support for enumerated properties and optional arguments of any data type, as well as a few minor enhancements.

The Class Builder Add-In is installed by the Visual Basic 6 setup routine, so you just have to open the Add-In Manager dialog box and double-click on the VB6 Class Builder Utility. When you close the window, a new item in the Add-In menu lets you invoke the utility.

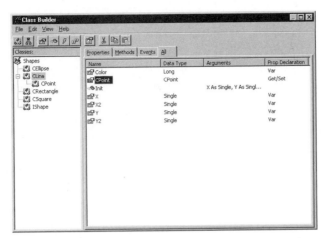

Figure 7-10. *The Class Builder Add-In. A child class (CPoint, in this case) always corresponds to a property in its parent class (CLine).*

Using the Class Builder Add-In is very simple, and I won't show in detail how you create new classes and their properties and methods. Its user interface is so clear that you won't have any problem using it. Instead, I focus on a few key points that can help you get the most from this utility.

■ You should use the Class Builder Add-In from the very start of your design process. This is important, because even if the add-in is able to recognize all the classes in the current project, it can establish the relationships among them only if you created them from within the add-in.

■ You can create top-level classes or dependent classes, depending on which item in the leftmost pane is highlighted when you invoke the New command from the File menu. If you create a child class, the Add-In automatically inserts in the parent a property that points to the new class. You can move a class around in the hierarchy by using drag-and-drop in the leftmost pane.

■ While the Class Builder doesn't support inheritance, you can create a class that's based on another existing class. In this case, the Class Builder copies all the necessary code from the existing class into the new class module.

■ The Class Builder utility is particularly useful for building collection classes: You simply point to the class that's to be contained in the collection, and the Add-In correctly creates the collection class with a suitable *Add* method, an *Item* default method, support for enumeration, and so on.

■ Finally, you have some degree of control over how child objects are created inside parent classes. You can have them instantiated in the parent *Initialize* event (which slows down the parent's creation but makes access more efficient), or you can have child objects created in the *Property Get* procedure of the parent if necessary (which speeds up the parent's creation but adds overhead to each access).

A drawback of the Class Builder is that you have no control over the code it generates. For example, it uses particular naming conventions for arguments and variables and adds a lot of pretty useless remarks, which you'll probably want to delete as soon as you can. Another issue is that once you begin to use it in a project, you're virtually forced to invoke it any time you want to add a new class—otherwise, it won't be able to correctly place the new class in the hierarchy. Even with these limitations, you'll find that creating hierarchies with the Class Builder Add-In is so simple that you can easily get carried away.

This chapter concludes our journey in object-oriented land. If you care about well-designed software and code reuse, you'll surely agree with me that OOP is a fascinating technology. When working with Visual Basic, however, a firm understanding of how classes and objects work is necessary to tackle many other technologies, including database, client/server, COM, and Internet programming. I'll frequently use, in the remaining sections of this book, all the concepts you've encountered in this chapter.

Chapter 8

Databases

All the surveys that I'm aware of among Visual Basic developers invariably conclude that the vast majority of Visual Basic programs are database and client/server applications. This isn't surprising because the language has a lot to offer developers. And this trend will surely grow now that Visual Basic 6 has introduced so many new tools for database and client/server (and, yes, Internet) programming.

In this chapter, I introduce you to database programming and show you how to use the ADO binding mechanism with bound controls and the ADO Data control, but the concepts underlying these technologies can be applied to other data consumers or sources.

Before showing what you can do with ADO in Visual Basic 6, however, I must quickly recapitulate database architectures and data access techniques.

THE DATA ACCESS SAGA

All the new database-related capacities in Visual Basic 6 are based on Microsoft ActiveX Data Objects (ADO), a technology that lets you access any database or data source, as long as someone has written an OLE DB provider that connects to that source.

Figure 8-1 on the next page summarizes the many ways you can get to a data source in Visual Basic 6. As you can see, data access methods differ greatly in the number of layers that sit between your application and the database you're connecting to. In this book, however, I concentrate on ADO technology and give you only glimpses of the others. Deciding not to cover popular data access techniques such as DAO and RDO has been a difficult choice, but I had to make it to keep this book a reasonable size. I was comforted in this choice by the fact that DAO and RDO haven't been improved at all in Visual Basic 6; so if you already mastered those techniques in Visual Basic 5, there's nothing new for you to see. Both these older technologies will be eventually replaced by ADO. You can find several good books and other information sources about DAO and RDO, such as the superb *Hitchhiker's Guide to Visual Basic and SQL Server* by William R. Vaughn (Microsoft Press, 1998). Although I don't have the space to describe DAO and RDO in depth, you need at least a broad understanding of how they work. To help you understand the benefits that ADO brings you, I must describe the tools that were available before it and how ADO relates to those older technologies.

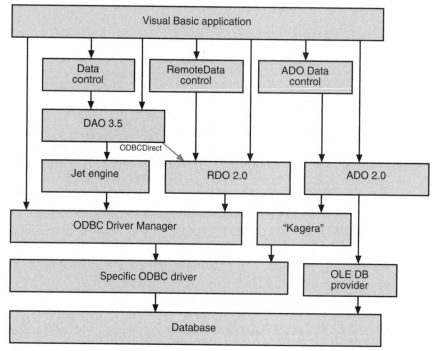

Figure 8-1. *Accessing a database using ODBC, DAO, RDO, and ADO.*

ODBC

ODBC stands for Open Database Connectivity and is a set of functions that lets you connect to a local or remote database. Microsoft launched this technology as a means of accessing several databases in different formats—dBASE, Microsoft FoxPro, Microsoft Access, Microsoft SQL Server, Oracle, or even plain comma-delimited text files—using a common API. The machine the application runs on connects to a DLL called the ODBC Driver Manager, which in turn sends commands to (and retrieves data from) an ODBC driver specific to the particular database you want to use. Visual Basic 2 was the first version of the language that was capable of connecting to an ODBC source. Since then the number of available ODBC drivers has grown very rapidly, to the point that it's nearly impossible to find a commercial database for which no ODBC driver exists.

The challenge of ODBC is to provide a common interface to all these different databases. In theory, you can prepare an application that uses ODBC to talk to an Access database and then upsize to an SQL Server database simply by changing the back-end ODBC driver and a few statements in the source code. You can do this because all the commands you send to the database are standard SQL statements. SQL (Structured Query Language) is a programming language specialized for working with databases. (See "Crash Course in SQL" later in this chapter for an introduction to SQL). In practice, however, while the ODBC layer does what it can to convert these standard SQL commands into the particular database's dialect, an ODBC programmer frequently has to bypass the ODBC translation engine and send commands directly to the database. (These are known as *pass-through* queries or commands.) Needless to say, having to do this hinders the portability of such an application to another database.

ODBC is efficient, at least compared with most other data access techniques. Another advantage of ODBC is that it supports both 16-bit and 32-bit APIs, so it's one of the few techniques available to Visual Basic 3 and Visual Basic 4/16 applications. ODBC version 3 has added several performance-boosting techniques, such as connection pooling, which means that an ODBC driver on the client side can reuse existing connections in a way that's transparent to your program. For example, your code can open and close multiple connections to a database, but the ODBC driver actually uses the same connection. Because opening a connection is a lengthy operation—it can take several seconds each time—connection pooling is bound to make your application much more responsive. Microsoft Transaction Server uses connection pooling to improve the performance of connections opened by ActiveX components that run under it.

Using ODBC, however, isn't easy, especially for Visual Basic programmers. The set of API functions is complex, and if you make a mistake you often crash your application with a fatal error. (If this occurs while you're in the IDE, you can't even save your code.) For this reason, relatively few Visual Basic programmers write applications that directly call ODBC functions. Interestingly, most other data access techniques available to Visual Basic can use ODBC drivers as intermediate layers, so sometimes you can augment other techniques (typically those based on RDO) with direct API calls. Unfortunately, you can't do that with ADO: Even though ADO internally uses an ODBC driver, you can't mix ADO code and ODBC API code for the same connection.

Even if you're not going to directly use ODBC API calls in your Visual Basic programs, you should become familiar with the basic concepts on which this technology is based. For example, one concept that you'll probably deal with even when working with ADO is the Data Source Name (DSN). A DSN is a set of values that an application needs to correctly connect to a database. It typically includes the name of the ODBC driver you want to use, the name of the machine that hosts the database server (if you're working with client-server engines such as SQL Server or Oracle), the name or path of the specific database, the timeout of the connection (that is, the number of seconds after which the ODBC driver gives up and returns an error to the calling application when trying to establish the connection), the name of the calling workstation and application, and so on.

You can create a DSN in several ways, inside or outside the Visual Basic 6 environment. The command center for ODBC is a Control Panel applet that lets you create DSNs and set other ODBC configuration values. You can choose from several types of DSNs. A *User DSN* is stored in the system Registry, can be used only by the current user, and can't therefore be shared with others. A *System DSN* is also stored in the Registry but is visible to all other users, including Microsoft Windows NT services. Finally, a *File DSN* is stored in a .dsn file and can be shared by all users (provided that the correct ODBC driver is installed on their machines). File DSNs can be easily copied on other machines, so they make the installation phase easier; on the other hand, the application needs to know where the DSN is located, so the code must provide the complete path to the .dsn file, and you need to store the path somewhere (in an INI file, for example). This is never an issue with User or System DSNs.

You aren't forced to work with DSNs if you don't want to. When you're working with ODBC, you can provide all the information needed for the connection—driver name, database name and path, and so on—right in your code. These are the so-called DSN-less connections, which are usually more efficient because you save the ODBC driver a trip to the Registry or to a File DSN. But DSN-less techniques require a bit more work from the developer.

The first three tabs of the ODBC Control Panel applet dialog box let you create, delete, and configure DSNs of all types. As you can see in Figure 8-2, creating a DSN often requires that you open several nested dialog boxes. The Drivers tab displays all the installed ODBC drivers and lets you compare version numbers (which is sometimes important when something doesn't work as expected on a customer's machine). Visual Basic 6 comes with several ODBC drivers (some of which are visible in Figure 8-3), but you can also purchase other drivers from third-party vendors.

You use the Tracing tab of the ODBC Data Source Administrator applet to define the path of the log file for all ODBC operations, which is a lifesaver when you're debugging ODBC-based applications. (This option is vital also when you are indirectly using ODBC through DAO, RDO, or ADO.) The latest version of the ODBC Data Source Administrator applet includes the ability to start Microsoft Visual Studio Analyzer, a tool that lets you monitor the activity of your programs over the network.

In the Connection Pooling tab, you can enable or disable connection pooling for each specific ODBC driver. You rarely need to change these settings, though, and

I suggest that you not play with them unless you're pretty sure about what you're doing. Finally, in the About tab, you can check the position and versions of all the code DLLs of the ODBC subsystem.

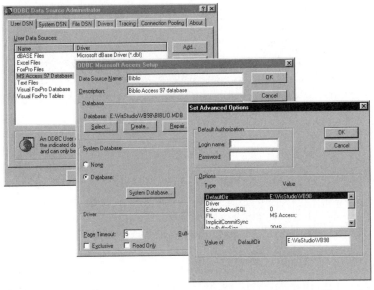

Figure 8-2. *Creating a User DSN for a Microsoft Jet database. The contents of nested dialog boxes depend on the ODBC driver you're connecting to.*

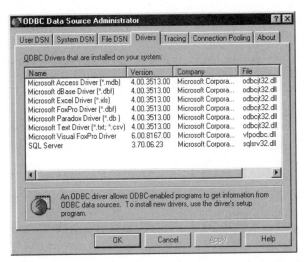

Figure 8-3. *Some of the ODBC drivers that can be installed by the Visual Basic 6 setup procedure.*

DAO

DAO, or Data Access Objects, has a place in the heart of all programmers who began to develop database applications with Visual Basic 3. DAO is an object-oriented interface to Microsoft Jet, the engine that powers Access. Developers can design an MDB database using Access and then use DAO from a Visual Basic application to open the database, add and retrieve records, and manage transactions. The best thing about DAO is that it doesn't limit you to Jet databases because you can directly open any database for which an ODBC driver exists. Or you can use Jet *attached tables,* which are virtual tables that appear to belong to an MDB database but actually retrieve and store data in other ODBC sources.

Even if you can use DAO to access non-Jet sources, you can clearly see that it was devised with Access databases in mind. For example, even if your application doesn't use MDB databases, you still have to load the entire Jet engine DLL in memory. (And you also have to distribute it to your users). Even worse, DAO doesn't expose many of the capabilities that you could use if working directly with ODBC API functions. For example, you can't perform asynchronous queries or connections using DAO, nor can you work with multiple result sets.

Visual Basic 3 also contained the first release of the Data control. This control lets you *bind* one or more controls on a form to a data source and offers buttons for navigating through the records of the database table you've connected to. At first, it seems that the Data control is a great tool because it lets you quickly create effective user interfaces to work with your data. After some testing, however, developers tend to abandon the Data control because its many limitations are difficult to overcome. Apart from performance considerations, the Data control has one serious disadvantage: It ties your front-end applications to the data in the back-end database. If you later want to access data in another database, you have to revise all the forms in your application. If you want to add complex validation rules to database fields, you must add code in every single module of the program. These (and other problems) are the typical defects of a 2-tier architecture, which in fact is being abandoned in favor of 3-tier (or n-tier) architectures, where one or more intermediate layers between the application and the database provide services such as data validation, business rules, workload balance, and security. Alas, if you want to embrace the n-tier philosophy, you should forget about the Data control.

Visual Basic 4 included the improved DAO 3.0 version, which features a special DLL that allows programmers who work with 32-bit technology to access 16-bit databases. Visual Basic 5 programmers can use DAO 3.5. In the Visual Basic 6 package, you'll find DAO 3.51, which is substantially similar to the previous one. This suggests that Microsoft doesn't plan to improve DAO further, even though version 4 has been announced for Microsoft Office 2000.

RDO

RDO, or Remote Data Objects, is the first attempt by Microsoft to combine the simplicity of DAO with the power of direct ODBC API programming. RDO is an object model vaguely patterned after DAO, but it bypasses the Jet Engine and the DAO DLL and works directly with the underlying ODBC drivers. Applications based on RDO load only a small DLL instead of the resource-hungry Jet engine. Even more important, RDO was specifically designed to work with ODBC sources, so it exposed functionality that couldn't be accessed from DAO. RDO is 32-bit technology, however, so you can't use it from 16-bit applications.

RDO 1 was introduced with Visual Basic 4, and the engine was improved in Visual Basic 5, which includes RDO 2. This latest version is a mature product and also supports a new programming model based on events, which is great for working with asynchronous operations. The development of RDO seems to have stopped, though, because Visual Basic 6 still includes version 2, with no apparent improvement over the version shipped with Visual Basic 5. So RDO could be another dead end. Although Microsoft seems committed to actively supporting RDO, it seems to be betting everything on ADO.

RDO 1 and 2 came with the RemoteData control, which works in much the same way as the Data control and lets you bind controls to remote data sources. In this sense, the RemoteData control shares all the advantages and disadvantages of the Data control, including its problems with n-tier architectures.

ODBCDirect

Visual Basic 5 included yet another data access technology, named ODBCDirect, which allowed programmers to employ RDO using a DAO syntax. ODBCDirect was conceived as a transition technique that would help Visual Basic programmers move their DAO/Jet applications to more powerful client/server architectures. In theory, by changing just a few properties, an existing DAO program that stores data in a Jet database might be converted to a client/server application that connects to any ODBC source. ODBCDirect shouldn't be regarded as a technology of its own. It's more like a trick that you can use to save time in converting applications, and nothing more. Most of the RDO 2 new features—the new event programming model, for example—can't be exploited by ODBCDirect because it has to be code-compatible with DAO. Besides, being based on RDO, ODBCDirect works only with 32-bit applications. For these reasons, unless you have very big and complex DAO/Jet Visual Basic applications to port to another database as quickly as possible, don't waste your time on ODBCDirect.

OLE DB

OLE DB is a low-level data access technology with which Microsoft intends to eventually replace ODBC as the primary means for connecting to databases. The OLE DB counterpart to ODBC drivers are the OLE DB providers, which work as bridges between applications and databases. Although OLE DB is a relatively recent technology, you can find OLE DB providers for most popular databases, and others will be released before long. In spite of their apparent similarities, ODBC and OLE DB technologies are profoundly different. First, OLE DB is based on COM, an architecture that has proven robust enough to move large quantities of data across the network. Second, OLE DB lends itself to the task of connecting any type of data source, not just relational and ISAM (indexed sequential access mode) databases, which are the natural field for ODBC drivers.

OLE DB is part of Microsoft's Universal Data Access (UDA) strategy, which enables you to read and process data where it is, without first converting it and importing it to a more traditional database. Using OLE DB providers, you can process data in e-mail messages, HTML pages, spreadsheet and text documents, and even in more exotic data sources. Visual Basic 6 itself comes with providers for Microsoft Jet, SQL Server, FoxPro, text files, and Oracle databases. You can download other OLE DB providers from the Microsoft Web site, and I've heard of other providers from third-party vendors.

In the transition between the ODBC and the OLE DB worlds, you can use a special OLE DB provider, named MSDASQL—also known by its code name, Kagera—that works as a bridge to any ODBC source. Instead of connecting directly to the database, you can use this special provider to connect to an ODBC driver, which in turn reads and writes data in the database. This additional layer has a performance hit, of course, but you should look at it as a short-term solution to a problem that will disappear when more providers are available.

ADO

ADO is the high-level interface to OLE DB. It fills more or less the same role that RDO does for the ODBC APIs. Like ODBC APIs, OLE DB is a low-level interface that can't be easily (or at all) accessed from high-level languages such as Visual Basic. ADO builds on OLE DB to provide functions that aren't available directly in OLE DB or that would make stringent demands on the coding abilities of a programmer. ADO matches most of RDO's capacities: Both can make asynchronous queries and connections and optimistic batch updates. ADO adds great new features such as file-based and stand-alone Recordsets, hierarchical Recordsets, and more.

The single most important feature of ADO is probably its extensibility. Instead of being a complex and monolithic object hierarchy as DAO and RDO are, ADO consists of fewer objects that can be combined in more ways. New features can be added to ADO in the form of special OLE DB providers, such as the MSDataShape provider, which offers hierarchical Recordset objects to other providers. Microsoft also is making new features available in ADO in the form of separate libraries that link dynamically to the core ADO library. For example, the new ADO 2.1 library includes support for Data Definition Language and security (that is, the creation of new database tables, users, and groups of users), Jet replicas, and multidimensional Recordsets. Because these additions are distinct libraries, you don't have to distribute them with your applications if you don't use them. This contrasts with DAO and RDO, each of which comprises one larger DLL that embeds all the features (and which you have to distribute in its entirety even if you use a small fraction of its potential).

Another nice ADO feature is that you can use it from within HTML pages in a browser such as Internet Explorer or on a server inside an Active Server Page hosted on Internet Information Server. One ADO subsystem, named Remote Data Services, even lets you send a bunch of records to a client browser or activate COM components remotely over the Internet.

The only relevant defect of ADO is that it's a recent technology that hasn't proven its robustness in a large number of real-world applications, as DAO and RDO have. For example, I found a few bugs in ADO 2, even though my experience is that most of these problems were caused by the OLE DB provider, not ADO itself. This distinction is important because you can often fix these bugs by simply updating the provider when a new version is released. In fact, I found that the providers for Microsoft Jet 4.0 and SQL Server 7.0 are noticeably better than the versions for Jet 3.51 and SQL Server 6.5. (The latter are the providers distributed with Visual Basic 6.) I expect that by the time you read this book, most major problems with ADO will be fixed. On the other hand, the only alternative to ADO is to continue to use DAO or RDO, but, as I've explained, these technologies aren't going to be improved significantly in the future.

You can see that choosing the data access technique to use is a complex matter. My suggestion is simple, though: If you're maintaining or updating an existing application based on DAO or RDO (or ODBC APIs, if you're a brave programmer), wait until you see where ADO is going. If you're beginning a new application, give ADO a try, especially if you plan to update and maintain it for several years or if you plan to eventually port it to the Internet.

The good news is that Visual Basic 6 includes several tools and facilities for creating ADO applications quickly and effectively. For this reason, the rest of this book focuses on ADO exclusively.

VISUAL DATABASE TOOLS

Visual Basic 5 Enterprise Edition was the first language version that integrated a suite of tools for working with databases from within the IDE. Before that, you had to switch to an external program, such as Access, SQL Server Enterprise Manager, or FoxPro, whenever you needed to create or edit a table, set a relationship between two tables, design a query, and so on. The Visual Database Tools suite has been inherited by Visual Basic 6, and most of its tools are also available in the Professional Edition. The new version of Visual Database Tools is better integrated in the environment, and in fact some menus in the IDE—most notably the Query menu, the Diagram menu, and some commands in the File, Edit, and View menus—become active only when a window of Visual Database Tools has the focus.

In this section, I review a few of these tools and show how you can use them to manage your databases. Remember that the Database Designer window and the Query Designer window are available only with Visual Basic 6 Enterprise Edition.

The DataView Window

The entry point for using Visual Database Tools is the DataView window, which you can display using the corresponding command in the View menu or by clicking on its yellow icon in the standard toolbar. This window is a repository for all the database connections you want to have available at all times; these connections are called *data links*. For example, the DataView window shown in Figure 8-4 on page 404 contains data links to the Biblio and NWind Jet databases and two connections to the Pubs SQL Server database, one of which connects through the native OLE DB provider for SQL Server while the other connects through the MSDASQL provider for ODBC sources. You can open these data link nodes and display all the tables, views, diagrams, and stored procedures in the database. (In an Oracle database, you'll see two more folders, Functions and Synonyms.) You can expand a table or a view node to see the individual fields that make up that particular table or view, and you can look at an object's properties by right-clicking on it and selecting the Properties menu command. Let me summarize what you can do with the DataView window:

- You can create new data links and add them to the DataView window by clicking on the rightmost icon on the DataView window's toolbar. You can also delete an existing data link—or any other object displayed in the window—by clicking on it and pressing the Del key or by right-clicking on it and selecting the Delete command from the pop-up menu. Data links are stored in the system Registry and aren't associated with any particular Visual Basic project.

- You can see the contents of a table or a view (as shown in Figure 8-5 on the next page) by double-clicking on it or by selecting the Open command from the pop-up menu. If you have the right permissions, you can even edit the values displayed in the grid and save your changes to the underlying database.

- You can create a new database table by right-clicking on the Tables folder and selecting the New Table menu command. In the same menu, you'll find other commands for showing or hiding system tables or for filtering tables according to their owner. Keep in mind that these capabilities aren't supported for all databases. For example, the SQL Server provider supports table creation whereas the Jet provider doesn't.

- You can change the layout of an existing table by right-clicking on it and selecting the Design menu command. Again, this feature isn't supported by the Jet providers in version 3.51 and 4.0. Interestingly, if you change the type of columns of a table or if you add or delete columns, the DataView window automatically moves existing data into the new layout.

- You can right-click on any object and select the Properties menu command to browse its attributes. This is especially useful for revising the values used for the connection, the owner of each table, and the type of columns. (See Figure 8-4.)

- You can create new stored procedures or edit existing ones. A stored procedure is a sequence of database commands that's stored in the database in a precompiled and optimized form. A stored procedure can (and often does) accept parameters and return a set of records. Stored procedures can be edited in the SQL Editor, another member of the Visual Database Tool suite. (See Chapter 14 for a description of the SQL Editor.)

- You can add a new trigger to an existing table by selecting the New Trigger command from the pop-up menu. Triggers are special stored procedures that are automatically executed whenever a record in the table is modified, inserted, or deleted.

- You can create a new database diagram or edit an existing one by selecting the corresponding command from the menu that pops up when you right-click the Database Diagram folder or on an existing database diagram object. Database diagrams are graphical views of part or all the tables in the database; they display all the relationships between these objects, and you can annotate these diagrams with your own comments.

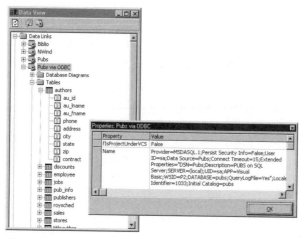

Figure 8-4. *Objects displayed in the DataView window can display a Properties dialog box.*

title	au_ord	au_lname	price	ytd_sales
The Busy Executive's Database Guide	2	Green	19.99	4095
The Busy Executive's Database Guide	1	Bennet	19.99	4095
Cooking with Computers: Surreptitious Balance Sheet	2	O'Leary	11.95	3876
Cooking with Computers: Surreptitious Balance Sheet	1	MacFeather	11.95	3876
You Can Combat Computer Stress!	1	Green	2.99	18722
Straight Talk About Computers	1	Straight	19.99	4095
Silicon Valley Gastronomic Treats	1	del Castillo	19.99	2032
The Gourmet Microwave	1	DeFrance	2.99	22246
The Gourmet Microwave	2	Ringer	2.99	22246
But Is It User Friendly?	1	Carson	22.95	8780
Secrets of Silicon Valley	1	Dull	20	4095
Secrets of Silicon Valley	2	Hunter	20	4095
Net Etiquette	1	Locksley	<NULL>	<NULL>
Computer Phobic AND Non-Phobic Individuals: Behavi	2	MacFeather	21.59	375
Computer Phobic AND Non-Phobic Individuals: Behavi	1	Karsen	21.59	375
Is Anger the Enemy?	2	Ringer	10.95	2045
Is Anger the Enemy?	1	Ringer	10.95	2045
Life Without Fear	1	Ringer	7	111

Figure 8-5. *The TitleView window, as seen in Visual Database Tools.*

A few of these operations are so important that they deserve a more detailed description.

Adding a new data link

Before working on a database with the DataView window, you must establish a data link to that database. A data link includes several pieces of information, including the name of the OLE DB provider used to connect to the database engine, the name of the particular database you want to access, and other login data such as the user name and password.

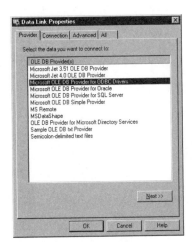

Figure 8-6. *To create a new data link, you must select an OLE DB provider.*

You can create a new data link by clicking on the rightmost icon in the DataView toolbar or by selecting the Add A Data Link command from the pop-up menu that appears when you right-click on the window. This command starts a four-step wizard, whose first page is visible in Figure 8-6. In this page, you select the OLE DB provider you want to use to connect to the database. By default, ADO uses the Microsoft OLE DB Provider for ODBC Drivers (MSDASQL), which lets you connect to virtually any relational and ISAM database in the world. For some data sources, you can get better performance and more features using providers specifically created for those particular data sources.

The content of the second page of the wizard depends on which provider you selected in the opening tab. For example, when connecting to a Jet database you have to select only the path of the MDB file and the user name and password to use at login. Figure 8-7 on the next page shows the options you have when connecting to a SQL Server database using the Microsoft OLE DB Provider for SQL Server 6.5: here you must select the server name, enter login data, and select, if you want, a database name. (This is what ADO calls the *initial catalog*.) Remember that if you have a blank password, you must tick the Blank Password check box because simply leaving the password field empty won't work. You don't need to specify a user name and password if you rely on Windows NT integrated security. In that case, SQL Server uses the name and password provided at login time to check whether you're granted access to the server. Click on the Test Connection button to be sure that everything is OK.

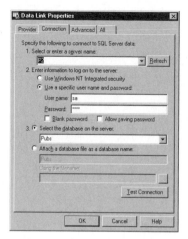

Figure 8-7. *The connection properties of the Microsoft OLE DB Provider for SQL Server.*

When you use the default Microsoft OLE DB Provider for ODBC Drivers, the second page of the wizard is different. In this case, you can opt for a DSN or use a connection string (which broadly corresponds to a DSN-less connection). If you've chosen to use a connection string, you can build one starting with an existing DSN or create one from scratch, and you can also enter other properties in a dialog box whose content depends on the ODBC driver you're using. If you fill in the user name, password, and database name fields in this dialog box (on the right in Figure 8-8), you don't need to type these values again in the corresponding fields of the wizard page (on the left in the same figure).

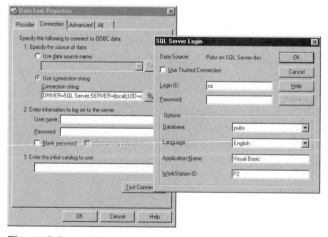

Figure 8-8. *Building a connection string.*

You seldom need to enter any values in the remaining two pages of the Data Link wizard. But you can optimize your application's performance if you specify in the Advanced page that you're opening the database for read-only operations exclusively, and you can prevent timeout errors by setting a higher value for the Connection Timeout property. In the last wizard page, named All, you see a summary of all the connection properties. Some of these attributes are also present in the previous pages, while others can be modified only here. In general, these are advanced settings, and you shouldn't alter their default values unless you know what you're doing. Because each OLE DB provider exposes a different set of properties, you should refer to the documentation of the specific provider for additional information.

> **TIP** If you're using the Microsoft OLE DB Provider for SQL Server 6.5, chances are that you can't list the database tables contained in a given SQL Server. This seems to be a bug in this version of the provider, and in fact everything works correctly if you upgrade to the Microsoft OLE DB Provider for SQL Server 7.0. (You need to upgrade just the provider, not the entire SQL Server engine). It turns out, however, that SQL Server 6.5 needs just a little help from us. Use the Find command to locate a copy of the INSTCAT.SQL file on your system. (You should find it in your \Windows\System directory and possibly in other directories as well.) Then import this file in ISQL_w and run the script; at the end of the execution, try again to create a data link, and you'll see that you are now able to correctly list all SQL Server databases.

Creating or editing a database table

You can create a new database table—if the underlying provider allows you to do so—by right-clicking an existing table object and selecting the New Table command from the pop-up menu. You'll be asked for the name of the new table, and then a window like the one in Figure 8-9 on the next page will appear. You must enter the name of each field in the new table in this window, together with its type (integer, floating-point number, string, and so on), size, precision, and default value. You must also decide whether the field can accept Null values and whether the field is the identity key for the table.

> **TIP** When you're building a table, you can create new fields by copying and pasting their attributes from other tables in the database. To select multiple field rows, click on the leftmost (gray) column while pressing the Ctrl or Shift key. (See Figure 8-9.) You can copy the selection using the Ctrl+C key combination and then paste it into another grid using Ctrl+V.

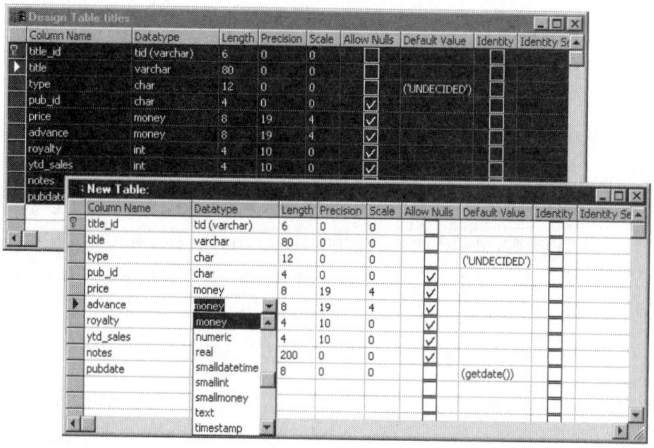

Figure 8-9. *When you create a new table or edit the design of an existing one, you can copy and paste field attributes from other tables.*

The next step you take when creating a table is deciding which field (or fields) should be the primary key, which can include multiple columns, if necessary. A primary key is useful for uniquely identifying each record in the table and for enforcing relational integrity rules. You also generally need a primary key to create updatable cursors on the table. To create a primary key, select the row that contains the field key (use Ctrl+mouse click to select multiple columns), and then right-click on the grid and select the Set Primary Key menu command. You can create only one primary key per table, and the involved columns can't allow Null values. A key icon will appear on the left border for all the fields that are part of the primary key.

If you right-click on the grid and select the Properties menu command, the dialog box shown in Figure 8-10 appears. Here you can define the constraints, the relationships, and the indices for this table.

A constraint is a simple validation rule that involves one or more fields in the table, for example:

```
price > 0
```

A table can have multiple constraints, and each constraint has a name. You can have the database enforce the constraint for all the records already in the table, for all subsequent insert and delete operations, and when the database is being replicated.

In the second page of the Properties dialog box, you define the attributes for the relationships this table is involved in.

In the third page of the Properties dialog box, you create and delete the indices associated with the table. Indices are database entities that permit you to quickly retrieve the information in a table if you know the value of one or more fields. Indices also serve to create relationships between tables and to enforce referential integrity constraints. You can define several types of indices. A *primary key* index is the main index for a table; none of its fields can have a Null value and their combination must have a unique value so that each row of the table can be uniquely identified. A *foreign key* index is based on one or more keys that are primary keys in another table, and it's used when the two tables participate in a relationship. A *unique* index is based on any field (or combination of fields) that has a unique value in all the rows of the table. A unique index differs from a primary index in that a unique index can accept Null values. You can also have *non-unique* indices, which are often used to speed up searches without enforcing any constraints on the fields upon which they're based. Some database engines also support *clustered* indices, which ensure that the records in the table are physically arranged in the same order as they are in the index. (You can have only one index of this type in each table.)

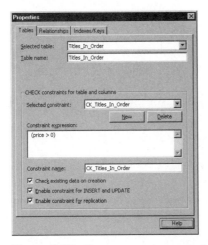

Figure 8-10. *You can create constraints in a table's Properties page.*

When you complete the definition of a new table or when you alter the layout of an existing table, you can select the Save Change Script command from the File menu. This creates a script containing a sequence of SQL commands that reproduce the edits you've just completed. You can save this script to use as a reference or to enable you to re-create the table in other SQL Server systems. You can't decide where the script is saved, though. For example, on my system all scripts are stored in files with .sql extensions, which are saved in the C:\Program Files\Microsoft Visual Studio\Vb98 directory.

The Database Diagram Window

As I mentioned earlier, database diagrams display all or part of the tables in your database, including their fields, their keys, and the relationships among them. You can create diagrams for SQL Server and Oracle databases by right-clicking on a database Diagram folder in the DataView windows and selecting the New Diagram menu command. This command brings up the Database Diagram window, another

Visual Database tool. You can drag-and-drop tables from the DataView window to the Database Diagram window, and when the diagram includes more tables the relationships among them are automatically displayed. You can also display all the tables that are related to a table already in the diagram by right-clicking on the table and selecting the Add Related Tables menu command. Figure 8-11 shows a diagram I created for the sample Pubs database that comes with SQL Server. Using the database diagram window, you can perform several interesting tasks:

- You can automatically arrange all tables, or just the selected tables, using the command in the Diagram menu.

- You can show or hide the names of the relationships using the Show Relationship Labels command in the Diagram menu or in the pop-up menu that appears when you right-click on the Database Diagram window background.

- You can add a text annotation using the New Text Annotation menu command, located in the Diagram menu or in the Database Diagram window pop-up menu. You can change the attributes of the text you enter using the Set Text Font command in the Diagram menu.

- You can select one or more tables in the diagram and change their appearance. You can decide to display just a table name, the key field names, all column names, or all column names and attributes, and you can even define a custom view to display only the column attributes you want.

- Because all the information in the tables is alive, you can change a table's layout without leaving the Database Diagram window, and you can also create and delete columns and select primary keys. (See the pop-up menu in Figure 8-11.) You can delete the table from the diagram or drop it from the database using the Delete Table from Database and Remove Table from Diagram menu commands respectively, so pay attention to which option you select. If you delete a table from the database, all the data it contains is gone forever.

- You can change the zoom factor of the diagram window, from the Zoom submenu in the Edit menu or from the pop-up menu that you display by right-clicking the window background.

- You can print the diagram using the Print command from the File menu. Before printing, you might want to recalculate and view page breaks using the corresponding commands in the Diagram menu or the pop-up menu. Unlike the Print Setup command in the File menu, the Print Setup command in the pop-up menu lets you select the zoom factor of the printed page.

■ Finally, you can save the diagram to the database with the Save and Save As commands in the File menu.

The nature of relationships between tables is a key factor in the design of a database. You can place tables in one-to-one relationships or in one-to-many relationships. An example of a one-to-one relationship is the relationship between the Publishers and Pub_info tables in the Pubs database. An example of a one-to-many relationship is that between the Publishers and Titles tables. You can revise the attributes of a relationship in the Database Diagram window by right-clicking on the line that connects two related tables and selecting the Properties menu command.

The Database Diagram window can also work as a source for drag-and-drop operations. For example, you can copy a subset of the tables in a diagram to another diagram by selecting the subset and dragging the tables to the other diagram's window. Using drag-and-drop, you can also assemble multiple diagrams into a larger one. These techniques are particularly useful when you're dealing with databases with a lot of tables.

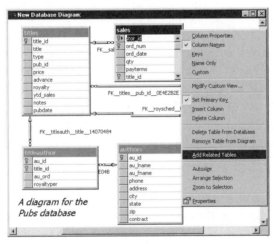

Figure 8-11. *A database diagram for the Pubs database.*

The Query Builder Window

If you right-click on a Views folder inside the Data View window, you can create a new view. A view is either a subset of all the rows from a database table or the logical join of two or more tables in the database. For example, the Titleview view in the Pubs database shows all the titles in the database together with their authors. To retrieve this information, the view has to collect data from three distinct tables, Authors, Titles, and TitlesAuthor. When you create a new view, or edit an existing one, the Query Builder window appears. This is another member of the Visual Database

Tools suite and is also one of the most useful because it lets you create queries and views using an intuitive user interface. The Query Builder window is subdivided into four panes, as you can see in Figure 8-12.

■ In the Diagram pane, you arrange tables dropped from the DataView or the Database Diagram windows, from which you can select the fields that should appear in the query. You can display four different pop-up menus from this pane, which arise from a right-click on a table caption, a field name, a relationship connecting line, or the pane's background. Some of these commands are also included in the Query top-level menu, which becomes active when the Query Builder window is the foreground window.

■ In the Grid pane, you can define the query or the view using a tabular format. For each field, you can define an alias name (that is, the name that field will appear under in the result set) and a criteria selection. For example, you can create a view that returns only the titles from a specific publisher or those whose price is below a given threshold.

■ In the SQL pane, you see the query in SQL syntax. You can modify the query using the Diagram or the Grid panes and see how the SQL string changes, but you can also change the SQL query and watch the other two panes update their contents and appearance. (Some queries are too complex for Query Builder to display graphically, though.) You can also have Query Builder verify the syntax of the SQL string that you've typed, using the Verify SQL Syntax command in the Query menu.

■ In the Result pane, you can see the result of the query or the view so that you have a chance to confirm that your query does exactly what you want. To populate this pane, you must select the Run command from the Query menu or from the pop-up menu that appears when you right-click anywhere in the Query Builder window. When you modify the query or view using one of the other three panes, the contents of this pane are grayed out to remind you that they aren't up to date.

You can hide and show individual panes using the Show Panes submenu in the View top-level menu. Commands in the Query menu let you add filters, sort or group the results based on a field value, and more. You can also use the Query Builder window to create SQL commands other than SELECT. You usually do this using the Change Type submenu from the Query menu, but these commands are disabled when you're creating or modifying a view (which can be based only on a SELECT command). For examples of other SQL commands, see "Crash Course in SQL" at the end of this chapter.

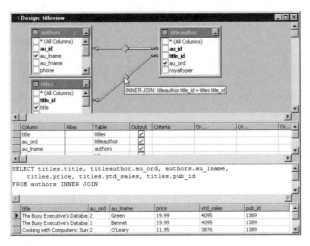

Figure 8-12. *The Query Builder open in the Titleview view of the Pubs database.*

ADO DATA BINDING

Historically, the first form of database support in Visual Basic (version 3) was the Data control and bound controls, as I explained in the first section of this chapter. This binding mechanism has undergone several refinements in Visual Basic 4 and 5, but it hadn't changed much until the ADO binding mechanism made its debut in Visual Basic 6.

First let me briefly remind you that binding is a technology that lets you place controls—such as TextBox, CheckBox, ListBox, and ComboBox controls—on a form and *bind* any or all of them to another control, called the Data control, which in turn is connected to a database. The Data control allows you to navigate through the records in the database: Each time a new record becomes current, its field values appear in the bound controls. Similarly, if the user updates one or more values in the bound controls, these changes are propagated to the database. You can therefore create simple user interfaces to database data without writing a single line of code. (This is in theory; in practice you should validate input data and often format data displayed in bound controls.)

The new ADO-based binding technology is a revolution in how you display data from a database. First of all, you don't always have a database to work with, not directly at least. In Visual Basic 6 you shouldn't talk about bound controls and Data controls; instead, you should talk about one or more *data consumers* that are bound to a *data source*. In Visual Basic 6, you can use many types of data consumers, such as an intrinsic or external control, a class, a COM component, a homemade ActiveX control (or UserControl), or the DataReport designer. You also have many data sources to choose from: the ADO Data control, a class, a COM component, a UserControl, or the DataEnvironment designer. (The DataEnvironment designer is described later in this chapter, whereas the DataReport designer is covered in Chapter 15.)

This assortment of data sources and consumers gives you an unparalleled flexibility in devising the most appropriate binding scheme for your application, and it also overcomes one of the most serious limitations of the original Data control (and its younger cousin, the RemoteData control). When you use ADO binding, you're not tied to a 2-tier architecture because you don't have to necessarily bind user interface elements to fields in a database. Rather, you can use one or more intermediate COM components, which consistently implement a more flexible 3-tier design. It isn't really important where these COM components reside; they might execute on the client machine, on the server machine, or on another machine. Don't forget that n-tier development is a state of mind: In a sense, you can do 3-tier development even when the client and the server are on the same machine (although in that case you surely don't take advantage of many of the 3-tier promises). The important point in n-tier architectures is that the front-end application isn't tightly tied to the back-end database so that you can—if the need arises—substitute the front end or the back end without having to rewrite the entire application.

The Binding Mechanism

You exploit the simplest form of ADO binding when you bind one or more controls to an ADO Data control, but the concepts I'll explain here can be applied to any type of data source or consumer. And you'll learn more about writing such data sources and consumers in Chapters 17 and 18.

Before using the ADO Data control, you must add it to the current project to have it available in the control Toolbox. You also need to add some items to the References dialog box, so let's take the following shortcut: Select the New Project command from the File menu, and then open the Data Project template from the Project gallery. This template adds several modules to the project (some of which aren't of interest to us right now). Above all, the template adds a reference to the Microsoft ActiveX Data Objects 2.0 Library (MSADO15.DLL) and a number of additional controls to the Toolbox, including the ADO Data control. If you already upgraded to the new ADO 2.1 version, the item added to the References dialog box is msado20.tlb.

Drop an instance of the ADO Data control on the only form in the project, frmDataEnv, and set its *Align* property to 2-vbAlignBottom so that it resizes with the form. You might set other properties from the regular Properties window, but it's much better to use the custom Property pages that pop up when you right-click on the control and select the ADODC Properties menu command. In the General page, you can specify which database you're connecting to using three different methods: a Data Link file, an ODBC Data Source Name (the old DSNs aren't dead in the ADO world, as you can see), or a custom connection string.

Data link files are the ADO equivalent of file-based DSNs. At first, you might wonder how to create a UDL file because no New or Add button is immediately apparent. The answer is in Figure 8-13: Click on the Browse button to bring up an Open dialog box that lets you browse through your directories looking for UDL files. Then right-click inside the (possibly empty) file list part of the dialog box, and select the New submenu and the Microsoft Data Link menu command. This creates a "blank" UDL file, which you can rename whatever you like. It's a simple task once you know how to do it; just don't call this process an intuitive user interface!

Creating the UDL file is only part of the job because you now have to specify which database this Data Link file is pointing to. You need to perform another counter-intuitive operation: Right-click on the UDL file that you've just created, and select the Properties menu command. This brings up a multipage Properties dialog box, which seems intimidating at first. A closer look reveals that the last four tabs are nothing new: They're the Provider, Connection, Advanced, and All pages you saw when we created a data link inside the Data View window. This shouldn't be a surprise. We're still talking about the same concepts here. Anyway, it's good to walk in familiar territory again.

By the way, you can also do without UDL files and create the connection string directly. If you click on the Build button in the ADODC Properties dialog box, once again you'll see those four pages that let you define an ADO connection. Suddenly, everything you learned when you were working with the Data View window makes sense in this context as well. For this example, let's connect to the NWind.mdb database, using any of the available methods.

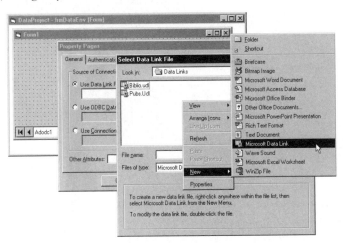

Figure 8-13. *The long path to Data Link file creation.*

Back to the ADODC Properties dialog box. Move on to the Authentication page, enter user name and password if your database requires them, and then click on the RecordSource page. This is where you define the database table, the stored procedure, or the SQL query that will feed data to bound controls. For this example, select the adCmdText option in the upper combo box, and then enter the following SQL query:

```
Select * from Products
```

Go back to the form and add four TextBox controls, four Labels, and one CheckBox control, as shown in Figure 8-14. Set the *DataSource* properties of the CheckBox control and all the TextBox controls to Adodc1, and then set their *DataField* properties to the name of the database field you want to bind the control to. You don't have to guess their names because a handy drop-down list in the Properties window contains all the field names in the Publishers table. For this example, use the ProductName, UnitPrice, UnitsInStock, UnitsOnOrder, and Discontinued fields.

You're finally ready to run this program and to navigate through the records using the four arrow buttons in the ADO Data control. Try to modify one or more fields, and then move to the next record and back to see whether the new values have persisted. As you can see, the mechanism really works without your having written a single line of Visual Basic code.

You can even add new records, still without writing a single line of code. Go back to design time, and set the ADO Data control's *EOFAction* property to the value 2-adDoAddNew. Then run the sample program again, click on the rightmost arrow button to move to the last record, and click on the second button from the right to move to the next record. All bound controls will be cleared, and you can enter a new record's field values. Remember that you need to move to another record to make your edits persistent. If you simply close the form, any changes you made to the current record are lost.

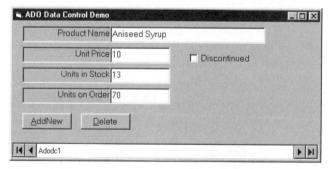

Figure 8-14. *The ADO Data control sample application uses the DataCombo control described in Chapter 15.*

Working with Bound Controls

Most of the Visual Basic 6 intrinsic controls support data binding, including the TextBox, Label, CheckBox, ListBox, ComboBox, PictureBox, and OLE controls. Typically, you use TextBox for editable string or numeric fields, Labels for non-editable fields, CheckBoxes for Boolean values, and ListBoxes and ComboBoxes to list valid values. In the Visual Basic 6 package, you'll also find some external ActiveX controls that support data binding, such as the ImageCombo, MonthView, DateTimePicker, MaskEdBox, RichTextBox, DataGrid, DataList, DataCombo, and Hierarchical FlexGrid controls. In this section, I've assembled a few tips and suggestions for making the best use of the intrinsic controls as bound controls; data-aware ActiveX controls are covered in Chapters 10, 11, 12, and 15.

> **NOTE** Visual Basic 6 includes some data-aware controls—namely the DBGrid, DBList, DBCombo, and MSFlexGrid controls—that aren't compatible with the ADO Data control and work only with older Data and RemoteData controls. All the intrinsic controls work with both the older Data controls and the newer ADO Data control.

All bound controls expose the *DataChanged* run-time–only Boolean property. Visual Basic sets this property to True when the end user (or the code) modifies the value in the control. The ADO binding mechanism uses this flag to check whether the current record has been edited and resets it to False after displaying a new record. This means that you can prevent the ADO Data control from moving a control's value to a database field by setting the control's *DataChanged* property to False yourself.

> **TIP** The *DataChanged* property is independent from the ADO binding mechanism and is correctly managed from Visual Basic even if the control isn't currently bound to a database field. For example, you can exploit this property when you want to determine whether a control's contents have been modified after you have loaded a value in it. If you didn't use this property, you would need to use a form-level Boolean variable and manually set it to True from within the control's *Change* or *Click* event procedure.

When you use a data-bound Label control, you should set its *UseMnemonics* property to False. If it's set to its True (default) value, all ampersand characters in database fields will be mistakenly interpreted as placeholders for hot key characters.

The CheckBox control recognizes a zero value as vbUnchecked, any nonzero value as vbChecked, and a Null value as vbGrayed. But when you modify the value in this field, The CheckBox control always stores 0 and –1 values in the database. For this reason, the CheckBox control should be bound only to a Boolean field.

> **CAUTION** You can't bind a PictureBox control to photographs stored in an Access database field of type OLE control. Instead, you must use an OLE control. A bound PictureBox control is fine for displaying a photograph stored in an SQL Server field of type Image.

The OptionButton control isn't data aware, so you need to resort to the following trick to bind it to an ADO Data control. Create an array of OptionButton controls and a hidden TextBox control, and bind the hidden TextBox control to the database field in question. Then write the code you see at the top of the next page in the form module.

```
Private Sub optRadioButton_Click(Index As Integer)
    ' Change hidden TextBox's contents when user clicks on radio buttons.
    txtHidden.Text = Trim$(Index)
End Sub

Private Sub txtHidden_Change()
    ' Select the correct radio button when the ADO Data control
    ' assigns a new value to the hidden TextBox.
    On Error Resume Next
    optRadioButton(CInt(txtHidden.Text)).Value = True
End Sub
```

The ideal solution would be to have an ActiveX control that displays an array of OptionButton controls and bind them to a single database field, and in fact a few commercial controls do exactly this. But now that Visual Basic supports the creation of ActiveX controls, you can create such a control yourself in a few minutes. See Chapter 17 to learn how you can create bound ActiveX controls.

Pay attention when you use ComboBox controls with *Style* set to 2-DropdownList and ListBox controls as bound controls. If the value in the database doesn't match one of the values in the list, you get a run-time error.

Visual Basic 6 lets you assign the *DataSource* property of a control at run time, so you can bind (or unbind) a control during execution:

```
' Bind a control at run time.
txtFirstName.DataField = "FirstName"
Set txtFirstName.DataSource = Adodc1
...
' Unbind it.
Set txtFirstName.DataSource = Nothing
```

Dynamic assignments of the *DataSource* property don't work with older Data and RemoteData controls.

The ADO Data Control

The ADO Data control embodies many features of the ADO Connection and Recordset objects, which I'll cover in Chapter 13. For this reason, in this section I'll only describe the few properties that you really need to set up a minimal sample application that uses this control.

The *ConnectionString* property is the string that contains all the information that's necessary to complete the connection, as I showed you in the previous section. You can set login data using the *UserName* and *Password* properties, and you can define a timeout for the connection attempt with the *ConnectionTimeout* property. *Mode* determines which operations are allowed on the connection. For additional information about these properties, read "The Connection Object" section in Chapter 13.

Most of the other properties of the ADO Data control are borrowed from the ADO Recordset object. *RecordSource* is the table, the stored procedure, or the SQL command that returns the records from the database. (It corresponds to the Recordset object's *Source* property.) *CommandType* is the type of query stored in the *Record-Source* property, and *CommandTimeout* is the timeout in seconds for the command to execute. *CursorLocation* specifies whether the cursor should be located on the client or on the server workstation, and *CursorType* determines the type of the cursor. *CacheSize* is the number of records that are read from the database in each data transfer, whereas *LockType* affects how the client application can update data in the database. I examine these properties in detail, along with cursor and locking options, in Chapters 13 and 14.

The ADO Data control also exposes a pair of properties that have no corresponding items in the Recordset object. The *EOFAction* property determines what happens when the user attempts to move past the last record: 0-adDoMoveLast means that the record pointer stays at the last record in the Recordset, 1-adStayEOF sets the EOF (End-Of-File) condition, and 2-adDoAddNew automatically adds a new record. The *BOFAction* property determines what happens when the user clicks on the left arrow button when the first record is the current record; 0-adDoMoveFirst leaves the pointer on the first record, and 1-adStayBOF sets the BOF (Begin-Of-File) condition.

At run time, the ADO Data control exposes one more property, the *Recordset* property, which returns a reference to the underlying Recordset object. This reference is essential for exploiting all the power of this control because it lets you add support for other operations. For example, you can create two CommandButton controls, set their *Caption* properties to *AddNew* and *Delete*, and write this code behind their *Click* events:

```
Private Sub cmdAddNew_Click()
    Adodc1.Recordset.AddNew
End Sub

Private Sub cmdDelete_Click()
    Adodc1.Recordset.Delete
End Sub
```

Keep in mind, however, that the preceding operations aren't always permitted; for example, you can't add new records or delete existing ones if the ADO Data control has opened the data source in read-only mode. Even if the data source has been opened in read-write mode, certain operations on a record might be illegal. For example, you can't delete a record in the Customers table when one or more records in the Orders table are referencing it.

The Recordset object is packed with properties and methods, and you can use all of them from the ADO Data control. You can, for example, sort or filter the displayed records, or set a bookmark to quickly return to a given record. The ADO Data control doesn't expose the underlying Connection object directly, but you can use the *ActiveConnection* property of the underlying Recordset. For example, you can implement transactions using the following code:

```
Private Sub Form_Load()
    ' Start a transaction when the form loads.
    Adodc1.Recordset.ActiveConnection.BeginTrans
End Sub

Private Sub Form_Unload(Cancel As Integer)
    ' Commit or roll back when the form unloads.
    If MsgBox("Do you confirm changes to records?", vbYesNo) = vbYes Then
        Adodc1.Recordset.ActiveConnection.CommitTrans
    Else
        Adodc1.Recordset.ActiveConnection.RollbackTrans
    End If
End Sub
```

If you roll back a transaction using the preceding *Form_Unload* routine, you need to invoke the control's *Refresh* method to see the previous values in records.

> **NOTE**   A *transaction* is a group of related database operations that should be logically considered as a single command, which can either succeed or fail as a whole. For example, when you move money from one bank account to another account you should enclose the two operations within a transaction so that if the second operation isn't successful, the first one is canceled as well. When you confirm a transaction, you should *commit* it. When you want to cancel the effect of all its commands, you should *roll it back*.

The ADO Data control also exposes several events borrowed from the Recordset, so I'm deferring the description of most of them until Chapter 13. I want to describe only three events here. The *MoveComplete* event fires when a new record has become the current record. You can exploit this event to display information that can't be retrieved with a simple bound control. For example, suppose that a field in the database, named PictureFile, holds the path of a BMP file. You can't directly display this bitmap using a bound control, but you can trap the *MoveComplete* event and manually load the image into a PictureBox control:

```
Private Sub Adodc1_MoveComplete(ByVal adReason As ADODB.EventReasonEnum, _
    ByVal pError As ADODB.Error, adStatus As ADODB.EventStatusEnum, _
    ByVal pRecordset As ADODB.Recordset)
    picPhoto.Picture = LoadPicture(Adodc1.Recordset("PictureFile"))
End Sub
```

The *WillChangeRecord* fires immediately before the ADO Data control writes data to the database. This is the best place to validate the contents of bound controls and cancel the operation if necessary:

```
Dim ValidationError As Boolean              ' A form-level variable

Private Sub Adodc1_WillChangeRecord(ByVal adReason As _
    ADODB.EventReasonEnum, ByVal cRecords As Long, adStatus As _
    ADODB.EventStatusEnum, ByVal pRecordset As ADODB.Recordset)
    ' Check that fields are valid, cancel the update if not.
    If txtProductName = "" Or Not IsNumeric(txtUnitPrice) Then
        MsgBox "Please enter valid field values", vbExclamation
        ValidationError = True
        adStatus = adStatusCancel
    End If
End Sub
```

The *Error* event is the only event that hasn't been inherited from the Recordset object. The ADO Data control fires it if an error occurs while there's no Visual Basic code running. Typically, this happens when the user clicks on one of the control's arrow buttons and the resulting operation fails (for example, when you're trying to update a record locked by another user). This event also fires when you cancel an operation in the *WillChangeRecord* event. By default, the ADO Data control displays a standard error message, but you can modify this standard behavior by assigning True to the *fCancelDisplay* parameter. This code snippet completes the previous example that performs field validation:

```
Private Sub Adodc1_Error(ByVal ErrorNumber As Long, Description As String,_
    ByVal Scode As Long, ByVal Source As String, ByVal HelpFile As String,_
    ByVal HelpContext As Long, fCancelDisplay As Boolean)
    ' Don't show validation errors (already processed elsewhere).
    If ValidationError Then
        fCancelDisplay = True
        ValidationError = False
    End If
End Sub
```

Formatting Data

One of the serious limitations of the original Data and RemoteData controls was that you couldn't format data for display on screen. For example, if you wanted to display a number with thousand separators, you had to write code. You also had to write code to display a date value in the long date format (such as "October 17, 1999") or some other more or less standard format. Well, it doesn't make sense to use bound controls if you have to write code even for such basic operations, does it?

The *DataFormat* property

The ADO binding mechanism effectively and elegantly solves this problem by adding the new *DataFormat* property to all bound controls. If you click on the *DataFormat* item in the Properties window, the property page shown in Figure 8-15 appears. Here you can interactively select from many basic format types (such as number, currency, date, and time), each one with several formatting options (number of decimal digits, thousand separators, currency symbol, date/time formats, and so on).

You can also set custom formatting, in which case you can specify a format string that follows the same syntax for the *Format* function (which I described in Chapter 5). But the ADO Data control can't correctly unformat values that were formatted using a complex format string, so it might store wrong data in the database. This problem can be overcome using StdDataFormat objects, as I explain in the next section.

The *DataFormat* property might not work correctly for a few controls. For example, when used with the DataCombo control this property doesn't affect the formatting of the items in the list portion. The DataGrid control exposes a DataFormats collection, where each item affects the format of a column of the grid.

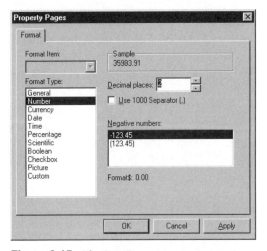

Figure 8-15. *The* DataFormat *property page.*

StdDataFormat objects

To be able to use StdDataFormat objects, you must add a reference to the Microsoft Data Formatting Object Library, and you must then distribute the corresponding MSSTDFMT.DLL file with all your applications.

The first use for these objects is to set the *DataFormat* property of a bound field at run time. You must do this, for example, when you create controls during execution using a control array (as explained in Chapter 3) or using the new Visual Basic 6 dynamic control creation feature (covered in Chapter 9). To modify how data is formatted in a bound control, you create a new StdDataFormat object, set its properties, and then assign it to the *DataFormat* property of the control, as in the following piece of code:

```
Private Sub Form_Load()
    ' Create a new formatting object and assign it to a bound field.
    Dim sdf As New StdDataFormat
    sdf.Type = fmtCustom
    sdf.Format = "mmm dd, yyyy"
    Set txtShippedDate.DataFormat = sdf
    ' Force the Data control to correctly display the first record.
    Adodc1.Recordset.Move 0
End Sub
```

The most important property of StdDataFormat objects is *Type*, which can be assigned one of the following values: 0-fmtGeneral, 1-fmtCustom, 2-fmtPicture, 3-fmtObject, 4-fmtCheckbox, 5-fmtBoolean, or 6-fmtBytes. If you're using a custom formatting option, you can assign the *Format* property a formatting string, which has the same syntax as the second argument of the VBA *Format* function.

When retrieving data from a Boolean field, you typically use a CheckBox control and the frmCheckbox setting. But you can also use a Label or a TextBox control that interprets the contents of the Boolean field and displays a meaningful description. In this case, you must assign strings to the *FalseValue*, *TrueValue*, and (optionally) *NullValue* properties:

```
Private Sub Form_Load()
    Dim sdf As New StdDataFormat
    sdf.Type = frmBoolean
    ' Set meaningful strings for False, True, and Null values.
    sdf.FalseValue = "In Production"
    sdf.TrueValue = "Discontinued"
    sdf.NullValue = "(unknown)"
    Set lblDiscontinued.DataFormat = sdf
    ' Force the Data control to correctly display the first record.
    Adodc1.Recordset.Move 0
End Sub
```

As a rule, you should use this technique only with Label, locked TextBox, and ListBox controls because the user shouldn't be allowed to enter a value other than the three strings assigned to the *FalseValue*, *TrueValue*, and *NullValue* properties.

The real power of StdDataFormat objects is their ability to raise events. You can think of an StdDataFormat object as something that sits between a data source and a data consumer. You're using an ADO Data control as a data source and a bound control as a data consumer in this case, but the StdDataFormat object can be used whenever the ADO binding mechanism is active. StdDataFormat objects let you actively intervene when the data is moved from the data source to the consumer and when the move occurs in the opposite direction. You do this thanks to the *Format* and *Unformat* events.

To trap these events, you must declare the StdDataFormat object as a form-level variable, using the *WithEvents* keyword. The *Format* event fires when a value is read from the database and displayed in a control. If the user modifies the value, an *Unformat* event fires when the ADO Data control saves the value back to the database. Both events receive a *DataValue* parameter, which is an object with two properties: *Value* is the value being transferred, and *TargetObject* is the bound control—or more generally, the data consumer—involved. Normally, if you manually format and unformat values inside these events you don't need to set any other property of the StdDataFormat object.

Figure 8-16 shows a sample program (also available on the companion CD) that displays data from the Orders table of the NWind.mdb database. The Freight amount can be expressed as dollars or euros, but the database stores the value only in dollars and therefore you need to do the conversion on the fly. This is the code that does the trick:

```
' How many euros in one dollar?
' (Of course, in a real program this would be a variable.)
Const DOLLARS_TO_EURO = 1.1734

Dim WithEvents sdfFreight As StdDataFormat

Private Sub Form_Load()
    Set sdfFreight = New StdDataFormat
    Set txtFreight.DataFormat = sdfFreight
    ' Force the Data control to correctly display the first record.
    Adodc1.Recordset.Move 0
End Sub

Private Sub sdfFreight_Format(ByVal DataValue As StdFormat.StdDataValue)
    ' Convert to euros if necessary.
    If optFreight(1) Then
        DataValue.Value = Round(DataValue.Value * DOLLARS_TO_EURO, 2)
    End If
End Sub

Private Sub sdfFreight_UnFormat(ByVal DataValue As StdFormat.StdDataValue)
    ' Convert back to dollars if necessary.
    If optFreight(1) Then
        DataValue.Value = Round(DataValue.Value / DOLLARS_TO_EURO, 2)
    End If
End Sub

Private Sub optFreight_Click(Index As Integer)
    If Index = 0 Then
```

```
    ' Convert from euros to dollars.
    txtFreight = Trim$(Round(CDbl(txtFreight) / DOLLARS_TO_EURO, 2))
Else
    ' Convert from dollars to euros.
    txtFreight = Trim$(Round(CDbl(txtFreight) * DOLLARS_TO_EURO, 2))
End If
End Sub
```

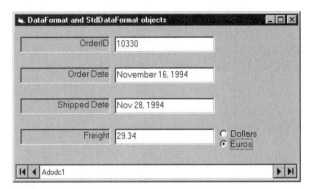

Figure 8-16. *Use StdDataFormat object to keep the display format independent of the value stored in the database.*

You can use the *DataValue.TargetObject* property to affect the appearance or the behavior of the bound control. For example, you can have the Freight amount appear in red when it's higher than 30 dollars:

```
Private Sub sdfFreight_Format(ByVal DataValue As StdFormat.StdDataValue)
    ' Show the value in red ink if >30 dollars.
    If DataValue.Value > 30 Then
        DataValue.TargetObject.ForeColor = vbRed
    Else
        DataValue.TargetObject.ForeColor = vbBlack
    End If
    ' Convert to euros if necessary.
    If optFreight(1) Then
        DataValue.Value = Round(DataValue.Value * DOLLARS_TO_EURO, 2)
    End If
End Sub
```

An interesting—though not adequately documented—feature of StdDataFormat objects is that you can assign the same instance to the *DataFormat* properties of more than one control. This is especially effective when you want to manage the formatting yourself in *Format* and *Unformat* events, so you have a single entry point to format multiple on-screen fields. You can use the *DataValue.TargetObject.Name* property to find out which bound control is requesting the formatting, as in the piece of code you see at the top of the next page.

```
Private Sub sdfGeneric_Format(ByVal DataValue As StdFormat.StdDataValue)
    Select Case DataValue.TargetObject.Name
        Case "txtFreight", "txtGrandTotal"
            ' These are currency fields.
            DataValue.Value = FormatCurrency(DataValue.Value)
        Case "ProductName"
            ' Display product names in uppercase characters.
            DataValue.Value = UCase$(DataValue.Value)
    End Select
End Sub
```

An StdDataFormat object exposes a third event, *Changed*, which fires when any property of the object has been changed. You usually react to this event by refreshing the contents of fields, as follows:

```
Private Sub sdfGeneric_Changed()
    ' This forces the ADO Data control to reread the current record.
    Adodc1.Recordset.Move 0
End Sub
```

Here are a few other bits of information about StdDataFormat objects:

- If you assign a complex formatting string to the *Format* property, the StdDataFormat object is unable to correctly unformat it, so you must do that manually in the *Unformat* event.

- The Visual Basic 6 online documentation warns that you should unbind a control and then rebind it if you want to change its StdDataFormat object's *Type* property. I've found that you don't need the unbind/rebind operation, but I must admit that I haven't tested all the possible combinations of properties and field types. So just be careful when you modify the *Type* property at run time.

- The *Unformat* event fires only if the value of the bound control has been modified since it was read from the database, that is, if its *DataChanged* property is True.

- At first, I believed that the *Unformat* event fires when the data is moved back to the database, but this isn't what actually happens. This event fires as soon as the user edits the value in a bound control and then moves the focus to another control. This is an important fact because when the *Unformat* event completes, the control's *DataChanged* property is set to False. So you can't rely on this property to determine whether any control has been modified. (If no StdDataFormat object is associated to the bound control, the *DataChanged* property stays True until the record is stored back in the database.)

The Data Form Wizard

The Data Form Wizard is a Visual Basic 6 add-in that automatically builds a form with a group of controls that are bound to a data source. It also creates a number of push buttons for common database operations, such as adding or deleting records. The Data Form Wizard was already included with Visual Basic 5, but it has been modified to work with the ADO Data control. It can also work without an ADO Data control simply by using an ADO Recordset as the data source, and it can even create an ad hoc data source class module.

Using the Data Form Wizard is really straightforward, so I won't describe each step in detail. Figure 8-17 displays an intermediate step, in which you decide the type of form you want to create and which type of binding should be used. You can generate a set of bound controls, a single DataGrid or Hierarchical FlexGrid control, a master/detail form, or an MSChart. The wizard is especially useful for creating single record and master/detail forms. For example, Figure 8-18 on the next page shows a form that displays orders in the upper part and information for each order in the lower grid.

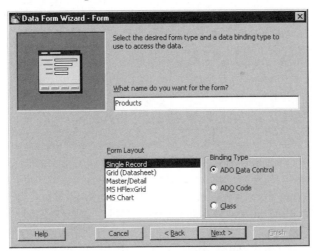

Figure 8-17. *The Data Form Wizard creates five different types of bound forms.*

In the next page, you select which table or view should be used as the record source. You also select which fields will be included in the result form and whether the output is to be sorted on a given column. If you are building a master/detail form, you have to select two different record sources, one for the master table and one for the detail table, and you also need to select one field from each table that links the two sources together. In the Control Selection tab you select which buttons will be placed on the form, choosing from the Add, Update, Delete, Refresh, and Close buttons. Finally, in the last page of the wizard, you have the opportunity to save all your settings in an RWP profile file so that you can later rerun the wizard without having to reenter all the options.

Figure 8-18. *A master/detail form based on the Orders and Order Details tables of the NWind.mdb database.*

It's highly likely that you'll need to fix the form or the code produced by the Data Form Wizard, if only for cosmetic reasons. But you might learn how to write good ADO code by simply running it and then browsing the results. Or you could use the wizard just to create a data source class. (Data source classes are described in Chapter 18.)

THE DATAENVIRONMENT DESIGNER

The DataEnvironment designer is one of the most intriguing new features of Visual Basic 6. In short, it's a design-time representation of the ADO objects that you would otherwise create at run time. This capability is *very* exciting because it brings the same programming paradigm to database development that Visual Basic itself introduced several years ago and that made Windows programming so easy and immediate.

When you use a form designer, you're actually defining at design time the forms and controls Visual Basic will create at run time. You make your choices in a visual manner, without worrying about what Visual Basic actually does when the program runs. Similarly, you can use the DataEnvironment designer to define the behavior of ADO Connections, Commands, and Recordset objects. You can set their properties at design time by pressing the F4 key to bring up the Properties window or by using their custom property pages, exactly as you would do with forms and controls.

The DataEnvironment designer is the descendent of the UserConnection designer, the first external designer ever created for Visual Basic. The UserConnection designer was included in the Enterprise Edition of Visual Basic 5 and could work exclusively with RDO connections, so only a fraction of Visual Basic developers ever used it or even were aware that a such a tool existed. The DataEnvironment designer is much more powerful than its ancestor. It works with any local and remote ADO connection and even supports multiple connections. Moreover, it qualifies as an ADO data source, so you can bind fields to it, as I'll show later.

Another advantage of using DataEnvironment objects defined at design time instead of ADO objects built through code is that—similarly to forms—a Data-Environment instance is a self-sufficient entity that contains other objects and the code to manage them. You can add public properties and methods to DataEnvironment designers, which greatly improves their reusability, as if they were class modules specialized to work with databases. I believe that DataEnviroment objects, properly used, will revolutionize the way database applications are built.

To add a DataEnvironment designer to the current project, you can choose the Add Data Environment command from the Project menu. This command appears only if you've added a reference to the Microsoft Data Environment Instance 1.0 library. You can also create a DataEnvironment designer from the DataView window. Finally, you can create a new Data Project from the project gallery. In this case, Visual Basic creates a project for you with all the necessary references and an instance of the DataEnvironment designer.

Connection Objects

The main object in a DataEnviroment designer is the Connection object. It broadly corresponds to the form object in the Form designer in the sense that it's the top-level object. Unlike forms, however, a DataEnvironment designer instance can contain multiple Connection objects.

You can create a Connection in many ways. When you create a DataEnvironment, it already contains a default Connection object, so you simply need to set its properties. You do this either by pressing F4 to display the standard Properties window, or (better) by right-clicking on the object and selecting the Properties menu command to display its custom property pages. (You get the same effect by clicking on the Properties button on the DataEnviroment toolbar.) I won't spend any time describing the Connection object's property pages because you're already familiar with them. The Provider, Connection, Advanced, and All pages are exactly the same ones that you encountered when setting data link's properties in the DataView window or when creating the *ConnectionString* property of an ADO Data control.

The standard Properties window contains a few properties that don't appear in the custom property pages. The *DesignUserName* and *DesignPassword* properties let you set the user name and password you want to use when you're creating the DataEnvironment object, while *RunUserName* and *RunPassword* are the user name and password you want to use when the program is executing. For example, you might develop the application using an Administrator identity and then check how the application behaves at run time when a guest user logs in. You can decide whether you want to see the prompt when the connection opens, and you can use different settings for design time and run time. The *DesignPromptBehavior* and *RunPromptBehavior* properties can take the following values: 1-adPromptAlways (always show the login dialog box, so the user is allowed to change login data), 2-adPromptComplete (show the login dialog box only if one or more required parameters are missing), 3-adPromptCompleteRequired (like the previous one, but allow user to enter only required parameters), and 4-adPromptNever (never show the login dialog box, and return an error to the application if one or more required parameters are missing). You usually set *DesignPromptBehavior* to adPromptComplete and *RunPromptBehavior* to adPromptNever; the latter prevents malicious users from logging on to other data sources or entering random user names and passwords until they manage to get into the system. Finally, the *DesignSaveAuthentication* and *RunSaveAuthentication* properties determine whether the login information described previously is saved in the VBP or the EXE file, respectively. A word of caution is in order here: User names and passwords in EXE files aren't encrypted, so determined hackers might load the file into a hex editor or parse it in some other way until they find that information.

Command Objects

A Command object in the DataEnvironment designer represents an action performed on a database. A command object is always a child of a Connection object, in much the same way a control is always a child of a form. More precisely, you can create a stand-alone Command object, but you can't use it until you make it a child of a Connection object.

Creating a Command object

The easiest way to create a Command object is by dragging a table, a view, or a stored procedure from the DataView window into the DataEnvironment window. Visual Basic then creates the Command object that corresponds to that table, view, or stored procedure, and it also creates a parent Connection, if necessary. A Command object can be a child only of a Connection that refers to its own database. You can also create one or more Command objects that map to stored procedures in a database by clicking on the Insert Stored Procedures button on the DataEnvironment toolbar. I used this shortcut to quickly create the Command objects visible in Figure 8-19.

There are two kinds of Command objects: ones that return Recordsets and ones that don't. The former are SQL queries, stored procedures, tables, or views that return a Recordset (which can be empty, if no records in the database meet the selection criteria). The latter are SQL commands or stored procedures that insert, delete, or modify values in the database but don't return a set of records. For example, you can create a Command named AuthorsInCA that returns all the authors that live in California by using the following SQL query:

```
SELECT * FROM Authors WHERE State = 'CA'
```

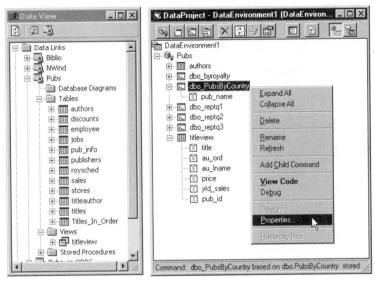

Figure 8-19. *You can drag tables, views, and stored procedures from the DataView window to the DataEnvironment designer to create Command objects, and right-click on them to display the custom property pages.*

Unlike Connection objects, all the properties of a Command object can be set in its custom property pages, and you never need to display the standard Properties window. In the General tab, you select the database object that the Command corresponds to—a table, a view, a stored procedure, or a synonym—or you enter the SQL text of a query. (You can also run the SQL Query Builder to build the query interactively.)

If you have a normal, nonparameterized and nonhierarchical command, you can skip all the intermediate tabs and go to the Advanced page, shown in Figure 8-20 on the next page. Here you decide the cursor type and location, the type of locking to be enforced, the size of the local cache (that is, the number of records read from the server when necessary), the timeout for the command, and the maximum number of records that the query should return. You can use this last value to prevent a query from returning hundreds of thousands of records and so bringing your workstation and your network to their knees. Don't worry if you don't understand the real meaning of most of these options; they directly map to properties of ADO Recordset and Command objects, so their purpose will be clear to you after you read Chapters 13 and 14.

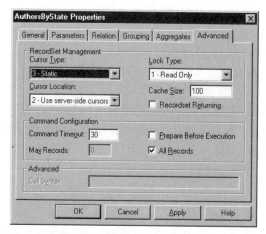

Figure 8-20. *The Advanced tab of the Command's property pages.*

The only attribute in this page that doesn't directly relate to an ADO property is the Recordset Returning check box. Most of the time, the DataEnvironment designer is able to determine whether you've added a Recordset returning or non-Recordset returning command, but if it makes a wrong assumption you can correct it by acting on this check box.

Parameterized commands

Using parameters adds a lot of flexibility to Command objects. You can create two types of parameterized Command objects: those based on a SQL query and those based on a stored procedure with parameters. For the first kind, you must enter a parameterized SQL query, using question marks as placeholders for parameters. For example, you can create a Command object named AuthorsByState, which corresponds to the following query:

```
SELECT * FROM Authors WHERE State = ?
```

After you've entered this query in the General tab of the Properties dialog box, switch to the Parameters tab and check that the DataEnvironment has correctly determined that the query embeds one parameter. In this tab, you can assign a name to each parameter, set its data type and size, and so on. All parameters in this type of query are input parameters.

To create a Command object that maps a stored procedure, you can click on the Insert Stored Procedure button and select the stored procedure you're interested in. The DataEnvironment is usually able to retrieve the stored procedure syntax and correctly populate the Command's Parameters collection. You should pay attention to the direction of the parameters because sometimes the DataEnvironment doesn't correctly recognize output parameters and you have to manually fix their *Direction* attribute. Also, double-check that all *string* parameters have nonzero sizes.

Data Binding with the DataEnvironment Designer

DataEnvironment designers can work as ADO data sources, so they appear in the DataSource combo box in the Properties window at design time. When you bind a control to a DataEnvironment designer, however, you must also set the *DataMember* property of a data-aware control to the name of the specific Command object you're binding it to. Only recordset-returning Command objects can work as data sources.

Fields and grids

You don't need to manually create controls on a form and bind them to the Data-Environment object because Visual Basic 6 allows you to do everything with drag-and-drop. To see how simple it is to use this feature, open a new form, click on a Command object in the DataEnvironment window, and drop it on the form. You'll immediately see the form being populated with many TextBox and (possibly) CheckBox controls, one for each field in the Command object, as shown in Figure 8-21. You can press F5 to check that the data binding mechanism is working correctly.

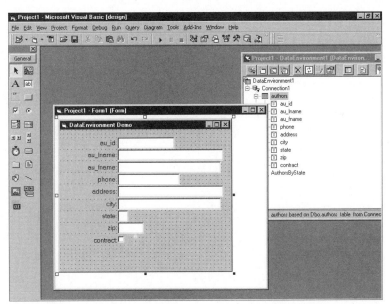

Figure 8-21. *A group of bound controls created by dropping a Command object on a form.*

Because you don't have a Data control on the form, you must provide the navigational buttons yourself. This is really easy: Just create two CommandButton controls, name them *cmdPrevious* and *cmdNext*, and then add the code you see at the top of the next page.

```
Private Sub cmdNext_Click()
    DataEnvironment1.rsAuthors.MoveNext
End Sub
Private Sub cmdPrevious_Click()
    DataEnvironment1.rsAuthors.MovePrevious
End Sub
```

The preceding code works because the DataEnvironment creates at run time, for each recordset-returning Command object, a Recordset whose name is *rs* followed by the Command's name. Using the same method, you can add buttons for deleting and inserting records, finding values, and so on. See Chapters 13 and 14 for all the properties, methods, and events of the ADO Recordset object.

You aren't restricted to creating simple controls, and you can even use bound grids to display a tabular view of your records. If you want to use bound grids, you must start the drag-and-drop operation using the right mouse button, release the button when the cursor is over the form, and select the Data Grid option from the pop-up menu. The sample application shown in Figure 8-22 demonstrates how you can use the parameterized AuthorsByState command to display a subset of all the records in the grid. This is the code behind the Filter push button:

```
Private Sub cmdFilter_Click()
    ' Run the query, passing the expected "State" parameter.
    DataEnvironment1.AuthorsByState txtState
    ' Ensure that the grid is bound to the DataEnvironment.
    Set DataGrid1.DataSource = DataEnvironment1
    DataGrid1.DataMember = "AuthorsByState"
End Sub
```

Or you can bind the grid directly to the Recordset produced by the parameterized query:

```
Set DataGrid1.DataSource = DataEnvironment1.rsAuthorsByState
```

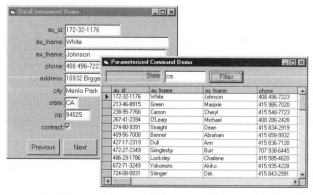

Figure 8-22. *The sample application shows a record-view and table-view of the Authors table, and it lets you filter records on their State fields.*

Selecting field types

When you drop a Command object (or an individual database field) onto a form, the DataEnvironment designer creates by default TextBox controls for all types of fields, except CheckBox controls for Boolean fields. You can change this default behavior in the following ways:

■ Click on the Options button on the DataEnvironment toolbar to bring up the dialog box shown in Figure 8-23, where you can select which control will be created when you drop a field of a given type. ADO field types are grouped by category, but you can tick the Show All Data Types check box to view individual data types. For each field type, you can select the corresponding control among all the intrinsic Visual Basic controls and all the ActiveX controls installed on the machine. The Drag And Drop Field Captions check box determines whether the DataEnvironment designer will also create Label controls for each field.

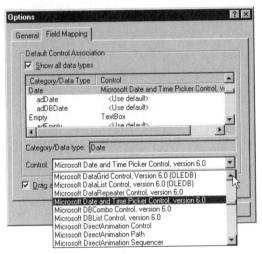

Figure 8-23. *The Field mapping tab of the Options dialog box lets you select which type of control will be created when you drop a field on a form.*

■ You can choose from two special field types. The Caption element lets you specify which control will be used to label the other fields. (The default is a Label control.) Multiple is the control to use when you drag a Command object using the left mouse button. You can specify a grid-like control if you want, but leaving the default value (TextBox control) won't hurt because you can always drop either a DataGrid or a Hierarchical FlexGrid control if you start dragging with the right mouse button.

■ For maximum flexibility, you can select the control to be used for each individual field of a particular Command object. Just right-click on a field in the DataEnvironment designer, issue the Properties menu command, and then select the control type and the caption to be used when the user drops that field on a form.

Hierarchical Commands

The DataEnvironment designer offers a design-time interface to one of the most powerful features of ADO, the ability to create hierarchical Recordsets. A hierarchical Recordset contains a set of records, which in turn might contain other child Recordsets. A practical example will clarify why this is a good thing. Let's say that you want to create a list of authors from the Biblio.mdb database, and for each author you want to display (and possibly update) the list of titles he or she has written. You can retrieve this information by executing an SQL JOIN query, or you can manually populate a form that shows this master/detail relationship by executing a distinct SQL SELECT query on the Title Author and Titles tables each time the user moves to a new record from the main Authors table. But neither of these approaches seems particularly satisfying, especially now that you can use a hierarchical Recordset instead. Let me show you how it works.

Relation hierarchies

You can create hierarchical Recordsets inside a DataEnvironment designer in a couple of different ways. The first one requires that you display the Relation property page of the Command object that corresponds to the main table in the relationship. To see how this technique works, open a connection to the Biblio.mdb database in the DataView window, and then drag its Authors and Title Author tables to the DataEnvironment window. To make the latter Command a child of the former one, display the Title_Author object's property pages and switch to the Relation tab. (See Figure 8-24.)

Click on the Relate To a Parent Command Object check box to activate the controls on this page, and then select the parent Command (Authors in this case) in the combo box. In the Relation Definition frame, you select the fields through which the two Command objects are related. These fields are the primary key in the parent Command and a foreign key in the child Command. In this particular example, the two fields have the same name in both tables, but this isn't generally the case. To complete our example, ensure that the Au_ID item is highlighted in both combo boxes, click on the Add button to add to the list of fields, and then click on the OK button to confirm. You will notice that the Title_Author Command has become a child of the Author Command, at the same level as the latter's fields. In fact, when the DataEnvironment designer creates this hierarchical Recordset at run time, its fourth field will actually contain the child Recordset.

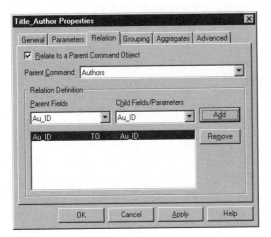

Figure 8-24. *The Relation tab of the Properties dialog box.*

To refine the example, we need to create a Titles Command and make it a child of the Title_Author object. This time we'll follow a different approach: Right-click on the Title_Author Command, and select the Add Child Command object. This creates an object called Command1 object. Rename it as Titles, bring up its property pages, specify that it takes its records from the Authors table in Biblio.mdb, and then switch to the Relation page to complete the relationship. The Title_Author and Titles Commands are related through their ISBN field, so you can click on the Add button and close the dialog box. You have completed the creation of a 3-level hierarchical Recordset.

To test-drive this new object, create a new form, drag the Authors Command onto it using the right mouse button, and then select the Hierarchical Flex Grid from the menu. This creates an instance of the Microsoft Hierarchical FlexGrid control on the form. Before running the program, you need to make a few columns invisible, so you should right-click on the grid, select the Retrieve Structure command, right-click again to display the Properties dialog box, and switch to the Bands tab. In this tab, you can define which fields are visible for each of the three Recordsets that participate in the relationship. In Band 0 (Authors), clear the Au_ID check box; in Band 1 (Title_Author), clear both the ISBN and Au_ID check boxes (which makes the band invisible); and in Band 2 (Titles), clear the Pub_ID, Description, Notes, and Comments check boxes. You can now run the application, which should display what appears in Figure 8-25 on the next page. Notice how you can expand and collapse rows using the plus and minus symbols near the grid's left border.

You can better this example by adding another level to the hierarchy, which you'd need to display information about the publisher of each title. You can add the level by dragging the Publishers table from the DataView window to the Data-Environment designer, making it a child Command of the Titles Command. I leave this to you as an exercise.

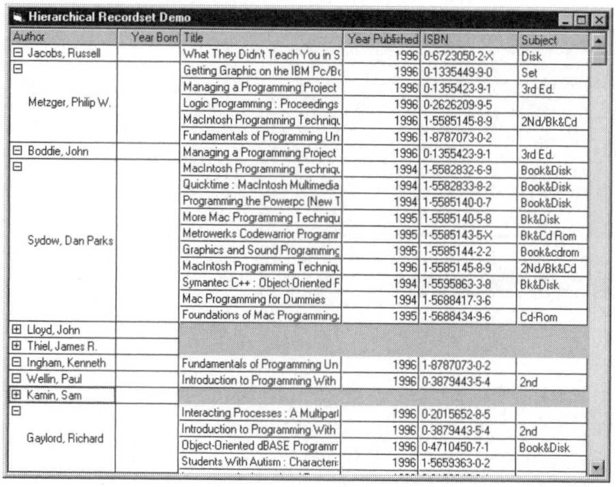

Figure 8-25. *The Hierarchical FlexGrid control displays hierarchical Recordsets and lets you expand and collapse individual rows in the parent Recordset.*

Grouping hierarchies

The DataEnvironment designer supports two more types of hierarchies, the Grouping and the Aggregate hierarchies. A grouping hierarchy is conceptually simple: You start with a Command object and build a parent Command that groups the records of the original Command according to one or more fields. To see what this means in practice, drop the Titles table on the DataEnvironment window, bring up its *Grouping* property page, tick the Group Command Object check box to enable the controls on this tab, move the Year Published field from the left list box to the right list box, and then close the dialog box to confirm your changes. You'll see that the Data-Environment designer now hosts a new Command object under the main Connection, named Titles1_grouped_using_Title1_Grouping, and two folders under it. One folder contains the Year Published field (the summary field), the other folder contains the fields of the original Titles1 Command. If you bind a Hierarchical FlexGrid control to the new parent Command, you'll see that the leftmost column displays different year numbers and all the other columns contain information about the titles published in that year.

Aggregate hierarchies

An aggregate field is a calculated field that computes an elementary expression (the count, the sum, the average, and so on) for a given field in all the rows of a Recordset. You often add an aggregate field when you already have a grouping hierarchy. To our previous example, we could add a TitleCount field that reports the number of books that were published in each year. In a more complex example, you might have all your orders grouped by month, with several aggregate fields reporting the order count, the sum of orders total, their average amounts, and so on.

You define aggregate fields in the Aggregates tab of the Properties dialog box. Click on the Add button to create a new aggregate, give it a meaningful name, and select a function among those available: COUNT, SUM, AVERAGE, MINIMUM, MAXIMUM, STANDARD DEVIATION, or ANY. (ANY returns the value common to all the fields in the selected records.) The Aggregate On combo box determines on which fields the aggregate field is evaluated and can be one of the following: Grouping, Grand Total, or the name of a child Command. (The actual content of the combo box depends on the type of the current Command.) If you select Grand Total, you can enter the name of the grand total field. In this case, a new folder is created under the main Command, and it will gather all the grand total fields in the Command. (See Figure 8-26.)

Figure 8-26. *A Command object that exploits all three types of hierarchies.*

CRASH COURSE IN SQL

If you want to work with databases, you must learn to speak their language. Databases speak Structured Query Language, better known as SQL, which was invented by E. F. Codd in the 1970s. Instead of working with tables one record at a time, SQL manages groups of records as a single entity, which makes it suitable for creating queries of any complexity. This language has been standardized, and now most database servers, and ADO itself, accept its ANSI-92 dialect.

SQL encompasses two distinct categories of statements: data definition language (DDL) and data manipulation language (DML). The DDL subset includes a group of statements that allow you to create database structures, such as tables, fields, indices, and so on. The DML subset includes all the commands that allow you to query and modify the data in the database, add new records, or delete existing ones. While both subsets are equally important, most of the time you'll use only DML statements to retrieve and update data stored in a database whose structure has been already defined in advance (possibly by another developer or the database administrator). For this reason, I focus in this section exclusively on the DML subset of the language. You need the information contained in this section to build queries that can't be created interactively using the SQL Query Builder (which permits you to create only the simplest queries).

Countless books have been written about SQL, so it's impossible to tell you anything new in a few pages. I'm writing this section only to enable those of you who've never worked with databases to understand the SQL queries that are used in the rest of the book. If you're already proficient with SQL, you can jump to the next chapter without any hesitation.

Most of the examples in the following sections are based on the Biblio.mdb or the NWind.mdb databases. On the companion CD, you'll find a sample application (shown in Figure 8-27) that lets you practice with SQL and immediately see the results of your query. You can recall previous queries using the less-than and greater-than buttons, and you can also safely perform action queries that delete, insert, or modify records because all your operations are wrapped in a transaction that's rolled back when you close the form.

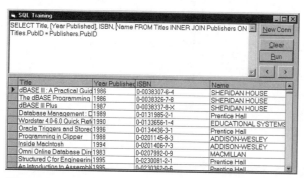

Figure 8-27. *The SQL Training sample application.*

The SELECT Command

The most frequently used SQL statement is undoubtedly the SELECT command, which returns a set of records based on selection criteria.

Basic selections

The simplest SELECT command returns all the records and all the fields from a database table:

```
SELECT * FROM Publishers
```

(In all the examples in this section, I use uppercase characters for SQL keywords, but you can write them in lowercase characters if you like.) You can refine a SELECT command by specifying the list of fields you want to retrieve. If the field name includes spaces or other symbols, you must enclose it within square brackets:

```
SELECT PubID, [Company Name], Address FROM Publishers
```

You can often speed up a query by retrieving only the fields you're actually going to use in your application. SQL supports simple expressions in the field list portion of a SELECT. For example, you determine the age of each author at the turn of the century using the following command:

```
SELECT Author, 2000-[Year Born] AS Age FROM Authors
```

Notice how the AS clause lets you assign a well-defined name to a calculated field, which would otherwise be labeled with a generic name such as *Expr1001*. You can also use aggregate functions such as COUNT, MIN, MAX, SUM, and AVG on the table field, as in this code:

```
SELECT COUNT(*) AS AuthorCnt, AVG(2000-[Year Born]) AS AvgAge FROM Authors
```

This statement returns only one record with two fields: AuthorCnt is the number of records in the Authors table, and AvgAge is the average of the age of all authors in the year 2000.

Aggregate functions generally consider only non-Null values in the database. For example, you can learn the number of authors for which the average has been evaluated using this statement:

```
SELECT COUNT([Year Born]) FROM Authors
```

The COUNT(*) syntax is an exception to the general rule in that it returns the number of all the records in the result. In a real application, you rarely retrieve all the records from a table, though, for a good reason: If the table contains thousands of records, you're going to add too much overhead to your system and the network. You filter a subset of the records in the table using the WHERE clause. For example, you might want to retrieve the names of all the publishers in California:

```
SELECT Name, City FROM Publishers WHERE State = 'CA'
```

You can also combine multiple conditions using AND and OR Boolean operators, as in the following query, which retrieves only the Californian publishers whose names begin with the letter *M*:

```
SELECT * FROM Publishers WHERE State = 'CA' AND Name LIKE 'M%'
```

In the WHERE clause, you can use all the comparison operators (=, <, <=, >, >=, and <>) and the LIKE, BETWEEN, and IN operators. The BETWEEN operator is used to select all the values in a range:

```
SELECT * FROM Titles WHERE [Year Published] BETWEEN 1996 AND 1998
```

The IN operator is useful when you have a list of values. The query on the next page returns all the publishers located in California, Texas, and New Jersey.

```
SELECT Name, State FROM Publishers WHERE State IN ('CA', 'TX', 'NJ')
```

SQL lets you embed strings in single quotes or in double quotes. Because you usually pass these statements as Visual Basic strings, using single quotes is often more practical. But when the string contains a single quote, you must use two consecutive single quotes. For example, to search for an author named *O'Hara*, you must use the following query:

```
SELECT * FROM Authors WHERE Author = 'O''Hara'
```

Sorting and grouping

The ORDER BY clause lets you affect the order in which records are retrieved. For example, you can display publishers in alphabetical order:

```
SELECT * FROM Publishers ORDER BY [Company Name]
```

You can also specify multiple sort keys by separating the keys with commas. Furthermore, for each sort key you can add the DESC keyword to sort in descending order. For example, you can list publishers sorted by state in ascending order and at the same time list all the publishers in the same state by city in descending order, as you can see in the following statement. (This is, admittedly, not a really useful thing to do, but it works as an example.)

```
SELECT * FROM Publishers ORDER BY State, City DESC
```

When the results are sorted, you can decide to take just the first records returned by the SELECT, which you do with the TOP clause. For example, you can retrieve the five titles published more recently using the following query:

```
SELECT TOP 5 * FROM Titles ORDER BY [Year Published] DESC
```

Keep in mind, however, that the TOP clause always returns all the records with a given value in the field for which the results are sorted. For example, the version of the Biblio.mdb database I'm working with includes seven titles published in the most recent year (1999), and therefore the preceding query will return seven records, not five.

You can define the number of returned records in terms of the percentage of the total number of the records that would be returned, using the TOP PERCENT clause:

```
SELECT TOP 10 PERCENT * FROM Titles ORDER BY [Year Published] DESC
```

The GROUP BY clause lets you create summary records that include aggregate values from groups of other records. For example, you can create a report with the number of titles published in each year by using the following query:

```
SELECT [Year Published], COUNT(*) As TitlesInYear FROM Titles
    GROUP BY [Year Published]
```

The next query displays the number of titles published in the last 10 years:

```
SELECT TOP 10 [Year Published], COUNT(*) As TitlesInYear FROM Titles
    GROUP BY [Year Published] ORDER BY [Year Published] DESC
```

You can prepare more sophisticated groupings with the HAVING clause. This clause is similar to the WHERE clause, but it acts on the fields produced by the GROUP BY clause and is often followed by an aggregate expression. The next query is similar to the previous one but returns a record only for those years when more than 50 titles have been published:

```
SELECT [Year Published], COUNT(*) As TitlesInYear FROM Titles
    GROUP BY [Year Published] HAVING COUNT(*)  > 50
```

You can have both a WHERE clause and a HAVING clause in the same query. If you use both, SQL applies the WHERE clause first to filter the records from the original table. The GROUP BY clause then creates the groups, and finally the HAVING clause filters out the grouped records that don't meet the condition it specifies.

The following statement returns the names of all the cities where there's at least one publisher:

```
SELECT City FROM Publishers
```

This query presents some problems in that it also returns records for which the City field is Null, and, in addition, it returns duplicate values when there's more than one publisher in a city. You can solve the first problem by testing the field with the ISNULL function, and you can filter out duplicates using the DISTINCT keyword:

```
SELECT DISTINCT City FROM Publishers WHERE NOT ISNULL(City)
```

Subqueries

All the examples I've shown you so far retrieved their records from just one table. Most of the time, however, the data you're interested in is distributed in multiple tables. For example, to print a list of titles and their publishers you must access both the Titles and the Publishers tables. You do this easily by specifying both table names in the FROM clause and then setting a suitable WHERE clause:

```
SELECT Titles.Title, Publishers.Name FROM Titles, Publishers
    WHERE Titles.PubID = Publishers.PubID
```

You use the *tablename.fieldname* syntax to avoid ambiguities when the two tables have fields with the same name. Here's another example, which retrieves all the titles published by a given publisher. You need to specify both tables in the FROM clause, even if the returned fields come only from the Titles table:

```
SELECT Titles.* FROM Titles, Publishers WHERE Publishers.Name = 'MACMILLAN'
```

But you can use another—and often more efficient—way to retrieve the same information, based on the fact that the SELECT statement can return a value, which you can use to the left of the = operator. The next query uses a nested SELECT query to get a list of all the titles from a given publisher:

```
SELECT * FROM Titles WHERE PubID =
    (SELECT PubID FROM Publishers WHERE Name = 'MACMILLAN')
```

If you aren't sure whether the subquery returns only one record, use the IN operator instead of the equal sign. You can make these subqueries as complex as you like. For example, the following query returns the titles published by all the publishers from California, Texas, and New Jersey:

```
SELECT * FROM Titles WHERE PubId IN
    (SELECT PubID FROM Publishers WHERE State IN ('CA', 'TX', 'NJ'))
```

You can also use aggregate functions, such as SUM or AVG. The next query returns all the items from the Orders table in NWind.mdb for which the Freight value is higher than the average Freight value:

```
SELECT * FROM Orders WHERE Freight > (SELECT AVG(Freight) FROM Orders)
```

Joins

The join operation is used to retrieve data from two tables that are related to each other through a common field. Conceptually, the result of the join is a new table whose rows consist of some or all the fields from the first table followed by some or all the fields from the second table; the expression in the ON clause in a JOIN command determines which rows from the second table will match a given row from the first table. For example, the following query returns information about all titles, including the name of their publisher. I already showed that you can complete this task using a SELECT command with multiple tables, but an INNER JOIN command is often better:

```
SELECT Titles.Title, Titles.[Year Published], Publishers.Name FROM Titles
    INNER JOIN Publishers ON Titles.PubID = Publishers.PubID
```

This is an important detail: the previous statement retrieves only those titles for which there is a publisher, that is, those whose PubID field isn't Null. While the INNER JOIN (also known as *equi-join*) is the most common form of join operation, SQL also supports two other types of joins, the LEFT JOIN and the RIGHT JOIN operations. The LEFT JOIN operation retrieves all the records in the first table, regardless of whether there's a corresponding record in the other table. For example, the following command retrieves all the titles, even if their publisher isn't known:

```
SELECT Titles.Title, Titles.[Year Published], Publishers.Name FROM Titles
    LEFT JOIN Publishers ON Titles.PubID = Publishers.PubID
```

The RIGHT JOIN operation retrieves all the records in the second table, even if there isn't a related record in the first table. The following statement selects all the publishers, whether or not they have published any titles:

```
SELECT Titles.Title, Titles.[Year Published], Publishers.Name FROM Titles
    RIGHT JOIN Publishers ON Titles.PubID = Publishers.PubID
```

Join operations can be nested. Here's an example that retrieves information about all authors and the books they've written. The two tables are related through the intermediate table Title Author, so we need a nested INNER JOIN operation:

```
SELECT Author, Title, [Year Published] FROM Authors INNER JOIN
    ([Title Author] INNER JOIN Titles ON [Title Author].ISBN = Titles.ISBN)
    ON Authors.Au_Id = [Title Author].Au_ID
```

Of course, you can filter records using a WHERE clause in both the nested and the external join. For example, you can return only titles published before 1960:

```
SELECT Author, Title, [Year Published] FROM Authors INNER JOIN
    ([Title Author] LEFT JOIN Titles ON [Title Author].ISBN = Titles.ISBN)
    ON Authors.Au_Id = [Title Author].Au_ID WHERE [Year Published] < 1960
```

Unions

You can append results to a SELECT command using the UNION keyword. Say that you want to send your Christmas greetings to all your customers and suppliers. You can retrieve their names and addresses using the following query:

```
SELECT Name, Address, City FROM Customers
    UNION SELECT CompanyName, Address, City FROM Suppliers
```

The two tables can have different structures, provided that the fields returned by each SELECT command are of the same type.

The INSERT INTO Command

The INSERT INTO command adds a new record to a table and sets its fields in one operation. You must provide a list of field names and values, as in the following statement:

```
INSERT INTO Authors (Author, [Year Born]) VALUES ('Frank Whale', 1960)
```

If the table has a key field that's automatically generated by the database engine—as is true for the Au_Id field in the Authors table—you don't have to include it in the field list. Null values are inserted in all the columns that you omit from the field list and that aren't automatically generated by the database engine. If you want to insert data that's already stored in another table, you can append a SELECT command to the INSERT INTO statement. For example, the following command copies all the records from a table called NewAuthors into the Authors table:

```
INSERT INTO Authors SELECT * FROM NewAuthors
```

You often need a WHERE clause to limit the number of records that are inserted. You can copy from tables with a different structure or with different name fields, but in this case you need to use aliases to make field names match. The statement at the top of the next page copies an entry from the Contact table to the Customer table but accounts for different field names.

```
INSERT INTO Customers SELECT ContactName AS Name, Address, City, State
   FROM Contacts WHERE Successful = True
```

The UPDATE Command

The UPDATE command modifies the values in one or more records. You often use a WHERE clause to restrict its action to the record(s) you're interested in:

```
UPDATE Authors SET [Year Born] = 1961 WHERE Author = 'Frank Whale'
```

You can also use expressions in SET clauses. For example, the following statement increments the discount for all the items in the Order Details table that have been ordered by customer *LILAS*. (Run this query against the NWind.mdb database.)

```
UPDATE [Order Details] INNER JOIN Orders
   ON [Order Details].OrderID = Orders.OrderID
   SET Discount = Discount + 0.10 WHERE CustomerID = 'LILAS'
```

The DELETE Command

The DELETE command lets you remove one or more records from a table. You must append a WHERE clause to this command unless you want to delete all the records in the table. For example, the following command deletes all the titles that were published before 1950:

```
DELETE FROM Titles WHERE [Year Published] < 1950
```

A DELETE operation can fire cascading delete operations in other tables if an integrity relationship is enforced between the two tables. For example, you can delete a record in the Orders table in NWind.mdb and the Jet engine automatically deletes all the related records in the Order Details table. In general, however, you can't delete a record in a table if a foreign key in another table points to it. For example, you can't delete a record in the Employees table until you delete the records in the Orders table whose EmployeeID values are pointing to the record you want to delete. You can do the latter operation using an INNER JOIN clause in the DELETE command. Keep in mind that when multiple tables are involved, you need to specify which one you want to delete records from immediately after the DELETE command:

```
DELETE Orders.* FROM Orders INNER JOIN Employees ON Orders.EmployeeID =
   Employees.EmployeeID WHERE Employees.LastName = 'King'
```

After that, you can delete the records in the Employees table:

```
DELETE FROM Employees WHERE Employees.LastName = 'King'
```

This chapter concludes the first part of this book, which has covered all the basic concepts you need before diving into more complex programming issues. We'll go back to database programming in Chapter 13, but in the meantime let's see how you can take advantage of the ActiveX controls that come in the Visual Basic package.

Part II
The User Interface

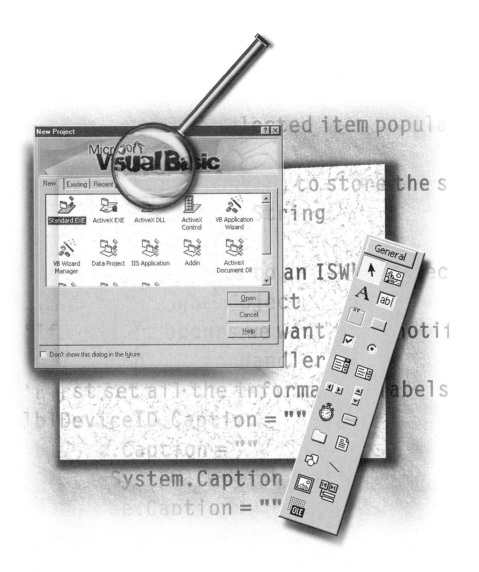

Chapter 9

Advanced Forms and Dialogs

Forms have evolved considerably since their first appearance in Microsoft Visual Basic 1, yet many programmers fail to take advantage of all their new features. In most cases, programmers deal with forms as they did in Visual Basic 3, not realizing that the inner workings of forms has changed.

In this chapter, I focus both on regular forms and MDI forms, and I also explain how to create parameterized form components and how to implement drag-and-drop. I also describe several new Visual Basic 6 features, including dynamic control creation and the capability to deliver data-driven forms that can be reused against different data sources.

STANDARD USAGE OF FORMS

In Chapter 2, I described the many properties, methods, and events of Visual Basic forms. In this chapter, I illustrate how forms fit into the object-oriented programming paradigm and how you can exploit them to build effective and bug-free applications.

Forms as Objects

The first step in getting the most out of Visual Basic forms is recognizing what they really are. In all versions from Visual Basic 4 on, in fact, a form is nothing but a class module plus a designer. As you might recall from Chapter 2, *designers* are modules integrated into the Visual Basic environment that let programmers visually design characteristics of objects to be instantiated at run time.

The form designer lets you define the aspect of your form at design time by placing child controls on its surface and setting their properties. When you launch the application, the Visual Basic runtime translates these pieces of information into a series of calls to Windows API functions that create the main window and then all its child controls. Translated into C or C++ code, a typical Visual Basic form with some controls on it would require several hundred lines of code, which gives you an idea why Visual Basic has quickly become the most popular language for building Windows software.

It's easy to prove that a form is nothing but an object with a user interface. Say that you have a form in your application named frmDetails. You can instantiate it as if it were a regular object using a standard New operator:

```
Dim frm As frmDetails
Set frm = New frmDetails
frm.Show
```

A consequence of forms being objects is that they can expose properties, methods, and events exactly as regular objects do. For instance, you can add to a form module one or more Public Property procedures that encapsulate values contained in the form's child controls, as in the following code:

```
' Inside the frmDetails form
Public Property Get Total() As Currency
    Total = CCur(txtTotal.Text)
End Property
```

Similarly, you can define Public methods that let the main application ask the form object to perform an action, for example, to print its contents on the printer:

```
' Note that Sub, Function, and Property procs are Public by default.
Sub PrintOrders()
    ' Here you place the code that prints the form's contents.
End Sub
```

From outside the form module, you access the form's properties and methods as you would do with any object:

```
Dim Total As Currency
Total = frm.Total()
frm.PrintOrders
```

The most important difference between form modules and regular class modules is that the former can't be made Public and accessed from another application through COM.

Hidden global form variables

The notion that a form is a special type of object leads to an apparent paradox. As you know, to use an object you must first initialize it. But you can (and usually do) reference a form directly without any prior explicit initialization. For example, in the following code snippet you don't need to explicitly create the frmDetails form:

```
Private Sub cmdDetails_Click()
    frmDetails.Show
End Sub
```

Since forms are objects, why doesn't this statement raise error 91: "Object variable or With block variable not set"? The reason is mostly historical. When Visual Basic 4 was released, Microsoft engineers were faced with the issue of backward compatibility with Visual Basic 3 and previous versions for which the preceding code was OK. Clearly, if Visual Basic 4 couldn't have imported existing Visual Basic 3 projects, it would have been a flop. The solution the engineers came up with is both simple and elegant. For each form in the current application, the compiler defines a hidden global variable, whose name coincides with that of the form class:

```
' (Note: you will never actually see these declarations.)
Public frmDetails As New frmDetails
Public frmOrders As New frmOrders
' (Same for every other form in the application)
```

When your code references the *frmDetails* entity, you aren't referring to the frmDetails form *class*, you're referring to a *variable* whose name happens to be the same as its class. Because this variable is declared to be auto-instancing, Visual Basic creates a new instance of that particular form class as soon as your code references the variable.

This ingenious trick, based on a hidden global form variable, has permitted developers to painlessly port their existing Visual Basic 3 applications to Visual Basic 4 and later versions. At the same time, as you'll see in a moment, these hidden variables introduce a few potential problems that you need to be aware of.

The "clean form instance" problem

To illustrate a problem that often manifests itself when working with forms, I'll create a simple frmLogin form, which asks the end user for his or her name and password and refuses to unload if the password isn't the correct one. This simple form has only two public properties, *UserName* and *Password*, which are set to the contents of the txtUserName and txtPassword controls, respectively, in the *Unload* event procedure. This is the complete source code of the frmLogin form module:

```
Public UserName As String
Public Password As String
```

(continued)

```
Private Sub cmdOK_Click()
    ' Unload this form only if password is OK.
    If LCase$(txtPassword) = "balena" Then Unload Me
End Sub

Private Sub Form_Load()
    ' Move property values into form fields.
    txtUserName = UserName
    txtPassword = Password
End Sub

Private Sub Form_Unload(Cancel As Integer)
    ' Move field contents back into public properties.
    UserName = txtUserName
    Password = txtPassword
End Sub
```

You can display the frmLogin form and read its properties to retrieve values entered by the end user:

```
' Code in frmMain form
Private Sub cmdShowLogin_Click()
frmLogin.Show vbModal
' Execution gets here only if password is OK.
MsgBox frmLogin.UserName & " logged in."
End Sub
```

To test that this form works correctly, run the main form, click on its cmdShowLogin button, and then enter the correct user name and password. (Mine is shown in Figure 9-1). When the frmMain form regains control, it greets you with a message box. Apparently, everything works as it should. But if you click again on the Login button, the frmLogin form appears again; however, this time the user name and password fields are already filled with the values from the previous call. This isn't what I'd call a secure way to manage passwords!

Figure 9-1. *The Login demo application.*

To understand what has happened, add the following statements to the frmLogin form module:

```
Private Sub Form_Initialize()
    Debug.Print "Initialize event"
End Sub
Private Sub Form_Terminate()
    Debug.Print "Terminate event"
End Sub
```

If you now run the program and repeat the same sequence of actions that I just described, you'll see that the *Initialize* event is called as soon as you reference the *frmLogin* variable in code, whereas the *Terminate* event is never invoked. In other words, the second time you show the frmLogin form, you're actually using the same instance created the first time. The form has been unloaded normally, but Visual Basic hasn't released the instance data area associated with the form instance—that is, the area where Private and Public variables are stored. For this reason, the value of *UserName* and *Password* properties persist from the first call, and you'll find them in the two TextBox controls. In a real application, this behavior can lead to bugs that are very difficult to discover because they aren't immediately visible in the user interface.

You can work around this issue by forcing Visual Basic into releasing the form instance so that the next time you reference the form a new instance will be created. You can choose from two methods to achieve this. The most obvious one is to set the form variable to Nothing after returning from the *Show* method:

```
Private Sub cmdShowLogin_Click()
    frmLogin.Show vbModal
    MsgBox frmLogin.UserName & " logged in."
    ' Set the hidden global form variable to Nothing.
    Set frmLogin = Nothing
End Sub
```

The other method is a more object-oriented way to achieve the same result. You simply need to explicitly create a local form variable with the same name as the hidden global variable so that the local variable takes precedence over the global variable:

```
Private Sub cmdShowLogin_Click()
    Dim frmLogin As New frmLogin
    frmLogin.Show vbModal
    MsgBox frmLogin.UserName & " logged in."
End Sub
```

If you now run the program, you'll see that when the form variable goes out of scope Visual Basic correctly invokes the form's *Form_Terminate* event, which is a confirmation that the instance is correctly destroyed: An interesting benefit of this technique is that you can create multiple instances of any nonmodal form, as you can see in Figure 9-2.

```
Private Sub cmdShowDocument_Click()
    Dim TextBrowser As New TextBrowser
    TextBrowser.Filename = txtFilename.Text
    ' Show the form, making it a child form of this one.
    TextBrowser.Show, Me
End Sub
```

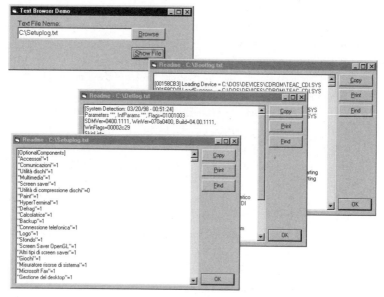

Figure 9-2. *Using explicit form variables, you can create and display multiple instances of the same form. All child forms are shown in front of their parent form, even if the parent form has the focus.*

TIP   The *Show* method supports a second, optional argument that permits you to specify the parent form of the form being shown. When you pass a value to this argument, you achieve two interesting effects: the child form is always shown in front of its parent, even if the parent has the focus, and when the parent form is closed or minimized, all its child forms are also automatically closed or minimized. You can take advantage of this feature to create floating forms that host a toolbar, a palette of tools, a group of icons, and so on. This technique is most effective if you set the *BorderStyle* property of the child form to 4–Fixed ToolWindow or 5-Sizable ToolWindow.

You can find the complete source code of the frmTextBrowser form module on the companion CD. Note that in this case you're working with modeless forms.

Consequently, when the form variable goes out of scope the form is still visible, which prevents Visual Basic from releasing the instance data area. When eventually the end user unloads the form, the Visual Basic runtime fires the *Form_Terminate* event immediately after the *Form_Unload* event. This seems to break the rule that any object is released as soon as the program destroys the last reference to it, but we haven't really destroyed the last reference, as I'll explain next.

The Forms collection

The Forms collection is a global collection that contains all the currently loaded forms. This means that all loaded forms are referenced by this collection, and this additional reference keeps the form alive even if the main application has released all the references to a form. You can exploit the Forms collection to retrieve a reference to any form, even though the application has set to Nothing all the other references to it. All you need is the following function:

```
Function GetForm(formName As String) As Form
    Dim frm As Form
    For Each frm In Forms
        If StrComp(frm.Name, formName, vbTextCompare) = 0 Then
            Set GetForm = frm
            Exit Function
        End If
    Next
End Function
```

If there are multiple occurrences of the same form, the preceding function returns the first reference to it in the Forms collection. You can use this function to reference a form by its name, as in this code:

```
GetForm("frmLogin").Caption = "Login Form"
```

You should be aware that the *GetForm* function returns a reference to a generic Form object. It therefore exposes the interface common to all forms, which includes properties such as *Caption* and *ForeColor* and methods such as *Move* and *Show*. You can't use this interface to access any custom method or property you have defined for a particular form class. Instead, you must *cast* the generic Form reference to a specific variable:

```
Dim frm As frmLogin
Set frm = GetForm("frmLogin") = "Login Form"
username = frm.UserName
```

Reusable Forms

The notion that forms are objects suggests that you can reuse them exactly as you reuse class modules. You can reuse forms many ways, the simplest one being to store them as templates, as I suggested in Chapter 2. But you can take advantage of more advanced and flexible techniques for form code reuse. I'll describe these techniques in the following sections.

Using custom properties and methods

Many business applications show a calendar for the user to select one or more dates. Visual Basic comes with a MonthView Microsoft ActiveX control (see Chapter 11), but a custom form has its advantages: Just to name a few, you can customize its size, the language used for months and the names of days of the week, and colors used for holidays. In general, a custom form gives you the greatest flexibility and control over the user interface. On the companion CD, you'll find the complete source code for the frmCalendar form module shown in Figure 9-3. The buttons with day numbers are arranged in an array of OptionButton controls whose *Style* property is set to 1-Graphical.

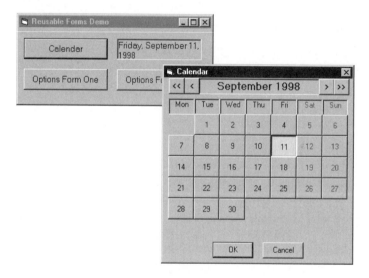

Figure 9-3. *A custom Calendar form that communicates with the main application through custom properties, methods, and events.*

The frmCalendar form exposes several properties that let you customize its interface, such as *DialogTitle* (the caption of the dialog box), *FirstDayOfWeek*, and *SaturdayIsHoliday* (useful for customizing the appearance of the calendar). There are also properties for retrieving the date selected by the user: *CancelPressed* (True if the end user hasn't selected any date), *SelectedDate* (a read/write Date value), *Day*, *Month*, and *Year* (read-only properties that return a given component of *SelectedDate*). The module exposes a single method, *ShowMonth*, that displays a given month in the dialog box, and optionally highlights a particular day:

```
Private Sub cmdCalendar_Click()
    Dim Calendar As New frmCalendar
    Calendar.DialogTitle = "Select a new date for the appointment"
    ' Highlight the current day/month/year.
    Calendar.ShowMonth Year(Now), Month(Now), Day(Now)
    ' Show the calendar as a modal dialog.
    Calendar.Show vbModal
    ' Get the result if the user didn't press Cancel.
    If Not Calendar.CancelPressed Then
        AppointmentDate = Calendar.SelectedDate
    End If
End Sub
```

In general, when working with a form as an object, you should provide the form with an interface that lets you avoid accessing the form's native properties. For example, the frmCalendar form module exposes the *DialogTitle* property, and client code should use it instead of the standard *Caption* property. This way, the client doesn't break the form object encapsulation, which in turn makes it possible for you to have control of what happens inside the form module. Alas, while you can build really robust class modules, you have no way to prevent the application from directly accessing the form's native properties or the controls on the form's surface. Nevertheless, you should exercise this discipline if you want to enjoy all the benefits of using forms as objects.

Adding custom events

In the previous code example, the frmCalendar form is displayed as a modal dialog box, which pauses the execution of the program until the dialog box is closed. When the dialog box closes, you can query the form's properties to retrieve the end user's choices. In many circumstances, however, you might want to display a form as a modeless dialog box. In this case, you need a way to learn when the user closes the form so that you can query its *SelectedDate* property. You can accomplish this by adding a couple of custom events to the form module:

```
Event DateChanged(newDate As Date)
Event Unload(CancelPressed As Boolean)
```

These custom events increase the usability of the frmCalendar module. To trap these custom events, you need a module-level *WithEvents* variable in the form that's showing the calendar dialog box, as you would for a regular object:

```
' In the frmMain form
Dim WithEvents Calendar As New frmCalendar

Private Sub cmdCalendar_Click()
    Set Calendar = New frmCalendar
```

(continued)

457

```
        Calendar.DialogTitle = "Select a new date for the appointment"
        Calendar.ShowMonth Year(Now), Month(Now), Day(Now)
        Calendar.Show                ' Show as a modeless dialog box.
    End Sub

    Private Sub Calendar_DateChanged(newDate As Date)
        ' Show the date currently selected on a Label control.
        lblStatus.Caption = Format(newDate, "Long Date")
    End Sub

    Private Sub Calendar_Unload(CancelPressed As Boolean)
        If CancelPressed Then
            MsgBox "Command canceled", vbInformation
        Else
            MsgBox "Selected date: " & Format$(Calendar.SelectedDate, _
                "Long Date"), vbInformation
        End If
        ' We don't need this variable any longer.
        Set Calendar = Nothing
    End Sub
```

> **NOTE**   You might wonder why you need a custom *Unload* event: since the *Calendar* variable is referencing the frmCalendar form, you might think it capable of trapping its *Unload* event. This assumption isn't correct because, in fact, the *Calendar* variable is pointing to the frmCalendar interface, whereas the *Unload* event as well as other form events such as *Resize*, *Load*, *Paint*, and so on are exposed by the *Form* interface and can't be trapped by the *frmCalendar* variable. If you want to trap standard form events, you should assign the form reference to a generic *Form* variable. In this particular case, adding a custom *Unload* event simplifies the structure of the client code.

As they do for regular class modules, custom events add a lot of flexibility to form modules. Adding a *Change*-like event—such as the *DateChanged* event in the frmCalendar module—lets you keep the application in sync with data entered by the end user in the form. You can add many other types of events, for instance a *Progress* event, for when the form module performs lengthy operations. For more information about events, see Chapter 7.

Parameterized forms

You can push the usability of form modules even further with the concept of *parameterized forms,* a name that I use for forms whose appearance heavily depends on how the main application sets the properties or invokes the methods of the form before actually showing it. To see what I mean, have a look at Figure 9-4: the two Options forms are actually the same form module, which adjusts itself according to what the main application has requested.

Parameterized forms are difficult to build, for two main reasons. First, you need to provide a reasonable set of properties and methods that let the client code customize the form appearance and contents and eventually retrieve all the values entered by the user. Second, you have to write a lot of code within the form to create controls on the fly and automatically place them in their appropriate positions on the form.

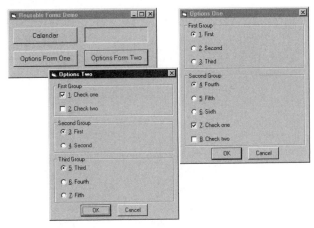

Figure 9-4. *Two distinct instances of a parameterized Options form.*

The frmOptions form exposes three key methods, which let you add a Frame control, a CheckBox control, and an OptionButton control:

```
Private Sub cdmOptionsOne_Click()
    Dim frm As New frmOptions

    ' Add a Frame control - the first argument to this and following
    ' methods is a unique ID code for the control being created.
    frm.AddFrame "F1", "First Group"
    ' Each subsequent AddOption and AddCheck method adds
    ' a control inside the current frame, until another AddFrame
    ' method is issued.
    frm.AddOption "O1", "&1. First", True    ' Set the value to True.
    frm.AddOption "O2", "&2. Second"
    frm.AddOption "O3", "&3. Third"

    ' Add a second frame, with three radio buttons and two check boxes.
    frm.AddFrame "F2", "Second Group"
    frm.AddOption "O4", "&4. Fourth", True   ' Set the value to True.
    frm.AddOption "O5", "&5. Fifth"
    frm.AddOption "O6", "&6. Sixth"
    ' Tick this check box control.
    frm.AddCheck "C1", "&7. Check one", True
    frm.AddCheck "C2", "&8. Check two"
    ' Show the form as a modal dialog.
    frm.Show vbModal
```

The form module exposes the *Value* method, which returns the value of a control given its ID code. You can use it as you would use the *Value* property for CheckBox and OptionButtons controls, or you can pass it the ID code of a Frame control to learn which OptionButton control is selected inside the frame itself:

```
' Continuing the cmdOptionsOne_Click procedure...
If frm.CancelPressed Then
    MsgBox "Command canceled", vbInformation
Else
    MsgBox "Option button in first frame: " & frm.Value("F1") _
        & vbCr &  "Option button in second frame: " _
        & frm.Value("F2") & vbCr _
        & "First checkbox : " & frm.Value("C1") & vbCr _
        & "Second checkbox: " & frm.Value("C2") & vbCr, _
        vbInformation, "Result of Options form"
    End If
End Sub
```

Have a look at the source code of the frmOptions form module to see how it resizes each Frame control to account for all its contained controls. You can also see how the form itself is resized to account for all the Frame controls on it.

You can build a huge number of parameterized forms like the frmOptions module. For example, you can use forms for showing custom message boxes with any number of buttons, any icon, any font for the main message text, and so on. The greatest advantage of parameterized forms is that you build them once and reuse them for forms and dialog boxes that behave in the same or a similar way, even if their appearance is different. This has a beneficial impact on the size of the EXE file and on the memory needed at run time.

Forms as Object Viewers

You can look at forms in yet another way. If your application extensively uses class modules for storing and processing data, you might build forms that work as specialized *object viewers*. For example, if you have a CPerson class module that holds personal data, you might build a frmPerson form module that exposes one custom object property—*Person*, of type CPerson. This approach greatly simplifies the structure of the client code because it just needs to assign one single property instead of many distinct, simpler properties (in this case, *Name*, *Address*, *City*, and *Married*):

```
' The client code that uses the frmPerson form
Dim Person1 As New CPerson
' Initialize properties for this instance.
Person1.Name = "John Smith"
Person1.Address = "12345 West Road"
...
```

```
' Display it on screen.
Dim frm As New frmPerson
Set frm.Person = Person1
frm.Show
```

The frmPerson form module has to correctly assign values to its fields when the *Person* property is set, as you can see in Figure 9-5 and in the code that follows it.

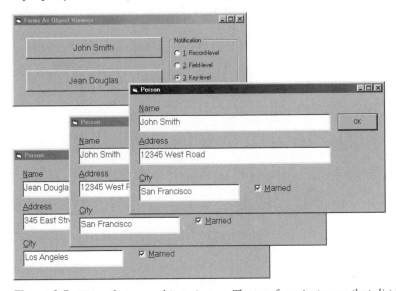

Figure 9-5. *Using forms as object viewers. The two form instances that display the same CPerson object are automatically synchronized.*

```
' Inside the frmPerson form module
Private WithEvents ThisPerson As CPerson

Property Get Person() As CPerson
    Set Person = ThisPerson
End Property
Property Set Person(newValue As CPerson)
    ' Initialize the private object and form fields.
    Set ThisPerson = newValue
    With ThisPerson
        txtName.Text = .Name
        txtAddress.Text = .Address
        txtCity.Text = .City
        chkMarried.Value = Abs(.Married)    ' Assign zero or one.
    End With
End Property
```

Another advantage of this technique is that the client code doesn't directly address the properties of the CPerson object. Thanks to this detail, you must add or remove statements in the frmPerson module if the interface exposed by this class changes, but you don't have to modify the code in the client application that instantiates the frmPerson module showing the object.

A third, more interesting advantage of this approach is this: Because the form has a direct link with the class that holds the data, the form can delegate all the data validation chores to the class itself, which is the right thing to do in an object-oriented application. The validation process usually occurs when the user clicks on the OK button:

```
' In the frmPerson form module...
Private Sub cmdOK_Click()
    On Error Resume Next
    ' Assign (and implicitly validate) the Name property.
    ThisPerson.Name = txtName.Text
    If Err Then
        ' If the class raised an error
        MsgBox Err.Description
        txtName.SetFocus
        Exit Sub
    End If

    ' Similar code for the Address, City, and Married properties.
    ...
End Sub
```

Forms used as object viewers have a fourth advantage, which is, in my opinion, also the most important and intriguing one. Since each form holds a reference to the actual object, you can have multiple forms pointing to the same object. This ensures that all form instances access the same data and that they don't display inconsistent values. To see what I mean, run the ObjView.Vbp sample application, click two or more times on the John Smith button, modify data in a form, and then click on OK to see the new value automatically propagated to all the other form instances. By selecting a different option in the Notification frame on the main form, you can also have new values propagated to other forms whenever the user exits each field (field-level notification) or even when the user presses a key (key-level notification). I added this capability to the demonstration program just to show you that it's possible to do it. But in most real-world applications, record-level notification is the most appropriate choice.

To implement this fourth feature, the CPerson class raises an event whenever one of its properties changes, as shown here:

```
' In the CPerson class module...
Event Change(PropertyName As String)
' A private variable that holds the value of the Name property
Private m_Name As String

Property Let Name(newValue As String)
    ' It's very important that the new value always be checked.
    If newValue = "" Then Err.Raise 5, , "Invalid Value for Name property"
    If m_Name <> newValue Then
        m_Name = newValue
        PropertyChanged "Name"
    End If
End Property


' Similar code for Property Let Address/City/Married
...


' This private method simply raises a Change event in client code.
Private Sub PropertyChanged(PropertyName As String)
    RaiseEvent Change(PropertyName)
End Sub
```

The frmPerson form module can trap the *Change* event because its *ThisPerson* Private instance pointing to the CPerson object is declared using the *WithEvents* keyword:

```
Private Sub ThisPerson_Change(PropertyName As String)
    Select Case PropertyName
        Case "Name"
            txtName.Text = ThisPerson.Name
        Case "Address"
            txtAddress.Text = ThisPerson.Address
        Case "City"
            txtCity.Text = ThisPerson.City
        Case "Married"
            chkMarried.Value = Abs(ThisPerson.Married)
    End Select
End Sub
```

Here are a couple of final notes about using forms as object viewers:

■ In your application, you can have forms from different classes pointing to the same object. For example, you can have a frmPerson form module that shows essential information about a person and a frmPerson2 form module that displays the same information plus additional confidential data. You can use both forms in the same application and open them so that they refer to the same CPerson instance at the same time. When you have multiple forms that display the same object, this technique dramatically reduces the amount of code because all the validation logic, as well as the code that reads data from a database and stores it back, is located in the class module and doesn't need to be duplicated in each form module.

■ You can have the same form module work as a viewer for multiple classes, as long as such classes have a common secondary interface. For example, your application can deal with CPerson, CCustomer, and CEmployee objects. If all of these objects implement the IPersonalData secondary interface, which gathers all the properties that are common to them, you can build a frmPersonalData form module that exposes a *PersonalData* property:

```
' Inside the frmPersonalData form module...
Private PersData As IPersonalData

Property Get PersonalData() As IPersonalData
    Set PersonalData = PersData
End Property

Property Set PersonalData(newValue As IPersonalData)
    Set PersData = newValue
    ' Initialize fields on the form.
    With PersData
        txtName = .Name
        ...
    End With
End Property
```

You can't receive events from the classes, however, because events aren't exposed by secondary interfaces. So you can use a single form that points to a secondary interface of multiple classes only when you don't need to keep multiple instances of the form in sync. You don't need to account for synchronization issues when all the forms are shown as modal dialog boxes.

Dynamic Control Creation

Dynamic control creation is one of the most exciting, new features of Visual Basic 6 and overcomes a serious limitation of the previous versions of the language. Using this new capability, you can create new controls on a form at run time by specifying their class name. This mechanism is much more flexible than the one based on control arrays (described in Chapter 3). In fact, creating a control at run time using control arrays forces you to place an instance of each type of control on the form at design time. This isn't necessary using Visual Basic 6's dynamic control creation features.

The *Add* method of the Controls collection

Under Visual Basic 6, the Controls collection has been enhanced to support the *Add* method, which lets you dynamically create controls at run time. This method uses the following syntax:

```
Set controlRef = Controls.Add(ProgID, Name [,Container])
```

where ProgID is the class name of the control in the format *libraryname.controlname*, and *Name* is the name you want to assign to the control (and which will be returned by its *Name* property). This name must be unique: If another control in the collection has the same name, Visual Basic raises an error 727—"There is already a control with the name 'ctrlname'". *Container* is an optional reference to a container control (for example, a PictureBox or a Frame control) inside which you want to place the control being created. If you omit this argument, the control is placed on the form's surface. *ControlRef* is an object variable that you use to reference the control's properties, invoke its methods, and trap its events. You can see from the following code how easy it is to create a CommandButton control and place it near the lower right corner of the form:

```
Dim WithEvents cmdCalendar As CommandButton

Private Sub Form_Load()
    Set cmdCalendar = Controls.Add("VB.CommandButton", "cmdButton")
    ' Assumes that form's ScaleMode is twips.
    cmdCalendar.Move ScaleWidth - 1400, ScaleHeight - 800, 1000, 600
    cmdCalendar.Caption = "&Calendar"
    ' All controls are created invisible.
    cmdCalendar.Visible = True
End Sub
```

Because you have declared *cmdCalendar* using the *WithEvents* clause, you can react to its events. For example, you can display a custom calendar when the user clicks on the button you just created:

```
Private Sub cmdCalendar_Click()
    Dim frm As New frmCalendar
    frm.ShowMonth Year(Now), Month(Now)
    frm.Show vbModal
End Sub
```

You can remove any control added dynamically using the Controls collection's *Remove* method, whose only argument is the name of the control (that is, the string passed as a second argument to the *Add* method):

```
Controls.Remove "cmdButton"
```

You get an error if the control specified doesn't exist on the form or if it wasn't added dynamically at run time.

Adding an external ActiveX control

Adding an external ActiveX control is similar to adding an intrinsic Visual Basic control. But you must pay particular attention to two important details.

■ For some external ActiveX controls, you can't use the ProgID as you read it in the object browser. When you try to use it, you get a run-time error. Fortunately, the error message clearly reports the correct ProgID. (See Figure 9-6.) For example, the TreeView control's actual ProgID is "MSComCtlLib.TreeCtrl.2", and this is the string you must pass as the first argument to the *Controls.Add* method.

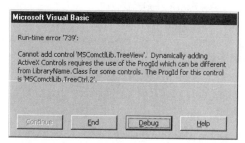

Figure 9-6. *The error message you get when you try to add a TreeView control using the ProgID string as found in the Object Browser.*

■ If you dynamically add an ActiveX control that's never been used on any form of the current project, Visual Basic raises a run-time error. (See Figure 9-7.) This happens because the Visual Basic compiler usually discards all the information about controls that are present in the Toolbox but not referenced in the project. This step optimizes the performance and reduces the size of the executable file. To circumvent this error, uncheck the Remove Information About Unused ActiveX Controls box in the Make tab of the Project Properties dialog box.

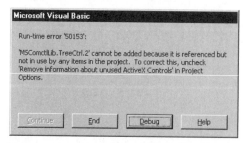

Figure 9-7. *You get this error message when you try to load an ActiveX control that appears in the Toolbox but isn't referenced in any other form of the application.*

> **NOTE** You can dynamically add any type of intrinsic Visual Basic control, except menu items. Unfortunately, this limitation prevents developers from devising customizable menu structures with top-level menus and submenus built on the fly.

The Windowless Controls Library

Visual Basic 6 comes with a new library of windowless controls that exactly duplicate the appearance and the features of most Visual Basic intrinsic controls. This library isn't mentioned in the main language documentation, and it must be installed manually from the Common\Tools\VB\Winless directory. This folder contains the Mswless.ocx ActiveX control and the Ltwtct98.chm file with its documentation. To install the library, you first copy this directory on your hard disk. Before you can use the control, you must register it using the Regsvr32.exe utility or from within Visual Basic, and then double-click on the Mswless.reg file, which creates the Registry keys that make the ActiveX control available to the Visual Basic environment.

Once you have completed the registration step, you can load the library into the IDE by pressing the Ctrl+T key and selecting the Microsoft Windowless Controls 6 item from the list of available ActiveX controls. After you do this, you'll find that a number of new controls have been added to the Toolbox. The library contains a replacement for the TextBox, Frame, CommandButton, CheckBox, OptionButton, ComboBox, ListBox, and the two ScrollBar controls. It doesn't include Label, Timer, or Image controls because the Visual Basic versions are already windowless. Nor does it contain PictureBox and OLE controls, which are containers and can't therefore be rendered as windowless controls.

The controls in the Windowless Controls Library don't support the *hWnd* property. As you might remember from Chapter 2, this property is the handle of the window on which the control is based. Since these controls are windowless, there's no such window and therefore the *hWnd* property doesn't make any sense. Other properties are missing, namely those that have to do with DDE communications. (DDE is, however, an outdated technology and isn't covered in this book.) Another difference is that the WLOption control (the windowless counterpart of the OptionButton intrinsic control) supports the new *Group* property, which serves to create groups of mutually exclusive radio buttons. (You can't create a group of radio buttons by placing them in a WLFrame control because this control doesn't work as a container.)

Apart from the *hWnd* property and the *Group* property, the controls in the library are perfectly compatible with Visual Basic's intrinsic controls in the sense that they expose the same properties, methods, and events as their Visual Basic counterparts. Interestingly, the library's controls offer a number of property pages that let the programmer set the properties in a logical manner, as you can see in Figure 9-8 on the following page.

Figure 9-8. *You can set the properties of controls in the Windowless library using handy property pages. Notice how the new controls appear in the Toolbox.*

The real advantage of using the controls in the Windowless library is that at run time they aren't subject to many of the limitations that the intrinsic controls are. In fact, *all* their properties can be modified during execution, including the *MultiLine* and *ScrollBars* properties of the WLText control, the *Sorted* and *Style* properties of the WLList and WLCombo controls, and the *Alignment* property of the WLCheck and WLOption controls.

The ability to modify any property at run time makes the Windowless library a precious tool when you're dynamically creating new controls at run time using the *Controls.Add* method. When you add a control, it's created with all properties set to their default values. This situation means that you can't use the *Controls.Add* method to create multiline intrinsic TextBox controls or sorted ListBox or ComboBox controls. The only solution is to use the Windowless Controls Library:

```
Dim WithEvents TxtEditor As MSWLess.WLText

Private Sub Form_Load()
    Set TxtEditor = Controls.Add("MSWLess.WLText", "txtEditor")
    TxtEditor.MultiLine = True
    TxtEditor.ScrollBars = vbBoth
    TxtEditor.Move 0, 0, ScaleWidth, ScaleHeight
    TxtEditor.Visible = True
End Sub
```

Unreferenced controls

So far, I've described what you have to do to add controls that are referenced at design time in the Toolbox. But you can do more with the dynamic control creation feature than I've shown you so far; its greater power lies in letting you create ActiveX controls that aren't referenced in the Toolbox. You can provide support for versions of ActiveX controls that don't exist yet at compile time, for example by storing the control's name in an INI file that you edit when delivering a new version of the control. This adds tremendous flexibility to your applications and lets you transform your forms into generic ActiveX control containers.

The first issue you must resolve when working with controls not referenced in the Toolbox is design-time licensing. Even if you're not actually using the control at design time, to dynamically load it at run time you must prove that you're legally allowed to do so. If there weren't any restrictions to dynamically creating ActiveX controls at run time, any programmer could "borrow" ActiveX controls from other commercial software and use them in his or her applications without actually purchasing the license for the controls. This is an issue only for ActiveX controls that aren't referenced in the Toolbox at design time; if you can load a control in the Toolbox, you surely own a design-time license for the control.

To dynamically create an ActiveX control not referenced in the Toolbox at compile time, you must exhibit your design-time license at run time. In this context, a license is a string of characters or digits that comes with the control and is stored in the system Registry when you install the control on your machine. Visual Basic doesn't force you to search for this string in the Registry because you can find it by means of the *Add* method of the Licenses collection:

```
' This statement works only if the MSWLess library is
' *NOT* currently referenced in the Toolbox.
Dim licenseKey As String
licenseKey = Licenses.Add("MSWLess.WLText")
```

After you have the license string, you must devise a way to make it available to the application at run time. The easier method is storing it in a file:

```
Open "MSWLess.lic" For Output As #1
Print #1, licenseKey
Close #1
```

The preceding code must be executed just once during the design process, and after you've generated the LIC file you can throw the code away. The application reads this file back into the Licenses collection, again using the *Add* method but this time with a different syntax:

```
Open "MSWLess.lic" For Input As #1
Line Input #1, licenseKey
Close #1
Licenses.Add "MSWLess.WLText", licenseKey
```

The Licenses collection also supports the *Remove* method, but you will rarely need to invoke it.

Late-bound properties, methods, and events

Once you resolve the licensing issue, you're ready to face another problem that comes up when you're working with ActiveX controls not referenced in the Toolbox at compile time. As you might imagine, if you don't know what control you'll load at run time, you can't assign the return value of the *Controls.Add* method to an object variable of a specific type. This means that you have no simple way to access properties, methods, or events of your freshly added control.

The solution offered by Visual Basic 6 is a special type of object variable named *VBControlExtender*. This represents a generic ActiveX control inside the Visual Basic IDE:

```
Dim WithEvents TxtEditor As VBControlExtender

Private Sub Form_Load()
    ' Add the license key to the Licenses collection (omitted).
    Set TxtEditor = Controls.Add("MSWLess.WLText", "TxtEditor")
    TxtEditor.Move 0, 0, ScaleWidth, ScaleHeight
    TxtEditor.Visible = True
    TxtEditor.Text = "My Text Editor"
End Sub
```

Trapping events from an ActiveX control not referenced in the Toolbox is a bit more complex than accessing properties and methods. In fact, the VBControlExtender object can't expose the events of the control it will host at run time. Instead, it supports only a single event, named *ObjectEvent*, which is invoked for all the events raised by the original ActiveX control. The *ObjectEvent* event receives one argument, an EventInfo object that in turn contains a collection of EventParameter objects. This collection enables the programmer to learn what arguments were passed to the event.

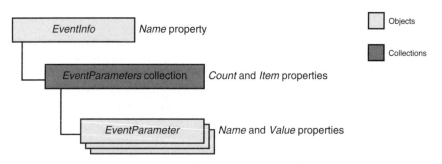

Inside the *ObjectEvent* event procedure, you usually test the *EventInfo.Name* property to discern which event was fired, and then you read, and sometimes modify, the value of each of its parameters:

```
Private Sub TxtEditor_ObjectEvent(Info As EventInfo)
    Select Case Info.Name
        Case "KeyPress"
            ' The Escape key clears the editor.
            If Info.EventParameters("KeyAscii") = 27 Then
                TxtEditor.Object.Text = ""
            End If
        Case "DblClick"
            ' Just to prove that we can trap any event
            MsgBox "Why have you double-clicked me?"
    End Select
End Sub
```

Events trapped in this way are called *late-bound events*. There's a group of *extender events* that you don't trap inside the *ObjectEvent* event. These extender events (one of which is shown in the following code snippet) are available as regular events of the VBControlExtender object. This group of events includes *GotFocus*, *LostFocus*, *Validate*, *DragDrop*, and *DragOver*. For more information about extender properties, methods, and events, see Chapter 17.

```
Private Sub TxtEditor_GotFocus()
    ' Highlight textbox's contents on entry.
    TxtEditor.Object.SelStart = 0
    TxtEditor.Object.SelLength = 9999
End Sub
```

Data-Driven Forms

Visual Basic's new dynamic control creation capabilities enable developers to create true *data-driven forms,* which are forms whose appearance is completely determined at run time by data read from a file or—if you're building a form that displays data from a database table—by the structure of the database itself. Imagine what degree of flexibility you get if you're able to modify the appearance of a Visual Basic form at run time without having to recompile the application:

■ You can add and remove fields to the database and have the form automatically update itself.

■ You can provide your users with the ability to customize the application's user interface in terms of colors, fonts, field position and size, new buttons that display other tables, and so on.

■ You can easily implement policies to make given fields invisible or read-only, depending on which user is currently logged in. For example, you can give access to confidential information only to people authorized to read it, and you can hide it from others.

To implement data-driven forms, however, you must first solve a problem. When you don't know in advance how many controls you're going to add to the form, how can you trap events from them? This problem arises because the *WithEvents* keyword is unable to trap events from an array of objects. As you'll see, this issue can be resolved, but the solution probably isn't as simple as you might think it should be. However, the technique that I'll describe is both interesting and flexible and can not only help you build data-driven forms but also more generally trap events from an undetermined number of objects, a problem I left unresolved in Chapter 7.

Trapping events from an array of controls

To trap events coming from an undetermined number of controls dynamically created at run time—or, in general, from an undetermined number of objects—you need to build two support classes, the first one a collection class that contains all the instances of the second class. In the sample program that you'll find on the companion CD, these classes are named ControlItems and ControlItem, respectively. The relationships among these classes and the main form are summarized in Figure 9-9.

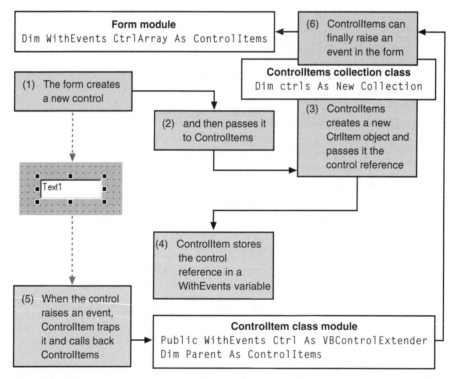

Figure 9-9. *You need two auxiliary classes and some tricky code to trap events raised by an array of controls dynamically created at run time.*

The events can be trapped as follows:

1. The main application holds a reference to an instance of the ControlItems collection class in a variable named *CtrlArray*. This variable is declared using the *WithEvents* clause because it will raise events in the main application.

2. After the form creates a new control, it passes a reference to that control to the *Add* method of the ControlItems collection class. This reference can be of a specific class (if you know at design time which type of controls you're creating) or it can be of a VBControlExtender object if you want to exploit late-bound events.

3. The *Add* method of the ControlItems collection class creates a new instance of the ControlItem class and passes it a reference to the control just created on the form. It also passes a reference to itself.

4. The ControlItem class instance stores the reference to the control in a *WithEvents* Public variable. It also stores a reference to the parent ControlItems collection class in the Private *Parent* object variable.

5. When the control eventually raises an event, the ControlItem class traps it and can therefore pass the event to the parent collection classes. This notification is performed by calling a Friend method in the ControlItems collection class. In general, you should provide one such method for each possible event trapped by the dependent class because each event has a different set of arguments.

6. Inside the notification event, the ControlItems class can finally raise an event in the parent form. The first argument passed to this event is a reference to the control that raised the event or a reference to the ControlItem object that trapped it.

As you can see, it's a long trip just to intercept an event. But now that you know how to do it, you can apply this technique in many interesting ways.

Database-driven data-entry forms

One of the many possible applications of dynamic control creation are forms that automatically map themselves to the structure of a database table or query. This is especially useful when you're writing large business applications with dozens or hundreds of queries, and you don't want to create customized forms for each one. This technique dramatically reduces development time and shrinks the size of the executable file as well as its requirements in terms of memory and resources.

On the companion CD, you'll find a complete Visual Basic application whose main form adapts itself to the structure of a database table of SQL SELECT query, as you can see in Figure 9-10.

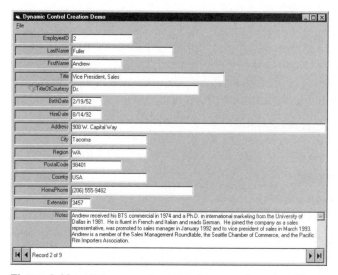

Figure 9-10. *All the controls on this form are dynamically created at run time, based on the structure of an ADO recordset. The program creates different controls according to the type of the database field and also provides validation for each.*

Space constraints prevent me from showing the complete source code in print, so I'll include only the most interesting routines:

```
' The collection of controls added dynamically (module-level
' variable)
Dim WithEvents ControlItems As ControlItems

' This is the most interesting routine, which actually
' creates the controls and passes them to the ControlItems
' collection class.
Sub LoadControls(rs As ADODB.Recordset)
    Dim index As Long, fieldNum As Integer
    Dim field As ADODB.field
    Dim ctrl As Control, ctrlItem As ControlItem, ctrlType As String
    Dim Properties As Collection, CustomProperties As Collection
    Dim top As Single, propItem As Variant
    Dim items() As String

    ' Start with a fresh ControlItems collection.
    Set ControlItems = New ControlItems
    ' Initial value for Top property
    top = 100

    ' Add controls corresponding to fields.
    ' This demo program supports only a few field types.
```

```
For Each field In rs.Fields
    ctrlType = ""
    Set Properties = New Collection
    Set CustomProperties = New Collection
    Select Case field.Type
        Case adBoolean
            ctrlType = "MSWLess.WLCheck"
            Properties.Add "Caption="
        Case adSmallInt    ' As Integer
            ctrlType = "MSWLess.WLText"
        Case adInteger     ' As Long
            ctrlType = "MSWLess.WLText"
            CustomProperties.Add "IsNumeric=-1"
            CustomProperties.Add "IsInteger=-1"
        Case adSingle, adDouble, adCurrency
            ctrlType = "MSWLess.WLText"
            CustomProperties.Add "Numeric=-1"
        Case adChar, adVarChar   ' As String
            ctrlType = "MSWLess.WLText"
            Properties.Add "Width=" & _
                (field.DefinedSize * TextWidth("W"))
        Case adLongVarChar    ' (Memo field)
            ctrlType = "MSWLess.WLText"
            Properties.Add "Width=99999"   ' Very large width
            Properties.Add "Height=2000"
            Properties.Add "Multiline=-1"
            Properties.Add "ScrollBars=2"   'vbVertical
        Case adDate
            ctrlType = "MSWLess.WLText"
            Properties.Add "Width=1000"
            CustomProperties.Add "IsDate=-1"
        Case Else
            ' Ignore other field data types.
    End Select

    ' Do nothing if this field type is not supported (ctrlType="").
    If ctrlType <> "" Then
        fieldNum = fieldNum + 1
        ' Create the label control with database field name.
        Set ctrl = Controls.Add("VB.Label", "Label" & fieldNum)
        ctrl.Move 50, top, 1800, 315
        ctrl.Caption = field.Name
        ctrl.UseMnemonic = False
        ctrl.BorderStyle = 1
        ctrl.Alignment = vbRightJustify
        ctrl.Visible = True
        ' Create the control, and move it to the correct position.
```

(continued)

475

```
                Set ctrl = Controls.Add(ctrlType, "Field" & fieldNum)
                ctrl.Move 1900, top, 2000, 315

                ' If the field is not updatable, lock it.
                If (field.Attributes And adFldUpdatable) = 0 Then
                    On Error Resume Next
                    ctrl.Locked = True
                    ' If the control doesn't support the Locked property,
                    ' disable it.
                    If Err Then ctrl.Enabled = False
                    On Error GoTo 0
                End If

                ' Set other properties of the field.
                For Each propItem In Properties
                    ' Split property's name and value.
                    items() = Split(propItem, "=")
                    CallByName ctrl, items(0), VbLet, items(1)
                Next
                ' Link it to the Data control, and make it visible.
                Set ctrl.DataSource = Adodc1
                ctrl.DataField = field.Name
                ctrl.Visible = True

                ' Add this control to the ControlItems collection.
                Set ctrlItem = ControlItems.Add(ctrl)
                ' Move the actual width into the custom Width property.
                ' This is used in the Form_Resize event.
                ctrlItem.Properties.Add ctrl.Width, "Width"
                ' Set its other custom properties.
                For Each propItem In CustomProperties
                    ' Split property name and value.
                    items() = Split(propItem, "=")
                    ctrlItem.Properties.Add items(1), items(0)
                Next
                ' Increment top.
                top = top + ctrl.Height + 80
            End If
        Next
        ' Force a Form_Resize event to resize longer controls.
        Call Form_Resize
        Adodc1.Refresh
End Sub

' A control added dynamically is asking for validation.
' Item.Control is a reference to the control.
' Item.GetProperty(propname) returns a custom property.
Private Sub ControlItems_Validate(Item As ControlItem, _
    Cancel As Boolean)
```

```
    If Item.GetProperty("IsNumeric") Then
        If Not IsNumeric(Item.Control.Text) Then
            MsgBox "Please enter a valid number"
            Cancel = True: Exit Sub
        End If
    End If
    If Item.GetProperty("IsInteger") Then
        If CDbl(Item.Control.Text) <> Int(CDbl(Item.Control.Text)) Then
            MsgBox "Please enter a valid Integer number"
            Cancel = True: Exit Sub
        End If
    End If
    If Item.GetProperty("IsDate") Then
        If Not IsDate(Item.Control.Text) Then
            MsgBox "Please enter a valid date"
            Cancel = True: Exit Sub
        End If
    End If
End Sub
```

Many points in the *LoadControls* routine are worth a closer look. First, it uses the Windowless Controls Library because it needs to modify properties such as TextBox control's *Multiline* (for example, for memo fields). Second, to streamline the structure of the code and make it easily extendable, each *Case* clause in the main *Select* block simply adds property names and values to a Properties collection: after the control is actually created, it uses the *CallByName* command to assign all the properties in a *For Each* loop. Third, it creates the *CustomProperties* collection, where it stores information that can't be directly assigned to the control's properties. This includes the "*IsNumeric*", "*IsInteger*", and "*IsDate*" custom attributes, which are later used when the code in the main form validates the value in the field.

Please refer to the complete project on the companion CD for the complete source code of the main form and the ControlItems and ControlItem class modules.

MDI FORMS

MDI stands for Multiple Document Interface and is the type of user interface used by most of the applications in the Microsoft Office suite, including Microsoft Word, Microsoft Excel, and Microsoft PowerPoint. Many applications lend themselves to implementation via an MDI user interface. Whenever you have an application that should be able to deal with multiple documents at the same time, an MDI interface is probably the best choice.

MDI Applications

Building Visual Basic MDI applications is simple, as long as you know how to make the best use of a few features of the language. You begin developing an MDI application by adding an MDIForm module to the current project. An MDIForm module is similar to a regular Form module, with just a few peculiarities:

■   You can have only one MDIForm module in each project; after you add one MDI module to the current project, the Add MDIForm command in the Project menu is disabled, as is the corresponding icon on the main toolbar.

■   You can't place most controls directly on an MDIForm surface. More specifically, you can create only menus, invisible controls (such as Timer and CommonDialog controls), and controls that support the *Align* property (such as PictureBox, Toolbar, and StatusBar controls). The only way to show any other control on an MDIForm object is to place it inside a container control, typically a PictureBox control.

■   You can't display text or graphics on an MDIForm surface. Again, you need to place a PictureBox control and display text or graphics inside it.

MDI child forms

An MDIForm object contains one or more child forms. To create such child forms, you add a regular form to the project and set its *MDIChild* property to True. When you do this, the form's icon in the Project Explorer window changes, as shown in Figure 9-11. You don't have to specify which MDI form this form is a child of because there can be only one MDIForm module per project.

An MDI child form can't be displayed outside its parent MDIForm. If an MDI child form is the startup form for an application, its parent MDI form is automatically loaded and displayed before the child form becomes visible. Apart from the startup form, all instances of the MDI child form are created using the *New* keyword:

```
' Inside the MDIForm module
Private Sub mnuFileNew_Click()
    Dim frmDoc As New frmDocument
    frmDoc.Show
End Sub
```

MDIForm modules support an additional property, *AutoShowChildren*. When this property is True (the default value), an MDI child form is displayed inside its parent MDI form as soon as you load the parent. In other words, you can't load an MDI child form and keep it hidden unless you set this property to False.

MDI child forms have other peculiarities as well. For example, they don't display menu bars as regular forms do: If you add one or more top-level menus to an

MDI child form, when the form becomes active its menu bar replaces the MDI parent form's menu bar. For this reason, it's customary for MDI child forms not to include a menu; you define menus only for the main MDIForm module.

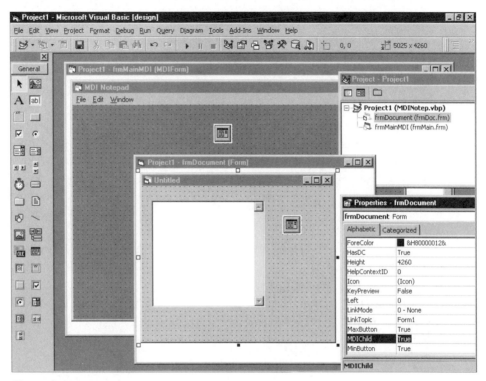

Figure 9-11. *The MDI Notepad application at design time.*

When a menu command is invoked in the MDIForm module, you normally apply it to the MDI child form that's currently active, which you do through the *ActiveForm* property. For example, here's how you execute the Close command on the File menu:

```
' In the MDI parent form
Private Sub mnuFileClose_Click()
    ' Close the active form, if there is one.
    If Not (ActiveForm Is Nothing) Then Unload ActiveForm
End Sub
```

You should always check for an *ActiveForm* because it's possible that no MDI child form is currently open, in which case *ActiveForm* returns Nothing. (It doesn't return a reference to the MDIForm itself, as you might expect.) If your MDI application supports different kinds of child forms, you often need to figure out which form is the active form, as in the code on the following page.

```
Private Sub mnuFilePrint_Click()
    If TypeOf ActiveForm Is frmDocument Then
        ' Print the contents of a TextBox control.
        Printer.Print ActiveForm.txtEditor.Text
        Printer.EndDoc
    ElseIf TypeOf ActiveForm Is frmImageViewer Then
        ' Print the contents of a PictureBox control.
        Printer.PaintPicture ActiveForm.picImage.Picture, 0, 0
        Printer.EndDoc
    End If
End Sub
```

The Window menu

MDIForm modules support an additional method that's not exposed by regular forms: the *Arrange* method. This method provides a quick way to programmatically arrange all the child forms in an MDI application. You can tile all child forms horizontally or vertically, you can arrange them in a cascading fashion, or you can line up all the minimized forms in an orderly fashion near the bottom of the MDI parent form. To this purpose, you usually create a Window menu with four commands: Tile Horizontally, Tile Vertically, Cascade, and Arrange Icons. This is the code behind these menu items:

```
Private Sub mnuTileHorizontally_Click()
    Arrange vbTileHorizontal
End Sub
Private Sub mnuTileVertically_Click()
    Arrange vbTileVertical
End Sub
Private Sub mnuCascade_Click()
    Arrange vbCascade
End Sub
Private Sub mnuArrangeIcons_Click()
    Arrange vbArrangeIcons
End Sub
```

It's also customary for the Window menu to include a list of all open MDI child forms and to let the user quickly switch to any one of them with a click of the mouse. (See Figure 9-12.) Visual Basic makes it simple to add this feature to your MDI applications: You only have to tick the WindowList option in the Menu Editor for the top-level Window menu. Alternatively, you can create a submenu with the list of all open windows by ticking the WindowList option for a lower level menu item. In any case, only one menu item can have this option ticked.

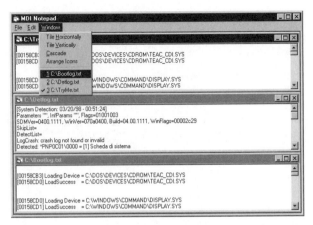

Figure 9-12. *The Window menu lets you tile and arrange all MDI child windows and quickly switch to any one of them with a click of the mouse.*

Adding properties to MDI child forms

In Visual Basic 3, writing MDI applications wasn't particularly easy because you had to keep track of the status of each MDI child form using an array of UDTs, and it was up to you to update this array whenever an MDI child form was created or closed. Things are much simpler in Visual Basic 4 and later versions because each form can support custom properties and you can store the data right in MDI child form modules without the need for a global array of UDTs.

Typically, all MDI child forms support at least two custom properties, *Filename* and *IsDirty* (of course, actual names can be different). The *Filename* property stores the name of the data file from where data was loaded, whereas *IsDirty* is a Boolean flag that tells whether data was modified by the user. Here's how these properties are implemented in the MDI Notepad sample program:

```
' Inside the frmDocument MDI child form
Public IsDirty As Boolean
Private m_FileName As String

Property Get Filename() As String
    Filename = m_FileName
End Property
Property Let Filename(ByVal newValue As String)
    m_FileName = newValue
    ' Show the filename on the form's Caption.
    Caption = IIf(newValue = "", "Untitled", newValue)
End Property

Private Sub txtEditor_Change()
    IsDirty = True
End Sub
```

You need the *IsDirty* property so that you can ask the user if he or she wants to save modified data when closing the form. This is done in the MDI child form's *Unload* event procedure:

```
Private Sub Form_Unload(Cancel As Integer)
    Dim answer As Integer
    If IsDirty Then
        answer = MsgBox("This document has been modified. " & vbCr _
            & "Do you want to save it?", vbYesNoCancel + vbInformation)
        Select Case answer
            Case vbNo
                ' The form will unload without saving data.
            Case vbYes
                ' Delegate to a procedure in the main MDI form.
                frmMainMDI.SaveToFile Filename
            Case vbCancel
                ' Refuse to unload the form.
                Cancel = True
        End Select
    End If
End Sub
```

Polymorphic MDI Containers

The MDI Notepad application described in the previous section is perfectly functional, but it can't be regarded as a good example of object-oriented design. In fact, the MDIForm object breaks the encapsulation of MDI child forms because it directly accesses the properties of the txtEditor control. This might appear to be a minor defect, but you know that good encapsulation is the key to reusable, easily maintainable, bug-free software. I'll demonstrate this concept by offering an alternate way to design an MDI application.

Defining the parent-child interface

If you don't want the parent MDI form to directly access controls on its child forms, the solution is to define an interface through which the two forms can talk to one another. For example, instead of loading and saving text by manipulating the txtEditor's properties, the parent MDI form should ask the child form to load or save a given file. Similarly, instead of directly cutting, copying, and pasting data on the txtEditor control, the parent MDI form should invoke a method in the child form that does the job. The parent MDI form should also query the MDI child form to learn which commands should be made available in the Edit menu.

After playing for a while with MDI projects, I came up with a simple interface that's generic enough to fit many MDI applications. In addition to the usual *Filename* and *IsDirty* properties, this interface includes properties such as *IsEmpty* (True if the MDI child form doesn't contain any data), *CanSave*, *CanCut*, *CanCopy*, *CanPaste*, and

CanPrint, as well as methods such as *Cut, Copy, Paste, PrintDoc, LoadFile, SaveFile,* and *AskFilename* (which uses a *FileOpen* or *FileSave* common dialog). This interface permits you to rewrite the MDI Notepad application without breaking the encapsulation of MDI child forms. For example, this is the code that implements the Save As command on the File menu in the MDI parent form:

```
Private Sub mnuFileSaveAs_Click()
    ' Ask the document to show a common dialog, and
    ' then save the file with the name selected by the user.
    On Error Resume Next
    ActiveForm.SaveFile ActiveForm.AskFilename(True)
End Sub
```

And this is how the MDI child form implements the *PrintDoc* method:

```
Sub PrintDoc()
    Printer.NewPage
    Printer.Print txtEditor.Text
    Printer.EndDoc
End Sub
```

As usual, the complete source code of this new version of the application is available on the companion CD. You'll notice that the overall amount of code is slightly larger than the original MDI Notepad application. But this new structure has several benefits, which will be apparent in a moment.

> **NOTE** In this sample program, I defined a set of properties and methods. Then I added them to the primary interface of the frmDocument MDI child form. Because the frmMain MDI parent form accesses all its child forms through the *ActiveForm* property, properties and methods of this interface are accessed through late binding, which means that you must protect each reference with an *On Error* statement. For a more robust implementation, define a secondary interface as an abstract class and implement it in each MDI child form module.

Changing the client form's implementation

Because this new version of the MDI parent form never breaks the encapsulation of the MDI child forms, you're free to change the implementation of MDI child forms without affecting the rest of the application. For example, you can turn the Notepad-like program into an MDI image viewer application. In this case, the MDI child form hosts a PictureBox control, so you have to modify the implementation of all the properties and methods of the interface used for the parent-child communication. For example, the *PrintDoc* method is now implemented as follows:

```
Sub PrintDoc()
    Printer.NewPage
    Printer.PaintPicture picBitmap.Picture, 0, 0
    Printer.EndDoc
End Sub
```

Surprisingly, you need to modify fewer than 20 lines of code to morph the MDI Notepad application into an image viewer application. But the most interesting detail is that you *don't need to modify one single line of code in the frmMain module*. In other words, you have created a reusable, polymorphic MDI parent form!

Alternatively, if you're willing to slightly modify the parent MDI form's code, you can have the same MDI container work for different types of child forms at the same time. Figure 9-13 shows this new version of the sample MDI application, which hosts text documents and images at the same time. You can add new types of child forms or expand the interface to take additional properties and methods into account.

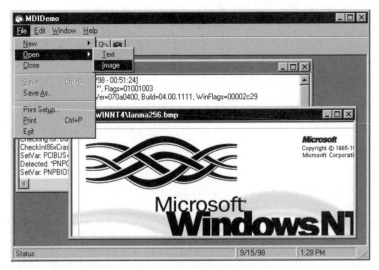

Figure 9-13. *You can reuse the frmMain.frm generic MDI form with different child forms, for example, mini word processors and image viewers.*

The Application Wizard

Visual Basic 6 comes with a revamped Application Wizard, which is more flexible than the one provided with Visual Basic 5 and is tightly integrated with the Toolbar Wizard and the Form Wizard.

The Application Wizard is automatically installed by the Visual Basic setup procedure, so you just need to make it available in the Add-In menu by selecting it in the Add-In Manager window. When you run the wizard, you can choose from among MDI, SDI (Single Document Interface, applications based on standard forms), and Windows Explorer–like applications, as you can see in Figure 9-14.

If you select the MDI option, you're asked to configure your menus (Figure 9-15): this tool is so simple to use and so intuitive that you'll probably wish you could have it when you're working with the standard Menu Editor.

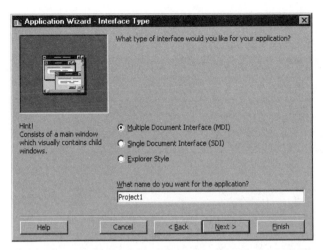

Figure 9-14. *The Application Wizard: Choosing the interface.*

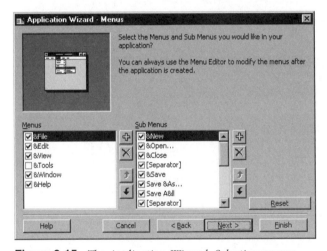

Figure 9-15. *The Application Wizard: Selecting menus.*

In the next step, you configure the program's toolbar (Figure 9-16) using an embedded wizard. This slick tool is also available outside the Application Wizard, and you'll find it in the Add-In menu under the name Toolbar Wizard.

In subsequent steps, the Application Wizard asks you whether you want to use resource files and whether you want to add an item in the Help menu that points to your Web site. You can then select additional forms to be added to the project (Figure 9-17), choosing among four standard forms and any form templates you have defined previously. Finally, you can create any number of data-bound forms: in this case, the wizard calls the Data Form wizard, which I illustrated in Chapter 8. In the last step, you can decide to save all the current settings to a configuration file so that the next time you run the Application Wizard you can speed up the process even more.

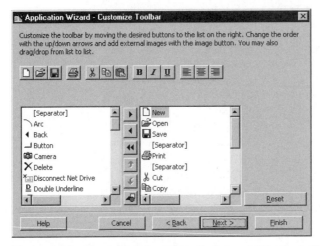

Figure 9-16. *The Application Wizard: Customizing the toolbar.*

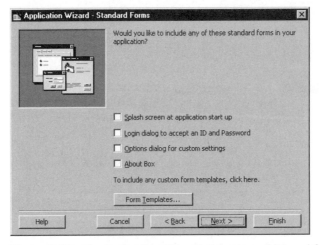

Figure 9-17. *The Application Wizard: Selecting additional forms.*

While the code delivered by the Application Wizard is a good starting point for building your own MDI application, in my opinion it leaves much to be desired. The MDI application created by the wizard uses a sample MDI child form that hosts a RichTextBox control to build a simple word processor–like application. On some occasions, however, the buttons on the toolbar don't work as they should, and the code for setting up all common dialogs isn't properly implemented, just to name a few shortcomings. Unfortunately, you have no control over the code generated by the wizard, so each time you run the wizard you must fix the resulting code by hand.

USING DRAG-AND-DROP

Visual Basic has included drag-and-drop capabilities since its early versions, but only Visual Basic 5 added a new set of properties, methods, and events that let developers implement a standard OLE-compliant mechanism and enable cross-application drag-and-drop. You can recognize these properties, methods, and events because their names begin with *OLE*. In this section, I'll illustrate a few possible applications of this powerful, and underutilized, feature.

Automatic Drag-and-Drop

Basically, a control can work as a source or as a destination of a drag-and-drop operation. Visual Basic supports two drag-and-drop modes, automatic or manual. In *automatic* mode, you just have to set a property at design time or at run time and let Visual Basic do everything. Conversely, in *manual* mode you have to respond to a number of events that occur while dragging is in progress, but in return you get better control over the process.

Most intrinsic Visual Basic controls, as well as a few external ActiveX controls, support OLE drag-and-drop in one form or another. A few controls can work only as destinations of the drag-and-drop operations; others can work both as sources and destinations. Only a few intrinsic controls can work in automatic mode. You decide how a control will actually behave as the source of a drag-and-drop operation by setting its *OLEDragMode* property. Similarly, you decide how a control behaves as the destination of a drag-and-drop operation by setting its *OLEDropMode* property. Table 9-1 summarizes the degree of OLE drag-and-drop support by intrinsic Visual Basic controls and some external ActiveX controls.

Controls	*OLEDragMode*	*OLEDropMode*
TextBox, PictureBox, Image, RichTextBox, MaskEdBox	vbManual, vbAutomatic	vbNone, vbManual vbAutomatic
ComboBox, ListBox, DirListBox, FileListBox, DBCombo, DBList, TreeView, ListView, ImageCombo, DataList, DataCombo	vbManual, vbAutomatic	vbNone, vbManual
Form, Label, Frame, CommandButton, DriveListBox, Data, MSFlexGrid, SSTab, TabStrip, Toolbar, StatusBar, ProgressBar, Slider, Animation, UpDown, MonthView, DateTimePicker, CoolBar	Not supported	vbNone, vbManual

Table 9-1. *You can classify controls according to their degree of support for OLE drag-and-drop features. Controls in the Windowless library support the same features as intrinsic controls.*

If a control supports automatic drag-and-drop, you simply set its *OLEDragMode* or its *OLEDropMode* property (or both) to vbAutomatic. For example, if you want your application to support drag-and-drop of RTF text, you just need to place a RichTextBox control on your form and ensure that both its *OLEDragMode* and *OLEDropMode* properties are set to 1-vbAutomatic. If you do so, you can drag portions of text to and from Microsoft Word, WordPad, and most other word processors. Of course, you can also drag-and-drop to other RichTextBox controls in your own application, as well as to TextBox and MaskEdBox controls, as you can see in Figure 9-18.

Other controls support the vbAutomatic setting for the *OLEDragMode* property. But in some cases the effect of such automatic drag-and-drop might not be what you expect. Just to name a few possibilities, you can drag selected items from a multiselect ListBox control into a multilined TextBox control, where the items are rendered as multiple lines of text separated by CR-LF pairs. Or you can drop a FileListBox's selected item onto another Windows application that supports that type of file. For example, use the demonstration application on the companion CD to drop a DOC or TXT file onto Microsoft Word. Note that although the DirListBox officially supports the automatic mode for *OLEDragMode*, no drag operation actually starts when you operate on its items.

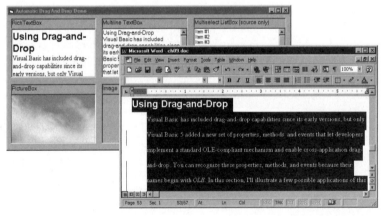

Figure 9-18. *This demo shows how you can drag-and-drop text and images to and from other Windows programs. Notice how the text is rendered differently on the RichTextBox and regular TextBox controls.*

When you perform automatic drag-and-drop, your application doesn't receive any events and you have no control over the process. You can initiate the drag-and-drop operation only with the left mouse button, and by default its effect is a Move command. (That is, the data is moved to the destination and then is deleted from the source control.) If you want to perform a Copy operation, you must keep the Ctrl key pressed, as you would do inside Windows Explorer.

Manual Drag-and-Drop

While automatic mode allows you to get interesting effects by simply setting some design-time properties, it's apparent that you need manual mode to tap the real power of drag-and-drop. As you'll see, this process requires you to write code in several event procedures, both for the source and target controls. Figure 9-19 summarizes the events that fire as the end user performs a drag-and-drop operation: You'll probably need to refer to this diagram while reading the rest of this section.

Figure 9-19. *All the events that fire when manual drag-and-drop is enabled.*

The demonstration application shown in Figure 9-20 on the following page consists of a RichTextBox control that works either as the source or the target for an OLE drag-and-drop operation. On the form you'll also find a ListBox control on which you can drop plain text, either from the RichTextBox control or another source (such as Microsoft Word). When you do this, the ListBox control will scan the text, find all unique words, sort them, and display the results to the user.

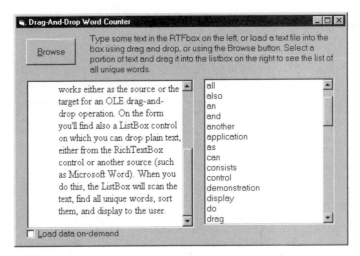

Figure 9-20. *This demonstration application shows how you can use OLE drag-and-drop capabilities to create a ListBox control that automatically searches the text you drop on it, finds unique words, and sorts them.*

Initiating a drag-and-drop operation

If you want a control to be able to initiate a drag-and-drop operation, you should set its *OLEDragMode* property to vbManual (the default value of this property for all controls except RichTextBox), and then start the drag process by invoking its *OLEDrag* method. You usually do this in the *MouseDown* event procedure:

```
Private Sub rtfText_MouseDown(Button As Integer, Shift As Integer, _
    x As Single, y As Single)
    ' Start a drag operation if right button is pressed.
    If Button = 2 Then rtfText.OLEDrag
End Sub
```

When you invoke the *OLEDrag* method, an *OLEStartDrag* event is fired for the source control. This event receives a DataObject object and an *AllowedEffects* parameter. You can think of the DataObject object as a recipient for the data you want to pass from the source to the target control. You store data in this object through its *SetData* method. As is the case with the Clipboard, you can store multiple data in different formats, as shown in Table 9-2. For example, a RichTextBox control is able to move or copy data in RTF or plain text format:

```
Private Sub rtfText_OLEStartDrag(Data As RichTextLib.DataObject, _
    AllowedEffects As Long)
    ' Use selected text, or all text if no text is currently selected.
    If rtfText.SelLength Then
        Data.SetData rtfText.SelRTF, vbCFRTF
        Data.SetData rtfText.SelText, vbCFText
    Else
```

```
        Data.SetData rtfText.TextRTF, vbCFRTF
        Data.SetData rtfText.Text, vbCFText
    End If
    AllowedEffects = vbDropEffectMove Or vbDropEffectCopy
End Sub
```

Constant	Value	Meaning
vbCFText	1	Text
vbCFBitmap	2	Bitmap (BMP)
vbCFMetafile	3	Metafile (WMF)
vbCFEMetafile	14	Enhanced metafile (.emf)
vbCFDIB	8	Device independent bitmap (DIB or BMP)
vbCFPalette	9	Color palette
vbCFFiles	15	List of files
vbCFRTF	-16639	Rich Text Format (RTF)

Table 9-2. *All the formats supported by the DataObject object.*

You should assign the *AllowedEffects* parameter a value that specifies all the effects that you want to support for the drag-and-drop operation. You can assign the value 1-vbDropEffectCopy or 2-vbDropEffectMove or their sum if you want to support both effects, as in the preceding piece of code.

Preparing to drop on the source control

If a drag operation is currently active, Visual Basic raises an *OLEDragOver* event for all the controls the mouse hovers on. This event receives the DataObject object and the *Effect* value, as set by the source control, plus information on the mouse position and button state. Based on this data, you assign to the *Effect* parameter the one effect corresponding to the action that will be performed when the end user releases the mouse on this control. This value can be 0-vbDropEffectNone, 1-vbDropEffectCopy, 2-vbDropEffectMove, or &H80000000-vbDropEffectScroll. (The latter value means that the target control will scroll its own contents, for example, when the mouse is on the scrollbar of a ListBox control). The *State* parameter holds a value that specifies whether the mouse is entering or leaving the control, and can be one of the following values: 0-vbEnter, 1-vbLeave, or 2-vbOver.

```
Private Sub lstWords_OLEDragOver(Data As DataObject, Effect As Long, _
    Button As Integer, Shift As Integer, X As Single, Y As Single, _
    State As Integer)
    If Data.GetFormat(vbCFText) Then
        Effect = Effect And vbDropEffectCopy
    Else
        Effect = vbDropEffectNone
```

(continued)

```
        End If
        ' As a demonstration, change the background of this ListBox when
        ' the mouse is over it.
        If State = vbLeave Then
            ' Restore background color on exit.
            lstWords.BackColor = vbWindowBackground
        ElseIf Effect <> 0 And State = vbEnter Then
            ' Change background color on entry.
            lstWords.BackColor = vbYellow
        End If
End Sub
```

The target control should test whether the DataObject object contains data in one of the formats the target supports. It performs this test by invoking the DataObject object's *GetFormat* method, as in the previous code snippet. In addition, you should always consider the *Effect* parameter to be a bit-field value. In the preceding case, the statement

```
Effect = Effect And vbDropEffectCopy
```

will set its value to 0 if the source control doesn't support the Copy operation. At first you might think that this caution is excessive because you know that the RichTextBox control does support the Copy operation. But you should keep in mind that once you enable the lstWords control as a target control for a drag-and-drop operation, it can receive values from any possible source of a drag-and-drop action, inside or outside the application it belongs to; therefore, you must be prepared to deal with such cases.

Immediately after the *OLEDragOver* event for the source control, Visual Basic raises an *OLEGiveFeedback* event for the source control. In this event, the source control learns which effect was selected by the target control and possibly modifies the mouse cursor:

```
Private Sub lstWords_OLEGiveFeedback(Effect As Long, _
    DefaultCursors As Boolean)
    ' If effect is Copy, use a custom cursor.
    If Effect = vbDropEffectCopy Then
        DefaultCursors = False
        Screen.MousePointer = vbCustom
        ' imgCopy is an Image control that stores a custom icon.
        Screen.MouseIcon = imgCopy.Picture
    Else
        DefaultCursors = True
    End If
End Sub
```

The *DefaultCursors* parameter should be explicitly set to False if you assign a different mouse cursor. You don't have to implement the *OLEGiveFeedback* event if you don't care about the cursor's shape.

Dropping data

When the user releases the mouse button over the target control, Visual Basic raises an *OLEDragDrop* event for the target control. Apart from the *State* parameter, this event receives the same parameters as the *OLEDragOver* event. In this case, the meaning of the *Effect* parameter is slightly different because it represents the action that was decided by the target control.

```
Private Sub lstWords_OLEDragDrop(Data As DataObject, Effect As Long, _
    Button As Integer, Shift As Integer, X As Single, Y As Single)
    ' Restore the correct background color.
    lstWords.BackColor = vbWindowBackground
    ' Select Copy action if possible, otherwise select Move.
    If Effect And vbDropEffectCopy Then
        Effect = vbDropEffectCopy
    ElseIf Effect And vbDropEffectMove Then
        Effect = vbDropEffectMove
    End If
    ' In either case, ask for the data - only plain text is supported.
    Dim text As String
    text = Data.GetData(vbCFText)

    ' Code for processing the text and loading the list of unique
    ' words in the lstWords listbox (omitted)...
End Sub
```

Immediately after the *OLEDragDrop* event is executed, Visual Basic fires the source control's *OLECompleteDrag* event. You need to write code for this event to delete highlighted data in the source code if the action was vbDropEffectMove or to restore the control's original appearance if it changed during the drag-and-drop process:

```
Private Sub rtfText_OLECompleteDrag(Effect As Long)
    If Effect = vbDropEffectMove Then
        ' If this was a Move operation, delete the highlighted text.
        rtfText.SelText = ""
    Else
        ' If it was a Copy command, just clear the selection.
        rtfText.SelLength = 0
    End If
End Sub
```

Loading data on demand

When the source control supports many formats, loading data in those formats into the DataObject object when the *OLEStartDrag* event fires isn't an efficient solution. Fortunately, Visual Basic supports another approach: Instead of loading the source data in the DataObject object when the drag operation begins, you just specify which formats the source control is willing to support.

```
' In the rtfText's OLEStartDrag event procedure
Data.SetData , vbCFRTF
Data.SetData , vbCFText
```

If the drag-and-drop operation isn't canceled, the target control eventually invokes the DataObject's *GetData* method to retrieve the data in a given format. When this happens, Visual Basic fires the *OLESetData* event for the source control:

```
Private Sub rtfText_OLESetData(Data As RichTextLib.DataObject, _
    DataFormat As Integer)
    ' This event fires only when the target control invokes the
    ' Data's GetData method.
    If DataFormat = vbCFText Then
        If rtfText.SelLength Then
            Data.SetData rtfText.SelText, vbCFText
        Else
            Data.SetData rtfText.text, vbCFText
        End If
    ElseIf DataFormat = vbCFRTF Then
        If rtfText.SelLength Then
            Data.SetData rtfText.SelRTF, vbCFRTF
        Else
            Data.SetData rtfText.TextRTF, vbCFRTF
        End If
    End If
End Sub
```

This event isn't invoked if you passed data to the *SetData* method's first argument when the drag-and-drop operation began.

Dragging and dropping files

As you know, Windows Explorer supports drag-and-drop of filenames, and many Windows applications can work as destinations of a file drag operation initiated inside Windows Explorer. In this section, I'll show how you can implement both these features—working as a source or a target for file drag-and-drop.

The key to these capabilities is the DataObject's *Files* property. If you want your application to work as a target for a file drag-and-drop operation, you check whether the DataObject object contains data in vbCFFiles format, and then you retrieve filenames by iterating on the Files collection. For example, you can load the names of the dropped files into a ListBox control using this code:

```
If Data.GetFormat(vbCFFiles) Then
    For i = 1 To Data.Files.Count
        lstFiles.AddItem Data.Files(i)
    Next
End If
```

Of course, you can also open the file and display its contents. The demonstration program shown in Figure 9-21 implements both possibilities.

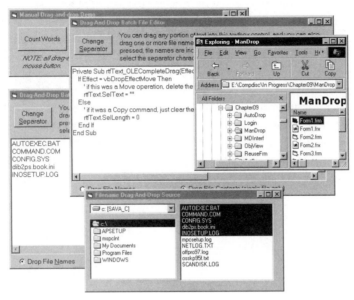

Figure 9-21. *The upper window is displaying the contents of the AutoDrop.Vbp file dropped by Windows Explorer, while the bottom window is displaying a list of filenames dropped by the file dialog on the right.*

Creating an application that behaves as a source for dragging and dropping files isn't difficult either. You just have to add items to the Files collection and set the vbCFFiles format. Just remember that target applications expect the Files collection to contain filenames with their complete paths. This code shows how you can use a FileListBox control as a source for a drag operation:

```
Private Sub File1_OLEStartDrag(Data As DataObject, AllowedEffects As Long)
    Dim i As Integer, path As String
    path = File1.path & IIf(Right$(File1.path, 1) <> "\", "\", "")
    ' Add all selected files to the Data.Files collection.
    Data.Files.Clear
    For i = 0 To File1.ListCount - 1
        If File1.Selected(i) Then
            Data.Files.Add path & File1.List(i)
        End If
    Next
    If Data.Files.Count Then
        ' Only if we actually added files
        Data.SetData , vbCFFiles
        AllowedEffects = vbDropEffectCopy
    End If
End Sub
```

Using custom formats

The OLE drag-and-drop mechanism is even more flexible than I've demonstrated in that it also supports moving data in a proprietary format. For example, you might have a form that's displaying an invoice, an order, or information about a customer, and you want to enable the user to drag-and-drop this data on another form of your application. Using a custom format also enables you to easily transfer information among different instances of your application, and at the same time it prevents your accidentally dropping it on other programs. In this way, you can move confidential data between applications without the risk of unauthorized people peeking at it.

The first step in using a custom format is registering it with Windows, which you do by invoking the *RegisterClipboardFormat* API function. This step must be executed by every application that needs to access data in a custom format. Windows guarantees that the first time this function is invoked with a given custom format name (*PersonalData* in the code below), a unique integer will be returned and all subsequent calls to that API function with the same argument will return the same value, even if called from other applications.

```
Private Declare Function RegisterClipboardFormat Lib "user32" _
    Alias "RegisterClipboardFormatA" (ByVal lpString As String) As Integer
Dim CustomFormat As Integer

Private Sub Form_Load()
    CustomFormat = RegisterClipboardFormat("PersonalData")
End Sub
```

At this point, you can store data using the *CustomFormat* identifier, exactly as you did with a standard format such as vbCFText or vbCFBitmap. The only difference is that custom data must be loaded into a Byte array before passing it to the *DataObject.SetData* method. The demonstration application in Figure 9-22 uses this technique to move or copy data about two forms:

```
' Code in the source application
Private Sub imgDrag_OLESetData(Data As DataObject, DataFormat As Integer)
    Dim i As Integer, text As String, bytes() As Byte
    ' Build a long string made up of field contents.
    For i = 0 To txtField.UBound
        If i > 0 Then text = text & vbNullChar
        text = text & txtField(i)
    Next
    ' Move to a byte array, and then assign it to DataObject.
    bytes() = text
    Data.SetData bytes(), CustomFormat
End Sub
```

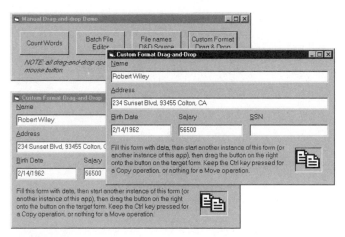

Figure 9-22. *You can move data in a custom format between distinct forms or even between distinct instances of your application, without the risk of dropping your confidential data somewhere else.*

The target form must retrieve the Byte array, rebuild the original string, and then extract the value of individual fields:

```
' Code in the target application
Private Sub imgDrag_OLEDragDrop(Data As DataObject, Effect As Long, _
    Button As Integer, Shift As Integer, X As Single, Y As Single)
    Dim bytes() As Byte, text() As String, i As Integer
    bytes() = Data.GetData(CustomFormat)
    ' Retrieve individual values, and then assign them to fields.
    text() = Split(CStr(bytes), vbNullChar)
    For i = 0 To txtField.UBound
        txtField(i) = text(i)
    Next
End Sub
```

Browse the source code of the demonstration application to see more information about this technique.

Now that you have mastered all the techniques concerning SDI and MDI forms, dialog boxes, and OLE drag-and-drop, you're ready to dive into the intricacies of the external ActiveX controls that come with Visual Basic. These controls are covered in the next three chapters.

Chapter 10

Windows Common Controls: Part I

Apart from the intrinsic controls described in Chapter 3, the Microsoft Windows common controls are probably the most widely used controls in Microsoft Visual Basic applications. The main reason for their popularity is that they contribute to creating the Windows look-and-feel more than any other group of controls. For example, a Windows Explorer–like application with a TreeView control on the left and a ListView control on the right immediately reminds users of Windows Explorer itself, thus making for a familiar interface.

Windows common controls were first introduced in Windows 95. The initial group of these controls included the TreeView, ListView, ImageList, Toolbar, StatusBar, TabStrip, and Slider controls. Visual Basic 4—the first 32-bit version of this language—offered an OLE Custom Control (OCX) that provided access to their features. After this initial release, Microsoft manufactured several new common controls as well as more powerful versions of the original ones. But the OCXs that came with Visual Basic 5 (and its three service packs) were never significantly updated, which meant that Visual Basic programmers couldn't use these newer controls in their applications (with the exceptions of the new Animation and UpDown controls). Until recently, to use such newer controls or to fully exploit the capabilities of the original controls, Visual Basic developers had to resort to third-party Microsoft ActiveX controls or to complex API programming.

Visual Basic 6 has remedied this problem. It now includes all the tools you need to fully take advantage of the features of nearly all existing common controls. A few

Windows common controls are still missing from the newer versions of the OCX files (most notably, the IP Address control), but in most cases you won't need to purchase any additional custom controls to give your Visual Basic applications a modern user interface.

Most of the Windows common controls come in the MsComCtl.ocx file. This file contains all the original common controls, plus the ImageCombo control. Another file, MsComCt2.ocx, includes the code for five additional controls: Animation, UpDown, MonthView, DateTimePicker, and FlatScrollBar. I describe these controls in Chapter 11. Note that these two files correspond to the outdated files ComCtl32.ocx and ComCt232.ocx that were distributed with Visual Basic 5. Visual Basic 6 doesn't replace the older OCX files and can peacefully coexist with Visual Basic 5 and applications developed with that version of the language.

Visual Basic 6 also includes a third OCX file, ComCt332.ocx, which adds support for yet another common control, the CoolBar control (also described in Chapter 11). This file has been available to Visual Basic 5 developers, who had to download it from the Microsoft web site, but the file is now included in the Visual Basic package.

OCX files that are distributed with Visual Basic 6 have an interesting feature. While the older ComCtl32.ocx and ComCt232.ocx files were just intermediaries between Visual Basic and the system DLLs that included the actual code for the controls, the newer versions are self-contained and include all the necessary code for manipulating the controls. Needless to say, newer files are bigger than their predecessors—MsComCtl.ocx is more than 1 MB—but this approach simplifies the distribution of Visual Basic applications and reduces the chance of conflicts with programs already installed on the end user's machine.

In this chapter, I describe the features of all the Windows common controls included in MsComCtr.ocx, while the next chapter covers all the controls in MsComCt2.ocx and ComCt232.ocx. To test the code presented here, you first make the controls available to your Visual Basic environment. To do so, execute the Components command from the Project menu (or just press the Ctrl+T key combination) to display the Components dialog box similar to the one in Figure 10-1, and then select the OCXs that interest you, as shown in Figure 10-2.

When you load into the Visual Basic 6 environment a project built with a previous version of the language that contains references to older versions of Windows common controls, a message box appears asking whether you want to upgrade those controls with their newer versions. For the maximum compatibility with existing applications, you might decide to continue to use the older controls, even though upgrading to the newer versions is the best choice if you want to improve the application's user interface and functionality. You can turn this warning off by deselecting the Upgrade ActiveX Controls check box on the General tab of the Project Properties dialog box.

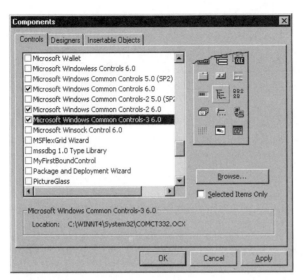

Figure 10-1. *The Components dialog box, with all the Windows common controls OCXs selected.*

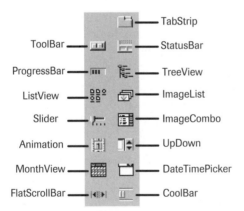

Figure 10-2. *The common controls in the Toolbox.*

THE IMAGELIST CONTROL

The ImageList control is most often used as a container for images and icons that are employed by other controls, such as TreeView, ListView, TabStrip, and ImageCombo controls. For this reason, it makes sense to describe it before any other controls. The ImageList control is invisible at run time, and to display one of the images it contains you must draw it on a form, a PictureBox control, or an Image control, or associate it with another control.

Using the ImageList control as a repository for images that are then used by other controls offers a number of advantages. Without this control, in fact, you would have to load images from disk at run time using a *LoadPicture* function, which slows down execution and increases the number of files to be distributed with your program, or an array of Image controls, which slows down form loading. It's much easier and more efficient to load all the images in the ImageList control at design time and then refer to them from the other controls or in source code.

Adding Images

The ImageList control exposes a ListImages collection, which in turn contains a number of ListImage objects. Each ListImage item holds an individual image. As with any collection, an individual ListImage object can be referenced through its numerical index or its string key (if it has one). Each ListImage object can hold an image in one of the following graphic formats: bitmap (.bmp), icon (.ico), cursor (.cur), JPEG (.jpg), or GIF (.gif). The latter two formats weren't supported by the ImageList control distributed with Visual Basic 5.

Adding images at design time

Adding images at design-time is easy. After you place an ImageList control on a form, right-click on it, select the Properties command from the pop-up menu, and switch to the Images tab, as shown in Figure 10-3. All you have to do now is click on the Insert Picture button and pick up your images from disk. You should associate a string key with each image so that you can refer to it correctly later, even if you add or remove other images in the future (which would affect its numerical index). Of course, all string keys must be unique in the collection. You can also specify a string for the *Tag* property of an image, for example, if you want to provide a textual description of the image or any other information associated with this image. Visual Basic never directly uses this property, so you're free to store any string data in it.

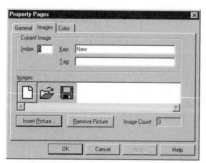

Figure 10-3. *The Images tab of the Properties window of an ImageList control.*

Images added to the ListImages collection can be of any size, with a caveat: If you're going to use these images inside another common control, all the images after the first one will be resized and stretched to reflect the size of the first image added to the control. This isn't an issue if you're going to display these images on a form, a PictureBox control, or an Image control.

If the ImageList control doesn't contain any images, you can set the size you want the images to be in the General tab of the Properties dialog box. Trying to do this when the control already contains one or more ListImage items raises an error.

Adding images at run time

Adding images at run time requires you to use the *Add* method of the ListImages collection, the syntax of which is the following:

```
Add([Index], [Key], [Picture]) As ListImage
```

If you omit the *Index* argument, you add the new image at the end of the collection. The following code creates a new ListImage item and associates it with a bitmap loaded from disk:

```
Dim li As ListImage
Set li = ImageList1.ListImages.Add(, "Cut", _
    LoadPicture("d:\bitmaps\cut.bmp"))
```

You don't need to assign the result value of the *Add* method to a ListImage object unless you want to assign a string to the *Tag* property of the object just created. Even in that case, you can do without an explicit variable:

```
With ImageList1.ListImages.Add(, "Cut", LoadPicture("d:\bitmaps\cut.bmp"))
    .Tag = "The Cut icon"
End With
```

You can remove individual ListImage objects (added either at design time or at run time) by using the *Remove* method of the ListImages collection.

```
' You can use a numerical index or a string key
' to remove the associated image.
ImageList1.ListImages.Remove "Cut"
```

You can also remove all the images in one operation by using the collection's *Clear* method:

```
' Remove all images.
ImageList1.ListImages.Clear
```

You can learn the size of the images currently stored in the control by using the ImageList's *ImageWidth* and *ImageHeight* properties. These properties are in pixels and can be written to only if the ListImages collection is empty; after you add the first image, they become read-only properties.

Extracting and Drawing Images

If you associate an ImageList control with another common control, you usually don't have to worry about extracting and showing individual images because everything is done automatically for you. But if you want to manually display or print images, you have to learn how to use a few properties and methods from the ImageList control and its ListImage dependent objects.

Extracting individual images

Each ListImage object exposes a *Picture* property, which lets you extract the image and assign it to another control, typically a PictureBox or Image control:

```
Set Picture1.Picture = ImageList1.ListImages("Cut").Picture
```

In general, you can use the *Picture* property of a ListImage object whenever you would use the *Picture* property of a PictureBox or an Image control, as in the following example:

```
' Save an image to a disk file.
SavePicture ImageList1.ListImages("Cut").Picture, "C:\cut.bmp"
' Display an image on the current form, zooming it by a factor
' of 4 along the X-axis, and 8 along the Y-axis.
With ImageList1
    PaintPicture .ListImages("Cut").Picture, 0, 0, _
        ScaleX(.ImageWidth, vbPixels) * 4, ScaleY(.ImageHeight, vbPixels) * 8
End With
```

Using the *PaintPicture* method, you can display any ListImage object on a form or in a PictureBox control, or you can print it to the Printer object. For more information about the *PaintPicture* method, see Chapter 2.

ListImage objects also expose an *ExtractIcon* method, which creates an icon out of the image and returns it to the caller. You can therefore use this method whenever an icon is expected, as in this code:

```
Form1.MouseIcon = ImageList1.ListImages("Pointer").ExtractIcon
```

Unlike standard collections, keys in the ListImages collection are dealt with in a case-sensitive way. In other words, "*Pointer*" and "*pointer*" are assumed to be different items.

Creating transparent images

The ImageList control has a *MaskColor* property whose value determines the color that should be considered transparent when you're performing graphical operations on individual ListImage objects or when you're displaying images inside other controls. By default, this is the gray color (&HC0C0C0), but you can change it both at design time in the Color tab of the Properties dialog box and at run time via code.

When a graphical operation is performed, none of the pixels in the image that are the color defined by *MaskColor* are transferred. To actually display transparent images, however, you must ensure that the *UseMaskColor* property is set to True, which is its default value. You can modify this value in the General tab of the Properties dialog box or at run time via code:

```
' Make white the transparent color.
ImageList1.MaskColor = vbWhite
ImageList1.UseMaskColor = True
```

Using the *Draw* method

ListImage objects support the *Draw* method, which has the following syntax:

```
Draw hDC, [x], [y], [Style]
```

where *hDC* is the handle of a device context (typically the value returned by the *hDC* property of a form, a PictureBox control, or the Printer object) and *x* and *y* are the coordinates in pixels where the image should be displayed in the target object. *Style* is one of the following values: 0-imlNormal (default, draw the image without any change), 1-imlTransparent (use the *MaskColor* property to account for transparent areas), 2-imlSelected (draw the image dithered with the system highlight color), or 3-imlFocus (as imlSelected, but create a hatched effect to indicate that the image has the focus):

```
' Show an image in the upper left corner of a PictureBox control.
ImageList1.ListImages("Cut").Draw Picture1.hDC, 0, 0
```

Creating composite images

The ImageList control also includes the ability to create composite images by overlaying two individual images held in ListImage objects. This can be accomplished using the *Overlay* method. Figure 10-4 shows two individual images and then what you can get by overlaying the second one on the first one:

```
PaintPicture ImageList1.ListImages(1).Picture, 0, 10, 64, 64
PaintPicture ImageList1.ListImages(2).Picture, 100, 10, 64, 64
PaintPicture ImageList1.Overlay(1, 2), 200, 10, 64, 64
```

Figure 10-4. *The effect of the* Overlay *method.*

The *Overlay* method implicitly uses the *MaskColor* property to determine which color is to be considered as the transparent color, so you must ensure that the *UseMaskColor* property is set to True.

THE TREEVIEW CONTROL

The TreeView control is probably the first Windows common control that users become acquainted with because it's the control Windows Explorer is based on. Basically, the TreeView control displays a hierarchy of items. A plus sign beside an item indicates that it has one or more child items. An item that has child items can be expanded to show them or collapsed to hide them. This can be done interactively by the user or via code.

The Visual Basic 6 version of the TreeView control has a number of improvements and now supports check boxes beside each item and full row selection. Moreover, individual nodes can have different *Bold*, *Foreground*, and *Background* attributes.

The TreeView control exposes a Nodes collection, which in turn includes all the Node objects that have been added to the control. Each individual Node object exposes a number of properties that let you define the look of the control. Typically, a TreeView control has one single root Node object, but you can also create multiple Node objects at the root level.

Setting Design-Time Properties

Immediately after creating a TreeView control on a form, you should display its Properties dialog box (shown in Figure 10-5), which you do by right-clicking on the control and selecting the Properties menu item. Of course, you can also set properties that appear in this page at run time, but you rarely need to change the appearance of a TreeView control once it has been displayed to the user.

The *Style* property affects which graphical elements will be used inside the control. A TreeView control can display four graphical elements: the text associated with each Node object, the picture associated with each Node object, a plus or minus sign beside each Node object (to indicate whether the Node is in collapsed or expanded state), and the lines that go from each Node object to its child objects. The *Style* property can be assigned one of eight values, each one representing a different combination of these four graphical elements. In most cases, you use the default value, 7-tvwTreelinesPlusMinusPictureText, which displays all graphical elements.

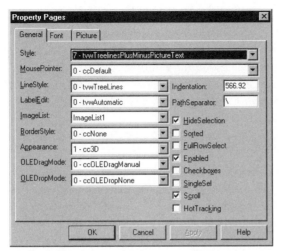

Figure 10-5. *The General tab of the Properties dialog box of a TreeView control.*

The *LineStyle* property affects how lines are drawn. The value 0-tvwTreeLines doesn't display lines among root Node objects (this is the default setting), whereas the value 1-tvwRootLines also displays lines among all root Nodes and makes them appear as if they were children of a fictitious Node located at an upper level. The *Indentation* property states the distance in twips between vertical dotted lines.

The *LabelEdit* property affects how the end user can modify the text associated with each Node object. If it's assigned the value 0-tvwAutomatic (the default), the end user can edit the text by clicking on the Node at run time; if it's assigned the value 1-tvwManual, the edit operation can be started only programmatically, by your issuing a *StartLabelEdit* method.

The ImageList combo box lets you select which ImageList control will be used to retrieve the images of individual Node objects. The combo box lists all the ImageList controls located on the current form.

TIP You can associate a TreeView control (or any control) with an ImageList control located on another form by making the assignment at run time, as shown in this code:

```
Private Sub Form_Load()
    Set TreeView1.ImageList = AnotherForm.ImageList1
End Sub
```

This technique allows you to use a group of bitmaps and icons in all the forms of your application without having to duplicate them and thus shrink the size of the EXE file. This way, you save memory and resources at run time.

The *HideSelection* property determines whether the selected Node object will continue to be highlighted when the TreeView control loses the focus. The *Path-Separator* property states which character or string should be used in the *FullPath* property of the Node object. The default value for the *PathSeparator* property is the backslash character. For example, if you have a root Node labeled "*Root*" and a child Node labeled "*FirstChild*", the *FullPath* property of the child Node will be "*Root\FirstChild*".

The *Sorted* property states whether Nodes in the control are automatically sorted in alphabetical order. The documentation omits an important detail: This property affects only how root Node objects are sorted but has no effect on the order of child Node objects at lower levels. If you want all the branches of the tree to be sorted, you should set the *Sorted* properties of all individual Node items to True.

The TreeView control that comes with Visual Basic 6 adds a few interesting properties not available in previous versions of the language. The *FullRowSelect* property, if True, causes a Node of the control to be selected if the user clicks anywhere on its row. (By default, this property is False, in which case an item can be selected only with a click over it or its plus or minus symbol.)

If you set the *Checkboxes* property to True, a check box appears beside each Node object so that the end user can select multiple Node objects.

By default, you need to double-click on Node items to expand or collapse them (or click on the plus or minus sign, if present), and you can expand and collapse any number of tree branches independently of one another. But if you set the *SingleSel* property to True, the control's behavior is different: You expand and collapse items with a single click—that is, as soon as you select them. Moreover, when you expand a Node, the item that was previously expanded is automatically collapsed.

The *Scroll* property determines whether the TreeView control displays a vertical or horizontal scroll bar if necessary. The default value is True, but you can set it to False to disable this behavior (even though, honestly, I can't find a reason why you would want to do that).

Finally the *HotTracking* property lets you create a Web-like user interface. If you set this property to True, the cursor changes into a hand when the mouse passes over the Node object and the TreeView control underlines the Node's *Text* property.

Run-Time Operations

To fully exploit the potential of the TreeView control, you must learn to deal with the Nodes collections and the many properties and methods of Node objects.

Adding Node objects

One of the shortcomings of the TreeView control is that you can't add items at design time as you can with ListBox and ComboBox controls. You can add Node objects only at run time using the *Add* method of the Nodes collection. The *Add* method's syntax is the following:

```
Add([Relative],[Relationship],[Key],[Text],[Image],[SelectedImage]) As Node
```

Relative and *Relationship* indicate where the new Node should be inserted. *Key* is its string key in the Nodes collection, *Text* is the label that will appear in the control, and *Image* is the index or the string key in the companion ImageList control of the image that will appear beside the Node. *SelectedImage* is the index or key of the image that will be used when the Node is selected. For example, if you're creating a TreeView control that mimics Windows Explorer and its directory objects, you might write something like this:

```
Dim nd As Node
Set nd  = Add(, , ,"C:\System", "Folder", "OpenFolder")
```

To place the new Node in a given position in the tree, you must provide the first two arguments. The first argument specifies an existing item in the Nodes collection by its numerical index or string key; the second argument states the relationship between the Node being added and its relative. Such a relationship can be 0-tvwFirst, in which the new Node becomes the first item at the level of its relative—in other words, it becomes the first sibling of the relative Node. Or the relationship can be 1-tvwLast (the new Node becomes the last sibling of the relative Node); 2-tvwNext (default, the new Node is added immediately after the relative Node, at the same level in the hierarchy); 3-tvwPrevious (the new Node is inserted immediately before the relative Node, at the same level in the hierarchy); or 4-tvwChild (the new Node becomes a child of the relative Node and is inserted after all existing child nodes).

Here's an example of a routine that fills a TreeView control with the structure of an MDB file—that is, the tables it contains and the fields for each table. The routine accepts a reference to the control in its second argument so that you can easily reuse it in your applications. The third argument passed to the routine is a Boolean value that states whether system tables should be displayed:

```
Sub ShowDatabaseStructure(MdbFile As String, TV As TreeView, _
    ShowSystemTables As Boolean)
    Dim db As DAO.Database, td As DAO.TableDef, fld As DAO.Field
    Dim nd As Node, nd2 As Node
    ' Clear the current contents of the TreeView control.
    TV.Nodes.Clear
```

(continued)

```
' Open the database.
Set db = DBEngine.OpenDatabase(MdbFile)
' Add the root Node, and then expand it to show the tables.
Set nd = TV.Nodes.Add(, , "Root", db.Name, "Database")
nd.Expanded = True

' Explore all the tables in the database.
For Each td In db.TableDefs
    ' Discard system tables if user isn't interested in them.
    If (td.Attributes And dbSystemObject) = 0 Or ShowSystemTables Then
        ' Add the table under the Root object.
        Set nd = TV.Nodes.Add("Root", tvwChild, , td.Name, "Table")
        ' Now add all the fields.
        For Each fld In td.Fields
            Set nd2 = TV.Nodes.Add(nd.Index, tvwChild, , _
                fld.Name, "Field")
            Next
        End If
Next
db.Close
End Sub
```

Note that the routine doesn't include any error handler: if the file doesn't exist or is an invalid or corrupted MDB archive, the error is simply returned to the caller. It's usual to show a TreeView control with the root object already expanded in order to save the end user a mouse click. The routine does this by setting the root Node object's *Expanded* property to True.

Appearance and visibility

You can control the appearance of individual Node objects by setting their *ForeColor*, *BackColor*, and *Bold* properties, the effects of which are shown in Figure 10-6. This new feature permits you to visually convey more information about each Node. Typically, you set these properties when you add an item to the Nodes collection:

```
With TV.Nodes.Add(, , , "New Node")
    .Bold = True
    .ForeColor = vbRed
    .BackColor = vbYellow
End With
```

Figure 10-6. *Effects of the* ForeColor, BackColor, *and* Bold *properties of Node objects, as well as of the* Checkboxes *property of the TreeView control.*

Each Node object has three images associated with it, and the Node's current state determines which image is displayed. The *Image* property sets or returns the index of the default image; the *SelectedImage* property sets or returns the index of the image used when the Node is selected; the *ExpandedImage* property sets or returns the index of the image used when the Node is expanded. You can set the first two properties in the Nodes collection's *Add* method, but you must explicitly assign the *ExpandedImage* property after you've added the item to the collection.

You can learn whether a particular Node is currently visible by querying its *Visible* property. A Node item can be invisible because it belongs to a tree branch that's in a collapsed state or because it has scrolled away from the visible portion of the control. This property is read-only, but you can force the visibility state of a Node by executing its *EnsureVisible* method:

```
' Scroll the TreeView, and expand any parent Node if necessary.
If aNode.Visible = False Then aNode.EnsureVisible
```

You can learn how many Nodes are visible in the control by executing TreeView's *GetVisibleCount* method.

You have two ways to determine whether a Node is currently the selected Node object in the control—either by querying its *Selected* property or by testing the TreeView's *SelectedItem* property:

```
' Check whether aNode is the Node currently selected (two
' equivalent ways).
' First way:
If aNode.Selected Then MsgBox "Selected"
' Second way:
If TreeView1.SelectedItem Is aNode Then MsgBox "Selected"

' Make aNode the currently selected Node (two equivalent ways).
' First way:
aNode.Selected = True
' Second way:
Set TreeView1.SelectedItem = aNode
```

Showing information about a Node

Users expect the program to do something when they click on a Node object in the TreeView control—for example, to display some information related to that object. To learn when a Node is clicked, you have to trap the *NodeClick* event. You can determine which Node has been clicked by looking at the *Index* or *Key* property of the Node parameter passed to the event procedure. In a typical situation, you store information about a Node in an array of String or UDT items:

```
Private Sub TreeView1_NodeClick(ByVal Node As MSComctlLib.Node)
    ' info() is an array of strings that hold nodes' descriptions.
    lblData.Caption = info(Node.Index)
End Sub
```

The *NodeClick* event differs from the regular *Click* event in that the latter fires whenever the user clicks on the TreeView control, whereas the former is activated only when the user clicks on a Node object.

The previous code snippet has a flaw: In general, the *Index* property of a Node object can't be trusted because it can change when other Node objects are removed from the Nodes collection. For this reason, you should rely exclusively on the *Key* property, which is guaranteed not to vary after the Node has been added to the collection. For example, you can use the *Key* property to search for an item in a standard Collection object, where you store information that's related to the Node. Here's a better technique: You store the data in the *Tag* property of the Node object so that you don't have to worry about removing items from the control's Node collection. The BrowMdb.vbp project on the companion CD includes a revised version of the *ShowDatabaseStructure* routine to show properties and attributes of all the Field and TableDef objects displayed in the TreeView control, as you can see in Figure 10-7.

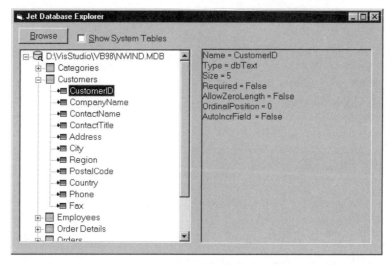

Figure 10-7. *A simple browser for Microsoft Jet databases.*

Editing Node text

By default, the user can click on a Node object to enter Edit mode and indirectly change the Node object's *Text* property. If you don't like this behavior, you can set the *LabelEdit* property to 1-tvwManual. In this case, you can enter Edit mode only by programmatically executing a *StartLabelEdit* method.

Regardless of the value of the *LabelEdit* property, you can trap the instant when the user begins editing the current value of the *Text* property by writing code in the *BeforeLabelEdit* event procedure. When this event fires, you can discover which Node is currently selected by using the TreeView's *SelectedItem* property, and you can cancel the operation by setting the event's *Cancel* parameter to True:

```
Private Sub TreeView1_BeforeLabelEdit(Cancel As Integer)
    ' Prevent the root Node's Text property from editing.
    If TreeView1.SelectedItem.Key = "Root" Then Cancel = True
End Sub
```

Similarly, you can find out when the user has completed the editing and reject, if you want to, the new value of the *Text* property by trapping the *AfterLabelEdit* event. Typically, you use this event to check whether the new value follows any syntactical rule enforced by the particular object. For example, you can reject empty strings by writing the following code:

```
Private Sub TreeView1_AfterLabelEdit(Cancel As Integer, _
    NewString As String)
    If Len(NewString) = 0 Then Cancel = True
End Sub
```

Using check boxes

To display a check box beside each Node in the TreeView control, you simply need to set the control's *Checkboxes* property to True, either at design time or run time. You can then query or modify the state of each Node using its *Checked* property:

```
' Count how many Node objects are checked, and then reset all check boxes.
Dim i As Long, SelCount As Long
For i = 1 To TreeView1.Nodes.Count
    If TreeView1.Nodes(i).Checked Then
        SelCount = SelCount + 1
        TreeView1.Nodes(i).Checked = False
    End If
Next
```

You can enforce tighter control over what happens when a Node is checked by writing code in the control's *NodeChecked* event. This event doesn't fire if you modify a Node's *Checked* property using code:

```
Dim SelCount As Long      ' The number of selected items

Private Sub TreeView1_NodeCheck(ByVal Node As MSComctlLib.Node)
    ' Display the number of selected Nodes.
    If Node.Checked Then
        SelCount = SelCount + 1
    Else
        SelCount = SelCount - 1
    End If
    lblStatus = "Selected Items = " & SelCount
End Sub
```

> **TIP** If you want to prevent the user from modifying the *Checked* state of a given Node object, you can't simply reset its *Checked* property within the *NodeCheck* event because all changes to this property are lost when the event procedure is exited. You can solve this problem by adding a Timer control on the form and writing this code:

```
Dim CheckedNode As Node                   ' A form-level variable

Private Sub TreeView1_NodeCheck(ByVal Node As MSComctlLib.Node)
    ' Prevent the user from checking the first Node.
    If Node.Index = 1 Then
        ' Remember which Node has been clicked on.
        Set CheckedNode = Node
        ' Let the Timer routine do the job.
        Timer1.Enabled = True
    End If
End Sub

Private Sub Timer1_Timer()
    ' Reset the Checked property, and then go to sleep.
    CheckedNode.Checked = False
    Timer1.Enabled = False
End Sub
```

> This technique is more effective if the Timer's *Interval* property is set to a small value, such as 10 milliseconds.

Advanced Techniques

The TreeView control is very flexible, but sometimes you have to resort to more advanced and less intuitive techniques to leverage its power.

Loading Nodes on demand

Theoretically, you can load thousands of items into a TreeView control, which is more than an average user is willing to examine. In practice, loading more than a few hundred items makes a program unacceptably slow. Take, for example, the task of loading a directory structure into a TreeView control the way Windows Explorer does it: This simple job requires a lot of time to scan the system's hard disk, and you simply can't have your user wait for this long. In these situations, you might need to resort to a *load on demand* approach.

Loading items on demand means that you don't add Node objects until you have to display them, one instant before their parent Node is expanded. You can determine when a Node is expanded by trapping the TreeView control's *Expand* event. (You can also find out when a Node object is collapsed by trapping the control's *Collapse* event.) The tricky detail is how to let the user know that a Node has one or more child objects without actually adding them. In other words, we need to show a plus sign beside each Node item with children.

It is easy to demonstrate that the TreeView common control is able to display a plus sign beside a Node without child Nodes: Just run Windows Explorer and look at the plus sign beside the icon for the A: floppy drive; it's there even if no subdirectories are on the diskette (and even if no diskette is in the A: drive). Unfortunately, the ability to display a plus sign without adding child Nodes hasn't been exposed in the OCX that comes with Visual Basic and requires some API programming. The technique I will show you, however, does the trick without any API call.

To show a plus sign beside a Node, all you have to do is add a child Node, *any* child Node. I'll call this a *dummy child Node*. You need to mark such a dummy Node item in an unambiguous way—for example, by storing a special value in its *Text* or *Tag* property. When a Node is eventually expanded, the program checks whether the Node has a dummy child item. If so, the code removes the dummy child and then adds all the actual child Nodes. As you see, the technique is simple, even if its implementation includes some nontrivial code.

Figure 10-8 shows the demonstration program at run time. Its complete source code is on the companion CD, so I'll just illustrate its key routines. The form contains the *tvwDir* TreeView control and uses the FileSystemObject hierarchy to retrieve the directory structure.

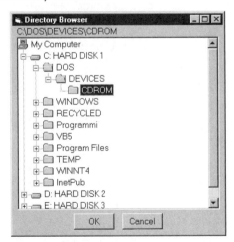

Figure 10-8. *A directory browser program that loads TreeView Nodes on demand.*

The following *DirRefresh* procedure is invoked from within the *Form_Load* event:

```
Private Sub DirRefresh()
    Dim dr As Scripting.Drive
    Dim rootNode As node, nd As Node
    On Error Resume Next
```

(continued)

```
        ' Add the "My Computer" root Node (expanded).
        Set rootNode = tvwDir.Nodes.Add(, , "\\MyComputer", _
            "My Computer", 1)
        rootNode.Expanded = True
        ' Add all the drives; display a plus sign beside them.
        For Each dr In FSO.Drives
            ' Error handling is needed to account for not-ready drives.
            Err.Clear
            Set nd = tvwDir.Nodes.Add(rootNode.Key, tvwChild, dr.Path & "\", _
                dr.Path & " " & dr.VolumeName, 2)
            If Err = 0 Then AddDummyChild nd
        Next
End Sub

Sub AddDummyChild(nd As node)
        ' Add a dummy child Node if necessary.
        If nd.Children = 0 Then
            ' Dummy nodes' Text property is "***".
            tvwDir.Nodes.Add nd.index, tvwChild, , "***"
        End If
End Sub
```

The previous routine ensures that the form is displayed with the "MyComputer" root Node and all the drives below it. When the user expands a Node, the following event fires:

```
Private Sub tvwDir_Expand(ByVal node As ComctlLib.node)
        ' A Node is being expanded.
        Dim nd As Node
        ' Exit if the Node had already been expanded or has no children.
        If node.Children = 0 Or node.Children > 1 Then Exit Sub
        ' Also exit if it doesn't have a dummy child Node.
        If node.Child.text <> "***" Then Exit Sub
        ' Remove the dummy child item.
        tvwDir.Nodes.Remove node.Child.index
        ' Add all the subdirs of this Node object.
        AddSubdirs node
End Sub
```

The *tvwDir_Expand* procedure uses the *Children* property of the Node object, which returns the number of its child Nodes, and the *Child* property, which returns a reference to its first child Node. The *AddSubdirs* procedure adds all the subdirectories below a given Node. Because each Node's *Key* property always holds the path corresponding to that Node, it's simple to retrieve the corresponding Scripting.Folder object and then iterate on its SubFolders collection:

```
Private Sub AddSubdirs(ByVal node As ComctlLib.node)
        ' Add all the subdirectories under a Node.
```

```
    Dim fld As Scripting.Folder
    Dim nd As Node
    ' The path in the Node is held in its key property, so it's easy
    ' to cycle on all its subdirectories.
    For Each fld In FSO.GetFolder(node.Key).SubFolders
        Set nd = tvwDir.Nodes.Add(node, tvwChild, fld.Path, fld.Name, 3)
        nd.ExpandedImage = 4
        ' If this directory has subfolders, add a plus sign.
        If fld.SubFolders.Count Then AddDummyChild nd
    Next
End Sub
```

Even if this code can be used only for loading and displaying a directory tree, you can easily modify it to work with any other type of data that you want to load on demand into a TreeView control.

A great way to use this technique is for browsing databases in a hierarchical format. Take the ubiquitous Biblio.Mdb as an example: You can load all the publishers' names in the TreeView control and show their related titles only when the user expands a Node. This is much faster than preloading all the data in the control and offers a clear view of how records are related. I've provided a sample program that uses this technique on the companion CD.

Searching the Nodes collection

When you need to extract information from a TreeView control, you have to search the Nodes collection. In most cases, however, you can't simply scan it from the first to the last item because this order would reflect the sequence in which Node objects were added to the collection and doesn't take into account the relationships among them.

To let you visit all the items in a TreeView control in a hierarchical order, each Node object exposes a number of properties that return references to its relatives. We have already seen the *Child* property, which returns a reference to the first child, and the *Children* property, which returns the number of child Nodes. The *Next* property returns a reference to the next Node at the same level (the next sibling Node), and the *Previous* property returns a reference to the previous Node at the same level (the previous sibling Node). The *FirstSibling* and the *LastSibling* properties return a reference to the first and last Node, respectively, that are at the same level as the Node being examined. Finally the *Parent* property returns a reference to the Node object one level above, and the *Root* property returns a reference to the root of the hierarchy tree that the Node being queried belongs to. (Remember, there can be multiple root Nodes.) You can use these properties to test where a given Node appears in the hierarchy. Here are a few examples:

```
' Check whether a Node has no children (two possible approaches).
If Node.Children = 0 Then MsgBox "Has no children"
If Node.Child Is Nothing Then MsgBox "Has no children"
```

(continued)

```
' Check whether a Node is the first child of its parent (two approaches).
If Node.Previous Is Nothing Then MsgBox "First Child"
If Node.FirstSibling Is Node Then MsgBox "First Child"
' Check whether a Node is the last child of its parent (two approaches).
If Node.Next Is Nothing Then MsgBox "Last Child"
If Node.LastSibling Is Node Then MsgBox "Last Child"
' Check whether a Node is the root of its own tree (two approaches).
If Node.Parent Is Nothing Then MsgBox "Root Node"
If Node.Root Is Node Then MsgBox "Root Node"
' Get a reference to the first root Node in the control.
Set RootNode = TreeView1.Nodes(1).Root.FirstSibling
```

Not surprisingly, the majority of routines you write to search the Nodes collection are recursive. Typically, you start with a Node object, get a reference to its first child Node, and then recursively call the routine for all its children. The following routine is an example of this technique. Its purpose is to build a text string that represents the contents of a TreeView control or of one of its subtrees. Each line in the string represents a Node object, indented with 0 or more tab characters that reflect the corresponding nesting level. The routine can return a string for all the Nodes or for just the items that are actually visible (that is, those whose parents are expanded):

```
' Convert the contents of a TreeView control into a string.
' If a Node is provided, it only searches a subtree.
' If last argument is False or omitted, all items are included.
Function TreeViewToString(TV As TreeView, Optional StartNode As Node, _
    Optional OnlyVisible As Boolean) As String
    Dim nd As Node, childND As Node
    Dim res As String, i As Long
    Static Level As Integer

    ' Exit if there are no Nodes to search.
    If TV.Nodes.Count = 0 Then Exit Function
    ' If StartNode is omitted, start from the first root Node.
    If StartNode Is Nothing Then
        Set nd = TV.Nodes(1).Root.FirstSibling
    Else
        Set nd = StartNode
    End If

    ' Output the starting Node.
    res = String$(Level, vbTab) & nd.Text & vbCrLf
    ' Then call this routine recursively to output all child Nodes.
    ' If OnlyVisible = True, do this only if this Node is expanded.
    If nd.Children And (nd.Expanded Or OnlyVisible = False) Then
        Level = Level + 1
        Set childND = nd.Child
        For i = 1 To nd.Children
```

```
                res = res & TreeViewToString(TV, childND, OnlyVisible)
                Set childND = childND.Next
        Next
        Level = Level - 1
    End If

    ' If searching the whole tree, we must account for multiple roots.
    If StartNode Is Nothing Then
        Set nd = nd.Next
        Do Until nd Is Nothing
            res = res & TreeViewToString(TV, nd, OnlyVisible)
            Set nd = nd.Next
        Loop
    End If
    TreeViewToString = res
End Function
```

Figure 10-9 shows a demonstration program that uses this routine and the resulting string loaded into Notepad. You can embellish the *TreeViewToString* procedure in many ways. For instance, you can create a routine that prints the contents of a TreeView control (including all connecting lines, bitmaps, and so on). Using a similar approach, you can build a routine that saves and restores the current state of a TreeView control, including the *Expanded* attribute of all Node objects.

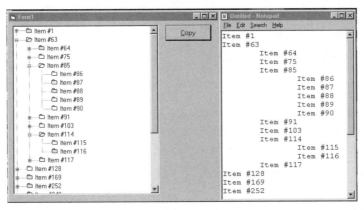

Figure 10-9. *A demonstration program that uses the* TreeViewToString *routine.*

Implementing drag-and-drop

Another common operation that you might want to perform on TreeView controls is drag-and-drop, typically to copy or move a portion of a hierarchy. Implementing a drag-and-drop routine isn't simple, though. First you have to understand which Node the drag operation starts and ends on, and then you have to physically copy or move a portion of the Nodes collection. You must also prevent incorrect operations, as Windows Explorer does when you try to drag a directory onto one of its subfolders.

The TreeView control does offer a few properties and methods that are particularly useful for implementing a drag-and-drop routine. You can use the *HitTest* method to determine which Node object is located at a given pair of coordinates. (Typically, you use this method in a *MouseDown* event to pinpoint the source Node of the drag operation.) During the drag operation, you use the *DropHighlight* property to highlight the Node that's under the mouse cursor so that you can provide the user with a clue to the potential target Node of the operation.

Figure 10-10 shows a demonstration program, provided on the companion CD, that lets you experiment with drag-and-drop between TreeView controls or within the same TreeView control. The two controls on the form belong to a control array, so the same code works whichever is the source or the target control.

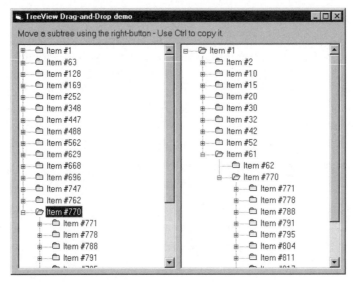

Figure 10-10. *You can use drag-and-drop to move or copy subtrees between controls or even within the same TreeView control.*

As usual, the drag operation is started in the *MouseDown* event procedure:

```
' The source control
Dim SourceTreeView As TreeView
' The source Node object
Dim SourceNode As Node
' The state of Shift key during the drag-and-drop operation
Dim ShiftState As Integer

Private Sub TreeView1_MouseDown(Index As Integer, _
    Button As Integer, Shift As Integer, x As Single, y As Single)
    ' Check whether we are starting a drag operation.
```

```
    If Button <> 2 Then Exit Sub
    ' Set the Node being dragged, or exit if there is none.
    Set SourceNode = TreeView1(Index).HitTest(x, y)
    If SourceNode Is Nothing Then Exit Sub
    ' Save values for later.
    Set SourceTreeView = TreeView1(Index)
    ShiftState = Shift
    ' Start the drag operation.
    TreeView1(Index).OLEDrag
End Sub
```

The *OLEStartDrag* event procedure is where you decide whether you're moving or copying items, depending on the state of the Ctrl key:

```
Private Sub TreeView1_OLEStartDrag(Index As Integer, _
    Data As MSComctlLib.DataObject, AllowedEffects As Long)
    ' Pass the Key property of the Node being dragged.
    ' (This value is not used; we can actually pass anything.)
    Data.SetData SourceNode.Key
    If ShiftState And vbCtrlMask Then
        AllowedEffects = vbDropEffectCopy
    Else
        AllowedEffects = vbDropEffectMove
    End If
End Sub
```

In the *OLEDragOver* event procedure, you offer feedback to the user by highlighting the Node under the mouse in the target control. (The source and the target controls might coincide.)

```
Private Sub TreeView1_OLEDragOver(Index As Integer, _
    Data As MSComctlLib.DataObject, Effect As Long, Button As Integer, _
    Shift As Integer, x As Single, y As Single, State As Integer)
    ' Highlight the Node the mouse is over.
    Set TreeView1(Index).DropHighlight = TreeView1(Index).HitTest(x, y)
End Sub
```

Finally you have to implement the *OLEDragDrop* routine, which is the most complex of the group. First you must figure out whether the mouse is over a Node in the target control. If so, the source Node becomes a child of the target Node; otherwise, the source Node becomes a root Node in the target control. If the source and target controls coincide, you must also ensure that the target Node isn't a child or grandchild of the source Node, which would trap you in an endless loop.

```
Private Sub TreeView1_OLEDragDrop(Index As Integer, _
    Data As MSComctlLib.DataObject, Effect As Long, Button As Integer, _
    Shift As Integer, x As Single, y As Single)
    Dim dest As Node, nd As Node
```

(continued)

```
    ' Get the target Node.
    Set dest = TreeView1(Index).DropHighlight

    If dest Is Nothing Then
        ' Add the Node as the root of the target TreeView control.
        Set nd = TreeView1(Index).Nodes.Add(, , , SourceNode.Text, _
            SourceNode.Image)
    Else
        ' Check that the destination isn't a descendant of the source
        ' Node.
        If SourceTreeView Is TreeView1(Index) Then
            Set nd = dest
            Do
                If nd Is SourceNode Then
                    MsgBox "Unable to drag Nodes here", vbExclamation
                    Exit Sub
                End If
                Set nd = nd.Parent
            Loop Until nd Is Nothing
        End If
        Set nd = TreeView1(Index).Nodes.Add(dest.Index, tvwChild, , _
            SourceNode.Text, SourceNode.Image)
    End If
    nd.ExpandedImage = 2: nd.Expanded = True

    ' Copy the subtree from source to target control.
    CopySubTree SourceTreeView, SourceNode, TreeView1(Index), nd
    ' If this is a move operation, delete the source subtree.
    If Effect = vbDropEffectMove Then
        SourceTreeView.Nodes.Remove SourceNode.Index
    End If
    Set TreeView1(Index).DropHighlight = Nothing
End Sub
```

The *CopySubTree* recursive procedure performs the actual Copy command. (A move operation consists of a copy operation followed by a delete operation.) It accepts a reference to source and target TreeView controls, so you can easily recycle it in other applications:

```
Sub CopySubTree(SourceTV As TreeView, sourceND As Node, _
    DestTV As TreeView, destND As Node)
    ' Copy or move all children of a Node to another Node.
    Dim i As Long, so As Node, de As Node
    If sourceND.Children = 0 Then Exit Sub
```

```
    Set so = sourceND.Child
    For i = 1 To sourceND.Children
        ' Add a Node in the destination TreeView control.
        Set de = DestTV.Nodes.Add(destND, tvwChild, , so.Text, _
            so.Image, so.SelectedImage)
        de.ExpandedImage = so.ExpandedImage
        ' Now add all the children of this Node in a recursive manner.
        CopySubTree SourceTV, so, DestTV, de
        ' Get a reference to the next sibling.
        Set so = so.Next
    Next
End Sub
```

You don't need a recursive procedure to delete a subtree because if you delete a Node object, all its child nodes are automatically deleted too.

THE LISTVIEW CONTROL

Together with the TreeView control, the ListView control has been made popular by Windows Explorer. Now many Windows applications use this pair of controls side by side, and they're therefore called Windows Explorer–like applications. In these applications, the end user selects a Node in the TreeView control on the left and sees some information related to it in the rightmost ListView control.

The ListView control supports four basic view modes: Icon, SmallIcon, List, and Report. To see how each mode is rendered, try the corresponding items in the Windows Explorer View menu. (The Report mode corresponds to the Details menu command.) To give you an idea of the flexibility of this control, you should know that the Windows desktop is nothing but a large ListView control in Icon mode with a transparent background. When used in Report mode, the ListView control resembles a grid control and lets you display well-organized information about each item.

The Visual Basic 6 version of the ListView control has many new features. It can display icons in column headers and grid cells; it supports hot tracking, full row selection, and reordering of columns; and its items can have independent *Bold* and *Color* attributes. The new ListView control can also show a background bitmap, grid lines, and check boxes beside each item.

The ListView control exposes two distinct collections: The ListItems collection comprises individual ListItem objects, each one corresponding to an item in the control, whereas the ColumnHeaders collection includes ColumnHeader objects that affect the appearance of the individual headers visible in Report mode. A third collection, ListSubItems, contains data for all the cells displayed in Report mode.

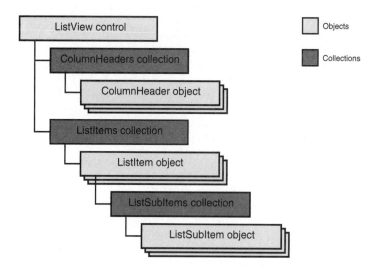

Setting Design-Time Properties

While you can use the regular Properties window to set most properties of a ListView control, it's surely preferable to use a ListView control's custom Properties dialog box, shown in Figure 10-11.

Figure 10-11. *The General tab of the Properties dialog box of a ListView control.*

General properties

I've already referred to the *View* property, which can be one of the following values: 0-lvwIcon, 1-lvwSmallIcon, 2-lvwList, or 3-lvwReport. You can change this property at run time as well as let the user change it (typically by offering four options in the View menu of your application). The *Arrange* property lets you decide whether icons are automatically aligned to the left of the control (1-lvwAutoLeft) or to the top of the control (2-lvwAutoTop), or whether they shouldn't be aligned at all (0-lvwNone, the default behavior). This property takes effect only when the control is in Icon or SmallIcon display mode.

The *LabelEdit* property determines whether the user can edit the text associated with an item in the control. If this property is set to 0-lvwAutomatic, the edit operation can be initiated only by code using a *StartLabelEdit* method. The *LabelWrap* Boolean property specifies whether longer labels wrap on multiple lines of text when in Icon mode. The *HideColumnHeaders* Boolean property determines whether column headers are visible when in Report mode. (The default value is False, which makes the columns visible.) If you assign the *MultiSelect* property the True value, the ListView control behaves much like a ListBox control whose *MultiSelect* property has been set to 2-Extended.

A few properties are new to Visual Basic 6. If you set *AllowColumnReorder* to True, users can reorder columns by dragging their headers when the control is in Report mode. You can change the appearance of the ListView control by setting the *GridLines* property to True (thus adding horizontal and vertical lines). The third new property designed to change the appearance of the ListView control, the *FlatScrollBar* property, seems to be buggy: If you set it to True, the scroll bars don't show. The ListView control shares a few new properties with the TreeView control. I've already described the *Checkboxes* property (which lets you display a check box beside each item) and the *FullRowSelect* property (for highlighting entire rows instead of a row's first item only). The *HotTracking* Boolean property, if True, changes the appearance of an item when the user moves the mouse cursor over it. The *HoverSelection* Boolean property, if True, lets you select an item by simply moving the mouse cursor over it. See Figure 10-12 for an example of what you can get with these new properties.

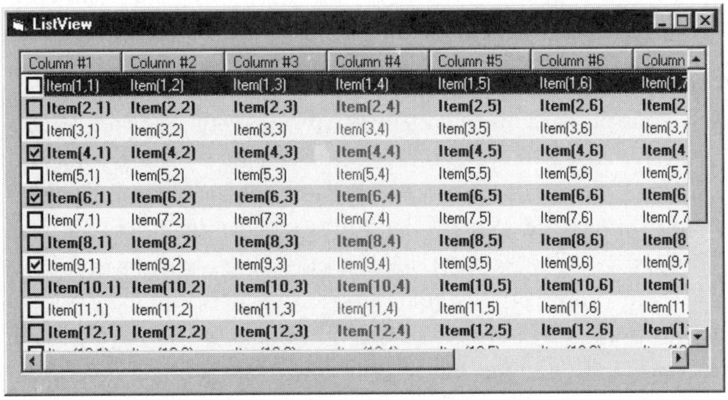

Figure 10-12. *A gallery of new features of ListView controls: Check boxes, grid lines, and* Bold *and* ForeColor *properties for individual items. The alternate row effect is achieved by means of a tiled background picture.*

You can associate up to three ImageList subsidiaries with a ListView control: The first ImageList is used when the control is in Icon mode, the second is used when the control is in any other display mode, and the third is used for icons in column headers. You can set these associated ImageList controls at design time in the Image Lists tab of the Properties dialog box, or you can set them at run time by assigning an ImageList control to the ListView's *Icons*, *SmallIcons*, and *ColumnHeaderIcons* properties, respectively.

The *ColumnHeaders* property is new to Visual Basic 6 because previous versions of the ListView control didn't support icons in column headers:

```
' You can use the same ImageList control for different properties.
Set ListView1.Icons = ImageList1
Set ListView1.SmallIcons = ImageList2
Set ListView1.ColumnHeaderIcons = ImageList2
```

You can automatically sort the items in the ListView control by setting a few properties in the Sorting tab of the Properties dialog box. Set the *Sorted* property to True if you want to sort items. *SortKey* is the index of the column that will be used for sorting (0 for the first column), and *SortOrder* is the sorting order (0-lvwAscending or 1-lvwDescending). You can also set these properties at run time.

Column headers

You can create one or more ColumnHeader objects at design time by using the Column Header tab of the Properties dialog box. You just have to click on the Insert Column button and then type the values of the *Text* property (which will be displayed in the header), the *Alignment* property (Left, Right, or Center, although the first column header can only be left-aligned), and the *Width* in twips. You can also specify a value for the *Key* and *Tag* properties and set the index of the icon to be used for this header. (It's an index referred to by the *ColumnHeaderIcons* property in the ImageList control, or it's 0 if this column header doesn't have any icons.)

Background image

The ListView control that comes with Visual Basic 6 supports a background bitmap. You can load an image into the control at design time by using the Picture tab of the Properties dialog box and then selecting the *Picture* property in the leftmost list box. You can load an image in any format supported by the PictureBox control. Two additional properties affect how a background image is displayed in the control, but you can set them only in the regular Properties window. The *PictureAlignment* property lets you align the image in one of the four corners of the control, center it, or tile it to spread over the entire control's internal area. The *TextBackground* property determines whether the background of ListView's items is transparent (0-lvwTransparent, the default value) or not (1-lvwOpaque); in the latter case, the background image will be visible only in the area not occupied by ListItem objects.

The background image offers a great method for displaying rows with alternate background colors, as shown in Figure 10-12. All you have to do is create a bitmap as tall as two rows and then set *PictureAlignment* = 5-lvwTile and *TextBackground* = 0-lvwTransparent.

Run-Time Operations

While you can define the appearance of a ListView control at design time, you can fill it with data only through code. In this section, I'll show how to add and manipulate data for this control.

Adding ListItem objects

You add new items to the ListView controls with the ListItems collection's *Add* method, which has the following syntax:

```
Add([Index], [Key], [Text], [Icon], [SmallIcon]) As ListItem
```

Index is the position at which you place the new item. (If you omit *Index*, the item is added to the end of the collection.) *Key* is the inserted item's optional key in the ListItems collection, *Text* is the string displayed in the control, *Icon* is an index or a key in the ImageList control pointed to by the *Icons* property, and *SmallIcon* is an index or a key in the ImageList control pointed to by the *SmallIcons* property. All these arguments are optional.

The *Add* method returns a reference to the ListItem object being created, which you can use to set those properties whose values can't be passed to the *Add* method itself, as in the following example:

```
' Create a new item with a "ghosted" appearance.
Dim li As ListItem
Set li = ListView1.ListItems.Add(, , "First item", 1)
li.Ghosted = True
```

ListItem objects support a number of new properties. The *Bold* and *ForeColor* properties affect the boldface and color attributes of the objects. The *ToolTipText* property allows you to define a different ToolTip for each item, and the *Checked* property sets or returns the state of the check box beside the item (if the ListView's *Checkboxes* property is True). When you have to assign multiple properties, you can use a *With* clause with the *Add* method:

```
With ListView1.ListItems.Add(, , "John Ross", 1)
    .Bold = True
    .ForeColor = vbRed
    .ToolTipText = "Manager of the Sales Dept."
End With
```

When working with ListView controls whose *MultiSelect* property is True, the user can select multiple items by clicking on them while pressing the Ctrl or the Shift key. You can modify the selection state of a ListItem object via code by assigning the appropriate value to the *Selected* property. With such ListView controls, you must also assign the *SelectedItem* property to make a ListItem the current item:

```
' Make the first ListItem object the current one.
Set ListView1.SelectedItem = ListView1.ListItems(1)
' Select it.
ListView1.ListItems(1).Selected = True
```

Adding ColumnHeaders objects

Often you don't know at design time what columns should be displayed in a ListView control. For example, you might be showing the result of a user-defined query, in which case you don't know the number and the names of the fields involved. In such circumstances, you must create ColumnHeader objects at run time with the *Add* method of the ColumnHeaders collection, which has this syntax:

```
Add([Index], [Key], [Text], [Width], [Alignment], [Icon]) _
    As ColumnHeader
```

Index is the position in the collection, *Key* is an optional key, *Text* is the string displayed in the header, and *Width* is the column's width in twips. *Alignment* is one of the following constants: 0-lvwColumnLeft, 1-lvwColumnRight, or 2-lvwColumnCenter. *Icon* is an index or a key in the ListImage control referenced by the *ColumnHeaderIcons* property. With the exception of the *Tag* property, these are the only properties that can be assigned when a ColumnHeader object is created, so you can usually discard the return value of the *Add* method:

```
' Clear any existing column header.
ListView1.ColumnHeaders.Clear
' The alignment for the first column header must be lvwColumnLeft.
ListView1.ColumnHeaders.Add , , "Last Name", 2000, lvwColumnLeft
ListView1.ColumnHeaders.Add , , "First Name", 2000, lvwColumnLeft
ListView1.ColumnHeaders.Add , , "Salary", 1500, lvwColumnRight
```

Adding ListSubItems

Each ListItem object supports a ListSubItems collection, which lets you create values displayed in the same row as the main ListItem object when the control is in Report mode. This collection replaces the *SubItems* array that was present in previous versions of the control. (The array is still supported for backward compatibility.) You can create new ListSubItem objects using the *Add* method of the ListSubItems collection:

```
Add([Index], [Key], [Text], [ReportIcon], [ToolTipText]) _
    As ListSubItem
```

Index is the position in the collection of the new item, *Key* is its optional key, *Text* is the string that will be displayed in the grid cell, *ReportIcon* is the index or the key of an icon in the ImageList control referenced by the *SmallIcons* property, and *ToolTipText* is the text of a ToolTip that appears when the user keeps the mouse hovering over this item. You can also assign individual *Bold* and *ForeColor* attributes to each ListSubItem:

```
' This ListItem goes under ColumnHeader(1).
With ListView1.ListItems.Add(, , "Ross", 1)
    .Bold = True
    ' This ListSubItem goes under ColumnHeader(2).
    With .ListSubItems.Add(, , "John")
        .Bold = True
    End With
    ' This ListSubItem goes under ColumnHeader(3).
    With .ListSubItems.Add(, , "80,000")
        .Bold = True
        .ForeColor = vbRed
    End With
End With
```

ListSubItem objects are actually displayed only if the ListView control is in Report mode and only if there are enough ColumnHeader objects. For example, if the ColumnHeaders collection includes only three elements, the ListView control will display only up to three items in each row. Because the leftmost ColumnHeader object is located above ListItem elements, only the first two elements in the ListSubItems collection will be visible.

ListSubItem objects also support the *Tag* property, which you can use to store additional information associated with the items.

Loading data from databases

The ListView control can't be automatically bound to a database through Data, RemoteData, or an ADO Data control. In other words, if you want to load database data into this control you're on your own. The task of filling a ListView control with data read from a recordset isn't conceptually difficult, but you have to account for a few details. First you must retrieve the list of fields contained in the recordset and create a corresponding number of ColumnHeader objects of a suitable width. You also have to discard fields that can't be displayed in ListView controls (for example, BLOB fields), and you must determine the best alignment for each field (to the right for numbers and dates, to the left for all others). A routine that does all this, which you can easily reuse in your applications, is shown on the following page.

```
Sub LoadListViewFromRecordset(LV As ListView, rs As ADODB.Recordset, _
    Optional MaxRecords As Long)
    Dim fld As ADODB.Field, alignment As Integer
    Dim recCount As Long, i As Long, fldName As String
    Dim li As ListItem

    ' Clear the contents of the ListView control.
    LV.ListItems.Clear
    LV.ColumnHeaders.Clear
    ' Create the ColumnHeader collection.
    For Each fld In rs.Fields
        ' Filter out undesired field types.
        Select Case fld.Type
            Case adBoolean, adCurrency, adDate, adDecimal, adDouble
                alignment = lvwColumnRight
            Case adInteger, adNumeric, adSingle, adSmallInt, adVarNumeric
                alignment = lvwColumnRight
            Case adBSTR, adChar, adVarChar, adVariant
                alignment = lvwColumnLeft
            Case Else
                alignment = -1       ' This means "Unsupported field type".
        End Select
        ' If field type is OK, create a column with the correct alignment.
        If alignment <> -1 Then
            ' The first column must be left-aligned.
            If LV.ColumnHeaders.Count = 0 Then alignment = lvwColumnLeft
            LV.ColumnHeaders.Add , , fld.Name, fld.DefinedSize * 200, _
                alignment
        End If
    Next
    ' Exit if there are no fields that can be shown.
    If LV.ColumnHeaders.Count = 0 Then Exit Sub

    ' Add all the records in the recordset.
    rs.MoveFirst
    Do Until rs.EOF
        recCount = recCount + 1
        ' Add the main ListItem object.
        fldName = LV.ColumnHeaders(1).Text
        Set li = LV.ListItems.Add(, , rs.Fields(fldName) & "")
        ' Add all subsequent ListSubItem objects.
        For i = 2 To LV.ColumnHeaders.Count
            fldName = LV.ColumnHeaders(i)
            li.ListSubItems.Add , , rs.Fields(fldName) & ""
        Next
        If recCount = MaxRecords Then Exit Do
        rs.MoveNext
    Loop
End Sub
```

The *LoadListViewFromRecordset* routine expects an ADO Recordset and an optional *MaxRecords* argument that lets you limit the number of records displayed. This is necessary, because—as opposed to what happens with bound controls, which load only the information that is actually displayed—this routine reads all the rows in the recordset, which might be a lengthy process. I suggest that you set *MaxRecords* to 100 or 200, depending on the type of connection you have to your database and the speed of your CPU.

Another problem you face when loading data from a database is that you might need to manually adjust the width of each column. The *LoadListViewFromRecordset* routine initializes the width of all ColumnHeader objects using the fields' maximum width, but in most cases values stored in database fields are considerably shorter than this value. Instead of leaving the burden of the manual resizing on your users, you can change all columns' width programmatically using the following routine:

```
Sub ListViewAdjustColumnWidth(LV As ListView, _
    Optional AccountForHeaders As Boolean)
    Dim row As Long, col As Long
    Dim width As Single, maxWidth As Single
    Dim saveFont As StdFont, saveScaleMode As Integer, cellText As String
    ' Exit if there aren't any items.
    If LV.ListItems.Count = 0 Then Exit Sub

    ' Save the font used by the parent form, and enforce ListView's
    ' font. (We need this in order to use the form's TextWidth
    ' method.)
    Set saveFont = LV.Parent.Font
    Set LV.Parent.Font = LV.Font
    ' Enforce ScaleMode = vbTwips for the parent.
    saveScaleMode = LV.Parent.ScaleMode
    LV.Parent.ScaleMode = vbTwips

    For col = 1 To LV.ColumnHeaders.Count
        maxWidth = 0
        If AccountForHeaders Then
            maxWidth = LV.Parent.TextWidth(LV.ColumnHeaders(col).Text)+200
        End If
        For row = 1 To LV.ListItems.Count
            ' Retrieve the text string from ListItems or ListSubItems.
            If col = 1 Then
                cellText = LV.ListItems(row).Text
            Else
                cellText = LV.ListItems(row).ListSubItems(col - 1).Text
            End If
```

(continued)

```
            ' Calculate its width, and account for margins.
            ' Note: doesn't account for multiple-line text fields.
            width = LV.Parent.TextWidth(cellText) + 200
            ' Update maxWidth if we've found a larger string.
            If width > maxWidth Then maxWidth = width
        Next
        ' Change the column's width.
        LV.ColumnHeaders(col).width = maxWidth
    Next
    ' Restore parent form's properties.
    Set LV.Parent.Font = saveFont
    LV.Parent.ScaleMode = saveScaleMode
End Sub
```

To determine the optimal width of all the values stored in a given column, the *ListViewAdjustColumnWidth* routine evaluates the maximum width of all the strings stored in that column. The problem is that the ListView control doesn't support the *TextWidth* method, so the routine relies on the *TextWidth* method exposed by the control's parent form. If a True value is passed in the second argument, the routine also accounts for the *Text* property of all ColumnHeader objects, so no header title is truncated.

The ListView control already allows you to automatically resize columns to fit their contents, even though this capability hasn't been exposed in the Visual Basic ActiveX control. In fact, you can interactively resize a column to fit the longest item it contains by double-clicking on its right border in the column header (as you would in the Details view mode of Windows Explorer). In the demonstration program on the companion CD, you'll find another version of the *ListViewAdjustColumnWidth* routine that does the resizing by using API calls instead of plain Visual Basic code. The following code sample shows how to use the *ListViewAdjustColumnWidth* routine to display all the records in the Orders table of the NorthWind.Mdb database, as shown in Figure 10-13:

```
Private Sub Form_Load()
    Dim cn As New ADODB.Connection, rs As New ADODB.Recordset
    ' WARNING: you might need to modify the DB path in the next line.
    cn.Open "Provider=Microsoft.Jet.OLEDB.3.51;" _
        & "Data Source=C:\VisStudio\VB98\NWind.mdb"
    rs.Open "Orders", cn, adOpenForwardOnly, adLockReadOnly
    LoadListViewFromRecordset ListView1, rs
    ListViewAdjustColumnWidth ListView1, True
End Sub
```

On my 233-MHz machine, this code takes about 15 seconds to complete, which is more than most customers are willing to wait. Therefore, you should use this technique judiciously and set an upper limit to the number of records that are read from a database.

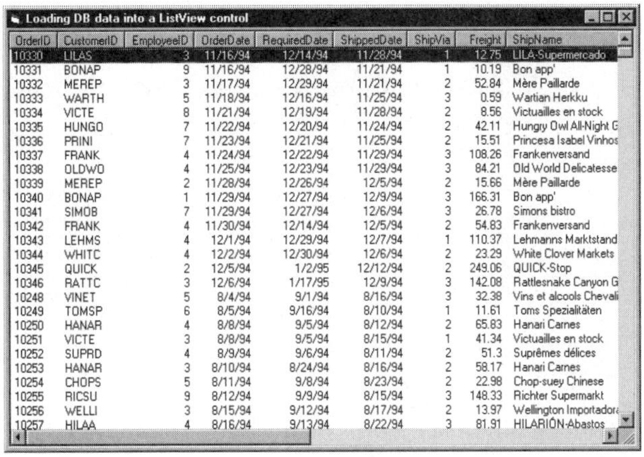

OrderID	CustomerID	EmployeeID	OrderDate	RequiredDate	ShippedDate	ShipVia	Freight	ShipName
10330	LILAS	3	11/16/94	12/14/94	11/28/94	1	12.75	LILA-Supermercado
10331	BONAP	9	11/16/94	12/28/94	11/21/94	1	10.19	Bon app'
10332	MEREP	3	11/17/94	12/29/94	11/21/94	2	52.84	Mère Paillarde
10333	WARTH	5	11/18/94	12/16/94	11/25/94	3	0.59	Wartian Herkku
10334	VICTE	8	11/21/94	12/19/94	11/28/94	2	8.56	Victuailles en stock
10335	HUNGO	7	11/22/94	12/20/94	11/24/94	2	42.11	Hungry Owl All-Night G
10336	PRINI	7	11/23/94	12/21/94	11/25/94	2	15.51	Princesa Isabel Vinhos
10337	FRANK	4	11/24/94	12/22/94	11/29/94	3	108.26	Frankenversand
10338	OLDWO	4	11/25/94	12/23/94	11/29/94	3	84.21	Old World Delicatesse
10339	MEREP	2	11/28/94	12/26/94	12/5/94	2	15.66	Mère Paillarde
10340	BONAP	1	11/29/94	12/27/94	12/9/94	3	166.31	Bon app'
10341	SIMOB	7	11/29/94	12/27/94	12/6/94	3	26.78	Simons bistro
10342	FRANK	4	11/30/94	12/14/94	12/5/94	2	54.83	Frankenversand
10343	LEHMS	4	12/1/94	12/29/94	12/7/94	1	110.37	Lehmanns Marktstand
10344	WHITC	4	12/2/94	12/30/94	12/6/94	2	23.29	White Clover Markets
10345	QUICK	2	12/5/94	1/2/95	12/12/94	2	249.06	QUICK-Stop
10346	RATTC	3	12/6/94	1/17/95	12/9/94	3	142.08	Rattlesnake Canyon G
10248	VINET	5	8/4/94	9/1/94	8/16/94	3	32.38	Vins et alcools Chevali
10249	TOMSP	6	8/5/94	9/16/94	8/10/94	1	11.61	Toms Spezialitäten
10250	HANAR	4	8/8/94	9/5/94	8/12/94	2	65.83	Hanari Carnes
10251	VICTE	3	8/8/94	9/5/94	8/15/94	1	41.34	Victuailles en stock
10252	SUPRD	4	8/9/94	9/6/94	8/11/94	2	51.3	Suprêmes délices
10253	HANAR	3	8/10/94	8/24/94	8/16/94	2	58.17	Hanari Carnes
10254	CHOPS	5	8/11/94	9/8/94	8/23/94	2	22.98	Chop-suey Chinese
10255	RICSU	9	8/12/94	9/9/94	8/15/94	3	148.33	Richter Supermarkt
10256	WELLI	3	8/15/94	9/12/94	8/17/94	2	13.97	Wellington Importador
10257	HILAA	4	8/16/94	9/13/94	8/22/94	3	81.91	HILARIÓN-Abastos

Figure 10-13. *This demonstration program loads NorthWind's Orders table into a ListView control and lets you sort on any field by clicking on the corresponding column's header.*

Sorting and reordering columns

I already explained how you can define a sort key and a sort order at design time. You can get the same effect at run time by setting the *Sorted*, *SortKey*, and *SortOrder* properties. Usually you do this when the end user clicks on a column header, an action that you can trap in the *ColumnClick* event:

```
Private Sub ListView1_ColumnClick(ByVal ColumnHeader As _
    MSComctlLib.ColumnHeader)
    ListView1.SortKey = ColumnHeader.Index - 1
    ListView1.Sorted = True
End Sub
```

Things are slightly more complicated if you want to offer the ability to sort in either direction: The first click sorts in ascending order, and the second click sorts in descending order. In this case, you must check to see whether the column being clicked is already sorted:

```
Private Sub ListView1_ColumnClick(ByVal ColumnHeader As _
    MSComctlLib.ColumnHeader)
    ' Sort according to data in this column.
    If ListView1.Sorted And _
        ColumnHeader.Index - 1 = ListView1.SortKey Then
        ' Already sorted on this column, just invert the sort order.
        ListView1.SortOrder = 1 - ListView1.SortOrder
    Else
        ListView1.SortOrder = lvwAscending
        ListView1.SortKey = ColumnHeader.Index - 1
    End If
    ListView1.Sorted = True
End Sub
```

The ListView control is able to sort string data exclusively. If you want to sort on columns that hold numeric or date information, you must resort to a trick. Create a new ColumnHeader object, fill it with string data derived from the numbers or dates you want to sort on, sort on that column, and finally delete those items. Here's a reusable routine that does all this for you:

```
Sub ListViewSortOnNonStringField(LV As ListView, ByVal ColumnIndex As _
    Integer, SortOrder As Integer, Optional IsDateValue As Boolean)
    Dim li As ListItem, number As Double, newIndex As Integer

    ' This speeds up things by a factor of 10 or more.
    LV.Visible = False
    LV.Sorted = False
    ' Create a new, hidden field.
    LV.ColumnHeaders.Add , , "dummy column", 1
    newIndex = LV.ColumnHeaders.Count - 1

    For Each li In LV.ListItems
        ' Extract a number from the field.
        If IsDateValue Then
            number = DateValue(li.ListSubItems(ColumnIndex - 1))
        Else
            number = CDbl(li.ListSubItems(ColumnIndex - 1))
        End If
        ' Add a string that can be sorted using the Sorted property.
        li.ListSubItems.Add , , Format$(number, "000000000000000.000")
    Next

    ' Sort on this hidden field.
    LV.SortKey = newIndex
    LV.SortOrder = SortOrder
    LV.Sorted = True
    ' Remove data from the hidden column.
    LV.ColumnHeaders.Remove newIndex + 1
    For Each li In LV.ListItems
        li.ListSubItems.Remove newIndex
    Next
    LV.Visible = True
End Sub
```

You can use the *ListViewSortOnNonStringField* routine from a *ColumnClick* event procedure, as I explained previously. The code I just showed you doesn't work with negative values, but the complete version on the companion CD solves this problem.

TIP When the *Sorted* property is True, insert and remove operations are unbearably long. It's much better to set the *Sorted* property to False, do whatever updates you want, and then reset it to True. Depending on how many items are in the ListView control, you can easily speed up your routines by an order of magnitude.

Columns can be moved and reordered at run time. You can let the user drag a column to a new position by setting the *AllowColumnReorder* property to True. However, you shouldn't do this when your ListView control has the property *Checkboxes* set to True. If the user moves the first column, the control's contents will look pretty unusual because the check boxes will move with the first column.

Reordering columns from your code ensures better control over which columns are moved and where. In this case, you only have to assign a new value to the *Position* property of a ColumnHeader object. For example, you can exchange the position of the first two columns with this code:

```
ListView1.ColumnHeaders(1).Position = ListView1.ColumnHeaders(1).Position _
    + 1
' You need to refresh after reordering one or more columns.
ListView1.Refresh
```

Searching items

You can quickly search for a string in a ListView control using the *FindItem* method, which has this syntax:

```
FindItem(Search, [Where], [Start], [Match]) As ListItem
```

Search is the string being searched. *Where* specifies in which property the string will be searched: 0-lvwText for the *Text* property of ListItem objects, 1-lvwSubItem for the *Text* property of ListSubItem objects, or 2-lvwTag for the *Tag* property of ListItem objects. *Start* is the index or the key of the ListItem object from which the search begins. *Match* can be 0-lvwWholeWord or 1-lvwPartial and defines whether an item that begins with the searched string makes for a successful search. (*Match* can be used only if *Where* = 0-lvwText.)

Note that you can't search in the *Tag* property of ListSubItem objects, nor can you restrict the search to a single column of ListSubItems. All search operations are case insensitive.

Other properties, methods, and events

The ListView control supports properties, methods, and events that are similar to those exposed by the TreeView control, so I won't describe them in detail here.

You can control when the user edits a value in the control using the *Before-LabelEdit* and *AfterLabelEdit* events. Regardless of where the user clicks on the row, the only item that can actually be edited is the one in the leftmost column. If you want to programmatically start an edit operation, you have to make a given ListItem object the selected one and then invoke the *StartLabelEdit* method:

```
ListView1.SetFocus
Set ListView1.SelectedItem = ListView1.ListItems(1)
ListView1.StartLabelEdit
```

If the control's *Checkboxes* property is set to True, you can read and modify the checked state of each row through the *Checked* property of individual ListItem objects. You can trap the action of ticking a check box by writing code in the *ItemCheck* event procedure. Similarly, the *ItemClick* event fires when a ListItem object is clicked.

ListItem objects expose an *EnsureVisible* method that, if necessary, scrolls the contents of the control to move the item into the visible area of the control. You can also query the ListView's *GetFirstVisible* method, which returns a reference to the first visible ListItem object.

The ListView's *HitTest* method returns the ListItem object at the specified coordinates. You typically use this method in drag-and-drop operations together with the *DropHighlight* property, as I explained in the section devoted to the TreeView control. By the way, there's no simple way to determine which column the mouse is on when the control is in Report mode.

THE TOOLBAR CONTROL

The majority of Windows applications include one or more toolbars, which offer the end user the convenience of executing the most common commands with a click of the mouse. Toolbars should never replace menus—and for good reason: menus can be operated with the keyboard; toolbars can't—but they surely make a program more usable and give it a modern look and feel.

Visual Basic comes with a Toolbar control that can contain buttons and other controls and that can be interactively customized by the end user. The Visual Basic 6 version adds the flat style made popular by Microsoft Internet Explorer and the support for building drop-down menus.

The Toolbar control exposes the Buttons collection, which in turn contains Button objects. Each Button object can be an actual push button, a separator, or a placeholder for another control placed on the toolbar (typically a TextBox control or a ComboBox control). In addition, a Button object exposes the ButtonsMenus collection, where each ButtonMenu object is an item of a drop-down menu. (If the Button object isn't a drop-down menu, this collection is empty.)

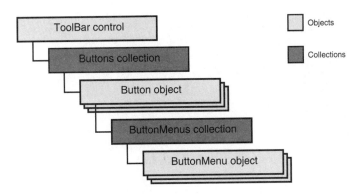

Setting Design-Time Properties

In most cases, you define the appearance of a Toolbar at design time and then simply react to user's clicks on its buttons. You have two ways to work with a Toolbar at design time: by using the Toolbar Wizard or by manually setting properties. The two methods aren't mutually exclusive: In most cases, in fact, you might find it convenient to create a first version of a Toolbar control using the wizard and then refine it in its Properties dialog box.

The Toolbar Wizard

The Toolbar Wizard is a new add-in provided with Visual Basic 6. But you won't find this wizard in the list of installable add-ins in the Add-In Manager dialog box. Instead, you have to install the Application Wizard add-in: After you do this, you'll find the Toolbar Wizard command in the Add-In menu. If you select this command, the wizard adds a new Toolbar control to the current form and lets you customize it. Or you can place a Toolbar control on the form yourself, and the wizard will be automatically activated.

Using the Toolbar Wizard is simple. You have a list of buttons in the leftmost list box (see Figure 10-14 on the following page) from which you select the buttons you want to add to the Toolbar control. You can move items between the two list boxes and change their order in the toolbar by using the provided push buttons, or you can use drag-and-drop. The wizard also creates the companion ImageList control on the form. When you complete a toolbar, you'll be asked whether you want to save it in an .rwp profile file, which lets you speed up the creation of similar toolbars in future applications.

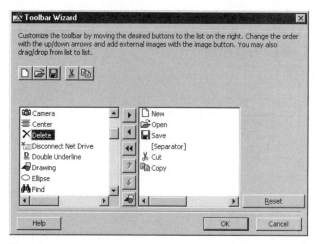

Figure 10-14. *Creating a toolbar using the Toolbar Wizard.*

General properties

After you create a toolbar, you can access its Property Pages by right-clicking on it and choosing Properties. The General tab of the Property Pages dialog box includes most of the design-time properties that let you control the fine points of the appearance and behavior of a Toolbar control, as shown in Figures 10-15 and 10-16. For example, you make the following decisions: Whether the end user can customize the toolbar at run time (*AllowCustomize* property), whether the toolbar will wrap on multiple lines when the form is resized (*Wrappable* property), whether ToolTips are visible (*ShowTips* property), and what the default size of buttons (*ButtonWidth* and *ButtonHeight* properties) is. If necessary, buttons are automatically enlarged to account for their caption or image, so in most cases you don't need to edit the default values of the latter two properties.

A few new properties let you access the most interesting features introduced in Visual Basic 6. You can create flat toolbars by setting the *Style* property to the value 1-tbrFlat, and you can use the *TextAlignment* property to modify the alignment of a button's caption with respect to the button's image (0-tbrTextAlignBottom or 1-tbrTextAlignRight).

A toolbar's button can be in three possible states: normal, disabled, or selected. (The selected state occurs when the mouse passes over the button if *Style* is 1-tbrFlat.) Instead of having three properties to point to different images of the same ImageList control, the Toolbar control uses a different approach: Each Button object exposes only one *Image* property—an index or a string key—and the state of the button implicitly affects which ImageList control will be used. You assign these three ImageList controls to the *ImageList*, *DisabledImageList*, and *HotImageList* properties either at design time or at run time. For example, you can mimic the behavior of Internet Explorer 4 by using a set of black-and-white icons for the normal state and a set of colorful icons for the selected state. If you don't assign the latter two properties, the Toolbar automatically creates a suitable image for the disabled or selected state.

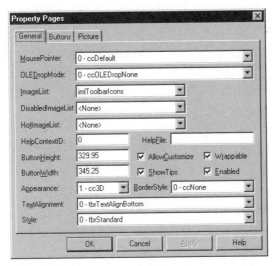

Figure 10-15. *The General tab of the Property Pages dialog box of a Toolbar control.*

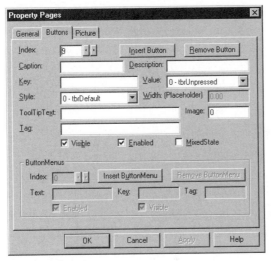

Figure 10-16. *The Buttons tab of the Property Pages dialog box of a Toolbar control.*

Button objects

A Toolbar control without any Button objects is useless. You can add Button objects using the Toolbar Wizard, as I explained previously, or you can do it in the Buttons tab of the Property Pages dialog box, as you can see in Figure 10-16. Each Button has a *Caption* property (use an empty string if you want to display only the icon), an optional *Description* that appears during a customization operation, a *Tag* property, a *Key* in the Buttons collection (optional, but use it to improve the readability of your code), a *ToolTipText* that appears if the Toolbar's *ShowTips* property is True, and an *Image* index or key to the associated ImageList controls.

Style is the most interesting property of a Button object. This property affects the appearance and behavior of the button and can be assigned one of the following values: 0-tbrDefault (a normal button, which behaves like a push button), 1-tbrCheck (a button that stays down when pressed, much like a CheckBox control), 2-tbrButtonGroup (a button that belongs to a group in which only one item can be in the selected state, similar to an OptionButton control), 3-tbrSeparator (a separator of fixed width), 4-tbrPlaceholder (a separator whose size depends on the *Width* property; this style is used to make room for another control placed on the toolbar), or 5-tbrDropDown (a button with a down arrow beside it, which displays a drop-down menu when clicked).

When the *Style* property is set to the value 5-tbrDropDown, you can add one or more ButtonMenu objects to the current Button. (You can create ButtonMenu items regardless of the button's style, but they're visible only when the style is tbrDropDown.) Each ButtonMenu object has a *Text* property (the caption of the menu line), an optional *Key* in the ButtonMenus collection, and a *Tag* property. Unfortunately, you can't associate an image with a ButtonMenu object: Drop-down menus are inherently text-only, which definitely contrasts with the graphical nature of the Toolbar control. See Figure 10-17 for an example of a Toolbar control whose first button has an associated drop-down menu.

Figure 10-17. *A toolbar with a drop-down menu.*

Run-Time Operations

Once you have added a Toolbar control to a form, you have to trap the user's actions on it. You might also need to programmatically build the control at run time or let the user customize it and save the new layout for subsequent sessions.

Creating Button and ButtonMenu objects

You can create new Button objects at run time using the *Add* method of the Buttons collection, which has the following syntax:

```
Add([Index], [Key], [Caption], [Style], [Image]) As Button
```

Index is the position at which the Button object will be inserted in the collection, *Key* is its optional string key, *Caption* is the text visible on the toolbar, *Style* determines the type of the button being added (0-tbrNormal, 1-tbrCheck, 2-tbrButtonGroup, 3-tbrSeparator, 4-tbrPlaceholder, or 5-tbrDropDown), and *Image* is the index or the key of an image in the three companion ImageList controls.

You might want to set a few additional properties when you're creating a Button object, such as *Width* (for placeholder buttons) and *ToolTipText*. Buttons whose style is tbrCheck or tbrButtonGroup can be created in a pressed state by assigning 1-tbrPressed to the *Value* property. Here's an example of code that adds a few buttons:

```
' A button that can be in an on or off state
Dim btn As Button
Set btn = Toolbar1.Buttons.Add(, , , tbrCheck, "Lock")
btn.Value = tbrPressed
' A separator
Toolbar1.Buttons.Add, , , tbrSeparator
' Two buttons that are mutually exclusive
Set btn = Toolbar1.Buttons.Add(, , , tbrButtonGroup, "Green")
Set btn = Toolbar1.Buttons.Add(, , , tbrButtonGroup, "Red")
btn.Value = tbrPressed
```

You can place any control in the toolbar by creating a Button object with the *Style* property set to tbrPlaceholder and then moving the control to the correct position. For example, let's say that you want to place the *cboFontSizes* control in the toolbar:

```
' Create a placeholder of proper width.
Dim btn As Button
Set btn = Toolbar1.Buttons.Add(, , , tbrPlaceholder)
btn.Width = cboFontSizes.Width
' Move the ComboBox control over the placeholder button.
Set cboFontSizes.Container = Toolbar1
cboFontSizes.Move btn.Left, btn.Top
```

If you create a Button object whose *Style* property is tbrDropDown, you can add one or more items to its ButtonMenus collection by using the collection's *Add* method:

```
Add ([Index], [Key], [Text]) As ButtonMenu
```

Index is the position in the collection, *Key* is an optional key, and *Text* is the caption of the menu item. The piece of code at the top of the next page adds one drop-down Button object with a menu of three items.

```
Dim btn As Button
Set btn = Toolbar1.Buttons.Add(, , , tbrDropDown, "New")
With btn.ButtonMenus
    .Add , , "File"
    .Add , , "Document"
    .Add , , "Image"
End With
```

Reacting to a user's actions

When the user clicks on a button, the Toolbar control fires a *ButtonClick* event, so it's easy to execute a piece of code when this happens:

```
Private Sub Toolbar1_ButtonClick(ByVal Button As MSComCtlLib.Button)
    Select Case Button.Key
        Case "New"
            Call mnuFileNew_Click
        Case "Save"
            Call mnuFileSave_Click
        ' And so on.
    End Select
End Sub
```

Visual Basic 6 introduces two new events, both of which are related to drop-down menus. The *ButtonDropDown* event fires when the user opens a drop-down menu. You can use this event to create or modify the menu on the fly—for example, by setting the *Visible* or *Enabled* property of its individual ButtonMenu items or by adding new menu lines:

```
Private Sub Toolbar1_ButtonDropDown(ByVal Button As MSComctlLib.Button)
    ' Make the "Open | Image" command unavailable if necessary.
    If Button.Caption = "Open" Then
        Button.ButtonMenus("Image").Enabled = ImagesAreEnabled
    End If
End Sub
```

The *ButtonMenuClick* event fires when the end user actually selects a command in a drop-down menu:

```
Private Sub Toolbar1_ButtonMenuClick(ByVal ButtonMenu As _
    MSComctlLib.ButtonMenu)
    Select Case ButtonMenu.Key
        Case "Document"
            Call mnuFileNewDocument
        Case "Image"
            Call mnuFileNewImage
    End Select
End Sub
```

Customizing the Toolbar control

You can allow for users to customize the Toolbar control if you want. You can choose from two ways to achieve this: You set the *AllowCustomization* property to True to let users enter customization mode by double-clicking on the toolbar, or you programmatically enter customization mode by executing the Toolbar's *Customize* method. The latter approach is necessary if you want to provide this capability only to a restricted group of users:

```
Private Sub Toolbar1_DblClick()
    If UserIsAdministrator Then Toolbar1.Customize
End Sub
```

Whatever method you choose, you end up displaying the Customize Toolbar dialog box, shown in Figure 10-18.

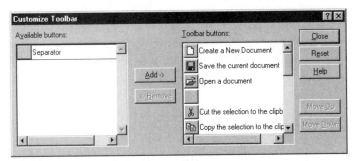

Figure 10-18. *The Customize Toolbar dialog box.*

When the user closes this dialog box, the Toolbar control raises a *Change* event. (Beware: This event occurs even if the user made no changes to the toolbar's layout.) Within this event procedure, you should execute a *SaveToolbar* method, which has the following syntax:

```
SaveToolbar Key, Subkey, Value
```

Key is the name of a Registry key, *SubKey* is the name of a Registry subkey, and *Value* is the name of a Registry value; together, these arguments define a location in the system Registry where the layout of the toolbar is stored. For example, you can use them to save different layouts depending on the application's name, the user currently logged in, and the particular toolbar:

```
Private Sub Toolbar1_Change()
    Toolbar1.SaveToolbar "MyApplication", UserName, "MainFormToolbar"
End Sub
```

You restore these settings using the *RestoreToolbar* method, typically in the *Form_Load* event procedure:

```
Private Sub Form_Load()
    Toolbar1.RestoreToolbar "MyApplication", UserName, "MainFormToolbar"
End Sub
```

> **NOTE** Oddly, the *RestoreToolbar* method raises a *Change* event. This behavior is usually harmless because the code in this event procedure proceeds to save the toolbar again in the Registry (adding just a little overhead to the form-loading process). However, if the Toolbar object's *Change* event procedure contains other, time-consuming statements, they might slow down your code and even cause an unexpected error.

When the Customize Toolbar dialog box is active, users can delete existing buttons, restore buttons that had been previously deleted, or change the order of buttons in the toolbar. If you want to let users add buttons, you must create such buttons at design time, run the application, invoke the Customize Toolbar, and delete these extra buttons. The deleted buttons will be available in the leftmost list box in the Customize Toolbar dialog box in case a user wants to restore them.

THE TABSTRIP CONTROL

Tabbed dialog boxes are standard these days among Windows applications. Visual Basic comes with two controls for implementing them: The TabStrip common control and the SSTab control. In this section, I describe the TabStrip control, whereas Chapter 12 covers the SSTab control.

The most important thing to learn about the TabStrip control is that it *isn't* a container. In other words, it offers a program only the ability to display a number of tabs and react to users' clicks on them. It's up to the developer to make a group of controls visible or invisible, depending on which tab is currently selected. This makes working with this control at design time a tedious job and is probably the reason why many developers prefer the SSTab control, which is a real container control and can swap pages at design time as well. In my opinion, this nuisance is balanced by the fact that TabStrip is more powerful in other areas.

The TabStrip control exposes a Tabs collection, which in turn contains Tab objects. You must be aware of this structure to exploit all the features of this control.

Setting Design-Time Properties

After you place a TabStrip control on a form, you have to set up a few general properties and then add a number of tabs. You can perform both operations from within the Properties custom dialog box, which you display by right-clicking on the control and selecting the Properties menu option.

General properties

You can set all general properties from the General tab of the Property Pages dialog box, as shown in Figure 10-19. The first property you might want to set is *Style*, which lets you change the appearance of the control. In most cases, you leave it with its default value 0-tabTabs (the control is rendered as a collection of tabbed pages), but you can also set it to 1-tabButtons (tabs are replaced by buttons, and no border is displayed) or 2-tabFlatButtons (same as tabButtons, but buttons are flat). In the latter two cases, you can opt for separators among buttons by setting the *Separators* property to True. A few combinations of these styles are visible in Figure 10-20.

The tabFlatButton setting has appeared for the first time in Visual Basic 6, together with the *Separator* property. Other new Visual Basic 6 properties are *TabMinWidth*, *Placement*, *TabStyle*, *HotTracking*, and *MultiSelect*.

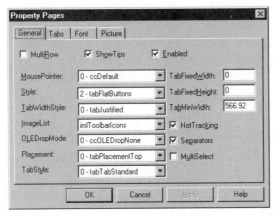

Figure 10-19. *The General tab of the Property Pages dialog box of a TabStrip control.*

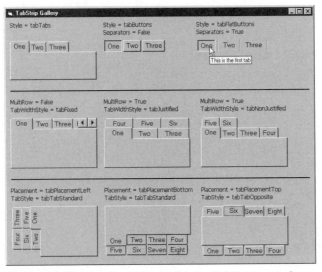

Figure 10-20. *A gallery of styles for the TabStrip control.*

If you're going to add more tabs than can appear in a single line, you can create multiple lines of tabs by setting the *MultiRow* property to True. You can choose different justification styles for the tabs by setting the *TabWidthStyle* property to 0-tabJustified, 1-tabNonJustified, or 2-tabFixed. If you're working with tabs of fixed width, you can assign a suitable value to the *TabFixedWidth* and *TabFixedHeight* properties. If you're working with tabs of variable width, you can set a minimum value for their size using the *TabMinWidth* property.

The *Placement* property lets you decide whether tabs should appear near the top (default), bottom, left, or right border of the control. The *TabStyle* property affects the run-time behavior of TabStrip controls with multiple rows: When you set this property to 1-tabTabOpposite, all the rows that precede the current one are displayed on the opposite side of the control.

A few other design-time Boolean properties can affect the appearance of the control. You can set the *HotTracking* property to True to activate the hot tracking feature (but only if *Style* is tabFlatButtons). If the *Multiselect* property is True, the user can select multiple tabs by clicking on them while pressing the Ctrl key (but only if *Style* is tabButtons or tabFlatButtons). Finally, if the *ShowTips* property is True, the control displays the *ToolTipText* associated with the tab over which the user moves the mouse.

Tab objects

Once you've set the most important general properties, you can create tabs in the Tabs tab (sounds a bit confusing, yes? It's the second tab…) of the Property Pages dialog box. The only property that isn't optional is the *Caption* property. The *Key* property is the value that identifies a tab in the Tabs collection, whereas *Tag* and *ToolTipText* have the usual meanings and effects.

You can display an icon in each tab. To do that, you have to load all the images into a companion ImageList control and then store a reference to this control in the TabStrip's *ImageList* property. At this point, you can assign a Tab's *Image* property the index of the image that should be displayed.

Preparing the child containers

Because the TabStrip control isn't a container control, you can't place child controls directly on its surface. This is probably the most serious limitation of this control: Even if it doesn't affect the control's run-time potential, it surely makes the design-time phase a little cumbersome. At run time, it's up to the programmer to show all the controls on the tab being clicked by the user and hide the child controls belonging to all other tabs.

In practice, the most convenient way to manage the child controls is to create a number of container controls on the form—for example, PictureBox or Frame controls. These controls should belong to a control array so that you can easily manipulate them as a group. It isn't really important where you place these containers on the form because you'll have to move and resize them at run time.

Let's say that you have a TabStrip control with three tabs. You create three PictureBox controls, such as those visible in Figure 10-21, and then place child controls inside each PictureBox. I suggest that you move the containers to different positions so that you can easily select them at design time and bring them to the front using the Ctrl+J key combination. Things are easier if you use containers with visible borders and then hide the borders at run time.

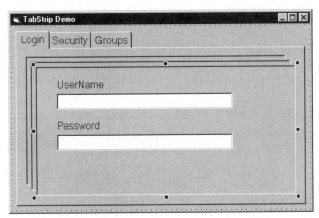

Figure 10-21. *Using PictureBoxes to contain child controls of a TabStrip control.*

Run-Time Operations

In most cases, you use only a fraction of the possibilities offered by the TabStrip control. In fact, the majority of applications just need to show the pages defined at design time and never need to create new ones. In this section, I describe the most common actions you can perform on this control using code.

Moving and resizing containers

If you have followed my advice about using Frame or PictureBox controls as containers for child controls, you need to move and resize them before the form becomes visible. You usually do it in the *Form_Load* event and exploit the properties *ClientLeft*, *ClientTop*, *ClientWidth*, and *ClientHeight* of the TabStrip control to learn where those containers should be moved. You also need to hide containers' borders, if they have any. The following code snippet assumes that all PictureBox container controls belong to the *picTab* control array:

```
Private Sub Form_Load()
    Dim pic As PictureBox
    For Each pic In picTab
        pic.Move TabStrip1.ClientLeft, TabStrip1.ClientTop, _
            TabStrip1.ClientWidth, TabStrip1.ClientHeight
        pic.BorderStyle = 0
    Next
End Sub
```

Selecting the current container

You react to the user's clicks by making the container control—the one that corresponds to the clicked tab—the only visible container. You can learn which tab has been clicked by querying the *SelectedItem* property:

```
Private Sub TabStrip1_Click()
    Dim pic As PictureBox
    For Each pic In picTab
        ' The expression on the right returns True for one picture box.
        ' (Control arrays are zero-based; Selected.Index is one-based.)
        pic.Visible = (pic.Index = TabStrip1.SelectedItem.Index - 1)
    Next
End Sub
```

When the *Click* event fires, the *SelectedItem* property has already been set to the tab that's now current. If you want to keep track of which tab was current before the click, you must store this value in a form-level variable. Alternatively, you can trap the user's action before the *Click* event in the *BeforeClick* event. This event offers the program an opportunity to validate data on the current tab before the user leaves it and possibly to cancel the click. Here's an example of this technique:

```
Private Sub TabStrip1_BeforeClick(Cancel As Integer)
    Select Case TabStrip1.SelectedItem.Index
        Case 1
            ' Refuse to move until the user types something in this field.
            If txtUserName.Text = "" Then Cancel = True
        Case 2
            ' Validation code for second tab
        Case 3
            ' Validation code for third tab
    End Select
End Sub
```

You can also select a tab programmatically, by assigning a value to the *SelectedItem* property. You can use one of these two syntax forms:

```
' Both statements select the second tab.
Set TabStrip1.SelectedItem = TabStrip1.Tabs(2)
TabStrip1.Tabs(2).Selected = True
```

The *BeforeClick* and *Click* events fire even when a tab is selected through code.

Multiple Tab objects can have their *Selected* property set to True if the TabStrip's *MultiSelect* property is also True. You can quickly deselect all tabs using the *DeselectAll* method. Finally, you can highlight one or more tabs without showing their contents by setting the *Highlighted* property to True:

```
' Highlight the second tab.
TabStrip1.Tabs(2).Highlighted = True
```

Creating and removing Tab objects

You can create new tabs at run time, using the *Add* method of the *Tabs* collection, which has the following syntax:

```
Add([Index], [Key], [Caption], [Image]) As Tab
```

The *Add* method's arguments are the *Index*, *Key*, *Caption*, and *Image* properties of the Tab object being created. Because this method returns a reference to the created object, you can set additional properties using the following technique:

```
With TabStrip1.Add(, , "Authentication")
    .ToolTipText = "Click here to change authentication settings"
    .Tag = "ABC123"
End With
```

You can remove an existing Tab object at run time using the Tabs collection's *Remove* method, and you can remove all the tabs using the collection's *Clear* method.

THE STATUSBAR CONTROL

Many applications employ the bottom portion of their windows for displaying information to the end user. The most convenient way to create this interface in Visual Basic is with a StatusBar control.

The StatusBar control exposes a Panels collection, which in turn contains Panel objects. A Panel object is an area of the status bar that can hold a piece of information in a given style. The StatusBar control offers several automatic styles (such as date, time, and state of shift keys), plus a generic Text style that lets you show any string in a Panel object. You can also have a StatusBar control work in SimpleText mode, whereby individual Panel objects are replaced by a wider area in which you can display long text messages.

Setting Design-Time Properties

The General tab of the Properties dialog box doesn't contain many interesting properties. In theory, you can set the *Style* property to 0-sbrNormal (the default) or 1-sbrSimpleText, and you can specify the *SimpleText* property itself, which will therefore appear as is in the StatusBar. In practice, however, you never change the default settings because you rarely need to create a StatusBar control merely to show a text message. In that case, in fact, you'd be better off with a simpler Label control or a PictureBox control with *Align* = vbAlignBottom. The only other custom property that appears on this tab is *ShowTips*, which enables the *ToolTipText* property of individual Panel objects.

Move on to the Panels tab of the Property Pages dialog box to create one or more Panel objects, as shown in Figure 10-22. Each Panel object has a number of properties that finely determine its appearance and behavior. The most interesting property is *Style*, which affects what's shown inside the Panel. The default value is 0-sbrText, which displays the string assigned to the *Text* property. You can use a Panel object as an indicator of the status of a particular shift key using one of the settings 1-sbrCaps, 2-sbrNum, 3-sbrIns, or 4-sbrScrl. You can also automatically display the current time or date using the 5-sbrTime or 6-sbrDate setting.

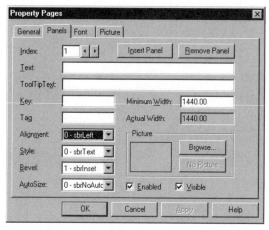

Figure 10-22. *The Panels tab of the Property Pages dialog box of a StatusBar control.*

As I mentioned previously, the *Text* property is the string that appears in the Panel object when *Style* is sbrText. *Key* is the optional key that identifies a Panel object in the Panels collection; *Tag* and *ToolTipText* have the usual meanings. The *Alignment* property determines the position of the Panel's contents (0-sbrLeft, 1-sbrCenter, or 2-sbrRight). The *Bevel* property affects the type of border drawn around the Panel: Its default value is 1-sbrInset, but you can change it to 2-sbrRaised or opt to have no 3-D border with 0-sbrNoBevel.

The *MinWidth* property is the initial size of the Panel object in twips. The *AutoSize* property affects the behavior of the Panel object when the form is resized: 0-sbrNoAutoSize creates a fixed-size Panel. The setting 1-sbrSpring is for Panels that resize with the parent form. (When there are multiple Panels with this setting, all of them shrink or expand accordingly.) The setting 2-sbrContents is for Panel objects whose widths are determined by their contents.

You can display an icon or a bitmap inside a Panel. At design time, you do this by loading an image from disk. Note that this is an exception among common controls, which usually refer to images by way of a companion ImageList control. The reason for this practice is that you might want to load images of different sizes in each Panel, whereas an ImageList control can contain images only of the same width and height.

Run-Time Operations

You won't want to perform many operations on a StatusBar control at run time. But you might need to change the *Text* property of a given Panel object whose *Style* property is 0-sbrText, as in the following example:

```
' Display a message in the third panel.
StatusBar1.Panels(3).Text = "Hello World!"
```

For longer messages, you can change the *Style* property of the StatusBar control and assign a string to its *SimpleText* property:

```
' Display a message in the entire status bar.
StatusBar1.Style = sbrSimple
StatusBar1.SimpleText = "Saving data to file..."
' A lengthy operation
' ...
' Remember to restore the Style property.
StatusBar1.Style = sbrText
```

Creating and removing Panel objects

You rarely create and destroy Panel objects at run time, but it's good to know that you can do it if you really need to. To accomplish this, use the *Add* method of the Panels collection, which has the following syntax:

```
Add([Index], [Key], [Text], [Style], [Picture]) As Panel
```

where each argument corresponds to a property of the Panel object being created. For example, this code creates a new Panel in the leftmost position in the StatusBar control:

```
' Use Index = 1 to place this item before all other Panels.
With StatusBar1.Panels.Add(1, "temporary", "Hello World", sbrText)
    .Alignment = sbrCenter
    .Bevel = sbrNoBevel
    .AutoSize = sbrContents
End With
```

You can remove a single Panel object using the *Remove* method of the Panels collection, and you can remove all Panel objects using the *Clear* method.

Reacting to a user's actions

The StatusBar control exposes a couple of custom events, *PanelClick* and *PanelDblClick*. As their names suggest, these events fire when the end user clicks or double-clicks on a Panel object. The Panel being clicked is passed as an argument to those events. The code at the top of the next page shows how you can let the user modify the contents of a panel by double-clicking on it.

```
Private Sub StatusBar1_PanelDblClick(ByVal Panel As MSComctlLib.Panel)
    Dim s As String
    If Panel.Style = sbrText Then
        s = InputBox("Enter a new text for this panel")
        If Len(s) Then Panel.Text = s
    End If
End Sub
```

Creating animated icons

Panel objects expose a *Picture* property. Usually, you assign this property at design time, but nothing prevents you from assigning images to this property dynamically through code. For example, you can use different images to create animated icons. The trick is to load all the images into an array of Image controls and then assign them in turn in the *Timer* event procedure of a Timer control. (See Figure 10-23.)

```
Private Sub Timer1_Timer()
    Static n As Integer
    ' Show the next image.
    StatusBar1.Panels("moon").Picture = imgMoon(n).Picture
    n = (n + 1) Mod 8
End Sub
```

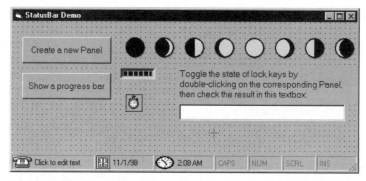

Figure 10-23. *The demonstration program lets you interactively edit Panel text and start a simple animation.*

Toggling the state of lock keys

Even if the StatusBar control can display the state of the Caps, Num, Scroll, and Insert key, it doesn't allow users to toggle it with a click of the mouse, which is probably what most users would expect. Fortunately, you only need a couple of API functions and some code in the *Click* or *DblClick* event procedures to do the magic:

```
' API declarations.
Declare Function GetKeyboardState Lib "user32" (KeyState As Byte) As Long
Declare Function SetKeyboardState Lib "user32" (KeyState As Byte) As Long
```

```
Private Sub StatusBar1_PanelDblClick(ByVal Panel As MSComctlLib.Panel)
    Select Case Panel.Style
        Case sbrCaps:  ToggleKey vbKeyCapital
        Case sbrNum:   ToggleKey vbKeyNumlock
        Case sbrScrl:  ToggleKey vbKeyScrollLock
        Case sbrIns:   ToggleKey vbKeyInsert
    End Select
    StatusBar1.Refresh
End Sub

Sub ToggleKey(vKey As KeyCodeConstants)
    Dim keys(255) As Byte
    ' Read the current state of the keyboard.
    GetKeyboardState keys(0)
    ' Toggle bit 0 of the virtual key we're interested in.
    keys(vKey) = keys(vKey) Xor 1
    ' Enforce the new keyboard state.
    SetKeyboardState keys(0)
End Sub
```

> **NOTE** While the *ToggleKey* routine always works correctly, I've found that on Windows NT systems the keyboard LED indicators don't change to reflect the new states of the toggled keys.

Hosting controls on the status bar

Even if the StatusBar control offers many properties, some things seem to be out of reach of the Visual Basic programmer. For example, you can't change the background color of individual Panel objects, nor can you show a progress bar inside a Panel, a feature that many Windows applications have. Fortunately, there's an easy trick that lets you overcome these limitations.

The StatusBar control can't work as a container, so you can't actually move another control—a ProgressBar, for example—*inside* a StatusBar. But you can move a control *over* a StatusBar, provided that you know exactly where it must appear. This is possible thanks to the *Left* and *Width* properties of the Panel object. The following code fragment moves a ProgressBar control over a specific Panel, simulates a growing progress bar, and then restores the original appearance of the Panel:

```
Private Sub cmdProgress_Click()
    Dim deltaY As Single, pnl As Panel, v As Single
    ' Account for two pixels around the Panel.
    deltaY = ScaleY(2, vbPixels, vbTwips)
    ' Get a reference to the Panel object, and hide its bevel.
    Set pnl = StatusBar1.Panels(1)
    pnl.Bevel = sbrNoBevel
```

(continued)

```
' Move the progress bar into position and in front of the status bar.
ProgressBar1.Move pnl.Left, StatusBar1.Top + deltaY, _
    pnl.Width, StatusBar1.Height - deltaY
ProgressBar1.Visible = True
ProgressBar1.ZOrder

' Let the progress bar grow.
For v = 1 To 100 Step 0.1
    ProgressBar1.Value = v
    DoEvents
Next
' Restore original visibility state and bevel.
ProgressBar1.Visible = False
pnl.Bevel = sbrInset
End Sub
```

This trick works perfectly if the form isn't resizable. In all other cases, you should also move the ProgressBar control when the form is resized, which you do by adding the proper code in the *Form_Resize* event. See the source code of the demonstration program on the companion CD for more details.

THE PROGRESSBAR CONTROL

The ProgressBar control is used to inform the user about the progress state of a lengthy operation. This control is the simplest one among those contained in the MsComCtl.OCX file because it doesn't have any dependent objects and it doesn't expose any custom events.

Setting Design-Time Properties

You have to set up a few properties at design time after you drop a ProgressBar control on a form; in most cases, you can accept the default values. The most important properties are *Min* and *Max*, which determine the minimum and maximum values that can be displayed by the progress bar.

The ProgressBar control that comes with Visual Basic 6 includes two new properties, *Orientation* and *Scrolling*. The former lets you create vertical progress bars; the latter lets you alternate between a standard segmented bar and a smoother bar, as you can see in Figure 10-24. You can change these values even at run time.

Run-Time Operations

There isn't much to say about run-time interaction with the ProgressBar control. In practice, the only thing you can do through code is set the *Value* property to a number in the range from *Min* to *Max*. Any value outside this interval fires an error 380 "Invalid property value." As I mentioned previously, the ProgressBar control doesn't expose any custom events.

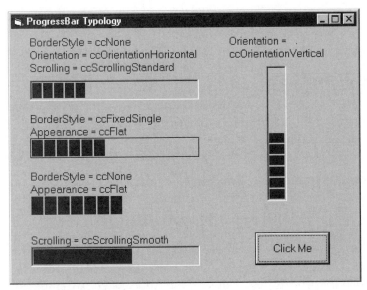

Figure 10-24. *The effects of the* Orientation, Scrolling, Appearance, *and* BorderStyle *properties on the ProgressBar control.*

Only two other properties affect the aspect of the control—*Appearance* and *BorderStyle*. Figure 10-24 shows a number of possible combinations of these properties.

THE SLIDER CONTROL

The Slider control provides a way for end users to select a numerical value in a range. Conceptually, it's akin to the ScrollBar control, with which it shares many properties and events. A major difference is that there's only one kind of Slider control, which can create both horizontal and vertical sliders. The Slider control can also work in select-range mode, allowing your users to select a range rather than a single value.

Setting Design-Time Properties

Once you drop a Slider control on a form, you should right-click it and select the Properties menu command. In the General tab of the Properties custom dialog box, you can set the *Min, Max, SmallChange,* and *LargeChange* properties, which have the same meaning and effects as in HScrollBar and VScrollBar controls. In this tab, you can also set the *SelectRange* property, but this operation is most often performed at run time. (See "Employing the SelectRange Mode" later in this section.)

In the Appearance tab, you set a few properties that are peculiar to this control. The *Orientation* property lets you set the direction of the slider. The *TickStyle* property lets you select whether the slider has unit ticks and where they appear. (Valid values are 0-sldBottomRight, 1-sldTopLeft, 2-sldBoth, and 3-sldNoTicks.) The *TickFrequency* property indirectly determines how many ticks will be displayed. For example, if *Min* is 0 and *Max* is 10 (the default settings), a *TickFrequency* that equals 2 displays 6 ticks. The *TextPosition* property lets you decide where the ToolTip appears. (See "Showing the Value as a ToolTip" later in this section.)

Run-Time Operations

For most practical purposes, you can deal with a Slider control at run time as if it were a scroll bar control: Slider controls expose the *Value* property and the *Change* and *Scroll* events, exactly as scroll bars do. The following brief sections describe two features of the Slider control that are missing from the scroll bar controls.

Showing the value as a ToolTip

Slider controls can display ToolTip text that follows the indicator when it's being dragged by the user. You can control this new Visual Basic 6 feature using two properties, *Text* and *TextPosition*. The former is the string that appears in the ToolTip window; the latter determines where the ToolTip appears with respect to the indicator. (Possible values are 0-sldAboveLeft and 1-sldBelowRight.) You can also set the *TextPosition* property at design time in the Appearance tab of the Property Pages dialog box.

You generally use these properties to show the current value in a ToolTip window near the indicator. To do so, you need just one statement in the *Scroll* event procedure:

```
Private Sub Slider1_Scroll()
    Slider1.Text = "Value = " & Slider1.Value
End Sub
```

Employing the SelectRange mode

The Slider control supports the ability to display a range instead of an individual value, as you can see in Figure 10-25. To display a range, you use a number of properties together. First of all, you enter select range mode by setting the *SelectRange* property to True—for example, when users click on the control while they're pressing the Shift key.

```
Dim StartSelection As Single

Private Sub Slider1_MouseDown(Button As Integer, Shift As Integer, _
    x As Single, y As Single)
    If Shift = vbShiftMask Then
        ' If the shift key is being pressed, enter select range mode.
        Slider1.SelectRange = True
        Slider1.SelLength = 0
        StartSelection = Slider1.Value
    Else
        ' Else cancel any active select range mode.
        Slider1.SelectRange = False
    End If
End Sub
```

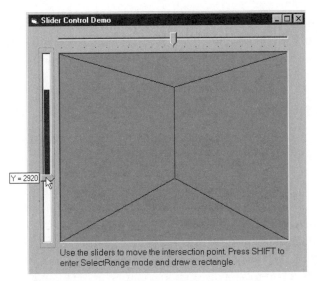

Figure 10-25. *You can use a Slider control to select a range, and you can also display a ToolTip beside the indicator being dragged.*

After you enter the select range mode, you can control the interval being high-lighted by means of the *SelStart* and *SelLength* properties. You do this in the *Scroll* event procedure. Because *SelLength* can't be negative, you must account for two distinct cases:

```
Private Sub Slider1_Scroll()
    If Slider1.SelectRange Then
        ' The indicator is being moved in SelectRange mode.
        If Slider1.Value > StartSelection Then
            Slider1.SelStart = StartSelection
            Slider1.SelLength = Slider1.Value - StartSelection
        Else
            Slider1.SelStart = Slider1.Value
            Slider1.SelLength = StartSelection - Slider1.Value
        End If
    End If
End Sub
```

THE IMAGECOMBO CONTROL

The ImageCombo control is new to Visual Basic and is one of the few controls introduced in Visual Basic 6. In a nutshell, the ImageCombo control is a combo box that supports images and a different indentation for each individual item. This is the same control that Windows uses internally for its file common dialog boxes.

From the programmer's point of view, the main difference between the ImageCombo control and the standard ComboBox control is that the ImageCombo control uses an object-oriented architecture and exposes the ComboItems collection, which in turn contains ComboItem objects.

Setting Design-Time Properties

An ImageCombo control is so similar to a standard ComboBox control that it makes sense to describe only the few differences between them. At design time, you need to set only two properties. The *ImageList* property is a reference to the ImageList control that contains the images to be displayed beside each ComboItem object. The *Indentation* property sets the default indentation for all ComboItem objects, expressed as a number of indentation units, where each unit is 10 pixels. Individual ComboItem objects can provide a different value for this property, thus overwriting the default value set in the Properties window at design time or through code at run time.

Like, ComboBox controls, ImageCombo controls can be bound to a data source and therefore support all the usual *Dataxxxx* properties.

Run-Time Operations

The ImageCombo control exposes many of the properties supported by the regular ComboBox control, including *ForeColor*, *BackColor*, *Text*, *SelText*, *SelStart*, *SelLength*, and *Locked*. The ImageCombo control doesn't expose any events other than the ones supported by ComboBox.

You see the difference between an ImageCombo control and a ComboBox control when it's time to add items to the control. The ImageCombo control doesn't support the *AddItem* method. Instead, you add items using the *Add* method of the ComboItems collection, which has the following syntax:

```
Add([Index],[Key],[Text],[Image],[SelImage],[Indentation]) As ComboItem
```

Index determines where the new ComboItem is inserted, *Key* is its key in the collection, *Text* is the string that appears in the control, *Image* is the associated image (an index or a key in the companion ImageList control), *SelImage* is the image displayed when the item is selected, and *Indentation* is the indentation level. (Each unit is 10 pixels.) This syntax allows you to add a new ComboItem and set all its properties in one operation. Here's a routine that loads all the drive letters and volume labels in an ImageCombo control, as you can see in Figure 10-26:

```
Sub LoadDrivesIntoImageCombo(ImgCombo As ImageCombo)
    Dim fso As New Scripting.FileSystemObject, dr As Scripting.Drive
    Dim drLabel As String, drImage As String
```

```
' Assume that the ImageCombo control is linked to an ImageList
' control that includes three icons with the following key names.
ImgCombo.ComboItems.Add , , "My Computer", "MyComputer"
For Each dr In fso.Drives
    ' Use a different image for each type of drive.
    Select Case dr.DriveType
        Case Removable:  drImage = "FloppyDrive"
        Case CDRom:      drImage = "CDDrive"
        Case Else:       drImage = "HardDrive"
    End Select
    ' Retrieve the letter and (if possible) the volume label.
    drLabel = dr.DriveLetter & ": "
    If dr.IsReady Then
        If Len(dr.VolumeName) Then drLabel = drLabel & "[" & _
            dr.VolumeName & "]"
    End If
    ' Add an indented item to the combo.
    ImgCombo.ComboItems.Add , dr.DriveLetter, drLabel, drImage, , 2
Next
' Select the current drive.
Set ImgCombo.SelectedItem = ImgCombo.ComboItems(Left$(CurDir$, 1))
End Sub
```

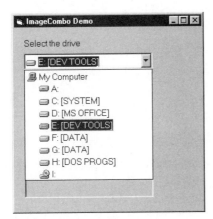

Figure 10-26. *The ImageCombo demonstration program shows information about all the drives in the system.*

You can choose from two ways to select a ComboItem object through code: You can use the *SelectedItem* property of the ImageCombo control (as shown in the preceding routine), or you can set the *Selected* property of an individual ComboItem object:

```
' Select the current drive (alternative method).
Set ImgCombo.ComboItems(Left$(CurDir$, 1)).Selected = True
```

An interesting effect of dealing with individual ComboItem objects is that you can modify their *Text* properties without having to remove and add them again, as you would do with a standard ComboBox:

```
' Change the text of the first item.
ImgCombo.ComboItems(1).Text = "My Computer"
```

You can delete an individual ComboItem using the *Remove* method of the ComboItems collection, and you can delete all the items using the collection's *Clear* method.

The ImageCombo control exposes only one custom method, *GetFirstVisible*, which returns a reference to the first ComboItem object in the list portion of the control. There isn't much that you can do with this method, however, because you have no way to set the first visible item and therefore you can't programmatically scroll the contents of the list area.

This concludes the description of all the controls embedded in the file MsComCtl.ocx. In the next chapter, I'll describe all the other Windows common controls provided with Visual Basic 6.

Chapter 11

Windows Common Controls: Part II

This chapter examines the Microsoft Windows common controls provided in the MsComCt2.ocx and ComCt332.ocx files. More specifically, the MsComCt2.ocx file embeds the Animation, UpDown, MonthView, DateTimePicker, and FlatScrollBar controls, whereas the ComCt332.ocx file includes only the CoolBar control.

THE ANIMATION CONTROL

The Animation control can play back AVI files so that you can add simple animations to your program. This control supports only AVI files that don't include sound and that aren't in compressed form or that have been compressed using Run-Length Encoding (RLE). Any attempt to play back an AVI file that doesn't follow these rules brings up error message 35752, "Unable to open AVI file."

The Animation control is especially useful for embedding simple animations, such as those that you find in the \Common\Graphics\AVIs subdirectory under the main Microsoft Visual Basic installation directory. For example, you can use this control to display sheets of paper that fly from one folder to another folder while you perform a file copy operation in the background, as shown in Figure 11-1 on the following page.

Figure 11-1. *A demonstration program provided on the companion CD-ROM lets you experiment with the Animation control.*

The Animation control exposes three main properties. Two of them, *Center* and *BackStyle*, can be set only at design time, and are read-only at run time. If the *Center* property is True, the AVI file is centered in the Animation control window (instead of being displayed near the upper left corner). The *BackStyle* property can be 0-cc2BackstyleTransparent (the default setting, which displays the background color of the control) or 1-cc2BackstyleOpaque (displays the background of the AVI file). The third property, *AutoPlay*, can be set at any time. You set it to True to automatically start the playback of any AVI file as soon as it's loaded in the control. (If you make this setting, you must set *AutoPlay* to False through code to stop playback).

No design-time property determines which AVI file is loaded and displayed at run time. To start an animation through code, you must first open the AVI file, which you do using the *Open* method:

```
Animation1.Open "d:\vb6\Graphics\AVIs\filecopy.avi"
```

If the *AutoPlay* property is True, the AVI file starts as soon as it has been loaded in the control. Otherwise, you have to start it through code with the *Play* method, which has the following syntax:

```
Play [RepeatCount], [StartFrame], [EndFrame]
```

RepeatCount is the number of times the animation must run. (The default is –1, which repeats the animation indefinitely.) *StartFrame* is the starting frame of the animation (the default is 0, the first frame). *EndFrame* is the ending frame of the animation (the default is –1, the last frame in the AVI file).

You can choose from two ways to stop an animation, and you must select one or the other according to the method you used to start it. If the animation is in AutoPlay mode, you can stop it only by setting the *AutoPlay* property to False; if you started the animation with the *Play* method, you can stop it with the *Stop* method. If you don't plan to restart the same AVI file immediately, you can release some memory by executing the *Close* method, as shown in the following code (which assumes that the *AutoPlay* property is False):

```
Private Sub cmdStart_Click()
    Animation1.Open "d:\vb5\graphics\AVIs\filecopy.avi"
```

```
    Animation1.Play
End Sub
Private Sub cmdStop_Click()
    Animation1.Stop
    Animation1.Close
End Sub
```

The Animation control doesn't expose any custom events. This means, for example, that you can't find out when an animation ends.

THE UPDOWN CONTROL

The UpDown control offers a simple but effective way to create those spin buttons that many Windows applications display to the right of numeric fields and that let users increment or decrement a field's value using mouse clicks. While it's a trivial matter to create such spin buttons yourself—using a tiny VScrollBar control, for example, or using two smaller buttons with *Style* = 1-Graphical—the UpDown control offers many advantages and is far easier to set up and use than any other solution.

The most intriguing characteristic of the UpDown control is that you can link it to another control—its *buddy control*—at design time, and you can even select which particular property of the buddy control is affected by the UpDown control. Add to this the ability to set the scrolling range and the increment, and you see that in most cases you don't even need to write code to make everything work as expected.

Setting Design-Time Properties

In the General tab of an UpDown control, you typically set the *Alignment* property, which determines where the UpDown control has to align with respect to its buddy control. (The values are 0-cc2AlignmentLeft and 1-cc2AlignmentRight.) In this tab, you also set the *Orientation* property (0-cc2OrientationVertical or 1-cc2OrientationHorizontal). The *Orientation* property can be set only at design time and is read-only at run time.

You select the buddy control in the Buddy tab of the Property Pages dialog box. (See Figure 11-2 on the following page.) You can either type the control's name in the first field or tick the *AutoBuddy* check box. In the latter case, the UpDown control automatically selects the previous control in the TabIndex sequence as its buddy control. After you've selected a buddy control, two other fields on the Property Pages dialog box become available. In the BuddyProperty combo box, you select which property of the buddy control is affected by the UpDown control. (If you don't select any, the buddy control's default property is used.) You can set the *SyncBuddy* property to True, which causes the UpDown control to automatically modify the selected property in its buddy control.

You usually select a TextBox control as the buddy control of an UpDown control and *Text* as the buddy property. But nothing prevents you from connecting an

UpDown control to other properties (for example, *Left* or *Width*) exposed by other types of controls. You can't use lightweight windowless controls as buddy controls, however.

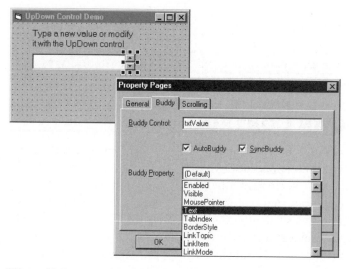

Figure 11-2. *The Buddy tab of the Property Pages dialog box of an UpDown control lets you select the buddy control and the buddy property.*

Finally, in the Scrolling tab of the Property Pages dialog box, you select the UpDown control's *Min* and *Max* properties, which identify the valid range for the *Value* property. The *Increment* property is the value that's added to or subtracted from the *Value* property when the user clicks on the UpDown control's spin buttons. If the *Wrap* property is set to True, the *Value* property wraps when it reaches the *Min* or *Max* value.

Run-Time Operations

If the UpDown control's *SyncBuddy* property is set to True, you don't need to write any code to manually change the property in the buddy control. There are cases, however, when you can't rely on this simple mechanism. For example, the UpDown control might have no buddy controls or perhaps it's supposed to affect multiple controls or multiple properties of the same control. (For example, you might need to enlarge or shrink another control by affecting its *Width* and *Height* properties at the same time.) In such cases, all you have to do is write code inside the *Change* event procedure, as you would do for a scroll bar control.

The UpDown control exposes two custom events that give you even more flexibility: The *DownClick* and *UpClick* events, which fire when the mouse is released (that is, after the *Change* event) on either one of the buttons that make up the UpDown control. These events fire even if the *Value* property has already reached its *Min* or *Max*, which makes *DownClick* and *UpClick* events useful when you don't want to enforce a limit to the range of valid values:

```
' Move all controls on the form pixel by pixel.
Private Sub UpDown1_DownClick()
    Dim ctrl As Control
    For Each ctrl In Controls
        ctrl.Top = ctrl.Top + ScaleY(1, vbPixels, vbTwips)
    Next
End Sub
Private Sub UpDown1_UpClick()
    Dim ctrl As Control
    For Each ctrl In Controls
        ctrl.Top = ctrl.Top - ScaleY(1, vbPixels, vbTwips)
    Next
End Sub
```

All the properties that you set at design time can also be modified at run time through code, with the exception of the *Orientation* property. For example, you can change the buddy control and the buddy property using this code:

```
Set UpDown1.BuddyControl = Text2
UpDown1.BuddyProperty = "Text"
```

The *BuddyControl* property can also be assigned the name of the buddy control, for example:

```
UpDown1.BuddyControl = "Text2"
' This syntax even works with items of control arrays.
UpDown1.BuddyControl = "Text3(0)"
```

When you change the buddy control at run time, the UpDown control automatically moves to a position beside its buddy control, which shrinks to make room for the UpDown control.

THE FLATSCROLLBAR CONTROL

The FlatScrollBar control is a replacement for the intrinsic HScrollBar and VScrollBar controls: You can substitute an HScrollBar or VScrollBar control with a FlatScrollBar control with the same name, and the program continues to work as before. This control can work as either a horizontal or a vertical scroll bar, according to the value of its *Orientation* property. This property can be also modified at run time.

You can set all the properties specific to the FlatScrollBar control at design time, as shown in Figure 11-3 on the following page. This control supports three graphic styles: flat, tridimensional (similar to intrinsic scroll bar controls), and Track3D (a flat scroll bar that becomes tridimensional when the mouse passes over it, much like the scroll bars in Microsoft Encarta). You can select the graphic style at design time by setting the *Appearance* property to one of these values: 0-fsb3D, 1-fsbFlat, or 2-fsbTrack3D.

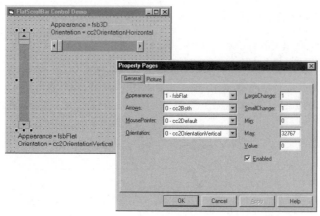

Figure 11-3. *The General tab of the Property Pages dialog box of a FlatScrollBar control.*

The *Arrows* property lets you selectively enable one or both arrows at the ends of the bar, using the values 1-cc2LeftUp or 2-cc2RightDown; the default value 0-cc2Both enables both arrows. The *Min*, *Max*, *LargeChange*, *SmallChange*, and *Value* properties have the same meaning they have with HScrollBar and VScrollBar controls.

At run time, you react to users' actions on a FlatScrollBar control as you would do with a regular scroll bar; that is, by executing code in *Change* and *Scroll* events. The only property of the FlatScrollBar that you might reasonably want to modify at run time is *Arrows*—for example, to disable the appropriate arrow when the scroll bar has reached it minimum or maximum value. You usually do this in the *Change* event procedure:

```
Private Sub FlatScrollBar1_Change()
    ' This is a horizontal FlatScrollBar.
    If FlatScrollBar1.Value = FlatScrollBar1.Min Then
        FlatScrollBar1.Arrows = cc2RightDown
    ElseIf FlatScrollBar1.Value = FlatScrollBar1.Max Then
        FlatScrollBar1.Arrows = cc2LeftUp
    Else
        FlatScrollBar1.Arrows = cc2Both
    End If
End Sub
```

THE MONTHVIEW CONTROL

Visual Basic 6 comes with two new common controls for dealing with dates: The MonthView control and the DateTimePicker control. The former is a calendarlike control, and the latter is a text box control for entering dates and times. The two are closely related in that the DateTimePicker control uses a MonthView control when the user drops down a calendar for selecting a date.

Setting Design-Time Properties

After you place a MonthView control on a form, you can right-click on it to display its custom Property Pages dialog box, shown in Figure 11-4. The *Value* property is the date highlighted in the control. (By the way, click on the Down arrow to the right of the *Value* field to get a taste of what a DateTimePicker control is.) *MinDate* and *MaxDate* set the range of valid dates that can be selected in the MonthView control; the *StartOfWeek* property determines the weekday that appears in the leftmost column in the calendar.

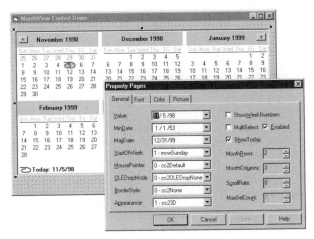

Figure 11-4. *Setting design-time properties of a MonthView control.*

A number of Boolean properties affect the appearance and the behavior of the control. If *ShowWeekNumbers* is True, the MonthView control displays the number of weeks elapsed since the beginning of the year. If *MultiSelect* is True, the user is allowed to select a range of dates: In this case, the maximum number of consecutive days that can be selected is equal to the value of the *MaxSelCount* property. (The default is one week.) The *ShowToday* property lets you decide whether the Today legend should be displayed.

The MonthView control can display up to 12 months, and the number of displayed months is the product of the properties *MonthRows* and *MonthColumns*. By default, when the user clicks on the arrow buttons the control scrolls a number of months equal to the months displayed in the control, but you can modify this behavior by assigning a nonzero value to the *ScrollRate* property.

The MonthView control exposes many properties that are related to foreground and background colors, and it's easy to confuse them. Refer to Figure 11-5 on the following page to understand how you can use the *ForeColor*, *TitleForeColor*, *TitleBackColor*, *MonthBackColor*, and *TrailingForeColor* properties. (*Trailing days* are those days that belong to previous or next months.) The *MonthBackColor* property also affects the color of weekday names and numbers. Oddly, the control also exposes the standard *BackColor* property, but it doesn't appear to have any other effect than coloring a line of pixels near the bottom and right borders.

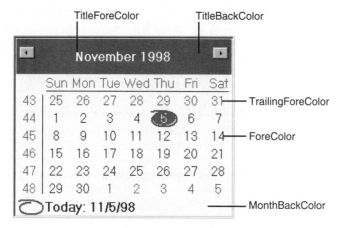

Figure 11-5. *You can modify the colors used by individual areas in a MonthView control.*

Among the many design-time properties, you might notice in particular the *DataSource, DataField, DataMember,* and *DataFormat* properties. In fact, MonthView is a data-aware control that can be bound to any *Date* field exposed by a standard Data control, a RemoteData control, or any ADO data source.

> **CAUTION**   If you're going to localize your application to other languages, you'll be glad to know that the MonthView control automatically adapts itself to the user's locale and correctly translates all the month and day names. There's only a minor bug in this implementation: The Today legend isn't localized, so you should set the *ShowToday* property to False and provide a legend elsewhere on the form.

Run-Time Operations

Users can act on the MonthView control in several ways, a few of which aren't immediately apparent. Most people can easily figure out that users can move to the next or previous month by clicking on one of the two arrows near the control's title and that they can select a date simply by clicking on it. Some users will even figure out that they can select a range of dates (if *MultiSelect* is True) by clicking on a date while pressing the Shift key. I doubt, however, that many users guess that a click on the month's name in the control's title displays a pop-up menu that lets them move to any month in the current year. Even more counter-intuitive is that a click on the year number displays two spin buttons that can take a user to any year, future or past. (See Figure 11-6.) Don't forget to mention these hidden features in your program's documentation, or even better, show their usage in a Label control on the same form as the MonthView control.

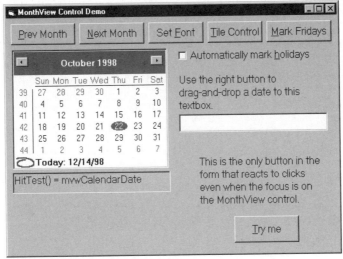

Figure 11-6. *The demonstration program lets you experiment with all the advanced features of the MonthView control. The spin buttons in the title area appear if you click on the year number.*

Retrieving the current Date value

Unless you need to perform special operations, using the MonthView control in code is straightforward. The control exposes the *Value* property, which you can assign to highlight a given date or read to retrieve the day selected by the user. You don't even need to extract the day, month, or year portions from the *Value* property because the control exposes also the *Day*, *Month*, and *Year* properties. Conveniently, these properties can be assigned too—for example, you can programmatically display the next month using this code:

```
If MonthView1.Month < 12 Then
    MonthView1.Month = MonthView1.Month + 1
Else
    MonthView1.Month = 1
    MonthView1.Year = MonthView1.Year + 1
End If
```

The *DayOfWeek* property returns the weekday number of the selected date. Also, this property is writable, so, for example, you can highlight Monday in the current week using the following single statement:

```
MonthView1.DayOfWeek = vbMonday
```

Be aware, however, that *Day*, *Month*, *Year*, and *DayOfWeek* properties can't be assigned if *MultiSelect* is True.

CAUTION   While experimenting with the MonthView control, I've discovered an unexpected behavior: If the control has the focus and you click on another control on the same form, the other control gets the focus but not the *Click* event. This might puzzle your users, much as it confused me when I realized that if the focus is on a MonthView control, a click on push buttons doesn't yield the expected results. This bug will probably be fixed in a future service pack. In the meantime, the workaround to this problem is really cumbersome, to say the least, and relies on the *MouseDown* event instead of the *Click* event:

```
Dim MousePressed As Boolean        ' A form-level variable

Private Sub cmdTryMe_MouseDown(Button As Integer, _
    Shift As Integer, X As Single, Y As Single)
    MousePressed = True
    Call DoSomething
End Sub
Private Sub cmdTryMe_MouseUp(Button As Integer, _
    Shift As Integer, X As Single, Y As Single)
    MousePressed = False
End Sub
Private Sub cmdTryMe_Click()
    ' This event might be called as a response to a hot key
    ' or a click when the focus isn't on the MonthView control.
    If Not MousePressed Then Call DoSomething
End Sub
Private Sub DoSomething()
    ' The code that must execute when the button is clicked
    MsgBox "Button has been clicked!"
End Sub
```

Reacting to range selections

You can set the *MinDate* and *MaxDate* property to limit the range of date values that the user can select. If the *MultiSelect* property is True, you can select a number of consecutive dates. You retrieve the selected range using the *SelStart* and *SelEnd* properties. (These properties return Date values.) The maximum number of days in the selected range depends on the value of the *MaxSelCount* property.

Each time the user selects a new date, a custom *SelChange* event fires. This event receives the start date and end date of the selected range and enables the programmer to cancel the operation. For example, you can refuse a selection that includes a weekend day:

```
Private Sub MonthView1_SelChange(ByVal StartDate As Date, _
    ByVal EndDate As Date, Cancel As Boolean)
    Dim d As Date
    ' A Date variable can be used to control a For loop.
```

```
    For d = StartDate To EndDate
        If Weekday(d) = vbSunday Or Weekday(d) = vbSaturday Then
            ' Cancel the selection if the day is Sunday or Saturday.
            Cancel = True
            Exit For
        End If
    Next
End Sub
```

> **CAUTION**   The MonthView control suffers from a bug. Unless the user has selected three or more dates, setting the *Cancel* parameter to True doesn't actually cancel the operation. This bug will probably be fixed in future versions of the control, but currently there isn't any simple workaround for it. (I'm currently using version 6.00.8177 of the MsComCt2.ocx file.)

Two other custom events, *DateClick* and *DateDblClick*, fire when the user selects a new date. When a user clicks on a date, your Visual Basic application receives a *SelChange* event and then a *DateClick* event. If a date is double-clicked, your code receives *SelChange*, *DateClick*, *DateDblClick*, and *DateClick* events, in this order, so you should account for the fact that a double-click also fires two *DateClick* events. Both events receive one argument, the date being clicked or double-clicked:

```
Private Sub MonthView1_DateDblClick(ByVal DateDblClicked As Date)
    Dim descr As String
    descr = InputBox("Enter a description for day " & _
        FormatDateTime(DateDblClicked, vbLongDate))
    If Len(descr) Then
        ' Save the description (omitted) ...
        ' ...
    End If
End Sub
```

Finding the optimal size

The MonthView control gives you several ways, apart from its many color properties, to affect the control's appearance. For example, you can show up to 12 months in the control by assigning suitable values to the *MonthRows* and *MonthColumns* properties. Changing these properties at run time, however, can cause a problem in that you have no control over a MonthView's size (which depends on the number of months displayed, the font used, the presence of a border, and other settings). To help you determine the best values for the *MonthRows* and *MonthColumns* properties, the MonthView control supports the *ComputeControlSize* method. This method takes as arguments the number of rows and columns and returns the computed width and height of the corresponding MonthView control in its third and fourth argument.

```
' Evaluate the size of a MonthView control with 2 rows and 3 columns
Dim wi As Single, he As Single
MonthView1.ComputeControlSize 2, 3, wi, he
```

The *ComputeControlSize* method comes in handy when you want to display the highest number of months in a form. The following routine has been extracted from the demonstration program provided on the companion CD:

```
Private Sub cmdTile_Click()
    ' Find the best value for MonthRows and MonthColumns.
    Dim rows As Integer, cols As Integer
    Dim wi As Single, he As Single
    For rows = 6 To 1 Step -1
        ' Note how we avoid creating more than 12 months.
        For cols = 12 \ rows To 1 Step -1
            MonthView1.ComputeControlSize rows, cols, wi, he
            If wi <= ScaleWidth - MonthView1.Left And _
                he < ScaleHeight - MonthView1.Top Then
                MonthView1.MonthRows = rows
                MonthView1.MonthColumns = cols
                Exit Sub
            End If
        Next
    Next
End Sub
```

Highlighting dates

The MonthView control lets the programmer draw attention to dates in the calendar by displaying them with a bold attribute. You could use this feature whenever the contents of the control changes by writing code in the *GetDayBold* event procedure, as in the following example:

```
' Display all Sundays and major holidays in boldface.
Sub MonthView1_GetDayBold(ByVal StartDate As Date, _
    ByVal Count As Integer, State() As Boolean)
    Dim i As Long, d As Date
    d = StartDate
    For i = 0 To Count - 1
        If Weekday(d) = vbSunday Then
            State(i) = True          ' Mark all Sundays.
        ElseIf Month(d) = 12 And Day(d) = 25 Then
            State(i) = True          ' Xmas time.
        Else
            ' Deal here with other holidays...
        End If
        d = d + 1
    Next
End Sub
```

The *GetDayBold* event receives three parameters: *StartDate* is a Date value that corresponds to the first day displayed in the control (this includes trailing days, which are the days that belong to the previous month), *Count* is the number of visible days, and *State* is a zero-based Boolean array with *Count* elements. Thus, to enforce a bold attribute to a given date, you only have to assign True to the corresponding item in the *State* array.

Alternatively, you can modify the bold attribute for any date that's currently displayed in the control by writing code outside the *GetDayBold* event procedure. You do this using *VisibleDays* and *DayBold* properties. The *VisibleDays* property accepts an index in the range from 1 to the number of visible days and returns the Date value that corresponds to that day. The problem with this property is that there's no easy way to know in advance how many days are visible in the control and therefore what the highest value for the index is. The Visual Basic documentation incorrectly states that the index must be in the range from 1 through 42, but this doesn't take into account the MonthView control's ability to display multiple months. The simplest way to deal with this issue is to set up an error handler, as in the following code:

```
Dim tmpDate As Date
' Exit the loop when the index isn't valid any longer.
On Error GoTo EndTheLoop
For i = 1 To 366
    ' Visit each day.
    tmpDate = MonthView1.VisibleDays(i)
Next
EndTheLoop:
    ' Get here when the index becomes invalid.
```

The *VisibleDays* property returns a Date value whose fractional portion is equal to the current time on your system. This undocumented behavior can get in the way when you compare the returned value to a Date constant or variable.

The *DayBold* property takes as an argument a Date value that corresponds to a visible day and sets or returns the bold attribute for that day. This property lets you mark a number of days at the same time even if you aren't processing a *GetDayBold* event. You typically use the *DayBold* property together with the *VisibleDays* property, as in the following piece of code:

```
Private Sub cmdMark_Click()
    Dim i As Integer
    On Error GoTo EndOfLoop
    For i = 1 To 999
        ' Mark all Fridays.
        If Weekday(MonthView1.VisibleDays(i)) = vbFriday Then
            MonthView1.DayBold(MonthView1.VisibleDays(i)) = True
        End If
    Next
EndOfLoop:
End Sub
```

Implementing drag-and-drop

The MonthView control is an ideal source for drag-and-drop operations because it permits you to copy a date value to any other control that accepts a string through this mechanism. The key for a correct implementation of drag-and-drop is the *HitTest* method, the syntax of which is the following:

```
Area = MonthView1.HitTest(X, Y, HitDate)
```

Area is an integer that indicates which area of the control the *x* and *y* coordinates correspond to. (See the Visual Basic documentation or the demonstration program's source code on the companion CD for a list of all possible return values.) When the function returns the value 4-mvwCalendarDay, the *HitDate* variable is assigned the Date value of the day in the calendar at *x* and *y* coordinates. With this method, you'll find it easy to implement an effective drag-and-drop routine. The following code is taken from the demonstration program shown in Figure 11-6:

```
' Start a drag-and-drop operation.
Private Sub MonthView1_MouseDown(Button As Integer, Shift As Integer, _
    X As Single, Y As Single)
    ' Exit if the right button isn't clicked.
    If Button <> vbRightButton Then Exit Sub
    ' Exit if mouse isn't over a valid date.
    If MonthView1.HitTest(X, Y, DraggedDate) <> mvwCalendarDay Then
        Exit Sub
    End If
    ' Now DraggedDate contains the date to be dragged,
    ' and we can start the drag operation.
    MonthView1.OLEDrag
End Sub

Private Sub MonthView1_OLEStartDrag(Data As MSComCtl2.DataObject, _
    AllowedEffects As Long)
    ' When this event fires, DraggedDate contains a valid date.
    Data.SetData Format(DraggedDate, "long date")
    AllowedEffects = vbDropEffectCopy
End Sub
```

The preceding code assumes that the *OLEDropMode* property of the control over which the mouse button is released is set to the value 2-Automatic.

THE DATETIMEPICKER CONTROL

The DateTimePicker control is a text box especially designed for Date or Time values. The text box is subdivided into subfields, one for each individual component (day, month, year, hour, minute, and second). This control supports all the usual date and time formats (including a custom format) and the ability to return a Null value (if the user doesn't want to select a particular date). You can even define your own custom subfields.

At run time, end users can advance through subfields using the Left and Right arrow keys and can increment and decrement their values using the Up and Down arrow keys. They can display a drop-down calendar (if the *UpDown* property is set to False) or modify the current value of the highlighted component using the companion spin buttons (if the value of *UpDown* is True).

Setting Design-Time Properties

By default, a Down arrow appears to the right of the control, much like a regular ComboBox control: A click on the arrow drops down a calendar, which lets users select a date without typing any keys. If you set the *UpDown* property to True, however, the Down arrow is replaced by a pair of spin buttons, which let users increment or decrement the value of individual subfields using only the mouse.

The *CheckBox* property, if True, displays a check box near the left border of the control: Users can deselect this check box if they don't intend to actually select any dates. (See Figure 11-7 on the following page.)

The DateTimePicker control shares a few properties with the MonthView control. For example, it exposes a *Value* property, which returns the Date value entered by the end user, and the *MinDate* and *MaxDate* properties, which define the interval of valid dates.

The drop-down calendar is nothing but a MonthView control that can show only one month at a time. Thus, the DateTimePicker control also exposes all the color properties of the MonthView control, even though each now has a different name: *CalendarForeColor, CalendarBackColor, CalendarTitleForeColor, CalendarTitleBackColor,* and *CalendarTrailingForeColor*. Oddly, the control doesn't expose the standard *ForeColor* and *BackColor* properties, so while you can modify the appearance of the drop-down calendar, you can't programmatically change the default colors of the edit portion of the control!

The *Format* property affects what's displayed in the control and can be one of the following values: 0-dtpLongDate, 1-dtpShortDate, 2-dtpTime, or 3-dtpCustom. If you select a custom format, you can assign a suitable string to the *CustomFormat* property. This property accepts the same formatting strings that you would pass to a *Format* function that works with date or time values. You can use this string:

```
'Date is' dddd MMM d, yyy
```

to display a value such as

```
Date is Friday Nov 5, 1999
```

As you see, you can include literal strings by enclosing them within single quotation marks. As I'll explain in a moment, the *CustomFormat* property can be used to create custom subfields too.

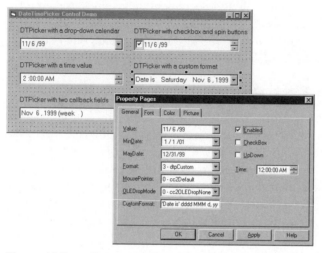

Figure 11-7. *Different styles of the DateTimePicker control.*

The DateTimePicker control can be bound to a data source, so it exposes the usual *DataSource*, *DataMember*, *DataField*, and *DataFormat* properties. The *DataFormat* property isn't supported when the control is bound to a standard Data or RemoteData control, but in either case you can modify the format of the displayed value using the *Format* and *CustomFormat* properties.

Run-Time Operations

At run time, you set and retrieve the contents in the DateTimePicker control through the *Value* property or by means of the *Year*, *Month*, *Day*, *DayOfWeek*, *Hour*, *Minute*, and *Second* properties. For example, you can programmatically increment the month portion of a date displayed in a DateTimePicker control with the following statements:

```
DTPicker1.Month = (DTPicker1.Month Mod 12) + 1
If DTPicker1.Month = 1 Then DTPicker1.Year = DTPicker1.Year + 1
```

If *CheckBox* is True and the user has deselected the check box, all date-related properties return Null.

The DateTimePicker control exposes many of the events supported by a standard TextBox control, including *Change*, *KeyDown*, *KeyPress*, *KeyUp*, *MouseDown*, *MouseMove*, *MouseUp*, *Click*, and *DblClick*. All keyboard and mouse events refer to the edit portion of the control and so don't fire when a calendar has been dropped down.

When the user clicks on the Down arrow, a *DropDown* event fires just before the drop-down calendar actually appears—that is, if the *UpDown* property is False (the default value). When the user selects a date in the drop-down calendar, a *CloseUp* event fires. These events aren't particularly useful, however, because you don't have much control over the calendar itself, apart from the colors it uses. When the user selects a date in the drop-down calendar, the *Change* event fires before the *CloseUp* event.

> **CAUTION** Because of a bug in the DateTimePicker control, you can't assign both the *MinDate* and *MaxDate* properties at run time. When you assign either one, the other is assigned the date 12/31/1999. The reason for this odd behavior and a possible workaround are explained in article Q198880 of Microsoft Knowledge Base.

Managing callback fields

The most intriguing feature of the DateTimePicker control is the capability to define custom subfields, also known as *callback fields*. To define a callback field, you use a string of one or more *X* characters in the value assigned to the *CustomFormat* property. You can define multiple callback fields by using strings with different numbers of *X*s. For example, the following format defines a date field with two callback fields:

```
DTPicker1.CustomFormat = "MMM d, yyy '(week 'XX')' XXX"
```

In the code sample that follows, the *XX* field is defined as the number of weeks since January 1, and the *XXX* field is the name of the holiday, if any, that occurs on the displayed date.

When you define a callback field, you're in charge of defining its maximum length, its current value, and its behavior (that is, what happens if the user presses a key when the caret is on it). You establish the maximum size of a callback field in the *FormatSize* custom event, which fires once for each callback field. If you have multiple fields, you must prepare a *Select Case* structure, as in the following code:

```
Private Sub DTPicker1_FormatSize(ByVal CallbackField As String, _
    Size As Integer)
    Select Case CallbackField
        Case "XX"
            ' The number of weeks since January 1st (max 2 digits)
            Size = 2
        Case "XXX"
            ' The name of a holiday, if any
            Size = 16
    End Select
End Sub
```

When the DateTimePicker control is about to display a date, it raises a *Format* event for each callback field. You return the value of the callback field in the *FormattedString* parameter:

```
Private Sub DTPicker1_Format(ByVal CallbackField As String, _
    FormattedString As String)
    Select Case CallbackField
        Case "XX"
            ' The number of weeks since January 1st (max 2 digits)
            FormattedString = DateDiff("ww", _
                DateSerial(DTPicker1.Year, 1, 1), DTPicker1.Value)
        Case "XXX"
            ' The name of a holiday, if any
            If DTPicker1.Month = 12 And DTPicker1.Day = 25 Then
                FormattedString = "Christmas"
            Else
                ' Deal here with other holidays.
            End If
    End Select
End Sub
```

You can process all the keys pressed when the caret is on a callback field by writing code in the *CallbackKeyDown* event procedure. This event receives information about the key being pressed, the state of shift keys, and the name of the callback field. Typically, you process the key by assigning a new Date value to the *CallbackDate* parameter:

```
Private Sub DTPicker1_CallbackKeyDown(ByVal KeyCode As Integer, _
    ByVal Shift As Integer, ByVal CallbackField As String, _
    CallbackDate As Date)
    If CallbackField = "XX" Then
        ' Move to the previous/next week when the Up/Down key is pressed.
        If KeyCode = vbKeyUp Then
            CallbackDate = DTPicker1.Value + 7
        ElseIf KeyCode = vbKeyDown Then
            CallbackDate = DTPicker1.Value - 7
        End If
    Else
        ' No keyboard support for the Holiday field
    End If
End Sub
```

THE COOLBAR CONTROL

The CoolBar control has been made popular by Microsoft Internet Explorer and consists of a collection of bands that can host other controls, typically flat Toolbar, TextBox, and ComboBox controls. Users can resize and move bands at run time using the mouse and can even change their order. A double-click on a band's handle expands the band as much as possible on the row to which it belongs.

The CoolBar control includes a Bands collection, which in turn contains one or more Band objects. Each Band object can work as the container for only one control, and such a contained control is automatically moved and resized when the user moves or resizes the Band container. You can't have a windowless control as a child control for a Band object, but you can place a windowless control in another container control—for example, a PictureBox control—and make the latter a child control of the Band. Similarly, you can't have more than one child control per Band object, but you can place multiple controls inside the child PictureBox. (In this case, you must write the code that resizes the controls inside the PictureBox's *Resize* event.)

The CoolBar control is the only control contained in the ComCt332.ocx file. Visual Basic 6 is the first version that includes this control, even though the control has been available to Visual Basic 5 programmers for downloading from the Microsoft site.

Setting Design-Time Properties

The CoolBar control is complex and exposes so many design-time properties that you'll probably need some time to master all of them.

General properties

After you drop a CoolBar control on a form, first align it to the form's border. You do this in the regular Properties window by setting the *Align* property to the value 1-vbAlignTop. All the other design-time properties can be modified within the custom Properties dialog box.

The *Orientation* property lets you set the aspect of the control to either 0-cc3OrientationHorizonal (the default value) or 1-cc3OrientationVertical. The *BandBorders* property can be set to False if you want to suppress the horizontal lines that mark the borders of each Band, but in most cases it's a better idea to leave it set to True.

Users can move and resize a Band object at run time by dragging its leftmost border, but you can ensure that users aren't allowed to alter the order of Band objects by setting the *FixedOrder* property to True. The *VariantHeight* Boolean property tells whether Band objects can have different heights: If True (the default value), the height of each row is determined by the largest *MinHeight* property of all the Band objects in that row; if False, all rows have the same height, which is determined by the largest *MinHeight* property of all the Band objects in the CoolBar control.

Band objects

By default, the CoolBar control has three Band objects, but you can add or remove Band objects in the Bands tab of the Property Pages dialog box, shown in Figure 11-8 on the following page. Each Band can be resizable (if the *Style* property is

0-cc3BandNormal) or not (if *Style* is 1-cc3BandFixedSize). A band of a fixed width doesn't display the leftmost resize handle.

A Band object can display a string (the *Caption* property); and it has an initial width (the *Width* property), a minimal width (*MinWidth* property), and a minimal height (*MinHeight* property). It also exposes a *Key* property, which lets you retrieve the Band object from the Bands collection, and a *Tag* property, in which you can store any information related to the Band itself.

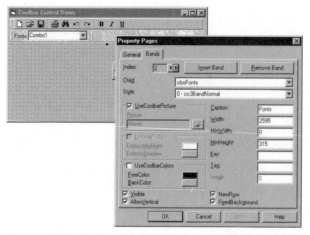

Figure 11-8. *The Bands tab of the Properties dialog box of a CoolBar control. Note that the background picture doesn't work well with a child Toolbar.*

The most important property of a Band object is *Child*, which holds a reference to the child control that's contained in that particular Band. To move a control into a Band object, you must first make the control a child of the CoolBar. The simplest way to do that is by creating it from the Toolbox inside the CoolBar control. After doing that, you'll find the control's name in the list of controls that can be made a child of the Band.

By default, a row of Bands hosts as many Bands as possible, and the position of each Band object depends on the order of Bands and their minimum widths. To change the position of a Band, you can set the *NewRow* property to True to move a Band to the beginning of the next row. Finally you can set the *AllowVertical* property to False to make a Band invisible when the CoolBar control changes its orientation to cc3OrientationVertical.

Image and color management

The CoolBar control supports advanced management of colors and pictures. If the *Picture* property hasn't been assigned, the aspect of the control depends on the standard *ForeColor* and *BackColor* properties. If you assign a bitmap or a metafile to the CoolBar's *Picture* property, this image spreads over all the Bands in the control and the *BackColor* property is ignored.

To let programmers create a user interface identical to the one exposed by Microsoft Internet Explorer, the CoolBar control includes three additional properties. The *EmbossPicture* Boolean property determines whether the image should be dithered to two colors; if this property is True, the colors used for embossing depend on the *EmbossHighlight* and *EmbossShadow* properties. The CoolBar control uses a dithering algorithm to decide which colors in the original image should be rendered with the lighter or with the darker color.

By default, all Band objects inherit the picture set for the parent CoolBar control and the picture tiles across all the bands regardless of whether the bands are resized or moved. You can set the *FixedBackground* property of a Band object to False, in which case the image remains fixed when that particular band is moved or resized.

Alternatively, you can set a different image for all or some Band objects by setting their *UseCoolbarPicture* properties to False and assigning a valid value to their *Picture* properties. You can even dither the image by setting the affected Bands' *EmbossProperty* to True and assigning suitable values to the *EmbossHighlight* and *EmbossShadow* properties, much as you do with the main CoolBar control.

Band objects also inherit the parent Coolbar's color properties, unless you set the Band's *UseCoolbarColors* to False. If you do that, you can select the color used for a particular Band by setting its *ForeColor* and *BackColor* properties. (But the latter is actually used only if the band doesn't display an image.)

Oddly, neither the CoolBar control nor the Band control expose the *Font* property, so the appearance of a Band's caption depends entirely on system settings, with the exception of its text color (which is affected by the *ForeColor* property). For greater control over text attributes, you can use a Label control and put it inside a PictureBox control used as a child control of the CoolBar. (Remember that Label controls and other lightweight controls can't be children of a Band object.)

Run-Time Operations

In most cases, you don't have to interact with a CoolBar control at run time: The CoolBar knows how to resize bands when the user moves them to another row and how to resize child controls inside each band. In a few particular circumstances, however, you might need to programmatically manipulate a CoolBar control.

Reacting to *Resize* events

When the user moves a Band object at run time and this action causes a row of bands to be created or destroyed, the CoolBar control raises a *Resize* event. You can take advantage of this event if you want to rearrange the position of other controls on the form or to programmatically hide or show Band objects.

But sometimes you shouldn't add code to the *Resize* event. For example, if the CoolBar control is itself contained in another control, the CoolBar's *Height* property might return incorrect values if queried from inside that event, or the *Resize* event might even be suppressed. For these reasons, it's preferable to write code inside the *HeightChanged* event procedure. This event fires when the *Height* property of a horizontal CoolBar or the *Width* property of a vertical CoolBar is modified.

Reacting to such events is important if the form contains other controls. Unless you take precautions, when the CoolBar grows in height other controls on the form might be covered by it. For this reason, you might want to gather all the other controls on the form inside a container control—for example, a PictureBox, so that you can move all of them by simply moving the container. If you follow this approach, you should also write code inside the form's *Resize* and PictureBox's *Resize* event procedures. This code snippet (taken from the demonstration program provided on the companion CD and shown in Figure 11-9) illustrates how this solution works:

```
' Resize the PictureBox when the form resizes.
Private Sub Form_Resize()
    Picture1.Move 0, CoolBar1.Height, ScaleWidth, _
        ScaleHeight - CoolBar1.Height
End Sub

' Resize and move the PictureBox when the Coolbar's height changes.
Private Sub CoolBar1_HeightChanged(ByVal NewHeight As Single)
    ' Assumes this Coolbar is aligned to the form's top border
    Picture1.Move 0, NewHeight, ScaleWidth, ScaleHeight - NewHeight
End Sub

' Resize the controls inside the PictureBox when the latter is resized.
Private Sub Picture1_Resize()
    Label1.Move 0, 0, Picture1.ScaleWidth, Label1.Height
    Text1.Move 0, Label1.Height, Picture1.ScaleWidth, _
        Picture1.ScaleHeight - Label1.Height
End Sub
```

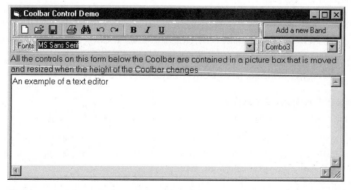

Figure 11-9. *The demonstration program shows how to deal with resizable CoolBar controls.*

Adding Band objects

From time to time, you might need to programmatically add Band objects at run time. You do this using the Bands collection's *Add* method, which has the following syntax:

```
Add([Index],[Key],[Caption],[Image],[NewRow],[Child],[Visible]) As Band
```

where each argument affects the Band property of the same name. The *Child* argument is a reference to the control that should go inside that Band. When you're using this technique for creating a Band object, the child control is probably being created dynamically, in which case you should make it a child of the CoolBar control before assigning it to the *Child* property of a Band object:

```
' Create a new ComboBox control.
Dim cb As ComboBox
Set cb = Controls.Add("VB.ComboBox", "NewCombo")
' Make it a child of the CoolBar1 control.
Set cb.Container = CoolBar1
' Create a new Band object, assigning the ComboBox to its
' Child property.
CoolBar1.Bands.Add , "NewBand" , cb.Name, , , cb
```

You can remove a Band object using the Bands collection's *Remove* method:

```
' Remove the Band object created with the previous code snippet.
CoolBar1.Bands.Remove "NewBand"
```

Using a Toolbar control as a child control

While a background image gives the CoolBar control an appealing appearance, you should be aware that it doesn't work well with some types of child controls, most notably Toolbar controls. In fact, the background image doesn't appear inside the Toolbar control, and the end result doesn't look very good. (See Figure 11-9.) Fortunately, there's a workaround, even though it isn't as simple as you might wish.

The solution I found is based on a file that, as I write this, is available on the Visual Studio Owner's Area of the Microsoft Web site, in the Coolbar Sample project. This sample project shows how to include a Toolbar control in the CoolBar control and uses an auxiliary TransTBWrapper module that magically creates a flat toolbar with a transparent background, which you can see in Figure 11-10 on the following page. This technique was necessary because the version of the Toolbar available on the Web to Visual Basic 5 programmers didn't support the flat style.

As you know, the Visual Basic 6 Toolbar control does support the flat style, so you can embed it in a CoolBar control and still achieve a consistent look. The new Toolbar still doesn't support a transparent background, however, which prevents you from using a background picture in the CoolBar control. It took me some minutes to modify the TransTBWrapper module and have it work with the new Toolbar control, but the results are worth the additional effort. You can use this new version of the module in your own applications, but remember that this file isn't supported by Microsoft.

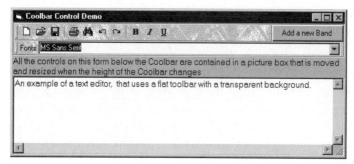

Figure 11-10. *A better version of the demonstration program uses the TransTBWrapper module to host a child Toolbar control with a transparent background.*

To achieve the transparent background effect shown in Figure 11-10, prepare your program as you would normally do and then add the TransTB.Ctl file to your project. This file includes the TransTBWrapper ActiveX control, so you can add an instance of this control on the form that contains the CoolBar and Toolbar controls. At this point, you just need a few statements in the form's *Load* and *Unload* event procedures:

```
Private Sub Form_Load()
    ' Put the toolbar wrapper controls in the CoolBar band.
    Set TransTBWrapper1.Container = CoolBar1
    ' This must be the same Band that hosts the toolbar.
    Set CoolBar1.Bands(1).Child = TransTBWrapper1
    ' Put the toolbar into the toolbar wrapper.
    Set TransTBWrapper1.Toolbar = Toolbar1
End Sub

Private Sub Form_Unload(Cancel As Integer)
    ' It is VERY important to set the wrapper's Toolbar property
    ' to Nothing before the form is unloaded.
    CoolBar1.Visible = False
    Set TransTBWrapper1.Toolbar = Nothing
End Sub
```

> **CAUTION**   Ensure that the *Form_Unload* event is always executed; otherwise, you risk an application crash. For this reason, when testing the application inside the Visual Basic IDE *always* terminate it by unloading the main form, and never execute an *End* statement. (An *End* statement would prevent the *Unload* event from firing.)

This chapter concludes the description of all the common controls provided with Visual Basic. There are a few other controls that Visual Basic programmers can use in their programs, and these will be described in the next chapter.

Chapter 12

Other ActiveX Controls

Microsoft Visual Basic applications can exploit any ActiveX control, whether it's provided with the product or purchased from a third-party vendor. And of course you can manufacture your own ActiveX controls, as explained in Chapter 17. In this chapter, I describe the most interesting controls included in the Visual Basic package. All these controls were included in Visual Basic 5.

THE MASKEDBOX CONTROL

The MaskEdBox control is a TextBox-like control with many additional features that are helpful, or even necessary, in building robust and bulletproof data entry procedures. This control is embedded in the MSMask32.ocx, so you have to distribute this file with all the applications that include one or more instances of the MaskEdBox control.

Setting Design-Time Properties

All the custom properties of the MaskEdBox control can be set in the General tab of the custom Property Pages dialog box, as shown in Figure 12-1. The *MaxLength* property is the maximum number of characters accepted in the control; if the *AutoTab* property is True, the focus automatically advances to the following field after the user has typed the allotted number of characters. The *PromptChar* property sets the prompt character, that is, the symbol used as a placeholder for an input character. (The default is the underscore character.) The *AllowPrompt* Boolean property determines whether the prompt character is also a valid input character. (The default is False.) The *PromptInclude* property determines whether the *Text* property returns prompt characters.

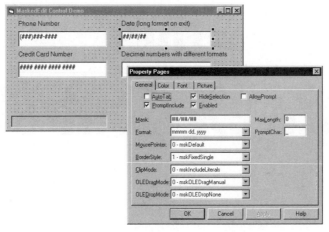

Figure 12-1. *The MaskEdBox control at design time.*

The key property of the MaskEdBox control is *Mask*, a string that tells you which characters are allowed in each position of the control's contents. This string can include special characters that specify whether the required character is a digit, a letter, a decimal or thousand separator, or another kind of character. (See Table 12-1 for a complete list of special characters.) For example, the following statement prepares a MaskEdBox control for accepting a phone number:

```
MaskEdBox1.Mask = "(###)###-####"
```

You can specify a date and time format using the appropriate separators, as shown here:

```
MaskEdBox1.Mask = "##/##/##"        ' A date value in mm/dd/yy format
MaskEdBox1.Mask = "##:##"           ' A time value in hh:mm format
```

In this case, however, the MaskEdBox control performs only a character-by-character validation, and it's up to you to check that the control contains a valid date in the *Validate* event procedure. For this reason, it's usually preferable to use a DateTimePicker control for date and time entry because this control performs all the validation chores automatically. If the *Mask* property is assigned an empty string, the control behaves like a regular TextBox control.

Character	Description
#	Required digit.
9	Optional digit.
.	Decimal separator.
,	Thousand separator.
:	Time separator.
/	Date separator.
&	Character placeholder. (All ANSI codes, except nonprintable characters, such as the tab character.)
C	Same as &. (Ensures compatibility with Microsoft Access.)
A	Alphanumerical required character (a–z, A–Z, 0–9).
a	Alphanumerical optional character (a–z, A–Z, 0–9).
?	Letter placeholder (a–z, A–Z).
>	Convert all characters that follow to uppercase.
<	Convert all characters that follow to lowercase.
\	Escape symbol: the character or symbol that follows is treated as a literal.
(Other)	Any other character in the mask is treated as a literal and is displayed in the control as is.

Table 12-1. *Special characters in the* Mask *property of a MaskEdBox control. The actual characters accepted for decimal, thousand, date, and time separators depend on the localization settings of your system.*

The *Format* property determines the appearance of the control when the focus leaves it. For example, you might have a date field that should be formatted as a long date when the user leaves the control. You can arrange this by assigning the *Format* property a suitable string either at design time or at run time:

```
MaskEdBox1.Format = "mmmm dd, yyyy"
```

You can pass the *Format* property any value that you would use with the VBA's *Format* function, except named formats such as *scientific* or *long date*. You can also pass up to four values to format positive, negative, zero, or Null values with different format substrings separated by a semicolon, as in this code:

```
' Show two decimal digits and the thousand separator, enclose
' negative numbers within parentheses, and show "Zero" when "0"
' has been entered.
MaskEdBox1.Format = "#,##0.00;(#,##0.00);Zero"
```

The fourth format substring is used when the control is bound to a database field that contains the Null value.

The only other custom property that you can set at design time is *ClipMode*, which determines what happens when the user copies or cuts the contents of the control to the Clipboard. If this property is 0-mskIncludeLiterals, the string being cut or copied includes all literal characters. If the property is 1-mskExcludeLiterals, all literal characters are filtered out before cutting or copying the string to the Clipboard. This property has no effect if *Mask* is an empty string.

Run-Time Operations

The MaskEdBox control is basically a supercharged TextBox control, and as such it supports many of the latter control's properties, methods, and events. There are a few differences, however, that you should take into account.

Working with the *Text* property

The MaskEdBox control supports the *Text* property, as well as related properties such as *SelStart*, *SelLength*, and *SelText*. The *Text* property returns the current contents of the control, including all literal characters, separators, and the underscores that are part of the mask. To filter out such extra characters, you can use the value returned by the *ClipText* read-only property:

```
' Work with a date control.
MaskEdBox1.Mask = "##/##/####"
' Assign a date using the Text property.
MaskEdBox1.Text = "12/31/1998"
' Read it back with the ClipText property.
Print MaskEdBox1.ClipText          ' Displays "1231998"
```

Don't forget that when you assign a value to the *Text* property, you're subject to the same constraints enforced when a string is entered in the control and that assigning an invalid string raises an error.

Fortunately, to retrieve the contents of a MaskEdBox control, you don't have to filter out separators yourself. When the *ClipMode* property is True, the value returned by the *SelText* property doesn't include literals and separators. Even more interesting, if you assign a value to this property, the control behaves as if the string had been pasted from the Clipboard or, if you prefer, as if each character had been manually typed in the control. This means that you don't have to include any literals or separators in your assignment statement:

```
' Read the contents of the control without any separator.
MaskEdBox1.ClipMode = mskExcludeLiterals
MaskEdBox1.SelStart = 0: MaskEdBox1.SelLength = 9999
MsgBox "The control's value is " & MaskEdBox1.SelText
' Assign a new date value. (Don't worry about date separators.)
MaskEdBox1.SelText = "12311998"
```

Another way to access the contents of a MaskEdBox control is through the *FormattedText* property, which returns the string that's displayed in the control when it doesn't have the input focus. If the *Mask* property is an empty string, this property is similar to the *Text* property, except that it's read-only. Note that if the *HideSelection* property has been set to False, the control doesn't format its contents when it loses the input focus; in this case, however, you can still retrieve the formatted value through the *FormattedText* property.

Validating user input

The MaskEdBox control raises a *ValidationError* event each time the user presses an invalid key or pastes an invalid string into the control. This event receives two parameters: InvalidText is the value that the *Text* property would assume if the invalid key had been accepted, and *StartPosition* is the index of the first invalid character in this string.

```
Private Sub MaskEdBox1_ValidationError(InvalidText As String, _
    StartPosition As Integer)
    ' StartPosition is zero-based.
    LblStatus.Caption = "'" & Mid$(InvalidText, StartPosition + 1, 1) _
        & "' is an invalid character"
End Sub
```

The previous code snippet has a defect, though, in that it doesn't work correctly if the invalid character is typed at the end of the current contents of the control. In that case, the *Mid$* function returns an empty string, and there's no way to retrieve the invalid character. For this reason, you might prefer to display a generic error message that doesn't contain the actual invalid character.

A shortcoming of the *ValidationError* event is that it seems impossible to show a message box from within it. If you try to show a message box, you're caught in an endless loop and the event is repeatedly invoked, until you press the Ctrl+Break key combination. (If you're working with a compiled application, you have to force its termination using Ctrl+Alt+Del.)

Starting with Visual Basic 6, the MaskEdBox control supports the standard *Validate* event, so it's now considerably simpler to enforce data entry validation.

THE COMMONDIALOG CONTROL

The CommonDialog control provides an easy and convenient way to invoke the Color, Font, Printer, FileOpen, and FileSave Windows common dialog boxes, and it also allows you to display a page in a help file. This control exposes only properties and methods—no events. In most cases, you don't set any properties at design time because it's often preferable to assign all of them at run time, especially when you use the same control to display different dialog boxes. The control is invisible during the execution, so it doesn't support properties such as *Left*, *Visible*, or *TabIndex*. This control is embedded in the ComDlg32.ocx file, which has to be distributed with any Visual Basic application that uses it.

The lack of a visible interface and the lack of events doesn't mean that this control is easy to use, though. As a matter of fact, using the CommonDialog control is a complex enterprise because it supports many options, some of which aren't always intuitive. Some properties have different meanings, depending on which common dialog box you're displaying. For example, the *Flags* property is a bit-field property, and the meaning of each bit is different for each of the various common dialog boxes.

One of the few properties that can have the same meaning regardless of which common dialog box you're displaying is *CancelError*. If this property is True, an end user closing the dialog box using the Cancel key causes error 32755 (equal to the constant *cdlCancel*) to be raised in the calling program. The CommonDialog control includes intrinsic constants for all the errors that can be generated at run time.

All common dialog boxes also share a few properties related to help support. You can display a Help button in the common dialog box and tell the CommonDialog control what page in what help file must be displayed when the user clicks the Help button. *HelpFile* is the complete name of the help file, *HelpContext* is the context ID of the requested page, and *HelpCommand* is the action that must be performed when the button is clicked. (It's usually assigned the value 1-cdlHelpContext.) Don't forget that to actually display the Help button, you must set a bit in the *Flags* property. The position of this bit varies with the particular common dialog box, for example:

```
' Show a Help button.
CommonDialog1.HelpFile = "F:\vbprogs\DlgMaste\Tdm.hlp"
CommonDialog1.HelpContext = 12
CommonDialog1.HelpCommand = cdlHelpContext
' The value for the Flags property depends on the dialog.
If ShowColorDialog Then
    CommonDialog1.Flags = cdlCCHelpButton
    CommonDialog1.ShowColor
ElseIf ShowFontDialog Then
    CommonDialog1.Flags = cdlCFHelpButton
    CommonDialog1.ShowFont
Else
    ' And so on
End If
```

For more information about help properties, see the section "Help Windows," later in this chapter.

The CommonDialog control exposes six methods: *ShowColor*, *ShowFont*, *ShowPrinter*, *ShowOpen*, *ShowSave*, and *ShowHelp*. Each method displays a different common dialog box, as explained in the following sections. On the companion CD, you'll find a complete demonstration program (part of which is visible in Figure 12-2) that shows in action all the common dialog boxes described in this section.

The Color Dialog

The Color common dialog box lets users select a color. It also permits them to define new custom colors, but you can keep this privilege from users by assigning the 4-cdlCCPreventFullOpen value to the *Flags* property. Alternatively, you can display the custom color section of the dialog box when the dialog appears by setting the 2-cdlCCFullOpen bit. (Custom color choices take up the right half of the dialog box shown in Figure 12-2.) You can initially highlight a color in the dialog box by assigning its RGB value to the *Color* property and setting the 1-cdlCCRGBInit bit in the *Flags* property, as in the following example:

```
' Let the user change the ForeColor of the Text1 control.
With CommonDialog1
    ' Prevent display of the custom color section
    ' of the dialog.
    .Flags = cdlCCPreventFullOpen Or cdlCCRGBInit
    .Color = Text1.ForeColor
        .CancelError = False
        .ShowColor
        Text1.ForeColor = .Color
End With
```

When you provide an initial color, you don't need to set the *CancelError* property to True; if the user clicks on the Cancel key, the value of the *Color* property doesn't change.

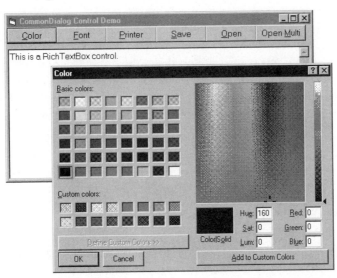

Figure 12-2. *The Color common dialog box, with the section for creating custom colors already opened, as it appears in the demonstration program.*

The Font Dialog

The Font dialog box lets users select font names and attributes. You can initialize the value shown in the dialog box, and you can decide which attributes can be modified. Of course, it's also up to you to apply the new attributes to controls and objects in your application. An example of a Font dialog box, with all the options enabled, is shown in Figure 12-3.

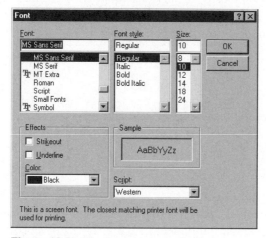

Figure 12-3. *The Font common dialog box.*

The font attributes can be initialized (and retrieved when the user closes the dialog box) through a number of properties whose names are self-explanatory: *FontName*, *FontSize*, *FontBold*, *FontItalic*, *FontUnderLine*, *FontStrikeThru*, and *Color*.

When used with the Font common dialog box, the *Flags* property accepts all the options that are summarized in Table 12-2. You use these flags to affect what fonts are listed in the dialog box and to restrict user selection. One of the bits that you should always include is cdlCFForceFontExist. Besides, at least one of the first four values in Table 12-2 must be specified; otherwise, the CommonDialog control raises an error 24574 "No fonts exist."

Constant	*Description*
cdlCFScreenFonts	Show screen fonts.
cdlCFPrinterFonts	Show printer fonts.
cdlCFBoth	Show both screen fonts and printer fonts. (This is the sum of cdlCFScreenFonts and cdlCFPrinterFonts.)
cdlCFWYSIWYG	Show only fonts that are available both on the screen and on the printer.

Table 12-2. *Values for the* Flags *property for a Font common dialog box.*

Constant	Description
cdlCFANSIOnly	Restrict selection to fonts that use ANSI character sets.
cdlCFFixedPitchOnly	Restrict selection to nonproportional (fixed pitch) fonts.
cdlCFNoVectorFonts	Restrict selection to nonvector fonts.
cdlCFScalableOnly	Restrict selection to scalable fonts.
cdlCFTTOnly	Restrict selection to TrueType fonts.
cdlCFNoSimulations	Restrict selection to fonts that aren't GDI font simulations.
cdlCFLimitSize	Restrict selection to font size in the range indicated by the *Min* and *Max* properties.
cdlCFForceFontExist	Raise an error if user selects a font or a style that doesn't exist.
cdlCFEffects	Enable the strikethrough, underline, and color fields in the dialog box.
cdlCFNoFaceSel	Don't select font name.
cdlCFNoSizeSel	Don't select font size.
cdlCFNoStyleSel	Don't select font style. (Can be tested on exit to determine whether user selected a style.)
cdlCFHelpButton	Display the Help button.

The following piece of code lets the user modify the font attributes of a TextBox control. It limits the user's selection to existing screen fonts and forces the font size in the range from 8 to 80 points:

```
With CommonDialog1
    .Flags = cdlCFScreenFonts Or cdlCFForceFontExist Or cdlCFEffects _
        Or cdlCFLimitSize
    .Min = 8
    .Max = 80
    .FontName = Text1.FontName
    .FontSize = Text1.FontSize
    .FontBold = Text1.FontBold
    .FontItalic = Text1.FontItalic
    .FontUnderline = Text1.FontUnderline
    .FontStrikethru = Text1.FontStrikethru
    .CancelError = False
    .ShowFont
    Text1.FontName = .FontName
    Text1.FontBold = .FontBold
    Text1.FontItalic = .FontItalic
```

(continued)

```
        Text1.FontSize = .FontSize
        Text1.FontUnderline = .FontUnderline
        Text1.FontStrikethru = .FontStrikethru
End With
```

In this particular case, you don't need to set the *CancelError* property to True because if the user clicks on the Cancel button the control doesn't modify any *Fontxxxx* properties and all *Fontxxxx* property values can be assigned back to the control without any undesirable effects.

When you don't want to initialize a field with a well-defined value, you have a more complex problem. Consider this situation: You're writing a word processor application, and you display a Font common dialog box to let the user select the font name, size, and attributes of the selection portion of text. If the selection contains characters with homogeneous attributes, you can (and should) initialize the corresponding fields in the common dialog box. On the other hand, if the selection includes characters of different fonts or with different sizes or attributes, you should leave these fields blank. You can do this by specifying the cdlCFNoFaceSel, cdlCFNoStyleSel, and cdlCFNoStyleSel bits of the *Flags* property. The following code lets the user modify the attributes of a RichTextBox control. (I describe this control in depth later in this chapter.)

```
On Error Resume Next
With CommonDialog1
    .Flags = cdlCFBoth Or cdlCFForceFontExist Or cdlCFEffects
    If IsNull(RichTextBox1.SelFontName) Then
        .Flags = .Flags Or cdlCFNoFaceSel
    Else
        .FontName = RichTextBox1.SelFontName
    End If
    If IsNull(RichTextBox1.SelFontSize) Then
        .Flags = .Flags Or cdlCFNoSizeSel
    Else
        .FontSize = RichTextBox1.SelFontSize
    End If
    If IsNull(RichTextBox1.SelBold) Or IsNull(RichTextBox1.SelItalic) Then
        .Flags = .Flags Or cdlCFNoStyleSel
    Else
        .FontBold = RichTextBox1.SelBold
        .FontItalic = RichTextBox1.SelItalic
    End If
    .CancelError = True
    .ShowFont
    If Err = 0 Then
        RichTextBox1.SelFontName = .FontName
        RichTextBox1.SelBold = .FontBold
        RichTextBox1.SelItalic = .FontItalic
```

```
        If (.Flags And cdlCFNoSizeSel) = 0 Then
            RichTextBox1.SelFontSize = .FontSize
        End If
        RichTextBox1.SelUnderline = .FontUnderline
        RichTextBox1.SelStrikeThru = .FontStrikethru
    End If
End With
```

The Printer Dialog

The CommonDialog control can display two distinct dialogs: the Print Setup dialog box that allows users to select a printer's attributes and the standard Print dialog that lets users select many options of a print job, such as which portion of the document should be printed (all, a page range, or the current selection), the number of copies, and so on. See Figures 12-4 and 12-5 for examples of these common dialog boxes.

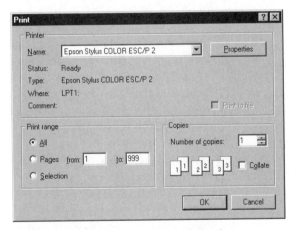

Figure 12-4. *The Print common dialog box.*

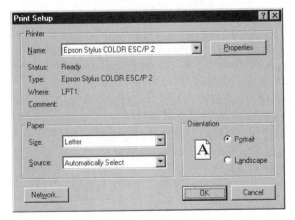

Figure 12-5. *The Print Setup common dialog box.*

You decide which dialog box appears by setting the *cdlPDPrintSetup* bit in the *Flags* property. The complete list of bits that can be set in the *Flags* property is summarized in Table 12-3.

Constant	Description
cdlPDPrintSetup	Display the Print Setup dialog box instead of the Print dialog box.
cdlPDNoWarning	Prevent an error message if there isn't any default printer.
cdlPDHidePrintToFile	Hide the Print To File check box.
cdlPDDisablePrintToFile	Disable the Print To File check box.
cdlPDNoPageNums	Disable the Pages option button.
cdlPDNoSelection	Disable the Selection option button.
cdlPDPrintToFile	The state of the Print To File check box. (Can be read upon exiting.)
cdlPDAllPages	The state of the All Pages option button. (Can be read upon exiting.)
cdlPDPageNums	The state of the Pages option button. (Can be read upon exiting)
cdlPDSelection	The state of the Selection option button. (Can be read upon exiting.)
cdlPDCollate	The state of the Collate check box. (Can be read upon exiting.)
cdlPDReturnDC	The *hDC* property returns the device context of the selected printer.
cdlPDReturnIC	The *hDC* property returns the information context of the selected printer.
cdlPDReturnDefault	Return default printer name.
cdlPDUseDevModeCopies	Set support for multiple copies.
cdlPDHelpButton	Display the Help button.

Table 12-3. *Values for the* Flags *property for a printer common dialog box. Most of these bits are meaningless if you're showing a Print Setup dialog box (*Flags = cdlPDPrintSetup*).*

When you're displaying a printer dialog box, the *Min* and *Max* properties are the minimum and maximum valid values for page numbers whereas *FromPage* and *ToPage* are the actual values displayed in the dialog box. You typically set the latter two properties upon entering and read them back upon exiting if the bit cdlPDPageNums is set. The *Copies* property reflects the number of copies entered by the user.

The *PrinterDefault* property determines whether the Visual Basic Printer object is automatically set to match the printer selected by the user. I recommend that you set this bit because it greatly simplifies subsequent print operations. If you don't set this bit, the only way you can retrieve information about the selected printer is through the Common Dialog's *hDC* property, which means that you need to perform your printing chores using API calls (not a simple thing to do).

When you're displaying a Print Setup dialog box, the *Orientation* property sets and returns the orientation selected for the printer job. (The settings can be 1-cdlPortrait or 2-cdlLandscape.) Neither the *Orientation* nor *Copies* properties are correctly set under Windows NT, however.

If you're showing a regular printer dialog box, you need to decide whether the Pages and the Selection option buttons should be enabled. For example, should a user want to print the contents of a TextBox control, you should enable the Selection option button only if the user actually selects a portion of text:

```
On Error Resume Next
With CommonDialog1
    ' Prepare to print using the Printer object.
    .PrinterDefault = True
    ' Disable printing to file and individual page printing.
    .Flags = cdlPDDisablePrintToFile Or cdlPDNoPageNums
    If Text1.SelLength = 0 Then
        ' Hide Selection button if there is no selected text.
        .Flags = .Flags Or cdlPDNoSelection
    Else
        ' Else enable the Selection button and make it the default
        ' choice.
        .Flags = .Flags Or cdlPDSelection
    End If
    ' We need to know whether the user decided to print.
    .CancelError = True
    .ShowPrinter
    If Err = 0 Then
        If .Flags And cdlPDSelection Then
            Printer.Print Text1.SelText
        Else
            Printer.Print Text1.Text
        End If
    End If
End With
```

The FileOpen and FileSave Dialogs

The FileOpen and FileSave common dialog boxes are very similar, and in fact the Visual Basic documentation explains them together. While this is a reasonable approach, I have found that dealing with them jointly tends to hide the many subtle differences between these two dialog box types. For this reason, I decided to describe their common properties first and then focus on each type of dialog box in a separate section.

Properties in common

You can choose from an impressive number of ways to customize the appearance and behavior of the FileOpen and FileSave dialog boxes. For example, the *DialogTitle* property determines the caption of the common dialog box, and *InitDir* is the directory displayed when the dialog appears. When the dialog box is invoked, the *FileName* property contains the name of the prompted file. And when the dialog closes, it contains the name of the file selected by the user. The *DefaultExt* property can be assigned the default extension of a filename so that the control can automatically return a complete name in the *FileName* property even if the user doesn't type the extension. Alternatively, you can set and retrieve the base filename (that is, the name of the file without the extension) by using the *FileTitle* property.

You can define the file filters available to the user when browsing the contents of a directory. You do this by assigning the *Filter* property a string that contains *(description, filter)* pairs, with items separated by a pipe (|) character. For example, when working with graphic files, you can define three filters in the following way:

```
' You can specify multiple filters by using the semicolon as a delimiter.
CommonDialog1.Filter = "All Files|*.*|Bitmaps|*.bmp|Metafiles|*.wmf;*.emf"
```

You decide which filter is initially selected using the *FilterIndex* property:

```
' Display the Bitmaps filter. (Filters are one-based.)
CommonDialog1.FilterIndex = 2
```

The real difficulty in working with FileOpen and FileSave dialog boxes is that they support a lot of flags, and most flags aren't adequately documented in the Visual Basic manuals. In some cases, I had to resort to the Windows SDK documentation to understand what a given flag actually does. All the flags supported by FileOpen and FileSave common dialog boxes are summarized in Table 12-4.

Constant	*Description*
cdlOFNReadOnly	The state of the Open As Read-Only check box (FileOpen only).
cdlOFNOverwritePrompt	Show a message before overwriting existing files. (FileSave only.)
cdlOFNHideReadOnly	Hide the Open As Read-Only check box. This bit should always be set in FileSave dialog boxes.
cdlOFNNoChangeDir	Don't modify the current directory. (By default, a File dialog box changes current drive and directory to match the path of the file selected by the user.)

Table 12-4. *Values of the* Flags *property for a FileOpen or FileSave common dialog box. Note that a few bits make sense only with one of the two dialog boxes.*

Constant	Description
cdlOFNNoValidate	Accept invalid characters in filenames. (Not recommended.)
cdlOFNAllowMultiselect	Enable multiple file selection. (FileOpen only.)
cdlOFNExtensionDifferent	The extension of the selected file is different from the value of the *DefaultExt* property. (To be tested upon exiting.)
cdlOFNPathMustExist	Refuse filenames with invalid or nonexistent paths. (Highly recommended.)
cdlOFNFileMustExist	Refuse to select files that don't exist. (FileOpen only.)
cdlOFNCreatePrompt	If the selected file doesn't exist, ask whether a new file should be created. Automatically set cdlOFNFileMustExist and cdlOFNPathMustExist. (FileOpen only.)
cdlOFNShareAware	Ignore network sharing errors. (Not recommended—use only if you're willing to solve sharing conflicts through code.)
cdlOFNNoReadOnlyReturn	Refuse to select read-only files or files that reside in a write-protected directory.
cdlOFNExplorer	Use a Windows Explorer–like interface in multiple-selection dialog boxes. (Multiple-selection FileOpen only; ignored in all other cases.)
cdlOFNLongNames	This flag *should* enable long filenames in multiple-selection dialog boxes that use the Windows Explorer style. However, it turns out that these dialog boxes always support long filenames, so this feature appears to be useless. (Multiple-selection FileOpen only.)
cdlOFNNoDereferenceLinks	Return the name and the path of the file selected by the user, even if this is a shortcut LNK file that points to another file. If this flag is omitted, when the user selects a LNK file the dialog box returns the name and path of the referenced file.
cdlOFNHelpButton	Show the Help button.
cdlOFNNoLongNames	Disallow long filenames.

When working with a FileOpen or a FileSave dialog box, you should always set the *CancelError* property to True because you need a way to find out whether the user canceled the file operation.

The FileSave dialog

Because the FileSave dialog box is the simpler of the two, I'll describe it first. Now you know enough to display a FileSave dialog box like the one shown in Figure 12-6. The next routine accepts a reference to a TextBox control and to a CommonDialog control: The routine uses the latter control to ask for a filename before it saves the contents of a TextBox control to the selected file. It returns the name of the file in the third argument:

```
' Returns False if the Save command has been canceled,
' True otherwise.
Function SaveTextControl(TB As Control, CD As CommonDialog, _
    Filename As String) As Boolean
    Dim filenum As Integer
    On Error GoTo ExitNow

    CD.Filter = "All files (*.*)|*.*|Text files|*.txt"
    CD.FilterIndex = 2
    CD.DefaultExt = "txt"
    CD.Flags = cdlOFNHideReadOnly Or cdlOFNPathMustExist Or _
        cdlOFNOverwritePrompt Or cdlOFNNoReadOnlyReturn
    CD.DialogTitle = "Select the destination file "
    CD.Filename = Filename
    ' Exit if user presses Cancel.
    CD.CancelError = True
    CD.ShowSave
    Filename = CD.Filename

    ' Write the control's contents.
    filenum = FreeFile()
    Open Filename For Output As #filenum
    Print #filenum, TB.Text;
    Close #filenum
    ' Signal success.
    SaveTextControl = True
ExitNow:

End Function
```

You can use the *SaveTextControl* routine as follows:

```
Dim Filename As String
If SaveTextControl(RichTextBox1, CommonDialog1, Filename) Then
    MsgBox "Text has been saved to file " & Filename
End If
```

Upon exiting a FileSave (and also a FileOpen) dialog box, you can test the cdlOFNExtensionDifferent bit of the *Flags* property, in case you need to know whether the selected file has an extension different from the one assigned to the *DefaultExt* property:

```
If CD.Flags And cdlOFNExtensionDifferent Then
    ' Process nonstandard extensions here.
End If
```

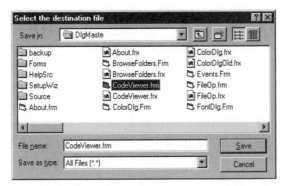

Figure 12-6. *The FileSave common dialog box.*

Don't forget to specify the cdlOFNHideReadOnly bit for FileSave dialog boxes: If you do forget, the Open As Read-Only check box will appear in the dialog box, which can confuse the user, who is saving a file, not opening it. Another convenient flag is cdlOFNNoReadOnlyReturn, which ensures that the file doesn't have the read-only attribute and therefore can be overwritten without raising an error.

The single-selection FileOpen dialog

The CommonDialog control supports both single- and multiple-selection FileOpen dialog boxes. The former type isn't substantially different from a FileSave dialog box, even though you usually specify different bits for the *Flags* property. Here's a reusable routine that loads the contents of a text file into a TextBox control:

```
' Returns False if the command has been canceled, True otherwise.
Function LoadTextControl(TB As Control, CD As CommonDialog, _
    Filename As String) As Boolean
    Dim filenum As Integer
    On Error GoTo ExitNow

    CD.Filter = "All files (*.*)|*.*|Text files|*.txt"
    CD.FilterIndex = 2
    CD.DefaultExt = "txt"
    CD.Flags = cdlOFNHideReadOnly Or cdlOFNFileMustExist Or _
        cdlOFNNoReadOnlyReturn
    CD.DialogTitle = "Select the source file "
    CD.Filename = Filename
```

(continued)

```
      ' Exit if user presses Cancel.
      CD.CancelError = True
      CD.ShowOpen
      Filename = CD.Filename

      ' Read the file's contents into the control.
      filenum = FreeFile()
      Open Filename For Input As #filenum
      TB.Text = Input$(LOF(filenum), filenum)
      Close #filenum
      ' Signal success.
      LoadTextControl = True
ExitNow:
End Function
```

If you don't specify the cdlOFNHideReadOnly bit in the *Flag* property, the common dialog box includes the Open As Read-Only check box. To discover whether the user has clicked that check box, you test the *Flags* property upon exiting as follows:

```
If CD.Flags And cdlOFNReadOnly Then
      ' The file has been opened in read-only mode.
      ' (For example, you should disable the File-Save command.)
End If
```

The multiple-selection FileOpen dialog

Multiple-selection FileOpen dialog boxes are a bit more complex than single-selection dialog boxes. You specify that you want to open a multiple-selection file dialog box by setting the cdlOFNAllowMultiselect bit of the *Flags* property: All the files selected by the user will be concatenated in an individual string and then returned in the *FileName* property.

Because the user can select dozens or even hundreds of files, the returned string can be very long. By default, however, the FileOpen dialog box can deal only with returned strings of 256 characters or less: If the combined length of the file names selected by the user exceeds this limit, the control raises an error 20476 "Buffer too small." To circumvent this error, you can assign a higher value to the *MaxFileSize* property. For example, a value of 10 KB should suffice for most practical purposes:

```
CommonDialog1.MaxFileSize = 10240
```

To preserve compatibility with 16-bit programs, multiple-selection FileOpen dialogs return the lists of selected files using the space as a separator. Unfortunately, because the space is a valid character inside long filenames and therefore potentially confusing, all filenames are rendered in the old 8.3 MS-DOS format, and the dialog itself uses the outdated look visible in Figure 12-7. To work around this problem, you must specify the cdlOFNExplorer bit in the *Flags* property, which displays a modern

Windows Explorer–like user interface and returns the list of selected files as long filenames separated by null characters. Note that the documentation is incorrect, and the cdlOFNLongNames flag can be safely omitted because Windows Explorer–like dialog boxes automatically support long filenames.

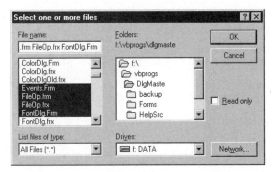

Figure 12-7. *A multiple-selection FileOpen common dialog box without the cdlOFNExplorer flag uses an outdated Windows 3.x look.*

Here's a reusable routine that asks the users for multiple files and then places all the filenames in a string array:

```
' Returns False if the command has been canceled, True otherwise.
Function SelectMultipleFiles(CD As CommonDialog, Filter As String, _
    Filenames() As String) As Boolean
    On Error GoTo ExitNow

    CD.Filter = "All files (*.*)|*.*|" & Filter
    CD.FilterIndex = 1
    CD.Flags = cdlOFNAllowMultiselect Or cdlOFNFileMustExist Or _
        cdlOFNExplorer
    CD.DialogTitle = "Select one or more files"
    CD.MaxFileSize = 10240
    CD.Filename = ""
    ' Exit if user presses Cancel.
    CD.CancelError = True
    CD.ShowOpen

    ' Parse the result to get filenames.
    Filenames() = Split(CD.Filename, vbNullChar)
    ' Signal success.
    SelectMultipleFiles = True
ExitNow:
End Function
```

After the user closes the dialog box, the *Filename* property might contain data in different formats, according to the number of files selected, for a couple of reasons.

■ If the user selected only one file, the *Filename* property returns the file's complete name (including the path), exactly as if this were a single-selection dialog box. In this case, the string doesn't contain any null character separators.

■ If the user selected multiple files, the *Filename* property contains a number of elements, which are separated by null characters (assuming that the cdlOFNExplorer bit has been set). The first element is the path, followed by the base names of selected files (but without the path portion).

The following code builds on the previously defined *SelectMultipleFiles* routine to find out which of these two cases occurred:

```
Dim Filenames() As String, i As Integer
If SelectMultipleFiles(CommonDialog1, "", Filenames()) Then
    If UBound(Filenames) = 0 Then
        ' The Filename property contained only one element.
        Print "Selected file: " & Filenames(0)
    Else
        ' The Filename property contained multiple elements.
        Print "Directory name: " & Filenames(0)
        For i = 1 To UBound(Filenames)
            Print "File #" & i & ": " & Filenames(i)
        Next
    End If
End If
```

Help Windows

You can use the CommonDialog control to display information from HLP files. In this case, no dialog box appears and only a few properties are used. You should assign the *HelpFile* property the filename and path, and the *HelpCommand* property an enumerated value that tells what you want to do with that file. Depending on which operation you're performing, you might need to assign a value to either the *HelpKey* or *HelpContext* property. Table 12-5 summarizes all the supported commands.

Constant	*Description*
cdlHelpContents	Show help contents page.
cdlHelpContext	Show the page whose context ID matches the value passed in the *HelpContext* property.
cdlHelpContextPopup	Same as cdlHelpContext, but the help page appears in a pop-up window.

Table 12-5. *All the possible values that can be assigned to the* HelpCommand *property when showing a help page.*

Constant	*Description*
cdlHelpKey	Show the page associated with the keyword passed in the *HelpKey* property.
cdlHelpPartialKey	Same as *cdlHelpKey*, but also searches for partial matches.
cdlHelpCommandHelp	Execute the help macro whose name has been assigned to the *HelpKey* property.
cdlHelpSetContents	The help page pointed to by the *HelpContext* property becomes the content page for the specified help file.
cdlHelpForceFile	Ensure that the help window is visible.
cdlHelpHelpOnHelp	Show the Help on Help page.
cdlHelpQuit	Close the help window.
cdlHelpIndex	Show help contents page (same as cdlHelpContents).
cdlHelpSetIndex	Set the current index for multi-index Help (same as cdlHelpSetContents).

The following code snippet shows how you can display the contents page associated with a help file:

```
' Show the contents page of DAO 3.5 help file.
With CommonDialog1
    ' Note: The path of this file may be different on your system.
    .HelpFile = "C:\WINNT\Help\Dao35.hlp"
    .HelpCommand = cdlHelpContents
    .ShowHelp
End With
```

You can also display a page associated with a keyword. If the keyword you provide in the *HelpKey* property doesn't match any particular page, the index of the help file is displayed instead:

```
With CommonDialog1
    .HelpFile = "C:\WINNT\Help\Dao35.hlp"
    .HelpCommand = cdlHelpKey
    .HelpKey = "BOF property"
    .ShowHelp
End With
```

You can also display a page associated with a given context ID, in which case you assign the cdlHelpContext constant to the *HelpCommand* property and the context ID to the *HelpContext* property. Of course, you must know which context ID corresponds to the particular page you're interested in, but this isn't a problem if you're the author of the help file. For more information about help context IDs, see the section "Showing Help" in Chapter 5.

THE RICHTEXTBOX CONTROL

The RichTextBox control is one of the most powerful controls provided with Visual Basic. In a nutshell, it's a text box that's able to display text stored in *Rich Text Format* (RTF), a standard format recognized by virtually all word processors, including Microsoft WordPad (not surprisingly, since WordPad internally uses the RichTextBox control). This control supports multiple fonts and colors, left and right margins, bulleted lists, and more.

You might need time to get used to the many features of the RichTextBox control. The good news is that the RichTextBox control is code-compatible with a regular multiline TextBox control, so you can often recycle code that you have written for a TextBox control. But unlike the standard TextBox control, the RichTextBox control has no practical limit to the number of lines of text it can contain.

The RichTextBox control is embedded in the RichTx32.ocx file, which you must distribute with all the applications that use this control.

Setting Design-Time Properties

You can set a few useful design-time properties in the General tab of the Property Pages dialog box as you can see in Figure 12-8. For example, you can type the name of a TXT or RTF file that must be loaded when the form is loaded and that corresponds to the *Filename* property.

The *RightMargin* property represents the distance in twips of the right margin from the left border of the control. The *BulletIndent* is the number of twips a paragraph is indented when the *SetBullet* property is True. The *AutoVerbMenu* is an interesting property that lets you prevent the standard Edit pop-up menu from appearing when the user right-clicks on the control. If you want to display your own pop-up menu, leave this property as False. All the other properties in this General page are also supported by standard TextBox controls, so I won't describe them here.

In the Appearance tab of the Properties dialog box, you find other properties, such as *BorderStyle* and *ScrollBars*, whose meaning should already be known to you. An exception is the *DisableNoScroll* property: When the *ScrollBars* property is assigned a value other than 0-rtfNone and you set the *DisableNoScroll* property to True, the RichTextBox control will always display the scroll bars, even if the current document is so short that it doesn't require scrolling. This is consistent with the behavior of most word processors.

The RichTextBox control is data-aware and therefore exposes the usual *Dataxxxx* properties that let you bind the control to a data source. In other words, you can write entire TXT or RTF documents in a single field of a database.

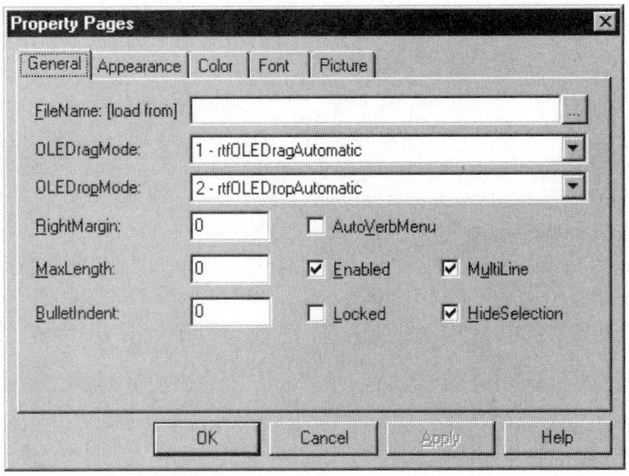

Figure 12-8. *The General tab of the Properties dialog box of a RichTextBox control.*

Run-Time Operations

The RichTextBox control exposes so many properties and methods that it makes sense to subdivide them in groups, according to the action you want to perform.

Loading and saving files

You can load a text file into the control using the *LoadFile* method, which expects the filename and an optional argument that specifies whether the file is in RTF format (0-rtfRTF, the default) or plain text (1-rtfText):

```
' Load an RTF file into the control.
RichTextBox1.LoadFile "c:\Docs\TryMe.Rtf", rtfRTF
```

The name of the file loaded by this method becomes available in the *FileName* property. You can also indirectly load a file into the control by assigning its name to the *FileName* property, but in this case you have no way of specifying the format.

You can save the current contents of the control using the *SaveFile* method, which has a similar syntax:

```
' Save the text back into the RTF file.
RichTextBox1.SaveFile RichTextBox1.FileName, rtfRTF
```

The *LoadFile* and *SaveFile* methods are a good solution when you want to load or save the entire contents of a file. At times, however, you might want to append the contents of the control to an existing file or store multiple portions of text in the same file. In such cases, you can use the *TextRTF* property with regular Visual Basic file commands and functions:

```
' Store the RTF text from two RichtextBox controls in the same file.
Dim tmp As Variant
Open "c:\tryme.rtf" For Binary As #1
```

(continued)

```
' Use an intermediate Variant variable to ease the process.
' (Don't need to store the length of each piece of data.)
tmp = RichTextBox1.TextRTF: Put #1, , tmp
tmp = RichTextBox2.Text RTF: Put #1, , tmp
Close #1


' Read the data back in the two controls.
Open "c:\tryme.rtf" For Binary As #1
Get #1, , tmp: RichTextBox1.TextRTF = tmp
Get #1, , tmp: RichTextBox2.TextRTF = tmp
Close #1
```

You can use this technique to save and reload the entire contents of the control in plain or RTF format (using the *Text* and *TextRTF* properties), and you can even save and reload just the text that's currently selected (using the *SelText* and *SelRTF* properties).

Changing character attributes

The RichTextBox control exposes many properties that affect the attributes of the characters in the selected text: These are *SelFontName*, *SelFontSize*, *SelColor*, *SelBold*, *SelItalic*, *SelUnderline*, and *SelStrikeThru*. Their names are self-explanatory, so I won't describe what each one does. You might find it interesting to note that all of the properties work as they would within a regular word processor. If text is currently selected, the properties set or return the corresponding attributes; if no text is currently selected, they set or return the attributes that are active from the insertion point onward.

The control also exposes a *Font* property and all the various *Fontxxxx* properties, but these properties affect the attributes only when the control is loaded. If you want to change the attribute of the entire document, you must select the whole document first:

```
' Change font name and size of entire contents.
RichTextBox1.SelStart = 0
RichTextBox1.SelLength = Len(RichTextBox1.Text)
RichTextBox1.SelFontName = "Times New Roman"
RichTextBox1.SelFontSize = 12
' Cancel the selection.
RichTextBox1.SelLength = 0
```

When you read the value of the *Selxxxx* properties, you see that they return the attributes of the selected text but can also return Null if the selection includes characters with different attributes. This means that you must take precautions when toggling the attributes of the selected text:

```
Private Sub cmdToggleBold_Click()
    If IsNull(RichTextBox1.SelBold) Then
        ' Test for Null values first to avoid errors later.
        RichTextBox1.SelBold = True
    Else
        ' If not Null, we can toggle the Boolean value using
        ' the Not operator.
```

```
        RichTextBox1.SelBold = Not RichTextBox1.SelBold
    End If
End Sub
```

A similar problem occurs when your application includes a toolbar whose buttons reflect the *Bold, Italic, Underline,* and other attributes of the selection. In this case, you need to use the *MixedState* property of the toolbar's Button objects and also exploit the fact that when the user selects or deselects text, the RichTextBox control fires a *SelChange* event:

```
Private Sub RichTextBox1_SelChange()
    ' Keep the toolbar's button in sync with current selection.
    If IsNull(RichTextBox1.SelBold) Then
        ToolBar1.Buttons("Bold").MixedState = True
    Else
        ToolBar1.Buttons("Bold").MixedState = False
        ToolBar1.Buttons("Bold").Value = IIf(rtfText.SelBold, _
            tbrPressed, tbrUnpressed)
    End If
    ' Add similar code that deals with Italic, Underline, and so on.
    ' ...
End Sub
```

The demonstration program shown in Figure 12-9 uses this technique. I built the skeleton of this program using the Application Wizard, but I had to manually edit the code generated by the wizard to account for the fact that many *Selxxxx* properties can return Null values. I also included a CoolBar that hosts a transparent Toolbar control, using the technique described in Chapter 11.

Figure 12-9. *The demonstration program is an MDI mini–word processor.*

SelProtect is an interesting property that lets you protect the selected text from being edited. Use it when the document includes crucial data that you don't want the user to accidentally delete or modify. If you want nothing in the entire document to be modified, however, you'd better set the *Locked* property to True.

Changing paragraph attributes

You can control the formatting of all the paragraphs that are included in the current selection. The *SelIndent* and *SelHangingIndent* properties work together to define the left indentation of the first line and all the following lines of a paragraph. The way these properties work differs from how word processors usually define these sorts of entities: The *SelIndent* property is the distance (in twips) of the first line of the paragraph from the left border, whereas the *SelHangingIndent* property is the indentation of all the following lines relative to the indentation of the first line. For example, this is the code that you must execute to have a paragraph that is indented by 400 twips and whose first line is indented by an additional 200 twips:

```
RichTextBox1.SelIndent = 600    ' Left indentation + 1st line indentation
RichTextBox1.SelHangingIndent = -200    ' A negative value
```

The *SelRightIndent* property is the distance of the paragraph from the right margin of the document (whose position depends on the *RightMargin* property). The following code moves the right margin about 300 twips from the right border of the control, and then sets a right indentation of 100 twips for the paragraphs that are currently selected:

```
' RightMargin is measured from the left border.
RichTextBox1.RightMargin = RichTextBox1.Width - 300
RichTextBox1.SelRightIndent = 100
```

You can control the alignment of a paragraph by means of the *SelAlignment* enumerated property, which can be assigned the values 0-rtfLeft, 1-rtfRight, or 2-rtfCenter. (The RichTextBox control doesn't support justified paragraphs.) You can read this property to retrieve the alignment state of all the paragraphs in the selection: In this case, the property returns Null if the paragraphs have different alignments.

The *SelCharOffset* property lets you create superscript and subscript text—in other words, position characters slightly above or below the text baseline. A positive value for this property creates a superscript, a negative value creates a subscript, and a zero value restores the regular text position. You shouldn't assign this property large positive or negative values, though, because they would make the superscript or subscript text unreadable (or even invisible)—the RichTextBox control doesn't automatically adjust the distance between lines if they contain superscript or subscript text:

```
' Make the selection superscript text.
RichTextBox1.SelCharOffset = 40
```

```
' Don't forget to reduce the characters' size.
RichTextBox1.SelFontSize = RichTextBox1.SelFontSize \ 2
```

The *SelBullet* Boolean property can be set to True to morph a normal paragraph into a bulleted paragraph. It returns the attribute of the paragraphs currently selected or Null if the selection includes paragraphs with different attributes:

```
' Toggle the bullet attribute of the selected paragraphs.
Private Sub cmdToggleBullet_Click()
    If IsNull(RichTextBox1.SelBullet) Then
        RichTextBox1.SelBullet = True
    Else
        RichTextBox1.SelBullet = Not RichTextBox1.SelBullet
    End If
End Sub
```

You can control the distance between the bullet and the paragraph body by using the *BulletIndent* property, which affects the entire document.

Managing the Tab key

Like a real word processor, the RichTextBox control is capable of managing tab positions on a paragraph-by-paragraph basis. This is achieved using the two properties *SelTabCount* and *SelTabs*: The former sets the number of tab positions in the paragraphs included in the selection, and the latter sets each tab position to a given value. Here's a simple example that shows how you can use these properties:

```
' Add three tabs, at 300, 600, and 1200 twips from left margin.
RichTextBox1.SelTabCount = 3
' The SelTabs property is zero-based.
' Tabs must be specified in increasing order, otherwise they are ignored.
RichTextBox1.SelTabs(0) = 300
RichTextBox1.SelTabs(1) = 600
RichTextBox1.SelTabs(2) = 1200
```

You can also read these properties to find the tab positions in selected paragraphs. Remember to account for Null values when the selection includes more paragraphs.

Here's one more issue that you should consider when working with tabs: The Tab key inserts a tab character only if there aren't any controls on the form whose *TabStop* property is set to True. In all other cases, the only way to insert a tab character in the document is by using the Ctrl+Tab key combination.

An easy way to work around this problem is to set the *TabStop* properties of all the controls to False when the focus enters the RichTextBox control and to reset them to True when the focus moves away from it. (Focus can move only when the user presses the hot key associated with another control or clicks on another control.) Here's a reusable routine that performs both jobs.

```
' In a BAS module
Sub SetTabStops(frm As Form, value As Boolean)
    Dim ctrl As Control
    On Error Resume Next
    For Each ctrl In frm.Controls
        ctrl.TabStop = value
    Next
End Sub

' In the form module that contains the RichTextBox control
Private Sub RichTextBox1_GotFocus()
    SetTabStops Me, False
End Sub
Private Sub RichTextBox1_LostFocus()
    SetTabStops Me, True
End Sub
```

Searching and replacing text

You can search text in a RichTextBox control by applying the *InStr* function to the value returned by the *Text* property. This control also supports the *Find* method, which makes the process even simpler and faster. The *Find* method has the following syntax:

```
pos = Find(Search, [Start], [End], [Options])
```

Search is the string being searched. *Start* is the index of the character from which the search should start (the index of first character is zero). *End* is the index of the character where the search should end. *Options* is one or more of the following constants: 2-rtfWholeWord, 4-rtfMatchCase, and 8-rtfNoHighlight. If the search is successful, the *Find* method highlights the matching text and returns its position; if the search fails, it returns –1. The matching string is highlighted even if the *HideSelection* property is True, and the control doesn't have the focus unless you specify the rtfNoHighlight flag.

If you omit the *Start* argument, the search starts from the current caret position and ends at the position indicated by the *End* argument. If you omit the *End* argument, the search starts from the position indicated by the *Start* argument and ends at the end of the document. If you omit both the *Start* and *End* arguments, the search is performed in the current selection (if there's selected text) or in the entire contents.

Implementing a Search and Replace function is simple. Because the Find method highlights the found string, all you have to do to replace it is assign a new value to the *SelText* property. You can also easily write a routine that replaces all the occurrences of a substring and returns the number of replacements:

```
Function RTFBoxReplace(rtb As RichTextBox, search As String, _
    replace As String, Optional options As FindConstants) As Long
    Dim count As Long, pos As Long
    Do
```

```
           ' Search the next occurrence.
           ' (Ensure that the rtfNoHighlight bit is off.)
           pos = rtb.Find(search, pos, , options And Not rtfNoHighlight)
           If pos = -1 Then Exit Do
           count = count + 1
           ' Replace the found substring.
           rtb.SelText = replace
           pos = pos + Len(replace)
       Loop
       ' Return the number of occurrences that have been replaced.
       RTFBoxReplace = count
End Function
```

The *RTFBoxReplace* routine is considerably slower than a plain VBA *Replace* function, but it preserves the original attributes of the replaced string.

Moving the caret and selecting text

The *Span* method extends the selection toward the start or the end of the document until a given character is found. Its syntax is the following:

```
Span CharTable, [Forward], [Negate]
```

CharTable is a string that contains one or more characters. *Forward* is the direction of the movement (True to move forward, False to move backward). *Negate* indicates where the movement terminates: If False (the default setting), it ends with the first character that doesn't belong to *CharTable* (and therefore the selection contains only characters that appear in *CharTable*). If True, the movement ends when any character contained in *CharTable* is encountered. (In this case, the selection contains only characters that don't appear in *CharTable*.) The *Span* method is useful for programmatically selecting a word or an entire sentence:

```
' Select from the caret to the end of the sentence.
' You need the CRLF to account for the paragraph's end.
RichTextBox1.Span " .,;:!?" & vbCrLf, True, True
```

To move the insertion point without selecting the text, you can use the *UpTo* method, which has the same syntax as *Span*:

```
' Move the caret to the end of the current sentence.
RichTextBox1.UpTo " .,;:!?" & vbCrLf, True, True
```

Another method that you might find useful is *GetLineFromChar*, which returns the line number that corresponds to a given offset from the beginning of the text. For example, you can use this method to display the number of the line on which the caret is currently located:

```
Private Sub RichTextBox1_SelChange()
    ' The return value from GetLineFromChar is zero-based.
```

(continued)

```
lblStatus.Caption = "Line " & (1 + RichTextBox1.GetLineFromChar _
    (RichTextBox1.SelStart))
End Sub
```

You can find out how many lines are in the current document by executing the following statement:

```
MsgBox (1 + RichTextBox1.GetLineFromChar(Len(RichTextBox1.Text))) _
    & " Lines"
```

Printing the current document

The RichTextBox control directly supports printing through the *SelPrint* method, which prints the current selection or the entire document if no text is selected. Its syntax is the following:

```
SelPrint hDC, [StartDoc]
```

hDC is the device context of the target printer, and *StartDoc* is a Boolean value that determines whether the method also sends StartDoc and EndDoc commands to the printer. The latter argument has been introduced with Visual Basic 6, and it's useful when you're working with printers that don't behave in the standard way. You can print the entire document on the current printer with just two statements:

```
RichTextBox1.SelLength = 0          ' Clear selection, if any.
RichTextBox1.SelPrint Printer.hDC   ' Send to the current printer.
```

A drawback of the *SelPrint* method is that you don't have any control over print margins. The demonstration program included on the companion CD shows how you can overcome this limit by using a technique based on Windows API calls.

Embedding objects

An intriguing feature of the RichTextBox control is its ability to embed OLE objects, which is similar to what you can do with the intrinsic OLE control. (The OLE control is briefly described in Chapter 3.) You exploit this capacity by means of the *OLEObjects* collection, which holds 0 or more OLEObject items. Each OLEObject item corresponds to an OLE object that has been embedded in the document. You can programmatically embed a new OLE object through the *OLEObject* collection's *Add* method, which has the following syntax:

```
Add ([Index], [Key], [SourceDoc], [ClassName]) As OLEObject
```

Index is the position in the collection where the object will be inserted. *Key* is an alphabetical key that will uniquely identify the object in the collection. *SourceDoc* is the filename of the embedded document that will be copied into the RichTextBox control. (It can be omitted to insert a blank document.) *ClassName* is the class name of the embedded object. (*ClassName* can be omitted if *SourceDoc* is specified.) For example, you can embed a blank Microsoft Excel worksheet at the current caret position by executing this code:

```
' This new object is associated to the "Statistics" key.
Dim statObj As RichTextLib.OLEObject
Set statObj = RichTextBox1.OLEObjects.Add(, "Statistics", _
    , "Excel.Sheet")
```

As soon as you add an OLEObject, it becomes active and is ready for input. OLEObject items expose a few properties and methods that let you (partially) control them through code. For example, the *DisplayType* property determines whether the object should display its contents (0-rtfDisplayContent) or its icon (1-rtfDisplayIcon):

```
' Show the object just added as an icon.
statObj.DisplayType = rtfDisplayIcon
```

Each embedded object supports a number of actions, called *verbs*. You can retrieve the verbs supported by the embedded object by using the *FetchVerbs* and then querying the *ObjectVerbs* and *ObjectVerbsCount* properties:

```
' Print the list of supported verbs to the Debug window.
statObj.FetchVerbs
For i = 0 To statObj.ObjectVerbsCount - 1
    ' These strings are printed as they might appear in a pop-up
    ' menu and can include an & character.
    Debug.Print Replace(statObj.ObjectVerbs(i), "&" , "")
Next
```

The list of supported verbs typically includes actions such as Edit or Open. You can execute one of these actions by using the *DoVerb* method, which accepts a verb name, an index in the *ObjectVerbs* property, or a negative value for common actions (−1-vbOLEShow, −2-vbOLEOpen, −3-vbOLEHide, −4-vbOLEUIActivate, −5-vbOLEIn-PlaceActivate, −6-vbOLEDiscardUndoState). You can determine whether a verb is available by testing the *ObjectVerbsFlags* property. For example, you can print the contents of an embedded object using this code:

```
Dim i As Integer
For i = 0 To statObj.ObjectVerbsCount - 1
    ' Filter out "&" characters.
    If Replace(statObj.ObjectVerbs(i), "&" , "") = "Print" Then
        ' A "Print" verb has been found, check its current state.
        If statObj.ObjectVerbFlags(i) = vbOLEFlagEnabled Then
            ' If the verb is enabled, start the print job.
            statObj.DoVerb i
        End If
        Exit For
    End If
Next
```

For more information about this feature, see the Visual Basic documentation.

THE SSTAB CONTROL

The SSTab control permits you to create tabbed dialog boxes almost the same way the TabStrip common control does it. The most important difference between the two controls is that the SSTab control is a real container, so you can place child controls directly on its surface. You can even switch among tabbed pages at design time, making the job of preparing the control much simpler and quicker than with the TabStrip control. Many programmers find it easier to work with the SSTab control because the control doesn't contain dependent objects, and the syntax of properties and events is more straightforward.

The SSTab control is embedded in the TabCtl32.ocx file, which must therefore be distributed with any Visual Basic application that uses this control.

Setting Design-Time Properties

The first thing to do after you drop an SSTab control on a form is to change its *Style* property from the default 0-ssStyleTabbedDialog value to the more modern 1-ssStylePropertyPage setting, which you can see in Figure 12-10. The tabs are usually displayed on the upper border of the control, but you can change this default setting by using the *TabOrientation* property.

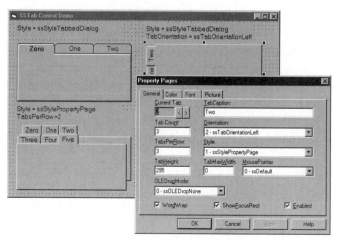

Figure 12-10. *The General tab of the Property Pages dialog box of an SSTab control.*

You can add new tabs (or delete existing ones) by typing a value in the TabCount field (which corresponds to the *Tabs* property), and you can create multiple rows of tabs by setting a suitable value for the *TabsPerRow* property. After you have created enough tabs, you can use the spin buttons to move from tab to tab and modify each one's *TabCaption* property. (This property is the only field in the dialog box whose value depends on the Current Tab field.) Tab captions can include & characters to define hot keys for a quick selection.

The *TabHeight* property is the height in twips of all the tabs in the control. The *TabMaxWidth* property is the maximum width of a tab. (A zero width means that the tab is just large enough to accommodate its caption.) The *WordWrap* property must be True to let longer captions wrap around. If *ShowFocusRect* is True, a focus rectangle is displayed on the tab that has the focus.

Each tab can display a little image. To set it at design time, you first set the current tab in the General page of the Properties dialog box, switch to the Picture tab, click on the Picture property in the leftmost listbox, and then select the bitmap or icon that you want to assign to the current tab. This bitmap can be referenced in code using the *TabPicture* property.

After you have created the tabs you need, you can place controls on each one of them. This operation is simple because you can select tabs even at design time. But you should be aware of an important detail: From Visual Basic's standpoint, all the controls you place on different tabs are contained in the SSTab control. In other words, the container is the SSTab control, not its tab pages. This has a number of implications—for example, if you have two groups of OptionButton controls on two different tab pages of the SSTab control, you should place each group in a separate Frame or another container, otherwise Visual Basic sees them as a single group.

Run-Time Operations

The main property of the SSTab control is *Tab*, which returns the index of the tab currently selected by the user. You can also set it to switch to another tab by means of code. The first tab has a 0 index.

Changing a tab's attributes

You don't need to make a tab current to modify its attributes because most properties expect an index. For example, you can read or modify a tab's caption using the *TabCaption* property, add a picture to a tab using the *TabPicture* property, enable or disable a tab with the *TabEnabled* property, and make it visible or invisible using the *TabVisible* property:

```
' Change caption and bitmap of the second tab. (Tabs' indexes are 0-based.)
SSTab1.TabCaption(1) = "Information"
' Note: The actual path of this file might be different on your system.
filename = "c:\VisStudio\Common\Graphics\Bitmaps\Assorted\balloon.bmp"
SSTab1.TabPicture(1) = LoadPicture(filename)
' Make the first tab invisible.
SSTab1.TabVisible(0) = False
```

The *Tabs* property returns the number of existing tabs:

```
' Disable all the tabs except the current one.
For i = 0 To SSTab1.Tabs - 1
    SSTab1.TabEnabled(i) = (i = SSTab1.Tab)
Next
```

Creating new tabs

You can create new tabs at run time by increasing the value of the *Tabs* property. You can append the new tab in one place only: following all the existing ones.

```
SSTab1.Tabs = SSTab1.Tabs + 1
SSTab1.TabCaption(SSTab1.Tabs - 1) = "Summary"
```

After you've created a new tab, you might want to add new controls to it. You can do that by dynamically creating new controls and then changing their *Container* properties. The control becomes a child of the tab that's currently selected:

```
' Create a TextBox control.
Dim txt As TextBox
Set txt = Controls.Add("VB.TextBox", "txt")
' Move it on the new tab. (You must select it first.)
SSTab1.Tab = SSTab1.Tabs - 1
Set txt.Container = SSTab1
txt.Move 400, 800, 1200, 350
txt.Visible = True
```

Reacting to tab selection

The SSTab control doesn't expose any custom events. The *Click* event, however, receives the index of the tab that was current previously. You can use this argument to validate the controls on the tab that lost the focus and to reset the *Tab* property to cancel the focus shift:

```
Private Sub SSTab1_Click(PreviousTab As Integer)
    Static Active As Boolean
    If Active Then Exit Sub
    ' Prevent recursive calls.
    Active = True
    Select Case PreviousTab
        Case 0
            ' Validate controls on first tab.
            If Text1 = "" Then SSTab1.Tab = 0
        Case 1
            ' Validate controls on the second tab.
            ' ...
    End Select
    Active = False
End Sub
```

Setting the *Tab* property in code fires a *Click* event, so you must protect your code from recursive calls to the event procedure using a Static flag (the *Active* variable in the previous routine).

Managing the input focus

You should be aware of a couple of issues concerning the way the SSTab control manages the input focus:

■   When the user presses the hot key that corresponds to a child control placed on a tab other than the current one, the input focus moves to that control. But the SSTab control doesn't automatically change the current tab to make the control visible.

■   When the user moves to another tab, the input focus doesn't automatically move to the first control on that tab.

The easiest solution to the first problem is to disable all controls that aren't on the current tab so that they don't receive the input focus if the user presses their hot keys. There's no documented way to learn which controls are on which pages, but it's easy to demonstrate that the SSTab control moves off screen all the child controls that don't belong to the current tab; this is achieved by setting a negative value for the *Left* property of each child. You can temporarily disable all such controls using the following approach:

```
' This routine can be reused for any SSTab controls in the application.
Sub ChangeTab(SSTab As SSTab)
    Dim ctrl As Control, TabIndex As Long
    TabIndex = 99999            ' A very high value.
    On Error Resume Next

    For Each ctrl In SSTab.Parent.Controls
        If ctrl.Container Is SSTab Then
            If ctrl.Left < -10000 Then
                ctrl.Enabled = False
            Else
                ctrl.Enabled = True
                If ctrl.TabIndex >= TabIndex Then
                    ' This control comes after our best candidate or
                    ' it doesn't support the TabIndex property.
                Else
                    ' This is the best candidate so far to get the focus.
                    TabIndex = ctrl.TabIndex
                    ctrl.SetFocus
                End If
            End If
        End If
    Next
End Sub

' Call from within the Click event procedure.
Private Sub SSTab1_Click(PreviousTab As Integer)
    ChangeTab SSTab1
End Sub
```

The *ChangeTab* routine also solves the second problem, mentioned previously, of moving the focus to the current tab. It does this by moving the focus to the control with the lowest value for the *TabIndex* property among all the child controls on the current tab. The only thing you have to do is assign an increasing value to the *TabIndex* properties of the child controls of a SSTab control. For more details, see the source code of the demonstration application provided on the companion CD.

THE SYSINFO CONTROL

The SysInfo control helps Visual Basic programmers create applications that are compliant with the Windows logo program. One of the prerequisites for such applications is the ability to react to systemwide events, such as when the screen resolution changes or when a plug-and-play device is connected to or disconnected from the system.

The SysInfo control is embedded in the SysInfo.ocx file, which must be distributed with any application that uses this control.

Properties

The SysInfo control is pretty easy to use: It doesn't expose any design-time properties or support any methods. You use a SysInfo control by querying its run time–only properties and writing code for its events. The properties of a SysInfo control can be subdivided into three groups: Properties that return information on the operating system, those that return information on screen settings, and those that return information about battery status. All the properties exposed by this control are read-only.

The first group includes the *OSPlatform*, *OSVersion*, and *OSBuild* properties. *OSPlatform* returns 1 if the application is being executed under Windows 95 or Windows 98, or it returns 2 if it's being executed under Windows NT. *OSVersion* returns the Windows version (as a Single value). *OSBuild* lets you distinguish among different builds of the same version.

The second group comprises these properties: *WorkAreaLeft*, *WorkAreaTop*, *WorkAreaWidth*, *WorkAreaHeight*, and *ScrollBarSize*. The first four properties return the position and the size (in twips) of the work area—that is, the portion of the desktop not occupied by the Windows taskbar. You can use this information to properly move and resize your forms. *ScrollBarSize* returns the system-defined width of vertical scrollbars: You can use this data to make your scroll bars look good at any screen resolution.

The third group includes the following properties: *ACStatus* (0 for batteries, 1 for AC power), *BatteryFullTime* (the estimated battery life), *BatteryLifePercent* (the estimated remaining battery life as a percentage), *BatteryLifeTime* (the estimated remaining battery life in seconds), and *BatteryStatus* (1 for High, 2 for Low, 4 for

Critical, 8 for Charging). All these properties return a special value (–1 for *ACStatus* and *BatteryStatus*, 255 for the other properties) when the requested information is unknown. For more information, see the source code of the demonstration program (shown in Figure 12-11) provided on the companion CD.

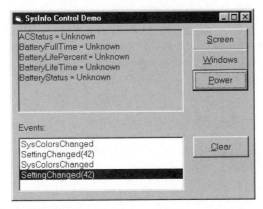

Figure 12-11. *The demonstration program shows how to leverage all the properties and events of the SysInfo control.*

Events

The SysInfo control exposes 18 custom events. They can be subdivided into the following four groups:

■ Events that fire when a plug-and-play device is connected or disconnected: *DeviceArrival, DeviceOtherEvent, DeviceQueryRemove, DeviceQuery-RemoveFailed, DeviceRemoveComplete*, and *DeviceRemovePending*.

■ Events that fire when the hardware configuration changes: *QueryChange-Config, ConfigChanged*, and *ConfigChangeCancelled*. You can cancel such changes by returning True in the *Cancel* parameter of a *QueryChangeConfig* event.

■ Events that fire when the power state changes: *PowerQuerySuspend, PowerResume, PowerStatusChanged*, and *PowerSuspend*. For example, you can react to a *PowerSuspend* event by saving all critical data to disk.

■ Events that fire when system settings change: *DisplayChanged, Sys-ColorsChanged, TimeChanged, SettingChanged*, and *DevModeChanged*. The last event fires when the configuration of a device is modified by the user or another program.

The simplest and most useful events are *DisplayChanged*, *SysColorChanged*, and *TimeChanged*, whose names are self-explanatory. Another interesting event is *SettingChanged*, which receives an integer that states which particular system setting has been modified. For example, your application can detect when the user has moved or resized the Windows taskbar in the following way:

```
Private Sub SysInfo1_SettingChanged(ByVal Item As Integer)
    Const SPI_SETWORKAREA = 47
    If Item = SPI_SETWORKAREA Then Call Resize_Forms
End Sub
```

Apart from the simplest cases, however, taking advantage of *SysInfo* events requires a thorough knowledge of the Windows operating system.

THE MSCHART CONTROL

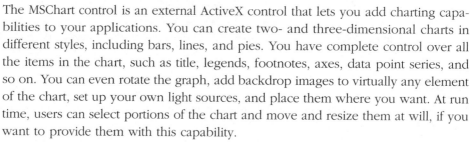

The MSChart control is an external ActiveX control that lets you add charting capabilities to your applications. You can create two- and three-dimensional charts in different styles, including bars, lines, and pies. You have complete control over all the items in the chart, such as title, legends, footnotes, axes, data point series, and so on. You can even rotate the graph, add backdrop images to virtually any element of the chart, set up your own light sources, and place them where you want. At run time, users can select portions of the chart and move and resize them at will, if you want to provide them with this capability.

The MSChart control is undoubtedly the most complicated ActiveX control ever provided with Visual Basic. Just to give you an idea of its complexity, consider that its type library includes 47 different objects, most of which have dozens of properties, methods, and events. A detailed description of this control would require 100 pages of text, if not more. For this reason, I'll illustrate only a few of its major characteristics and provide just a few code samples. If you dare to dive into the intricacies of this hierarchy, you'll find Figure 12-12 some help in keeping you from getting lost in this maze.

The topmost object of this hierarchy is MSChart, which lets you set the general characteristics of the chart and also exposes several custom events. All the other objects in the hierarchy are dependents of MSChart.

The DataGrid object is where you store the data that you want to display graphically. The Plot object is a compound object (that is, an object with other child objects) that contains all the graphical information about the data series (color, markers, backdrop pattern, position and attributes of light sources, and so on). The Title, Legend, and Footnote objects are compound objects with similar structures and control over the features of the relevant elements of the chart (text, color, position, and so on).

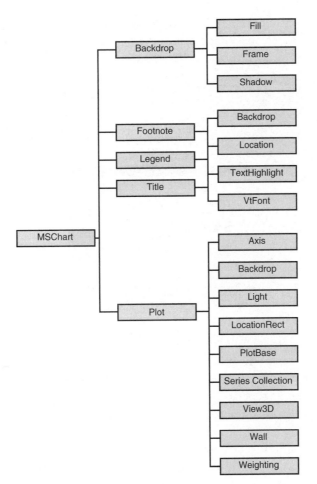

Figure 12-12. *The top levels of the MSChart hierarchy.*

Setting Design-Time Properties

The MSChart control has the richest Property Pages dialog box among the controls provided in the Visual Basic package (see Figure 12-13 on the following page), with eight tabs.

The Chart tab is where you decide which type of graphic you want to display, whether you want to stack series, and whether you show legends that explain what each data series is. These settings correspond to the *ChartType*, *Chart3d*, *Stacking*, and *ShowLegend* properties of the MSChart object.

The Axis tab is where you select the attributes of the axis of the chart: line width and color, whether the scale is displayed, and whether the scale is determined automatically by the control (the recommended setting) or manually by the programmer. In the latter case, you have to set minimum and maximum values and the frequency of divisions. Two-dimensional charts have three axes (*x*-axis, *y*-axis, and secondary *y*-axis), while three-dimensional charts have an additional fourth axis (*z*-axis). Your code can modify these properties using the Axis object, a child of the Plot object.

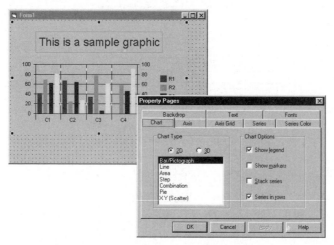

Figure 12-13. *The Chart tab of the Property Pages dialog box of the MSChart control.*

The AxisGrid tab lets you modify the style lines of axis grids; these settings correspond to the properties of the AxisGrid object, a child of the Axis object.

In the Series tab, you define how each data series should be displayed. You can hide a series (but reserve the space for it on the chart), exclude it (this also reuses its space on the chart), show its markers, and draw it on the secondary *y*-axis. If you are drawing a two-dimensional Line chart, you can also display statistical data, such as minimum and maximum values, mean, standard deviation, and regression. You can modify these features through code by acting on the SeriesCollection and the Series objects.

You refine the appearance of each data series in the SeriesColor tab, where you select the color and the style of the edge and the interior of each series. (The latter isn't available for Line and X-Y charts.) Your code can manipulate these properties through the DataPoint object.

All the main objects in the control—MsChart, Plot, Title, Legend, and Footnote—can have a backdrop pattern. You define the color and style of each backdrop in the Backdrop tab of the Property Pages window. The title, the legends, and the axis in your graph expose a Title, and you can set its properties in the Text and the Font tabs.

Run-Time Operations

Unless you want to give users the ability to modify some key properties of your charts, you can define all the key properties at design time using the Property Pages dialog box so that at run time you only have to feed the MSChart control the actual data to be displayed. You achieve this using the DataGrid object.

You can think of the DataGrid object as a multidimensional array that holds both data and its associated labels. You define the size of the array by assigning a value to the DataGrid's *RowCount* and *ColumnCount* properties, and you define the number of labels with the *RowLabelCount* and *ColumnLabelCount* properties. For example, you might have 12 rows of data to which you add a label at every third data point:

```
' 12 rows of data, with a label every third row
MSChart1.DataGrid.RowCount = 12
MSChart1.DataGrid.RowLabelCount = 4
' 10 columns of data, with a label on the 1st and 6th column
MSChart1.DataGrid.ColumnCount = 10
MSChart1.DataGrid.ColumnLabelCount = 2
```

Alternatively, you can set these four properties in one operation using the *SetSize* method:

```
' Syntax is: SetSize RowLabelCount, ColLabelCount, RowCount, ColCount
MSChart1.DataGrid.SetSize 4, 2, 12, 10
```

You define the label text using the *RowLabel* and *ColumnLabel* properties, which accept two arguments: the row or column number and the number of the label you want to assign.

```
' Set a label every three years.
MSChart1.DataGrid.RowLabel(1, 1) = "1988"
MSChart1.DataGrid.RowLabel(4, 2) = "1991"
MSChart1.DataGrid.RowLabel(7, 3) = "1994"
' And so on.
```

You can set the value of individual data points using the *SetData* method, which has the following syntax:

```
MSChart.DataGrid.SetData Row, Column, Value, NullFlag
```

where *Value* is a Double value and *NullFlag* is True if the data is Null. You can easily (and quickly) insert or delete rows or columns using a number of methods exposed by the DataGrid object. Among these are *InsertRows, DeleteRows, Insert-Columns, DeleteColumns, InsertRowLabels, DeleteRowLabels, InsertColumnLabels,* and *DeleteColumnLabels.* You can also fill the grid with random values (useful for providing the user with visual feedback even without actual data values) with the method *RandomDataFill.*

You can learn a lot about the MSChart control by studying the Chrtsamp.vbp sample project that comes with Visual Basic 6 and is shown in Figure 12-14 on the following page.

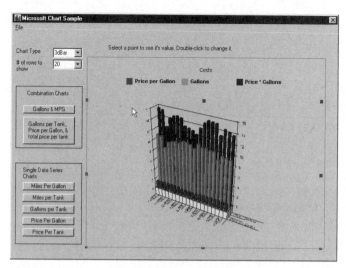

Figure 12-14. *The sample Microsoft Chart program.*

The Visual Basic package includes other controls that you might find useful in your applications. Unfortunately, I don't have room to explore all of them in depth. The controls that I have illustrated in this chapter and in Chapters 10 and 11, however, should suffice to help you create sophisticated Windows applications with great user interfaces.

This chapter concludes a series dedicated to building the user interface of your applications. Creating a good-looking and logical user interface is a requirement for a successful Windows application, but appearance isn't everything. In fact, the real value of an application is in its ability to process data, so the majority of the programs you'll write in Visual Basic have to read, write, and process the information stored in a database. In Part III of this book, I show you how to do all that in the most efficient way.

Part III
Database Programming

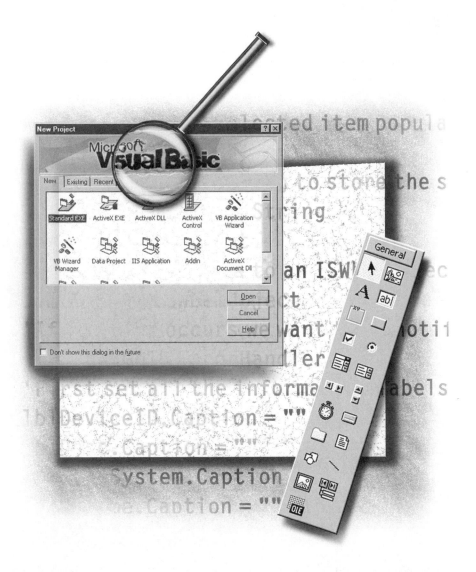

Chapter 13

The ADO
Object Model

The Microsoft ActiveX Data Objects (ADO) architecture is considerably less complicated than that of the DAO or RDO object model. The relative simplicity of the ADO architecture doesn't mean that learning ADO is simple, however. Even though the ADO object model has fewer objects and collections than DAO and RDO, those elements it has are often more complex than their DAO or RDO counterparts because they expose more methods and properties. A few ADO objects also expose events, which weren't implemented in DAO.

Figure 13-1 on the following page depicts the complete ADO 2.0 object model. As you can see, ADO has three main independent objects—the Connection object, the Recordset object, and the Command object—each of which exposes two collections. The Connection, Recordset, and Command objects aren't related explicitly. You create relationships among them implicitly within the running code—for example, by assigning a Connection object to the *ActiveConnection* property of a Recordset object. This ability to create relationships among database objects gives you an unparalleled flexibility that's unknown to DAO and RDO developers.

In this chapter, I focus on the properties, methods, and events of the objects in the ADO hierarchy. (In Chapter 14, I describe how you use these objects in database applications.) To demonstrate how ADO works, I've prepared an ADO Workbench application that lets you interactively create Connection, Command, and Recordset objects; execute their methods; see how their properties change; and watch their events fire. (See Figure 13-2 on page 631.) The program is complex, with 10 modules and about 2000 lines of code, but you'll find it a very useful way to practice with ADO without having to write a single line of code. In fact, as I was using this program, I discovered several interesting details about ADO that I'll share with you in this chapter and in Chapter 14.

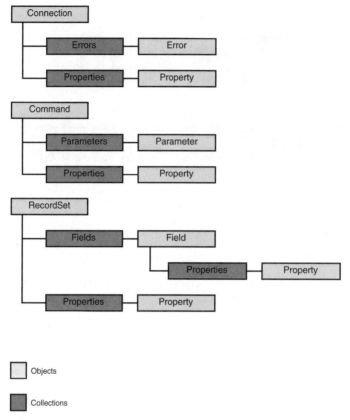

Figure 13-1. *The ADO 2.0 object model.*

One reason the ADO object model is simpler than the DAO and RDO object models is that it has fewer collections, which abound in DAO and RDO. For example, in ADO you can create any number of Connection and Recordset objects, but they are stand-alone objects and the object hierarchy won't maintain a reference to them for you. At first glance, you might believe that having to keep track of all the active objects and store them in your own collections if you want to use them later is going to make your job a bit more difficult. But when you take a closer look, you'll realize that dealing with stand-alone objects greatly simplifies the structure of your programs because in most cases you don't have to write cleanup code: When an object goes out of scope, ADO takes care of its correct termination and automatically closes open Recordsets and connections if necessary. This approach reduces memory leaking and delivers applications that require fewer resources.

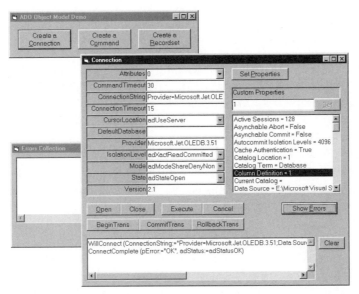

Figure 13-2. *The ADO Workbench application in action.*

As you'll see in the rest of this chapter, ADO compensates for its fewer objects by having each object expose more properties than comparable objects in the DAO and RDO models do. All main ADO objects expose a Properties collection, which includes any number of *dynamic properties* that are specific to a given OLE DB provider and that account for the particular features of that provider. You shouldn't confuse these dynamic properties, whose availability depends on the OLE DB Provider, with the *built-in* properties that use the standard dot syntax and that are always available, regardless of the provider you're using.

THE CONNECTION OBJECT

The ADO Connection object represents an open connection to a data source. This data source might be a database, an ODBC source, or any other source for which an OLE DB provider exists. The Connection object lets you specify all the necessary parameters—for example, the server and the database names, the user's name and password, and the timeout—before opening the data source. Connection objects are also important because they serve as containers for transactions. Each connection belongs to a given client application and is closed only when you explicitly close it, when you set the object variable to Nothing, or when your application ends.

Properties

The Connection object doesn't expose many properties. Rather than list each property individually, I've grouped them according to their purposes: preparing for the connection, managing transactions, and determining the state of the connection and what version of ADO is running.

Preparing for the connection

A group of properties lets you specify which database should be open and in which mode. All these properties can be written to before the connection is opened, but they become read-only after the connection has been established. The *Provider* property is the name of the OLE DB provider for the connection—for example, "SQLOLEDB" for the Microsoft SQL Server OLE DB Provider. If you leave this property unassigned, the default MSDASQL provider is used, which is the OLE DB Provider for ODBC Drivers, a sort of bridge that permits you to connect to almost any relational database on earth even if an OLE DB provider hasn't been developed for it yet (provided that an ODBC driver exists for that database, of course). MSDASQL is also known by the code name "Kagera."

Instead of assigning a value to the *Provider* property, you can pass the provider's name in the *ConnectionString* property together with other parameters the OLE DB provider expects. For example, this connection string opens the Biblio.mdb database:

```
Dim cn As New ADODB.Connection
cn.ConnectionString = "Provider=Microsoft.Jet.OLEDB.3.51;" _
    & "Data Source=C:\Microsoft Visual Studio\Vb98\Biblio.mdb"
```

The following connection string opens the Pubs SQL Server database on a server named "ServerNT". (The connection string also contains the user's name and password.)

```
cn.ConnectionString = "Provider=SQLOLEDB;Server=ServerNT;" _
    & "User ID=MyID;Password=MyPWD;Data Source=Pubs"
```

You shouldn't specify the provider name in the *ConnectionString* property and the *Provider* property at the same time because the results are unpredictable.

A simple way to build a connection string is to drop an ADO Data control on a form, open its property pages, select the Use Connection String option, and click on the Build button. A new dialog box appears, in which you can select the provider, the user name, the user password, and all the provider-dependent dynamic properties, as shown in Figure 13-3 on page 634. When you've finished, the complete connection string appears in the General tab of the Property Pages dialog box.

Mastering the syntax for specifying the *ConnectionString* property can be difficult because the string can include many different arguments in the form *argname=value*. This task is made more complex by the fact that when you're connecting to an ODBC source, the *ConnectionString* property also supports ODBC attributes that can coexist with newer OLE DB attributes. Table 13-1 lists a few of the most common attributes that you can specify in this string.

Argument	Description
Data Source	The name of the SQL Server or the name of the MDB database to which you want to connect. When connecting to an ODBC source, this argument can also be the name of a Data Source Name (DSN).
DSN	An ODBC source name registered on the current machine; this argument can replace the *Data Source* argument.
Filename	A file that contains information about the connection; this argument can be an ODBC DSN file or a Microsoft Data Link (UDL) file.
Initial Catalog	The name of the default database. When connecting to an ODBC source, you can also use the *Database* argument.
Password	The user's password. When connecting to an ODBC source, you can use the *PWD* argument. You don't need to pass your user ID and password if you're connecting to SQL Server and you use integrated security.
Persist Security Info	True if ADO stores the user ID and the password in the data link.
Provider	The name of the OLE DB provider; the default value is MSDASQL, the provider for ODBC sources.
User ID	The user's name. When connecting to an ODBC source, you can use the UID argument instead.

Table 13-1. *Some of the arguments you can use in the* ConnectionString *property.*

The *DefaultDatabase* property is the name of the default database for the connection. Many ADO dialog boxes refer to this property with the name Initial Catalog. This property isn't available until the connection has been opened, and it's read-only afterward.

The Connection object exposes two properties that let you tailor your application to the speed of the network and the database server. The *ConnectionTimeout* property specifies the number of seconds that ADO will wait before raising a timeout error when trying to establish a connection. (The default value is 15 seconds.) The *CommandTimeout* property specifies the number of seconds that ADO waits for a database command or a query to complete. (The default is 30 seconds.) This value is used for all the queries performed on the Connection object only; it isn't inherited by a Command object that uses the same connection. (A Command object is affected only by its own *CommandTimeout* property.)

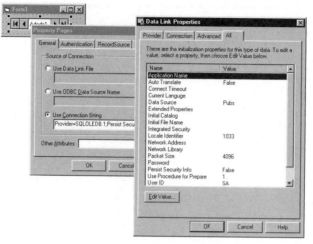

Figure 13-3. *You can interactively create a connection string using the custom property pages of an ADO Data control. The All page gathers all the custom properties exposed by the selected OLE DB provider (SQLOLEDB in this case).*

The *CursorLocation* property specifies whether a cursor is to be created, and if so, where. The possible values for this property are 2-adUseServer for server-side or driver-supplied cursors and 3-adUseClient for client-side cursors, including dissociated Recordsets. (Dissociated Recordsets are those that aren't associated with an active Connection object.)

The *Mode* property indicates the permissions on the connection. It can take a value from the following list:

Value	Description
1-adModeRead	Allows read-only data access
2-adModeWrite	Allows write-only data access
3-adModeReadWrite	Allows both read and write data access
4-adModeShareDenyRead	Prevents other clients from opening a connection with read permissions
8-adModeShareDenyWrite	Prevents other clients from opening a connection with write permissions
12-adModeShareExclusive	Prevents other clients from opening a connection to the same data source
16-adModeShareDenyNone	Allows other clients to open a connection with any permissions

If you don't assign a value to this property, it defaults to 0-adModeUnknown. You can write to this property only when the connection is closed; on an open connection, this property is read-only.

Managing transactions

The *IsolationLevel* property affects how transactions are executed in the connection. This is a bit-field property that can be the sum of one or more of the following values:

Value	Description
&H10-adXactChaos	You can't overwrite pending changes from more highly isolated transactions.
&H100-adXactBrowse	You can view changes in other transactions even before they are committed.
&H1000-adXactCursorStability	You can't view changes in other transactions until they have been committed.
&H10000-adXactRepeatableRead	You can't see changes in other transactions, but you will see them if you repeat the query.
&H100000-adXactIsolated	Transactions are isolated from other transactions.
−1-adXactUnspecified	The isolation level can't be determined.

The *IsolationLevel* property is read/write, but any change you make to its value will take effect only when the next *BeginTrans* method is issued. Providers don't necessarily support all the isolation levels listed previously: If you request an unsupported isolation level, the provider usually enforces the next greater level.

The *Attributes* property contains two bits that affect what happens when a transaction is committed or rolled back. The bit &H20000-adXactCommitRetaining automatically starts a new transaction after every *CommitTrans* method, and the bit &H40000-adXactAbortRetaining starts a new transaction after every *RollbackTrans* method. Not all providers allow you to automatically start a new transaction after every *CommitTrans* and *RollbackTrans* method, however.

Testing the state and the version

The *State* property is a read-only, bit-field property that reports the current state of the connection. It can be the sum of one or more of the following values:

Value	Description
0-adStateClosed	The connection is closed.
1-adStateOpen	The connection is open.
2-adStateConnecting	The connection is being opened.
4-adStateExecuting	The connection is executing a command.
8-adStateFetching	A Recordset is being retrieved.

You should query this property when you aren't sure about a Connection object's state because when the object is closed or is fetching data, many of its properties aren't usable.

The last property of the Connection object, *Version*, returns a read-only string that identifies the version of ADO in use. For example, under ADO 2.0, this property returns "2.0."

Methods

The methods of the Connection object let you do four things: open a connection, run a command, manage transactions on the active connection, and determine the structure of the database tables.

Establishing the connection

The most important method of the Connection object is *Open*, which establishes the connection. Its syntax is as follows:

```
Open [ConnectionString], [UserID], [Password], [Options]
```

The first argument has the same meaning as the *ConnectionString* property, *UserID* is the user's login name, and *Password* is the user's password. If *Options* is set to 16-adAsyncConnect, the connection is opened in asynchronous mode and it won't be available until the *ConnectComplete* event fires. All arguments are optional, but if you pass the *UserID* and *Password* arguments, you shouldn't specify them also in the *ConnectionString* argument or property. For example, the following statement opens an asynchronous connection to the Pubs database of SQL Server and specifies the "sa" user name with a blank password:

```
Dim cn As New ADODB.Connection
cn.Open "Provider=SQLOLEDB;Data Source=MyServer;Initial Catalog=Pubs;" _
    & "User ID=sa;Password=;", , , adAsyncConnect
```

You close an open connection using the *Close* method, which takes no arguments.

Executing database commands and queries

The *Execute* method performs an action query or a select query on the connection. The syntax of this method depends on the type of the action; if you're executing an action that doesn't return a Recordset (for example, an INSERT, UPDATE, or DELETE SQL statement), this is the correct syntax:

```
Execute CommandText, [RecordsAffected], [Options]
```

CommandText is the name of a stored procedure, a table, or the text of an SQL query. *RecordsAffected* is a Long variable that receives the number of records that have been affected by the command. *Options* is an enumerated value that indicates how the string in *CommandText* should be interpreted and can be one of the following constants:

Value	Description
1-adCmdText	The text of an SQL query
2-adCmdTable	A database table
4-adCmdStoredProc	A stored procedure
8-adCmdUnknown	Unspecified; the provider will determine the correct type
512-adCmdTableDirect	A database table that should be opened directly (an operation that you should avoid on SQL Server databases)

If you pass the value adCmdUnknown or omit the *Options* argument, the OLE DB provider is usually able to find out the type of the operation, but at the expense of some overhead. For this reason, you should always pass a correct value in this argument.

If you're executing a command that returns a Recordset, the syntax of the *Execute* method is slightly different:

```
Execute(CommandText, [RecordsAffected], [Options]) As Recordset
```

You should assign the result of this method to a Recordset object so that you can later browse the results. The *Execute* command can create Recordset objects with default settings only—that is, read-only, forward-only Recordsets with the cache size equal to 1.

You can perform asynchronous commands by adding the 16-adAsyncExecute constant to the *Options* argument. You might also decide to populate the Recordset asynchronously by adding the value 32-adAsyncFetch. Whether or not you've specified an asynchronous option, an *ExecuteComplete* event is raised in your code when the *Execute* command completes.

You can cancel an asynchronous operation any time by issuing the *Cancel* method. This method doesn't take any arguments. You never need to specify which operation you want to cancel because only one asynchronous operation can be active on a given connection.

Starting and committing transactions

The *BeginTrans*, *CommitTrans*, and *RollbackTrans* methods let you control when a transaction begins and ends. You start a transaction by issuing a *BeginTrans* method:

```
level = cn.BeginTrans
```

This method returns the transaction level: 1 for top-level transactions that aren't nested in any other transactions, 2 for transactions nested in a top-level transaction, and so on. The *BeginTrans*, *CommitTrans*, and *RollbackTrans* methods all return an error if the provider doesn't support transactions. You can find out if the provider supports transactions by checking whether the Connection object exposes a custom property named *Transaction DDL*:

```
On Error Resume Next
value = cn.Properties("Transaction DDL")
If Err = 0 Then
    level = cn.BeginTrans
    If level = 1 Then
        MsgBox "A top-level transaction has been initiated"
    Else
        MsgBox "A nested transaction has been initiated"
    End If
Else
    MsgBox "This provider doesn't support transactions"
End If
```

The *CommitTrans* method commits the current transaction—that is, it makes all the changes in the database permanent. Conversely, the *RollbackTrans* method rolls back the current transaction, thus undoing all changes that the code performed while the transaction was active. You can be certain that a *CommitTrans* method permanently writes data to the database only if the transaction is a top-level transaction: In all other cases, the current transaction is nested in another transaction that could be rolled back.

The value of the *Attributes* property affects what happens when you commit or roll back a transaction. If the *Attributes* property has the adXactCommitRetaining bit set, the provider automatically starts a new transaction immediately after a *CommitTrans* method; if the *Attributes* property has the adXactAbortRetaining bit set, the provider starts a new transaction after every *RollbackTrans* method.

Determining the structure of database tables

The only method I haven't described yet is *OpenSchema*. This method queries a data source and returns a Recordset that contains information about its structure (table names, field names, and so on). I don't expect that you'll use this method often, however, because ADO 2.1 specifications extend the ADO object model with items that let you get information about the structure of a data source using a less cryptic object-oriented approach, as I explain at the end of this chapter. If you do use this method, be aware of a bug: It doesn't work with server-side Recordsets, which unfortunately are the default in ADO. Therefore, if you use the *OpenSchema* method, remember to set the Connection's *CursorLocation* property to adUseClient before opening a Recordset.

Events

The Connection object exposes nine events. Not all the events have the same syntax, but a few patterns do recur, and it makes more sense to describe the patterns than to examine each event individually.

Most ADO events are grouped in pairs. For example, the Connection object exposes the *WillConnect* and *ConnectComplete* events, which fire immediately before and immediately after a connection is established, respectively. Another pair, *WillExecute* and *ExecuteComplete*, lets you run code immediately before a command is executed on the connection and immediately after it has completed. The key to these *Willxxxx* and xxxx*Complete* events is the *adStatus* parameter.

On entry to a *Willxxxx* event, this parameter can be 1-adStatusOK (no errors), 2-adStatusErrorsOccurred (an error has occurred), or 3-adStatusCantDeny (no errors, and the operation can't be canceled). Your event procedure can modify the value of the *adStatus* parameter to 4-adStatusCancel if you want to cancel the operation or 5-adStatusUnwantedEvent if you don't want to receive the event from the ADO object any longer. You can't use the adStatusCancel value if the event procedure receives *adStatus* equal to adStatusCantDeny.

The same status values are used for xxxx*Complete* events, but in this case, the operation has already been completed so you can't set *adStatus* to adStatusCancel. Even if you cancel an operation in the *Willxxxx* event, the corresponding xxxx*Complete* event will fire, but it will receive the value adStatusCancel in *adStatus*. When you cancel an operation, the program receives error 3712, "Operation canceled by the user," even if you reset the Errors collection or the *adStatus* argument while inside the xxxx*Complete* event procedure.

You'll see that many ADO events receive in their last parameter a pointer to the object that's raising the event. This argument is never necessary in Visual Basic: Because you can trap only events coming from individual objects, you must already have a reference to the object itself. In other languages—for example, Microsoft Visual C++— you can write event procedures that trap events raised from multiple objects, in which case the object reference is necessary to figure out where the event comes from.

Connection events

Let's take a quick look at the events of the Connection object. The *WillConnect* event fires when an *Open* method has been attempted on the connection. It receives the four arguments passed to the *Open* method plus the *adStatus* parameter and a pointer to the Connection object itself, as you can see in the code at the top of the next page.

```
Private Sub cn_WillConnect(ConnectionString As String, UserID As String, _
    Password As String, Options As Long, _
    adStatus As ADODB.EventStatusEnum, _
    ByVal pConnection As ADODB.Connection)
```

You can use this method to modify the connection string, the user ID, or the password on the fly. When a connect operation is completed—whether or not it succeeded—the Connection object raises a *ConnectComplete* event, which receives an Error object and the ubiquitous *adStatus* parameter:

```
Private Sub cn_ConnectComplete(ByVal pError As ADODB.error, _
    adStatus As ADODB.EventStatusEnum, _
    ByVal pConnection As ADODB.Connection)
```

The Connection object also exposes the *Disconnect* event, which (obviously) fires when the connection is closed:

```
Private Sub cn_Disconnect(adStatus As ADODB.EventStatusEnum, _
    pConnection As Connection)
```

Setting the *adStatus* parameter to adStatusUnwantedEvent has no effect on *Connect-Complete* and *Disconnect* events.

Execution events

The *WillExecute* event fires before any command is attempted on the connection:

```
Private Sub cn_WillExecute(Source As String, _
    CursorType As ADODB.CursorTypeEnum, LockType As ADODB.LockTypeEnum, _
    Options As Long, adStatus As ADODB.EventStatusEnum, _
    ByVal pCommand As ADODB.Command, _
    ByVal pRecordset As ADODB.Recordset, _
    ByVal pConnection As ADODB.Connection)
```

Source is an SQL string or the name of a stored procedure. *CursorType* identifies the type of cursor. (For more information about the *CursorType* property of the Recordset object, see the "Working with Cursors" section later in this chapter.) *LockType* is the type of lock to be enforced on the returned Recordset. (See the *LockType* property of the Recordset object.) *Options* corresponds to the argument with the same name that was passed to the *Execute* method. If the command won't return a Recordset, then *CursorType* and *LockType* parameters are set to -1. Because all these parameters are passed by reference, you can modify them if you want to. The last three arguments are pointers to the Connection, Command, and Recordset objects that are the source of the event. The *pConnection* parameter always points to the active Connection object. This event fires whenever a Connection's *Execute* method, a Command's *Execute* method, or a Recordset's *Open* method is attempted.

The *ExecuteComplete* event fires when the execution of a stored procedure or an SQL query comes to an end:

```
Private Sub cn_ExecuteComplete(ByVal RecordsAffected As Long, _
    ByVal pError As ADODB.error, adStatus As ADODB.EventStatusEnum, _
    ByVal pCommand As ADODB.Command, ByVal pRecordset As ADODB.Recordset, _
    ByVal pConnection As ADODB.Connection)
```

RecordsAffected is the number of records that have been affected by the operation (the same value that is returned in the *Execute* method's second argument). *pError* and *adStatus* have the usual meanings. The last three parameters are pointers to the objects that are raising the event.

Transaction events

The *BeginTransComplete* event fires when a *BeginTrans* method has completed its execution. The first parameter contains the value that is about to be returned to the program—that is, the level of the transaction just initiated. The meanings of all the other arguments should be self-explanatory.

```
Private Sub cn_BeginTransComplete(ByVal TransactionLevel As Long, _
    ByVal pError As ADODB.error, adStatus As ADODB.EventStatusEnum, _
    ByVal pConnection As ADODB.Connection)
```

The syntax of the *CommitTransComplete* and *RollbackTransComplete* events is similar to that of *BeginTransComplete*, but no information about the transaction level is passed to the event:

```
Private Sub cn_CommitTransComplete(ByVal pError As ADODB.error, adStatus _
    As ADODB.EventStatusEnum, ByVal pConnection As ADODB.Connection)
```

```
Private Sub cn_RollbackTransComplete(ByVal pError As ADODB.error, adStatus _
    As ADODB.EventStatusEnum, ByVal pConnection As ADODB.Connection)
```

Other events

The only other event exposed by the Connection object is *InfoMessage*. This event fires when the database engine sends a message or a warning or when a stored procedure executes a PRINT or RAISERROR SQL statement:

```
Private Sub cn_InfoMessage(ByVal pError As ADODB.error, adStatus As _
    ADODB.EventStatusEnum, ByVal pConnection As ADODB.Connection)
```

In most cases, you'll want to test the *pError* parameter or examine the elements in the Errors collection to understand what exactly happened.

The Errors Collection

The Connection object exposes the *Errors* property, which returns a collection of all the errors that have occurred on the connection itself. More precisely, each time an error occurs, the Errors collection is cleared and then filled with the errors raised by all the layers that sit between your program and the data source, including the ODBC driver (if you're using the MSDASQL OLE DB Provider) and the database engine itself. You can examine all the items in this collection to find out where the error originated and how the layers have interpreted it. You won't find ADO errors—for example, the errors that occur when you pass an invalid value to an ADO property or method—in this collection, because those errors are considered to be regular Visual Basic errors and should be managed by a standard error-trapping handler.

Each Error object in the collection exposes several properties that let you understand what exactly went wrong. The *Number, Description, HelpFile*, and *HelpContext* properties have the same meanings as they do in the Visual Basic Error object. The *Source* property is especially important if you want to track down where the error occurred. The *SQLState* and *NativeError* properties return information about errors in SQL data sources. An ODBC source returns errors as defined in the ODBC 3 specifications.

ADO clears the Errors collection when the code executes the *Clear* method. ADO clears the Errors collection of the Connection object, however, only when an error actually occurs. For this reason, you might find it convenient to manually clear the collection before invoking methods of the Connection object that can potentially raise errors.

THE RECORDSET OBJECT

The Recordset object contains all the data that you read from a database or that you're about to send to it. A Recordset can include several rows and columns of data. Each row is a record, and each column is a field in the record. You can access only one row at a time, the so-called current row or current record. You navigate through a Recordset by changing the current record.

ADO Recordset objects are much more versatile than their DAO and RDO counterparts. For example, you can create an ADO Recordset object yourself, without being connected to a database. Or you can retrieve a Recordset from a database, close the connection, modify the data in the Recordset, and finally reestablish the connection to send all your updates to the server. (These optimistic batch updates were possible in RDO but not in DAO.) You can even save an ADO Recordset to a disk file so that you can restore it later.

The ADO Workbench application provided on the companion CD lets you play with the many properties of the Recordset object. You can also execute its methods and see which events fire. The application decodes the meaning of all the symbolic constants exposed by the ADODB library, as shown in Figure 13-4.

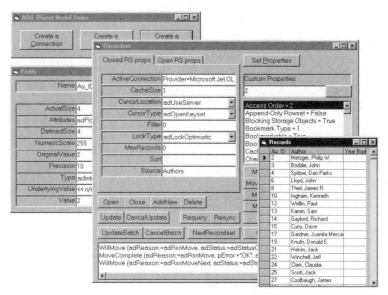

Figure 13-4. *You can use the ADO Workbench application to look at a Recordset's properties, execute its methods, and see its events fire; other windows let you browse the Fields collection and the actual contents of the records.*

Properties

The Recordset object is the richest object in the ADO object model in terms of properties. Again, I'll group the properties according to their functionality rather than by name.

Setting the Recordset's source

The most significant property of the Recordset object is probably the *Source* property, which holds the name of the table, the name of the stored procedure, or the text of the SQL query used to populate the Recordset. This property is declared as Variant, which permits you to assign a Command object to it. If you assign a Command object to this property, it returns the contents of the *CommandText* property of the Command object, not a reference to the Command object itself. The *Source* property is read/write for closed Recordset objects and read-only after the Recordset has been opened. Here's an example of the *Source* property:

```
' Edit this constant to match your directory structure.
Const DBPATH = "C:\Program Files\Microsoft Visual Studio\Vb98\NWind.mdb"
Dim cn As New ADODB.Connection, rs As New ADODB.Recordset
cn.Open "Provider=Microsoft.Jet.OLEDB.3.51;Data Source=" & DBPATH
rs.Source = "Employees"
rs.Open , cn
```

You can make your code more concise if you pass the value of this property as the first argument of the *Open* method:

```
rs.Open "Employees", cn
```

When you assign an ADO Command object to the *Source* property, you can later retrieve a reference to this object through the *ActiveCommand* property.

To open a Recordset, you must associate it with an existing connection. You can explicitly create this Connection object and assign it to the *ActiveConnection* property, or you can create it implicitly by assigning a connection string to the *ActiveConnection* property:

```
' Edit this constant to match your directory structure.
Const DBPATH = "C:Program Files\Microsoft Visual Studio\VB98\NWind.mdb"

' First method: explicit Connection object
cn.Open "Provider=Microsoft.Jet.OLEDB.3.51;Data Source=" & DBPATH_
Set rs.ActiveConnection = cn
rs.Source = "Employees"
rs.Open

' Second method: implicit Connection object
rs.ActiveConnection = "Provider=Microsoft.Jet.OLEDB.3.51;" _
    & "Data Source= " & DBPATH
rs.Source = "Employees"
rs.Open
```

When you create an implicit Connection object, you can later reference it through the *ActiveConnection* property (for example, to access the Connection's Errors collection). The *ActiveConnection* property is read-only after the record has been opened or when a Command object has been assigned to the *ActiveCommand* property.

Yet another way to select the location from which the Recordset should retrieve its data is with the *DataSource* and *DataMember* properties. For example, you can link a Recordset object to an ADO Data control by using the following statement:

```
Set rs.DataSource = Adodc1
```

You don't need to set any other property, nor do you have to call the *Open* method (which in fact raises an error). If the data source is a DataEnvironment object, you also need to assign a valid string to the *DataMember* property; otherwise, an error will occur when setting the *DataSource* property.

The Recordset's *State* property returns the current state of the Recordset as a set of bits that can be tested individually:

Value	Description
0-adStateClosed	The Recordset is closed.
1-adStateOpen	The Recordset is open.
2-adStateConnecting	The Recordset is connecting.
4-adStateExecuting	The Recordset is executing a command.
8-adStateFetching	The rows of the Recordset are being fetched.

The last three values apply only when the Recordset object is executing an asynchronous method.

Working with cursors

A cursor is a set of records that represent the results of a query. Cursors can contain the actual data or just pointers to records in the database, but the mechanism that retrieves the data is transparent to the programmer. You can specify where the cursor should be created (on the client or on the server workstation), the cursor type, and the locking option.

The *CursorLocation* property specifies where the cursor is to be created. This property can have one of two values: 2-adUseServer or 3-adUseClient. The value of this property is inherited from the Connection object and can be changed only for closed Recordsets. When you're working with the OLE DB Provider for ODBC Drivers and for SQL Server, the default cursor is a forward-only cursor created on the server. (This type of cursor is also the most efficient.) You need to switch to client-side cursors if you want to create dissociated Recordsets and use an optimistic batch update strategy. Client-side cursors are often a good choice when you have a DataGrid control or another complex control that is bound to the Recordset. In all other cases, server-side cursors are often preferable because they offer better performance and additional cursor types.

The *CursorType* property tells which type of cursor should be created and is one of the following constants: 0-adOpenForwardOnly, 1-adOpenKeyset, 2-adOpenDynamic, or 3-adOpenStatic. Server-side cursors support all these options, whereas client-side cursors support only 3-adOpenStatic. But if you use a different setting for a client-side cursor, a static cursor is automatically created without raising an error.

A forward-only cursor is the default for server-side cursors and is available only for server-side cursors. As I just mentioned, this type of cursor is the most efficient, especially if you set *LockType* = adReadOnly and *CacheSize* = 1. Many programmers and authors refer to this last type of cursor as a "noncursor." In *The Hitchhiker's Guide to Visual Basic and SQL Server*, William R. Vaughn defines this as a "fire-hose" cursor, to emphasize how fast it is at tossing data to the client application. You don't have to do anything special to use this cursor (or noncursor) because it's the default for ADO. You can navigate a forward-only Recordset only by using the *MoveNext* method. If you want to get the best performance for an application that needs to update records, you should do all your updates through SQL commands or stored procedures.

Dynamic cursors consist of a set of bookmarks to the actual data in the data source. Any time the client requests a record, ADO uses the bookmark to read the current value, which means that the application always reads the latest value stored by other users. Dynamic cursors are automatically updated when other users add or delete a record or change any record, already in the Recordset. Not surprisingly, these cursors are the most expensive cursors in terms of performance and LAN traffic because any time you move to another record, a trip to the server is required to re-trieve the current values. You can always update data and perform all kinds of navi-gational methods on dynamic Recordsets, including using bookmarks if the provider supports them. This type of cursor is available only as server-side cursors.

NOTE Microsoft Jet Engine doesn't support dynamic cursors, so if you attempt to open dynamic cursors with the Jet OLE DB Provider you always get a keyset.

Keyset cursors are similar to dynamic cursors, but they don't include records added by other users. (Changes other users have made to records in the Recordset are visible, though.) You can read and modify all the records in the cursor, but you get an error if you access a record that another user has deleted. The keyset cursor is available only as a server-side cursor.

Static cursors create a fully scrollable snapshot of all the records identified by the *Source* property, and they are the only type possible for client-side cursors. Be-cause a static cursor is actually a copy of the data coming from the database, changes that other users make aren't visible. Whereas these cursors are less efficient than forward-only cursors and increase the workload on the computer where they reside, their performance is reasonable and they're a good choice, especially when the Recordset doesn't include too many records. A static cursor is usually the best choice for retrieving data from a stored procedure. Depending on the provider and on other settings, this Recordset can even be updatable. You should create client-side static cursors only when the client workstation has enough memory.

The *MaxRecords* property sets a limit to the number of records that will be re-turned in the Recordset when you're working with a cursor. The default value is 0, which means that all records will be returned. This property can be written to when the Recordset is closed and is read-only when the Recordset is open.

The *CacheSize* property sets and returns the number of records that ADO will cache locally when working with cursors. You can adjust the value of this property to fine-tune your application, trading memory for performance. You can assign a new value to this property at any moment, but if the Recordset is already open, the new setting will be used only when ADO needs to fill the local cache—that is, when you move the pointer to the current record to point to a record that isn't in the cache.

> **NOTE**   Most programmers like cursors—especially dynamic and keyset cursors—because they're so powerful and versatile. Unfortunately, cursors are often the worst choice in terms of performance, resources, and scalability. You should use cursors only when you're working with small Recordsets or when you're using bound controls. (Bound controls need cursors to support backward and forward navigation.) When you employ cursors, remember to build the *Source* property so that you reduce the number of rows fetched and to use a WHERE clause that exploits one or more indexes. Another effective technique to improve the performance of your application is to execute a *MoveLast* method to quickly populate the Recordset and release any lock on the data source as soon as possible.

Working with concurrency

All multiuser databases enforce some type of locking strategy. Locks are necessary to prevent multiple users from performing changes on the same record at the same moment, which would probably result in an inconsistent database. Locks are extremely expensive in terms of scalability; when a lock is enforced on a record being modified by a user, no other user can access the same record. Depending on how you write your applications, a lock can significantly degrade performance and can even cause fatal errors if you don't implement a good lock-resolving strategy.

The *LockType* property indicates which type of lock should be enforced on the data in the database. This enumerated property can be assigned one of the following values: 1-adLockReadOnly, 2-adLockPessimistic, 3-adLockOptimistic, and 4-adLockBatchOptimistic.

The default value for this property is adLockReadOnly, which creates nonupdatable Recordsets. This is the most efficient option because it doesn't impose a write lock on data. It's also the best choice as far as scalability is concerned. Again, a good strategy is to rely on forward-only, read-only noncursors (the default in ADO) when reading data and to do all updates through SQL statements or stored procedures.

When you're using pessimistic locking, ADO tries to lock the record as soon as you enter edit mode, which occurs when you modify one field in the Recordset. It releases the lock only when you issue an *Update* method or move to another record. While a record is locked, no other user can access it for writing, which severely reduces the potential for the scalability of the application. For this reason, you should *never* use pessimistic locking when the user interface of your application lets the user freely navigate in the Recordset (unless you want to block all users when any one of them takes a coffee break!). Pessimistic locking is available only for server-side cursors.

Optimistic locking scales up better than pessimistic locking does, but it requires more attention from the programmer. With optimistic locking, ADO locks the current record only while it's being updated, which usually takes a small amount of time.

Optimistic batch locking is a special mode that's available only for client-side static cursors. In optimistic batch locking, you download all the data on the client machine, let the user perform all the necessary changes (including adding and deleting records), and then resubmit all the changes in one single operation. If you decided to go with client-side cursors, optimistic batch locking is the most efficient mode because it reduces network traffic. However, you'll need to implement a strategy for handling conflicts (for example, when two users update the same record), which won't be a trivial task.

For more information about the various types of locking, read the "Locking Issues" section in Chapter 14.

Reading and modifying fields' values

The ultimate purpose in opening a Recordset is to read the values of its rows and columns and possibly to modify them. Recordsets allow you to read and write only the values in the current record, so you need to navigate through the Recordset to access all the records you're interested in.

You can read the values of the fields of the current record through the Fields collection. You can specify which field you're interested in by passing a numeric index or the name of the field:

```
' Print the names and values of all the fields in the Recordset.
Dim i As Integer
For i = 0 To rs.Fields.Count - 1     ' The Fields collection is zero-based.
    Print rs.Fields(i).Name & " = " & rs.Fields(i).Value
Next
```

You can also use the *For Each* statement to iterate on all the fields. You can omit the *Value* property because it's the default property for the Field object.

```
Dim fld As ADODB.Field
For Each fld In rs.Fields
    Print fld.Name & " = " & fld
Next
```

Unlike DAO and RDO, ADO doesn't support an *Edit* method, and you can start updating one or more fields of the current record simply by assigning new values to the Field object you want to modify. Moreover, you don't need to explicitly issue an *Update* method because ADO will automatically execute it for you when you move to another record in the Recordset. These features simplify the structure of the code that reads and updates all the records in a Recordset:

```
' Convert the contents of the LastName field to uppercase.
rs.MoveFirst
Do Until rs.EOF
    rs("LastName") = UCase$(rs("LastName"))
    rs.MoveNext
Loop
```

You can determine the editing status of a Recordset by querying its *EditMode* property, which returns one of the following values:

Value	Description
0-adEditNone	No editing operation is in progress.
1-adEditInProgress	One or more fields have been modified, but new values haven't been saved yet.
2-adEditAdd	A new record has been added, but it hasn't been saved to the database yet.
3-adEditDelete	The current record has been deleted.

Setting and retrieving the position in the Recordset

A number of properties help you understand where you are in the Recordset so that you can enable or disable certain operations or set bookmarks to quickly return to a record you've visited previously. The property in this group that you'll probably use most frequently is *EOF*, which returns True when the pointer to the current record is positioned after the end of the Recordset. You typically use this property when looping on all the records in the Recordset:

```
' Count all employees hired before January 1, 1994.
rs.MoveFirst
Do Until rs.EOF
    If rs("HireDate") < #1/1/1994# then count = count + 1
    rs.MoveNext
Loop
```

BOF is a similar property. It returns True when the record pointer is positioned before the beginning of the Recordset. It's often crucial to know the values of *EOF* and *BOF* properties: When either one returns True, most of the Recordset's methods and properties return an error because there's no current record. For example, you can't retrieve a Field's value if the current record is before the beginning or after the end of the Recordset. If both *BOF* and *EOF* properties are True, the Recordset is empty.

The *Bookmark* property lets you retrieve a Variant value that identifies the current record; you can later move back to this record simply by reassigning the same value to the *Bookmark* property, as this code demonstrates:

```
Dim mark As Variant
mark = rs.Bookmark            ' Remember where you are.
rs.MoveLast                   ' Move to the last record.
rs("HireDate") = #12/10/1994# ' Assign a new value to the HireDate field.
rs.Bookmark = mark            ' Return to the marked record.
```

ADO bookmarks are stored internally as Double values. Even if they are numeric values, you shouldn't assume that you can compare them as if they were numbers.

The only arithmetic operation that makes sense with bookmarks is a test for equality, as in the following code:

```
' Print the names of the employees who were hired on the same
' day as (or later than) the employee whose record is current in the Recordset.
Dim mark As Double, curHireDate As Date
mark = rs.Bookmark: curHireDate = rs("HireDate")
rs.MoveFirst
Do Until rs.EOF
    If rs.Bookmark <> mark Then
        ' Don't consider the current employee.
        If rs("HireDate") >= curHireDate Then Print rs("LastName")
    End If
    rs.MoveNext
Loop
' Move the record pointer back to the record that was current.
rs.Bookmark = mark
```

Moreover, bookmarks can be compared for equality only if they come from the same Recordset object or from a clone Recordset. (See the description of the *Clone* method later in this chapter.) In all other cases, you shouldn't compare the *Bookmark* properties of two distinct Recordset objects, even if they are pointing to the same rowset in the same database. For more information about comparing bookmarks, see the description of the *CompareBookmarks* method in the section "Navigating the Recordset," later in this chapter.

The *RecordCount* read-only property returns the number of records in the Recordset. Depending on the database engine, the provider, and the type of Recordset, this property can also return –1. This property isn't supported by forward-only Recordsets, for example. If the property is supported, reading its value forces ADO to perform an implicit *MoveLast* method, so this operation can add a lot of overhead if used with large Recordsets.

The *AbsolutePosition* property sets or returns a Long value that corresponds to the ordinal position of the current record in the Recordset. (The first record returns 1; the last record returns RecordCount.) It can also return one of the following values: –1-adPosUnknown (position is unknown), –2-adPosBOF (BOF condition), or –3-adPosEOF (EOF condition).

You should never use this property in place of the record number or, worse, instead of the *Bookmark* property, because the *AbsolutePosition* property varies when records are added to or removed from the Recordset. The most reasonable way to use this property is when you want to provide a scroll bar or a Slider control that lets the user quickly move in the Recordset. In this case, you should set the scroll bar's *Min* property to 1 and its *Max* property to *rs.RecordCount* and then add this code in the scroll bar's *Change* or *Scroll* event procedure:

```
Private Sub HScrollBar1_Change()
    On Error Resume Next
```

```
    rs.AbsolutePosition = HScrollBar1.Value
End Sub
```

Remember that a scroll bar's *Max* value can't be higher than 32,767; if you have to deal with more records than that, you should either scale that value or use a Slider control.

Each Recordset is subdivided into pages, and each page can contain a fixed number of records (except the last page, which can be filled only partially). The *PageSize* property returns the number of records in each page, whereas the *PageCount* property returns the number of pages in the Recordset. The *AbsolutePage* property sets or returns the page number of the current record. This property is conceptually similar to the *AbsolutePosition* property (and supports the same negative values to indicate unknown, BOF, and EOF conditions), but it works with page numbers instead of record numbers. It's most useful when you're implementing advanced strategies to buffer records being read from the database.

Sorting and filtering records

You can sort the records in a Recordset by assigning a field list to the *Sort* property, as in the following example:

```
' Sort the Recordset on the LastName and FirstName fields.
rs.Sort = "LastName, FirstName"
```

The first field name is the primary sort key, the second field name is the secondary sort key, and so on. By default, records are sorted in ascending order for the selected keys; however, you can opt for descending order by using the *DESC* qualifier:

```
' Sort in descending order on the HireDate field. (The employees hired
' most recently should be listed first.)
rs.Sort = "HireDate DESC"
```

> **NOTE** The documentation incorrectly states that you should use the *ASCEND-ING* and *DESCENDING* qualifiers. It turns out, however, that they cause an error 3001. This bug will probably be fixed in a future version of ADO.

This property doesn't affect the order of the records in the data source, but it does affect the order of the records in the Recordset. You can restore the original order by assigning an empty string to this property. I found out that the *Sort* method works only with client-side static cursors, at least with the OLE DB providers for ODBC, Microsoft Jet, and SQL Server. If you sort on fields that aren't indexed, ADO creates a temporary index for them and deletes the index when you close the Recordset or assign an empty string to the *Sort* property.

You can filter the records in a Recordset by using the *Filter* property. You can assign three types of values to this property: an SQL query string, an array of bookmarks, or a constant that indicates which records should appear in the Recordset. The most intuitive way to use this property is to assign it an SQL string. This string is similar to the WHERE clause of a SELECT command, but you have to omit the WHERE. A few examples are shown on the following page.

```
' Filter out all employees hired before January 1, 1994.
rs.Filter = "HireDate >= #1/1/1994#"
' Include only employees born in the 1960s.
rs.Filter = "birthdate >= #1/1/1960# AND birthdate < #1/1/1970#"
' Filter in only employees whose last names start with the letter C.
rs.Filter = "LastName LIKE 'C*'"
```

You can use the comparison operators (<, <=, >, >=, =, <>) and the LIKE operator, which supports the * and % wildcards but only at the end of the string argument. You can connect simpler statements using AND and OR logical operators, but you can't perform other operations (such as string concatenations). You can group simpler expressions using parentheses. If a field name contains spaces, you must enclose the name within square brackets. You can use the *Filter* property in this way with server-side cursors if the provider supports filtering; in all other cases, you should use client-side cursors. Because ADO performs the filtering, you should stick to ADO syntax rules; for example, date values must be enclosed in # symbols, strings must be enclosed in single quotes, and quotes embedded in a string must be doubled. (Here's a brief tip: Use the *Replace* function to prepare the string quickly.)

If you want to filter a group of records that can't be specified using a simple SQL string, you can pass an array of bookmarks to the *Filter* property:

```
' Filter out those employees who were hired when they were over age 35.
ReDim marks(1 To 100) As Variant
Dim count As Long
' Prepare an array of bookmarks. (Assume that 100 bookmarks are enough.)
Do Until rs.EOF
    If Year(rs("HireDate")) - Year(rs("BirthDate")) > 35 Then
        count = count + 1
        marks(count) = rs.Bookmark
    End If
    rs.MoveNext
Loop
' Enforce the new filter using the array of bookmarks.
ReDim Preserve marks(1 To count) As Variant
rs.Filter = marks
```

Finally, you can assign the *Filter* property one of these enumerated constants:

Value	Description
0-adFilterNone	Remove the current filter (same as assigning an empty string).
1-adFilterPendingRecords	In batch update mode, view only records that have been modified but not sent to the server yet.

Value	Description
2-adFilterAffectedRecords	View records affected by the most recent *Delete, Resync, UpdateBatch,* or *CancelBatch* method.
3-adFilterFetchedRecords	View only the records in the local cache.
5-adFilterConflictingRecords	In batch update mode, view only the records that failed to be committed to the server.

Setting the *Filter* property to the value 2-adFilterAffectedRecords is the only way to see the records that have been deleted.

Other properties

The *MarshalOption* property affects how you send back rows to the server. It can be assigned two enumerated constants: 0-adMarshalAll (ADO sends all the rows to the server, which is the default) or 1-adMarshalModifiedOnly (ADO sends only the records that have been modified). This property is available only on client-side ADOR Recordsets, which are described in the "Remote Data Services" section in Chapter 19.

The *Status* property is a bit-field value that returns the status of the current record after a batch update operation or another bulk operation has completed. You can test its individual bits using the enumerated properties listed in Table 13-2 on the next page.

The only Recordset property I haven't yet described is *StayInSync*, which applies to the child Recordsets of a hierarchical Recordset object. To understand what this property does, you must consider that hierarchical Recordsets expose Field objects that contain child Recordset objects. By default, ADO automatically updates these child Recordsets when the record pointer of the parent Recordset moves to another record. This default behavior is what you want in the vast majority of cases, but at times you'd like to save the contents of a child Recordset for later; and in a sense, you want to detach it from its parent Recordset. Well, you can separate the parent and child Recordsets by setting the child Recordset's *StayInSync* property to False. Another way to reach the same result is to use the *Clone* method to create a copy of the child Recordset: If you use this method, the cloned Recordset won't be updated when the parent Recordset moves to another record. For more information, see the section "Hierarchical Recordsets" in Chapter 14.

Methods

The Recordset object exposes several methods. Again, I'll describe them in groups, according to their purpose.

Constant	Value	Description
adRecOK	0	The record was successfully updated.
adRecNew	1	The record is new.
adRecModified	2	The record was modified.
adRecDeleted	4	The record was deleted.
adRecUnmodified	8	The record wasn't modified.
adRecInvalid	&H10	The record wasn't saved because its bookmark is invalid.
adRecMultipleChanges	&H40	The record wasn't saved because it would affect multiple records.
adRecPendingChanges	&H80	The record wasn't changed because it refers to a pending insert.
adRecCanceled	&H100	The record wasn't saved because the operation was canceled.
adRecCantRelease	&H400	The record wasn't saved because of existing record locks.
adRecConcurrencyViolation	&H800	The record wasn't saved because optimistic concurrency was in use.
adRecIntegrityViolation	&H1000	The record wasn't saved because it would violate integrity constraints.
adRecMaxChangesExceeded	&H2000	The record wasn't saved because there were too many pending changes.
adRecObjectOpen	&H4000	The record wasn't saved because of a conflict with an open storage object.
adRecOutOfMemory	&H8000	The record wasn't saved because of an out-of-memory error.
adRecPermissionDenied	&H10000	The record wasn't saved because the user had insufficient permissions.
adRecSchemaViolation	&H20000	The record wasn't saved because it doesn't match the structure of the database.
adRecDBDeleted	&H40000	The record had already been deleted from the database.

Table 13-2. *The constants to use when testing the* Status *property.*

Opening and closing the Recordset

If you want to read the data in a Recordset, you must open it first, which you do with the *Open* method:

```
Open [Source], [ActiveConnection], [CursorType], [LockType], [Options]
```

The arguments of the *Open* method have the same meaning as the properties with the same names: *Source* is the name of a table or a stored procedure, an SQL query, or a reference to an ADO Command object; *ActiveConnection* is a reference to an ADO Connection object or to a connection string that identifies the provider and the data source; *CursorType* specifies which type of cursor you want to create (forward-only, static, keyset, or dynamic); and *LockType* is the type of locking you want to enforce (read-only, pessimistic, optimistic, or optimistic batch). *Options* is the only argument that doesn't correspond to a *Recordset* property: It explains to ADO what you're passing in the *Source* argument and can be one of the following enumerated constants:

Value	*Description*
1-adCmdText	Textual SQL query
2-adCmdTable	Database table
4-adCmdStoredProc	Stored procedure
8-adCmdUnknown	Unspecified; the provider will determine the correct type
256-adCmdFile	A persistent Recordset
512-adCmdTableDirect	A database table opened directly

Even if in most cases the provider can understand what the source of the Recordset is without your help, you can often speed up the *Open* method by assigning a correct value to this argument.

All these arguments are optional. However, ADO can't open the Recordset if you don't provide enough information. For example, you can omit the *Source* argument if you've assigned a value to the *Source* property, and you can omit the *ActiveConnection* argument if you've assigned a value to the *ActiveConnection* property or if you're using an ADO Command object as the source for this Recordset (in which case the *ActiveConnection* argument is inherited from that Command object). If you omit the third or fourth argument, by default, the *Open* method creates a forward-only, read-only Recordset, which is the most efficient Recordset type that ADO supports. You can't specify the cursor position in the *Open* method, and if you want to create a client-side cursor, you must assign the adUseClient constant to the *CursorLocation* property before opening the Recordset. A few examples that show the *Open* method in action are on the following page.

```
' Edit this constant to match your directory structure.
Const DBPATH = "C:\Program Files\Microsoft Visual Studio\VB98\NWind.mdb"
' All the following examples use these variables.
Dim cn As New ADODB.Connection, rs As New ADODB.Recordset
Dim connString As String, sql As String
connString = "Provider=Microsoft.Jet.OLEDB.3.51;Data Source=" & DBPATH

' Open the Recordset using an existing Connection object.
cn.Open connString
rs.Open "Employees", cn, adOpenStatic, adLockReadOnly, adCmdTable

' Open the Recordset using a Connection object created on the fly.
' This creates a forward-only, read-only Recordset.
rs.Open "Employees", connString, , , adCmdTable
' After the Recordset has been opened, you can query the properties
' of the implicit Connection object.
Print "Current Connection String = " & rs.ActiveConnection.ConnectionString

' Select only the employees who were born in the 1960s or later.
sql = "SELECT * FROM Employees WHERE BirthDate >= #1/1/1960#"
rs.Open sql, connString, , , adCmdText
```

You can also open a record that you previously saved to a disk file using the *Save* method: In this case, the first argument of the *Open* method is the complete name and path of the file, and you should pass the adCmdFile constant to the *Options* argument.

The *Options* argument supports two more constants for asynchronous operations. The value 16-adAsyncExecute executes the query asynchronously: The control goes back to the application immediately, and ADO continues to populate the Recordset until the local cache is filled with data. The value 32-adAsyncFetch tells ADO that after filling the local cache with data, it should fetch the remaining records asynchronously. When all the records have been retrieved, ADO fires a *FetchComplete* event.

You can cancel an asynchronous operation at any moment by issuing a *Cancel* method. If no asynchronous operations are pending, this method does nothing and no error is raised.

When you're done with a Recordset, you should close it using its *Close* method. This method doesn't take any argument. ADO automatically closes a Recordset when no more variables are pointing to it. When a Recordset is closed, ADO releases all the locks and the memory allocated to its cursor (if it has one). You can't close a Recordset if an edit operation is in progress (that is, if you modified the value of one or more fields and haven't committed the changes). You can reopen a closed Recordset by using the same or different values for its *Source*, *CursorType*, *MaxRecords*, *CursorPosition*, and *LockType* properties. (These properties are read-only while the Recordset is open.)

You can create a Recordset also by using the *Clone* method to create a copy of an existing Recordset:

```
Dim rs2 As ADODB.Recordset
Set rs2 = rs.Clone(LockType)
```

The optional *LockType* argument tells which type of lock you want to enforce on the new Recordset. The cloned record can be opened only with the same lock type as the original record has (in this case, you just omit the argument) or in read-only mode (you pass the adLockReadOnly constant). Cloning a Recordset is more efficient than creating another Recordset against the same data source. Any modified value in one Recordset is immediately visible to all its clones regardless of their cursor type, but all the Recordsets in the group can be scrolled and closed independently from one another. If you issue a *Requery* method against the original Recordset, its clones aren't synchronized any longer. (The opposite isn't true, however: If you *Requery* the clones, they are still synchronized with the original Recordset.) Keep in mind that only Recordsets that support bookmarks can be cloned and that you can compare bookmarks defined in a Recordset and its clones.

Refreshing the Recordset

ADO offers two methods for repopulating a Recordset without closing and reopening it. The *Requery* method reexecutes the Recordset query. This method is especially useful with parameterized queries against an SQL Server database when you aren't using a Command object because it tells ADO to reuse the temporary stored procedure that SQL Server created when the Recordset was opened the first time. The *Requery* method accepts the adAsyncExecute option to run the query asynchronously. When the query completes, a *RecordsetChangeComplete* event fires. The *Requery* method lets you reexecute the query, but you can't modify any property that affects the type of the cursor (*CursorType*, *CursorLocation*, *LockType*, and so on) because these properties are read-only when the Recordset is open. To change these properties, you must close and then reopen the Recordset.

The *Resync* method refreshes the Recordset from the underlying database without actually reexecuting the query. Its syntax is as follows:

```
Resync [AffectRecords], [ResyncValues]
```

AffectRecords tells which records should be refreshed and can be one of the following constants:

Value	*Description*
1-adAffectCurrent	Refreshes the current record only
2-adAffectGroup	Refreshes the records that satisfy the current *Filter* property, which should have been assigned one of the supported enumerated constants
3-adAffectAll	Refreshes the entire Recordset (the default)

ResyncValues can be one of the following values:

Value	Description
1-adResyncUnderlyingValues	Reads the most recent values from the database and puts them in the *UnderlyingValue* properties of the Field objects
2-adResyncAllValues	Reads the most recent values and puts them in the *Value* properties of the Field objects (the default)

The effect of these two options is completely different: adResyncUnderlyingValues preserves the old data and doesn't cancel pending changes; adResyncAllValues cancels pending changes (as if a *CancelBatch* method had been issued).

Because the *Resync* method doesn't reexecute the query, you'll never see new records added by other users in the meantime. This method is especially useful with forward-only or static cursors when you want to be sure you're working with the most recent values. Any conflict during the resynchronization process—for example, another user has deleted a record—fills the Errors collection with one or more warnings. When using client-side cursors, this method is available only for updatable Recordsets.

Retrieving data

To read the values of the current record, you simply query the Fields collection as shown here:

```
' Print employee's first and last name.
Print rs.Fields("FirstName").Value, rs.Fields("LastName").Value
```

Because *Fields* is the default property for the Recordset object, you can omit it and access the field simply by using its name or its index. Similarly, you can drop the *Value* property because it's the default member of the Field object:

```
Print rs("FirstName"), rs("LastName")
```

You display the values of all the fields in the current record by iterating on the Fields collection. You can use the Field's index in a *For...Next* loop or a Field object variable in a *For Each...Next* loop:

```
' The first method uses a regular For...Next loop.
For i = 0 To rs.Fields.Count - 1
    Print rs.Fields(i).Name & " = " & rs(i)
Next

' The second method uses a For Each...Next loop.
Dim fld As ADODB.Field
```

```
For Each fld In rs.Fields
    Print fld.Name & " = " & fld.Value
Next
```

ADO also offers more efficient ways to retrieve data. The *GetRows* method returns a two-dimensional array of Variants, where each column corresponds to a record in the Recordset and each row corresponds to a field in the record. This method has the following syntax:

```
varArray = rs.GetRows([Rows], [Start], [Fields])
```

Rows is the number of records you want to read; use −1 or omit this argument if you want to retrieve all the records in the Recordset. *Start* is a bookmark that indicates the first record to be read; it can also be one of the following enumerated constants: 0-adBookmarkCurrent (the current record), 1-adBookmarkFirst (the first record), or 2-adBookmarkLast (the last record).

Fields is an optional array of field names that serves to restrict the quantity of data to read. (You can also specify a single field name, a single field index, or an array of field indexes.) When you set *Rows* to a value less than the number of records in the Recordset, the first unread record becomes the current record. If you omit the *Rows* argument or set it to −1-adGetRowsRest or to a value greater than the number of records still unread, the *GetRows* method reads all the records and leaves the Recordset in the EOF condition, without raising any error.

When processing the data in the target Variant array, you should remember that data is stored somewhat counterintuitively: The first subscript in the array identifies the Recordset's field (which is usually thought of as a column), and the second subscript identifies the Recordset's record (which is usually thought of as a row). Here's an example that loads three fields from all the records in the Recordset:

```
Dim values As Variant, fldIndex As Integer, recIndex As Integer
values = rs.GetRows(, , Array("LastName", "FirstName", "BirthDate"))
For recIndex = 0 To UBound(values, 2)
    For fldIndex = 0 To UBound(values)
        Print values(fldIndex, recIndex),
    Next
    Print
Next
```

The *GetRows* method is usually noticeably faster than an explicit loop that reads one record at a time, but if you use this method you must ensure that the Recordset doesn't contain too many records; otherwise, you can easily fill up all your physical memory with a very large Variant array. For the same reason, be careful not to include any BLOB (Binary Large Object) or CLOB (Character Large Object) fields in the field list; if you do, your application will almost surely bomb, especially with larger Recordsets.

Finally, keep in mind that the Variant array returned by this method is zero-based; the number of returned records is *UBound(values,2)+1*, and the number of returned fields is *UBound(value, 1)+1*.

The *GetString* method is similar to *GetRows*, but it returns multiple records as a single string. *GetString* has the following syntax:

```
GetString([Format], [NumRows], [ColDelimiter], [RowDelimiter], [NullExpr])
```

Format is the format for the result. *GetString* potentially supports more formats, but the only format currently supported is 2-adClipString, so you don't really have any choice. *NumRows* is the number of rows to retrieve. (Use −1 or omit this argument to read all the remaining records.) *ColDelimiter* is the delimiter character for the columns. (The default is the Tab character.) *RowDelimiter* is the delimiter character for the records. (The default is the carriage return.) *NullExpr* is the string to be used for Null fields. (The default is the empty string.) The documentation states that the last three arguments can be used only if *Format* = adClipString, but this warning doesn't make much sense because, as I just mentioned, this format is the only one currently supported. Here's an example that uses the *GetString* method to export data in a semicolon-delimited text file:

```
Dim i As Long
Open "datafile.txt" For Output As #1
For i = 0 To rs.Fields.Count - 1              ' Export field names.
    If i > 0 Then Print #1, ";";
    Print #1, rs.Fields(i).Name;
Next
Print #1, ""
rs.MoveFirst                                  ' Export data.
Print #1, rs.GetString(, , ";", vbCrLf);  ' Don't add an extra CR-LF here.
Close #1
```

The *GetString* method doesn't permit you to export only a subset of the fields, nor does it permit you to modify the order of the exported fields. If you need these additional capabilities, you should use the *GetRows* method and build the result string yourself.

Navigating the Recordset

When you open a Recordset, the current record pointer points to the first record unless the Recordset is empty (in which case, both the *BOF* and *EOF* properties return True). To read and modify values in another record, you must make that record the current record, which you usually do by executing one of the *Move*xxxx methods exposed by the Recordset object. *MoveFirst* moves to the first record in the Recordset, *MoveLast* moves to the last record, *MovePrevious* moves to the previous record, and *MoveNext* moves to the next record. You typically provide users with four buttons that let them navigate the Recordset. Executing a *MovePrevious* method when *BOF* is True or executing a *MoveNext* method when *EOF* is True raises an error; therefore, you have to trap these conditions before moving to the previous or next record:

```
Private Sub cmdFirst_Click()
    rs.MoveFirst
End Sub

Private Sub cmdPrevious_Click()
    If Not rs.BOF Then rs.MovePrevious
End Sub

Private Sub cmdNext_Click()
    If Not rs.EOF Then rs.MoveNext
End Sub

Private Sub cmdLast_Click()
    rs.MoveLast
End Sub
```

The *MoveFirst* and *MoveNext* methods are commonly used in loops that iterate on all the records in the Recordset, as shown in the following example:

```
rs.MoveFirst
Do Until rs.EOF
    total = total + rs("UnitsInStock") * rs("UnitPrice")
    rs.MoveNext
Loop
Print "Total of UnitsInStock * UnitPrice = " & total
```

ADO also supports a generic *Move* method, whose syntax is:

```
Move NumRecords, [Start]
```

NumRecords is a Long value that specifies the number of records to skip toward the end (if positive) or the beginning (if negative) of the Recordset. The move is relative to the record identified by the *Start* argument, which can be a bookmark value or one of the following enumerated constants:

Value	*Description*
0-adBookmarkCurrent	The current record
1-adBookmarkFirst	The first record in the Recordset
2-adBookmarkLast	The last record in the Recordset

As you can see on the following page, the *Move* method embodies the functionality of the four *Move*xxxx methods I've described previously.

```
rs.Move 0, adBookmarkFirst          ' Same as MoveFirst
rs.Move -1                          ' Same as MovePrevious
rs.Move 1                           ' Same as MoveNext
rs.Move 0, adBookmarkLast           ' Same as MoveLast
rs.Move 10, adBookmarkFirst         ' Move to the tenth record.
rs.Move -1, adBookmarkLast          ' Move to the next to the last record.
rs.Move 0                           ' Refresh the current record.
```

If you specify a negative offset that points to a record before the first record, the *BOF* property becomes True and no error is raised. Similarly, if you specify a positive offset that points to a record after the last record, the *EOF* property is set to True and no error is raised. Interestingly, you can specify a negative offset even with forward-only Recordsets: If the target record is still in the local cache, no error occurs. (You can't use *MovePrevious* with forward-only Recordsets, regardless of whether the previous record is in the cache.)

You can also navigate a Recordset using the *Bookmark* and *AbsolutePosition* properties. ADO also provides a *CompareBookmarks* method that lets you compare bookmarks coming from the same Recordset or from a cloned Recordset. This method has the following syntax:

```
result = CompareBookmarks(Bookmark1, Bookmark2)
```

result can receive one of these values:

Value	Description
0-adCompareLessThan	The first bookmark refers to a record that precedes the record the second bookmark refers to.
1-adCompareEqual	The two bookmarks point to the same record.
2-adCompareGreaterThan	The first bookmark refers to a record that follows the record the second bookmark refers to.
3-adCompareNotEqual	The two bookmarks refer to different records, but the provider can't determine which one comes first.
4-adCompareNotComparable	The bookmarks can't be compared.

Updating, inserting, and deleting records

ADO differs from DAO and RDO in that the *Update* method isn't really necessary: All you have to do to modify a record is assign a new value to one or more Field objects and then move to another record. The ADO *Update* method supports the capability to update multiple fields at once, using the following syntax:

```
Update [fields] [, values]
```

fields is a Variant containing a single field name, a field index, or an array of field names or indexes. *values* is a Variant containing a single value or an array of values. These arguments are optional, but you can't omit just one of the two: If provided, they must contain the same number of arguments. The following example demonstrates how you can update multiple fields using this syntax:

```
' Update four fields in one operation.
rs.Update Array("FirstName", "LastName", "BirthDate", "HireDate"), _
    Array("John", "Smith", #1/1/1961#, #12/3/1994#)
```

Because an update operation is automatically performed if one or more fields in the current record have been modified, ADO provides the *CancelUpdate* method to cancel such changes and leave the current record unmodified. You can use the *Update* and *CancelUpdate* methods together to offer the user a chance to confirm or cancel changes to the current record:

```
If rs.EditMode = adEditInProgress Then
    If MsgBox("Do you want to commit changes?", vbYesNo) = vbYes Then
        rs.Update
    Else
        rs.CancelUpdate
    End If
End If
```

You can add new records to the Recordset with the *AddNew* method. This method is similar to the *Update* method in that it supports two syntax forms, with or without arguments. If you don't pass an argument, you create a new record at the end of the Recordset and you're supposed to assign values to its fields using the Fields collection:

```
rs.AddNew
rs("FirstName") = "Robert"
rs("LastName") = "Doe"
rs("BirthDate") = #2/5/1955#
rs.Update
```

You don't need an explicit *Update* method after an *AddNew* method—any *Movexxxx* method will do. In the second syntax form, you pass the *AddNew* method a list of fields and a list of values; in this case, no update is necessary because values are immediately committed to the database:

```
' This statement has the same effect as the previous code snippet.
rs.AddNew Array("FirstName", "LastName", "BirthDate"), _
    Array("Robert", "Doe", #2/5/1955#)
```

After you commit changes with an *Update* method, the record you've just added becomes the current record. If you issue a second *AddNew* method, you commit changes automatically to the record added just before, as if you had executed a *Movexxxx* method. Depending on the type of cursor, it's possible that the record you've added doesn't appear in the Recordset immediately and that you'll have to execute a *Requery* method to see it.

You can delete the current record by executing the *Delete* method. This method accepts an optional argument:

```
rs.Delete [AffectRecords]
```

If *AffectRecords* is 1-adAffectCurrent or is omitted, only the current record is deleted. When you delete a record, it's still the current record but it can't be accessed any longer, so you'd better move on to another record:

```
rs.Delete
rs.MoveNext
If rs.EOF Then rs.MoveLast
```

You can delete a group of records by assigning an enumerated constant to the *Filter* property and then issuing a *Delete* method with the *AffectRecords* argument set to 2-adAffectGroup:

```
' After a batch update attempt, delete all the records that failed
' to be transferred to the server.
rs.Filter = adFilterConflictingRecords
rs.Delete adAffectGroup
rs.Filter = adFilterNone        ' Remove the filter.
```

You should nest your delete operations in a transaction if you want to give your users the chance to undelete them.

Finding records

The *Find* method provides a simple way to move to a record in the Recordset that matches search criteria. This method has the following syntax:

```
Find Criteria, [SkipRecords], [SearchDirection], [Start]
```

Criteria is a string that contains the search condition, which consists of a field name followed by an operator and a value. The supported operators are = (equal), < (less than), > (greater than), and LIKE (pattern matching). The value can be a string enclosed by single quotes, a number, or a date value enclosed by # characters. *SkipRecord* is an optional number that indicates how many records should be skipped before starting the search: Positive values skip forward (toward the end of the Recordset), and negative values skip backward (toward the beginning of the Recordset). *SearchDirection* indicates the direction in which the search must proceed; you can use the values 1-adSearchForward (the default) or −1-adSearchBackward. *Start* is an optional bookmark that specifies the record from which the search should begin. (The default is the current record.)

In most cases, you can omit all the arguments except the first one, which results in a search that starts from the current record (included) and goes toward the end of the database. If the search is successful, the record that matches the search criteria becomes the current record; if the search fails, the current record is past the last record in the Recordset (or before the first record, if *Search* = adSearchBackward). Passing a nonzero value to the *SkipRecord* argument is necessary when you want to restart the search after you've found a match, as the following code snippet demonstrates:

```
' Search all the employees who were hired after January 1, 1994.
rs.MoveFirst
rs.Find "HireDate > #1/1/1994#"
Do Until rs.EOF
    Print rs("LastName"), rs("BirthDate"), rs("HireDate")
    ' Search the next record that meets the criteria, but skip the current one.
    rs.Find "HireDate > #1/1/1994#", 1
Loop
```

The LIKE operator accepts two wildcard symbols: * (asterisk) matches zero or more characters, and _ (underscore) matches exactly one character. Comparisons aren't case sensitive and aren't affected by the *Option Compare* directive. Here are a few examples:

```
rs.Find "FirstName LIKE 'J*'"      ' Matches "Joe" and "John".
rs.Find "FirstName LIKE 'J__'"     ' Matches "Joe" but not "John".
rs.Find "FirstName LIKE '*A*'"     ' Matches "Anne", "Deborah", and "Maria".
rs.Find "FirstName LIKE '*A'"      ' This gives an error: a bug?
```

Updating records in batch mode

If you open a Recordset with the adLockBatchOptimistic option, all the rules stated so far about record updating are void. When working with optimistic batch updates, you're actually working with a cursor on the client workstation. You can read it even if the connection with the server doesn't exist anymore, and you can modify it without committing the changes to the server (not immediately at least). In optimistic batch mode, the implicit or explicit *Update* method affects only the local cursor, not the real database. This helps keep the network traffic to a minimum and greatly improves overall performance.

When you're ready to commit the changes to the database on the server, you issue an *UpdateBatch* method, which has the following syntax:

```
UpdateBatch [AffectRecords]
```

You should assign the *AffectRecords* argument one of the constants listed on the following page.

Value	Description
1-adAffectCurrent	Updates only the current record
2-adAffectGroup	Updates all the modified records that satisfy the current *Filter* property, which must have been assigned one of the supported enumerated constants
3-adAffectAll	Updates all modified records in the Recordset (the default)
4-adAffectAllChapters	Updates all the chapters in a hierarchical Recordset

The adAffectAll setting is hidden in the ADODB type library. If you issue the *UpdateBatch* method while in edit mode, ADO commits the changes to the current record and then proceeds with the batch update.

The Visual Basic documentation states that if there is a conflict and one or more records can't be successfully updated, ADO fills the Errors collection with warnings but doesn't raise an error in the application. ADO raises an error only if all the records fail to update. Some tests prove, however, that when there is one conflicting record, the error &H80040E38, "Errors occurred," is returned to the application. You can then set the *Filter* property to the adFilterConflictingRecords value to see which records weren't updated successfully.

You can cancel a batch update using the *CancelBatch* method, which has the following syntax:

```
CancelBatch [AffectRecords]
```

AffectRecords has the same meaning here as it has with the *UpdateBatch* method. If the Recordset hasn't been opened with the adLockBatchOptimistic option, any value other than 1-adAffectCurrent raises an error. If you're in edit mode, the *CancelBatch* method cancels the updates to the current record first and then cancels the changes to the records affected by the *AffectRecords* argument. After a *CancelBatch* method is completed, the current record position might be undetermined, so you should use the *Move*xxxx method or the *Bookmark* property to move to a valid record.

When performing batch update operations on the client machine, you don't need to keep the connection to the database active. In fact, you can set the Recordset's *ActiveConnection* property to Nothing, close the companion Connection object, let your user browse and update the data, and then reestablish the connection when he or she is ready to post the updates to the database. For more information about batch updates, see the section "Optimistic Client-Batch Updates" in Chapter 14.

Implementing persistent Recordsets

One of the most intriguing features of the ADO Recordset object is that you can save it to a regular disk file and then reopen it when necessary. This feature is advantageous in many situations—for example, when you're performing batch updates or when you want to postpone the processing of a Recordset. You don't even need to reopen the Recordset with the same application that saved it. For example, you can save a Recordset to a file and later process it with a report application that sends the output to a printer during off hours. The key to this capability is the *Save* method, which has the following syntax:

```
Save [FileName], [PersistFormat]
```

The first argument is the name of the file in which the Recordset should be saved, and the second argument is the format in which the Recordset should be saved. ADO 2.0 supports only the Advanced Data TableGram (ADTG), so you should specify the constant 0-adPersistADTG or omit the argument. Although the syntax of the *Save* method is rather intuitive, it includes some subtle details that you must account for when you're working with persistent Recordsets:

- In general, persistent Recordsets should use client-side cursors, so you should change the value of the *CursorLocation* property, whose default value is adUseServer. Some providers might support this capability with server-side cursors, however.

- You need to specify the filename only the first time you save the Recordset to a file; in all subsequent saves, you must omit the first argument if you want to save to the same data file. If you don't omit the argument, a run-time error occurs.

- An error occurs if the file already exists, so you should test for its existence before issuing the *Save* method and manually delete it if necessary.

- *Save* doesn't close the Recordset, so you can continue to work with it and save the most recent changes by issuing additional *Save* methods without the *FileName* argument. The file is closed only when the Recordset is also closed; in the meantime, other applications can read the file but can't write to it.

- After you've saved to a file, you can specify a different filename to save to a different file; however, this operation doesn't close the original file. Both files remain open until the Recordset is closed.

- If the *Filter* property is in effect, only the records that are currently visible are saved. This feature is useful for postponing the processing of records that failed to be committed to the database during a batch update operation.

- If the *Sort* property isn't an empty string, the records will be saved in the sorted order.

■   If the *Save* method is issued while an asynchronous operation is in progress, the method doesn't return until the asynchronous operation is completed.

■   After a *Save* operation, the current record will be the first record in the Recordset.

When opening a persistent Recordset, you should use the adCmdFile value in the *Option* argument of the *Open* method:

```
' Save a Recordset to a file, and then close both the file
' and the Recordset.
rs.Save "C:\datafile.rec", adPersistADTG
rs.Close
'...
' Reopen the persistent Recordset.
rs.Open "C:\datafile.rec", , , , adCmdFile
```

> **NOTE**   Because the ADTG is a binary format, you can't easily edit a Recordset that has been saved in this format. The ADODB type library already includes the hidden constant 1-adPersistXML, even though this constant isn't supported in ADO 2.0. The good news is that ADO 2.1 fully supports Recordset persistence in XML format; this option is tantalizing because XML is a text-based format, and so you can edit the saved file using an editor.

Managing multiple Recordsets

ADO Recordsets support multiple queries in the *Source* property or in the *Source* argument of the *Open* method if the provider also supports multiple queries. You specify multiple SELECT queries, or even SQL action queries, by using the semicolon as a separator, as shown here:

```
rs.Open "SELECT * FROM Employees;SELECT * FROM Customers"
```

When the *Open* method completes its execution, the Recordset object contains all the records from the first query, and you can process these records as you would with a regular Recordset. When you're done with the records, you can retrieve them from the second query using the *NextRecordset* method:

```
Dim RecordsAffected As Long
Set rs = rs.NextRecordset(RecordsAffected)
```

The argument is optional; if specified, it should be a Long variable. This variable receives the number of records that have been affected by the current operation (which might also be an SQL command that doesn't return a Recordset). Although the syntax permits you to assign the result of the *NextResult* method to another Recordset variable, as of this writing, no provider supports this functionality and the original contents of the Recordset are always discarded. If this functionality becomes available, it will be possible to assign each Recordset object to a distinct object variable and process all the Recordsets simultaneously.

Here are a few details to be aware of when you're working with multiple Recordsets:

- Each query is executed only when the *NextRecordset* method requests it; therefore, if you close the Recordset before processing all the pending commands, the corresponding queries or action commands are never executed.

- If a row-returning query doesn't return any record, the resulting Recordset is empty. You can test this condition by checking whether both the *BOF* and *EOF* properties return True.

- If the pending SQL command doesn't return any row, the resulting Recordset will be closed. You can test this condition with the *State* property.

- When no more commands are pending, the *NextRecordset* method returns Nothing.

- You can't call the *NextResult* method if an edit operation is in progress; to avoid errors, you should issue an *Update* or *CancelUpdate* method first.

- If one or more of the SQL commands or queries require parameters, you should fill the Parameters collection with all the required parameter values, and they should be in the order expected by the commands or queries.

- The provider must support multiple queries. For example, the provider for Microsoft Jet databases doesn't support them. The providers for SQL Server seem to support this functionality only with static client-side cursors or with server-side "cursorless" Recordsets.

Here's an example of a code framework that you can use when working with multiple Recordsets:

```
Dim RecordsAffected As Long
rs.Open
Do
    If rs Is Nothing Then
        ' No more Recordsets, so exit.
        Exit Do
    ElseIf (rs.State And adStateOpen) = 0 Then
        ' It was a non-row-returning SQL command.
        ...
```

(continued)

```
    Else
        ' Process the Recordset here.
        ...
    End If
    Set rs.NextRecordset(RecordsAffected)
Loop
```

Testing for features

Not all types of Recordsets support all the features that I've described so far. Instead of having you guess which features are supported and which aren't, the ADO Recordset object exposes the *Supports* method, which accepts a bit-field argument and returns True only if the Recordset supports all the features indicated in the argument. For example, you can test whether the Recordset supports bookmarks using the following code:

```
If rs.Supports(adBookmark) Then currBookmark = rs.Bookmark
```

The argument to the *Supports* method can include one or more of the constants listed in Table 13-3. You don't need to issue multiple *Supports* methods if you want to test multiple features:

```
If rs.Supports(adAddNew Or adDelete Or adFind) Then
    ' The Recordset supports the AddNew, Delete, and Find methods.
End If
```

Don't forget that if this method returns True you're only sure that ADO supports the requested operation, not that the OLE DB provider necessarily supports it under all circumstances.

Constant	*Value*	*Description*
adHoldRecords	&H100	Support for reading more records or changing the next retrieve position without committing pending changes
adMovePrevious	&H200	Support for the *MoveFirst* and *MovePrevious* methods and for *Move* and *GetRows* with backward moves
adBookmark	&H2000	Support for the *Bookmark* property
adApproxPosition	&H4000	Support for the *AbsolutePosition* and *AbsolutePage* properties
adUpdateBatch	&H10000	Support for the *UpdateBatch* and *CancelBatch* methods
adResync	&H20000	Support for the *Resync* method

Table 13-3. *The arguments for the* Supports *method.*

Constant	Value	Description
adNotify	&H40000	Support for notifications
adFind	&H80000	Support for the *Find* method
adAddNew	&H1000400	Support for the *AddNew* method
adDelete	&H1000800	Support for the *Delete* method
adUpdate	&H1008000	Support for the *Update* method

Events

The ADO Recordset object exposes 11 events. These events allow you to take complete control of what's happening behind the scenes. By writing code for these events, you can leverage asynchronous queries, trap the instant when a field or a record is modified, and even add data when the user reaches the end of the Recordset. The ADO Workbench application is especially helpful when watching events because it automatically converts all the enumerated constants to their symbolic names.

Data retrieval events

The *FetchProgress* event is fired periodically during a lengthy asynchronous operation. You can use it to show the user a progress bar that indicates the percentage of records retrieved:

```
Private Sub rs_FetchProgress(ByVal Progress As Long, _
    ByVal MaxProgress As Long, adStatus As ADODB.EventStatusEnum, _
    ByVal pRecordset As ADODB.Recordset)
```

The *Progress* parameter is the number of records retrieved so far. *MaxProgress* is the total number of expected records. *adStatus* is the usual status parameter. *pRecordset* is a reference to the Recordset object that is raising the event. (In Visual Basic, you never need to use this argument because you already have a reference to the Recordset.)

When the retrieval of records is completed, ADO fires a *FetchComplete* event. If the *adStatus* parameter is equal to adStatusErrorsOccurred, you can query the error through the *pError* parameter:

```
Private Sub rs_FetchComplete(ByVal pError As ADODB.error, _
    adStatus As ADODB.EventStatusEnum, _
    ByVal pRecordset As ADODB.Recordset)
End Sub
```

Navigation events

Each time the current record changes, a *WillMove* event fires, soon followed by a *MoveComplete* event, as you can see in the code at the top of the next page.

```
Private Sub rs_WillMove(ByVal adReason As ADODB.EventReasonEnum, _
    adStatus As ADODB.EventStatusEnum, _
    ByVal pRecordset As ADODB.Recordset)
```

The *adReason* parameter tells why this event has been fired. It can be one of the constants listed in Table 13-4. Unless *adStatus* is set to adStatusCantDeny, you can cancel the operation by assigning the value adStatusCancel to *adStatus*.

When the move operation has completed (or when it has been canceled), a *MoveComplete* event fires:

```
Private Sub rs_MoveComplete(ByVal adReason As ADODB.EventReasonEnum, _
    ByVal pError As ADODB.error, adStatus As ADODB.EventStatusEnum, _
    ByVal pRecordset As ADODB.Recordset)
```

The *adReason* and *adStatus* parameters have the same meanings as they have in the *WillMove* event: If *adStatus* is equal to adStatusErrorOccurred, the *pError* object contains information about the error; otherwise, *pError* is Nothing. You can cancel further notifications by setting *adStatus* to adStatusUnwantedEvent.

Value	Constant		Value	Constant
1	adRsnAddNew		9	adRsnClose
2	adRsnDelete		10	adRsnMove
3	adRsnUpdate		11	adRsnFirstChange
4	adRsnUndoUpdate		12	adRsnMoveFirst
5	adRsnUndoAddNew		13	adRsnMoveNext
6	adRsnUndoDelete		14	adRsnMovePrevious
7	adRsnRequery		15	adRsnMoveLast
8	adRsnResynch			

Table 13-4. *The values of the* adReason *parameter in Recordset's events.*

When the program attempts to move past the end of the Recordset, possibly as a result of a *MoveNext* method, an *EndOfRecordset* error fires:

```
Private Sub rs_EndOfRecordset(fMoreData As Boolean, _
    adStatus As ADODB.EventStatusEnum, _
    ByVal pRecordset As ADODB.Recordset)
```

ADO lets you add new records to the Recordset when this event fires. If you want to take advantage of this opportunity, just execute an *AddNew* method, fill the Fields collection with data, and then set the *fMoreData* parameter to True to let ADO know that you've added new records. As usual, you can cancel the operation that caused the move by setting the *adStatus* parameter to adStatusCancel, unless the *adStatus* parameter contains the value adStatusCantDeny.

Update events

Any time ADO is about to modify one or more fields in a Recordset, it fires the *WillChangeField* event:

```
Private Sub rs_WillChangeField(ByVal cFields As Long, _
    ByVal Fields As Variant, adStatus As ADODB.EventStatusEnum, _
    ByVal pRecordset As ADODB.Recordset)
```

cFields is the number of fields that are about to be modified, and *Fields* is an array of Variants that contains one or more Field objects with pending changes. You can set *adStatus* to adStatusCancel to cancel the pending update operation, unless it contains the adStatusCantDeny value.

When the update operation is completed, ADO fires a *FieldChangeComplete* event, which receives the same parameters plus the pError object that lets you investigate any error raised in the meantime (if *adStatus* is equal to adStatusErrorOccurred):

```
Private Sub rs_FieldChangeComplete(ByVal cFields As Long, _
    ByVal Fields As Variant, ByVal pError As ADODB.error, _
    adStatus As ADODB.EventStatusEnum, _
    ByVal pRecordset As ADODB.Recordset)
```

When one or more records are about to change, ADO fires a *WillChangeRecord* event:

```
Private Sub rs_WillChangeRecord(ByVal adReason As ADODB.EventReasonEnum, _
    ByVal cRecords As Long, adStatus As ADODB.EventStatusEnum, _
    ByVal pRecordset As ADODB.Recordset)
```

adReason is one of the enumerated constants listed in Table 13-4, *cRecords* is the number of records that are going to be modified, and *adStatus* is the parameter that you can set to adStatusCancel to cancel the operation (unless the *adStatus* parameter contains the adStatusCantDeny value).

When the update operation is completed, ADO fires a *RecordChangeComplete* event:

```
Private Sub rs_RecordChangeComplete( _
    ByVal adReason As ADODB.EventReasonEnum, ByVal cRecords As Long, _
    ByVal pError As ADODB.error, adStatus As ADODB.EventStatusEnum, _
    ByVal pRecordset As ADODB.Recordset)
```

All the parameters have the same meanings as they do in the *WillChangeRecord* event. If *adStatus* is adStatusErrorOccurred, you can query the *pError* object to find out what went wrong, and you can reject further notifications by setting *adStatus* to adStatusUnwantedEvent. These two events can occur because of an *Update*, *UpdateBatch*, *Delete*, *CancelUpdate*, *CancelBatch*, or *AddNew* method. During this event, the *Filter* property is set to the value adFilterAffectedRecords and you can't change it.

Whenever ADO is about to perform an operation that's going to change the contents of the Recordset as a whole—such as *Open*, *Requery*, and *Resync* methods—a *WillChangeRecordset* event fires:

```
Private Sub rs_WillChangeRecordset( _
    ByVal adReason As ADODB.EventReasonEnum,
    adStatus As ADODB.EventStatusEnum, _
    ByVal pRecordset As ADODB.Recordset)
```

adReason is one of the constants listed in Table 13-4, and *adStatus* has the usual meaning. If this parameter isn't equal to adStatusCantDeny, you can cancel the operation by setting it to the value adStatusCancel.

When the update operation is complete, ADO fires a *RecordsetChangeComplete* event:

```
Private Sub rs_RecordsetChangeComplete( _
    ByVal adReason As ADODB.EventReasonEnum, _
    ByVal pError As ADODB.error, _
    adStatus As ADODB.EventStatusEnum, ByVal pRecordset As ADODB.Recordset)
```

The parameters here mean the same as they do in the *WillChangeRecordset* event. One undocumented behavior you should keep in mind is that with a forward-only Recordset, the *WillChangeRecordset* and *RecordsetChangeComplete* events also fire whenever you execute the *MoveNext* method because you're working with a cursorless Recordset; each time you move to another record, ADO re-creates the Recordset object. In general, with any Recordset that doesn't support bookmarks, these events fire whenever the local cache has to be refilled (with a frequency that therefore depends on the *CacheSize* property).

THE FIELD OBJECT

The Recordset object exposes the Fields collection, which in turn contains one or more Field objects. Each Field object represents one column in the data source and exposes 12 properties and 2 methods.

Properties

The properties of a Field object can be divided into two distinct groups: properties that describe the attributes and the characteristics of the field (and that are available also when the Recordset is closed) and properties that describe the contents of a field in the current record. (These properties are available only when the Recordset is open and the current record isn't invalid.)

Describing the field's characteristics

All the properties that describe the Field object's characteristics (which are also known as *metadata* properties) are read/write if you're adding the Field object to a standalone Recordset and read-only after the Recordset has been opened.

The *Name* property is the name of the database column the Field object takes data from and writes data to. Because this property is also the key associated with the Field object in the Fields collection, you can refer to a particular field in one of three ways, using the following syntax:

```
' Full syntax
rs.Fields("LastName").Value = "Smith"
' Fields is the Recordset's default property.
rs("LastName").Value = "Smith"
' Value is the Field's default property.
rs("LastName") = "Smith"
```

You usually enumerate the fields in a Recordset using a *For...Next* or *For Each...Next* loop:

```
For i = 0 To rs.Fields.Count - 1
    lstFieldNames.AddItem rs.Fields(i).Name
Next
```

The *Type* property returns an enumerated constant that defines which kind of values can be stored in the field. All the types that ADO supports are listed in Table 13-5, but you should be aware that not all OLE DB providers and database engines support all these data types. The *Type* property also indirectly affects *NumericScale*, *Precision*, and *DefinedSize*.

> **CAUTION** A few constants in Table 13-5 apply only to Parameter objects (which are described later in this chapter)—at least, this is what the Visual Basic documentation states. I found, however, that some of these values are also used for Field objects. For example, the *Type* property of a string field in an MDB database returns the value adVarChar.

Constant	Value	Description
adEmpty	0	No value specified
adSmallInt	2	2-byte signed integer
adInteger	3	4-byte signed integer
adSingle	4	Single-precision floating point value
adDouble	5	Double-precision floating point value

Table 13-5. *The constants used for the* Type *property of the Field, Parameter, and Property objects.*

(continued)

Table 13-5. *continued*

Constant	Value	Description
adCurrency	6	Currency value
adDate	7	Date value (stored in a Double value, in the same format as Visual Basic's Date variables)
adBSTR	8	Null-terminated Unicode string
adIDispatch	9	Pointer to an *IDispatch* interface of an OLE object
adError	10	32-bit error code
adBoolean	11	Boolean value
adVariant	12	Variant value
adIUnknown	13	Pointer to an *IUnknown* interface of an OLE object
adDecimal	14	Numeric value with fixed precision and scale
adTinyInt	16	1-byte signed integer
adUnsignedTinyInt	17	1-byte unsigned integer
adUnsignedSmallInt	18	2-byte unsigned integer
adUnsignedInt	19	4-byte unsigned integer
adBigInt	20	8-byte signed integer
adUnsignedBigInt	21	8-byte unsigned integer
adGUID	72	Globally Unique Identifier (GUID)
adBinary	128	Binary value
adChar	129	String value
adWChar	130	Null-terminated Unicode character string
adNumeric	131	Exact numeric value with fixed precision and scale
adUserDefined	132	User-defined variable
adDBDate	133	Date value in format "yyyymmdd"
adDBTime	134	Time value in format "hhmmss"
adDBTimeStamp	135	Date and time stamp in format "yyyymmddhhmmss" plus a fraction in billionths
adChapter	136	Chapter (a dependent Recordset in a hierarchical Recordset)
adVarNumeric	139	Variable-length exact numeric value with fixed precision and scale
adVarChar	200	String value (Parameter object only)

Constant	Value	Description
adLongVarChar	201	Long variable-length character string (Parameter object only)
adVarWChar	202	Null-terminated Unicode character string (Parameter object only)
adLongVarWChar	203	Long variable-length Unicode character string (Parameter object only)
adVarBinary	204	Binary value (Parameter object only)
adLongVarBinary	205	Long variable-length binary data (Parameter object only)

The *DefinedSize* property returns the maximum capacity that was defined when the field was created. The *NumericScale* property indicates the scale of numeric values (in other words, the number of digits to the right of the decimal point that will be used to represent the value). The *Precision* property is the degree of precision for numeric values in a numeric Field object (that is, the maximum total number of digits used to represent the value). The *Attributes* property is a bit-field value that returns information about the field. It can contain one or more of the constants listed in Table 13-6.

Constant	Value	Description
adFldMayDefer	2	A deferred field—that is, a field whose value is retrieved only when the field is explicitly referenced in the code. BLOB and CLOB fields are often fields of this type.
adFldUpdatable	4	The field is updatable.
adFldUnknownUpdatable	8	The provider can't determine whether the field is writable.
adFldFixed	&H10	The field contains fixed-length data.
adFldIsNullable	&H20	The field accepts Null values.
adFldMayBeNull	&H40	The field can contain Null values (but doesn't necessarily accept them).
adFldLong	&H80	The field is a long binary field (for example, a BLOB or a CLOB), and you can use the *AppendChunk* and *GetChunk* methods on it.

Table 13-6. *Constants used for the* Attributes *property of the Field object.*   *(continued)*

Table 13-6. *continued*

Constant	Value	Description
adFldRowID	&H100	The field contains a record identifier that can't be written to and that has no meaningful value except for identifying the row (for example, a record number or a unique identifier).
adFldRowVersion	&H200	The field contains some kind of date stamp or time stamp that is used to track record updates.
adFldCacheDeferred	&H1000	The field is cached the first time it is read from the database, and all subsequent reads fetch the data from the cache.
adFldKeyColumn	&H8000	The field is part of the key.

Describing the field's value

The *Value* property sets or returns the contents of the field. It is also the default property of the Field object, so you can omit it if you want to:

```
rs.Fields("BirthDate") = #4/12/1955#
```

The *ActualSize* property is a read-only property that returns the number of bytes taken by the current value in the field. Don't confuse this property with the *DefinedSize* property, which returns the declared maximum length of the field. This property is especially useful with BLOB and CLOB fields. If the provider can't determine the size of the field, it returns that value −1. (The Visual Basic documentation states that in this case this property returns the constant adUnknown; however, this constant doesn't appear in the ADODB type library.)

The *OriginalValue* property returns the value that was in the field before any changes were made. If you're in immediate update mode, this is the value that the *CancelUpdate* method uses to restore the field's contents; if you're in batch update mode, this is the value that was valid after the last *UpdateBatch* method and is also the value that the *CancelBatch* method uses to restore the field's contents.

The *UnderlyingValue* property is the value that is currently stored in the database. This value might be different from the *OriginalValue* property if another user has updated the field since you last read it. A *Resync* method would assign this value to the *Value* property. You typically use this property together with the *OriginalValue* property to resolve conflicts arising from batch updates.

You can assign the *DataFormat* property a StdDataFormat object so that you can control how values coming from the data source are formatted in the field. For more information on this property, see the section, "The *DataFormat* Property" in Chapter 8.

Methods

The Field object supports only two methods, both of which are used only with large binary fields such as BLOB or CLOB fields. (These are the fields whose *Attributes* property has the adFldLong bit set.) Because these fields can be several kilobytes—or even hundreds of kilobytes—long, writing to them and reading them back in smaller chunks is often more practical.

The *AppendChunk* method writes a chunk of data to a Field and expects a Variant argument that contains the data to be written. Usually, you write the contents of a file in chunks of 8 KB or 16 KB, and in most cases, you want to store a large amount of data that you have in a file, such as a long document or a bitmap. Here's a reusable routine that moves the contents of a file into a field that supports the *AppendChunk* method:

```
Sub FileToBlob(fld As ADODB.Field, FileName As String, _
    Optional ChunkSize As Long = 8192)
    Dim fnum As Integer, bytesLeft As Long, bytes As Long
    Dim tmp() As Byte
    ' Raise an error if the field doesn't support GetChunk.
    If (fld.Attributes And adFldLong) = 0 Then
        Err.Raise 1001, , "Field doesn't support the GetChunk method."
    End If
    ' Open the file; raise an error if the file doesn't exist.
    If Dir$(FileName) = " " Then Err.Raise 53, , "File not found"
    fnum = FreeFile
    Open FileName For Binary As fnum
    ' Read the file in chunks, and append data to the field.
    bytesLeft = LOF(fnum)
    Do While bytesLeft
        bytes = bytesLeft
        If bytes > ChunkSize Then bytes = ChunkSize
        ReDim tmp(1 To bytes) As Byte
        Get #1, , tmp
        fld.AppendChunk tmp
        bytesLeft = bytesLeft - bytes
    Loop
    Close #fnum
End Sub
```

When you first call this method for a given field, it overwrites the current contents of the field; each subsequent call to this method appends data to the current value of the field. If you read or write another field in the record and then go back to again append data with the *AppendChunk* method, ADO assumes that you're appending a new value and overwrites the field's contents. ADO also overwrites the contents of the field when you start to work with another field in a Recordset clone, but not when you work with a field in another Recordset that isn't a clone of the current one.

You can use the *GetChunk* method to read back the data stored in a Field that contains a long binary value. This method takes one argument: the number of bytes that must be read from the Field object. The problem with this method is that if you read too many bytes, ADO will pad the returned string with spaces. Such spaces are usually something you don't want to retrieve, especially when you're working with images or other binary data. For this reason, you should test the *ActualSize* property to ensure that you don't read more bytes than necessary. I've prepared a reusable routine that does this testing for you automatically:

```
Sub BlobToFile(fld As ADODB.Field, FileName As String, _
    Optional ChunkSize As Long = 8192)
    Dim fnum As Integer, bytesLeft As Long, bytes As Long
    Dim tmp() As Byte
    ' Raise an error if the field doesn't support GetChunk.
    If (fld.Attributes And adFldLong) = 0 Then
        Err.Raise 1001, , "Field doesn't support the GetChunk method."
    End If
' Delete the file if it exists already, and then open a new one for writing.
    If Dir$(FileName) <> "" Then Kill FileName
    fnum = FreeFile
    Open FileName For Binary As fnum
    ' Read the field's contents, and write the data to the file
    ' chunk by chunk.
    bytesLeft = fld.ActualSize
    Do While bytesLeft
        bytes = bytesLeft
        If bytes > ChunkSize Then bytes = ChunkSize
        tmp = fld.GetChunk(bytes)
        Put #fnum, , tmp
        bytesLeft = bytesLeft - bytes
    Loop
    Close #fnum
End Sub
```

> **NOTE** The *FileToBlob* and *BlobToFile* routines are included in the library of functions in the companion CD, as are most of the other routines in this chapter and Chapter 14.

Multiple *GetChunks* methods continue to retrieve data starting from where the previous *GetChunk* method left off. But if you read or write the value of another field in the same Recordset (or in a clone of the Recordset), the next time you execute a *GetChunk* method on the original field ADO will restart from the beginning of the field. Also, remember that BLOB fields should be the last fields in SELECT queries against SQL Server data sources.

The Fields Collection

You can use the Fields collection in two distinct ways. The simplest and most intuitive way is by iterating on its items to retrieve information about the fields of a Recordset—for example, when you want to create a list of field names and values:

```
' Error trapping accounts for values, such as BLOB fields, that
' can't be converted to strings.
On Error Resume Next
For i = 0 To rs.Fields.Count - 1
    lstFields.AddItem rs.Fields(i).Name & " = " & rs.Fields(i).Value
Next
```

The Fields collection also supports the *Append* method, which creates a new Field object and appends it to the collection. This method is useful when you want to manufacture a Recordset object in memory without necessarily connecting it to a data source (not immediately at least). You can use this method only with client-side Recordsets (*CursorLocation* = adUseClient) and only if the Recordset is closed and isn't currently associated with a Connection (*ActiveConnection* = Nothing). The *Append* method has the following syntax:

```
Append(Name, Type, [DefinedSize], [Attrib]) As Field
```

The arguments define the properties of the Field object being created. The following reusable routine creates a new stand-alone Recordset that has the same field structure of another Recordset:

```
Function CopyFields(rs As ADODB.Recordset) As ADODB.Recordset
    Dim newRS As New ADODB.Recordset, fld As ADODB.Field
    For Each fld In rs.Fields
        newRS.Fields.Append fld.Name, fld.Type, fld.DefinedSize, _
            fld.Attributes
    Next
    Set CopyFields = newRS
End Function
```

Here's another routine that creates a new stand-alone record that not only duplicates the field structure of an existing Recordset but also duplicates all the records that it contains (but without being a clone Recordset):

```
Function CopyRecordset(rs As ADODB.Recordset) As ADODB.Recordset
    Dim newRS As New ADODB.Recordset, fld As ADODB.Field
    Set newRS = CopyFields(rs)
    newRS.Open     ' You must open the Recordset before adding new records.
    rs.MoveFirst
    Do Until rs.EOF
        newRS.AddNew                      ' Add a new record.
        For Each fld In rs.Fields         ' Copy all fields' values.
```

(continued)

681

```
                    newRS(fld.Name) = fld.Value      ' Assumes no BLOB fields
            Next
            rs.MoveNext
        Loop
        Set CopyRecordset = newRS
    End Function
```

The Fields collection also supports the *Delete* method, which removes a field in a stand-alone record before opening it, and the *Refresh* method.

> **NOTE** Alas, it seems that you can't create hierarchical stand-alone Recordsets. In fact, if you try to create a Field whose *Type* property is adChapter, an error arises.

THE COMMAND OBJECT

The ADO Command object defines a command or a query that you can execute on a data source. Command objects are useful when you plan to execute the same command or query several times (on the same or on a different data source) and when you want to run stored procedures or parameterized queries. Recall from earlier in this chapter that you can execute SQL queries and commands using the *Execute* method of a Connection object or the *Open* method of a Recordset object. In a real application, you're more likely to use Command objects for these tasks. When you're working with SQL Server, for example, Command objects automatically reuse the temporary stored procedure that SQL Server creates the first time you execute it, and you can pass different arguments each time you execute the query.

You can create stand-alone Command objects that aren't associated with a Connection object; you can then establish the connection by assigning a valid connection object to the *ActiveConnection* property. By doing so, you can reuse the same command on multiple connections.

Properties

The Command object supports nine properties, but only two of them are really necessary for carrying out a query or a command.

Setting the query

The most important property of the Command object is *CommandText*, which sets or returns the SQL command or query, the name of a table, or the name of a stored procedure. If you use an SQL query, it should be in the dialect of the database engine you're connecting to. Depending on the string that you assign to this property and on the particular provider you're using, ADO might change the contents of this property. For this reason, after assigning a value to *CommandText*, you might be wise to read it back to check the actual value that will be used for the query. Here's an example of how you use this property:

```
Dim cmd As New ADODB.Command
cmd.CommandText = "SELECT * FROM Employees WHERE BirthDate > #1/1/1960"
```

If you're going to repeat the query or the command with different arguments, it's convenient to prepare a parameterized Command object, which you do by inserting ? (question mark) symbols in the *CommandText* property:

```
Dim cmd As New ADODB.Command
cmd.CommandText = "SELECT * FROM Employees WHERE BirthDate > ? " _
    & "AND HireDate > ?"
```

The *CommandText* property tells the Command object what to do, and the *ActiveConnection* property specifies on which data source the command should be carried out. This property can be assigned a connection string (that follows the syntax of the *ConnectionString* of the Connection object) or a Connection object that already points to a data source. When you set this property to Nothing, you disconnect the Command object and release all the resources allocated on the server. If you attempt to run the *Execute* method before assigning a connection string or a Connection object to this property, a run-time error occurs. An error also occurs if you assign a closed Connection object to this property. Some providers require you to set this property to Nothing before switching to another connection.

You can share the connection among multiple ADO Command objects only if you assign the same Connection object to their *ActiveConnection* properties. Simply assigning the same connection string creates distinct connections. Here's an example that leverages this capability:

```
' Edit this constant to match your directory structure.
Const DBPATH = "C:\Program Files\Microsoft Visual Studio\Vb98\NWind.mdb"
' Create the first Command object.
Dim cmd As New ADODB.Command, rs As New ADODB.Recordset
cmd.ActiveConnection = "Provider=Microsoft.Jet.OLEDB.3.51;" _
    & "Data Source= " & DBPATH
cmd.CommandText = "SELECT FirstName, LastName FROM Employees"
Set rs = cmd.Execute()
' Create a second Command object on the same database connection.
Dim cmd2 As New ADODB.Command, rs2 As New ADODB.Recordset
Set cmd2.ActiveConnection = cmd.ActiveConnection
cmd2.CommandText = "SELECT * FROM Customers"
Set rs2 = cmd2.Execute()
```

Setting the *ActiveConnection* property to Nothing can affect the Parameters collection. More precisely, if the provider has populated the Parameters collection automatically, the collection will be cleared when the *ActiveConnection* is set to Nothing. If the Parameters collection has been manually populated through code, setting the *ActiveConnection* to Nothing doesn't affect it.

Optimizing the execution

The *CommandType* property lets you optimize execution speed by indicating what the *CommandText* string contains. It can be one of the following enumerated constants:

Value	Description
1-adCmdText	The text of an SQL query.
2-adCmdTable	A database table.
4-adCmdStoredProc	A stored procedure.
8-adCmdUnknown	The provider will determine the correct type (the default).
512-adCmdTableDirect	A database table opened directly.

If you don't specify a value for this property, or if you use adCmdUnknown, you force ADO to figure out by itself what the *CommandText* string is, an operation that usually adds considerable overhead. The adCmdStoredProc option can also improve performance because it prevents ADO from creating a temporary stored procedure before executing the query. If the value you assign to the *CommandType* property doesn't match the type of the *CommandText* string, a run-time error occurs.

The *Prepared* property lets you leverage the real power of the Command object. When this property is True, the provider creates a compiled (prepared) version of the query passed in the *CommandText* property and then uses it to run the query each time this command is reexecuted. Creating a compiled procedure takes some time, so you should set this property to True only if you plan to execute the query two or more times. If the data source doesn't support prepared statements, what happens depends on the provider: It can raise an error, or it can just ignore the assignment.

The *CommandTimeout* property sets or returns the number of seconds ADO will wait when a command executes before raising an error. The default value is 30 seconds. If you set this property to 0, ADO will wait forever. This value isn't inherited from the *CommandTimeout* property of the Connection object to which the Command object is connected. In addition, not all providers support this property.

State is a read-only property that can be queried to understand what the Command is currently doing. It can return the value 0-adStateClosed (the Command object is inactive) or 4-adStateExecuting (the Command object is executing a command).

Methods

The most important method of the Command object is the *Execute* method, which runs the query or the command stored in the *CommandText* property. This method is similar to the Connection object's *Execute* method, but the syntax is slightly different because the text of the query can't be passed as an argument:

```
Execute([RecordsAffected], [Parameters], [Options]) As Recordset
```

If the *CommandText* property contains a row-returning query, the *Execute* method returns an open Recordset (which doesn't necessarily contain any row, however). Conversely, if the *CommandText* property specifies an action query, this method returns a closed Recordset. In the latter case, you can effectively use *Execute* as a procedure instead of as a function and ignore its return value.

If you pass a Long variable as the *RecordsAffected* argument, the *Execute* method returns in the variable the number of records that were affected by the action query command. This argument is optional, so you aren't obliged to pass anything, and it doesn't return any meaningful value with row-returning queries. If you're running a parameterized command or query, *Parameters* is a Variant that contains the value of a parameter or an array of all the expected parameters:

```
' Edit this constant to match your directory structure.
Const DBPATH = "C:\Program Files\Microsoft Visual Studio\Vb98\NWind.mdb"
Dim cmd As New ADODB.Command, rs As New ADODB.Recordset
cmd.ActiveConnection = "Provider=Microsoft.Jet.OLEDB.3.51;" _
    & "Data Source= " & DBPATH
cmd.CommandText = "SELECT * FROM Employees WHERE BirthDate > ? " _
    & "AND HireDate > ?"
cmd.CommandType = adCmdText
' You can pass multiple parameters without using a temporary array.
Set rs = cmd.Execute(, Array(#1/1/1960#, #1/1/1994#))
```

The parameters you pass in this way are valid only for the current execution of the command, and they don't affect the Parameters collection. If you omit one or more arguments in the *Execute* method, ADO uses the corresponding values in the Parameters collection. Here's an example that passes only the second argument and implicitly uses the first item in the Parameters collection:

```
Set rs = cmd.Execute(, Array(, #1/1/1994#))
```

> **CAUTION**   Although you can pass any number of parameters using this method, you can't retrieve output parameters in this way. If you want to execute a stored procedure with output parameters, you can retrieve their values only by using the Parameters collection.

The *Option* argument can contain the same value that you assign to the *CommandType* property plus one or more of the following constants:

Value	*Description*
16-adAsyncExecute	Runs the command asynchronously in a separate thread
32-adAsyncFetch	Fetches the results asynchronously for Recordsets based on client-side cursors

(continued)

continued

Value	Description
64-adAsyncFetchNonBlocking	Similar to adAsyncFetch, but the calling program is never blocked
128-adExecuteNoRecords	Specifies that a command of type adCmdText or adCmdStoredProc is an action query and doesn't return a Recordset

There are subtle differences among the adAsyncExecute, adAsyncFetch, and adAsyncFetchNonBlocking options. All of them execute the command asynchronously and set AffectedRecords to –1 because when the method returns, the command hasn't completed yet and ADO doesn't know how many records will be affected. If you specify adAsyncExecute, the command is executed asynchronously, and when the provider completes it, ADO fires an *ExecutionComplete* event in your program. If you specify adAsyncFetch on a Recordset based on a client-side cursor, when the execution of the command completes, ADO starts fetching the result rows asynchronously: When the code asks for a row that hasn't been retrieved yet, the application is blocked until the data is available (and when this occurs, a *FetchComplete* event fires). The adAsyncFetchNonBlocking option is similar to adAsyncFetch but with an important difference: When the code asks for a row that hasn't been retrieved yet, the application isn't blocked and the Recordset's *EOF* property is set to True. The code can therefore try again later or wait for the *FetchComplete* event to determine when data is finally available.

You can cancel the execution of an asynchronous operation by using the Command object's *Cancel* method. This method raises an error if no asynchronous option was specified for the most recent *Execute* method.

The third method the Command object supports is *CreateParameter*. With this method, you can create the Parameters collection entirely in code, without a round-trip to the server. The syntax of this method is as follows:

```
CreateParameter([Name], [Type], [Direction], [Size], [Value]) As Parameter
```

Each argument you pass to this method is assigned to a property of the Parameter object being created. We'll go over these properties in more detail in the next section.

THE PARAMETER OBJECT

A Parameter object represents a parameter in the parameterized command or stored procedure on which a Command object is based. In theory, a provider might not support parameterized commands, but in practice, all major providers do. Parameter objects can represent input values for a command or a query or output values or return values from a stored procedure. All the Parameter objects related to a Command object are contained in the Command's Parameters collection.

ADO is really smart at dealing with the Parameters collection. It automatically builds the collection when you reference the *Parameters* property of a Command object. But ADO also gives you the capability to create the collection yourself through code, which is something that isn't possible in DAO or RDO. Usually you can get better performance if you create the Parameters collection yourself because you save ADO a round-trip to the server just to determine the names and the types of all the parameters. On the other hand, if you want ADO to retrieve all the parameters' names and attributes, you only have to perform the *Refresh* method of the Parameters collection of a Command object, as here:

```
cmd.Parameters.Refresh
```

Calling the *Refresh* method is optional, however, because if you access the Parameters collection without having created its elements yourself, ADO will refresh the collection automatically.

Properties

The Parameter object exposes nine properties. Most of them are similar to properties with the same names as those exposed by the Field object. Because of the similarities, I won't describe these properties in depth here. For example, each Parameter object has a *Name*, *Type*, *Precision*, and *NumericScale* property, exactly as Field objects have. Table 13-5 on page 675 lists all the possible values for the *Type* property. (Notice that Parameter objects support a few types that Field objects don't support.)

The Parameter object also supports the *Value* property. This property is also the default for this object, so you can omit it if you want to:

```
cmd.Parameters("StartHireDate") = #1/1/1994#
```

The *Direction* property specifies whether the Parameter object represents an input parameter, an output parameter, or the return value from a stored procedure. It can be one of the following enumerated constants:

Value	*Description*
0-adParamUnknown	Unknown direction
1-adParamInput	An input parameter (the default)
2-adParamOutput	An output parameter
3-adParamInputOutput	An input/output parameter
4-adParamReturnValue	A return value from a stored procedure

This property is read/write, which is useful when you're working with a provider that can't determine the direction of the parameters in a stored procedure.

The *Attributes* property specifies a few characteristics of the Parameter object. This is a bit-field value that can be the sum of the following values:

Value	Description
16-adParamSigned	The parameter accepts signed values.
64-adParamNullable	The parameter accepts Null values.
128-adParamLong	The parameter accepts long binary data.

The *Size* property sets and returns the maximum size of the value of a Parameter object. If you're creating a Parameter object of a variable-length data type (for example, a string type), you must set this property before appending the parameter to the Parameters collection; if you don't, an error occurs. If you've already appended the Parameter object to the Parameters collection and you later change its type to a variable-length data type, you must set the *Size* property before invoking the *Execute* method.

The *Size* property is also useful if you let the provider automatically populate the Parameters collection. When the collection includes one or more variable-length items, ADO can allocate memory for those parameters based on their maximum potential dimension, which might cause an error later. You can prevent such errors by explicitly setting the *Size* property to the correct value before executing the command.

Methods

The only method the Parameter object supports is *AppendChunk*. This method works exactly as it does in the Field object, so I won't repeat its description here. You can test the adParamLong bit of the Parameter object's *Attributes* property to test whether the parameter supports this method.

The Parameters Collection

Each Command object exposes a *Parameters* property that returns a reference to a Parameters collection. As I mentioned earlier in the chapter, you can let ADO automatically populate this collection or you can save ADO some work by creating Parameter objects and adding them manually to the collection. You add objects manually with the *CreateParameter* method of the Command object in conjunction with the *Append* method of the Parameters collection, as this code demonstrates:

```
' Edit this constant to match your directory structure.
Const DBPATH = "C:\Program Files\Microsoft Visual Studio\Vb98\NWind.mdb"
Dim cmd As New ADODB.Command, rs As New ADODB.Recordset
cmd.CommandText = "Select * From Employees Where BirthDate > ? " _
```

```
      & "AND HireDate > ?"
cmd.ActiveConnection = "Provider=Microsoft.Jet.OLEDB.3.51;" _
      & "Data Source= " & DBPATH
' You can use a temporary Parameter variable.
Dim param As ADODB.Parameter
Set param = cmd.CreateParameter("BirthDate", adDate, , , #1/1/1960#)
cmd.Parameters.Append param
' Or you can do everything in one operation.
cmd.Parameters.Append cmd.CreateParameter("HireDate", adDate, , , _
      #1/1/1993#)
Set rs = cmd.Execute(, , adCmdText)
```

Parameterized queries and commands are especially useful when you're going to perform the operation more than once. In all subsequent operations, you need to modify only the values of the parameters:

```
' You can reference a parameter by its index in the collection.
cmd.Parameters(0) = #1/1/1920#
' But you deliver more readable code if you reference it by its name.
cmd.Parameters("HireDate") = #1/1/1920#
Set rs = cmd.Execute()
```

You can use the *Delete* method of the Parameters collection to remove items from it, and you can use its *Count* property to determine how many elements it contains. When the Command object refers to a stored procedure that has a return value, *Parameters(0)* always refers to the return value.

THE PROPERTY OBJECT

The Connection, Recordset, Command, and Field objects expose Properties collections, which contain all the dynamic properties that the ADO provider has added to the built-in properties that are referenced using the standard dot syntax. You can't add dynamic properties yourself; thus, the Properties collection exposes only the *Count* and *Item* properties and the *Refresh* method.

Dynamic properties are important in advanced ADO programming because they often provide supplemental information about an ADO object. Sometimes you can even modify the behavior of a provider by assigning different values to such dynamic properties. Each provider can expose a different set of dynamic properties, even though the OLE DB specifications list a few properties that should have the same meaning across different providers. Here's a routine that fills a ListBox control with the values of all the dynamic properties associated with the object passed as an argument:

```
Sub ListCustomProperties(obj As Object, lst As ListBox)
    Dim i As Integer, tmp As String
    On Error Resume Next
```

(continued)

```
        lst.Clear
        For i = 0 To obj.Properties.Count - 1
            lst.AddItem obj.Properties(i).Name & " = " & obj.Properties(i)
        Next
End Sub
```

The Properties collection contains one or more Property objects, which expose four properties: *Name*, *Value*, *Type*, and *Attributes*. The *Type* property can be an enumerated value chosen from those listed in Table 13-5 on page 675. The *Attributes* property is a bit-field value given by the sum of one or more of the following constants:

Value	*Description*
1-adPropRequired	The user must specify a value for this property before the data source is initialized.
2-adPropOptional	The user doesn't need to specify a value for this property before the data source is initialized.
512-adPropRead	The user can read the property.
1024-adPropWrite	The user can assign a value to the property.

If the *Attributes* property returns the value 0-adPropNotSupported, it means that the provider doesn't support this property.

ADO 2.1 DDL AND SECURITY EXTENSIONS

The beauty of ADO is that it is an extensible architecture. It's not the monolithic (and overly complex) object model that DAO is. Microsoft can easily add new features to ADO without breaking existing applications and without forcing developers to learn a new object model at each new release. In fact, although ADO 2.1 contains several improvements to the ADO 2.0 model, all the new features are provided in the form of distinct object trees that are linked dynamically—that is, at run time—to the object in the standard ADO hierarchy.

In the remainder of this chapter, I'll illustrate the objects in the Microsoft Extension 2.1 for DDL and Security (ADOX) library, which extends the standard ADODB library with data definition language capabilities, giving you, for example, the ability to enumerate the tables, views, and stored procedures in a database as well as the ability to create new ones. This library also contains security objects that permit you to determine and modify the permissions granted to an individual or to groups of users. ADO 2.1 contains other extensions, such as the ADOMD library for online analytical processing (OLAP) operations and the support for Microsoft Jet replications, but I won't cover those topics in this book.

Figure 13-5 depicts the ADOX hierarchy. This object tree includes more items than ADODB, but the relationships among the nodes are still fairly intuitive. Whereas the standard ADO library deals mostly with the data in databases, the ADOX library is interested only in the structure of the tables, the views, and the procedures stored in the database as well as in the users and the groups of users that can access these items. Working with the ADOX library is simple because you don't have to account for recordsets, cursors, timeout errors, locks, transactions, and all the usual issues you have to resolve when writing a standard database application based on ADO. All the objects in the hierarchy also support the Properties collection, which includes all the dynamic properties.

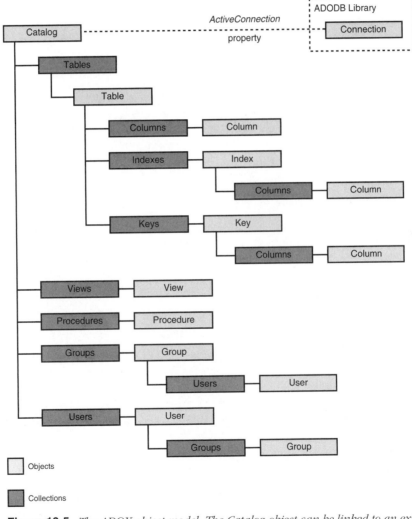

Figure 13-5. *The ADOX object model. The Catalog object can be linked to an existing ADODB.Connection object through the Catalog's* ActiveConnection *property.*

> **CAUTION**   Not all providers support all the DDL capabilities mentioned in this section. For example, a provider might support the enumeration of database objects but not the creation of new ones. For this reason, it is essential for you to make sure that all the code that accesses these objects is protected against unanticipated errors.

The Catalog Object

The Catalog object is the entry point of the ADOX hierarchy. It represents the database and includes all the tables, stored procedures, views, users, and groups of users. The Catalog object allows you to perform two distinct operations: enumerate the objects in an existing database or create a new database from scratch.

When you just want to explore an existing database, you have to create a stand-alone ADODB.Connection object, open it, and then assign it to the *ActiveConnection* property of the Catalog object. By doing so, you link the ADODB and the ADOX hierarchies together:

```
' Edit this constant to match your directory structure.
Const DBPATH = "C:\Program Files\Microsoft Visual Studio\Vb98\Biblio.mdb"
Dim cn As New ADODB.Connection, cat As New ADOX.Catalog
' Open the connection.
cn.Open "Provider=Microsoft.Jet.OLEDB.4.0;Data Source=" & DBPATH
' Link the catalog to the connection.
Set cat.ActiveConnection = cn
```

After you've linked the Catalog object to an open Connection object, you can enumerate the objects in the database by using the Tables, Procedures, Views, Groups, and Users collections:

```
' Fill a list box with the names of the stored procedures in the database.
Dim proc As ADOX.Procedure
For Each proc In cat.Procedures
    List1.AddItem proc.Name
Next
```

On the companion CD, you'll find a complete project that lists all the objects in a Catalog and the values of all their properties, as shown in Figure 13-6.

The Catalog object exposes two methods, *GetObjectOwner* and *SetObjectOwner*, which let you read and modify the owner of a database object, as in the following example:

```
On Error Resume Next     ' Not all providers support this capability.
owner = cat.GetObjectOwner("Authors", adPermObjTable)
```

When you create a new (empty) database, you don't need a stand-alone Connection object. Instead, you can carry out the task by using the Catalog object's *Create* method. This method takes as its only argument the connection string that defines both the provider and the database name:

```
' The next line fails if the database already exists.
cat.Create "Provider=Microsoft.Jet.OLEDB.4.0;User ID=Admin;" _
    & "Data Source=C:\Microsoft Visual Studio\Vb98\BiblioCopy.mdb"
```

The *Create* method isn't supported by the OLE DB providers for SQL Server, Oracle, and ODBC drivers.

Regardless of whether you've created a new database or opened an existing one, you can add or remove objects using the Catalogs collections. For example, here's the code that creates a new table with two fields and adds it to the database:

```
Dim tbl As New ADOX.Table
tbl.Name = "Customers"                      ' Create a table.
tbl.Columns.Append "CustID", adInteger      ' Add two fields.
tbl.Columns.Append "Name", adWVarChar, 50
cat.Tables.Append tbl                       ' Append the table to
                                            ' the collection.
```

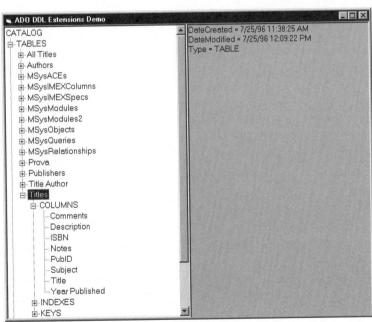

Figure 13-6. *This ADOX application shows all the objects in a Catalog and the relationships among them.*

The Table Object

The Table object is the most complex object in the ADOX hierarchy. It exposes four simple properties—*Name*, *Type*, *DateCreated*, and *DateModified*—and the Columns, Indexes, Keys, and Properties collections. These names are fairly self-explanatory, so I won't describe them in depth. The Table object doesn't expose any methods.

All the tables in the database are contained in the Tables collection. This collection exposes the usual *Item* and *Count* properties and the *Append*, *Delete*, and

Refresh methods. For example, you can enumerate all the tables in the database and all the columns in each table by using the following code:

```
Dim tbl As ADOX.Table, col As ADOX.Column
For Each tbl in cat.Tables
    Print "TABLE " & tbl.Name
    Print "Created on " & tbl.DateCreated
    Print "Modified on " & tbl.DateModified
    Print "Field List ------"
    For Each col In tbl.Columns
        Print "    " & col.Name
    Next
Next
```

You can't append or delete tables using the OLE DB providers for Oracle and ODBC drivers.

The Column Object

The Column object and the corresponding Columns collection appear in several places in the ADOX hierarchy, namely, as a dependent object of the Table, Index, and Key objects. The Column object exposes several properties, even though not all of them make sense in all cases. When the Column object is a dependent of a Table object, you can read the *Name*, *Type*, *DefinedSize*, *NumericScale*, and *Precision* properties, which have the same meaning as the properties with the same names exposed by the ADODB.Field object. The Column object also supports the *Attributes* bit-field property, which can be 1-adColFixed or 2-adColNullable.

If the Column object is a dependent of a Key object, you can also set or retrieve the *RelatedColumn* property, which specifies the name of the related field in the related table. If the Column object is a dependent of an Index object, you can set the *SortOrder* property with the values 1-adSortAscending or 2-adSortDescending.

You can add a Column object to a table, an index, or a key by using the *Append* method of the respective Columns collections. This method takes as arguments the name of the column, its type, and (optionally) the value of the *DefinedSize* property of the Column object to be created:

```
' Add two fields to the Customers table.
Dim tbl As ADOX.Table
Set tbl = cat.Tables("Customers")
tbl.Columns.Append "CustID", adInteger
tbl.Columns.Append "Name", adVarChar, 255
```

The Index Object

You can enumerate the indexes of a table through its Indexes collection. The Index object exposes a few properties whose names are self-explanatory: *Name*, *Clustered* (True if the index is clustered), *Unique* (True if the index is unique), and *PrimaryKey*

(True if the index is the primary key for the table). The only property that requires a more detailed description is *IndexNulls*, which specifies whether records with Null values appear in the index. This property can take one of the following values:

Value	Description
0-adIndexNullsAllow	Null values are accepted.
1-adIndexNullsDisallow	The index raises an error if a key column has a Null value.
2-adIndexNullsIgnore	Columns with Null values are ignored and are not added to the index.
4-adIndexNullsIgnoreAny	In a multicolumn index, records are not indexed if any of the index columns has a Null value.

To add an index to a table, you create a stand-alone Index object, set its properties as required, add one or more items to its Columns collection, and finally add the Index to the Indexes collection of a Table object:

```
Dim tbl As ADOX.Table, ndx As New ADOX.Index
' Create a new index.
ndx.Name = "YearBorn_Author"
ndx.Unique = True
' Append two columns to it.
ndx.Columns.Append "Year Born"
ndx.Columns("Year Born").SortOrder = adSortDescending
ndx.Columns.Append "Author"
' Add the index to the Authors table.
Set tbl = cat.Tables("Authors")
tbl.Indexes.Append ndx
```

You can modify all the properties of an Index object only before the Index is appended to the Indexes collection of a Table object. When you add a field to the Columns collection of an Index object, an error occurs if the column doesn't already exist in the Table object or if the Table object hasn't already been added to the Tables collections of the Catalog object.

The Key Object

The Key object represents a key column in a table. You can enumerate the Keys collection of a Table object to determine its key columns, or you can use the collection's *Append* method to add new keys. When a key hasn't yet been appended to the collection, you can set its *Name* and *Type* properties. The *Type* property defines the type of the key and can be one of the following values: 1-adKeyPrimary (the primary key), 2-adKeyForeign (a foreign key), or 3-adKeyUnique (a unique key).

If the key is a foreign key, three other properties come into play. The *RelatedTable* property contains the name of the related table, and the *UpdateRule* and *DeleteRule* properties determine what happens to the foreign key if the record in the related table is updated or deleted, respectively. The *UpdateRule* and *DeleteRule* properties can contain one of the following values:

Value	Description
0-adRINone	No action is taken.
1-adRICascade	Changes are cascaded.
2-adRISetNull	The key is assigned a Null value.
3-adRISetDefault	The key is assigned its default value.

Each Key object exposes a Columns collection, which contains all the columns that make up the key. The following code shows how you can add a new key to a table:

```
' Add a foreign key to the Orders table, and make the key point
' to the EmployeeID field of the Employees table.
Dim tbl As ADOX.Table, key As New ADOX.Key
Set tbl = cat.Tables("Orders")
' Create the key, and set its attributes.
key.Name = "Employee"
key.Type = adKeyForeign
key.RelatedTable = "Employees"
key.UpdateRule = adRICascade
' Add a column to the key, and set its RelatedColumn attribute.
key.Columns.Append tbl.Columns("EmployeeId")
key.Columns("EmployeeId").RelatedColumn = "EmployeeId"
' Append the key to the table's Keys collection.
tbl.Keys.Append key
```

The View and Procedure Objects

The View object and the Procedure object are similar. They represent a view and a stored procedure in the database, respectively. They also expose the same set of four properties: *Name*, *DateCreated*, *DateModified*, and *Command*. The *Command* property provides the maximum flexibility to these objects, without making the ADOX hierarchy more complex than strictly required. In fact, the *Command* property returns a reference to an ADODB.Command object that can execute the view or the stored procedure, so you can determine the underlying SQL command as well as the name and the type of any parameters using this Command object's properties. The following code example demonstrates how you can extract this information:

```
Dim cmd As ADODB.Command
Set cmd = cat.Views("All Titles").Command
MsgBox cmd.CommandText
```

You also use the auxiliary Command object when you want to create a new view or a stored procedure, as shown in the following code snippet:

```
' Edit this constant to match your directory structure.
Const DBPATH = "C:\Program Files\Microsoft Visual Studio\Vb98\Biblio.mdb"
Dim cn As New ADODB.Connection, cmd As New ADODB.Command
' Note the version number of the Jet OLE DB Provider.
cn.Open "Provider=Microsoft.Jet.OLEDB.4.0;Data Source=" & DBPATH
Set cmd.ActiveConnection = cn
cmd.CommandText = "Select * From Authors Where [Year Born] = [Year]"
cmd.Parameters.Append cmd.CreateParameter("Year", adInteger, adParamInput)
' Open the Catalog, and create the new procedure.
Set cat.ActiveConnection = cn
cat.Procedures.Append "AuthorsByYear", cmd
```

Views aren't supported by the OLE DB Provider for SQL Server. The providers for ODBC and Oracle support them, but you can only enumerate them—you can't add or delete individual View objects. None of these providers can create or delete Procedure objects.

The Group and User Objects

The Catalog object exposes the Groups and Users collections, which include the groups of users and the individual users that can access some or all of the objects in the database. These two objects are tightly connected to each other in that each User object exposes a Groups collection (all the groups the user belongs to), and each Group object exposes a Users collection (all the users that belong to that group).

You can retrieve the permissions assigned to a User object or a Group object using their *GetPermissions* method. Because this method returns a bit-field value, you must use the AND Boolean operator to understand which operations are allowed:

```
' Displays which permissions on the Customers table
' have been granted to the users in the Guests group.
Dim grp As ADOX.Group, permissions As Long
Set grp = cat.Groups("Guests")
permissions = grp.GetPermissions("Customers", adPermObjTable)
If permissions And adRightExecute Then Print "Execute"
If permissions And adRightRead Then Print "Read"
If permissions And adRightUpdate Then Print "Update"
If permissions And adRightInsert Then Print "Insert"
If permissions And adRightDelete Then Print "Delete"
If permissions And adRightReference Then Print "Reference"
If permissions And adRightCreate Then Print "Create"
If permissions And adRightWriteDesign Then Print "Design"
If permissions And adRightWithGrant Then Print "Grant Permissions"
```

The *SetPermission* method lets you set, grant, deny, or revoke permissions on a given database object to a User or a Group:

```
' Revoke the Guests group the permission to read the Customers table.
cat.Users("Guests").SetPermissions "Customers", adPermObjTable, _
    adAccessRevoke, adRightRead
' Give the Managers group full permissions on the Employees table.
cat.Users("Managers").SetPermissions "Employees", adPermObjTable, _
    adAccessSet, adRightFull
```

The Groups and the Users collections aren't supported by the OLE DB Provider for SQL Server, Oracle, and ODBC drivers.

In this chapter, I described all the objects in the ADO hierarchy and their many properties, methods, and events. Although I've shown you how to use ADO to carry out some complex tasks, I haven't yet illustrated in practice how you can build complete database applications that exploit ADO's most advanced features. We'll focus on how to use these objects in Chapter 14.

Chapter 14

ADO at Work

ADO is so rich, powerful, and flexible that I decided to devote two chapters to it. Chapter 13 contains an in-depth description of its objects and their properties, methods, and events. In this chapter, I show you how to put in practice those concepts and also how to work around a few ADO quirks that could make your programming efforts harder than strictly necessary.

A preliminary note: ADO is an evolving technology, and the good news is that Microsoft is committed to continuously improving it. It's therefore possible that a few problems I encountered will have been resolved by the time you read these pages. Moreover, ADO behavior is heavily affected by the underlying OLE DB provider, so many problems can depend on which database you're connecting to and can also disappear if you install a more recent version of the provider. When possible, I tried the code with several providers, but I surely couldn't test all the possible combinations. Take this into account when you test the code I show you in this chapter.

SETTING UP A CONNECTION

The great flexibility of the ADO programming model is apparent from the very first action you perform in every database-oriented application—that is, setting up a connection to your database. In fact, while the most obvious choice is to create a stand-alone Connection object, it surely isn't the only available one. For example, you can also create a stand-alone Recordset object and assign a connection string to its *Open* method. Or you can create a stand-alone Command object and assign a connection string to its *ActiveConnection* property. You don't even need to create an ADO object to establish the connection, if you use the ADO Data control or the DataEnvironment designer.

Building the Connection String

Regardless of the object you use to connect to an ADO data source, you must build a connection string. This will be the string that you assign to the *ConnectionString* property of a Connection object or to the *ActiveConnection* property of a Recordset or Command object, or it will be the string that you pass to the *Execute* method of a Connection object or to the *Open* method of a Recordset object. So you need to understand how to correctly build this string and how to exploit all the options you have.

The connection string can contain one or more elements in the form *argument=value*. The list of valid arguments depends on the provider to which you're connecting, but two arguments are always supported: the *Provider* and the *File Name*. For a list of supported arguments, see Table 13-1 in Chapter 13.

Determining which arguments are valid with which provider is the most difficult job in building a connection string. When I began to explore this unknown territory, I found that the best approach was to drop an ADO Data control on a form, set a connection using its property pages, and then see the final value of the *ConnectionString* property. I also discovered that I could modify the values in the All property page, and my settings were reflected in the *ConnectionString* property.

The simplest way to connect to any database is based on Microsoft Data Link files (I explained how to create these files in "The Binding Mechanism" section in Chapter 8). The UDL file contains all the information needed by ADO to connect to the database, including the name of the provider, and you only need to use the *File Name* argument. In fact, if you use both the *Provider* and *File Name* arguments, you get an error. The following example assumes that you have prepared a UDL file that points to the Biblio.mdb database:

```
Dim cn As New ADODB.Connection
cn.Open "File Name=C:\Program Files\Common Files\System\ole db" _
    & "\Data Links\Biblio.udl"
```

You can also use the *File Name* argument to point to a file-based DSN, in which case you're implicitly using the default MSDASQL provider for ODBC sources:

```
cn.Open "File Name=C:\Program Files\Common Files\ODBC\Data Sources\" _
    & "Pubs.dsn"
```

If you're using a user or system ODBC Data Source Name, you simply have to specify its name with a *Data Source* or *DSN* argument. The following code assumes that you've created a system or user DSN that points to the Pubs database on Microsoft SQL Server and shows how you can open a Recordset without first creating an explicit Connection object:

```
Dim rs As New ADODB.Recordset
rs.Open "Authors", "Provider=MSDASQL.1;User ID=sa;Data Source=Pubs"
' You can omit the name of the provider because it's the default.
rs.Open "Authors", "DSN=Pubs"
```

If you aren't using DSNs or UDL files, you must build the connection string yourself. This is the ADO equivalent of a DSN-less connection: On one hand, it simplifies the installation of the application (because you don't have to create the DSN or UDL file on your customer's machine); on the other, it makes the programmer's job a little harder. When connecting to a Microsoft Jet database, you need only the name of the provider and the path of the MDB database:

```
cn.Open "Provider=Microsoft.Jet.OLEDB.3.51;" _
    & "Data Source=E:\Microsoft Visual Studio\VB98\Biblio.mdb
```

The job is a bit more complex when you're connecting to an SQL Server database either through the dedicated OLE DB provider or through the default MSDASQL provider. This is the connection string to connect to the Pubs database on the SQL Server located on the MyServer workstation, using Windows NT integrated security:

```
cn.Open "Provider=SQLOLEDB.1;Integrated Security=SSPI;" _
    & " Data Source=MyServer;Initial Catalog=Pubs;"
```

In this case, *Data Source* is the name of the server, and you specify that you want to use integrated security by setting the *Integrated Security* argument to the *SSPI* value. The following statement opens a connection to the same SQL Server database, this time using an explicit user ID and password:

```
cn.Open "Provider=SQLOLEDB.1;Data Source=MyServer;User ID=sa;" _
    & "Password=mypwd;Initial Catalog=Pubs"
```

Connection Timeout is another handy connection string argument. You usually don't need it when you're opening a connection using a Connection object because this object exposes the *ConnectionTimeout* property that lets you set a timeout when opening the connection. You do need it, however, when you create an implicit Connection object in the *Open* method of a Recordset or the *Execute* method of a Command:

```
rs.Open "Authors", "Provider=SQLOLEDB.1;Data Source=MyServer;User ID=sa;" _
    & "Connection Timeout=10;Initial Catalog=Pubs"
```

When you're working with an SQL Server source, you can use many additional arguments to fine-tune your connection. For example, the *PacketSize* argument sets the size of data block sent through the network. (The default is 4096 bytes.) The *Use Procedure for Prepare* argument specifies whether ADO should create stored procedure by default. The possible values are 0=No, 1-Yes And Drop Them When You Disconnect (the default), or 2=Yes And Drop Them When You Disconnect And As

Appropriate While You're Connected. The *Locale Identifier* argument sets the international locale. The *Network Address* and *Network Library* arguments should be specified when you're accessing SQL Server with a method other than named pipes; the *Workstation ID* argument identifies the machine from which you're connecting.

If you're connecting through the default MSDASQL provider, you must specify several additional arguments, the most important of which is the ODBC driver that you want to use:

```
cn.ConnectionString = "Provider=MSDASQL.1;User ID=sa;" _
    & "Extended Properties=""DRIVER=SQL Server;SERVER=ServerNT;" _
    & "MODE=Read;WSID=P2;DATABASE=pubs"""
```

As you see, when working with the OLE DB Provider for ODBC you can insert the same ODBC argument list you used with RDO by enclosing it between double quotes and assigning it to the *Extended Properties* argument. This string is passed to the provider without ADO trying to interpret it. When you're using this argument in a Visual Basic statement, as in the previous statement, you must use two consecutive double quotes characters. As I mentioned previously, however, you can also pass arguments using the old ODBC syntax and ADO interprets them correctly anyway:

```
' You can omit the Provider argument because you're using MSDASQL.
cn.ConnectionString = "DRIVER={SQL Server};SERVER=MyServer;" _
    & "UID=sa;DATABASE=pubs"
```

You can pass a user's name and password using either the ADO syntax (*User Id* and *Password* arguments) or the ODBC syntax (*UID* and *PWD* arguments). If you pass both, the ADO syntax wins.

When working with the Microsoft Jet OLE DB Provider, you can pass additional login information, either in the connection string or as dynamic properties of the Connection object. Jet *OLEDB:System Database* is the path and name of the file with the information on the workgroup, *Jet OLEDB:Registry Path* is the Registry key that holds values for the Jet engine, and *Jet OLEDB:Database Password* is the database password:

```
cn.Properties("Jet OLEDB:Database Password") = "mypwd"
```

Opening the Connection

After you have built a correct connection string, the operations you must perform to actually open the connection depend on the object you want to use.

Explicit Connection objects

Most often you build a connection using a stand-alone Connection object, which you can reuse for all the queries and commands on that data source during the life of your application. You should assign reasonable values to the Connection object's *Mode* and *ConnectionTimeout* properties and also to its *Provider* property (unless the connection string contains the *Provider* or *File Name* argument):

```
' Prepare to open a read-only connection.
Dim cn As New ADODB.Connection
cn.ConnectionTimeout = 30     ' Default for this property is 15 seconds.
cn.Mode = adModeRead          ' Default for this property is adModeUnknown.
```

At this point, you can choose from several ways to open the connection. You can assign the connection string to the *ConnectionString* property and then invoke the *Open* method:

```
cn.ConnectionString = "Provider=SQLOLEDB.1;Data Source=MyServer;" _
    & "Initial Catalog=Pubs"
' The second and third arguments are the user name and the password.
cn.Open , "sa", "mypwd"
```

Alternatively, you can pass the connection string as the first argument to the *Open* method. In the following example, the user name and the password are embedded in the connection string, so you shouldn't specify them as separate arguments. (If you do so, the results are unpredictable.)

```
cn.Open "Provider=SQLOLEDB.1;Data Source=MyServer;User ID=sa;" _
    & "Password=mypwd;Initial Catalog=Pubs"
```

You should know one more thing about the *ConnectionString* property: If you assign a value to it and then open the connection, reading its value back will probably return a different string, one that often contains many additional values put there by the provider. This is perfectly normal. When you eventually close the Connection object, the *ConnectionString* property will be restored to the value that you originally assigned to it.

Implicit Connection objects

From time to time, you might prefer not to create a stand-alone Connection object and instead directly use a Recordset or Command object. This is mostly a matter of programming style, however, because even if you don't explicitly create a Connection object, ADO does it for you. So you aren't actually saving any resources, either on the server or the client workstation. The only savings you get is in terms of lines of code. For example, you need only two statements to execute an SQL query on any database:

```
Dim rs As New ADODB.Recordset
rs.Open "Authors", "Provider=SQLOLEDB.1;Data Source=MyServer;User ID=sa;" _
    & "Password=mypwd;Initial Catalog=Pubs"
```

You can use a similar technique to open an implicit connection with a Command object, but in this case you need to write more code because you must set the *ActiveConnection* and *CommandText* properties before opening the connection and carrying out command with the *Execute* method, as you can see in the code at the top of the next page.

```
Dim cmd As New ADODB.Command
cmd.ActiveConnection = "Provider=SQLOLEDB.1;Data Source=MyServer;" _
    & "user ID=sa;Password=mypwd;Initial Catalog=Pubs"
cmd.CommandText = "DELETE FROM Authors WHERE State = 'WA'"
cmd.Execute
```

When you open a connection with a Recordset or Command object in one of the ways described previously, you can access the implicit Connection object that ADO creates for you by querying the Recordset's or Command's *ActiveConnection* property, as in the following code snippet:

```
' Display the errors in the connection created by the previous example.
Dim er As ADODB.Error
For Each er In cmd.ActiveConnection.Errors
    Debug.Print er.Number, er.Description
Next
```

When you open an implicit Connection object using a Recordset or Command object, you inherit all the default values for the Connection object's properties. This is often too limiting and is a good reason to prefer explicit Connection objects. By default, ADO uses a *ConnectionTimout* equal to 15 seconds and creates server-side, forward-only, and read-only cursors with *CacheSize*=1 (also called noncursors).

The Properties collection

I haven't yet covered one important aspect of the Connection object: What happens if the information in the connection string isn't sufficient to set up the connection? If you're working with the standard OLE DB provider for an ODBC source, this behavior can be controlled by the dynamic *Prompt* property, which appears in the Connection's Properties collection. This property can be set to the following values: 1-adPromptAlways (always displays the login dialog box), 2-adPromptComplete (displays the login dialog box only if some required values are missing in the connection string), 3-adPromptCompleteRequired (similar to adPromptComplete, but the user can't enter any optional value), and 4-adPromptNever (never displays the login dialog box). The default value for this property is adPromptNever: If the connection string doesn't include enough information to carry out the operation, no login dialog box is displayed and the application receives an error. Use the following code to change this default behavior:

```
' Display the login dialog box if necessary.
Dim cn As New ADODB.Connection
cn.Properties("Prompt") = adPromptComplete
cn.Open "Provider=MSDASQL.1;Data Source=Pubs"
```

The *Prompt* dynamic property works in this way with the MSDASQL provider only.

The Properties collection contains many other interesting bits of information. For example, your application can determine the name and the version of the database it's working with by using the *DBMS Name* and *DBMS Version* dynamic properties and the name of the server by using the *Data Source Name* property. Another group of properties returns information about the provider: *Provider Name* returns the name of the DLL, *Provider Friendly Name* is the string that you see when selecting the provider from the list of all the OLE DB providers installed on the machine, and *Provider Version* is a string that identifies its version. You might want to print this information to a log file if your application isn't working properly on a customer's machine.

Asynchronous Connections

All the connection examples you've seen so far have one thing in common: They're performed synchronously. This means that the Visual Basic program won't execute the statement that follows the *Open* method until the connection is established, the connection times out, or another error occurs. In the meantime, the application won't respond to a user's actions, which is a situation that you should avoid, especially if you set a high value for the *ConnectionTimeout* property.

Fortunately, ADO solves this problem in a simple and elegant way. In fact, you can keep the Visual Basic program from waiting by passing the adAsyncConnect value to the *Options* argument of the *Open* method. When you open a connection asynchronously, you must determine when the connection is ready (or when an error occurs). This can be achieved in two ways: by polling the Connection's *State* property or by using events. Polling the *State* property is the simplest solution, but it's often inadequate if you need to perform complex operations while the connection is being attempted:

```
Dim cn As New ADODB.Connection
On Error Resume Next
cn.Open "Provider=sqloledb;Data Source=MyServer;Initial Catalog=pubs;" _
    & "User ID=sa;Password=;", , , adAsyncConnect
' State is a bit-field value, so you need the And operator to test one bit.
Do While (cn.State And adStateConnecting)
    ' Perform your operations here.
    ...
    ' Let the user interact with the program's user interface.
    DoEvents
Loop
' Check whether the connection has been successful.
If cn.State And adStateOpen Then MsgBox "The connection is open."
```

A better solution is to use the *ConnectComplete* event. You declare the Connection object variable using the *WithEvents* keyword and create a new instance of it when you're ready to open the connection, as you can see in the code at the top of the next page.

```
Dim WithEvents cn As ADODB.Connection

Private Sub cmdConnect_Click()
    Set cn = New ADODB.Connection
    cn.ConnectionTimeout = 20
    cn.Open "Provider=sqloledb;Data Source=MyServer;" _
        & "Initial Catalog=pubs;", "sa", , adAsyncConnect
End Sub

Private Sub cn_ConnectComplete(ByVal pError As ADODB.Error, adStatus As _
    ADODB.EventStatusEnum, ByVal pConnection As ADODB.Connection)
    If adStatus = adStatusOK Then
        MsgBox "The connection is open"
    ElseIf adStatus = adStatusErrorsOccurred Then
        MsgBox "Unable to open the connection" & vbCr & Err.Description
    End If
End Sub
```

The Connection object also fires the *WillConnect* event, though its usefulness
is limited. For example, you can use it to modify the connection string to specify the
provider you're connecting to (instead of modifying the string in multiple points of
the application's source code), or you can give users the ability to select a server, enter
their password, and so on:

```
Private Sub cn_WillConnect(ConnectionString As String, UserID As String, _
    Password As String, Options As Long, adStatus As _
    ADODB.EventStatusEnum, ByVal pConnection As ADODB.Connection)
    If UserID <> "" And Password = "" Then
        ' Ask for user's password.
        Password = InputBox("Please enter your password")
        If Password = "" Then
            ' If not provided, cancel the command if possible.
            If adStatus <> adStatusCantDeny Then adStatus = adStatusCancel
        End If
    End If
End Sub
```

When you're working with the *WillConnect* event, keep in mind that its parameters exactly match the values assigned to the corresponding arguments of the *Open*
method. This implies, for example, that the *UserID* and *Password* parameters both
receive an empty string if the user name and password were passed in the connection string. If you set the *adStatus* parameter to the adStatusCancel value, an error is
returned to the *Open* method and the connection isn't even attempted.

The *WillConnect* and *ConnectComplete* events fire when the connection isn't
opened in asynchronous mode, and the *ConnectComplete* fires also if you canceled
the operation in the *WillConnect* event. In this case, the *ConnectComplete* event receives *adStatus* set to adStatusErrorsOccurred and *pError.Number* set to error 3712,
"Operation has been canceled by the user."

PROCESSING DATA

After you've successfully opened a connection, your next step will probably be to read some records from the data source. You can accomplish this in several ways, but all of them involve the creation of a Recordset object.

Opening a Recordset Object

Before you open a Recordset, you must decide which records you want to retrieve, which type of cursor you want to create (if any), the cursor's location, and so on.

The source string

The most important property of a Recordset object is its *Source* property, which indicates which records should be retrieved. This property can be the name of a database table or view, the name of a stored procedure, or the text of a SELECT command. When you're working with file-based Recordsets, the *Source* property can also be the name and path of a file. (File-based Recordsets are described later in this chapter.) Here are a few examples:

```
' Select a different source, based on an array of option buttons.
Dim rs As New ADODB.Recordset
If optSource(0).Value Then          ' Database table
    rs.Source = "Authors"
ElseIf optSource(1).Value Then      ' Stored procedure
    rs.Source = "reptql"
ElseIf optSource(2) Then            ' SQL query
    rs.Source = "SELECT * FROM Authors" WHERE au_lname LIKE 'A*'"
End If
```

When you open a Recordset, you must specify the connection that you want used. You can do this in at least four ways:

■   You create a stand-alone Connection object with all the properties you want (connection timeout, user name and password, and so on), you open it, and then you assign it to the Recordset's *ActiveConnection* property before opening the Recordset.

■   You create a stand-alone Connection object as described in the previous point and pass it as the second argument of the Recordset's *Open* method. The effects of this sequence are identical, but it lets you save one statement.

■   You pass a connection string as the second argument of the Recordset's *Open* method. In this scenario, ADO creates an implicit Connection object that you can later access through the Recordset's *ActiveConnection* property. This method is the most concise of the four, in that it requires only one executable statement.

■ You create a stand-alone Connection object as shown in the first two points. Then you pass the source string as the first argument to its *Execute* method and assign the returned value to a Recordset variable. This means of specifying a connection is the least flexible of the group because you have little control over the type of the returned Recordset.

I'll describe a few other ways to open a Recordset, based on the Command object, in the "Using Command Objects" section, later in this chapter. Here are some code examples, all of which open the Authors table of the Pubs database on the SQL Server named P2:

```
' Method 1: explicit Connection assigned to the ActiveConnection property.
Dim cn As New ADODB.Connection, rs As New ADODB.Recordset
cn.ConnectionTimeout = 5
cn.Open "Provider=sqloledb;Data Source=P2;Initial Catalog=pubs;", "sa"
Set rs.ActiveConnection = cn
rs.Open "Authors"

' Method 2: explicit Connection passed to the Open method.
Dim cn As New ADODB.Connection, rs As New ADODB.Recordset
cn.ConnectionTimeout = 5
cn.Open "Provider=sqloledb;Data Source=P2;Initial Catalog=pubs;", "sa"
rs.Open "Authors", cn

' Method 3: implicit Connection created in the Recordset's Open method.
' Note that you need to embed additional connection attributes (such as
' connection timeout and user ID) in the connection string.
Dim rs As New ADODB.Recordset
rs.Open "Authors", "Provider=sqloledb;Data Source=P2;" _
    & "Initial Catalog=pubs;User ID=sa;Connection Timeout=10"

' Method 4: the Execute method of the Connection object. By default, it
' opens a server-side forward-only, read-only Recordset with CacheSize=1.
Dim cn As New ADODB.Connection, rs As New ADODB.Recordset
cn.Open "Provider=sqloledb;Data Source=P2;Initial Catalog=pubs;", "sa"
Set rs = cn.Execute("Authors")
```

Notice a substantial difference among all these approaches: The first, the second, and the fourth methods let you easily share the same connection among multiple Recordsets, whereas if you open multiple Recordsets using the third method each Recordset would use a different connection even if you use the same connection string for all of them.

> **TIP** If you have used a connection string to open a Recordset and then you want to reuse the same implicit Connection object to open another Recordset, you can exploit the *ActiveConnection* property of the first Recordset, as follows:

```
' Open a new Recordset on the same connection as "rs".
Dim rs2 As New ADODB.Recordset
rs2.Open "Publishers", rs.ActiveConnection
```

You can pass many types of strings to the *Open* method or the *Source* property and let ADO determine what they represent. This has a price, however, because you force ADO to send one or more queries to the database just to find out whether the source string is the name of a table, a view, a stored procedure, or the text of an SQL command. You can avoid these additional trips to the server by assigning a correct value to the last argument of the *Open* method, as in the following examples:

```
' Select a different source, based on an array of option buttons.
If optSource(0).Value Then        ' Database table
    rs.Open "Publishers", , , , adCmdTable
Else optSource(1).Value Then       ' Stored procedure
    rs.Open "reptql", , , , adCmdStoredProc
ElseIf optSource(2) Then         ' SQL query
    rs.Open "SELECT * FROM Authors", , , , adCmdText
End If
```

Cursors and concurrency

Recordsets can greatly differ in functionality and performance. For example, a Recordset can be updatable or read-only; it can support only the MoveNext command or be fully scrollable. Another key difference is in whether the Recordset contains the actual data or is just a collection of bookmarks that are used to retrieve the data from the database when necessary. It goes without saying that a client-side Recordset based on bookmarks takes fewer resources in the client application but might generate more network traffic when new data needs to be retrieved. Incidentally, this makes it almost impossible to compare the performance of different data retrieval techniques because they depend on too many factors.

The kinds of operations supported by a Recordset heavily depend upon the cursor on which the Recordset is based. Cursors are a collection of records that can be stored and maintained by the server database or by the client application. As you know from Chapter 13, ADO supports four types of cursors: forward-only read-only, static, keyset, and dynamic.

Cursors aren't very popular among professional programmers because of their appetite for resources and CPU time. Moreover, cursors often use locks on the database, which further reduces their scalability. Most heavy-duty client/server applications rely on cursorless Recordsets for retrieving data, and then update and insert records using SQL commands or, even better, stored procedures.

So, what are cursors good for? For one, when you're retrieving small sets of data—some hundreds of records, for example—a cursor is a reasonable choice. Cursors are also necessary when you want to enable your users to browse data and scroll back and forth through it, and you must use a cursor when your user interface is based on bound controls. In some cases, you're more or less forced to use cursors (in particular, client-side cursors) because a few interesting ADO features are available only with them. For example, persistent file-based Recordsets and hierarchical Recordsets can be based only on client-side static cursors, and you can use the *Sort* method only on this type of Recordset.

If you decide that cursors meets your requirements, you should at least attempt to reduce their overhead, which you do by adopting some simple but effective techniques. First, reduce the number of records in the cursor using an appropriate WHERE clause, and consider using the *MaxRecords* property to avoid huge cursors. Second, move to the last row of the Recordset as soon as possible, in order to free the locks on the data pages and index pages on the server. Third, always set the Recordset's *CursorLocation*, *CursorType*, and *LockType* properties so that the cursor isn't more powerful (and therefore less efficient) than what you actually need.

Speaking of *CursorType* and *LockType*, you should remember from Chapter 13 that you can also set these properties by passing values to the third and fourth arguments of the *Open* method, as the following code demonstrates:

```
' Open a server-side dynamic cursor.
' (Assumes that the ActiveConnection property has been set already.)
rs.CursorType = adOpenDynamic
rs.Open "SELECT * FROM Authors", , , , adCmdText

' Open a server-side keyset cursor, with a single statement.
rs.Open "SELECT * FROM Authors", , adOpenKyset, adLockOptimistic, adCmdText
```

You can create client-side static cursors by simply setting the *CursorLocation* to adUseClient before opening the Recordset. This property, in fact, seems to have a higher priority than *CursorType*: Whatever cursor type you specify in the latter property or as an argument to the *Open* method, ADO always creates a Recordset based on a static cursor, which is the only cursor available on the client side:

```
' Open a client-side static cursor.
rs.CursorLocation = adUseClient
rs.CursorType = adOpenStatic        ' This statement is optional.
rs.Open "SELECT * FROM Authors", , , , adCmdText
```

Client-side static cursors offer a decent scalability because they use resources from each client and not from the server. The only resource used on the server is the open connection, but later in this chapter I'll show how you can work around this issue, using dissociated Recordsets and optimistic batch updates.

Server-side cursors have their advantages. They let you use less powerful client workstations and offer more choices in terms of cursor types and locking options. For example, a keyset or dynamic cursor can reside only on the server, server-side static cursors can be read-write, and client-side static cursors can only be read-only or use optimistic batch updates. Another point in favor of cursors is that SQL Server lets you have multiple active statements on a connection only if you're using server-side cursors. On the other hand, server-side cursors drain resources from the server, so scalability is often an issue. Each cursor you create on the server uses room in the TempDB database, so you must ensure that TempDB can accommodate all the cursors requested by client applications. Finally, server-side cursors usually generate high network traffic because each time the client needs a different record, a round-trip to the server is performed.

> **TIP** The Visual Basic documentation incorrectly states that the Recordset returned by a Connection object's *Execute* method is always a server-side cursorless Recordset. The truth is that you can also create client-side static cursors if you set the Connection's *CursorLocation* property to adUseClient before creating the Recordset:

```
' This code creates a client-side static cursor.
Dim cn As New ADODB.Connection, rs As New ADODB.Recordset
cn.Open "Provider=sqloledb;Data Source=P2;" & _
    "Initial Catalog=pubs;", "sa"
cn.CursorLocation = adUseClient
Set rs = cn.Execute("Authors")
```

> I didn't find a way, however, to have an *Execute* method return a server-side cursor other than the default noncursor.

Stand-alone Recordset objects

ADO Recordset objects are much more flexible than DAOs and RDOs, in that you don't even need an open connection to create a Recordset. In fact, ADO provides support for two different types of Recordsets: stand-alone Recordsets created from scratch and file-based Recordsets.

Stand-alone Recordsets are conceptually simple. You create a new Recordset object, append one or more fields to its Fields collection, and finally open it. What you get is a client-side Recordset based on a static cursor and optimistic batch locking:

```
' Creates a dissociated Recordset with three fields
Dim rs As New ADODB.Recordset
rs.Fields.Append "FirstName", adChar, 40, adFldIsNullable
rs.Fields.Append "LastName", adChar, 40, adFldIsNullable
rs.Fields.Append "BirthDate", adDate
rs.Open
```

After you have opened the Recordset, you can add records to it and you can even assign it to the *Recordset* property of an ADO Data control or to the *DataSource* property of any bound control. This lets you bind a control to data of any type, even if it isn't stored in a database. For example, you can display the contents of a semicolon-delimited text file in a DataGrid control, as shown in Figure 14-1, by using the following code. (See the companion CD for the complete application.)

```
Dim rs As New ADODB.Recordset
Dim lines() As String, fields() As String
Dim i As Long, j As Long

' Open the Publishers.dat text file.
Open "Publishers.dat" For Input As #1
' Read the contents of the file, and process each individual line.
lines() = Split(Input(LOF(1), 1), vbCrLf)
Close #1
' Process the first line, which contains the list of fields.
fields() = Split(lines(0), ";")
For j = 0 To UBound(fields)
    rs.fields.Append fields(j), adChar, 200
Next
rs.Open

' Process all the remaining lines.
For i = 1 To UBound(lines)
    rs.AddNew
    fields() = Split(lines(i), ";")
    For j = 0 To UBound(fields)
        rs(j) = fields(j)
    Next
Next
' Display the recordset in the DataGrid control.
rs.MoveFirst
Set DataGrid1.DataSource = rs
```

Using similar code, you can display the contents of a two-dimensional array of strings, of an array of User Defined Type structures, or even less traditional data sources, such as information coming from the serial port or an HTML page downloaded from the Internet.

ADO also supports saving the contents of a client-side Recordset to a disk file. This capability can greatly increase the functionality and the performance of your applications. For example, you can create local copies of small lookup tables and update them only when necessary. Or you can save a Recordset to a directory and let another program create a report out of it, possibly during off-hours. Or you can enable your users to save the current state of the application—including any Recordset being processed—and restore it in a later session. I have described file-based Recordset in detail in the "Implementing Persistent Recordsets" section in Chapter 13.

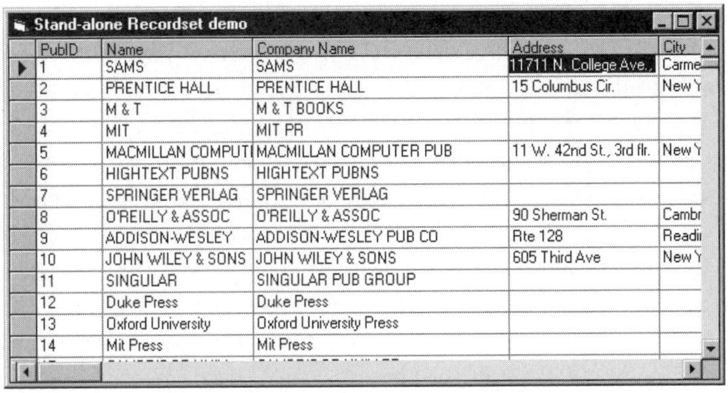

Figure 14-1. *You can bind data-aware controls to any type of data, using stand-alone Recordsets.*

Basic Operations on a Database

The ultimate purpose in connecting to a database is to read the data it contains and possibly modify it. As you'll see in a moment, ADO offers several ways to perform these tasks.

Read records

After you've created a Recordset, reading the data in it is as simple as iterating on all its records using a *Do...Loop* structure similar to the following one:

```
' Fill a list box with the names of all the authors.
Dim rs As New ADODB.Recordset
rs.Open "Authors", "Provider=sqloledb;Data Source=P2;" _
    & "Initial Catalog=pubs;User ID=sa;Connection Timeout=10"
Do Until rs.EOF
    lstAuthors.AddItem rs("au_fname") & " " & rs("au_lname")
    rs.MoveNext
Loop
rs.Close
```

The previous code works regardless of the type of Recordset you're working with, because all Recordsets—including cursorless ones—support the *MoveNext* method. You can reference the values in the current record using the more verbose syntax:

```
rs.Fields("au_fname").Value
```

but in most cases you'll omit both *Fields* (the default property for the Recordset object) and *Value* (the default property for the Field object) and use the most concise form:

```
rs("au_fname")
```

Reading the *Value* property of a Field object might fail if the field is a large binary object (BLOB), such as an image or a long memo stored in a database field. In this situation, you should retrieve the value using the Field object's *GetChunk* method, as described in the "The Field Object" section in Chapter 13. Similarly, you should write data to a BLOB field using the *AppendChunk* method.

ADO supports two other ways to retrieve data from an open Recordset. The first one is based on the *GetRows* method, which returns a Variant containing a two-dimensional array of values. The second one is based on the *GetString* method, which returns a long string where fields and records are separated using the characters you specify. In general, these methods are *much* faster than using a loop based on the *MoveNext* method, even though the actual speed improvement depends on many factors, including the type of cursor and the system memory available on the client machine. You can find a description of these methods in the "Retrieving Data" section of Chapter 13.

Insert, delete, and update records

Provided that the Recordset is updatable, you can insert new records using the Recordset's *AddNew* method. Use the *Supports* method to determine whether you can add new records to the Recordset:

```
If rs.Supports(adAddNew) Then...
```

I've shown how you can use the *AddNew* method to add records to a stand-alone Recordset, and the same technique applies to a regular Recordset. If you've grown up with DAO and RDO, you might find ADO's *AddNew* method disconcerting at first because it doesn't require that you confirm the addition of the new record. In fact, any operation that moves the record pointer to another record—including another *AddNew* method—confirms the insertion of the new record. If you want to cancel the operation, you must call the *CancelUpdate* method, as this code demonstrates:

```
rs.AddNew
rs.Fields("Name") = "MSPress"
rs.Fields("City") = "Seattle"
rs.Fields("State") = "WA"
If MsgBox("Do you want to confirm?", vbYesNo) = vbYes Then
    rs.Update
Else
    rs.CancelUpdate
End If
```

Remember that you can't close a Recordset if an *AddNew* method hasn't been resolved with an *Update* method (implicit or explicit) or a *CancelUpdate* method.

Another feature of the *AddNew* method that's missing in DAO and RDO is its ability to pass an array of field names and values. To give you an idea of which sort of speed improvement you can get using this feature, I rewrote the loop that adds new records in the code snippet shown in the "Stand-Alone Recordset Objects" section, earlier in this chapter:

```
' Build the FieldNames() variant array. (You need to do this only once.)
ReDim fieldNames(0 To fieldMax) As Variant
For j = 0 To fieldMax
    fieldNames(j) = fields(j)
Next
' Process the text lines, but use an array of values in AddNew.
For i = 1 To UBound(lines)
    fields() = Split(lines(i), ";")
    ReDim fieldValues(0 To fieldMax) As Variant
    For j = 0 To UBound(fields)
        fieldValues(j) = fields(j) ' Move values into the Variant array.
    Next
    rs.AddNew fieldNames(), fieldValues()
Next
```

While the amount of code is more or less the same, passing arrays of field names and values to the *AddNew* method makes this code run about *three times faster* than the original loop. This gives you an idea of the overhead you incur whenever you reference an item in the Fields collection.

ADO lets you modify field values in the current record without explicitly entering edit mode. In fact, unlike DAO and RDO, ADO Recordset objects expose no *Edit* method and you implicitly enter edit mode when you modify a field's value:

```
' Increment unit prices of all products by 10%.
Do Until rs.EOF
    rs("UnitPrice") = rs("UnitPrice") * 1.1
    rs.MoveNext
Loop
```

If you aren't sure whether ADO has initiated an edit operation, you can query the *EditMode* property:

```
If rs.EditMode = adEditInProgress Then...
```

The *Update* method is similar to *AddNew* in that it also supports a list of field names and values. This feature is especially convenient when the same subset of values must be inserted in multiple records. Don't forget that the *Update* method might not be supported by the Recordset, depending on its type, location, and concurrency option. When in doubt, use the *Supports* method:

```
If rs.Supports(adUpdate) Then...
```

The syntax of the *Delete* method is simple: Depending on the argument you pass to this method, you can either delete the current record (the default) or all the records that are currently visible because of an active *Filter* property. In most cases, you'll use the default option. Remember that after you invoke this method, the current record becomes invalid, so you should move the record pointer to point to a valid record immediately after the delete operation:

```
rs.Delete
rs.MoveNext
If rs.EOF The rs.MoveLast
```

Locking issues

Even if the Recordset is updatable, you can't be sure that the *Update* method will succeed. In fact, an updatable record might be (possibly temporarily) made non-updatable because it's being edited by another user. This is an issue only when you open the Recordset using a locking option other than the adLockReadOnly value. If you open a Recordset in read-only mode, you're not using locks at all and can happily go back and forth through your Recordset (only forth, if not scrollable) without caring about locking.

Different users can access the same set of records using different lock options. For example, user A might use pessimistic locking and user B might use optimistic locking. In this case, user A might lock the record even if user B is already editing it, in which case user B will be locked out until user A completes the update operation. If you use pessimistic locking, you should trap errors only when you start editing the record, whereas if you use optimistic locking you should trap errors only when you implicitly or explicitly update the record. If you're using optimistic batch locking, you must solve update conflicts, as I explain later in this chapter.

When you're using pessimistic locking and your edit operation fails, you get an error &H80004005, "Couldn't update; currently locked by user *<username>* on machine *<machinename>*." You get the same error when the Update command fails for a Recordset opened with optimistic locking. In both cases, you should implement a strategy for solving these locking problems: Typically you can either retry automatically after a while or notify the user that the edit or update operation failed and let him or her decide whether the command should be attempted again:

```
' Update strategy for optimistic locking.
On Error Resume Next
Do
    Err.Clear
    rs.Update
    If Err = 0 Then
        Exit Do
    ElseIf MsgBox("Update command failed:" & vbCr & Err.Description, _
        vbRetryCancel + vbCritical) = vbCancel Then
        Exit Do
    End If
Loop
```

> **CAUTION** The OLE DB Provider for Microsoft Jet version 3.51 has a serious bug: If you're using optimistic locking and the implicit or explicit *Update* method fails, you get a cryptic error &H80040E21, "Errors occurred." This isn't very helpful. What's worse with optimistic updates, however, is that you get this error only the first time you attempt the update operation. If you retry the update later and the record is still locked, you get no error and the code incorrectly assumes that the update succeeded. This bug has been fixed in version 4.0 of the provider, which returns the correct error code &H80004005. The OLE DB Provider for SQL Server 6.5 also returns the incorrect error code, but at least the error correctly persists if you retry the *Update* operation again on the same locked record.

Many database engines—including Microsoft Jet and SQL Server 6.5 and earlier—don't support locking at the record level and use locks that affect entire pages that can contain multiple records. (For example, Microsoft Jet supports 2-KB pages.) This means that a record can be locked even if it isn't being updated by a user but merely because a user has locked another record in the same page. Microsoft SQL Server 7 and Oracle databases support record-level locking. The locking mechanism also works on pages of indexes, so you might be prevented from updating a record because another user has locked the index page that contains a pointer to the record you're working with.

Updates through SQL commands

As you know, the most efficient Recordsets are those built on forward-only, read-only noncursors, which are nonupdatable Recordsets. Even if you opt for other types of cursors, for a better scalability I advise you to open the Recordset in read-only mode, which avoids locking and delivers applications that scale better. You must, however, implement a strategy for adding, inserting, and deleting records if such operations are needed. If the Recordset isn't updatable, your only choice is to send an SQL command to the database or to execute a stored procedure that you've created previously. In this section, I show you how to use plain SQL commands without parameters. The concepts, by the way, can be applied to other circumstances as well, which you'll see when I describe parameterized queries in the "Parameterized Commands and Queries" section, later in this chapter.

If you're working with a read-only Recordset, you can update an individual row using an UPDATE command as long as you can uniquely identify the current record. Usually you do that using the value of the primary key in the WHERE clause:

```
' Ask the end user for a new price for each product that costs more
' than $40.
Dim rs As New ADODB.Recordset, cn As New ADODB.Connection
Dim newValue As String
cn.Open "Provider=Microsoft.Jet.OLEDB.4.0;" _
    & "Data Source=C:\Program Files\Microsoft Visual Studio\VB98\NWind.mdb"
```

(continued)

```
rs.Open "Products", cn
Do Until rs.EOF
    If rs("UnitPrice") > 40 Then
        ' In a real-world application, you will surely use a better UI.
        newValue = InputBox("Insert a new price for product " & _
            rs("ProductName"), , rs("UnitPrice"))
        If Len(newValue) Then
            cn.Execute "UPDATE Products SET UnitPrice=" & newValue & _
                " WHERE ProductID =" & rs("ProductID")
        End If
    End If
    rs.MoveNext
Loop
```

Deleting a record using an SQL command is similar, but you have to use the DELETE command instead:

```
' Ask users if they want to selectively delete suppliers from Italy.
Dim rs As New ADODB.Recordset, cn As New ADODB.Connection
cn.Open "Provider=Microsoft.Jet.OLEDB.4.0;" _
    & "Data Source=E:\Microsoft Visual Studio\VB98\NWind.mdb"
rs.Open "Suppliers", cn
Do Until rs.EOF
    If rs("Country") = "Italy" Then
        If MsgBox("Do you want to delete supplier " & rs("Company Name") _
            & "?", vbYesNo) = vbYes Then
            cn.Execute "DELETE FROM Suppliers WHERE SupplierID =" _
                & rs("SupplierID")
        End If
    End If
    rs.MoveNext
Loop
```

Update and delete operations can fail for several reasons, so you should always protect them from unanticipated errors. For example, the previous DELETE command fails if the deleted record is referenced by any record in the Products table, unless a cascading delete relationship has been established between the two tables.

Adding new records requires an INSERT INTO command:

```
cn.Execute "INSERT INTO Employees (LastName, FirstName, BirthDate) " _
    & "VALUES ('Smith', 'Robert', '2/12/1953')"
```

When you retrieve the values from controls, you must build the SQL string programmatically, as in this code:

```
cn.Execute "INSERT INTO Employees (LastName, FirstName, BirthDate) " _
    & "VALUES ('" & txtLastName & "', '" & txtFirstName _
    & "', '" & txtBirthDate & "')"
```

You can write less code and make it more readable by defining a routine that replaces all the placeholders in a string:

```
' Replace all @n arguments with provided values.
Function ReplaceParams(ByVal text As String, ParamArray args() As Variant)
    Dim i As Integer
    For i = LBound(args) To UBound(args)
        text = Replace(text, "@" & Trim$(i + 1), args(i))
    Next
    ReplaceParams = text
End Function
```

Here's how you can rewrite the previous INSERT command using the *Replace-Params* routine:

```
sql = "INSERT INTO Employees (LastName, FirstName, BirthDate) " _
    & "VALUES ('@1', '@2', '@3')"
cn.Execute ReplaceParams(sql, txtLastName, txtFirstName, txtBirthDate)
```

Optimistic Client-Batch Updates

Until now, I haven't described in detail how optimistic batch updates work for a reason: They require a completely different programming logic and deserve a section of their own.

Disconnecting the Recordset

In a nutshell, ADO lets you create Recordsets on which you can perform all the commands you want to—including deletes, inserts, and updates—without immediately affecting the original rows in the database. You can even disconnect the Recordset from the database by setting its *ActiveConnection* property to Nothing and optionally close the companion Connection object. When you're finally ready to confirm the updates to the database, you simply have to reconnect the Recordset and issue an UpdateBatch command. Or you can use the *CancelBatch* method to cancel the pending changes. The following snippet is similar to a code example you saw in the previous section, but it uses optimistic batch updates instead of UPDATE SQL commands:

```
Dim rs As New ADODB.Recordset, cn As New ADODB.Connection
' Open the recordset with optimistic batch locking.
cn.ConnectionString = "Provider=Microsoft.Jet.OLEDB.4.0;" _
    & "Data Source=C:\Microsoft Visual Studio\VB98\NWind.mdb"
cn.Open
rs.CursorLocation = adUseClient
rs.Open "Products", cn, adOpenStatic, adLockBatchOptimistic
' Disconnect the recordset from the data source and free the connection.
Set rs.ActiveConnection = Nothing
cn.Close
```

(continued)

```
Do Until rs.EOF
    If rs("UnitPrice") > 40 Then
        ' In a real-world application, you'll surely use a better UI.
        newValue = InputBox("Insert a new price for product " & _
            rs("ProductName"), , rs("UnitPrice"))
        If Len(newValue) Then rs("UnitPrice") = newValue
    End If
    rs.MoveNext
Loop

' Ask for confirmation of all changes.
If MsgBox("Send updates to the database?", vbYesNo) = vbYes Then
    ' Reestablish the connection, and send the updates.
    cn.Open
    Set rs.ActiveConnection = cn
    rs.UpdateBatch
Else
    rs.CancelBatch
End If
```

Notice how the program closes the connection while it isn't being used by the Recordset and reopens it only if necessary. This detail can probably improve the scalability of your application more than any other technique you've seen so far.

Resolving the conflicts

The previous code example omits an essential part of any optimistic batch update routine—conflict handling. In fact, the *optimistic* in the name means that you *hope* that no other user has updated the same record while you were processing the Recordset locally. In practice, you must always trap errors and resolve any conflicts manually. These conflicts can occur because the records you've updated have been deleted by another user in the meantime, or because the fields that you've updated have been updated by another user. By default, ADO signals a conflict only if two users modify the same field, not when they modify different fields in the same record. For the best results, you should ensure that the table being updated has a primary key. Otherwise, you might accidentally update more records than you meant to.

To see which records caused the conflicts, you set the *Filter* property to the value adFilterConflictingRecords and then loop on the Recordsets, testing each record's *Status* property:

```
' A skeletal code that resolves batch update conflicts
On Error Resume Next
rs.UpdateBatch
rs.Filter = adFilterConflictingRecords
If rs.RecordCount > 0 Then
    ' Resolve the conflicts here.
End If
```

```
' Go back to the regular recordset.
rs.Filter = adFilterNone
```

Next, you need a way to solve the conflicts you've found. First of all, you can visit each record in the Recordset and query its *Status* property. If it returns the value adRecModified, it means that another user has changed the same fields that the current user has edited, whereas it returns the value adRecDeleted if the record has been deleted. Often, the adRecConcurrencyViolation bit is set in case of errors. See Table 13-2 in Chapter 13 for the complete list of values that can be returned by the *Status* property. Keep in mind that this is a bit-field value, so you should test individual bits using the And operator, as in this code:

```
If rs.Status And adRecModified Then...
```

If a record has been modified, you must decide what to do. Unfortunately, there are no universally valid rules. Automatic conflict-solving strategies are always dangerous; usually the best thing to do is to let users decide. To let them reach a meaningful decision, however, you should display the new value that has been stored in the database. Unfortunately, simply querying the Field object's *UnderlyingValue* property won't work because it returns the same value as the *OriginalValue* property (that is, the value that was in that field when the Recordset was opened). To achieve the correct value for the *UnderlyingValue* property, you must run the Recordset's *Resync* method.

You can pass the *Resync* method two optional arguments. The first argument determines which records are resynchronized, and can be one of the following values: adAffectAllChapters (the default, affect all records), adAffectGroup (affect only the records made visible by the current filter), or adAffectCurrent (affect only the current record). For our purposes, the adAffectGroup value is usually the best choice. The second argument to the *Resync* method determines how Field object's properties are affected: The value we need is adResyncUnderlyingValues, which sets the *UnderlyingValue* property to the value read from the database. If you mistakenly use the adResyncAllValues for the second argument (the default), you overwrite the *Value* property and therefore lose what the user has entered. The following code puts all these concepts together and displays the list of all the conflicting records, with details about the involved fields:

```
On Error Resume Next
rs.UpdateBatch
rs.Filter = adFilterConflictingRecords
If rs.RecordCount Then
    Dim fld As ADODB.Field
    ' Resync the Recordset to retrieve correct values for UnderlyingValue.
    rs.Resync adAffectGroup, adResyncUnderlyingValues
```

(continued)

```
' Loop on all the conflicting records. Note that setting the Filter
' property implicitly performs a MoveFirst method.
Do Until rs.EOF
    Print "Conflict on record: " & rs("ProductName")
    For Each fld In rs.Fields
        ' Display fields whose local and underlying values don't match.
        If fld.Value <> fld.UnderlyingValue Then
            Print "Field: " & fld.Name _
                & "- Original value = " & fld.OriginalValue _
                & "- Value now in database = " & fld.UnderlyingValue _
                & "- Local value = " & fld.Value
        End If
    Next
    rs.MoveNext
Loop
End If
rs.Filter = adFilterNone
```

ADO signals a conflict even if the underlying value is equal to the local value. In other words, ADO signals a conflict if two users attempted to store the same value in the same field of a record. After you or your users have all the information needed to reach a decision, you should resolve the conflict in one of the following ways:

- You can accept the value currently in the database, which you do by assigning the Field's *UnderlyingValue* property to its *Value* property.

- You can force the local value into the database, by reexecuting the *UpdateBatch* method. In this case, no error will be raised unless another user has modified those fields (or other fields) in the meantime.

To watch optimistic batch updates in action, run two instances of the BatchUpd project on the companion CD, modify the same records in both instances, and then click on the Update button. In the first instance, you get an OK message; in the other instance, you get an error and have the opportunity to browse conflicting records, resynchronize the Recordset, and see the relevant properties of all fields, which are visible in Figure 14-2. The application works with the Pubs SQL Server database and with the Biblio.mdb Jet database.

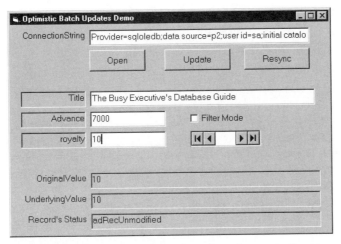

Figure 14-2. *The Optimistic Batch Updates demonstration program.*

The *Update Criteria* property

As I've mentioned before, ADO by default raises a conflict when different users modify the same field: In other words, if two users read the same record but modify different fields, no error occurs. This behavior is very dangerous and might lead to inconsistencies in the database. Fortunately, you can change this default action through the *Update Criteria* dynamic property of the Recordset object. This property affects the fields used by ADO to locate the record to be updated. You can set this property to one of the following four values: 0-adCriteriaKey (ADO uses only the primary key), 1-adCriteriaAllCols (ADO uses all the columns in the Recordset), 2-adCriteriaUpdCols (the default, ADO uses the key and the updated fields), and 3-adCriteriaTimeStamp. (ADO uses a TIMESTAMP column, if available; otherwise, it uses adCriteriaAllCols.)

Because *Update Criteria* is a dynamic property, you set it through the Properties collection, as in the following example:

```
rs.Properties("Update Criteria") = adCriteriaTimeStamp
```

In general, setting this property to the value adCriteriaTimeStamp offers the best performance if the table includes a TIMESTAMP field; otherwise, this setting reverts to adCriteriaAllCols, which is the least efficient of the group (although it's also the safest one). Note that you don't need to retrieve the TIMESTAMP field just to use the adCriteriaTimeStamp setting. For more information, see article Q190727 in the Microsoft Knowledge Base.

Using Command Objects

We've seen how you can execute commands with a Connection's *Execute* method and retrieve a set of records using a Recordset's *Open* method. You can write many useful applications with just those two simple techniques, but you need the power of the Command object for more demanding tasks. Command objects are the best choice when you want to run parameterized queries and are the only viable solution when you want to call stored procedures with parameters and return values.

Action commands

A Command object represents a command that you intend to perform on a data source. You need an open connection to actually perform the command, but you don't need to have it available when you create the Command object. In other words, you can create a stand-alone Command and set its properties and then associate it with an open Connection object through the Command's *ActiveConnection* property, which works similarly to the Recordset property of the same name. Here's an example of a simple Command that performs an UPDATE SQL statement on the Publishers table of the Pubs SQL Server's sample database:

```
' Prepare the Command object's properties.
Dim cmd As New ADODB.Command
cmd.CommandText = "UPDATE Publishers SET city = 'London' " _
    & "WHERE Pub_ID = '9999'"
cmd.CommandTimeout = 10
cmd.CommandType = adCmdText          ' This saves ADO some work.

' When you're ready, open the connection and fire the command.
Dim cn As New ADODB.Connection
Dim recs As Long
cn.Open "Provider=sqloledb;Data source=p2;user id=sa;initial catalog=pubs"
Set cmd.ActiveConnection = cn
cmd.Execute recs
Print "RecordsAffected = " & recs
```

Alternatively, you can assign a string to the Command's *ActiveConnection* property, in which case ADO creates an implicit Connection object for you. I recommend that you not use this latter technique because it gives you little control on the Connection itself—for example, you can't trap events from it—but here's an example of this technique for those of you who like concise code:

```
cmd.ActiveConnection = "Provider=sqloledb;Data Source=p2;User Id=sa;" _
    & "Initial Catalog=pubs"
cmd.Execute recs
```

Row-returning queries

You can use a Command object to run a row-returning query in three distinct ways. They're equivalent, and you can choose one depending on the particular task or your coding style. In the first technique, you simply assign a Recordset object the return value of a Command's *Execute* method:

```
' This code assumes that Command's properties have been set correctly.
Dim rs As ADODB.Recordset
cmd.CommandText = "SELECT * FROM Publishers WHERE country = 'USA'"
Set rs = cmd.Execute
' At this point, the Recordset is already open.
```

Using the second technique, you assign the Command object to a Recordset's *Source* property, as in the following code:

```
Set rs.Source = cmd
rs.Open
```

The third technique is the most concise of the group:

```
rs.Open cmd
```

When you pass a Command object to a Recordset's *Open* method, the Recordset inherits the Command's active connection. For this reason, if you also pass a distinct Connection object or a connection string to the *Open* method, an error occurs. You also get an error if you pass a Command object that isn't associated with an open connection. After you have associated a Command with a Recordset, you can get a reference to the original Command using the Recordset's *ActiveCommand* property. Don't try to assign a Command to this property, however, because it's read-only.

Parameterized commands and queries

In the code you've seen so far, there is no advantage in using Command objects instead of plain SQL commands. The real power of these objects becomes apparent when the command or the query contains one or more parameters. For example, let's say that you often have to select publishers in a given country. This is how you can prepare such a query using a Command object:

```
Dim cmd As New ADODB.Command, rs As ADODB.Recordset
cmd.ActiveConnection = "Provider=sqloledb;Data source=p2;user id=sa;" _
    & "initial catalog=pubs"
' Use question marks as placeholders for parameters.
cmd.CommandText = "SELECT * FROM Publishers WHERE country = ?"
' You can pass CommandType as the Execute's third argument.
Set rs = cmd.Execute(, "USA", adCmdText)
```

When you create multiple parameters, you must pass their values in an array of Variants, which you can do using an *Array* function:

```
cmd.CommandText = "SELECT * FROM Publishers WHERE country = ? " _
    & " AND Pub_Name LIKE ?"
' Note that the LIKE operator follows the SQL Server syntax.
Set rs = cmd.Execute(, Array("USA", "N%"), adCmdText)
```

You can write more elegant code if you assign parameters' values through the Parameters collection:

```
cmd.Parameters.Refresh              ' Create the collection (optional).
cmd.Parameters(0) = "USA"
cmd.Parameters(1) = "N%"
Set rs = cmd.Execute()
```

The Parameters collection's *Refresh* method is optional because as soon as you reference any property or method of the collection (except *Append*), ADO parses the query text and builds the collection for you, at the expense of some overhead. Fortunately, it isn't difficult to create the collection yourself and save this overhead, using the Command's *CreateParameter* method:

```
' Create the collection of parameters. (Do this only once.)
With cmd.Parameters
    .Append cmd.CreateParameter("Country", adChar, adParamInput, 20)
    .Append cmd.CreateParameter("Name", adChar, adParamInput, 20)
End With
' Assign a value to parameters.
cmd.Parameters("Country") = "USA"
cmd.Parameters("Name") = "N%"
Set rs = cmd.Execute()
```

The Command object's *Prepared* property plays a key role in optimizing your parameterized queries. If this property is True, ADO creates a temporary stored procedure on the server the first time you invoke the *Execute* method of the Command object. This adds a little overhead to the first execution, but it noticeably speeds up all subsequent calls. The temporary stored procedure is automatically deleted when the connection is closed. One note: By tracing SQL calls, I found that this property doesn't work very well with SQL Server 6.5 SP3 or earlier.

Using the DataEnvironment Designer

You can greatly simplify your coding by using Connection and Command objects defined at design time through the DataEnvironment designer. As you'll see in a moment, the amount of necessary code is dramatically reduced because most of the properties of these objects can be set interactively at design time, using a RAD approach that isn't conceptually different from what you routinely do with forms and controls.

Connections and commands

You can use a reference to a Connection object to open a database, start a transaction, and so on. In many cases, however, you don't even need to explicitly open a connection because the run-time instance of the DataEnvironment will do it for you whenever you reference a Command object that's a child of that connection. In practice, you reference a Connection only if you need to set some of its properties—for example, the user name and the password:

```
' This code assumes that DataEnvironment1 has a Connection object named
' "Pubs" and a Command object named ResetSalesReport under it.
Dim de As New DataEnvironment1
de.Pubs.Open userid:="sa", Password:="mypwd"
de.ResetSalesReport
```

Remember that you can decide whether a login dialog box is shown to the user by setting the *RunPromptBehavior* property appropriately. All the Command objects you have defined at design time become methods of the DataEnvironment. The following code example directly executes the Command object, without first explicitly opening the Connection because all the login information has been specified at design time:

```
' You can hardly write code more concise than this!
DataEnvironment1.ResetSalesReport
```

The previous two code snippets differ significantly in this respect: The former explicitly creates an instance—named *de*—of the DataEnvironment1 designer, while the latter uses its global name. It turns out that Visual Basic manages DataEnvironment designers a bit like form designers, in that you can use the class name as a variable. (This detail is covered in Chapter 9.) Keep this in mind because you might accidentally create more instances of the designer without realizing that you're wasting memory and resources.

At run-time, the DataEnvironment designer object exposes three collections: Connections, Commands, and Recordsets. You can use them to let your users select the query they want to run against the database:

```
' Fill a list box with the names of all supported Commands.
' BEWARE: just referencing the Commands collection opens the connection.
Dim cmd As ADODB.Command
For Each cmd In DataEnvironment1.Commands
    List1.AddItem cmd.Name
Next
```

Recordsets

An instance of the designer exposes a collection of Connections and Commands and also exposes one Recordset object for each Command that returns a result set. The name of this Recordset is formed using the *rs* prefix followed by the name of the Command that generates it. For example, if you have defined a Command object named Authors that performs a query, the DataEnvironment object will also expose a property named *rsAuthors* of type Recordset. By default, this Recordset is closed, so before using it you need to run the associated Command:

```
' Fill a list box with authors' names.
Dim de As New DataEnvironment1
de.Authors                        ' Run the query.
Do Until de.rsAuthors.EOF
    List1.AddItem de.rsAuthors("au_fname") & " " & de.rsAuthors("au_lname")
    de.rsAuthors.MoveNext
Loop
de.rsAuthors.Close
```

Alternatively, you can explicitly open the Recordset object. This latter technique is more flexible because you can set the Recordset's properties before opening it:

```
Dim rs As ADODB.Recordset
' Get a reference to the Recordset, and open it with an optimistic lock.
Set rs = DataEnvironment1.rsAuthors
rs.Open LockType:=adLockOptimistic
Do Until rs.EOF
    List1.AddItem rs("au_fname") & " " & rs("au_lname")
    rs.MoveNext
Loop
rs.Close
```

Of course, you can declare the *rs* variable using the *WithEvents* keyword so that you can trap all the events raised by the Recordset object.

Parameterized queries

If a Command object expects one or more parameters, you can just pass them after the Command name. To test this feature, create a Command object named AuthorsByState under a Connection object to the Pubs SQL Server database, based on the following query:

```
SELECT au_lname, au_fname, address, city, zip, state FROM authors
    WHERE (state =?)
```

and then run this code:

```
DataEnvironment1.AuthorsByState "CA"
' Show the results in a DataGrid control.
Set DataGrid1.DataSource = DataEnvironment1.rsAuthorsByState
```

Things are more complex when you're running a parameterized stored procedure because ADO sometimes is unable to determine the right type for its parameters, and you probably have to adjust what the DataEnvironment designer displays in the Parameters tab of the Command object's Property Pages dialog box. Also, if you're working with SQL Server 6.5, be sure that you've installed its Service Pack 4 (which you can find on the Visual Studio CD), which has fixed several problems in this area. Let's say that you need to call an SQL Server stored procedure named *SampleStoredProc*, which takes one input parameter and one output parameter and has a return value. This is what the Visual Basic documentation suggests:

```
Dim outParam As Long, retValue As Long
retValue = DataEnvironment1.SampleStoredProc(100, outParam)
Set DataGrid1.DataSource = DataEnvironment1.rsSampleStoredProc
Print "Output parameter = " & outParam
Print "Return value = " & retValue
```

I found many problems using this syntax. Even worse, you can't use this approach when you want to omit one or more parameters. To work around these problems, you can resort to the Parameters collection of the ADO Command object. To get a reference to this object, you must query the DataEnvironment's *Commands* property, as in the following piece of code:

```
With DataEnvironment1.Commands("SampleStoredProc")
    ' This is the "royalty" parameter.
    .Parameters(1) = 100
    Set DataGrid1.DataSource = .Execute
    ' Retrieve the output parameter.
    Print "Output parameter = " & .Parameters(2)
    ' The return value is always in Parameters(0).
    Print "Return value = " & .Parameters(0)
End With
```

An important point: When you use the Commands collection to retrieve the ADO Command object, you're in a sense bypassing the Recordset-returning mechanism offered by the DataEnvironment designer. For this reason, you can retrieve the Recordset only by reading the return value of the *Execute* method, and you can't rely on the *rsSampleStoredProc* property of the designer. Finally, you can also pass input parameters directly to the *Execute* method and retrieve output parameters and return values using the Parameters collection:

```
Dim recordsAffected As Long
With DataEnvironment1.Commands("SampleStoredProc")
    ' The array of parameters passed to the Execute method must account for
    ' the return value, which is always the first parameter.
    Set DataGrid1.DataSource = .Execute(recordsAffected, Array(0, 100))
    Print "Output parameter = " & .Parameters(2)
    Print "Return value = " & .Parameters(0)
End With
```

Reusable modules

Up to this point, I've illustrated the virtues of the DataEnvironment designer to create Connection, Command, and Recordset objects that you can use from code without having to define them at run time. However, you shouldn't forget that you can also write code *inside* the designer itself. This code might respond to events raised by the

Connection and Recordset objects created by the DataEnvironment itself. In addition, you can add public properties, methods, and events as you can do with any type of class module. These capabilities let you encapsulate some complex programming logic inside a DataEnvironment module and reuse it in many other applications.

One possible use for such public properties is to offer meaningful names for the parameters that you should pass to a Command's Parameters collection, as in the following code:

```
' Inside the DataEnvironment module
Public Property Get StateWanted() As String
    StateWanted = Commands("AuthorsByState").Parameters("State")
End Property

Public Property Let StateWanted(ByVal newValue As String)
    Commands("AuthorsByState").Parameters("State") = newValue
End Property
```

Here's another example—a property named *InfoText*, which gathers all the output coming from the Connection's *InfoMessage* event:

```
Private m_InfoText As String

Public Property Get InfoText() As String
    InfoText = m_InfoText
End Property

Public Property Let InfoText(ByVal newValue As String)
    m_InfoText = newValue
End Property

' Add a new text line to the InfoText property.
Private Sub Connection1_InfoMessage(ByVal pError As ADODB.Error, _
    adStatus As EventStatusEnum, ByVal pConnection As ADODB.Connection)
    m_InfoText = m_InfoText & "pError = " & pError.Number & " - " & _
        pError.Description & vbCrLf
End Sub
```

The dark side of the DataEnvironment object

I was thrilled when I first saw the DataEnvironment object in action, and I think I have expressed my enthusiasm many times in these pages. But it wouldn't be fair if I failed to mention that the DataEnvironment designer still has a few serious problems, which sometimes prevent it from being used in production applications. Here's a brief list of my disappointing discoveries:

■   The DataEnvironment isn't very good at dealing with parameterized stored procedures, especially those that take output parameters and return a value. In particular, sometimes you can't call these procedure using the Command's name as a method of the DataEnvironment object—as in the *DataEnvironment1.SampleStoredProc* example I showed you previously—and you're forced to pass parameters through the Command's Parameters collection.

■ When you use the DataEnvironment designer as a data source for one or more bound controls, you can't rely on the automatic connection mechanism provided by the DataEnvironment. In fact, if the connection fails, no error is returned to the program: You'll just find no data in bound controls and won't be given a clue about what went wrong. If the Connection object's *RunPromptBehavior* property is set to adPromptNever (the preferred setting for most real-world applications), your users have no way to correct the problem. For this reason, you should always test to see whether the connection is open in the *Form_Load* event procedure, as in this code:

```
Private Sub Form_Load()
    If (DataEnv1.Connection1.State And adStateOpen) = 0 Then
        ' In a real application you'll do something smarter
        ' than just showing a message box.
        MsgBox "Unable to open the connection", vbCritical
    End If
End Sub
```

■ In general, you can't be sure that the data source path entered at design time will match your users' directory structures. So you must provide a means of configuring the application with the correct path—by reading it from a Registry or an INI file, for example—and then enforcing it before showing data coming from the database, as in the following code:

```
Private Sub Form_Load()
    If (DataEnv1.Connection1.State And adStateOpen) = 0 Then
        Dim conn As String
        conn = "Provider=Microsoft.Jet.OLEDB.3.51;"_
            & "Data Source=???"
        ' ReadDataBasePathFromINI is defined elsewhere.
        conn = Replace(conn, "???", ReadDataBasePathFromINI())
        DataEnv1.Connection1.ConnectionString = conn
        DataEnv1.Connection1.Open
    End If
End Sub
```

■ Under some circumstances, the DataEnvironment object opens more connections than it really needs. For example, if you have two or more instances of the same DataEnvironment designer, each instance opens a distinct connection. If you don't pay attention to this behavior, you might easily consume all the available connections, especially if you're working with SQL Server Developer Edition (which allows a lower number of connections than the "real" product).

■ While the DataEnvironment designer behaves like a class module in most regards, its implementation shows a few dangerous quirks. For example, I found that if you use the global DataEnvironment instance to implicitly open a Connection, that connection is *never* closed while the program is executing. More precisely, a trip to the SQL Server trace confirms that the connection is indeed closed, but this seems to happen after the program has already terminated its execution. It's a minor detail, but it implies that you can't rely on the Connection's *Disconnect* event to execute your cleanup code. Even more inexplicable is this: The global DataEnviroment instance doesn't even receive a *Terminate* event, as all objects do when the application terminates, so you can't count on this event to close the connection in an orderly way. This bug manifests itself both in the IDE and in compiled programs.

The bottom line is this: Don't blindly assume that the DataEnvironment designer will work as expected, and always test its behavior in "extreme" conditions, such as when connections aren't guaranteed or are scarce.

ADVANCED TECHNIQUES

Now that you're familiar with the basic techniques for data retrieval in ADO, let's tackle a few advanced topics, such as asynchronous operations and hierarchical Recordsets.

Recordset Events

If you've worked with RDO, you might believe that you need to cope with events only when you're performing asynchronous operations. The truth is that, while events play a pivotal role in asynchronous operations, they can be useful on many other occasions. In fact, ADO fires events whether or not the operation is asynchronous. I illustrate asynchronous queries and fetch operations in the next section, but here I want to introduce a few Recordset events that you might find useful when doing synchronous operations.

The Recordset object exposes 11 events, comprising 4 pairs of *Will/Complete* events plus the *FetchProgress*, *FetchComplete*, and *EndOfRecordset* events. The Visual Basic documentation isn't very helpful, and you can learn how events really work only by writing sample code or playing with the ADO Workbench program introduced in Chapter 13. I had to do both to discover a few undocumented (or insufficiently documented) bits of information about events. For example, I found that ADO sometimes fires more events than I expected, as I'll show in a moment. First, let's start with the basics.

ADO can fire the following pairs of *Will/Complete* Recordset's events:

■ A *WillChangeField/FieldChangeComplete* pair of events when you modify the value of a field using the Field object (but not when you're using an SQL command or stored procedure).

■ A *WillChangeRecord/RecordChangeComplete* pair of events when an operation modifies one or more records—for example, as a consequence of an *Update, UpdateBatch, AddNew,* or *Delete* method.

■ A *WillMove/MoveComplete* pair of events when another record becomes the current record. It can be caused by a *Movexxxx, Open, AddNew,* or *Requery* method, or an assignment to the *Bookmark* or *AbsolutePage* property.

■ A *WillChangeRecordset/RecordsetChangeComplete* pair of events when an operation affects the entire Recordset—for example, an *Open, Requery,* or *Resync* method.

While the syntax of these events differs, they have a lot in common. For example, all of them receive an *adStatus* parameter. On entry to a *Willxxxx* event, the *adStatus* parameter can be adStatusOK or adStatusCantDeny: In the former case, you can set it to adStatusCancel if you want to cancel the operation that causes the event. All xxxx*Complete* events receive the *adStatus* parameter and a *pError* parameter containing information about errors that have occurred.

Field validation

The ability to cancel the operation that caused the event is especially useful when you want to validate the value of a field: Instead of spreading the validation code all over the program, you just write it in the *WillChangeField* event. This event receives the number of fields in the *cFields* parameter and an array of Field objects in the *Fields* parameter. The following code example shows how you can use this event to validate values being stored in fields:

```
Private Sub rs_WillChangeField(ByVal cFields As Long,
    ByVal Fields As Variant, adStatus As ADODB.EventStatusEnum,
    ByVal pRecordset As ADODB.Recordset)
    Dim fld As ADODB.Field, i As Integer
    ' If we can't cancel this event, there's no point in
    ' validating fields.
    If adStatus = adStatusCantCancel Then Exit Sub
    ' Note that we can't use a For Each loop.
```

(continued)

```
    For i = 0 To UBound(Fields)
        Set fld = Fields(i)
        Select Case fld.Name
            Case "FirstName", "LastName"
                ' These fields can't be empty strings or Null.
                If (fld.Value & "") = "" Then adStatus = adStatusCancel
            Case "GrandTotal"
                ' This field must be positive.
                If fld.Value < 0 Then adStatus = adStatusCancel
            ' Add Case blocks for other fields here.
        End Select
    Next
End Sub
```

The *WillChangeField* event fires also if you're assigning the same value that is already contained in the field. You can probably save ADO some time—especially on networks with a narrow bandwidth—if you catch this case and cancel the operation. Just keep in mind that the main program should be ready to deal with the error &H80040E4E: "The change was canceled during notification; no columns are changed."

It would be great if you could trap incorrect values and fix them in the *WillChangeField* event procedure. Unfortunately, it seems impossible to *modify* the value of a field within this event: You can only accept or reject the value set by the main program. This event receives multiple fields when the main program has called an *Update* method with a list of fields' names and values. You don't really need the *cFields* parameter because you can use *UBound(Fields)+1* instead.

The *FieldChangeComplete* event has limited use, at least as far as field validation is concerned. You might use it to update values on screen if you aren't using bound controls. If you're using bound controls, you might want to use this event to update other (unbound) controls that contain calculated values. Be aware, however, that this event—and all the *xxxxComplete* events, for that matter—fires even if the corresponding operation was canceled by the program or because of an error raised by ADO. For this reason, you should always check the *adStatus* parameter first:

```
Private Sub rs_FieldChangeComplete(ByVal cFields As Long, _
    ByVal Fields As Variant, ByVal pError As ADODB.Error, _
    adStatus As ADODB.EventStatusEnum, ByVal pRecordset As ADODB.Recordset)
    If adStatus <> adStatusErrorsOccurred Then
        ' Update your unbound controls here.
    End If
End Sub
```

If you have absolutely no use for this event, you can (slightly) improve execution speed by asking ADO not to fire it again:

```
Private Sub rs_FieldChangeComplete(…)
    ' This event will be invoked only once.
```

```
        adStatus = adStatusUnwantedEvent
End Sub
```

Record validation

In general, individual field validation isn't sufficient to ensure that the database contains valid data. As a rule, you need to validate all fields just before the record is written to the database. This is the ideal job for the *WillChangeRecord* event.

On entry to this event, *adReason* holds a value that indicates why the record is being changed, and *cRecords* holds the number of affected records. (For a list of values that *adReason* can receive, see Table 13-4 in Chapter 13.) The first time you update a field in the current record, ADO fires a *WillChangeRecord* event (and its *RecordChangeComplete* companion event) with *adReason* set to adRsnFirstChange, to give you the opportunity to prepare for a record update (and possibly reject it). When the record is ready to be written to the database, ADO fires another *WillChangeRecord/RecordChangeComplete* pair of events, this time with a more specific value in *adReason*. You should take values in Table 13-4 with a grain of salt, however. For example, I noticed that even if the record is updated because of a *MoveNext* method, the *WillChangeRecord* event receives *adReason* equal to adRsnUpdate. This is the implicit *Update* method that ADO invokes for you when you change one or more fields and then move to another record.

Inside the *WillChangeRecord* event, you can't modify the value of the Recordset's fields, so you can't use this event to provide default values to fields, automatically fix invalid values, force to uppercase or lowercase, and so on. You can only test the fields' values and reject the update operation as a whole if you find some value incorrect or incomplete. Because of the extra event fired when the first field is being modified, you must always test the value of the *adReason* parameter:

```
Private Sub rs_WillChangeRecord(ByVal adReason As ADODB.EventReasonEnum, _
    ByVal cRecords As Long, adStatus As ADODB.EventStatusEnum, _
    ByVal pRecordset As ADODB.Recordset)
    If adReason <> adRsnFirstChange Then
        ' These two fields can't both be empty strings.
        If rs("CustAddress") = "" And rs("ShipAddress") = "" Then
            adStatus = adStatusCancel
        End If
    End If
End Sub
```

Displaying data with unbound controls

If your application displays data without using bound controls, you must write the code that retrieves data from the Recordset and shows it on screen as well as code that moves data from a control to the database. Typically, you use the *WillMove* event to move data from controls to the database and use the *MoveComplete* event to move data from the database to controls. Let's start with the latter event, the code for which is shown at the top of the next page.

```
' Assumes that the form contains two TextBox controls.
Private Sub rs_MoveComplete(ByVal adReason As ADODB.EventReasonEnum, _
    ByVal pError As ADODB.Error, adStatus As ADODB.EventStatusEnum, _
    ByVal pRecordset As ADODB.Recordset)
    ' Move data from the Recordset to on-screen controls.
    txtFirstName.Text = rs("FirstName")
    txtLastName.Text = rs("LastName")
    ' Clear the controls' "modified" flag.
    txtFirstName.DataChanged = False
    txtLastName.DataChanged = False
End Sub
```

As you see in the preceding code snippet, you can use the *DataChanged* property even in unbound controls. In fact, this property is perfectly functional with regular controls in that Visual Basic automatically sets it to True when the contents of the control changes. The only substantial difference is in how the *DataChanged* property is reset: When you're using bound controls, Visual Basic resets this property to False automatically, but when you're using unbound controls you must do that manually. You can then test the value of the *DataChanged* property in the *WillMove* event to understand whether you really need to move values from the on-screen controls to the database:

```
Private Sub rs_WillMove(ByVal adReason As ADODB.EventReasonEnum, _
    adStatus As ADODB.EventStatusEnum, ByVal pRecordset As ADODB.Recordset)
    ' Move data to Recordset only if user modified the controls' contents.
    If txtFirstName.DataChanged Then rs("FirstName") = txtFirstName.Text
    If txtLastName.DataChanged Then rs("LastName") = txtLastName.Text
End Sub
```

In a more robust implementation of this concept, you should test the *adReason* parameter and react accordingly. For example, you can decide whether you should save values to the database when the Recordset is being closed. Or you can load default values in controls when the *MoveComplete* event has fired because of an *AddNew* method. Unlike *WillChangeField* and *WillChangeRecord* events, the *WillMove* event does permit you to assign values to the Recordset's fields, so you can use this event to provide default values or calculated fields:

```
' In the WillMove event
If txtCountry.Text = "" Then rs("country") = "USA"
```

Dealing with multiple events

One single operation on the Recordset fires a lot of (nested) events. For example, the following table shows which events fire because of a simple sequence of methods:

Method	*Events*
rs.Open	WillExecute
	WillMove (adReason = adRsnMove)
	MoveComplete (adReason = adRsnMove)
	ExecuteComplete
rs("FirstName") = "John"	WillChangeRecordset (adReason = adRsnMove)
	RecordsetChangeComplete (adReason = adRsnMove)
	WillMove (adReason = adRsnMove)
	MoveComplete (adReason = adRsnMove)
	WillChangeRecord (adReason = adRsnFirstChange)
	WillChangeField
	FieldChangeComplete
	RecordChangeComplete (adReason = adRsnFirstChange)
rs("LastName") = "Smith"	WillChangeField
	ChangeFieldComplete
rs.MoveNext	WillMove (adReason = adRsnMoveNext)
	WillChangeRecord (adReason = adRsnUpdate)
	RecordChangeComplete (adReason = adRsnUpdate)
	WillChangeRecordset (adReason = adRsnMove)
	RecordsetChangeComplete (adReason = adRsnMove)
	MoveComplete (adReason = adRsnMoveNext)

For the most part, the preceding sequence is clear and reasonable. It offers, however, a few surprises. For example, the *MoveNext* method fires a *WillChange-Recordset/RecordsetChangeComplete* pair of events. This shouldn't happen, according to the Visual Basic documentation. There's some evidence that this extra pair of events has to do with ADO filling the local cache. In fact, if you set *CacheSize* to a value greater than 1—say 4—these events are fired every four *MoveNext* operations. In other words, each time ADO refills the local cache it rebuilds the Recordset object. Store this information somewhere in your long-term memory—someday it might prove useful.

Other events can't be explained so easily. For example, why does the assignment to the *FirstName* field fire an extra *WillMove/MoveComplete* pair of events? After all, the first record is already the current record, isn't it? Honestly, I can't answer this one. Just pay attention to what code you write inside *WillMove* and *MoveComplete* events because it might execute more often than you expect.

See what happens to the previous sequence if you cancel one event. For example, if you set *adStatus* to adStatusCancel in the *WillMove* event that immediately follows the *MoveNext* method, all the other events are suppressed and ADO fires only the matching *MoveComplete* event. On the other hand, if you cancel the command in the *WillChangeRecord* event, ADO suppresses only the *WillChangeRecordset/RecordsetChangeComplete* pair of events. In general, after you set *adStatus* to adStatusCancel, this value goes unmodified through all the subsequent events, until the error is returned to the main program.

Asynchronous Operations

ADO offers several types of asynchronous operations, all of which help to make your application more responsive to the user. I already showed that you can set up an asynchronous connection, so it's time to see how you can execute a lengthy command without having your code wait until ADO completes it.

Asynchronous commands

The simplest form of asynchronous operation is a command performed through the Connection object. In this case, all you have to do is pass the adAsyncExecute value to the *Options* argument of the Connection's *Execute* method, as in the following example:

```
Dim cn As New ADODB.Connection, recs As Long
cn.Open "Provider=Microsoft.Jet.OLEDB.4.0;" _
    & "Data Source=E:\Microsoft Visual Studio\VB98\Biblio.mdb"
cn.Execute "DELETE FROM Publishers WHERE State = 'WA'", _
    recs, adAsyncExecute
Debug.Print recs & " records affected"         ' Displays -1.
```

When you run a command in this way, ADO fires a *WillExecute* event before returning the control to the statement that follows the *Execute* statement. Because the command hasn't completed yet, the *recs* variable receives the special value −1. This is the syntax of the *WillExecute* event:

```
Private Sub cn_WillExecute(Source As String, _
    CursorType As ADODB.CursorTypeEnum, LockType As ADODB.LockTypeEnum, _
    Options As Long, adStatus As ADODB.EventStatusEnum, _
    ByVal pCommand As ADODB.Command, ByVal pRecordset As ADODB.Recordset, _
    ByVal pConnection As ADODB.Connection)
    MsgBox "About to execute command " & Source
End Sub
```

Because all arguments are passed by reference, you can modify them if it makes sense to do so. You can also cancel the command, by setting the *adStatus* parameter to the value adStatusCancel, unless it's already set to the value adStatusCantDeny:

```
' Put this code inside the WillExecute event.
If adStatus <> adStatusCantDeny Then
    If MsgBox("About to execute statement " & Source & vbCr & "Confirm?", _
        vbYesNo + vbInformation) = vbNo Then
        adStatus = adStatusCancel
    End If
End If
```

When the ADO completes the command, an *ExecuteComplete* event fires, with the actual number of affected records in its first parameter:

```
Private Sub cn_ExecuteComplete(ByVal RecordsAffected As Long, _
    ByVal pError As ADODB.Error, adStatus As ADODB.EventStatusEnum, _
    ByVal pCommand As ADODB.Command, ByVal pRecordset As ADODB.Recordset, _
    ByVal pConnection As ADODB.Connection)
    If adStatus = adStatusOK Then
        MsgBox "Execution of the command has been completed" & vbCr _
            & RecordsAffected & " record(s) were affected", vbInformation
    ElseIf adStatus = adStatusErrorsOccurred Then
        MsgBox "Execution error: " & pError.Description, vbCritical
    End If
End Sub
```

In the *WillExecute* event, you can determine whether you're executing a row-returning command by checking the value in *CursorType* or *LockType*: If either contains −1, this is an action command. When the *ExecuteComplete* event fires because of a Recordset's *Open* statement, you find a reference to the Recordset object in *pRecordset*, which isn't very exciting because you already have a reference to the Recordset being opened. The *pRecordset* parameter is more useful when you complete a row-returning *Execute* command of a Connection's object because it contains the results of the query. So, for instance, you can assign it to an ADO Data control or process it in any way you prefer.

As you would expect, the *pCommand* parameter in the *WillExecute* event contains a reference to a Command object if the event has been fired because of a Command's *Execute* method; otherwise, the parameter contains Nothing. Interestingly, even if you aren't using a Command object, ADO manufactures a temporary Command object to perform the query and passes a reference to this temporary object in the *pCommand* parameter of the *ExecuteComplete* event. This temporary object lets you retrieve information such as the *Source* string, which isn't otherwise available after the query has completed:

```
' In the ExecuteComplete event
' The next statement works with *any* type of command or query.
Debug.Print "Statement " & pCommand.CommandText & " has been completed"
```

A more interesting (and advanced) use for this capability is repeating a command or a query that failed, for example, because of a timeout. In a situation like this, you simply run the Command object's *Execute* method and pay some attention to reentrancy problems.

> **TIP**   While the database is executing the command, your application can continue its execution as usual. If you need to know whether the operation has completed, you might set a global flag from the *ExecuteComplete* event or, more simply, test the Connection's *State* property. Because this property is a bit field, you should use the AND operator, as in the following line of code:
>
> ```
> If cn.State And adStateExecuting Then...
> ```
>
> When you're working with SQL Server databases, you should be aware that you can generally execute multiple asynchronous commands only if there's no pending transaction and the active command is an action query or is a recordset-returning query that creates a client-side cursor. If these conditions are met, SQL Server silently creates a new connection to serve the new command; otherwise, an error occurs.

Asynchronous fetches

ADO gives you an additional degree of control over asynchronous queries with the adAsyncFetch value. You can pass this value to a Connection's *Execute* method and to a Recordset's *Open* or *Requery* methods. While the adAsyncExecute value tells ADO that the query should be performed asynchronously, the adAsyncFetch value informs ADO that it should fetch data from the data source to the Recordset in asynchronous mode. Accordingly, ADO executes the query and immediately fills the local cache with the first group of result records and then fetches all remaining records asynchronously.

If the fetch operation takes some time, ADO fires a *FetchProgress* event, which you can use to display a progress bar to your end users. When the fetch is complete, ADO fires a *FetchComplete* event. For more information about the adAsyncFetch and adAsychFetchNonBlocking options, see the description of the Command's *Execute* method in Chapter 13.

Stored Procedures

Client/server applications based on SQL Server or Oracle implement much of their functionality using *stored procedures*. A stored procedure is a procedure written in the SQL dialect of the hosting database and is compiled to improve execution speed. Stored procedures let the developer enforce better security while improving performance, just to mention a couple of outstanding advantages. As you'll see in a moment, both ADO and Visual Basic 6 Enterprise Edition have a lot to offer when you're working with stored procedures.

The SQL Editor and the T-SQL Debugger

If you open the DataView window and select a data link to an SQL Server or Oracle database, you'll find a subfolder named Stored Procedures, inside of which is the list of all the stored procedures available for that database. You can open the node corresponding to a stored procedure to see its return value and arguments (if any), and you can double-click on an argument node to see its properties. The property window of a parameter displays the ADO data type for that parameter, which is vital information when you have to create the Parameters collection of the Command object that runs this stored procedure.

Double-click on the name of a stored procedure to bring up the SQL Editor, which lets you edit a stored procedure without leaving the Visual Basic IDE. You can use this editor to create triggers as well. Curiously, there's a minor bug in this feature's implementation: When you display the SQL Editor, the Data View window's font is changed to match the font in the editor, as you can see in Figure 14-3 on the following page. It's a rather harmless bug, and I even found a use for it: When I'm teaching a class and someone complains that the DataView window is hardly readable, I bring up the Stored Procedure Editor and immediately close it, just to switch to a larger font.

As if the integrated editor weren't enough, if you're working with SQL Server (but not with Oracle) you can debug your stored procedures right in the Visual Basic environment. This works even with remote servers and uses OLE Remote Automation to physically connect to the database. You can also use the T-SQL Debugger add-in to execute system or batch stored procedures. The T-SQL Debugger lets you set breakpoints, step in and out of nested procedures, watch local and global variables, display the call stack, and so on. When you're developing a complex application, this feature alone can save you dozens of hours.

Setting up the TSQL Debugger isn't intuitive, so here are a few tips that should prove useful. First, the debugger works only with SQL Server 6.5 Service Pack 3 or later. (Visual Basic 6 comes with SQL Server 6.5 Service Pack 4.) Second, you must tick the SQL Server Debugging option when you're installing BackOffice immediately after you've installed Visual Basic 6 Enterprise Edition. Third, the SQL Server service should be configured to log in as a user with sufficient permissions; logging in as a Windows NT system account won't work. Finally, ensure that OLE Remote Automation is working and correctly configured on your machine.

You can invoke the editor from the SQL Editor or from the Add-Ins menu if you have installed and activated the T-SQL Debugger add-in. In the latter instance, you have to specify a DSN and the database you're logging in to, as shown in Figure 14-4 on the following page, but you can also debug batch stored procedures. If you want to debug stored procedures and triggers when they're invoked by your code, select the T-SQL Debugging Options command in the Tools menu and tick the Automatically Step Into Stored Procedures Through RDO And ADO Connections option. (See Figure 14-5 on page 743.)

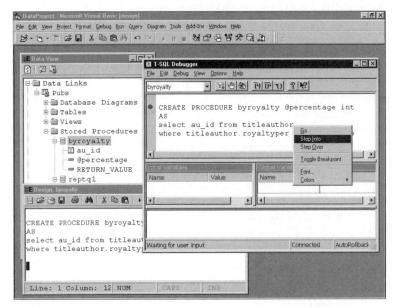

Figure 14-3. *Visual Basic 6 Enterprise Edition lets you edit SQL Server stored procedures and even debug them.*

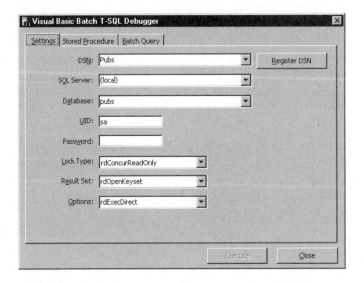

Figure 14-4. *The T-SQL Debugger add-in.*

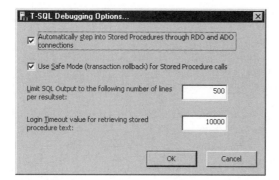

Figure 14-5. *The T-SQL Debugger Options dialog box. Notice that the timeout value is in milliseconds.*

Parameterized stored procedures

I've already shown you how you can use ADO Command objects to run parameterized SQL queries and how you can build their Parameters collection or let ADO build them for you. Working with parameterized stored procedures isn't much different, provided that you're alert to some quirks.

You can let ADO automatically build the Command's Parameters collection. You do this by simply referencing the Parameters collection in code or by issuing an explicit Parameters.Refresh command. This solution has many benefits, including fewer errors in your code because ADO correctly retrieves the names and the types of all the parameters and automatically accounts for the return value by creating a Parameter object whose name is RETURN_VALUE. A particular advantage of this solution is that if you later modify the type of a parameter, you don't have to change your Visual Basic code. Unfortunately, ADO needs a trip to the server to retrieve information about the stored procedure. This extra command is performed only the first time you reference the Parameters collection, however, so in most cases this overhead is negligible as long as you keep the Command object alive for the entire session. A potential problem is that ADO might be confounded by output parameters and mistakenly believe that they're input/output parameters. If this happens, you can simply set the parameter's *Direction* property to a correct value. Conveniently, this property is read/write even after the parameter has been added to the collection.

If you want to save ADO a trip to the server, you can build the Parameters collection yourself. The following code example invokes the *byroyalty* stored procedure that comes with the sample SQL Server Pubs database:

```
Dim cn As New ADODB.Connection, cmd As New ADODB.Command
Dim rs As ADODB.Recordset
' Establish the connection.
cn.Open "Provider=sqloledb;Data source=p2;user id=sa;initial catalog=pubs"
```

(continued)

```
Set cmd.ActiveConnection = cn
' Define the stored procedure.
cmd.CommandText = "byroyalty"
cmd.CommandType = adCmdStoredProc
' Save ADO some work by creating the parameter yourself.
cmd.Parameters.Append cmd.CreateParameter("@percentage", adInteger, _
    adParamInput)
' Set a value to this parameter, and execute the query.
cmd.Parameters("@percentage") = 100
Set rs = cmd.Execute()
```

When you're manually building the Parameters collection, you must pay attention to an important detail: If the stored procedure returns a value, it must be the first parameter. To see how you can work with return values and output parameters, double-click on the *byroyalty* stored procedure in the DataView window to bring up the SQL Editor and modify the text of the procedure as follows. (Added or modified code is in boldface.)

```
CREATE PROCEDURE byroyalty2 @percentage int, @totalrecs Int Output
AS
select @totalrecs= count(*) from titleauthor
select au_id from titleauthor
where titleauthor.royaltyper = @percentage
return (@@rowcount)
```

Here's the Visual Basic code that prepares the Parameters collection, runs the query, and prints the results:

```
cmd.CommandText = "byroyalty2"
cmd.CommandType = adCmdStoredProc
' Create the Parameters collection
With cmd.Parameters
    .Append cmd.CreateParameter("RETVAL", adInteger, adParamReturnValue)
    .Append cmd.CreateParameter("@percentage", adInteger, adParamInput)
    .Append cmd.CreateParameter("@totalrecs", adInteger, adParamOutput)
End With
' Set a value for input parameters, and run the stored procedure.
cmd.Parameters("@percentage") = 100
Set rs = cmd.Execute()
' Dump the contents of the recordset.
Do Until rs.EOF
    Print "Au_ID=" & rs("au_id")
    rs.MoveNext
Loop
rs.Close
' Print the values of the output parameter and the return value.
Print "Records in titleauthor = " & cmd.Parameters("@totalrecs")
Print "Records returned by the query = " & cmd.Parameters("RETVAL")
```

Here are a couple of points worth noting. First, you can use any name for the return value parameter as long as it's the first item in the collection. Second, and most important, you must close the Recordset (or set it to Nothing to have it closed by ADO) before accessing return values and output parameters. This holds true for forward-only, read-only Recordsets returned by SQL Server and can possibly apply to other cursor types and providers. According to official documentation, ADO reads output parameters and the return value only once from the provider, so if you try to read them before they're available you won't have a second chance.

Multiple result sets

The next great feature of ADO is its ability to work with multiple result sets. In Chapter 13, I explained how you can use the *NextRecordset* method, but here I'll show you practical examples. This is the Visual Basic code that you can use to explore multiple result sets:

```
' This code assumes that all properties have been correctly initialized.
Set rs = cmd.Execute()
Do Until rs Is Nothing
    If rs.State = adStateClosed Then
        Print "---- Closed Recordset"
    Else
        Do Until rs.EOF
            For Each fld In rs.Fields
                Print fld.Name & "="; fld & ", ";
            Next
            Print
            rs.MoveNext
        Loop
        Print "---- End of Recordset"
    End If
    Set rs = rs.NextRecordset
Loop
```

To see how SQL Server and ADO deal with a stored procedure, right-click on the Stored Procedures folder in the DataView window, select the New Stored Procedure menu command, and then enter the following code in the SQL Editor:

```
Create Procedure PubsByCountry As
Select pub_name From Publishers where country='USA'
Select pub_name From Publishers where country='France'
Select pub_name From Publishers where country='Germany'
Select pub_name From Publishers where country='Italy'
```

When you run the *PubsByCountry* stored procedure using the Visual Basic code that I showed you previously, you get the result shown on the following page.

```
pub_name=New Moon Books
pub_name=Binnet & Hardley
pub_name=Algodata Infosystems
pub_name=Five Lakes Publishing
pub_name=Ramona Publishers
pub_name=Scootney Books
---- End of Recordset
pub_name=Lucerne Publishing
---- End of Recordset
pub_name=GGG&G
---- End of Recordset
---- End of Recordset
```

The last SELECT statement returns a Recordset object that doesn't contain any records. If you then execute the *NextRecordset* method one more time, you get Nothing and the loop exits. Let's see another example of a query that returns multiple Recordsets. This is the source code of the *reptq1* stored procedure that comes with the Pubs sample database:

```
CREATE PROCEDURE reptq1 AS
select pub_id, title_id, price, pubdate from titles
where price is NOT NULL order by pub_id
COMPUTE avg(price) BY pub_id
COMPUTE avg(price)
```

This is the output that the previous routine produces when you execute the *reptq1* stored procedure. As you see, the first *COMPUTE* statement generates a separate Recordset for each publisher, whereas the second *COMPUTE* statement generates a final Recordset with the average price for all the publishers:

```
pub_id=0736, title_id=BU2075, price=2.99, pubdate=6/30/91,
pub_id=0736, title_id=PS2091, price=10.95, pubdate=6/15/91,
pub_id=0736, title_id=PS2106, price=7, pubdate=10/5/91,
pub_id=0736, title_id=PS3333, price=19.99, pubdate=6/12/91,
pub_id=0736, title_id=PS7777, price=7.99, pubdate=6/12/91,
---- End of Recordset
avg=9.784,
---- End of Recordset
pub_id=0877, title_id=MC2222, price=19.99, pubdate=6/9/91,
pub_id=0877, title_id=MC3021, price=2.99, pubdate=6/18/91,
pub_id=0877, title_id=PS1372, price=21.59, pubdate=10/21/91,
pub_id=0877, title_id=TC3218, price=20.95, pubdate=10/21/91,
pub_id=0877, title_id=TC4203, price=11.95, pubdate=6/12/91,
pub_id=0877, title_id=TC7777, price=14.99, pubdate=6/12/91,
---- End of Recordset
avg=15.41,
---- End of Recordset
pub_id=1389, title_id=BU1032, price=19.99, pubdate=6/12/91,
```

```
pub_id=1389, title_id=BU1111, price=11.95, pubdate=6/9/91,
pub_id=1389, title_id=BU7832, price=19.99, pubdate=6/22/91,
pub_id=1389, title_id=PC1035, price=22.95, pubdate=6/30/91,
pub_id=1389, title_id=PC8888, price=20, pubdate=6/12/94,
---- End of Recordset
avg=18.976,
---- End of Recordset
avg=14.7662,
---- End of Recordset
```

In theory, you might retrieve multiple result sets and assign them to different Recordset variables, or at least the syntax of the *NextRecordset* method seems to make it possible. Unfortunately, as of this writing no OLE DB provider supports this capability, so you're forced to retrieve and process one Recordset at a time. Or you can use the *Clone* method (if the Recordset is capable of being cloned) to retrieve all Recordsets, assign them to items of an array, and process them later:

```
Dim cn As New ADODB.Connection, rs As ADODB.Recordset
' We can reasonably assume that 100 Recordset items will suffice.
Dim recs(100) As ADODB.Recordset, recCount As Integer
' Open the connection, and retrieve the first Recordset.
cn.Open "Provider=sqloledb;Data source=p2;user id=sa;" _
    & "initial catalog=pubs"
Set rs = New ADODB.Recordset
rs.Open "PubsByCountry", cn
' Retrieve all Recordsets, and clone them.
Do
    recCount = recCount + 1
    Set recs(recCount) = rs.Clone
    Set rs = rs.NextRecordset
Loop Until rs Is Nothing
' Now the recs() array contains one clone for each Recordset.
```

Unfortunately, it seems impossible to use this technique to update fields in the database: Any attempt to send data back to SQL Server through the Recordsets now stored in the *recs()* array raises an error &H80004005, "Insufficient base table information for updating or refreshing." You can't even disconnect the Recordset and close the connection because all the Recordsets in the array are immediately closed, even if the original Recordset was configured to use optimistic batch updates. In short, you can store cloned Recordsets in an array, but in practice this is only useful when you want to process their contents at the same time (for example, when you want to compare the records in them). Here are a few additional tips concerning multiple result sets:

■ Multiple statements that aren't row-returning commands generate closed Recordsets. You should test for this using the *State* property.

■ All the queries following the first one are executed when you invoke the
   NextRecordset method; if you close the Recordset before retrieving all the
   pending result sets, the corresponding queries will never execute.

■ If you specify the adAsyncFetch option, only the first Recordset is retrieved
   asynchronously; all the subsequent ones are fetched synchronously.

■ All the Recordsets created by the NextRecordset command use the same
   cursor type and location as the original one. Most of the time, you'll need
   a client-side cursor to process multiple SQL statements or server-side
   cursorless Recordsets.

■ Don't use an auto-instancing variable for the Recordset object; if you do,
   the *Is Nothing* test will never be successful.

Hierarchical Recordsets

If I were asked to choose the feature of ADO that has impressed me most, I would
undoubtedly pick the ability to create hierarchical Recordset objects. Hierarchical
Recordsets can contain child Recordset objects, much like a folder can contain other
folders. For example, you can create a Recordset from the Publishers table, where
each record contains data about an individual publisher plus a child Recordset that
contains the list of titles published by that company. Each record in this child Recordset
can contain information about each title, plus another child Recordset that contains
data about that book's authors, and so on. You can nest hierarchical Recordset objects without any limit—theoretically, anyway—to the number of nesting levels. Creating hierarchical Recordsets is also known as *data shaping*.

You can build hierarchical Recordsets in two distinct ways. The easiest method
is to interactively build a Command object at design time using the DataEnvironment
designer, as I showed you in Chapter 8. The more difficult technique—which is also
the more flexible one—is to create the hierarchical Recordset through code at run time.

The MSDataShape provider

The first thing to do when creating a hierarchical Recordset is to select the right provider. You need a specific provider designed for doing data shaping. This provider
will in turn connect to the OLE DB provider that actually accesses the data source.
Currently, the only provider that offers data shaping capabilities is the MSDataShape
provider, but in theory any vendor might create another provider of this type in the
future. When you're working with the MSDataShape provider, you specify the actual
data source using the *Data Provider* argument in the connection string:

```
Dim cn As New ADODB.Connection
cn.Open "Provider=MSDataShape.1;Data Provider=Microsoft.Jet.OLEDB.4.0;" _
    & "Data Source= " & DBPATH
```

The SHAPE APPEND command

The MSDataShape provider supports two commands, the SHAPE APPEND keyword and the SHAPE COMPUTE keyword. The SHAPE APPEND keyword lets you create the relationship between two SQL commands that return records. Its syntax is the following:

```
SHAPE {parent_command} [[AS] table-alias]
APPEND {child_command} [[AS] table-alias]
RELATE(parent_column TO child_column) [[AS] table-alias]
```

where *parent_command* is the SQL command that returns the main Recordset, and *child_command* is the SQL command that returns the child Recordset. The two commands must have one column in common (although the column can have a different name in each table), and you specify that name or names in the RELATE clause. The following is a simple SHAPE APPEND command, which returns a hierarchical Recordset containing all Publishers and a child Recordset that lists all the titles by the current publisher:

```
Dim cn As New ADODB.Connection, rs As New ADODB.Recordset
cn.Open "Provider=MSDataShape.1;Data Provider=Microsoft.Jet.OLEDB.4.0;" _
    & "Data Source=C:\Microsoft Visual Studio\vb98\biblio.mdb"
Set rs.ActiveConnection = cn
rs.Open "SHAPE {SELECT * FROM Publishers} " _
    & "APPEND ({SELECT * FROM Titles} " _
    & "RELATE PubID TO PubID) AS Titles"
```

The name used in the AS clause after the RELATE clause becomes the name of the field that contains the child Recordset. To display the contents of a hierarchical Recordset, you can assign it to the *DataSource* property of a Hierarchical FlexGrid control, as in this line of code:

```
Set MSHFlexGrid1.DataSource = rs
```

You can nest multiple SHAPE APPEND commands to set a relationship between multiple pairs of commands. For example, the following code snippet is the command that builds a three-level hierarchical Recordset to contain all the authors in Biblio.mdb. Each record contains a field named *Title_Author*, which contains a child Recordset with one record for each title written by that author. In turn, this Recordset has a child Recordset containing one single record: the record from the Titles table that corresponds to a particular title. I have indented the SHAPE APPEND commands to make their relationship as clear as possible:

```
SHAPE {SELECT * FROM Authors} AS [Authors With Titles]
APPEND
    (( SHAPE {SELECT * FROM [Title Author]}
    APPEND ({SELECT * FROM Titles}
    RELATE ISBN TO ISBN) AS Titles1)
RELATE Au_ID TO Au_ID) AS Title_Author
```

The name after the first AS clause—*Authors With Titles,* in this example—is the name of the hierarchical command created, and usually it can be omitted when you pass the string to the *Open* method of a Recordset object or to the *CommandText* property of a Command object. The fields listed in the RELATE clause can have different names as long as they refer to the same information. If you don't provide a name after the parenthesis that closes the RELATE clause, the default field name *chapter* is used.

A hierarchical Recordset can have more than one child Recordset. For example, the following SHAPE APPEND command is similar to the previous one but adds another child Recordset that lists all the authors that are born in the same year as the author pointed to by the parent Recordset. Notice that the APPEND keyword isn't repeated and subsequent child commands at the same nesting level are separated by a comma:

```
SHAPE {SELECT * FROM Authors}
APPEND (( SHAPE {SELECT * FROM [Title Author]}
    APPEND ({SELECT * FROM Titles}
    RELATE ISBN TO ISBN) AS Titles1) AS Title_Author
RELATE Au_ID TO Au_ID) AS Title_Author,
({SELECT * FROM Authors}
RELATE [Year Born] TO [Year Born]) AS AuthorsBornSameYear
```

The SHAPE COMPUTE command

While the SHAPE APPEND command creates a child Recordset starting from the parent (main) Recordset, the SHAPE COMPUTE command works the other way around: It executes an aggregate function on the rows of a Recordset to create a parent Recordset. For example, you can start with a Recordset that contains the records in the Titles table and build a parent Recordset where the titles are grouped by their Year Published field. In this instance, the parent Recordset has two fields: the first is Year Published, and the second is a Recordset that contains all the titles published in that year. The syntax of the SHAPE COMPUTE command is as follows:

```
SHAPE {child_command} [[AS] table_alias]
COMPUTE aggregate_command_field_list
[BY grp_field_list]
```

where *child_command* is the Recordset you start with and typically is a SELECT statement that returns a group of records; *table_alias* is the name of the field in the parent Recordset that will contain the child Recordset; *aggregate_command_field_list* is the list of fields on which the aggregate function operates; and *grp_field_list* is the list of fields the child Recordset is grouped by.

In the simplest situation, you group records in the child Recordset according to the value of one field. For example, you can group Titles by the Year Published field using this command:

```
' You can enclose field and table names within
' single quotes or square brackets.
rs.Open "SHAPE {SELECT * FROM Titles} AS Titles " _
    & "COMPUTE Titles BY 'Year Published'"
```

The name following the COMPUTE keyword must coincide with the alias name assigned to the child Recordset. You can group by multiple fields, using the comma as a separator after the BY keyword:

```
' Group titles by publishers and year of publication.
rs.Open "SHAPE {SELECT * FROM Titles} AS Titles " _
    & "COMPUTE Titles BY PubID, 'Year Published'"
```

The COMPUTE command can be followed by a list of fields or functions among those listed in Table 14-1. Typically you append an AS clause to indicate the name of the aggregate field in the parent Recordset:

```
' Group titles by publishers, and add a field named TitlesCount that
' holds the number of titles by each publisher.
rs.Open "SHAPE {SELECT * FROM Titles} AS Titles " _
    & "COMPUTE Titles, COUNT(Titles.Title) AS TitlesCount BY PubID"
```

Function Syntax	Action/Returned Value
COUNT(alias[.fieldname])	The number of rows in the child Recordset
SUM(alias.fieldname)	The sum of all values in the specified field
MIN(alias.fieldname)	The minimum value in the specified field
MAX(alias.fieldname)	The maximum value in the specified field
AVG(alias.fieldname)	The average of all values in the specified field
STDEV(alias.fieldname)	The standard deviation of all the values in the specified field
ANY(alias.fieldname)	The value of a column (where the value of the column is the same for all rows in the child Recordset)
CALC(expression)	The result of an expression that uses values from the current row only
NEW(fieldtype, [width | scale [, precision])]	Adds an empty column of the specified type to the Recordset

Table 14-1. *Functions supported by SHAPE COMPUTE.* Alias *is the name of the child Recordset as it appears in the command.*

You can use the CALC function to evaluate an arbitrary expression that contains fields from the current row in the parent Recordset. For example, you can group titles by publisher and also add three fields with the year a publisher began to publish books, the year it published its most recent book, and the difference between these values:

```
rs.Open " SHAPE {SELECT * FROM Titles} AS Titles2 " _
    & "COMPUTE Titles2, MIN(Titles2.[Year Published]) AS YearMin, " _
    & "MAX(Titles2.[Year Published]) AS YearMax, " _
    & "CALC(YearMax - YearMin) AS YearDiff BY PubID"
```

Using hierarchical Recordset objects

Hierarchical Recordsets can be browsed in much the same way as regular Recordsets. The only difference is in the way you deal with Field objects that contain child Recordsets. To retrieve data in those Recordsets, you must first assign the Field's *Value* property to a Recordset variable, as the following code demonstrates:

```
Dim cn As New ADODB.Connection, rs As New ADODB.Recordset
Dim rsTitles As ADODB.Recordset
cn.Open "Provider=MSDataShape.1;Data Provider=Microsoft.Jet.OLEDB.4.0;" _
    & "Data Source=" & DBPATH
Set rs.ActiveConnection = cn
rs.Open "SHAPE {SELECT * FROM Titles} AS Titles " _
    & "COMPUTE Titles, COUNT(Titles.Title) AS TitlesCount BY PubID"
' Have the rsTitles variable always point to the child Recordset.
' (The StayInSync property's default value is True.)
Set rsTitles = rs("Titles").Value

' Browse the parent Recordset.
Do Until rs.EOF
    ' Show information in summary fields.
    Debug.Print "PubID=" & rs("PubID")
    Debug.Print "TitlesCount=" & rs("TitlesCount")
    ' For each row in the parent, browse the child recordset.
    Do Until rsTitles.EOF
        Debug.Print "   " & rsTitles("Title")
        rsTitles.MoveNext
    Loop
    rs.MoveNext
Loop
```

If the parent Recordset is updatable, you can use standard ADO commands to update values in the child Recordset as well. You can distinguish Fields that contain a child Recordset from regular Fields because their *Type* property returns the value 136-adChapter.

The parent Recordset's *StayInSync* property affects how object variables pointing to child Recordsets are updated when the record pointer in the main Recordset moves to another record. The default value for this property is True, which means that once you have assigned the Field object to a Recordset variable (*rsTitle*, in the previous code example), this variable correctly points to child records even when the parent Recordset moves to another row. This setting simplifies the navigation in the hierarchical Recordset and slightly optimizes execution speed because you don't have to reexecute the Set command after each Move*xxxx* command. Under certain circumstances, you might want to set *StayInSync* to False, which detaches the object variable from the parent Recordset.

The real advantage in building hierarchical Recordsets in code instead of using DataEnvironment's Command objects defined at design time is the greater flexibility you have when building complex SHAPE commands. For example, you can add WHERE clauses in the nested SELECT commands, as in the following snippet:

```
Dim cn As New ADODB.Connection, rs As New ADODB.Recordset,
Dim cmd As New ADODB.Command, source As String
cn.Open "Provider=MSDataShape.1;Data Provider=Microsoft.Jet.OLEDB.4.0;" _
    & "Data Source=C:\Microsoft Visual Studio\Vb98\biblio.mdb"
source = "SHAPE {SELECT * FROM Titles WHERE [Year Published] = 1990} " _
    & "AS Titles COMPUTE Titles BY PubID"
Set cmd.ActiveConnection = cn
cmd.CommandText = source
Set rs = cmd.Execute()
```

I didn't manage to have the Command object work with ? parameters embedded in SHAPE commands, so it seems that you have to forgo parameterized queries when you're working with the MSDataShape provider. This isn't as bad as it might sound at first, though, because hierarchical Recordsets are inherently client-side and are never compiled on the server. You can create pseudoparameterized SHAPE commands using placeholders and the *ReplaceParams* routine I introduced earlier in this chapter:

```
source = "SHAPE {SELECT * FROM Titles WHERE [Year Published] = @1} " _
    & "AS Titles COMPUTE Titles BY PubID"
cmd.CommandText = ReplaceParams(source, "1990")
Set rs = cmd.Execute()
```

You can also decide at run time the names of chapter fields and the expression in the WHERE condition, which is impossible when using design-time DataEnvironment objects.

Parameterized commands

When you use hierarchical Recordsets, ADO downloads all the data from the main table and the child table and builds the relationship on the client workstation. Needless to say, when you're working with large tables—as all real applications do—this adds considerable overhead, both in terms of network traffic and resources on the client workstation. You can reduce this overhead by using the special parameterized syntax shown on the following page for the *Source* property or argument of a hierarchical Recordset.

```
Dim cn As New ADODB.Connection, rs As New ADODB.Recordset
cn.Open "Provider=MSDataShape.1;Data Provider=sqloledb.1;" _
    & "Data Source=p2;user id=sa;initial catalog=pubs"
Set rs.ActiveConnection = cn
rs.Open "SHAPE {SELECT * FROM Publishers} " _
    & "APPEND ({SELECT * FROM Titles WHERE pub_id = ?} " _
    & "RELATE pub_id TO PARAMETER 0) AS Titles"
```

When you use this syntax, ADO doesn't download the entire Titles table. Instead, it downloads only the Publisher table (unless you add a suitable WHERE clause to the first SELECT, of course). Then it uses the value of the Pub_Id key field to retrieve only the items in Titles that correspond to that value. Each time you move to another record in Publisher, ADO issues another SELECT against the Titles table, so only a fraction of this table is downloaded each time.

This technique is extremely efficient also because ADO automatically builds a temporary stored procedure on the server to retrieve chunks of the child table. But the *overall* execution time is higher than with the standard technique because of the multiple queries, so there's no point in using these parameterized commands when you're going to assign the result Recordset to a Hierarchical FlexGrid control. The parameterized command might be more convenient, though, because ADO optimizes the access to the child Recordset and retrieves its records only if the application actually references one of its properties and events, as the following code demonstrates:

```
' Continuing the previous code example...
' Print the number of titles for US publishers. (This is just an example:
' in a real program you should add a WHERE clause to the Open method.)
Dim rs2 As ADODB.Recordset
Set rs2 = rs("titles").Value      ' Make the assignment just once.
Do Until rs.EOF
    If rs("country") = "USA" Then
        ' The next statement actually retrieves the records from Titles.
        Print rs("pub_name"), rs2.RecordCount
    End If
rs.MoveNext
Loop
```

Fields that are retrieved only when referenced in code are called *deferred fields*. Even if you're going to process all the records in the child Recordset, using a parameterized command can help if the client workstation is short on system memory.

DataEnvironment Commands objects

If you've defined a hierarchical Command object at design time in a DataEnvironment designer, using it from code is really straightforward: You only have to retrieve it using the Commands collection and assign it to a regular ADODB.Command object variable, as in this code:

```
Dim cmd As ADODB.Command, rs As ADODB.Recordset
Set cmd = DataEnvironment1.Commands("Authors")
Set rs = cmd.Execute
Set MSHFlexGrid1.DataSource = rs
```

Or you can execute the query and then retrieve the result Recordset using custom methods of the DataEnvironment object:

```
DataEnvironment1.Authors
Set MSHFlexGrid1.DataSource = DataEnvironment1.rsAuthors
```

Even if you don't plan to use DataEnvironment objects in your code, the DataEnvironment designer is helpful for building SHAPE commands. In fact, you can interactively design a hierarchical Command object, and then right-click on it and select the Hierarchy Information menu command, as shown in Figure 14-6.

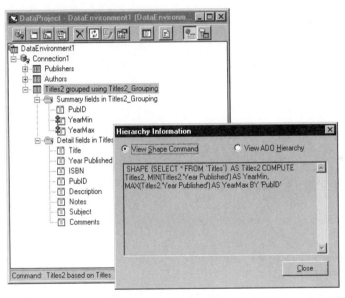

Figure 14-6. *Let the DataEnvironment designer build complex SHAPE commands for you.*

This chapter and Chapter 13 together offer an in-depth description of how ADO works and how you can work around its few limitations and quirks. All the code seen so far, however, has focused on data retrieval exclusively. In the next chapter, I show you how you can use bound grid controls and the DataReport designer to display the result of queries to your users.

Chapter 15

Tables and Reports

In preceding chapters, you learned how to use design-time tools such as the DataEnvironment designer or pure ADO code to deal with databases. Now it's time to complete this overview of database programming and see how to display this data to users in the most effective way, both on screen and in print.

THE DATACOMBO AND DATALIST CONTROLS

Visual Basic 6 includes two controls that can be used only as bound controls: DataList and DataCombo. These controls are variants of the regular ListBox and ComboBox controls and are special because they can be bound to two different ADO Data controls. The first Data control determines the value to be selected in the control (as is the case for regular ListBox and ComboBox controls); the second Data control fills the list portion.

The DataList and DataCombo controls are often used to provide lookup tables. A *lookup table* is a secondary table that typically contains the human-friendly description of an entity and is used to transform an encoded value into an intelligible form. For example, the Products table in the NWind.mdb database includes the CategoryID field, which is a number that corresponds to a value in the CategoryID field of the Categories table. Therefore, to display information about a product, you have to perform an INNER JOIN command to retrieve all the requested data:

```
SELECT ProductName, CategoryName FROM Products INNER JOIN Categories
    ON Products.CategoryID = Categories.CategoryID
```

While this approach works when you're processing data via code, it often isn't a viable solution when you're using bound controls. For example, what happens if users are allowed to modify the category of a product? In this case a bullet-proof interface would require that you load all the values in the Categories table into a ListBox or ComboBox control so that users couldn't enter an incorrect category name. This task requires you to open a secondary Recordset, as this code illustrates:

```
' This code assumes that cn already points to a valid connection.
Dim rsCat As New ADODB.Recordset
rsCat.Open "SELECT CategoryID, CategoryName FROM Categories", cn
lstCategories.Clear
Do Until rsCat.EOF
    lstCategories.AddItem rsCat("CategoryName")
    lstCategories.ItemData(lstCategories.NewIndex) = rsCat("CategoryID")
    rsCat.MoveNext
Loop
rsCat.Close
```

Of course, you then have to write the code that highlights the correct item in the ListBox when the user navigates through the records in the Products table, as well as the code that modifies the value of the CategoryID field in the Products table when users select a different item in the list. As you see, this deceptively simple job requires more code than you probably thought was necessary. Fortunately, if you set a few design-time properties, the DataCombo and DataList controls can easily accomplish this task.

The DataCombo and DataList controls are included in the MSDATLST.OCX file, which must therefore be distributed with any application that uses these controls.

NOTE   The DataCombo and DataList controls are functionally similar to the DBCombo and DBList controls introduced by Visual Basic 5 (and still supported by Visual Basic 6). The main difference is that the DataCombo and DataList controls work only with the ADO Data control, while the DBCombo and DBList controls work only with the old Data and RemoteData controls.

Setting Design-Time Properties

To implement a lookup table with the DataCombo and DataList controls, you need to place two ADO Data controls on the form, one that points to the main table (Products, in the previous example) and one that points to the lookup table (Categories, in the previous example). Then set, at a minimum, the following properties for the DataCombo and DataList controls:

- *DataSource*   a reference to the main ADO Data control, which in turn points to the main database table.

- *DataField*   the name of the field in the table referred to by the *DataSource* property and to which this control is bound. This field is updated when a new value is selected in the list.

- ■ *RowSource*   a reference to the secondary ADO Data control, which in turn points to the lookup table. The list portion of the control will be filled with data coming from the lookup table.

- ■ *ListField*   the name of a field in the lookup table. The list portion of the control will be filled with values coming from this field.

- ■ *BoundColumn*   the name of a field in the lookup table. When the user selects a value in the list, the *DataField* field in the main table receives a value from this column. If you don't assign any value to this property, it will use the same field name as the *ListField* property.

Let's implement the example described previously. Create an ADO Data control (Adodc1), set it to point to the Products table in NWind.mdb, and add some bound TextBox controls that display fields from that table. Then add another ADO Data control (Adodc2), and set it to retrieve data from the Categories table. Finally, add a DataList control and set its properties as follows: *DataSource* = Adodc1, *DataField* = CategoryID, *RowSource* = Adodc2, *ListField* = CategoryName, and *BoundColumn* = CategoryID.

The Products table contains another foreign key, SuppliersID, that points to the Suppliers table. You can implement another lookup mechanism by adding a third ADO Data control (Adodc3), which points to the Suppliers table, and a DataCombo control whose properties should be set as follows: *DataSource* = Adodc1, *DataField* = SupplierID, *RowSource* = Adodc3, *ListField* = CompanyName, and *BoundColumn* = SupplierID. You can now run the application, as shown in Figure 15-1 on the following page.

> **NOTE** The DataCombo and DataList controls expose two additional properties, *DataMember* and *RowMember*, that are assigned only when you use a DataEnvironment designer's Command object as the main or secondary data source.

The DataCombo and DataList controls support other design-time properties, but since in most cases they are the same properties as exposed by the regular ListBox and ComboBox controls, you should already be familiar with them. The only other property you might want to set at design time is *MatchEntry*, which can take the values 0-dblBasicMatching or 1-dblExtendedMatching. In basic matching mode, when the user presses a key while the focus is on the control, the control highlights the item in the list that begins with the pressed character. In extended matching mode, each character entered is appended to a search string, which is then used to highlight the first matching item, if any. (The search string is automatically reset after a few seconds, or when the BackSpace key is pressed.)

As with all bound controls, DataCombo and DataList expose the *DataFormat* property, but this property won't deliver the results you probably expect. For example, you can't use *DataFormat* to change the format of the items in the list. This isn't a bug, however; *DataFormat* works on the *DataField* column, whose value is normally hidden from the user when you use these controls. For this reason, the *DataFormat* property is of limited use with these two controls. The following tip explains how you can format the items in the list.

> **TIP** Often you need to display a combination of fields in the list portion of a DataCombo or DataList control. For example, you might want to display the supplier's name and city instead of just the name. You can accomplish this by using the SELECT command with a calculated field as the *RecordSource* property of the secondary ADO Data control:
>
> ```
> Adodc3.RecordSource = "SELECT SupplierID, CompanyName + ' (' " _
>     & "+ City + ')' AS NameCity FROM Suppliers"
> ```
>
> Don't forget to include the key field in the SELECT command; otherwise, you can't assign it to the *BoundColumn* property. You can use the same trick to sort the list or to format the list in a nonstandard way. For example, you can sort the suppliers list and convert their names to uppercase using the following query:
>
> ```
> Adodc3.RecordSource = "SELECT SupplierID, UCase(CompanyName + ' (' " _
>     & "+ City + ')') AS NameCity FROM Suppliers ORDER BY CompanyName"
> ```

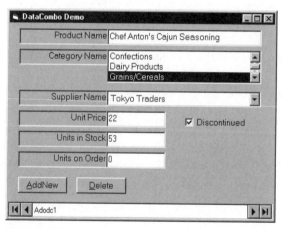

Figure 15-1. *A bound form with two lookup tables.*

Run-Time Operations

Working with the DataCombo and DataList controls at run time is similar to working with regular ListBox and ComboBox controls, with a few essential differences. For example, there are no *ListIndex* and *ListCount* properties, nor is there an *AddItem* method to add items to the list at run time. The only way to fill the list portion of these controls is by using an ADO Data control or another data source, such as a Recordset or DataEnvironment instance.

The DataList and DataCombo controls also expose a few peculiar properties. The *MatchedWithList* read-only property returns True if the value in the edit portion of a DataCombo control matches one of the elements in the list. This property is always True with DataList and DataCombo controls whose *Style* property is 2-dbcDropDownList. The *BoundText* property returns or sets the value of the field named by the *BoundColumn* property—that is, the value that will be assigned to the *DataField* column in the main table.

Displaying additional lookup information

The *SelectedItem* property returns a bookmark to the lookup table that corresponds to the highlighted item in the list portion. You usually use this property to display additional information about the selected item. For example, suppose that you want to display the value of the ContactName field from the Suppliers table whenever a new supplier is selected from the list. To do so, create a Label control named *lblSupplierData* and add the following code to the form module:

```
Private Sub DataCombo1_Click(Area As Integer)
    ' Move to the correct record in the lookup table.
    ' NOTE: The ContactName field must be included in the list
    '       of fields returned by the Adodc3 data control.
    If Area = dbcAreaList Then
        Adodc3.Recordset.Bookmark = DataCombo1.SelectedItem
        lblSupplierData = Adodc3.Recordset("ContactName")
    End If
End Sub
```

The DataCombo's *Click* and *DblClick* events receive an *Area* parameter that states which portion of the control has been clicked. Possible values for this parameter are 0-dbcAreaButton, 1-dbcAreaEdit, and 2-dbcAreaList.

The problem with the preceding approach is that the DataList or DataCombo controls' *Click* event doesn't fire when the user displays a new record in the form. For this reason, you must trap the primary ADO Data control's *MoveComplete* event:

```
Private Sub Adodc1_MoveComplete(ByVal adReason As ADODB.EventReasonEnum, _
    ByVal pError As ADODB.Error, adStatus As ADODB.EventStatusEnum, _
    ByVal pRecordset As ADODB.Recordset)
    ' You need to manually assign a value to BoundText because the
    ' SelectedItem property hasn't been updated yet when this event fires.
    DataCombo1.BoundText = Adodc1.Recordset("SupplierID")
    ' Simulate a Click to keep the control in sync.
    DataCombo1_Click dbcAreaList
End Sub
```

The *VisibleCount* property returns the number of visible items in the list portion. It's intended to be used together with the *VisibleItems* property, which returns an array of bookmarks to the lookup table that correspond to all the visible items in the list. For example, you might place a lstDescription ListBox control to the right of the DataList1 control and load it with additional information from the lookup table, as you can see in the code at the top of the next page.

```
Dim i As Long
lstDescription.Clear
For i = 0 To DataList1.VisibleCount - 1
    Adodc2.Recordset.Bookmark = DataList1.VisibleItems(i)
    lstDescription.AddItem Adodc2.Recordset("Description")
Next
```

The problem here is that you can execute this code whenever a new record be-comes current, but it's impossible to keep the lstDescription ListBox in sync with the DataList1 control because the latter lacks a *Scroll* event. A better use for the *VisibleCount* and *VisibleItems* properties is to implement a ToolTip mechanism:

```
' This code assumes that DataList1.IntegralHeight = True.
Private Sub DataList1_MouseMove(Button As Integer, Shift As Integer, _
    x As Single, y As Single)
    ' Determine the item over which the mouse cursor is placed.
    Dim item As Long
    item = Int(y / DataList1.Height * DataList1.VisibleCount)
    ' Retrieve the description for the category under the cursor, and
    ' prepare a ToolTip in case the user doesn't move the mouse.
    Adodc2.Recordset.Bookmark = DataList1.VisibleItems(item)
    DataList1.ToolTipText = Adodc2.Recordset("Description")
End Sub
```

> **CAUTION**   When you use the properties and methods of the Recordset ex-posed by an ADO Data control, or of a Recordset that is directly bound to data-aware controls, you might get error H80040E20. You can usually get rid of this error by using a static client-side cursor, or by preceding the statement that causes the error with this line:
>
> ```
> ADODC1.Recordset.Move 0
> ```
>
> For additional information, see article Q195638 in the Microsoft Knowl-edge Base.

Saving connections

One of the problems of the original Data control, which has been inherited by the newer ADO Data control, is that each instance of the control opens its own connection to the database, with two undesirable consequences. First, if you have multiple Data controls, they can't share the same transaction space. Second, each connection takes resources from the server. If a form uses numerous lookup tables based on DataCombo and DataList controls, your application is going to consume more resources than neces-sary and might incur problems if there is a shortage of available connections.

When working with ADO data-aware controls, you can often avoid this waste of resources. In fact, your DataCombo and DataList controls don't typically need a visible Data control because the user never actually navigates the lookup table. There-fore, you can obtain the same results using a plain ADO Recordset object. Set the prop-erties of the DataCombo and DataList controls as if they were bound to an ADO Data control for the lookup table, but leave their *RowSource* property blank. Assign this property at run time, after creating a Recordset object that shares the main ADO Data control's connection:

```
Dim rsCategories As New ADODB.Recordset
Dim rsSuppliers As New ADODB.Recordset

Private Sub Form_Load()
    rsCategories.Open "Categories", Adodc1.Recordset.ActiveConnection
    Set DataList1.RowSource = rsCategories
    rsSuppliers.Open "Suppliers", Adodc1.Recordset.ActiveConnection
    Set DataCombo1.RowSource = rsSuppliers
End Sub
```

Updating the lookup table

So far we've assumed that the lookup table's contents are fixed. In practice, however, the user often needs to add new items to the table, as when he or she inserts a product that comes from a company not yet in the Suppliers table. You can deal with this situation by using DataCombo controls with *Style* = 0-dbcDropdownCombo. When the main ADO Data control is about to write values to the Products table, your code can check whether the Supplier name is already in the Suppliers table and, if it isn't, ask the user if a new supplier should be created. Here's the minimal code that implements this feature:

```
Private Sub Adodc1_WillChangeRecord(ByVal adReason As _
    ADODB.EventReasonEnum, ByVal cRecords As Long, adStatus As
    ADODB.EventStatusEnum, ByVal pRecordset As ADODB.Recordset)
    ' Exit if data in DataCombo hasn't been modified
    ' or if it matches an item in the list.
    If Not DataCombo1.DataChanged Or DataCombo1.MatchedWithList Then
        Exit Sub
    End If
    ' Ask if the user wants to add a new supplier; cancel operation if not.
    If MsgBox("Supplier not found." & vbCr & "Do you want to add it?", _
        vbYesNo + vbExclamation) = vbNo Then
        adStatus = adStatusCancel
    End If

    ' Add a new record to the Recordset. In a real application, you should
    ' display a complete data entry form.
    rsSuppliers.AddNew "CompanyName", DataCombo1.Text
    rsSuppliers.Update
    ' Ensure that the new record is visible in the Recordset.
    rsSuppliers.Requery
    rsSuppliers.Find "CompanyName = '" & DataCombo1.Text & "'"
    ' Refill the DataCombo and make the correct item the current one.
    DataCombo1.ReFill
    DataCombo1.BoundText = rsSuppliers("SupplierID")
End Sub
```

The preceding code automatically adds a new record to the Suppliers table in a simplified way; a real application should display a complete data entry form in which the user can enter additional data about the new supplier.

THE DATAGRID CONTROL

Probably the most usual way to display data in a database table is with a grid control. Visual Basic 6 comes with several grid controls, but only two of them can work with the newer ADO Data control and other ADO data sources: the DataGrid control and the Hierarchical FlexGrid control. I'll describe the DataGrid control in this section and the Hierarchical FlexGrid control in the next section.

Before looking at the individual properties, methods, and events supported by the DataGrid control, you should be familiar with its object model. As you can see in Figure 15-2, this is a simple object model, with the DataGrid control at the top of the hierarchy and the Columns and Splits collections under it. You can split a DataGrid control into two or more sections and navigate through them independently or in a synchronized manner. The DataGrid control is included in the MSDATGRD.OCX file, which must therefore be distributed with any application that uses this control.

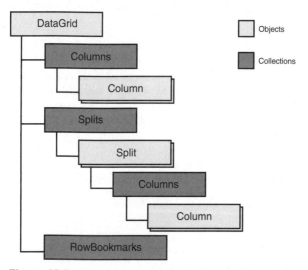

Figure 15-2. *The object model for the DataGrid control.*

NOTE   The DataGrid is source-code compatible with the older DBGrid control, which, though still included in Visual Basic 6, doesn't support the newer ADO Data control and data sources. Thanks to this compatibility, the DataGrid control can be used as a drop-in substitute for the DBGrid control. The only relevant difference between the two controls is that the newer DataGrid control doesn't work in unbound mode. But because you can bind this control to any ADO data source—including your own classes, as explained in Chapter 18—nothing prevents you from creating a class that encapsulates an in-memory data structure, such as an array of UDTs or a two-dimensional array of Strings or Variants.

Setting Design-Time Properties

Since the DataGrid control can work only as a bound control to an ADO data source, the first thing to do is prepare such a source. This can be a design-time source such as an ADO Data control or a DataEnvironment object, or it can be a run-time source such as an ADO Recordset or an instance of a custom class that qualifies as a data source. Working with design-time sources is definitely preferable, because you can retrieve the field structure at design time and adjust column width and other attributes in a visual manner, without writing code.

NOTE You can bind complex controls, such as the DataGrid and Hierarchical FlexGrid controls, only to Recordsets based on static or keyset cursors.

Editing the Column layout

After you have bound the DataGrid control to an ADO Data control or to a DataEnvironment's Command object through the DataGrid's *DataSource* property, you can right-click on the control and select the Retrieve Fields menu command. This prepares a column layout at design time, with each column taking its caption and width directly from the database field to which it maps. You can then right-click again on the control and select the Edit menu command, which puts the grid in edit mode. In this mode, you can adjust the column width, scroll the grid horizontally by using the scroll bar at the bottom, and right-click on the control to display a menu of commands. These commands allow you to add and remove columns, split the grid into two or more sections, cut and paste columns to rearrange their order, and so on. To modify other properties, however, you must right-click once again on the control and select the Properties command, which brings up a Property Pages dialog box with as many as eight tabs, as shown in Figure 15-3 on the following page.

Contrary to what the documentation states, it seems impossible in practice to have distinct column layouts for different split sections. In fact, if you delete an existing column or add a new column to a split, all the other splits are affected as well. A possible workaround for this problem is to set a column's *Visible* property to False. Because this attribute can be set on a split-by-split basis (as explained in "The Layout Tab" section later in this chapter), you can effectively hide a column in all the splits where it shouldn't appear.

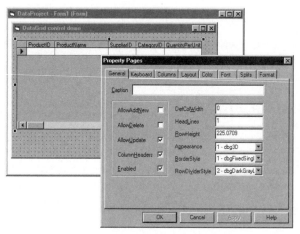

Figure 15-3. *The DataGrid control at design time, after displaying its Property Pages dialog box.*

The General and Keyboard tabs

By default, the grid has no caption, but you can enter a custom string in the General tab of the Property Pages dialog box; if a nonempty string is specified for the *Caption* property, it will appear in a gray section above the column headers. The *AllowAddNew*, *AllowDelete*, and *AllowUpdate* Boolean properties determine which operations are allowed on the grid. The *ColumnHeaders* property can be set to False to hide the gray row containing the column headers. Note that in the Font tab you can set the *HeadFont* property, which determines the character font used for column headers.

The *DefColWidth* property is the default width of the grid's columns: If set to 0 (its default value), the width of each column is the largest value between the underlying field's size and the column header's width. The *HeadLines* property is an integer between 0 and 10, and corresponds to the number of rows used for column headings; you can use 0 to remove column headers, but it's preferable to set the *ColumnHeaders* property to False to achieve the same result. The *RowHeight* property is the height of each row in twips. The DataGrid control doesn't support rows of different heights.

You can set the *BorderStyle* property to 0-dbgNoBorder to suppress the fixed border around the grid. The *RowDividerLine* property determines the style used to draw the dividing lines between the rows and can be one of the following enumerated values: 0-dbgNoDividers, 1-dbgBlackLine, 2-dbgDarkGrayLine (the default), 3-dbgRaised, 4-dbgInset, or 5-dbgUseForeColor. If 3-dbgRaised or 4-dbgInset is used, the color of the dividing line depends on the Microsoft Windows settings.

The Keyboard tab allows you to set some properties that affect how keys behave when the DataGrid control has the focus. If the *AllowArrows* property is True, the user can visit all the cells in the grid using the arrow keys; if *WrapCellPointer* is also True, pressing the right arrow key at the end of a row moves the focus rectangle to the first cell in the next row and pressing the left arrow key at the beginning of a row moves the focus rectangle to the last cell in the previous row.

The *TabAction* property decides what happens when the Tab key or Shift+Tab key combination is pressed and the DataGrid control is the active control. The default action is 0-dbgControlNavigation, in which case the next control (or the previous control, if Shift+Tab is pressed) on the form receives the focus. If you set this property to 1-dbgColumnNavigation, pressing the Tab key moves the focus rectangle to the next column unless the current cell is the last (or the first, if Shift+Tab is pressed) of its row. In this case, pressing this key causes the focus to move to the next (or previous) control in the TabIndex order. Finally, the setting 2-dbgGridNavigation is similar to the previous one, but the Tab key never moves the focus rectangle to another control and the behavior at the beginning or end of the row depends on the *WrapCellPointer* property.

By default, tab and arrow keys never move the focus rectangle to another split in the same grid. You can, however, set the *TabAcrossSplit* property to True to let the user navigate through splits by using the Tab key. In this case, the value of the *WrapCellPointer* and *TabAction* properties are ignored, unless the user presses the Tab key when the current cell is in the last column of the rightmost split or presses the Shift+Tab key combination when the current cell is in the first column of the leftmost split.

The Columns and Format tabs

The Columns tab allows you to set the *Caption* property of each individual Column object, as well as its *DataField* property, which contains the name of the field in the data source to which the column is bound.

The Format tab allows you to set the *DataFormat* property of each Column object, using the same dialog box used for individual bound controls. Typically, you use this tab to format numbers, currency values, dates, and times. You can also use a custom format, if needed. The settings on this tab are reflected in the *DataFormat* property of individual Column objects at run time. A few other properties of Column objects, which will be described later, are set on the Layout tab.

The Splits tab

If the grid is subdivided into two or more split areas, you can set the attributes for these areas in the Splits tab. You can't create new splits in this property page, but you act on the fields in this page to set each split's appearance and behavior. (Creating a new split is described in the "Editing the Column Layout" section earlier in this chapter.)

To modify the attributes of a split, you have to select it in the upper drop-down list. If the grid isn't split, there will be only one item in the drop-down list, the *Split 0* item, and your setting will affect the entire grid control. You can set the *Locked* property to True to turn the DataGrid into a read-only control. The *AllowFocus* property determines whether the split can receive the focus (it's similar to the *TabStop* property of individual Visual Basic controls). The *AllowSizing* property determines whether the split can be interactively resized with the mouse at run time. If *AllowRowResizing* is True, the user can resize rows in this split by using the mouse. (Resize operations affect all the rows in all the splits because the DataGrid control doesn't support rows with different heights.) The *RecordSelectors* property determines whether there is a gray column for displaying record selectors on the left side of the split (or the whole grid).

You can control whether multiple splits vertically scroll together or independently of one another by using the *ScrollGroup* property of the Split object, which is an integer greater than or equal to 1. All the splits with the same value scroll together, so you can create splits that scroll independently by assigning different values to this property. The *ScrollBars* property affects the presence or absence of scroll bars in a particular split and takes one of the following values: 0-dbgNone, 1-dbgHorizontal, 2-dbgVertical, 3-dbgBoth, and 4-dbgAutomatic. (The default is 4-dbgAutomatic—show a scroll bar only if necessary.) If you have a group of Split objects that scroll together and the *ScrollBars* property of each is set to 4-dbgAutomatic, only the rightmost split of the group will show a vertical scroll bar.

The *MarqueeStyle* property determines how the DataGrid control highlights the currently selected cell. This property can have one of the following values: 0-dbgDottedCellBorder (a dotted border around the cell, also known as a focus rectangle, is used), 1-dbgSolidCellBorder (a solid border is used, which is usually more visible than a dotted border), 2-dbgHighlightCell (text and background color are inverted), 3-dbgHighlightRow (the entire row is highlighted—this is useful only when the grid or the split isn't editable), 4-dbgHighlightRowRaiseCell (similar to the previous one, but the current cell appears to be raised), 5-dbgNoMarquee (the current cell isn't highlighted in any way), or 6-dbgFloatingEditor (the default—the current cell is highlighted using a floating editor window with a blinking cursor, as in Microsoft Access).

The *AllowRowSizing*, *MarqueeStyle*, and *RecordSelectors* properties are exposed by the DataGrid control as well as its Split objects. Setting one of these properties for the DataGrid control has the same effect as setting the same property for all its Split objects.

The last two properties shown in the Splits tab work together to determine how many columns are visible in the split and whether they are resized to fit in the visible area. More precisely, the *Size* property can be assigned a numeric value whose meaning depends on the *SizeMode* property. If *SizeMode* is 0-dbgScalable, *Size* contains an integer that corresponds to the width of that split with respect to other scalable splits; for example, if you have two splits with *Size* = 1 and *Size* = 2, respectively, the first split will take one third of the grid's width and the second split will take the remaining two thirds. If *SizeMode* is 1-dbgExact, then *Size* is a floating-point number that corresponds to the split's exact width in twips; this setting ensures that the split always has the same width, whether other splits are added or removed.

The Layout tab

In the Layout tab, you can set column attributes on a split-by-split basis. The DataGrid control, in fact, allows you to display the same column with different attributes in different splits. For example, a column can be read-write in one split and read-only in another; or it can be invisible in some of the splits and visible in others. You set the read-only attribute with the *Locked* property and the visibility attribute with the *Visible* property. The *AllowSizing* Boolean property determines if the right border of the column can be dragged to resize the column's width. The *WrapText* Boolean property causes the text in the cell to wrap to the next row if necessary: You can use this property with the *RowHeight* property to produce multiline displays. The *Button* property, if set to True, causes a button for a drop-down menu to appear in the cell when it gets the focus. When the user clicks on this button, the DataGrid control receives a *ButtonClick* event, to which you typically react by dropping down a list of values using a standard ComboBox, a bound ListBox, or even another DataGrid control.

The *DividerStyle* property affects the style of the vertical line on the right border of a column and can be one of the following values: 0-dbgNoDividers, 1-dbgBlackLine, 2-dbgDarkGrayLine (the default), 3-dbgRaised, 4-dbgInset, 5-dbgUseForeColor, or 6-dbgLightGrayLine. The *Alignment* property sets the alignment of the contents of the column and can be 0-dbgLeft, 1-dbgRight, 2-dbgCenter, or 3-dbgGeneral. (By default, text is left-aligned and numbers are right-aligned.) The *Width* property specifies the width of each Column object, expressed in the units of the DataGrid's container.

Run-Time Operations

The DataGrid control is complex and is likely to demand some time from you before you're familiar with it. I'll outline the most common operations that you might want to perform on it, together with a few tricks to get the most out of this object.

Working with the current cell

The most important run-time properties of the DataGrid control are *Row* and *Col*, which set or return the position of the cell in the focus rectangle. The first row and the leftmost column return zero values. Once you make a given cell the current cell, you can retrieve and modify its contents using the DataGrid's *Text* property:

```
' Convert the current cell's contents to uppercase.
Private Sub cmdUppercase_Click()
    DataGrid1.Text = UCase$(DataGrid1.Text)
End Sub
```

The *EditActive* property returns True if the current cell is being edited and False otherwise; you can also assign a value to this property to enter or exit edit mode programmatically. When the edit mode is entered, a *ColEdit* event is triggered:

```
' Save the current cell value before editing.
Private Sub DataGrid1_ColEdit(ByVal ColIndex As Integer)
    ' SaveText is a module-level variable.
    SaveText = DataGrid1.Text
End Sub
```

You can determine whether the current cell has been modified by querying the *CurrentCellModified* property, and you can also set this property to False and then set *EditActive* to False to completely cancel the edit operation. The *CurrentCellVisible* property is exposed by both the DataGrid and Split objects; it returns True if the current cell is visible in the object. If you set a Split's *CurrentCellVisible* property to True, the Split scrolls until the cell becomes visible; if you set the DataGrid control's *CurrentCellVisible* property to True, all the splits scroll to make the cell visible. While the current cell is being edited, you can also read and modify the grid's *SelStart, SelLength,* and *SelText* properties, as you would do with a regular TextBox control.

Because the DataGrid control is always bound to an ADO data source, the *Bookmark* property, which sets or returns the bookmark to the current record, is often more useful than the *Row* property. Even more interesting, whenever the user moves to another row, the current record in the underlying Recordset object automatically changes to reflect the new current cell. Thus, you can retrieve additional fields from the Recordset by simply querying the Recordset's Fields collection. The following code assumes that the DataGrid control is bound to an ADO Data control:

```
' Display the current product's unit price in Euro currency.
' The RowColChange event fires when a new cell becomes current.
Private Sub DataGrid1_RowColChange(LastRow As Variant, _
    ByVal LastCol As Integer)
    ' The DOLLAR_TO_EURO_RATIO variable is defined elsewhere in the module.
    lblEuroPrice = Adodc1.Recordset("UnitPrice") * DOLLAR_TO_EURO_RATIO
End Sub
```

The DataGrid control's *Split* property returns an integer in the range 0 through *Splits.Count-1*, which points to the split section that contains the current cell. You can also assign a new value to this property to move the focus to another split. When a grid is split into more sections, a few properties of the DataGrid control—such as *RecordSelectors* and *FirstRow*—are equivalent to the same properties exposed by the current split. In other words:

```
' The following statements are equivalent.
DataGrid1.RecordSelectors = True
DataGrid1.Splits(DataGrid1.Split).RecordSelectors = True
```

Accessing other cells

There are a few properties that let you retrieve and set the properties of any cell in the grid, but you have to use them in a way that isn't always intuitive. Each column object exposes the *Text* and *Value* properties: The former sets or returns the text displayed in the column for the current row, while the latter is the actual value in the column for the current row before it's formatted for display to the user. The Column object also exposes the *CellText* and *CellValue* methods, which return the contents of a cell in that column for any row, given its bookmark. There are several ways to retrieve the bookmark relative to a row, as I'll show you in a moment.

VisibleRows and *VisibleCols* are read-only properties that return the number of visible rows and columns, respectively. There are no properties that directly return the total number of rows and columns. You can use the *ApproxCount* property, which returns the approximate number of rows; this number might differ from the actual value. To retrieve the number of columns, you must query the *Count* property of the Columns collection.

The DataGrid object exposes two methods that let you access the bookmark of any row in the control. *GetBookmark* returns a bookmark of a row relative to the current row: *GetBookmark(0)* is the same as the *Bookmark* property, *GetBookmark(−1)* is the bookmark of the row preceding the current row, *GetBookmark(1)* is the bookmark of the row following the current row, and so on. The other available method, *RowBookmark*, returns the bookmark of any visible row: *RowBookmark(0)* is the bookmark of the first visible row, and *RowBookmark(VisibleRows−1)* is the bookmark of the last visible row.

The bookmark of the first row is also returned by the *FirstRow* property. According to the documentation, you can assign a new bookmark to this property to programmatically scroll the grid's contents, but I found that I always get an "Invalid bookmark" error when I try to assign a value to it. The *LeftCol* property holds the index of the first visible column, so you can programmatically display the upper left corner of the grid using the code shown on the following page.

```
DataGrid1.LeftCol = 0
Adodc1.Recordset.MoveFirst
DataGrid1.CurrentCellVisible = True
```

The *FirstRow*, *LeftCol*, and *CurrentCellVisible* properties are also exposed by the Split object; here, also, assigning a value to the *FirstRow* property without raising an error appears impossible.

You can use the value returned by any of the preceding bookmark methods as an argument of the Column object's *CellText* and *CellValue* methods, described previously. For example, this code displays the difference in the Total field between the current row and the row that precedes the current row:

```
Private Sub DataGrid1_RowColChange(LastRow As Variant, _
    ByVal LastCol As Integer)
    Dim gcol As MSDataGridLib.Column
    If DataGrid1.Row > 0 Then
        ' Get a reference to the current column.
        Set gcol = DataGrid1.Columns("Total")
        ' Display the difference between the values in the "Total" column
        ' of the current row and the cell immediately above it.
        Label1 = gcol.CellValue(DataGrid1.GetBookmark(-1)) - gcol.Value
    Else
        Label1 = "(First Row)"
    End If
End Sub
```

Managing cell selections

Users can select any number of adjacent columns by clicking on the column headers while keeping the Shift key pressed; they can also select any number of rows—even nonadjacent ones—by clicking on the leftmost gray column while keeping the Ctrl key pressed. (Multiple row selection, therefore, requires that the grid's or the split's *RecordSelectors* property is set to True.) The *SelStartCol* and *SelEndCol* properties set and return the indices for the first and last selected columns, respectively. You can clear the column selection by setting these properties to –1, or by invoking the *ClearSelCols* method. These properties and this method are also exposed by the Split object.

Because the user can select nonadjacent rows, the system to determine which rows are currently highlighted is based on the DataGrid control's *SelBookmarks* collection, which contains the bookmarks of all the selected rows. For example, to select the current row, execute the following statement:

```
DataGrid1.SelBookmarks.Add DataGrid1.Bookmark
```

You can iterate on all the selected rows using a *For Each* loop. For example, the following code takes advantage of the *SelChange* event—which fires any time a column or a row is selected or deselected—to update a Label control with the sum of all the cells in the Total column for the rows that are currently selected:

```
Private Sub DataGrid1_SelChange(Cancel As Integer)
    Dim total As Single, bmark As Variant
    For Each bmark In DataGrid.SelBookmarks
        total = total + DataGrid.Columns("Total").CellValue(bmark)
    Next
    lblGrandTotal = total
End Sub
```

There's no method that programmatically clears selected rows; you can do this only by removing all the items in the *SelBookmark* collection, as in the following code:

```
Do While DataGrid1.SelBookmarks.Count
    DataGrid1.SelBookmarks.Remove 0
Loop
```

Monitoring edit operations

The DataGrid control has a rich collection of events that let you trap nearly every user action. Almost all these events are in the form *Beforexxxx* and *Afterxxxx*, where *Beforexxxx* events receive a *Cancel* parameter that you can set to True to cancel the operation. We've already seen the *ColEdit* event, which fires whenever a value in a cell is edited by pressing a key. This event is actually preceded by the related *BeforeColEdit* event, which lets you selectively make a cell read-only:

```
' Refuse to edit a cell in the first column if it already contains a value.
Private Sub DataGrid1_BeforeColEdit(ByVal ColIndex As Integer, _
    ByVal KeyAscii As Integer, Cancel As Integer)
    ' Note how you can test Null values and empty strings at the same time.
    If ColIndex = 0 And DataGrid1.Columns(ColIndex).CellValue _
        (DataGrid1.Bookmark) & "" <> "" Then
        Cancel = True
    End If
End Sub
```

If you cancel the edit operation in the *BeforeColEdit* event, the control doesn't receive any other event for this operation, which might be disorienting if you're accustomed to the ADO way of raising events, where a postnotification event fires even if the code in the prenotification event cancels the operation. The *KeyAscii* parameter contains the code of the key pressed to enter edit mode, or 0 if the user entered edit mode with a click of the mouse. Because this parameter is passed by value, you can't alter it. This isn't a problem, however, because the grid also receives all the usual *KeyDown*, *KeyPress*, and *KeyUp* events, which let you modify the value of the parameter that contains the code for the key the user pressed.

Any time you modify a value in a cell, the DataGrid control receives a *Change* event; if the edit operation actually modifies the value in a cell—that is, if you don't cancel it with the Esc key—the control also receives the *BeforeColUpdate* and *AfterColUpdate* events:

```
Private Sub DataGrid1_BeforeColUpdate(ByVal ColIndex As Integer, _
    OldValue As Variant, Cancel As Integer)
    ' Trap invalid values here.
End Sub
```

But watch out for a quirk in the procedure. You can't access the value that is about to be entered in the grid by using the *Text* or *Value* properties of the DataGrid or the Column, because within this event procedure these properties return the value that was originally in the grid cell—that is, the same value returned by the *OldValue* parameter. It turns out that the DataGrid's *Text* property returns the string entered by the user only when the *EditActive* property is True, but this property has already been reset to False when processing the *BeforeColUpdate* event. The solution is to declare a form-level variable and assign it a value from within the *Change* event. For example, this code correctly checks that the value being entered isn't duplicated in any other record of the Recordset:

```
Dim newCellText As String

' Remember the most recent value entered by the user.
Private Sub DataGrid1_Change()
    newCellText = DataGrid1.Text
End Sub

' Check that the user isn't entering a duplicate value for that column.
Private Sub DataGrid1_BeforeColUpdate(ByVal ColIndex As Integer, _
    OldValue As Variant, Cancel As Integer)
    Dim rs As ADODB.Recordset, fldName As String
    ' Retrieve the field name for the current column.
    fldName = DataGrid1.Columns(ColIndex).DataField
    ' Search for the new value in the Recordset. Use a clone Recordset
    ' so that the current bookmark doesn't change.
    Set rs = Adodc1.Recordset.Clone
    rs.MoveFirst
    rs.Find fldName & "='" & newCellValue & "'"
    ' Cancel the operation if a match has been found.
    If Not rs.EOF Then Cancel = True
End Sub
```

NOTE   This "quirk" is officially a bug, described in article Q195983 of the Microsoft Knowledge Base. However, the workaround shown here is simpler than the solution suggested in that article, which relies on the grid's *hWndEditor* property and the *GetWindowText* API function.

When the user moves to another row, a pair of *BeforeUpdate* and *AfterUpdate* events fire, and you have an opportunity to perform record-level validation and optionally reject the update. Here's the complete sequence of events that fire when the user edits a value in a column and then moves to the next or previous grid row:

KeyDown	The user presses a key.
KeyPress	
BeforeColEdit	The grid enters edit mode.
ColEdit	
Change	Now you can read the new value using the Text property.
	Here the *ActiveEdit* property becomes True.
KeyUp	The first key is released.
KeyDown	Another key is pressed.
KeyPress	
Change	
KeyUp	
	Other keys are pressed.
BeforeColUpdate	The user moves to another column.
AfterColUpdate	
AfterColEdit	
RowColChange	This event fires only when the move is complete.
BeforeUpdate	The user moves to another row.
AfterUpdate	
RowColChange	This event fires only when the move is complete.

CAUTION Be very careful with the code you place in the event procedures of a DataGrid control. To begin with, a few of these events, such as *RowColChange*, might fire multiple times if the grid is currently split into two or more areas, so you should avoid executing the same statements more than once. The *RowColChange* event, moreover, doesn't fire if the current record changes programmatically to a row that isn't fully visible; in this case, the grid correctly scrolls to make the new current record visible, but the event doesn't fire. This problem also occurs when the user moves to a record that isn't fully visible by using the buttons of the companion ADO Data control.

Performing insert and delete operations

The user can delete one or more rows by selecting them and then pressing the Delete key. This operation fires the *BeforeDelete* event (where you can cancel the command) and *AfterDelete* event, and then a *BeforeUpdate* and *AfterUpdate* pair of events. For example, you can write code in the *BeforeDelete* event procedure that checks whether the current record is the master record in a master-detail relationship, and either cancels the operation (as the following code illustrates) or automatically deletes all the related detail records.

```
Private Sub DataGrid1_BeforeDelete(Cancel As Integer)
    Dim rs As ADODB.Recordset, rsOrderDetails As ADODB.Recordset
    ' Get a reference to the underlying Recordset
    Set rs = Adodc1.Recordset
    ' Use the connection to perform a SELECT command that checks whether
    ' there is at least one record in the Order Details table that has
    ' a foreign key that points to the ProductID value of current record.
    Set rsOrderDetails = rs.ActiveConnection.Execute _
        ("Select * FROM [Order Details] WHERE [Order Details].ProductID=" _
        & rs("ProductID"))
    ' If EOF = False, there is a match, so cancel the delete command.
    If Not rsOrderDetails.EOF Then Cancel = True
End Sub
```

If you cancel the delete command, the DataGrid control displays an error message. You can suppress this and other error messages from the control by trapping its *Error* event:

```
Private Sub DataGrid1_Error(ByVal DataError As Integer, _
    Response As Integer)
    ' DataError = 7011 means "Action canceled"
    If DataError = 7011 Then
        MsgBox "Unable to delete this record because there are " _
            & "records in the Order Details table that point to it."
        ' Cancel the standard error processing by setting Response = 0.
        Response = 0
    End If
End Sub
```

Upon entry into this event, the *DataError* parameter contains the error code, whereas the *Response* parameter contains 1; you can prevent the grid from displaying the standard error message by setting the *Response* parameter to 0, as the previous example demonstrates. You can also test the standard error message by means of the DataGrid's *ErrorText* property.

If the *AllowAddNew* property is True, the DataGrid control displays a blank row at its bottom, marked with an asterisk, and the user can enter a new row—and therefore a new record in the underlying recordset—simply by typing a character in one of the cells in this row. When this happens, the control fires a *BeforeInsert* event, immediately followed by an *AfterInsert* event (unless you cancel the command), and then an *OnAddNew* event. The exact event sequence is as follows:

BeforeInsert	The user clicks on the last row.
AfterInsert	
OnAddNew	
RowColChange	This event fires only when the move is complete.
BeforeColEdit	The user types a key.
ColEdit	
Change	
Other Change and Keyxxx events	
BeforeColUpdate	The user moves to another column on the same row.
AfterColUpdate	
AfterColEdit	
RowColChange	This event fires only when the move is complete. The user enters values in other cells on the same row.
BeforeUpdate	The user moves to another row.
AfterUpdate	
RowColChange	This event fires only when the move is complete.

You can monitor the current status using the *AddNewMode* property, which can be assigned one of the following values: 0-dbgNoAddNew (no AddNew command is in progress), 1-dbgAddNewCurrent (the current cell is on the last row, but no AddNew command is pending), 2-dbgAddNewPending (the current row is in the next-to-last row as a result of a pending AddNew command). An AddNew command can be initiated either by the user or by code, as the result of assignment to the *Text* or *Value* properties.

Trapping mouse events

The DataGrid control exposes all the usual mouse events, which are passed the mouse coordinates and the state of the shift keys. Unfortunately, the DataGrid control doesn't support OLE drag-and-drop operations, so you won't find the usual *OLExxxx* properties, methods, and events. When working with the mouse, you're likely to use three methods exposed by the control: the *RowContaining* method, which returns the visible row over which the mouse cursor is located; the *ColContaining* method, which returns the corresponding column number; and finally the *SplitContaining* method, which returns the split number. If the mouse is outside the grid area—for example, when the mouse is over the record selectors area—these methods return −1. Here is an example that uses the *ToolTipText* property to display a ToolTip with the underlying value of the cell under the mouse, which can be especially useful if the column is too narrow to display longer strings:

```
Private Sub DataGrid1_MouseMove(Button As Integer, Shift As Integer, _
    X As Single, Y As Single)
```

(continued)

```
    Dim row As Long, col As Long
    On Error Resume Next
    row = DataGrid1.RowContaining(Y)
    col = DataGrid1.ColContaining(X)
    If row >= 0 And col >= 0 Then
        DataGrid1.ToolTipText = DataGrid1.Columns(col).CellValue _
            (DataGrid1.RowBookmark(row))
    Else
        DataGrid1.ToolTipText = ""
    End If
End Sub
```

Changing the grid layout

You can programmatically change the layout of a DataGrid control by using one of the many properties and methods of the Splits and Columns collections. For example, you can add a new column using the *Columns.Add* method, as follows:

```
' Add a Product Name column. (It will become the 4th column.)
With DataGrid1.Columns.Add(3)
    .Caption = "Product Name"
    .DataField = "ProductName"
End With
' You need to rebind the grid after adding a bound column.
DataGrid1.ReBind
```

You can also remove a column from the layout, using the *Columns.Remove* method:

```
' Remove the column added by the previous code snippet.
DataGrid1.Columns.Remove 3
```

Adding a split requires that you use the *Splits.Add* method. The argument you pass to this method is the position of the new split (0 for the leftmost split in the grid):

```
' Add a new split to the left of all existing splits.
DataGrid1.Splits.Add 0
```

After you create a split, you have to decide which columns are visible in it. Because each new split inherits all the columns from the grid, removing a column from one split would remove it from all the other splits, as described in the "Editing the Column Layout" section earlier in this chapter. Rather than deleting unwanted columns, make them invisible, as illustrated by the following code:

```
' Add a new split to the right of the existing split.
With DataGrid1.Splits.Add(1)
    ' Ensure that the two splits divide the grid's width in half.
    ' Assumes that the existing split's SizeMode property is 0-dbgScalable.
    ' (Always set SizeMode before Size!)
    .SizeMode = dbgScalable
    .Size = DataGrid1.Splits(0).Size
```

```
    ' This new split can be scrolled independently.
    .ScrollGroup = DataGrid1.Splits(0).ScrollGroup + 1
    ' Hide all the columns except the one labeled "ProductName".
    For Each gcol In .Columns
        gcol.Visible = (gcol.Caption = "ProductName")
    Next
End With
```

Dealing with lookup values

Often a value retrieved from a database table isn't meaningful in itself and is only useful because it's a foreign key to another table where the real information is. For example, the Products table in NWind.mdb includes a SupplierID field, which contains the value of a key in the Suppliers table, where you can find the name and the address of the supplier for that particular product. When you're displaying the Products table in a DataGrid control, you might use a suitable JOIN statement for the ADO Data control's *RecordSource* property so that the grid automatically displays the correct supplier name instead of its key.

The ADO binding mechanism, however, provides you with a better alternative. The trick is to declare a custom StdDataFormat object, assign it to the *DataFormat* property of a Column object, and then use the *Format* event to transform the numeric key values coming from the data source into more descriptive strings of text. The following routine loads all the values from the secondary table (also known as the *lookup table*) into a hidden ComboBox control. The routine then uses the contents of that control in the *Format* event of the custom StdDataFormat object to translate the SupplierID key into the supplier's CompanyName field:

```
Dim WithEvents SupplierFormat As StdDataFormat

Private Sub Form_Load()
    ' Load all the values from the Supplier lookup table into the
    ' hidden cboSuppliers ComboBox control.
    Dim rs As New ADODB.Recordset
    rs.Open "Suppliers", Adodc1.Recordset.ActiveConnection
    Do Until rs.EOF
        cboSuppliers.AddItem rs("CompanyName")
        ' The SupplierID value goes into the ItemData property.
        cboSuppliers.ItemData(cboSuppliers.NewIndex) = rs("SupplierID")
        rs.MoveNext
    Loop
    rs.Close

    ' Assign the custom format object to the SupplierID column.
    Set SupplierFormat = New StdDataFormat
    Set DataGrid1.Columns("SupplierID").DataFormat = SupplierFormat
```

(continued)

```
        ' Make the row height equal to the ComboBox's height.
        DataGrid1.RowHeight = cboSuppliers.Height
End Sub

Private Sub SupplierFormat_Format(ByVal DataValue As _
    StdFormat.StdDataValue)
    Dim i As Long
    ' Search the key value in the cboSuppliers ComboBox.
    For i = 0 To cboSuppliers.ListCount - 1
        If cboSuppliers.ItemData(i) = DataValue Then
            DataValue = cboSuppliers.List(i)
            Exit For
        End If
    Next
End Sub
```

Using the ComboBox control as a repository for the contents of the lookup table isn't a casual decision. In fact, with some wizardry we can even use the ComboBox to let the user select a new value for the SupplierID field. All we have to do is make the ComboBox control appear in front of the DataGrid control, exactly over the cell edited by the user, and then update the underlying SupplierID field when the user selects a new value from the list. For the best visual effect, you also need to trap a few events so that the ComboBox is always in the correct position, as in Figure 15-4 on page 782. Here's the code that does the trick:

```
Private Sub MoveCombo()
    ' In case of error, hide the ComboBox.
    On Error GoTo Error_Handler
    Dim gcol As MSDataGridLib.Column
    Set gcol = DataGrid1.Columns(DataGrid1.col)

    If gcol.Caption = "SupplierID" And DataGrid1.CurrentCellVisible Then
        ' Move the ComboBox inside the SupplierID column
        ' if it is the current column and it is visible.
        cboSuppliers.Move DataGrid1.Left + gcol.Left, _
            DataGrid1.Top + DataGrid1.RowTop(DataGrid1.row), gcol.Width
        cboSuppliers.ZOrder
        cboSuppliers.SetFocus
        cboSuppliers.Text = gcol.Text
        Exit Sub
    End If
Error_Handler:
    ' In all other cases, hide the ComboBox.
    cboSuppliers.Move -10000
    If DataGrid1.Visible Then DataGrid1.SetFocus
End Sub
```

```
Private Sub cboSuppliers_Click()
    ' Change the value of the underlying grid cell.
    DataGrid1.Columns("SupplierID").Value = _
        cboSuppliers.ItemData(cboSuppliers.ListIndex)
End Sub

Private Sub DataGrid1_RowColChange(LastRow As Variant, _
    ByVal LastCol As Integer)
    MoveCombo
End Sub

Private Sub DataGrid1_RowResize(Cancel As Integer)
    MoveCombo
End Sub

Private Sub DataGrid1_ColResize(ByVal ColIndex As Integer, _
    Cancel As Integer)
    MoveCombo
End Sub

Private Sub DataGrid1_Scroll(Cancel As Integer)
    MoveCombo
End Sub

Private Sub DataGrid1_SplitChange()
    MoveCombo
End Sub
```

This code requires that the DataGrid control's *RowHeight* property match the ComboBox's *Height* property. Because the latter is read-only at run time, execute the following statement in the *Form_Load* event procedure:

```
' Have the row height match the ComboBox's height.
DataGrid1.RowHeight = cboSuppliers.Height
```

Another approach to lookup tables is based on the *Button* property of the Column object and the *ButtonClick* event. In this case, however, you get a better visual result if you display a ListBox (or DataList) control just under the current cell, rather than displaying a ComboBox or DataCombo control over the cell. Since the implementation of this latter method is similar to what I've shown previously, I leave it to you as an exercise.

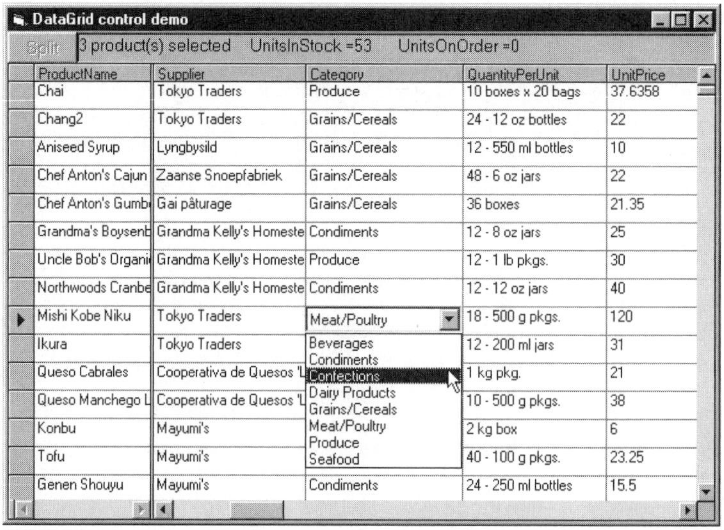

Figure 15-4. *The demonstration application uses lookup fields with drop-down ComboBoxes and supports splits, sort commands, and more.*

Sorting data

The DataGrid control doesn't offer any built-in functionality for sorting data. However, thanks to its *HeadClick* event and the ADO Recordset's *Sort* property, sorting data is an easy task that requires only a handful of statements:

```
Private Sub DataGrid1_HeadClick(ByVal ColIndex As Integer)
    ' Sort on the clicked column.
    Dim rs As ADODB.Recordset
    Set rs = Adodc1.Recordset

    If rs.Sort <> DataGrid1.Columns(ColIndex).DataField & " ASC" Then
        ' Sort in ascending order; this block is executed if the
        ' data isn't sorted, is sorted on a different field,
        ' or is sorted in descending order.
        rs.Sort = DataGrid1.Columns(ColIndex).DataField & " ASC"
    Else
        ' Sort in descending order.
        rs.Sort = DataGrid1.Columns(ColIndex).DataField & " DESC"
    End If
    ' No need to refresh the contents of the DataGrid.
End Sub
```

The only limitation of this approach is that it doesn't work well if the column contains lookup values.

THE HIERARCHICAL FLEXGRID CONTROL

The Hierarchical FlexGrid control is another grid control included in Visual Basic 6. Unlike the DataGrid control, the Hierarchical FlexGrid control can merge contiguous cells in different rows if they contain the same values. This control really shines when you assign a hierarchical ADO Recordset to its *DataSource* property, because it can correctly display multiple bands—where each band is a set of data columns—that come from a different child Recordset in the hierarchical data structure, as shown in Figure 15-5. The only serious limitation of this control is that it's read-only—the cells can't be directly edited by the user.

The easiest way to create a Hierarchical FlexGrid control is to build a hierarchical Command object in a DataEnvironment designer, use the right mouse button to drop it on a form, and select the Hierarchical Flex Grid command from the pop-up menu. This operation adds the necessary references to the control's type library and links the newly created Hierarchical FlexGrid control to the Command object. All the examples in this section—as well as in the demonstration program on the CD—are based on the hierarchical Recordset obtained by setting a relationship among the Authors, Title, and Titles tables of the Biblio.mdb database.

NOTE The Hierarchical FlexGrid control is source-code compatible with the older FlexGrid control, which is still included in Visual Basic 6, but doesn't support the newer ADO Data control and data sources. Thanks to this compatibility, the Hierarchical FlexGrid control can be used as a substitute for the older FlexGrid control. The minor differences between the controls will be highlighted in the following sections.

The Hierarchical FlexGrid control is included in the MSHFLXGD.OCX file, which must therefore be distributed with any application that uses this control.

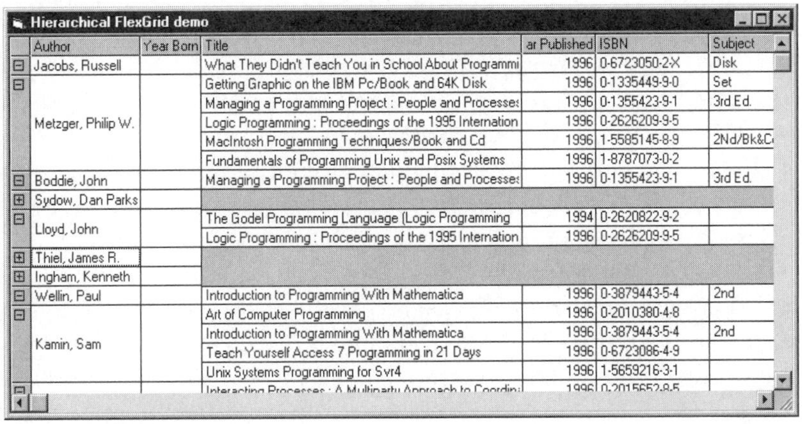

Figure 15-5. *A Hierarchical FlexGrid control showing a three-level hierarchical ADO Recordset (the Authors, Title, and Titles tables in Biblio.mdb).*

Setting Design-Time Properties

After you've created a bound Hierarchical FlexGrid control, you can right-click on it and select the Retrieve Structure menu command, which fills the grid with column headers, each one referring to a different field in the data source. Unfortunately, this grid doesn't expose an Edit command, so you can't use the mouse to modify the column layout and widths at design time. Unlike the DataGrid control, the Hierarchical FlexGrid doesn't expose an object model.

The General tab

The General tab, shown in Figure 15-6, allows you to assign a value to the control's *Rows* and *Cols* properties, which—as you probably expect—determine the number of rows and columns in the grid. These properties, however, affect the appearance of the control only in unbound mode—that is, when its *DataSource* doesn't point to an ADO data source. In all other cases, the dimensions of the grid depend on the number of records and fields in the source. The *FixedRows* and *FixedCols* properties affect how many fixed (nonscrollable) rows and columns are displayed at the left and on the upper borders of the grid. If the *AllowBigSelection* property is True, clicking on a row or column header selects the entire row or column.

The *Highlight* property affects the appearance of selected cells and can be one of the following enumerated values: 0-flexHighlightNever, 1-flexHighlightAlways (the default—selected cells are always highlighted), and 2-flexHighlightWithFocus (selected cells are highlighted only when the control has the focus). The *FocusRect* property determines which kind of border appears around the current cell: 0-flexFocusNone (no border), 1-flexFocusLight (the default), or 2-flexFocusHeavy.

The *BandDisplay* property can change how bands are displayed in the control and can be either 0-flexBandDisplayHorizontal (the default, all bands corresponding to a record are displayed on the same row) or 1-flexBandDisplayVertical (each band is displayed in a separate row). Under normal circumstances, setting the grid's *Text* property or another cell-formatting property affects only the current cell; you can change this default behavior by changing the value of the *FillStyle* property from 0-flexFillSingle to 1-flexFillRepeat, in which case all the selected cells will be affected by the assignment. The *SelectionMode* property decides whether you can select any cell (0-flexSelectionFree, the default) or are forced to select entire rows (1-flexSelectionByRow) or entire columns (2-flexSelectionByColumn).

The *AllowUserResizing* property determines whether the user can resize rows or columns with the mouse and takes one of the following values: 0-flexResizeNone (no resizing is allowed), 1-flexResizeColumns, 2-flexResizeRows, or 3-flexResizeBoth (the default). If this property is set to 2-flexResizeRows or 3-flexResizeBoth, you can limit the effect of a row resize with the *RowSizingMode* property, which can be 0-flexRowSizeIndividual (only the resized row is affected—this is the default) or 1-flexRowSizeAll (all rows are resized).

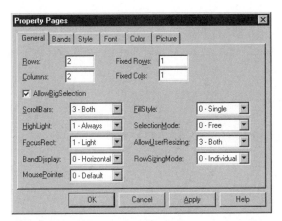

Figure 15-6. *The General tab of the Property Pages dialog box of a Hierarchical FlexGrid control.*

The Bands tab

The Bands tab is probably the most important tab in the Property Pages dialog box of the Hierarchical FlexGrid control, because here you decide which fields in the parent and child Recordsets are visible in the grid. Typically, you should hide those numeric key fields that are meaningless to the user and repeated occurrences of foreign keys. For example, in the demonstration program I hid the Au_ID and ISBN fields in Band 1 (the band that refers to the intermediate Title Author table), because the Au_ID is meaningless to the user and the ISBN field is already displayed in Band 2 (the band that refers to the Titles table). Because all the fields in Band 1 are invisible, the grid actually displays only two bands. You can also change the column caption of any visible field, as shown in Figure 15-7 on the following page.

The Bands tab also allows you to set a few other Band attributes. In the GridLines field, you can select the type of line to draw between the current band and the next one. This value corresponds to the *GridLinesBand* property and can be one of the following values: 0-flexGridNone, 1-flexGridFlat (the default—the color is determined by the *GridColor* property), 2-flexGridInset, 3-flexGridRaised, 4-flexGridDashes, or 5-flexGridDots.

In the TextStyle combo box, you can select the 3-D effect used for displaying text in the band. This corresponds to the *TextStyleBand* property and can be one of the following values: 0-flexTextFlat (the default), 1-flexTextRaised, 2-flexTextInset, 3-flexTextRaisedLight, or 4-flexTextInsetLight. Settings 1 and 2 work best for larger bold fonts, while settings 3 and 4 work better for smaller fonts. The *TextStyleHeader* property can take the same values but affects the style of the text in column headers.

The *BandIndent* property sets the number of columns by which a band is indented; this property has an effect only when the *BandDisplay* property is set to 1-flexBandDisplayVertical. The *BandExpandable* Boolean property specifies whether the band can be expanded or collapsed; a plus or minus symbol is displayed in the first column of the band, unless the band is the last one on its row. The last property on this tab, *ColumnHeaders*, determines whether the grid displays column headers above the band.

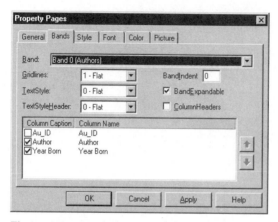

Figure 15-7. *The Bands tab lets you decide which fields are visible in each band and what their captions are.*

The other tabs

The Style tab allows you to set a few other properties that affect the appearance of the grid. The *GridLinesFixed* property corresponds to the style of the grid lines (allowed values are the same as for the *GridLinesBand* property). The *TextStyleFixed* property determines the 3-D style used for text in the fixed rows and columns (using the same values as for the *TextStyleBand* property).

The *MergeCells* property determines how adjacent cells with similar values can be merged; this property is used only when the grid is manually filled with values and has no effect when the control is bound to a hierarchical ADO Recordset. (See the Visual Basic online documentation for further information.)

The *RowHeightMin* property is the minimum height for rows, in twips. The *GridLinesUnpopulated* property affects the style of cells that don't contain any values. The *WordWrap* property should be set to True if you want the text in cells to wrap if longer than the cell's width.

The Hierarchical FlexGrid control exposes many color and font properties that you can assign in the Color and Font tabs, respectively. See the Visual Basic documentation for additional details on these properties.

Run-Time Operations

The Hierarchical FlexGrid control has nearly 160 properties, and their thorough description would require more pages than we can afford here. But since most of these properties affect minor details of the control's appearance, they aren't tremendously interesting. What you really need is a guided tour through the most important properties, methods, and events.

Working with the current cell

The most significant run-time properties of the Hierarchical FlexGrid control are *Row*, *Col*, and *Text*, which set and return the coordinates and contents of the current cell. Remember that this control is inherently read-only: You can programmatically change the contents of any cell in the grid, but the new value won't be stored in the database. Also keep in mind that the grid automatically merges cells with the same values. For example, in the grid displayed in Figure 15-4, the cells in column 1 and rows 2 through 5 have the same value, and you can change this value by setting the *Text* property for any one of the cells that were merged together.

The control exposes a number of read-only properties that return information about the current cell. For example, you can find out what band the current cell belongs to by querying the *BandLevel* property, and you can determine the type of the current cell by querying the grid's *CellType* property, which returns one of the following values: 0-flexCellTypeStandard, 1-flexCellTypeFixed, 2-flexCellTypeHeader, 3-flexCellTypeIndent, or 4-flexCellTypeUnpopulated.

Unlike the DataGrid control, the Hierarchical FlexGrid control allows you to completely determine the appearance of the current cell, through properties such as *CellBackColor*, *CellForeColor*, *CellFontName*, *CellFontSize*, *CellFontBold*, *CellFontItalic*, *CellFontUnderline*, *CellFontStrikeThrough*, and *CellFontWidth*. For example, the following code lets the user highlight any cell by double-clicking on it to change its background to red:

```
Private Sub MSHFlexGrid1_DblClick()
    If MSHFlexGrid1.CellBackColor = vbWindowBackground Then
        ' Highlight a cell with white text on red background.
        MSHFlexGrid1.CellBackColor = vbRed
        MSHFlexGrid1.CellForeColor = vbWhite
    Else
        ' Restore default colors.
        MSHFlexGrid1.CellBackColor = vbWindowBackground
        MSHFlexGrid1.CellForeColor = vbWindowText
    End If
End Sub
```

The *CellTextStyle* property determines the 3-D aspect of the text in the current cell. The *CellAlignment* property sets and returns the alignment attribute for the text in the currently selected cells; it can have one of the following values: 0-flexAlignLeftTop, 1-flexAlignLeftCenter, 2-flexAlignLeftBottom, 3-flexAlignCenterTop, 4-flexAlign-CenterCenter, 5-flexAlignCenterBottom, 6-flexAlignRightTop, 7-flexAlignRightCenter,

8-flexAlignRightBottom, 9-flexAlignGeneral (the default setting—strings to the left, numbers to the right).

You can also display an image in the current cell by assigning a suitable value to the *CellPicture* property and specifying the image's alignment through the *CellPicture-Alignment* property. For example, you can display a string of text in the upper left corner and a picture in the lower right corner:

```
MSHFlexGrid1.CellAlignment = flexAlignLeftTop
MSHFlexGrid1.Text = "This is an arrow"
MSHFlexGrid1.CellPictureAlignment = flexAlignRightBottom
' You might need to edit the path to this icon file.
Set MSHFlexGrid1.CellPicture = LoadPicture( _
    "C:\Microsoft Visual Studio\Graphics\Icons\Arrows\Arw02rt.ico")
```

Accessing other cells

If the *FillStyle* property has been set to 1-flexFillRepeat, most of the properties already mentioned will affect all the cells in the selected range. These include the *CellPicture*, *CellPictureAlignment*, and all the *CellFontxxxx* properties. You therefore have a way to change the formatting of a group of cells by assigning the same properties you would assign for a single cell. A word of caution: Although you can assign a value to the *Text* property to fill all the selected cells with the same string, I found that on some occasions this action raises the error "Method 'Text' of 'IMSHFlexGrid' failed." For this reason, you shouldn't assign a value to the *Text* property when more than one cell is selected, or you should at least protect such an assignment with an *On Error* statement.

To make the best use of the capacity to affect multiple cells with the assignment to a single property, you must learn how to use the *RowSel* and *ColSel* properties to retrieve the coordinates of the current selected range. These properties return the row and column of the cell at one corner of the rectangular selection area. The cell at the opposite corner is always the active cell and is therefore pointed to by the *Row* and *Col* properties. This means that to iterate on all the cells in the current selection you must write code such as the following:

```
' Evaluate the sum of all the cells in the current selection.
Dim total As Double, r As Long, c As Long
Dim rowMin As Long, rowMax As Long
Dim colMin As Long, colMax As Long
' Determine the minimum and maximum row and column.
If MSHFlexGrid1.Row < MSHFlexGrid1.RowSel Then
    rowMin = MSHFlexGrid1.Row
    rowMax = MSHFlexGrid1.RowSel
Else
    rowMin = MSHFlexGrid1.RowSel
    rowMax = MSHFlexGrid1.Row
End If
```

```
If MSHFlexGrid1.Col < MSHFlexGrid1.ColSel Then
    colMin = MSHFlexGrid1.Col
    colMax = MSHFlexGrid1.ColSel
Else
    colMin = MSHFlexGrid1.ColSel
    colMax = MSHFlexGrid1.Col
End If
' Loop on all the selected cells.
On Error Resume Next
For r = rowMin To rowMax
    For c = colMin To colMax
        total = total + CDbl(MSHFlexGrid1.TextMatrix(r, c))
    Next
Next
```

This code uses the *TextMatrix* property, which returns the contents of any cell in the grid. The code works correctly even if a cell spans multiple rows or columns, because in this case *TextMatrix* returns a nonempty value only for the row/column combination corresponding to the top left corner of the merged cell, so you never count the same number more than once.

The *Clip* property offers an efficient way to assign the contents of the cells that are currently selected. First, prepare a tab-delimited string, where individual rows are separated by vbCr characters and individual columns by vbTab characters. Then adjust the *RowSel* and *ColSel* properties to select a range of cells, and finally assign the string to the *Clip* property:

```
Dim clipString As String
clipString = "TopLeft" & vbTab & "TopRight" & vbCr & "BottomLeft" _
    & vbTab & "BottomRight" & vbCr
' Range must be 2 rows by 2 columns to match the clipString.
MSHFlexGrid1.RowSel = MSHFlexGrid1.Row + 1
MSHFlexGrid1.RowCol = MSHFlexGrid1.Col + 1
MSHFlexGrid1.Clip = clipString
```

According to the documentation, this property should also return the contents of the current range as a tab-delimited string; unfortunately, there must be a bug somewhere because this property always returns an empty string. The *Clip* property works correctly in an MSFlexGrid control, so watch out when porting older Visual Basic 5 programs to Visual Basic 6. Until this bug is fixed, you can simulate the *Clip* property by using the following routine:

```
' Return the Clip property for an MSHFlexGrid control.
Function MSHFlexGrid_Clip(FlexGrid As MSHFlexGrid) As String
    Dim r As Long, c As Long, result As String
    Dim rowMin As Long, rowMax As Long
    Dim colMin As Long, colMax As Long
```

(continued)

```
' Find minimum and maximum row and column in selected range.
If FlexGrid.Row < FlexGrid.RowSel Then
    rowMin = FlexGrid.Row
    rowMax = FlexGrid.RowSel
Else
    rowMin = FlexGrid.RowSel
    rowMax = FlexGrid.Row
End If
If FlexGrid.Col < FlexGrid.ColSel Then
    colMin = FlexGrid.Col
    colMax = FlexGrid.ColSel
Else
    colMin = FlexGrid.ColSel
    colMax = FlexGrid.Col
End If
' Build the clip string.
For r = rowMin To rowMax
    For c = colMin To colMax
        result = result & FlexGrid.TextMatrix(r, c)
        If c <> colMax Then result = result & vbTab
    Next
    result = result & vbCr
Next
MSHFlexGrid_Clip = result
End Function
```

The *Clip* property is also useful to work around a known problem in the Hierarchical FlexGrid control: the control can't display more the 2048 rows when used in bound mode. When you bind the grid to a data source with more than 2048 records, the *Rows* property contains the correct number of records, but only the first 2048 records are displayed in the grid. To display all the records in the data source, you can use the ADO Recordset's *GetString* property to retrieve all the records and assign its result to the grid's *Clip* property. For additional information, see article Q194653 in the Microsoft Knowledge Base.

Changing column attributes

You can choose among several properties that affect the attributes of a column. The *ColAlignment* property affects how all the values in standard cells in a column are displayed:

```
' Align the contents of all standard cells in column 2 to center and bottom.
' Column indexes are zero-based.
MSHFlexGrid1.ColAlignment(2) = flexAlignCenterBottom
```

The *ColAlignmentFixed* property does the same, but it affects the cells in the fixed rows:

```
' Align column headers to left and center.
MSHFlexGrid1.ColAlignmentFixed(2) = flexAlignLeftCenter
```

The *ColWordWrapOption* property can be set to True to enable word wrapping in all the standard cells in a column, whereas the *ColWordWrapOptionFixed* property affects the wrapping status of the column header cells:

```
' Enable word wrapping in all cells in column 5.
MSHFlexGrid1.ColWordWrapOption(4) = True
MSHFlexGrid1.ColWordWrapOptionFixed(4) = True
```

The Hierarchical FlexGrid control offers a nonstandard way to set column and row headers. You can set them individually, using the *TextMatrix* property, but you can assign them in a single operation by using the *FormatString* property. In this case, you have to pass the column headers separated by pipe characters (|). You can precede column headers with special characters that affect their alignment (< for left, ^ for center, and > for right); you can also add a section to the format string, separated by a semicolon, containing the headers for all the strings. Here's an example:

```
' Display year numbers in column headers and month names in row headers.
MSHFlexGrid1.FormatString = "Sales|>    1998|>    1999|>    2000" _
    & ";Sales|Jan|Feb|Mar|Apr|May|Jun|Jul|Aug|Sep|Oct|Nov|Dec"
```

The width of each column caption indirectly affects the width of the column itself. For a more precise setting, use the *ColWidth* property. A bug in the implementation of this property makes the Hierarchical FlexGrid control ignore the formatting characters when used with fixed columns. Everything works well with a regular FlexGrid control. (For additional information, see article Q197362 in the Microsoft Knowledge Base.)

Making the grid editable

While the Hierarchical FlexGrid control is inherently a read-only control, it doesn't take much effort to add some basic editing capabilities to it. The trick, as you might have guessed, is to superimpose a TextBox control over the current cell so that it appears as if it belongs to the grid. You need to trap a few events to keep the TextBox in sync with the grid, but on the whole it doesn't require much code.

To make this technique work, add a TextBox control to the form and then set its *Visible* property to False, its *MultiLine* property to True, and its *BorderStyle* property to 0-None. These routines cause the phantom TextBox (named txtCellEditor) to appear and disappear as needed:

```
' These variables keep track of the cell that was active
' when edit mode was entered.
Dim cellRow As Long, cellCol As Long
```

(continued)

```
Sub ShowCellEditor()
    With MSHFlexGrid1
        ' Cancel range selection, if any.
        .RowSel = .Row
        .ColSel = .Col
        ' Move the cell editor into place by making it one pixel smaller
        ' than the current cell.
        txtCellEditor.Move .Left + .CellLeft, .Top + .CellTop, _
            .CellWidth - ScaleX(1, vbPixels, vbTwips), _
            .CellHeight - ScaleY(1, vbPixels, vbTwips)
        ' Transfer the contents of the current cell into the TextBox.
        txtCellEditor.Text = .Text
        ' Move the TextBox in front of the grid.
        txtCellEditor.Visible = True
        txtCellEditor.ZOrder
        txtCellEditor.SetFocus
        ' Remember current coordinates for later.
        cellRow = .Row
        cellCol = .Col
    End With
End Sub

Sub HideCellEditor(Optional Cancel As Boolean)
    ' Hide the TextBox control if necessary.
    If txtCellEditor.Visible Then
        ' If the operation hasn't been canceled, transfer the contents
        ' of the TextBox into the cell that was active.
        If Not Cancel Then
            MSHFlexGrid1.TextMatrix(cellRow, cellCol) = txtCellEditor.Text
        End If
        txtCellEditor.Visible = False
    End If
End Sub
```

The *ShowCellEditor* routine can move the TextBox into place, thanks to the grid's *CellLeft*, *CellTop*, *CellWidth*, and *CellHeight* properties. The next step is to determine when cell editing is activated. In the demonstration program, this happens when the grid is double-clicked or when the user presses an alphanumeric key when the grid has the input focus:

```
Private Sub MSHFlexGrid1_DblClick()
    ShowCellEditor
End Sub

Private Sub MSHFlexGrid1_KeyPress(KeyAscii As Integer)
    ShowCellEditor
    ' If it's an alphanumeric key, it is passed to the TextBox.
    If KeyAscii >= 32 Then
```

```
        txtCellEditor.Text = Chr$(KeyAscii)
        txtCellEditor.SelStart = 1
    End If
End Sub
```

Edit mode is terminated when the TextBox loses the focus (for example, when the user clicks elsewhere in the grid), or when either the Enter or Esc key is pressed:

```
Private Sub txtCellEditor_LostFocus()
    HideCellEditor
End Sub

Private Sub txtCellEditor_KeyPress(KeyAscii As Integer)
    Select Case KeyAscii
        Case 13
            HideCellEditor
        Case 27
            HideCellEditor True      ' Also cancel the edit.
    End Select
End Sub
```

It should be noted that this simple example modifies only the contents of the Hierarchical FlexGrid control without affecting the underlying ADO hierarchical Recordset. Updating the underlying ADO hierarchical Recordset is a more complex task, but the grid offers all the properties you need to determine which field in which record should be modified.

THE DATAREPORT DESIGNER

Visual Basic 6 is the first version that includes a report writer completely integrated in the IDE. Compared to the more popular Crystal Report, you'll probably find—especially for simpler reports—the new report designer easier to use. But it still lacks several features and can't reasonably replace Crystal Report or other third-party report writers for heavy-duty tasks. By the way, Crystal Report is still included in the package, even though you have to install it manually.

Before using the DataReport designer, you must make it accessible from the IDE, which you do by issuing the Components command from the Project menu, switching to the Designer tab, and ticking the Data Report check box. Alternatively, you can create a new Data Project and let Visual Basic create an instance of the DataReport designer for you.

The DataReport designer works in bound mode only, in the sense that it's able to automatically retrieve the data to be sent to the printer or simply displayed in the preview window. It can export a report to a text file or an HTML file and also supports custom format layouts. The DataReport designer comes with a set of custom controls that you can drop on its surface in the same way as you do with forms and other designers. These controls include lines, shapes, images, and also function fields, which you can use to create summary fields in your reports. Another intriguing feature of this designer is its ability to print in asynchronous mode, which lets the user perform other tasks while the printing proceeds.

Design-Time Operations

The simplest way to create a report using the DataReport designer is in conjunction with the DataEnvironment designer. The DataReport designer supports drag-and-drop operations of DataEnvironment's Command objects, including hierarchical Command objects. The only limitation is that the report can account for just one child Recordset at each nesting level. For all the examples in this chapter, I'll use a hierarchical Command object based on the Orders and Order Details tables in the NWind.mdb database. As usual, the complete sample application is provided on the companion CD.

Binding to a Command object

Here are the steps you should follow to create a report based on the sample hierarchical Command object:

1. Create a hierarchical Command, named Orders, that contains a child Command named Order Details. Ensure that it retrieves the information you're interested in—for example, by binding it to a Hierarchical FlexGrid control on a form and running the application.

2. Create a new instance of the DataReport designer, or use the one provided by default with a Data Project type of Visual Basic project.

3. Bring up the Properties window, let the DataReport's *DataSource* property point to *DataEnvironment1* (or whatever the name of your DataEnvironment is), and then set its *DataMember* property to *Orders*.

4. Right-click on the Report Header of the DataReport designer, and select the Retrieve Structure menu command; this will create a Group Header and Group Footer section labeled Orders_Header and Orders_Footer, respectively; between them is a Detail section labeled Order_Details_Detail.

   A section represents a block of data that will be repeated for each record in the parent Command object. The first section corresponds to the parent Command object, the second section to its child Command, and so on until you reach the Detail section, which corresponds to the innermost Command object. All the sections except the Detail section are divided into a header section and a footer section, which are printed before and after the information related to the sections pertaining to objects at an inner level. The DataReport designer also includes a Report section (which prints information at the beginning and end of the report) and a Page section (which prints information at the beginning and end of each page). If you don't see these two sections, right-click anywhere on the DataReport designer and select the appropriate menu command.

5. Drag the fields you need from the Orders Command object in the DataEnvironment to the Orders_Header section of the DataReport. Whenever you release the mouse button, a pair of controls, RptLabel and a RptTextBox, appear in the DataReport. When the report is eventually displayed, the RptLabel control produces a constant string with the name of the field (or whatever you assigned to its *Caption* property), while the RptTextBox control is replaced by the actual contents of the corresponding database field. You can then arrange the fields in the Orders_Header section and delete the RptLabel controls that you don't want to display.

6. Click on the Order Details Command object and drag it onto the DataReport; Visual Basic creates one RtpLabel-RptTextBox control pair for each field in the corresponding Recordset. You can then delete the OrderID field and arrange the others in a row, as displayed in Figure 15-8 on the following page.

7. Adjust each section's height so that it doesn't take more room than strictly necessary. This is especially important for the Detail section, because it will be repeated for each single record in the Order Detail table. You can also reduce all the sections that don't contain any fields to a null height.

8. What you've done so far is sufficient to see the DataReport in action. Bring up the Project Property Pages dialog box, select DataReport1 as the start-up object, and then run the program.

Before moving on to another topic, a couple of notes about the placement of controls are in order. First, you can drop any control in the section that corresponds to the Command object it belongs to, as well as in any section with a deeper nesting level. For example, you can drop the OrderID field from the Orders Command in both the Orders section and the Order_Details section. You can't, however, move the UnitPrice field from the inner Order_Details section to the Order section. Second, you shouldn't drop binary fields or fields containing images from the DataEnvironment onto the DataReport designer; Visual Basic won't generate an error, but it will create a RptTextBox control that contains meaningless characters at run time.

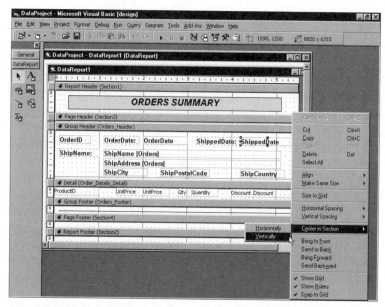

Figure 15-8. *The DataReport designer at design time, with the pop-up menu that appears when you right-click on a control.*

Setting control properties

The controls you have dropped on the DataReport's surface are similar to the standard controls you place on a form, but they belong to a different control library. In fact, you can't drop a standard intrinsic control on a DataReport designer, nor can you place a control from the DataReport control library on a form or another designer. But you can move DataReport controls and align them as you would do with any regular control. You can't use the commands in the standard Format menu, though, and you have to right-click on the control and use the commands in the pop-up menu, as shown in Figure 15-8.

DataReport controls react to the F4 key in the same way regular controls do, by displaying the Properties window. Because the RptLabel and RptTextBox controls are so similar to their standard counterparts, you should already be familiar with most of the properties you find in this window. For example, you can change the *DataFormat* properties of the txtOrderDate and txtShippedDate controls so that they display their values in long date format. Or you can change the txtOrderID control's *BackStyle* property to 1-rptBkOpaque and its *BackColor* property to gray (&HE0E0E0) so that order identifiers are highlighted in the report. RptLabel controls don't expose any *Dataxxxx* property; they're just cosmetic controls that insert fixed strings in the report.

The only custom property that we haven't seen yet is *CanGrow*, which applies to both the RptLabel and RptTextBox controls. If this property is True, the control is allowed to expand vertically when its content exceeds the control's width. The default value for this property is False, which causes longer strings to be truncated to the control's width.

Adding controls

Nothing prevents you from adding new controls to the DataReport from the Toolbox rather than from the DataEnvironment designer. In fact, the Toolbox includes a DataReport tab, which contains all the controls in the MSDataReportLib library. In addition to the RptLabel and RptTextBox controls, this library also contains the following items:

- The RptLine and RptShape controls, which allow you to add lines and other elementary shapes to the report, including squares and rectangles (also with round corners), circles, and ovals. You can't change a line's width, but you can create horizontal and vertical lines of any width by using rectangular RptShape controls whose *BackStyle* property is set to 1-rptBkOpaque.

- The RptImage control, which adds static images to the report, such as a company logo. Unfortunately this control can't be bound to a data source, so you can't use it to display images stored in database binary fields.

- The RptFunction control, a textbox variant that can automatically evaluate simple aggregate functions, such as count, sum, average, minimum, maximum, and standard deviation. (This control is described further in the next section.)

For example, drop a horizontal line in the Orders_Footer group, as shown in Figure 15-8. This control will draw a line to separate each group of detail information about an order. Using the *BorderStyle* property, you can also draw several types of dotted lines.

Displaying calculated fields

There are two ways to display calculated fields. The first way, which is suitable for calculated values that depend on other values in the same record, requires that you modify the SELECT command to include the calculated field in the list of fields to be retrieved. In the Orders example, you might have the inner Order Details Command object work with the following SELECT query:

```
SELECT OrderID, ProductID, UnitPrice, Quantity, Discount,
    ((UnitPrice*Quantity)*(1-Discount)) AS Total FROM [Order Details]
```

Then you might add a Total field in the Detail section that lists the total price for each record from the Order Details table. Remember to align the field to the right and allow for the correct number of digits after the decimal point. This way of implementing calculated fields is fairly versatile because you can use all the functions offered by SQL. But it can only work on a record-by-record basis.

Another way to take advantage of SQL is to use a JOIN clause in the SELECT command to retrieve information from other tables. For example, you might transform the ProductID field in the Order Details table into the product's name from the Products table, using the following SELECT in the Order Details Command object:

```
SELECT [Order Details].OrderID, [Order Details].ProductID,
    [Order Details].UnitPrice, [Order Details].Quantity,
    [Order Details].Discount, (([Order Details].UnitPrice*[Order
    Details].Quantity)*(1-[Order Details].Discount))  AS Total,
    Products.ProductName FROM [Order Details] INNER JOIN Products
    ON [Order Details].ProductID = Products.ProductID
```

You can use the same technique to display the customer's name in the Orders_Header section. The sample application, however, achieves the same result by using a different technique, which I'll explain in the "Adding Dynamic Formatting and Lookup Fields" section at the end of this chapter.

The second technique for adding a calculated field is based on RptFunction controls and is suitable for summary fields. For example, let's add a field that evaluates the total value of each order. This requires calculating the sum of the values of the Total field in the Order_Details Command. To do this, you must drop a RptFunction control into the Orders_Footer section—that is, the first footer after the section where the data to be summed is displayed. Then set the new control's *DataMember* property to Order_Details, its *DataField* property to Total, its *FunctionType* to 0-rptFuncSum, and its *DataFormat* property to Currency. Using the same approach, you can add a summary field with the total number of distinct products in the order, by setting *DataField* to ProductID and *FunctionType* to 4-rptFuncRCnt.

You're not forced to place a RptFunction control in the footer section that immediately follows the section where the data field is. For example, to evaluate the sum of the Total fields from the Order_Details Command, you can add a RptFunction control in the Report Footer section, and you can add another RptFunction control to calculate the sum of the Freight fields from the Orders section. In any case, you only have to set these controls' *DataMember* properties to point to the correct Command object. Unfortunately, you can't place a RptFunction control in a Page Footer section, so you can't have totals at the end of each page.

Thanks to the capabilities of the DataEnvironment designer, there is nothing special about preparing a report that groups records. For example, to display a list of customers grouped by country, all you have to do is create a Command object linked to the Customers table, switch to the Grouping tab of its Property Pages dialog box, and group the Command object by its Country field. This operation creates a new Command object with two folders. You can then assign this Command to the

DataMember property of a DataReport designer and issue the Retrieve Structure command to let the designer automatically create the necessary sections. The sample application on the companion CD includes a report built using this technique.

Managing page footers and page breaks

You can place controls in a Page Header or Page Footer section, typically to display information about the current page number, the total number of pages, the date and time of the report, and so forth. To do this, right-click in the section of interest, select the Insert Control menu command, and then from a pop-up menu select the information you want to display.

A control created in this way is a RptLabel, which contains special characters in its *Caption* property. Table 15-1 on the next page summarizes the characters with a special meaning when inside a RptLabel control. You can create the control yourself and set a suitable *Caption* property—for example, *Page %p of %P* to display the current and the total number of pages—in the same RptLabel control. Figure 15-9 displays the area near the bottom border of a report that includes a page footer, summary fields, and other embellishments that we've seen so far.

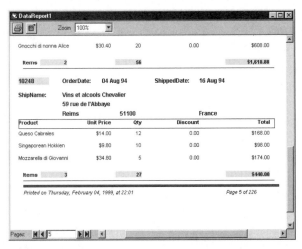

Figure 15-9. *The DataReport designer at run time; the controls in the window let you print the report, export it to a file, and navigate through its pages.*

All the Section objects expose two properties that affect how page breaks are inserted in the report. The *ForcePageBreak* property determines if a new page should be started before or after the section and can take one of the following values: 0-rptPageBreakNone (the default), 1-rptPageBreakBefore (add a page break before printing the section), 2-rptPageBreakAfter (add a page break immediately after the section), or 3-rptPageBreakBeforeAndAfter (add a page break immediately before and after the section).

The other property that affects the page breaks added to the report is the *KeepTogether* Boolean property. If you set this property to True, the DataReport designer will automatically insert a page break before the section if its contents would overflow to the next page. Both these properties are also exposed by the Report and Page sections, but they're ignored in these cases.

Symbol	Description	Symbol	Description
%d	Current date (Short format)	%p	Current page number
%D	Current date (Long format)	%P	Total number of pages
%t	Current time (Short format)	%i	The title of the report
%T	Current time (Long format)	%%	Percentage symbol

Table 15-1. *The special characters accepted in a RtpLabel's* Caption *property.*

Other report properties

The DataReport designer exposes many design-time properties, which you can modify in the Properties window as you would do with any other designer. Most of these properties are also exposed by forms—for example, *Caption, Font, WindowState,* and *ShowInTaskbar*—therefore, you already know how to use them. Some of these properties (such as *Caption* and *BorderStyle*) affect only the preview window; others (for example, *Font*) also affect the printed report.

Only a few properties are peculiar to the DataReport designer. The *LeftMargin, RightMargin, TopMargin,* and *BottomMargin* properties set and return the size of the printed report margins, whereas *ReportWidth* determines the width of the printed page. The *GridX* and *GridY* properties affect the distance between the division of the control grid at design time and are ignored at run time. All these measures are expressed in twips. The only other custom property of the DataReport designer is *Title,* which is used to replace the *%i* placeholder in RptLabel controls, as explained in the previous section, and is also used when displaying dialog boxes at run time.

> **CAUTION** You can make the DataReport window an MDI child window by setting its *MDIChild* property to True. Just be aware that there is a bug that sometimes makes the DataReport window disappear from the WindowList menu of the MDI application. For additional information and a workaround for this problem, see article Q195972 in the Microsoft Knowledge Base.

Run-Time Operations

While you can prepare great reports by merely dropping some controls on a DataReport designer, don't forget that because this is an object that exposes properties, methods, and events, it can be controlled through code at run time. The code can be placed outside the designer—for example, in the form that starts the reporting process—or inside the DataReport module itself. The latter approach lets you create a complex report and encapsulate all the code that manages it in the designer module so that you can easily reuse it in other projects.

Printing the report

The easiest way to print the report is to let the user start the operation interactively by clicking on the leftmost button in the DataReport preview window. Users can pick a printer from the list of installed ones and select a page range and the number of copies they want. They can even print to a file so that they can do the actual printing later. When you enable interactive printing, all you need to do is display the DataReport window, which you can do by using the *Show* method or (as is rarely done) by designating the DataReport designer as the startup object of the current project. You can use several properties to modify the default appearance of the preview window:

```
' Display the DataReport in a modal maximized window.
DataReport1.WindowState = vbMaximized
DataReport1.Show vbModal
```

You can fine-tune the printing process if you start the print process yourself through code. You will need the *PrintReport* method of the DataReport designer, which accepts several arguments and returns a Long value:

```
Cookie = PrintReport([ShowDialog], [Range], [PageFrom], [PageTo])
```

ShowDialog is a Boolean value that determines whether the designer will display the Print dialog box, and *Range* can be one of the following values: 0-rptRangeAllPages or 1-rptRangeFromTo. If you want to print a page range, you should pass the number of the first and last page to the *PageFrom* and *PageTo* arguments, respectively. The *PrintReport* method starts an asynchronous print process and returns a cookie value, which can be used to refer to the particular print operation. Here's an example:

```
' Print the first 10 pages of the report without showing a dialog.
Dim Cookie As Long
Cookie = DataReport1.PrintReport(False, rptRangeFromTo, 1, 10)
```

Taking advantage of asynchronous processing

Producing the report consists of three subprocesses: the query; the creation of a temporary file; and the actual print, preview, or export operation. The first two are synchronous operations; the third is asynchronous. While the DataReport designer is performing an asynchronous operation, it periodically fires a *ProcessingTimeout* event, approximately once every second. You can trap this event to let the user cancel a lengthy operation, using a block of code similar to the one shown on the following page.

```
Private Sub DataReport_ProcessingTimeout(ByVal Seconds As Long, _
    Cancel As Boolean,ByVal JobType As MSDataReportLib.AsyncTypeConstants,_
    ByVal Cookie As Long)
    ' Display a message every 20 seconds.
    Const TIMEOUT = 20
    ' The value of Seconds when we displayed the last message.
    Static LastMessageSecs As Long

    ' Reset LastMessage if a new print operation is in progress.
    If Seconds < LastMessageSecs Then
        LastMessageSecs = 0
    ElseIf LastMessageSecs + TIMEOUT <= Seconds Then
        ' A new timeout interval has elapsed.
        LastMessageSecs = Seconds
        ' Ask the user whether the operation should be canceled.
        If MsgBox("This operation has been started " & Seconds _
            & " seconds ago." & vbCr & "Do you want to cancel it?", _
            vbYesNo + vbExclamation) = vbYes Then
            Cancel = True
        End If
    End If
End Sub
```

The *JobType* argument is the type of operation in progress and can be one of the following values: 0-rptAsyncPreview, 1-rptAsyncPrint, or 2-rptAsyncExport. *Cookie* identifies the particular operation and corresponds to the Long value returned by a *PrintReport* or *ExportReport* method.

If you're simply interested in displaying a progress indicator without canceling an asynchronous operation, you can use the *AsyncProgress* event, which is fired every time a new page is sent to the printer or exported to a file:

```
Private Sub DataReport_AsyncProgress(ByVal JobType As
    MSDataReportLib.AsyncTypeConstants, ByVal Cookie As Long, _
    ByVal PageCompleted As Long, ByVal TotalPages As Long)
    ' Display the progress in a Label control on the main form.
    frmMain.lblStatus = "Printing page " & PageCompleted _
        & " of " & TotalPages
End Sub
```

If the DataReport designer can't continue its operations because of an error, it raises an *Error* event. In this event, you can determine which operation failed and suppress the standard error message by setting the *ShowError* parameter to False:

```
Private Sub DataReport_Error(ByVal JobType As
    MSDataReportLib.AsyncTypeConstants, ByVal Cookie As Long,
    ByVal ErrObj As MSDataReportLib.RptError, ShowError As Boolean)
    ' Display your own custom error message box.
    If JobType = rptAsyncPrint Or JobType = rptAsyncExport Then
```

```
        MsgBox "Error #" & ErrObj.ErrorNumber & vbCr _
            & ErrObj.Description, vbCritical
        ShowError = False
    End If
End Sub
```

Exporting a report

Users can export the current report by clicking on the second button from the left in the DataReport preview window. In the dialog box that appears, they must select a file name, a file type, and a page range, as shown in Figure 15-10. The DataReport designer supports four types of export formats: HTML Text, Unicode, HTML, and Unicode Text. Note that the dialog doesn't display the correct number of total pages; this value depends on the export format and generally doesn't match the number of pages in the preview window (which depends on the Font used in the window itself). Also note that the exported report can't include graphics originated by RptImage and RptShape controls. Horizontal lines are acceptable in HTML reports and appear as rows of hyphens in text reports. Table 15-2 on the following page lists the indices, symbolic constants, and string values that you can use to identify the four predefined export formats.

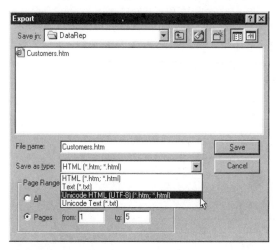

Figure 15-10. *The Export dialog box lets you export a report in one of four predefined formats.*

The *ExportReport* method allows you to programmatically export a report, and has the following syntax:

```
Cookie = ExportReport([FormatIndexOrKey], [FileName], [Overwrite],
    [ShowDialog], [Range], [PageFrom], [PageTo])
```

FormatIndexOrKey is a numerical index or a string key that identifies one of the predefined export formats, *FileName* is the name of the output file, *Overwrite* is a Boolean value that determines whether an existing file can be overwritten (the default is True), and *ShowDialog* is a Boolean value that specifies whether the standard export dialog box should be displayed. The remaining arguments have the same meaning as in the *PrintReport* method. The *ExportReport* method returns a Long value that can be used to identify this particular operation in a *ProcessingTimeout*, *AsyncProgress*, or *Error* event.

The *FormatOrIndexKey* is one of the values found in the first three columns of Table 15-2. In fact, you can pass a number in the range from 1 to 4, a *rptKey*xxxx symbolic constant, or its corresponding string value. If you omit either the export format or the file name, the Export dialog box is displayed even if you set *ShowDialog* to False:

```
' Export all pages to an HTML file in the application's directory.
Cookie = DataReport1.ExportReport rptKeyHTML, App.Path & "\Orders", True
```

The export dialog is also displayed if you specify the name of an existing file and pass *Overwrite* set to False. You can omit the file extension because the export filter adds the correct extension automatically.

> **CAUTION**   The exporting features of the DataReport designer probably need some refinement. On many occasions, executing the preceding code caused a crash in the IDE. This problemn shows up randomly, and I've not been able to find a recurring pattern or a workaround for it.

Index	Symbolic Constant	String	File Filter	Description
1	rptKeyHTML	"key_def_HTML"	*.htm, *.html	HTML
2	rptKeyUnicode-HTML_UTF8	"key_def_Unicode-HTML_UTF8"	*.htm, *.html	Unicode HTML
3	rptKeyText	"key_def_Text"	*.txt	Text
4	rptKeyUnicode-Text	"key_def_Unicode-Text"	*.txt	Unicode text

Table 15-2. *Indexes, symbolic constants and string values that identify the four predefined export formats.*

Creating custom export formats

The export mechanism is fairly sophisticated. In fact, you can define your own export format by adding an ExportFormat object to the ExportFormats collection. The

Add method of this collection expects five arguments, which correspond to the properties of the ExportFormat object being created:

```
ExportFormats.Add Key, FormatType, FileFormatString, FileFilter, Template
```

Key is the string key that will identify the new export format in the collection. *FormatType* is one of the following constants: 0-rptFmtHTML, 1-rptFmtText, 2-rptFmtUnicodeText, or 3-rptFmtUnicodeHTML_UTF8. *FileFormatString* is the description that will appear in the File Filter combo box within the Export dialog box, *FileFilter* is the file filter used for this type of report, and *Template* is a string that determines how the report is arranged:

```
Private Sub DataReport_Initialize()
    ' Create a custom export format.
    Dim template As String
    template = "My Custom Text Report" & vbCrLf & vbCrLf _
        & rptTagTitle & vbCrLf & vbCrLf _
        & rptTagBody
    ExportFormats.Add "Custom Text", rptFmtText, _
        "Custom text format (*.txt)", "*.txt", template
End Sub
```

When creating the *Template* property, you can use two special strings that will work as placeholders to be replaced by the actual report elements. The DataReport library exposes such strings as symbolic constants: The rptTagTitle constant is replaced by the report title (much like a RptLabel control whose *Caption* property is set to %i), while rptTagBody is replaced by the report body. When you create template strings for HTML formats, you can enforce any text attribute, as in the following code:

```
Private Sub DataReport_Initialize()
    ' Create a custom HTML format for exporting this report.
    Dim template As String
    Title = "Orders in May 1999"
    template = "<HTML>" & vbCrLf & _
        "<HEAD>" & vbCrLf & _
        "<TITLE>" & rptTagTitle & "</TITLE>" & vbCrLf & _
        "<BODY>" & vbCrLf _
        & rptTagBody & vbCrLf & _
        "</BODY>" & vbCrLf & _
        "</HTML>"
    ExportFormats.Add "Custom HTML", rptFmtHTML, _
        "Custom HTML format (*.htm)", "*.htm;*.html", template
End Sub
```

Once you've added a custom ExportFormat object, it appears in the Export dialog box's combo box, and you can select it programmatically as you would a built-in export format:

```
' Export the first page to an HTML report in custom format.
Cookie = DataReport1.ExportReport "Custom Text", App.Path & "\Orders", _
    True, False, rptRangeFromTo, 1, 1
```

Changing the report layout at run time

You often need to create several similar reports, such as one report that displays all the information in the Employees table and another that hides the confidential data. Because the DataReport is a programmable object, you can, in most cases, accommodate such minor differences with a few lines of code. In fact, you can reference all the controls that make up the report and consequently move them around, change their size and visibility, or assign new values to properties such as *Caption*, *ForeColor*, and so on.

Before looking at the implementation details, you must learn how to reference a Section object, using the Sections collection, and to reference a control inside a given section:

```
' Hide the footer section corresponding to the Orders Command.
DataReport1.Sections("Orders_Footer").Visible = False
' Change the background color of the lblTitle control.
DataReport1.Sections("Section1").Controls("lblTitle").Caption = "May 99"
```

You can reference a particular section using its numerical index or its name. When the DataReport is initially created, the default sections have generic names: Section1 is the Report Header, Section2 is the Report Footer, Section3 is the Page Header, and Section4 is the Page Footer. The sections that contain database fields take the names of the Command objects from which they retrieve data. In all cases, however, you can change the section's *Name* property in the Properties window.

Alas, you can't add controls at run time because the DataReport's Controls collection doesn't support the *Add* method (unlike the form's Controls collection). To work around this limitation, you have to incorporate all the possible fields when preparing a report and then hide those fields that aren't needed in a particular version of the report. You can also hide an entire section by using the section's *Visible* property, and you can shrink a section by using its *Height* property. There's a peculiarity, however: You can't reduce a section's height if the operation would leave one or more controls partially invisible. (This holds true even if the control's *Visible* property is False.) For this reason, after you make a control invisible, you have to decrease its *Top* property if you also want to shrink the section it belongs to.

The program on the companion CD puts all these techniques together to create a report in two versions (shown in Figure 15-11 on the following page), with and without details on each order. To make the report a reusable entity, I've added a Public Boolean property named *ShowDetails*, which can be assigned from outside the DataReport module before invoking its *Show*, *PrintReport*, or *ExportReport* methods. This is the code inside the DataReport module that implements this feature:

```
' A private member variable.
Dim m_ShowDetails As Boolean

Public Property Get ShowDetails() As Boolean
    ShowDetails = m_ShowDetails
End Property

Public Property Let ShowDetails(ByVal newValue As Boolean)
    Dim newTop As Single
    m_ShowDetails = newValue
    ' This property affects the visibility of the innermost section.
    Sections("Order_Details_Detail").Visible = m_ShowDetails
    ' It also affects the visibility of a few fields in the Orders section.
    ' This is the actual Top value if controls are visible; 0 otherwise.
    newTop = IIf(m_ShowDetails, 1870, 0)

    With Sections("Orders_Header")
        .Controls("lblProduct").Visible = m_ShowDetails
        .Controls("lblProduct").Top = newTop
        .Controls("lblUnitPrice").Visible = m_ShowDetails
        .Controls("lblUnitPrice").Top = newTop
        .Controls("lblQty").Visible = m_ShowDetails
        .Controls("lblQty").Top = newTop
        .Controls("lblDiscount").Visible = m_ShowDetails
        .Controls("lblDiscount").Top = newTop
        .Controls("lblTotal").Visible = m_ShowDetails
        .Controls("lblTotal").Top = newTop
        .Controls("shaDetailHeader").Visible = m_ShowDetails
        .Controls("shaDetailHeader").Top = newTop
        ' Setting the section's Height to 0 shrinks it as much as possible.
        .Height = IIf(m_ShowDetails, 2200, 0)
    End With
End Property
```

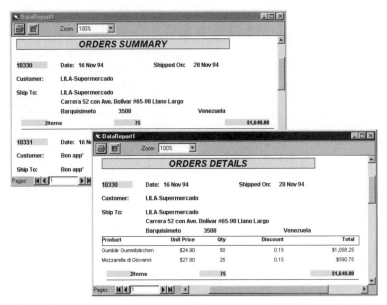

Figure 15-11. *Two versions of the demonstration report, with and without detail data on each order.*

Adding dynamic formatting and lookup fields

At first sight, it seems that the DataReport design has little to offer highly experienced Visual Basic programmers who have learned to use more powerful report writers such as Crystal Report. The truth is, however, that when you combine the DataReport with the standard ADO binding mechanism, its potential increases markedly.

The key to such power isn't obvious until you remember that you can control the format of bound fields through the *Format* event of a StdDataFormat object. Because this event fires each time a value is read from the data source, it offers a way to execute your custom code each time a record is about to be displayed on the report. The following example shows how you can use this technique to omit null discount values:

```
' This is used to trap the instant when a new record is read.
Dim WithEvents DiscountFormat As StdDataFormat

Private Sub DataReport_Initialize()
    ' Create a StdDataFormat object, and assign it to the txtDiscount field.
    Set DiscountFormat = New StdDataFormat
    Set Sections("Order_Details_Detail").Controls("txtDiscount"). _
        DataFormat = DiscountFormat
End Sub
```

```
Private Sub DiscountFormat_Format(ByVal DataValue As _
    StdFormat.StdDataValue)
    ' If the discount is zero, use a Null value instead.
    If CDbl(DataValue.Value) = 0 Then DataValue.Value = Null
End Sub
```

Unfortunately, the code inside a *Format* event procedure can't directly modify a control's properties, such as *Visible*, *ForeColor*, or *BackColor*. Nor can it dynamically assign an image to a RptImage control while the report is being processed, which would enable you to overcome the designer's inability to display bitmaps stored in a database. If these limitations were addressed, the DataReport designer would become a tool suitable even for most demanding reporting jobs.

The only other (minor) problem I found with this approach is that the *DataValue.TargetObject* property contains Nothing when the event fires, so you can't assign the same StdDataFormat object to the *DataFormat* properties of multiple controls, because you wouldn't have any means to tell which field is being processed.

The demonstration program also shows how you can implement lookup fields using a variant of this mechanism. In its *Initialize* event, the DataReport opens a Recordset that points to the lookup table, and in the *Format* event, it transforms the CustomerID value in the Orders table into the value of the CompanyName field in the Customers table:

```
Dim WithEvents CustFormat As StdDataFormat
' Used to look up the CustomerID field in the Customers table
Dim rsCust As New ADODB.Recordset

Private Sub DataReport_Initialize()
    ' Create a new format object, and assign it to the txtCustomer field.
    Set CustFormat = New StdDataFormat
    Set Sections("Orders_Header").Controls("txtCustomerName").DataFormat _
        = CustFormat
    ' Open a Recordset on the Customers table.
    rsCust.Open "Customers", DataEnvironment1.Connection1, adOpenStatic, _
        adLockReadOnly, adCmdTable
End Sub

Private Sub DataReport_Terminate()
    ' Close the Recordset.
    rsCust.Close
    Set rsCust = Nothing
End Sub

Private Sub CustFormat_Format(ByVal DataValue As StdFormat.StdDataValue)
    ' Transform a CustomerID value into the customer's CompanyName.
```

(continued)

```
        rsCust.MoveFirst
        rsCust.Find "CustomerID='" & DataValue.Value & "'"
        If rsCust.EOF Then
            DataValue.Value = Null                    ' Match not found.
        Else
            DataValue.Value = rsCust("CompanyName")   ' Match found.
        End If
    End Sub
End Sub
```

This chapter concludes the part of the book devoted to database programming. At this point, you probably know more than you ever dreamed of knowing about ADO, and above all you're aware of its incredible power and some of its shortcomings. In the next part of the book, I describe how you can take advantage of what you have learned about classes and objects to create ActiveX components and controls. If you're a database programmer, you'll find additional material in Chapter 18 about the inner workings of ADO, including directions for building your own data source classes and OLE DB providers.

Part IV
ActiveX
Programming

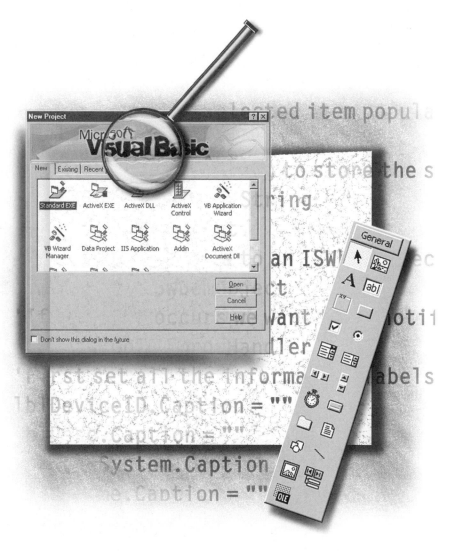

Chapter 16

ActiveX Components

A feature that greatly contributed to making Visual Basic one of the most popular languages for Microsoft Windows programming is its ability to create ActiveX components and controls. As you'll see in this chapter, creating an ActiveX component is an easy process, and in most cases you can turn a class-based application into a component simply by changing a few project settings. This shouldn't be a surprise; after all, classes were introduced in Visual Basic 4 with their main (or only) purpose being to help in the delivery of COM components. This move was necessary because Microsoft intended to propose Visual Basic as a language for developing complex multitier client/server applications.

INTRODUCING COM

I don't want to dive into the technical details of COM, but to understand the potential of Visual Basic in this area you need at least to understand a few key concepts.

A Long Story Made Short

When Microsoft launched Windows, its first operating system able to execute multiple applications at the same time, everyone could see that Microsoft needed to devise a system for those applications to exchange data and communicate with one another. The Clipboard was good for doing simple cut-and-paste operations, but it was too primitive and didn't address the most demanding requirements that Windows now posed.

The first serious attempt in the right direction was DDE (Dynamic Data Exchange), a communication protocol that let applications call each other. DDE wasn't very successful, probably because of its lack of reliability. Even though it was extended to work on LANs (Network DDE) and was therefore able to connect applications on different workstations, few Windows applications implemented it. (Visual Basic offers limited support of DDE, but I don't cover it in this book.)

The first version of OLE (Object Linking and Embedding) for Windows 3.1 appeared in 1992 and used DDE as the underlying means for interapplication communications. OLE was the first protocol that enabled users and programmers to create *compound documents*—that is, documents that contain data from different applications (for example, an Excel worksheet inside a Word document). Depending on the application's needs, compound documents can completely encapsulate other simpler documents (embedding) or contain simply a reference to existing documents (linking). When the user clicks on an embedded or linked document inside a compound document, Windows runs the application that's capable of dealing with that particular type of document.

OLE 2 was released in 1993, and for the first time it included the support for *in-place activation,* which gave a user the ability to edit compound documents without opening a different window. For example, OLE 2 lets you edit an Excel worksheet embedded in a Word document without leaving the Word environment. But you see only the Excel menus, which replace Word's menus when you're editing the embedded data. OLE 2 was an important step also because it abandoned DDE as the communication protocol and relied instead on a new component-based architecture: COM (Component Object Model).

It gradually became apparent that the COM infrastructure was even more important than linking and embedding technologies. While the ability to create compound documents is remarkable from the user's standpoint, developers found that they could build great applications just using COM. In fact, COM promotes the concept of component-based development, which lets you subdivide large applications into smaller pieces that you can maintain and deploy more easily than you can a monolithic application. The portion of OLE that lets programs talk to each other is known as *OLE Automation*. Many programming languages can work as *OLE Automation clients,* which control other applications known as *OLE Automation servers*. For example, you can drive Excel and Word from the outside using Visual Basic 3 and later versions as well as VBScript.

The potential for this new programming paradigm became evident when Microsoft shipped Visual Basic 4 Enterprise Edition, which included the support for Remote Automation. Not only were Visual Basic programmers finally able to create COM components, they were also the pioneers who could launch and execute a component located on a computer across the network, using that machine's CPU, memory, and other resources. Distributed computing had made its debut on Windows platforms.

At the time Visual Basic 4 was released, another type of component appeared for the first time: OLE controls. These were the successors to the VBX controls, which had greatly contributed to the popularity of Visual Basic. The problem with VBX controls was that they were based on a proprietary architecture, namely, the Visual Basic environment, which made it nearly impossible to use them with different languages. When switching to 32-bit platforms, Microsoft decided to create a new type of controls based on OLE that could be adopted and supported by other manufacturers as well.

Remote Automation was just the test drive for the next technology, Distributed COM, or DCOM for short. DCOM was officially released with Microsoft Windows NT 4 in 1996. Many programmers continued to use Remote Automation for a while, until in 1997 Microsoft released DCOM95.EXE, which added support for DCOM even on Windows 95 systems. DCOM proved to be more efficient and reliable than Remote Automation, which Microsoft no longer revises. The only advantage of Remote Automation is its ability to communicate with 16-bit platforms. On the other hand, if you're writing Visual Basic 5 and 6 applications you're inherently addressing only 32-bit platforms, and you won't have much use for Remote Automation.

The latest technology released from Microsoft's labs is ActiveX. In a sense, ActiveX is Microsoft's answer to the new challenges of the Internet. For example, OLE controls were too heavy to be easily transferred through the Net, so Microsoft needed to devise a new type of control. Nowadays, ActiveX has become a sort of synonym for OLE, and you can refer to COM components as ActiveX components. With the advent of ActiveX, OLE Automation has been renamed simply Automation. ActiveX also introduced new words to the ever-growing developers' dictionary: ActiveX controls and ActiveX documents. ActiveX controls have replaced OLE controls, while ActiveX documents have replaced OLE documents and permit programmers to create active documents that can be opened inside a container (for example, Microsoft Internet Explorer). Visual Basic 5 and 6 can create both ActiveX controls and documents.

Types of COM Components

You can classify COM code components into three types, according to where the component runs.

In-process servers (DLL)

The simplest type of COM component is a DLL that executes in the same address space as the application that's using it. Because each process under 32-bit platforms has its own address space, each one works with a distinct instance of the component. These components communicate directly with their clients, without the aid of COM, which makes them the most appropriate choice when speed really matters. Their main disadvantage is that the client isn't protected from the server's malfunctioning, and vice versa: If the component comes to a fatal error, its client application also crashes.

ActiveX controls are a special category of in-process components that can be hosted by an ActiveX container, such as a Visual Basic form. To qualify as an ActiveX control, a component must implement a number of interfaces defined by the ActiveX specifications. As a Visual Basic programmer, however, you don't have to worry about these additional interfaces because Visual Basic does everything for you. ActiveX controls are described in Chapter 17.

Local out-of-process servers (EXE)

You can also compile an ActiveX component as an EXE program. This is convenient when you want to create an application that can work as a stand-alone program and offer programmable objects to the outside at the same time. The best examples of such servers are the applications in the Microsoft Office suite: You can use Excel or Word either as independent applications or as providers of components that you can use from within your own programs. EXE servers execute in their own address spaces, which makes the communication with their clients slower than with in-process components. On the other hand, ActiveX EXE servers are somewhat safer than in-process servers. If a component crashes, the client application is usually able to recover.

Remote out-of-process servers (EXE)

Remote servers are EXE programs that run on a machine different from the one that is running the client application. The client and the server communicate through DCOM (or Remote Automation). Needless to say, the communication is even slower than with local servers, but remote components offer the ability to create true distributed applications. A server executing on a remote machine doesn't take processor time or memory away from the client application, so you can subdivide complex tasks among all the machines in your network. Moreover, if you have to complete a task that heavily uses a resource located elsewhere in the network (for example, a complex query on a database engine or a lengthy print job), it's more convenient to delegate the task to a remote component that executes on the machine where the resource is physically located.

A great thing about remote servers is that they aren't different at all from regular local EXE servers. In fact, the same server can provide its services to applications on the machine where it resides (thus working as a local server) and to applications that run on other machines (thus working as a remote server).

You can also run a DLL as a remote server. To allow a DLL to live an independent life, you need to be sure that the DLL is hosted in a *DLL surrogate process* on the remote machine. This is the principle upon which components for Microsoft Transaction Server are based. I don't cover MTS programming in this book, though.

Using existing components

To let you taste the power of component-based programming, I'll show you how simple it is to add a spell checker to your Visual Basic application. Developing a spell checker program isn't a trivial task, and it could take you several months to do it, if not years. Fortunately, Microsoft Word already includes a good spell checker and, most important, Word exposes it as a programmable object through Automation. All you have to do is take advantage of this capability and create an application that uses Word as a server.

The first step for using any Automation component is to add a reference to the library in the References dialog box, which you can reach from the Project menu. Browse the list of available references, and tick "Microsoft Word 8.0 Object Library". (This example assumes that you have installed Microsoft Word 97 on your system.) After you do this, you can explore all the objects exposed by the Word library using the Object Browser, and you can even ask for help with or information about a specific method or property if you installed the VBAWRD8.hlp file. (See Figure 16-1.)

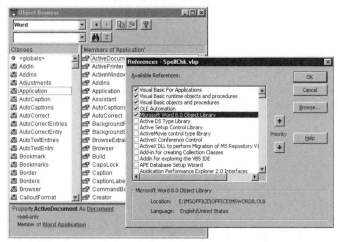

Figure 16-1. *The References dialog box with the Microsoft Word library selected and the Object Browser that displays the contents of the library itself.*

You can get your project to work as an Automation client even if you don't add a reference to the library. In that case, however, you must create objects using the *CreateObject* function instead of the *New* keyword. And you must store object references in generic *As Object* variables rather than in specific variables, which means that you can use only the less efficient late binding instead of early binding. All clients written in Visual Basic 3 and VBScript can access Automation servers only through this method.

After you've added a reference to the Word library, you can proceed as if its objects were local to your application. For example, you can declare a variable and create a new instance of the Word.Application object when your main form loads:

```
Dim MSWord As Word.Application

Private Sub Form_Load()
    ' Create the instance of Word that will be used later.
    Set MSWord = New Word.Application
End Sub
```

When an object of the Word library is created, the Word application itself is invisible. This lets you use its objects without your users even noticing that you use any external library. Of course, you can make Word visible, if you want to:

```
MSWord.Visible = True
```

The demonstration program I've prepared, however, uses Microsoft Word but hides it from users. Figure 16-2 shows what users actually see. Its main routine is the one that actually performs the spell checking and, if a word is found to be incorrect, fills the ListBox control with a list of suggestions to replace it:

```
Private Sub cmdCheck_Click()
    Dim text As String
    Dim suggestion As Word.SpellingSuggestion
    Dim colSuggestions As Word.SpellingSuggestions

    ' Add a document if there aren't any (needed to get suggestions).
    If MSWord.Documents.Count = 0 Then MSWord.Documents.Add
    text = Trim$(txtWord.text)

    lstSuggestions.Clear
    If MSWord.CheckSpelling(text) Then
        ' The word is correct.
        lstSuggestions.AddItem "(correct)"
    Else
        ' The word is incorrect. Get the list of suggested words.
        Set colSuggestions = MSWord.GetSpellingSuggestions(text)
        If colSuggestions.Count = 0 Then
            lstSuggestions.AddItem "(no suggestions)"
        Else
            For Each suggestion In colSuggestions
                lstSuggestions.AddItem suggestion.Name
            Next
        End If
    End If
End Sub
```

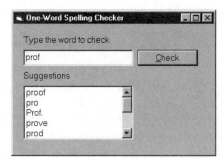

Figure 16-2. *The sample application that uses Microsoft Word to check the spelling of individual words.*

The key method in the *cmdCheck_Click* routine is *CheckSpelling*, which returns True if the word passed as an argument is correct and False otherwise. In the latter case, the program calls the *GetSpellingSuggestions* method, which returns a collection that contains 0 or more SpellingSuggestion objects. If there are any suggestions, they're enumerated using a *For Each* loop and loaded in the ListBox control.

The preceding routine creates an instance of the Word.Application class using the *New* keyword, exactly as if the class were internal to the current project. But when you're working with COM objects, you can also use the *CreateObject* function, which accepts the name of the class:

```
' An alternative way to create a Word.Application object
Set MSWord = CreateObject("Word.Application")
```

The *CreateObject* function is inherently more versatile than the *New* keyword because you can create the class name string at run time instead of hard coding it in the client's source code. Other subtle differences between these two ways of creating COM objects are covered in this chapter.

As you see, using external Automation objects is almost trivial, provided that you know how to exploit the methods, properties, and events exposed by the component. Besides, this simple example demonstrates the *language-neutral* nature of COM. Your Visual Basic program can use COM to access components written in any other language, and the opposite is also true: You can write components in Visual Basic and then use them from other development environments.

> **CAUTION** When declaring and creating an object that belongs to an external library, you can use the full *Servername.Classname* syntax instead of the plain *Classname*. This might be necessary to resolve any ambiguities—for example, when the application is referencing multiple external components, and two or more of them expose objects with the same name. Having two external components that expose objects with the same name is more frequent than you might expect, and if you don't take precautions you might have to face some subtle bugs. For example, both the Excel library and the Word library expose

the Application object. Now, consider what happens when Visual Basic executes these statements:

```
Dim x As New Application
x.Visible = True
```

What window will appear, Excel's or Word's? The answer is: It depends on which library is listed first in the References dialog box. It's for this reason that this dialog box includes two Priority buttons, which let you modify the position of an item in the list. Be aware, however, that this flexibility can cause some subtle errors. For example, if you copy this code in another project that has a different list of referenced libraries, the code won't work as expected anymore. For this reason, I suggest that you always specify the full name of an external object, unless you're 100 percent sure that your application doesn't use other libraries that expose objects with the same name.

CREATING AN ACTIVEX EXE SERVER

If you have a Visual Basic program that's already structured in classes, converting it to an ActiveX server requires just a few mouse clicks. As you'll see in a moment, you don't even need to compile the application into an actual EXE file to test the component, and you can debug it inside the Visual Basic IDE using all the tools that the environment gives you.

Of course, you can also start an ActiveX component from scratch by issuing the New Project command from the File menu and then selecting the ActiveX EXE item from the project gallery. In this situation, Visual Basic creates a project that contains one Public class module instead of a form.

The Basic Steps

It's customary, when showing how to implement a new technology, to start with a simple example. In this case, however, we can recycle one of the class-based samples that we developed in Chapter 7, the CFileOp application.

Setting the project properties

The first thing to do is unload all the modules that aren't really necessary. When you're transforming the CFileOp application into an ActiveX server, you don't need the Form1 form any longer, so you can remove it from the project. Don't delete it from the disk, however, because you'll need it again soon.

The next step is to turn this project into an ActiveX EXE application, which you do from within the General tab of the Project Properties dialog box. (See Figure 16-3.) You should also give a meaningful name to the project—for example, FileOpSvr. This becomes the name of the library that client programs have to reference to use the objects exposed by this application. Select (none) in the Startup Object field, and add a description for the project—in this case, "A component for file operations." This description will appear in the References dialog box of client programs.

Finally, go to the Component tab of the dialog box and make sure that the StartMode setting is ActiveX Component. This setting tells the Visual Basic environment that you want to test the current project as if it were invoked as a component from another application. Don't forget that ActiveX EXE applications can also be run as regular Windows applications; to test how they behave in that case, set the StartMode option to Standalone.

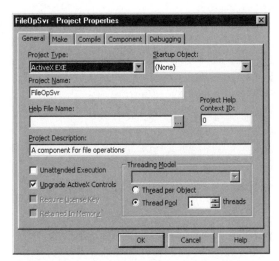

Figure 16-3. *The Project Properties dialog box with all the properties set to create the FileOpSvr server application.*

Setting class properties

The FileOpSvr project is almost ready to run, but Visual Basic will refuse to actually execute it until it contains at least one Public creatable class. Because you converted a Standard EXE project, the *Instancing* property of the CFileOp class module is set to 1-Private, and private classes aren't visible to the outside. To comply with Visual Basic requirements, you must change this property to 5-MultiUse, which means that the class is Public and its instances can be created from client applications. (You need to know more about the *Instancing* property, and you will in the next section.)

Running the server project

At this point, you're ready to run the server application. If you press F5, however, a dialog box appears; this is the Debugging page of the Project Properties dialog box. Ensure that the "Wait For Components To Be Created" option is selected, and then click on the OK button to start the server. If all the settings are correct, you'll see that the program is running, but nothing else happens. This is the normal behavior: Visual Basic is waiting for a client application to request an object from this component.

TIP   When running an ActiveX EXE or DLL project, you should deselect the Compile On Demand option in the General tab of the Options dialog box. This setting ensures that no compilation or syntax errors can occur while the program is providing its objects to client applications, which in most cases would force you to stop both the client and the server applications, fix the error, and restart. If you don't want to modify this IDE setting, you can force a full compilation by pressing the Ctrl+F5 combination instead of the F5 key or by issuing the Run With Full Compile command from the Run menu.

Creating the client application

It's time to recycle the Form1 form that you discarded from the ActiveX EXE project. Launch another instance of the Visual Basic environment, select a Standard EXE project type, if necessary, and then remove the Form1 module that Visual Basic automatically creates. You must do this to prevent name conflicts.

At this point, you can issue an Add File command from the Project menu to add the CFileOp.Frm file to the project. (You can use the Ctrl+D key shortcut.) You need to make this form the Startup Object for this project, which you do from within the General tab of the Project Properties dialog box. If you now run the client project, you'll get a compiler error ("User-defined type not defined"), caused by the following line in the declaration section of the Form1 module:

```
Dim WithEvents Fop As CFileOp
```

The reason should be evident: The CFileOp object is now external to the current application, and for Visual Basic to find it you must add a reference to it in the References dialog box of the application. Selecting the FileOpSvr project is simple because its description, "A component for file operations," appears early in the alphabetical list of all the components registered on the system. If you're in doubt, however, just check the Location field near the bottom of the dialog box. This string should point to the VBP project file or, if you haven't saved the project yet, to a temporary file in the Windows TEMP directory. Checking this value might be necessary when you search among multiple components with the same description, as often occurs when there are different versions of the same component.

Testing the client

After you add a reference to the FileOpSvr project, you can finally run the client application and see that it behaves like the original class-based program. The invisible difference, however, is that all the objects are external to the application and communicate with the application through COM. What's even more exciting is that you can debug this COM-based application as if it were a standard Visual Basic project. In fact, you can trace any cross-application call using the F8 function key, and you'll be transported from the client project's source code into the server's source code and back. This apparently minor feature is actually a great lifesaver, which can save you hours when testing your ActiveX clients and servers.

When you're finished with the testing phase, you should close the client application's form and then stop the server application by clicking on the End button on the toolbar. (This is one of the few circumstances when it's OK to stop a running application using the End button.) If you try to perform these actions in the reverse order, a warning appears when you try to stop the server, as you can see in Figure 16-4. If you click on the Yes button to confirm the termination of the server application, the client program raises an error when it tries to use the object pointed to by the *Fop* variable.

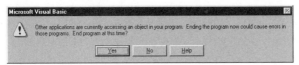

Figure 16-4. *You shouldn't end a server application if a client is currently using its objects.*

The *Instancing* Property

The *Instancing* property of a class module determines how objects of that class can be created and referenced from client applications via COM. This property can be assigned six different values, even though not all of them are available within the four types of projects, listed in Table 16-1, that you can build with Visual Basic.

	Standard EXE	ActiveX EXE	ActiveX DLL	ActiveX Control
1-Private	✓	✓	✓	✓
2-PublicNotCreatable		✓	✓	✓
3-SingleUse		✓		
4-Global SingleUse		✓		
5-MultiUse		✓	✓	
6-Global MultiUse		✓	✓	

Table 16-1. *The available values for the* Instancing *property in different types of projects.*

Selecting the most appropriate setting

You need to understand the differences among the possible settings of the *Instancing* property. At run time, you can neither read nor modify the values of the properties of a class listed in the Properties window. Unlike properties of controls, properties of classes are design-time–only properties. The possible settings of the *Instancing* property are listed on the next page.

Private   Private class modules aren't visible outside the current project. In other words, not only can't client applications create classes of this type, they can't even reference these objects. In fact, the server application isn't allowed to pass an instance of a Private class to its client (for example, as a return value of a function or through an argument of a procedure). All class modules in Standard EXE projects are Private, and for this reason the *Instancing* property isn't available in those projects.

PublicNotCreatable   These classes are visible from outside the project, but client applications can't directly create their instances. It means that clients can declare variables of their types and can assign these references using the Set command but can't use the *New* keyword or the *CreateObject* function to create instances of these classes. The only way for a client to get a valid reference to a PublicNotCreatable class is by asking the server to return it—for example, through a method of another class. For this reason, Visual Basic requires that all ActiveX projects contain at least one creatable class.

SingleUse   SingleUse objects are public and creatable, so clients can both declare variables of their type and create the instances using *New* or *CreateObject*. When a new object is created by the client, COM loads a new instance of the server, each time in a different address space. For example, if a client application creates 10 SingleUse objects, COM runs 10 different processes, each one providing one instance of the object.

MultiUse   MultiUse objects are public and creatable, but unlike SingleUse objects one single instance of the component provides all the objects requested by client applications. This is the default setting for class modules added to an ActiveX EXE or ActiveX DLL project, and is also the most reasonable setting in most cases.

GlobalSingleUse and GlobalMultiUse   These are variants of the SingleUse and MultiUse settings, respectively. Global objects are described later in this chapter.

Private and Public objects

The most important feature of a class is its scope. If the *Instancing* property is 1-Private, none of the instances of the class can be seen from outside the server. In all other cases, these objects can be manipulated by client applications and can be freely passed from the server to the client and vice versa—for example, as arguments to methods or as the return value of properties and functions.

If a client application were able to get a reference to a private object of the server, a series of nasty things might happen, including fatal errors or even GPF errors. Fortunately, you don't run any serious risk because the Visual Basic compiler prohibits the server from returning a Private object to its clients. For example, if your server component defines a Private class, and you create a Public class with a Public method that returns an instance of the Private class, the Visual Basic compiler raises the error message shown in Figure 16-5. The same thing happens when you attempt to pass clients a UDT defined in a BAS module of the component because everything defined in a BAS module is considered to be Private to the component, even if it's declared with the Public keyword.

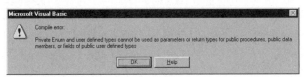

Figure 16-5. *It isn't legal for a server to pass Private objects and data structures to its clients.*

MultiUse and SingleUse objects

To understand the differences between SingleUse and MultiUse objects, you must keep in mind that Visual Basic creates single-threaded components unless you explicitly request that it build a multithreaded component. (Multithreading is covered in the section "Multithreaded ActiveX Components" later in this chapter.)

A single-threaded MultiUse component can serve only one client at a time; in other words, even if the component provides many objects to its clients, only one object can execute code in a given moment. So if two clients each request an object from the component and then execute a method at the same time, only one of the clients will be served immediately, and the other has to wait until the method in the first object completes its execution. No request is lost, however, because COM automatically serializes all clients' requests; requests are postponed and placed in a queue. Each request will remain in the queue until the server has completed all the tasks that were queued before it.

This one-thing-at-a-time limitation has been addressed by multithreaded MultiUse components, which can create multiple threads of execution, where each thread can provide a different object. Multithreaded components can therefore serve more clients without one client blocking the activity of other clients.

Conversely, each SingleUse object is provided by a different process. The main advantage of SingleUse objects is that they can multitask. In other words, each client can instantiate an object in a different process, and it never has to compete for the component with other clients. On the other hand, because each individual instance of a SingleUse class runs in a separate process, SingleUse objects require more memory and system resources than MultiUse objects. By and large, you can assume that each additional instance of a SingleUse object takes about 800 KB of memory, so it's clear that you can't use SingleUse objects when you envision the creation of hundreds or thousands of objects. In practice, you can't run more than one or two dozen SingleUse objects even on a high-end system. This is so because when too many processes are running, your CPU spends more time switching from one process to the other than actually executing code in the processes themselves.

Another problem with SingleUse components is that you can't completely test them inside the Visual Basic environment. The IDE can provide only one SingleUse object, and when the client requests a second object the Visual Basic instance that's providing the SingleUse component displays a warning message. A few seconds after the warning, the client application receives an error 429, "ActiveX component can't create object." To fully test a SingleUse component, you must compile it to an EXE file and have your clients reference this EXE file instead of the component provided by the Visual Basic environment.

All things considered, your best choice usually is to create single-threaded or multithreaded MultiUse objects. This is also the more *scalable* solution, in the sense that you can provide 10, 100, or even 10,000 objects without consuming all the memory and the CPU time of your system. You have no choice when working with in-process ActiveX. Because an ActiveX DLLs runs in the address space of its client, it isn't possible to create multiple instances of the component in different address spaces. For this reason, ActiveX DLL projects don't support the SingleUse attribute.

Whatever your decision is, the most important point is that you should *never* mix MultiUse and SingleUse objects (or their Global variants) in the same ActiveX EXE server. If you do, you have no control over which particular instance of the component is providing MultiUse objects and a given client could have its objects supplied by different instances, which is usually something that you should avoid.

In practice, if a SingleUse component exposes a hierarchy of objects, you make the root of the hierarchy the only creatable object and you make all the other Public objects in the hierarchy PublicNotCreatable. You must also provide your client with a number of constructor methods to have the server create an instance of each of such dependent objects. For more information about object hierarchies and constructor methods, see Chapter 7.

Internal instancing

An ActiveX server can instantiate an object defined in its own Visual Basic project. In this situation, the rules that affect how the object is created and used are slightly different:

- If the server creates its own object using the *New* operator, Visual Basic uses the so-called *internal instancing*: The object is created internally, without passing through COM. The *Instancing* property is ignored—otherwise, it wouldn't be possible to instantiate Private objects.

- If the server creates its own object using the *CreateObject* function, the request goes through COM and is subject to the rules enforced by the class's *Instancing* property, which means that the operation will be successful only if the class is Public and creatable.

Given all the COM overhead, it shouldn't be surprising that using *CreateObject* to instantiate a Public object defined in the same project is 4 or 5 times slower than using the *New* operator. So, in general, *CreateObject* should be avoided. (See "Multi-threaded Visual Basic Applications" later in this chapter for an exception to this rule.)

Global objects

The only difference between global and nonglobal SingleUse and MultiUse objects is that you can omit a declaration of a global object when referring to its methods or properties. Let me explain this with an example.

Let's say that you have an object that includes methods for doing math calculations, such as

```
' In the Math class of the VBLibrary project
Function Max(x As Double, y As Double) As Double
    If x > y Then Max = x Else Max = y
End Function
```

If you make this class GlobalMultiUse or GlobalSingleUse, you can reference the *Max* function from within a Visual Basic client application without explicitly creating an object variable that points to an instance of the class:

```
' In the client application
Print Max(10, 20)                        ' This works!
```

In other words, you can create a class that exposes *Sub* and *Function* methods, and you can see them from within your clients as if the methods were commands and functions, respectively. This is a great convenience because it makes the library a sort of extension of the Visual Basic language. You aren't limited to methods because your class can expose properties, and its clients see the properties as if they were variables. For example, you can add the π constant to Visual Basic:

```
' A read-only property in the VB2TheMax.Library class
Property Get Pi() As Double
    Pi = 3.14159265358979
End Property


' In the client program
Circumference = Diameter * Pi
```

You should, however, be aware of the following important detail. Even if you can skip declaring a variable that points to a global object and still access its properties and methods, the omission of this step is just a syntactical convenience that Visual Basic offers you. Behind the scenes, in fact, the language creates a hidden object variable of the proper type and uses that variable each time it invokes one of the class's members. This action means that your using a global object won't speed up your code at all. On the contrary: The hidden reference is implemented as an auto-instancing variable, so a little overhead accrues when your code accesses its methods and properties because Visual Basic has to decide whether a new instance should be instantiated.

Moreover, since you have no control over this hidden variable you can't even set it to Nothing, so the object it points to will be destroyed only when the application ends. This detail is usually irrelevant but can become meaningful if the object takes a lot of memory and resources.

Interestingly, you might have used Global objects for years without knowing it. In fact, the VBA library is nothing but a collection of global objects; you can explore the VBA library using the Object Browser, and you'll see a number of modules named Math, Strings, and so on. Each of these modules exposes several methods. Because each module is marked as Global, you can use those methods inside Visual Basic applications as if they were native functions. Similarly, the Visual Basic library (labeled *VB* in the Object Browser) includes a Global module, which exposes the global objects supported by the language, such as App, Printer, and Clipboard. For more information, see "Subclassing the VBA Language" in Chapter 7.

Because global objects are typically used to create libraries of functions, they're often implemented as in-process ActiveX components. On the companion CD, you'll find a nontrivial example of this concept, the VB2TheMax component, which includes 17 classes and over 170 methods that extend the Visual Basic language with many math, date, time, string, and file functions and commands.

Here are two more important details about global objects you need to know. First, such objects are global only outside the component: Inside the component's project, they're regular objects that must be declared and instantiated as usual. Second, as of the time of this writing, Visual Basic is the only development environment that creates clients supporting global objects. You can use your library of global objects with other COM-compliant languages, but in those other languages your global objects are considered to be regular SingleUse or MultiUse objects.

Passing Data Between Applications

The beauty of COM is that components and their clients can pass information back and forth without your having to worry about all the nitty-gritty details of the communication. You can surely write better programs, however, if you understand a bit of what COM does for you behind the scenes.

Marshaling

Marshaling is the operation that COM executes each time data has to be passed from a client to an out-of-process server and back. Marshaling is a complex procedure: Because ActiveX EXE servers and their clients reside in different address spaces, the variables stored in the client's address space aren't immediately visible to the component, and vice versa. Consider what happens when the client executes these statements:

```
Dim x As New MyServer.MyClass, value As Long
value = 1234
x.MyMethod value
```

When you pass a variable by reference, the called procedure receives the address of the variable. This address is then used to retrieve and possibly modify the variable's value. When the call originates in another process, however, the called procedure won't be able to access the actual variable's value because the variable is located in another address space and the address received would be meaningless in the context of the procedure. But you know that passing a value to an out-of-process server does work, and it works thanks to COM marshaling. Describing exactly how marshaling works is outside the scope of this book, but the following explanation should suffice for our purposes. (See Figure 16-6.)

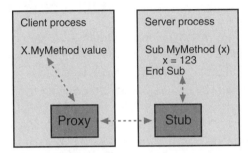

Figure 16-6. *How COM marshaling works.*

1. When a client application creates an object exposed by an ActiveX EXE server component, COM creates a special *proxy* module in the client's address space. All calls to the object are redirected to this proxy module, which has the same interface as the original object, with all its methods and properties. As far as the client is concerned, the proxy module *is* the object.

2. When the proxy module receives a call from the client application, it finds all the arguments on the stack, so it can easily retrieve their values. Variables passed by reference are no problem because the proxy module is in client's address space, so it can access all client variables.

3. The proxy module packs all the values received from the client and sends them to a *stub* module, which is located in the server's address space. The stub module unpacks all the data, retrieves the values of all arguments, and then calls the method in the server's code. As far as the server is concerned, it's being called by the client, not by the stub module. The actual mechanism used for sending data to another process is a complex one, and I won't describe its details here. Let's say that it's one of the magic tricks that COM does for you.

4. When the method completes its execution, the control is returned to the stub module. If there are values that must be passed back to the client (for example, the return value of a function or an argument passed by reference), the stub packs them and send them back to the proxy module.

5. Finally, the proxy module unpacks the data received by the stub module and passes the control back to the client's code.

Marshaling is necessary only when you're working with ActiveX EXE components. Because in-process components execute in the client's address space, they can directly access and modify all the client's variables. This explains why ActiveX DLL components are so much faster than out-of-process components.

The marshaling mechanism is quite sophisticated. For example, if a value is passed by reference, the stub creates a temporary variable in the server's address space and passes the address of this variable to the method. The code in the method can therefore read and modify this value. When the method returns, the stub module reads the new value of the variable, packs it, and sends it back to the proxy module, which in turn stores this value at the original variable's memory location.

In addition to allowing the exchange of data, the marshaling mechanism promotes the concept of *location transparency,* which is essential in the component world. The client code doesn't have to know where the server is located, and at the same time the server doesn't know from what place it's being called. In fact, the same method in the component can be called from outside or inside the component itself, and it will work in the same way in both cases.

The location transparency concept is important because it ensures that the component continues to work even when it's deployed remotely on another machine in the network. In that case, the communication between the proxy and the stub modules is even slower and more complex because it has to rely on the RPC (Remote Procedure Call) protocol to work across machines. But COM takes care of all this. Your client and your server applications will continue to work as before.

Simple data types

To correctly marshal data back and forth, it's mandatory that COM know the format in which the data is stored. Take Visual Basic strings, for example: When the client passes a string to a method, it's really passing a 32-bit pointer to the actual data. The proxy method knows that it's receiving a string and can therefore peek into the client's address space to retrieve the actual characters.

All Visual Basic simple data types are compatible with COM in the sense that COM knows how to marshal them. This means that a server can pass back to its client any numeric, string, or Variant value. Starting with Visual Basic 6, a server can directly return arrays of any type as well. (Servers written with previous versions of Visual Basic could only return arrays stored in Variants.)

Components compiled with Visual Basic 4 or 5 weren't able to pass back UDTs to their clients. Visual Basic 6 does permit components to pass a UDT, provided that the UDT is defined in a Public class and that you have installed DCOM98 or the Service Pack 4 for Windows NT 4. DCOM98 is automatically installed with Windows 98. Even though Windows 2000 hasn't been released as of this writing, it's reasonable to expect that it will support this feature without having to install a service pack.

Don't forget that DCOM98 or the Service Pack 4 must also be installed on your customers' machines. If it isn't, Visual Basic raises the run-time error 458, "Variable uses an Automation Type not supported in Visual Basic." You should trap this error and display a more meaningful message to your users, suggesting that they should upgrade their operating system to support this feature.

Because the UDT must be defined in a Public class, you can't pass UDTs defined in the client application to the server unless the client is an ActiveX EXE program itself. Finally, note that DCOM98 or the Service Pack 4 is required only when your component is passing a UDT to an out-of-process process server. When you're working with ActiveX DLL components, no marshaling takes place and UDTs can be passed back to the client even on plain Windows 95 or Windows NT 4 systems.

Private and Public objects

A server and a client can pass to each other any Public object. This includes both objects defined in the server and objects exposed by other external libraries, such as the Microsoft Word or Microsoft Excel object libraries.

I'll touch on a few more details concerning the marshaling of objects. In addition to the objects defined by class modules in the project, a Visual Basic application deals with objects exposed by three libraries: the Visual Basic, VBA, and VBRUN libraries. These three libraries can deceive you by seeming similar, but they aren't alike, at least for what concerns the visibility of objects.

All the objects exposed by the Visual Basic library (for example, the Form object, the App object, and all the intrinsic controls) are private to that library and so can't be passed to another application, even if that other application is written in Visual Basic. For example, if a Public class in your server includes the following code

```
' This function can't appear in a Public class module.
Function CurrentForm() As Form
    Set CurrentForm = Form1
End Function
```

the compiler will refuse to run the application. Conversely, the objects exposed by the VBA and VBRUN libraries are Public and so can be freely passed between different processes. These include the ErrObject and Collection objects (in the VBA library).

Many programmers find the inability to pass ordinary objects, such as forms and controls, between the server and the client a serious limitation and often look for a way to work around it. Such a workaround actually exists; just declare the argument or the return value of the method using *As Object* or *As Variant* instead of the actual specific type:

```
' In the MyClass public module of the MyServer ActiveX EXE project
' Assumes that the project contains a Form1 form and a Text1 text box on it
Function CurrentField() As Object
    Set CurrentField = Form1.Text1
End Function


' In the client project
Dim x As New MyServer.MyClass
Dim txt As Object
Set txt = x.CurrentField
txt.Text = "This string comes from the client"
```

The client application declares a generic *As Object* variable to receive the result of the *CurrentField* method, which means that you're doing late binding. As you know, late binding is less efficient and prevents you from using the *WithEvents* keyword.

Things are slightly better with in-process ActiveX servers, which let the client application declare objects using specific object variables. But you should be aware that DLLs created in this way might not work correctly under certain circumstances, so sticking to *As Objects* variables is usually advisable even when you're working with in-process components. And don't forget that you can use this method only if the client is itself written in Visual Basic.

Now that I've shown you the workaround, let me add that Microsoft explicitly discourages this technique and has warned that it might not work in future versions of Visual Basic. So you use this workaround at your own risk.

This problem raises an interesting question, though: How can the client application access forms and controls hosted in the server application? The answer is that a client should *never* directly access a private object in the server because that would break the component's encapsulation. If the client needs to manipulate a server's private object, the server should implement a number of methods and properties that provide the required capabilities, for example:

```
Property Get CurrentFieldText() As String
    CurrentFieldText = Form1.Text1.Text
End Function
Property Let CurrentFieldText(newValue As String)
    Form1.Text1.Text = newValue
End Property
```

Notice that Friend methods and properties don't appear in the Public interface of a component and therefore can't be called from outside the current project. For this reason, they never require marshaling, and you can always pass a Private object or a UDT as an argument or the return type of a Friend member.

NOTE Don't forget that when you marshal an object, you're actually passing a reference, not the object itself. While the client can invoke all the properties and methods of this object, the actual code for these properties and methods runs in the component. This distinction is important especially when you're working with remote components because each time the client uses the object variable, a round-trip to the remote component takes place.

Type libraries

You might wonder how COM can create proxy and stub modules for letting the client communicate with the server. The answer is in the *type library*, which gathers all the information about the Public classes exposed by the component, including the syntax of individual methods, properties, and events. The type library is usually stored in a file with the extension TLB or OLB, but it can also be embedded in the same EXE, DLL, or OCX file that hosts the component itself. For example, the type library of a component authored with Visual Basic is stored in the component's EXE or DLL file.

If a component has a type library, you can select it in the References dialog box and then explore it using the Object Browser. The References dialog box lists all the type libraries that have been registered in the Registry. If you have a type library that hasn't been registered yet, you can add it to the References dialog box by clicking on the Browse button.

In general, you can use an object without first adding its library to the References dialog box, but you're forced to create it using the *CreateObject* function and to reference it only through generic *As Object* variables. Without a type library, in fact, Visual Basic hasn't enough information to let you declare a specific object variable, so you're stuck with late binding. To use specific variables (and therefore early binding), the *New* keyword, and IntelliSense, you have to add the server's type library to the list of references.

TIP Visual Basic can create stand-alone type libraries, but you need the Enterprise Edition to do so. The trick is simple: In the Component tab of the Project Properties dialog box, tick the Remote Server Files check box, and then recompile the project. Visual Basic produces a TLB file with the same base name as the project's EXE file.

Performance tips

Now that you know how data is marshaled between the client and the server, you can understand a number of handy techniques that let you improve the performance of your ActiveX EXE components.

A very effective trick that you should always use is to declare methods arguments using *ByVal* rather than *ByRef* (unless the routine actually modifies the value and you want it to be returned to the client). Arguments passed by value are never marshaled back to the client because COM knows that they can't change during the call. The ideal situation is when you call a *Sub* procedure and all arguments are declared using *ByVal* because in this case no data needs to be marshaled back to the client. You're likely to experience the best improvement when passing long strings. For example, I found that passing a string of 1,000 characters using *ByVal* is about 20 percent faster than using *ByRef*.

Cross-process calls are inherently slow. Calling a method with four arguments is almost four times slower than setting four properties. For this reason, your servers should expose methods that let clients quickly set and retrieve properties. For example, let's say that your server exposes the *Name*, *Address*, *City*, and *State* properties. Besides providing the usual Property procedure pairs, you might write the following *GetProperties* and *SetProperties* methods:

```
' In the MyClass module of the MyServer project
Public Name As String, Address As String
Public City As String, State As String

Sub SetProperties(Optional Name As String, Optional Address As String, _
    Optional City As String, Optional State As String)
    If Not IsMissing(Name) Then Me.Name = Name
    If Not IsMissing(Address) Then Me.Address = Address
    If Not IsMissing(City) Then Me.City = City
    If Not IsMissing(State) Then Me.State = State
End Sub
Sub GetProperties(Optional Name As String, Optional Address As String, _
    Optional City As String, Optional State As String)
    If Not IsMissing(Name) Then Name = Me.Name
    If Not IsMissing(Address) Then Address = Me.Address
    If Not IsMissing(City) Then City = Me.City
    If Not IsMissing(State) Then State = Me.State
End Sub
```

The client application can therefore set and retrieve all properties (or a subset of them) in a single statement:

```
' Set all properties in one statement.
Dim x As New MyServer.MyClass
x.SetProperties "John Smith", "1234 East Road", "Los Angeles", "CA"
' Read just the City and State properties.
Dim city As String, state As String
x.GetProperties city:=city, state:=state
```

You can greatly improve the readability of your client's code using named arguments, as shown in the preceding code snippet.

Another way to reduce the number of cross-process calls is by passing a larger amount of data in an array. You can use an array of Variants because they enable you to pass values of different types. Of course, both the client and the server must agree on the meaning of data passed in the array. This approach is most effective when you don't know how many items you want to pass to the server. For example, suppose that the server exposes a Public collection class with its usual *Add, Remove, Count,* and *Item* methods. You might considerably speed up the application if you provide an *AddMulti* method that lets the client add more than a single item per call:

```
' In the MyCollection modules of the MyServer project
Private m_myCollection As New Collection

Sub AddMulti(values As Variant)
    Dim v As Variant
    For Each v In values
        m_myCollection.Add v
    Next
End Sub
```

Note that the *values* argument is declared as a Variant instead of as an array of Variants, as you might expect, and that the procedure iterates on its members using a *For Each...Next* loop. This gives this method unparalleled flexibility because you can pass it nearly anything: an array of Strings, an array of Variants, an array of objects, a Variant that contains an array of Strings, Variants, or objects, even a Collection:

```
' In the client application
Dim x As New MyServer.MyCollection
' Pass an array of Variants built on the fly.
x.AddMulti Array("First", "Second", "Third")
```

Similarly, if the client application needs to retrieve all the values stored in the *MyCollection* module, you can speed up things by implementing a method that returns all the items in the collection as an array of Variants:

```
Function Items() As Variant()
    Dim i As Long
    ReDim result(1 To m_myCollection.Count) As Variant
    For i = 1 To m_myCollection.Count
        ' Object values require the Set command.
        If IsObject(m_myCollection(i)) Then
            Set result(i) = m_myCollection(i)
        Else
            result(i) = m_myCollection(i)
        End If
    Next
    Items = result
End Function
```

You can get an idea of how you can streamline the interface of your server to provide better performance by having a look at how the Dictionary object is implemented. (See the "Dictionary Objects" section in Chapter 4.)

Finally, you can pass data back and forth from the client to the component by using a UDT that's declared as Public in the component.

Error Handling

An important part of COM programming has to do with error handling. Dealing with errors is always important, of course, but when you're working with ActiveX components you must correctly account for all unanticipated errors.

Error handling in the server component

Errors raised in a component behave exactly like errors that occur in a regular program; if the current procedure isn't protected by an active error handler, the procedure is exited immediately and the control is returned to the caller. If the caller has no active error handler, the control is returned to its caller, and so on until the application encounters a calling procedure with an active error handler or until there's no calling procedure (that is, the topmost procedure was reached and the error was not caught). In this latter case, the error is fatal and the application is terminated.

Properties and methods in an ActiveX component *always* have a caller—namely the client application—so in a sense all the code inside a procedure is always protected from fatal errors because all errors are returned to the client. The exception to this rule is that event procedures have no direct callers, so you should ensure that nothing can go wrong inside *Class_Initialize* and *Class_Terminate* event procedures.

Even if errors in methods and procedures are returned to the client, a well-behaved programmer might want to process them first. Basically, you can follow one of three strategies:

- The component is able to solve the problem that caused the error. In this case, the component should continue its job without notifying the client that anything was wrong.

- The component can't solve the problem, and it returns the error to the client without processing it first. This is convenient when the error code is unambiguous and can be successfully processed by the client to remedy the problem. For example, if the component exposes a method called *Evaluate* and a "Division by zero" error occurs, this error can be safely returned to the client because its meaning is evident in this context.

- The component can't solve the problem, and it returns the error to the client after processing it. For example, if the *Evaluate* method fails because the component can't find an initialization file, returning a raw "File not found" error to the client isn't the best solution because the client would probably be unaware that the method does try to open a file. In this case, it's preferable to raise a custom error and provide a more meaningful description of what happened.

When returning custom errors to the client, you can decide to stick to the COM guidelines for dealing with them. According to such guidelines, all custom errors should be in the range of 512 through 65535 so as not to be confused with COM's own errors, and should be added to the hexadecimal value &H80040000 (or −2,147,221,504). Visual Basic defines a symbolic constant for this value, vbObjectError, so a typical error handler inside an ActiveX server might resemble the following code:

```
Function Evaluate() As Double
    On Error GoTo ErrorHandler
    ' Open an initialization file (omitted).
    ' ...
    ' Evaluate the result. (This is just a sample expression.)
    Evaluate = a * b(i) / c
    Exit Function
ErrorHandler:
    Select Case Err
        Case 6, 11              ' Overflow or division-by-zero error
            Err.Raise Err.Number  ' can be returned to clients as is.
        Case 53
            Err.Raise 1001 + vbObjectError, , _
                "Unable to load initialization data"
        Case Else
            ' It's always good to provide a generic error code.
            Err.Raise 1002 + vbObjectError, , "Internal Error"
    End Select
End Function
```

Whatever strategy you decide to adopt, there's one thing that you absolutely shouldn't do—namely, show a message box. In general, the component should delegate the error to the client and let the client decide whether the user should be informed of what went wrong. Showing a message box from within a component is considered a bad programming practice because it prevents the application from running the component remotely.

Error handling in the client application

A correct error handler in the client application is more important than the handler in the server because in most cases the client has no caller to which it can delegate the error. So all errors must be resolved locally. Even if you're absolutely sure that the code in the server can't raise an error (for example, when you're simply retrieving a property), I strongly advise you to provide an error handler anyway. The reason is that when working with ActiveX components, you also have to account for errors raised by COM itself. The list on the following page describes a few errors that COM can raise.

- Error 429 ("ActiveX can't create the component") occurs when the object can't be instantiated. This error has many causes—for example, when the path of the component stored in the Registry doesn't point to the EXE file (which might have been moved, renamed, or deleted). Often you can solve this problem by registering the component again. (See the "Registering a Component" section later in this chapter.) When the component runs inside the Visual Basic component, this error can occur when the server's project is in break mode and so can't respond to clients' requests.

- Error 462 ("The remote server machine does not exist or is unavailable") typically occurs when the component that was providing the object has been terminated in an abnormal way (for example, by means of the Windows Task Manager) or when a machine where the remote component was running has been switched off or disconnected from the network.

- Error 430 ("Automation Error") is a generic error that is returned to the client when COM has been unable to connect the client with the server.

This list shouldn't be considered exhaustive, and you should always account for other errors in your error handler. In summary, a typical error handler in a client application should account for errors raised by three different sources: the server, COM, and the client itself. Here's a possible error handler for a Visual Basic client:

```
Private Sub cmdEvaluate()
    Dim x As New MyServer.MyClass, res As Double
    On Error GoTo ErrorHandler
    res = x.Evaluate()
    Exit Function
ErrorHandler:
    Select Case Err
        Case 429     ' ActiveX can't create the component.
            MsgBox "Please reinstall the application", vbCritical
            End
        Case 430     ' Automation error.
            MsgBox "Unable to complete the operation at this time. " _
                & "Please try again later.", vbCritical
        Case 462     ' The remote server machine is unavailable.
            MsgBox "Please ensure that the server machine " _
                & "is connected and functioning", vbCritical
        Case 1001 + vbObjectError
            MsgBox "Please copy the file VALUES.DAT in the " _
                & "application directory.", vbCritical
        Case 1002 + vbObjectError
            MsgBox "Unknown error. Please contact the manufacturer.", _
                vbCritical
```

```
        Case Else
            ' This might be a standard Visual Basic error or COM error.
            ' Do whatever is more appropriate for your application.
    End Select
End Sub
```

Component Busy and Component Request Pending

As I mentioned previously, COM serializes all the requests coming from clients so that the server can complete them on a first-come, first-served basis. But in certain cases, COM can't accept the client's request; this is the so-called *component busy* condition. For example, this could happen when your program is using Microsoft Excel as a server and Excel is currently showing a modal dialog box.

Visual Basic assumes that this is a temporary problem and automatically retries periodically. If the problem persists, after 10 seconds Visual Basic displays the Component Busy dialog box, shown in Figure 16-7. The Switch To button activates the other application and brings its window on top of all other windows so that you can correct the problem. (This option has no effect with ActiveX servers that don't have a user interface.) The Retry button lets you retry the operation for an additional 10 seconds. Finally, if you click on the Cancel button you revoke the request, in which case an error &H80010001 (decimal −2,147,418,111) is returned to the client. This is another error you should account for in your error handler.

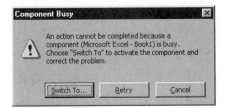

Figure 16-7. *The Component Busy dialog box.*

A different problem occurs when COM has accepted the client's request but the component takes too long to complete it. For example, this could happen when the component is waiting for a query to complete, or when it has displayed a message box and is waiting for the user to close it. This problem produces the *component request pending* condition, which is rather common in the debugging phase, when the server often stops for an unanticipated error.

Because COM has already accepted the request, Visual Basic doesn't have to resubmit it. But until the method returns, the client application is inactive and can't accept input from the user. After 5 seconds, if the user tries to interact with the client application a dialog box like the one you see in Figure 16-8 on the following page appears. This is similar to the Server Busy dialog box, but the Cancel button is disabled because the request can't be revoked.

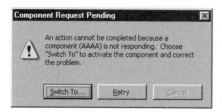

Figure 16-8. *The Component Request Pending dialog box.*

A few properties of the Application object affect the behavior and the appearance of these dialog boxes. The *App.OLEServerBusyTimeout* property is the timeout in milliseconds after which the Component Busy dialog box is shown. (The default is 10,000 milliseconds.) The *App.OLEServerBusyMsgText* and *App.OLEServerBusyMsgTitle* properties let you customize the contents and the caption of the dialog box shown to the user. If you assign a nonempty string to both these properties, the standard Component Busy dialog box is replaced by a regular message box containing just the OK and Cancel buttons. You can ask Visual Basic not to show the Component Busy dialog box by setting the *App.OleServerBusyRaiseError* property to True. In this case, no message is displayed and an error &H80010001 is immediately returned to the client. (This is the same error raised when the user clicks on the Cancel button in a Component Busy dialog box.)

A set of similar properties lets you customize Component Request Pending dialog boxes: *App.OleRequestPendingTimeout* (the default value is 5,000—that is, 5 seconds), *App.OleRequestPendingMsgText*, and *App.OleRequestPendingMsgTitle*.

Customizing the Component Busy and Component Request Pending dialog boxes is especially important when your application is dealing with remote components. The default timeouts are often insufficient, so the dialog box is quite likely to appear. When working with remote components, the Switch To button has no effect, so you should provide an alternate message that explains to your users what's happening.

Components with User Interfaces

One of the key advantages of ActiveX EXE servers is that the user can launch them as if they were standard Windows applications. This adds a lot of flexibility but creates a few problems as well.

Determining the StartMode

For example, the program must determine whether it's being run by the user or by the COM subsystem. In the former case, it should display a user interface, which it can do by loading the application's main form. An ActiveX EXE component can distinguish between the two conditions it might be in by querying the App object's *StartMode* property in the *Sub Main* procedure:

```
Sub Main
    If App.StartMode = vbSModeStandalone Then
        ' Being launched as a stand-alone program
        frmMain.Show
    Else  ' StartMode = vbSModeAutomation
        ' Being launched as a COM component
    End If
End Sub
```

For the previous code to work, you should set *Sub Main* as the Startup Object in the General tab of the Project Properties dialog box. A word of caution: When the server is started by COM, Visual Basic executes the *Sub Main* procedure and instantiates the object, and then COM returns the object to the client application. If the code in the *Sub Main* procedure or in the *Class_Initialize* event procedure takes too long, the call could fail with a timeout error. For this reason, you should never execute lengthy operations in these procedures, such as querying a database.

Showing forms

An ActiveX EXE component can display one or more forms as if it were a regular application. For example, the component might be a database browser that can work both as a stand-alone program or as a component to be invoked from other applications.

When the program is working as a COM component (*App.StartMode* = vbSModeAutomation), however, the client is the foreground application and its windows are likely to cover the server's forms. This raises a problem, and unfortunately Visual Basic has no means of ensuring that a given form becomes the topmost window in the system. For example, the Form object's *ZOrder* method brings a form in front of all other forms in the same application but not necessarily in front of windows belonging to other applications. The solution to this problem is a call to the *SetForegroundWindow* API function:

```
' In the server application
Private Declare Function SetForegroundWindow Lib "user32" _
    (ByVal hwnd As Long) As Long
' A method that displays a modal window
Sub DisplayDialog()
    frmDialog.Show
    SetForegroundWindow frmDialog.hWnd
End Sub
```

Unfortunately, Microsoft changed the way this function works under Windows 98, so the preceding approach might not work on that operating system. A solution to this problem, devised by Karl E. Peterson, appeared in the "Ask the VB Pro" column of the February 1999 issue of Visual Basic Programmer's Journal.

Visual Basic 6 supports the new vbMsgBoxSetForeground flag for the *MsgBox* command, which ensures that the message box appears on top of all the windows that belong to other applications.

Another issue concerns forms in ActiveX EXE components. You often want the form to behave like a modal form, but because modality doesn't work across process boundaries, the user is always able to activate the client's forms using a mouse click. On the other hand, if the server is showing a modal window, the method invoked by the client hasn't returned yet, and the client is therefore unable to react to clicks on its windows. The result is that after a 5-second timeout, a Component Request Pending dialog box appears, explaining that the operation can't be completed because the component isn't responding. (Which is rather misleading, since it's the client that isn't responding, not the server.)

The simplest way to solve this problem is to disable all the forms in the client application before calling the component's method that displays a modal form. This can be done quite easily, thanks to the Forms collection:

```
Private Sub cmdShowDialogFromComponent_Click()
    SetFormsState False
    x.DisplayDialog
    SetFormsState True
End Sub

' The same routine can disable and reenable all forms.
Sub SetFormsState(state As Boolean)
    Dim frm As Form
    For Each frm In Forms
        frm.Enabled = state
    Next
End Sub
```

Limiting the user's actions

An instance of an ActiveX EXE component can serve an interactive user and a client program at the same time. For example, when the user launches the program and then a client requests an object supplied by that server, the server that's currently running provides the object. The opposite isn't generally true; if a client program has created an object and then the user launches the program, a new, distinct instance of the server is loaded in memory.

When the server displays a form as a result of a request from a client application, the server should prevent the user from closing the form. You enforce this by setting a Public property in the form that tells why the form has been displayed and by adding some code to the *QueryUnload* event procedure:

```
' In the frmDialog form module
Public OwnedByClient As Boolean

Private Sub Form_QueryUnload(Cancel As Integer, UnloadMode As Integer)
    If UnloadMode = vbFormControlMenu Then
        ' The form is being closed by the user.
        If OwnedByClient Then
```

```
            MsgBox "This form can't be closed by the end user"
            Cancel = True
        End If
    End If
End Sub
```

Of course, you must correctly set the *OwnedByClient* property before showing the form, as in the following code:

```
' If the form is being displayed because a client requested it
frmDialog.OwnedByClient = True
frmDialog.Show vbModal
```

In more complex scenarios, the same form might be used by both the user and one or more client applications. In these situations, you should implement a form's property to act as a counter and tell when it's safe to unload the form.

One last word about a component with a user interface. Such a component is inherently a local component and can't run remotely on another machine, for obvious reasons. This means that you're building a solution that won't be scaled easily. Take this detail into account when deciding whether you should add a user interface to your component. One exception to this rule is when the component displays one or more forms for administrative and debugging purposes exclusively and when these forms aren't modal dialog boxes and therefore don't stop the normal execution flow of calls coming from clients.

Compatibility Issues

We human programmers reason in terms of readable names: Each class has a complete name, in the form of *servername.classname*. This complete name is called the *ProgID*. Of course, no programmer would purposely create two different classes with the same ProgID, so it seems that name conflicts should never happen. But COM is meant to manage components written by different programmers, so it's too optimistic to assume that no two programmers would create classes with the same ProgID. For this reason, COM uses special identifiers to label components and each class and interface that they expose.

Such identifiers are called GUIDs (Globally Unique Identifiers), and the algorithm that generates them ensures that no two identical GUIDs will ever be generated by two different machines anywhere in the world. GUIDs are 128-bit numbers and are usually displayed in a readable form as groups of hexadecimal digits enclosed within curly brackets. For example, this is the GUID that identifies the Excel.Application (Excel 97 version) object:

```
{00024500-0000-0000-C000-000000000046}
```

When Visual Basic compiles an ActiveX server, it generates distinct identifiers for each of its classes and the interfaces they expose. A class identifier is called a CLSID and an interface identifier is called an IID, but each is just a regular GUID with a different name. All these GUIDs are stored in the type library that Visual Basic creates for the component and registers in the system Registry. The type library is itself assigned another unique identifier.

The role of the Registry

A good COM programmer should have at least a general understanding of the Registry, how COM components are registered, and what happens when a client instantiates a component.

To run a component, Visual Basic has to convert the ProgID of the component's class into its actual CLSID. To do so, it calls a function in the COM run-time library that searches the ProgID in the HKEY_CLASS_ROOT subtree of the Registry. If the search is successful, the CLSID subkey of the found entry contains the identifier of the class. (See Figure 16-9.) This search is performed at run time when the program instantiates the component using the *CreateObject* function or at compile time when the component is created using the New operator. Incidentally, this explains why the New operator is slightly faster than *CreateObject*: When New is used, the executable already contains the CLSID of the class, which saves a time-consuming trip to the Registry. (You get better performance if you use specific variables instead of generic ones.)

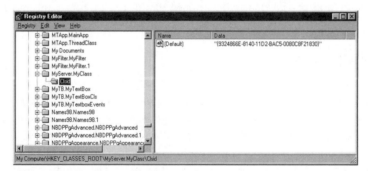

Figure 16-9. *The RegEdit program shows where COM can find the CLSID of the MyServer.MyClass component.*

At this point, COM can search in the HKEY_CLASS_ROOT\CLSID subtree of the Registry for the CLSID of the component. If the component is correctly registered, COM finds all the information it needs under this key. (See Figure 16-10.) In particular, the value of the *LocalServer32* key is the path of the EXE file that actually provides the component. Other important information is stored in the *TypeLib* key, which contains the GUID of the type library. COM uses this GUID for another search in the Registry to learn where the type library is located. (In this particular case, the type library is in the same EXE file that provides the component, but in general it can be stored in a separate file with a .tlb extension.)

Figure 16-10. *COM uses the CLSID of the component to retrieve the path of the executable file.*

Compatible components

In theory, a careful assessment of your project's requirements would enable you to create a COM component that already includes all the classes and the methods that are necessary for facing the challenges of the real world. In this ideal scenario, you never have to add classes or methods to the component or change its public interface in any way. These components would never raise any compatibility problem: When the Visual Basic compiler converts a method's name into an offset in the VTable, that offset will always be valid and will always point to the same routine in the component.

As you probably suspect, this scenario is too perfect to be true. The reality is that you often need to modify your component, to fix bugs, and to add new capabilities. These changes are likely to cause problems with existing clients. More precisely, if your new version of the component modifies the order in which methods are listed in the VTable, nasty things will happen when an existing client tries to invoke a method at the wrong offset. Similar problems can occur when the same routine expects a different number of arguments or arguments of a different type.

Visual Basic defines three levels of compatibility:

Version Identical   The new component has the same project name and the same interfaces as its previous version. For example, this happens if you change the internal implementation of methods and properties but don't modify their names, arguments, and return types. (You can't even add optional arguments to existing methods because that would change the number of values on the stack when the method is invoked.) In this case, Visual Basic compiles the new component using the same CLSIDs and IIDs used in its previous version, and existing clients won't even be aware that the component has actually changed.

Version Compatible   If you add new methods and properties but don't modify the interface of existing members, Visual Basic can create a new component that's compatible with its previous version in the sense that all the methods and properties preserve their positions in the VTable. Therefore, existing clients can safely call them. The VTable is extended to account for the new members, which will be used only by the clients that are compiled against the new version. The name of the component's EXE or DLL file can be the same as its previous version, and when you install this component on customers' machines it will overwrite the previous version.

Version Incompatible When you modify the interface of existing methods and properties—for example, by adding or removing arguments (including optional arguments) or by changing their type or the type of the return value—you end up with a component that's incompatible with its previous version. Visual Basic 6 sometimes produces incompatible components even if you change a setting in the Procedure Attributes dialog box. In this case, you must change the name of the EXE or DLL file that hosts the component so that it can coexist with the previous version on your customers' machines. Older client applications can continue to use the previous version of the component, whereas new clients use the new version.

If clients create objects from the component using the *New* operator, they reference them through their CLSIDs; in this way, no confusion can arise when two different (incompatible) components with the same ProgID are installed on the same machine. But it's preferable that different versions of the component also have distinct ProgIDs, which you accomplish by changing the project name of the newer version.

Let's consider what actually happens when you create a version-compatible component. You might believe that Visual Basic simply creates a new component that inherits the CLSIDs and IIDs from the previous version of the component, but that's not what happens. Instead, Visual Basic generates new identifiers for all the classes and the interfaces in the component. This conforms to COM guidelines, which state that once you publish an interface you should never change it.

The new component, however, also contains information about all the CLSIDs and IIDs of its previous version so that clients that were built for that older version can continue to work as before. When an old client requests an object from the newer component, COM searches the old CLSID in the Registry, which still references the same EXE file. You need to understand how this mechanism works because it explains why a version-compatible component accumulates multiple sets of CLSIDs and IIDs in the executable file and also tends to fill the Registry (both your customers' and your own) with many entries.

Version compatibility in the Visual Basic environment

You know enough to fully understand how you can create compatible components and when you should do it. The Visual Basic environment doesn't permit you to select the CLSIDs of your classes as other languages do; all class and interface identifiers are automatically generated for you. But you can decide whether a new version of the component should preserve the CLSIDs generated for a previous version. Visual Basic offers three settings that affect how identifiers are generated, as you can see in Figure 16-11.

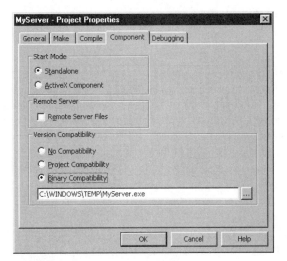

Figure 16-11. *Version compatibility settings in the Visual Basic IDE.*

No Compatibility   Each time you run the project in the environment (or compile it to disk), Visual Basic discards all existing identifiers and regenerates them. This includes all the classes, the interfaces, and the component's type library. This means that clients that worked with previous versions of the component won't work with the new one.

Project Compatibility   When you select this mode, you must also select a VBP, EXE, or DLL file with which you must preserve compatibility. In this case, Visual Basic discards all the identifiers for classes and interfaces but preserves the GUID of the component's type library. This setting is useful during the development process because a client application loaded in another instance of Visual Basic won't lose the reference to the server's type library in the References dialog box. When the Visual Basic environment loses a reference to a type library, the corresponding entry in the References dialog box is preceded by a *MISSING:* label. When this happens, you need to deselect it, close the dialog box, reopen the dialog box, and select the new reference with the same name that has been added.

Of course, just retaining the type library's GUID isn't sufficient for existing clients to continue to work with the new version of the component, but this is hardly a problem because during the test phase you haven't released any compiled clients yet. When you create an ActiveX EXE or DLL project, Visual Basic defaults to project compatibility mode.

Binary Compatibility   When you set binary compatibility with an existing component, Visual Basic tries to preserve all the identifiers for the component's type library, classes, and interfaces. You should enforce this mode after you've delivered the component (and its client applications) to your customers because it ensures that you can replace the component without also recompiling all the existing clients. You need to provide the path of the executable file that contains the previous version of the component and that Visual Basic will use to retrieve all the identifiers it needs.

> **CAUTION**   A common mistake is to select as the reference file for binary compatibility the same executable file that's the target of the compilation process. If you make this mistake, each time you compile a new version of your component a new set of GUIDs is added to the EXE file. These identifiers are of no use because they come from compilations in the development phase, and they increase the size of the executable file and add new keys to your Registry that will never be used. Moreover, under certain circumstances you can get a compiler error when the target of the compilation and the file used as a reference for binary compatibility coincide.
>
> Instead, you should prepare an initial version of your component with all the classes and methods already in place (even if empty), and then create an executable file and use it as a reference for all subsequent compilations. In this way, you can select the Binary Compatibility mode but avoid the proliferation of GUIDs. Of course, as soon as you release the first public version of your server, it should become the new reference for binary compatibility. Remember to store such EXE or DLL files in a separate directory so that you don't accidentally overwrite them when you compile the project to disk.

When you're in binary compatibility mode, Visual Basic just *tries* to maintain the compatibility with the compiled component used as a reference. In fact, at some point during the development of the new version of the component, you might purposely or accidentally break the compatibility—for example, by changing the project's name, the name of a class or a method, or the number or the type of a method's arguments. (See the "Version Incompatible" section, earlier in this chapter.) When you later run or compile the project, Visual Basic displays the dialog box shown in Figure 16-12 and gives you three options:

- You can undo changes to source code so that compatibility is preserved; you do this by clicking on the Cancel button. Unfortunately, you have to undo changes manually or load a previous version of the project's source code because Visual Basic doesn't offer an automatic way to do it.

- You can break the compatibility by selecting the Break Compatibility option button and clicking on the OK button. Visual Basic generates a new set of GUIDs, which make this component incompatible with clients compiled against the previous version. At the end of the compilation process, Visual Basic suggests that you change both the name of the executable file and the project's name (and therefore the ProgID of the component). You should also increment the Major version number in the Make tab of the Project Properties dialog box.

- You can select the Preserve Compatibility option button to ignore the warning, and keep the same CLSIDs and IIDs in the new version of the component. This option is only for advanced users and should be selected with great care because all existing clients will probably crash when they try to use the new component. For example, you can select this option when you have changed the syntax of a method but you're absolutely sure that no existing client ever calls it. This option wasn't available in previous versions of Visual Basic.

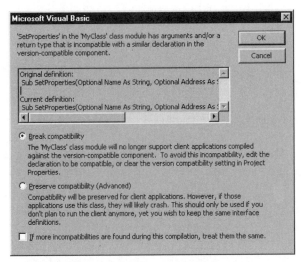

Figure 16-12. *The dialog box for specifying how to handle an incompatible component in Binary Compatibility mode.*

At times, you might want to purposely break the binary compatibility with previous versions of the component. This is a useful tactic, for example, when you're going to deploy both the client application and all the components it uses and therefore you're sure that no older client exists on the customer's machine. You can break the binary compatibility by manually resetting the compatibility setting to No Compatibility mode and recompiling the application. The component you obtain doesn't include all the GUIDs from its previous version and therefore is smaller and doesn't fill the Registry with keys and values that would never be used anyway.

Design tips

It's nearly impossible to design a nontrivial component so that you never need to break its compatibility with previous versions when the requirements change. But here are a few tips that can help you preserve compatibility.

First, carefully select the best data type for each method or property. Use Longs rather than Integers because the former provide a larger range of values without hurting performance. Similarly, use Double instead of Single arguments. Using Variant arguments also helps to preserve compatibility when your requirements change.

Second, try to anticipate how your methods could be extended. Even if you aren't willing to write the code that implements those additional capabilities, provide all the necessary methods and arguments that might become necessary later. You can use the *Optional* and *ParamArray* keywords to make your methods flexible without affecting the simplicity of existing clients.

Another trick you can use to help you preserve compatibility with older components is to include a sort of do-everything method that can perform different tasks depending on what you pass to it. Such a method might be implemented as follows:

```
Function Execute(Action As String, Optional Args As Variant) As Variant
    ' No code is here in the initial version of the component.
End Function
```

Any time you want to add more intelligence to your class but you don't want to break the compatibility with your existing clients, just add some code inside the *Execute* method, and then recompile without breaking the binary compatibility. For example, you might add the capability to save and load initialization data from a file:

```
Function Execute(Action As String, Optional Args As Variant) As Variant
    Select Case Action
        Case "LoadData"      ' LoadData and SaveData are private procedures
            LoadData args    ' defined elsewhere in the project.
        Case "SaveData"
            SaveData args
    End Select
End Function
```

The *Args* parameter is a Variant, so you can even pass multiple arguments to it using an array. For example, you can implement a function that evaluates the number of pieces sold within an interval of dates:

```
' Inside the Evaluate method
Case "EvalSales"
    ' Check that two arguments have been passed.
    If IsArray(Args) Then
        If UBound(Args) = 1 Then
            ' The arguments are the start and end date.
            Evaluate = EvalSales(Args(0), Args(1))
            Exit Function
        End If
    End If
    Err.Raise 1003, , "A two-element array is expected"
```

You could then call the *Evaluate* method as follows:

```
' Load initialization data.
obj.Evaluate "LoadData", "c:\MyApp\Settings.Dat"
' Build a 2-element array on the fly, and pass it to the Evaluate method.
SoldPieces = obj.Evaluate("EvalSales", Array(#1/1/98#, Now))
```

Registering a Component

As I've shown previously, much crucial data about a component is stored in the Registry. This information is physically recorded there when the component undergoes a process called *registration*. When you run an ActiveX project in the IDE, Visual Basic performs a temporary registration of the component so that COM will call Visual Basic itself when a client requests an object from the interpreted component. When you stop the running project, Visual Basic immediately unregisters the component.

When you install a component on the customer's machine, though, you need to perform a permanent registration. There are three ways to permanently register an ActiveX server:

- All Visual Basic EXE servers accept the */REGSERVER* switch on the command line; when you specify this switch, the program registers itself in the Registry and then exits immediately. This is the simplest way to silently register an out-of-process server and can be used from inside installation procedures.

- Even if you don't specify a switch on the command line, all Visual Basic EXE servers automatically register themselves in the Registry before starting their regular execution. This method differs from the previous one because the program must be closed manually, so it isn't appropriate for automated installation procedures.

- You register an ActiveX DLL server using the Regsvr32 utility provided with Visual Basic. (You can find it in the Common\Tools\Vb\RegUtils directory.) Just pass the complete path of the server executable file on the command line:

  ```
  regsvr32 <filename>
  ```

From time to time, you might want to unregister a component. For example, it's always a good idea to unregister a component before you delete it because you will remove all the component's entries in the Registry. If you keep your Registry clean, you have a more efficient system and reduce the number of unanticipated "ActiveX can't create the component" errors that make many COM programmers so nervous. You can unregister a component in two ways, as shown on the following page.

■   Run the ActiveX EXE server with the */UNREGSERVER* switch on the command line; the program unregisters itself from the Registry and then exits immediately.

■   Run the Regsvr32 utility with the */U* switch on the command line to unregister an ActiveX DLL server:

```
regsvr32 /U <filename>
```

TIP   You can cut down the time necessary to register a DLL server using the following trick. Open Windows Explorer and navigate to the C:\Windows\SendTo directory (assuming that your operating system is installed in the C:\Windows directory). Then create a shortcut to the Regsvr32.exe file and label it *Register-ActiveX DLL*, or whatever you prefer. After you've done this, you can easily register any DLL component by right-clicking on it and selecting the Register command from the SendTo menu. To easily unregister a DLL, you can create the following two-line batch file:

```
C:\VisStudio\Common\Tools\Vb\Regutils\regsvr32 /U %1
Exit
```

and add a shortcut to it in the SendTo menu. (Remember to use a path that matches your system directory configuration, of course.)

Shutting Down the Server

After you have used an object, you must correctly unload the component when you don't need it any longer. If you neglect to do so, your component will continue to hang around in your system, wasting memory, resources, and CPU time. An out-of-process ActiveX component is correctly unloaded when all of the following conditions are met:

■   The variables in a client application that point to objects in the component have been set to Nothing, explicitly through code or implicitly because they went out of scope. (All object variables are automatically set to Nothing when the client application terminates.)

■   No request for a component's object is in the queue waiting to be served.

■   The server has no form currently loaded, either visible or invisible.

■   The server isn't executing any code.

Don't forget that only object variables in client applications keep the component alive. If a component has one or more private variables that point to its own objects, they won't prevent COM from destroying the component when no clients are using its objects.

Meeting the last two conditions for unloading a component requires that you pay attention to what the code in the component actually does. For example, many components use hidden forms to host a Timer control that provides background processing capabilities. Consider this deceptively innocent routine:

```
' In the MyClass module of the MyServer component
Sub StartBackgroundPrinting()
    frmHidden.Timer1.Enabled = True
End Sub
```

Such a hidden form is enough to keep the component alive even after all its clients have been terminated, until the user resets the system or explicitly kills the server's process from the Task Manager or another similar utility. What's worse is that the component isn't visible, so you won't notice that it's still running unless you look for it in the list of active processes. Of course, the solution to this problem is to explicitly unload the form in the *Terminate* event procedure of the class, which is always executed when the client releases all the references to the component:

```
' In the MyClass module of the MyServer component
Private Sub Class_Terminate()
    Unload frmHidden
End Sub
```

If the server is executing code—for example, a loop that continuously polls the availability of data from a serial port—you must devise a way to stop it when all references are released. Most of the time, you can solve this problem in the same way you solve the hidden form problem, which is by explicitly stopping the code from within the *Terminate* event procedure. Some complex servers expose a method, such as *Quit* or *Close*, that clients can use to indicate that they don't need the component any longer and are therefore about to set all the references to Nothing. For example, this is the approach used by Microsoft Excel and Microsoft Word. (See the spell checker code sample at the beginning of this chapter.)

One last note: A server must not terminate until all of its clients are done with it. Even if a server exposes a method such as *Quit*, it should never try to force its own termination. If a server abruptly terminates itself—for example, by using an *End* statement—all the clients that still have one or more references to it receive an error 440, Automation error. The *Quit* method should be regarded only as a request to the server to prepare to close itself by unloading all of its forms and stopping any background activity.

Persistence

Visual Basic 6 has added the capacity for creating *persistable objects,* which are objects whose state can be saved and then restored later. The key to object persistence is the new *Persistable* class attribute and stand-alone PropertyBag objects. Only public creatable objects can be made persistent, so the *Persistable* attribute appears in the list of class attributes only if *Instancing* is MultiUse or SingleUse (or their Global variants).

Saving and restoring state

When you set the *Persistable* attribute of a public creatable class to 1-Persistable, the class module supports three new internal events: *InitProperties*, *WriteProperties*, and *ReadProperties*. In the *InitProperties* event, the class is expected to initialize its properties, which often means assigning the object's properties their default values. This event fires immediately after the *Initialize* event:

```
' A persistable CPerson class with just two properties
Public Name As String
Public Citizenship As String
' Default values
Const Name_Def = ""
Const Citizenship_Def = "American"

Private Sub Class_InitProperties()
    Name = Name_Def
    Citizenship = Citizenship_Def
End Sub
```

The *Class_WriteProperties* event fires when an object is asked to save its internal status. This event procedure receives a PropertyBag object, a virtual bag that should be filled with the current values of the object's properties. You fill the bag by using the PropertyBag's *WriteProperty* method, which accepts the name of the property and its current value:

```
Private Sub Class_WriteProperties(PropBag As PropertyBag)
    PropBag.WriteProperty "Name", Name, Name_Def
    PropBag.WriteProperty "Citizenship", Citizenship, Citizenship_Def
End Sub
```

Finally, the *Class_ReadProperties* event fires when the class is asked to restore its previous state. The PropertyBag object passed to the event procedure contains the values of properties that were saved previously, and the object can extract them using the PropertyBag's *ReadProperty* method:

```
Private Sub Class_ReadProperties(PropBag As PropertyBag)
    Name = PropBag.ReadProperty("Name", Name_Def)
    Citizenship = PropBag.ReadProperty("Citizenship", Citizenship_Def)
End Sub
```

The last argument passed to both *WriteProperty* and *ReadProperty* methods is the property's default value. This value is used to optimize the resources used by the PropertyBag object: If the value of the property coincides with its default value, the property isn't actually stored in the PropertyBag object. This argument is optional, but if you use it you must use the same value within all three event procedures. For this reason, it's advisable to use a symbolic constant.

The PropertyBag object

To have an object save its state, you must create a stand-alone PropertyBag and pass the persistable object to the PropertyBag's *WriteProperty* method, as shown in the following code snippet:

```
' Inside a form module
Dim pers As New CPerson, pb As New PropertyBag

' Initialize a CPerson object.
Private Sub cmdCreate_Click()
    pers.Name = "John Smith"
    pers.Citizenship = "Australian"
End Sub
' Save the CPerson object in a PropertyBag.
Private Sub cmdSave_Click()
    ' This statement fires a WriteProperties event in the CPerson class.
    pb.WriteProperty "APerson", pers
End Sub
```

If the class's *Persistable* attribute isn't 1-Persistable, you get an error 330, "Illegal Parameter. Can't write object because it doesn't support persistence" when you try to save or restore an object from that class.

Restoring the object's state is easy, too:

```
Private Sub cmdRestore_Click()
    ' To prove that persistence works, destroy the object first.
    Set pers = Nothing
    ' The next statement fires a ReadProperties event
    ' in the CPerson class.
    Set pers = pb.ReadProperty("APerson")
End Sub
```

When you pass objects to the *WriteProperty* and *ReadProperty* methods, you don't specify a default value. If you omit the last argument and the PropertyBag doesn't contain a corresponding value, Visual Basic raises an error 327, "Data value named '*property name*' not found." This is the symptom of a logical error in your program; typically, you have misspelled the name of the property, or you have specified a default value when you saved the object and have omitted it when restoring its state.

Once you have loaded a PropertyBag object with the values of one or more properties, you can also save those values to disk so that you can restore the object's state in subsequent sessions. You do this using the PropertyBag's *Contents* property, a Byte array that contains all the information about the values stored in the PropertyBag, as the code on the following page demonstrates.

```
' Save the PropertyBag to a binary file.
Dim tmp As Variant
Open App.Path & "\Propbag.dat" For Binary As #1
tmp = pb.Contents
Put #1, , tmp
Close #1
```

The previous routine uses a temporary *Variant* variable to simplify the saving of the Byte array. You can use the same trick when it's time to reload the contents of the file:

```
' Reload the PropertyBag object from file.
Dim tmp As Variant
Set pb = New PropertyBag
Open App.Path & "\Propbag.dat" For Binary As #1
Get #1, , tmp
pb.Contents = tmp
Close #1
```

> **CAUTION** If you're testing the application in the IDE, you might find that you're unable to reload the state of an object saved to disk in a previous session because of an error 713 "Class not registered." This happens because the property bag embeds the CLSID of the object being saved. By default, each time you rerun the application in the IDE, Visual Basic generates a new CLSID for each class in the project, so it won't be able to reload the state of an object with a different CLSID. To work around this issue, you should enforce the Binary Compatibility mode, as explained in the "Version Compatibility in the Visual Basic Environment" section earlier in this chapter.

Persistent object hierarchies

The persistence mechanism can also work with object hierarchies; each object in the hierarchy is responsible for saving its dependent objects in its *WriteProperties* event procedure and restoring them in its *ReadProperties* procedure. Everything works as long as all the objects in the hierarchy have their *Persistable* attribute set to 1-Persistable. For example, you can extend the CPerson class with a Children collection that contains other CPerson objects, and you can account for this new property in the *WriteProperties* and *ReadProperties* event procedures:

```
Public Children As New Collection       ' A new public property

Private Sub Class_WriteProperties(PropBag As PropertyBag)
    Dim i As Long
    PropBag.WriteProperty "Name", Name, Name_Def
    PropBag.WriteProperty "Citizenship", Citizenship, Citizenship_Def
    ' First, save the number of children (default = 0).
    PropBag.WriteProperty "ChildrenCount", Children.Count, 0
    ' Next, save all the children, one by one.
```

```
    For i = 1 To Children.Count
        PropBag.WriteProperty "Child" & i, Children.Item(i)
    Next
End Sub

Private Sub Class_ReadProperties(PropBag As PropertyBag)
    Dim i As Long, ChildrenCount As Long
    Name = PropBag.ReadProperty("Name", Name_Def)
    Citizenship = PropBag.ReadProperty("Citizenship", Citizenship_Def)
    ' First, retrieve the number of children.
    ChildrenCount = PropBag.ReadProperty("ChildrenCount", 0)
    ' Next, restore all the children, one by one.
    For i = 1 To ChildrenCount
        Children.Add PropBag.ReadProperty("Child" & i)
    Next
End Sub
```

Interestingly, the resulting PropertyBag object contains many properties labeled *Name*, *Citizenship*, *Child1*, *Child2*, and so on, but this isn't a problem because they are encapsulated in a hierarchy of properties so that no confusion can arise. In other words, the *Name* value stored in the *Child1* subtree is distinct from the *Name* value stored in the *Child2* subtree, and so on. If you want to study this technique further, you can browse the code of the demonstration program on the companion CD.

> **CAUTION** You need to be sure that the hierarchy doesn't contain any circular references. Or at least you need to be certain that the references are dealt with correctly when you're storing and restoring objects. To explain why this is such an important consideration, suppose that the CPerson class exposes a *Spouse* property that returns a reference to a person's wife or husband, and then think of what would happen if each object attempts to save the state of this property. Mr. Smith saves the state of Mrs. Smith, who in turn saves the state of Mr. Smith, who in turn saves the state of Mrs. Smith...and so on, until you get an "out of stack space" error.
>
> Depending on the nature of the relationship, you must devise a different strategy to avoid being caught in such endless loops. For example, you could decide that you'll save just the *Name* of a person's consort instead of its entire state, but then you have to correctly rebuild the relationship in the *ReadProperties* event procedure.

Using the PropertyBag with any class module

I've explained that the *Persistable* property is available only if the class is Public and creatable. In a sense, this is a requirement of COM, not of Visual Basic. This doesn't mean, however, that you can't take advantage of the PropertyBag object—and its capability to store data in all the Automation-compliant formats—to implement a sort of object persistence. In fact, the only thing you can't really do is implement custom class events, such as *WriteProperties* and *ReadProperties*. But you can add a special property of the class that sets and returns the current state of the object and uses a private PropertyBag object for the low-level implementation of the serialization mechanism. In the following example, I have a CPerson class module that exposes a special property called *ObjectState*:

```
' The CPerson class module
Public FirstName As String, LastName As String

Property Get ObjectState() As Byte()
    Dim pb As New PropertyBag
    ' Serialize all the properties into the PropertyBag.
    pb.WriteProperty "FirstName", FirstName, ""
    pb.WriteProperty "LastName", LastName, ""
    ' Return the PropertyBag's Contents property.
    ObjectState = pb.Contents
End Property

Property Let ObjectState(NewValue() As Byte)
    Dim pb As New PropertyBag
    ' Create a new PropertyBag with these contents.
    pb.Contents = NewValue()
    ' Deserialize the class's properties.
    FirstName = pb.ReadProperty("FirstName", "")
    LastName = pb.ReadProperty("LastName", "")
End Property
```

When implementing this form of persistence, the code in the client application is slightly different:

```
Dim p As New CPerson, state() As Byte

p.FirstName = "Francesco"
p.LastName = "Balena"
' Save the state into a Byte array.
state() = p.ObjectState
' ...
' Create a new object, and restore its state from the Byte array.
Dim p2 As New CPerson
p2.ObjectState = state()
Print p2.FirstName & " " & p2.LastName       ' Displays "Francesco Balena".
```

Of course, if the object has dependent objects, they must expose the *ObjectState* property as well so that the main object can correctly serialize the state of its child objects. A cleaner approach would be to define the *IObjectState* interface and have this interface be implemented by all the classes that you want to make persistent. Notice that this technique works because the object being deserialized is created by the component's code, not by the PropertyBag object, so there's no restriction about its

Instancing property. This technique also works inside Standard EXE programs and is actually one of the most useful unknown tricks that you can perform with the PropertyBag object.

Persistent ADO Recordsets

One fact that you won't find in the Visual Basic documentation is that under certain conditions you can even pass an ADO Recordset to a PropertyBag object. More precisely, any ADO Recordset that can be saved to a file using its *Save* method—for example, a Recordset with *CursorLocation* set to adUseClient—can be also be passed to the *WriteProperty* method of a PropertyBag. This gives you unparalleled flexibility in exchanging data among your applications. For example, instead of saving the contents of one single Recordset to a file using a *Save* method, you can store multiple related Recordsets inside one PropertyBag object, and then save its *Contents* property to file.

CREATING AN ACTIVEX DLL SERVER

Creating in-process DLL components in Visual Basic isn't significantly different from creating out-of-process components, so the majority of the techniques described in the preceding section, "Creating an ActiveX EXE Server," are also valid for ActiveX DLL components. In this section, I'll focus on the few differences between the two types of components.

> **CAUTION** If you haven't done it already, download the most recent Service Pack for Visual Basic. Although the Service Pack doesn't add any new features to the language, it fixes a number of serious bugs that occurred with ActiveX DLL components—in particular, those that occurred when the application was using more than seven or eight in-process servers.

In-Process Components in the Visual Basic IDE

In-process components can be created from the Project Properties dialog box by turning a class-based Standard EXE project into an ActiveX DLL project, much as you do with out-of-process components. Alternatively, you can create a new ActiveX DLL project from the Project Gallery dialog box that appears when you issue the New Project command from the File menu.

The main difference between creating out-of-process and in-process components is that the latter ones can be built in the same instance of the IDE as their client. Visual Basic 5 and 6 development environments support the concept of *project groups* and can host multiple projects in the same instance. To create a project group, you first load or create a project as usual, and then you issue the Add Project command from the File menu to create additional projects or you load existing projects from disk. This ability lets you create a project group made up by one standard EXE and one or more ActiveX DLLs so that you can test one or more in-process components at the same time. You can also save the project group in a file with a .vbg extension so that you can quickly reload all your projects with one Open menu command.

When you issue the Run command, the project that has been marked as the Startup project (see Figure 16-13) begins its execution. This is usually the standard EXE project that works as the client application and that later instantiates one or more objects from the ActiveX DLL projects. You don't need to explicitly run ActiveX DLL projects (as you do with out-of-process components running in separate instances of the Visual Basic IDE), but you still have to add a reference to the DLL in the References dialog box of the standard EXE project.

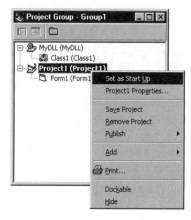

Figure 16-13. *You can make a project the Startup project by right-clicking on it in the Project window.*

Be aware that a few commands in the IDE implicitly refer to the current project—that is, the project being highlighted in the Project properties. For example, the contents of the References dialog box is different depending on which project is highlighted, and the Project Properties dialog box lets you see and modify only the attributes of the current project. When the current project is the standard EXE, the Object Browser shows only the Public classes and members of another ActiveX DLL project and doesn't allow you to change the member's attributes. To display all private members or modify the attributes and the descriptions of the DLL's methods and properties, you must make that ActiveX DLL the active project.

Running the DLL in the same environment as its client isn't a limitation because an ActiveX DLL can only have one client. It's loaded in the client's address space and therefore can't be shared with other applications. If two distinct client applications request objects from the same in-process component, COM instantiates two different DLLs, each one in the address space of the client that made the request. For this reason, using an ActiveX DLL is much simpler than using an ActiveX EXE component; the component serves only one client and therefore all requests can be immediately fulfilled. Client applications don't need to account for timeout conditions.

An ActiveX DLL project can't contain SingleUse or GlobalSingleUse classes. The reason for this is that such a DLL runs in the same process as its client and doesn't have a process of its own. So COM can't create a new process for the DLL when the client creates a second object from the component.

Differences Between In-Process and Out-of-Process Components

ActiveX DLL components can't do everything. In most cases, their limitations are caused by their in-process nature and aren't dictated by Visual Basic.

Error handling

You deal with errors in in-process components as you do within ActiveX EXE servers. In a sense, however, error handling inside in-process components is even more important because any fatal error in the server also terminates the client and vice versa because the two are actually the same process.

User interface

ActiveX DLLs can show their own forms, as out-of-process components do. Interestingly, a form coming from an in-process component is automatically placed in front of forms from its client application, so you don't need to resort to the *SetForegroundWindow* API function to achieve the right behavior. Depending on the client's capabilities, however, an in-process component might not be able to display nonmodal forms. For example, programs written in Visual Basic 5 or 6, all the applications in the Microsoft Office 97 suite (or later versions), and all the third-party applications that have licensed the VBA language support nonmodal forms displayed by in-process components. On the other hand, programs written with Visual Basic 4 and all the applications found in previous versions of Microsoft Office raise an error 369 when a DLL component tries to display a nonmodal form.

Visual Basic enables you to test whether a client supports nonmodal forms through the *App.NonModalAllowed* read-only property. Microsoft suggests that you test this property before showing a nonmodal form from within a component, and degrade gracefully by showing a modal form if necessary:

```
If App.NonModalAllowed Then
    frmChart.Show
Else
    frmChart.Show vbModal
End If
```

If you consider that the vbModal constant is 1 and that the *App.NonModalAllowed* returns 0 or –1, you can do everything in just one statement:

```
frmChart.Show (1 + App.NonModalAllowed)
```

Unfortunately, you can't test this feature without compiling the component into an actual ActiveX DLL because the *App.NonModalAllowed* property always returns True when the program runs in the Visual Basic environment.

Shutting down the server

The rules that state when an in-process component is terminated are different from those you've seen for out-of-process components. The main difference is that an in-process component always follows the destiny of its client: When the client terminates, the component also terminates even if it has visible forms. When the client is still executing, an in-process component is terminated if all of the following conditions are true:

- No object variable points to an object in the component, either in the client or *in the component itself*. (ActiveX EXE servers aren't kept alive by object variables owned by the component.)

- No request for a component's object is in the queue waiting to be served.

- The server has no visible form. (ActiveX EXE servers are kept alive even by forms that are loaded but invisible.)

- The server isn't executing any code.

The fact that an in-process server is kept alive also by internal references to its own objects raises a nontrivial problem. For example, if the component includes two objects that have references to each other, the component will never be shut down when the client releases all the references to it. In other words, circular references can keep an in-process component alive until the client terminates. There's no simple way to solve this problem, and it's up to the programmer to avoid creating circular references. (For more information about the circular reference problem, see Chapter 7.)

Another important detail in the behavior of in-process components might disorient many programmers. While ActiveX EXE components are terminated as soon as the client releases all the references to them (provided that all the other necessary conditions are met), in-process components aren't released immediately. In general, Visual Basic keeps them alive for a couple of minutes (the exact delay may vary, though) so that if another request comes from the client, COM doesn't have to reload the server. If this timeout expires, the DLL is silently unloaded and its memory is released. A new request coming from the client at this point will take a little more time because COM has to reload the component.

> **CAUTION**   Only references to public objects can keep a component alive. Even if an in-process DLL manages to pass its client a pointer to a private object (for example, by using an *As Object* argument or return value), this reference won't keep the component alive. So if the client releases all the references to the

component's public objects, after some time the component will be unloaded. The variable owned by the client becomes invalid and crashes the application as soon as it's used in any way. For this reason, a component should *never* pass a private object to its client.

Reentrancy issues

Calls to an in-process component's methods or properties are served immediately, even if the component is currently serving another request. This differs from how out-of-process components behave and raises a number of issues that you must account for:

- If the client calls a method while the component is servicing a previous request, the first call is suspended until the second request is completed. This means that requests are served in the opposite order of their arrival. (ActiveX EXE servers always serialize clients' requests.)

- If the component is displaying a modal form, it can't serve any requests coming from the client. (ActiveX EXE servers don't have this problem.)

As you see, both problems are caused by the fact that the client calls the component while it's serving a previous request. This can happen if the component executes a DoEvents command that lets the client become active again, if the component raises an event in its client application, or if the client calls the component from within a Timer control's *Timer* event procedure. If you avoid these circumstances, you should never experienced reentrancy problems. Alternatively, you can implement a semaphore, a global variable in the client that keeps track of when it's safe to call the component.

Differences between ActiveX DLL and standard EXE programs

You should be aware of a few more features of the behavior of an in-process component; these are important when you convert some classes from a standard Visual Basic application into an ActiveX DLL component. For example, a number of objects and keywords refer to the component's environment, not the client's:

- The *Command* function always returns an empty string if used inside an in-process component because the DLL is never called with an argument on the command line.

- The App and Printer objects and the Forms collection are private to the component and aren't affected by the objects with the same name in the client application.

- The main application and the ActiveX component don't share file numbers, so you can't open a file in the main application and have the DLL send data to it.

- The *Screen.ActiveForm* and *Screen.ActiveControl* properties can't see across the component boundaries; therefore, they return Nothing even if the client is displaying a form, and they can return a reference to a visible form or control in the DLL even if they aren't currently active.

A few other features don't work as they normally do:

- In-process components don't support DDE (Dynamic Data Exchange) operations.

- Any reference to the *App.OLEServerxxxx* properties causes an error 369, "Operation not valid in an ActiveX DLL."

- When a client terminates, no *QueryUnload* or *Unload* event is raised for the component's forms that are still loaded.

Embedding Forms in a DLL

ActiveX DLL servers offer a great way to reuse common forms and dialog boxes. As you know, form modules can't be Public, so they can't be visible from outside the project. But you can create a class that wraps around a form and exposes the same interface and then make the class Public so that you can create it from other applications. Existing applications need minor or no modifications at all to use the component instead of the form. The only requirement for doing this, in fact, is that an application never directly references controls on the form, which is something that you should not do anyway to preserve the form's encapsulation. (For more information about this issue, see Chapter 9.)

Say that you have created a frmLogin form that accepts a user's name and password and validates them. In this simple example, the only valid user name is *francesco*, which corresponds to the *balena* password. The form has two TextBox controls, named txtUsername and txtPassword, and one cmdOK CommandButton control. The form also exposes one event, *WrongPassword*, that's raised when the user clicks on the OK button and the user name or the password is invalid. This event can be trapped by the client code to show a message box to the user, as you can see in Figure 16-14. This is the complete source code of the form module:

```
Event WrongPassword(Password As String)
Public UserName As String
Public Password As String

Private Sub cmdOK_Click()
    ' Validate the password.
    If LCase$(txtUserName= "francesco" And LCase$(txtPassword) = _
        "balena" Then
        Unload Me
```

```
      Else
          RaiseEvent WrongPassword(txtPassword)
      End If
End Sub

Private Sub Form_Load()
    txtUserName = UserName        ' Load properties into fields.
    txtPassword = Password
End Sub
Private Sub Form_Unload(Cancel As Integer)
    UserName = txtUserName        ' Load field values into properties.
    Password = txtPassword
End Sub
```

You can use this form as if it were a class, without ever directly referencing the controls on its surface. This is the code of the main form in the demonstration program on the companion CD:

```
Dim WithEvents frmLogin As frmLogin

Private Sub Command1_Click()
    Set frmLogin = New frmLogin
    frmLogin.Show vbModal
    MsgBox "User " & frmLogin.UserName & " logged in", vbInformation
End Sub
Private Sub frmLogin_WrongPassword(password As String)
    MsgBox "Wrong Password"
End Sub
```

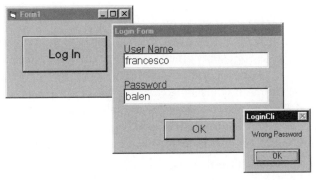

Figure 16-14. *An in-process component can conveniently encapsulate a reusable form and expose its events to client applications.*

Because the form can be used without accessing its controls, you can now wrap a CLogin class module around the frmLogin form and encapsulate both the class and the form modules in a LoginSvr DLL that exposes the form's functionality to the outside. The source code of the CLogin class is shown on the following page.

```
Event WrongPassword(Password As String)
Private WithEvents frmLogin As frmLogin

Private Sub Class_Initialize()
    Set frmLogin = New frmLogin
End Sub

Public Property Get UserName() As String
    UserName = frmLogin.UserName
End Property

Public Property Let UserName(ByVal newValue As String)
    frmLogin.UserName = newValue
End Property

Public Property Get Password() As String
    Password = frmLogin.Password
End Property

Public Property Let Password(ByVal newValue As String)
    frmLogin.Password = newValue
End Property

Sub Show(Optional mode As Integer)
    frmLogin.Show mode
End Sub

Private Sub frmLogin_WrongPassword(Password As String)
    RaiseEvent WrongPassword(Password)
End Sub
```

As you see, the *UserName* and *Password* properties and the *Show* method of the class simply delegate to the form's members with the same name. Moreover, the class traps the *WrongPassword* event coming from the form and raises an event with the same name in its client application. In short, the class exposes exactly the same interface as the original form. If you set the class's *Instancing* attribute to 5-MultiUse, the class (and hence the form) can be reused by any client application. You only have to change a couple of lines of code in the original client application to have it work with the CLogin class instead of the frmLogin class. (The modified code is in boldface.)

```
Dim WithEvents frmLogin As CLogin

Private Sub Command1_Click()
    Set frmLogin = New CLogin
    frmLogin.Show vbModal
    MsgBox "User " & frmLogin.UserName & " logged in", vbInformation
End Sub
Private Sub frmLogin_WrongPassword(password As String)
    MsgBox "Wrong Password"
End Sub
```

You can use this technique to create both modal and modeless reusable forms. You can't, however, use forms embedded in a DLL as MDI child forms in an MDI application.

Performance

You can improve the performance of your ActiveX DLL servers the following ways.

Passing data

Because the DLL runs in the same address space as its client, COM doesn't need to marshal data being passed from the client to the component and back. Actually, the role of COM with in-process components is much simpler than with out-of-process servers because COM only has to make sure that the DLL is correctly instantiated when the client requests an object from it. From that point onward, the client communicates directly with the component. COM will become active again only to ensure that the DLL is released when the client doesn't need it any longer.

The process switch that occurs any time a client calls an out-of-process component considerably slows down ActiveX EXE components. For example, calling an empty procedure without any arguments in an out-of-process component is *about 500 times slower* than calling an empty procedure in an in-process DLL! Surprisingly, a method in a DLL takes more or less the same time as a method in a Private class of the client application, which proves that the overhead for a call to an in-process component is negligible.

The absence of marshaling also suggests that the optimization rules for passing data to an in-process DLL might differ from those you should follow when working with out-of-process EXE servers. For example, there's no significant difference between passing a number to an in-process procedure using *ByRef* or *ByVal*. But you'd better pass longer strings by reference rather than by value: I built a simple benchmark program (which you can find on the companion CD) that compares the performance of in-process and out-of-process servers. I found that passing a 1000-character string by value can be 10 times slower than passing it by reference. And the longer the string is, the slower passing it by value is.

Setting the DLL Base Address

If you have multiple clients that are using the same in-process component at the same time, a separate instance of the DLL is loaded in each client's address space. This might result in a waste of memory unless you take some precautions.

Thanks to advanced features of the Windows virtual memory subsystem, you can load the same DLL in distinct address spaces without using more memory than required by a single instance of the DLL. More precisely, multiple client applications can share the same image of the DLL loaded from disk. This is possible, however, only if all the instances of the DLL are loaded at the same address in the memory space of the different processes and if this address coincides with the DLL's base address.

The *base address* of a DLL is the default address at which Windows tries to load the DLL within the address space of its clients. If the attempt is successful, Windows can load the DLL quickly because it just has to reserve an area of memory and load the contents of the DLL file there. On the other hand, if Windows can't load the DLL at its base address (most likely because that area has been allocated to another DLL), Windows has to find a free block in memory that's large enough to contain the DLL, and then it must *relocate* the DLL's code. The relocation process changes the addresses of jump and call instructions in the DLL's binary code to account for the different load address of the DLL.

Summarizing, it's far preferable that a DLL be loaded at its base address for two reasons:

1. The loading process is usually slightly faster because no relocation is necessary.

2. Windows can save memory if other processes have to load the same DLL because multiple instances of the DLL share one physical block of memory that holds the image of the DLL as it is stored on disk.

Visual Basic lets you select the base address for an in-process DLL server in the Compile tab of the Project Properties dialog box, as you see in Figure 16-15. The default value for this address is H11000000, but I strongly advise you to modify it before you compile the final version of your component. If you don't, your DLL base address will conflict with other DLLs written in Visual Basic. Only one DLL can win, and all the others will be relocated.

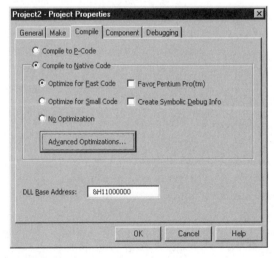

Figure 16-15. *You can improve the performance of an ActiveX DLL by changing its base address.*

Fortunately, other languages have different default values. For example, DLLs written in Microsoft Visual C++ default to address H10000000, so even if their programmers didn't modify this default setting, these DLLs won't conflict with those authored in Visual Basic.

When you're deciding which base address you should specify for a Visual Basic DLL, take the following points into account:

- DLLs use an integer number of 64-KB pages, so you should leave the four least significant digits as 0 (64 KB = &H10000).

- Each Windows process can use a 4-GB address space, but the area below 4 MB and above 2 GB is reserved for Windows.

- Windows executables are loaded starting at address 4 MB (&H400000).

For example, a base address greater than 1 GB (&H40000000) accommodates the largest client application that you can ever build and still leaves one gigabyte for your DLLs. Even after accounting for the 64-KB page size, this leaves you with 16,384 different values to choose from when assigning a base address to your DLL.

Extending an Application with Satellite DLLs

ActiveX DLL servers are very useful to augment the functionality of an application through so-called Satellite DLLs. To understand why satellite DLLs are so advantageous, let's see first what resource files are.

Resource files

Resource files are files, usually with the .res extension, that can contain strings, images, and binary data used by an application. You create resource files in two steps. First of all, you prepare a text file (usually with the .rc extension) that contains the description of the contents of the resource file. This text file must follow a well-defined syntax. For example, here's a fragment of an RC file that defines two strings and one bitmap:

```
STRINGTABLE
BEGIN
    1001    "Welcome to the Imaging application"
    1002    "Do you want to quit now?"
END
2001        BITMAP c:\windows\clouds.bmp
```

In the second step, you compile the .rc file into a .res file, using the Rc.exe resource compiler with the /r switch on the command line. (This utility comes with Visual Basic.)

```
RC /r TEST.RC
```

At the end of the compilation, you obtain a .res file with the same base name as the .rc file (test.res in this example). You can now load this new file into the Visual Basic environment using the Add File command in the Project menu.

NOTE   Visual Basic 6 greatly simplifies the resource file creation and compilation phases using a new add-in, the VB Resource Editor, shown in Figure 16-16. This add-in also supports multiple string tables, which let your application conform to the user's language automatically. A Visual Basic 5 version of this add-in is also available for downloading from Microsoft's Web site.

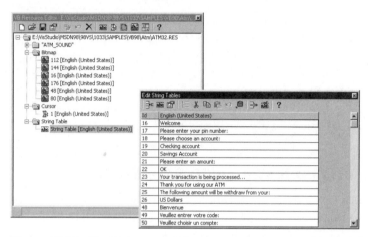

Figure 16-16. *The VB Resource Editor can create resource files with bitmaps, icons, sounds, and multiple string tables.*

After you create a .res file, your code can reference the resources it contains using the *LoadResString*, *LoadResPicture*, and *LoadResData* functions, as the following example shows:

```
' Print a welcome message.
Print LoadResString(1001)
' Load an image into a PictureBox control.
Picture1.Picture = LoadResString(2001, vbResBitmap)
```

Resource files are a great choice when you're creating an application that must be localized for other countries. The source code is completely independent of all the strings and pictures used by the program, and when you want to create a new version of the application for a different country you only have to prepare a different resource file. To learn more about resource files, have a look at the ATM.VBP sample project that comes with Visual Basic 6.

Even with the help of the VB Resource Editor add-in, however, working with resource files is rather cumbersome for the following reasons:

■ A Visual Basic project can include only one resource file; if an application has to support multiple languages at the same time, you must devise an indexing scheme. (See the ATM Visual Basic sample application for an example of this technique.)

■ You can't change the resource file of an application without recompiling the application.

Both these problems can be solved using satellite DLLs.

Satellite DLLs

The concept on which satellite DLLs are based is simple: Instead of loading strings and other resources from resource files, you load them from an ActiveX DLL. The trick is that you instantiate an object from the DLL using *CreateObject* instead of the New operator, and therefore you can select the DLL you load at run time. This approach lets you ship a DLL to your customers even after they've installed the main application, so you can effectively add support for new languages as soon as you prepare new DLLs. The user can switch from one DLL to another at run time—for example, with a menu command.

I've prepared a demonstration application that uses satellite DLLs to create a simple database program whose interface adapts itself to the nationality of the user. (See Figure 16-17.) When the application starts, it selects the DLL that matches the version of the Windows operating system in use or defaults to the English version if no DLL for the current language is found.

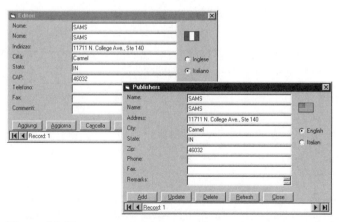

Figure 16-17. *A multiple-language application that uses satellite DLLs to support both English and Italian.*

A satellite DLL that exports strings, bitmaps, and binary data must expose at least three functions. To make satellite DLLs look like resource files, you can name them LoadResString, LoadResPicture, and LoadResData. Here's a portion of the source code of the DLL provided with the sample application:

```
' The Resources class module in the Application000 project
Enum ResStringID
    rsDataError = 1
    rsRecord
    rsPublishers
    ' (Other enumerated values omitted...)
End Enum
Enum ResPictureID
    rpFlag = 1
End Enum
Enum ResDataID
    rdDummy = 1          ' This is a necessary placeholder.
End Enum

Function LoadResString(ByVal ID As ResStringID) As String
    Select Case ID
        Case rsPublishers: LoadResString = "Publishers"
        Case rsClose: LoadResString = "&Close"
        Case rsRefresh: LoadResString = "&Refresh"
        ' (Other Case clauses omitted...)
    End Select
End Function

Function LoadResPicture(ByVal ID As ResPictureID, _
    Optional Format As Long) As IPictureDisp
    ' Loads images from the frmResources form
    Select Case ID
        Case rpFlag: Set LoadResPicture = _
            frmResources000.imgFlag.Picture
    End Select
End Function

Function LoadResData(ByVal ID As ResDataID, _
    Optional Format As Long) As Variant
    ' Not used in this sample program
End Function
```

This particular DLL includes only one bitmap and doesn't include any binary data. For simplicity's sake, the bitmap has been loaded at design time in an Image control on the frmResources form. This form is never displayed and works only as a container for the bitmap. You can use this approach also for storing icons and cursors. If you need to store other types of binary data, however, you can use a resource file. In this instance, however, each satellite DLL has its own resource file.

The trick in using satellite DLLs is to use the primary DLL (namely, the DLL that provides the resources for the default language—English in this example) as the interface that DLLs for other languages must implement. Let's see how the Italian DLL is implemented:

```
' The Resources class module in the Application410 project
Implements MyApplication000.Resources

Private Function Resources_LoadResString(ByVal ID As _
    MyApplication000.ResStringID) As String
    Dim res As String
    Select Case ID
        Case rsPublishers: res = "Editori"
        Case rsClose: res = "&Chiudi"
        Case rsRefresh: res = "&Aggiorna"
        ' (Other Case clauses omitted...)
    End Select
    Resources_LoadResString = res
End Function

Private Function Resources_LoadResPicture(ByVal ID As _
    MyApplication000.ResPictureID, Optional Format As Long) _
    As IPictureDisp
    Select Case ID
        Case rpFlag: Set Resources_LoadResPicture = _
            frmResources410.imgFlag.Picture
    End Select
End Function

Private Function Resources_LoadResData(ByVal ID As _
    MyApplication000.ResDataID, Optional Format As Long) As Variant
    ' Not used in this program
End Function
```

Notice that this class has no members in its primary interface. The Italian DLL is stored in a project named MyApplication410.vbp, whereas the default DLL is stored in a project named MyApplication000.vbp. The reason for this naming scheme will be clear in a moment.

Locale-aware client applications

Let's have a look at how a client application can leverage the power and flexibility of satellite DLLs to automatically adapt itself to the locale of users while still providing them with the capability to switch to a different language at run time. The secret is in an API function, *GetUserDefaultLangID*, which returns the locale identifier of the current interactive user. The client application uses this value to build the name of the DLL and then passes it to the *CreateObject* function, as the code on the following page demonstrates.

```
' The main BAS module in the client application
Declare Function GetUserDefaultLangID Lib "kernel32" () As Long

Public rs As New MyApplication000.Resources

Sub Main()
    InitLanguage              ' Load the satellite DLL.
    frmPublishers.Show        ' Show the startup form.
End Sub

' Load the satellite DLL that corresponds to the current user's locale.
Sub InitLanguage()
    Dim LangId As Long, ProgID As String
    ' Get the default language.
    LangId = GetUserDefaultLangID()
    ' Build the complete class name.
    ProgID = App.EXEName & Hex$(LangId) & ".Resources"
    ' Try to create the object, but ignore errors. If this statement
    ' fails, the RS variable will point to the default DLL (English).
    On Error Resume Next
    Set rs = CreateObject(ProgID)
End Sub
```

The key to this technique is in the *InitLanguage* procedure, where the application dynamically builds the name of the DLL that would provide the resources for the current locale. For example, when executed under an Italian version of Windows, the *GetUserDefaultLangID* API function returns the value 1040, or &H410.

You can create satellite DLLs for other languages and ship them to your foreign customers. This approach always works perfectly, provided that you assign a project a name like MyApplication*XXX*, where *XXX* is the hexadecimal locale identifier. (For a list of locale identifiers, see the Windows SDK documentation.) The first portion of the project name must match the client application's project name (*MyApplication*, in this example), but you can devise other effective ways to dynamically build the DLL's name.

If the *CreateObject* function fails, the *rs* variable won't be initialized in the *InitLanguage* procedure, but because it's declared as an auto-instancing variable it automatically instantiates the default MyApplication000.Resource component. The key point here is that all the satellite DLLs for this particular application implement the same interface, so the *rs* variable can hold a reference to any satellite using early binding. See how the *rs* variable is used within a form of the client application:

```
Private Sub Form_Load()
    LoadStrings
End Sub
Private Sub LoadStrings()
    Me.Caption = rs.LoadResString(rsPublishers)
```

```
        cmdClose.Caption = rs.LoadResString(rsClose)
        cmdRefresh.Caption = rs.LoadResString(rsRefresh)
        ' (Other string assignments omitted...)
        Set imgFlag.Picture = rs.LoadResPicture(rpFlag)
End Sub
```

Because the MyApplication000.Resource class declares enumerated constants for all the strings and other resources in the satellite DLL, you can use IntelliSense to speed up the development phase and produce a more readable and self-documenting code at the same time.

MULTITHREADED ACTIVEX COMPONENTS

Both Visual Basic 5 and 6 can create multithreaded ActiveX components. Components built with the first release of Visual Basic 5, however, could only support multithreading if they had no user interface, which is a serious limitation in some cases. This restriction was lifted in Service Pack 2.

Threading Models

In a nutshell, multithreading is the ability to execute different code portions of an application at the same time. Many popular Windows applications are multithreaded. For example, Microsoft Word uses at least two threads, and the Visual Basic environment uses five threads. Multiple threads are a good choice when you need to execute complex tasks in the background (for example, paginating a document) or when you want to keep the user interface responsive even when your application is doing something else. Multiple threads are especially necessary when you're building *scalable* remote components that have to serve hundreds of clients at the same time.

There are two main types of threading models: *free threading* and *apartment threading*. In the free-threading model, each thread can access the entire process's data area and all threads share the application's global variables. Free threading is powerful and efficient, but it's a nightmare even for most experienced programmers because you must arbitrate among all the shared resources, including variables. For example, even an innocent statement such as

```
If x > 1 Then x = x - 1    ' X should always be greater than 1.
```

can create problems. Imagine this scenario: Thread A reads the value of the *x* variable and finds that it is 2, but before it executes the Then portion of the statement, the CPU switches to Thread B. Thread B happens to be executing the same statement (an unlikely but not impossible circumstance), finds that *x* is 2, and therefore decrements it to 1. When Thread A regains the control of the CPU, it decrements the variable to 0, which is an invalid value that will probably cause other logic errors later in the program's life.

The apartment-threading model solves these problems by encapsulating each thread in an *apartment*. Code executed in a given apartment can't access variables belonging to other apartments. Each apartment has its own set of variables, so if two threads are accessing the *x* variable at the same time, they're actually referencing two different memory locations. This mechanism neatly solves the synchronization problem described earlier, and for this reason the apartment-threading model is inherently safer than the free-threading model. In Visual Basic, you can build ActiveX components that support the apartment model only.

Multithreaded ActiveX EXE Components

Visual Basic 5 and 6 let you create out-of-process servers that create an additional thread when a client instantiates a new object. All you need to do to transform a regular ActiveX EXE component into a multithreaded component is select an option in the General tab of the Project Properties dialog box. (See Figure 16-18.) There are three possible settings. The default setting is the Thread Pool option with 1 thread; this corresponds to a single-threaded component.

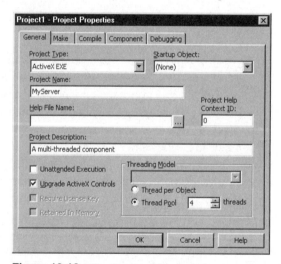

Figure 16-18. *Create a multithreaded component with a few mouse clicks in the Project Properties dialog box.*

If you select the Thread Per Object option, you build a multithreaded component that creates a new thread for every object requested by its clients. Because all objects are executed in their own threads, no client can ever block another client, so these components are highly responsive. The disadvantage of this approach is that too many threads can bring even a powerful system to its knees because Windows has to spend a lot of time just switching from one thread to the other.

Thread pools

If you select the Thread Pool option and enter a value greater than 1 in the Threads field, you build a multithreaded component that's allowed to create only a limited number of threads. This is a scalable solution in the sense that you can increase the size of the thread pool when you deploy your application on a more powerful system. (You need to recompile the application, though.) This setting prevents the system from wasting too much time on thread management because the pool can't grow larger than the limit you set. To assign threads to objects, the pool uses a *round robin* algorithm, which always tries to assign the first available thread to each new request for an object.

Let's say that you created a multithreaded component with a pool size of 10 threads. When the first client makes a request for an object, COM loads the component, which returns the created object in its first thread. When a second client makes a request, the component creates an object in a second thread, and so on, until the tenth client gets the last available thread in the pool. When the eleventh request comes, the component has to return an object in one of the threads that have been created previously. The thread used for this new object can't be determined in advance because it depends on several factors. For this reason, the round robin algorithm is said to be a nondeterministic algorithm.

Here are a few interesting points that concern object pooling. First, when there are more objects than threads, each thread can serve more objects, possibly owned by different clients. In this situation, a given thread can't execute an object's method if it's already serving another object. In other words, an object pool doesn't completely prevent objects from blocking one another (as components with one thread per object do), even if this problem happens less frequently than with single-threaded components.

Second, once an object has been created in a thread, it must execute in that thread; this is a requirement of apartment threading. Therefore, a client might be blocked by another client even if the component has some unallocated threads. Imagine this scenario: You have a pool with 10 threads, and you instantiate 20 objects. In an ideal situation, the pool is perfectly balanced and each thread serves exactly two objects. But suppose that all the objects served by threads 1 through 9 are released while the two objects served by thread 10 aren't. In this case, the pool has become highly unbalanced and the two objects will block each other, even if the pool has nine available threads.

Finally, even if the apartment model ensures that all apartments have a different set of variables, objects in the same thread share the same apartment and therefore share the same global values. This might appear to be a cheap way to exchange data among objects, but in practice you can't use this technique because you can't predict which objects will share the same thread.

The multithreading advantage

Many programmers mistakenly believe that multithreading is always a good thing. The truth, however, is that most computers have only one CPU, which has to execute all the threads in all the processes in the system. Multithreading is always a good thing if you're executing your component on a Windows NT machine with multiple CPUs; in this situation, the operating system automatically takes advantage of the additional processors to balance the workload. In the most common case, however, you're working with a single-processor machine and you might find that multithreading can even make your performance worse. This is a somewhat counter-intuitive concept, so I'll explain it with an example.

Let's say that you have two threads that execute two different tasks, each one taking 10 seconds to complete. In a single-threaded environment, one of the two tasks completes in 10 seconds, and the other waits for the first one to complete and therefore takes 20 seconds in total. The result is that the average time is 15 seconds per task. In a multithreaded environment, the two tasks would execute in parallel and will complete more or less at the same time. Unless you have two CPUs, in this case the average time is 20 seconds, which is worse than in the single-threaded case.

In summary, multithreading isn't always the best solution. Sometimes, however, it clearly offers advantages over single-threading:

- When you're executing tasks of different duration, multithreading is often preferable. For example, if you have a task that takes 10 seconds and another task that takes only 1 second, in a single-thread environment the shorter task might take 1 second or 11 seconds to complete, which results in an average time of 6 seconds, while in a multithreaded environment it doesn't take more than 2 seconds on average. By comparison, the longer task takes 10 or 11 seconds to complete in the single-threaded scenario (10.5 seconds on average), whereas it always requires 11 seconds in the multithreaded scenario. So the multithreaded scenario is slightly disadvantageous for longer tasks, but the user will hardly notice the difference.

- When you have some tasks, such as user-interface tasks, that have to be responsive, it's better to execute them in a multithreaded environment.

- When you have background tasks with low priority, multithreading is also a good choice. A typical example is formatting and spooling a document.

When you're deciding between single- and multithreading, don't forget that Visual Basic applications implicitly use multithreading for some tasks—for example, when printing data. Moreover, some database engines (most notably, the Microsoft Jet engine) internally use multithreading.

User-interface issues

Visual Basic 6 lets you create multithreaded components that expose a user interface. (You need Service Pack 2 to have this feature work under Visual Basic 5.) You can achieve this because all the forms and the ActiveX controls that you create are *thread safe*, which means that multiple instances of them can independently execute in different threads. The same is true for ActiveX documents and designers, such as the DataEnvironment designer, as well as the majority of the ActiveX controls that are in the package—for example, the MaskEdBox control and all the Windows common controls.

But a few ActiveX controls are inherently single-threaded and can't be safely used inside multithreaded components—for example, the Microsoft Chart (MSCHRT20.OCX) and Microsoft Data Bound Grid (DBGRID32.OCX) controls. If you attempt to add these controls to an ActiveX DLL project whose threading model is Apartment Threaded or to an ActiveX EXE project whose threading model is Thread Per Object or Thread Pool with a number of threads greater than 1, you get an error and the control isn't added to the Toolbox. You also get an error if you have a project that already includes one or more single-threaded controls and you change the project type to a value that isn't compatible with such controls. When you buy a third-party control, check with its vendor to learn whether it supports multithreading.

> **CAUTION** You can force Visual Basic to accept a single-threaded ActiveX control in a multithreaded project by manually editing the VBP file. There are many reasons not to do that, however. Single-threaded controls running in a multithreaded application perform poorly and, above all, can cause many problems and unexpected behavior. For example, the Tab key and Alt+*key* combinations don't work as they should, and a click on the control might not activate the form. Moreover, there might be some properties (most notably, the *Picture* property) whose values can't be marshaled between different threads, and any attempt to do so raises a run-time error.

Here are other minor issues concerning forms inside multithreaded components:

- When you use a hidden form variable that Visual Basic creates for each form in the application, you're implicitly using a variable that's global to the thread but not shared among all the threads. Thus, each thread creates a different instance of the form. To avoid confusion, you might want to use explicit form variables, as suggested in Chapter 9.

- MDI forms aren't allowed in multithreaded EXEs or DLLs because the Visual Basic MDI form engine isn't thread safe. For this reason, the Add MDI Form command in the Project menu is grayed inside these types of projects.

- A form can be modal only with respect to other forms in the same thread, but it's modeless with respect to forms displayed by other threads. Consequently, a modal form blocks only the code in its own thread, not the code in other threads.

- In a multithreaded component, the *Sub Main* procedure is executed whenever a new thread is created. For this reason, if you need to display a form when the component is first created, you can't simply invoke a form's *Show* method from this procedure, and you need to distinguish the first component's thread from all the others. See the "Determining the Main Thread" section later in this chapter.

- DDE between forms works only if the two forms are in the same thread. (DDE isn't covered in this book.)

Unattended execution

If your component doesn't include a form, UserControl, or UserDocument module, you can tick the Unattended Execution check box in the General tab of the Project Properties dialog box. This indicates that your component is meant to execute without any user interaction, a reasonable option when you're creating a component to run remotely on another machine.

The Unattended Execution option suppresses any message boxes or other kinds of user interface (including error messages) and redirects them to a log file or the Windows NT Application Event Log. You can also send your own messages to this log file. Using this option is important with remote components because any message box would stop the execution of the component until the user closes it, but when a component is running remotely no interactive user can actually close the dialog box.

The *StartLogging* method of the App object lets you select where your messages will be sent. Its syntax is as follows:

```
App.StartLogging LogFile, LogMode
```

where *LogFile* is the name of the file that will be used for logging, and *LogMode* is one of the values listed in Table 16-2. The vbLogOverwrite and vbLogThreadID settings can be combined with the other values in the table. When you're sending a message to the Windows NT Application Event Log, "VBRunTime" is used as the application source and the *App.Title* property appears in the description. When you're running under Windows 95 or 98, messages are sent by default to a file named Vbevents.log.

> **CAUTION**   Watch out for two bugs. First, if you specify an invalid filename, no errors are raised and logged messages silently go to default output. Also, the vbLogOverwrite option makes the *StartLogging* method behave as if the vbLogAuto option were specified. So you should always manually delete the log file and not rely on the vbLogOverwrite option.

Constant	*Value*	*Description*
vbLogAuto	0	If running under Windows 95 or 98, messages are logged to the file specified by the *LogFile* argument; if running under Windows NT, messages are logged to the Windows NT Application Event Log.
vbLogOff	1	Messages aren't logged anywhere and are simply discarded; message boxes have no effect.
vbLogToFile	2	Forces logging to file, or turns off logging if no valid file name is passed in the *LogFile* argument. (In the latter case, the *LogMode* property is set to vbLogOff.)
vbLogToNT	3	Forces logging to the Windows NT Application Event Log; if not running under Windows NT or the Event Log is unavailable, it turns off logging and resets the *LogMode* property to vbLogOff.
vbLogOverwrite	16	When logging to a file, it re-creates the log file each time the application starts; it has no effect when logging to the Application Event Log. It can be combined with other values in this table using the OR operator.
vbLogThreadID	32	The current thread ID is added to the beginning of the message in the form "[T:0nnn]"; if this value is omitted, the thread ID is shown only if the message comes from a multithreaded application. It can be combined with other values in this table using the OR operator.

Table 16-2. *All the values for the* LogMode *argument of the App object's* StartLogging *method; these are also the possible return values of the* LogMode *read-only property.*

Once you have set up logging, you can log messages using the App object's *LogEvent* method, which has the following syntax:

```
App.LogEvent LogMessage, EventType
```

LogMessage is the text of the message, and *EventType* is an optional argument that states the type of the event (one of the following values: 1-vbLogEventTypeError, 2-vbLogEventTypeWarning, or 4-vbLogEventTypeInformation). For example, the following piece of code

```
App.StartLogging "C:\Test.Log", vbLogAuto
App.LogEvent "Application Started", vbLogEventTypeInformation
App.LogEvent "Memory is running low", vbLogEventTypeWarning
App.LogEvent "Unable to find data file", vbLogEventTypeError
MsgBox "Press any key to continue", vbCritical
```

sends its output to the C:\TEST.LOG file if run under Windows 95 or 98 or to the Application Event Log if run under Windows NT. (See Figure 16-19.)

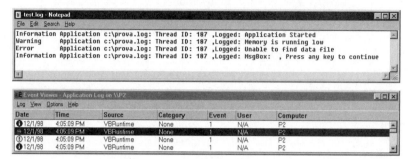

Figure 16-19. *Logged messages coming from a Visual Basic application as they appear in a log text file (top window) or in the Windows NT Application Event Log (bottom window).*

You can test the Unattended Execution attribute from code using the read-only *UnattendedApp* property of the App object. Likewise, you can retrieve the current log file and log mode using the App object's *LogPath* and *LogMode* properties, respectively. When you've compiled the code using the Unattended Execution attribute, all the MsgBox commands send their output to the log file or the Windows NT Application Event Log, as if a *LogEvent* method with the vbLogEventTypeInformation argument were issued.

One last note: If you run the program under the Visual Basic IDE, the Unattended Execution setting has no effect; all message boxes appear on screen as usual, and the *App.StartLogging* and *App.LogEvent* methods are ignored. To activate logging, you must compile your application to a stand-alone program.

Multithreaded ActiveX DLL Components

You can also create multithreaded ActiveX DLLs using Visual Basic 6. Unlike ActiveX EXE servers, however, Visual Basic's DLLs can't create new threads and can only use the threads of their clients. For this reason, multithreaded DLLs are most useful with multithreaded client applications. Because an ActiveX DLL doesn't actually create any thread, the options you have in the Project Properties dialog box are simpler than those offered by an ActiveX EXE project. In practice, you only have to decide if you want to create a Single Threaded or Apartment Threaded server. (See Figure 16-20.)

Both single- and multithreaded components are thread safe, which means that when an object in a thread is called by another thread, the calling thread is blocked until the called method returns. This prevents most reentrancy problems and greatly simplifies the job of the programmer.

While it's perfectly safe to use a single-threaded DLL with a multithreaded client, only one thread in the main application can directly call the methods of an object created by the DLL. This particular thread is the first thread created in the client application, or more precisely, the first thread that internally called the *OleInitialize* function. All the objects exposed by a single-threaded DLL are created in this thread; when they are used from another thread in the client application, arguments and return values undergo the so-called *cross-thread marshaling*, which is almost as slow as cross-process marshaling.

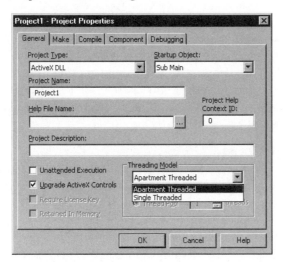

Figure 16-20. *Selecting the Threading Model option in the Project Properties dialog box.*

When you don't know how your DLL will be used, selecting an Apartment Threaded option is usually the best choice. In fact, a multithreaded DLL can be used by single-threaded clients without any problem and without any noticeable overhead. In one case a single-threaded DLL can be conveniently used with a multithreaded client, namely, when you want to offer a simple way for all the threads in the client to communicate and share data with each other. An example of this technique is described in the "Testing a Multithreaded Application" section later in this chapter.

Multithreaded Visual Basic Applications

Many programmers aren't aware that Visual Basic can create multithreaded regular applications, not just components. To be honest, creating such multithreaded applications isn't as straightforward as using other Visual Basic advanced features, and you have to account for a number of important issues.

The trick to creating a multithreaded application is simple: The application must be a multithreaded ActiveX EXE server that exposes one or more objects that run in different threads. To build such an application, the conditions shown on the following page must be fulfilled.

■   The application must be an ActiveX EXE server compiled with the Thread Per Object setting.

■   The code for the task that is intended to run in a different thread is embedded in a MultiUse class.

■   You create the new object using the *CreateObject* function instead of the *New* operator.

When you create an object exposed by the current application using the *New* operator, Visual Basic uses internal instancing, which bypasses COM and creates the object using a more efficient mechanism that doesn't undergo any restriction. (In fact, you can even create objects from Private or PublicNotCreatable classes.) Conversely, when you use *CreateObject*, Visual Basic always creates the object through COM. For this reason, the object should be creatable (MultiUse).

Determining the main thread

As I stated previously, the *Sub Main* procedure in a multithreaded Visual Basic application is executed each time a new thread is created. This isn't usually a problem for multithreaded EXE or DLL components, but it's an issue when you're creating an ActiveX EXE project that must work as a multithreaded application. In this case, it's crucial that you distinguish the first execution from all the subsequent ones: The first time the *Main* procedure executes, the program must create its main window, whereas in all other cases the procedure shouldn't display any user interface. More precisely, when the procedure is being executed as a result of a request for a new object, it should exit as soon as possible to avoid having the request fail with a timeout error. For the same reason, you should never execute lengthy operations inside the *Class_Initialize* event procedure.

Understanding whether the *Main* procedure has never been executed before isn't as trivial a task as it might appear at first. You can't simply use a global variable as a flag because that variable can't be seen from a thread in another apartment. Creating a temporary file in the *Main* procedure isn't a viable solution either because the application might terminate with a fatal error and never delete the file.

There are at least two ways to solve this problem. The first one is based on the *FindWindow* API function and is described in the Visual Basic documentation. In the following pages, I'll show you an alternative method, which I believe is less complex and slightly more efficient because it doesn't require that you create a window. This method is based on *atom objects,* which are sort of global variables managed by the Windows operating system. The Windows API provides functions that let you add a new atom, delete an existing atom, or query for an atom's value.

In the *Main* procedure of a multithreading application, you test whether a given atom exists. If it doesn't exist, this is the first thread of the application, and you need to create the atom. To have the mechanism work, you must also destroy the atom when you exit the application. This task is ideal for a class that creates the atom in its *Class_Initialize* procedure and destroys it in its *Class_Terminate* procedure. Here's the complete source code of the CThread class in the demonstration application on the companion CD:

```
Private Declare Function FindAtom Lib "kernel32" Alias "FindAtomA" _
    (ByVal atomName As String) As Integer
Private Declare Function AddAtom Lib "kernel32" Alias "AddAtomA" _
    (ByVal atomName As String) As Integer
Private Declare Function DeleteAtom Lib "kernel32" _
    (ByVal atomName As Integer) As Integer
Private atomID As Integer

Private Sub Class_Initialize()
    Dim atomName As String
    ' Build an atom name unique for this instance of the application.
    atomName = App.EXEName & App.hInstance
    ' Create the atom if it doesn't exist already.
    If FindAtom(atomName) = 0 Then atomID = AddAtom(atomName)
End Sub
Private Sub Class_Terminate()
    ' Delete the atom when this thread terminates.
    If atomID Then DeleteAtom atomID
End Sub

Function IsFirstThread() As Boolean
    ' This is the first thread if it was the one which created the atom.
    IsFirstThread = (atomID <> 0)
End Function
```

The name of the atom is built using the application's name and the instance handle (the *App.hInstance* property). The latter value is different for each distinct instance of the same application, which ensures that this method works correctly even when the user launches multiple instances of the same executable. The CThread class module exposes only one property, *IsFirstThread*. The following code shows how you can use this class in a multithreaded application to understand whether it's executing the first thread:

```
' This is global because it has to live for the entire application's life.
Public Thread As New CThread

Sub Main()
    If Thread.IsFirstThread Then
        ' First thread, refuse to be instantiated as a component.
        If App.StartMode = vbSModeAutomation Then
```

(continued)

```
        Err.Raise 9999, , "Unable to be instantiated as a component"
     End If
     ' Show the user interface.
     frmMainForm.Show
   Else
     ' This is a component instantiated by this same application.
   End If
End Sub
```

Implementing multithreading

Creating a new thread using the *CreateObject* function doesn't suffice to actually implement a multithreaded Visual Basic application. In fact, the synchronization mechanism offered by Visual Basic, which usually prevents a series of nasty problems, in this case gets in the way. When the program invokes a method of an object in another thread, the calling thread is blocked until the method returns. So you might have multiple threads, but only one of them is executing at a given time, which obviously isn't what you want.

The easy way to work around this issue is using a Timer control to "awaken" an object in a separate thread after it has returned the control back to the calling thread. You don't need a visible form to achieve this; an invisible form with a Timer control on it can do the job. You can take advantage of the new *CallByName* function to create a form module that you can easily reuse in all your applications that need this sort of callback mechanism. This is the complete source code of the CCallBack form module that encapsulates this functionality:

```
Dim m_Obj As Object
Dim m_MethodName As String

Public Sub DelayedCall(obj As Object, Milliseconds As Long, _
    MethodName As String)
    Set m_Obj = obj                        ' Save the arguments.
    m_MethodName = MethodName
    Timer1.Interval = Milliseconds         ' Start the timer.
    Timer1.Enabled = True
End Sub

Private Sub Timer1_Timer()
    Timer1.Enabled = False                 ' We need just one call.
    Unload Me
    CallByName m_Obj, m_MethodName, VbMethod    ' Do the callback.
End Sub
```

The CCallBack form can be used as a class module in other portions of the application. On the companion CD, you'll find a sample multithreaded application that creates and displays multiple count-down forms. (See Figure 16-21.) This is a partial listing of the class that the main application instantiates when it needs to create a new count-down form in a separate thread. (The statements that implement the callback mechanism are in boldface.)

```
Private Declare Sub Sleep Lib "kernel32" (ByVal dwMilliseconds As Long)

Dim frm As frmCountDown
Dim m_Counter As Integer

' The Counter property. Values > 0 display the form and start
' the countdown.
Property Get Counter() As Integer
    Counter = m_Counter
End Property
Property Let Counter(newValue As Integer)
    Dim cbk As New CCallBack
    m_Counter = newValue
    cbk.DelayedCall Me, 50, "Start"
End Property

Sub Start()
    Static active As Boolean
    If active Then Exit Sub              ' Prevent reentrancy.
    active = True
    ' The code that shows the countdown form (omitted...)
    ' ...
    active = False
End Sub
```

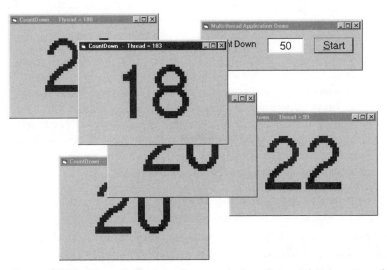

Figure 16-21. *The sample countdown multithreading application. Note that each window shows a different thread ID in its caption.*

This is the code in the main form of the count-down sample application:

```
Private Sub cmdStart_Click()
    Dim x As CCountDown
    ' Create a new CCountDown object in another thread.
    Set x = CreateObject("MThrApp.CCountDown")
    ' Set the counter using the value currently in the TextBox control.
    x.Counter = Val(txtSeconds)
    Set x = Nothing
    Beep
End Sub
```

CAUTION   There's an undocumented detail in the way Visual Basic imple-ments multithreading that deserves your attention. If the client code sets the last reference to the object to Nothing either explicitly or implicitly while the ob-ject is executing some code, the client has to wait until the routine in the object terminates. This is far from being irrelevant. If you delete the *Set x = Nothing* state-ment in the previous code routine, for example, the *x* variable will be set to Noth-ing after the *Beep* statement when the object has already been awakened by the callback procedure and is currently executing the count-down code. This means that the client has to wait as long as 10 seconds until the object can be completely destroyed, and during that time the main form can't react to the user's actions. You can choose from two ways to work around this problem:

- You explicitly set to Nothing any object reference immediately after the other thread is started, and in the call to the *DelayedCall* method of the CCallBack form module, you use a timeout value that's large enough to let the main application destroy its reference before the callback fires. This is probably the simplest solution, but it can't be used when the main program needs a reference to the object in the other thread (for example, to set its properties or invoke its methods).

- You keep the object alive until you don't need it anymore by using global variables instead of local ones. This solution lets you use the object's prop-erties and methods, but in this case it's your responsibility to understand when the object should be destroyed. Each object that you keep alive with-out any real reason consumes one thread and therefore adds some over-head to the system even if the thread isn't active.

Testing a multithreaded application

Debugging a multithreaded application or component isn't as simple as testing a regular program. For one thing, you have to compile your application as a stand-alone EXE file because the Visual Basic IDE supports only single-threaded applications and components. This means that you have to forgo all the amenities offered by the environment, including breakpoints, the Watch window, the Locals window, and the step-by-step trace capabilities. For this reason, you should thoroughly test the logic of your application in the environment before turning to multithreading.

When testing a compiled multithreaded application, you must devise alternate debugging strategies. For example, since you can't write values to the Immediate window using *Debug.Print* methods, you have to resort to logging to file or use plain MsgBox commands. One good idea is to display the thread ID in your messages so that you can learn which particular thread is issuing them:

```
MsgBox "Executing the Eval proc", vbInformation, "Thread: " & App.ThreadID
```

Single-threaded ActiveX DLL servers offer a better solution to this problem. As you might remember, you can safely use single-threaded DLLs with multithreaded clients, be they stand-alone applications or other components. For example, you can implement a DLL that exposes a CLog object that gathers trace information from its clients and redirects it to a window. Implementing such a DLL isn't difficult. Here's the source code of the CLog class. (The demonstration application found on the companion CD includes the complete version with additional capabilities.)

```
' If this property is nonzero, the ThreadID is added to the message.
Public ThreadID As Long

Sub StartLogging(LogFile As String, LogMode As Integer)
    ' Note that this refers to the global hidden form reference.
    ' This form will therefore be shared by all the instances
    ' of the class.
    frmLog.Show
End Sub

Sub LogEvent(ByVal LogText As String)
    If ThreadID Then
        LogText = "[" & Hex$(ThreadID) & "] " & LogText
    End If
    frmLog.LogText.SelStart = Len(frmLog.LogText.Text)
    frmLog.LogText.SelText = LogText & vbCrLf
End Sub
```

The frmLog form belongs to the ActiveX DLL project and includes the txtLog TextBox control that displays the text messages coming from the multithreaded client application, a CheckBox control that lets the user activate and deactivate the logging, and a CommandButton control that clears the contents of the txtLog control. Figure 16-22 on the following page shows a new version of the sample multithreaded application that has been enhanced with trace capabilities. The revised code in the main BAS module of the application is shown at the top of the following page.

```
Public Log As New CLog

Sub Main()
    Log.StartLogging "", 0              ' Initialize the CLog object.
    Log.ThreadID = App.ThreadID
    Log.LogEvent "Entering Sub Main"
    ' Here is the code that displays the main form (omitted...)
    ' ...
    Log.LogEvent "Exiting Sub Main"
End Sub
```

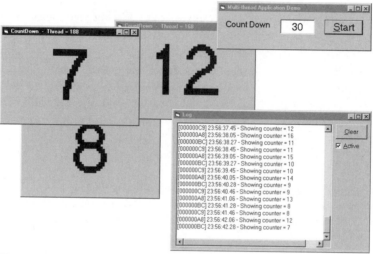

Figure 16-22. *Adding trace capabilities to a multithreaded application using a single-threaded ActiveX DLL. Each message includes the ID of the thread that sent it.*

For a more sophisticated test session, you might want to tick the Create Symbolic Debug Info option in the Compile tab of the Project Properties dialog box, and then recompile the application and execute it under a real debugger, such as the one included in Microsoft Visual C++.

REMOTE ACTIVEX COMPONENTS

ActiveX components can be executed remotely on another machine. Such a machine can be in the same or in a different room, in a different building, or even in a distant city. Thanks to the location transparency capabilities of COM, the client application always works as if the component executed locally. The only clue that the execution occurs remotely is that all calls to an object's properties and methods are much slower.

The portion of COM that deals with remote activation of a component is called *Distributed COM*, or DCOM for short. As I explained in the introduction to this chapter,

DCOM was first introduced with Windows NT 4, and it should be made clear that Windows NT is the operating system of choice when using remote components because it's the only one that provides the necessary security in a multiuser environment. In a production-distributed environment, Windows 95 and 98 machines should work only as DCOM clients.

Visual Basic also supports another limited form of remote activation, *Remote Automation*. I won't cover this outdated technology in detail because it's slower and less reliable than DCOM. Nowadays, the only reason to use Remote Automation is for supporting 16-bit clients, which isn't possible in DCOM because it's a 32-bit only technology.

The remaining part of this chapter deals with remote ActiveX EXE components. You can also remotely execute ActiveX DLLs, either by using a standard surrogate process such as DllHost.Exe or by using Microsoft Transaction Server (MTS). The creation of components for MTS isn't covered in this book.

> **NOTE** While a Windows 95 or 98 machine isn't good as a DCOM server in a production environment, you can still use it as a server in the development stage. The solution isn't very efficient and has other drawbacks as well. For example, there's no launch capability, and the COM component must be already running to accept remote requests. For more information, see the Microsoft Knowledge Base article Q165101.

Creating and Testing a Remote Component

If you have created and tested an ActiveX EXE component on the local machine, turning it into a remote component doesn't require a recompilation. All you have to do is modify a few keys in the Registry of the local machine so that all requests for the objects are automatically redirected to another machine. In theory, you can deliver remote components also with the Professional Edition of Visual Basic. In practice, however, only the Enterprise Edition includes all the tools that let you deploy remote components easily.

Compiling for remote activation

The first thing you have to do when creating a component that you envision using as a remote server is tick the Remote Server Files check box in the Component tab of the Project Properties dialog box, as shown in Figure 16-23 on the following page. If this option is enabled, Visual Basic creates two additional files when you compile the project. The files have the same name as the executable but different extensions: the .tlb type library and the .vbr registration file. These files are later used to register the component in a client workstation's Registry without physically installing the EXE file.

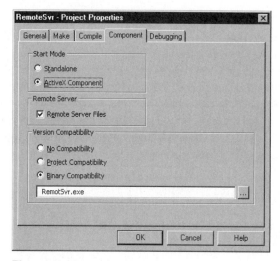

Figure 16-23. *Preparing an ActiveX EXE component for remote execution.*

Configuring the server

The next step is the installation and registration of the component on the server workstation. You accomplish this by copying the EXE file on a local disk of the machine and then running it with the */REGSERVER* switch on the command line. It's advisable that the EXE file be on a local drive instead of a networked drive because this setting raises fewer security issues. After the component has been registered, you can proceed to make it available to remote clients. You can choose from several tools to accomplish this.

The first and simplest tool of the group is the Remote Automation Connection Manager. This program has a dual purpose: You can employ it to make a local component available to remote clients using the commands on the Client Access tab, and you can run it on a client machine to modify the entry in the Registry so that all requests for a specific component's object are redirected to the server machine.

When the Remote Automation Connection Manager starts, it displays a list of all the components that are registered on the machine, as you can see in Figure 16-24. Using the option buttons on the Client Access tab, you can decide whether individual components should be available for remote activation.

Disallow All Remote Creates   This setting makes all the registered components unavailable to remote clients.

Allow Remote Creates By Key   You can make individual components available for remote activation; the state of each component depends on the Allow Remote Activation check box near the bottom border of the dialog box. This is a good choice under Windows 95 and 98 because these operating systems don't support ACLs. (See the next option.)

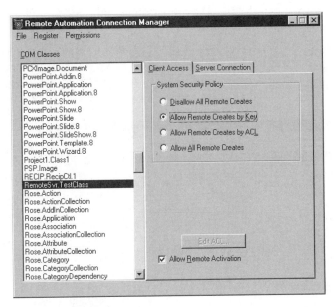

Figure 16-24. *The Client Access tab of the Remote Automation Connection Manager.*

Allow Remote Creates By ACL   This setting is available only under Windows NT systems and lets you decide which users are granted or denied the permission to use the component currently highlighted in the leftmost list box.

Allow All Remote Creates   All the registered components are available for remote activation; this setting should be used only under the development and debugging phase because it would make the server machine too vulnerable to attacks from malicious clients.

Testing the client

A quick way to test how your component works remotely is to install it on a client machine as if it were a local component (that is, by copying the EXE file and running it using the */REGSERVER* switch). Launch the client application, and make sure that everything works as expected. This step is important to sort out problems that don't have to do with remote activation.

Now you can run the Remote Automation Connection Manager to modify the Registry so that all object requests will be redirected to the server. In this case, you have to use the Server Connection tab of the program, shown in Figure 16-25 on the following page, where you select the Distributed COM setting and then make the object remote by using the Ctrl+R shortcut key or by using the Remote command in the Register menu or the pop-up menu that displays when you right-click on the window. To complete the registration procedure, you have to specify the name of the server machine where the object will be instantiated. When you're working with DCOM, this utility doesn't allow you to specify a network protocol or an authentication level.

Run the client again and ensure that everything is working; if you didn't make any errors, the object will now be instantiated on the server. You might not see the remote component on the server's monitor, but you can check that it appears in the list of processes when the client makes the request.

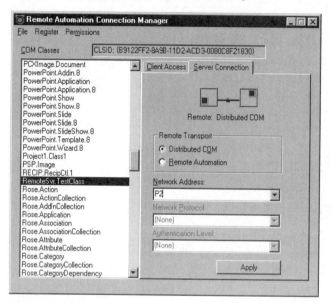

Figure 16-25. *The Server Connection tab of the Remote Automation Connection Manager.*

The *CreateObject* function

Visual Basic 6 improves the *CreateObject* function with the support of a second optional argument, which gives the client the ability to instantiate the component on a specific remote workstation, as in the following code:

```
Set x = CreateObject("RemoteSvr.TestClass", "ServerNT")
```

This feature makes it possible to write smarter clients that can implement a fault-tolerant mechanism and instantiate an object on an alternate workstation if the machine the Registry points to is currently unavailable. Thanks to this capability, a distributed application can also implement a sophisticated load-balancing algorithm so that heavy-duty components run on the machines that are currently idle.

Deploying the component

While the Remote Automation Connection Manager is fine for testing that the client application correctly connects to the component, its interactive nature gets in the way when it's time to actually deploy the application on multiple workstations. The solution to this problem lies in the Client Configuration utility, CliReg32.Exe. You can find this program in the Common\Tools\CliReg directory in your Visual Studio main directory, and you should ensure that it's in the client installation package.

You (or your installation routine) have to run the CliReg32 program and pass it the name of the VBR file that was produced when the component was compiled. The VBR file is nothing but a REG file with a different extension and a different header. The CliReg32 utility reads this file, customizes it using the settings found on the command line, and finally adds all the relevant keys to the Registry. Its syntax is the following:

```
CliReg32 <vbrfile> <options>
```

where all the available options are listed in Table 16-3.

Option	Description
-d	Use DCOM instead of Remote Automation.
-t <typelib>	Specify a type library file.
-a	Specify an authentication security level. (*n* can be in the range 0 through 6, corresponding to the values listed in Table 16-4.)
-s <address>	Specify a network address.
-p <protocol>	Specify a network protocol.
-u	Uninstall the VBR file.
-l	Log error information to file CLIREG.LOG.
-q	Suppress the dialog box; if you omit this option, CliReg32 displays a dialog box for letting the user enter missing values.
-nologo	Suppress the copyright dialog box.
-h or -?	Show this list of options.

Table 16-3. *The options for the CliReg32 utility.*

Configuring DCOM

DCOMCNFG is the main utility that you use to configure DCOM. When you run it for the first time, it quickly scans all the registered components in the system and prepares them for execution as remote components by adding their identifiers under the HKEY_CLASSES_ROOT\AppID key in the Registry. This portion of the Registry gathers all the information about component security. While a few components register themselves under this key, this doesn't happen with all the components authored in Visual Basic. Note that DCOMCNFG displays one AppID for each ActiveX server, even if the server exposes multiple classes.

DCOMCNFG also activates or deactivates DCOM as a whole. In the Default Properties tab shown in Figure 16-26 on the next page, you should tick the Enable Distributed COM On This Computer check box. This option must be selected to have the current machine work either as a server or as a client in a DCOM connection. You might need to reboot to enforce a new setting for this option.

Default authentication and impersonation levels

DCOMCNFG enables you to set both the DCOM default security settings and the security settings for each particular component. This sort of security is named *declarative security,* and it can be assigned from outside the component itself. DCOM also supports *programmatic security,* which enables the programmer to dynamically modify the security settings of the component at run time, and even set a different security level on a per-method basis. Unfortunately, programmatic security is beyond the capabilities of Visual Basic.

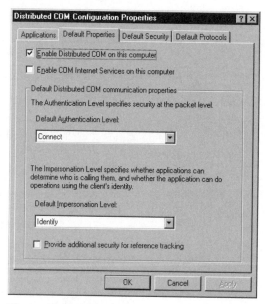

Figure 16-26. *The Default Properties tab of the DCOMCNFG utility.*

The Default Authentication Level option tells DCOM how it should check that data sent to the component is actually coming from the client. Higher security levels protect the server from data tampering, but at the same time they slow down the communication with its clients. The authentication levels supported by DCOM are listed in Table 16-4.

Value	Level	Description
0	Default	Corresponds to Connect authentication.
1	None	DCOM doesn't authenticate data in any way.
2	Connect	DCOM authenticates the client only when it first connects to the server.

Table 16-4. *DCOM authentication levels.*

Value	Level	Description
3	Call	DCOM authenticates the client at the beginning of each call to a method or property.
4	Packet	DCOM authenticates each packet of data coming from the client.
5	Packet integrity	Similar to previous level, but a checksum mechanism ensures that data hasn't been altered on the way from the client to the server.
6	Packet privacy	Similar to previous level, but data is also encrypted to ensure that it isn't read by unauthorized programs.

The impersonation level defines what the component can do on behalf of its clients. The lower the impersonation level is, the more protected the client is from misbehaving components. The Default Impersonation Level field determines the impersonation level assigned to all components that don't override this setting with a different value. DCOM supports four impersonation levels, which are summarized in Table 16-5.

Value	Level	Description
1	Anonymous	The server doesn't know anything about the client and therefore can't impersonate it. (This level isn't currently supported and is automatically promoted to Identify.)
2	Identify	The server has enough information about the client to impersonate it in ACL checking but can't access system objects as the client.
3	Impersonate	The server can impersonate the client while acting on its behalf.
4	Delegate	The server can impersonate the client when calling other servers on the behalf of the client. (Supported only in Windows 2000.)

Table 16-5. *DCOM impersonation levels. The default setting is Identify.*

Default access and launch permissions

In the Default Security tab, you select the list of users that are enabled to run or use all the components that don't provide a customized list of authorized users. To use a component, a user must be included in the Access Permission list, while to launch the component the user must be included in the Launch Permission list. Both of them are Windows NT Access Control Lists, as shown in Figure 16-27. You shouldn't modify these lists; instead, you should modify the individual ACLs associated with each component, as I'll explain in a moment. It's important that the SYSTEM user be included in both the access and launch lists; otherwise, the component can't be launched at all.

The Default Configuration Permission list includes all the users who are allowed to change the security settings of all the components that don't provide a customized list of authorized users. You shouldn't modify these settings because restricting the access to the Registry might cause problems to components written in Visual Basic, which register themselves each time they're launched.

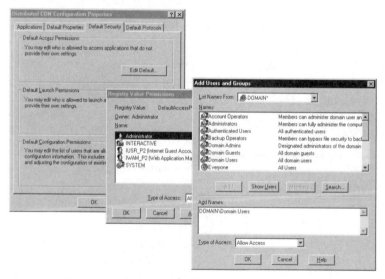

Figure 16-27. *The Default Security tab of the DCOMCNFG utility.*

Identity settings

If you switch to the Applications tab of the DCOMCNFG utility and double-click on a component's name, another window appears; this window is where you modify the security settings and other properties of that particular component. For example, in the General tab, you can set a custom Authentication level for the component, whereas in the Security tab, you define exactly which users can access or launch this component or can modify its configuration permissions.

The most interesting settings are in the Identity tab, as shown in Figure 16-28.

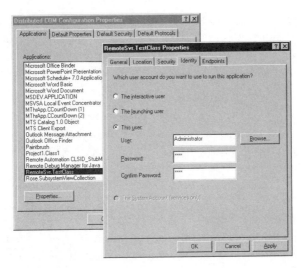

Figure 16-28. *The Identity tab of the DCOMCNFG utility for a specific component.*

Here you decide under which user account the component will run. DCOM provides the following three choices:

Run as The Interactive User   This option assigns the component the security credential of the user who is currently logged on the machine. This generally isn't a wise choice in a real distributed system because the permissions granted to the component vary depending on who is logged on. If no user has logged on, the component can't even run. In practice, this option makes sense only when you're testing the component.

All components that run in an account different from the interactive user's account execute in a *noninteractive window station* and aren't visible on the desktop. If you want to see the output of a component, it must run under the identity of the interactive user. For the same reason, unless you're 100 percent sure that your component will be run under the interactive user account, you should compile it using the Unattended Execution option. If you don't and an error occurs, the component will wait forever because no user can click on its error message box.

Run as The Launching User   This option assigns the security credentials of the user who is running the client application. This option usually isn't a good choice because different clients instantiate remote objects that must run under different credentials, and this is possible only by running multiple instances of the component. In this case, the component acts more or less as a SingleUse component even if it was compiled with the MultiUse attribute. Moreover, if a component is running under the account of a remote client, the component won't be able to make calls to components that run on another machine, at least on Windows NT 4 (which doesn't support the Delegate impersonation level).

Run as This User This option lets you assign a specific user's security credentials to the component. In a production environment, this is often the best choice because only one instance of a MultiUse component will be created. In practice, the best thing to do is create a new user just for this purpose, give it proper access rights to system resources, and then let the component run with this new user's credentials. In this way, you can modify the access rights of one or more components by simply changing the rights of this fictitious user.

It's important that this user be assigned the permission to log on as a batch job, otherwise the logon process that invisibly starts when the component is launched will fail. DCOMCNFG automatically assigns this right to the user in the Run As This User field, and you only have to avoid accidentally revoking this right from within the Windows NT User Manager utility.

Implementing a Callback Technique

An area in which you can greatly improve the performance of your remote components is event notification. While your ordinary event notifications work under DCOM (but not under Remote Automation), they're so inefficient that I strongly discourage you from using them. Instead, you should implement a callback technique.

The callback mechanism works as follows: When the client calls a lengthy method of the component, it passes a reference to an object defined in the client itself, and the component stores this reference in a local variable. This variable is then used when the component needs to call back the client to inform it that something has occurred.

Early-bound and late-bound callbacks

Callback techniques have been available to Visual Basic programmers since version 4 of the language. But only late-binding callbacks were possible in Visual Basic 4. Let me describe a concrete example of the callback technique. Say that you have created a generic reusable report printing engine: Any client application can instantiate it and start a print job. The server then calls back the client when the job has been completed or when an error occurs.

In this scenario, the print server doesn't know at compile time the type of the object passed by the client application because different types of clients expose different classes. The component can store a reference to the client only in a variable declared using *As Object,* which means that the notification occurs through late binding. The client and the component must agree on the name and the syntax of a method in the class used for callback. Any syntax error in the client or in the server will manifest itself only at run time. As you know, late binding is also less efficient than early binding, so you should avoid it if possible.

In Visual Basic 5 and 6, the *Implements* keyword allows you to enforce a stricter contract between the client and the component. The component includes a PublicNot-Creatable class that defines the callback interface, and any client that wants to receive callback notifications from the server has to expose a PublicNotCreatable class that implements that interface. The component can therefore store a reference to such an object in a specific variable, and all the notifications use early binding.

An example

On the companion CD-ROM, you can find the complete source code of a multi-threaded component that implements a callback mechanism to communicate with its clients. This component performs a (simulated) printing job and tells the client how the job progresses and when it completes. The component includes the CPrinterCBK PublicNotCreatable class that defines the callback interface:

```
' The CPrinterCBK class module.
Sub Complete(ErrCode As Long)
    '
End Sub
Sub Progress(percent As Integer)
    '
End Sub
```

This is the source code of the CPrinter class, which simulates the actual printing:

```
' The CPrinter class module.
Private Declare Sub Sleep Lib "kernel32" (ByVal dwMilliseconds As Long)

Dim SaveCBK As CPrinterCBK
Dim frmTimer As frmTimer

Sub StartPrintJob(Filename As String, cbk As CPrinterCBK)
    ' Save the callback object for later.
    Set SaveCBK = cbk
    ' Activate the timer that will restart this thread.
    Set frmTimer = New frmTimer
    With frmTimer
        Set .Owner = Me
        .Timer1.Interval = 100
        .Timer1.Enabled = True
    End With
End Sub
```

(continued)

```
Friend Sub StartIt()
    Dim totalTime As Single, percent As Integer
    Dim t As Single, startTime As Single

    ' This code is executed when the timer fires.
    ' Unload the form, and destroy it completely.
    Unload frmTimer
    Set frmTimer = Nothing

    ' Simulate the printing process.
    totalTime = Rnd * 10 + 5
    startTime = Timer
    Do
        ' Inform the client that something has happened.
        percent = ((Timer - startTime) / totalTime) * 100
        SaveCBK.Progress percent
        ' In this demo, just go to sleep for one second.
        Sleep 1000
    Loop Until Timer - startTime > totalTime
    ' Inform the client that the process has been completed.
    SaveCBK.Complete 0
    ' IMPORTANT: destroy the reference to the client
    ' so that it won't be kept alive forever.
    Set SaveCBK = Nothing
End Sub
```

The component also includes a frmTimer form with a Timer control on it; the only purpose of this form is to wake the component a few milliseconds after it has returned the control to its client from the *StartPrintJob* method:

```
' The frmTimer form module.
Public Owner As CPrinter

Private Sub Timer1_Timer()
    ' This procedure is executed only once.
    Timer1.Interval = 0
    Timer1.Enabled = False
    ' Yield to the companion CPrinter instance.
    Owner.StartIt
End Sub
```

On the CD-ROM, you can also find a client application that uses this component and that performs a CPU intensive task (finding prime numbers) while waiting for the simulated printing job to complete. If you don't have a network of computers, you can run multiple instances of this application and see that they can multitask without affecting one another, as shown in Figure 16-29.

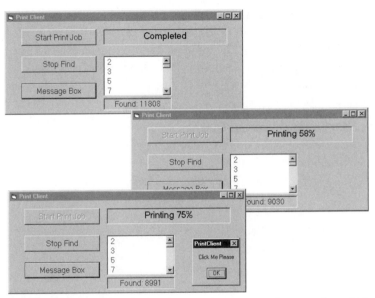

Figure 16-29. *Multiple clients that communicate with a sample multithreading component through callbacks.*

The client application includes a PublicNotCreatable callback class module, which is passed to the server component:

```
' The CallbackCls class module.
Implements PrintServer.CPrinterCBK

' This class directly references controls on the main form.
Private Sub CPrinterCBK_Complete(ErrCode As Long)
    frmClient.lblStatus = "Completed"
    frmClient.cmdStart.Enabled = True
End Sub
Private Sub CPrinterCBK_Progress(percent As Integer)
    frmClient.lblStatus = "Printing " & percent & "%"
End Sub
```

The only portion of the main form in the client application that's relevant in this context is the point at which it instantiates the component and passes it a reference to a CallbackCls object:

```
Private Sub cmdStart_Click()
    Dim prn As PrintServer.CPrinter
    ' Ask the CPrinter server to spool a fictitious file.
    Set prn = New PrintServer.CPrinter
    prn.StartPrintJob "a dummy filename", New CallbackCls
End Sub
```

Note that the client doesn't need to store a reference to the CallbackCls object in a local variable because this object is kept alive by the server component. Moreover, the CallbackCls class module can work to implement a callback mechanism from multiple servers, each one defining its own callback interface. In this case, the class has to include multiple *Implements* statements, one for each supported callback interface.

Comparing callbacks and events

The callback mechanism is undoubtedly more complex than a notification method based on events. For one thing, the client must be an ActiveX EXE itself to expose a public COM object, and the component must have sufficient rights to call a method in this object. On the other hand, callbacks have many advantages over events:

- Calling a method in the client uses VTable binding, whereas events use a less efficient ID binding.

- Callbacks let you control which clients get the notification and in which order. You can also provide a *Cancel* argument that clients can set to True to suppress notifications to other clients, which is something that you can't do with events.

- The callback method can be a function, which gives you broader control over how values are marshaled and lets you fine-tune your component for better performance.

Note that the callback technique described here isn't just for remote components and can be effectively used with local components as well.

Now you know everything you need to know to create great in-process, local, and remote components. But Visual Basic 6 also lets you create another type of component, namely ActiveX controls. They're covered in the next chapter.

Chapter 17

ActiveX Controls

ActiveX controls are the descendants of the first OCX controls that appeared when Visual Basic 4 was released. While they retain the same file extension, they're very different beneath the surface. The original OCX controls included a lot of low-level functionality (and consequently had to support many COM interfaces), and therefore were heavy and relatively slow. The new ActiveX controls were specifically redesigned to be embedded in HTML pages and delegate much of their functionality to their container, be it Microsoft Internet Explorer, a Visual Basic form, or any other ActiveX-compliant environment. Thanks to this different approach, ActiveX controls are generally slimmer than old OCXs, download faster, and load in memory more rapidly.

ACTIVEX CONTROL FUNDAMENTALS

Visual Basic 5 and 6 give you all the tools you need to create powerful ActiveX controls, which you can then reuse in all your projects. More precisely, you can create two different types of ActiveX controls:

- Private ActiveX controls that can be included in any type of Visual Basic project. They're saved in files with the .ctl extension, and you can reuse them in any other Visual Basic project merely by adding the file to the project. (This is reuse at the source-code level.)

- Public ActiveX controls that can be included only in ActiveX control projects; you have to compile them into OCX files, and then you can use them in any other Microsoft Windows application written in Visual Basic, Microsoft Visual C++, or any other development environment that supports ActiveX controls. (This is reuse at the binary level.)

Visual Basic 5 was the first language that permitted programmers to create ActiveX controls using a visual approach. As you'll see in a moment, you can create powerful controls by simply grouping simpler controls together: These controls are known as *constituent controls*. By putting together a PictureBox and two scroll bar controls, for example, you can create an ActiveX control that can scroll its contents. Visual Basic also allows you to create an ActiveX control without using any constituent controls. These are the so-called *owner-drawn* ActiveX controls.

You should also keep this in mind when working with ActiveX controls: You're used to distinguishing between two distinct types of people interacting with your program—the developer and the user. To better understand how ActiveX controls behave, you need to take another role into account, the *author* of the control itself. The author's job is to prepare a control that will be used by the developer to deliver an application to the user. As you'll see, the author's and developer's perspectives are sometimes different, even though the two roles might be occupied by the same person. (That is, you might act as the author of the control and then as the developer who uses it.)

Creating the UserControl Module

In this section, I'll show you how to create a sort of super-TextBox control that adds extra capabilities to the regular TextBox control, such as filtering out invalid characters. The steps that you have to take any time you create a new Public ActiveX control are the following ones:

1. Add a new ActiveX control project to the environment. This new project already includes a UserControl module. (Alternatively, manually add a UserControl module from the Project menu if you're creating a Private ActiveX control.)

2. Give the project a meaningful name and a description. The former becomes the name of the control's library, and the latter is the string that appears in the Components dialog box for all the projects that use this control. In this example, we'll use the project's name *SuperTB* and the description *An enhanced TextBox control.*

3. Click on the UserControl designer's window to give it the focus, and then enter a value for the *Name* property of the control in the Properties window. In this example, you can enter *SuperTextBox*.

4. Place one or more constituent controls on the surface of the UserControl designer. In this example, you need to add a Label control and a TextBox control, as shown in Figure 17-1.

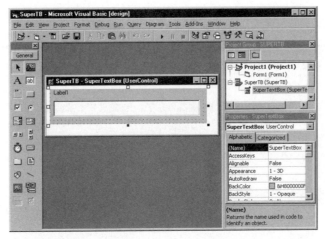

Figure 17-1. *The SuperTextBox control at design time.*

You can use any intrinsic control as a constituent control of an ActiveX control except the OLE Container control (whose Toolbox icon is disabled when an ActiveX control designer has the focus). You can also use external ActiveX controls as constituent controls, but if you use one you should ascertain that you have the legal right to encapsulate it in your own control. All the ActiveX controls in the Visual Basic package except DBGrid can be freely reused in your own ActiveX control. Always carefully read the license agreements for third-party controls before encapsulating any in your own controls. You'll find more advice about these matters in the "Licensing" section near the end of this chapter. Finally, you can create ActiveX controls that don't use constituent controls, such as the SuperLabel control that you can find on the companion CD in the same directory as the SuperText project.

Now you can close the UserControl designer's window and switch to the Standard EXE project that you are using as a test client program. You'll notice that a new icon is now active in the Toolbox. Select it, and drop an instance of your brand new control on the form, as shown in Figure 17-2 on the following page.

Congratulations! You've just created your first ActiveX control.

I want to draw your attention to one specific point in the previous description. You need to explicitly close the ActiveX control designer window before using the control on the test container form. If you omit this step, the icon in the Toolbox stays inactive. In fact, Visual Basic activates the ActiveX control and prepares it for *siting* only when you close the designer window. Siting refers to the instant an ActiveX control is placed on its container's surface.

You need to keep in mind that you have to deal with two different instances of the control, the design-time instance and the run-time instance. Unlike other Visual Basic modules, a UserControl module must be active even when the test project is in design mode. This is necessary because the control must react to the programmer's actions, such as entering the value of a property in the Properties window or resizing the control on the parent form. When you're working with the ActiveX control designer open, however, the control itself is in design mode and therefore can't be used in a form. To run an ActiveX control, you need to close its designer window, as I explained earlier.

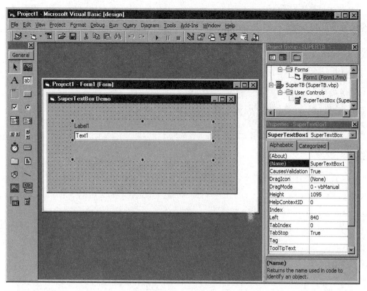

Figure 17-2. *An instance of the SuperTextBox control on a test form. The Properties window includes a number of properties that have been defined for you by Visual Basic.*

Running the ActiveX Control Interface Wizard

Our first version of the SuperTextBox control doesn't do anything useful yet, but you can run the client application and ensure that everything is working and that no error is raised. To turn this first prototype into a useful control, you need to add properties and methods and write the code that correctly implements the new features.

To complete the SuperTextBox control, you need to add all the properties that the user of this control expects to find, such as *ForeColor*, *Text*, and *SelStart*. A few of these properties must appear in the Properties window; others are run time–only properties. You also need to add other properties and methods that expand the basic TextBox functionality—for example, the *FormatMask* property (which affects how the control's contents is formatted) or the *Copy* method (which copies the control's contents to the Clipboard).

In most cases, these properties and methods map directly to properties and methods of constituent controls: for example, the *ForeColor* and the *Text* properties map directly to the Text1 constituent control's properties with the same names, whereas the *Caption* property corresponds to the *Caption* property of the Label1 constituent control. This is similar to the concept of inheritance by delegation that you saw in Chapter 7.

To facilitate the task of creating the public interface of an ActiveX control and writing all the delegation code, Visual Basic includes the ActiveX Control Interface Wizard. This add-in is installed with the Visual Basic package, but you might need to explicitly load it from within the Add-In Manager dialog box.

In the first step of the wizard, you select the interface members, as shown in Figure 17-3. The wizard lists the properties, methods, and events that are exposed by the constituent controls and lets you select which ones should be made available to the outside. In this case, accept all those that are already in the rightmost list except *BackStyle*, and then add the following items: *Alignment, Caption, Change, hWnd, Locked, MaxLength, MouseIcon, MousePointer, PasswordChar, SelLength, SelStart, SelText, Text*, plus all the *OLExxxx* properties, methods, and events. These members ensure that the SuperTextBox control matches nearly all the capabilities of a regular TextBox control. A few properties have been left out—namely, *MultiLine* and *ScrollBars*. The reason for these exclusions will be clear later.

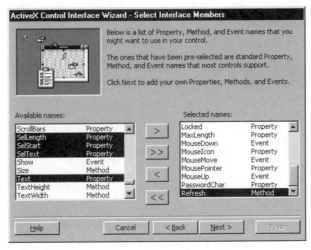

Figure 17-3. *The first step of the ActiveX Control Interface Wizard. You can also highlight multiple items and add all of them in one operation.*

NOTE Unfortunately, the ActiveX Control Interface Wizard lets you include many properties, methods, and events that you should never add to the public interface of your controls—for example, the *ToolTipText, CausesValidation, WhatsThisHelpID*, and *Validate* event. As a matter of fact, Visual Basic automatically adds these members to any ActiveX control that you create, so you don't need to specify them unless you plan to use the control in environments other than Visual Basic. More on this later.

In the next step, you define all the custom properties, methods, and events that your ActiveX control exposes. You should add the *FormatMask*, *FormattedText*, *CaptionFont*, *CaptionForeColor*, and *CaptionBackColor* properties; the *Copy*, *Clear*, *Cut*, and *Paste* methods; and the *SelChange* event.

In the third step, you define how the public members of the ActiveX control are mapped to the members of its constituent controls. For example, the *Alignment* public property should be mapped to the Text1 constituent control's *Alignment* property. The same holds true for the majority of the members in the list, and you can speed up mapping operations by selecting all of members and assigning them to the Text1 control, as shown in Figure 17-4.

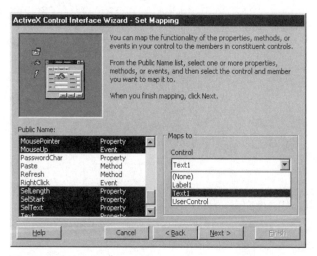

Figure 17-4. *In the third step in the ActiveX Control Interface Wizard, you can map multiple members by highlighting them in the leftmost list and then selecting a constituent control in the Control combo box on the right.*

A few members—for example, the *Caption* property—map to the Label1 constituent control. You must specify the name of the original member in the constituent control when the two names differ, as in the case of the *CaptionForeColor*, *CaptionBackColor*, and *CaptionFont* properties that correspond to the Label1's *ForeColor*, *BackColor*, and *Font* properties, respectively. At other times, you have to map a public member to the UserControl itself—for example, the *Refresh* method.

There might be members that can't be directly mapped to any constituent control, and in the fourth step of the wizard you define how such members behave. For example, you declare that the *Copy*, *Cut*, *Clear*, and *Paste* methods are *Sub*s by setting their return type to *Empty*. Similarly, you specify that *FormatMask* is a String property that can be read and modified either at design time or run time, whereas the *FormattedText* isn't available at design time and is read-only at run time. You should also specify an empty string as the default value for these three properties because even if you change the property type to String, the wizard doesn't automatically change the value *0* that it initially set as the default. You must enter the argument list for all methods and events, as well as a brief description for each member, as shown in Figure 17-5.

The otherwise excellent ActiveX Control Interface Wizard has some limitations, though. For example, you can neither define properties with arguments, nor can you enter a description for all the custom properties—the *CaptionFont* and *CaptionForeColor* properties in this case—that are mapped to constituent controls.

CAUTION Beware, international programmers! Being written in Visual Basic, the ActiveX Control Interface Wizard inherits a curious bug from the language if the Regional Setting established in the Control Panel isn't English. When Boolean constants True and False are concatenated in a string, the value you obtain is the localized string corresponding to that value. (For example, in Italian you get the strings "Vero" and "Falso", respectively.) Thus, in these circumstances the wizard doesn't produce correct Visual Basic code, and you might have to edit it manually to run it. Or, if you prefer, you can set the Regional Setting to English if you plan to run the wizard often in a programming session.

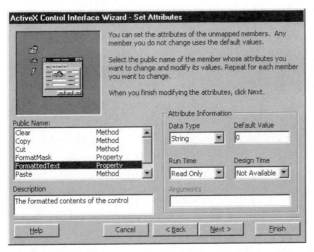

Figure 17-5. *In the fourth step in the ActiveX Control Interface Wizard, you decide the syntax of methods and events and whether properties are read/write or read-only at run time.*

You're finally ready to click on the Finish button and generate all the code for the SuperTextBox control. If you go back to the instance of the control on the test form, you'll notice that the control has been grayed. This happens each time you change the public interface of the control. You can make the ActiveX control active again by right-clicking on its parent form and selecting the Update UserControls menu command.

Adding the Missing Pieces

Looking at the code that the ActiveX Control User Interface wizard generates is a good starting point for learning how ActiveX controls are implemented. Most of the time, you'll see that a UserControl module isn't different from a regular class module. One important note: The wizard adds several commented lines that it uses to keep track of how members are implemented. You should follow the warnings that come along with these lines and avoid deleting them or modifying them in any way.

Delegated properties, methods, and events

As I already explained, most of the code generated by the wizard does nothing but delegate the real action to the inner constituent controls. For example, see how the *Text* property is implemented:

```
Public Property Get Text() As String
    Text = Text1.Text
End Property
Public Property Let Text(ByVal New_Text As String)
    Text1.Text() = New_Text
    PropertyChanged "Text"
End Property
```

The *PropertyChanged* method informs the container environment—Visual Basic, in this case—that the property has been updated. This serves two purposes. First, at design time Visual Basic should know that the control has been updated and has to be saved in the FRM file. Second, at run time, if the *Text* property is bound to a database field, Visual Basic has to update the record. Data-aware ActiveX controls are described in the "Data Binding" section, later in this chapter.

The delegation mechanism also works for methods and events. For example, see how the SuperTextBox module traps the Text1 control's *KeyPress* event and exposes it to the outside, and notice how it delegates the *Refresh* method to the UserControl object:

```
' The declaration of the event
Event KeyPress(KeyAscii As Integer)

Private Sub Text1_KeyPress(KeyAscii As Integer)
    RaiseEvent KeyPress(KeyAscii)
End Sub

Public Sub Refresh()
    UserControl.Refresh
End Sub
```

Custom properties

For all the public properties that aren't mapped to a property of a constituent control, the ActiveX Control Interface Wizard can't do anything but create a private member variable that stores the value assigned from the outside. For example, this is the code generated for the *FormatMask* custom property:

```
Dim m_FormatMask As String

Public Property Get FormatMask() As String
    FormatMask = m_FormatMask
End Property

Public Property Let FormatMask(ByVal New_FormatMask As String)
    m_FormatMask = New_FormatMask
    PropertyChanged "FormatMask"
End Property
```

Needless to say, you decide how such custom properties affect the behavior or the appearance of the SuperTextBox control. In this particular case, this property changes the behavior of another custom property, *FormattedText*, so you should modify the code generated by the wizard as follows:

```
Public Property Get FormattedText() As String
    FormattedText = Format$(Text, FormatMask)
End Property
```

The *FormattedText* property had been defined as read-only at run time, so the wizard has generated its *Property Get* procedure but not its *Property Let* procedure.

Custom methods

For each custom method you have added, the wizard generates the skeleton of a Sub or Function procedure. It's up to you to fill this template with code. For example, here's how you can implement the *Copy* and *Clear* methods:

```
Public Sub Copy()
    Clipboard.Clear
    Clipboard.SetText IIf(SelText <> "", SelText, Text)
End Sub

Public Sub Clear()
    If SelText <> "" Then SelText = "" Else Text = ""
End Sub
```

You might be tempted to use *Text1.Text* and *Text1.SelText* instead of *Text* and *SelText* in the previous code, but I advise you not to do it. If you use the public name of the property, your code is slightly slower, but you'll save a lot of time if you later decide to change the implementation of the *Text* property.

Custom events

You raise events from a UserControl module exactly as you would from within a regular class module. When you have a custom event that isn't mapped to any event of constituent controls, the wizard has generated only the event declaration for you because it can't understand when and where you want to raise it.

The SuperTextBox control exposes the *SelChange* event, which is raised when either the *SelStart* property or the *SelLength* property (or both) change. This event is useful when you want to display the current column on the status bar or when you want to enable or disable toolbar buttons depending on whether there's any selected text. To correctly implement this event, you must add two private variables and a private procedure that's called from multiple event procedures in the UserControl module:

```
Private saveSelStart As Long, saveSelLength As Long

' Raise the SelChange event if the cursor moved.
Private Sub CheckSelChange()
    If SelStart <> saveSelStart Or SelLength <> saveSelLength Then
        RaiseEvent SelChange
        saveSelStart = SelStart
        saveSelLength = SelLength
    End If
End Sub

Private Sub Text1_KeyUp(KeyCode As Integer, Shift As Integer)
    RaiseEvent KeyUp(KeyCode, Shift)
    CheckSelChange
End Sub

Private Sub Text1_Change()
    RaiseEvent Change
    CheckSelChange
End Sub
```

In the complete demonstration project that you can find on the companion CD, the *CheckSelChange* procedure is called from within Text1's *MouseMove* and *MouseUp* event procedures and also from within the *Property Let SelStart* and *Property Let SelLength* procedures.

Properties that map to multiple controls

Sometimes you might need to add custom code to correctly expose an event to the outside. Take, for example, the *Click* and *DblClick* events: You mapped them to the Text1 constituent control, but the UserControl module should raise an event also when the user clicks on the Label1 control. This means that you have to manually write the code that does the delegation:

```
Private Sub Label1_Click()
    RaiseEvent Click
End Sub

Private Sub Label1_DblClick()
    RaiseEvent DblClick
End Sub
```

You might also need to add delegation code when the same property applies to multiple constituent controls. Say that you want the *ForeColor* property to affect both the Text1 and Label1 controls. Since the wizard can map a property only to a single control, you must add some code (shown as boldface in the following listing) in the *Property Let* procedure that propagates the new value to the other constituent controls:

```
Public Property Let ForeColor(ByVal New_ForeColor As OLE_COLOR)
    Text1.ForeColor = New_ForeColor
    Label1.ForeColor = New_ForeColor
    PropertyChanged "ForeColor"
End Property
```

You don't need to modify the code in the corresponding *Property Get* procedure, however.

Persistent properties

The ActiveX Control Interface Wizard automatically generates the code that makes all the control's properties persistent via FRM files. The persistence mechanism is identical to the one used for persistable ActiveX components (which I explained in Chapter 16). In this case, however, you never have to explicitly ask an ActiveX control to save its own properties because the Visual Basic environment does it for you automatically if any of the control's properties have changed during the editing session in the environment

When the control is placed on a form, Visual Basic fires its *UserControl_InitProperties* event. In this event procedure, the control should initialize its properties to their default values. For example, this is the code that the wizard generates for the SuperTextBox control:

```
Const m_def_FormatMask = ""
Const m_def_FormattedText = ""

Private Sub UserControl_InitProperties()
    m_FormatMask = m_def_FormatMask
    m_FormattedText = m_def_FormattedText
End Sub
```

When Visual Basic saves the current form to an FRM file, it asks the ActiveX control to save itself by raising its *UserControl_WriteProperties* event:

```
Private Sub UserControl_WriteProperties(PropBag As PropertyBag)
    Call PropBag.WriteProperty("FormatMask", m_FormatMask, m_def_FormatMask)
    Call PropBag.WriteProperty("FormattedText", m_FormattedText, _
        m_def_FormattedText)
    Call PropBag.WriteProperty("BackColor", Text1.BackColor, &H80000005)
    Call PropBag.WriteProperty("ForeColor", Text1.ForeColor, &H80000008)
    ' Other properties omitted....
End Sub
```

The third argument passed to the PropertyBag object's *WriteProperty* method is the default value for the property. When you're working with color properties, you usually pass hexadecimal constants that stand for system colors. For example, &H80000005 is the vbWindowBackground constant (the default background color), and &H80000008 is the vbWindowText constant (the default text color). Unfortunately, the wizard doesn't generate symbolic constants directly. For a complete list of supported system colors, use the Object Browser to enumerate the SystemColorConstants constants in the VBRUN library.

When Visual Basic reloads an FRM file, it fires the *UserControl_ReadProperties* event to let the ActiveX control restore its own properties:

```
Private Sub UserControl_ReadProperties(PropBag As PropertyBag)
    m_FormatMask = PropBag.ReadProperty("FormatMask", m_def_FormatMask)
    m_FormattedText = PropBag.ReadProperty("FormattedText", _
        m_def_FormattedText)
    Text1.BackColor = PropBag.ReadProperty("BackColor", &H80000005)
    Text1.ForeColor = PropBag.ReadProperty("ForeColor", &H80000008)
    Set Text1.MouseIcon = PropBag.ReadProperty("MouseIcon", Nothing)
    ' Other properties omitted....
End Sub
```

Again, the last argument passed to the PropertyBag object's *ReadProperty* method is the default value of the property being retrieved. If you manually edit the code created by the wizard, be sure that you use the same constant in the *InitProperties*, *WriteProperties*, and *ReadProperties* event procedures.

The wizard does a good job of generating code for properties persistence, but in some cases you might need to fix it. For example, the preceding code directly assigns values to constituent controls' properties. While this approach is OK in most cases, it fails when the same property maps multiple controls, in which case you should assign the value to the Public property name. On the other hand, using the Public property name invokes its *Property Let* and *Set* procedures, which in turn call the *PropertyChanged* method and cause properties to be saved again even if they weren't modified during the current session. I'll show you how you can avoid this problem later in this chapter.

Moreover, the wizard creates more code than strictly necessary. For example, it generates the code that saves and restores properties that aren't available at design time (*SelStart*, *SelText*, *SelLength*, and *FormattedText* in this particular case). Dropping the corresponding statements from the *ReadProperties* and *WriteProperties* procedures makes your FRM files shorter and speeds up save and load operations.

The UserControl's *Resize* event

The UserControl object raises several events during the lifetime of an ActiveX control, and I'll describe all of them later in this chapter. One event, however, is especially important: the *Resize* event. This event fires at design time when the programmer drops the ActiveX control on the client form and also fires whenever the control itself is resized. As the author of the control, you must react to this event so that all the constituent controls move and resize accordingly. In this particular case, the position and size of constituent controls depend on whether the SuperTextBox control has a nonempty *Caption*:

```
Private Sub UserControl_Resize()
    On Error Resume Next
    If Caption <> "" Then
        Label1.Move 0, 0, ScaleWidth, Label1.Height
        Text1.Move 0, Label1.Height, ScaleWidth, _
            ScaleHeight - Label1.Height
    Else
        Text1.Move 0, 0, ScaleWidth, ScaleHeight
    End If
End Sub
```

The *On Error* statement serves to protect your application from errors that occur when the ActiveX control is shorter than the Label1 constituent control. The preceding code must execute also when the *Caption* property changes, so you need to add a statement to its *Property Let* procedure:

```
Public Property Let Caption(ByVal New_Caption As String)
    Label1.Caption = New_Caption
    PropertyChanged "Caption"
    Call UserControl_Resize
End Property
```

THE USERCONTROL OBJECT

The UserControl object is the container in which constituent controls are placed. In this sense, it's akin to the Form object, and in fact it shares many properties, methods, and events with the Form object. For example, you can learn its internal dimension using the *ScaleWidth* and *ScaleHeight* properties, use the *AutoRedraw* property to create persistent graphics on the UserControl's surface, and add a border using the *BorderStyle* property. UserControl objects also support all the graphic properties and methods that forms do, including *Cls*, *Line*, *Circle*, *DrawStyle*, *DrawWidth*, *ScaleX*, and *ScaleY*.

UserControls support most of the Form object's events, too. For example, *Click*, *DblClick*, *MouseDown*, *MouseMove*, and *MouseUp* events fire when the user activates the mouse over the portions of UserControl's surface that aren't covered by constituent controls. UserControl objects also support *KeyDown*, *KeyUp*, and *KeyPress* events, but they fire only when no constituent control can get the focus or when you set the UserControl's *KeyPreview* property to True.

The Life Cycle of a UserControl Object

UserControl are objects, and as such they receive several events during their lifetime. ActiveX controls actually have a double life because they're also alive when the environment is in design mode.

Creation

Initialize is the first event that a UserControl receives. In this event, no Windows resources have been allocated yet so you shouldn't refer to constituent controls, exactly as you avoid references to controls on a form in the form's *Initialize* event. For the same reason, the Extender and AmbientProperties objects aren't available in this event. (These objects are described in the following sections.)

After the *Initialize* event, the UserControl creates all its constituent controls and is ready to be sited on the client form's surface. When the siting completes, Visual Basic fires an *InitProperties* or *ReadProperties* event, depending on whether the control has been just dragged on the form from the Toolbox or the form is being reopened from a previous session. During these events, the Extender and the Ambient objects are finally available.

Just before becoming visible, the UserControl module receives the *Resize* event, and then the *Show* event. This event is more or less equivalent to the *Activate* event, which isn't exposed by UserControl modules. Finally the UserControl module receives a *Paint* event (unless its *AutoRedraw* property is True).

When a control is re-created at design time because its parent form is closed and then reopened, the complete sequence is repeated with the only differences being that the *InitProperties* event never fires and the *ReadProperties* event fires instead, immediately after the *Resize* event.

Termination

When the developer closes the parent form at design time, or when the program switches to run-time mode, Visual Basic destroys the design-time instance of the ActiveX control. If the developer modified one or more properties in the control, the UserControl module receives a *WriteProperties* event. During this event, Visual Basic doesn't write anything to the FRM file and simply stores values in the PropertyBag object kept in memory. This event fires only if the programmer modified the attributes of any control on the form (or of the form itself), but not necessarily the UserControl you're working with. A control informs you that one of its properties has changed and that the FRM file needs to be updated by calling the *PropertyChanged* method. When the control is removed from its container, a *Hide* event occurs. (ActiveX controls in HTML pages receive this event when the user navigates to another page.) This event broadly corresponds to a form's *Deactivate* event: The ActiveX control is still in memory, but it isn't visible any longer.

The last event in the life of an ActiveX control is *Terminate*; during this event, you usually close any open files and return any system resources that you allocated in the *Initialize* event procedure. The code in this event can't access the Extender and AmbientProperties objects.

Other event sequences

When the developer runs the program, Visual Basic destroys the design-time instance of the ActiveX control, and creates a run-time instance so that the control can receive all the events described previously. The main difference between design-time and run-time instances is that the latter ones never receive a *WriteProperties* event.

When you reopen the project, you start another special sequence of events: Now a new instance of the control is created, and it receives all the usual events that fire during creation plus a *WriteProperties* event that serves to update the PropertyBag object in memory.

Finally, when a form module is compiled, Visual Basic creates a hidden instance of it and then queries the properties of all its ActiveX controls so that the compiled program can use the most recent property values. Each ActiveX control receives the *Initialize, Resize, ReadProperties, Show, WriteProperties, Hide,* and *Terminate* events. You don't need to perform any special actions during these events. I mention this information only because if your code contains breakpoints or *MsgBox* commands, they might interfere with the compilation process.

The Extender Object

When you created a UserControl module and you placed an instance of it on a client form, you might have noticed that the Properties window isn't empty, as shown in Figure 17-2. Where did those properties come from?

It turns out that Visual Basic's forms don't use the ActiveX control directly. Instead, they wrap the control within an intermediate object known as the Extender object. This object exposes to the programmer all the properties defined in the ActiveX control, plus a number of properties that Visual Basic adds for its own purposes. For example, *Name, Left, Top,* and *Visible* are Extender properties and so you don't have to implement them in the UserControl module. Other Extender properties are *Height, Width, Align, Negotiate, Tag, Parent, Container, ToolTipText, DragIcon, DragMode, CausesValidation, TabIndex, TabStop, HelpContextID,* and *WhatsThisHelpID*.

The Extender object also provides methods and events of its own. For example, the *Move*, *Drag*, *SetFocus*, *ShowWhatsThis*, and *ZOrder* methods are provided by the container (and in fact, all of them are related to Extender properties in one way or another), as are the *GotFocus*, *LostFocus*, *Validate*, *DragDrop*, and *DragOver* events. The perspective of the programmer who uses the ActiveX control is different from the perspective of the control's author, who sees fewer properties, methods, and events.

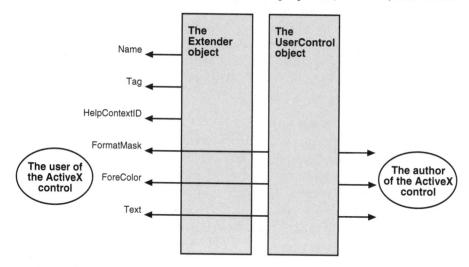

Reading Extender properties

At times, however, you need to access Extender properties from within the UserControl module. You can do this by means of the *Extender* property, which returns an object reference to the same Extender interface that's used by the programmer using the control. A typical example of why this might be necessary is when you want your ActiveX control to display its *Name* property, as most Visual Basic controls do as soon as they're created. To add this feature to the SuperTextBox ActiveX control, you simply need a statement in the *InitProperties* event procedure:

```
Private Sub UserControl_InitProperties()
    On Error Resume Next
    Caption = Extender.Name
End Sub
```

You might wonder why you need an error handler to protect a simple assignment like the preceding one. The reason is that you can't anticipate the environments in which your ActiveX control will be used, so you have no guarantee that the host environment will support the *Name* property. If it doesn't, the *Extender.Name* reference fails, and the error will prevent developers from using your control in those environments. In general, different hosts add different Extender members. Visual Basic is probably the most generous environment in terms of Extender properties.

The Extender object is built at run time by the host environment, so the *Extender* property is defined to return a generic Object. As a result, all the Extender members such as *Name* or *Tag* are referenced through late binding. This circumstance explains why accessing those members tends to slow down the code inside your UserControl module and at the same time makes it less robust. Because you can't be sure about which members the Extender object will expose at run time, you shouldn't let your ActiveX control heavily rely on them, and you should always arrange for your control to degrade gracefully when it runs under environments that don't support the features you need.

Finally, keep in mind that a few Extender properties are created only under certain conditions. For example, the *Align* and *Negotiate* properties are exposed only if the UserControl's *Alignable* property is set to True, and the *Default* and *Cancel* properties exist only if the UserControl's *DefaultCancel* property is True. Likewise, the *Visible* property is unavailable if the *InvisibleAtRuntime* property is True.

Setting Extender properties

In general, modifying an Extender property from within the UserControl module is considered bad programming practice. I found that under Visual Basic 6 all the Extender properties can be written to, but this might not be true for other environments or for previous versions of Visual Basic itself. In some cases, setting an Extender property provides added functionality. For example, see how you can implement a method that resizes your ActiveX control to fit its parent form:

```
Sub ResizeToParent()
    Extender.Move 0, 0, Parent.ScaleWidth, Parent.ScaleHeight
End Sub
```

This routine is guaranteed to work only under Visual Basic because other environments might not support the *Move* Extender method, and also because you can't be sure that, if a Parent object actually exists, it also supports the *ScaleWidth* and *ScaleHeight* properties. If any of the preceding conditions aren't met, this method raises an error 438, "Object doesn't support this property or method."

From the container's point of view, Extender properties have a higher priority than the UserControl's own properties. For example, if the UserControl module exposes a *Name* property, the client code—at least the client code written in Visual Basic—will actually refer to the Extender property with the same name. For this reason, you should carefully pick the names of your custom properties and stay clear of those automatically added by the most popular containers, such as Visual Basic and the products in the Microsoft Office suite.

> **TIP** You might intentionally expose properties that are duplicated in the Extender object so that users of your ActiveX control can find that property regardless of what programming language they're using. For example, you can define a *Tag* property (of type String or Variant) so that your control provides it even when it runs in an environment other than Visual Basic.

The *Object* property

This visibility rule raises an interesting question: How can the user of the ActiveX control directly access its interface and bypass the Extender object? This is possible thanks to the *Object* property, another Extender property that returns a reference to the inner UserControl object. This property is sometimes useful to developers who are using the ActiveX control, as in this code:

```
' Set the Tag property exposed by the UserControl module.
' Raises an error if such property isn't implemented
SuperTextBox1.Object.Tag = "New Tag"
```

You never need to use the *Extender.Object* property from within the UserControl module because it returns the same object reference as the *Me* keyword.

The AmbientProperties Object

An ActiveX control often needs to gather information about the form on which it has been placed. For example, you might want to adapt your ActiveX control to the locale of the user or to the font that's used by the parent form. In some cases, you can gather this information using the Extender or Parent object (for example, using *Parent.Font*). But there's a better way.

Conforming to the parent form settings

The UserControl object's *Ambient* property returns a reference to the AmbientProperties object, which in turn exposes several properties that provide information about the environment in which the ActiveX control runs. For example, you can find out what font is being used by the parent form using the *Ambient.Font* property, and you can determine which colors have been set for the parent form using the *Ambient.ForeColor* and *Ambient.BackColor* properties. This information is especially useful when you create the control and you want to conform to the parent form's current settings. See how you can improve the SuperTextBox control so that it behaves like Visual Basic's own controls:

```
Private Sub UserControl_InitProperties()
    ' Let the label and the text box match the form's font.
    Set CaptionFont = Ambient.Font
    Set Font = Ambient.Font
    ' Let the label's colors match the form's colors.
    CaptionForeColor = Ambient.ForeColor
    CaptionBackColor = Ambient.BackColor
End Sub
```

The AmbientProperties object is provided by the Visual Basic runtime, which always accompanies the ActiveX control, rather than by the Extender object, which is provided by the host environment. References to the AmbientProperties object rely on early binding, and the Visual Basic runtime automatically supplies a default value for those properties that aren't available in the environment. This detail has two consequences: Ambient properties are faster than Extender properties, and you don't need an error handler when referring to an Ambient property. For example, the AmbientProperties object exposes a *DisplayName* property, which returns the name that identifies the control in its host environment and lets you initialize the caption of your control:

```
Private Sub UserControl_InitProperties()
    Caption = Ambient.DisplayName
End Sub
```

This code should always be preferred to the method based on the *Extender.Name* property because it delivers a reasonable result under any environment and doesn't require an *On Error* statement.

Another ambient property that you might find useful is *TextAlign*, which indicates the preferred text alignment for the controls on the form. It returns one of the following constants: 0-General, 1-Left, 2-Center, 3-Right, 4-FillJustify. If the host environment doesn't provide any information about this feature, *Ambient.TextAlign* returns 0-General (text to the left, numbers to the right).

If your control contains a PictureBox control, you should set its *Palette* property equal to the *Ambient.Palette* property if possible so that the bitmaps on your control don't look strange when the PictureBox constituent control doesn't have the input focus.

The *UserMode* property

The *UserMode* property is probably the most important Ambient property because it lets the author of the ActiveX control know whether the control is being used by the developer (*UserMode* = False) or the user (*UserMode* = True). Thanks to this property, you can enable different behaviors at design time and run time. If you find it difficult to remember the meaning of the return value of this property, just recall that the "user" in *UserMode* is the user. See the "Read-Only Properties" section later in this chapter for an example that shows how this property can be useful.

The *AmbientChanged* event

You can immediately find out when an ambient property changes by trapping the *AmbientChanged* event. This event receives a string argument equal to the name of the ambient property being changed. For instance, you can allow the *BackColor* property of your UserControl to automatically match the background color of the parent form by writing this code:

```
Private Sub UserControl_AmbientChanged(PropertyName As String)
    If PropertyName = "BackColor" Then BackColor = Ambient.BackColor
End Sub
```

Here's an exception: If you change the parent form's *FontTransparent* or *Palette* properties, the ActiveX controls on the form don't receive any notification. The

AmbientChanged event is raised both at design time and at run time, so you might need to use the *Ambient.UserMode* property to differentiate between the two cases.

The *AmbientChanged* event is most important within user-drawn controls that expose a *Default* property. These controls must repaint themselves when the value of this property changes:

```
Private Sub UserControl_AmbientChanged(PropertyName As String)
    If PropertyName = "DisplayAsDefault" Then Refresh
End Sub
```

Localizing ActiveX controls

The *Ambient.LocaleID* property returns a Long value that corresponds to the locale of the program that's hosting the ActiveX control. This value lets you display localized messages in the language of the user—for example, by loading them from a string table, a resource file, or a satellite DLL. But you must account for some rough edges.

When you compile your application, the Visual Basic locale becomes the default locale for the application. But the application that's hosting the control might automatically adapt itself to the language of the user and change its locale accordingly. Inside the *Initialize* event procedure of the UserControl, the siting procedure hasn't completed yet, so the value returned by the *LocaleID* ambient property reflects the default locale of the Visual Basic version that compiled it. For this reason, if you want to use this property to load a table of localized messages, you should follow this schema:

```
Private Sub UserControl_Initialize()
    ' Load messages in the default (Visual Basic's) locale.
    LoadMessageTable Ambient.LocaleID
End Sub

Private Sub UserControl_InitProperties()
    ' Load messages in the user's locale.
    LoadMessageTable Ambient.LocaleID
End Sub

Private Sub UserControl_ReadProperties(PropBag As PropertyBag)
    ' Load messages in the user's locale.
    LoadMessageTable Ambient.LocaleID
End Sub

Private Sub UserControl_AmbientChanged(PropertyName As String)
    ' Load messages in the new user's locale.
    If PropertyName = "LocaleID" Then LoadMessageTable Ambient.LocaleID
End Sub

Private Sub LoadMessageTable(LocaleID As Long)
    ' Here you load localized strings and resources.
End Sub
```

You need to load the message in both the *InitProperties* and *ReadProperties* event procedures because the former is invoked when the control is first placed on the form's surface, whereas the latter is invoked any time the project is reopened or the application is executed.

Other ambient properties

The *Ambient.ScaleMode* property returns a string corresponding to the unit measure currently used in the container form (for example, *twip*). This value might be useful within messages to the user or the developer. For a way to easily convert from the form's and UserControl's units, see the section "Converting Scale Units."

The *Ambient.DisplayAsDefault* property is useful only within user-drawn controls whose *DefaultCancel* property is True. These controls must display a thicker border when their *Default* extender property becomes True. You usually trap changes to this property in the *AmbientChanged* event.

The *Ambient.SupportsMnemonics* property returns True if the environment supports hot keys, such as those that you indicate in a *Caption* property using the ampersand character. Most containers support this feature, but you can improve the portability of your control if you test this property in the *Show* event procedure and filter out ampersand characters in your captions if you find that the environment doesn't support hot keys.

The *Ambient.RightToLeft* property specifies whether the control should display text from right to left, as it might be necessary under Hebrew or Arabic versions of Windows. All the remaining ambient properties—namely, *MessageReflect*, *ShowGrabHandles*, *ShowHatching*, and *UIDead*—are of no practical use with controls developed with Visual Basic and can be safely ignored.

Implementing Features

The UserControl object exposes many properties, methods, and events that have no equivalent in form modules. In this section, I describe most of them and briefly hint at items that I examine in depth later in the chapter.

Managing the input focus

Understanding how UserControl objects manage the input focus can be a nontrivial task. Several events are related to input focus:

- The UserControl object's *GotFocus* and *LostFocus* events. These events can fire only if the UserControl doesn't contain any constituent controls that can get the input focus (typically, a user-drawn UserControl). In most cases, you don't have to write any code for these events.

- The constituent controls' *GotFocus* and *LostFocus* events. These events fire when the focus enters or exits a constituent control.

■ The UserControl's *EnterFocus* and *ExitFocus* events. These events fire when the input focus enters or exits the UserControl as a whole but don't fire when the focus moves from one constituent control to another.

■ The Extender's *GotFocus* and *LostFocus* events. These are the events that an ActiveX control activates in its container application.

The simplest way to see what actually happens at run time is to create a trace of all the events as they occur when the user visits the constituent controls by pressing the Tab key. I created a simple UserControl named *MyControl1* with two TextBox constituent controls on it—named *Text1* and *Text2*—and then added *Debug.Print* statements in all the event procedures related to focus management. This is what I found in the Immediate window (with some remarks manually added later):

```
UserControl_EnterFocus    ' The user has tabbed into the control.
MyControl1_GotFocus
Text1_GotFocus
Text1_Validate            ' The user has pressed the Tab key a second time.
Text1_LostFocus
Text2_GotFocus
MyControl1_Validate       ' The user has pressed the Tab key a third time.
Text2_LostFocus
UserControl_ExitFocus
MyControl1_LostFocus

...                       ' The user presses Tab several times
UserControl_EnterFocus    ' until the focus reenters the UserControl
MyControl1_GotFocus       ' and the sequence is repeated.
Text1_GotFocus
```

As you see, the UserControl object gets an *EnterFocus* just before the ActiveX control raises a *GotFocus* event in its parent form. Similarly, the UserControl receives an *ExitFocus* one instant before the ActiveX control raises a *LostFocus* in the form.

When the focus shifts from one constituent control to another, the control that loses the focus receives a *Validate* event, but this doesn't happen when the focus leaves the UserControl module. To force the *Validate* event of the last control in the UserControl, you must explicitly call the *ValidateControls* method in the UserControl's *ExitFocus*, which isn't really intuitive. If the ActiveX control includes several controls, it sometimes doesn't make sense to validate them individually in their *Validate* events. Moreover, if you use the *ValidateControls* method, you might incorrectly force the validation of a constituent control when the form is being closed (for example, when the user presses Cancel). For all these reasons, it's much better to validate the contents of a multifield ActiveX control only upon a request from the parent form, or more precisely, in the *Validate* event that the ActiveX control raises in the parent form. If the control is complex, you might simplify the life of programmers by providing a method that performs the validation, as in the following piece of code:

```
Private Sub MyControl1_Validate(Cancel As Boolean)
    If MyControl1.CheckSubFields = False Then Cancel = True
End Sub
```

> **TIP** The Visual Basic documentation omits an important detail about focus management inside ActiveX controls with multiple constituent controls. If the ActiveX control is the only control on the form that can receive the focus and the user presses the Tab key on the last constituent control, the focus won't automatically shift on the first constituent control as the user would expect. So to have such an ActiveX control behave normally, you should add at least one other control on the form. If you don't want to display another control, you should resort to the following trick: Create a CommandButton (or any other control that can get the focus), move it out of sight using a large negative value for the *Left* or *Top* property, and then add these statements in its *GotFocus* event procedure:

```
Private Sub Command1_GotFocus()
    MyControl1.SetFocus    ' Manually move the focus
                           ' to the ActiveX control.
    End Sub
```

Invisible controls

The *InvisibleAtRuntime* property permits you to create controls that are visible only at design time, as are the Timer and CommonDialog controls. When the *InvisibleAtRuntime* property is True, the Extender object doesn't expose the *Visible* property. You usually want the controls to have a fixed size at design time, and you ensure this result by using the *Size* method in the UserControl's *Resize* event:

```
Private Sub UserControl_Resize()
    Static Active As Boolean
    If Not Active Then Exit Sub        ' Avoid nested calls.
    Active = True
    Size 400, 400
    Active = False
End Sub
```

Hot keys

If your ActiveX control includes one or more controls that support the *Caption* property, you can assign each of them a hot key using the ampersand character, as you would do in a regular Visual Basic form. Such hot keys work as you expect, even if the input focus isn't currently on the ActiveX control. As an aside, keep in mind that it's considered bad programming practice to provide an ActiveX control with fixed captions, both because they can't be localized and because they might conflict with other hot keys defined by other controls on the parent form.

If your ActiveX control doesn't include a constituent control with a *Caption* property, your control responds to the hot keys assigned to the *AccessKeys* property.

For example, you might have a user-drawn control that exposes a *Caption* property and you want to activate it if the user types the Alt+*char* key combination, where *char* is the first character in the *Caption*. In this circumstance, you must assign the *AccessKeys* property in the *Property Let* procedure as follows:

```
Property Let Caption(New_Caption As String)
    m_Caption = New_Caption
    PropertyChanged "Caption"
    AccessKeys = Left$(New_Caption, 1)
End Property
```

When the user presses a hot key, an *AccessKeyPressed* event fires in the UserControl module. This event receives the code of the hot key, which is necessary because you can associate multiple hot keys with the ActiveX control by assigning a string of two or more characters to the *AccessKeys* property:

```
Private Sub UserControl_AccessKeyPress(KeyAscii As Integer)
    ' User pressed the Alt + Chr$(KeyAscii) hot key.
End Sub
```

You can create ActiveX controls that behave like Label controls by setting the *ForwardFocus* property to True. When the control gets the input focus, it automatically moves it to the control on the form that comes next in the TabIndex order. If the *ForwardFocus* property is True, the UserControl module doesn't receive the *AccessKeyPress* event.

Accessing the parent's controls

An ActiveX control can access other controls on its parent form in two distinct ways. The first approach is based on the Controls collection of the Parent object, as this code example demonstrates:

```
' Enlarge or shrink all controls on the parent form except this one.
Sub ZoomControls(factor As Single)
    Dim ctrl As Object
    For Each ctrl In Parent.Controls
        If Not (ctrl Is Extender) Then
            ctrl.Width = ctrl.Width * factor
            ctrl.Height = ctrl.Height * factor
        End if
    Next
End Sub
```

The items in the Parent.Controls collection are all Extender objects, so if you want to sort out the ActiveX control that's running the code you must compare each item with the *Extender* property, not with the *Me* keyword. The problem with this approach is that it works only under Visual Basic (more precisely, only under environments for which there is a Parent object that exposes the Controls collection).

The second approach is based on the *ParentControls* property. Unlike the Parent.Controls collection, this property is guaranteed to work with all containers. The items in the Parent.Controls collection contain the parent form itself, but you can easily filter it out by comparing each reference with the Parent object (if there is one).

Converting scale units

In the interaction with the container application, the code in the ActiveX control often has to convert values from the UserControl's coordinate system to the parent form's system by using the *ScaleX* and *ScaleY* methods. This is especially necessary in mouse events, where the container expects that the *x* and *y* coordinates of the mouse are measured in its current *ScaleMode*. While you can use the *Parent.ScaleMode* property to retrieve a Visual Basic form's *ScaleMode*, this approach fails if the control is running inside another container—for example, Internet Explorer. Fortunately, the *ScaleX* and *ScaleY* methods also support the vbContainerPosition constant:

```
' Forward the MouseDown event to the container, but convert measure units.
Private Sub UserControl_MouseDown(Button As Integer, Shift As Integer, _
    X As Single, Y As Single)
    RaiseEvent MouseDown(Button, Shift, _
        ScaleX(X, vbTwips, vbContainerPosition), _
        ScaleY(Y, vbTwips, vbContainerPosition))
End Sub
```

When you're raising mouse events from within a constituent control, things are a bit more complicated because you also need to keep the control's offset from the upper left corner of the UserControl's surface:

```
Private Sub Private Sub Text1_MouseDown(Button As Integer, _
    Shift As Integer, X As Single, Y As Single)
    RaiseEvent MouseDown(Button, Shift, _
        ScaleX(Text1.Left + X, vbTwips, vbContainerPosition), _
        ScaleY(Text1.Top + Y, vbTwips, vbContainerPosition))
End Sub
```

The *ScaleX* and *ScaleY* methods support an additional enumerated constant, vbContainerSize, that you should use when converting a size value (as opposed to a coordinate value). The vbContainerPosition and vbContainerSize constants deliver different results only when the container uses a custom *ScaleMode*. The ActiveX Control Interface Wizard doesn't address these subtleties, and you must manually edit the code that it produces.

Other properties

If the *Alignable* property is True, the ActiveX control—more precisely, its Extender object—exposes the *Align* property. Similarly, you should set *DefaultCancel* to True if the control has to expose the *Default* and *Cancel* properties. This setting is necessary when the ActiveX control should behave like a standard CommandButton and works only if *ForwardFocus* is False. If the ActiveX control's *Default* property is True and the user presses Enter, the click will be received by the constituent control whose *Default* property is also True. If there aren't any constituent controls that support the *Default* or *Cancel* properties, you can trap the Enter or Escape key in the *AccessKeyPress* event.

If the *CanGetFocus* is False, the UserControl itself can't get the input focus and the ActiveX control won't expose the *TabStop* property. You can't set this property to False if one or more constituent controls can receive the focus. The opposite is also true: You can't place constituent controls that can receive the focus on a UserControl whose *CanGetFocus* property is False.

The *EventsFrozen* property is a run-time property that returns True when the parent form ignores events raised by the UserControl object. This happens, for instance, when the form is in design mode. At run time, you can query this property to find out whether your *RaiseEvent* commands will be ignored so that you can decide to postpone them. Unfortunately, there's no safe way to find out when the container is again ready to accept events, but you can learn when a paused program has restarted by watching for a change in the *UIDead* property in the *AmbientChanged* event.

You can create controls that can be edited at design time by setting the *EditAtDesignTime* property to True. You can right-click on such controls at design time and select the Edit command to enter edit mode. While the control is in edit mode, it reacts exactly as it does at run time although it doesn't raise events in its container. (The *EventsFrozen* property returns True.) You exit edit mode when you click anywhere on the form outside the control. In general, writing a control that can be edited at design time isn't a simple task: for example, you must account for all the properties that aren't available at design time and that raise an error if used when *Ambient.UserMode* returns False.

The *ToolboxBitmap* property lets you assign the image that will be used in the Toolbox window. You should use 16-by-15-pixel bitmaps, but bitmaps of different size are automatically scaled. You shouldn't use icons because they don't scale well to that dimension. The lower left pixel in the bitmap defines its transparent color.

The *ContainerHwnd* property is available only through code and returns the Windows handle of the ActiveX control's container. If the control is hosted in a Visual Basic program, this property corresponds to the value returned by the *Extender.Container.hWnd* property.

The UserControl object exposes a few other properties, which let you create windowless controls, container controls, and transparent controls. I'll cover them later in this chapter.

REFINING THE ACTIVEX CONTROL

Adding a UserControl object to the current project and placing some constituent controls on it is just the first step toward the creation of a full-fledged, commercial-quality ActiveX control. In this section, I'll show you how to implement a robust user interface, add binding capabilities and property pages, create user-drawn controls, and prepare your controls for the Internet.

Custom Properties

You've already seen how you can add custom properties using pairs of property procedures. This section explains how to implement some special types of properties.

Design-time and run-time properties

Not all properties are available both at design time and at run time, and it's interesting to see how you write the code in the UserControl module to limit the visibility of properties. The easiest way to create a run-time–only property, such as the *SelText* property of a TextBox or the *ListIndex* property of a ListBox, is by ticking the Don't Show In Property Browser option in the Attributes section of the Procedure Attributes dialog box. (You can access this dialog box by choosing it from the Tools menu.) If this check box is selected, the property doesn't appear in the Properties window at design time.

The problem with this simple approach, however, is that it also hides the property in the other property browser that Visual Basic provides, namely the Locals window. To have the property listed in the Locals window at run time but not in the Properties window, you must raise an error in the *Property Get* procedure at design time, as this code demonstrates:

```
Public Property Get SelText() As String
    If Ambient.UserMode = False Then Err.Raise 387
    SelText = Text1.SelText
End Property
```

Error 387 "Set not permitted" is the error that by convention you should raise in this case, but any error will do the trick. If Visual Basic—or more generally, the host environment—receives an error when reading a value at design time, the property isn't displayed in the properties browser, which is precisely what you want. Creating a property that's unavailable at design time and read-only at run time is even simpler because you need merely to omit the *Property Let* procedure, as you would do with any read-only property. Visual Basic doesn't show such a property in the Properties window because it couldn't be modified in any way.

Another common situation concerns properties that are available at design time and read-only at run time. This is similar to the *MultiLine* and *ScrollBars* properties of the Visual Basic TextBox control. You can implement such properties by raising Error 382 "Set not supported at runtime" in their *Property Let* procedures, as shown in the following code:

```
' This property is available at design time and read-only at run time.
Public Property Get ScrollBars() As Integer
    ScrollBars = m_ScrollBars
End Property
Public Property Let ScrollBars(ByVal New_ScrollBars As Integer)
    If Ambient.UserMode Then Err.Raise 382
    m_ScrollBars = New_ScrollBars
    PropertyChanged "ScrollBars"
End Property
```

When you have design-time properties that are read-only at run time, you can't call the *Property Let* procedure from within the *ReadProperties* event procedure because you would get an error. In this case, you're forced to directly assign the private member variable or the constituent control's property, or you have to provide a module-level Boolean variable that you set to True on entering the *ReadProperties* event and reset to False on exit. You then query this variable before raising errors in the *Property Let* procedure. You can also use the same variable to skip an unnecessary call to the *PropertyChanged* method, as in this code example:

```
Public Property Let ScrollBars(ByVal New_ScrollBars As Integer)
    ' The ReadingProperties variable is True if this routine is being
    ' called from within the ReadProperties event procedure.
    If Ambient.UserMode And Not ReadingProperties Then Err.Raise 382
    m_ScrollBars = New_ScrollBars
    If Not ReadingProperties Then PropertyChanged "ScrollBars"
End Property
```

Enumerated properties

You can define enumerated properties using either *Enum* blocks in code or Visual Basic's own enumerated types. For example, you can modify the code produced by the wizard and improve the *MousePointer* property as follows:

```
Public Property Get MousePointer() As MousePointerConstants
    MousePointer = Text1.MousePointer
End Property
Public Property Let MousePointer(ByVal New_MousePointer _
    As MousePointerConstants)
    Text1.MousePointer() = New_MousePointer
    PropertyChanged "MousePointer"
End Property
```

Enumerated properties are useful because their valid values appear in the Properties window in a combo box, as shown in Figure 17-6. Keep in mind, however, that

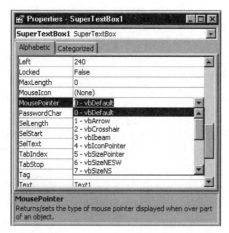

Figure 17-6. *Use enumerated properties to offer a list of valid values in the Properties window.*

you should always protect your ActiveX control from invalid assignments in code, so the previous routine should be rewritten as follows:

```
Public Property Let MousePointer(ByVal New_MousePointer _
    As MousePointerConstants)
    Select Case New_MousePointer
        Case vbDefault To vbSizeAll, vbCustom
            Text1.MousePointer() = New_MousePointer
            PropertyChanged "MousePointer"
        Case Else
            Err.Raise 380    ' Invalid Property Value error
    End Select
End Property
```

There's a good reason for not defining properties and arguments using Visual Basic and VBA enumerated constants, though: If you use the control with environments other than Visual Basic, these symbolic constants won't be visible to the client application.

TIP Sometimes you might want to add spaces and other symbols inside an enumerated value to make it more readable in the Properties window. For example, the *FillStyle* property includes values such as *Horizontal Line* or *Diagonal Cross*. To expose similar values in your ActiveX controls, you have to enclose Enum constants within square brackets, as in the following code:

```
Enum MyColors
    Black = 1
    [Dark Gray]
    [Light Gray]
    White
End Enum
```

> **TIP** Here's another idea that you might find useful: If you use an enumerated constant name whose name begins with an underscore, such as *[_HiddenValue]*, this value won't appear by default in the Object Browser. However, this value does appear in the Properties window, so this trick is especially useful for enumerated properties that aren't available at design time.

Picture and Font properties

Visual Basic deals in a special way with properties that return a Picture or Font object. In the former instance, the Properties window shows a button that lets you select an image from disk; in the latter, the Properties window includes a button that displays a Font common dialog box.

When working with Font properties, you should keep in mind that they return object references. For example, if two or more constituent controls have been assigned the same Font reference, changing a font attribute in one of them also changes the appearance of all the others. For this reason, *Ambient.Font* returns a copy of the parent form's font so that any subsequent change to the form's font doesn't affect the UserControl's constituent controls, and vice versa. (If you want to keep your control's font in sync with the form's font, you simply need to trap the *AmbientChanged* event.) Sharing object references can cause some subtle errors in your code. Consider the following example:

```
' Case 1: Label1 and Text1 use fonts with identical attributes.
Set Label1.Font = Ambient.Font
Set Text1.Font = Ambient.Font

' Case 2: Label1 and Text1 point to the *same* font.
Set Label1.Font = Ambient.Font
Set Text1.Font = Label1.Font
```

The two pieces of code look similar, but in the first instance the two constituent controls are assigned different copies of the same font, so you can change the font attributes of one control without affecting the other. In the latter case, both controls are pointing to the same font, so each time you modify a font attribute in either control the other one is affected as well.

It's a common practice to provide all the alternate, old-styled *Fontxxxx* properties, namely *FontName*, *FontSize*, *FontBold*, *FontItalic*, *FontUnderline*, and *FontStrikethru*. But you should also make these properties unavailable at design time, and you shouldn't save them in the *WriteProperties* event if you also save the *Font* object. If you decide to save individual *Fontxxxx* properties, it's important that you retrieve them in the correct order (first *FontName*, and then all the others).

One more thing to keep in mind when dealing with font properties: You can't restrict the choices of the programmer who's using the control to a family of fonts— for example, to nonproportional fonts or to printer fonts—if the *Font* property is exposed in the Properties window. The only way to restrict font selection is to show a

Font Common Dialog box from a Property Page. See the "Property Pages" section later in this chapter for details about building property pages.

Font properties pose a special challenge to ActiveX control programmers. If your control exposes a *Font* property and the client code modifies one or more font attributes, Visual Basic calls the *Property Get Font* procedure but not the *Property Set Font* procedure. If the *Font* property delegates to a single constituent control, this isn't usually a problem because the control's appearance is correctly updated. Things are different in user-drawn ActiveX controls because in this case your control gets no notification that it should be repainted. This problem has been solved in Visual Basic 6 with the *FontChanged* event of the StdFont object. Here's a fragment of code taken from a Label-like, user-drawn control that correctly refreshes itself when the client modifies an attribute of the *Font* property:

```
Private WithEvents UCFont As StdFont

Private Sub UserControl_InitProperties()
    ' Initialize the Font property (and the UCFont object).
    Set Font = Ambient.Font
End Sub

Public Property Get Font() As Font
    Set Font = UserControl.Font
End Property
Public Property Set Font(ByVal New_Font As Font)
    Set UserControl.Font = New_Font
    Set UCFont = New_Font          ' Prepare to trap events.
    PropertyChanged "Font"
    Refresh                        ' Manually perform the first refresh.
End Property

' This event fires when the client code changes a font's attribute.
Private Sub UCFont_FontChanged(ByVal PropertyName As String)
    Refresh                        ' This causes a Paint event.
End Sub
' Repaint the control.
Private Sub UserControl_Paint()
    Cls
    Print Caption;
End Sub
```

Object properties

You can create ActiveX controls with properties that return objects, such as a TreeView-like control that exposes a Nodes collection. This is possible because ActiveX control projects can include PublicNotCreatable classes, so your control can internally create them using the New operator and return a reference to its clients through a read-only property. Object properties can be treated as if they were regular properties in most circumstances, but they require particular attention when you need to make them persistent and reload them in the *WriteProperties* and *ReadProperties* procedures.

Even if Visual Basic 6 does support persistable classes, you can't save objects that aren't creatable, as in this case. But nothing prevents you from manually creating a PropertyBag object and loading it with all the properties of the dependent object. Let me demonstrate this technique with an example.

Suppose that you have an AddressOCX ActiveX control that lets the user enter a person's name and address, as shown in Figure 17-7. Instead of many properties, this AddressOCX control exposes one object property, named *Address*, whose class is defined inside the same project. Rather than having the main UserControl module save and reload the individual properties of the dependent object, you should create a Friend property in the PublicNotCreatable class. I usually call this property *AllProperties* because it sets and returns the values of all the properties in one Byte array. To serialize the properties into an array, I use a private stand-alone PropertyBag object. Following is the complete source code of the Address class module. (For the sake of simplicity, properties are implemented as Public variables.)

```
' The Address.cls class module
Public Name As String, Street As String
Public City As String, Zip As String, State As String

Friend Property Get AllProperties() As Byte()
    Dim PropBag As New PropertyBag
    PropBag.WriteProperty "Name", Name, ""
    PropBag.WriteProperty "Street", Street, ""
    PropBag.WriteProperty "City", City, ""
    PropBag.WriteProperty "Zip", Zip, ""
    PropBag.WriteProperty "State", State, ""
    AllProperties = PropBag.Contents
End Property
Friend Property Let AllProperties(value() As Byte)
    Dim PropBag As New PropertyBag
    PropBag.Contents = value()
    Name = PropBag.ReadProperty("Name", "")
    Street = PropBag.ReadProperty("Street", "")
    City = PropBag.ReadProperty("City", "")
    Zip = PropBag.ReadProperty("Zip", "")
    State = PropBag.ReadProperty("State", "")
End Property
```

Rather than saving and reloading all the individual properties in the *WriteProperties* and *ReadProperties* event procedures of the main AddressOCX module, you simply save and restore the *AllProperties* property of the Address object.

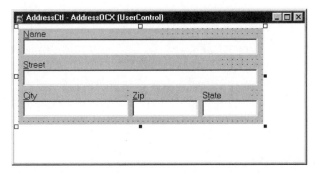

Figure 17-7. *An AddressOCX ActiveX control that exposes each of the Address properties as an individual Address, PublicNotCreatable object.*

```
' The AddressOCX code module (partial listing)
Dim m_Address As New Address

Public Property Get Address() As Address
    Set Address = m_Address
End Property
Public Property Set Address(ByVal New_Address As Address)
    Set m_Address = New_Address
    PropertyChanged "Address"
End Property

Private Sub UserControl_ReadProperties(PropBag As PropertyBag)
    m_Address.AllProperties = PropBag.ReadProperty("Address")
End Sub

Private Sub UserControl_WriteProperties(PropBag As PropertyBag)
    Call PropBag.WriteProperty("Address", m_Address.AllProperties)
End Sub
```

All the individual constituent controls must refer to the corresponding property in the Address object. For example, this is the code in the *Change* event procedure of the txtName control:

```
Private Sub txtName_Change()
    Address.Name = txtName
    PropertyChanged "Address"
End Sub
```

The ActiveX control should also expose a *Refresh* method that reloads all the values from the Address object into the individual fields. Alternatively, you might implement an event that the Address object raises in the AddressOCX module when any of its properties is assigned a new value. This problem is similar to the one I described in the "Forms as Object Viewers" section of Chapter 9.

Properties that return UDTs

ActiveX controls can expose properties and methods that return user-defined types or that accept UDTs as arguments. Because ActiveX controls are in-process COM components, you can always marshal UDTs regardless of the operating system version. For more details, see the "Passing Data Between Applications" section of Chapter 16.

This feature hasn't been completely ironed out, however. You can't use a property that returns a UDT in a *With* block without crashing the Visual Basic environment. I hope this bug will be fixed in a future service pack.

Special OLE data types

Properties can also return a few special data types. For example, the Wizard declares all the color properties using the OLE_COLOR type, as in this code:

```
Public Property Get BackColor() As OLE_COLOR
    BackColor = Text1.BackColor
End Property
```

When a property is declared as returning an OLE_COLOR value, programmers can pick its value from a palette of colors in the Properties window, exactly as they can with the *ForeColor* and *BackColor* properties of Visual Basic's own controls. For any other purpose, an OLE_COLOR property is treated internally as a Long.

Visual Basic supports three other special data types:

- OLE_TRISTATE is used for CheckBox-like controls that can be in three states. This enumerated property can return the values 0-Unchecked, 1-Checked, and 2-Gray.

- OLE_OPTEXCLUSIVE is used for OptionButton-like controls. When you build an ActiveX control that must behave like an OptionButton, you should have it expose a *Value* property of type OLE_OPTEXCLUSIVE and make it the default property for the control. The container ensures that when the *Value* property of one control in a group is assigned the True value, the *Value* properties of all other controls in the group are automatically set to False. (You need to call the *PropertyChanged* method in the property's *Property Let* procedure to have this mechanism work correctly.)

- OLE_CANCELBOOL is used for the *Cancel* argument in event declarations when you want to give clients the opportunity to cancel the event notification.

Procedure IDs

A few ActiveX control properties have special meanings. You define such special properties by assigning specific procedure IDs in the Advanced section of the Procedure Attributes dialog box.

As I already explained in the "Attributes" section of Chapter 6, you can make a property or a method the default member of a class by typing *0* (zero) or by selecting the (default) option from the list in the Procedure ID field. An OLE_OPTEXCLUSIVE property must be the default property to have the ActiveX control correctly behave like an OptionButton control.

If you have a *Text* or *Caption* property, you should assign it the Text or Caption procedure ID, respectively. These settings make these properties behave as they do in Visual Basic: When the programmer types their values in the Properties window, the control is immediately updated. Behind the scenes, the Properties window calls the *Property Let* procedure at each key press instead of calling it only when the programmer presses the Enter key. You can use these procedure IDs for any property, regardless of its name. However, your control can't have more than two properties that behave in this way.

> **TIP** Because you can select only one item in the procedure ID field, it seems to be impossible to duplicate the behavior of Visual Basic's TextBox and Label controls, which expose a *Text* or *Caption* property that's immediately updated by the Properties window and is the default property at the same time. You can work around this problem by defining a hidden property, make it the default property, and have it delegate to the *Text* or *Caption* property:

```
' Make this property the default property, and hide it.
Public Property Get Text_() As String
    Text_ = Text
End Property

Public Property Let Text_(ByVal newValue As String)
    Text = newValue
End Property
```

You should assign the Enabled procedure ID to the *Enabled* property of your ActiveX control so that it works correctly. This is a necessary step because the *Enabled* property behaves differently from any other property. When you disable a form, the form also disables all its controls by setting their Extender's *Enabled* property to False (so that controls appear disabled to the running code), but without setting their inner *Enabled* properties to False (so that controls repaint themselves as if they were enabled). To have Visual Basic create an Extender's *Enabled* property, your UserControl module must expose a Public *Enabled* property marked with the Enabled procedure ID:

```
Public Property Get Enabled() As Boolean
    Enabled = Text1.Enabled
End Property
```

(continued)

```
Public Property Let Enabled(ByVal New_Enabled As Boolean)
    Text1.Enabled() = New_Enabled
    PropertyChanged "Enabled"
End Property
```

The ActiveX Control Interface Wizard correctly creates the delegation code, but you have to assign the Enabled procedure ID manually.

Finally, you can create an About dialog box for displaying copyright information about your control by adding a Public *Sub* in its UserControl module and assigning the AboutBox procedure ID to it:

```
Sub ShowAboutBox()
    MsgBox "The SuperTextBox control" & vbCr _
        & "(C) 1999 Francesco Balena", vbInformation
End Sub
```

When the ActiveX control exposes a method with this procedure ID, an (About) item appear in the Properties window. It's common practice to hide this item so that programmers aren't encouraged to call it from code.

The Procedure Attributes dialog box

A few more fields in the Procedure Attributes dialog box are useful for improving the friendliness of your ActiveX controls. Not one of these setting affects the functionality of the control.

I've already described the Don't Show In Property Browser field in the "Design-Time and Run-Time Properties" section earlier in this chapter. When this check box is selected, the property won't appear in the Properties window at design time or in the Locals window at run time.

The Use This Page In The Property Browser combo box lets you associate the property with one generic property page provided by Visual Basic (namely StandardColor, StandardDataFormat, StandardFont, and StandardPicture) or with a property page that's defined in the ActiveX control project. When a property is associated with a property page, it appears in the Properties window with a button that, when clicked, brings up the property page. Property pages are described later in this chapter.

Use the Property Category field to select the category under which you want the property to appear in the Categorized tab of the Properties window. Visual Basic provides several categories—Appearance, Behavior, Data, DDE, Font, List, Misc, Position, Scale, and Text—and you can create new ones by typing their names in the edit portion of this combo box.

The User Interface Default attribute can have different meanings, depending on whether it's applied to a property or to an event. The property marked with this attribute is the one that's selected in the Properties window when you display it after creating the control. The event marked with the User Interface Default attribute is the one whose template is built for you by Visual Basic in the code window when you double-click the ActiveX control on the form's surface.

Limitations and workarounds

Creating ActiveX controls based on simpler constituent controls is an effective approach, but it has its limits as well. The one that bothers me most is that there's no simple way to create controls that expand on TextBox or ListBox controls and correctly expose all of their original properties. Such controls have a few properties—for example, *MultiLine*, *ScrollBars*, and *Sorted*—which are read-only at run time. But when you place an ActiveX control on a form at design time, the ActiveX control is already running, so you can't modify those particular properties in the Properties window of the application that's using the control.

You can use a few tricks to work around this problem, but none of them offers a definitive solution. For example, sometimes you can simulate the missing property with code, such as when you want to simulate a ListBox's *Sorted* property. Another well-known trick relies on an array of constituent controls. For example, you can implement the *MultiLine* property by preparing both a single-line and multiline TextBox control and make visible only the one that matches the current property setting. The problem with this approach is that the number of needed controls grows exponentially when you need to implement two or more properties in this way. You need 5 TextBox controls to implement the *MultiLine* and *ScrollBars* properties (one for single-line TextBox controls and 4 for all the possible settings of the *ScrollBar* property), and 10 TextBoxes if you also want to implement the *HideSelection* property.

A third possible solution is to simulate the control that you want to implement with simpler controls. For example, you can manufacture a ListBox-like ActiveX control based on a PictureBox and a companion VScrollBar. You simulate the ListBox with graphic methods of the PictureBox, so you're free to change its graphic style, add a horizontal scroll bar, and so on. Needless to say, this solution isn't often simple.

I want merely to hint of a fourth solution, undoubtedly the most complex of the lot. Instead of using a Visual Basic control, you create a control from thin air using the *CreateWindowEx* API function. This is the C way, and following this approach in Visual Basic is probably even more complicated than working in C because the Visual Basic language doesn't offer facilities, such as pointers, that are helpful when you're working at such a low level.

After hearing all these complaints, you'll be happy to know Visual Basic 6 has elegantly solved the problem. In fact, the new Windowless control library (described in Chapter 9) doesn't expose a single property that's read-only at run time. The only drawback of this approach is that controls in that library don't expose an *hWnd* property, so you can't augment their functionality using API calls, which I describe in the Appendix.

Container Controls

You can create ActiveX controls that behave like container controls, as PictureBox and Frame controls do. To manufacture a container control, all you have to do is set the UserControl's *ControlContainer* property to True. Keep in mind, however, that not all host environments support this feature. If the container doesn't support the *ISimpleFrame* interface, your ActiveX control won't be able to contain other controls, even if it works normally as far as other features are concerned. Visual Basic's forms support this interface, as do PictureBox and Frame controls. In other words, you can place an ActiveX control that works as a container inside a PictureBox or Frame control, and it will work without a glitch.

You can place controls on a container control both at design time (using drag-and-drop from the ToolBox) or at run time (through the *Container* property). In both cases, the ActiveX control can find out which controls are placed on its surface by querying its *ContainedControls* property. This property returns a collection that holds references to the Extender interface of the contained controls.

On the companion CD, you'll find a simple container ActiveX control named Stretcher, which automatically resizes all the contained controls when it's resized. The code that implements this capability is unbelievably simple:

```
' These properties hold the previous size of the control.
Private oldScaleWidth As Single
Private oldScaleHeight As Single

' To initialize the variables, you need to trap both these events.
Private Sub UserControl_InitProperties()
    oldScaleWidth = ScaleWidth
    oldScaleHeight = ScaleHeight
End Sub

Private Sub UserControl_ReadProperties(PropBag As PropertyBag)
    oldScaleWidth = ScaleWidth
    oldScaleHeight = ScaleHeight
End Sub

Private Sub UserControl_Resize()
    ' When the UserControl resizes, move and resize all container controls.
    Dim xFactor As Single, yFactor As Single
    ' Exit if this is the first resize.
    If oldScaleWidth = 0 Then Exit Sub
    ' This accounts for controls that can't be resized.
    On Error Resume Next
    ' Determine the zoom or factor along both axis.
    xFactor = ScaleWidth / oldScaleWidth
    yFactor = ScaleHeight / oldScaleHeight
    oldScaleWidth = ScaleWidth
```

```
    oldScaleHeight = ScaleHeight

    ' Resize all controls accordingly.
    Dim ctrl As Object
    For Each ctrl In ContainedControls
        ctrl.Move ctrl.Left * xFactor, ctrl.Top * yFactor, _
            ctrl.Width * xFactor, ctrl.Height * yFactor
    Next
End Sub
```

The ContainedControls collection includes only the contained controls that had been placed directly on the UserControl's surface. For example, if the ActiveX control contains a PictureBox, which in turn contains a TextBox, the PictureBox appears in the ContainedControls collection but the TextBox doesn't. Using Figure 17-8 as a reference, this means that the preceding code stretches or shrinks the Frame1 control contained in the Stretcher ActiveX control, but not the two OptionButton controls

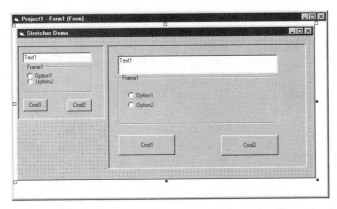

Figure 17-8. *The Stretcher ActiveX control resizes all its contained controls, both at design time and at run time.*

inside it. To have the resizing code work as well for the innermost controls, you need to modify the code in the *UserControl_Resize* event procedure as follows (added statements are in boldface):

```
Dim ctrl As Object, ctrl2 As Object
    For Each ctrl In ContainedControls
        ctrl.Move ctrl.Left * xFactor, ctrl.Top * yFactor, _
            ctrl.Width * xFactor, ctrl.Height * yFactor
        For Each ctrl2 In Parent.Controls
            ' Look for controls on the form that are contained in Ctrl.
            If ctrl2.Container Is ctrl Then
                ctrl2.Move ctrl2.Left * xFactor, ctrl2.Top * yFactor,_
                    ctrl2.Width * xFactor, ctrl2.Height * yFactor
            End If
        Next
    Next
```

You should know a few other bits of information about container ActiveX controls authored in Visual Basic:

- If the host application doesn't support container controls, any reference to the *ContainedControls* property raises an error. It's OK to return errors to the client, except from within event procedures—such as *InitProperties* or *Show*—because they would crash the application.

- The ContainedControls collection is distinct from the Controls collection, which gathers all the constituent controls on the UserControl. If a container ActiveX control contains constituent controls, they'll appear on the background, below all the controls that the developer put on the UserControl's surface at design time.

- Don't use a transparent background with container controls because this setting makes contained controls invisible. (More precisely, contained controls will be visible only on the areas where they overlap a constituent control.)

A problem with container controls is that the UserControl module doesn't receive any events when a control is added or removed at design time. If you need to react to these actions—for example, to automatically resize the contained control—you must use a Timer control that periodically queries the ContainedControls.Count collection. While this approach isn't elegant or efficient, you usually need to activate the Timer only at design time, and therefore you experience no impact on the run-time performance.

Transparent Controls

Visual Basic offers you many ways to create irregularly shaped controls. To begin with, if you set the *BackStyle* property of the UserControl object to 0-Transparent, the background of the control—that is, the portion of the control that isn't occupied by constituent controls—becomes transparent and lets the user see what's behind the control itself. When a control has a transparent background, all the mouse events go directly to the container form or to the control that happens to be under the ActiveX control in the z-order. In addition, Visual Basic ignores the *BackColor* and *Picture* properties for such an ActiveX control and all the output from graphic methods is invisible. Not surprisingly, transparent controls are also more demanding in terms of CPU time because, while repainting, Visual Basic has to clip all the areas that don't belong to the controls.

Using Label and Shape controls

If your transparent control includes one or more Label controls that use a TrueType font and whose *BackStyle* property is also set to 0-Transparent, Visual Basic clips all the pixels around the characters in the Label. Only the caption of the Label is considered to belong to the ActiveX control, and all the other pixels in the Label are transparent. For example, if you click inside a letter *O* in the caption, a *Click* event is raised in the parent form or in the control that shows through. I noticed that this feature works decently only with larger font sizes, however.

You can create a large variety of nonrectangular controls using Shape controls as constituent controls. (You can see one example on the companion CD.) If you set the Shape control's *BackStyle* property to 0-Transparent, all the pixels that fall outside the Shape control are transparent. For example, to create an elliptical radio button, you drop a Shape1 constituent control, set its *Shape* property to 2-Oval, and set both the UserControl's and Shape control's *BackStyle* property to 0-Transparent. Then you need only some code that resizes the Shape control when the UserControl resizes and that refreshes the control's appearance when the *Value* property changes. Following is a partial listing for the UserControl code module.

```
' Change the color when the control is clicked.
Private Sub UserControl_Click()
    Value = True
    RaiseEvent Click
End Sub

Private Sub UserControl_Resize()
    Shape1.Move 0, 0, ScaleWidth, ScaleHeight
End Sub

Public Sub Refresh()
    ' TrueColor and FalseColor are Public properties.
    Shape1.BackColor = IIf(m_Value, TrueColor, FalseColor)
    Shape1.FillColor = Shape1.BackColor
End Sub

' Value is also the default property.
Public Property Get Value() As OLE_OPTEXCLUSIVE
    Value = m_Value
End Property
Public Property Let Value(ByVal New_Value As OLE_OPTEXCLUSIVE)
    m_Value = New_Value
    Refresh
    PropertyChanged "Value"
End Property
```

The problem with using Shape controls to define irregularly shaped controls is that you can't easily use graphic methods to draw over them. The reason is that Visual Basic redraws the Shape control after raising the *Paint* event, so the Shape control covers the graphic you've produced in the *Paint* event. An easy way to work around this limitation is to activate a Timer in the *Paint* event and let the drawing occur in the Timer's *Timer* procedure, some milliseconds after the standard *Paint* event. Use this code as a guideline:

```
Private Sub UserControl_Paint()
    Timer1.Interval = 1        ' One millisecond is enough.
    Timer1.Enabled = True
End Sub

Private Sub Timer1_Timer()
    Timer1.Enabled = False     ' Fire just once.
    ' Draw some lines, just to show that it's possible.
    Dim i As Long
    For i = 0 To ScaleWidth Step 4
        Line (i, 0)-(i, ScaleHeight)
    Next
End Sub
```

As far as I know, the only other way to solve this problem is by subclassing the UserControl to run some code after the standard processing of the *Paint* event. (Subclassing techniques are described in the Appendix.)

Using the *MaskPicture* and *MaskColor* properties

If the shape of your transparent control is too irregular to be rendered with one Shape control (or even with a group of Shape controls), your next best choice is to assign a bitmap to the *MaskPicture* property and then to assign the color that should be considered as transparent to the *MaskColor* property. The bitmap is used as a mask, and for each pixel in the bitmap whose color matches *MaskColor*, the corresponding pixel on the UserControl becomes transparent. (Constituent controls are never transparent, even if they fall outside the mask region.) You also need to set the *Backstyle* property to 0-Transparent for this technique to work correctly.

Using this process, you can create ActiveX controls of any shape, including ones that have holes in them. Probably the only serious limitation of this approach is that you can't easily create a mask bitmap that resizes with the control because you can assign the *MaskPicture* property a bitmap, GIF, or JPEG image, but not a metafile.

Lightweight Controls

Visual Basic 6 permits you to write lightweight ActiveX controls that consume fewer resources at run time and therefore load and unload faster. The UserControl object exposes two new properties that let you fine-tune this capability.

The *HasDC* and *Windowless* properties

The *HasDC* property determines whether the UserControl creates a permanent Windows device context or uses a temporary device context when the control is redrawn and during event procedures. Setting this property to *False* can improve performance on systems with less memory. For more information about this property, see the "Fine-Tuning the Performance of Forms" section in Chapter 2.

Setting the *Windowless* property to True creates an ActiveX control that doesn't actually create a window and therefore consumes even fewer resources. A windowless control has a couple of limitations, however. It must be user-drawn or contain only other windowless controls, and it can't work as a container for other controls. You can't place regular constituent controls on a windowless ActiveX control, and you can't set the *Windowless* property to True if the UserControl already includes non-windowless constituent controls. Image, Label, Shape, Line, and Timer are the only intrinsic controls that you can place over a windowless UserControl. If you need features that these controls don't provide, have a look at the Windowless control library mentioned in the "Limitations and Workarounds" section earlier in this chapter.

Not all containers support windowless controls. Among the environments that do are Visual Basic 5 and 6, Internet Explorer 4 or later, and all the environments based on Visual Basic for Applications. Interestingly, when a windowless control runs in an environment that doesn't support this feature, the windowless control automatically turns into a regular control that's backed up by a real window.

A windowless control doesn't expose an *hWnd* property, so you can't call API functions to augment its functionality. (In some cases, you can use the *ContainerHwnd* property instead.) Moreover, the *EditAtDesign* and *BorderStyle* properties are disabled for windowless ActiveX controls. The *HasDC* property is usually ignored as well because windowless controls never have a permanent device context. But you should set this property to False because if the control runs in an environment that doesn't support windowless ActiveX controls, it won't, at least, use resources for a permanent device context.

Transparent windowless controls

You can create a windowless control that has a transparent background by setting its *BackStyle* property to 0-Transparent and assigning a suitable bitmap to the *MaskPicture*. But you should also consider the new *HitTest* event and the *HitBehavior* and *ClipBehavior* properties.

Before I show you how to use these new members, you need to understand what the four regions associated with a control are. (See Figure 17-9 on the following page.) The *Mask* region is the nontransparent portion of a control, which includes all the constituent controls and other areas that contain the output from graphic methods. (In regular controls, this is the only existing region.) The *Outside* region is the area outside the Mask region, while the *Transparent* region is any area inside the Mask region that doesn't belong to the control (the holes in the control). Finally, the *Close* region is an area that encircles the Mask region and whose width is determined by the author of the ActiveX control.

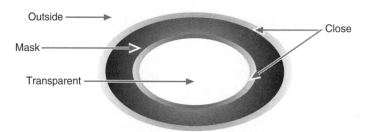

Figure 17-9. *The four regions associated with a transparent control.*

The problem with managing mouse actions over a transparent control is that Visual Basic doesn't know anything about the Close and Transparent regions, and it can only determine whether the mouse cursor is on the Mask region or in the Outside region. The problem is even worse when there are multiple overlapping controls, each one with its own Close or Transparent region, because Visual Basic has to decide which one will receive the mouse event. To let the control decide whether it wants to manage the mouse action, Visual Basic fires one or more *HitTest* events in all the controls that are under the mouse cursor, in their z-order. (That is, it fires the first event in the control that's on top of all others.) The *HitTest* event receives the *x* and *y* coordinates of the mouse cursor and a *HitTest* argument:

```
Sub UserControl_HitTest(X As Single, Y As Single, HitResult As Integer)
    ' Here you manage the mouse activity for the ActiveX control.
End Sub
```

The possible values for *HitResult* are 0-vbHitResultOutside, 1-vbHitResultTransparent, 2-vbHitResultClose, and 3-vbHitResultHit. Visual Basic raises the *HitTest* event multiple times, according to the following schema:

- A first pass is made through the controls from the topmost to the bottom-most control in the z-order; if any control returns *HitResult* = 3, it receives the mouse event and no more *HitTest* events are raised.

- If no control returns *HitResult* = 3, a second pass is performed; if any control returns *HitResult* = 2, it receives the mouse event and no more *HitTest* events are raised.

- If no control returns *HitResult* = 2, one more pass is performed; if any control returns *HitResult* = 1, it receives the mouse event.

- Otherwise, the parent form or the container control receives the mouse event.

Since Visual Basic knows only about the Mask and Outside regions, the value of *HitResult* that it passes to the *HitTest* event can only be 0 or 3. If you want to notify Visual Basic that your control has a Close or Transparent region, you must do so by code. In practice, you test the *x* and *y* coordinates and assign a suitable value to *HitResult*, as shown in the following code:

```
' A control with a circular transparent hole in it.
Sub UserControl_HitTest(X As Single, Y As Single, HitResult As Integer)
    Const HOLE_RADIUS = 200, CLOSEREGION_WIDTH = 10
    Const HOLE_X = 500, HOLE_Y = 400
    Dim distance As Single
    distance = Sqr((X - HOLE_X) ^ 2 + (Y - HOLE_Y) ^ 2)
    If distance < HOLE_RADIUS Then
        ' The mouse is over the transparent hole.
        If distance > HOLE_RADIUS - CLOSEREGION_WIDTH Then
            HitResult = vbHitResultClose
        Else
            HitResult = vbHitResultTransparent
        End If
    Else
        ' Otherwise use the value passed to the event (0 or 3).
    End If
End Sub
```

Not surprisingly, all these operations can add considerable overhead and slow down the application. Moreover, Visual Basic needs to clip the output accounting for the mask defined by *MaskPicture* for constituent controls and the output of graphic methods. To keep this overhead to a minimum, you can modify Visual Basic's default behavior by means of the *ClipBehavior* and *HitBehavior* properties.

The *ClipBehavior* property affects how Visual Basic clips the output of graphic methods. The default value is 1-UseRegion, which means that the output of a graphic method is clipped to fit the Mask region. The value 0-None doesn't perform clipping at all, and graphic output is visible also on the Mask and Transparent regions.

The *HitBehavior* property determines how the *HitResult* argument is evaluated before calling the *HitTest* event. When *HitBehavior* = 1-UseRegion (the default value), Visual Basic sets *HitResult* = 3 only for points inside the Mask region. If you set *HitBehavior* = 2-UsePaint, Visual Basic also considers the points produced by graphic methods in the *Paint* event. Finally, if *HitBehavior* = 0-None, Visual Basic doesn't even attempt to evaluate *HitResult* and always passes a 0 value to the *HitTest* event.

If your Mask region isn't complex and you can easily describe it in code, you can often improve the performance of your ActiveX control by setting *HitBehavior* = 0-UseNone. In this case, Visual Basic always passes 0 to the *HitResult* argument, and you change it to account for your Mask, Close, and Transparent regions. If the Mask region is complex and includes irregular figures, you should set *ClipBehavior*

= 0-None, thus saving Visual Basic the overhead needed to distinguish between the Mask and Outside regions.

You can easily create controls with hot spots using *ClipBehavior* = 0-None and *HitBehavior* = 1-UseRegion. In practice, you draw your control over its entire client area and use the *MaskPicture* property to define the areas that react to the mouse.

Data Binding

You can add data-binding capabilities to an ActiveX control with little more than a few mouse clicks. As is not the case for intrinsic controls, you can create controls that bind multiple properties to database fields. All you have to do is tick the Property Is Data Bound check box in the Data Binding section of the Procedure Attributes dialog box, shown in Figure 17-10, for all the properties that you want to make data aware.

You can create as many data-bound properties as you like, but you must select the This Property Binds To DataField option for one of them only. If no property is bound to the *DataField* property, the Extender object won't expose all the *Dataxxxx* properties that are necessary to actually bind the control. Because such properties are exposed by the Extender object, their availability depends on the host environment.

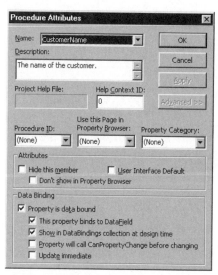

Figure 17-10. *The Procedure Attributes dialog box includes all the options for creating data-aware properties.*

PropertyChanged and *CanPropertyChange* methods

To support data binding in code, you don't have to do anything more than you already do for persistent properties. In each *Property Let* procedure, you must call the *PropertyChanged* method, which informs Visual Basic that the property has changed and that the database field should be updated before the record pointer moves to another record. If you omit this call, the database field won't be updated. You can also update the field immediately if you select the Update Immediate option in the Procedure Attributes dialog box.

Visual Basic also provides the *CanPropertyChange* method, which queries the data source to determine whether it's safe to update the field. You could use the following code in the *Property Let* procedure of a property called *CustomerName*. (The statements that have been added to the code by the wizard are in boldface.)

```
Public Property Let CustomerName(New_CustomerName As String)
    If CanPropertyChange("CustomerName") Then
        txtCustomerName.Text = New_CustomerName
        PropertyChanged "CustomerName"
    End If
End Sub
```

You should be aware, however, that you don't strictly need to call the *CanPropertyChange* method because under Visual Basic 5 and 6 it always returns True, even if the database field can't be updated. You should use this function only for compatibility with future versions of the language that might implement it. For all the properties that call this method before doing the update, you should also select the Property Will Call *CanPropertyChange* Before Changing option in the Procedure Attributes dialog box. Again, at this time there's no point in doing that, but it doesn't cause any harm either. The choice is yours.

To correctly support data binding, the constituent controls must update the corresponding bound property when their contents change. Typically this is done in the *Change* or *Click* event procedure, as in the following code snippet:

```
Private Sub txtCustomerName_Change()
    PropertyChanged "CustomerName"
End Sub
```

The DataBindings collection

As I mentioned before, only one property can be bound to the *DataField* Extender property. Because you can bind multiple properties, you need to provide developers with a method for associating each bound property to the corresponding database field. This association can be done either at design time or during execution.

For each property that you want to make bindable at design time, you must select the Show In DataBindings Collection At Design Time option in the Procedure Attributes dialog box. If this option is selected for one or more properties, the *DataBindings* item appears in the Properties window. When you click on it, Visual Basic brings up the dialog box shown in Figure 17-11 on the following page. Note that it's OK that the property bound to the *DataField* property also appears in the DataBindings collection.

Visual Basic 6 permits you to bind properties in the DataBindings collection to fields in different Data Sources, and you can also select a distinct *DataFormat* for each one of them. In Visual Basic 5, you could bind properties only to the same Data Source.

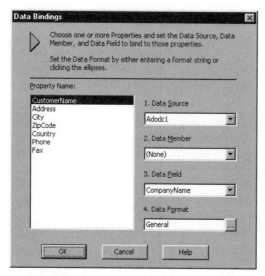

Figure 17-11. *The DataBindings dialog box lets developers associate properties with database fields at design time.*

All the bound properties appear in the DataBindings collection at run time, regardless of whether they appear in the collection at design time. You can't add new items to this collection through code, but you can change the database field to which a property is bound:

```
' Bind the CustomerName property to the CompanyName database field.
Customer1.DataBindings("CustomerName").DataField = "CompanyName"
```

Another common task for the DataBindings collection is to cancel changes in fields so that the database record won't be updated:

```
Dim dtb As DataBinding
For Each dtb In Customer1.DataBindings
    dtb.DataChanged = False
Next
```

For more information about the DataBindings collection, see the online Visual Basic documentation.

The DataRepeater control

Visual Basic 6 lets you create custom grid-like controls, using the DataRepeater control (contained in the Msdatrep.ocx file). This control works as a container of other ActiveX controls: It can host any type of controls, but it's especially useful with custom ActiveX controls.

Say that you want to display a table of records, but you don't want to use a standard Visual Basic grid control—such as the DataGrid or Hierarchical FlexGrid control—because you need maximum flexibility for interaction with the user or because you want to display information that can't be embedded in a regular grid (images, for example). Figure 17-12 shows a custom grid built on the DataRepeater

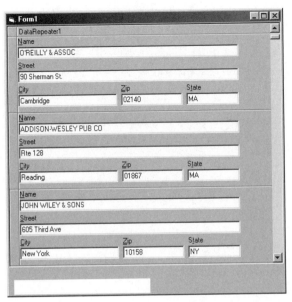

Figure 17-12. *The DataRepeater control lets you create custom views of your database tables.*

control that displays the Publisher table from the Biblio.mdb database. To create such a custom grid, you must execute these basic steps:

1. Create an AddressOCX control that contains all the fields you need; this is the object that will be replicated in the DataRepeater control.

2. For all the properties that you want to expose in the DataRepeater control—that is, Name, Street, City, Zip, and State—make the property data bound and have it appear in the DataBindings collection at design time.

3. Save the project, compile it into a stand-alone OCX file, and load the client application where you want to display the custom grid.

4. Drop an ADO Data control on the client form, and then set its *ConnectionString* and *RecordSource* properties to point to the table in the database that provides the data. (You can also use any other ADO data source, including a DataEnvironment object.)

5. Drop a DataRepeater control on the form, have its *DataSource* property pointing to the ADO Data control, and select the AddressOCX ActiveX control from the list that appears when you click on the *Repeated-ControlName*. (This list includes all the OCXs that are registered in your system.)

6. Bring up the DataRepeater control's custom property page, switch to the RepeaterBindings tab, and associate the bound properties exposed by the

inner ActiveX control with the database fields. You can also set in the Format tab the *DataFormat* property for each field.

The complete source code of the demonstration program is on the companion CD. The DataRepeater control has some rough edges, and you must pay attention to many details to have it working properly:

■ The UserControl must be compiled into an OCX file; otherwise, it can't be hosted in the DataRepeater control. You can't use an intrinsic Visual Basic control with a DataRepeater.

■ All the bound properties in the inner ActiveX control should return String values; you can then format these values using the DataFormat options offered by the DataRepeater control. Moreover, all the properties must be visible in the DataBindings collection at design time; otherwise, the DataRepeater control won't see them.

■ The constituent controls on the child form should call the *PropertyChanged* method whenever the user changes their values; otherwise, the database won't be updated correctly.

■ The DataRepeater control creates only one instance of the control; this control is used to let the user edit values for the current record, whereas all other rows are just images of the control. You might notice some incorrect repaints every now and then.

The DataRepeater control exposes several properties, methods, and events that augment its potential and flexibility. For example, you can directly access the active instance of the child control to set additional properties (*RepeatedControl* property), find the line number of the current record (*ActiveRow* property), change the DataRepeater's appearance (by assigning the *Caption, CaptionStyle, ScrollBars, RowIndicator,* and *RowDividerStyle* properties), get or set a bookmark to the current or the visible records (using the *CurrentRecord* and *VisibleRecords* properties), and so on. You can also monitor users' actions—for example, when they scroll the contents of the list (*ActiveRowChanged* and *VisibleRecordsChanged* events) or select another row (*CurrentRecordChanged* event).

Interestingly, it's even possible to load a different child ActiveX control at run time by assigning a new value to the *RepeatedControlName* property. In this case, you must associate the bound property with fields by using the properties of the *RepeaterBindings* collection. (You can provide the user with a list of bindable properties using the *PropertyNames* property.) Whenever a new child control is loaded at run time, the DataRepeater fires a *RepeatedControlLoaded* event, which the programmer can use to correctly initialize the new control.

What's missing

The data binding mechanism offered by Visual Basic is fairly complete, although a few features aren't directly supported and you have to implement them yourself.

For example, there's no direct support for controls that bind a *list* of values to a secondary Data source, as the DataList and DataCombo controls do. You can implement this feature by exposing a custom property—such as *RowSource*—to which developers can assign the secondary Data control (or another ADO-compliant data source). Here the problem to solve is: You can't display a custom list in the Properties window, so how do you let the developer select the data source at design time? The answer is based on custom property pages, which are described in the next section.

One thing that at first seems to be impossible is to decide at run time which property binds to the DataField Extender property. In this situation, the solution is actually simpler than it might appear: Create an additional property that binds to DataField and that delegates to one of the other properties exposed by the control. This mechanism can be made extremely flexible by means of the new *CallByName* function. For example, let's say that you want to give developers the ability to bind any property among those exposed by the Customer control. You need to create two additional properties: *BoundPropertyName,* which holds the name of the bound property, and *BoundValue,* which does the actual delegation. This is the code in the *Property Get* and *Let* procedures for the latter property:

```
' BoundValue binds directly to DataField, but the value actually stored
' in the database depends on the BoundPropertyName property.
Public Property Get BoundValue() As Variant
    BoundValue = CallByName(Me, BoundPropertyName, vbGet)
End Property

Public Property Let BoundValue (New_BoundValue As Variant)
    CallByName Me, BoundPropertyName, vbLet, New_BoundValue
End Property
```

You should make *BoundValue* hidden so that developers are discouraged from using it directly.

Property Pages

The majority of ActiveX controls that you find in the Visual Basic package or buy from third-party vendors are equipped with one or more custom property pages. In this section, you'll see how easy it is to create property pages for your own ActiveX controls.

Even if the Visual Basic's Properties window is usually sufficient to enter property values at design time, there are at least three reasons why you should create custom property pages. First, they greatly simplify the job of the programmers that are using your control because all properties can be grouped in a logical way. Second, and more important, property pages give you much greater influence over how properties are set at design time. For example, you can't show a combo box in the Properties window with a list of values built dynamically, nor can you let developers drop down a mini-editor to enter multiple values (as they do when editing the *List* property of ListBox and ComboBox controls). These restrictions are easily overcome with property pages. Third, property pages permit you to localize the design-time user interface of your controls for different languages.

So that you can see property pages in action, I created a SuperListBox ActiveX control, an expanded ListBox that exposes an *AllItems* property (which returns all the items separated by a carriage return character) and allows you to enter new items at run time using a pop-up menu. My control also gives the programmer the ability to bind either the *Text* property or the *ListIndex* property to the DataField, thus overcoming one of the few limitations of the data binding mechanism in Visual Basic. This control employs a number of interesting programming techniques—such as API functions to implement a columnar format—and you might want to browse its source code on the companion CD.

Running the Property Page Wizard

You can add a property page to an ActiveX Control project with the Add Property Page command from the Project menu, but you can save a lot of work and time using the Property Page Wizard. (You have to install this add-in from the Add-In Manager dialog box.) In the first step of the wizard, you can create custom property pages, select their order, and decide whether you want to keep standard property pages. (See Figure 17-13.) Visual Basic automatically adds the StandardColor, StandardFont, and StandardPicture pages (for properties that return OLE_COLOR, StdFont, and StdPicture values, respectively), but you can also decide to deactivate them if you want.

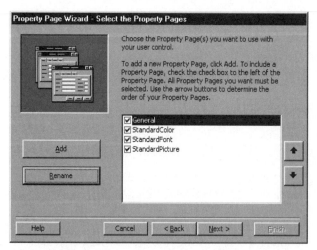

Figure 17-13. *The first step of the Property Page Wizard is the point at which you create new pages and change the order of selected pages.*

In the second step of the wizard, you decide on which page each custom prop-erty will be displayed. All the properties that you leave in the leftmost list box (as shown in Figure 17-14) won't be displayed on any property page.

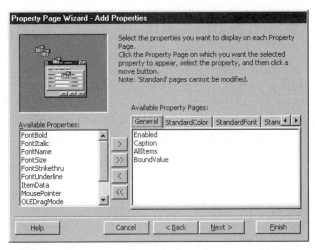

Figure 17-14. *In the second step of the Property Page Wizard, you decide which properties will be shown on which page.*

When you click on the Finish button, the wizard creates one or more PropertyPage modules. For each property that you assigned to the page, the wizard generates a Label control (whose *Caption* is the name of the property) and a TextBox control that holds the value of the property, or a CheckBox control if the property returns a Boolean value. If you want a fancier user interface—for example, ComboBox controls for enumerated properties—you have to modify what the wizard has pro-duced. Figure 17-15 shows the General property page for the SuperListBox control after I rearranged the controls and converted a couple of TextBox controls into ComboBox controls.

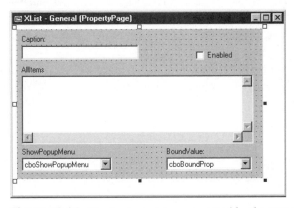

Figure 17-15. *The property page generated by the Property Page Wizard, after some retouching.*

The PropertyPage object

Just browsing the code produced by the wizard is sufficient to understand how property pages work. The PropertyPage object is similar to a form and supports many of the Form object's properties, methods, and events, including *Caption*, *Font*, and all the keyboard and mouse events. You might even implement property pages that work as drag-and-drop servers or clients if you need to.

Property pages have their peculiarities, of course. For one, you can control the size of the page using the *StandardSize* property, which can be assigned one of the values 0-Custom (the size is determined by the object), 1-Small (101-by-375 pixels), or 2-Large (179-by-375 pixels). Microsoft suggests that you create custom-sized pages that aren't larger than the space that you actually need because values other than 0-Custom might display incorrectly at different screen resolutions.

You might notice in Figure 17-15 that the property page doesn't include the OK, Cancel, and Apply buttons that you usually find on standard property pages. Those buttons, in fact, are provided by the environment, and you don't have to add them yourself. The communication between the property page and the environment occurs through properties and events of the PropertyPage object. If the project is associated with a help file, a Help button is also displayed.

When the page loads, the PropertyPage object receives the *SelectionChanged* event. In this event, your code should load all the controls in the page with the current values of the corresponding properties. The SelectedControls collection returns a reference to all the controls in the form that are currently selected and that will be affected by the property page. For example, this is the code in the *SelectionChanged* event procedure for the General page of the SuperListBox control:

```
Private Sub PropertyPage_SelectionChanged()
    txtCaption.Text = SelectedControls(0).Caption
    txtAllItems.Text = SelectedControls(0).AllItems
    chkEnabled.Value = (SelectedControls(0).Enabled And vbChecked)
    cboShowPopupMenu.ListIndex = SelectedControls(0).ShowPopupMenu
    cboBoundPropertyName.Text = SelectedControls(0).BoundPropertyName
    Changed = False
End Sub
```

When the contents of any field on the page is modified, the code in its *Change* or *Click* event should set the PropertyPage's *Changed* property to True, as in these examples:

```
Private Sub txtCaption_Change()
    Changed = True
End Sub


Private Sub cboShowPopupMenu_Click()
    Changed = True
End Sub
```

Setting the *Change* property to True automatically enables the Apply button. When the user clicks on this button (or simply switches to another property page), the PropertyPage object receives an *ApplyChanges* event. In this event, you must assign the values on the property page to the corresponding ActiveX control's properties, as in the following example:

```
Private Sub PropertyPage_ApplyChanges()
    SelectedControls(0).Caption = txtCaption.Text
    SelectedControls(0).AllItems = txtAllItems.Text
    SelectedControls(0).Enabled = chkEnabled.Value
    SelectedControls(0).ShowPopupMenu = cboShowPopupMenu.ListIndex
    SelectedControls(0).BoundPropertyName = cboBoundPropertyName.Text
End Sub
```

One more custom event is associated with PropertyPage objects—the *EditProperties* event. This event fires when the property page is displayed because the developer clicked on the ellipsis button beside a property name in the Properties window. (This button appears if the property has been associated with a specific property page in the Procedure Attributes dialog box.) You usually take advantage of this property to automatically move the focus on the corresponding control on the property page:

```
Private Sub PropertyPage_EditProperty(PropertyName As String)
    Select Case PropertyName
        Case "Caption"
            txtCaption.SetFocus
        Case "AllItems"
            txtAllItems.SetFocus
        ' etc. (other properties omitted...)
    End Select
End Sub
```

You might also want to disable or hide all other controls on the page, but this is rarely necessary or useful.

Working with multiple selections

The code produced by the Property Page Wizard accounts for only the simplest situation—that is, when only one ActiveX control is selected on the form. To build robust and versatile property pages, you should make them work also with multiple controls. Keep in mind that property pages aren't modal, and therefore the developer is allowed to select (or deselect) controls on the form even when the page is already visible. Each time a new control is added to or removed from the SelectedControls collection, a *SelectionChanged* event fires.

The standard way to deal with multiple selections is as follows. If the selected controls on the form share the same value for a given property, you fill the corresponding field on the property page with that common value; otherwise, you leave the field blank. This is a modified version of the *SelectionChanged* event that accounts for multiple selections:

```
Private Sub PropertyPage_SelectionChanged()
    Dim i As Integer
    ' Use the property of the first selected control.
    txtCaption.Text = SelectedControls(0).Caption
    ' If there are other controls, and their Caption property differs from
    ' the Caption of the first selected control, clear the field and exit.
    For i = 1 To SelectedControls.Count - 1
        If SelectedControls(i).Caption <> txtCaption.Text Then
            txtCaption.Text = ""
            Exit For
        End If
    Next

    ' The AllItems property is dealt with in the same way (omitted ...).

    ' The Enabled property uses a CheckBox control. If values differ, use
    ' the special vbGrayed setting.
    chkEnabled.Value = (SelectedControls(0).Enabled And vbChecked)
    For i = 1 To SelectedControls.Count - 1
        If (SelectedControls(i).Enabled And vbChecked) <> chkEnabled.Value
            Then
            chkEnabled.Value = vbGrayed
            Exit For
        End If
    Next

    ' The ShowPopupMenu enumerated property uses a ComboBox control.
    ' If values differ, set the ComboBox's ListIndex property to -1.
    cboShowPopupMenu.ListIndex = SelectedControls(0).ShowPopupMenu
    For i = 1 To SelectedControls.Count - 1
        If SelectedControls(i).ShowPopupMenu <> cboShowPopupMenu.ListIndex
            Then
            cboShowPopupMenu.ListIndex = -1
            Exit For
        End If
    Next

    ' The BoundPropertyName property is dealt with similarly (omitted ...).

    Changed = False
    txtCaption.DataChanged = False
    txtAllItems.DataChanged = False
End Sub
```

The *DataChange* properties of the two TextBox controls are set to False because in the *ApplyChange* event you must determine whether the developer entered a value in either of those fields:

```
Private Sub PropertyPage_ApplyChanges()
    Dim ctrl As Object
    ' Apply changes to Caption property only if the field was modified.
    If txtCaption.DataChanged Then
        For Each ctrl In SelectedControls
            ctrl.Caption = txtCaption.Text
        Next
    End If
    ' The AllItems property is deal with in the same way (omitted ...).

    ' Apply changes to the Enabled property only if the CheckBox control
    ' isn't grayed out.
    If chkEnabled.Value <> vbGrayed Then
        For Each ctrl In SelectedControls
            ctrl.Enabled = chkEnabled.Value
        Next
    End If

    ' Apply changes to the ShowPopupMenu property only if an item
    ' in the ComboBox control is selected.
    If cboShowPopupMenu.ListIndex <> -1 Then
        For Each ctrl In SelectedControls
            ctrl.ShowPopupMenu = cboShowPopupMenu.ListIndex
        Next
    End If
    ' The BoundPropertyName property is dealt with similarly (omitted ...).
End Sub
```

Advanced techniques

I want to mention a few techniques that you can use with property pages and that aren't immediately obvious. For example, you don't need to wait for the *ApplyChanges* event to modify a property in selected ActiveX controls: You can update a property right in the *Change* or *Click* event of the corresponding control on the property page. You can therefore achieve in the property page the same behavior that you can implement in the Properties window by assigning a property the Text or Caption procedure ID.

Another easy-to-overlook feature is that the PropertyPage object can invoke Friend properties and methods of the UserControl module because they're in the same project. This gives you some additional flexibility: For example, the UserControl module can expose one of its constituent controls as a Friend *Property Get* procedure so that the Property Page can directly manipulate its attributes, as you can see in the code at the top of the next page.

```
' In the SuperListBox UserControl module
Friend Property Get Ctrl_List1() As ListBox
    Set Ctrl_List1 = List1
End Property
```

A minor annoyance of this approach is that the PropertyPage code accesses the UserControl through the SelectedControls collection, which returns a generic Object, whereas Friend members can only be accessed through specific object variables. You can work around this issue by casting the elements of the collection to specific object variables:

```
' In the PropertyPage module
Dim ctrl As SuperListBox
' Cast the generic control to a specific SuperListBox variable.
Set ctrl = SelectedControls(0)
' Now it is possible to access Friend members.
ctrl.Ctrl_List1.AddItem "New Item"
```

The last technique that I'm showing you is likely to be useful when you're developing complex UserControls with many properties and constituent controls, such as the Customer ActiveX control that I introduced earlier in this chapter. Surprisingly, it turns out that you can use the UserControl even on a property page that's associated with itself. Figure 17-16 shows an example of this technique: The General property page uses an instance of the Customer ActiveX control to let the developer assign the properties of the Customer control itself!

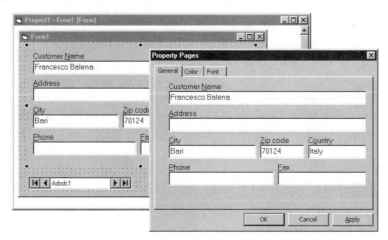

Figure 17-16. *A property page that uses an instance of the UserControl object defined in its own project.*

The beauty of this approach is how little code you need to write in the PropertyPage module. This is the complete source code of the property page shown in Figure 17-16:

```
Private Sub Customer1_Change(PropertyName As String)
    Changed = True
End Sub

Private Sub PropertyPage_ApplyChanges()
    ' Read all properties in one loop.
    Dim propname As Variant
    For Each propname In Array("CustomerName", "Address", "City", _
        "ZipCode", "Country", "Phone", "Fax")
        CallByName SelectedControls(0), propname, VbLet, _
            CallByName(Customer1, propname, VbGet)
    Next
End Sub

Private Sub PropertyPage_SelectionChanged()
    ' Assign all properties in one loop.
    Dim propname As Variant
    For Each propname In Array("CustomerName", "Address", "City", _
        "ZipCode", "Country", "Phone", "Fax")
        CallByName Customer1, propname, VbLet, _
            CallByName(SelectedControls(0), propname, VbGet)
    Next
End Sub
```

Notice how the code takes advantage of the *CallByName* function to streamline multiple assignments to and from the properties in the UserControl.

The Tricks of the Masters

At this point, you know everything you need to create ActiveX controls that match or even exceed the quality of commercial controls. There are a few advanced techniques, however, that even many experienced programmers aren't aware of. As I'll prove in this section, you don't always need to know all the intricacies of Windows and ActiveX programming to deliver efficient controls because, in most cases, Visual Basic is all you need.

Callback methods

Raising an event in the parent form from within an ActiveX control is easy, but it isn't the only method you can use to let the two objects communicate with each other. In Chapter 16, I showed you how an object can notify another object that something has occurred by using callback methods. Callback methods have several advantages over events: They're about 5 or 6 times faster on average and, more important, they aren't blocked when the client form is showing a message box in an interpreted program.

On the companion CD, you'll find the complete source code for the SuperTimer ActiveX control, which implements a Timer that can communicate with its parent form using a callback mechanism based on the *ISuperTimerCBK* interface (a PublicNotCreatable class contained in the ActiveX control project). When a form or any other container implements this interface, it can have the SuperTimer control send its notifications through that interface's only member, the *Timer* method. This is the source code for a typical form that uses this SuperTimer control:

```
Implements ISuperTimerCBK

Private Sub Form_Load()
    Set SuperTimer1.Owner = Me
End Sub

Private Sub ISuperTimerCBK_Timer()
    ' Do whatever you want here.
End Sub
```

The SuperTimer control contains a Timer1 constituent control that raises a *Timer* event in the UserControl module; in this procedure, the control decides whether it has to raise an event or invoke a callback method:

```
Public Owner As ISuperTimerCBK

Private Sub Timer1_Timer()
    If Owner Is Nothing Then
        RaiseEvent Timer       ' Fire a regular event.
    Else
        Owner.Timer            ' Fire a callback method.
    End If
End Sub
```

Interestingly, in an interpreted program the *Timer* event in a standard Timer control doesn't fire if the client form is showing a message box. (Timers are never blocked in compiled programs, though.) You don't suffer from this limitation if you use the ISuperTimerCBK interface of the SuperTimer OCX control, which therefore proves to be more powerful than a regular Timer control. (See Figure 17-17.) But you have to compile the SuperTimer control into an OCX file for this feature to work properly. (When the UserControl module runs in the Visual Basic IDE, modal windows in the client applications block events also in the ActiveX control.)

> **TIP** The demonstration program of the SuperTimer control displays different messages if the application is running in the IDE or as a compiled program. The Visual Basic language lacks a function that lets you distinguish between the two modes, but you can take advantage of the fact that all the methods of the Debug object aren't compiled in EXE programs and therefore are executed only when the application is running in the IDE. Here's an example of this technique:

```
Function InterpretedMode() As Boolean
    On Error Resume Next
    Debug Print 1/0                  ' This causes an error
    InterpretedMode = (Err <> 0)     ' but only inside the IDE.
    Err Clear                        ' Clear the error code.
End Function
```

The preceding code is based on a routine that appeared in the Tech Tips supplement of the Visual Basic Programmer's Journal.

Figure 17-17. *A compiled SuperTimer control can send callback methods to the parent form even if a message box is being displayed.*

Faster calls with VTable binding

As you know, all references to external ActiveX controls—but not intrinsic Visual Basic controls—implicitly use their Extender objects. What you probably don't know is that all references to the Extender use early ID binding instead of the most efficient VTable binding. This means that calling a method in an ActiveX control is slower than calling the same method if the object were encapsulated in an ActiveX DLL component because objects in DLLs are referenced through VTable binding.

In general, ID binding doesn't seriously impair the performance of your ActiveX control because most properties and methods implement the user interface and are sufficiently fast even on low-end machines. But sometimes you might need more speed. Say that you have a ListBox control that you want to fill as rapidly as possible with data read from a database or an array in memory: in this situation, you need to call a property or a method several thousand times, and the overhead of ID binding wouldn't be negligible.

A solution to this problem is conceptually simple. You add a PublicNotCreatable class to your ActiveX Control project that exposes the same properties and methods as those exposed by the ActiveX control. The class does nothing but delegate the execution of the properties and methods to the main UserControl module. Whenever the ActiveX control is instantiated, it creates a companion Public object and exposes it as a read-only property. The client form can store the return value of this property in a specific object variable and call the ActiveX control's members through this secondary object. This object doesn't use the Extender object and therefore can be accessed through VTable binding instead of ID binding.

I found that accessing UserControl's properties through this companion object can be about 15 times faster than through the regular reference to the ActiveX control. On the companion CD, you'll find a demonstration project whose only purpose is to show you what kind of performance you can get using this approach. You can use it as a model to implement this technique in your own ActiveX control projects.

Secondary interfaces

An alternative way to use VTable binding for super-fast ActiveX controls is to have the ActiveX control implement a secondary interface and have the client form access the secondary interface instead of the primary interface. This approach is even faster than the one based on a secondary PublicNotCreatable object because you don't need a separate class that delegates to the main ActiveX control module. Another benefit of this approach is that the same interface can be shared by multiple ActiveX controls so that you can implement a VTable-based polymorphism among different but related ActiveX controls.

The implementation of this approach isn't difficult, but beware of one difficulty. Say that you create an ActiveX control that contains an *Implements IControlInterface* statement at the beginning of its code module. Your goal is to take advantage of this common interface in the client form by assigning a specific ActiveX control instance to an interface variable. Unfortunately, the following sequence of statements raises an error:

```
' In the client form
Dim ctrl As IControlInterface
Set ctrl = MyControl1                        ' Error "Type Mismatch"
```

The problem, of course, is that the MyControl1 object in the client code uses the ActiveX control's Extender interface, which doesn't inherit the IControlInterface interface. To access that interface, you need to bypass the Extender object, as follows:

```
Set ctrl = MyControl1.Object
```

Trapping events with multicasting

Multicasting lets you trap events raised by any object that you can reference through an object variable. (I described multicasting in Chapter 7, so you might want to review those pages before reading what follows.) The good news is that multicasting also works with ActiveX controls, even if a control has been compiled into a standalone OCX file. In other words, your ActiveX control can trap events fired by the parent form, or even by other controls on the form itself.

To give you a taste of what you can do with this technique, I have prepared a simple ActiveX control that automatically resizes itself to cover the entire surface of its parent form. If it weren't for multicasting, this feature would be extremely difficult to implement because it requires you to subclass the parent form to be notified when it's being resized. Thanks to multicasting, the amount of code you need to implement this feature is amazingly little:

```
Dim WithEvents ParentForm As Form

Private Sub UserControl_ReadProperties(PropBag As PropertyBag)
    On Error Resume Next          ' In case parent isn't a form.
    Set ParentForm = Parent
End Sub

' This event fires when the parent form resizes.
Private Sub ParentForm_Resize()
    Extender.Move 0, 0, Parent.ScaleWidth, Parent.ScaleHeight
End Sub
```

The multicasting technique has an infinite number of applications. For example, you can build an ActiveX control that always displays the sum of the values contained in TextBox controls on the form. For this task, you need to trap those controls' *Change* events. When trapping the events of an intrinsic control, your UserControl module must declare a *WithEvents* variable of a specific object type, but when trapping events from external ActiveX controls—for example, a TreeView or MonthView control—you can use a generic VBControlExtender object variable and rely on its one-size-fits-all *ObjectEvent* event.

ACTIVEX CONTROLS FOR THE INTERNET

Many programmers believe that the Internet is the natural habitat for ActiveX controls, so you might have been surprised that I haven't described Internet-specific features until the end of the chapter. The plain truth is that, Microsoft's plans notwithstanding, Microsoft Internet Explorer still is, as I write these pages, the only popular browser that natively supports ActiveX controls, at least without any plug-in modules. So if you heavily use ActiveX controls in HTML pages, you automatically reduce the number of potential users of your Web site. You see, ActiveX controls probably aren't very useful for the Internet, even though they might find their way into intranets, where administrators can be sure about which browser is installed on all client machines. As far as the Internet is concerned, however, Dynamic HTML and Active Server Pages seem to offer a better solution for building dynamic and "smart" pages, as I explain in the section devoted to Internet programming.

Programming Issues

In general, ActiveX controls in HTML pages can exploit the additional features provided by the browser in which they're running. In this section, I briefly describe the new methods and events that such controls can use. But first of all, you need to understand how an ActiveX control is actually placed in an HTML page.

ActiveX controls on HTML pages

You can place a control in a page using a number of HTML Page editors. For example, following is the code that Microsoft FrontPage produces for an HTML page that includes my ClockOCX.ocx control, whose source code is available on the companion CD. Notice that the control is referenced through its CLSID, not its more readable ProgID name. (The HTML code that refers to the ActiveX control is in boldface.)

```
<HTML>
<HEAD>
<TITLE>Home page</TITLE>
</HEAD>
<BODY BGCOLOR="#FFFFFF">
<H1>A web page with an ActiveX Control on it.</H1>
<OBJECT CLASSID="clsid:27E428E0-9145-11D2-BAC5-0080C8F21830"
    BORDER="0" WIDTH="344" HEIGHT="127">
    <PARAM NAME="FontName" VALUE="Arial">
    <PARAM NAME="FontSize" VALUE="24">
</OBJECT>
</BODY>
</HTML>
```

As you can see, all the information concerning the control is enclosed by the <OBJECT> and </OBJECT> tags, and all initial properties values are provided in <PARAM> tags. These values are made available to the control in its *ReadProperties* event procedure. (If there are no <PARAM> tags, the control could receive an *InitProperties* event instead, but the exact behavior depends on the browser.) ActiveX controls intended to be used on Web pages should always expose *Fontxxxx* properties instead of, or together with, the *Font* object property because assigning object properties in an HTML page isn't simple.

When you're using an ActiveX control on a Web site, many things can go wrong—for example, references to Extender properties that aren't available under the browser. Visual Basic 6 offers a couple of ways to reduce the guesswork when it's time to fix these errors. The first option is to start the component from within the IDE and wait until the browser creates an instance of the control. The second option is to have Visual Basic create an empty HTML page with just the ActiveX control on it and automatically load it into the browser. You can select these options in the Debugging tab of the Project Properties dialog box, as shown in Figure 17-18.

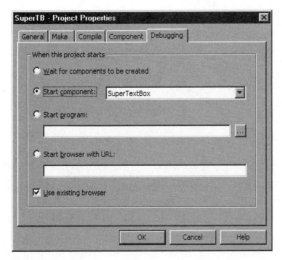

Figure 17-18. *The Debugging tab of the Project Properties dialog box.*

Hyperlinking

The UserControl object exposes the *Hyperlink* property, which returns a Hyperlink object that you can use to navigate to other HTML pages. The Hyperlink object exposes three methods, the most important of which is the *NavigateTo* method:

```
Hyperlink.NavigateTo Target, [Location], [FrameName]
```

Target is the URL to which you navigate, *Location* is an optional argument that points to a specific location in an HTML page, and *FrameName* is the optional name of a frame in a page. If the ActiveX control is running inside a browser, the new page is shown within the browser itself; if the control isn't running in a browser, the default browser is automatically launched.

The Hyperlink object exposes two more methods, *GoBack* and *GoForward*, which let you navigate the browser's history list. Unless you're absolutely sure that the history list isn't empty, you should always protect these methods with an *On Error* statement:

```
Private Sub cmdBack_Click()
    On Error Resume Next
    Hyperlink.GoBack
    If Err Then MsgBox "History is empty!"
End Sub
```

> **TIP** You can navigate many kinds of documents, not just HTML pages. For example, Internet Explorer can display Microsoft Word and Microsoft Excel files, so you can use it as a document browser, as the following code demonstrates:
> ```
> Hyperlink.NavigateTo "C:\Documents\Notes.Doc"
> ```

Asynchronous download

ActiveX controls authored in Visual Basic support asynchronous downloading of properties. Let's say that you have a PictureBox-like ActiveX control that can read its contents from a GIF or BMP file. Instead of waiting for the image to be completely downloaded, you'll do better to start an asynchronous download operation and immediately return the control to the user. The key to asynchronous downloading is the *AsyncRead* method of the UserControl object, whose syntax is this:

```
AsyncRead Target, AsyncType, [PropertyName], [AsyncReadOptions]
```

Target is the URL of the property to be downloaded. *AsyncType* is the type of the property and can be one of the following values: 0-vbAsyncTypePicture (an image that can be assigned to a *Picture* property), 1-vbAsyncTypeFile (a file created by Visual Basic), or 2-vbAsyncTypeByteArray (a Byte array). *PropertyName* is the name of the property whose value is being downloaded and is useful when there are many properties that can be downloaded asynchronously. But keep in mind that there can be only one *AsyncRead* operation active at one time.

The *AsyncRead* method supports a new *AsyncReadOptions* argument, a bitfielded integer that accepts the values listed in Table 17-1. Using this value, you can fine-tune the performance of your asynchronous download operation and decide whether the control can use the data in the local cache.

Constant	Value	AsyncRead *Behavior*
vbAsyncReadSynchronousDownload	1	Returns only when the down load is complete (synchronous download)
vbAsyncReadOfflineOperation	8	Uses only the locally cached resource
vbAsyncReadForceUpdate	16	Forces the download from the remote Web server, ignoring any copy in the local cache
vbAsyncReadResynchronize	512	Updates the copy in the local cache only if the version on the remote Web server is more recent
vbAsyncReadGetFromCacheIfNetFail	&H80000	Uses the copy in the local cache if the connection to the remote Web server fails

Table 17-1. *The available values for the* AsyncReadOptions *argument of the* AsyncRead *method.*

On the companion CD, you'll find the complete source code of a Scrollable-PictureBox ActiveX control, which supports scrolling of large images as well as their asynchronous downloading from the Internet. (See Figure 17-19.) The asynchronous download feature is provided in the form of a *PicturePath* property that, when assigned, starts the downloading process:

```
Public Property Let PicturePath(ByVal New_PicturePath As String)
    m_PicturePath = New_PicturePath
    PropertyChanged "PicturePath"
    If Len(m_PicturePath) Then
        AsyncRead m_PicturePath, vbAsyncTypePicture, "Picture"
    End If
End Property
```

You can cancel an asynchronous download operation at any moment using the *CancelAsyncRead* method:

```
CancelAsyncRead "Picture"
```

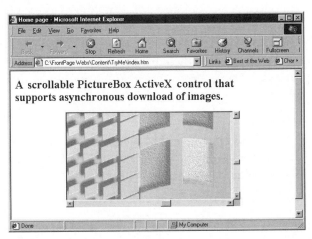

Figure 17-19. *The ScrollablePictureBox control running inside Internet Explorer.*

When the asynchronous download terminates, Visual Basic fires an *AsyncRead-Complete* event in the UserControl module. This event receives an AsyncProperty object, whose most important properties are *PropertyName* and *Value*:

```
Private Sub UserControl_AsyncReadComplete(AsyncProp As AsyncProperty)
    If AsyncProp.PropertyName = "Picture" Then
        Set Image1.Picture = AsyncProp.Value
    End If
End Sub
```

The AsyncProperty object has been greatly enhanced in Visual Basic 6 and now includes properties such as *BytesMax, ByteRead, Status,* and *StatusCode.* For additional information, see the language documentation. Visual Basic 6 also exposes the

AsyncReadProgress event, which fires when new data is available locally. You can use this event to display a progress bar that informs the user about the status of the operation:

```
Private Sub UserControl_AsyncReadProgress(AsyncProp As AsyncProperty)
    If AsyncProp.PropertyName = "Picture" Then
        Dim percent As Integer
        If AsyncProp.BytesMax > 0 Then
            percent = (AsyncProp.BytesRead * 100&) \ AsyncProp.BytesMax
        End If
    End If
End Sub
```

The *AsyncReadProgress* and *AsyncReadComplete* events fire immediately if the data is stored on a local disk (in this case, *PicturePath* is the path of a file) or if it is in the local cache. If you aren't downloading an image (therefore, *AsyncProp.AsyncType* is 1-vbAsyncTypeFile or 2-vbAsyncTypeByteArray), you can read and process the data while it's being downloaded. This arrangement slows the process slightly, but usually the overhead isn't noticeable. If you open a file, you must close it before exiting the event procedure, and you must avoid calling *DoEvents* to avoid reentrancy problems. The *AsyncReadProgress* and *AsyncReadComplete* events occur when the download is complete: You can learn when this happens in the *AsyncReadProgress* event by checking that the *AsyncProp.StatusCode* property returns the value 6-vbAsyncStatusCodeEndDownloadData.

Accessing the browser

A control on an HTML page can do more than simply modify its appearance and behavior: It can manipulate the attributes of the page itself and of the other controls on it. You can access the container page using the Parent object, as this code does:

```
' Changing the HTML page's foreground and background colors
With Parent.Script.document
    .bgColor = "Blue"
    .fgColor = "White"
End With
```

You can also access and manipulate all the controls on the page using the ParentControls collection. But this method requires that you set the *ParentControlsType* property of ParentControls collection to the value vbNoExtender. This setting is necessary because Internet Explorer exposes an Extender object that can't be used from Visual Basic code.

I don't have enough room to describe all the things that you can do once you have a reference to the page that contains the ActiveX control. If you're interested, you should look for additional information on the Internet Explorer Scripting Object Model on the Microsoft Web site.

> **TIP** If you're writing a control that can be used on both regular forms and HTML pages, you need to know which container it's running in. You can do this by looking at the object returned by the Parent object:
>
> ```
> ' Test if the control runs in an HTML page.
> If TypeName(Parent) = "HTMLDocument" Then ...
> ```

Show and *Hide* events

The *Show* event fires in the UserControl module when the page that contains it becomes visible, while the *Hide* event fires when the page becomes invisible but is still in the cache. Eventually, the page might become visible again, thus firing another *Show* event, or the browser might remove the page from the cache (for example, when the browser itself is closed), in which case the control receives a *Terminate* event.

Multithreaded ActiveX controls

If you're going to use the ActiveX control with Microsoft Explorer or a multithreaded Visual Basic application, you should make the control apartment-threaded by selecting the corresponding Threading Model option on the General tab of the Project Properties dialog box. Beware, however, of a documented bug: Multithreaded controls don't fire the *Hide* event when they run under Internet Explorer 4.0. For an ActiveX control to behave correctly, you must mark it as single-threaded and enable the Active Desktop option. For more information, see article Q175907 of the Microsoft Knowledge Base.

Component Download

When you're creating an HTML page that contains one or more ActiveX controls, you must provide a way for the browser to download and install the ActiveX control if it isn't already registered on the client machine.

Creating a package for deployment

The mechanism used for deploying the ActiveX controls on client machines is based on Cabinet (CAB) files. CAB files are compressed files that can include multiple ActiveX controls (as well as other types of files, such as EXEs and DLLs) and that can be digitally signed if necessary. You create CAB files by running the Package and Deployment Wizard and selecting Internet Package in its second step. The wizard also creates a sample HTM file that you can use as a model for the page that will host the control. This file contains the correct value for the CODEBASE attribute, which informs the browser of the name of the CAB file and the version of the ActiveX control. The browser then downloads the CAB file if the control with that CLSID isn't registered on the client machine or if its version is older than the one specified in the HTML page. This is a portion of the sample HTML file created for the ClockOCX control:

```
<OBJECT ID="Clock"
CLASSID="CLSID:27E428E0-9145-11D2-BAC5-0080C8F21830"
CODEBASE="ClockOCX.CAB#version=1,0,0,0">
</OBJECT>
```

CAB files can embed all the ancillary files that the ActiveX control needs to work properly, including data files and satellite DLLs. The list of dependencies of an ActiveX control is described in an INF file, which is produced by the Package and Deployment Wizard and also included in the CAB file itself.

ActiveX controls authored in Visual Basic also require the Visual Basic runtime files. The default option in the Package and Deployment Wizard instructs the installing procedure to download the runtime files from the Microsoft Web site. This setting ensures that the user always receives the most recent version of those files and also reduces the burden on your Web site.

Safety

When an ActiveX control is running in the browser, it could do all sort of evil things to the user's system, such as deleting system files, trashing the Registry, or stealing confidential data. You must, therefore, assure users that not only are your controls not so rude, but also that no other developer can use your controls to damage the machines they're running on.

To broadcast the promise that your control doesn't (and can't) misbehave, you can mark it as "Safe for initialization" or "Safe for scripting." If you declare that your control is safe for initialization, you're telling the browser that there's no way for an HTML page author to accidentally or intentionally do any harm by assigning values to the control's properties through the <PARAM> tags in the <OBJECT> section of the page. If you mark your control as safe for scripting, you're going a bit further because you're declaring that there's no way for a script on the page to set a property or call a method that can damage the system. By default, Microsoft Internet Explorer refuses to download components that aren't marked as safe for initialization and safe for scripting.

Marking your control as safe for initialization or safe for scripting isn't a decision that you should take lightly. The fact that your control doesn't purposely do any damage isn't enough in most cases. Just to give you an idea of the subtleties that you must account for, imagine these scenarios:

- You provide a method that lets developers save data to any path. The control isn't safe for scripting because a malicious developer might use this feature to overwrite important system files.

- You decide the location in which a temporary file is stored, but you leave developers free to write any amount of data to it. Again, the control isn't safe for scripting because a developer might deliberately consume all the free space on disk and bring Windows to an abrupt crash.

You mark your component as safe for initialization or safe for scripting in the Package and Deployment Wizard, as shown in Figure 17-20.

TIP You can quickly learn which ActiveX controls on your machine are safe for initialization or for scripting by using the OleView utility that comes with Visual Studio. This is the portion of the Registry that marks a control as safe:

```
HKEY_CLASSES_ROOT
  \CLS
    \<your control's CLSID>
      \Implemented Categories
        \{7DD95802-9882-11CF-9FA9-00AA006C42C4}
        \{7DD95801-9882-11CF-9FA9-00AA006C42C4}
```

The last two lines of the listing indicate safe for initialization and safe for scripting, respectively. Once you know how this information is recorded in the Registry, you can use the Regedit utility to modify these setting by adding or removing these keys.

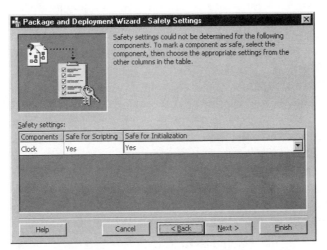

Figure 17-20. *The Package and Deployment Wizard lets you mark your controls as Safe For Initialization and Safe For Scripting.*

A more sophisticated way to address the safety problem is through the IObjectSafety ActiveX interface, which allows your component to programmatically specify which methods and properties are safe. This approach offers greater flexibility than just marking the component as safe. This is an advanced topic, however, and I won't cover it in this book.

Digital signatures

It's obvious that marking a control to be safe isn't enough for most users. After all, anyone can mark a control as safe. Even if they trust your good intentions and your ability as a programmer, they can't be absolutely sure that the control is actually coming from you or that it hasn't been tampered with after you compiled it.

Microsoft has solved this problem by making it possible for you to add a digital signature to ActiveX controls by using a public key encryption algorithm. To digitally sign a control, you need a private encoding key, which you obtain from a company that issues digital certificates—for example, VeriSign Inc. You must pay a fee to obtain such certificates, but they are quite affordable even for individual developers. For more information, pay a visit to *http://www.verisign.com*. Once you have obtained a certificate, you can sign your control—or, most likely, its CAB file—using the SignCode utility which is included in the ActiveX SDK. You can add a digital signature to EXE, DLL, and OCX files, but you need to do so only if you plan to distribute them without packaging them in a CAB file.

Licensing

ActiveX controls can be sold as part of a business application to users or as stand-alone components to other developers. In the latter case, your customers should be able to use the control at design time and also redistribute it with their own applications. If you don't want *their* customers to be able to redistribute your control, you need to add a license key to your control.

The Require License Key option

If you tick the Require License Key option on the General tab of the Project Properties dialog box and then compile the ActiveX control, Visual Basic generates a VBL (Visual Basic License) file that contains the license for the control. For example, this is the VBL file generated for the ClockOCX control:

```
REGEDIT
HKEY_CLASSES_ROOT\Licenses = Licensing: Copying the keys may be a violation
of established copyrights.
HKEY_CLASSES_ROOT\Licenses\27E428DE-9145-11D2-BAC5-0080C8F21830 =
geierljeeeslqlkerffefeiemfmfglelketf
```

As you see, a VBL file is nothing but a script for the Registry. When you create a standard installation procedure, the Wizard includes this file in the package. When other developers buy your control and install it on their machines, the installation routine uses this file to patch their Registries but won't copy the file on their hard disks. For this reason, when they redistribute your control as part of their applications, the VBL isn't included in the deployment package and their customers won't be able to use the control at design time (unless, of course, they buy a license from you).

A control that requires a license key always looks for this key when it's instantiated. If the control is used in a compiled program, the license key is included in the executable EXE file. But if the control is used in an interpreted environment, no executable file can provide the key and the control has to look for it in the Registry. This means that to use the control on a Visual Basic form or in a Microsoft Office application (or another VBA-powered environment), you need the license to be installed in the Registry.

If your control includes other ActiveX controls as constituent controls, you should license them for distribution as well; otherwise, your control won't correctly work at design time. Of all the controls included in the Visual Basic package, the only one that you can't redistribute is the DBGrid control. Note, however, that the Microsoft License Agreement specifies that you can use Microsoft controls in your ActiveX control only if you significantly expand their functionality. I never found anywhere how that "significantly" can be measured, though.

License keys for controls on Web pages

The mechanism that I've just described doesn't address the particular nature of ActiveX controls on a Web page. In fact, it doesn't make sense to require that the user machine have the control's license key installed in the Registry. Nor do you want to send the license key with the control in a readable form in the HTML page. The solution to this difficulty comes in the form of a License Package File (or LPK file for short). You create this file by using the Lpk_Tool.Exe utility that you can find in the \Common\Tools\Vb\Lpk_Tool subdirectory. (See Figure 17-21.) Once you have created an LPK file, you reference it with a parameter to the <PARAM> tag, as follows:

```
<PARAM NAME="LPKPath" VALUE="ClockOCX.lpk">
```

This parameter tells the browser where it can download the license key of the ActiveX control; the license key is transferred each time the page is downloaded because the license keys of ActiveX controls found on HTML pages are never added to the client machine's Registry. The value of the *LPKPath* parameter can be a relative or absolute URL, but in the latter case you might have problems when moving the HTM file to another location of your site. The owner of the Web site must have purchased a license for your ActiveX control to be able to send it in HTML pages. In other words, as far as the license mechanism is concerned, Web site owners are regarded as developers.

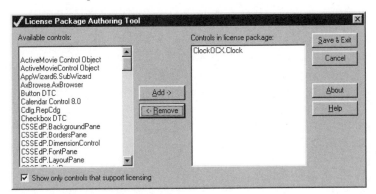

Figure 17-21. *The Lpt_Tool utility can create an LPK file containing the license keys of one or more ActiveX controls.*

NOTE   It should be made clear that the license mechanism provided by Visual Basic isn't bulletproof. After all, a malicious developer has only to copy the VBL from the installation diskette or—if that file is no longer available—retrieve the relevant information from the Registry and re-create the VBL file. Actually, the only thing you can be sure of is that the license key won't be accidentally included in an installation procedure. If you need a more secure system, you should devise an alternative method based on alternate locations of the Registry or custom license files loaded in system directories.

If you have carefully read Chapter 16 and this chapter, you might be surprised to see how few features Visual Basic 6 has added to those already available in Visual Basic 5. But you see the real potential of components and controls when you add ADO to the equation and begin to build data-aware classes and components. These new capabilities are described in the next chapter.

Chapter 18

ADO Components

Regular COM components are great when you're working with single blocks of data held in memory—for example, all the information you have about a customer. But COM components are awkward to work with when your data is to be read from and written to a database. Yes, you can implement a persistence mechanism based on custom *Load* and *Save* methods (or based on the new persistable classes in Microsoft Visual Basic 6), but this means a lot of additional work for the author of the component and for the programmer who uses it.

Visual Basic 6 offers a novel solution to this problem, based on new binding capabilities in ADO. In this chapter, I show you how to create data source classes that read data from a database. I also show you how to create consumer classes that bind themselves to data sources to retrieve data and automatically receive notifications when another record becomes current. You can then turn these classes into COM components so that you can reuse them more easily. I also illustrate how to create a custom version of the ADO Data control, a feat that wasn't possible in Visual Basic 5 (whose binding capabilities permitted you to create data consumer controls only, not data sources). All the data-aware classes you create can be used exactly as data-aware objects provided by Visual Basic itself, such as the DataEnvironment designer and the ADO Data control.

DATA SOURCE CLASSES

To create a data source class, you need to follow a few elementary steps. First add a reference to the Microsoft ActiveX Data Objects 2.0 (or 2.1) Library. Then set the *DataSourceBehavior* attribute of the class to 1-vbDataSource, which automatically adds a reference to the Microsoft Data Source Interfaces type library (Msdatsrc.tlb). You can now use a new *GetDataMember* event, the *DataMembers* property, and the

DataMemberChanged method of the class. You can set the *DataSourceBehavior* attribute to the value 1-vbDataSource in Private classes in any type of project or in Public classes in ActiveX DLL projects, but you can't do that in ActiveX EXE projects because the data source interfaces can't work across processes. You can also create a data source class by selecting the appropriate template when you add a new class module to the current project: In this case, you'll get a class with some skeleton code already present, but you have to add a reference to the Msdatsrc.tlb library manually. You can also create a data source class using the Data Form Wizard.

The *GetDataMember* Event

The key to building a data source is the code that you write in the *GetDataMember* event. This event receives a *DataMember* argument—a string that identifies which particular member the data consumer is requesting—and a *Data* argument declared as Object. In the simplest case, you can ignore the first argument and return an object that supports the necessary ADO interfaces in the *Data* argument. You can return an ADO Recordset, another data source class, or an OLEDBSimpleProvider class that you've created elsewhere in the application (as described in the "OLE DB Simple Providers" section later in this chapter).

I've prepared a demonstration program that builds on an ArrayDataSource class, whose source code is on the companion CD. The purpose of this class is to let you browse the contents of a two-dimensional array of Variants using bound controls: You can load data into an array, pass the array to the *SetArray* method of the class, and then display its contents in a DataGrid or another data-aware control. The user can modify existing values, delete records, and even add new ones. When the editing is completed, the client code can call the class's *GetArray* method to retrieve the new contents of the array.

The ArrayDataSource class, like most data source classes, incorporates an ADO Recordset object. The *SetArray* method creates the Recordset, adds the fields whose names have been passed in the *Fields* array argument, and then fills the Recordset with the data contained in the *Values* array passed as an argument to the method:

```
Private rs As ADODB.Recordset       ' Module-level variable

Sub SetArray(Values As Variant, Fields As Variant)
    Dim row As Long, col As Long
    ' Build a new ADO Recordset.
    If Not (rs Is Nothing) Then
        If rs.Status = adStateOpen Then rs.Close
    End If
    Set rs = New ADODB.Recordset
    ' Create the Fields collection.
    For col = LBound(Fields) To UBound(Fields)
        rs.Fields.Append Fields(col), adBSTR
    Next
```

```
' Move data from the array to the Recordset.
rs.Open
For row = LBound(Values) To UBound(Values)
    rs.AddNew
    For col = 0 To UBound(Values, 2)
        rs(col) = Values(row, col)
    Next
Next
rs.MoveFirst
' Inform consumers that the data has changed.
DataMemberChanged ""
End Sub
```

The call to the *DataMemberChanged* method informs bound controls (more generally, data consumers) that a new data set is available. Both arguments to the *SetArray* method are declared as Variants, so you can pass them an array of any data type. After the Recordset has been created, it can be safely returned in the *GetDataMember* event. This event fires the first time a data consumer asks for data and whenever the *DataMemberChanged* method is called:

```
' Return the Recordset to the data consumer.
Private Sub Class_GetDataMember(DataMember As String, Data As Object)
    Set Data = Recordset
End Sub


' Provides "Safe" access to the Recordset,
' in that it raises a meaningful error if the Recordset is set to Nothing.
Property Get Recordset() As ADODB.Recordset
    If rs Is Nothing Then
        Err.Raise 1001, , "No data array has been provided"
    Else
        Set Recordset = rs
    End If
End Property
```

The event procedure references the Private *rs* variable through the Public *Recordset* property; this raises an error with a meaningful message instead of the standard "Object variable or With block variable not set" error message that would be raised if the client code assigns the data source to a bound control before calling the *SetArray* method. A data source class should also expose all the properties and methods that you expect from an ADO source, including all the navigational *Movexxxx* methods, the *AddNew* and *Delete* methods, the *EOF* and *BOF* properties, and so on. The following code simply delegates to the inner *rs* variable through the *Recordset* property, which ensures that proper error checking is performed:

```
' Partial listing of properties and methods
Public Property Get EOF() As Boolean
```

(continued)

```
        EOF = Recordset.EOF
End Property

Public Property Get BOF() As Boolean
        BOF = Recordset.BOF
End Property

Public Property Get RecordCount() As Long
        RecordCount = Recordset.RecordCount
End Property

Sub MoveFirst()
        Recordset.MoveFirst
End Sub

Sub MovePrevious()
        Recordset.MovePrevious
End Sub
' And so on...
```

The code in the class needs to convert the data stored in the Recordset back into a Variant array when the client application requests it. This conversion occurs in the *GetArray* method:

```
Function GetArray() As Variant
    Dim numFields As Long, row As Long, col As Long
    Dim Bookmark As Variant
    ' Remember the current record pointer.
    Bookmark = Recordset.Bookmark

    ' Create the result array, and fill it with data from the Recordset.
    numFields = rs.Fields.Count
    ReDim Values(0 To rs.RecordCount - 1, 0 To numFields - 1) As String
    ' Fill the array with data from the Recordset.
    rs.MoveFirst
    For row = 0 To rs.RecordCount - 1
        For col = 0 To numFields - 1
            Values(row, col) = rs(col)
        Next
        rs.MoveNext
    Next
    GetArray = Values
    ' Restore the record pointer.
    rs.Bookmark = Bookmark
End Function
```

The complete version of the class on the companion CD supports additional properties, including the *BOFAction* and *EOFAction* properties, which let the class behave similarly to a Data control. To test-drive the ArrayDataSource class, create a form with three TextBox controls and a set of navigational buttons, as shown in Figure 18-1. Then add this code in the *Form_Load* event procedure:

```
Dim MyData As New ArrayDataSource          ' Module-level variable

Private Sub Form_Load()
    ReDim Fields(0 To 2) As String          ' Create the Fields array.
    Fields(0) = "ID"
    Fields(1) = "Name"
    Fields(2) = "Department"

    ReDim Values(0 To 3, 0 To 2) As String  ' Create the Values array.
    Values(0, 0) = 100                       ' ID field
    Values(0, 1) = "Christine Johnson"       ' Name field
    Values(0, 2) = "Marketing"               ' Department field
    ' Fill other records (omitted...)
    MyData.SetArray Values, Fields           ' Initialize the data source.

    ' Bind the controls.
    Set txtID.DataSource = MyData
    txtID.DataField = "ID"
    Set txtName.DataSource = MyData
    txtName.DataField = "Name"
    Set txtDepartment.DataSource = MyData
    txtDepartment.DataField = "Department"
End Sub
```

When the client program needs to retrieve the data edited by the user, it invokes the *GetArray* method:

```
Dim Values() As String
Values = MyData.GetArray()
```

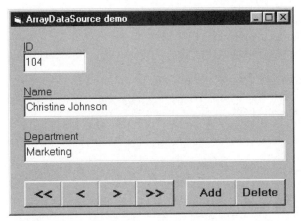

Figure 18-1. *A client form to test-drive the ArrayDataSource class.*

Support for the *DataMember* Property

The ArrayDataSource class is the simplest type of data source class that you can build with Visual Basic 6 and doesn't take into account the *DataMember* argument passed to the *GetDataMember* event. You can greatly enhance your class by adding support for the *DataMember* property in bound controls. All you have to do is build and return a different Recordset, depending on the *DataMember* you receive.

I've prepared a sample data source class, named FileTextDataSource, which binds its consumers to the fields of a semicolon-delimited text file. If you want to bind one or more controls to such a class, you must specify the name of the text file in the control's *DataMember* property:

```
' Code in the client form
Dim MyData As New TextFileDataSource

Private Sub Form_Load()
    ' This is the path for data files.
    MyData.FilePath = DB_PATH
    ' Bind the text controls. (Their DataField was set at design time.)
    Dim ctrl As Control
    For Each ctrl In Controls
        If TypeOf ctrl Is TextBox Then
            ctrl.DataMember = "Publishers"
            Set ctrl.DataSource = MyData
        End If
    Next
End Sub
```

The TextFileDataSource class module contains more code than the simpler ArrayDataSource class does, but most of it is necessary just to parse the text file and move its contents into the private Recordset. The first line in the text file is assumed to be the semicolon-delimited list of field names:

```
Const DEFAULT_EXT = ".DAT"          ' Default extension for text files
Private rs As ADODB.Recordset
Private m_DataMember As String, m_File As String, m_FilePath As String

Private Sub Class_GetDataMember(DataMember As String, Data As Object)
    If DataMember = "" Then Exit Sub
    ' Re-create the Recordset only if necessary.
    If DataMember <> m_DataMember Or (rs Is Nothing) Then
        LoadRecordset DataMember
    End If
    Set Data = rs
End Sub


Private Sub LoadRecordset(ByVal DataMember As String)
```

```
    Dim File As String, fnum As Integer
    Dim row As Long, col As Long, Text As String
    Dim Lines() As String, Values() As String

    On Error GoTo ErrorHandler
    File = m_FilePath & DataMember
    If InStr(File, ".") = 0 Then File = File & DEFAULT_EXT

    ' Read the contents of the file in memory.
    fnum = FreeFile()
    Open File For Input As #fnum
    Text = Input$(LOF(fnum), #fnum)
    Close #fnum

    ' Close the current Recordset, and create a new one.
    CloseRecordset
    Set rs = New ADODB.Recordset
    ' Convert the long string into an array of records.
    Lines() = Split(Text, vbCrLf)
    ' Get the field names, and append them to the Fields collection.
    Values() = Split(Lines(0), ";")
    For col = 0 To UBound(Values)
        rs.Fields.Append Values(col), adBSTR
    Next

    ' Read the actual values, and append them to the Recordset.
    rs.Open
    For row = 1 To UBound(Lines)
        rs.AddNew
        Values() = Split(Lines(row), ";")
        For col = 0 To UBound(Values)
            rs(col) = Values(col)
        Next
    Next
    rs.MoveFirst

    ' Remember DataMember and File for the next time.
    m_DataMember = DataMember
    m_File = File
    Exit Sub
ErrorHandler:
    Err.Raise 1001, , "Unable to load data from " & DataMember
End Sub

' If the Recordset is still open, close it.
Private Sub CloseRecordset()
    If Not (rs Is Nothing) Then rs.Close
    m_DataMember = ""
End Sub
```

The Visual Basic documentation suggests that you return the same Recordset when multiple consumers ask for the same *DataMember*. For this reason, the class stores the *DataMember* argument in the *m_DataMember* private variable and reloads the text file only if strictly necessary. When I traced the source code, however, I found that the *GetDataMember* event is called just once with a nonempty string in the *DataMember* argument when the client program assigns the instance of the class to the *DataSource* property of the first bound control. Each time after that, the event receives an empty string.

The TextFileDataSource class on the companion CD includes many other features that I don't have room to describe here. Figure 18-2 shows the demonstration program, which loads two forms, a record-based view of a text file and a table-based view of the same file. Because the controls on both forms are bound to the same instance of the TextFileDataSource class, any time you move the record pointer or edit a field value in one form the contents of the other form are immediately updated. The class also exposes a *Flush* method, which writes the new values back to disk. This method is automatically invoked during the *Class_Terminate* event, so when the last form unloads and the data source object is released, the *Flush* method automatically updates the data file.

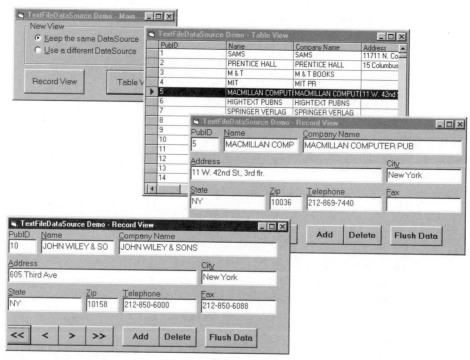

Figure 18-2. *The demonstration program of the TextFileDataSource class can open different views of the same data file. If the views use the same instance of the class, they're automatically synchronized.*

The TextFileDataSource class also offers an example of how you can add items to the DataMembers collection to inform data consumers about the available DataMembers items. The class module implements this feature in the *Property Let FilePath* procedure, where it loads the collection with all the data files in the specified directory:

```
Public Property Let FilePath(ByVal newValue As String)
    If newValue <> m_FilePath Then
        m_FilePath = newValue
        If m_FilePath <> "" And Right$(m_FilePath, 1) <> "\" Then
            m_FilePath = m_FilePath & "\"
        End If
        RefreshDataMembers
    End If
End Property

' Rebuild the DataMembers collection.
Private Sub RefreshDataMembers()
    Dim File As String
    DataMembers.Clear
    ' Load all the file names in the directory.
    File = Dir$(m_FilePath & "*" & DEFAULT_EXT)
    Do While Len(File)
        ' Drop the default extension.
        DataMembers.Add Left$(File, Len(File) - Len(DEFAULT_EXT))
        File = Dir$()
    Loop
End Sub
```

The TextFileDataSource class is bound to its consumers at run time. Therefore, there's no point in filling the DataMembers collection because the clients can't query this information. But this technique becomes useful when you're creating ActiveX controls that work as data sources because the list of all available DataMembers items appears right in the Properties windows of the controls that are bound to the ActiveX control.

Custom ActiveX Data Controls

Creating a custom Data control is simple because ActiveX controls can work as data sources exactly as classes and COM components can. So you can create a user interface that meets your needs, such as the one depicted in Figure 18-3, set the UserControl's *DataSourceBehavior* attribute to 1-vbDataSource, and add all the properties and methods that developers expect from a Data control, such as *ConnectionString*, *RecordSource*, *EOFAction*, and *BOFAction*. If you exactly duplicate the ADO Data interface, you might even be able to replace a standard ADO control with your custom Data control without changing a single line of code in client forms.

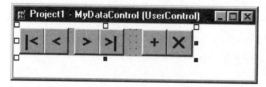

Figure 18-3. *A custom Data control that includes buttons to add and delete records.*

A custom Data control that connects to regular ADO sources doesn't need to manufacture an ADO recordset itself, as the data source classes I've shown you so far have. Instead, it internally creates an ADO Connection object and an ADO Recordset object based on the values of Public properties and then passes the Recordset to consumers in the *GetDataMember* event. The following code is a partial listing of the MyDataControl UserControl module. (The complete source code is on the companion CD.)

```
Private cn As ADODB.Connection, rs As ADODB.Recordset
Private CnIsInvalid As Boolean, RsIsInvalid As Boolean

Private Sub UserControl_GetDataMember(DataMember As String, Data As Object)
    On Error GoTo Error_Handler
    ' Re-create the connection if necessary.
    If cn Is Nothing Or CnIsInvalid Then
        ' If the Recordset and the connection are open, close them.
        CloseConnection
        ' Validate the ConnectionString property.
        If Trim$(m_ConnectionString) = "" Then
            Err.Raise 1001, , "ConnectionString can't be an empty string"
        Else
            ' Open the connection.
            Set cn = New ADODB.Connection
            If m_Provider <> "" Then cn.Provider = m_Provider
            cn.Open m_ConnectionString
            CnIsInvalid = False
        End If
    End If

    ' Re-create the Recordset if necessary.
    If rs Is Nothing Or RsIsInvalid Then
        Set rs = New ADODB.Recordset
        rs.CursorLocation = m_CursorLocation
        rs.Open RecordSource, cn, CursorType, LockType, CommandType
        rs.MoveFirst
        RsIsInvalid = False
    End If
    ' Return the Recordset to the data consumer.
    Set Data = rs
    Exit Sub
```

```
Error_Handler:
    Err.Raise Err.Number, Ambient.DisplayName, Err.Description
    CloseConnection
End Sub

' Close the Recordset and the connection in the correct way.
Private Sub CloseRecordset()
    If Not rs Is Nothing Then
        If rs.State <> adStateClosed Then rs.Close
        Set rs = Nothing
    End If
End Sub

Private Sub CloseConnection()
    CloseRecordset
    If Not cn Is Nothing Then
        If cn.State <> adStateClosed Then cn.Close
        Set cn = Nothing
    End If
End Sub
```

A custom Data control also differs from data source classes in that the code to navigate the Recordset is included in the UserControl module. In the MyDataControl module, the six navigational buttons belong to the *cmdMove* control array, which slightly simplifies their management:

```
Private Sub cmdMove_Click(Index As Integer)
    If rs Is Nothing Then Exit Sub    ' Exit if the Recordset doesn't exist.
    Select Case Index
        Case 0
            rs.MoveFirst
        Case 1
            If rs.BOF Then
                Select Case BOFAction
                    Case mdcBOFActionEnum.mdcBOFActionMoveFirst
                        rs.MoveFirst
                    Case mdcBOFActionEnum.mdcBOFActionBOF
                        ' Do nothing.
                End Select
            Else
                rs.MovePrevious
            End If
        Case 2
            If rs.EOF = False Then rs.MoveNext
            If rs.EOF = True Then
                Select Case EOFAction
                    Case mdcEOFActionEnum.mdcEOFActionAddNew
                        rs.AddNew
```

(continued)

```
                    Case mdcEOFActionEnum.mdcEOFActionMoveLast
                        rs.MoveLast
                    Case mdcEOFActionEnum.mdcEOFActionEOF
                        ' Do nothing.
                End Select
            End If
        Case 3
            rs.MoveLast
        Case 4
            rs.AddNew
        Case 5
            rs.Delete
    End Select
End Sub
```

Each time the client assigns a value to a property that affects the Connection or the Recordset, the code in the MyDataControl module resets the *cn* or the *rs* variables to Nothing and sets the *CnIsInvalid* or *RsIsInvalid* variables to True so that in the next *GetDataMember* event the connection or the Recordset is correctly rebuilt:

```
Public Property Get ConnectionString() As String
    ConnectionString = m_ConnectionString
End Property

Public Property Let ConnectionString(ByVal New_ConnectionString As String)
    m_ConnectionString = New_ConnectionString
    PropertyChanged "ConnectionString"
    CnIsInvalid = True
End Property
```

Remember to close the connection when the control is about to terminate:

```
Private Sub UserControl_Terminate()
    CloseConnection
End Sub
```

DATA CONSUMER CLASSES

A *data consumer* is a class or a component that binds itself to a data source. There are two types of data consumer objects: simple consumer and complex consumer. A simple consumer class or component binds one or more of its properties to the current row in the data source and so resembles an ActiveX control with multiple bindable properties. A complex consumer can bind its properties to multiple rows in the data source and resembles a grid control.

Simple Data Consumers

When you're transferring data from sources to consumers, consumers are passive entities. The object that actively moves data from the source to the consumer and back is the BindingCollection object.

The BindingCollection object

To create a BindingCollection object, you need to reference the Microsoft Data Binding Collection library in the References dialog box. The BindingCollection's most important members are the *DataSource* property and the *Add* method. To set up a connection between a data source and a data consumer, you need to assign the data source object to the BindingCollection's *DataSource* property and then call the *Add* method for each data consumer that must be linked to the source. The complete syntax for the *Add* method follows:

```
Add(BoundObj, PropertyName, DataField, [DataFormat], [Key]) As Binding
```

BoundObj is the data consumer object, *PropertyName* is the name of the property in the data consumer that's bound to a field of the data source, *DataField* is the name of the field in the source, *DataFormat* is an optional StdDataFormat object that affects how data is formatted during the transfer to and from the consumer, and *Key* is the key of the new Binding object in the collection. You can call multiple *Add* methods to bind multiple consumers or multiple properties of the same consumer.

A common data source is the ADO Recordset object, but you can also use a DataEnvironment object, an OLE DB Simple Provider, and any data source class or component that you've defined in code. The following code shows how you can bind two TextBox controls to fields of a database table through an ADO Recordset:

```
Const DBPath = "C:\Program Files\Microsoft Visual Studio\Vb98\NWind.mdb"
Dim cn As New ADODB.Connection, rs As New ADODB.Recordset
Dim bndcol As New BindingCollection

' Open the Recordset.
cn.Open "Provider=Microsoft.Jet.OLEDB.3.51;Data Source=" & DBPATH
rs.Open "Employees", cn, adOpenStatic, adLockReadOnly
' Use the BindingCollection object to bind two TextBox controls to the
' FirstName and LastName fields of the Employees table.
Set bndcol.DataSource = rs
bndcol.Add txtFirstName, "Text", "FirstName", , "FirstName"
bndcol.Add txtLastName, "Text", "LastName", , "LastName"
```

You can control how data is formatted in the consumer by defining a StdDataFormat object, setting its *Type* and *Format* properties, and then passing it as the fourth argument of a BindingCollection's *Add* method, as the code on the following page demonstrates.

```
Dim DateFormat As New StdDataFormat
DateFormat.Type = fmtCustom
DateFormat.Format = "mmmm dd, yyyy"
' One StdDataFormat object can serve multiple consumers.
bndcol.Add txtBirthDate, "Text", "BirthDate", DateFormat, "BirthDate"
bndcol.Add txtHireDate, "Text", "HireDate", DateFormat, "HireDate"
```

If the data source exposes multiple DataMember objects, as is the case for DataEnvironment objects, you select which one is bound to data consumers by using the BindingCollection's *DataMember* property, exactly as you do when you bind controls to an ADO Data control.

The BindingCollection object exposes a few other properties and methods that give you more control over the binding process. The *UpdateMode* enumerated property determines when data is updated in the data source: For the default value, 1-vbUpdateWhenPropertyChanges, the source is updated as soon as a property's value changes, whereas the value 2-vbUpdateWhenRowChanges causes the updates to the source only when the record pointer moves to another record. When the value is 0-vbUsePropertyAttributes, the decision when to update the source depends on the state of the Update Immediate option in the Procedure Attributes dialog box.

Each time you execute an *Add* method, you actually add a Binding object to the collection. You can later query the Binding object's properties to acquire information about the binding process. Each Binding object exposes the following properties: *Object* (a reference to the bound data consumer), *PropertyName* (the name of the bound property), *DataField* (the field in the source), *DataChanged* (True if data in the consumer has been changed), *DataFormat* (the StdDataFormat object used to format data), and *Key* (the key of the Binding object in the collection). For example, you can determine whether the value in a consumer has changed by executing the following code:

```
Dim bind As Binding, changed As Boolean
For Each bind in bndcol
    changed = changed Or bndcol.DataChanged
Next
If changed Then Debug.Print "Data has been changed"
```

If you assigned a key to a Binding object, you can directly read and modify its properties:

```
' Set the ForeColor of the TextBox control bound to the HireDate field.
bndcol("HireDate").Object.ForeColor = vbRed
```

The *UpdateControls* method of the BindingCollection object updates all the consumers with values from the current row in the data source and resets the *DataChanged* properties of all Binding objects to False.

Finally, you can trap any error that occurs in the binding mechanism by using the BindingCollection's *Error* event. To trap this event from a BindingCollection object, you must have declared it using a *WithEvents* clause:

```
Dim WithEvents bndcol As BindingCollection

Private Sub bndcol_Error(ByVal Error As Long, ByVal Description As String,_
    ByVal Binding As MSBind.Binding, fCancelDisplay As Boolean)
    ' Deal here with binding errors.
End Sub
```

Error is the error code, *Description* is the error description, *Binding* is the Binding object that caused the error, and *fCancelDisplay* is a Boolean argument that you can set to False if you don't want to display the standard error message.

> **CAUTION**   When binding a property of a control to a field in the data source, you should ensure that the control correctly sends the necessary notification to the binding mechanism when the property changes. For example, you can bind the *Caption* property of a Label or Frame control to a data source, but if you then change the value of the *Caption* property through code the control doesn't inform the source that the data has changed. Consequently, the new value isn't written to the database. In this case, you must force the notification yourself by using the BindingCollection object's *DataChanged* property.

Data consumer classes and components

To create a simple data consumer class, you only need to set the *DataBindingBehavior* attribute of the class to the value 1-vbSimpleBound in the Properties window. This setting adds two new methods that you can use from within the class module: *PropertyChange* and *CanPropertyChange*.

Implementing a simple data consumer class or component is similar to creating an ActiveX control that can be bound to a data source. In the *Property Let* procedures of all the bound properties, you must make sure that a property value can change by invoking the *CanPropertyChange* function. Then you call the *PropertyChange* method to inform the binding mechanism that the value has indeed changed. (Be aware that the *CanPropertyChange* method always returns True in Visual Basic, as I explained in the "*PropertyChanged* and *CanPropertyChange* Methods" section of Chapter 17.) The following code is taken from the demonstration program on the companion CD and shows how the sample CEmployee data consumer class implements its *FirstName* property:

```
' In the CEmployee class module
Dim m_FirstName As String

Property Get FirstName() As String
    FirstName = m_FirstName
End Property
```

(continued)

```
Property Let FirstName(ByVal newValue As String)
    If newValue <> m_FirstName Then
        If CanPropertyChange("FirstName") Then
            m_FirstName = newValue
            PropertyChanged "FirstName"
        End If
    End If
End Property
```

You bind the properties of a data consumer class to the fields in a data source using a BindingCollection object. The binding operation can be performed in the client form or module (as you saw in the previous section) or inside the data consumer class itself. The latter solution is usually preferable because it encapsulates the code in the class and prevents it from being scattered in all its clients. If you follow this approach, you must provide a method that lets clients pass a data source to the class: This can be a data source class, an ADO Data control or Recordset, or a DataEnvironment object. The class can use this reference as an argument to the *DataSource* property of an internal BindingCollection object:

```
' In the CEmployee class module
Private bndcol As New BindingCollection

Property Get DataSource() As Object
    Set DataSource = bndcol.DataSource
End Property

Property Set DataSource(ByVal newValue As Object)
    Set bndcol = New BindingCollection
    Set bndcol.DataSource = newValue
    bndcol.Add Me, "FirstName", "FirstName", , "FirstName"
    bndcol.Add Me, "LastName", "LastName", , "LastName"
    bndcol.Add Me, "BirthDate", "BirthDate", , "BirthDate"
End Property
```

The following code shows how a client form can bind the CEmployee class to a Recordset:

```
Dim cn As New ADODB.Connection, rs As New ADODB.Recordset
Dim employee As New CEmployee
cn.Open "Provider=Microsoft.Jet.OLEDB.3.51;" _
    & "Data Source=C:\Program Files\Microsoft Visual Studio\Vb98\NWind.mdb"
rs.Open "Employees", cn, adOpenKeyset, adLockOptimistic
Set employee.DataSource = rs
```

When the program modifies a value of a bound property in the data consumer class, the corresponding field in the data source is updated, provided that the data source is updatable. But the precise moment the field is updated depends on the *UpdateMode* setting of the BindingCollection object. If *UpdateMode* is 2-vbUpdateWhenRowChanges, the data source is updated only when another record becomes the current record, whereas if the setting is 1-vbUpdateWhenPropertyChanges the Recordset is updated immediately. If you set *UpdateMode* = 0-vbUsePropertyAttributes, the data source is updated immediately only if the property is marked with the *Update Immediately* attribute in the Procedure Attributes dialog box.

> **NOTE** Even if the data source is an ADO Recordset linked to a database, updating the data source doesn't mean that the database is immediately updated, but only that the new value is assigned to the Field's *Value* property. A way to force the update of the underlying database is to execute the Recordset's *Move* method using 0 as the argument. This doesn't actually move the record pointer but flushes to the database the current contents of the Fields collection. Oddly, the Recordset's *Update* method doesn't work in this situation.

Here's another peculiarity in the implementation of this feature: The setting 0-vbUpdateWhenPropertyChanges doesn't seem to work as the documentation states, and it doesn't immediately update the value in the Recordset. The only way to update the Recordset when a property changes is by using the setting 0-vbUsePropertyAttributes and ticking the Update Immediate check box in the Procedure Attributes dialog box.

Complex Data Consumers

Building a complex data consumer is slightly more difficult than building a simple data consumer. The reason for the additional difficulty is mostly the lack of good and complete documentation sources. The first step in creating a complex data consumer class is to set the *DataBindingBehavior* to the value 2-vbComplexBound. Alternatively, you can select the Complex Data Consumer template from the template gallery when you create a new class module. In both cases, you'll find that a couple of properties—*DataMember* and *DataSource*—have been added to the class module:

```
Public Property Get DataSource() As DataSource
End Property
Public Property Set DataSource(ByVal objDataSource As DataSource)
End Property

Public Property Get DataMember() As DataMember
End Property
Public Property Let DataMember(ByVal DataMember As DataMember)
End Property
```

When you set *DataBindingBehavior* to 2-vbComplexBound in a UserControl module, Visual Basic doesn't create the templates for these two properties for you— you must do it manually.

ActiveX controls that work as complex data consumers are typically gridlike controls. They expose the *DataMember* and *DataSource* properties, but unlike ActiveX controls that behave as simple data consumers, these properties aren't Extender properties. You can't count on the automatic binding mechanism that you can specify in the Procedure Attributes dialog box, and you must implement these two properties all by yourself.

Now you need to add a few type libraries in the References dialog box. When you're building a complex data consumer, you need the Microsoft Data Sources Interfaces (Msdatsrc.tlb), the Microsoft Data Binding Collection (msbind.dll), and, of course, the Microsoft ActiveX Data Objects 2.0 (or 2.1) Library. The first of these libraries exposes the DataSource interface, which is supported by all the objects that can work as data sources, such as the ADO Recordset, the ADO Data control, and the DataEnvironment object.

On the companion CD, you'll find the complete source code for the ProductGrid ActiveX control, shown in Figure 18-4. This ActiveX control builds on a ListView control to give you a custom view of the Products table of the NWind.mdb database. I used the ActiveX Control Interface Wizard to create most of the properties and events of this control, such as *Font*, *BackColor*, *ForeColor*, *CheckBoxes*, *FullRowSelection*, and all the mouse and keyboards events. The only routines I had to write manually are those that implement the binding mechanism. The declaration section of the Product-Grid module contains the following private variables:

```
Private WithEvents rs As ADODB.Recordset
Private bndcol As New BindingCollection
Private m_DataMember As String
```

Implementing the *DataMember* property is as easy as creating a wrapper around the private *m_DataMember* string variable:

```
Public Property Get DataMember() As String
    DataMember = m_DataMember
End Property
Public Property Let DataMember(ByVal newValue As String)
    m_DataMember = newValue
End Property
```

The *Property Let DataSource* procedure is where the binding process actually takes place. This procedure is called when the class or the control is bound to its data source. The binding can be done explicitly via code, or it can be done implicitly at form loading if you set the *DataSource* property in the Properties window of an ActiveX control that works as a complex data consumer. This is the implementation of the *DataSource* property for the CustomerGrid control:

```
Public Property Get DataSource() As DataSource
    ' Simply delegate to the Recordset's DataMember property.
    If Not (rs Is Nothing) Then
        Set DataSource = rs.DataSource
    End If
End Property
```

```
Public Property Set DataSource(ByVal newValue As DataSource)
    If Not Ambient.UserMode Then Exit Property
    If Not (rs Is Nothing) Then
        ' If the new value equals the old one, exit right now.
        If rs.DataSource Is newValue Then Exit Property
        If (newValue Is Nothing) Then
            ' The Recordset is being closed. (The program is shutting
            ' down.)  Flush the current record.
            Select Case rs.LockType
                Case adLockBatchOptimistic
                    rs.UpdateBatch
                Case adLockOptimistic, adLockPessimistic
                    rs.Update
                Case Else
            End Select
        End If
    End If
    If Not (newValue Is Nothing) Then
        Set rs = New ADODB.Recordset        ' Re-create the Recordset.
        rs.DataMember = m_DataMember
        Set rs.DataSource = newValue
        Refresh                             ' Reload all data.
    End If
End Property
```

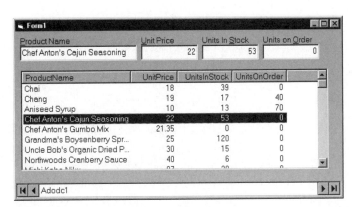

Figure 18-4. *The grid on this form is an instance of the ProductGrid ActiveX control.*

Notice that the previous routines don't include any reference to the UserControl's constituent controls. In fact, you can reuse them in nearly every class or component without changing a single line of code. The code specific to each particular component is located in the *Refresh* method:

```
Sub Refresh()
    ' Exit if in design mode.
    If Not Ambient.UserMode Then Exit Sub
```

(continued)

```
' Clear the ListView, and exit if the Recordset is empty or closed.
ListView1.ListItems.Clear
If rs Is Nothing Then Exit Sub
If rs.State <> adStateOpen Then Exit Sub
' Move to the first record, but remember the current position.
Dim Bookmark As Variant, FldName As Variant
Bookmark = rs.Bookmark
rs.MoveFirst

' Load the data from the Recordset into the ListView.
Do Until rs.EOF
    With ListView1.ListItems.Add(, , rs("ProductName"))
        .ListSubItems.Add , , rs("UnitPrice")
        .ListSubItems.Add , , rs("UnitsInStock")
        .ListSubItems.Add , , rs("UnitsOnOrder")
        ' Remember the Bookmark of this record.
        .Tag = rs.Bookmark
    End With
    rs.MoveNext
Loop
' Restore the pointer to the current record.
rs.Bookmark = Bookmark

' Bind the properties to the Recordset.
Set bndcol = New BindingCollection
bndcol.DataMember = m_DataMember
Set bndcol.DataSource = rs
For Each FldName In Array("ProductName", "UnitPrice", "UnitsInStock", _
    "UnitsOnOrder")
    bndcol.Add Me, FldName, FldName
Next
End Sub
```

This is a rather simple implementation of a data-aware grid ActiveX control based on the ListView common control. A more sophisticated control would probably avoid loading the entire Recordset all at once in the ListView and would instead exploit a buffering algorithm to improve performance and reduce memory consumption.

A complex data consumer has to do a couple of things to meet the user's expectations. First, it should change the current record when the user clicks on another grid row. Second, it should highlight a record when it becomes the current record. In the ProductGrid control, the first goal is met by code in the ListView's *ItemClick* event; this code exploits the fact that the control stores the value of the *Bookmark* property for each record in the Recordset in the *Tag* property of all the ItemList elements:

```
Private Sub ListView1_ItemClick(ByVal Item As MSComctlLib.ListItem)
    rs.Bookmark = Item.Tag
End Sub
```

To highlight a different row in the ListView control when it becomes the current record, you need to write code in the Recordset's *MoveComplete* event:

```
Private Sub rs_MoveComplete(ByVal adReason As ADODB.EventReasonEnum, _
    ByVal pError As ADODB.Error, adStatus As ADODB.EventStatusEnum, _
    ByVal pRecordset As ADODB.Recordset)
    Dim Item As ListItem
    ' Exit if in a BOF or EOF condition.
    If rs.EOF Or rs.BOF Then Exit Sub
    ' Highlight the item corresponding to the current record.
    For Each Item In ListView1.ListItems
        If Item.Tag = rs.Bookmark Then
            Set ListView1.SelectedItem = Item
            Exit For
        End If
    Next
    ' Ensure that the item is visible.
    If Not (ListView1.SelectedItem Is Nothing) Then
        ListView1.SelectedItem.EnsureVisible
    End If
    ListView1.Refresh
End Sub
```

The source code for the demonstration program exploits a technique that avoids running the code in the *MoveComplete* event procedure if the move was caused by an action inside the UserControl (in which case, the control already knows which row in the grid should be highlighted).

You can use the ProductGrid ActiveX control exactly as you would use a DataGrid or another data-aware grid control. I found, however, that the binding mechanism still has some rough edges. For example, if you refresh an ADO Data control, a complex data consumer authored in Visual Basic doesn't seem to get any notification. Therefore, if you need to change one or more properties in an ADO Data control and then execute its *Refresh* method, you also have to reassign the ADO Data control to the *DataSource* property of the ProductGrid control:

```
Adodc1.ConnectionString = "Provider=Microsoft.Jet.OLEDB.3.51;" _
    & "Data Source=C:\Program Files\Microsoft VisualStudio\Vb98\NWind.mdb"
Adodc1.Refresh
Set ProductGrid1.DataSource = Adodc1
```

OLE DB SIMPLE PROVIDERS

Visual Basic 6 provides you with the capability of building OLE DB Simple Providers— that is, components that can be registered in the system and that can be used by standard data sources to connect to data in a proprietary format. This capability can be useful in countless situations. For example, during the porting of a legacy application from MS-DOS to Microsoft Windows, you often need to continue to read data in the old format. Thanks to a custom OLE DB Simple Provider, you can access the old data from the new program using standard syntax and you can switch to a standard (and more efficient) OLE DB provider when the porting of the code is complete and you're ready to convert the database data to SQL Server or another major database engine for which a standard OLE DB provider exists.

Before you get too enthusiastic, keep in mind that Visual Basic doesn't allow you to write full-fledged OLE DB providers such as those that Microsoft has created for the Microsoft Jet Database engine, SQL Server, or Oracle. An OLE DB Simple Provider doesn't support transactions, Command objects, and batch updates, just to mention a few of its limitations. Another problem with these providers is that they don't expose information about the structure of the data: They can return the name of a column, but they don't expose a column's data type or maximum length. OLE DB Simple Providers are especially good at exposing table data that can be stored in an array in memory. These restrictions don't keep you from doing interesting things with OLE DB Simple Providers, however. For example, you can create a provider that accesses data encrypted with a proprietary algorithm or a provider that loads data from Microsoft Excel or Microsoft Outlook programs, or from any other program that you can control through Automation.

> **NOTE**   From the perspective of an OLE DB provider, *data consumers* are the components that we've called *data sources* in the earlier parts of this chapter. In other words, the clients of an OLE DB provider are the objects that a Visual Basic program perceives as data sources, such as the ADO Data control or the DataEnvironment object.

To illustrate the concepts underlying the construction of an OLE DB Simple Provider, I built a sample provider that connects to a semicolon-delimited text file. It expects that the first line of the file contains all the field names. When the provider is invoked, it opens the data file and loads it into an array in memory. This example is similar to the one found in the Visual Basic documentation, but my solution is more concise and more efficient because it uses an array of arrays to store individual records. (See Chapter 4 for a complete description of arrays of arrays.) The code is highly generic, and you can recycle most of the routines in other types of providers. You can find the full code on the companion CD.

The Structure of an OLE DB Simple Provider

The three pieces that make up an OLE DB Simple Provider are the Msdaosp.dll library, which is provided with Visual Basic 6 (more precisely, it belongs to the OLE DB SDK), and two classes that you write in Visual Basic: the OLE DB Simple Provider class and the data source class.

Msdaosp.dll is what data consumers actually see. Its primary job is to add all the functionality of a full-fledged OLE DB provider that's missing in the OLE DB Simple Provider class that you write in Visual Basic. When the DLL is invoked by a data consumer, it instantiates the data source class exposed by your project and calls one of its methods. The data source class returns the DLL an instance of the OLE DB Simple Provider class; from then on, the DLL communicates with the OLE DB Simple Provider through the OLEDBSimpleProvider interface.

To implement the sample OLE DB Simple Provider, you start by creating an ActiveX DLL project and assigning it the name TextOLEDBProvider. Add two type libraries to the References dialog box: the Microsoft Data Source Interface library (Msdatsrc.tlb) and the Microsoft OLE DB Simple Provider 1.5 Library (Simpdata.tbl). You can optionally add a reference to the OLE DB Errors Type Library (Msdaer.dll), which includes all the symbolic constants for error codes.

When all the references are in place, you can add two Public classes to the project. The first class module—named TextOSP—will implement the OLE DB Simple Provider; the second class module—named TextDataSource—will implement the Data Source object. Let's see how to build these two classes.

The OLE DB Simple Provider Class

The most complicated piece of code in the sample OLE DB Simple Provider project is TextOSP, a PublicNotCreatable class module that implements all the functions that the Msdaosp.dll calls when the consumer reads or writes data. Because the communication between the class and the DLL occurs through the OLEDBSimpleProvider interface, the class must contain an *Implement* keyword in its declaration section:

```
Implements OLEDBSimpleProvider

Const DELIMITER = ";"            ' Change this at will.
Const E_FAIL = &H80004005        ' A typical error code for OLE DB providers

Dim DataArray() As Variant       ' An array of arrays
Dim RowCount As Long             ' Number of rows (records)
Dim ColCount As Long             ' Number of columns (fields)
Dim IsDirty As Boolean           ' True if data has changed
Dim m_FileName As String         ' The path of the data file

Dim Listeners As New Collection
Dim Listener As OLEDBSimpleProviderListener
```

DataArray is an array of Variants that will store the data. Each element corresponds to a record and contains a string array that holds the values of all the fields. The element *DataArray(0)* holds the array with the field names. The *RowCount* and *ColCount* module-level variables hold the number of records and the number of fields, respectively. Whenever a field is written to, the *IsDirty* flag is set to True, so the class knows that it has to update the data file before terminating. The *LoadData* routine loads the data file in memory, and the contents of the file are assigned to the *DataArray* variable:

```
Sub LoadData(FileName As String)
    Dim fnum As Integer, FileText As String
    Dim records() As String, fields() As String
    Dim row As Long, col As Long

    ' Read the file in memory.
    m_FileName = FileName          ' Remember the file name for later.
    fnum = FreeFile
    On Error GoTo ErrorHandler
    Open m_FileName For Input Lock Read Write As #fnum
    FileText = Input(LOF(fnum), #fnum)
    Close #fnum

    ' Split the file into records and fields.
    records = Split(FileText, vbCrLf)
    RowCount = UBound(records)
    ColCount = -1
    ReDim DataArray(0 To RowCount) As Variant

    For row = 0 To RowCount
        fields = Split(records(row), DELIMITER)
        DataArray(row) = fields
    Next
    ' The first record sets ColCount.
    ColCount = UBound(DataArray(0)) + 1
    Exit Sub

ErrorHandler:
    Err.Raise E_FAIL
End Sub
```

The *SaveData* routine writes data back to the text file. This routine is automatically invoked from within the *Class_Terminate* event procedure if the *IsDirty* variable is True:

```
Sub SaveData()
    Dim fnum As Integer, FileText As String
    Dim records() As String, fields() As String
    Dim row As Long, col As Long

    For row = 0 To UBound(DataArray)
        FileText = FileText & Join(DataArray(row), DELIMITER) & vbCrLf
    Next
```

```
' Drop the last CR-LF character pair.
FileText = Left$(FileText, Len(FileText) - 2)
' Write the file.
fnum = FreeFile
On Error GoTo ErrorHandler
Open m_FileName For Output Lock Read Write As #fnum
Print #fnum, FileText;
Close #fnum
IsDirty = False
Exit Sub
ErrorHandler:
Err.Raise E_FAIL
End Sub
```

The rest of the class module implements the OLEDBSimpleProvider interface, which includes 14 functions. Keep in mind that after the *LoadData* routine has loaded the data into *DataArray*, you manipulate data exclusively through this array. Therefore, you can prepare a number of providers by simply modifying the code in the *LoadData* and *SaveData* procedures. The first two methods of the OLEDBSimpleProvider interface return the number of rows and columns in the data source:

```
' Return the exact number of rows.
Private Function OLEDBSimpleProvider_getRowCount() As Long
    OLEDBSimpleProvider_getRowCount = RowCount
End Function

' Return the number of columns.
Private Function OLEDBSimpleProvider_getColumnCount() As Long
    OLEDBSimpleProvider_getColumnCount = ColCount
End Function
```

The *getLocale* method returns information about the locale; if the provider doesn't support international settings, you can return an empty string:

```
' Return a string that determines the system's international settings
' or an empty string if the provider doesn't support different locales.
' (This one doesn't.)
Private Function OLEDBSimpleProvider_getLocale() As String
    OLEDBSimpleProvider_getLocale = ""
End Function
```

Three methods of the OLEDBSimpleProvider interface are useful when your provider supports asynchronous data transfers. In this example, we return False in the *isAsync* method, so we don't need to worry about the other two methods, *getEstimatedRows* and *stopTransfer*, because they're never called. (But you must provide them anyway because of the *Implements* keyword.)

```
' Return a nonzero value if the rowset is populated asynchronously.
Private Function OLEDBSimpleProvider_isAsync() As Long
    OLEDBSimpleProvider_isAsync = False
End Function

' Return the estimated number of rows or -1 if unknown.
' This method is used in asynchronous data transfers.
Private Function OLEDBSimpleProvider_getEstimatedRows() As Long
    ' The following statement is for demonstration purposes only because
    ' this method will never be called in this provider.
    OLEDBSimpleProvider_getEstimatedRows = RowCount
End Function

' Stop asynchronous transfer.
Private Sub OLEDBSimpleProvider_stopTransfer()
    ' Do nothing in this provider.
End Sub
```

The following two methods, *addOLEDBSimpleProviderListener* and *remove-OLEDBSimpleProviderListener*, are very important. They're called whenever a new consumer binds to this instance of the Provider class. The provider must keep track of all the consumers that are listening to this instance because whenever data is added, removed, or changed the provider must send a notification to all of these consumers. The TextOSP sample class records all the consumers using the Listeners module-level collection variable:

```
' Add a Listener object to the Listeners collection.
Private Sub OLEDBSimpleProvider_addOLEDBSimpleProviderListener( _
    ByVal pospIListener As MSDAOSP.OLEDBSimpleProviderListener)
    If Not (pospIListener Is Nothing) Then Listeners.Add pospIListener
End Sub

' Remove a Listener from the Listeners collection.
Private Sub OLEDBSimpleProvider_removeOLEDBSimpleProviderListener( _
    ByVal pospIListener As MSDAOSP.OLEDBSimpleProviderListener)
    Dim i As Long
    For i = 1 To Listeners.Count
        If Listeners(i) Is pospIListener Then
            Listeners.Remove i
            Exit For
        End If
    Next
End Sub
```

The *getRWStatus* method is invoked when the consumer requests information about the read/write status of the data source. When this method is called with *iRow* = −1, you must return the status of the column whose number is passed in *iColumn*; when the *iColumn* argument is −1, you must return the status of the record whose number is passed in *iRow*. When both arguments are positive, you must return the status of a field in a given row. In all cases, you can return one of the following values: OSPRW_READWRITE (data can be read and modified), OSPRW_READONLY (data can only be read), or OSPRW_MIXED (undetermined status). In this simple example, all fields are writable, so you don't have to test *iRow* and *iCol*:

```
' Return the read/write status of a value.
Private Function OLEDBSimpleProvider_getRWStatus(ByVal iRow As Long, _
    ByVal iColumn As Long) As MSDAOSP.OSPRW
    ' Make all fields read/write.
    OLEDBSimpleProvider_getRWStatus = OSPRW_READWRITE
End Function
```

The *getVariant* method returns an existing value. This method receives a *format* parameter, which indicates the format in which the value should be returned to the consumer. Possible values are OSPFORMAT_RAW (the default; data isn't formatted), OSPFORMAT_FORMATTED (data is a string contained in a Variant), or OSPFORMAT_HTML (data is an HTML string). In this sample provider, the *format* parameter is ignored and data is returned as it's stored in the *DataArray* array:

```
' Read a value at given row and column coordinates.
Private Function OLEDBSimpleProvider_getVariant(ByVal iRow As Long, _
    ByVal iColumn As Long, ByVal format As MSDAOSP.OSPFORMAT) As Variant
    ' Use (iColumn - 1) because the iColumn parameter is 1-based
    ' whereas values are stored in 0-based string arrays.
    OLEDBSimpleProvider_getVariant = DataArray(iRow)(iColumn - 1)
End Function
```

In the *setVariant* method, you're expected to write the value in the *Var* parameter to the private array. Before assigning the value, you must notify all listeners that data is about to change (prenotification). Similarly, after you make the assignment, you must inform all listeners that data has actually changed (postnotification). You do both the notifications through methods of the OLEDBSimpleProvider object stored in the Listeners collection:

```
' Write a value at given row/column coordinates.
Private Sub OLEDBSimpleProvider_setVariant(ByVal iRow As Long, _
    ByVal iColumn As Long, ByVal format As MSDAOSP.OSPFORMAT, _
    ByVal Var As Variant)
    ' Prenotification
    For Each Listener In Listeners
        Listener.aboutToChangeCell iRow, iColumn
    Next
    DataArray(iRow)(iColumn - 1) = Var
    ' Postnotification
    For Each Listener In Listeners
        Listener.cellChanged iRow, iColumn
    Next
    IsDirty = True
End Sub
```

The *insertRows* and *deleteRows* methods are called when a consumer adds a new record or deletes an existing record, respectively. Thanks to the array of arrays structure, performing these operations is straightforward. In both cases, you must send a prenotification and a postnotification to all the consumers that are listening to this provider:

```
' Insert one or more rows.
Private Function OLEDBSimpleProvider_insertRows(ByVal iRow As Long, _
    ByVal cRows As Long) As Long
    Dim row As Long
    ' Validate iRow - (RowCount + 1), and account for AddNew commands.
    If iRow < 1 Or iRow > (RowCount + 1) Then Err.Raise E_FAIL
    ReDim emptyArray(0 To ColCount) As String
    ReDim Preserve DataArray(RowCount + cRows) As Variant

    ' Prenotification
    For Each Listener In Listeners
        Listener.aboutToInsertRows iRow, cRows
    Next
    ' Make room in the array.
    If iRow <= RowCount Then
        For row = RowCount To iRow Step -1
            DataArray(row + cRows) = DataArray(row)
            DataArray(row) = emptyArray
        Next
    Else
        For row = RowCount + 1 To RowCount + cRows
            DataArray(row) = emptyArray
        Next
    End If
    RowCount = RowCount + cRows

    ' Postnotification
    For Each Listener In Listeners
        Listener.insertedRows iRow, cRows
    Next
    ' Return the number of inserted rows.
    OLEDBSimpleProvider_insertRows = cRows
    IsDirty = True
End Function

' Delete one or more rows.
Private Function OLEDBSimpleProvider_deleteRows(ByVal iRow As Long, _
    ByVal cRows As Long) As Long
    Dim row As Long
    ' Validate iRow.
    If iRow < 1 Or iRow > RowCount Then Err.Raise E_FAIL
    ' Set cRows to the actual number, which can be deleted.
    If iRow + cRows > RowCount + 1 Then cRows = RowCount - iRow + 1
```

```
' Prenotification
For Each Listener In Listeners
    Listener.aboutToDeleteRows iRow, cRows
Next
' Shrink the array.
For row = iRow To RowCount - cRows
    DataArray(row) = DataArray(row + cRows)
Next
RowCount = RowCount - cRows
ReDim Preserve DataArray(RowCount) As Variant

' Postnotification
For Each Listener In Listeners
    Listener.deletedRows iRow, cRows
Next
' Return the number of deleted rows.
OLEDBSimpleProvider_deleteRows = cRows
IsDirty = True
End Function
```

The last method, *Find*, is invoked when the consumer searches for a value. It receives the searched value in the *val* parameter, the starting row number in the *iStartRow* parameter, and the number of the column in which the value must be searched in *iColumn*. *Find* is the most complex method of the OLEDBSimpleProvider interface because it has to account for several flags and search options. The *findFlags* parameter is bit-coded: 1-OSPFIND_UP means that the search goes from the end to the beginning of the data file, and 2-OSPFIND_CASESENSITIVE means that the search is case sensitive. The *compType* parameter indicates which condition must be met: 1-OSPCOMP_EQ (equal), 2-OSPCOMP_LT (less than), 3-OSPCOMP_LE (less than or equal to), 4-OSPCOMP_GE (greater than or equal to), 5-OSPCOMP_GT (greater than), and 6-OSPCOMP_NE (not equal). The *Find* method must return the row number in which the match has been found, or −1 if the search failed. The following routine accounts for all these different settings:

```
Private Function OLEDBSimpleProvider_Find(ByVal iRowStart As Long, _
    ByVal iColumn As Long, ByVal val As Variant, ByVal findFlags As _
    MSDAOSP.OSPFIND, ByVal compType As MSDAOSP.OSPCOMP) As Long
    Dim RowStop As Long, RowStep As Long
    Dim CaseSens As Long, StringComp As Boolean
    Dim result As Long, compResult As Integer, row As Long

    ' Determine the end row and the step value for the loop.
    If findFlags And OSPFIND_UP Then
        RowStop = 1: RowStep = -1
    Else
        RowStop = RowCount: RowStep = 1
    End If
```

(continued)

```
' Determine the case-sensitive flag.
If findFlags And OSPFIND_CASESENSITIVE Then
    CaseSens = vbBinaryCompare
Else
    CaseSens = vbTextCompare
End If
' True if we're dealing with strings
StringComp = (VarType(val) = vbString)
' -1 means not found.
result = -1
' iColumn is 1-based, but internal data is 0-based.
iColumn = iColumn - 1

For row = iRowStart To RowStop Step RowStep
    If StringComp Then
        ' We're comparing strings.
        compResult = StrComp(DataArray(row)(iColumn), val, CaseSens)
    Else
        ' We're comparing numbers or dates.
        compResult = Sgn(DataArray(row)(iColumn) - val)
    End If
    Select Case compType
        Case OSPCOMP_DEFAULT, OSPCOMP_EQ
            If compResult = 0 Then result = row
        Case OSPCOMP_GE
            If compResult >= 0 Then result = row
        Case OSPCOMP_GT
            If compResult > 0 Then result = row
        Case OSPCOMP_LE
            If compResult <= 0 Then result = row
        Case OSPCOMP_LT
            If compResult < 0 Then result = row
        Case OSPCOMP_NE
            If compResult <> 0 Then result = row
    End Select
    If result <> -1 Then Exit For
Next
' Return the row found or -1.
OLEDBSimpleProvider_find = result
End Function
```

The Data Source Class

The OLE DB Simple Provider project contains a Public MultiUse class named
TextDataSource. This class is the component that Msdaosp.dll instantiates when a
consumer uses your provider. TextDataSource must expose two Public methods:
msDataSourceObject and *addDataSourceListener*. The *msDataSourceObject* method
creates a new instance of the Provider class, asks it to load a data file, and returns

the instance to the caller. From that point on, Msdaosp.dll will communicate directly with the TextOSP Provider class. In this simple implementation, you can simply return zero in the *addDataSourceListener* method:

```
Const E_FAIL = &H80004005


' The DataMember passed to this function is the path of the text file.
Function msDataSourceObject(DataMember As String) As OLEDBSimpleProvider
    ' Raise an error if the member is invalid.
    If DataMember = "" Then Err.Raise E_FAIL
    ' Create an instance of the OLE DB Simple Provider component,
    ' load a data file, and return the instance to the caller.
    Dim TextOSP As New TextOSP
    TextOSP.LoadData DataMember
    Set msDataSourceObject = TextOSP
End Function

Function addDataSourceListener(ByVal pospIListener As DataSourceListener) _
    As Long
    addDataSourceListener = 0
End Function
```

Now that you've seen all the relevant properties and methods, you're finally ready to compile the DLL. Your job isn't finished, however, because now you must register your DLL as an OLE DB Simple Provider.

The Registration Step

To register your OLE DB Simple Provider, you must add a few entries to the Registry. Usually, you create a REG file and include it in the installation procedure of your provider so that you can easily register the provider on any machine by double-clicking it or by running the Regedit utility. Here's the contents of the TextOSP.Reg file that registers the sample provider that comes on the companion CD:

```
REGEDIT4
[HKEY_CLASSES_ROOT\TextOSP_VB]
@="Semicolon-delimited text files"
[HKEY_CLASSES_ROOT\TextOSP_VB\CLSID]
@="{CDC6BD0B-98FC-11D2-BAC5-0080C8F21830}"
[HKEY_CLASSES_ROOT\CLSID\{CDC6BD0B-98FC-11D2-BAC5-0080C8F21830}]
@="TextOSP_VB"
[HKEY_CLASSES_ROOT\CLSID\{CDC6BD0B-98FC-11D2-BAC5-
0080C8F21830}\InprocServer32]
@="c:\\Program Files\\Common Files\\System\\OLE DB\\MSDAOSP.DLL"
"ThreadingModel"="Both"
[HKEY_CLASSES_ROOT\CLSID\{CDC6BD0B-98FC-11D2-BAC5-0080C8F21830}\ProgID]
@="TextOSP_VB.1"
```

(continued)

```
[HKEY_CLASSES_ROOT\CLSID\{CDC6BD0B-98FC-11D2-BAC5-
0080C8F21830}\VersionIndependentProgID]
@="TextOSP_VB"
[HKEY_CLASSES_ROOT\CLSID\{CDC6BD0B-98FC-11D2-BAC5-
0080C8F21830}\OLE DB Provider]
@="Semicolon-delimited text files"
[HKEY_CLASSES_ROOT\CLSID\{CDC6BD0B-98FC-11D2-BAC5-
0080C8F21830}\OSP Data Object]
@="TextOLEDBProvider.TextDataSource"
```

Each OLE DB Simple Provider has two entries in the Registry. The entry HKEY_CLASSES_ROOT\<*YourProviderName*> contains the description of the provider (the string that appears when a programmer asks for all the OLE DB providers registered on the system) and the provider's CLSID. Don't confuse this CLSID with the CLSID of the DLL that we just created—this CLSID serves solely to uniquely identify the provider. You have to create this CLSID yourself—for example, by using the Guidgen.exe utility provided with Microsoft Visual Studio, as shown in Figure 18-5.

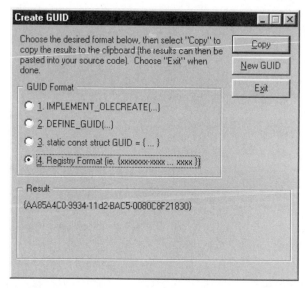

Figure 18-5. *The Guidgen.exe utility provides new GUIDs in different formats.*

The HKEY_CLASSES_ROOT\CLSID\<*YourProviderClsid*> entry gathers all the other information about the provider, including the path of the Msdaosp.dll file and the complete name of the data source class that must be instantiated when a consumer connects to the provider. The latter value is the *projectname.classname* name of the data source class that you've included in your Visual Basic project.

To help you in creating your customized Registry files, I prepared a template REG file, named Model_osp.reg. You can reuse this template for all the OLE DB Simple Providers you create by following this procedure:

1. Run the Guidgen.exe utility, select the Registry Format option, click on the Copy button, and then close the utility.

2. Load the Model_osp.reg file into a word processor or an editor. (If you're running Windows 95 or Windows 98, Notepad isn't a good choice because it lacks search-and-replace capabilities.) Then replace all the occurrences of "$ClsId$" with the CLSID (which you stored in the Clipboard at the end of step 1).

3. Search for the two occurrences of the "$Description$" string, and replace them with a textual description of your provider—for example, "Semicolon-delimiter Text Files"; this is the string that identifies your provider in the list of all the OLE DB providers installed on the machine.

4. Find and replace all the occurrences of the "$ProviderName$" string with the name of your provider; this name is a string that identifies your provider in the Registry and is used as the *Provider* attribute in the *ConnectionString* property of an ADO Connection object. For example, the name of the sample provider that you'll find on the companion CD is "TextOSP_VB".

5. Search for the only occurrence of the "$DataSource$" string, and replace it with the complete name of the data source class in the OLE DB provider project; in the sample project, this string is "TextOLEDB-Provider.TextDataSource".

6. Ensure that the Msdaosp.dll is located in the C:\Program Files\Common Files\System\OLE DB; if it's not, modify the value of the InprocServer32 key in the REG file to point to the correct location of that file.

7. Save the file with a different name so that you don't modify the template REG file.

8. Double-click on the REG file to add all the necessary keys to the Registry.

Testing the OLE DB Simple Provider

You can use the OLE DB Simple Provider that you just built as you would use any other OLE DB provider. For example, you can open a Recordset and loop through its records using the following code:

```
Dim cn As New ADODB.Connection, rs As New ADODB.Recordset

cn.Open "Provider=TextOSP_VB;Data Source=TextOLEDBProvider.TextDataSource"
rs.Open "C:\Employees.Txt", cn, adOpenStatic, adLockOptimistic
rs.MoveFirst
```

(continued)

```
Do Until rs.EOF
    Print rs("FirstName") & " " & rs("LastName")
    rs.MoveNext
Loop
rs.Close
cn.Close
```

You can't test the provider inside the Visual Basic IDE, and you have to compile it to a stand-alone ActiveX component. This means that you have to forgo all the debug tools that work only in the environment and can rely only on *MsgBox* and *App.LogEvent* statements.

THE DATA OBJECT WIZARD

The Data Object Wizard is an add-in that can help you to quickly generate data-aware class and UserControl modules. This wizard is probably the most sophisticated add-in provided with Visual Basic 6. Unfortunately, it's also one of the least intuitive to use. In the remainder of this chapter, I'll briefly introduce this utility. (Space doesn't permit me to explain all its capabilities in depth.)

Preparing for the Wizard

The Data Object Wizard works in conjunction with the DataEnvironment designer. Instead of entering all the necessary information about the data source when the Data Object Wizard is executing, you have to prepare a DataEnvironment object with one or more Command objects before running the add-in. Each Command object represents one of the actions that you can perform on the data source: select, insert, update, or delete records, lookup values, and so on. Once you run the wizard, you can't go back to the Visual Basic IDE, so you need to prepare all the Command objects in advance.

In this section, I guide you through a simple example based on the Products table of the NWind.mdb database. Frankly, the Data Object Wizard works best when used on SQL Server and Oracle databases. Even so, I opted for an example based on a local MDB database for those of you who don't have a client/server system available. These are the preparatory steps that you have to follow before running the wizard:

1. Open the DataView window, and create a data link to the NWind.mdb database (if you don't have one already). Select the OLE DB Provider for ODBC, not the Provider for Microsoft Jet databases, if you want to be in sync with the following description. Test that the connection is working, and then expand the Tables subfolder under the NWind data link you just created.

2. Click the Add A DataEnvironment button in the DataView window to create a new DataEnvironment designer, and then delete the default Connection1 node that Visual Basic automatically adds to all DataEnvironment modules.

3. Drag the Products table from the DataView window into the DataEnvironment window. Visual Basic automatically creates a new Connection1 node and a Command object beneath it, named Products. The Recordset returned by this Command object doesn't necessarily have to be updatable because all the insert, update, and delete operations are performed by means of other Command objects.

4. Click on the Add Command button on the DataEnvironment toolbar to create a new Command object named Command1, and then click on the Properties button to show its Properties dialog box. Change the name of the Command object to Products_Insert, select the SQL Statement option, and enter the following SQL query string into the multiline text box under it, as shown in Figure 18-6:

```
INSERT INTO Products(ProductName, CategoryID, SupplierID, QuantityPerUnit,
UnitPrice, UnitsInStock, UnitsOnOrder, ReorderLevel, Discontinued)
VALUES (?, ?, ?, ?, ?, ?, ?, ?, ?)
```

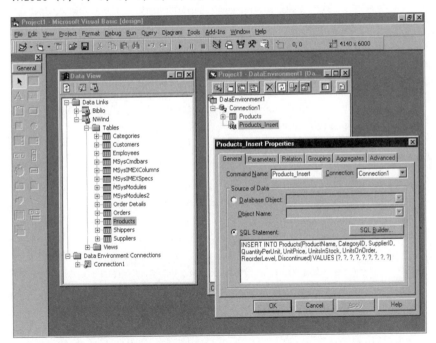

Figure 18-6. *The Properties dialog box of the Products_Insert Command object.*

5. Switch to the Parameters tab of the Properties dialog box, and assign a meaningful name to the nine parameters of the preceding SQL command. Each parameter should be assigned the name of the corresponding field—that is, *ProductName*, *CategoryID*, and so on. The majority of parameters are Long integers, so in most cases you don't need to modify the default

settings. The exceptions are two string parameters (*ProductName* and *QuantityPerUnit*), one Currency parameter (*UnitPrice*), and one Boolean parameter (*Discontinued*). Set a greater-than-zero value for the *Size* attribute of string parameters; if you don't, the Command object won't be created correctly.

6. Create another Command object, assign it the name Products_Update, and enter the following string in the SQL Statement field:

```
UPDATE Products SET ProductName = ?, CategoryID = ?, SupplierID = ?,
QuantityPerUnit = ?, UnitPrice = ?, UnitsInStock = ?, UnitsOnOrder = ?,
ReorderLevel = ?, Discontinued = ? WHERE (ProductID = ?)
```

Then switch to the Parameters tab and assign meaningful names and types for all the parameters, exactly as you did in step 5. (Unfortunately, there's no way to copy and paste this information between Command objects.)

7. Create a fourth Command object, name it Products_Delete, and enter the following string in the SQL Statement field:

```
DELETE FROM Products WHERE ProductID = ?
```

Then switch to the Parameters tab and assign the *ProductID* name to the only parameter, without changing the other attributes.

8. Drag the Categories and Suppliers tables from the DataView window to the DataEnvironment window. This creates two Command objects, named *Categories* and *Suppliers*, that the Data Object Wizard will use to create lookup tables for the CategoryID and SupplierID fields, respectively.

All these steps shouldn't take more than 5 or 10 minutes. If you prefer, you can start with a blank Standard EXE project and then just load the DE1.dsr file from the project on the companion CD. This file already contains all the Command objects ready to be used by the Data Object Wizard.

Most of the time required to build these Command objects is spent manually entering the names and other attributes of the many parameters in the Products_Insert and Products_Update commands. You can't avoid this step when working with MDB databases because the OLE DB provider doesn't correctly recognize any parameterized QueryDef object stored in the database. The good news is that when you work with SQL Server you can create Command objects that link to stored procedures. In this case, the DataEnvironment designer is able to deduce the name and type of parameters without your help, which dramatically reduces the amount of time necessary to complete these preparatory steps.

Creating the Data-Bound Class

You're now ready to run the Data Object Wizard. If you haven't loaded it yet, select the Add-In Manager command from the Add-Ins menu, double-click on its name in the list of available add-ins, and click on the OK button. Now the wizard should be available in the Add-Ins menu. Run it, and then follow these steps:

1. Click on the Next button to get past the introduction page; in the Create Object page, select the kind of object you want to create. The Data Object Wizard can create data consumer classes that bind to a data source or UserControl modules that bind to a data consumer class (which you must have created previously with the wizard). The first time you run the wizard, you have no choice; you must select the first option, A Class Object To Which Other Objects Can Bind Data. Click Next to advance to the next page.

2. In the Select Data Environment Command page, you select the source Command object—namely, the command that should be used by the class to fetch data. In this example, you select the Products command, which retrieves data directly from a database table; in real-world applications, you'll probably select a command that reads data using a stored procedure or an SQL SELECT query.

3. In the Define Class Field Information page, you indicate which fields are the primary keys in the Recordset and which fields can't be Null (required values). In this particular example, the ProductID field is the primary key, and the ProductName, SupplierID, and CategoryID fields can't be Null.

4. In the Define Lookup Table Information page, you define the lookup fields in the source command. As you know, a lookup field is a field whose value is used as a key into another table to retrieve data. For example, you can display the CompanyName field from the Suppliers table instead of the SupplierID field. In this case, you define SupplierID as a lookup field into the Suppliers table. To let the wizard generate the correct code, you must enter the following data into the page:

   ❏ Select SupplierID as the Source field (that is, the lookup field in the source command).

   ❏ Select Suppliers as the Lookup command. (This tells the wizard which Command object should be used to map the lookup value onto a more readable string to be displayed to the user.)

❑   Select CompanyName in the Display Field combo box. (This is the field in the Lookup Command object that provides the decoded value.)

❑   Tick the SupplierID entry in the Lookup On Field(s) list box. (This is the name of the lookup field as it appears in the Lookup command; it might or might not be the same as the name of the field in the source Command.) Click on the Add button to proceed.

Repeat the same four operations to define CategoryID as another lookup field, as shown in Figure 18-7.

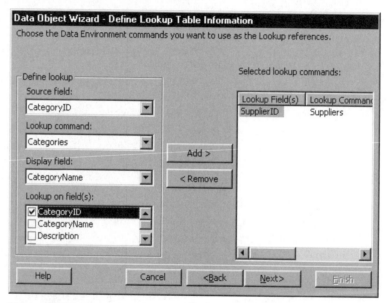

Figure 18-7. *The Define Lookup Table Information page, after you've added the SupplierID field to the list of lookup fields and just before you add the CategoryID field.*

5.   In the next page, Map Lookup Fields, you define how the fields in the source Command object map onto the fields in the Lookup Command object; there are two consecutive pages for this purpose because you defined two Lookup Command objects. Because the field names are the same in the two Command objects, the wizard can do the mapping correctly all by itself, so you can click on the Next button without modifying the values in the grid.

6.   In the Define And Map Insert Data Command page, you select which DataEnvironment Command, if any, should be used for adding new records to the source Recordset. In this example, you should select the Products_Insert Command object. You can then define the mapping

between the fields in the source Command and the parameters in the Insert Command. Because we picked parameters' names that are the same as the fields' names, the wizard is able to do the correct mapping by itself, and you don't have to modify the proposed mapping scheme. (See Figure 18-8.)

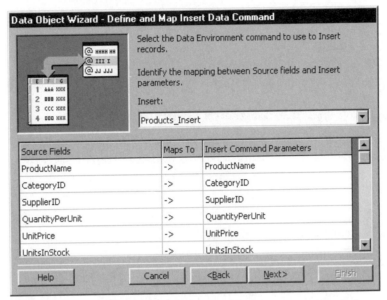

Figure 18-8. *Mapping field names to parameter names is crucial when you define Command objects for inserting, updating, and deleting records, but in most cases the wizard is able to do the mapping automatically.*

7. In the next page, Define And Map Update Data Command, you select the Command object that should be used for updating the source Command (the Products_Update Command in this example). You can also tick the Use Insert Command For Update check box when you have a stored procedure that can both append a new record and update an existing one. Again, in this example, the wizard is able to correctly map field names to parameter names, so you can skip to the next page.

8. In the Define And Map Delete Data Command page, you select which Command object should be used to delete a record from the source Command (the Products_Delete Command in this example). Again, you don't need to manually map fields; the wizard does the mapping automatically.

9. You're about to complete running the wizard. In the last page, enter a name for the class and click on the Finish button. The class name you provide is automatically prefixed with the *rscls* characters. For example, if you enter *Products*, the wizard will create the rsclsProducts class module.

Going through the preceding steps might seem complex at first, but after some practice you'll see that using the wizard really takes no more than a couple of minutes. When the wizard completes its execution, you'll find that two new classes have been added to the current project: the clsDow class and the rsclsProducts class. The clsDow class module contains only the *EnumSaveMode* enumerated constants, which define the values that can be assigned to the *SaveMode* property of the rsclsProducts class: 0-adImmediate, if you want the class to save values in the source Recordset as soon as the record pointer moves to another record, or 1-adBatch, if the class should update the Recordset only when you invoke the class's *Update* method.

Creating the Data-Bound UserControl

You could use the rsclsProducts class module created by the wizard directly from your applications, but you'll find it more convenient to use it through a custom UserControl. The great news is that you can create such a UserControl in a matter of seconds, again using the Data Object Wizard.

1. Run the wizard again, and in its Create Object page, select the A User-Control Object Bound To An Existing Class Object option.

2. In the next page, select the data class to use as the data source for the UserControl (the rsclsProducts class in this example).

3. In the Select User Control Type page, decide which type of UserControl you want to create. The wizard lets you choose among Single Record (a collection of individual fields), Data Grid (a DataGrid-like control), ListBox, and ComboBox. For this first run, select the Single Record option.

4. In the next page, decide which database fields are visible in the User-Control and which control type is to be used for each visible field. For example, you should select *(None)* for the ProductID field because this is an auto-increment primary key field that's meaningless to the user, and you should use a ComboBox field for the CategoryName and SupplierName lookup fields (as shown in Figure 18-9).

5. In the next page, you select a base name for the control. In most cases, you can accept the default name (*Products* in this example) and click on the Finish button. The actual name the wizard uses depends on which type of UserControl you selected in step 3. For example, if you selected a Single Record type of control, the UserControl module that the wizard generates is named uctProductsSingleRecord.

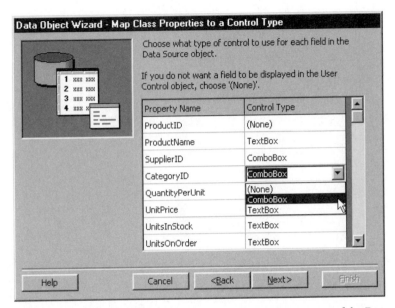

Figure 18-9. *The Map Class Properties To A Control Type page of the Data Object Wizard.*

You're now ready to use the control in the application. Close the UserControl module so that its icon in the Toolbox becomes active, create an instance of the control on a form, and add a few navigational buttons, as shown in Figure 18-10 on the following page. The code behind these buttons is really simple:

```
Private Sub cmdPrevious_Click()
    uctProductsSingleRecord1.MovePrevious
End Sub
Private Sub cmdNext_Click()
    uctProductsSingleRecord1.MoveNext
End Sub
Private Sub cmdAddNew_Click()
    uctProductsSingleRecord1.AddRecord
End Sub
Private Sub cmdUpdate_Click()
    uctProductsSingleRecord1.Update
End Sub
Private Sub cmdDelete_Click()
    uctProductsSingleRecord1.Delete
End Sub
```

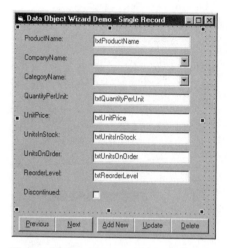

Figure 18-10. *The ActiveX control generated by the Data Object Wizard can be tested with a few navigational buttons on its parent form.*

The Data Object Wizard isn't particularly efficient when used with the OLE DB Provider for Microsoft Jet. After some experiments, I found that if you want to add new records, you *must* set the UserControl's *SaveMode* property to 1-adBatch, and therefore you have to invoke the *Update* method after entering a new record. Everything works unproblematically when you create classes and UserControls that bind to a SQL Server database.

When you understand the mechanism, creating the other types of UserControls is easy. For example, restart the wizard and create a DataGrid-like control. If you then place the control on a form and set its *GridEditable* property to True, you'll see that not only can you edit field values in the grid but you can also select the value of a lookup field from a drop-down list, as shown in Figure 18-11. The DataList-like and DataCombo-like controls are even simpler because they're just lists of values and don't use the Insert, Update, Delete, and Lookup Command objects.

You can create more flexible classes and controls if the original source Command object is based on a parameterized query or a stored procedure, such as this one:

```
SELECT * FROM Products WHERE ProductName LIKE ?
```

In this case, the resulting class and UserControl modules expose a property whose name is obtained by concatenating the name of the source Command and the name of the parameter in the query (for example, *Products_ProductName*). You can set this property at design time and let the UserControl initialize the internal Recordset as soon as the control is created at run time. Or you can set the *ManualInitialize* property to True so that you can assign this property using code and then manually invoke the *Init*xxxx method exposed by the control (*InitProducts* in this example). The sample application shown in Figure 18-11 uses this technique to narrow the number of records displayed in the grid. This is the only code in the form module:

```
Private Sub cmdFetch_Click()
    uctProductsDataGrid1.Products_FetchProductName = txtProductName & "%"
    uctProductsDataGrid1.InitProducts2
End Sub
```

The Data Object Wizard is a great add-in, and it produces very good code. In fact, I suggest that you study the generated code to learn how to get the maximum benefit from this utility and also to learn new tricks for building better data-aware classes and UserControls. The wizard also has some defects, however. Apart from those that I've already mentioned (and that are mostly caused by bugs in the OLE DB Provider for Microsoft Jet), the one that bothers me most is that the UserControl module tends to go out of sync with its instances on forms, so you often need to right-click on forms and invoke the Update UserControls menu command. This is a minor nuisance, however, when compared to the time the wizard saves.

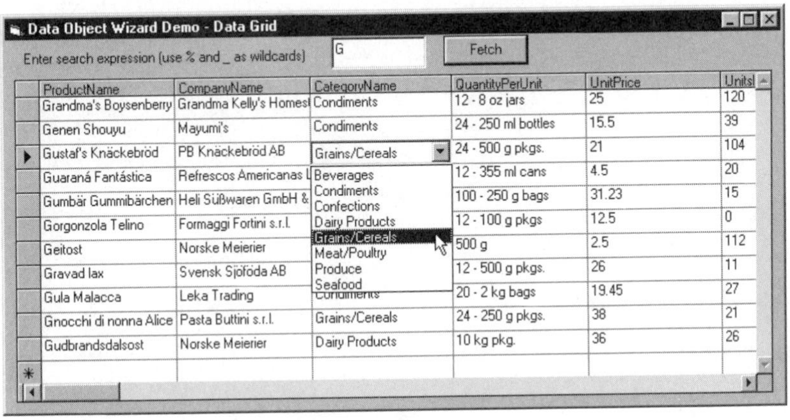

Figure 18-11. *DataGrid-like UserControls also let you select values from drop-down lists.*

In this chapter, you've seen that ADO permits you to build many new types of classes and components: data consumers, data sources, and OLE DB Simple Providers. You can build another type of database component with Visual Basic, a Remote Data Services (RDS) component. You normally use these when you're accessing a database through the HTTP protocol, and for this reason I'll describe this type of component in the next chapter, together with the new Visual Basic features in the Internet area.

Part V
Internet Programming

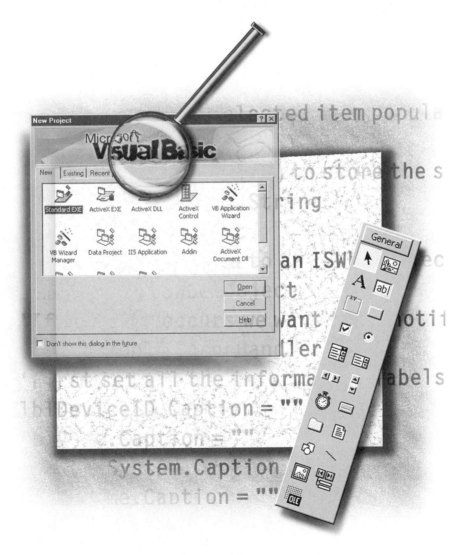

Chapter 19

Dynamic HTML Applications

In the beginning, there was just HTML (Hypertext Markup Language). All Web pages were inherently static, but they were appealing enough to fuel Web mania. Then came Common Gateway Interface (CGI) applications, external applications that ran on the server and, for the first time, allowed for pages whose content wasn't fixed. The next step toward dynamic content was client-side scripting routines or simple programs written in macro languages that execute inside the browser, such as Microsoft Visual Basic, Scripting Edition (VBScript), or scripting languages complying with the ECMAScript specification. Microsoft has delivered newer proprietary technologies for creating dynamic content in the browser, such as ActiveX controls and ActiveX documents, whereas other vendors have focused mostly on applets written in Java. The most interesting, powerful, and widely accepted server-side technology is based on server-side scripting and Active Server Pages (ASP). The most powerful way to create dynamic pages on the client side is based on Dynamic HTML (DHTML).

All these technologies have some flaws, however. CGI applications aren't very efficient, they can't be easily scaled to hundreds of clients, and they aren't powerful enough for large Internet or intranet applications. Client-side scripting is definitely more suitable for a Visual Basic programmer, especially if the programmer uses VBScript. Alas, VBScript isn't currently supported by Netscape Navigator; therefore, you should use it only for intranet installations. Neither does Netscape Navigator support ActiveX controls and ActiveX documents. Many Internet developers consider Active Server Pages (ASP) the best way to deliver pure HTML dynamic pages to any browser, but it's a fact that building and maintaining a large ASP-based application isn't a trivial task. In addition, scripts on the server become a less efficient solution as the number of clients increases.

Visual Basic 6 introduces two fresh approaches to Internet programming that might be the answer to all your needs because they combine the flexibility of proven Internet technologies with the power and ease of the Visual Basic language. *DHTML applications* are in-process components (DLLs) that run on the client machine inside Microsoft Internet Explorer and trap events fired by the elements on the DHTML page, such as when the user clicks on a button or follows a hyperlink. *IIS applications* (also known as *WebClasses*) are DLLs that run on the server machine inside Microsoft Internet Information Server (IIS) and intercept the requests coming from the client browsers. Neither approach can be considered a brand-new technology because they simply expand what's already available. But the ability to write an entire Internet application using the full-featured Visual Basic language (instead of just a limited script language), test it inside the IDE, and then produce optimized and highly scalable native code (as opposed to less efficient script code) is very appealing to most developers.

In this chapter, I explain how to create DHTML applications. (I cover WebClasses in Chapter 20.) But before diving into the most interesting stuff, we need to go over a few basic concepts.

A QUICK COURSE ON HTML

Before you can start to create a DHTML application, you need to know at least some rudiments of HTML, such as how an HTML page is created and the most important and frequently used HTML tags. If you're already familiar with HTML syntax, you can safely skip this section.

Even though the HTML language has its own logic, it isn't as structured as high-level programming languages such as Visual Basic. For this reason, many programmers find HTML syntax rules somewhat strange. As always, nothing beats hands-on practice, so I prepared the DHTML Cheap Editor that lets you write an HTML fragment and immediately see how the browser renders it. I wrote this piece of software using the WebBrowser control, which is nothing less than Internet Explorer embedded in an ActiveX control.

Although this simple editor can't compete with Microsoft FrontPage or even the simplest freeware HTML editor, it does offer some useful features. First, it allows you to swap from the editor to the preview window with the touch of a button (F4 for the editor, F5 for the preview window). Second, it provides several shortcut key combinations that you can use to add the most common HTML tags and even to enter more complex structures such as tables and controls. All these shortcuts are listed in the Insert menu, as shown in Figure 19-1. The source code for this editor is on the companion CD, and you're welcome to improve it to add support for additional HTML tags or other capacities.

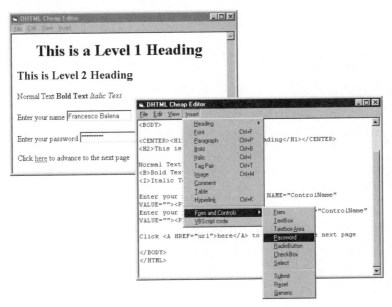

Figure 19-1. *Two instances of the DHTML Cheap Editor: one in editor mode and one in preview mode.*

Headings and Paragraphs

An HTML page is a file that consists of plain text plus tags that tell the browser how the page should be rendered on the client's screen. This is the skeleton of an HTML page:

```
<HTML>
<HEAD>
<TITLE>The title of this page</TITLE>
</HEAD>
<BODY>
Welcome to HTML
</BODY>
</HTML>
```

This code displays the string "Welcome to HTML" near the top border of an otherwise blank page. Notice that all the elements in the page are enclosed within a pair of tags and each tag is enclosed between angle brackets. For example, the title of the page—the string that Internet Explorer displays in the caption of its main window—is enclosed between the <TITLE> and </TITLE> tags. The <BODY> and </BODY> tags enclose the text that appears inside the page.

Typically, the body of a page contains one or more headings. HTML supports six levels of headings, where level 1 corresponds to the most important heading and level 6 to the least important one. Headings are useful for giving subtitles to sections of the page:

```
<BODY>
<H1>This is a level 1 heading</H1>
Some normal text here
<H2>This is a level 2 heading</H2>
Text under level 2 heading
</BODY>
```

An important characteristic of the HTML language is that carriage return characters and line feed characters in the source text don't affect the appearance of the page. Apart from headings and a few other tags, which add a CR-LF pair automatically, one way to start a new line is to insert a <P> tag manually, as here:

```
This is a paragraph.<P>As is this.<P>
```

The <P> tag forces a new line and also inserts a blank line between the current paragraph and the next one. If you need to break the current line but you don't want an extra blank line, you can use the <BR> tag:

```
This paragraph is subdivided<BR>into two distinct lines.<P>
```

To add a horizontal line of space between two paragraphs, you can also use the <HR> tag:

```
Two paragraphs separated<HR>by a horizontal line<P>
```

The <PRE> and </PRE> pair of tags is an exception to the rule that carriage returns in HTML source text are ignored: Everything between these tags is rendered as monospaced text (typically using the Courier font), and all embedded CR-LF character pairs are inserted in the resulting output. These tags are often used to insert text as is (for example, a source code listing):

```
<PRE>First line
second line</PRE>
```

By default, all text is aligned to the left, but you can use the tags <CENTER> and </CENTER> to center a portion of text:

```
<CENTER>A centered paragraph<P>
Another centered paragraph</CENTER>
```

> **NOTE**   If you're using the DHTML Cheap Editor, you can center any portion of text by highlighting its source code, pressing Ctrl+T to enter a tag pair, and then typing *CENTER* in the input box. You can use the same method for any tag pair, such as <PRE> and </PRE>. Other commands in the Insert menu—for example, the Bold, Italic, and Hyperlink commands—automatically add a pair of tags at the beginning and end of the selected text.

Creating lists of bulleted or numbered items is easy in HTML. You create bulleted items by using the <LI> and </LI> tags to mark the beginning and end of individual items and then enclosing the entire list within <UL> and </UL>:

```
<UL>
<LI>First bulleted paragraph</LI>
<LI>Second bulleted paragraph</LI>
<LI>Third bulleted paragraph</LI>
</UL>
```

You create a list of numbered items in much the same way. The only difference is that you must enclose the list within the <OL> and </OL> pair of tags:

```
<OL>
<LI>First you must do this.</LI>
<LI>Then you must do that.</LI>
</OL>
```

Attributes

Most HTML tags can embed special attributes that affect how the text between the tags is rendered. For example, by default, headings are left-aligned, but you can modify the alignment of a given heading by adding the ALIGN attribute:

```
<H1 ALIGN=center>This is a centered level 1 heading</H1>
<H2 ALIGN=right>This is a right-aligned level 2 heading</H2>
```

The TEXT attribute defines the color of the text for a page element. If you use this attribute for the BODY tag, the color affects the entire page:

```
<BODY BGCOLOR="cyan" TEXT="#FF0000">
Text on this page is red over a cyan background.
</BODY>
```

You can specify a color attribute using the #RRGGBB format, which is similar to the Visual Basic *RGB* function, or you can use one of the following 16 color names accepted by Internet Explorer: Black, Maroon, Green, Olive, Navy, Purple, Teal, Gray, Silver, Red, Lime, Yellow, Blue, Fuchsia, Aqua, and White. The BODY tag also supports other color attributes, such as LINK (used for hyperlinks), ALINK (to render an active hyperlink), and VLINK (to mark visited hyperlinks).

You can make text boldface by enclosing it within the <B> and </B> pair of tags. Similarly, you can italicize a portion of text with the <I> and </I> pair:

```
<B>This text is boldface.</B><P>
<I>This text is italic.</I><P>
<B>This sentence in boldface has an <I>italicized</I> word in it.</B>
```

You can use the <U> and </U> tag pair to underline text. This isn't usually a good idea, however, because the underline attribute should be reserved for hyperlinks.

You can apply attributes to an entire paragraph by enclosing them between the <P> and </P> tags, as in the following example:

```
<P ALIGN=center>Centered paragraph</P>
```

To modify the attributes of the text, you can use the <FONT> tag, which takes three attributes: FACE, SIZE, and COLOR. The COLOR attribute is specified in the same way as before. The FACE attribute is the name of a font. This attribute even accepts a comma-delimited list of font names if you want to provide alternate choices in case the preferred font isn't available on the user's machine:

```
<FONT FACE="Arial, Helvetica" SIZE=14 COLOR="red">Red text</FONT>
```

This statement attempts to use the Arial font, but it reverts to Helvetica if Arial isn't installed on the user's system. The SIZE attribute is the font size in points. This attribute also accepts a number preceded by a plus or minus sign to indicate a size relative to the default font size:

```
Text in regular size<P>
<FONT SIZE=+4>Text 4 points taller</FONT><P>
<FONT SIZE=-2>Text 2 points smaller</FONT>
```

Images

To insert an image in an HTML page, you need the <IMG> tag, whose SRC attribute specifies the path to the image to be displayed; such a path can be absolute or relative to the path of the page itself. For example, the following code loads a GIF image located in the same directory as the HTML source file:

```
<IMG SRC="mylogo.gif">
```

Images are typically in GIF or JPEG format. GIF images can be *interlaced*, in which case the browser first downloads every other line of pixels and then downloads the remaining lines.

As you can for text strings, you can center an image horizontally by enclosing the <IMG> tab within the <CENTER> and </CENTER> tags or by using the ALIGN attribute. If you know the size of the image being downloaded, you can specify it using the WIDTH and HEIGHT attributes so that the browser can correctly position the text around the image before actually downloading it. The image's width and height are expressed in pixels:

```
This is a right-aligned image 200 pixels wide and 100 pixels high.
<IMG ALIGN=right WIDTH=200 HEIGHT=100 SRC="mylogo.gif">
```

If necessary, the browser will stretch or shrink the original image to fit the size you've specified. This feature is often exploited to insert graphical elements that separate areas on the page. For example, you can create a horizontal separator by using an image with a gradient background and a HEIGHT attribute of just a few pixels.

You can control how much white space is left around the image by using the HSPACE and VSPACE attributes, for horizontal and vertical space, respectively. By default, a 2-pixel transparent border is drawn around all images, but you can suppress it (by setting the BORDER attribute to *none*) or specify a different width:

```
A right-aligned image with 10 pixels of horizontal white space
and 20 pixels of vertical space
<IMG VSPACE=20 ALIGN=right SRC="mylogo.gif" HSPACE=10>
```

Finally, the ALT attribute is used to provide a textual description of the image; this description is displayed in the browser while the image is being downloaded, and it completely replaces the image if the user has turned off images.

Hyperlinks

HTML supports three types of hyperlinks: a hyperlink to another location on the same page, a hyperlink to another page on the same server, and a hyperlink to a page in another Internet domain. In all cases, you use the <A> and </A> tags to define which portion of the text will appear to be underlined. These tags are always accompanied by the HREF attribute, which points to the hyperlink's target:

```
Click <A HREF="PageTwo.htm">here</A> to proceed to the next page, or click
<A HREF="toc.htm">here</A> to go to the table of contents.
```

If the destination of the hyperlink is inside the same page, you need a way to label it. You do this with the <A> tag and the NAME attribute:

```
<A NAME="Intro">Introduction</A>
```

(You don't need to insert a string between the opening and closing tags.) You can place this tag, also known as the *anchor*, before the first line of the target portion of HTML source code. To refer to an anchor inside the same page, you use the # symbol for the value of the HREF attribute:

```
Click <A HREF="#Intro">here</A> to go to the introduction.
```

(Warning: intra-page hyperlinks aren't supported by the Cheap DHTML Editor demo on the companion CD.) You can have a hyperlink point to an anchor inside another page by using the following syntax:

```
Click <A HREF="Chap1.htm#Intro">here</A> to go to the book's introduction.
```

You can also have the hyperlink point to any page on another server by providing the fully qualified URL to it:

```
Jump to the <A HREF="http://www.vb2themax.com/index.htm">
VB-2-The-Max</A> Web site.
```

You can even use images as hyperlinks. The syntax is the same, and you only have to insert an <IMG> tag instead of plain text inside the <A> and </A> tag pair, as shown in the code on the following page.

```
<A HREF="http://www.vb2themax.com"><IMG SRC="mylogo.gif"></A>
```

You can create clickable images linked to an *image map*. In this case, the image includes multiple hot spots, each one pointing to a different target. This advanced technique is beyond the scope of this HTML tutorial, so I won't elaborate on image maps here.

Tables

The HTML language has a rich assortment of tags and keywords for creating and formatting tables. Tables are important in plain HTML because they offer a way to precisely position and align text and image elements. All the data pertaining to a table is enclosed between a pair of <TABLE> and </TABLE> tags. Each new row is marked with a <TR> tag, and each column by a <TD> tag. You can also use the <TH> tag for cells in header rows. The </TR>, </TD>, and </TH> closing tags are optional. The following example displays a table with two columns and three rows, the first of which is a header row:

```
<TABLE BORDER=1>
<TR>
    <TH> HeadRow 1, Column 1</TH>
    <TH> HeadRow 1, Column 2</TH>
</TR><TR>
    <TD> Row 1, Column 1</TD>
    <TD> Row 1, Column 2</TD>
</TR><TR>
    <TD> Row 2, Column 1</TD>
    <TD> Row 2, Column 2</TD>
</TR></TABLE>
```

The BORDER attribute specifies the border's width; if this attribute is omitted, the table doesn't display a border. You can change the border's color using the BORDERCOLOR attribute, and you can even create a 3-D effect with the BORDERCOLORLIGHT and BORDERCOLORDARK attributes. The table can have a background color (the BGCOLOR attribute), or it can use a background image specified by the BACKGROUND attribute.

Each cell can contain text, an image, or both. You can change the horizontal alignment of the contents of a cell by using the ALIGN attribute (which can take the values *left*, *center*, or *right*), and you can control the vertical alignment with the VALIGN attribute (which can be assigned the values *top*, *middle*, or *bottom*). By default, a cell is wide enough to display its contents, but you can set any size you want with the WIDTH and HEIGHT attributes, whose values are in pixels. For the WIDTH attribute, you can also specify a percentage of the table's width. You can apply most of these attributes to the <TR>, <TD>, and <TH> tags alike. The following example shows how to apply these tags; the result is shown in Figure 19-2:

```
<TABLE BORDER=1>
<TR >
    <TH HEIGHT=100> A row 100 pixels tall</TH>
    <TH> <IMG SRC="mylogo.gif"></TH>
</TR>
<TR>
    <TD WIDTH=200 HEIGHT= 90 ALIGN=center VALIGN=bottom>
    Text aligned to center, bottom</TD>
    <TD WIDTH=50%> This cell takes half of the table's width. </TD>
</TR>
<TR VALIGN=bottom>
    <TD> This row is bottom-aligned.</TD>
    <TD ALIGN=right> This one is right-aligned.</TD>
</TR></TABLE>
```

A cell can also contain a hyperlink or an image that works as a hyperlink. By default, a table is wide enough to show its contents, but you can use the WIDTH attribute of the <TABLE> tag to specify an absolute width in pixels or a percentage of the window's width:

```
<TABLE BORDER=1 WIDTH=90%>
```

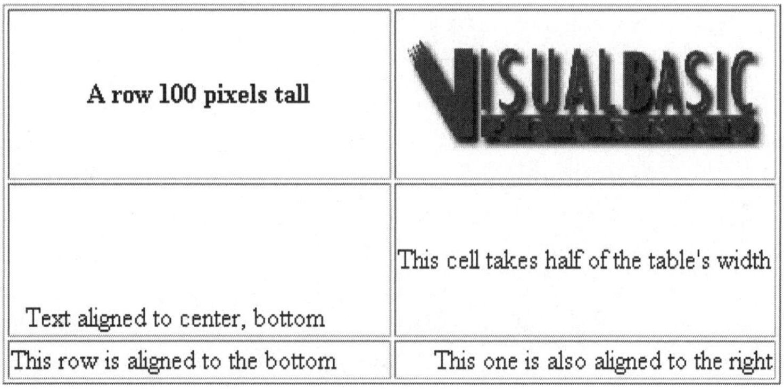

A row 100 pixels tall	VISUALBASIC
Text aligned to center, bottom	This cell takes half of the table's width
This row is aligned to the bottom	This one is also aligned to the right

Figure 19-2. *A table with an embedded image and different formatting and alignment options.*

Styles

Styles offer a way to define the appearance of an HTML tag in an HTML page. If you don't specify a style, a given heading is always displayed with its default attributes—for example, an <H1> heading always uses a black New Times Roman font 14 points tall. You can modify this default setting by using a surrounding <FONT> tag, as in this code:

```
<FONT FACE="Arial" SIZE=20 COLOR="red"><H1>Level 1 Heading</H1></FONT>
```

The problem with the preceding approach is that if all your Level 1 headings need to be rendered with nondefault attributes, you must update all the individual occurrences of the <H1> tag. And when you later want to change to another color or font size, you need to revise all the tags once again.

Conversely, if you define and then apply a style, you need to redefine the <H1> tag just once and your change will affect the entire document. You can even take a further step and keep your style definitions in a separate file—a Cascading Style Sheet file, or CSS—that can be referenced by all the HTML pages that make up your application. This approach gives you an effective way to keep the contents of an HTML document separated from its appearance so that you can easily modify either one of them independently from the other. While it's common practice to keep styles in a separate file, for the sake of clarity in the following examples I'll embed the definition of the style in the HTML page that uses it.

You can define a new style using the <STYLE> and </STYLE> pair of tags. For example, see how you can redefine the <H1> and <H2> tags:

```
<STYLE>
H1 {FONT-FAMILY=Arial; FONT-SIZE=20; COLOR="red"}
H2 {FONT-FAMILY=Arial; FONT-SIZE=16; FONT-STYLE=italic; COLOR="green"}
</STYLE>
<H1>This is a Red heading</H1>
<H2>This is a Green italic heading</H2>
```

The name of the tag that you want to redefine is followed by a semicolon-delimited list of *ATTRIBUTE=value* pairs enclosed within braces. In most cases, you can also omit the double quotes that surround a string value—for example, when you're specifying a color attribute. You can redefine as many tags as you want within a single <STYLE> and </STYLE> tag pair.

Style sheets even let you define contextual behaviors. Take, for instance, the definition of the <H2> tag above, which renders all the level 2 headings as green italicized text. Such a style actually nullifies the effect of an <I> tag inside the heading because the text is already italic. You can remedy this by specifying that <I> tags inside an <H2> and </H2> pair should produce normal (nonitalic) characters in the color red. You enforce this behavior by adding this definition to the style (the added line is in boldface):

```
<STYLE>
H1 {FONT-FAMILY=Arial; FONT-SIZE=20; COLOR="red"}
H2 {FONT-FAMILY=Arial; FONT-SIZE=16; FONT-STYLE=italic; COLOR="green"}
H2 I {FONT-STYLE=normal; COLOR="blue"}
</STYLE>
<H2>This is a heading with a <I>Normal Blue</I> portion in it</H2>
```

Instead of redefining the appearance of all the tags with a given name, you can set the style for a specific tag using the STYLE attribute, as in this code:

```
<H3 STYLE="FONT-STYLE=bold;COLOR=blue">A blue and bold Level 3 Heading</H3>
```

A great feature of style sheets is that they allow you to define new classes of style attributes. This way, you can label an item in the page according to its meaning and specify its appearance elsewhere in the page or (better) in a separate style sheet. This approach is similar to the one you follow when you define a new style in a word processor such as Microsoft Word. For example, suppose that some of your headings are book titles, and you want all book titles in your HTML pages formatted as bold green text. All you have to do is create the booktitle style class, and then apply it when you need it using the CLASS attribute:

```
<STYLE>
.booktitle {FONT-FAMILY=Arial; FONT-STYLE=bold; COLOR="green"}
</STYLE>
<H3 CLASS=booktitle>Programming Microsoft Visual Basic 6</H3>
```

The CLASS attribute really shines when used with the <DIV> and </DIV> tags to apply a particular style class to a portion of the page. (For additional information about the <DIV> tag, see the "Tags" section later in this chapter.)

```
<STYLE>
.listing {FONT-FAMILY=Courier New; FONT-SIZE=12}
</STYLE>

<DIV CLASS=listing>
' A Visual Basic listing <BR>
Dim x As Variant
</DIV>
```

Finally, here's one way to store a style definition in a separate file, based on the *@import* directive:

```
<STYLE>
@import URL("http://www.vb2themax.com/stylesheet.css");
</STYLE>
```

Forms

HTML forms offer a way to let the user enter information in a page. A form can contain controls, including single-line and multiline text boxes, check boxes, radio buttons, push buttons, list boxes, and combo boxes. These controls can't compete with their Visual Basic counterparts, but they're sufficiently powerful for most purposes. All the controls in an HTML form must be enclosed between the <FORM> and </FORM> tags. The <FORM> tag accepts several attributes, the most important of which is NAME, because you need to assign a name to the form if you want to access its controls from script routines. You can place controls outside a form, as, for example, when you plan to process them through scripts and don't plan to post their contents to the Web server.

Most of the controls in a form are inserted using the <INPUT> tag. The TYPE attribute determines the type of control, and the NAME attribute is the name of the control. For example, the following code builds a form with one CheckBox control:

```
<FORM NAME="formname">
<INPUT TYPE=Checkbox NAME=Shipped CHECKED>The product has been shipped.<BR>
</FORM>
```

The NAME attribute vaguely corresponds to the Visual Basic controls' *Name* property. The CHECKED attribute displays a mark in the control. The text that follows the > character corresponds to the caption of the control, but as far as HTML is concerned, it's just text that happens to follow the control in the page.

The NAME attribute is more important for RadioButton controls because all the controls with the same name belong to the same group of mutually exclusive choices. You can select one of the controls in the group by adding the CHECKED attribute:

```
Select the type of malfunction observed:<BR>
<INPUT TYPE=Radio NAME="Problem" CHECKED>Wrong Results<BR>
<INPUT TYPE=Radio NAME="Problem">Fatal Error<BR>
<INPUT TYPE=Radio NAME="Problem">General Protection Fault<BR>
```

HTML supports three types of push buttons: the Submit button, the Reset button, and the generic, programmable button. The first two buttons are similar, differing only for the value of the TYPE attribute:

```
<INPUT TYPE=Submit VALUE="Submit">
<INPUT TYPE=Reset VALUE="Reset values">
```

In both cases, the VALUE attribute determines the caption of the button. The effect of the Submit button is to send the contents of all the controls on the form to the server. The effect of the Reset button is to clear the contents of all the controls on the form and restore their initial values. The third type of button is used in combination with a script, as I explain in the following section.

HTML forms can contain three types of TextBox controls: the standard single-line control, the control for entering passwords, and the multiline control. A single-line control has a TYPE attribute equal to *Text*, can contain a VALUE attribute to specify the initial contents of the control, and also supports the SIZE attribute (the width in characters) and the MAXLENGTH attribute (the maximum number of characters):

```
Enter book title: <BR>
<INPUT TYPE=Text NAME="BookTitle" SIZE=40 MAXLENGTH=60
VALUE="Programming Microsoft Visual Basic 6">
```

The Password control is functionally identical to the regular TextBox control and supports the same attributes. It corresponds to a Visual Basic TextBox whose *PasswordChar* property has been set to an asterisk:

```
Enter your password:
<INPUT TYPE=Password NAME="UserPwd" SIZE=40 MAXLENGTH=60><BR>
```

The TextArea control corresponds to a Visual Basic's multiline TextBox control. This control is an exception to the general rule, however, because it uses the <TEXTAREA> tag instead of the <INPUT> tag; you can determine the control's size using the ROWS and COLS attributes, and the initial contents of the control can be inserted before the closing </TEXTAREA> tag:

```
<TEXTAREA NAME="Comments" ROWS=5 COLS=30 MAXLENGTH=1000>
Enter your comments here.
</TEXTAREA>
```

The text between the <TEXTAREA> and </TEXTAREA> tags is inserted in the control as is, including carriage returns. If a line is wider than the control's width, the user has to scroll the control to see its rightmost portion.

HTML forms support single-choice and multiple-choice list box controls, which are named *Select* controls in the HTML jargon. A Select control is defined by means of the <SELECT> and </SELECT> tags, which accept the SIZE attribute for specifying the control's height (in number of rows), and the MULTIPLE attribute if the control accepts multiple choices. Each individual item of the list requires an <OPTION> and </OPTION> tag pair. You can insert the SELECT attribute if the item is initially selected, and a VALUE attribute to specify the string that will be sent to the server when the form is submitted. The following code creates a multiple-choice Select control that's 4 rows tall and whose first item is initially highlighted:

```
<SELECT NAME="Products" SIZE=4 MULTIPLE>
    <OPTION SELECTED VALUE=1>Computers</OPTION>
    <OPTION VALUE=2>Monitors</OPTION>
    <OPTION VALUE=3>Hard disks</OPTION>
    <OPTION VALUE=4>CD-ROM drives</OPTION>
</SELECT>
```

If you omit the MULTIPLE attribute and specify SIZE=1 (or omit it), the Select control turns into a combo box control.

Scripting

Now that you know how to prepare an HTML page and an HTML form, understanding how scripting fits in is really straightforward. First, you need the <SCRIPT> and </SCRIPT> tags to reserve a section of the HTML document for your script code, as in this code:

```
<SCRIPT LANGUAGE="VBScript">
    ' Your VBScript code goes here.
</SCRIPT>
```

You can also specify another script language in the LANGUAGE attribute—for example, JavaScript—but given the typical reader of this book, all my examples use VBScript.

VBScript vs. Visual Basic for Applications

The VBScript language is an extensive subset of Visual Basic for Applications (VBA) and differs from its more powerful cousin in relatively few features:

- Specific data types aren't supported. Everything in VBScript is a variant, so the *As* clause in the *Dim* statements and argument lists isn't allowed. UDTs are missing in VBScript, so you can't use the *Type...End Type* keywords.

- For the same reason, specific object variables are missing in VBScript, as is the *New* operator. You create a new external object using the *CreateObject* function and access it using a Variant variable and late binding. *TypeOf* tests and *With...End With* blocks aren't supported either.

- VBScript doesn't support Property procedures, Optional arguments, Static variables, constants, labels, *Goto* and *Gosub* commands, and the *On Error Goto* statement. (*On Error Resume Next* is supported, though.)

- All the string functions are supported, except *StrConv*, the *Like* operator, and the *LSet*, *RSet*, and *Mid$* commands.

- VBScript doesn't offer file I/O commands and functions. You can use the FileSystemObject library to manipulate directories and files and the Dictionary object to account for the fact that VBScript doesn't support collections.

> **NOTE**   All the examples in this book are written with VBScript version 3.0. As this book is going to print, VBScript 5 is in public beta. This new version supports classes, property procedures, specific object variables, and the *New* operator. It also provides sophisticated search and replace capabilities. VBScript 5 will be distributed with Internet Explorer 5.

Executing code at page load

Most of the time, the code between the <SCRIPT> and </SCRIPT> tags consists of routines that are invoked from elsewhere in the page. Code can be placed outside any routine, however, in which case it's executed immediately after the page has been downloaded from the server but before it's rendered in the browser's window:

```
<SCRIPT LANGUAGE="VBScript">
    MsgBox "About to display a page"
</SCRIPT>
```

You can also achieve the same result by writing code for the *onload* event of the Window object, as in this snippet:

```
<SCRIPT LANGUAGE="VBScript">
' A variable declared outside any routine is global to the page.
```

```
Dim loadtime
Sub Window_onload()
    ' Remember when the page has been loaded.
    loadtime = Now()
End Sub
</SCRIPT>
```

Accessing form controls

VBScript code can access any control in the form by using the syntax *form-name.controlname* and can also read and modify attributes of controls by using the dot syntax, exactly as in regular Visual Basic. The following code snippet shows you how to assign a string to the VALUE attribute of a TextBox control when the form loads:

```
<FORM NAME="DataForm">
<INPUT TYPE=Text NAME="UserName" VALUE="">
</FORM>
<SCRIPT LANGUAGE="VBScript">
DataForm.UserName.Value = "Francesco"
</SCRIPT>
```

If you want to access controls on the form when the page loads, the <SCRIPT> tag must follow the <FORM> tag; otherwise, the script attempts to reference a control that doesn't exist yet. You can retrieve the status of a CheckBox control through its *Checked* property, and the index of the selected item in a Select control using its *SelectedIndex* property. To check the state of a radio button, you use the following syntax:

```
If DataForm.RadioButton.Item(0).Checked Then …
```

You frequently use VBScript code to react to events raised by controls. For example, buttons, CheckBox controls, and RadioButton controls raise an *onclick* event when they're clicked. You can react to such events as you would in standard Visual Basic. The following example uses a TextBox, one Button, and two RadioButton controls; when the push button is clicked, the code converts the TextBox's contents to uppercase or lowercase, according to the RadioButton currently selected:

```
<FORM NAME="DataForm">
<INPUT TYPE=Text NAME="UserName" VALUE=""><BR>
<INPUT TYPE=Radio NAME="Case" CHECKED>Uppercase
<INPUT TYPE=Radio NAME="Case">Lowercase<BR>
<INPUT TYPE=BUTTON NAME="Convert" VALUE="Convert">
</FORM>

<SCRIPT LANGUAGE="VBScript">
Sub Convert_Onclick()
    If DataForm.Case.Item(0).Checked Then
        DataForm.UserName.Value = UCase(DataForm.UserName.Value)
```

(continued)

```
     Else
         DataForm.UserName.Value = LCase(DataForm.UserName.Value)
     End If
End Sub
</SCRIPT>
```

Another way to specify which VBScript routine should execute when the user acts on a control is to add an *onclick* attribute in the definition of the control and set its value to reference the code that has to be executed when the control is clicked. For example, the following code defines two RadioButtons that, when clicked, modify the contents of a TextBox control:

```
<FORM NAME="UserData">
<INPUT TYPE=Text NAME="UserName" VALUE=""><BR>
<INPUT TYPE=Radio NAME="Case" onClick="Convert(0)" CHECKED>Uppercase<BR>
<INPUT TYPE=Radio NAME="Case" onClick="Convert(1)">Lowercase<BR>
</FORM>

<SCRIPT LANGUAGE="VBScript">
Sub Convert(index)
    If index = 0 Then
        UserData.Username.Value = UCase(UserData.Username.Value)
    Else
        UserData.Username.Value = LCase(UserData.Username.Value)
    End If
End Sub
</SCRIPT>
```

Usually, the value of the *onclick* attribute is the name of the procedure that must be called, together with its arguments (*index*, in this case), but in general it can be any valid piece of VBScript code.

TextBox, TextArea, and Select controls raise an *onchange* event when the user types something in them or selects a new item.

Scripts are often used to add items to a Select control at run time. The sequence of actions necessary for reaching this goal will probably seem contorted to a Visual Basic programmer: You must use the *CreateElement* method of the Document object, set its *Text* and *Value* properties, and finally add it to the Options collection of the Select control. The following example creates a form with a Select control and a push button. Initially, the Select control contains only one item, but you can add two more items by clicking on the button:

```
<FORM NAME="UserForm">
<SELECT NAME="Countries" SIZE=1>
    <OPTION VALUE=1>US</OPTION>
</SELECT>
<INPUT TYPE=BUTTON NAME="AddCountries" VALUE="Add Countries">
</FORM>
```

```
<SCRIPT LANGUAGE="VBScript">
Sub AddCountries_onclick()
    Dim e
    Set e = Document.createElement("OPTION")
    e.Text = "Italy"
    e.Value = 2
    Userform.Countries.Options.Add e
    Set e = Document.createElement("OPTION")
    e.Text = "Germany"
    e.Value = 3
    Userform.Countries.Options.Add e
End Sub
</SCRIPT>
```

Generating HTML code

VBScript lets you generate a new HTML page on the fly, using the *Write* method of
the Document object. I explain the Document object (and all the other objects available to HTML programmers) later in this chapter, but a simple example can give you
a taste of what you can do:

```
<FORM NAME="UserData">
<INPUT TYPE=Text NAME="Rows" VALUE="10">
<INPUT TYPE=Text NAME="Cols" VALUE="10"><BR>
<INPUT TYPE=Button NAME="Generate" VALUE="Generate Table">
</FORM>

<SCRIPT LANGUAGE="VBScript">
Sub Generate_onclick()
    Dim rows, cols
    ' We need to store these values in variables before the form is
    ' destroyed when a new document is created.
    rows = UserData.Rows.Value
    cols = UserData.Cols.Value

    Document.Open
    Document.Write "<H1>Multiplication Table</H1>"
    Document.Write "<TABLE BORDER=1>"
    For r = 1 to rows
        Document.Write "<TR>"
        For c = 1 to cols
            Document.Write "<TD> " & (r*c) & " </TD>"
        Next
        Document.Write "</TR>"
    Next
    Document.Write "</TABLE>"
End Sub
</SCRIPT>
```

This code programmatically creates a new HTML page, which contains a multiplication table whose size is specified by the user in two text box controls. (See Figure 19-3.) As soon you issue the *Open* method of the Document object, the *UserData* form doesn't exist any longer, so you need to cache the values of those text box controls in the *rows* and *cols* local variables before you create the new page.

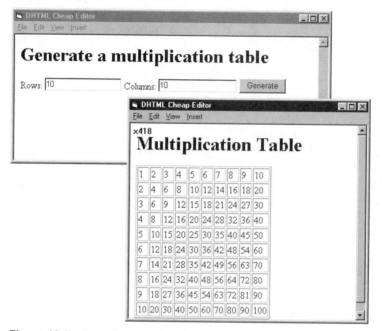

Figure 19-3. *An HTML page that dynamically creates a multiplication table with a given number of rows and columns.*

This concludes our quick course on HTML and VBScript. Now you're ready to move on to Dynamic HTML and appreciate its great flexibility and increased power.

AN INTRODUCTION TO DYNAMIC HTML

Entire books have been devoted to Dynamic HTML (DHTML), and I strongly advise you to get one of them if you're seriously interested in producing DHTML programs. As I've done with plain HTML, in this chapter I can only outline the most important features of this language.

In theory, Dynamic HTML should be considered as HTML 4.0—that is, the next version of HTML. In practice, Microsoft Internet Explorer and Netscape Navigator currently support different versions of DHTML, so it's difficult to write DHTML pages that work equally well with both browsers. From our particular point of view as Visual Basic programmers, however, this issue isn't really relevant because DHTML applications actually require Internet Explorer 4.01 Service Pack 1 or later, and they can't run inside another browser. The problem isn't the DHTML language itself, but the fact that only the most recent versions of the Microsoft browser expose DHTML events to the outside, where a DLL written in Visual Basic 6 can trap them and react accordingly.

Main Features

Dynamic HTML isn't radically different from regular HTML. All the old tags are still supported, and scripts inside the page can exploit an expanded object model that's compatible with the previous version, so they'll continue to work as before. In a sense and at the risk of oversimplifying, we can say that the real difference between regular HTML and Dynamic HTML is in how the page is interpreted by the browser when the page is being downloaded from the remote server.

Among the new features of DHTML, the following ones deserve special mention:

- Dynamic redrawing of the page, which means that you can change the style, the color or any other attribute of an element of the page—including its visibility—and the page automatically redraws itself without the user needing to download it again. This means faster response time, less workload on the server, and above all, really dynamic behavior.

- The DHTML object model gives you access to any element of the page, including tags, images, and paragraphs, down to the individual word or character if necessary. You can therefore manipulate the appearance of the page in its tiniest details.

- Styles and style sheets have been expanded with more attributes, and so they give you more control over the page elements.

- You can enforce absolute position of elements, which means that, if necessary, you can prepare the layout of your pages with the highest accuracy. Moreover, each element has a *z-index* attribute (similar to Visual Basic's *ZOrder* property) that can be used to simulate 3-D appearance. Because elements' coordinates can be dynamically modified, it's easy to create animation effects using simple scripts.

- The new event model adds flexibility in how a user's actions can be processed by scripts in the page. This includes the event bubbling feature, which lets scripts process events when it's more convenient to do so.

■   Visual filters offer many eye-catching ways to render any element on the page and permit you to create shadowed and 3-D text. Transition filters let you display a portion of the page using fading effects. Internet Explorer offers 13 built-in transition filters, but you can also use third-party filters.

■   DHTML includes many other improvements over traditional HTML, such as better control over the creation of tables and support for additional graphic formats (such as PNG, or Portable Network Graphics, the successor of the GIF format).

Let's see the most important new features in more detail.

Tags

You've already seen how you can use the <DIV> and </DIV> tags to group multiple elements and create a portion of the page that can be assigned a common style. For example, you can use these tags to create rectangular areas with text and background colors that are different from the other elements:

```
<DIV STYLE=" WIDTH=300; HEIGHT=100; COLOR=white; BACKGROUND=red;">
A red block with white text<BR>
Another line in the same block
</DIV>
```

When you're working with DHTML, you might need to process items that are smaller than the heading or the paragraph. You can reference such items using the <SPAN> and </SPAN> pair of tags, which subdivide an element into smaller chunks so that each portion can have different attributes:

```
<DIV STYLE="WIDTH=300; HEIGHT=150; COLOR=white; BACKGROUND=red;">
A red block with white text<BR>
<SPAN STYLE="COLOR=yellow">Some words in yellow,</SPAN>
<SPAN STYLE="COLOR=blue">Other words in blue</SPAN>
</DIV>
```

An important difference between the <DIV> tag and the <SPAN> tag is that the former always adds a carriage return after the closing </DIV> tag, which means that you can't continue to insert text on the same line. Conversely, the </SPAN> tag doesn't insert a carriage return, so, for example, the previous code snippet produces two lines of text, not three. The importance of the <DIV> and <SPAN> tags will be more evident when you see how you can use scripts to create dynamic pages.

The <BUTTON> and </BUTTON> tags allow you to add more versatile button controls on a form. While the standard <INPUT TYPE=Button> tag supports only a text caption, these new tags let you embed anything in the text, including an image:

```
<BUTTON ID="Button1" STYLE="height=80; width=180">
Click Here
<IMG SRC="www.vb2themax.com/mylogo.gif">
</BUTTON>
```

DHTML includes a sort of Frame control, which can draw a border around other controls. You create such a control using the <FIELDSET> tag and specify its caption using the <LEGEND> tag. Actually, this frame control is even more powerful than its Visual Basic counterpart because you can embed nearly everything between the <LEGEND> and </LEGEND> tag pair:

```
<FIELDSET>
<LEGEND>Select a product<IMG SRC="mylogo.gif"></LEGEND>
<INPUT TYPE=Radio NAME="Product" CHECKED>Tape
<INPUT TYPE=Radio NAME="Product">Music CD
<INPUT TYPE=Radio NAME="Product">Videotape
</FIELDSET>
```

Dynamic HTML also adds several new attributes that you can use with certain tags. For example, the TABINDEX attribute lets you specify the tab order of controls on the page exactly as the Visual Basic property does. The ACCESSKEY attribute works with some types of page elements to provide a hot key for easy Alt+*key* selection. The difference is that DHTML doesn't highlight the selected key in any way—you have to do it yourself. While this failure to highlight a selected key seems to be a flaw in DHTML, it actually gives you a lot of flexibility when building your user interface:

```
' A "Click Here" button that you click using the Alt+H key combination
<BUTTON ID="Button1" ACCESSKEY="H">Click <B>H</B>ere</BUTTON>
```

Finally, the DISABLED attribute lets you selectively disable (and reenable) controls and other elements. You just need to remember that it works in a way opposite to the Visual Basics *Enabled* property:

```
<INPUT TYPE=Radio ID="optMusicCD" NAME="Product" DISABLED>Music CD

<SCRIPT LANGUAGE="VBScript">
Sub Button1_onclick()
    ' Reenable the option button.
    optMusicCD.disabled = False
End sub
</SCRIPT>
```

Properties

Dynamic HTML adds some new properties to the <STYLE> tag. These properties are useful in themselves, but above all they add a new dimension to scripting because they allow a script routine to move, hide, and change the relative z-order of the elements on the page, thereby making the page a truly dynamic one.

The *position* property permits you to accurately place an element on the page; by default, this property is set to the value *static*, which means that the element is positioned according to the usual rules of HTML. But if you set the *position* property to *absolute*, you can specify the coordinates of an object with respect to the upper left corner of the window, using the *left* and *top* properties. Here's an example that displays white text inside a rectangle with a red background. The rectangle is 300 pixels wide and 150 pixels high:

```
<DIV STYLE="POSITION=absolute; TOP=50; LEFT=100; WIDTH=300; HEIGHT=150;
COLOR=white; BACKGROUND=red;">A red block with white text</DIV>
```

If the object is contained within another object—for example, another <DIV> section—the left and top coordinates are measured with respect to the container's upper left corner. For example, the following piece of code creates a red rectangle and a blue rectangle within it:

```
<DIV STYLE="POSITION=absolute; TOP=100; LEFT=100; WIDTH=300; HEIGHT=150;
COLOR=white; BACKGROUND=red;">
Outer rectangle
    <DIV STYLE="POSITION=absolute; TOP=20; LEFT=40; WIDTH=220; HEIGHT=110;
    COLOR=white; BACKGROUND=Blue;">Inner rectangle</DIV>
</DIV>
```

If *position* is set to *relative*, the *left* and *top* properties refer to the upper left corner of the element in the page that immediately precedes the current one. You typically use the relative mode to move a portion of text or an image to a given distance from the last piece of text in the page:

```
A string of text followed by a green rectangle
<DIV STYLE="POSITION=relative; TOP:10; LEFT=0; WIDTH=300; HEIGHT=10;
BACKGROUND=green;"></DIV>
```

When you have overlapping objects on the page, you can determine their visibility using the *z-order* property, by means of which a higher value puts an object in front of objects with lower values:

```
<DIV STYLE="POSITION=absolute; TOP=100; LEFT=100; WIDTH=300;
HEIGHT=150; COLOR=white; BACKGROUND=red; Z-INDEX=2">
This rectangle overlaps the next one.</DIV>
<DIV STYLE="POSITION=absolute; TOP=120; LEFT=120; WIDTH=300;
HEIGHT=150; COLOR=white; BACKGROUND=green; Z-INDEX=1"></DIV>
```

You can't use the *z-order* property to change the relative z-ordering of an object and its container because the container will always appear behind the objects it contains. If you omit the *z-order* property, objects stack according to the order in which they appear in the HTML source code. (That is, each object covers the object defined before it in code.)

The *visibility* property specifies whether the object is visible. It takes the values *hidden* or *visible*. This property is most useful when it's controlled via script. Another new intriguing property is *display*: When you set it to *none*, the element becomes invisible and the browser reclaims the space this element occupied to rearrange the other elements on the page (unless they use absolute positioning). You can make the element visible again by setting the *display* property back to an empty string. For an example of this property, see the "The First Example: A Dynamic Menu" section later in this chapter.

Properties and Scripting

The "dynamic" in Dynamic HTML means that you can modify one or more attributes of the page at run time and have the browser immediately render the new contents of the page without needing to reload the page from the server. For this reason, you must create script procedures to exploit the potential of DHTML.

You can programmatically control any attribute of any item on the page, provided that the item can be referenced in code. In plain HTML, you can reference only a few items—for example, the controls in a form—but in Dynamic HTML, you can reference any item that has an ID attribute. For example, the following code contains a <DIV> portion of the page associated with the *rectangle* ID, and a push button that, when clicked, executes a VBScript routine that modifies the background color of the <DIV> section:

```
<DIV ID="rectangle" STYLE="POSITION=absolute; LEFT=100;
TOP=50; WIDTH=200; HEIGHT=100; BACKGROUND=red">
Click the button to change background color
</DIV>
<FORM>
<INPUT TYPE=BUTTON NAME="ChangeColor" VALUE="Change Color">
</FORM>

<SCRIPT LANGUAGE="VBScript">
' Randomly change the color of the rectangle.
Sub ChangeColor_onclick()
    Rectangle.style.background = "#" & RndColor() & RndColor() & RndColor()
End Sub

' Return a random two-digit hexadecimal value.
Function RndColor()
    RndColor = Right("0" & Hex(Rnd * 256), 2)
End Function
</SCRIPT>
```

You need to pass through the intermediate style object to get to the *background* property. This makes sense because *background* is a property of the STYLE attribute. Likewise, you can control other properties of the style object, such as these:

■ The *fontFamily*, *fontStyle*, and *fontSize* properties determine the style of the characters. (Notice that property names are similar to names of style attributes but don't include the hyphen.)

■ The *left*, *top*, *width*, and *height* properties set and return a string that contains the position and size of the object (for example, *10px* for 10 pixels); there are also the *posLeft*, *posTop*, *posWidth*, and *posHeight* properties, which don't append the *px* string to the numeric value and are therefore more useful in regular programming.

■ The padding property is the distance in pixels between the contents of an element and its border. You can use the properties *paddingLeft*, *paddingTop*, *paddingRight*, and *paddingBottom* to specify the distance from the individual borders on the four sides.

■ The *textAlign* property affects the horizontal alignment of text in an element and can be set to left, center, or right.

■ The *visibility* property affects whether the element is displayed (can be hidden or visible). The *zIndex* property sets or returns a number that determines whether the object is displayed in front of or behind other elements; positive values move the element in front of the other objects on the page, and negative values move the element behind others on the page. The <BODY> element has *zIndex* equal to 0.

■ The *cssText* property sets and returns the argument of the STYLE attribute as a string.

To fine-tune the position and size of an item, you can strip the *px* characters appended to the value returned by the *left*, *top*, *width*, and *height* properties. Using the *posxxxx* properties is usually better, however, because they return numerical values. The following example shows how you can move an element to the right:

```
rectangle.style.posLeft = rectangle.style.posLeft + 10
```

If a property isn't defined in the STYLE attribute, it returns Null. The *posxxxx* properties are an exception to this rule because they always return numeric values.

NOTE Use the *style.color* and *style.backgroundColor* properties to adjust the text and background color of any element on the page except the Document object, for which you should use the *fgcolor* and *bgcolor* properties.

Text Properties and Methods

Because a DHTML document is an active entity, you often want to modify its contents at run time. You can make run-time modifications in many ways—for example, by using the TextRange object (which is described later in this chapter). Most visible page elements, however, support four properties and two methods that make this an easy job.

The four properties are *innerText*, *outerText*, *innerHTML*, and *outerHTML*. The *innerText* returns the portion of the document contained in the element as text. (All HTML tags are automatically filtered out.) The *outerText* property returns the same value as *innerText*, but you get a different result when you assign a string to it, as you'll see in a moment. The *innerHTML* property returns the HTML code between the opening and closing tags. The *outerHTML* property returns the HTML code of the element, including its opening and closing tags.

To experiment with these properties, let's define an element that contains some HTML tags inside it, such as

```
<H1 ID=Heading1>Level <I>One</I> Heading</H1>
```

which is rendered on your browser as **Level *One* Heading**. Now see what the preceding properties return when applied to this element:

```
MsgBox Heading1.innerText   ' Level One Heading
MsgBox Heading1.outerText   ' Level One Heading
MsgBox Heading1.innerHTML   ' Level <I>One</I> Heading
MsgBox Heading1.outerHTML   ' <H1 ID=Heading1>Level <I>One</I> Heading</H1>
```

Assigning a value to the *innerText* substitutes the text between the opening and closing tags; the new value isn't parsed, so it shouldn't include HTML tags. For example, the statement

```
Heading1.innerText = "A New Heading"
```

completely replaces the text between the <H1> and </H1> tags, and the new heading appears in your browser as **A New Heading**. Even if the *outerText* property always return the same string as the *innerText* property, it behaves differently when a new value is assigned to it because the substitution also affects the surrounding tags.

Hence the statement

```
Heading1.outerText = "A New Heading"
```

actually destroys the <H1> and </H1> tags and transforms the heading element into plain text (unless it was contained in another pair of tags). What's worse is that now the object has no ID attribute associated with it, so you can't programmatically access it any longer. For this reason, the *outerText* property has limited practical use, and in most cases you'll use it just to delete the tags that surround an element:

```
' A reusable VBScript routine
Sub DeleteOuterTags(anyElement)
    anyElement.outerText = anyElement.innerText
End Sub
```

If you want to replace the portion of a page inside a pair of tags with some HTML text, you should use that element's *innerHTML* property, as in this line of code:

```
Heading1.innerHTML = "A <U>New</U> Heading"
```

In this case, the string passed to the property is parsed and all HTML tags affect the result. For example, after the previous assignment the result displayed in the browser is **A <u>New</u> Heading**.

The last property of this group, *outerHTML*, works like *innerHTML*, but the substitution also affects the surrounding tags. This means that you can modify the type and ID of the element you're referencing, and you can change the level of a heading and the formatting of its contents, for example, in one operation:

```
Heading1.outerHTML = "<H2 ID=Heading1>Level <U>Two</U> Heading</H2>"
```

Or you can center the heading using this code:

```
Heading1.outerHTML = "<CENTER>" & Heading1.outerHTML & "</CENTER>"
```

Thanks to the string manipulation capabilities of VBScript, you can create a reusable routine that lets you change the level of any heading in the page without altering either its ID or its contents:

```
Sub ChangeHeadingLevel(element, newLevel)
    html = element.outerHTML
    pos1 = Instr(UCase(html), "<H")
    level = Mid(html, pos1 + 2, 1)
    pos2 = InstrRev(UCase(html), "</H" & level, -1, 1)
    ' You must type the next two lines as a single statement.
    html = Left(html, pos1 + 1) & newLevel & Mid(html, pos1 + 3,
        pos2 - pos1) & newLevel & Mid(html, pos2 + 4)
    element.outerHTML = html
End Sub
```

If you modify an element's ID, the event procedure you've written for it won't work any longer. For this reason, you should always keep the same ID, or you should dynamically add the code to manage events from the new element. Also keep in mind that not all visible elements support all these four properties, the most notable exception being table cells (which expose only the *innerText* and *innerHTML* properties).

While the four properties I've described so far let you *replace* a portion of the document, most elements also support two methods that enable you to *add* new contents to the document. The *insertAdjacentText* method inserts a portion of plain text immediately before or after the opening or closing tag of the element. The *insertAdjacentHTML* method does the same, but its argument is parsed and all HTML is correctly recognized and affect the result. Here are a few examples:

```
' Append plain text at the end of the heading.
Heading1.insertAdjacentText "BeforeEnd", " (added dynamically)"
' As above, but appends italicized text.
Heading1.insertAdjacentHTML "BeforeEnd", " <I>(added dynamically)</I>"
' Add new text before the first word of the heading.
Heading1.insertAdjacentText "AfterBegin", "This is a "
' Add a level 2 heading immediately after this heading.
Heading1.insertAdjacentHTML "AfterEnd", "<H2>New Level 2 Heading</H2>"
' Insert italicized text right before this heading.
Heading1.insertAdjacentHTML "BeforeBegin", "<I>Introducing...</I>"
```

Events

Each page element with which you've associated an ID attribute can raise an event. The majority of DHTML events are similar to Visual Basic events, even though their names are different. All the DHTML events begin with the two characters *on*, such as *onclick*, *onkeypress*, and *onchange*. For example, when the hyperlink

```
Click <A ID="Details" HREF="www.vb2themax.com/details">here</A> for details
```

is clicked, you can trap the user's action with the following VBScript code:

```
Sub Details_onclick()
    MsgBox "About to be transferred to another site"
End Sub
```

The handling of DHTML events differs significantly in a couple of ways from the Visual Basic way of managing events, though. First, event procedures don't take arguments. Second, an event is received by the object that raised it (which is like the innermost of a set of Russian dolls) and, in turn, by all the page elements that contain the object that raised the event. This feature, known as *event bubbling*, is explained in the following section.

All the arguments that make sense inside an event can be retrieved as (and possibly assigned to) properties of the event object. For example, when an *onkeypress* event is received, you can determine which key has been pressed by looking at the *event.keycode* property, and you can also "eat" the key by setting this property to 0. For example, see how you can convert to uppercase all the text entered in a TextBox control:

```
<INPUT TYPE=Text NAME="txtCity" VALUE="">

<SCRIPT LANGUAGE="VBScript">
Sub txtCity_onkeypress()
    window.event.keycode = Asc(UCase(Chr(window.event.keycode)))
End Sub
</SCRIPT>
```

Inside any event procedure, you can retrieve a reference to the object the event is bound to by using the *Me* keyword, as in the following piece of code:

```
Sub txtCity_onkeypress()
    ' Clear the text box if the spacebar is pressed.
    If window.event.keycode = 32 Then
        Me.Value = ""
        window.event.keycode = 0        ' Also eat the key.
    End If
End Sub
```

Event bubbling

The event bubbling feature of DHTML events lets you process an event in multiple places on the page, which isn't something you can do in Visual Basic. A DHTML event is first received by the object acted on by the user, it's next raised for its container and then for the container's container, and so on until the event reaches the highest tag in the hierarchy. For example, if the user clicks on a hyperlink inside a table, the *onclick* event is first fired for the hyperlink object and then for the table, for the Body object, and finally for the Document object.

The following example makes use of the event bubbling feature to write one event procedure that manages the keys pressed in three distinct TextBox controls, which have been grouped together under a <DIV> tag. The example also demonstrates that the event is generated for the Body object (provided that you label it with an ID attribute) and for the Document object:

```
<BODY ID="Body">
<DIV ID=Textboxes>
<INPUT TYPE=Text NAME="txtName" VALUE="">
<INPUT TYPE=Text NAME="txtCity" VALUE="">
<INPUT TYPE=Text NAME="txtCountry" VALUE="">
</DIV>
```

```
<SCRIPT LANGUAGE="VBScript">
Sub Textboxes_onkeypress()
    ' Convert to uppercase.
    window.event.keycode = Asc(UCase(Chr(window.event.keycode)))
End Sub

Sub Body_onkeypress()
    ' The Body element also gets the event.
End Sub

Sub Document_onkeypress()
    ' The Document element also gets the event.
End Sub
</SCRIPT>
</BODY>
```

By setting the *event.cancelBubble* property to True, you can cancel the bubbling in any event procedure. For example, if you set this property to True in the *Body_onclick* procedure, the Document object won't receive the event.

In any event procedure in the event chain, you can retrieve a reference to the element that started the event by querying the *event.srcElement* property. This permits you to create generalized event procedures and at the same time to account for special cases, as in the following example:

```
Sub Textboxes_onkeypress()
    ' Convert all textboxes to uppercase except txtName.
    If window.event.srcElement.Name <> "txtName" Then
        window.event.keycode = Asc(UCase(Chr(window.event.keycode)))
    End If
End Sub
```

Don't confuse the *srcElement* property with the *Me* keyword, which returns a reference to the object the event procedure is bound to. The two objects coincide only inside the first event procedure fired by the event bubbling mechanism.

Canceling the default effect

Most user actions on a page element produce default results. For example, a mouse click on a hyperlink causes a jump to another HTML page, and a key pressed when the focus is on a TextBox control causes the character to be added to the control's current contents. You can cancel this default action by assigning False to the *event.returnValue* property, as in this example:

```
Click <A ID="Link1" HREF="http://www.vb2themax.com">here</A>

<SCRIPT LANGUAGE="VBScript">
Sub Link1_onclick()
    ' Prevent the hyperlink from firing.
    window.event.returnValue = False
End Sub
</SCRIPT>
```

1053

Another way to cancel the default action of an event is to transform the event procedure into a Function and assign False to the return value, as here:

```
Function Link1_onclick()
    Link1_onclick = False
End Function
```

Timer events

Even if HTML doesn't provide a Timer control, it's possible—indeed simple—to create routines that are executed at regular intervals. You can choose from two types of timer routines: one that fires repeatedly and one that fires only once. (This in fact is a standard HTML feature, so you don't need DHTML for using the code in this section.) You activate a timer routine using the *setTimeout* (for one-shot timers) or *setInterval* (for regular timers) method of the *window* object. These methods have a similar syntax:

```
window.setTimeout "routinename", milliseconds, language
window.setInterval "routinename", milliseconds, language
```

You normally invoke these methods from within the *window_onload* routine or outside any routine. (In both cases, the methods are executed as soon as the page is downloaded.) For example, the following code moves a button to the right by 20 pixels twice per second.

```
<INPUT TYPE=BUTTON NAME="Button1" VALUE="Button Caption"
    STYLE="POSITION=absolute" >

<SCRIPT LANGUAGE="VBScript">
' This line is executed when the page is loaded.
window.setInterval "TimerEvent", 500, "VBScript"

' The following routine is executed every 500 milliseconds.
Sub TimerEvent()
    Button1.style.posLeft = Button1.style.posLeft+5
End Sub
</SCRIPT>
```

You can cancel the effect of a *setTimeout* or *setInterval* method by using the *clearTimeout* or *clearInterval* method, respectively.

Event summary

We can subdivide DHTML events into a few categories according to their functions.

Keyboard events include *onkeypress*, *onkeydown*, and *onkeyup*. These are similar to the Visual Basic events of the same names. The event object's *keycode* property contains the code of the pressed key, and you can read the state of shift keys by means of the *altKey*, *ctrlKey*, and *shiftKey* properties of the event object.

Dynamic HTML supports the same mouse events as Visual Basic, including *onclick*, *ondblclick*, *onmousedown*, *onmouseup*, and *onmousemove*. The *onclick* event also fires when the user presses Enter while a push button has the focus. Inside a mouse event, you can query the *event.button* property to learn which button was pressed. (The bit-coded value you get is similar to the argument received by Visual Basic's mouse events.)

Several DHTML events have no counterparts in Visual Basic: *onmouseover* fires when the mouse cursor enters an element, and *onmouseout* fires when the mouse abandons an element. Inside these event procedures, you can use the *fromElement* and *toElement* properties of the event object to learn which element has been entered or abandoned.

The *onfocus* and *onblur* events are similar to Visual Basic's *GotFocus* and *LostFocus* events, but they also fire when the focus goes to another window or another application. The *onchange* event is similar to the corresponding Visual Basic event, but it fires only when the focus leaves the control.

The *onselectstart* event fires when the user clicks on the page and starts selecting a portion of text or other elements; when the mouse moves and the selected area changes accordingly, an *onselect* event is fired. The *ondragstart* event fires when a drag operation starts: By trapping this event, you can cancel its default action, which is copying the selected text elsewhere.

A few events are global to the entire page. The *onreadystatechange* event fires when the state of the page changes (for example, when the download has completed and the page is about to become interactive). The *onresize* event fires when the page is resized. The *onunload* and *onbeforeunload* events are similar to Visual Basic's *Unload* and *QueryUnload*, and they fire when the page is about to be unloaded because the user is navigating to another page or closing the browser. The *onscroll* event occurs when the document (or a page element) is scrolled. The *onhelp* event fires when the user presses the F1 key. The *onerror* event fires when a script error occurs or when the download of a page element (for example, an image) fails.

A few events can't be trapped from a DHTML Visual Basic application: *onabort* (the user clicks on the Stop button on the browser's toolbar), *onreset* (the user clicks on the Reset button), and *onsubmit* (the user clicks on the Submit button).

THE DHTML OBJECT MODEL

To write effective Dynamic HTML applications, you must become familiar with the object model exposed by the browser that hosts the DHTML page. Figure 19-4 on the following page shows the complete Window object hierarchy. I'm not going to dissect every property, method, and event in this hierarchy; instead, I'll focus on the objects that are the most interesting and useful to a Visual Basic programmer.

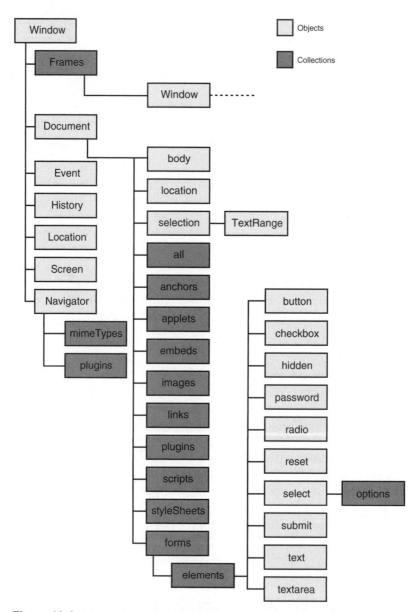

Figure 19-4. *The DHTML object model.*

The Window Object

The Window object is the root of the DHTML hierarchy. It represents the window inside which the HTML page (which is represented by the Document object) is displayed.

Properties

If a window contains frames, you can access them by using the Frames collection, which contains other Window objects. Several other properties return a reference to Window objects. If the window is itself inside a frame, you can get a reference to its container window with the *parent* property. The *top* property returns a reference to the topmost window. In general, you can't anticipate which window is referenced by the latter two properties because the user might have loaded the page in a frame created by another HTML page external to your application. The *opener* property returns a reference to the window that opened the current one.

You can query the open or closed state of the window using the *closed* property. The *status* property sets and returns the text displayed in the browser's status bar, and *defaultStatus* is the default string in the status bar.

Methods

The Window object exposes several methods. The *open* method loads a new document in the window, and the *showModalDialog* method loads an HTML page in a modal window:

```
' Jump to another page.
window.open "http://www.vb2themax.com/tips"
```

You can close the window using the *close* method. A few other methods—*alert*, *confirm*, and *prompt*—display message box and input box dialog boxes, but you usually get a better result using Visual Basic's *MsgBox* and *InputBox* commands.

The *focus* method is similar to Visual Basic's *SetFocus* method. The *blur* method moves the input focus to the next window, as if the user had pressed the Tab key. The *scroll* method accepts an *x-y* pair of coordinates and scrolls the window to ensure that the specified point is visible in the browser:

```
' Scroll the window to the top.
window.scroll 0, 0
```

The *execScript* method adds a lot of flexibility to your program because it lets you manufacture a piece of script code and execute it on the fly. The following example uses this method to implement a cheap calculator with just a bunch of lines of code (see Figure 19-5 on the following page):

```
Insert your expression here:
<INPUT TYPE=Text NAME="Expression" VALUE=""><BR>
Then click to evaluate it:
<INPUT TYPE=BUTTON NAME="Evaluate" VALUE="Evaluate">
<INPUT TYPE=Text NAME="Result" VALUE="">

<SCRIPT LANGUAGE="VBScript">
Sub Evaluate_onclick
```

(continued)

```
      If Expression.Value = "" Then
          MsgBox "Please enter an expression in the first field"
          Exit Sub
      End If

      On Error Resume Next
      window.execScript "Result.value = " & Expression.Value, "VBScript"
      If Err Then
          MsgBox "An error occurred - please type a valid expression"
      End If
  End Sub
</SCRIPT>
```

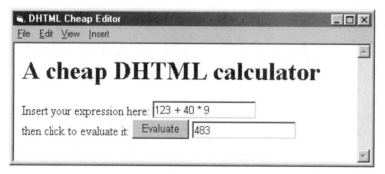

Figure 19-5. *An expression evaluator built with DHTML code.*

Don't forget to pass the "VBScript" string as a second argument to the *execScript* function because the default language is JavaScript.

This powerful method can even add script procedures to the page. The following example demonstrates this feature by creating a table of values using an expression the user entered in a TextBox control. (This is something that would be very difficult to do in Visual Basic!)

```
Enter an expression:   FN(x) =
<INPUT TYPE=Text NAME="Expression" VALUE="x*x"><P>
Click here to generate a table of values:
<INPUT TYPE=BUTTON NAME="CreateTable" VALUE="Create Table">

<SCRIPT LANGUAGE="VBScript">
Sub CreateTable_onclick()
' Create the FUNC() function.
' (Enter the following two lines as a single VBScript statement,)
window.execScript "Function FUNC(x): FUNC = "
    & Expression.Value & ": End Function", "VBScript"
' Create the HTML code for the table.
code = "<H1>Table of values for FN(x) = " & Expression.Value & "</H1>"
code = code & "<TABLE BORDER>"
code = code & "<TR><TH>  x  </TH><TH>  FN(x)  </TH></TR>"
```

```
For n = 1 To 100
    code = code & "<TR><TD> " & n & " </TD>"
    code = code & "<TD> " & FUNC(n) & " </TD></TR>"
Next
code = code & "</TABLE>"

' Write the code to a new HTML page.
window.document.clear
window.document.open
window.document.write code
window.document.close
End Sub
</SCRIPT>
```

I've already explained the remaining methods of the Window object: *setInterval*, *setTimeout*, *clearInterval*, and *clearTimeout*. (See the "Timer Events" section earlier in this chapter.)

The History object

The History object represents all the URLs that the user has visited in the current session. It exposes only one property and three methods.

The *length* property returns the number of URLs stored in the object. The *back* and *forward* methods load the page at the previous and next URL in the history list and therefore correspond to a click on the Back and Forward buttons on the browser's toolbar. They're useful for adding buttons on the page that perform the same function, as shown here:

```
Sub cmdPrevious_onclick()
    window.history.back
End Sub
```

The only other method of this object is *go*, which loads the URL at the *n*th position in the history list:

```
' Display the third page in the history list.
window.history.go 3
```

The Navigator object

The Navigator object represents the browser program and provides information about it capabilities. The *appCodeName*, *appName*, and *appVersion* properties return the code name, the product name, and the version of the browser. The *cookieEnabled* property returns True if the browser supports cookies; *userAgent* is the browser name sent as a string to the server in the HTTP request. You can use the following VBScript code to display some information about your browser:

```
' Dynamically create an HTML page with all the requested information.
Set doc = window.document
```

(continued)

```
Set nav = window.navigator
doc.open
doc.write "<B>appCodeName</B> = " & nav.appCodeName & "<BR>"
doc.write "<B>appName</B> = " & nav.appName & "<BR>"
doc.write "<B>appVersion</B> = " & nav.appVersion & "<BR>"
doc.write "<B>cookieEnabled</B> = " & nav.cookieEnabled & "<BR>"
doc.write "<B>userAgent</B> = " & nav.userAgent & "<BR>"
doc.close
```

A few other properties return information about the browser, including *cpuType*, *userLanguage*, *systemLanguage*, and *platform*. The only method worth noting is *javaEnabled*, which returns True if the browser supports the Java language.

The Navigator object also exposes two collections: The mimeTypes collection includes all the document and file types that the browser supports, and the plugins collection contains all the objects in the page.

The Location object

The Location object represents the URL of the page currently displayed in the browser. Its most important property is *href*, which returns the complete URL string. All the other properties contain a portion of the URL string: *hash* (the portion following the # symbol), *hostname* (the name of the host), *host* (the *hostname:port* portion of the URL), *port* (the port number), *protocol* (the first part of the URL that holds the protocol name), and *search* (the portion following the ? symbol in the URL).

This object also exposes three methods: *assign* (loads a different page), *replace* (loads a page and substitutes the current entry in the history list), and *replace* (reloads the current page).

The Screen object

The Screen object exposes properties about the screen and doesn't support any methods. The *width* and *height* properties are the dimensions of the screen in pixels and can be useful when you're deciding where to place a new window. The *colorDepth* property is the number of color planes supported and is typically used when the server site contains several similar images and you want to download the one that best fits the number of colors supported by the user's video card. The *bufferDepth* is a writable property that corresponds to the color depth of the off-screen buffer that the browser uses to display images. This property lets you display an image with a color depth different from its original color depth. The *updateInterval* property can be assigned the interval at which the browser redraws the page. (This is especially useful to reduce flickering when you're doing animations.)

Internet Explorer also supports the *availWidth* and *availHeight* properties, which return the size of the screen that isn't occupied by visible taskbars (such as the Microsoft Windows and Microsoft Office taskbars), and the *fontSmoothingEnabled* Boolean property, which specifies whether the browser should use smoother fonts if necessary.

The Event object

I explained many features of the Event object earlier in this chapter. This object is used within VBScript event procedures to read and possibly modify event arguments, to specify whether the default action should be canceled, and to cancel event bubbling. The Event object exposes only properties, no methods.

Four pairs of properties return the coordinates of the mouse cursor. The *screenX* and *screenY* properties give you the position relative to the upper left corner of the screen; *clientX* and *clientY* give you the position relative to the upper left corner of the browser's client area; *x* and *y* give you the position relative to the container of the object that fired the event; and *offsetX* and *offsetY* give you the position relative to the object that fired the event. A ninth property, *button*, returns the state of the mouse button as a bit-fielded value (1=left button, 2=right button, 4=middle button).

Four properties have to do with the state of the keyboard: The *keycode* property is the ASCII code of the key that was pressed (and you can assign it to modify the effect of a key press), whereas *altKey*, *ctrlKey*, and *shiftKey* return the state of the corresponding shift key.

Three properties return a reference to an element of the page. The scrElement object is the item that originally fired the event; it can be different from the Me object if you're trapping the event within the event procedure of an object that's higher in the hierarchy. The *fromElement* and *toElement* properties return the element being left and entered, respectively, during *onmouseout* or *onmouseover* events.

You can set the *cancelBubble* property to False to cancel event bubbling. You can set the *returnValue* property to False to cancel the default action associated with the event. The *type* property returns the name of the event without the leading *on* characters (such as *click*, *focus*, and so on).

The Document Object

The Document object represents the contents of the page currently loaded in the browser. It's probably the richest DHTML object in terms of properties, methods, events, and functionality.

Properties

Several properties return information about the state of the document and the page loaded in it. The *title* property contains the title of the document (the string defined by the <TITLE> tag); *URL* holds the Uniform Resource Locator of the page (such as *http://www.vb2themax.com*); *domain* returns the security domain of the document; and *lastModified* returns the date and time of the most recent edit operation for the document. The *referrer* property is the URL of the page that referred the current one.

Some properties set or return color values. For example, *fgcolor* and *bgcolor* give you the text and background colors of the page; changing these properties has an immediate effect on the page (except in the areas where specific color settings have been defined). Three properties control the color of hyperlinks: *linkColor* returns the color for links that haven't been visited yet; *vLinkColor* tells you the color for visited links, and *alinkColor* returns the color for active links (that is, links under the cursor when the mouse button is pressed).

A number of properties return references to other objects in the page. The *body* property gives you a reference to the Body object; *parentWindow* returns a reference to the Window object that this document belongs to; *location* is a reference to the Location object exposed by the parent Window; and *activeElement* is a reference to the page element that has the focus. (When you've just downloaded the page, this property returns a reference to the Body element.)

The *readyState* property returns a string that describes the current download state of the document. This is valuable information because it lets you avoid the errors that would occur if you referenced an object—such as an image—while the page was still downloading:

```
If document.readyState = "complete" Then
    ' Fill the text box control only if the page has been completely
    ' downloaded.
    MyTextBox.Value = "Good morning dear user!"
End If
```

This property is so important that the Document object fires a special event, *onReadyStateChange*, when its value changes. Thanks to this event, you don't have to continuously poll this property to determine when it's safe to act on page elements.

Methods

We have already seen several methods of the Document object—namely, the *clear*, *open*, *write*, and *close* methods that we've used to dynamically create new HTML pages. The *writeln* method is a variant of the *write* method that adds newline characters and supports multiple arguments:

```
document.writeln "First Line<BR>", "Second Line"
```

Remember that the added newline character usually has no effect if the output is pure HTML unless you're inserting text inside a pair of <PRE> and </PRE> tags or <TEXTAREA> and </TEXTAREA> tags.

The *elementFromPoint* method returns the element that corresponds to a given pair of coordinates (It's therefore similar to the *HitTest* method exposed by a few Visual Basic controls.) You can use this method inside a mouse event procedure to display a description of the object under the mouse cursor:

```
Sub Document_onmousemove()
    On Error Resume Next     ' Not all elements have a Name property.
    ' Fill a text box with the description of the element under the mouse cursor.
    Set element = document.elementFromPoint(window.event.x, window.event.y)
```

```
    Select Case element.Name
        Case "txtUserName"
            txtDescription.Value = "Enter your username here"
        Case "txtEmail"
            txtDescription.Value = "Enter your e-mail address here"
        ' And so on.
    End Select
End Sub
```

Earlier in this chapter, I showed you how to use the Document's *createElement* method to create new Option objects and dynamically fill a Select control at run time. You can also use this method to create new <IMG> tags and <AREA> tags. (The latter tags create image maps, which aren't covered in this book, however.)

Child collections

The Document object exposes several child collections, which let you iterate on all the elements in the page. These collections aren't disjoint, so an element can belong to more than one collection. For example, the *all* collection gathers all the tags and elements in the body of the document, but the Document object also exposes the *anchors*, *images*, and *links* collections, whose names are self-explanatory. The *scripts* collection contains all the <SCRIPT> tags, *forms* is the collection of existing forms, and *styleSheets* gathers all the styles defined for the document. A few collections concern objects that I haven't covered in this chapter, such as the *frames*, *embeds*, and *plugins* collections.

Working with these collections is similar to working with Visual Basic's collections. You can refer to an element in the collection using its index (collections are zero-based) or key (in most cases, the key corresponds to the name of the element). The most relevant difference is that DHTML collections support the *length* property instead of the *Count* property. You can iterate on all the items of a collection using a *For Each…Next* loop, and you can determine the type of an element by peeking at its *tagName* property:

```
' Print the tags of all the items in the page.
For Each x In document.all
    text = text & x.tagName & ", "
Next
text = Left(text, Len(text) - 2)        ' Drop the last comma.
MsgBox text
```

If you want to retrieve only elements with a given tag, you can filter the collection using its *tags* method, which accepts the name of the tag you're filtering on:

```
' Display the names of all <INPUT> elements.
For Each x In document.all.tags("INPUT")
    text = text & x.Name & ", "
next
MsgBox Left(text, Len(text) - 2)        ' Drop the last comma.
```

The *tags* method returns a collection, so you can store its return value in a variable for later. Or you can query its *length* property:

```
Set imgCollection = document.all.tags("IMG")
MsgBox "Found " & imgCollection.length & " images."
```

The *forms* collection is special in that it exposes the child *elements* collection, which in turn contains all the controls in the form. A page can contain multiple forms, even though all the examples in this chapter use only one form:

```
' List the names of all the controls on the first form in the page.
For Each x In document.forms(0).elements
    text = text & x.name & ", "
Next
MsgBox Left(text, Len(text) - 2)

' Move the input focus on the control named "txtUserName"
' of the form named "UserData."
document.forms("UserData").elements("txtUserName").focus
```

The Selection object

The Selection object represents the portion of the document that's currently highlighted by the user. Its only property is *type*, which returns a string that tells which kind of elements are selected. (The choices are *none* or *text*.)

The Selection object supports three methods. The *empty* method cancels the selection and reverts its *type* property to *none*. The *clear* method actually deletes the contents of the selection. If the selection includes text, controls, or an entire table, they are physically removed from the document and the page is automatically refreshed. (The *empty* method doesn't delete tables that are only partially selected, however):

```
' Delete the selected portion of the document
' when the user presses the "C" key.
Sub Document_onkeypress()
    If window.event.keycode = Asc("C") Then
        document.selection.clear
    End If
End Sub
```

The last method of the Selection object is *createRange*, which returns a reference to the TextRange object that describes the text currently selected. I'll explain what to do with such a TextRange object in the next section.

The TextRange Object

The TextRange object represents a portion of the document. This can be the area currently selected by the user or an area defined programmatically. The TextRange object lets you access the contents of a portion of the page—either as HTML source code or as text visible to the user—and exposes several methods that let you define the size and position of the range itself.

You can create a *TextRange* property from the Selection object, as we've just seen, or you can use the *createTextRange* methods of the Body object or a Button, TextArea, or TextBox element:

```
Set bodyTxtRange = document.body.createTextRange
Set inputTxtRange = document.all("txtUserName").createTextRange
```

Properties

The TextRange object exposes only two properties, *text* and *htmlText*. The former can set or return the textual contents of the portion of the document defined by the object but doesn't let you specify its formatting. The latter property is read-only and returns the portion of the document in HTML format. The following piece of VBScript code displays the HTML contents of the selected text when the user presses the *C* key and converts the text to uppercase when the user presses the *U* key:

```
Sub Document_onkeypress()
    If window.event.keycode = Asc("C") Then
        MsgBox document.selection.createRange.htmlText
    ElseIf window.event.keycode = Asc("U") Then
        ' Type the following two-line statement as one line.
        document.selection.createRange.text =
            UCase(document.selection.createRange.text)
    End If
End Sub
```

The *htmlText* property always returns syntactically correct HTML code. For example, if the TextRange object comprises only the starting <B> tag of a portion of bold text, the value returned by this property correctly includes the closing </B> tag, so you can safely reuse it in the same or another document without any problem. The value returned by this property also includes <SCRIPT> tags inside the area.

The *text* property always returns the characters in a TextRange object, but an assignment to it works only if the area doesn't extend over portions of the document with different attributes.

Methods

The TextArea object exposes 27 methods, but I'll explain just the most useful ones. The first method to get familiar with is *select*, which makes the TextRange object appear to be selected: It's useful for getting visual feedback about what you're doing to the object.

The *moveStart*, *moveEnd*, and *move* methods change the position of the starting point, the ending point, or both ends of the area. You can move these points by the specified number of characters, words, and whole sentences as shown in the code on the following page.

```
' Extend the selection 10 characters to the right.
Set selRange = document.selection.createRange
selRange.moveEnd "character", 10
' Extend it one word to the left.
' (Negative values move toward the beginning of the document.)
selRange.moveStart "word", -2
selRange.select
' Extend it one sentence to the right. (The value "1" can be omitted.)
selRange.moveEnd "sentence"
selRange.select
' Restore it as it was.
selRange.move "textedit"
```

The *collapse* method reduces the size of a TextRange method to either its start point (if the method's argument is True) or to its ending point (if the argument is False):

```
selRange.collapse True        ' Reduce the range to its starting point.
```

The *moveToElementText* method is useful when you want the TextRange object to move over a particular element in the page. This method works only if the TextRange already includes the element, so you often create a TextRange object from the body element and then shrink it to the desired element, as in the following code:

```
' Create a TextRange corresponding to the "MyControl" element.
Set range = document.body.createTextRange
range.moveToElementText document.all("MyControl")
```

You can use the *moveToPoint* method to have the TextRange point to a given *x-y* pair of coordinates, typically the mouse coordinates:

```
' Retrieve the word the user clicked on.
Sub Document_onclick()
    Set range = document.body.createTextRange
    range.moveToPoint window.event.x, window.event.y
    range.expand "word"
    MsgBox range.text
End Sub
```

Use the *findText* method to have a TextRange move over a given text string in the page. In its simplest form, this method takes one argument, the string being searched, and returns True if the search succeeds (in which case, the range has moved over the searched text). Otherwise, it returns False:

```
Set range = document.body.createTextRange
If range.findText("ABC") Then
    range.select
Else
    Msgbox "Text not found"
End If
```

Concerning the remaining methods of the TextRange object, it's worth mentioning *scrollIntoView* (which ensures that the text range is visible in the browser's window), *parentElement* (which returns a reference to the element that completely contains the text range), *pasteHTML* (which replaces the contents of the text range with HTML code), and *duplicate* (which creates a new TextRange object that points to the same range).

The Table Object

In Dynamic HTML, tables are defined exactly as they are in pure HTML—that is, with the <TABLE> and </TABLE> tag pair and a series of <TR> and <TD> tags. The real difference is that in DHTML a table exposes the *rows* and *cells* collections, which let you access individual cells without having to assign them a specific ID attribute. More precisely, the table object exposes a *rows* collection, and each row object exposes a *cells* collection. The following piece of code extracts the contents of the table as a tab-delimited string that's ready to be exported to a text file:

```
Set table = document.all("Table1")
For each thisRow in table.rows
    For each thisCell In thisRow.cells
        text = text & thisCell.innerText & Chr(9)
    Next
    ' Replace the last tab char with a CR-LF pair.
    text = Left(text, Len(text) - 1) & Chr(13) & Chr(10)
Next
MsgBox text
```

You can directly reference a cell using this syntax:

```
' Modify the first cell in the third row. (Row and column indices are
' zero-based.)
table.rows(2).cells(0).innerText = "New Value"
```

Because individual cells don't support the *innerHTML* property, to modify the attributes of a given cell you must create a TextRange object and use its *pasteHTML* method instead:

```
Set thisCell = table.rows(2).cells(0)
Set range = document.body.createTextRange
range.moveToElementText thisCell
range.pasteHTML "<B>New Value in Boldface</B>"
```

Even more exciting than this is your ability to add new rows and columns, thanks to the *insertRow* method of the table object and the *insertCell* method of the row object:

```
' Add a row as the fifth row of the table.
set newRow = table.insertRow(4)
```

(continued)

```
' Insert a cell in the first column, and set its contents.
set newCell = newRow.insertCell(0)
newCell.innerText = "New Cell in Column 1"
' Add other cells, using a more concise syntax.
newRow.insertCell(1).innerText = "New cell in Column 2"
newRow.insertCell(2).innerText = "New cell in Column 3"
```

You can also delete cells or entire rows using the row object's *deleteCell* method and the table object's *deleteRow* method, respectively. The table, row, and cell objects have a few properties in common—such as *align*, *vAlign*, and *borderColor*—that let you format data they contain.

THE DHTMLPAGE DESIGNER

 The big news about Visual Basic 6 is that you can write DHTML code using your favorite language, thanks to the DHTMLPage designer. Like all designers, the DHTMLPage designer exposes a visual part (the HTML page) and a code section. When you compile the program, you produce an ActiveX DLL that runs inside Internet Explorer 4.01 or later versions. Being able to access the DHTML object from a compiled DLL written in Visual Basic has a lot of advantages:

■ The appearance of the page is completely separated from the code that manages it, which permits a better subdivision of the work among the programmer and the page author.

■ You enjoy source code protection: the code is embedded in a DLL and can't be peeked at by just reading the contents of the page.

■ Visual Basic compiled code is typically faster than routines written in VBScript or other script languages. The speed advantage is even more noticeable if you compile to native code with some degree of optimization turned on.

■ You don't have to guess the names of the properties and methods of each object in the hierarchy because IntelliSense is there to help you. Ditto for the syntax of event procedures, which are created for you by the DHTMLPage designer code editor.

■ The DHTMLPage designer is well integrated in the environment, so you can modify the initial properties of any element by using the Properties window rather than by inserting cryptic HTML tags.

A First Look at the DHTMLPage Designer

The fastest way to show you the DHTMLPage designer in action is to select the DHTML Application template from the project gallery. This template adds one instance of the

DHTMLPage designer and one standard BAS module, which contains some useful routines. In a typical DHTML application, you'll create several DHTMLPage designers, one for each DHTML page your program consists of.

Figure 19-6 shows the DHTMLPage designer, with a treeview pane on the left and a detail pane on the right. The two panes are actually different representations of the contents of the page: In the treeview pane, you see the hierarchical relationships of the elements of the page, and in the detail pane you see (and arrange) the elements as if they were controls on a form. The designer doesn't provide access to the HTML code behind the page, so you can't add script routines or HTML tags directly. Fortunately, you don't really need to use scripts any longer because you'll be using Visual Basic, and you can use an external editor to author an HTML page and then import it into the designer.

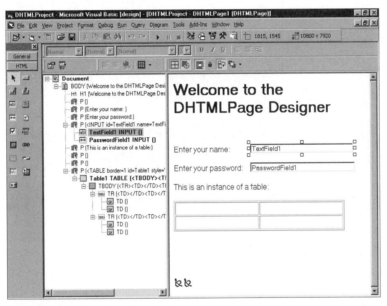

Figure 19-6. *The DHTMLPage designer.*

When the designer is active, a new tab appears in the Toolbox window, containing all the HTML controls that you can drop in the detail pane. All the controls we've seen so far are included in the toolbox, plus a few new ones: hidden TextBox controls, InputImage controls, and FileUpload controls. To simplify the developer's job, you have distinct icons for the one-line Select control and for the multiline (and optionally multiselect) List control, even though they're rendered using the same HTML tags. The toolbox also contains a few items which aren't controls in the stricter sense of the word: the HorizontalRule element (for drawing horizontal lines) and the Hyperlink element. You can also create a Hyperlink by selecting a portion of text and clicking on the Make Selection Into Link button on the toolbar. Moreover, if you write text that's formatted as a Web address (such as *www.microsoft.com*) the designer automatically turns it into a hyperlink.

As you know, an HTML page can contain ActiveX controls, and the DHTMLPage designer supports this capability too. You can drop an external ActiveX control on the page, such as a TreeView or ActiveX control you've authored in Visual Basic and compiled as a stand-alone OCX file. You can't use intrinsic Visual Basic controls, nor can you use UserControl objects that are private in the current project.

The topmost portion of the DHTMLPage designer toolbar (visible in Figure 19-7) gives you the ability to format the text or the element currently selected. The second combo box from the left is filled with all the styles defined for the current page, including those defined in an external Cascading Style Sheet that the page refers to. Because you can't define a style in the DHTMLPage designer, this combo box can contain elements only if you've imported an external HTML page written with a more powerful editor.

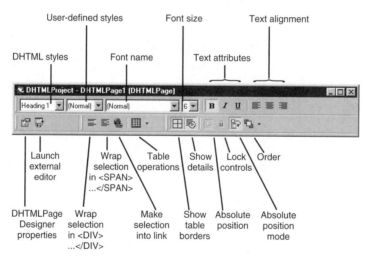

Figure 19-7. *The toolbar of the DHTMLPage designer.*

Using the DHTMLPage Designer Properties button, you can decide whether the HTML page being built should be saved together with the current project or as a separate HTM file. Each choice has its advantages, but because the designer can't compete with more powerful HTML editors, such as Microsoft FrontPage, I suggest that you use the latter option so that you can use an external HTML editor to embellish the page.

The Launch Editor button lets you edit the current page using the external editor of your choice. By default, this editor is Notepad, which hardly qualifies as an HTML editor but is used by many HTML programmers nonetheless. You can define a better editor in the Advanced tab of the Options dialog of the Visual Basic IDE. You can edit the page in an external editor only if you saved it as an external HTM file. When you click on this button, Visual Basic automatically saves the project with the most recent edits, and then runs the external editor. Visual Basic continuously checks the file's date and time, and as soon as you save the page in the editor Visual Basic asks whether you want to reload it in the DHTMLPage designer.

As with all designers, you can click on a control (in either of the two panes) and then press the F4 key to bring up the Properties window. In the DHTMLPage designer, you can modify the attributes of *any* element, including plain text. I suggest that you create an empty HTML page and drop an instance of each control in the toolbox and then press F4 to become familiar with the properties it exposes. In the Properties window, you can read the type of each element according to the name classification used by the designer. For example, many of the controls dropped from the toolbox are of type *DispIHTMLInputElement* and are further classified by their *type* property (which can be *text*, *password*, *image*, and so on). The class of Hyperlink elements is *DispHTMLAnchorElement*. Tables are of class *DispHTMLTable*, and they contain elements whose class is *DispHTMLTableCell*.

Speaking of tables, you have a lot of options when creating and editing tables— for example, you can use the drop-down menu from the designer's toolbar or right-click on the table itself in the detail pane. The pop-up menu includes the Properties command, which brings up the Properties dialog box shown in Figure 19-8. In this dialog box, you can set a lot of attributes, and you can also span cells to take multiple rows and columns. Also notice that a button on the toolbar lets you show and hide table borders at design time, without affecting the actual *Border* attribute. Having a table with visible borders at design time usually simplifies your editing chores.

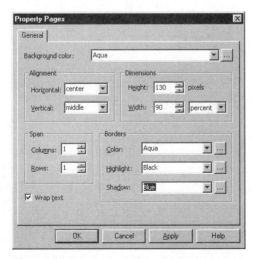

Figure 19-8. *The Properties dialog box of a DispHTMLTable object.*

If you click on an external ActiveX control and press the F4 key, you get the list of supported HTML attributes, not the usual list of properties specific to that control. To edit the intrinsic properties of an external ActiveX control, you must right-click on it and bring up its Properties dialog box. The List and Select DHTML controls support a custom Properties dialog box as well, so you can use it for specifying the list of items these controls contain.

The designer can work in two position modes, relative or absolute. In *relative* mode, you let the browser position all the elements in the page when the page itself is resized, as it happens for all the (non-Dynamic) HTML pages. In *absolute* mode, the element stays where you drop it. On the toolbar, two buttons affect position mode: One button affects the current mode, and the other affects the absolute position attribute of the element that's currently selected. The latter button is disabled when you select text elements because you can modify the position of a text element only by pressing the Enter key to add empty lines, as you do in a word processor. Because hyperlinks are just text elements, they're subject to the same rules for positioning. All the other elements can be moved with the mouse, but you have to grab them from their border. You can control the z-order position of page elements by using the Order submenu on the designer's toolbar.

Setting text properties in the internal designer isn't the most intuitive action. In fact, a <P> element doesn't initially expose any font or style property. To force it to expose such attributes, you must change its appearance using the topmost toolbar—for example, by modifying the font size. When you change the standard appearance of a paragraph, a <FONT> element appears in the treeview as a child of the <P> item. You can then select this new item and press the F4 to display the Properties window, and then change other attributes, such as *color* and *face*.

Programming DHTML Elements

To exploit the dynamic capabilities of DHTML, you must write code that reacts to events raised by the page or its elements. In a Visual Basic 6 DHTML application, you write code that reacts to events raised by the page and its elements, exactly as you write code behind the controls on a form. When you then compile the application, Visual Basic creates one or more HTM files and a DLL that contains the compiled code you've written inside event procedures. This DLL will be loaded in the address space of Internet Explorer and can trap DHTML events exposed to the outside by that browser.

All Visual Basic 6 DHTML applications are actually ActiveX DLL applications, whose threading model is apartment threading. You shouldn't use the DHTMLPage designer inside single-threaded ActiveX projects. All the HTM files produced when you compile the application contain an OBJECT tag with a reference to the corresponding DLL. The first time the user navigates to the page, the DLL is automatically downloaded from the server and installed in the client's system. This mechanism is identical to the one used for downloading an ActiveX control in an HTML page.

The DHTMLPage object

The DHTMLPage object represents the component in the DLL that's bound to a particular HTM page. Like all objects, it exposes an *Initialize* and *Terminate* event, which fire the first time the page is used and immediately before the DLL is unloaded, respectively. It also exposes two events, *Load* and *Unload*, which fire when the page is loaded and unloaded, respectively.

The DHTMLPage object exposes four design-time properties. The *SourceFile* property is the path of the HTM file that contains the HTML source of the page being built or an empty string if you aren't editing the page using an external editor. The *BuildFile* property is the path of the HTM file that will be built during the compilation process and that should be distributed with the DLL. (It's initially the same value as the *SourceFile* property.) The *AsynchLoad* property specifies whether the page should be loaded asynchronously. (See more on this in the "Loading a Page Asynchronously" section later in this chapter.) Specifying the *id* property makes the page programmable. In the Properties window, you'll also find a fifth property, *Public*, but you can't actually count it because it's set to True and can't be changed. (You can't have private DHTMLPage objects.)

These properties are available only at design time. At run time, the DHTMLPage object exposes a different set of properties: *BaseWindow*, *Document*, and *DHTMLEvent* (as shown in Figure 19-9). They return a reference to the all-important DHTML Window, Document, and Event objects, respectively, and so they're the links between the Visual Basic program and the Dynamic HTML object mode. Notice that while you can access DHTML objects from within the DHTMLPage designer module, you can't access the designer from a script inside the HTML page. The page is oblivious to the fact that it's being processed by a DLL.

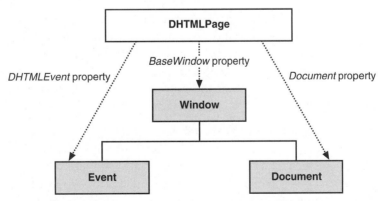

Figure 19-9. *The runtime properties of the DHTMLPage object.*

When inside a DHTML module, you can directly reference the DHTMLPage object's properties in code, exactly as you do with a form's properties inside a form code module. The following example demonstrates this concept:

```
' (This code must run inside a DHTMLPage code module.)
' Change the background color of the page.
Document.bgcolor = "red"
' Retrieve the state of the Alt key inside an event procedure.
If DHTMLEvent.altKey Then …
```

The *id* property

Not all the page elements can be associated with event procedures. In order to be programmable, a page element must have a nonempty *id* property. This *id* becomes the name by which you refer to that element in code. This requirement can mislead Visual Basic programmers because many HTML elements also support a *Name* property, which is usually meaningless in pure HTML programming. As I explained in the HTML tutorial at the beginning of this chapter, the *Name* property is mostly used for grouping mutually exclusive Option controls. In DHTML applications, you need different *id* values even for the items in a group of Option controls if you want to refer to them individually.

Under standard DHTML, the *id* properties of multiple controls don't need to be different. Within a DHTML application written in Visual Basic, however, all the *id*s in a page must be unique. When you import an existing .hml file into the designer, Visual Basic checks all the *id* values, and if necessary, it automatically appends a number to them to ensure that their values are unique in the page. So always double-check the *id* assigned to an element when you import an HTM page.

Not all the elements in the page need to have an *id* property. In most cases they don't: Only the elements that you want to write code for have to be assigned an *id*. The treeview in the leftmost pane shows such programmable elements in boldface. The designer automatically creates an *id* for all the elements and controls that you drop from the Toolbox. To assign an *id* to an element, select it in the treeview, switch to the Properties window, and type a unique value for the *id* property. You can also select a page element in the combo box controls at the top of the Properties window. (Use this method to change the properties of the DHTMLPage object itself.) Moreover, you can always access the properties and methods of a page element through the *All* property and other collections of the Document object.

The first example: A dynamic menu

To show you how you can leverage what you learned about DHTML programming, let's build a practical example: a dynamic menu consisting of items that appear and disappear when you click on the menu header and that are rendered as boldface text when the mouse passes over them.

To begin with, create a new DHTML page, save it in an HTM file, and then add a few paragraphs as shown in Figure 19-10. Set these paragraphs' *id* properties to *MainMenu*, *MenuItem1*, *MenuItem2*, and *MenuItem3*, respectively. You can change the color of each paragraph by changing its font size from the toolbar, and then editing the properties of the <FONT> item that the designer creates for you.

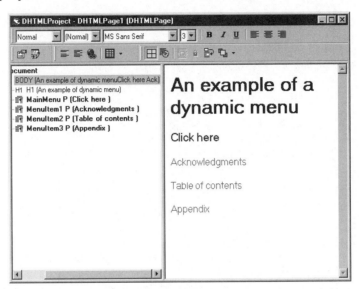

Figure 19-10. *The first DTHML application: a dynamic menu.*

Now you can finally write code for managing these items. You write code behind a page element the same way you write code for a control on a regular form: You double-click on the element (in the treeview pane) to access the code window, and then select the event procedure in the rightmost combo box. You can also access the code window by pressing the F7 function key or by selecting the View Code command from the menu that appears when you right-click on the designer window. This is the code you should enter in the code module. (Or you can load the sample application from the companion CD.)

```
Private Sub DHTMLPage_Load()
    ' Make the submenu choices invisible when the page loads.
    SetVisibility False
End Sub

' Change the display attribute of all the menu items.
Private Sub SetVisibility(newValue As Boolean)
    MenuItem1.Style.display = IIf(newValue, "", "none")
    MenuItem2.Style.display = IIf(newValue, "", "none")
    MenuItem3.Style.display = IIf(newValue, "", "none")
End Sub
```

(continued)

```
' When the MainMenu paragraph is clicked,
' switch menu items from hidden to visible and back.
Private Function MainMenu_onclick() As Boolean
    If MenuItem1.Style.visibility = "hidden" Then
        SetVisibility True
    Else
        SetVisibility False
    End If
End Function


' Change the boldface attribute of the element under the mouse, but only
' if this element is one of the three MenuItem  paragraphs.
Private Sub Document_onmouseover()
    Select Case DHTMLEvent.srcElement.innerText
        Case "Click here", "Acknowledgments", "Table of contents", _
            "Appendix"
            DHTMLEvent.srcElement.Style.fontWeight = "800"
    End Select
End Sub


' Restore the original font attribute when the mouse leaves the element.
Private Sub Document_onmouseout()
    Select Case DHTMLEvent.srcElement.innerText
        Case "Click here", "Acknowledgments", "Table of contents", _
            "Appendix"
            DHTMLEvent.srcElement.Style.fontWeight = ""
    End Select
End Sub
```

In its simplicity, the preceding code is a good example of how you can put DHTML features to good use. Because all the menu items behave in a similar way, it doesn't make any sense to repeat the same code inside their *onmouseover* and *onmouseout* event procedures. In fact, it's much better to exploit the event bubbling features of Dynamic HTML and trap those events at the Document level. This is something that you couldn't do if this were a regular Visual Basic form.

This approach has its drawbacks, however, because you need to be sure that the *onmouseover* and *onmouseout* events were raised by one of the four <P> elements you're interested in, and not by something else on the page. The Event object exposes an *srcElement* property that returns a reference to the object that first originated the event. The problem is this: How can you determine whether this object is one of the four <P> items that make up the menu? At first I believed that I could compare the *id* properties of those four items with the value returned by the *DTHMLEvent.srcElement.id* property, but—to my surprise—I discovered that the latter property always returns an empty string and so can't be used for this purpose. Fortunately, you can solve the problem with the *innerText* property. If multiple elements on the page have the same value for the *innerText* property, you should assign them a unique *Name* and use this property to find out which element is raising the event.

Using DIV and SPAN tags

In most cases, you don't need to resort to the unusual technique based on *id*, *innerText*, or some other property to figure out whether you're interested in the event because under Dynamic HTML you can precisely delimit the range of event bubbling by creating an area of the document that exactly contains only the items you're interested in. If you don't have a container that holds all the elements you want to receive events from (and only them), you can group the elements you're interested in using a <DIV> and </DIV> pair of tags.

For the dynamic menu example, you need to create a DIV section that comprises the four menu items. This is really simple: In the pane on the right side of the DHTMLPage designer, select the four paragraphs and then click on the third button from the left in the lower line of buttons in the designer's toolbar. This action creates a DIV section, but you need to assign it a nonempty *id* property to make it programmable. So type *DynMenu* in the Properties window, and then go to the code window to enter this code:

```
Private Sub DynMenu_onmouseover()
    DHTMLEvent.srcElement.Style.fontWeight = "800"
End Sub

Private Sub DynMenu_onmouseout()
    DHTMLEvent.srcElement.Style.fontWeight = ""
End Sub
```

As you see, you don't need to test the *srcElement.innerText* property because you're sure that the event comes from one of those four <P> items.

As an exercise, let's see how you use the <SPAN> tag, which is often useful for referencing smaller portions of the HTML page. Let's suppose that you want to change the text of the *MainMenu* element to *Click here to close the menu* when the menu is open, and you want to restore it to *Click here* when the menu is closed. One way to obtain this behavior is to extend the text of the *MainMenu* element to *Click here to close the menu*, select the last four words, and click the fourth button on the designer toolbar to turn this small portion of text into a <SPAN> section. To refer to this section from within code, you need to assign this <SPAN> object an *id* (*CloseMenu*, for example) and then update the code as follows. (Added statements are in boldface.)

```
Private Function MainMenu_onclick() As Boolean
    If MenuItem1.Style.visibility = "hidden" Then
        SetVisibility True
        MenuClose.Style.visibility = "visible"
```

(continued)

```
    Else
        SetVisibility False
        MenuClose.Style.visibility = "hidden"
    End If
End Function
```

As you see, Dynamic HTML lets you achieve eye-catching results with a small amount of code.

DHTML event procedures

If you look carefully at the code in the sample application, you'll notice that many (but not all) event routines are functions rather than procedures. As I explained in the "Canceling the Default Effect" section earlier in this chapter, all DHTML events expect a return value that, if False, cancels the default action for the event. To return a value, the event procedure must be declared as a function.

The way you return a value from an event inside a DHTMLPage designer is different from the technique used within script routines inside the HTM file. In VBScript, you must explicitly set the return value of a procedure to False to cancel the default action of a given event, or you must set the *event.returnValue* property to False to reach the same result. In Visual Basic, however, False is the default value for any function, and DHTML event procedures are no exception to this rule. In other words, if you write an event procedure, you must explicitly set its return value to True if you don't want to cancel the default action.

To explain this concept with an example, let's say that you have a hyperlink and you want to ask for a confirmation before letting the user navigate to the specified URL. This is the code you have to write in the Hyperlink object's *onclick* event procedure:

```
Private Function Hyperlink1_onclick() As Boolean
    If MsgBox("Do you really want to jump there?", vbYesNo) = vbYes Then
        Hyperlink1_onclick = True
    End If
End Function
```

> **NOTE** Setting the *DHTMLEvent.returnValue* property to True doesn't work.

The MSHTML library

All DHTML applications include a reference to the MSHTML type library, which contains all the objects that make up the Dynamic HTML object model. You'll probably need some time to get acquainted with this huge library—the version that comes with Internet Explorer 5 includes about 280 classes and interfaces! Its elements also have names that are different from what you might expect. For example, the Window object corresponds to the HTMLWindow2 class, the Document object derives from the HTMLDocument class, the Event object is of class CeventObj, and so on. I don't have enough room to describe all the classes and their properties, methods, and events here, so I can only suggest that you spend some time with the Object Browser to see the most relevant features of each object.

DHTML Applications

When programming Visual Basic 6 DHTML applications, you have to solve a new class of problems. In this section, I illustrate a few of them.

Navigating to other pages

You can let the user navigate to other pages by simply placing one or more hyperlinks on the page and carefully preventing any of the hyperlinks from returning False in their *onclick* event procedures. If you're building the target URL in a dynamic way, however, you can't assign it to the <HREF> tag of a hyperlink at design time, and you need to follow one of the following methods:

■ You can use the Navigate method of the Window object to get a reference to the object using the *BaseWindow* property of the DHTMLPage global object. This is the code that you need to execute:

```
' Note: This is an absolute URL.
BaseWindow.Navigate "http://www.vb2themax.com"
```

■ If you're inside the *onclick* event procedure of a Hyperlink object, you can change this object's *href* property and then confirm that you want to follow the hyperlink by assigning True to the event procedure's return value:

```
Private Function Hyperlink1_onclick() As Boolean
    ' This code assumes that the global InternetIsUnavailable
    ' variable has been set to True if you're connected to the Internet
    ' and False if you're navigating on your private intranet.
    If InternetIsUnavailable Then
        Hyperlink1.href = "localpage.htm"
    End If
    ' In all cases, you need to return True to enable the jump.
    Hyperlink1_onclick = True
End Function
```

■ Finally, when you can, navigate to another page in your DHTML application using this syntax:

```
BaseWindow.Navigate "DHTMLPage2.htm"
```

where the argument is the name of the HTM file to which you saved the target DHTML page. (The previous code assumes that all HTM files that make up the application have been deployed in the same directory on the Web server.)

Whatever method you choose, you should pay attention to how you use relative and absolute paths. In general, all the references to other pages in your application—

whether or not they're associated with a DHTMLPage designer—should be relative so that you can easily deploy your application to a new Web site without having to recompile the source code. Conversely, all the references to pages outside your Web site should be absolute and preceded by the *http://* prefix.

Loading a page asynchronously

The first time a DHTMLPage is referenced in code, it fires an *Initialize* event. You should use this element exclusively to initialize local variables. Because all the page elements haven't been created yet, an error occurs if you reference them.

By default, a DHTMLPage object becomes active when the page has been completely downloaded from the Web server. At this point, this object fires the *Load* event. Because all the elements now exist, you can reference them without any problem. The problem with this simple approach, however, is that the download phase of complex pages with several objects in them—large images, for example—can take a long time to complete. Until the page has been completely downloaded, users are locked out because the controls on the page won't react to their actions.

You can activate an asynchronous download by setting the DHTMLPage object's *AsyncLoad* property to True. In this situation, the *Load* event fires when the download phase begins and not all the elements on the page have been downloaded yet. This means that you might reference a page element before it's available, which would result in an error. Here are a few techniques that you can use when you turn on the asynchronous loading feature:

- In general, you shouldn't reference any object from within an event procedure, except the object that fired the event. You can't even reference other objects that appear earlier in the page than the one that's raising the event in the HTML page because the browser can load elements in random order.

- If the logic of your application forces you to reference other objects, always add an *On Error* statement to protect your code from unanticipated errors.

- Don't access any object (except the one that's raising the event) until the Document's *readyState* property returns the value *complete*. You can poll this property before accessing any object, or you can wait for the Document's *onreadystatechange* event and check the property there.

Most of the time, you'll have to mix all three techniques. For example, when the page is loaded asynchronously, don't execute critical code in the *DHTMLPage_Load* event but move it to the *Document_onreadystatechange* event instead:

```
Private Sub Document_onreadystatechange()
    If Document.readyState = "complete" Then
```

```
        ' Here you can safely access all the elements in the page.
    End If
End Sub
```

If you can't wait for the *onreadystatechange* event, you must protect your code from unanticipated errors that would occur when a user tries to access a nonexistent object, or you can use the following routine:

```
' A reusable function that checks whether an element is available
Function IsAvailable(ByVal id As String) As Boolean
    On Error Resume Next
    id = Document.All(id).id
    IsAvailable = (Err = 0)
End Function
```

For example, a click on the MainMenu element should be ignored until the menu items are ready:

```
Private Function MainMenu_onclick() As Boolean
    If Not IsAvailable("MenuItem1") Then Exit Function
    ' Don't execute this code if the menu items aren't available yet.
    ...
End Function
```

Managing the state

DHTML applications are different from regular Visual Basic applications for an important reason: Because the user is free to navigate from one page to another page—including pages for which you don't provide a hyperlink—you can't be certain about the order in which pages will be visited. This situation contrasts with the usual Visual Basic programming model, which let's you decide which forms can be visited at a given moment.

Another key difference between DHTML and Visual Basic applications is that Internet applications are *stateless*, in the sense that the HTTP protocol doesn't store any information between requests; it's up to you to maintain the state, if necessary. You can do this using the *PutProperty* and *GetProperty* routines that you find in the modDHTML.Bas module included in the DHTML Application template project. This is the source code of the two routines, after stripping out some comment lines:

```
Sub PutProperty(objDocument As HTMLDocument, strName As String, _
    vntValue As Variant, Optional Expires As Date)
    objDocument.cookie = strName & "=" & CStr(vntValue) & _
        IIf(CLng(Expires) = 0, "", "; expires=" & _
        Format(CStr(Expires), "ddd, dd-mmm-yy hh:mm:ss") & " GMT")
End Sub

Function GetProperty(objDocument As HTMLDocument, strName As String) _
    As Variant
```

(continued)

```
    Dim aryCookies() As String
    Dim strCookie As Variant
    On Local Error GoTo NextCookie

    ' Split the document cookie object into an array of cookies.
    aryCookies = Split(objDocument.cookie, ";")
    For Each strCookie In aryCookies
        If Trim(VBA.Left(strCookie, InStr(strCookie, "=") - 1)) = _
            Trim(strName) Then
            GetProperty = Trim(Mid(strCookie, InStr(strCookie, "=") + 1))
            Exit Function
        End If
NextCookie:
        Err = 0
    Next strCookie
End Function
```

As you see, both routines are nothing more than an interface to the Document object's *cookie* property, so you can directly access this property from your code for some special tasks (for example, to enumerate all the defined cookies). To save a value in a persistent way, call the *PutProperty* routine:

```
' Store the name of the user in the "UserName" cookie.
PutProperty Document, "UserName", txtUserName.Value
```

You can also set an expiration date for the cookie, for example:

```
' The user password is valid for one week.
PutProperty Document, "UserPwd", txtPassword.Value, Now() + 7
```

If you don't set an expiration date, the cookie is automatically deleted at the end of the session, when the browser is closed. You can retrieve a cookie using the *GetProperty* function:

```
' This returns an empty string if the cookie doesn't exist.
txtUserName.Value = GetProperty(Document, "UserName")
```

The sample application PropBag.vbp on the Visual Basic CD demonstrates how you can use these routines to pass data between two pages in your project.

> **NOTE**   The PropBag.vbp demo project raises an error when you run it on a system on which Internet Explorer 5 is installed. The error is caused by slight differences in the browser object model. You can fix it by substituting *WindowBase.Document* with just *Document* in the code that calls the *PutProperty* and *GetProperty* routines. I'm testing this with a late beta of Internet Explorer 5, so it's possible that the error will disappear in the official release.

You typically save a page's state in the *Unload* event. Don't wait until the *Terminate* event because when this event fires the page has already been destroyed, and you can't reference its elements any longer. This is similar to the situation you have in the *Initialize* event.

One last note: The PropBag.vbp demo application might make you believe that you need a cookie any time you're passing data between two pages of your DHTML application, but it isn't strictly necessary. In fact, when you're directly calling another page of your application—using one of the methods outlined in the "Navigating to Other Pages" section earlier in this chapter—you just need to store the value in a global variable of your ActiveX DLL project. You actually need to resort to a cookie (directly, or indirectly through the routines in the modDHTML.Bas module) only if you want to make some data available to another page that you aren't calling directly or if you want to preserve data among subsequent sessions. (In this latter case, you should specify a suitable value for the *Expires* argument of the *PutProperty* routine.)

Creating elements

While you're programming in Visual Basic, you shouldn't forget that you can leverage all the power of Dynamic HTML. To give you an idea of what you can do with Visual Basic and DHTML together in the same application, I'll show you how you can use Visual Basic to query an ADO data source and then dynamically build a table of results right in the browser using the many HTML methods that modify the contents of a page already loaded in the browser. (See the "Text Properties and Methods" section earlier in this chapter.)

When you plan to fill a portion of the page at run time, for example, with the results of a database query, you need to place a <DIV> section in the proper place. This section should be associated with a nonempty *id* property so that you can reference it from code. Figure 19-11 shows a typical search page, with two TextBox controls in which the user enters search criteria, and a Search button that starts the search.

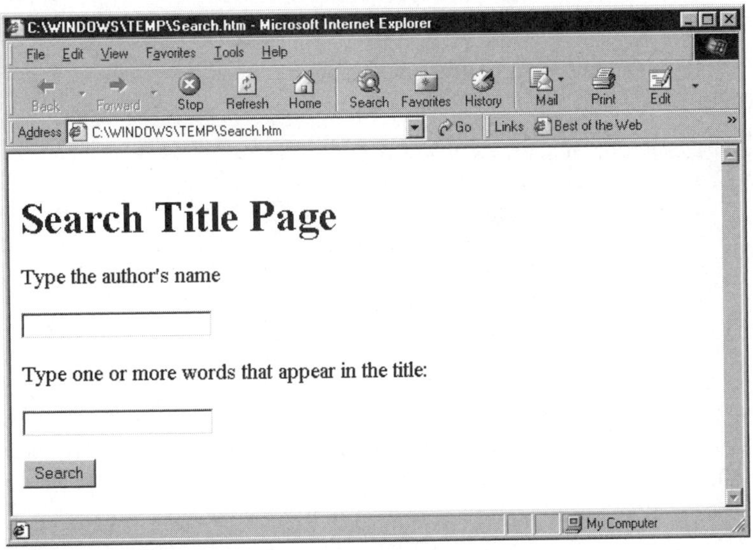

Figure 19-11. *A simple search page.*

The button is followed in the HTML source by an empty (and therefore invisible) <DIV> section whose *id* is *divResults*. When the user clicks on the button, the Visual Basic code executes the query and builds an ADO Recordset:

```
' Edit this constant to match your directory structure.
Const DB_PATH = "C:\Program Files\Microsoft Visual Studio\Vb98\Biblio.mdb"

Private Function cmdSearch_onclick() As Boolean
    Dim rs As New ADODB.Recordset
    Dim conn As String, sql As String
    Dim AuthorSearch As String, TitleSearch As String
    Dim resText As String, recIsOK As Boolean, recCount As Long

    On Error GoTo Error_Handler

    ' Prepare the query string.
    AuthorSearch = txtAuthor.Value
    TitleSearch = txtTitle.Value
    sql = "SELECT Author, Title, [Year Published] AS Year FROM Titles " _
        & "INNER JOIN ([Title Author] INNER JOIN Authors " _
        & "ON [Title Author].Au_ID = Authors.Au_ID) " _
        & "ON Titles.ISBN = [Title Author].ISBN"
    ' You can filter author names right in the SQL query string.
    If Len(AuthorSearch) Then
        sql = sql & " WHERE Author LIKE '" & AuthorSearch & "%'"
    End If
    ' Open the Recordset.
    conn = "Provider=Microsoft.Jet.OLEDB.3.51;Data Source=" & DB_PATH
    rs.Open sql, conn, adOpenStatic, adLockReadOnly
```

At this point, you start to build a table, with a header row that displays the names of the fields:

```
' Prepare the header of the table.
resText = "<TABLE BORDER>" _
    & "<TR ALIGN=left>" _
    & "<TH WIDTH=150>Author</TH>" _
    & "<TH WIDTH=300>Title</TH>" _
    & "<TH WIDTH=80>Year</TH>" _
    & "</TR>" & vbCrLf
```

You can loop through the Recordset and filter out all the records that don't contain the specified string in the Title field (if the user actually entered some text in the *txtTitle* control). For each record that matches the criteria, this code adds a row to the table:

```
Do Until rs.EOF
    recIsOK = True
    ' Filter out unwanted records.
    If Len(TitleSearch) Then
        If InStr(1, rs("Title"), TitleSearch, vbTextCompare) = 0 Then
            recIsOK = False
        End If
    End If
    ' If the record meets the search criteria, add it to the page.
    If recIsOK Then
        recCount = recCount + 1
        resText = resText & "<TR>" _
            & "<TD>" & rs("Author") & "</TD>" _
            & "<TD>" & rs("Title") & "</TD>" _
            & "<TD>" & rs("Year") & "</TD>" _
            & "</TR>" & vbCrLf
    End If
    rs.MoveNext
Loop
rs.Close
```

When the Recordset has been completely processed, you need simply to append a </TABLE> tag and prepare a simple message that informs about the number of records found. This is the remaining part of the routine:

```
If recCount = 0 Then
    ' If no record matched the search criteria, drop the table.
    resText = "<I>No record matches the search criteria</I>"
Else
    ' Otherwise add the number of found records and complete the table.
    resText = "Found " & recCount & IIf(recCount = 1, _
        " record", " records") & ".<P>" & vbCrLf & resText _
        & "</TABLE>" & vbCrLf
End If
' Substitute the current contents of the divResults section.
divResults.innerHTML = resText
Exit Function

Error_Handler:
    MsgBox "Error #" & Err.Number & vbCr & Err.Description, vbCritical
End Function
```

Figure 19-12 shows the program in action, after a query has been successfully completed. You can refine this first version in countless ways—for example, by adding a maximum number of returned records or by creating Next and Previous buttons to let the user navigate through pages of results. (Here's some advice: Prepare Next and Previous buttons on the page and make them visible when needed.)

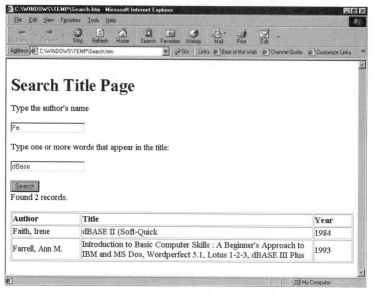

Figure 19-12. *The result of a successful database search.*

A problem that you must solve when dynamically adding new controls (as opposed to just plain text elements) is how to reference them in code and trap their events. As an example, I'll show you how you can add two controls at the right of each element in the result table: a CheckBox control that lets the user add that particular title to the order, and a Button control that lets him or her ask for additional details, such as the image of the cover, the table of contents, and so on.

Dynamically creating the controls while the code is building the table isn't difficult, and in fact you only have to ensure that each new control is assigned a unique value for its *id* property. You must assign this *id* to later get a reference to the control. Here's the code that adds one table row for each record that meets the search criteria (added lines are in boldface):

```
recCount = recCount + 1
bookmarks(recCount) = rs.Bookmark
resText = resText & "<TR>" _
    & "<TD>" & rs("Author") & "</TD>" _
    & "<TD>" & rs("Title") & "</TD>" _
    & "<TD>" & rs("Year") & "</TD>" _
    & "<TD><INPUT TYPE=BUTTON ID=cmdDetails" & Trim$(recCount) _
    & " VALUE=""Details""></TD>" _
    & "<TD><INPUT TYPE=Checkbox ID=Buy" & Trim$(recCount) _
    & " NAME=Buy?></TD>" _
    & "</TR>" & vbCrLf
```

The *bookmarks* array holds the bookmarks for all the records that meet the search criteria; it's defined as a module-level variable, so it's accessible from any routine in the DHTMLPage module.

The next step is to trap the *onclick* event from the Detail buttons, which at first seems impossible because you've created the buttons dynamically and no code exists for them in the DHTMLPage designer. Fortunately, thanks to event bubbling, you just need to trap the *onclick* event for the Document object and check whether the event comes from one of the controls you've added dynamically:

```
Private Function Document_onclick() As Boolean
    Dim index As Long, text As String
    ' Not all the elements support the Name or ID property.
    On Error GoTo Error_Handler
    ' Check the ID of the element that fired the event.
    If InStr(DHTMLEvent.srcElement.id, "cmdDetails") = 1 Then
        ' Retrieve the index of the button.
        index = CLng(Mid$(DHTMLEvent.srcElement.id, 11))
        ' Move the Recordset's pointer to that element.
        rs.Bookmark = bookmarks(index)
        ' Show the title of the selected book. (This is just a demo!)
        MsgBox "You requested details for title " & rs("Title")
    Else
        ' Return True to enable the default action of Checkbox controls.
        Document_onclick = True
    End If
End Function
```

Notice how you can test whether the *onclick* event was raised by one of the Detail buttons and how you extract the index of the control.

Your next task is to prepare a list of all the titles that have been flagged for ordering, which you accomplish using the following piece of code:

```
Dim text As String
For index = 1 To UBound(bookmarks)
    If Document.All("Buy" & Trim$(index)).Checked Then
        rs.Bookmark = bookmarks(index)
        text = text & rs("Title") & vbCr
    End If
Next
If Len(text) Then
    text = "Confirm the order for the following title(s)" & vbCr & text
    If MsgBox(text, vbYesNo + vbExclamation) = vbYes Then
        ' In a real application, you would insert the code that processes
        ' the order right here.
        MsgBox "Order filed!", vbInformation
    Else
        MsgBox "Order canceled!", vbCritical
    End If
End If
```

For more information, see the demonstration application provided on the companion CD. The project includes two distinct DHTMLPage modules: One does a simple search, and the other builds a more complex page with Button and CheckBox controls inside the grid. (See Figure 19-13.) Select the page to run in the Debugging tab of the Project Properties dialog box. I explain how to do this in the next section.

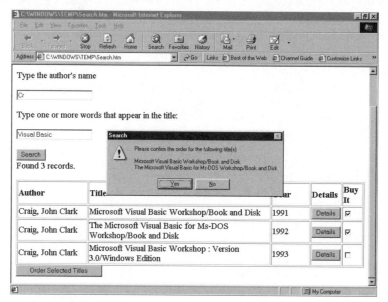

Figure 19-13. *A DHTML page that dynamically builds its own array of controls.*

Testing DHTML applications

The beauty of DHTML applications is that you can test your code inside the IDE, using all the tools that make debugging Visual Basic applications a relatively easy job. You're so used to such debugging features that you've probably missed a rather important point: You're executing your DHTML application inside the environment but Internet Explorer is behaving as if you compiled your code to an ActiveX DLL that runs inside Internet Explorer's address space. This little bit of magic is made possible by the VB6Debug DLL, a file that you find in the main Visual Basic installation directory. Be careful not to delete it, or you won't be able to do such cross-process debugging any longer.

When you test a DHTML application, you can take advantage of all the options you find in the Debugging tab of the Project Properties dialog box, shown in Figure 19-14 on page 1090. This tab is new to Visual Basic 6 and is disabled in Standard EXE projects because it's useful only when you're developing ActiveX components intended for consumption by client programs such as Internet Explorer. The options this tab offers (which I'll describe shortly) greatly simplify the testing of such components because they let you automatically start the client application that uses them. You can choose one of four actions when the current project starts its execution inside the environment:

Wait for Components to be Created   This is the default action: The Visual Basic IDE silently waits until the client asks the COM subsystem to create the component.

Start Component   You start one of the components defined in the current project and let it decide what to do. The default behavior for DHTMLPage designers is to load the HTM source file into Internet Explorer so that the component is automatically activated immediately afterward. If you select a UserControl or UserDocument, Visual Basic creates a temporary HTM page that contains a reference to it and then loads the page into the browser; this option lets you test how the control behaves in an HTML page. The component you select in this combo box control doesn't interfere with the selection you make in the Startup Object combo box in the General tab of the same dialog box. For example, you can select a DHTMLPage designer as a Start component and still have the *Sub Main* procedure automatically execute when the component is instantiated.

Start Program   This option lets you specify the path of the executable to launch when you run the project. Select this option when you know that the selected program will in turn create an instance of the component being developed. For example, you can create another application in Visual Basic that creates an instance of the component under development.

Start Browser With URL   You can start the default browser and load an HTML page in it. This option enables you to test an ActiveX Control or DLL referenced in an existing HTM page, as opposed to the blank temporary page that Visual Basic automatically creates when you select the Start Component option.

The page also contains a check box that you can tick if you want to use the existing instance of the browser (if one is already running), or clear if you want to start a new instance each time you run the project.

To have Internet Explorer automatically create an instance of the ActiveX DLL that's being developed in the IDE, Visual Basic adds an <OBJECT> tag at the beginning of the HTM page that contains all the elements defined in the DHTMLPage designer:

```
<OBJECT
ID="DHTMLPage1" CLASSID="clsid:8F0A368F-C5BC-11D2-BAC5-0080C8F21830"
WIDTH=0 HEIGHT=0></OBJECT>
```

Figure 19-14. *The Debugging tab of the Project Properties dialog box.*

Deploying a DHTML application

Once you've thoroughly tested your DHTML application, you must prepare a distribution package for it. This package comprises the following elements:

- The main DLL that contains all the compiled code of the application

- The Visual Basic 6 and OLE Automation runtime files

- The HTM files that make up the application—both those that host the ActiveX DLL and other regular HTML pages

- Other files referenced by the HTM files, such as images, data files, and so on

You create the distribution package using the Package and Deployment Wizard, which you can run as a Visual Basic add-in or as a stand-alone program. This is the sequence of actions you should perform:

1. In the topmost field in the Package and Deployment Wizard, select the DHTML project, and click on the Package button. The wizard asks whether you want to recompile the project if it finds that the DLL file is older than any of the source code files.

2. In the Select Type page, select the Internet Package type and click Next.

3. In the Package Folder page, enter the path of a directory in which you want the wizard to place the distribution package.

4. In the Included Files page, you'll see a list of all the files that make up the application, including Visual Basic and OLE Automation libraries but excluding .hml files and data files needed by the application.

5. In the File Source page (see Figure 19-15), specify the site from which each file should be downloaded. By default, all the Visual Basic, ADO, and other system files are downloaded from the Microsoft Web site, which is often the best choice.

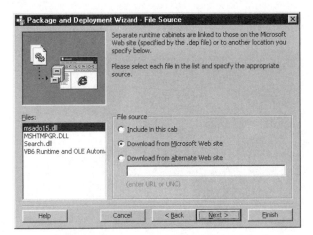

Figure 19-15. *The File Source page of the Package and Deployment Wizard.*

6. In the Safety Setting tab, you decide whether the components included in the DLL are Safe For Scripting and Safe For Initialization. (For more information about these terms, see the "Component Download" section in Chapter 17.)

7. In the last page of the wizard, you can assign a name to the current script so that you can easily repeat these steps in the future.

The wizard creates a new directory and puts in it a CAB file (which contains the DLL) and all the HTM files belonging to your application. You now need to deploy these files to a Web server, and you can use the Package and Deployment Wizard to achieve this:

1. Click on the Deploy button, and select the script name you entered in step 7 of the previous sequence.

2. In the Deployment Method page, select the Web Publishing option.

3. In the Items To Deploy page, select which files should be deployed. The first time you run the wizard, you normally deploy all the files except those that are on the Microsoft Web site, but in subsequent deployment operations you can omit the files that haven't changed in the meantime.

4. In the Additional Items To Deploy page, you can select files and entire folders for deployment. Here you select all the ancillary files, such as images, data files, WAV files, and so on.

5. In the Web Publishing Site page (see Figure 19-16), you must enter the complete URL of the site to which items should be deployed (for example, *www.yoursite.com*).You also enter the Web publishing protocol to be used (FTP or HTTP Post). Tick the Unpack And Install Server-Side Cab option if you want the CAB file to be unpacked after deployment. When you press the Next button, the wizard asks whether you want to save information about this site in the Registry.

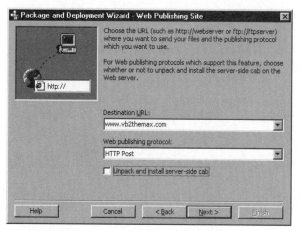

Figure 19-16. *The Web Publishing Site page of the Package and Deployment Wizard.*

6. In the last page of the wizard, you can give a name to this deployment script and click the Finish button to initiate the deployment phase.

When deployment is complete, uninstall the ActiveX DLL from your system, and use your browser to navigate to the main HTM page of the application. The browser should download the CAB file, install the DLL, and start your compiled DHTML application. The browser knows from what site the DLL can be downloaded because the Package and Deployment wizard has patched the <OBJECT> tags inside all the HTM pages with a CODEBASE attribute. (The text added by the wizard is in boldface.)

```
<OBJECT CODEBASE=Search.CAB#Version1,0,0,0
ID="DHTMLPage2" CLASSID="clsid:8F0A368F-C5BC-11D2-BAC5-0080C8F21830"
WIDTH=0 HEIGHT=0></OBJECT>
```

As you can see in the preceding HTML fragment, the Package and Deployment Wizard produces an incorrect CODEBASE attribute; the version number should be preceded by an equal sign. So you need to manually edit it, like this:

```
<OBJECT CODEBASE=Search.CAB#Version=1,0,0,0
```

Troubleshooting

I conclude this section with a few tips for building better DHTML applications:

- Ensure that your DHTML page works correctly even if the user has disabled image downloading.

- Always use relative URLs when referencing another page in the same Web site so that you can then deploy your project to another location without breaking the code in it.

- Use separate style sheets for keeping the appearance of all your pages uniform.

- Don't forget that page elements inherit most, but not all, the attributes of their containers. For example, paragraphs inherit the font of the Document, but they don't inherit its background color.

- When working with an external HTML editor, ensure that all the programmable elements have been assigned unique values for the *id* property. If there are any duplicates, the DHTMLPage designer adds a digit to make them unique, but script code in the page that references that item won't work any longer.

REMOTE DATA SERVICES

In a previous example, I showed you how a DHTML application can use ADO to perform a search on an MDB database and display the results as a table in an HTML page. When creating real-world Internet applications, however, you obviously can't use the approach shown in that example because the database isn't local and you don't have a path to it.

Another problem that you must solve when a client communicates with a Web browser is that HTTP is a *stateless* protocol, which means that no information is retained between consecutive requests from the browser. This sharply contrasts with the ADO way of doing things, which in general expects that the client is always in touch with the data source, from its logon and until the connection is closed. The ADO objects that get closer to the concept of a connectionless state are disconnected Recordsets, which update data through optimistic batch updates.

How can you read data from and write data to a database located on a remote Web server? The answer to this question is provided by Remote Data Services (RDS). You can choose one of two ways to use such objects: You can use bound DHTML controls or "pure" ADO code.

DHTML Data Binding

The simplest way to display data coming from a data source on an HTML page is to place an RDS.DataControl object on the page and bind one or more controls to it. This is conceptually similar to having bound controls on a regular Visual Basic form, but the actions you have to undertake are different.

Creating the RDS.DataControl object

The first thing you have to do is add an RDS.DataControl to the HTML page. This object is an ActiveX component exposed by the RDS library, and you can place it on an HTML page with the following <OBJECT> tag in the body of the page:

```
<OBJECT CLASSID=clsid:BD96C556-65A3-11D0-983A-00C04FC29E33
    ID=dcPublishers HEIGHT=1 WIDTH=1>
    <PARAM NAME="Server" VALUE="http://www.yourserver.com">
    <PARAM NAME="Connect" VALUE="DSN=Pubs">
    <PARAM NAME="SQL" VALUE="SELECT * FROM Publishers">
</OBJECT>
```

You must set at least three properties of the RDS.DataControl object: The *Server* property is the URL of the server where the data source resides, the *Connect* property points to the data source on that server, and *SQL* is the text of the query. You can also create the RDS.DataControl dynamically, which is especially useful when you want to assign these properties at run time, when the page has already been loaded. You can dynamically create an RDS.DataControl object using plain VBScript code placed in the *Window_onload* event or outside any VBScript procedure:

```
<SCRIPT LANGUAGE="VBScript"
' This code executes when the page loads.
Dim dcPublishers
Set dcPublishers = CreateObject("RDS.DataControl")
dcPublishers.Server = "http://www.yourserver.com"
dcPublishers.Connect = "DSN=Pubs"
dcCustomer.SQL = "SELECT * From Publishers"
dcCustomer.Refresh
</SCRIPT>
```

The *Server* property can point to an HTTP URL address or to an HTTPS URL address for a secure protocol (HTTPS is the Secure Hypertext Transfer Protocol). In both cases, the URL can include a port number. If you're retrieving data through DCOM, you can assign the name of the machine where the data source is. Finally, if you're working with a local database (typically, during earlier debug phases), you can assign an empty string to this property or omit it in the <OBJECT> tab. If you don't specify the server, the RDS.DataControl object is instantiated as an in-process object. All the demonstration applications on the companion CD use a local NWind.mdb, so this property is always left blank. Remember to assign it a meaningful value when you move the application to your local network or intranet.

Binding DHTML elements

You can bind many types of DHTML elements to an RDS.DataControl object, some of which are listed in Table 19-1. All bindable elements support three properties:

- DATASRC is the name of the RDS.DataControl the element is bound to and is preceded by a # sign—for example, *#dcPublishers*. (It corresponds to the *DataSource* property of a Visual Basic bound control.)

- DATAFLD is the name of the field in the data source that this element binds to. (It corresponds to Visual Basic's *DataField* property.)

- DATAFORMATAS can be *text* or *HTML*, depending on whether the contents of the source field must be interpreted as plain text or HTML code. The default for this property is *text*, and you can use *HTML* only for the controls that support the *innerHTML* property.

Here's an example of TextBox controls that are bound to the *dcPublishers* RDS.DataControl created previously:

```
Publisher Name: <BR>
<INPUT ID="txtPubName" DATASRC="#dcPublishers" DATAFLD="Pub_Name"><BR>
City: <BR>
<INPUT ID="txtCity" DATASRC="#dcPublishers" DATAFLD="City"><BR>
```

Element	Bound Property	Updatable
A	*href*	No
BUTTON	*innerText/innerHTML*	Yes
DIV	*innerText/innerHTML*	Yes
IMG	*src*	No
INPUT	*value* or *checked* (depending on the TYPE attribute)	Yes
SELECT	the text of the selected OPTION tag	Yes
SPAN	*innerText/innerHTML*	Yes
TEXTAREA	*value*	Yes

Table 19-1. *Some of the HTML elements that can be bound to an RDS.DataControl object.*

Navigating and updating the Recordset

Unlike the standard ADO Data control, the RDS.DataControl object doesn't have a visible interface, so you must provide the buttons for navigating the Recordset. Such buttons use the methods of the Recordset exposed by the RDS.DataControl object. This VBScript code assumes that you've created the four *btnMovexxxx* buttons, plus the *btnDelete* and *btnAddNew* controls:

```
Sub btnMoveFirst_onclick()
    dcPublishers.Recordset.MoveFirst
End Sub
```

(continued)

```
Sub btnMovePrevious_onclick()
    dcPublishers.Recordset.MovePrevious
    If dcPublishers.Recordset.BOF Then dcPublishers.Recordset.MoveFirst
End Sub

Sub btnMoveNext_onclick()
    dcPublishers.Recordset.MoveNext
    If dcPublishers.Recordset.EOF Then dcPublishers.Recordset.MoveLast
End Sub

Sub btnMoveLast_onclick()
    dcPublishers.Recordset.MoveLast
End Sub

Sub btnDelete_onclick()
    dcPublishers.Recordset.Delete
    dcPublishers.Recordset.MoveNext
    If dcPublishers.Recordset.EOF Then dcPublishers.Recordset.MoveLast
End Sub

Sub btnAddNew_onclick()
    dcPublishers.Recordset.AddNew
End Sub
```

The RDS.DataControl object works with disconnected Recordsets, so all the changes you make to it through bound controls are cached locally. When you're ready to send the changes to the data source, you execute the RDS.DataControl's *SubmitChanges* method. You typically invoke this method in the *Window_onunload* event or from the *onclick* event of a button:

```
Sub btnUpdate_onclick()
    dcPublishers.SubmitChanges
End Sub
```

You can cancel all pending updates using the *CancelUpdate* method. On the companion CD, you'll find an application that uses bound HTML controls to connect to the Customers table of a local copy of NWind.mdb; you'll probably have to change the *Connect* property of the RDS.DataControl to have it point to a valid path on your system.

All bound controls can raise two events, which you can trap from a script in the page or from Visual Basic code in a DHTML application. The *onbeforeupdate* event fires before a modified value is transferred from the control to the data source; if you don't cancel it, the control fires an *onafterupdate* event immediately after the update operation finishes executing. You can use these events to validate the data that the user has entered in bound controls, as you can see in Figure 19-17.

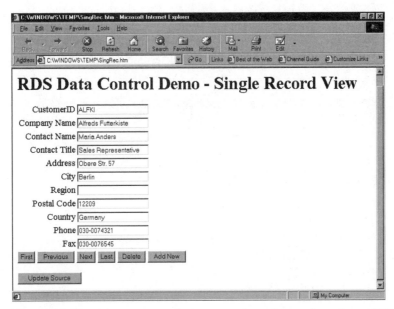

Figure 19-17. *This DHTML application uses bound controls and some VBScript code behind the navigational buttons.*

Tabular binding

If you prefer displaying the result of a query in tabular format, you can take advantage of the special binding features of the DHTML tables. In this case, you have to assign the DATASRC property in the <TABLE> tag and then prepare one single row of table cells containing <SPAN> tags with appropriate DATAFLD attributes. The following code is taken from the demonstration program (shown in Figure 19-18 on the following page) provided on the companion CD:

```
<TABLE DATASRC="#dcCustomers" BORDER=1>
 <THEAD><TR>
    <TH>Company Name</TH>
    <TH>Address</TH>
    <TH>City</TH>
    <TH>Region</TH>
    <TH>Country</TH>
  </TR></THEAD>
 <TBODY><TR>
    <TD><B><SPAN DATAFLD="CompanyName"></SPAN><B></TD>
    <TD><SPAN DATAFLD="Address"></SPAN></TD>
    <TD><SPAN DATAFLD="City"></SPAN></TD>
    <TD><SPAN DATAFLD="Region"></SPAN></TD>
    <TD><SPAN DATAFLD="Country"></SPAN></TD>
  </TR> </TBODY>
</TABLE>
```

For each record in the source, the RDS.DataControl object generates a new row of cells. For such dynamically generated rows, RDS.DataControl uses the HTML template included between the <TBODY> and </TBODY> tags. You can format and align individual columns by using standard HTML tags. For example, the sample application displays the CompanyName field in boldface.

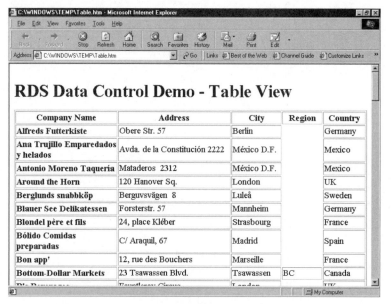

Figure 19-18. *Bound DHTML tables automatically resize their columns to display the contents of their cell in the most appropriate way.*

More on the RDS.DataControl object

The RDS.DataControl object exposes several other properties and methods that can be used for fine-tuning your application. For example, the *InternetTimeout* property gives you the timeout in milliseconds for HTTP transmissions, while the *SortColumn* and the *SortDirection* properties let you sort data in the underlying Recordset:

```
' Sort on the City field in ascending order.
dcPublishers.SortDirection = True
dcPublishers.SortColumn = "City"
dcPublishers.Reset
```

The *FilterColumn*, *FilterCriterion*, and *FilterValue* properties work together to apply a filter on the retrieved data:

```
' Display only U.S. publishers.
dcPublishers.FilterColumn = "Country"
' FilterCriterion supports the following operators: < <= > >= = <>.
dcPublishers.FilterCriterion = "="
dcPublishers.FilterValue = "USA"
dcPublishers.Reset
```

By default, the RDS.DataControl executes the query and fetches the Recordset asynchronously. You can control how queries are executed using the *ExecuteOptions* property, which can be 1-adcExecSync or 2-adcExecAsync. Similarly, you can determine how the Recordset is fetched using the *FetchOptions* property, which can take one of the following values: 1-adcFetchUpFront (synchronous execution, the control is returned to the application when the Recordset has been completely populated); 2-adcFetchBackground (the control is returned to the application when the first batch of records is returned, and the remaining data is retrieved asynchronously); or 3-adcFetchAsync (the default mode, all the records are retrieved in the background).

When the RDS.DataControl is working asynchronously, you must test the *ReadyState* property, which returns one of the following values: 2-adcReadyStateLoaded (the Recordset is open but no data has been retrieved yet); 3-adcReadyStateInteractive (the Recordset is being populated); 4-adcReadyStateComplete (the Recordset has completed retrieving data). When this property receives a new value, the RDS.DataControl fires an *onreadystatechange* event. You can cancel an asynchronous operation using the *Cancel* method.

When an error occurs and no VBScript code is executing, the RDS.DataControl object raises an *onerror* event.

Using RDS Objects

While binding is always great for creating a prototype, in most cases you must write code if you want to remain in control of the whole process. The RDS library comprises a few objects that make it possible for a disconnected client to exchange data using a stateless protocol. More precisely, when developing applications based on RDS, you use objects from *three* different libraries. (See Figure 19-19.)

■ *RDS.DataSpace* is a component that runs in the client application and represents a link to the server on which the data actually resides. This object is exposed by the Microsoft Remote Data Services library (Msadco.dll).

■ *RDSServer.DataFactory* is a component that runs on the server. It queries the data source and optionally updates it with data coming from the client. This object is exposed by the Microsoft Remote Data Services Server library (Msadcf.dll). You don't need to install this library on client workstations.

■ *RDS.DataControl* (described in the previous section) is an ActiveX component that you can drop on an HTML page. It allows you to bind one or more elements on the page to the remote data source. This object is included in the Msadco.dll library and encompasses the functionality in both RDS.DataSpace and RDSServer.DataFactory.

■ *ADOR.Recordset* is functionally similar to a regular ADO Recordset, but it takes fewer resources and is therefore a better choice when the application runs inside the browser and doesn't need the full power and versatility of ADO. This object is exposed by the Microsoft ActiveX Data Object Recordset library (Msador15.dll). The ADOR library also includes the Field and Property objects, but not the Connection and Command objects. This library is automatically installed with Internet Explorer, so it never requires you to download and install it on the client workstation.

NOTE Just to give you an idea about the relative weight of the ADOR library compared to the regular ADO library, compare these facts: The Msador15.dll file is a mere 37 KB in size, whereas the full-fledged Msado15.dll file is 332 KB.

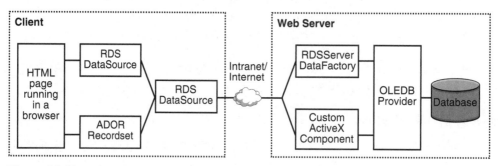

Figure 19-19. *All the objects that partake of a typical RDS session.*

Establishing a connection

If you're accustomed to the ADO way of doing things, the approach you must follow with RDS to establish a connection might at first seem unnatural and unnecessarily complex. But it has its inner logic and also offers a lot of flexibility.

Before trying the code that follows in the Visual Basic IDE, add a reference to the RDS and ADOR libraries in the References dialog box. The next step is to create an instance of the RDS.DataSource object; use its *CreateObject* method to create an instance of the remote RDSServer.DataFactory object. You don't need to add a reference to the RDSServer library because you're going to assign the return value of the *CreateObject* method to a generic Object variable.

```
Dim ds As New RDS.DataSpace
Dim df As Object
Set df = ds.CreateObject("RDSServer.DataFactory", _
    "http://www.yourserver.com")
```

NOTE All the examples in this section are written in Visual Basic code running inside a standard Visual Basic application or a DHTMLPage designer module. You can easily convert the code so that it runs as a script in an HTML page by dropping the *As* clause in all the *Dim* statements and using the *CreateObject* method instead of the *New* keyword.

The second argument of the RDS.DataSpace's *CreateObject* method can be an HTTP or HTTPS URL address, the name of another computer in the network, or an empty string if you're instantiating a DataFactory object on the same machine on which the program is running.

After you've obtained a reference to a valid RDSServer.DataFactory object, you can use its *Query* method to actually retrieve the Recordset object that contains the result of the query:

```
Dim rs As ADOR.Recordset
Set rs = df.Query("DSN=Pubs", "SELECT * FROM Publishers")
```

The first argument of the *Query* method is the connection string that the DataFactory object will use to connect to the data source, so you can use all the arguments you would use for the *ConnectionString* property of an ADO.Connection object. Don't forget that this connection string will be used by a component that already runs on the server (so you don't need a lengthy timeout value), and ensure that you're referring to a DSN or other connection attributes that are valid for that particular server.

Displaying and updating data

You can use the ADOR.Recordset object as you would use a regular ADO Recordset because the differences between the two objects are minimal. (See the ADO documentation for more details.) You can navigate the Recordset and update its fields, but all your changes are cached locally. Because you don't have bound controls, you must provide the code that moves data to and from the Recordset and the fields in the page. It turns out that you can take advantage of the *dataFld* property even when the control isn't bound to a data source. In fact, you can assign the name of the field that you want to display in the control to this property and then move data back and forth using the following routines:

```
' You can reuse these routines in any DHTMLPage module.
Sub GetFieldData()
    ' Move data from the Recordset to the fields in the page.
    ' All the "pseudo-bound" controls have a nonempty DataFld property,
    ' so you just need to iterate on the "all" collection.
    Dim ctrl As Object
    On Error Resume Next
    For Each ctrl In Document.All
        If Len(ctrl.dataFld) = 0 Then
            ' Empty or unsupported DataFld property.
```

(continued)

```
            Else
                ' Append an empty string to account for Null values.
                ctrl.Value = rs(ctrl.dataFld) & ""
            End If
        Next
    End Sub

    Sub PutFieldData()
        ' Move data from the fields in the page to the Recordset.
        Dim ctrl As Object
        On Error Resume Next
        For Each ctrl In Document.All
            If Len(ctrl.dataFld) = 0 Then
                ' Empty or unsupported DataFld property
            ElseIf rs(ctrl.dataFld) & "" <> ctrl.Value Then
                ' Don't update the Recordset if it isn't necessary.
                rs(ctrl.dataFld) = ctrl.Value
            End If
        Next
    End Sub
```

Thanks to these routines, it's easy to write the code associated with navigational buttons. For example, this is the code that executes when the user clicks on the Next button:

```
Private Function btnMoveNext_onclick() As Boolean
    PutFieldData                        ' Save current values.
    rs.MoveNext                         ' Move to the next record.
    If rs.EOF Then rs.MoveLast          ' Go back if you moved too far.
    GetFieldData                        ' Display the current record.
End Function
```

When you're ready to submit changes to the server, you must invoke the *SubmitChanges* method of the RDSServer.DataFactory object. This method expects the connection string and a reference to the Recordset that must be marshaled back to the data source:

```
' Specify that you want to marshal only modified values.
rs.MarshalOptions = adMarshalModifiedOnly
' Send modified values to the server.
df.SubmitChanges conn, rs
```

The *SubmitChanges* method fails if there were conflicts in just one single record. In this circumstance, the RDS library is far less sophisticated than the ADO library because in the ADO library you can manage conflicts on a record-by-record basis.

Custom Business Components

Remote Data Services technology promises much more than a way to move a Recordset back and forth between the server and the client. In fact, the DataSource's *CreateObject* method can instantiate *any* ActiveX component that resides on the Web server. In a sense, you might consider RDS the extension of DCOM to the HTTP and HTTPS protocols. This new technique opens up a new world of opportunities for the brave programmer.

From this perspective, the RDSServer.DataFactory object is just one of the many components that can be instantiated on the Web server and deserves special attention only because it's provided in the RDS package. But when you dive into the production of real world applications, you see that this component has one defect: Once the client has created a link to the server, it can query *any* database on that server, provided that it has a correct user name and password. In fact, using a trial-and-error approach, a client equipped this way can discover user names and passwords it doesn't have. This security scheme is inadequate for a Web server, which is exposed to attack from any browser in the world.

> **NOTE** RDS allows a (limited) customization of the behavior of the RDSServer.DataFactory object through a default handler object named MSDFMAP.Handler or through a custom handler object that you provide. The default handler can be controlled by editing the msdfmap.ini configuration file in the Windows directory. Open this file with an editor to get an idea of what you can achieve with this object, and read the RDS documentation for additional details.

The solution to the security problem is to build a custom ActiveX component and install it on the Web server. Such a component can expose—through its properties and methods—only the data that you want to make available to the outside. Additionally, because client workstations access the database through this custom component, you have all the benefits of a three-tier architecture:

- The code in client applications is simplified because the custom component can expose higher level methods that access and process data.

- The clients never see the physical structure of the database on the server, so you can change the implementation of the database without worrying about any adverse impact on clients.

- The component can process data locally on the server before returning a result to a client, which often makes for better overall performance.

Writing a custom component

A custom component intended to be instantiated via an RDS.DataSpace's *CreateObject* method isn't really different from a regular ActiveX component, so you can make use of all you've learned in Chapter 16. The component should expose methods that enable the client to execute a query and send new and updated records back to the component.

On the companion CD, you'll find a simple ActiveX DLL component named NWindFactory.Shipper. This component lets a Web client query the Shippers table in the NWind.mdb database installed on the server computer. The component exposes just three methods: *GetShippers* returns a disconnected ADOR.Recordset with all the records in the Shippers table, *UpdateShippers* updates the table with values from the ADOR.Recordset passed to it in its argument, and *GetEmptyShippers* returns an empty ADOR.Recordset that the client can use to insert information about new shippers. This is the complete source code of the component:

```
' This is the path of the NWind.mdb database on the server.
Const DBPATH = "C:\Program Files\Microsoft Visual Studio\Vb98\NWind.mdb"
Dim conn As String

Private Sub Class_Initialize()
    ' Initialize the connection string.
    conn = "Provider=Microsoft.Jet.OLEDB.3.51;Data Source=" & DBPATH
End Sub


' Return the Shippers table in a Recordset object.
Function GetShippers() As ADOR.Recordset
    Dim rs As New ADOR.Recordset
    ' Query the Shippers table.
    rs.CursorLocation = adUseClient
    rs.Open "SELECT * FROM Shippers", conn, adOpenStatic, _
        adLockBatchOptimistic
    ' Disconnect the Recordset.
    Set rs.ActiveConnection = Nothing
    Set GetShippers = rs
End Function


' Update the Shippers table with data contained in a Recordset.
Function UpdateShippers(rs As ADOR.Recordset) As Boolean
    On Error Resume Next
    rs.ActiveConnection = conn           ' Reconnect the Recordset.
    rs.UpdateBatch                       ' Perform the updates.
    Set rs.ActiveConnection = Nothing    ' Disconnect it once again.
    UpdateShippers = (Err = 0)           ' Return True if everything is OK.
End Function


' Return an empty Recordset.
Function GetEmptyShippers() As ADOR.Recordset
```

```
      Dim rs As New ADOR.Recordset
      ' Retrieve an empty Recordset from the Shippers table.
      rs.CursorLocation = adUseClient
      ' Notice the WHERE clause in the following SQL SELECT command.
      rs.Open "SELECT * FROM Shippers WHERE 0", conn, adOpenStatic, _
          adLockBatchOptimistic
      ' Disconnect the Recordset.
      Set rs.ActiveConnection = Nothing
      Set GetEmptyShippers = rs
End Function
```

For better results, you should compile your custom ActiveX DLL components using the Unattended Execution option and the Apartment Threading model. Both these options are in the General tab of the Project Properties dialog box.

Registering the component

To make the ActiveX custom component available for installation through RDS, you have to take one more step. Not all the components installed on the server can be instantiated from an Internet client because it would be difficult to enforce decent security. Only the components that are listed under a given key in the server's Registry can be instantiated through RDS. More precisely, you must create the following key in the server's Registry:

```
HKEY_LOCAL_MACHINE\System\CurrentControlSet\Services\W3SVC\Parameters\
    ADCLaunch\<servername.classname>
```

Notice that this key has no value. Moreover, a component for RDS should be marked as Safe For Scripting and Safe For Initialization, which means adding two more keys to the Registry, as explained in the "Component Download" section in Chapter 17.

When you're building the installation package of a component, the best way to go is to prepare a REG file that patches the Registry automatically. For example, the next code snippet is the REG file for the sample NWindFactory.Shippers component. The first entry marks the component as an object that can be instantiated through the RDS.DataSpace's *CreateObject* method, whereas the remaining two entries mark it with the Safe For Scripting and Safe For Initialization settings. When you create a REG file for your own component, you have to substitute the "NWindFactory.Shippers" string with the component's ProgID, and the string {03C410F7-C7FD-11D2-BAC5-0080C8F21830} with the component's CLSID.

```
REGEDIT4
[HKEY_LOCAL_MACHINE\System\CurrentControlSet\Services\W3SVC\Parameters\
    ADCLaunch\NWindFactory.Shippers]
[HKEY_CLASSES_ROOT\CLSID\{03C410F7-C7FD-11D2-BAC5-0080C8F21830}\
    Implemented Categories\{7DD95801-9882-11CF-9FA9-00AA006C42C4}]
[HKEY_CLASSES_ROOT\CLSID\{03C410F7-C7FD-11D2-BAC5-0080C8F21830}\
    Implemented Categories\{7DD95802-9882-11CF-9FA9-00AA006C42C4}]
```

You don't need to create a key for the RDSServer.DataFactory object because the Registry patching is part of the RDS installation package on the server.

Using the component

Using a custom component via RDS is similar to using the RDSServer.DataFactory object. You just have to create an instance of your component through the RDS.DataSpace object's *CreateObject* and then use your component's methods to retrieve and update the Recordset. Because your clients never have to directly perform queries on the database, they simply need to reference the ADOR lightweight library instead of the full-fledged ADO library.

Figure 19-20 shows the demonstration client application. Its three TextBox controls are dynamically bound to the Recordset retrieved from the component. This is a partial listing of the code in the main form of the application:

```
' Modify this constant to point to your Web server,
' or use an empty string to connect to a local component.
Const WEB_SERVER = "www.yourserver.com"

Dim ds As New RDS.DataSpace
Dim myObj As Object
Dim rs As ADOR.Recordset

Private Sub Form_Load()
    ' Create the remote component.
    Set myObj = ds.CreateObject("NWindFactory.Shippers", WEB_SERVER)
End Sub

Private Sub cmdGetShippers_Click()
    ' Ask the component to query the table and then return a Recordset.
    Set rs = myObj.GetShippers()
    ' Bind the controls to this Recordset.
    SetDataSource rs
End Sub

Private Sub cmdGetEmptyShippers_Click()
    ' Ask the component to create an empty Recordset.
    Set rs = myObj.GetEmptyShippers()
    ' Bind the controls to this Recordset.
    SetDataSource rs
End Sub

Private Sub cmdUpdateShippers_Click()
    ' This optimizes the update operation.
    rs.MarshalOptions = adMarshalModifiedOnly
    ' Pass the updated Recordset to the component, and test the result.
    If myObj.UpdateShippers(rs) Then
        MsgBox "Update successful", vbExclamation
    Else
        MsgBox "Unable to update!", vbCritical
```

```
    End If
End Sub

Sub SetDataSource(obj As Object)
    ' Use the Recordset as a data source for the fields.
    Set txtShipperID.DataSource = obj
    Set txtCompanyName.DataSource = obj
    Set txtPhone.DataSource = obj
End Sub
```

Figure 19-20. *A demonstration application using dynamically bound controls.*

You can optimize the update process using the Recordset's *MarshalOptions* property; if you set this property to 1-adMarshalModifiedOnly, only the records that have been modified, added, or deleted are transferred back to the server. If the update operation fails, you can figure out what happened by checking the *Status* property for each record in the Recordset. For all the records that weren't successfully updated, this property returns a value different from adRecUnmodified.

An RDS component can marshal only Recordsets that contain a single result set, so, for example, you can't send back to the client the result of a stored procedure that returns multiple results sets. Similarly, you can return a Variant that contains an array of values and even an array of arrays, but you can't return an array that contains multiple result sets. On the other hand, it's OK to return a hierarchical Recordset.

> **NOTE** Don't forget that offering a custom component for querying and manipulating a database on the Web server doesn't mean that you've solved all your security problems. For example, a client might connect through the standard RDSServer.DataFactory object, and if he or she happens to know a valid login name and password, your data is at stake. For this reason, you might decide to disable the remote instantiation of the RDSServer.DataFactory object by deleting the corresponding entry in the ADCLaunch key of the Registry.

THE DHTML EDIT CONTROL

Relatively few Visual Basic programmers are aware that Microsoft has made publicly available part of the technology on which the DHTMLPage designer is based, in the form of a DHTML Edit control. This control can be downloaded for free from the Microsoft Web site at *http://www.microsoft.com/workshop/author/dhtml/edit/download.asp*. (The site also contains a version that works with earlier versions of Internet Explorer.) The control includes all the functionality found in the rightmost pane of the DHTMLPage designer and so makes it possible for you to add a Dynamic HTML editor to your application.

Installation

Run the EXE file you've downloaded, and select a target installation directory. At the end of the unpacking process, you'll find several files, including the complete documentation and a few interesting samples. You'll also find some include files, but they're of no interest to Visual Basic programmers. (The package also includes a version for the C++ language)

Run the Visual Basic IDE, press the Ctrl+T key to bring up the list of installed ActiveX controls, and select the new DHTML Edit Control component. This operation adds two new icons to the Toolbox window. Each icon corresponds to a different flavor of the control: One is the complete version, and the other is marked as Safe For Scripting and Safe For Initialization and doesn't permit a few operations—for example, saving files. In general, you'll use the former version in your Visual Basic applications and the latter one in HTML pages or in DHTML applications that run inside a browser.

To get a feeling of what this control gives you, drop an instance of it on a form and run the program. You can type any text in the control's window as if the window were a standard TextBox. Unlike a standard TextBox control, however, you can format the selected text with bold, italic, and underline attributes (using the Ctrl+B, Ctrl+I, and Ctrl+U key combinations, respectively). The control supports many other operations through shortcut keys: You can insert a hyperlink by pressing the Ctrl+L key combination, increase and decrease paragraph indentation by using the Ctrl+T and Ctrl+Shift+T key combinations, and display the Find dialog box by using the Ctrl+F key combination. The control also supports multilevel undo and redo features by means of the Ctrl+Z and Ctrl+Y key combinations, respectively, and some sophisticated drag-and-drop capabilities for moving elements on the page.

Properties and Methods

The rest of the DHTML Edit control's functionality, however, can be reached only through its methods and properties. For example, you can create a new document, load an existing HTM file, or save the contents of the control to a file using the *NewDocument*, *LoadDocument*, and *SaveDocument* methods, respectively. (The latter two methods can also display a common dialog box for file selection.) Or you can load an HTM file from a URL using the *LoadURL* method, as shown here:

```
DHTMLEdit1.LoadURL = "http://www.vb2themax.com/index.htm"
```

You can also load and save HTML source code without using a file by assigning a string to the *DocumentHTML* property. This property gives you an effective way to store and retrieve a formatted document stored in a database field or build a sophisticated DHTML editor that lets you enter plain HTML source code, a feature that's missing even in the DHTMLPage designer. As an exercise, you might revise the DHTMLEd.vbp project on the companion CD to use the DHTML Edit control instead of the WebBrowser control. Just a warning: Using the *DocumentHTML* property raises an error if a document is being loaded, a condition that you can test using the *Busy* property.

The DHTML Edit control can also work in preview mode, in which you see how the page you're building will appear inside a browser. You can switch to and from preview mode by setting the *BrowserMode* property to True or False, respectively.

The DHTML Edit control supports formatting commands in an unusual way. Instead of exposing dozens of properties or methods, one for each available option, you issue commands through the all-in-one *ExecCommand* method, whose first argument is a constant that tells the method what to do. I counted over 50 commands, for changing text attributes, inserting or deleting table cells, performing cut-and-paste operations, changing the z-order or the alignment of an element, and so on. For example, the following code shows how you can change the font size of the current selected text:

```
' The second argument suppresses the default dialog box.
' The third argument is the new font's size.
DHTMLEdit1.ExecCommand DECMD_SETFONTSIZE, OLECMDEXECOPT_DONTPROMPTUSER, fs
```

The *DOM* property of the DHTML Edit control returns a reference to the Document object of the page hosted in the control. Thanks to this property, you can do virtually anything to the document being edited. For example, you can change the background color of the HTML page with this code:

```
DHTMLEdit1.DOM.bgColor = "red"
```

The DHTML Edit control also exposes several events that let you react to actions of the user who's editing the document. The most important event is *DisplayChange*, which fires any time the user selects a new element or simply moves the insertion point. You typically react to this event by updating a status bar and the state of the buttons on a toolbar. The *DocumentComplete* event fires when the page has been completely loaded and is ready for editing. The *ShowContextMenu* and *ContextMenuAction* events let you decide what appears when users right-click on the control and what happens when they select a menu command.

I was surprised by how many sample programs are provided with this control. VBEdit.vbp is a complete WYSIWYG editor for Dynamic HTML pages, and its source code provides a great occasion for you to see how you can exploit the features of the DHTML Edit control. (See Figure 19-21.) The VBDom.vbp project shows you how to access the Document Object Model of the document hosted in the control. Finally, in the Web subdirectory, you'll find many examples of HTML pages that host the DHTML Edit control.

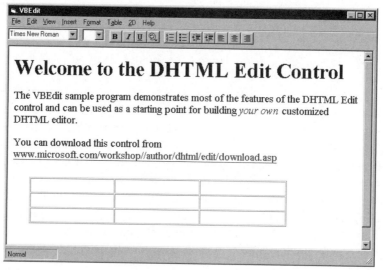

Figure 19-21. *The VBEdit.vbp sample application.*

This chapter has been a long one, but we had a lot of ground to cover. You've seen what HTML and Dynamic HTML are, how you can exploit the power of the new HTMLPage designer, and how you can take advantage of RDS and remote Automation over the Internet. You're now ready for the final leap: You can build Visual Basic applications that run inside a Web server. This topic is covered in the next chapter.

Chapter 20

Internet Information Server Applications

In Chapter 19, you learned how to create client applications that connect to a Web server through the Internet or an intranet. It's now time to find out how you can leverage your Visual Basic expertise to build applications and components that run on the server, right inside Microsoft Internet Information Server (IIS) and its Active Server Pages (ASP). Before we delve into the nitty-gritty details of Web server programming, however, you need to have at least a general idea of what IIS is and how you can do ASP programming without using Visual Basic.

AN INTRODUCTION TO INTERNET INFORMATION SERVER 4

There are several Web server programs on the market, from various vendors. Some of them are expensive; others are free. Internet Information Server 4 is Microsoft's offering in this area, and it belongs to the "free" group. In fact, it's part of the Microsoft Windows NT 4 Option Pack, together with other all-important applications such as Component Services (formerly known as Transaction Server, or MTS), Microsoft Message Queue Server (MSMQ), and Microsoft Index Server. You can install the Windows NT 4 Option Pack from a Visual Studio CD, or you can download it from Microsoft's Web site. All these products, in addition to other strategic software—such as Microsoft SQL Server, Microsoft Exchange Server, Microsoft Systems Management Server (SMS), Microsoft Cluster Server, and Microsoft SNA Server—make up the Microsoft BackOffice platform upon which you can create efficient, scalable, and robust enterprise solutions.

Main Features

Even if your primary job is programming a Web site rather than administering it, you still need to have at least a basic understanding of what IIS can do. To put it simply, when you run IIS, you're transforming your Windows NT machine into a Web server that is able to accept and process requests from clients on an intranet or the Internet.

IIS 4 fully supports the HTTP 1.1 protocol, but it can also accept requests through the older and less efficient HTTP 1.0 protocol. In addition, it supports other widely accepted Internet standards, such as File Transfer Protocol (FTP) for file downloading and Simple Mail Transport Protocol (SMPT) for sending e-mail messages from within a Web application.

IIS 4 is a departure from its previous versions in that it can run as an MTS component. This has a substantial impact on its performance and robustness. In fact, a script that runs inside an ASP page can instantiate an ActiveX DLL that runs as an MTS component and still consider the DLL as an in-process component. In comparison, a script running under IIS 3 had to cross its process boundaries to access components inside MTS, and you know how slow out-of-process components are. You need MTS components to build reliable component-based transactional applications. If you care for robustness more than performance, however, you can run a Web application in a separate process. That way, if the application breaks with an error or some other malfunction, the other applications aren't affected.

IIS 4 includes support for multiple Web sites, and it even supports different administrators, one for each Web site. Individual Web administrators have full control of the sites they're in charge of—they can grant permissions, assign content rating and expiration, activate log files, and so on. But they're prevented from modifying global settings that would affect other sites hosted inside IIS, such as the Web site name or the bandwidth assigned to each Web site.

In spite of its power, IIS can be administered using a simple and user-friendly interface based on the Microsoft Management Console. You can also configure IIS to accept administrative commands through a Web-based Internet Service Manager (which lets an administrator work remotely using a regular browser), and you can even write your own applications that manipulate IIS through the COM object model that it exposes. Thanks to the tight integration between IIS and Windows NT, administrators can also manage users and groups using the system tools they're already familiar with and can use standard debug utilities such as Event Viewer and Performance Monitor.

The Microsoft Management Console

As just mentioned, you can administer IIS—as well as most other components of the BackOffice platform—through the Microsoft Management Console (MMC), which is shown in Figure 20-1. This utility doesn't do anything in itself; it works only as a container for one or more *snap-in* applications. You can install and remove snap-in applications for other programs from the Add/Remove Snap-in command in the Console menu.

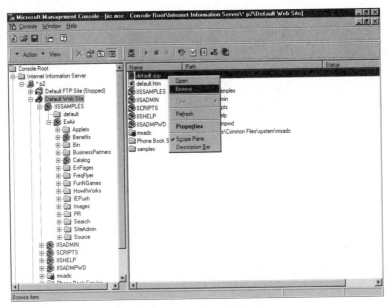

Figure 20-1. *The Microsoft Management Console.*

Computers and directories

The MMC utility can manage multiple computers on your LAN. Under the name of each computer in the leftmost pane, you'll find all the Web and FTP sites hosted on that computer. You can create a new site by right-clicking on a computer node and selecting the Web Site command from the New menu. A wizard starts, asking you for the site's description, its IP address and port number, the path to a directory that will act as the home directory for the site, and the access permissions for the home directory. You can leave the "(All Unassigned)" default value for the IP address during the development phase, but you should assign a different port number to each Web site defined on a given machine.

When working with a Web site, you need to account for several types of directories. The *home directory* is a local directory (or a directory located on another computer in the LAN) that is the entry point for the Web site when it is accessed through the Internet. For example, on my machine, the URL *http://www.vb2themax.com* is mapped to the directory C:\inetpub\vb2themax. All the subdirectories of the home directory can be accessed as subdirectories in the URL. For example, *http://www.vb2themax.com/tips* is mapped to C:\inetpub\vb2themax\tips.

A *virtual directory* is a directory that doesn't physically belong to the directory tree that originates under the home directory but that will appear as if it did. For example, I might have the *www.vb2themax.com/buglist* URL subdirectory mapped to the D:\KnowledgeBase\VbBugs physical directory. You create a virtual directory by right-clicking on a Web site node and selecting the Virtual Directory command from the New menu. The physical and virtual directories are marked with different icons in the leftmost pane of the MMC.

Web site, directory, and file properties

You can modify the properties of a Web site by right-clicking on its node and selecting the Properties menu command (or by clicking the Properties button on the toolbar). The Properties dialog box has nine tabs:

■ In the Web Site tab (shown in Figure 20-2), you can modify the IP address and port number of the site, the number of allowed connections, the connection timeout (the number of seconds after which the server disconnects an inactive user), and logging settings.

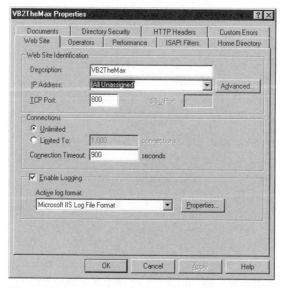

Figure 20-2. *The Web Site tab of the Properties dialog box of an IIS Web site.*

■ In the Operators tab, you select which Windows NT users are granted operator privileges on this site—in other words, who is the administrator of this site. By default, Windows NT administrators are also the Web site administrators, but this isn't a requirement.

■   The Performance tab lets you fine-tune the Web site performance by tailoring it to the number of expected hits per day. In this tab, you can also enable one of the most useful features of IIS for multiple site management, *bandwidth throttling,* which lets you limit the bandwidth of one site so that it doesn't affect the performance of other sites hosted on the same machine.

■   In the ISAPI Filters tab, you select which ISAPI filters this Web site uses. You often don't need to specify any filter here because all Web sites inherit the filters defined for the computer (which you can set using the Properties dialog box of the Computer node).

■   In the Home Directory tab (shown in Figure 20-3), you establish the mapping between the URL path and a physical directory on the local machine or on another machine on the LAN, and you establish the read and write permissions on the directory. In the Application Settings frame, you decide whether this directory is the starting point of a Web application.

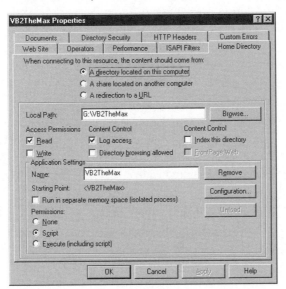

Figure 20-3. *The Home Directory tab of the Properties dialog box of an IIS Web site.*

A *Web application* is defined as the files and the subdirectories contained in a directory marked as an application starting point. Click the Configure button to specify which ISAPI application will process files with nonstandard extensions (such the Asp.dll for managing ASP files). A Web application can optionally run as an isolated process, which means that other IIS applications and the Web server itself won't be affected if this application fails. Finally, you can set the execute permissions for the files in this directory. The options are None, Script (only scripts are allowed to execute), or Execute (scripts, DLLs, and EXEs can execute in this directory).

- The Documents tab lets you select one or more default files for the Web site's home directory. The default document is the one sent to client browsers when they access the directory without specifying a particular file. This file is typically named index.html, default.htm, or default.asp, but you can add other filenames and even set priorities for them.

- The Directory Security tab contains push buttons that let you open other dialog boxes. In the Authentication Methods secondary dialog box, you decide whether clients can log in to this Web site using anonymous access, a basic authentication method based on user names and passwords (which are sent as plain text); or the Windows NT Challenge/Response method, in which access is restricted using Windows NT File System's Access Control Lists and information is exchanged in encrypted form.

  In the IP Address And Domain Name Restriction secondary dialog box, you select which computers are granted or denied access to this Web site. When publishing a Web site, you obviously have to grant access to anyone. But you can enforce stricter access permissions for selected portions of the site. All the settings in this tab are inherited from the properties of the parent computer node.

- The HTTP Headers tab lets you set an expiration date or interval for the documents in the Web site. This setting is crucial because it tells the client browser whether it can reuse the information in its local cache, thereby reducing download times dramatically.

- The Custom Errors tab lets you specify which page of your server the client browser is redirected to when an HTTP error occurs. You don't usually need to alter the settings in this tab, unless you want to override the default action or localize the error message to a different language.

You can modify the properties of a physical or virtual directory by right-clicking on the corresponding node in either pane of the MMC and selecting the Properties menu command. The Properties dialog box contains a subset of the tabs that are found in the Web site's Properties dialog box. For this reason, I won't describe them again. The same thing happens with the Properties dialog box of individual document files.

Just to remind you, IIS lets you define the behavior and the attributes of each individual element in the computer/site/directory/file hierarchy. At the same time, it saves you a lot of time by automatically assigning to an object all the attributes of its parent. The tabs in the Properties dialog boxes for these elements are identical, and the user interface is logical and coherent.

> **TIP** Make sure that the NTFS security settings for a file or a directory don't differ from the settings in the Properties dialog box of that object. If the two sets of security settings don't match, IIS will use the more limiting ones.

Browsing the Web site

To browse the pages hosted in a Web site, you must activate the site first, either by clicking on it and selecting the Start command from its context menu or by clicking on the Start Item button on the toolbar. You can also stop or pause a Web site using other menu commands or toolbar buttons.

To see how a page will appear in a client's browser, right-click on an HTM or ASP document in the rightmost pane and select the Browse menu command. Browsing a page from within the MMC rather than directly from within Windows Explorer might deliver completely different results, because if the page contains server-side scripts they will be executed correctly. This approach permits you to test your ASP programs on the same machine on which you're developing them.

> **TIP** If you're using Microsoft Internet Explorer 4.0 to browse pages hosted in a local IIS, you get an error if the browser is configured to connect to the Internet using a modem. If you get an error, bring up the Internet Options dialog box and make sure that the Connect To The Internet Using A Local Area Network option is selected.

The context menu that appears when you right-click a file also contains an Open command, which loads the file into the application that has registered itself as the default HTML editor. For example, if you have Microsoft InterDev installed, this command will load the HTM or ASP file into InterDev for editing.

Active Server Pages

In a nutshell, an ASP page is a document that resides on the Web server and that contains a mixture of HTML code and server-side scripts. Such scripts process requests coming from client browsers and can build a response page for that particular client— for example, by querying a database through ADO. This capability is very important because it lets you create "dynamic" HTML pages that can be downloaded by any browser that supports plain HTML. For this reason, ASP can play a key role in Internet applications, whereas DHTML should be used only in more controlled environments— such as a company intranet—in which all clients can standardize on Internet Explorer.

Don't let the adjective "dynamic" confuse you. We're not talking about dynamic pages in the DHTML sense. The ASP technology doesn't deliver pages with animation and transition effects. Rather, with it you can create pages on the fly that are customized for each client. For example, you can have the server accept a request from a client, perform a query on a database, and then return the results of the query as a standard HTML table to that particular client.

> **NOTE**   You can develop ASP applications using the Personal Web Server 4
> that runs on Windows 95 and Windows 98. For serious Web development, how-
> ever, you absolutely need the "real" IIS that runs on Windows NT or Windows
> 2000 Server family. All the examples in this book were developed on Windows NT
> Server.

ASP basics

An HTML page can contain two types of scripts: *server-side* scripts, which are executed
on the server and contribute to creating the HTML document sent back to the browser,
and *client-side* scripts, such as VBScript or JScript procedures executed within the
client browser. The two types of scripts require different tags in an ASP page because
the ASP filtering mechanism must execute server-side scripts without sending them to
the browser but has to send client-side scripts to the browser without interpreting them.

You can insert a server-side script inside an ASP page in two ways. The first way
is to use the <SCRIPT> tag with the RUNAT attribute, as here:

```
<SCRIPT LANGUAGE="VBScript" RUNAT="Server">
' Add server-side VBScript code here.
</SCRIPT>
```

You can specify either VBScript or JScript in the LANGUAGE attribute. Unlike client-
side scripts, however, the default script language for ASP is VBScript, so you can safely
omit the language specification. The second way to insert server-side scripts is to use
the <% and %> delimiters. For example, the following statement assigns the current
server time to the *currTime* variable:

```
<% currTime = Now() %>
```

I won't show ASP examples written in JScript, but for the sake of completeness,
I'll show you how you can change the default script language for all server-side script
fragments enclosed in the <% and %> delimiters:

```
<%@ LANGUAGE = JScript %>
```

Two types of statements can be enclosed between the script delimiters: those
that execute a command and those that return a value. For statements that return a
value, you must insert an equal sign (= character) immediately after the opening
delimiter, as here:

```
<% = Now() %>
```

(Note that you can insert comments in statements that execute a command, but not
in those that return a value.) The value returned by the VBScript expression is in-

serted in the HTML page exactly where the code snippet is. This means that you can (and often do) mix plain HTML text and server-side script code in the same line. For example, here is the source code for a complete ASP document that displays the current date and time on the server:

```
<HTML>
<HEAD><TITLE>Your first ASP document</TITLE></HEAD>
<BODY>
<H1>Welcome to the XYZ Web server</H1>
Today is <% = FormatDateTime(Now, 1) %>. <P>
Current time on this server is <% = FormatDateTime(Now, 3) %>.
</BODY>
</HTML>
```

You can use the <SCRIPT> tag to enclose individual statements and entire routines:

```
<SCRIPT RUNAT="Server">
Function RunTheDice()
    RunTheDice = Int(Rnd * 6) + 1
End Function
</SCRIPT>
```

The routine defined in the page can be called elsewhere in the script:

```
<% Randomize Timer %>
First die shown <% = RunTheDice %> <P>
Second die shown <% = RunTheDice %>
```

You can also embed a VBScript statement within <% and %> delimiters, but without the = symbol. The following example is more complex than the previous ones in that it alternates plain HTML and server-side statements:

```
<% h = Hour(Now)
If h <= 6 Or h >= 22 Then %>
Good Night
<% ElseIf h <= 12 Then %>
Good Morning
<% ElseIf h <= 18 Then %>
Good Afternoon
<% Else %>
Good Evening
<% End If %>
```

Server-side VBScript programming

Server-side scripting isn't a lot different from client-side scripting, at least syntactically. The real difficulty in writing ASP code is in trying to anticipate what your script produces when IIS executes it.

The only relevant difference between regular VBScript code and server-side VBScript code is that a few statements are prohibited in the latter, most notably those statements that show a dialog box on the screen. This prohibition is understandable, though. After all, the script will be executed on an unattended server; no one will be there to click the OK button in a message box. So just stay clear of the *MsgBox* and *InputBox* statements when you're writing server-side VBScript code.

Server-side scripts support *include files*—that is, files that reside on the server and that are included as-is in the HTML page being generated. This is the syntax for inserting an include file:

```
<!-- #include file="Routines.inc " -->
```

The filename can be either a physical path (such as C:\Vbs\Routines.inc) and in this case can be absolute or relative to the current file, or it can be virtual, but in this case you need a slightly different syntax:

```
<!-- #include virtual="/Includes/Routines.inc" -->
```

There's no restriction on the file's extension, but it's common practice to use the .inc extension to differentiate these files from other files on the Web site. The include file can contain virtually anything: plain text, HTML code, server-side scripts, and so on. The only restriction is that it can't contain incomplete portions of scripts, such as an opening <SCRIPT> tag without the corresponding </SCRIPT> tag.

A typical use for include files is to make a number of constants available to your ASP scripts. But if these constants come from a type library, as all the ADO constants do, there's a better way to work: Just include the following directive at the beginning of a page or in the Global.asa file. (For more information about this file, see the "The Global.asa File" section later in this chapter.)

```
<!--METADATA TYPE="typelib"
    FILE="C:\Program Files\Common Files\system\ado\msado15.dll" -->
```

Server-side ActiveX components

If ASP pages were only able to run server-side scripts written in VBScript or JScript, they would hardly qualify as a viable means for writing complex Internet applications. Fortunately, you can augment the power of plain VBScript by instantiating external ActiveX components, either standard or custom ones. For example, a server-side script can query a database by instantiating an ADO Recordset object and then using its properties and methods. To create ActiveX components, you have to use the *Server.CreateObject* method instead of the simpler CreateObject command, but apart from this detail, you can process the returned object reference as you would in plain VBScript (or Visual Basic, for that matter). The following ASP code snippet demonstrates how you can use this capability to dynamically build a table with the results of a query on the Authors table of a copy of the Biblio.mdb database stored on the server machine:

```
<%
Dim rs, conn, sql
Set rs = Server.CreateObject("ADODB.Recordset")
' Modify the next lines to match your directory structure.
conn = "Provider=Microsoft.Jet.OLEDB.3.51;"
conn = conn & "Data Source=C:\Microsoft Visual Studio\Vb98\Biblio.mdb"
' Return all the authors whose birth year is known.
sql = "SELECT * FROM Authors WHERE NOT ISNULL([Year Born])"
rs.Open sql, conn
%>

<H1>A query on the Authors Table</H1>
<TABLE WIDTH=75% BGCOLOR=LightGoldenrodYellow BORDER=1
CELLSPACING=1 CELLPADDING=1>
    <TR>
        <TH ALIGN=center>Author ID</TH>
        <TH>Name</TH>
        <TH ALIGN=Center>Year Born</TH>
    </TR>
<%  Do Until rs.EOF %>
    <TR>
        <TD ALIGN=center> <%= rs("Au_Id")%>        </TD>
        <TD>                <%= rs("Author")%>      </TD>
        <TD ALIGN=center> <%= rs("Year Born") %> </TD>
    </TR>
<%  rs.MoveNext
    Loop
    rs.Close %>
</TABLE>
```

The result of this ASP code is shown in Figure 20-4. An important point is that the browser on the client receives a plain HTML table and doesn't see a single line of server-side script code. Unlike client-side scripts, no one can peek at the code that makes your application work.

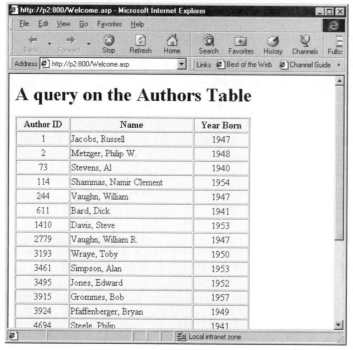

Figure 20-4. *You can process a database query on the server and send the results as a pure HTML table to the client browser.*

THE ASP OBJECT MODEL

As you've seen, the basic concepts of ASP programming are simple, especially if you're already familiar with scripting and ADO programming. To build complete and effective ASP applications, you only need to learn how to use the ASP object model, which isn't that complex, at least compared with other object hierarchies you've mastered.

The ASP object model, which is outlined in Figure 20-5, consists of just six main objects, which I'll describe in depth in the next sections. As you can see in the figure, this model isn't a hierarchy because there are no direct relationships among the six objects.

The Request Object

The Request object represents the data coming from the client browser. It exposes six properties (*QueryString*, *Form*, *ServerVariables*, *Cookies*, *ClientCertificate*, and *TotalBytes*), the first five of which are actually collections, and one method (*BinaryRead*). All the properties are read-only, which makes sense because the ASP running on the server has no way to affect the data the client sends.

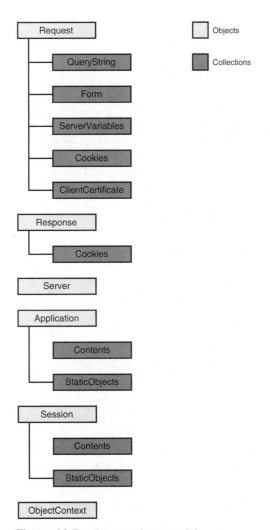

Figure 20-5. *The ASP object model.*

Sending data to the server

To fully understand the Request object's features, you need to know how data is sent from the client. An HTML form in the client browser can send data in two distinct ways: using the GET method or using the POST method. The method chosen depends on the METHOD attribute of the <FORM> tag. For example, the following form sends some values using the GET method. (It is part of the form shown in Figure 20-6.)

```
<H1>Send data through the GET method</H1>

<FORM ACTION="http://www.yourserver.com/Get.asp" METHOD=get NAME=FORM1><P>
Your Name: <INPUT name=txtUserName >
```

(continued)

```
Your Address: <INPUT name=txtAddress >
Your City: <INPUT name=txtCity >
<INPUT NAME=reset1 TYPE=reset VALUE=Reset>
<INPUT NAME=submit1 TYPE=submit VALUE=Submit>
</FORM>
```

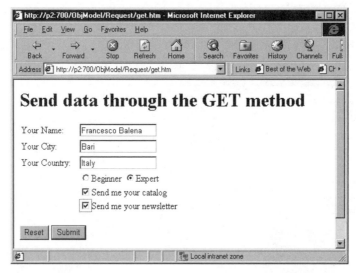

Figure 20-6. *A form that sends a few values over the Internet using the GET method.*

The value of the ACTION attribute is the URL of another page that will be executed and will receive the values in the three TextBox controls. When the user clicks on the Submit button of a form that uses the GET method, the values of the controls in the form are appended to the URL specified in the ACTION parameter:

```
http://www.yourserver.com/Get.asp?txtUserName=Francesco+Balena
    &txtCity=Bari&txtCountry=Italy&submit1=Submit
```

Notice that a question mark is appended immediately after the URL and that ampersand characters are used as delimiters for the *controlname=value* pairs sent to the server. When the user clicks on the Submit button, the above string will appear in the browser's Address combo box when the browser finishes downloading the target page. Once you understand how the URL is built, nothing prevents you from building it yourself—for example, by using a client-side VBScript routine that fires when a button is clicked. If you choose to do so, you'll need to add the expected delimiters yourself, and you'll also have to replace all the spaces and other special characters with valid symbols:

```
<SCRIPT LANGUAGE=VBScript>
' This is a client-side script routine.
Sub btnSendData_onclick()
```

```
    url = "http://www.yourserver.com/get.asp?"
    url = url & "txtUserName=" & Replace(Form1.txtUserName.Value, " ", "+")
    url = url & "&txtCity=" & Replace(Form1.txtCity.Value, " ", "+")
    url = url & "&txtCountry=" & Replace(Form1.txtCountry.Value, " ", "+")
    Window.Navigate url
End Sub
</SCRIPT>
```

As you can see, this approach requires more code, but it's also more flexible than sending data via the GET method of a form because the client-side script can validate and preprocess the data before sending it. At times, you don't even need a script. For example, you can have two or more hyperlinks on the same page, and all of them can point to the same URL in spite of your having appended different values to that URL:

```
<A HREF="http://www.yourserver.com/Get.asp?Request=Titles>
Show me the titles</A>
<A HREF="http://www.yourserver.com/Get.asp?Request=Authors>
Show me the authors</A>
```

Building a URL via code does have one drawback, however: a few characters have a special meaning when they appear in a URL. For example, you should replace all spaces with + symbols, and you should use % characters only as escape characters. For additional information about characters with special meanings, see the section "Encoding HTML Text and URLs" later in this chapter.

The GET method for sending data has two drawbacks. First, because of limitations of the HTTP protocol, a browser can send only about 1000 characters with the URL, so the data might be truncated. Second, data is sent as text over the Internet, which makes intercepting it easier. (This second problem is less serious if you build the URL yourself because you can encrypt the data being sent.)

If you want to work around the first problem and make your data harder to get at, you can use the POST method of sending data. In this method, the data is sent in the HTTP header, and the user doesn't see anything in the browser's Address combo box. To send data through the POST method instead of the GET method, you have to change only the value of the METHOD attribute of the <FORM> tag:

```
<FORM ACTION="http://www.yourserver.com/Get.asp" METHOD=post NAME=FORM1><P>
```

Receiving data from the client

On the client side, the only difference between the two methods of sending data is the value of the METHOD attribute, but the code in the ASP page that has to process the incoming data is completely different in the two cases. When data has been sent through the GET method (or by manually appending data to the URL), you can retrieve it by using the Request object's *QueryString* property. This property has a dual nature; it can work both as a regular property and as a collection. When used as a collection, you can pass it the name of a control on the form and it will return the value of that argument. What follows is the Get.asp page that retrieves the data being passed by the form:

```
<H1>This is what the ASP script has received:</H1>
<B>The entire Request.QueryString: </B> <% = Request.QueryString %>

<P><I>The string can be broken as follows:</I><P>
<B>UserName:</B>  <% = Request.QueryString("txtUserName") %> </BR>
<B>City:</B>  <% = Request.QueryString("txtCity") %> </BR>
<B>Country:</B>  <% = Request.QueryString("txtCountry") %> </BR>
```

If the argument passed to the *QueryString* doesn't match the name of a control sent on the URL, the property returns an empty string without raising an error. You can also take advantage of the collection nature of the *QueryString* property and enumerate all the values it contains using a *For Each...Next* loop:

```
<% For Each item In Request.QueryString %>
<B><% = item %></B> = <% Request.QueryString(item) %><BR>
<% Next %>
```

When the client sends data through the POST method, the *QueryString* property returns an empty string and you have to retrieve data using the Form collection:

```
<B>UserName:</B>  <% = Request.Form("txtUserName") %> </BR>
```

You can also retrieve the values in all the controls in the form using a *For Each...Next* loop:

```
<% For Each item In Request.Form %>
<B><% = item %></B> = <% Request.Form(item) %><BR>
<% Next %>
```

When working with the controls on a form, you have to account for controls that have the same name. You need to consider two cases—when the controls with the same name are radio buttons and when they are something else. When the controls are radio buttons, the rule is simple: Only the single radio button control the user has selected is returned in the *QueryString* or *Form* property. For example, if you have the following controls in your form

```
<INPUT TYPE=radio NAME=optLevel VALUE=1>Beginner
<INPUT TYPE=radio NAME=optLevel VALUE=2>Expert
```

the script statement *Request.QueryString("optLevel")*—or *Request.Form("optLevel")*, if the form sends data with the POST method—will return 1 or 2, depending on the selected control.

When you have multiple controls with the same name and a type other than Radio, the QueryString or Form collection will include a subcollection that holds all the controls whose value isn't empty. This detail is important to remember: If the form contains two controls named *chkSend*, the *Request.QueryString("chkSend")* or

Request.Form("chkSend") element might contain zero, one, or two elements, depending on how many check boxes the user has flagged:

```
<INPUT TYPE=checkbox NAME=chkSend VALUE="Catalog">Send me your catalog
<INPUT TYPE=checkbox NAME=chkSend VALUE="News">Send me your newsletter
```

If you have two or more check boxes with the same name, you can distinguish among the many cases using the *count* property, as follows:

```
<% If Request.QueryString("chkSend").Count = 1 Then %>
    <B>Send:</B> <% = Request.QueryString("chkSend") %><BR>
<% Else
    For i = 1 To Request.QueryString("chkSend").Count %>
        <B>Send:</B> <% = Request.QueryString("chkSend")(i) %><BR>
<% Next
    End If %>
```

The preceding source code is meant for use with the GET method. The source code for the server-side script that reads data sent using POST is similar, except it will use the Form collection instead of the QueryString collection. The companion CD includes two examples of HTM pages that send data to an ASP page: one using the GET method and another using the POST method. An example of a result from the ASP page is shown in Figure 20-7.

Figure 20-7. *This page has been dynamically created by an ASP server-side script and sent back to the client; notice the URL in the browser's Address combo box.*

The ServerVariables collection

Each request from the client browser carries a lot of information in the HTTP header, including critical information about the user, the client browser, and the document itself. You can access this information using the ServerVariables collection of the Request object. To test this capability, you can write a short server-side script that lists the contents of this collection. The following code is an excerpt from the ServerVa.asp file on the companion CD:

```
<H1>The ServerVariables collection</H1>
<TABLE BORDER=1 WIDTH = 90%>
<TR>
    <TH>Variable</TH>
    <TH>Value</TH>
</TR>
<% For Each item In Request.ServerVariables  %>
<TR>
    <TD><B>  <% = item %>                         </B></TD>
    <TD>     <% = Request.ServerVariables(item) %>    </TD>
</TR>
<% Next %>
</TABLE>
```

A few items in this collection are particularly useful. For example, you can use the following code to determine the method the page used to send data:

```
<% Select Case UCase(Request.ServerVariables("REQUEST_METHOD"))
    Case "GET"
        ' Data is being sent through the GET method.
    Case "POST"
        ' Data is being sent through the POST method.
    Case ""
        ' No data is being sent from the client.
End Select %>
```

Another important item in this collection is HTTP_USER_AGENT, which holds the name of the client browser, thereby permitting you to filter out unsupported HTML statements. For example, you might return DHTML code to Internet Explorer 4 or later versions, but stick to standard HTML code in all other cases:

```
<%  Supports_DHTML = 0     ' Assume that the browser doesn't support DHTML.
    info = Request.ServerVariables("HTTP_USER_AGENT")
    If InStr(info, "Mozilla") > 0 Then
        ' This is a Microsoft Internet Explorer browser.
        If InStr(info, "4.") > 0 Or InStr(info, "5.") > 0 Then
            ' You can safely send DHTML code.
            Supports_DHTML = True
        End If
    End If
%>
```

Other items of interest in the ServerVariables collection are APPL_PHYSICAL_PATH (the physical path of the application), SERVER_NAME (the name or IP address of the server), SERVER_PORT (the port number used on the server), SERVER_SOFTWARE (the name of the Web server software—for example, MicrosoftIIS 4.0), REMOTE_ADDR (the client's IP address), REMOTE_HOST (the client's host name), REMOTE_USER (the client's user name), URL (the URL of the current page, which might be useful for referencing other files on the server), HTTP_REFERER (the URL of the page that contains the link the user clicked to get to the current page), HTTPS (returns *on* if you're using a secure protocol), and HTTP_ACCEPT_LANGUAGE (a list of natural languages the client browser supports).

The Cookies collection

Cookies are pieces of information stored as individual files on the client machine. The browser sends this information to the server with each request, and an application running on the server can use the cookies to store data about that specific client. This method of storing data is necessary because HTTP is a stateless protocol and therefore the server can't associate a given set of variables with a given client. Actually, the server can't even find out whether this is the first time the client is accessing one of its pages. To obviate this problem, the server can send a cookie to the client, which will store the cookie and resubmit it to the server at the next request. Depending on the expiration date set at creation time, the cookie can expire at the end of the current session or at a given date and time—or it can never expire. For example, Web servers that let their clients customize the home page often use cookies that never expire.

From within ASP code, you can access cookies in two ways: as a collection of the Request object or as a collection of the Respond object. The difference between the two modes of access is important. The Request.Cookies collection is read-only because the server is just accepting a request from the client and can only examine the cookies that come with it. Conversely, you can create and send new cookies to a client only through the Response.Cookies collection (which is explained in the section "The Response Object" later in this chapter). You can retrieve the contents of a cookie within an ASP script by using the following syntax:

```
User Preference: <% = Request.Cookies("UserPref") %>
```

You can also use a *For Each...Next* loop to enumerate all the cookies sent by the client. But you must account for an added difficulty—the fact that a cookie can have multiple values, which are held in a secondary collection. You can test whether a cookie has multiple values by checking its *HasKeys* Boolean property. The following code prints the contents of the Cookies collection and all its subcollections:

```
<%
For Each item In Request.Cookies
```

(continued)

```
       If Request.Cookies(item).HasKeys = 0 Then %>
           <% = item %> = <% Request.Cookies(item) %>
  <% Else
           For Each subItem In Request.Cookies(item) %>
               <% = item & "(" & subItem & ")" %> =
               <% Request.Cookies(item)(subItem> %>
  <%     Next
      End If
  Next %>
```

Other properties and methods

The Request object supports two more properties and one method. The ClientCertificate collection lets you transfer data using the more secure HTTPS protocol rather than the simpler HTTP protocol. Security over the Internet is a complex and delicate matter, however, and well beyond the scope of this book.

The remaining property and the only method of the Request object are almost always used together. The *TotalBytes* property returns the total number of bytes received from the client as a result of a POST method, and the *BinaryRead* method performs a low-level access to the raw data sent by the client:

```
<%  bytes = Request.TotalBytes
    rowData = Request.BinaryRead(bytes)    %>
```

The *BinaryRead* method can't be used with the Form collection, so you have to choose one or the other. In practice, you won't often use this method.

The Response Object

The Response object represents the data being sent from the Web server to the client browser. It exposes five properties (*Expires*, *ContentType*, *CharSet*, *Status*, and *Pics*), four methods (*Write*, *BinaryWrite*, *IsClientConnected*, and *AppendToLog*), and one collection (Cookies).

Sending data to the browser

The *Write* method of the Response object sends a string or an expression right to the client's browser. This method isn't strictly necessary because you can always use the <%= delimiter. For example, the following three statements are equivalent:

```
<B>Current Time is <% = Time %> </B>
<% = "<B>Current Time is " & Time & "</B>" %>
<% Response.Write "<B>Current Time is " & Time & "</B>" %>
```

Choosing one over another is mostly a matter of programming style. When you're already inside a server-side script block, however, using the *Response.Write* method often delivers more readable code—at least to Visual Basic programmers.

The *Buffer* property gives you control over when the browser receives the page. The default for this property is False, which means that the browser receives the page while it's being built. If you set this property to True, all the data the ASP page produces is stored in a buffer and then sent to the client as a block of data when you invoke the Response object's *Flush* method. This buffering capability has a couple of advantages. First, in some cases, your ASP page will appear to be faster than it really is. Second, and most important, at any moment you can decide to discard what you've produced by using a *Response.Clear* method. For example, you might have a database query that sends output to the buffer; at the end of the process, you can check whether an error has occurred and cancel the results built up to that point:

```
<%  ' Here you execute the query.
    ...
    If Err Then
        Response.Clear
        Response.Write "An error has occurred"
    Else
        ' Send the result of the query to the client.
        Response.Flush
    End If
%>
```

You can also use the Response object's *End* method, which stops processing the ASP page and returns the page built up to that point to the browser.

The Response object also supports another method for sending data to a client, the *BinaryWrite* method. This method is rarely used, though. One situation in which you would use it is when you're sending nonstring data to a custom application.

Cookies

The Response object's *Cookies* property (unlike that of the Request object) lets you create and modify the value of a cookie. The Cookies collection behaves much like a Dictionary object, so you can create a new cookie simply by assigning a new value to this property:

```
<%  ' Remember the user's login name.
    Response.Cookies("LoginName") = Request.Form("txtLoginName")  %>
```

As I explained in the section "The Cookies Collection" earlier in the chapter, a cookie can have multiple values. For example, an Internet shopping site might have a shopping bag in which you can put multiple values:

```
<%  ' Add a new item to the Bag cookie.
    product = Request.Form("txtProduct")
    quantity = Request.Form("txtQty")
    Response.Cookies("Bag")(product) = quantity       %>
```

Remember that cookies are sent back to the client in the HTTP header, and for this reason they must be assigned before sending the first line of text to the client—otherwise, an error will occur. When it's impractical to assign a cookie before sending the first line of HTML text—and it often is—you can activate buffering before sending any text to the client. By default, cookies are stored on the client's machine only during the current session and are deleted when the browser is closed. You can change this default behavior by assigning a value to the *Expires* property of the cookie, as in the following code snippet:

```
<%  ' This cookie is valid until December 31, 1999.
    Response.Cookies("LoginName").Expires = #12/31/1999#  %>
```

The Cookie object has other important properties as well. You can set the *Domain* property to a specific domain so that only the pages in that domain will receive that particular cookie. The *Path* property lets you be even more selective and decide that only the pages in a given path in that domain receive the cookie. Finally, the *Secure* Boolean property lets you specify whether the cookie should be transmitted exclusively over a Secure Sockets Layer (SSL) connection. Here's an example that uses all the properties of the Cookie object:

```
<%  ' Create a secure cookie that expires after one year and that
    ' is valid only on the /Members path of the vb2themax.com site.
    Response.Cookies("Password") = Request.Form("txtPassword")
    Response.Cookies("Password").Expires = Now() + 365
    Response.Cookies("Password").Domain = "/vb2themax.com"
    Response.Cookies("Password").Path = "/members"
    Response.Cookies("Password").Secure = True    %>
```

A final example demonstrates how a page can keep track of whether or not the user has already visited the site and also shows how an ASP page can query the user for missing values and then take the control again:

```
<%  ' We're going to create cookies, so we need to turn on buffering.
    Response.Buffer = True  %>
```

```
<HTML>
<HEAD></HEAD>
<BODY>

<H1>Using Cookies to manage login forms</H1>

<% If Request.Cookies("LoginName") <> "" Then
    ' This isn't the first time the user has visited this site. %>

    It's nice to hear from you again, <% = Request.Cookies("LoginName") %>.

<% Elseif Request.Form("txtLoginName") <> "" Then
    ' This is the user's first visit to this site, and
    ' she has just filled out the login form.
    ' Save the user's login name as a cookie for subsequent sessions.
    Response.Cookies("LoginName") = Request.Form("txtLoginName")
    Response.Cookies("LoginName").expires = Now() + 365    %>

    Welcome to this site, <% = Request.Form("txtLoginName") %>
<% Else
    ' This is the user's first visit to this site,
    ' so prepare a login form.    %>
    This is the first time you've logged in. Please enter your name:<P>
<% url = Request.ServerVariables("URL") %>
    <FORM ACTION="<%= url %>" METHOD=POST NAME=form1>
    <INPUT TYPE="text" NAME=txtLoginName>
    <INPUT TYPE="submit" VALUE="Submit" NAME=submit1>
    </FORM>
<%  End If %>
</BODY>
</HTML>
```

The preceding page can work in three different ways. The first time this page is accessed, it sends back an HTML form that asks for the user's name, as shown in the top portion of Figure 20-8 on the following page. This information is then reposted to the page—notice how it builds the ACTION attribute of the <FORM> tag—which retrieves the contents of the txtLoginName control and stores it in a cookie that expires after one year. (See the middle part of Figure 20-8.) Finally, when the user navigates again to this page, the server is able to recognize the user and display a different "Welcome back" greeting. (See the bottom part of Figure 20-8.)

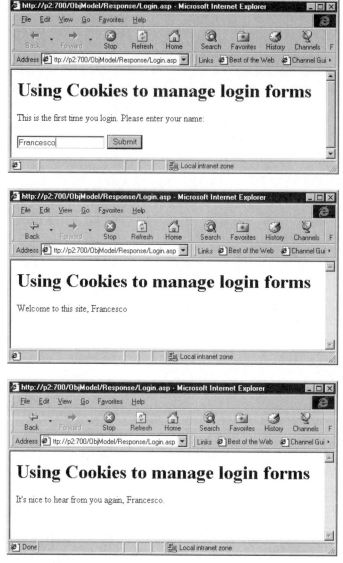

Figure 20-8. *An ASP script can behave differently, according to whether a cookie is stored on the client side.*

Page attributes

Some properties of the Response object let you control important attributes of the page sent back to the client. All these attributes are transmitted to the client in the HTTP header and therefore must be set before sending the contents of the page (or you have to activate the page buffering).

The *expires* property determines how many minutes the returned page can be held in the client browser's local cache. For example, if your page contains stock exchange data, you might want to set a relatively short expiration timeout:

```
<%  ' This page expires after 5 minutes.
    Response.Expires = 5     %>
```

In other circumstances, you might need to set an absolute expiration date and time, which you do through the *ExpiresAbsolute* property:

```
<%  ' This page expires 1 minute before the year 2000.
    Response.expiresabsolute = #12/31/1999  23:59:00#  %>
```

You can decide whether the page can be held in a proxy server's cache by setting the *CacheControl* property to *public*; you set it to *private* to disable this kind of caching.

In most cases, the ASP code sends back HTML text to the client browser, but this isn't a requirement. In fact, you can produce any MIME (Multipurpose Internet Mail Extensions) contents the browser supports, provided that you inform the client what's going to arrive. You notify the browser by assigning a suitable value to the *ContentType* property, such as *text/plain* for plain text or *text/richtext* for MIME Rich Text format. You can also send back data in binary format, such as *image/tiff* or *image/gif* for an image extracted from a database. (If you use a binary format, you need to send the data using the *BinaryWrite* method.)

The *CharSet* property lets the ASP code inform the client browser that the text uses a given character set. The value of this property instructs the browser to use the right code page and ensures that the characters are displayed correctly on the client's screen. For example, to use the Greek code page, you execute this statement at the beginning of the page:

```
<% Response.CharSet = "windows-1253" %>
```

The properties listed so far allow you to set some of the data that is sent to the client in the HTTP header. If you want to, you can modify any standard header information and even create custom header data, using the *AddHeader* method.

Redirection

You can redirect the browser to another page using the *redirect* method. A typical use for this method is to redirect the browser to a particular page after reading one or more of the values stored in its ServerVariables collection. For example, a company that has international customers can prepare multiple home pages, one for each language, and automatically redirect the (potential) customer to the proper page:

```
<%  If InStr(Request.ServerVariables("HTTP_ACCEPT_LANGUAGE"), "it") Then
        ' If the browser supports Italian, go to a specific page.
        Response.Redirect "Italy.asp"
```

(continued)

```
    Else
        ' If the browser doesn't support Italian, use the standard page.
        Response.Redirect "English.asp"
    End If
%>
```

You must use the *Redirect* method before sending any contents because redirection is achieved by sending an HTTP header back to the browser.

Other properties and methods

The Response object has two properties and two methods remaining: the *Status* and *Pics* properties and the *IsClientConnected* and *AppendToLog* methods. The *Status* property sets or returns the HTTP status line returned to the browser. For example, it returns *200 OK* if everything is correct or *404 Page not found* if the page requested isn't available. The *Pics* property lets you add a value to the PICS-Label field in the HTTP header, which in turn lets the browser filter out pages whose content doesn't conform to the rules set in the browser's Content Advisor dialog box.

The *IsClientConnected* function returns False if the client has disconnected after the most recent *Response.Write* operation. This property is useful if the server-side script is engaged in a lengthy operation and you want to ensure that the client is still connected and waiting for an answer. Finally, the *AppendToLog* method writes a string to the Web Server log file, provided that logging has been enabled in IIS. Because this log file is comma-delimited, you shouldn't use commas in the string passed as an argument:

```
<% Response.AppendToLog "This page was loaded at " & Now()  %>
```

The Server Object

As you can deduce from its name, the Server object represents the Web server application. Although it has just one property (*ScriptTimeout*) and four methods (*CreateObject*, *HTMLEncode*, *URLEncode*, and *MapPath*), the Server object plays a key role in most ASP applications.

The *ScriptTimeout* property sets or returns the number of seconds after which the server-side script is forced to terminate and an error is returned to the client. This property, whose default value is 90 seconds, is very useful to terminate extremely long queries or programming errors such as infinite loops.

Creating external objects

You've already seen the Server object's *CreateObject* method in action. Recall that this method permits you to instantiate an external COM object, either from a standard library such as ADODB or from a custom component you've written yourself or bought from a third-party vendor. This method is especially useful with the Scripting library to create a FileSystemObject or Dictionary object to make up for a few deficiencies of the VBScript language. (VBScript doesn't support collections or file I/O statements.) Here's an interesting example of an ASP page that dynamically builds a list of hyperlinks to all the other HTM documents in its directory:

```
<H1>CreateObject demo</H1>
This page demonstrates how you can use a FileSystemObject object
to dynamically create hyperlinks to all the other pages in
this directory.<P>

<%
Set fso = Server.CreateObject("Scripting.FileSystemObject")
' Get a reference to the folder that contains this file.
aspPath = Request.ServerVariables("PATH_TRANSLATED")
Set fld = fso.GetFile(aspPath).ParentFolder
' For each file in this folder, create a hyperlink.
For Each file In fld.Files
    Select Case UCase(fso.GetExtensionName(file))
        Case "HTM", "HTML"
            Response.Write "<A HREF=""" & file & """>" & file & "</A><BR>"
    End Select
Next
%>
```

Don't forget that the object being created must be correctly registered on the machine the Web server application is running on. It's a good idea to protect all the *Server.CreateObject* methods with an *On Error Resume Next* statement.

Even if you create objects in ASP scripts following a method similar to the one you follow under Visual Basic or VBScript, you must pay attention to an important difference: The scope of all such objects is the page, and the objects are released only when the page has been completely processed. This means that setting an object variable to Nothing won't destroy the object because ASP retails a reference to the object and therefore keeps the object alive. This may have many nasty consequences. Take for example the following code:

```
Dim rs
Set rs = Server.CreateObject("ADODB.Recordset")
rs.Open "Authors", "DSN=Pubs"
...
Set rs = Nothing
```

In regular Visual Basic or VBScript, the last statement would close the Recordset and release all the associated resources. In an ASP script, however, this doesn't happen, unless you explicitly close the Recordset:

```
rs.Close
Set rs = Nothing
```

Encoding HTML text and URLs

As you know, HTML uses angle brackets as special characters for defining tags. Although this way of encoding information is simple, it can cause problems when you're sending data read from somewhere else, such as from a database or a text file. In fact, any < character found in the database field would make the browser mistakenly believe that an HTML tag is arriving. The easiest way to work around this issue is by resorting to the Server object's *HTMLEncode* method, which takes a string and returns the corresponding HTML code that makes that string appear in the browser. The following code example relies on this method to display values from a hypothetical database of math formulas (which are highly likely to contain special symbols):

```
<%
Set rs = Server.CreateObject("ADODB.Recordset")
rs.Open "SELECT * FROM Formulas", "DSN=MathDB"
Do Until rs.EOF
    Response.Write Server.HTMLEncode(rs("Formula")) & "<BR>"
Loop
%>
```

This method is also useful when you want to show HTML code in a page rather than having it interpreted by the browser. For example, the following ASP code displays the contents of the *htmltext* variable without interpreting the HTML tags it contains:

```
This is the typical beginning of an HTML page<P>
<%  htmltext = "<HTML><BODY>"
    Response.Write Server.HTMLEncode(htmltext)
%>
```

This is what is actually sent to the client, as you can see by using the View command from the Source menu of the browser:

```
This is the typical beginning of an HTML page<P>
&lt;HTML&gt;&lt;BODY;&gt<P>
```

It's then rendered into this in the browser's window:

```
This is the typical beginning of an HTML page
<HTML><BODY>
```

Sending the special <% and %> pair of characters is a bit more complex because these characters confuse the ASP script parser. For example, say that you want to send the following string to the browser:

```
<% Set obj = Nothing %>
```

Unfortunately, you can't simply use the following ASP script because it raises an error, "Unterminated string constant":

```
<%  ' CAUTION: This doesn't work!
    Response.Write Server.HTMLEncode("<% Set obj = Nothing %>")
%>
```

One way to avoid this problem is to keep the two characters of the %> pair apart, using the concatenation operator:

```
<%  ' This works!
    Response.Write Server.HTMLEncode("<% Set obj = Nothing %" & ">")
%>
```

Another solution is to use the backslash (\) character to inform the ASP script that the character that comes next is to be taken literally:

```
<%  ' This works too!
    Response.Write Server.HTMLEncode("<% Set obj = Nothing %\>")
%>
```

The *URLEncode* method lets you solve similar problems caused by the unusual way in which HTML formats URLs. We first encountered this problem in the section "Sending Data to the Server", when we were building client-side scripts that use the *Window.Navigate* method to open a new page and send it additional values via its URL. Sometimes you also have to solve this problem when you're writing server-side scripts—but in this case, the solution is simple. For example, you can dynamically create a hyperlink that jumps to another page and passes the contents of a database field via the URL:

```
<%  ' This code assumes that rs contains a reference to an open Recordset.
Do Until rs.EOF
    Response.Write "<A HREF=""Select.asp?Name="
    Response.Write Server.URLEncode(rs("Name")) & """>"
    Response.Write rs("Name") & "</A></BR>"
    rs.MoveNext
Loop
%>
```

Mapping paths

The final method of the Server object is *MapPath*, which converts a logical path as seen by the client browser into a physical path on the server machine. If the argument passed to this method has a leading / or \ character, the path is considered to be absolute with respect to the application's root directory; without such a leading character, it is considered to be relative to the directory where the current ASP document is. For example, the following code redirects the browser to the default.asp page located in the root directory:

```
<%  Response.Redirect Server.MapPath("\default.asp") %>
```

This code redirects the browser to the two.asp page in the same directory where the current page is:

```
<%  Response.Redirect Server.MapPath("two.asp") %>
```

You can determine the name of the root directory, the current directory, and the parent directory using the following code:

```
<%  rootDir = Server.MapPath("\")
    curDir = Server.MapPath(".")
    parentDir = Server.MapPath("..")      %>
```

The Application Object

The Application object represents the Web server application running inside IIS. This is a global object shared by all the clients that are accessing one of the pages that make up the application in a given moment. An Application object comes to life when the first client accesses one of its pages and ends only when the administrator stops the Web server or when the server machine crashes. If the Application object runs in its own address space, you can also terminate it by clicking the Unload button in the Directory tab of the Application object's Property Pages dialog box.

The Application object has a rather simple interface, with just one property (*Value*), two collections (Contents and StaticObjects), and two methods (*Lock* and *Unlock*). Unlike all the other objects examined so far (but similar to the Session object, which is described a little later in this chapter), the Application object exposes events (*OnStart* and *OnEnd*).

Sharing data among clients

The main use for the Application object is storing data that should be available to all the scripts that are serving client requests in a given moment. Examples of such data include the location of a database file or a flag that indicates whether a given resource is accessible. Such shared data is available through the Application object's *Value* property, which expects the name of the variable you want to read or set. Because this is the default property of the Application object, in most cases it is omitted:

```
<%  ' Increment a global counter. (WARNING: This might not work correctly.)
    Application("GlobalCounter") = Application("GlobalCounter") + 1
%>
```

This code snippet has a problem, though. Because the Application object is shared among all the ASP scripts that are serving the currently connected clients, a server-side script might execute the same statement at exactly the same moment as another script. This would cause incorrect values for the Application variable. To avoid such undesirable situations, any time you're going to access one or a group of Application object's variables, you should bracket the code within a *Lock* and *Unlock* pair of methods:

```
<%  ' Increment a global counter. (This code always works correctly.)
    Application.Lock
    Application("GlobalCounter") = Application("GlobalCounter") + 1
    Application.Unlock
%>
```

When you use this approach, only one script can execute the code in the critical section between the two methods. The second script that encounters the *Lock* method will patiently wait until the first script executes the *Unlock* method. It goes without saying that you should avoid inserting any lengthy operation after the *Lock* method and that you should invoke the *Unlock* method as soon as possible.

> **CAUTION** In general, you should invoke the *Lock* and *Unlock* methods even when just *reading* an Application object's variables. This precaution might seem excessive, but remember that under Windows NT and Windows 2000 Server a thread can be preempted at any time. When you're dealing with variables that hold objects, locking is even more important because many properties and methods of the object might not be reentrant.

The Global.asa file

The *OnStart* and *OnEnd* events of the Application object fire—not surprisingly—when the Web application starts and ends, respectively. The problem with these events is that when the Application object is created, no ASP document is active yet. For this reason, the code for these events must be located in a special file, named Global.asa, that *must* reside in the root directory of the application. Here's an example of a Global.asa file that records the time the application starts:

```
<SCRIPT LANGUAGE=vbscript RUNAT=Server>
Sub Application_OnStart()
    Application("StartTime") = Now()
End Sub
</SCRIPT>
```

> **NOTE** The events in the Global.asa file fire only when the client accesses an ASP file. The events don't fire when an HTM or HTML file is read.

You can't use the <% and %> delimiters in the Global.asa. The only valid way to insert VBScript code is by using the <SCRIPT RUNAT=Server> tag. *OnStart* events are often useful for creating an instance of an object when the application starts so that individual scripts don't need to invoke a *Server.CreateObject* method. For example, you might create an instance of the FileSystemObject class and use it inside ASP scripts, which will speed up the execution of individual scripts:

```
<SCRIPT LANGUAGE=vbscript RUNAT=Server>
Sub Application_OnStart()
    Set fso = Server.CreateObject("Scripting.FileSystemObject")
    ' This is an object, so we need a Set command.
    Set Application("FSO") = fso
End Sub
</SCRIPT>
```

The *OnEnd* event is less useful than the *OnStart* event. You typically use it to release resources—for example, to close a connection opened in the *OnStart* event. Another common use is to permanently store on a database the value of a global variable (such as a counter that keeps track of how many visitors a given page has had) that you don't want to reinitialize the next time the application is started.

> **CAUTION**   Because the Global.asa file must reside in the home directory of an application, two distinct applications share the same Global.asa file if they share the home directory. Needless to say, this can be the source of countless problems. For example, if you modify the Global.asa for one application, the other one is also affected. I strongly advise you to assign a different home directory to each application.

The Contents and StaticObjects collections

Because the *Value* property isn't a collection, you can't enumerate all the Application object's variables. However, the Application object does provide you with two collections that let you retrieve information about global values available to all the scripts.

The Contents collection contains references to all the elements that have been added to the Application object via a script and can be accessed by ASP code. This collection includes simple values and objects created with the *Server.CreateObject* method. You can therefore enumerate all the Application's variables using the following code:

```
<%  For Each item In Application.Contents
        If IsObject(Application.Contents(item)) Then
            objClass = TypeName(Application.Contents(item))
            Response.Write item & " = object of class " & objClass
        Else
            Response.Write item & " = " & Application.Contents(item)
        End If
    Next
%>
```

The StaticObjects collection is similar to the Contents collection, but it contains only the objects that have been created with an <OBJECT> tab in the Application's scope. Because you're guaranteed that this collection contains only objects, you can iterate through the objects using a simple loop:

```
<%  For Each item In Application.StaticObjects
        objClass = TypeName(Application.StaticObjects(item))
        Response.Write item & " = object of class " & objClass
    Next
%>
```

The Session Object

The Session object represents the connection between a given client and the Web server. Whenever a client accesses one of the ASP documents on the server, a new Session object is created and is given a unique ID. This object will live as long as the client keeps the browser open. By default, it's destroyed when the server doesn't receive a request from that client within a given timeout interval. The default for this timeout is 20 minutes, but you can change it by assigning a new value to the Session's *Timeout* property. For example, you might want to reduce this value if your Web site is receiving too many requests and you want to release the resources allocated to users as often as possible:

```
<%   ' Reduce the timeout to 10 minutes.
     Session.Timeout = 10 %>
```

The Session object resembles the Application object in that both expose the Contents and StaticObjects collections, the *Value* property, and the *OnStart* and *OnEnd* events. The main difference between the two objects is that IIS creates only one Application object for each application but as many Session objects as the number of users that are connected at a given moment.

Sharing data among pages

The Session object's *Value* property lets you store and retrieve values with a session scope, which means that only the pages requested by a given client can share a particular set of values. The difference between variables with application scope and those with session scope is illustrated in Figure 20-9.

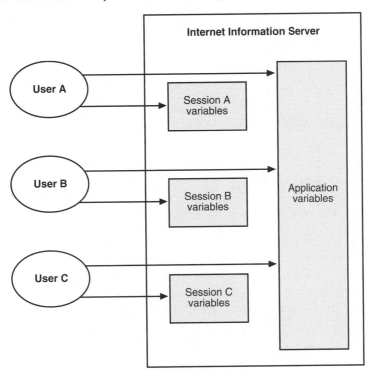

Figure 20-9. *Application variables and session variables.*

Session variables are especially important because all the variables declared in an ASP script are destroyed when the browser jumps to another page. Session variables bring state management to the stateless HTTP protocol. At first, it might seem impossible for the Web browser to keep information pertinent to one user distinct from the information belonging to another user because the protocol doesn't even maintain information about who's making the request. The solution to this problem is provided by a special cookie that the Web server sends to the client browser and that the browser sends back to the server at each subsequent request. Because this cookie has no specific expiration date, it expires when the browser is closed or after the timeout. You can also force the Session object to terminate using its *Abandon* method.

You reference Session object's variables by using the *Value* property, which is the default property for this object and therefore can be omitted:

```
<%  ' Remember the user's name while the session is open.
    Session("UserName") = Request.Form("txtUserName")   %>
```

Session objects are great, but they have an adverse impact on the performance and the scalability of the application. Each Session object consumes resources on the server, and some session operations are serialized, so each session must wait for its turn. You can minimize these problems by creating Session objects only if you really need them. You can limit the number of Session objects created by adding the following line at the beginning of all your ASP scripts:

```
<%@ EnableSessionState = False %>
```

Alternatively, you can disable Session variables for the ASP subsytem by changing the AllowSessionState value of the HKEY_LOCAL_MACHINE\SYSTEM\CurrentControlSet \Services\W3SVC\ASP\Parameters Registry key from 1 to 0.

When a client accesses a page that doesn't support a session state, no Session object is created and the *Session_OnStart* event procedure isn't executed. This means that you can't store values in the Session object any longer and that you must implement your own persistence scheme—for example, one based on a real, multiuser database.

Session events

As I mentioned in the previous section, the Session object exposes the *OnStart* and *OnEnd* events. As is the case with the Application object, because you write the code for these events in the Global.asa file, all the Sessions objects share the same event procedures. Typically, you use the *OnStart* event to create a resource that is to be used during the entire session, such as an ADO Connection object. The following code demonstrates how you can make the Application and Session objects cooperate:

```
<SCRIPT LANGUAGE=vbscript RUNAT=Server>
Sub Application_OnStart()
```

```
    ' Initialize the Connect string that points to the shared database.
    ' In a real application, the string might be read from an INI file.
    conn = "Provider=SQLOLEDB;Data Source=MySrv;User ID=sa;Password=MyPwd"
    Application("ConnString") = str
End Sub

Sub Session_OnStart()
    Set cn = Server.CreateObject("ADODB.Connection")
    cn.Open Application("ConnString")
    ' Make this Connection object available to all the ASP scripts
    ' in the session.
    Set Session("Connection") = cn
End Sub

Sub Session_OnEnd()
    ' Release all the resources in an orderly way.
    Set cn = Session("Connection")
    cn.Close
    Set cn = Nothing
End Sub
</SCRIPT>
```

Here's another example that uses the *OnStart* and *OnEnd* events to keep track of how many sessions are currently active:

```
<SCRIPT LANGUAGE=vbscript RUNAT=Server>
Sub Application_OnStart()
    Application("SessionCount") = 0
End Sub

Sub Session_OnStart()
    Application.Lock
    Application("SessionCount") = Application("SessionCount") + 1
    Application.Unlock
End Sub

Sub Session_OnEnd()
    Application.Lock
    Application("SessionCount") = Application("SessionCount") - 1
    Application.Unlock
End Sub
</SCRIPT>
```

Locale-aware properties

The Session object exposes two properties that permit you to create Web sites that can accommodate international users. The *LCID* property sets or returns the locale ID that will be used when sorting and comparing strings, and for all the date-related and time-related functions. For example, the code snippet on the following page displays the current date and time using the Italian format and then restores the original locale ID.

```
<%  currLocaleID = Session.LCID
    ' The locale ID of Italy is hex 410.
    Session.LCID = &H410
    Response.Write "Current date/time is " & Now()
    ' Restore the original locale ID.
    Session.LCID = currLocaleID
%>
```

The other property that lets you add an international flavor to a Web site is *CodePage*, which sets or returns the code page used when reading text from or writing text to the browser. For example, most Western languages use code page 1252, and Hebrew uses code page 1255.

Session collections

The Session object exposes the Contents and StaticObjects collections in the same way that the Application object does, so I won't describe those collections again here. (See the section "The Contents and StaticObjects Collections" earlier in this chapter for details about these collections.) These collections contain only elements with a session scope, which raises an interesting question: How can you have a session-scoped <OBJECT> tag in the Global.asa file? The answer is in the SCOPE attribute:

```
<OBJECT RUNAT=Server SCOPE=Session ID=Conn ProgID="ADODB. Connection">
```

The ObjectContext Object

The sixth and final object in the ASP object model is the ObjectContext object. This object is used only when an ASP script runs in a transaction and is managed by Microsoft Transaction Server. Such transaction pages contain a <%@ TRANSACTION %> directive at the beginning of the script.

The ObjectContext object exposes two methods, *SetComplete* and *SetAbort*, which commit and abort the transaction, respectively. It also exposes two events, *OnTransactionCommit* and *OnTransactionAbort*, which fire after a transaction is completed successfully or is aborted, respectively. Because this book doesn't cover MTS programming, I won't explain these methods and events in detail.

> **NOTE**   As I'm writing this, Internet Information Server 5.0 is in beta, so it's possible to get an idea of the new features of ASP technology, although the final release may still change some of the details. The Server object has been enhanced with three new methods. The *Execute* method executes another ASP document and then returns to the current ASP script. The *Transfer* method is similar to the *Response.Redirect* method but is more efficient because no data is sent to the client browser. The *GetLastError* method returns a reference to the new ASPError object, which contains detailed information about errors. The Application and Session's Contents collections have been improved with the *Remove* and *RemoveAll* methods, which let you delete one or all of the elements of the collection. Finally, the ASP parser is more efficient, so pages will be processed faster.

ASP COMPONENTS

As you know, ASP scripts can instantiate and use ActiveX components, which can add tremendous flexibility and power to ASP scripts.

Using Components in ASP Scripts

There are two ways to instantiate ActiveX components in ASP scripts: by using the *Server.CreateObject* method and by using an <OBJECT> tag with the SCOPE attribute set to *server*. The former technique is more likely to appeal to Visual Basic programmers, whereas the latter will sound more natural to HTML programmers.

In at least one case, however, it makes sense even for Visual Basic programmers to use an <OBJECT> tag—namely, to create an object reference that has application scope or session scope. Let's say that you want to create an ADO Connection object that is shared by all the scripts in the session. You can achieve this by creating the object in the *Session_OnStart* event procedure and then storing the reference in a Session variable:

```
<SCRIPT LANGUAGE=vbscript RUNAT=Server>
Sub Session_OnStart()
    ' Create the ADO Connection object.
    Set conn = Server.CreateObject("ADODB.Connection")
    ' Open it.
    connStr = "Provider=SQLOLEDB;Data Source=MyServer;Initial Catalog=Pubs"
    conn.Open connStr, "sa", "myPwd"
    ' Make it available to all ASP scripts.
    Set Session("conn") = conn
End Sub
</SCRIPT>
```

An ASP script can use this session-scoped Connection object, but it has to extract it from the Session object:

```
<%  ' Inside an ASP script
    Set conn = Session("conn")
    conn.BeginTrans                %>
```

Let's see what happens when the object is declared in Global.asa using a <SCRIPT> tag with a proper SCOPE attribute:

```
<OBJECT RUNAT=server SCOPE=Session ID="Conn" PROGID="ADODB.Connection">
</OBJECT>
<SCRIPT LANGUAGE=vbscript RUNAT=Server>
Sub Session_OnStart()
```

(continued)

1147

```
      ' Open the connection (no need to create it).
      connStr = "Provider=SQLOLEDB;Data Source=MyServer;Initial Catalog=Pubs"
      conn.Open connStr, "sa", "myPwd"
End Sub
</SCRIPT>
```

When an object is declared in this way, you can reference it from any session in the application just by using its name, as in the following ASP script:

```
<%  conn.BeginTrans %>
```

Objects can be defined this way with Application scope as well as with Session scope. In both cases, they appear in the StaticObjects collection of the corresponding object.

> **NOTE**   Most components designed for ASP pages are in-process components. From time to time, however, you might need to create out-of-process components. To do so, you must manually modify the AllowOutOfProcCmpts value in the HKEY_LOCAL_MACHINE\SYSTEM\CurrentControlSet\Services\W3SVC \ASP \Parameters Registry key from 0 (the default value) to 1.

Using Custom ASP Components

You can use any ActiveX component from an ASP page, including those written in Visual Basic. For example, you can write a component that augments VBScript in the areas in which this script language is weak, such as file management, fast math calculations, string routines, and so on. These components can't really be classified as ASP components, however, because they don't interact with the ASP object model. What we need is a component that can read data coming from an HTML form through the Request object and write data using the Response object.

Writing ASP components in Visual Basic

Writing an ASP component in Visual Basic is surprisingly simple—except for one detail, it's exactly like writing a standard ActiveX component. The first thing you do is start an ActiveX DLL project, set the threading model to Apartment model, and check the Unattended Execution option in the General tab of the Project Properties dialog box.

Visual Basic 6 offers a new option for components marked for unattended execution, the Retained In Memory flag. (See Figure 20-10.) When this option is enabled, the component is held in memory until the client process terminates. This capability is especially useful when you expect that your component will often be loaded in memory and then discarded because it saves Windows the overhead of continuously loading it from disk. When the component is running inside IIS or MTS, which typically serve hundreds or even thousands of clients, this option is going to speed up the overall performance noticeably.

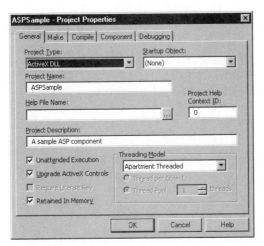

Figure 20-10. *The suggested project settings for a typical ASP component.*

Now you have to add a reference to the ASP type library. Two such libraries are registered in a system on which IIS has been installed: the Microsoft Active Server Pages Object Library and the Microsoft Active Server Pages 2.0 ObjectContext Class Type Library. The former library includes the five main ASP objects, and the latter includes only the definition of the ObjectContext object, which you need only when developing ASP components that must run under MTS. Both type libraries are contained in the Asp.dll file.

As you see, up to this point there isn't really anything special about an ASP component. The only problem left to be resolved is this: How can the component get a reference to one of the five main ASP objects? Well, the script code might pass such an object to a property or a method of the component, soon after creating it, but this technique isn't necessary if you know the little secret about writing ASP components in Visual Basic.

As soon as the component is created by an ASP script, IIS invokes the component's *OnStartPage* method, if the component exposes such a method. Therefore, the only thing to do is to add the code for this method:

```
' This is a class-level variable.
Dim sc As ASPTypeLibrary.ScriptingContext

Sub OnStartPage(AspSC As ASPTypeLibrary.ScriptingContext)
    ' Save the reference for later.
    Set sc = AspSC
End Sub
```

The ScriptingContext object passed to the *OnStartPage* method is nothing but the root object of the ASP type library. A quick trip to the object browser reveals that this object exposes five properties—*Application, Request, Response, Server,* and *Session*—which are just the main elements of the ASP object model. So it's simple to set or retrieve a Session or Application variable or send HTML text by using the *Response.Write* method:

```
' Inside the component
Sub IncrementCounter(CounterName As String)
    sc.Application.Lock
    sc.Application(CounterName) = Application(CounterName) + 1
    sc.Application.Unlock
End Sub
```

When the page that instantiated the component is about to be unloaded, the component receives an *OnEndPage* event, in which you close the connection and release the resources that you allocated in the *OnStartPage* event. But you'd usually use the *Terminate* event instead.

A real, useful component

Now that you're nearing the end of this huge book about Visual Basic programming, you're ready for something more complex than an unsophisticated Hello World–like ASP component. On the companion CD, you'll find the complete source code for the ASPSample.QueryToTable component, which accepts a connection string and a query string and automatically builds an HTML table that contains the result of the query against the specified data source. It even supports alignment and formatting on a field-by-field basis.

Before describing the source code, let me show you how you can use this custom component from an ASP script:

```
<%
Set tbl = Server.CreateObject("ASPSample.QueryToTable")
' Enter the next two lines as a single VBScript statement.
conn = "Provider=SQLOLEDB;Data Source=MyServer;" & _
    "Initial Catalog=Pubs;User ID=sa;Password=MyPwd"
tbl.Execute conn, "SELECT * FROM Authors WHERE State = 'CA'"
tbl.GenerateHTML
%>
```

It couldn't be simpler! The *Execute* method expects the connection string and the text of the SQL query, and the *GenerateHTML* method sends the generated HTML text to the page being built. You can fine-tune the format of the output table by using the component's *ShowRecNumbers* property (set it to True to display record numbers in the leftmost column) and *AddField* method, which lets you decide which fields appear in the table, the horizontal and vertical alignment attributes of the corresponding cells in the table, and the formatting of their values. The syntax of the *AddField* method follows:

```
AddField FldName, Caption, HAlign, VAlign, PrefixTag, PostfixTag
```

To display a field using default options, you just need to pass the field's name:

```
<%  tbl.AddField "au_lname"
    tbl.AddField "au_fname"     %>
```

You can specify the caption of the column header (if it's different from the field's name) and the horizontal and vertical alignment attributes of the table cells like this:

```
<%  tbl.AddField "au_lname", "Last Name", "center", "middle"
    tbl.AddField "au_fname", "First Name", "center", "middle"    %>
```

Finally, you can format the cells by using the *PrefixTag* and *PostfixTag* arguments, as here:

```
<%  ' Display the State field using boldface characters.
    tbl.AddField "State", , "center", , "<B>", "</B>"
    ' Display the ZIP field using boldface and italic attributes.
    tbl.AddField "ZIP", , "center", , "<B><I>", "</I></B>"    %>
```

The component doesn't validate the last two arguments; you must ensure that the tags you're passing form a valid HTML sequence. The field layout that you set with a sequence of *AddField* methods is preserved across consecutive queries, but you can clear the current layout by using the *ResetFields* method.

Implementing the component

Now that you know what the component does, understanding how its source code works shouldn't be too difficult. The component holds all the information about the columns to be displayed in the Fields array of UDTs. The *AddField* method does nothing but store its arguments in this array. If the script calls the *Execute* method without first calling the *AddField* method, the component builds a default field layout.

```
' Public Properties ----------------------
' True if Record numbers must be displayed
Public ShowRecNumbers As Boolean

' Private Members --------------------------
Private Type FieldsUDT
    FldName As String
    Caption As String
    HAlign As String
    VAlign As String
    PrefixTag As String
    PostfixTag As String
End Type

' A reference to the ASP library entry point
Dim sc As ASPTypeLibrary.ScriptingContext
' The Recordset being opened
Dim rs As ADODB.Recordset
' Array information about the fields
Dim Fields() As FieldsUDT
' Number of elements in the Fields array
Dim FieldCount As Integer
```

When the component is instantiated by an ASP script, its *OnStartPage* method is called. In this method, the component stores a reference to the ASPTypeLibrary .ScriptingContext object and initializes the Fields array:

```
' This event fires when the component is instantiated
' from within the ASP script.
Sub OnStartPage(AspSC As ASPTypeLibrary.ScriptingContext)
    ' Save the reference for later.
    Set sc = AspSC
    ResetFields
End Sub


' Reset the field information.
Sub ResetFields()
    Dim Fields(0) As FieldsUDT
    FieldCount = 0
End Sub
```

The *Execute* method is just a wrapper around the ADO Recordset's *Open* method:

```
' Execute an SQL query.
Function Execute(conn As String, sql As String)
    ' Execute the query
    Set rs = New ADODB.Recordset
    rs.Open sql, conn, adOpenStatic, adLockReadOnly
End Function
```

The *AddField* method does a minimal validation of its arguments and stores them in the first available element in the *Fields* array:

```
' Add a field to the table layout.
Sub AddField(FldName As String, Optional Caption As String, _
    Optional HAlign As String, Optional VAlign As String, _
    Optional PrefixTag As String, Optional PostfixTag As String)
    ' Check the values.
    If FldName = "" Then Err.Raise 5

    ' Add to the internal array.
    FieldCount = FieldCount + 1
    ReDim Preserve Fields(0 To FieldCount) As FieldsUDT
    With Fields(FieldCount)
        .FldName = FldName
        .Caption = Caption
        .HAlign = HAlign
        .VAlign = VAlign
        .PrefixTag = PrefixTag
        .PostfixTag = PostfixTag

        ' The default caption is the field's name.
        If .Caption = "" Then .Caption = FldName
```

```
        ' The default horizontal alignment is "left."
        Select Case LCase$(.HAlign)
            Case "left", "center", "right"
            Case Else
                .HAlign = "left"
        End Select
        .HAlign = " ALIGN=" & .HAlign

        ' The default vertical alignment is "top."
        Select Case LCase$(.VAlign)
            Case "top", "middle", "bottom"
            Case Else
                .VAlign = "top"
        End Select
        .VAlign = " VALIGN=" & .VAlign
    End With
End Sub
```

The heart of the QueryToTable component is the *GenerateHTML* method, which uses the contents of the Recordset and the layout information held in the *Fields* array to build the corresponding HTML table. Although this code might seem complex at first, it took me just a few minutes to build it. I obtained cleaner code by using a private *Send* procedure, which actually sends the HTML code to the Response object:

```
' Generate the HTML text for the table.
Sub GenerateHTML()
    Dim i As Integer, recNum As Long, f As FieldsUDT

    ' Initialize the Fields array if not done already.
    If FieldCount = 0 Then InitFields
    ' Restart from the first record.
    rs.MoveFirst

    ' Output the table header and the border.
    Send "<TABLE BORDER=1>"
    Send "  <THEAD>"
    Send "    <TR>"
    ' Insert a column for the record number if requested.
    If ShowRecNumbers Then
        Send "      <TH ALIGN=Center>Rec #</TH>"
    End If
    ' These are the fields' captions.
    For i = 1 To UBound(Fields)
        f = Fields(i)
        Send "      <TH" & f.HAlign & ">" & f.Caption & "</TH>"
    Next
    Send "    </TR>"
    Send "  </THEAD>"
    Send "  <TBODY>"
```

(continued)

```
      ' Output the body of the table.
      Do Until rs.EOF
          ' Add a new row of cells.
          Send "   <TR>"
          ' Add the record number if requested.
          recNum = recNum + 1
          If ShowRecNumbers Then
              Send "    <TD ALIGN=center>" & recNum & "</TD>"
          End If

          ' Send all the fields of the current record.
          For i = 1 To UBound(Fields)
              f = Fields(i)
              Send "    <TD" & f.HAlign & f.VAlign & ">" & f.PrefixTag & _
                  rs(f.FldName) & f.PostfixTag & "</TD>"
          Next
          Send "   </TR>"
          ' Advance to the next record.
          rs.MoveNext
      Loop

      ' Close the table.
      Send "  </TBODY>"
      Send "</TABLE>"
End Sub

' Send a line of text to the output stream.
Sub Send(Text As String)
      sc.Response.Write Text
End Sub

' Initialize the Fields() array with suitable values.
Private Sub InitFields()
      Dim fld As ADODB.Field
      ResetFields
      For Each fld In rs.Fields
          AddField fld.Name
      Next
End Sub
```

On the companion CD, you'll find the complete source code for this component and a Test.asp page that uses it. The great thing about writing ASP components in Visual Basic 6 is that you can debug them without having to compile them to a DLL. This is a little magic that the Visual Basic IDE does for us: IIS believes that the script is executing an in-process DLL while you're comfortably testing it in the environment, using the full range of debugging tools that Visual Basic provides. (See Figure 20-11.) An example of a table produced by the component is shown in Figure 20-12. I encourage you to augment the component's versatility by adding other properties and methods—for example, to control cell color, value formatting, and so on.

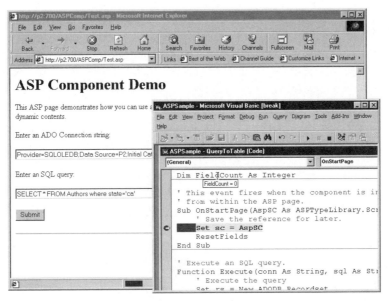

Figure 20-11. *Add a breakpoint in the* OnStartPage *procedure, and then press F8 to single-step through the component's source code as the ASP script invokes its methods.*

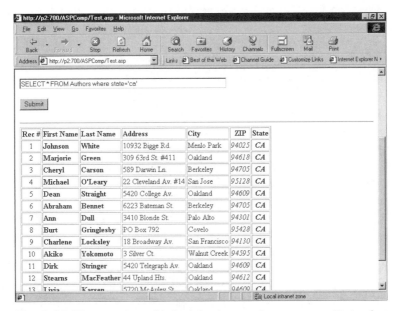

Figure 20-12. *An HTML table built by the sample component. Notice that you can refine and reexecute the query by entering text in the controls in the upper portion of the page.*

WEBCLASSES

Visual Basic 6 adds a new tool to your bag of Internet programming techniques: the WebClass component. A WebClass is an in-process component that runs inside IIS and that intercepts and then processes all the requests that clients make to an ASP document. Figure 20-13 diagrams how a WebClass works.

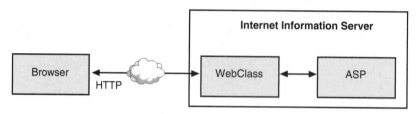

Figure 20-13. *A WebClass acts as an intermediary between the browser and ASP.*

Before diving into the details, let me clarify one point: WebClasses can't do anything that you can't do already with an ASP script and a custom component written in Visual Basic (or another language capable of delivering ActiveX DLLs). The difference is in how the technologies work at a lower level and in how the programmer uses them. In a standard ASP application, the ASP script takes the control when the client browser requests an ASP document and relinquishes it when the resulting HTML page is sent back to the client. In a WebClass application, the WebClass comes into existence when the client browser references a page in the application, and from that point on it reacts to the actions that the user performs on the page, such as clicking on a hyperlink or a Submit button.

A key advantage of WebClasses over traditional script-based and component-based ASP programming is that you develop a WebClass application entirely within the Visual Basic environment, so you have all the usual debugging tools at hand. Because a WebClass usually comprises multiple pages, it should be considered a higher level component. For example, a single WebClass can implement an entire online order management system and can therefore be reused in another application much easier than a collection of loosely coupled ASP pages can. Other evidence of WebClasses' higher level of abstraction is that you don't need to do anything special to maintain the state of a session between consecutive requests from users—such as use cookies or Session variables—because the WebClass does everything for you, even if at the expense of some scalability. (You can decide to disable this option and produce more scalable but stateless WebClass components.) Finally, unlike ASP scripts, the code for the WebClass is isolated from the HTML code that affects the appearance of its pages; therefore, it's easier to partition the task of building the application among developers and HTML authors.

First Impressions

You create a WebClass by using a special designer provided with Visual Basic 6. Unlike the DHTMLPage designer, which lets you create an entire page from scratch without resorting to an external HTML editor, the WebClass designer is meant to import HTML pages created outside the Visual Basic environment. What the designer does is graphically display all the items in an HTML page that are capable of sending requests to the server, such as the ACTION attribute of a FORM tag or the HREF attribute of a hyperlink element. In general, all the tags and attributes that can contain a URL are candidates for being the source of a request to the server. You can then associate such items with actions that the WebClass will perform when that particular request is received. In a sense, this scenario is nothing but the Visual Basic event-driven programming model applied to IIS and ASP applications.

Creating an IIS project

You create a WebClass by selecting the IIS Application project type from the project gallery. This template project includes one WebClass module and has all of the necessary project attributes already set for you. An IIS project is an ActiveX DLL project whose threading model is set to Apartment Threading and that contains one or more WebClass designer modules. In the General tab of the Project Properties dialog box, you'll also find that this project is marked for unattended execution (which makes sense, because it will run under IIS) and that the Retained In Memory flag is set. When this flag is set, the Visual Basic run-time library won't be unloaded even if no WebClass components are currently running in IIS. This arrangement allows the components to be instantiated very quickly when a request comes from a client.

WebClass modules have some properties of their own. They have a *Name* property (the name used inside the current project to reference the WebClass from Visual Basic code), a *NameInURL* property (the name used when referencing this class from HTML and ASP code), a *Public* property (can only be True), and a *StateManagement* property.

The *StateManagement* property indicates what happens between consecutive requests from a client. If this property is set to 1-wcNoState (the default value), the WebClass component is automatically destroyed after it sends a response to the client browser; if this property is set to 2-wcRetainInstance, the WebClass component is kept alive between consecutive requests from the same client. Each option has its pros and cons. If the instance of the WebClass is retained, all the variables in the WebClass module are automatically preserved between consecutive requests, which makes the programmer's job much easier. On the other hand, each component running on the server takes memory and CPU resources, so setting 1-wcNoState creates more scalable solutions—but at the cost of some added complexity in programming. (See the section "State Management" later in this chapter for more details.)

A WebClass contains and manages one or more *WebItems*. Each WebItem corresponds to an HTML page that is sent back to the client browser. There are two types of WebItems: HTML template WebItems and custom WebItems. An HTML template WebItem is based on an existing HTML page that's used as a template for building the response page. This page is then sent to the client browser, usually after substituting one or more placeholders with data. A custom WebItem doesn't correspond to any existing HTML page, and it builds the page returned to the client browser using only code, typically with a series of *Response.Write* commands. A WebClass can contain only HTML template WebItems, only custom WebItems, or (more often) a mixture of the two types.

The first thing to do when working on an IIS application is to establish the directory structure of the project. To separate all the items in the project in an orderly manner, you need at least three directories:

- A directory for the HTML pages that will serve as the templates of your WebClass.

- A directory for the Visual Basic source files. In this directory, the WebClass designer stores the modified HTML templates—that is, the HTML pages whose URL tags have been replaced with references to WebItems in the project.

- A directory for deployment, in which you store the DLL produced by the compilation process, the main ASP document, all the HTM files that must be distributed, and other ancillary files, such as the images used by HTML pages. This directory will also contain the main ASP file that represents the entry point for the WebClass application. When a browser references this file, the WebClass DLL is activated and the application starts its execution.

You can use a single directory for the three types of files used by the project if you want to, though it isn't usually a good idea. If you create an HTML template file in the same directory where the WebClass source file is located, the designer will automatically create a new HTML file whose name is obtained by appending a number to the original name. For example, if you have an Order.htm template file, the designer will create an Order1.htm file in the same directory. Such a rename operation doesn't occur if the original template file is located in a directory different from the one in which the WebClass project is stored. If you work with numerous template files, you'll prefer having those generated by the WebClass differentiated.

Adding HTML Template WebItems

HTML Template WebItems are undoubtedly the simplest WebItems to work with. To create such a WebItem, you must have prepared an HTML template file using an HTML editor such as Microsoft FrontPage or Microsoft InterDev. When creating such a template file, you don't need to pay attention to the destination of hyperlinks and other URLs in the page because they'll be replaced by the WebClass designer anyway. The same applies to the ACTION attribute of forms, to the SRC attribute of the IMG tag, and other HTML attributes that can be assigned a URL. You can't directly associate an event with a button on a form, but you need to associate an event with the ACTION attribute of the form that contains that button. The type of the button must be SUBMIT.

Before importing any HTML template file, you must first save the IIS application to disk. This step is necessary because Visual Basic must know where the modified HTML template file is to be stored. As mentioned in the previous section, it's usually a good idea to keep the original HTML files in a separate directory so that you don't force Visual Basic to create a different name for the modified template file. After you've saved the project, you can import an HTML template file by clicking on the fifth button from the left in the WebClass designer's toolbar. This operation creates a new HTML Template WebItem, which you can rename with a meaningful name: This is the name that will be used in code to refer to that WebItem.

Figure 20-14 shows the WebClass designer after importing two HTML template files. As you can see, the StartPage WebItem contains three items that can send requests to the server and that can raise an event in the WebClass: the BACKGROUND attribute of the BODY element and two hyperlinks. Even if the designer displays all the possible sources for requests, in most cases, you can focus on just a small subset of them—such as the hyperlinks, ACTION attributes in FORM tags, and SRC attributes in IMG tags. If the tag in the original HTML file is associated with an ID, this ID will be used to identify the tag in the designer; otherwise, the designer automatically generates unique IDs for each tag capable of raising an event. For example, the first hyperlink in the page that doesn't have an ID is assigned the *Hyperlink1* ID, the second hyperlink without an ID is assigned the *Hyperlink2* ID, and so on. Such IDs are temporary and aren't stored in the HTML file unless you connect the tag to an event. If you connect these tags to a WebItem, the ID becomes permanent and is stored in the HTML file.

> **NOTE** If the HTML template file contains errors—for example, unmatched opening and closing tags—you get an error when importing the template into the designer. In addition, you can only import forms whose METHOD attributes are set to POST because only forms of this type send the server a request that can be trapped by the WebClass. If you add an HTML template WebItem containing a form that uses the GET method, the WebClass designer displays a warning and then automatically modifies the form's METHOD attribute to the POST value.

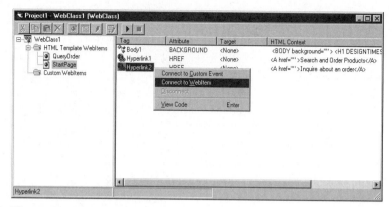

Figure 20-14. *The WebClass designer after creating two HTML Template WebItems.*

Connecting a WebItem

To activate one of these potential sources for requests (requests that become events in the WebClass), you must connect it to a WebItem or a custom event, which you do by right-clicking on such a source in the right pane of the WebClass designer. For now, let's focus on the Connect To WebItem menu command, which brings up the dialog box shown in Figure 20-15. In this dialog box, you can select any of the WebItems currently defined in the WebClass. (You can't connect an attribute to a WebItem defined in another WebClass.) After you close the dialog box, the selected WebItem's name appears in the Target column in the right pane of the designer, near the attribute it has been connected to.

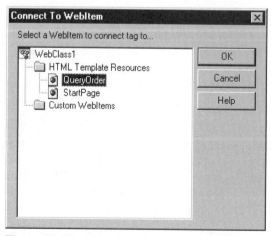

Figure 20-15. *This dialog box appears when you connect an attribute of a tag in an HTML template to a WebItem defined in the WebClass.*

You can't edit the original HTML template from inside the Visual Basic project, but you can quickly invoke your favorite HTML editor on that page, using a button on the designer's toolbar. You can configure which editor should be launched by setting the External HTML Editor option in the Advanced tab of the Options dialog box of the Tools menu. The Visual Basic environment continuously monitors the date and time of HTML template files, and as soon as it finds that one of them has changed, it asks you if you want to reload and parse the new version of the file into the designer. You can also refresh a template in another way, by right-clicking on an HTML Template WebItem and choosing the Refresh HTML Template command from the pop-up menu. This command is useful if for some reason the Visual Basic environment doesn't correctly recognize that the HTML template file has been changed. The designer is usually able to maintain all the associations you set previously, so you don't have to reconnect attributes to WebItems each time you edit the HTML template file.

If the HTML file references other HTML files, these files should be manually copied in the same directory as the WebClass project or in one of its subdirectories. For the same reason, all URLs need to be relative to the current directory so that you can freely copy these files to the deployment directory without having to edit them. Using absolute URLs is acceptable in only two cases: when you refer to files that are always in the same position in your Web site and when you refer to files located at another Web site.

Writing code

You must write some code inside the WebClass designer before running the project. This code is necessary because the WebClass doesn't know what to do when it is activated, and it doesn't know which WebItem should be sent to the client when the WebClass application is first activated.

You decide what happens when the WebClass application is activated—that is, when the browser references its main ASP file—by writing code in the WebClass's *Start* event. In this event, you typically redirect the browser to a WebItem by assigning a WebItem reference to the WebClass's *NextItem* property, as in the following piece of code:

```
' This event fires when the WebClass is activated for the first time,
' that is, when a client browser references its main ASP file.
Private Sub WebClass_Start()
    Set NextItem = StartPage
End Sub
```

Starting the processing of a WebItem doesn't automatically send it to the client's browser. In fact, when a WebItem is assigned to the *NextItem* property, the WebClass fires the WebItem's *Respond* event. In this event procedure, you might want to do additional processing—for example, you might query a database and retrieve the values that must be displayed in the client's browser. The assignment to the *NextItem* property doesn't alter the execution flow immediately because Visual Basic fires the target WebItem's *Respond* event only when the current event procedure has completed.

When you're ready to send the data to the browser, you can invoke the WebItem's *WriteTemplate* method as in the following piece of code:

```
' This event fires when the user jumps to the StartPage page.
Private Sub StartPage_Respond()
    StartPage.WriteTemplate
End Sub
```

At this point, the client's browser displays the StartPage.htm page. In this particular case, the start page doesn't contain any portions that are to be substituted, so the WebClass sends it unmodified to the client. (This case isn't the norm, however.) When the user clicks on a hyperlink, the WebClass receives the *Respond* event of the WebItem that is connected to that hyperlink. Again, you reply to this event by executing the *WriteTemplate* method of the involved WebItem:

```
' This event fires when the user clicks the hyperlink on the
' StartPage page that is linked to the QueryOrder WebItem.
Private Sub QueryOrder_Respond()
    QueryOrder.WriteTemplate
End Sub
```

At first you might be puzzled by the amount of code you have to write just to run a simple application like this one. Don't forget, however, that the WebClass designer really shines when the pages sent back to the client contain dynamic data.

You can run the application built so far: The Visual Basic environment will start IIS and will load the start page into Internet Explorer. Set a breakpoint in the *WebClass_Start* event to see what happens when you click on a hyperlink. Remember that you can debug a WebClass only on the machine where IIS is running. Also, it is generally preferable to have only one instance of the browser running during the debug phase because Visual Basic doesn't keep track of which instance is showing the output coming from the WebClass, and all the instances might be affected during the debug session.

Extending the example

The best way to learn how to use WebClasses is to see a complete example in action. For this reason, I've prepared a nontrivial IIS application based on the NorthWind database that comes with SQL Server 7. This sample application lets users do three different things:

- Users can query the Products database, filter products on their categories, and search them by product name or supplier name.

- After they've found a product of interest, they can specify how many items they want to order and then add the product to their shopping bag list. When the order is complete, the users can confirm it by specifying their name, address, and other data requested. The customer's data is automatically added to the Customers table (if it isn't already there). When the order is completed, the system assigns an ID to it.

■ At any time, the user can track down the current status of an order placed previously by using the ID obtained when the order was completed.

Figure 20-16 sketches the outline of the sample application. As you can see, there are eight template WebItems and two custom WebItems. The figure doesn't show all the possible hyperlinks, such as the hyperlinks that bring users back to the StartPage WebItem at the end of a search or after the confirmation or cancellation of an order.

NOTE To have the sample application work correctly, you must create a system DSN named "NorthWind" that points to the NorthWind SQL Server 7 database. If you don't have SQL Server 7 installed, you can create a version of this database that works in a SQL Server 6.5 database using Access's Upsizing Wizard to convert the NWind.mdb database.

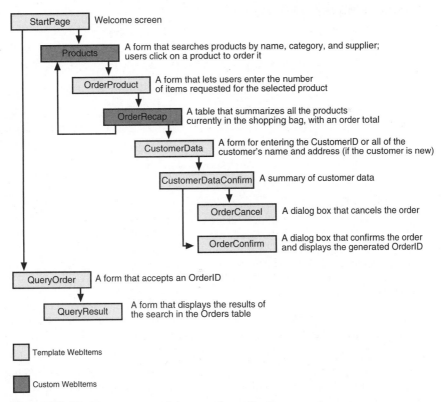

Figure 20-16. *The structure of the sample application.*

The most complex WebItem in the application is Products, for many reasons. This WebItem has to display the input fields for entering search criteria and then display a table with the results of the current search. In general, if the page contains an HTML table with a variable number of rows, you need a custom WebItem because you have to generate the table dynamically using the *Response.Write* method, exactly as you would in a regular ASP application that doesn't rely on WebClasses.

> **NOTE** As I'm writing this, Microsoft is launching a new Web site at *http://vblive.rte.microsoft.com*. This site is completely written using WebClasses, and it's the best place to see the potential this technology offers. Even more astonishing is that you can download the complete Visual Basic source code of the site, so you can learn dozens of tricks to make the best use of WebClasses.

WebClass Basic Techniques

Now that you have a basic idea of what a WebClass is, let's see how you can use it to solve the most common problems you'll encounter when developing IIS applications.

Accessing the ASP object model

One of the advantages of the WebClass programming model is that all the objects in the ASP object model are accessible as properties of the WebClass itself. For example, to write HTML code to the output stream, you can use the Response object, as follows:

```
Response.Write "<BODY>" & vbCrLf
```

Besides the main ASP objects—that is, Request, Response, Server, Application, and Session—the WebClass also makes another object available: the BrowserType object. This object lets the WebClass query the capabilities of the client browser, such as its support for ActiveX controls, cookies, and VBScript. All these capabilities are exposed as properties, as here:

```
If BrowserType.VBScript Then
    ' Send VBScript code to the client browser.
    ...
ElseIf BrowserType.JavaScript Then
    ' Send JavaScript code to the client browser.
    ...
End If
```

Other supported properties, whose names are self-explanatory, are *Frames*, *Tables*, *Cookies*, *BackgroundSounds*, *JavaApplets*, *ActiveXControls*, *Browser* (can return "IE" or "Netscape"), *Version*, *MajorVersion*, *MinorVersion*, and *Platform* (can return "Win95" or "WinNT"). This object relies on the Browscap.ini file that is installed with IIS in its main directory. Load it into an editor to get an idea of which properties are supported and the possible values they can have. Also remember to periodically visit

Microsoft's Web site to download the most recent version of this file, which includes information on the newer browsers. You can also find an up-to-date version of this file at other Web sites, such as *http://www.cyscape.com/browscap*.

WebClass events

As with all classes, WebClass modules have their own life cycle. These are the relevant events in the life of a WebClass:

■ The *Initialize* event fires when the WebClass is first instantiated. If the *StateManagement* property is set to wcNoState, the WebClass is re-created each time a request comes from the client browser; otherwise, this event fires only at the first request coming from a given client. Remember that in the latter case the same instance of the WebClass will serve only the requests coming from a given client.

■ The *BeginRequest* event fires immediately after the *Initialize* event, and in general it is invoked any time the WebClass receives a request from the client browser. Typically, you use this event to retrieve state information if the *StateManagement* property is set to wcNoState. (See the "State Management" section later in this chapter for additional information on this issue.)

■ The *Start* event fires when the client browser activates the WebClass application for the first time—that is, when it requests to download the main ASP file that hosts the WebClass and that represents the entry point for the application. In general, you shouldn't count on this event, however, because the client might reference an HTML page that corresponds to a template WebItem. If this happens, the *Start* event doesn't fire and the WebClass fires the *Respond* event for the corresponding WebItem instead.

■ The *EndRequest* event fires when the WebClass has finished processing an HTTP request and has sent a page back to the client browser. You can use this event to release any resource allocated in the *BeginRequest* event procedure, to close any database, and to perform other cleanup tasks.

■ The *Terminate* event fires immediately before the WebClass is destroyed. Depending on the value of the *StateManagement* property, this event might occur only once during the interaction with a given client browser (if *StateManagement* is set to wcRetainInstance), or it can occur after each *EndRequest* event (if *StateManagement* is set to wcNoState). If *State-Management* is set to wcRetainInstance, a WebClass instance is released when the WebClass invokes the *ReleaseInstance* method.

■ The *FatalErrorResponse* event fires when a fatal error occurs—for example, because of an internal error in the run-time DLL or because the WebClass can't find the appropriate WebItem to send back to the client. In these cases, you can use this event to send a custom error message to the client, but you can't prevent the application from being shut down.

WebClasses offer no *Load* and *Unload* events; you can use the *BeginRequest* and *EndRequest* events for performing the tasks that you would typically perform in the *Load* and *Unload* events, respectively.

Tag replacement

One of the advantages of WebClasses over plain ASP programming is that you don't need to bury script code inside the HTML body of a page to create dynamic contents. At least for the simplest cases, WebClasses offer a better way.

If you need to send back to the client browser an HTML page that contains one or more variable parts—such as the name of the user, the total amount of an order, or the details about a product—you just need to insert a pair of special tags in the HTML template page. When the WebClass processes the template, typically as the result of a *WriteTemplate* method, the corresponding WebItem object receives a series of *ProcessTag* events, one for each pair of the special tags. Inside this event, you can assign a value to a parameter, and that value will replace the text between the tags.

NOTE   The *WriteTemplate* method supports an optional *Template* argument, which lets you specify a different template to be returned to the client. This argument is useful when you have to choose among several templates with a number of events in common.

By default, the special tags that fire the *ProcessTag* events are <WC@tagname> and </WC@tagname>. *WC@* is the tag prefix and is the same for all the tags of a given WebItem; *tagname* can vary from tag to tag and is used inside the *ProcessTag* event procedure to identify which particular pair of tags is to be replaced. Here's a fragment of an HTML template page that contains two pairs of such tags, which will be replaced by the user name and the current date and time:

```
<HTML><BODY>
Welcome back, <WC@USERNAME>Username</WC@USERNAME>. <P>
Current date/time is <WC@DATETIME></WC@DATETIME>
</BODY></HTML>
```

The text embedded between the opening and closing WC@ tag is the tag contents. Here's the code in the WebClass module that processes these tags and replaces them with meaningful information:

```
' This code assumes that the previous template is associated
' with a WebItem named WelcomeBack.
Private Sub WelcomeBack_ProcessTag(ByVal TagName As String, _
```

```
        TagContents As String, SendTags As Boolean)
    Select Case TagName
        Case "WC@USERNAME"
            ' Replace with the user's name, held in a Session variable.
            TagContents = Session("UserName")
        Case "WC@DATETIME"
            ' Replace with the current date and time.
            TagContents = Format$(Now)
    End Select
End Sub
```

On entry to the event, the *TagContents* parameter holds the text found between the opening and closing WC@ tags. In most cases, you use this parameter only to output the replacement value, but nothing prevents you from using it to discern which kind of replacement should be done. For example, the QueryResults WebItem in the sample application on the companion CD uses a single tag—WC@FIELD—and uses the value of the *TagContents* parameter to retrieve the name of the database field that will be used to fill the various cells of a table. As you can see in the following code snippet, this approach simplifies the structure of the *ProcessTag* event procedure because you don't need to test the *TagName* parameter:

```
' The module-level rs variable points to the record that holds the results.
Private Sub QueryResults_ProcessTag(ByVal TagName As String, _
    TagContents As String, SendTags As Boolean)
    If rs.EOF Then
        ' Don't display anything if there isn't a current record.
        TagContents = ""
    ElseIf TagContents = "Freight" Then
        ' This field needs special formatting.
        TagContents = FormatCurrency(rs(TagContents))
    Else
        ' All other fields can be output as they are, but we need to
        ' account for Null fields.
        TagContents = rs(TagContents) & ""
    End If
End Sub
```

An example of a result HTML page sent to the client browser is shown in Figure 20-17 on the following page. Here are a few other details that concern tag substitution inside the *ProcessTag* event:

■ You can change the WC@ tag prefix if you want to. This string corresponds to the *TagPrefix* property of the WebItem object and can be changed both at design time in the Properties window and at run time through code, as here:

```
        QueryResults.TagPrefix = "QR@"
```

The readmevb.htm file that comes with Visual Basic 6 suggests changing the default tag prefix to *WC:* (but without explaining the reason for doing so). In the sample application, I retained the default WC@ without any adverse effects, but in production code you should probably follow this suggestion.

■   If an HTML template doesn't contain any replacement tag, you can improve the execution speed slightly by setting the *TagPrefix* property to an empty string; this informs the WebClass that no replacements are needed, and the parsing process is skipped.

■   The *SendTags* parameter is set to False on entry to the *ProcessTag* event procedure, which means that the opening and closing tags are discarded and aren't sent to the output stream. If you set this parameter to True, the replacement tags are included in the output stream. Even if these tags don't usually affect the appearance of the text displayed in the browser, there's no point in setting the *SendTags* parameter to True unless you also set the *ReScanReplacements* property to True. (See the next entry.)

■   The *ProcessTag* event fires once for each pair of replacement tags found in the HTML template. In some cases, you might want to do multiple passes—for example, when in the first pass you leave the original replacement tags or add new ones. To force the WebClass to make multiple passes, you must set the WebItem's *ReScanReplacements* property to True. You can set this property both at design time and at run time.

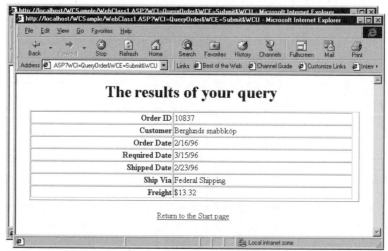

Figure 20-17. *The results of a successful query on an OrderID, as they appear in the client's browser.*

Custom events

Not all the requests the browser sends to the server can be directly mapped to a WebItem. In most cases, in fact, you'll probably want to process the request with some custom code and then decide which WebItem should be processed. In some cases, you don't even want to move to another WebItem—for example, when you process the data in a form and find that the information the user entered is incomplete or incorrect. In these situations, you need a custom event.

To create a custom event, you must right-click in the right pane of the WebClass designer on an attribute that is a candidate as an event source and select the Connect To Custom Event menu command. This operation creates the custom event and links the attribute to it in a single operation. You can then rename the custom event in the left pane of the designer, and the right pane will automatically update to reflect the new name. After you've created the custom event, you can double-click on it to enter some code for processing it. (You can also issue the View Code command from the pop-up menu.)

In the sample application provided on the companion CD, any time I need to process the Submit button in a form, I create a *Submit* custom event that processes the data the user entered and redisplays the same page—but with a suitable error message—if the data is incomplete or incorrect. For example, the following code in the *Submit* event of the QueryOrder WebItem checks whether the OrderID the user entered is an empty string and then retrieves the record in the Orders table that contains the information about that particular order. Notice that if the OrderID is empty or doesn't correspond to an existing order, the routine stores an error message in the *QueryOrderMsg* variable and then reprocesses the QueryOrder WebItem. This WebItem contains one replacement tag, which serves to display the error message (if an error message was stored in the *QueryOrderMsg* variable):

```
' The message that appears on top of the QueryOrder page
Dim QueryOrderMsg As String


' This event fires when the user enters an OrderID in the Query
' page and clicks the Submit button.
Private Sub QueryOrder_Submit()
    ' Don't accept a query with an empty order ID.
    If Request.Form("txtOrderID") = "" Then
        QueryOrderMsg = "Please insert an Order ID"
        QueryOrder.WriteTemplate
        Exit Sub
    End If

    OpenConnection
    ' This Recordset has to retrieve data from three different tables.
    rs.Open "SELECT OrderID, Customers.CompanyName As CompanyName," _
        & " OrderDate, RequiredDate, ShippedDate, Freight, " _
        & " Shippers.CompanyName As ShipVia, " _
```

(continued)

```
              & "FROM Orders, Customers, Shippers " _
              & "WHERE Orders.CustomerID = Customers.CustomerID " _
              & "AND Orders.ShipVia = Shippers.ShipperID " _
              & "AND Orders.OrderID = " & Request.Form("txtOrderID")
        If rs.EOF Then
            ' No record matches the search criteria.
            CloseConnection
            QueryOrderMsg = "OrderID not found"
            QueryOrder.WriteTemplate
            Exit Sub
        End If
        ' If everything is OK, display the results.
        Set NextItem = QueryResults
End Sub


Private Sub QueryResults_Respond()
        ' Show the results, and then close the connection.
        QueryResults.WriteTemplate
        CloseConnection
End Sub
```

(See the previous section for the source code of the *QueryResults_ProcessTag* event procedure.) Two separate routines perform the actual opening and closing of the database connection:

```
' Open the connection to the database.
Private Sub OpenConnection()
        ' Close the Recordset if necessary.
        If rs.State And adStateOpen Then rs.Close
        ' If the connection is closed, open it.
        If (cn.State And adStateOpen) = 0 Then
            cn.Open "DSN=NorthWind"
            Set rs.ActiveConnection = cn
        End If
End Sub


' Close the Recordset and the connection.
Private Sub CloseConnection()
        If rs.State And adStateOpen Then rs.Close
        If cn.State And adStateOpen Then cn.Close
End Sub
```

Here's an important point to keep in mind: In general, you shouldn't store information in WebClass variables to share values among distinct event procedures, because if the *StateManagement* property is set to wcNoState, the WebClass is destroyed between consecutive calls and so are the values in the variables. The code above seems to violate this rule because it stores information in the *QueryOrderMsg*, *cn*, and *rs* variables. If you look more closely, however, you'll see that this information is never maintained across consecutive requests from clients, so this method of passing data is safe. For example, the *QueryOrder_Submit* event assigns a string to the *QueryOrderMsg* variable and then invokes the *QueryOrder.WriteTemplate* method. This method immediately fires the *QueryOrder_ProcessTag* event procedure in which that variable is used. The same reasoning applies to the ADO Recordset that is opened in the *QueryOrder_Submit* event and closed in the *QueryResults_Respond* event.

Custom WebItems

As I mentioned earlier, there are two types of WebItems: template WebItems and custom WebItems. Whereas template WebItems are always associated with an HTML template file, custom WebItems are made of Visual Basic code and generate an HTML page by using plain *Response.Write* methods. Needless to say, working with custom WebItems is more difficult than using template WebItems. Nevertheless, using custom WebItems pays off in terms of greater flexibility. For example, a custom WebItem is usually necessary when you want to create a table of results and you don't know in advance how many rows the table has.

A custom WebItem can be the target of an event from a template WebItem, and it exposes the *Respond* event and custom events as template WebItems do. For example, the Products custom WebItem in the sample application is the target of a hyperlink in the StartPage WebItem. The purpose of the Products WebItem is to provide a form in which the user can select a product category from a combo box control and enter the first characters of the desired product's name. (See Figure 20-18 on page 1173.) At first, you might think that you can display such a form using a template WebItem, but a closer look reveals that you need a custom WebItem because you have to fill the products combo box with the list of the product categories, something you can't do with the simple replacement approach permitted by template WebItems. The *Products_Respond* event procedure uses an auxiliary routine, named *BuildProductsForm*, that actually creates the form; the reason for using a separate procedure will become clear later:

```
' This event fires when the Products WebItem is reached
' from the Start page.
Private Sub Products_Respond()
    ' Display the Products form.
    BuildProductsForm False
End Sub


' Dynamically build the Products form; if the argument is True,
' the three controls are filled with data coming from Session variables.
Private Sub BuildProductsForm(UseSessionVars As Boolean)
    Dim CategoryID As Long, ProductName As String, SupplierName As String
    Dim selected As String
    If UseSessionVars Then
        CategoryID = Session("cboCategory")
        ProductName = Session("txtProduct")
        SupplierName = Session("txtSupplier")
```

(continued)

```
        Else
            CategoryID = -1
        End If

        ' Build the page dynamically.
        Send "<HTML><BODY>"
        Send "<H1>Search the products we have in stock</H1>"
        Send "<FORM action=""@@1"" method=POST id=frmSearch name=frmSearch>", _
            URLFor("Products", "ListResults")
        Send "Select a category and/or type the first characters of the " _
            & "product's name or the supplier's name<P>"
        Send ""
        ' We need a table for alignment purposes.
        Send "<TABLE border=0 cellPadding=1 cellSpacing=1 width=75%>"
        Send "<TR>"
        Send "  <TD><DIV align=right>Select a category  </DIV></TD>"
        Send "  <TD><SELECT name=cboCategory style=""HEIGHT: 22px; " _
            & "WIDTH: 180px"">"

        ' Fill the combo box with category names.
        ' The first item is selected only if CategoryID is -1.
        selected = IIf(CategoryID = -1, "SELECTED ", "")
        Send "<OPTION " & selected & "VALUE=-1>(All categories)"
        ' Then add all the records in the Categories table.
        OpenConnection
        rs.Open "SELECT CategoryID, CategoryName FROM Categories"
        ' Add all the categories to the combo box.
        Do Until rs.EOF
            selected = IIf(CategoryID = rs("CategoryID"), "SELECTED ", "")
            Send "    <OPTION @@1 value=@@2>@@3</OPTION>", selected, _
                rs("CategoryID"), rs("CategoryName")
            rs.MoveNext
        Loop
        rs.Close
        Send "</SELECT>"
        Send "</TD></TR>"

        ' Add the txtProduct text box, and fill it with the correct value.
        Send "<TR>"
        Send " <TD><DIV align=right>Product name  </DIV></TD>"
        Send " <TD><INPUT name=txtProduct value=""@@1"" style=""HEIGHT: " _
            & " 22px; WIDTH: 176px""></TD></TR>", ProductName
        Send "<TR>"
        Send " <TD><DIV align=right>Supplier </DIV>"
        Send " <TD><INPUT name=txtSupplier value=""@@1"" style=""HEIGHT: " _
            & "22px; WIDTH: 177px"">", SupplierName
        Send "<TR><TD><TD>"
        Send "<TR>"
```

```
Send " <TD><DIV align=right> </DIV></TD>"
Send " <TD><INPUT type=submit value=""Search"" id=submit1 " _
    & "style=""HEIGHT: 25px; WIDTH: 90px"">"
If BrowserType.VBScript Then
    Send "    <INPUT type=button value=""Reset fields"" id=btnReset" _
        & " Name=btnReset style=""HEIGHT: 25px; WIDTH: 90px"">"
End If
Send "</TD></TR></TABLE></P><P></P>"
Send "</TABLE>"
Send "</FORM>"
Send "<HR>"

' Insert client-side script for the Reset Fields button.
If BrowserType.VBScript Then
    Send "<SCRIPT LANGUAGE=VBScript>"
    Send "Sub btnReset_onclick()"
    Send "   frmSearch.cboCategory.Value = -1"
    Send "   frmSearch.txtProduct.Value = """""
    Send "   frmSearch.txtSupplier.Value = """""
    Send "End Sub"
End If
Send "</SCRIPT>"

' If this is a blank form, we must complete it.
If Not UseSessionVars Then
    Send "<P><A HREF=""@@1"">Go Back to the Welcome page</A>", _
        URLFor(Default)
    Send "</BODY></HTML>"
End If
End Sub
```

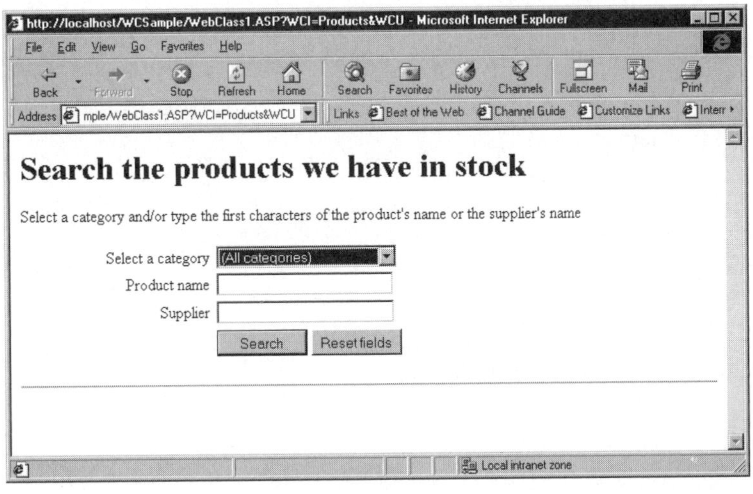

Figure 20-18. *The form produced by the Products custom WebItem. The combo box control contains all the categories in the Categories table in the NorthWind database.*

You'll probably agree that this isn't what you'd call "readable code." Still, it didn't take me much effort to create it. In fact, I just ran Microsoft InterDev (you can use your HTML editor of choice, of course) and created a sample form with three controls inside a table. (I used a table only for alignment purposes.) Then I imported the code in the Visual Basic code editor and wrote some code "around" the static HTML text. The entire process took about 10 minutes.

The previous routine has many interesting characteristics. First of all, to streamline the Visual Basic code, I created an auxiliary routine, named *Send*, which sends data to the output stream by using the *Response.Write* method. But the *Send* routine does a lot more; it also provides a way to dynamically replace variable portions in the output string, based on numbered placeholders. The routine is even capable of dealing with replaced arguments that occur inside a quoted string. These arguments must be processed in a special way because any double quote character inside them must be doubled in order to be displayed correctly on the client's browser. The complete source code of the routine follows. As you can see, the code isn't specific to this particular program and can therefore be easily reused in any other WebClass application.

```
' Send a string to the output stream, and substitute @@n placeholders
' with the arguments passed to the routine. (@@1 is replaced by the
' first argument, @@2 by the second argument, and so on.) Only one
' substitution per argument is permitted. If the @@n placeholder
' is enclosed with double quotes, any double quote is replaced by
' two consecutive double quotes.
Private Sub Send(ByVal Text As String, ParamArray Args() As Variant)
    Dim i As Integer, pos As Integer, placeholder As String
    For i = LBound(Args) To UBound(Args)
        placeholder = "@@" & Trim$(Str$(i + 1))
        ' First search the quoted placeholder.
        pos = InStr(Text, """" & placeholder)
        If pos Then
            ' Double all the quotes in the argument.
            pos = pos + 1
            Args(i) = Replace(Args(i), """", """""")
        Else
            ' Else, search the unquoted placeholder.
            pos = InStr(Text, placeholder)
        End If
        If pos Then
            ' If a placeholder found, substitute it with an argument.
            Text = Left$(Text, pos - 1) & Args(i) & Mid$(Text, pos + 3)
        End If
```

```
    Next
    ' Send the result text to the output stream.
    Response.Write Text & vbCrLf
End Sub
```

Another intriguing technique used in the *BuildProductsForm* routine is sending a piece of VBScript code to be processed on the client workstation when the user clicks the Reset Fields button. You can't rely on a standard button with TYPE=Reset because such a button would restore the contents that the fields have when the form is received from the server, and in some cases the server doesn't send blank fields to the client. For this reason, the only way to enable users to clear the fields on the form is to provide a button and associate a client-side script with it. Mixing server-side and client-side code is a powerful technique, and it also provides maximum scalability because it frees the server from the tasks that the client machine can conveniently perform. The client browser might not be capable of executing VBScript code, however, and for this reason the WebClass sends the client-script code only if the *BrowserType.VBScript* property returns True. A better approach is to send JavaScript code, which both Microsoft and Netscape browsers should accept.

The *URLFor* method

The last point of interest in the *BuildProductsForm* routine is where it defines what happens when the user clicks the Search button. As you know, both template WebItems and custom WebItems can expose custom events, which appear in the left pane of the WebClass designer. The way you create and invoke such custom events, however, is different for the two types of WebItems. When working with template WebItems, you implicitly create a custom event when you select the Connect To Custom Event menu command in the right pane of the designer. A custom WebItem creates its HTML code dynamically at run time, and therefore the designer can't display anything in the right pane. For this reason, you can create custom events for custom WebItems only manually—that is, by right-clicking on the WebItem and selecting the Add Custom Event menu command. (You can manually add a custom event to a template WebItem as well, if necessary—but you rarely need to.)

The Products WebItem in the sample application exposes two custom events, *ListResults* and *RestoreResults*, in addition to its standard *Respond* event. (See Figure 20-19 on the following page.) The *ListResults* event fires when the user clicks the Search button, whereas the *RestoreResults* event fires when the user goes back to the Products page from the OrderRecap page. (See Figure 20-16.) When the user clicks the Search button, the Products WebItem uses the values in the form to dynamically build a table with all the products that match the search criteria and appends this table to the form itself.

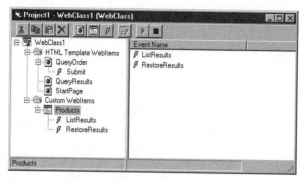

Figure 20-19. *The WebClass designer, after adding the custom Products WebItem and its* ListResults *and* RestoreResults *custom events.*

So here's the problem: How can you have the WebClass module fire the *ListResults* event in the Products WebItem when the user clicks the Search button? The answer to this question is the following line of code in the *BuildProductsForm* procedure:

```
Send "<FORM action=""@@1"" method=POST id=frmSearch name=frmSearch>", _
    URLFor("Products", "ListResults")
```

The *URLFor* method expects two arguments, the name of a WebItem and the name of an event, and generates a URL that—when the request is sent to the server—will fire that particular event for that particular WebItem. You can omit the second argument for this method; if you do, the WebClass will activate the default *Response* event.

> **TIP** The first argument of the *URLFor* method is defined as type Variant and can accept either a reference to a WebItem object or its name. For performance reasons, always pass the WebItem's name, as in the following example:
> ```
> ' The following two lines yield the same results, but the second
> ' line is slightly more efficient.
> Response.Write URLFor(Products, "ListResults")
> Response.Write URLFor("Products", "ListResults")
> ```

You respond to custom events in a custom WebItem as you would in a template WebItem. For example, the following code is executed when the user clicks the Search button in the Products WebItem. As you can see, it reuses the *BuildProductsForm* routine and then runs another auxiliary routine, *BuildProductsTable*, which generates the HTML table containing the results of the search.

```
' This event fires when the Product WebItem is invoked
' from the Search button on the form itself.
Private Sub Products_ListResults()
    ' Move data from controls on the form to Session variables.
    ' This allows you to return to the page later and reload these
    ' values in the controls.
    Session("cboCategory") = Request.Form("cboCategory")
```

```
        Session("txtProduct") = Request.Form("txtProduct")
        Session("txtSupplier") = Request.Form("txtSupplier")
        ' Rebuild the Products form, and then generate the result table.
        BuildProductsForm True
        BuildProductsTable
End Sub


' This private procedure builds the table that contains the
' result of the search on the Products table.
Private Sub BuildProductsTable()
        Dim CategoryID As Long, ProductName As String, SupplierName As String
        Dim selected As String, sql As String
        Dim records() As Variant, i As Long
        ' Retrieve the values from the Session variables.
        CategoryID = Session("cboCategory")
        ProductName = Session("txtProduct")
        SupplierName = Session("txtSupplier")


        ' Dynamically build the query string.
        sql = "SELECT ProductID, ProductName, CompanyName, QuantityPerUnit, " _
            & "UnitPrice FROM Products, Suppliers " _
            & "WHERE Products.SupplierID = Suppliers.SupplierID "
        If CategoryID <> -1 Then
            sql = sql & " AND CategoryID = " & CategoryID
        End If
        If ProductName <> "" Then
            sql = sql & " AND ProductName LIKE '" & ProductName & "%'"
        End If
        If SupplierName <> "" Then
            sql = sql & " AND CompanyName LIKE '" & SupplierName & "%'"
        End If
        ' Open the Recordset.
        OpenConnection
        rs.Open sql


        If rs.EOF Then
            Send "<B>No records match the specified search criteria.</B>"
        Else
            ' Read all the records in one operation.
            records() = rs.GetRows()
            ' Now we know how many products meet the search criteria.
            Send "<B>Found @@1 products.<B><P>", UBound(records, 2) + 1
            Send "You can order a product by clicking on its name."


            ' Build the result table.
            Send "<TABLE BORDER WIDTH=90%>"
            Send " <TR>"
            Send "  <TH WIDTH=35% ALIGN=left>Product</TH>"
```

(continued)

```
          Send "  <TH WIDTH=30% ALIGN=left>Supplier</TH>"
          Send "  <TH WIDTH=25% ALIGN=left>Unit</TH>"
          Send "  <TH WIDTH=20% ALIGN=right>Unit Price</TH>"
          Send " </TR>"
          ' Add one row of cells for each record.
          For i = 0 To UBound(records, 2)
              Send " <TR>"
              Send "  <TD><A HREF=""@@1"">@@2</A></TD>", _
                  URLFor("OrderProduct", CStr(records(0, i))), records(1, i)
              Send "  <TD>@@1</TD>", records(2, i)
              Send "  <TD>@@1</TD>", records(3, i)
              Send "  <TD ALIGN=right>@@1</TD>", _
                  FormatCurrency(records(4, i))
              Send " </TR>"
          Next
          Send "</TABLE>"
      End If
      CloseConnection

      ' Complete the HTML page.
      Send "<P><A HREF=""@@1"">Go Back to the Welcome page</A>", _
          URLFor("StartPage")
      Send "</BODY></HTML>"
  End Sub
```

An example of the result of this event procedure is shown in Figure 20-20.

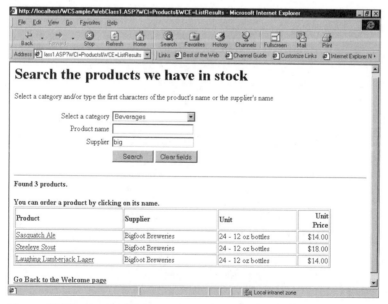

Figure 20-20. *A successful search in the Products table.*

The *UserEvent* event

Let's continue analyzing the code in the *BuildProductsTable*. Notice that each product name in the leftmost column of the result table is a hyperlink created using this statement:

```
Send "  <TD><A HREF=""@@1"">@@2</A></TD>", _
    URLFor("OrderProduct", CStr(records(0, i))), records(1, i)
```

The second argument passed to the *URLFor* method is the ProductID of the product whose name is made visible to the user. Obviously, the OrderProduct WebItem can't expose one event for each possible ProductID value, and in fact it doesn't need to. When the WebClass raises a WebItem event whose name doesn't correspond to either a standard event (such as *Respond*) or a custom event defined at design time, the WebItem element receives a *UserEvent* event. This event receives an *EventName* parameter that contains the name of the event specified as the second argument of the *URLFor* method. In this particular example, when the user clicks on a product name in the result table, the WebClass fires the *OrderProduct_UserEvent* event and passes it the ID of the selected product:

```
' This event fires when the user clicks on a product's name
' in the Products page, asking to order a given product.
' The name of the event is the ID of the product itself.
Private Sub OrderProduct_UserEvent(ByVal EventName As String)
    Dim sql As String
    ' Build the query string, and open the Recordset.
    sql = "SELECT ProductID, ProductName, CompanyName, QuantityPerUnit," _
        "UnitPrice FROM Products INNER JOIN Suppliers " _
        & " ON Products.SupplierID = Suppliers.SupplierID " _
        & "WHERE ProductID = " & EventName
    OpenConnection
    rs.Open sql
    ' Use the URLData property to send the ProductID to the page
    ' being shown in the browser. This value is then sent
    ' to the OrderRecap WebItem if the user confirms the inclusion
    ' of this product in the shopping bag.
    URLData = CStr(rs("ProductID"))
    ' Write the template. (This fires an OrderProduct_ProcessTag event.)
    OrderProduct.WriteTemplate
    CloseConnection
End Sub
```

Because OrderProduct is a template WebItem, the *UserEvent* procedure can execute the WebItem's *WriteTemplate* method, which in turn fires a *ProcessTag* event. The code inside this event procedure performs a tag replacement and fills a one-row table with data about the selected product. (See Figure 20-21 on the following page.)

```
' The WebClass fires this event when the OrderProduct template is
' being interpreted. The only WC@ tag in this template is WC@FIELD, and the
' TagContents corresponds to the database field that must be displayed.
Private Sub OrderProduct_ProcessTag(ByVal TagName As String, _
    TagContents As String, SendTags As Boolean)
    If TagContents = "UnitPrice" Then
        TagContents = FormatCurrency(rs("UnitPrice"))
    Else
        TagContents = rs(TagContents)
    End If
End Sub
```

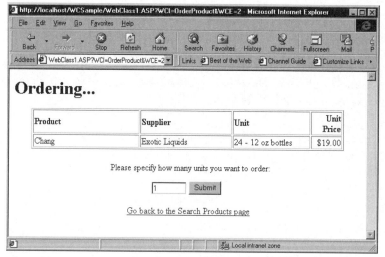

Figure 20-21. *The result of the processing of the OrderProduct WebItem.*

The *URLData* property

When the user enters the number of units of a given product to buy, the control jumps to the OrderRecap custom WebItem, which displays the list of all the items that are included in the current order and evaluates the total value of the order so far. To correctly implement this WebItem, you must solve a minor problem: how to pass the ID of the product selected by the user in the OrderProduct page. If the *StateManagement* property is set to wcRetainInstance, you can simply store it in a WebClass variable; but if the WebClass component is destroyed after the page has been sent back to the browser, you have to take a different approach.

Among the many techniques that you can adopt to preserve data among client requests, one of the simplest ones is based on the *URLData* property. When you assign a string to this property, the string is sent to the browser. When the browser sends the next request, the string is sent back to the server, and the WebClass can read it by querying the *URLData* property. In other words, the string assigned to this property isn't stored anywhere and continues to be pinged from the server to the client and back. This statement sets the *URLData* property in the *OrderProduct_UserEvent* procedure:

```
URLData = CStr(rs("ProductID"))
```

The ProductID value is then retrieved in the *OrderRecap_Respond* event procedure, where the application adds the new product to the current contents of the user's shopping bag. Such a shopping bag is implemented as a two-dimensional array stored in a Session variable:

```
Private Sub OrderRecap_Respond()
    ' The shopping bag is a two-dimensional array in a Session variable.
    ' This array has three rows: row 0 holds ProductID, row 1 holds
    ' Quantity, and row 2 holds UnitPrice. Each new product appends
    ' a new column.
    Dim shopBag As Variant, index As Integer, sql As String
    ' Retrieve the current shopping bag.
    shopBag = Session("ShoppingBag")

    If URLData <> "" Then
        ' Add a new product to the shopping bag.
        If IsEmpty(shopBag) Then
            ' This is the first product in the bag.
            ReDim shopBag(2, 0) As Variant
            index = 0
        Else
            ' Else extend the bag to include this product.
            index = UBound(shopBag, 2) + 1
            ReDim Preserve shopBag(2, index) As Variant
        End If
        ' Store the product in the array.
        shopBag(0, index) = URLData
        shopBag(1, index) = Request.Form("txtQty")
    End If

    ' Dynamically build the response page.
    Send "<HTML><BODY>"
    Send "<CENTER>"
    If IsEmpty(shopBag) Then
        ' No items are in the bag.
        Send "<H1>Your shopping bag is empty</H1>"
```

(continued)

```
Else
    ' Open the Products table to retrieve the products in the order.
    sql = "SELECT ProductID, ProductName, CompanyName, " _
        & "QuantityPerUnit, UnitPrice " _
        & "FROM Products INNER JOIN Suppliers " _
        & "ON Products.SupplierID = Suppliers.SupplierID "
    For index = 0 To UBound(shopBag, 2)
        sql = sql & IIf(index = 0, " WHERE ", " OR ")
        sql = sql & "ProductID = " & shopBag(0, index)
    Next
    OpenConnection
    rs.Open sql

    ' Build the table with the products in the shopping bag.
    Send "<H1>Your shopping bag contains the following items: </H1>"
    Send "<TABLE BORDER WIDTH=100%>"
    Send " <TR>"
    Send "   <TH WIDTH=5% ALIGN=center>Qty</TH>"
    Send "   <TH WIDTH=30% ALIGN=left>Product</TH>"
    Send "   <TH WIDTH=25% ALIGN=left>Supplier</TH>"
    Send "   <TH WIDTH=20% ALIGN=left>Unit</TH>"
    Send "   <TH WIDTH=10% ALIGN=right>Unit Price</TH>"
    Send "   <TH WIDTH=10% ALIGN=right>Price</TH>"
    Send " </TR>"

    ' Loop on all the records in the Recordset.
    Dim total As Currency, qty As Long
    Do Until rs.EOF
        ' Retrieve the quantity from the shopping bag.
        index = GetBagIndex(shopBag, rs("ProductID"))
        ' Remember the UnitPrice for later so that you don't need to
        ' reopen the Recordset when the order is confirmed.
        shopBag(2, index) = rs("UnitPrice")

        ' Get the requested quantity.
        qty = shopBag(1, index)
        ' Update the running total. (No discounts in this demo!)
        total = total + qty * rs("UnitPrice")
        ' Add a row to the table.
        Send " <TR>"
        Send "   <TD ALIGN=center>@@1</TD>", qty
        Send "   <TD ALIGN=left>@@1</TD>", rs("ProductName")
        Send "   <TD ALIGN=left>@@1</TD>", rs("CompanyName")
        Send "   <TD ALIGN=left>@@1</TD>", rs("QuantityPerUnit")
        Send "   <TD ALIGN=right>@@1</TD>", _
```

```
                FormatCurrency(rs("UnitPrice"))
            Send "  <TD ALIGN=right>@@1</TD>", _
                FormatCurrency(qty * rs("UnitPrice"))
            Send " </TR>"
            rs.MoveNext
        Loop
        CloseConnection

        ' Store the shopping bag back in the Session variable.
        Session("ShoppingBag") = shopBag
        ' Add a row for the total.
        Send " <TR>"
        Send "  <TD></TD><TD></TD><TD></TD><TD></TD>"
        Send "  <TD ALIGN=right><B>TOTAL</B></TD>"
        Send "  <TD ALIGN=right>@@1</TD>", FormatCurrency(total)
        Send " </TR>"
        Send "</TABLE><P>"
        ' Add a few hyperlinks.
        Send "<A HREF=""@@1"">Confirm the order</A><P>", _
            URLFor("CustomerData")
        Send "<A HREF=""@@1"">Cancel the order</A><P>", _
            URLFor("OrderCancel")
    End If

    Send "<A HREF=""@@1"">Go back to the Search page</A>", _
        URLFor("Products", "RestoreResults")
    Send "</CENTER>"
    Send "</BODY></HTML>"
End Sub
```

The preceding routine uses an auxiliary function that searches for a ProductID value in the shopping bag and returns the corresponding column index, or –1 if the ProductID isn't found:

```
Function GetBagIndex(shopBag As Variant, ProductID As Long) As Long
    Dim i As Integer
    GetBagIndex = -1
    For i = 0 To UBound(shopBag, 2)
        If shopBag(0, i) = ProductID Then
            GetBagIndex = i
            Exit Function
        End If
    Next
End Function
```

The result of the processing of the OrderRecap WebItem is shown in Figure 20-22.

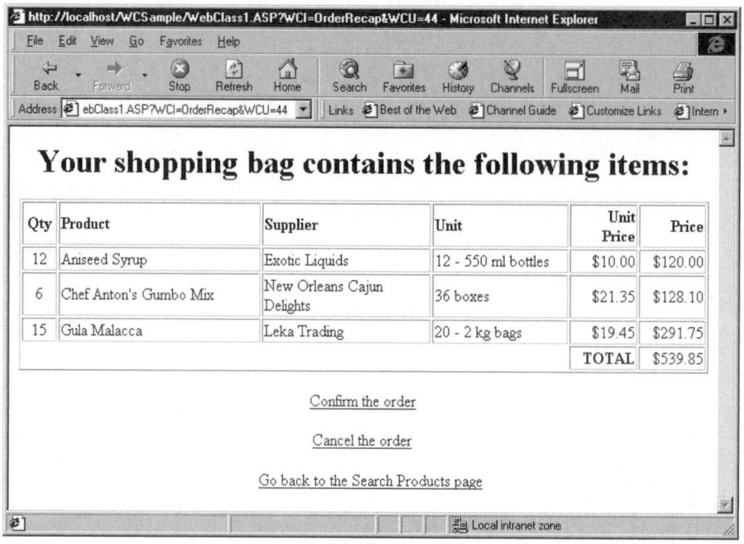

Figure 20-22. *The result of the processing of the OrderRecap WebItem, showing the current contents of the shopping bag.*

The Professional Touch

With what you've learned so far, you can build fairly complex and powerful WebClass components. To create highly efficient and scalable applications, however, you need to learn a few additional details.

Navigation

A WebClass application differs from a standard application in many respects. One area in which the differences are remarkable is in navigating from one WebItem to another. In a traditional application, the programmer can control what the user can do at any moment, and no form in the program can be reached if the developer doesn't provide the user with a means to display it. In an Internet application, on the other hand, the user can navigate to any page by simply typing its URL in the browser's address field. This fact has a number of implications in the way you define the structure of the program:

■ In general, you have no guarantee that the first page loaded in the WebClass application is its main ASP file, and therefore you can't be sure that the WebClass's *Start* event fires. For example, the user can jump directly to a WebItem by referencing it in the address field of the browser:

```
http://www.myserver.com/MyWebClass.asp?WCI=Products
```

For this reason, if you need to read some initialization data or perform any other kind of initialization chores, you should rely on the *Initialize* or *BeginRequest* event instead of on the *Start* event.

■ Don't start a transaction in one page on the assumption that you can close it in the following page because you can't be sure that the user will proceed in that direction. For example, the user might click on the Back button or type another URL in the browser's address field, in which case the transaction would never be completed and data and index pages on the database would be locked.

■ When a user returns to a page that he's already visited, you should restore the previous contents of the page—for example, by reloading all the values in the fields in an HTML form. (The sample application uses this technique for the Products custom WebItem.) An exception to this rule is when a user has completed a transaction—for example, by confirming an order—in which case, clicking on the Back button should display a blank form, which will make it clear that the operation has been completed and can't be undone.

■ The preferred way to navigate among WebItems is by means of the *NextItem* property. Keep in mind that assignments to this property are ignored in the *ProcessTag*, *EndRequest*, and *FatalErrorResponse* events.

■ In applications that consist of multiple WebClass modules, you might want to jump from one WebClass to another. You can do this using the *Response.Redirect* method:

```
' Assumes that the WebClass2's main directory is the same
' as the current WebClass's directory.
Response.Redirect "WebClass2.asp"
```

You can also use this method to jump to a custom event of a WebItem in the same application:

```
Response.Redirect URLFor("Products", "RestoreResults")
```

State management

State management plays an important role in the development of WebClass applications. As you know, the HTTP protocol is inherently stateless, which means that it doesn't "remember" information from previous requests. As for regular ASP applications, when working with WebClasses you have several ways to overcome this issue, and each solution has advantages and disadvantages.

If the *StateManagement* property of the WebClass is set to wcRetainInstance, you can safely store all the information in the WebClass's variables because the instance of the WebClass is kept alive between client requests and will be destroyed only when the code explicitly invokes the *ReleaseInstance* method. You pay for this convenience with reduced scalability of the IIS application. Also, because WebClass components use the apartment threading model and can run only in the thread in which they were created, when a subsequent client request arrives, it might have to wait until that particular thread becomes available.

> **TIP**   By default, IIS initially allocates 2 threads to ASP and increases this number as necessary, up to 10 threads per processor. You can modify the default values by assigning different numbers to the values for NumInitialThreads and ProcessorMaxThreads of the HKEY_LOCAL_MACHINE\SYSTEM\Current-ControlSet\Services\W3SVC\ASP\Parameters Registry key. The highest valid number for the ProcessorMaxThreads setting is 200.

You can store values in Application and Session variables so that they persist among client requests even if the WebClass component is destroyed and then re-created. If you have to store a lot of information, you might create a server-side component that stores the data and then assign it to an Application or Session variable. In general, if the server-side component uses the apartment threading model—as all components authored in Visual Basic do—you shouldn't store them in an Application variable.

If you have to store a lot of data, you can resort to a database on the server machine. This solution permits the sharing of data among multiple clients, but it requires that you set up a connection and open a Recordset each time you need to read or write a value. Opening and closing a connection isn't as inefficient as it might sound, though, because database connections are pooled.

You can use the *URLData* property to move data back and forth between the server and the client, as explained in the "The *URLData* Property" section earlier in this chapter. This technique is equivalent to using the *Request.QueryString* property, but its implementation is considerably simpler. One of its advantages is that the data is stored in the page itself; therefore, if the user clicks the Back button and then resubmits the form, the WebClass receives the same data originally sent to the page. Another advantage is that the *URLData* property works even with browsers that don't support cookies. This technique isn't without disadvantages, however. You can't store more than about 2 KB of data in the *URLData* property, and moving data back and forth in this way slightly slows down each request. You can't use this technique if the HTML page includes a form whose METHOD attribute is set to GET, but this isn't a real limitation because WebClasses only work with forms that use the POST method.

You can use cookies, as you would in a regular ASP application—that is, through the Request.Cookies and Response.Cookies collections. As is the case for the *URLData* property, you can pass only a limited amount of data through cookies. Even worse, the user might have disabled cookies for security reasons, or the browser might not support them at all (a rare occurrence, though). Moreover, you have a performance hit when moving many cookies with a lot of information in them, so you might be best off using cookies only to store the ID of a record that you later load from a database.

Another way to store state information in the page is by using an HTML Hidden Control, which the WebClass initializes when it creates the page and reads back when the page is resubmitted to the server, through the Request.Form collection of variables. The problems with this approach are that you can use it only when the page includes a form and that the contents of such hidden fields are visible in the source code of the page. If this visibility is a problem, you should encrypt the data stored in these fields.

Testing and deployment

Testing a WebClass application isn't much different from testing any ASP component in the sense that you can take advantage of all the debug tools offered by the Visual Basic environment. A couple of additional WebClass features are very useful in the debug phase.

The *Trace* sends a string to the *OutputDebugString* Windows API function. A few debugging tools, such as the DBMON utility, can intercept such strings. Using the *Trace* method with a debugger in this way is especially useful after you've compiled the WebClass because you can't rely on other ways for displaying messages. Remember that WebClass applications use the Unattended Execution option; therefore, you can't use *MsgBox* statements to display a message on the screen. However, you can use the methods of the App object to write to a log file or to the Windows NT event log.

When the WebClass application raises a fatal error (and therefore can't continue), the code receives a *FatalErrorResponse* event. You can react to this event by sending your custom message to the client browser using the *Response.Write* method, after which you should set the *SendDefault* argument to False to suppress the WebClass standard error message:

```
Private Sub WebClass_FatalErrorResponse(SendDefault As Boolean)
    Response.Write "A fatal error has occurred.<P>"
    Response.Write "If the problem persists, please send an e-mail"
    Response.Write "message to the Web administrator."
    SendDefault = False
End Sub
```

Inside a *FatalErrorResponse* event, you can query the WebClass's Error object, which returns detailed information through its *Number*, *Source*, and *Description* properties. This object always returns Nothing outside the *FatalErrorResponse* event. All the fatal errors that can occur correspond to one of the wcrErr*xxxx* enumerated constants exposed by the WebClass library, such as wcrErrCannotReadHtml or wcrErrSystemError.

Fatal errors are automatically registered in the Windows NT event log, but you can disable this feature by changing the LogErrors value of the HKEY_LOCAL _MACHINE\SOFTWARE\Microsoft\Visual Basic\6.0\WebClass Registry key from 1 to 0. Under Windows 95 and Windows 98, a log file is created in the Windows directory.

Finally, you should account for some behavioral differences between the interpreted and the compiled versions of the WebClass component:

- In the compiled version, only system DSNs will work; all other types of DSNs work only in the interpreted version.

- MDB databases work in the interpreted version but not in the compiled version. The readmevb.htm file that comes with Visual Basic mentions this issue, and in fact I experienced all sorts of problems when trying to access an MDB file from a compiled WebClass. But I can't be sure that no compiled WebClass will work with MDB databases.

- When accessing an SQL Server database from within a compiled WebClass, you'll find that the component can't correctly log in unless you've granted login access to the user corresponding to the identity of the WebClass component. You can set this identity in the Directory Security tab of the Property Pages dialog box of the directory that contains the WebClass application.

- An interpreted program can store a reference to a WebClass object in an Application variable without any problem, but this operation causes an error in compiled applications.

- You can deploy a WebClass application using the Package And Deployment Wizard. But keep in mind that the wizard doesn't automatically recognize all the ASP, HTM, and images files used by the application, so you have to manually add them to the list of distribution files.

To have a compiled WebClass component execute correctly under IIS, you must distribute the special WebClass run-time file, which is contained in the Mswcrun.dll file.

We've finally come to the end of this long journey through Internet Information Server, ASP applications, and WebClass components. This chapter is the last one about Internet programming technologies. Both DHTML applications and WebClass components require a different approach than traditional programming, but in return you get the capability to write great Internet and intranet applications while still using your favorite programming language. Internet programming would also be the last topic covered in this book, but there are so many interesting ways to expand the Visual Basic language using Windows API functions that I couldn't resist the temptation to include an Appendix exclusively devoted to these advanced techniques.

Appendix

Windows API Functions

The Visual Basic language provides a rich set of functions, commands, and objects, but in many cases they don't meet all the needs of a professional programmer. Just to name a few shortcomings, Visual Basic doesn't allow you to retrieve system information—such as the name of the current user—and most Visual Basic controls expose only a fraction of the features that they potentially have.

Expert programmers have learned to overcome most of these limitations by directly calling one or more Windows API functions. In this book, I've resorted to API functions on many occasions, and it's time to give these functions the attention they deserve. In contrast to my practice in most other chapters in this book, however, I won't even try to exhaustively describe all you can do with this programming technique, for one simple reason: The Windows operating system exposes several thousand functions, and the number grows almost weekly.

Instead, I'll give you some ready-to-use routines that perform specific tasks and that remedy a few of the deficiencies of Visual Basic. You won't see much theory in these pages because there are many other good sources of information available, such as the Microsoft Developer Network (MSDN), a product that should always have a place on the desktop of any serious developer, regardless of his or her programming language.

A WORLD OF MESSAGES

The Microsoft Windows operating system is heavily based on messages. For example, when the user closes a window, the operating system sends the window a WM_CLOSE message. When the user types a key, the window that has the focus receives a WM_CHAR message, and so on. (In this context, the term *window* refers to both top-level windows and child controls.) Messages can also be sent to a window or a control to affect its appearance or behavior or to retrieve the information it contains. For example, you can send the WM_SETTEXT message to most windows and controls to assign a string to their contents, and you can send the WM_GETTEXT message to read their current contents. By means of these messages, you can set or read the caption of a top-level window or set or read the *Text* property of a TextBox control, just to name a few common uses for this technique.

Broadly speaking, messages belong to one of two families: They're *control messages* or *notification messages*. Control messages are sent by an application to a window or a control to set or retrieve its contents, or to modify its behavior or appearance. Notification messages are sent by the operating system to windows or controls as the result of the actions users perform on them.

Visual Basic greatly simplifies the programming of Windows applications because it automatically translates most of these messages into properties, methods, and events. Instead of using WM_SETTEXT and WM_GETTEXT messages, Visual Basic programmers can reason in terms of *Caption* and *Text* properties. Nor do they have to worry about trapping WM_CLOSE messages sent to a form because the Visual Basic runtime automatically translates them into *Form_Unload* events. More generally, control messages map to properties and methods, whereas notification messages map to events.

Not all messages are processed in this way, though. For example, the TextBox control has built-in undo capabilities, but they aren't exposed as properties or methods by Visual Basic, and therefore they can't be accessed by "pure" Visual Basic code. (In this appendix, *pure Visual Basic* means code that doesn't rely on external API functions.) Here's another example: When the user moves a form, Windows sends the form a WM_MOVE message, but the Visual Basic runtime traps that message without raising an event. If your application needs to know when one of its windows moves, you're out of luck.

By using API functions, you can work around these limitations. In this section, I'll show you how you can send a control message to a window or a control to affect its appearance or behavior, while in the "Callback and Subclassing" section, I'll illustrate a more complex programming technique, called *window subclassing*, which lets you intercept the notification messages that Visual Basic doesn't translate to events.

Before you can use an API function, you must tell Visual Basic the name of the DLL that contains it and the type of each argument. You do this with a *Declare* statement, which must appear in the declaration section of a module. *Declare* statements must be declared as Private in all types of modules except BAS modules (which also accept Public *Declare* statements that are visible from the entire application). For additional information about the *Declare* statement, see the language documentation.

The main API function that you can use to send a message to a form or a control is *SendMessage*, whose *Declare* statement is this:

```
Private Declare Function SendMessage Lib "user32" Alias "SendMessageA" _
    (ByVal hWnd As Long, ByVal wMsg As Long, _
    ByVal wParam As Long, lParam As Any) As Long
```

The *hWnd* argument is the handle of the window to which you're sending the message (it corresponds to the window's *hWnd* property), *wMsg* is the message number (usually expressed as a symbolic constant), and the meaning of the *wParam* and *lParam* values depend on the particular message you're sending. Notice that *lParam* is declared with the *As Any* clause so that you can pass virtually anything to this argument, including any simple data type or a UDT. To reduce the risk of accidentally sending invalid data, I've prepared a version of the *SendMessage* function, which accepts a Long number by value, and another version that expects a String passed by value. These are the so called type-safe *Declare* statements:

```
Private Declare Function SendMessageByVal Lib "user32" _
    Alias "SendMessageA" (ByVal hWnd As Long, ByVal wMsg As Long, _
    ByVal wParam As Long, Byval lParam As Long) As Long

Private Declare Function SendMessageString Lib "user32" _
    Alias "SendMessageA" ByVal hWnd As Long, ByVal wMsg As Long, _
    ByVal wParam As Long, ByVal lParam As String) As Long
```

Apart from such type-safe variants, the *Declare* functions used in this chapter, as well as the values of message symbolic constants, can be obtained by running the API Viewer utility that comes with Visual Basic. (See Figure A-1 on the following page.)

> **CAUTION** When working with API functions, you're in direct touch with the operating system and aren't using the safety net that Visual Basic offers. If you make an error in the declaration or execution of an API function, you're likely to get a General Protection Fault (GPF) or another fatal error that will immediately shut down the Visual Basic environment. For this reason, you should carefully double-check the *Declare* statements and the arguments you pass to an API function, and you should always save your code before running the project.

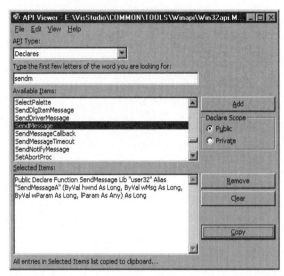

Figure A-1. *The API Viewer utility has been improved in Visual Basic 6 with the capability to set the scope of* Const *and* Type *directives and* Declare *statements.*

Multiline TextBox Controls

The *SendMessage* API function is very useful with multiline TextBox controls because only a small fraction of their features is exposed through standard properties and methods. For example, you can determine the number of lines in a multiline TextBox control by sending it an EM_GETLINECOUNT message:

```
LineCount = SendMessageByVal(Text1.hWnd, EM_GETLINECOUNT, 0, 0)
```

or you can use the EM_GETFIRSTVISIBLELINE message to determine which line is the first visible line. (Line numbers are zero-based.)

```
FirstVisibleLine = SendMessageByVal(Text1.hWnd, EM_GETFIRSTVISIBLELINE, 0, 0)
```

> **NOTE** All the examples shown in this appendix are available on the companion CD. To make the code more easily reusable, I've encapsulated all the examples in Function and Sub routines and stored them in BAS modules. Each module contains the declaration of the API functions used, as well as the *Const* directives that define all the necessary symbolic constants. On the CD, you'll also find demonstration programs that show all the routines in action. (See Figure A-2.)

The EM_LINESCROLL message enables you to programmatically scroll the contents of a TextBox control in four directions. You must pass the number of columns to scroll horizontally in *wParam* (positive values scroll right, negative values scroll left) and the number of lines to scroll vertically in *lParam* (positive values scroll down, negative values scroll up).

```
' Scroll one line down and (approximately) 4 characters to the right.
SendMessageByVal Text1.hWnd, EM_LINESCROLL, 4, 1
```

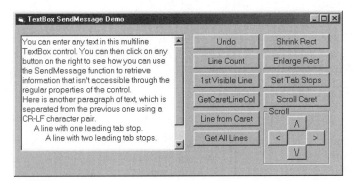

Figure A-2. *The program that demonstrates how to use the routines in the TextBox.bas module.*

Notice that the number of columns used for horizontal scrolling might not correspond to the actual number of characters scrolled if the TextBox control uses a nonfixed font. Moreover, horizontal scrolling doesn't work if the *ScrollBars* property is set to 2-Vertical. You can scroll the control's contents to ensure that the caret is visible using the EM_SCROLLCARET:

```
SendMessageByVal Text1.hWnd, EM_SCROLLCARET, 0, 0
```

One of the most annoying limitations of the standard TextBox control is that there's no way to find out how longer lines of text are split into multiple lines. Using the EM_FMTLINES message, you can ask the control to include the so-called *soft line breaks* in the string returned by its *Text* property. A soft line break is the point where the control splits a line because it's too long for the control's width. A soft line break is represented by the sequence CR-CR-LF. Hard line breaks, points at which the user has pressed the Enter key, are represented by the CR-LF sequence. When sending the EM_FMTLINES message, you must pass True in *wParam* to activate soft line breaks and False to disable them. I've prepared a routine that uses this feature to fill a String array with all the lines of text, as they appear in the control:

```
' Return an array with all the lines in the control.
' If the second optional argument is True, trailing CR-LFs are preserved.
Function GetAllLines(tb As TextBox, Optional KeepHardLineBreaks _
    As Boolean) As String()

    Dim result() As String, i As Long
    ' Activate soft line breaks.
    SendMessageByVal tb.hWnd, EM_FMTLINES, True, 0
    ' Retrieve all the lines in one operation. This operation leaves
    ' a trailing CR character for soft line breaks.
    result() = Split(tb.Text, vbCrLf)
    ' We need a loop to trim the residual CR characters. If the second
    ' argument is True, we manually add a CR-LF pair to all the lines that
    ' don't contain the residual CR char (they were hard line breaks).
```

(continued)

```
        For i = 0 To UBound(result)
            If Right$(result(i), 1) = vbCr Then
                result(i) = Left$(result(i), Len(result(i)) - 1)
            ElseIf KeepHardLineBreaks Then
                result(i) = result(i) & vbCrLf
            End If
        Next
        ' Deactivate soft line breaks.
        SendMessageByVal tb.hWnd, EM_FMTLINES, False, 0
        GetAllLines = result()
End Function
```

You can also retrieve one single line of text, using the EM_LINEINDEX message to determine where the line starts and the EM_LINELENGTH to determine its length. I've prepared a reusable routine that puts these two messages together:

```
Function GetLine(tb As TextBox, ByVal lineNum As Long) As String
    Dim charOffset As Long, lineLen As Long
    ' Retrieve the character offset of the first character of the line.
    charOffset = SendMessageByVal(tb.hWnd, EM_LINEINDEX, lineNum, 0)
    ' Now it's possible to retrieve the length of the line.
    lineLen = SendMessageByVal(tb.hWnd, EM_LINELENGTH, charOffset, 0)
    ' Extract the line text.
    GetLine = Mid$(tb.Text, charOffset + 1, lineLen)
End Function
```

The EM_LINEFROMCHAR message returns the number of the line given a character's offset; you can use this message and the EM_LINEINDEX message to determine the line and column coordinates of a character:

```
' Get the line and column coordinates of a given character.
' If charIndex is negative, it returns the coordinates of the caret.
Sub GetLineColumn(tb As TextBox, ByVal charIndex As Long, line As Long, _
    column As Long)
    ' Use the caret's offset if argument is negative.
    If charIndex < 0 Then charIndex = tb.SelStart
    ' Get the line number.
    line = SendMessageByVal(tb.hWnd, EM_LINEFROMCHAR, charIndex, 0)
    ' Get the column number by subtracting the line's start
    ' index from the character position.
    column = tb.SelStart - SendMessageByVal(tb.hWnd, EM_LINEINDEX, line, 0)
End Sub
```

Standard TextBox controls use their entire client area for editing. You can retrieve the dimension of such a formatting rectangle using the EM_GETRECT message, and you can use EM_SETRECT to modify its size as your needs dictate. In each instance, you need to include the definition of the RECT structure, which is also used by many other API functions:

```
Private Type RECT
    Left As Long
    Top As Long
    Right As Long
    Bottom As Long
End Type
```

I've prepared two routines that encapsulate these messages:

```
' Get the formatting rectangle.
Sub GetRect(tb As TextBox, Left As Long, Top As Long, Right As Long, _
    Bottom As Long)
    Dim lpRect As RECT
    SendMessage tb.hWnd, EM_GETRECT, 0, lpRect
    Left = lpRect.Left: Top = lpRect.Top
    Right = lpRect.Right: Bottom = lpRect.Bottom
End Sub

' Set the formatting rectangle, and refresh the control.
Sub SetRect(tb As TextBox, ByVal Left As Long, ByVal Top As Long, _
    ByVal Right As Long, ByVal Bottom As Long)
    Dim lpRect As RECT
    lpRect.Left = Left: lpRect.Top = Top
    lpRect.Right = Right: lpRect.Bottom = Bottom
    SendMessage tb.hWnd, EM_SETRECT, 0, lpRect
End Sub
```

For example, see how you can shrink the formatting rectangle along its horizontal dimension:

```
Dim Left As Long, Top As Long, Right As Long, Bottom As Long
GetRect tb, Left, Top, Right, Bottom
Left = Left + 10: Right = Right - 10
SetRect tb, Left, Top, Right, Bottom
```

One last thing that you can do with multiline TextBox controls is to set their tab stop positions. By default, the tab stops in a TextBox control are set at 32 dialog units from one stop to the next, where each dialog unit is one-fourth the average character width. You can modify such default distances using the EM_SETTABSTOPS message, as follows:

```
' Set the tab stop distance to 20 dialog units
' (that is, 5 characters of average width).
SendMessage Text1.hWnd, EM_SETTABSTOPS, 1, 20
```

You can even control the position of each individual tab stop by passing this message an array of Long elements in *lParam* as well as the number of elements in the array in *wParam*. Here's an example:

```
Dim tabs(1 To 3) As Long
' Set three tab stops approximately at character positions 5, 8, and 15.
tabs(1) = 20: tabs(2) = 32: tabs(3) = 60
SendMessage Text1.hWnd, EM_SETTABSTOPS, 3, tabs(1)
```

Notice that you pass an array to an API function by passing its first element by reference.

ListBox Controls

Next to TextBox controls, ListBox and ComboBox are the intrinsic controls that benefit most from the *SendMessage* API function. In this section, I describe the messages you can send to a ListBox control. In some situations, you can send a similar message to the ComboBox control as well to get the same result, even if the numeric value of the message is different. For example, you can retrieve the height in pixels of an item in the list portion of these two controls by sending them the LB_GETITEMHEIGHT (if you're dealing with a ListBox control) or the CB_GETITEMHEIGHT (if you're dealing with a ComboBox control). I've encapsulated these two messages in a polymorphic routine that works with both types of controls. (See Figure A-3.)

```
' The result of this routine is in pixels.
Function GetItemHeight(ctrl As Control) As Long
    Dim uMsg As Long
    If TypeOf ctrl Is ListBox Then
        uMsg = LB_GETITEMHEIGHT
    ElseIf TypeOf ctrl Is ComboBox Then
        uMsg = CB_GETITEMHEIGHT
    Else
        Exit Function
    End If
    GetItemHeight = SendMessageByVal(ctrl.hwnd, uMsg, 0, 0)
End Function
```

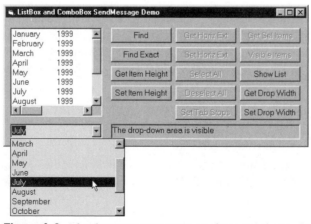

Figure A-3. *The demonstration program for using the* SendMessage *function with* ListBox *and ComboBox controls.*

You can also set a different height for the list items by using the LB_ SETITEMHEIGHT or CB_SETITEMHEIGHT message. While the height of an item isn't valuable information in itself, it lets you evaluate the number of visible elements in a ListBox control, data that isn't exposed as a property of the Visual Basic control. You can evaluate the number of visible elements by dividing the height of the internal area of the control—also known as the *client area* of the control—by the height of each item. To retrieve the height of the client area, you need another API function, *GetClientRect*:

```
Private Declare Function GetClientRect Lib "user32" (ByVal hWnd As Long, _
    lpRect As RECT) As Long
```

This is the function that puts all the pieces together and returns the number of items in a ListBox control that are entirely visible:

```
Function VisibleItems(lb As ListBox) As Long
    Dim lpRect As RECT, itemHeight As Long
    ' Get client rectangle area.
    GetClientRect lb.hWnd, lpRect
    ' Get the height of each item.
    itemHeight = SendMessageByVal(lb.hWnd, LB_GETITEMHEIGHT, 0, 0)
    ' Do the division.
    VisibleItems = (lpRect.Bottom - lpRect.Top) \ itemHeight
End Function
```

You can use this information to determine whether the ListBox control has a companion vertical scroll bar control:

```
HasCompanionScrollBar = (Visibleitems(List1) < List1.ListCount)
```

Windows provides messages for quickly searching for a string among the items of a ListBox or ComboBox control. More precisely, there are two messages for each control, one that performs a search for a partial match—that is, the search is successful if the searched string appears at the beginning of an element in the list portion—and one that looks for exact matches. You pass the index of the element from which you start the search to *wParam* (−1 to start from the beginning), and the string being searched to *lParam* by value. The search isn't case sensitive. Here's a reusable routine that encapsulates the four messages and returns the index of the matching element or −1 if the search fails. Of course, you can reach the same result with a loop over the ListBox items, but the API approach is usually faster:

```
Function FindString(ctrl As Control, ByVal search As String, Optional _
    startIndex As Long = -1, Optional ExactMatch As Boolean) As Long
    Dim uMsg As Long
    If TypeOf ctrl Is ListBox Then
        uMsg = IIf(ExactMatch, LB_FINDSTRINGEXACT, LB_FINDSTRING)
```

(continued)

```
    ElseIf TypeOf ctrl Is ComboBox Then
        uMsg = IIf(ExactMatch, CB_FINDSTRINGEXACT, CB_FINDSTRING)
    Else
        Exit Function
    End If
    FindString = SendMessageString(ctrl.hwnd, uMsg, startIndex, search)
End Function
```

Because the search starts with the element after the *startIndex* position, you can easily create a loop that prints all the matching elements:

```
' Print all the elements that begin with the "J" character.
index = -1
Do
    index = FindString(List1, "J", index, False)
    If index = -1 Then Exit Do
    Print List1.List(index)
Loop
```

A ListBox control can display a horizontal scroll bar if its contents are wider than its client areas, but this is another capability that isn't exposed by the Visual Basic control. To make the horizontal scroll bar appear, you must tell the control that it contains elements that are wider than its client area. (See Figure A-3.) You do this using the LB_SETHORIZONTALEXTENT message, which expects a width in pixels in the *wParam* argument:

```
' Inform the ListBox control that its contents are 400 pixels wide.
' If the control is narrower, a horizontal scroll bar will appear.
SendMessageByVal List1.hwnd, LB_SETHORIZONTALEXTENT, 400, 0
```

You can add a lot of versatility to standard ListBox controls by setting the positions of their tab stops. The technique is similar to the one used for TextBox controls. If you add to that the ability to display a horizontal scroll bar, you see that the ListBox control becomes a cheap means for displaying tables—you don't have to resort to external ActiveX controls. All you have to do is set the tab stop position to a suitable distance and then add lines of tab-delimited elements, as in the following code:

```
' Create a 3-column table using a ListBox.
' The three columns hold 5, 20, and 25 characters of average width.
Dim tabs(1 To 2) As Long
tabs(1) = 20: tabs(2) = 100
SendMessage List1.hWnd, LB_SETTABSTOPS, 2, tabs(1)
' Add a horizontal scroll bar, if necessary.
SendMessageByVal List1.hwnd, LB_SETHORIZONTALEXTENT, 400, 0
List1.AddItem "1" & vbTab & "John" & vbTab & "Smith"
List1.AddItem "2" & vbTab & "Robert" & vbTab & "Doe"
```

You can learn how to use a few other ListBox messages by browsing the source code of the demonstration program provided on the companion CD.

ComboBox Controls

As I explained in the previous section, ComboBox and ListBox controls supports some common messages, even though the names and the values of the corresponding symbolic constants are different. For example, you can read and modify the height of items in the list portion using the CB_GETITEMHEIGHT and CB_SETITEMHEIGHT messages, and you can search items using the CB_FINDSTRINGEXACT and CB_FINDSTRING messages.

But the ComboBox control also supports other interesting messages. For example, you can programmatically open and close the list portion of a drop-down ComboBox control using the CB_SHOWDROPDOWN message:

```
' Open the list portion.
SendMessageByVal Combo1.hWnd, CB_SHOWDROPDOWN, True, 0
' Then close it.
SendMessageByVal Combo1.hWnd, CB_SHOWDROPDOWN, False, 0
```

and you can retrieve the current visibility state of the list portion using the CB_GETDROPPEDSTATE message:

```
If SendMessageByVal(Combo1.hWnd, CB_GETDROPPEDSTATE, 0, 0) Then
    ' The list portion is visible.
End If
```

One of the most useful messages for ComboBox controls is CB_SETDROPPEDWIDTH, which lets you set the width of the ComboBox drop-down list although values less than the control's width are ignored:

```
' Make the drop-down list 300 pixels wide.
SendMessageByVal cb.hwnd, CB_SETDROPPEDWIDTH, 300, 0
```

(See Figure A-3 for an example of a ComboBox whose drop-down list is wider than usual.)

Finally, you can use the CB_LIMITTEXT message to set a maximum number of characters for the control; this is similar to the *MaxLength* property for TextBox controls, which is missing in ComboBox controls:

```
' Set the maximum length of text in a ComboBox control to 20 characters.
SendMessageByVal Combo1.hWnd, CB_LIMITTEXT, 20, 0
```

SYSTEM FUNCTIONS

Many internal Windows values and parameters are beyond Visual Basic's capabilities, but they're just an API function call away. In this section, I show how you can retrieve some important system settings and how you can augment Visual Basic support for the mouse and the keyboard.

Windows Directories and Versions

Even though Visual Basic hides most of the complexities of the operating system, as well as the differences among the many Windows versions around, sometimes you must distinguish one from another—for example, to account for minor differences between Windows 9x and Windows NT. You can do this by examining the higher-order bit of the Long value returned by the *GetVersion* API function:

```
Private Declare Function GetVersion Lib "kernel32" () As Long

If GetVersion() And &H80000000 Then
    MsgBox "Running under Windows 95/98"
Else
    MsgBox "Running under Windows NT"
End If
```

If you need to determine the actual Windows version, you need the *GetVersionEx* API function, which returns information about the running operating system in a UDT:

```
Type OSVERSIONINFO
    dwOSVersionInfoSize As Long
    dwMajorVersion As Long
    dwMinorVersion As Long
    dwBuildNumber As Long
    dwPlatformId As Long
    szCSDVersion As String * 128
End Type

Private Declare Function GetVersionEx Lib "kernel32" Alias _
    "GetVersionExA" (lpVersionInformation As OSVERSIONINFO) As Long

Dim os As OSVERSIONINFO, ver As String
' The function expects the UDT size in the UDT's first element.
os.dwOSVersionInfoSize = Len(os)
GetVersionEx os
ver = os.dwMajorVersion & "." & Right$("0" & Format$(os.dwMinorVersion), 2)
Print "Windows Version = " & ver
Print "Windows Build Number = " & os.dwBuildNumber
```

Windows 95 returns a version number 4.00, and Windows 98 returns version 4.10. (See Figure A-4.) You can use the build number to identify different service packs.

All tips and tricks collections show how you can retrieve the path to the main Windows and System directories, which are often useful for locating other files that might interest you. These functions are helpful for another reason as well: They show you how to receive strings from an API function. In general, no API function directly returns a string; instead, all the functions that return a string value to the calling program require that you create a receiving string buffer—typically, a string filled with spaces or null characters—and you pass it to the routine. Most of the time, you must pass the buffer's length in another argument so that the API function doesn't accidentally write in the buffer more characters than allowed. For example, this is the declaration of the *GetWindowsDirectory* API function:

```
Private Declare Function GetWindowsDirectory Lib "kernel32" Alias _
    "GetWindowsDirectoryA" (ByVal lpBuffer As String, _
    ByVal nSize As Long) As Long
```

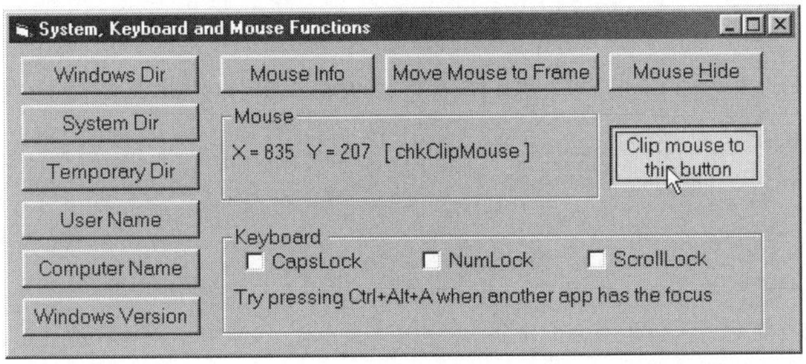

Figure A-4. *The sample program demonstrates several system, keyboard, and mouse API functions.*

You use this function by allocating a large-enough buffer, and then you pass it to the function. The return value of the function is the actual number of characters in the result string, and you can use this value to trim off characters in excess:

```
Dim buffer As String, length As Integer
buffer = Space$(512)
length = GetWindowsDirectory(buffer, Len(buffer))
Print "Windows Directory = " & Left$(buffer, length)
```

You can use the same method to determine the path of the Windows\System directory, using the *GetSystemDirectory* API function:

```
Private Declare Function GetSystemDirectory Lib "kernel32" Alias _
    "GetSystemDirectoryA" (ByVal lpBuffer As String, _
    ByVal nSize As Long) As Long

Dim buffer As String, length As Integer
buffer = Space$(512)
length = GetSystemDirectory(buffer, Len(buffer))
Print "System Directory = " & Left$(buffer, length)
```

The *GetTempPath* API function uses a similar syntax—although the order of arguments is reversed—and returns a valid directory name for storing temporary files, including a trailing backslash character (such as C:\WINDOWS\TEMP\):

```
Private Declare Function GetTempPath Lib "kernel32" Alias "GetTempPathA" _
    (ByVal nBufferLength As Long, ByVal lpBuffer As String) As Long

Dim buffer As String, length As Integer
buffer = Space$(512)
length = GetTempPath (Len(buffer), buffer)
Print "Temporary Directory = " & Left$(buffer, length)
```

The *GetUserName* function returns the name of the user currently logged in. At first glance, this function appears to use the same syntax as the functions I've just described. The documentation reveals, however, that it doesn't return the length of the result but just a zero value to indicate a failure or 1 to indicate the success of the operation. In this situation, you must extract the result from the buffer by searching for the Null character that all API functions append to result strings:

```
Private Declare Function GetUserName Lib "advapi32.dll" Alias _
    "GetUserNameA" (ByVal lpBuffer As String, nSize As Long) As Long

Dim buffer As String * 512, length As Long
If GetUserName buffer, Len(buffer) Then
    ' Search the trailing Null character.
    length = InStr(buffer, vbNullChar) - 1
    Print "User Name = " & Left$(buffer, length)
Else
    Print "GetUserName function failed"
End If
```

The *GetComputerName* API function, which retrieves the name of the computer that's executing the program, uses yet another method: You must pass the length of the buffer in a *ByRef* argument. On exit from the function, this argument holds the length of the result:

```
Private Declare Function GetComputerName Lib "kernel32" Alias _
    "GetComputerNameA" (ByVal lpBuffer As String, nSize As Long) As Long

Dim buffer As String * 512, length As Long
length = Len(buffer)
If GetComputerName(buffer, length) Then
    ' Returns nonzero if successful, and modifies the length argument
    MsgBox "Computer Name = " & Left$(buffer, length)
End If
```

The Keyboard

Visual Basic's keyboard events let you know exactly which keys are pressed and when. At times, however, it's useful to determine whether a given key is pressed even when you're not inside a keyboard event procedure. The pure Visual Basic solution is to store the value of the pressed key in a module-level or global variable, but it's a solution that negatively impacts the reusability of the code. Fortunately, you can easily retrieve the current state of a given key using the *GetAsyncKeyState* function:

```
Private Declare Function GetAsyncKeyState Lib "user32" _
    (ByVal vKey As Long) As Integer
```

This function accepts a virtual key code and returns an Integer value whose high-order bit is set if the corresponding key is pressed. You can use all the Visual Basic vbKey*xxxx* symbolic constants as arguments to this function. For example, you can determine whether any of the shift keys is being pressed using this code:

```
Dim msg As String
If GetAsyncKeyState(vbKeyShift) And &H8000 Then msg = msg & "SHIFT "
If GetAsyncKeyState(vbKeyControl) And &H8000 Then msg = msg & "CTRL "
If GetAsyncKeyState(vbKeyMenu) And &H8000 Then msg = msg & "ALT "
' lblKeyboard is a Label control that displays the shift key states.
lblKeyboard.Caption = msg
```

An interesting characteristic of the *GetAsynchKeyState* function is that it works even if the application doesn't have the input focus. This capability lets you build a Visual Basic program that reacts to hot keys even if users press them while they're working with another application. To use this API function to trap hot keys, you need to add some code into a Timer control's *Timer* event procedure and set the Timer's *Interval* property to a small-enough value—for example, 200 milliseconds:

```
' Detect the Ctrl+Alt+A key combination.
Private Sub Timer1_Timer()
    If GetAsyncKeyState(vbKeyA) And &H8000 Then
        If GetAsyncKeyState(vbKeyControl) And &H8000 Then
            If GetAsyncKeyState(vbKeyMenu) And &H8000 Then
                ' Process the Ctrl+Alt+A hot key here.
            End If
        End If
    End If
End Sub
```

You can streamline your code by taking advantage of the following reusable routine, which can test the state of up to three keys:

```
Function KeysPressed(KeyCode1 As KeyCodeConstants, Optional KeyCode2 As _
    KeyCodeConstants, Optional KeyCode3 As KeyCodeConstants) As Boolean
    If GetAsyncKeyState(KeyCode1) >= 0 Then Exit Function
    If KeyCode2 = 0 Then KeysPressed = True: Exit Function
    If GetAsyncKeyState(KeyCode2) >= 0 Then Exit Function
    If KeyCode3 = 0 Then KeysPressed = True: Exit Function
    If GetAsyncKeyState(KeyCode3) >= 0 Then Exit Function
    KeysPressed = True
End Function
```

The three arguments are declared as KeyCodeConstant (an enumerated type defined in the Visual Basic runtime library) so that IntelliSense automatically helps you write the code for this function. See how you can rewrite the previous example that traps the Ctrl+Alt+A hot key:

```
If KeysPressed(vbKeyA, vbKeyMenu, vbKeyControl) Then
    ' Process the Ctrl+Alt+A hot key here.
End If
```

You can also modify the current state of a key, say, to programmatically change the state of the CapsLock, NumLock, and ScrollLock keys. For an example of this technique, see the "Toggling the State of Lock Keys" section in Chapter 10.

The Mouse

The support Visual Basic offers to mouse programming is defective in a few areas. As is true for the keyboard and its event procedures, you can derive a few bits of information about the mouse's position and the state of its buttons only inside a *MouseDown*, *MouseUp*, or *MouseMove* event procedure, which makes the creation of reusable routines in BAS modules a difficult task. Even more annoying, mouse events are raised only for the control under the mouse cursor, which forces you to write a lot of code just to find out where the mouse is in any given moment. Fortunately, querying the mouse through an API function is really simple.

To begin with, you don't need a special function to retrieve the state of mouse buttons because you can use the *GetAsyncKeyState* function with the special vbKeyLButton, vbKeyRButton, and vbKeyMButton symbolic constants. Here's a routine that returns the current state of mouse buttons in the same bit-coded format as the *Button* parameter received by *Mousexxxx* event procedures:

```
Function MouseButton() As Integer
    If GetAsyncKeyState(vbKeyLButton) < 0 Then
        MouseButton = 1
    End If
    If GetAsyncKeyState(vbKeyRButton) < 0 Then
        MouseButton = MouseButton Or 2
    End If
    If GetAsyncKeyState(vbKeyMButton) < 0 Then
        MouseButton = MouseButton Or 4
    End If
End Function
```

The Windows API includes a function for reading the position of the mouse cursor:

```
Private Type POINTAPI
    X As Long
    Y As Long
End Type
```

```
Private Declare Function GetCursorPos Lib "user32" (lpPoint As POINTAPI) _
    As Long
```

In both cases, the coordinates are in pixels and relative to the screen:

```
' Display current mouse screen coordinates in pixels using a Label control.
Dim lpPoint As POINTAPI
GetCursorPos lpPoint
lblMouseState = "X = " & lpPoint.X & "   Y = " & lpPoint.Y
```

To convert screen coordinates to a pair of coordinates relative to the client area of a window—that is, the area of a window inside its border—you can use the *ScreenToClient* API function:

```
Private Declare Function ScreenToClient Lib "user32" (ByVal hWnd As Long, _
    lpPoint As POINTAPI) As Long


' Display mouse screen coordinates relative to current form.
Dim lpPoint As POINTAPI
GetCursorPos lpPoint
ScreenToClient Me.hWnd, lpPoint
lblMouseState = "X = " & lpPoint.X & "   Y = " & lpPoint.Y
```

The *SetCursorPos* API function lets you move the mouse cursor anywhere on the screen, something that you can't do with standard Visual Basic code:

```
Private Declare Function SetCursorPos Lib "user32" (ByVal X As Long, _
    ByVal Y As Long) As Long
```

When you use this function, you often need to convert from client coordinates to screen coordinates, which you do with the *ClientToScreen* API function. The following code snippet moves the mouse cursor to the center of a push button:

```
Private Declare Function ClientToScreen Lib "user32" (ByVal hWnd As Long, _
    lpPoint As POINTAPI) As Long


' Get the coordinates (in pixels) of the center of the Command1 button.
' The coordinates are relative to the button's client area.
Dim lpPoint As POINTAPI
lpPoint.X = ScaleX(Command1.Width / 2, vbTwips, vbPixels)
lpPoint.Y = ScaleY(Command1.Height / 2, vbTwips, vbPixels)
' Convert to screen coordinates.
ClientToScreen Command1.hWnd, lpPoint
' Move the mouse cursor to that point.
SetCursorPos lpPoint.X, lpPoint.Y
```

In some circumstances, for example, during drag-and-drop operations, you might want to prevent the user from moving the mouse outside a given region. You can achieve this behavior by setting up a rectangular *clipping area* with the *ClipCursor* API function. You'll often need to clip the mouse cursor to a given window, which you can do by retrieving the window's client area rectangle with the *GetClientRect* API function and convert the result to screen coordinates. The following routine does everything for you:

```
Private Declare Function ClipCursor Lib "user32" (lpRect As Any) As Long

Sub ClipMouseToWindow(ByVal hWnd As Long)
    Dim lpPoint As POINTAPI, lpRect As RECT
    ' Retrieve the coordinates of the upper-left corner of the window.
    ClientToScreen hWnd, lpPoint
    ' Get the client screen rectangle.
    GetClientRect hWnd, lpRect
    ' Manually convert the rectangle to screen coordinates.
    lpRect.Left = lpRect.Left + lpPoint.X
    lpRect.Top = lpRect.Top + lpPoint.Y
    lpRect.Right = lpRect.Right + lpPoint.X
    lpRect.Bottom = lpRect.Bottom + lpPoint.Y
    ' Enforce the clipping.
    ClipCursor lpRect
End Sub
```

Here's an example that uses the previous routine and then cancels the clipping effect:

```
' Clip the mouse cursor to the current form's client area.
ClipMouseToWindow Me.hWnd
...
' When you don't need the clipping any longer. (Don't forget this!)
ClipCursor ByVal 0&
```

(Remember that a window automatically loses the mouse capture if it executes a *MsgBox* or *InputBox* statement.) Windows normally sends mouse messages to the window under the cursor. The only exception to this rule occurs when the user presses a mouse button on a window and then drags the mouse cursor outside it. In this situation, the window continues to receive mouse messages until the button is released. But sometimes it's convenient to receive mouse notifications even when the mouse is outside the window's boundaries.

Consider the following situation: You want to provide the user with a visual clue when the mouse cursor enters the area of a control—for example, by changing the control's background color. You can achieve this effect simply by changing the control's *BackColor* property in its *MouseMove* event because this event fires as soon as the mouse cursor hovers over the control. Unluckily, Visual Basic doesn't fire an event in a control when the mouse cursor exits its client area, so you don't know when to restore the original background color. Using pure Visual Basic, you're forced to write code inside the *MouseMove* events of the forms and of all the other controls on the form's surface, or you must have a Timer that periodically monitors where the mouse is. By no means is this an elegant or efficient solution.

A better approach would be to capture the mouse when the cursor enters the control's client area, using the *SetCapture* API function. When a form or a control captures the mouse, it receives mouse messages until the user clicks outside the form or the control or until the mouse capture is explicitly relinquished through a *ReleaseCapture* API function. This technique permits you to solve the problem by writing code in one single procedure:

```
' Add these declarations to a BAS module.
Private Declare Function SetCapture Lib "user32" (ByVal hWnd As Long) _
    As Long
Private Declare Function ReleaseCapture Lib "user32" () As Long
Private Declare Function GetCapture Lib "user32" () As Long


' Change the BackColor of Frame1 control to yellow when the mouse enters
' the control's client area, and restore it when the mouse leaves it.
Private Sub Frame1_MouseMove(Button As Integer, Shift As Integer, _
    X As Single, Y As Single)
    ' Set the mouse capture unless the control already has it.
    ' (The GetCapture API function returns the handle of the window that
    ' has the mouse capture.)
    If GetCapture <> Frame1.hWnd Then
        SetCapture Frame1.hWnd
        Frame1.BackColor = vbYellow
    ElseIf X < 0 Or Y < 0 Or X > Frame1.Width Or Y > Frame1.Height Then
        ' If the mouse cursor is outside the Frame's client area, release
        ' the mouse capture and restore the BackColor property.
        ReleaseCapture
        Frame1.BackColor = vbButtonFace
    End If
End Sub
```

You can see this technique in action in the demonstration program shown in Figure A-4. Anytime the user moves the mouse onto or away from the topmost Frame control, the control's background color changes.

The *WindowsFromPoint* API function often comes in handy when you're working with the mouse because it returns the handle of the window at given screen coordinates:

```
Private Declare Function WindowFromPointAPI Lib "user32" Alias _
    "WindowFromPoint" (ByVal xPoint As Long, ByVal yPoint As Long) As Long
```

This routine returns the handle of the window under the mouse cursor:

```
Function WindowFromMouse() As Long
    Dim lpPoint As POINTAPI
    GetCursorPos lpPoint
    WindowFromMouse = WindowFromPoint(lpPoint.X, lpPoint.Y)
End Function
```

For example, you can quickly determine from within a form module which control is under the mouse cursor using the following approach:

```
Dim handle As Long, ctrl As Control
On Error Resume Next
handle = WindowFromMouse()
For Each ctrl In Me.Controls
    If ctrl.hWnd <> handle Then
        ' Not on this control, or hWnd property isn't supported.
    Else
        ' For simplicity's sake, this routine doesn't account for elements
        ' of control arrays.
        Print "Mouse is over control " & ctrl.Name
        Exit For
    End If
Next
```

For more information, see the source code of the demonstration application on the companion CD.

THE WINDOWS REGISTRY

The Windows Registry is the area where the operating system and most applications store their configuration values. You must be able to read as well as to write data into the Registry in order to build flexible applications that adapt themselves to their environment.

Visual Basic Built-In Functions

Unfortunately, the support for the Registry offered by Visual Basic leaves much to be desired and is limited to the following four commands and functions:

```
' Save a value.
SaveSetting AppName, Section, Key, Setting
' Read a value. (The Default argument is optional.)
value = GetSetting(AppName, Section, Key, Default)
' Return a list of settings and their values.
values = GetAllSettings(AppName, Section)
' Delete a value. (Section and Key arguments are optional.)
DeleteSetting AppName, Section, Key
```

These four commands can't read and write to an arbitrary area in the Registry but are limited to the *HKEY_CURRENT_USER\Software\VB and VBA Program Settings* subtree of the Registry. For example, you can use the *SaveSetting* function to store the initial position and size of the main form in the MyInvoicePrg application:

```
SaveSetting "MyInvoicePrg", "frmMain", "Left", frmMain.Left
SaveSetting "MyInvoicePrg", "frmMain", "Top", frmMain.Top
```

```
SaveSetting "MyInvoicePrg", "frmMain", "Width", frmMain.Width
SaveSetting "MyInvoicePrg", "frmMain", "Height", frmMain.Height
```

You can see the result of this sequence of statements in Figure A-5.

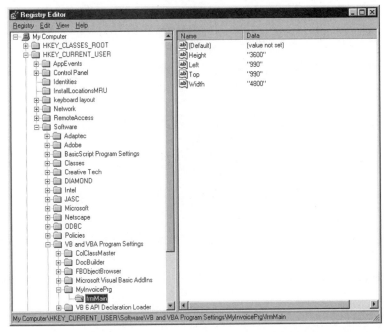

Figure A-5. *All Visual Basic Registry functions read and write values in the* HKEY_CURRENT_USER\Software\VB and VBA Program Settings *subtree.*

You can then read back these settings using the *GetSetting* function:

```
' Use the Move method to avoid multiple Resize and Paint events.
frmMain.Move GetSetting("MyInvoicePrg", "frmMain", "Left", "1000"), _
    GetSetting("MyInvoicePrg", "frmMain", "Top", "800"), _
    GetSetting("MyInvoicePrg", "frmMain", "Width", "5000"), _
    GetSetting("MyInvoicePrg", "frmMain", "Height", "4000")
```

If the specified key doesn't exist, the *GetSetting* function either returns the values passed to the *Default* argument or it returns an empty string if that argument is omitted. *GetAllSettings* returns a two-dimensional array, which contains all the keys and values under a given section:

```
Dim values As Variant, i As Long
values = GetAllSettings("MyInvoicePrg", "frmMain")
' Each row holds two items, the key name and the key value.
For i = 0 To UBound(settings)
    Print "Key =" & values(i, 0) & "  Value = " & values(i, 1)
Next
```

The last function of the group, *DeleteSetting*, can delete an individual key, or it can delete all the keys under a given section if you omit its last argument:

```
' Delete the "Left" key for the frmMain form.
DeleteSetting "MyInvoicePrg", "frmMain", "Left"
' Delete all the settings for the frmMain form.
DeleteSetting "MyInvoicePrg", "frmMain"
```

The demonstration program shown in Figure A-6 demonstrates how you can use the Visual Basic built-in Registry functions to save and to restore form settings.

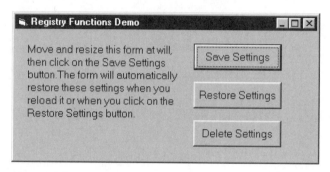

Figure A-6. *The demonstration program contains reusable routines for saving and restoring form settings to the Registry.*

The API Functions

While the Visual Basic built-in functions are barely versatile enough for saving and restoring program configuration values, they entirely lack the functionality for accessing any region of the Registry, which you must have to read some important settings of the operating system. Luckily, the Windows API contains all the functions you need to perform this task.

> **WARNING** You must be very careful when you play with the Registry in this way because you might corrupt the installation of other applications or the operating system itself, and you might even be forced to reinstall them. But in general, you can't do much harm if you simply read values in the Registry and don't write to it. To reduce risks, however, you might want to back up your system Registry so that you have a copy to restore if something goes wrong.

Predefined keys

Before starting to play with API functions, you must have a broad idea of how the Registry is arranged. The system Registry is a hierarchical structure that consists of keys, subkeys, and values. More precisely, the Registry has a number of predefined top-level keys, which I've summarized in Table A-1.

Key	Value	Description
HKEY_CLASSES_ROOT	&H80000000	The subtree that contains all the information about COM components installed on the machine. (It's actually a subtree of the HKEY _LOCAL_MACHINE key but also appears as a top-level key.)
HKEY_CURRENT_USER	&H80000001	The subtree that contains the preferences for the current user. (It's actually a subtree of the HKEY_USERS key but also appears as a top-level key.)
HKEY_LOCAL_MACHINE	&H80000002	The subtree that contains information about the physical configuration of the computer, including installed hardware and software.
HKEY_USERS	&H80000003	The subtree that contains the default user configuration and also contains information about the current user.
HKEY_PERFORMANCE_DATA	&H80000004	The subtree that collects performance data; data is actually stored outside the Registry, but appears to be part of it. (It's available only in Windows NT.)
HKEY_CURRENT_CONFIG	&H80000005	The subtree that contains data about the current configuration. (It corresponds to a subtree of the HKEY_LOCAL_MACHINE key but also appears as a top-level key.)
HKEY_DYN_DATA	&H80000006	The subtree that collects performance data; this portion of the Registry is reinitialized at each reboot. (It's available only in Windows 95 and 98.)

Table A-1. *The predefined Registry keys.*

Each Registry key has a name, which is a string of up to 260 printable characters that can't include backslash characters (\) or wildcards (? and *). Names beginning with a period are reserved. Each key can contain subkeys and values. In Windows 3.1, a key could hold only one unnamed value, while 32-bit platforms allow an unlimited number of values. (But unnamed values, called *default values*, are maintained for backward compatibility.)

> **NOTE** In general, Windows 9x and Windows NT differ in how they deal with the Registry. In Windows NT, you must account for additional security issues, and in general you have no guarantee that you can open an existing Registry key or value. In this section, I stayed clear of such details and focused on those functions that behave the same way for all the Windows platforms. For this reason, I've sometimes used "old" Registry functions instead of newer ones, which you recognize by the *Ex* suffix in their names, a suffix that stands for "extended."

Working with keys

Navigating the Registry is similar to exploring a directory tree: To reach a given file, you must open the directory that contains it. Likewise, you reach a Registry subkey from another open key at a higher level in the Registry hierarchy. You must open a key before reading its subkeys and its values, and to do that you must supply the handle of another open key in the Registry. After you've worked with a key, you must close it, as you do with files. The only keys that are always open and that don't need to be closed are the top-level keys listed in Table A-1. You open a key with the *RegOpenKeyEx* API function:

```
Declare Function RegOpenKeyEx Lib "advapi32.dll" Alias "RegOpenKeyExA" _
    (ByVal hKey As Long, ByVal lpSubKey As String, ByVal ulOptions As _
    Long, ByVal samDesired As Long, phkResult As Long) As Long
```

hKey is the handle of an open key and can be one of the values listed in Table A-1 or the handle of a key that you've opened previously. *lpSubKey* is the path from the *hKey* key to the key that you want to open. *ulOptions* is a reserved argument and must be 0. *samDesired* is the type of access you want for the key that you want to open and is a symbolic constant, such as KEY_READ, KEY_WRITE, or KEY_ALL_ACCESS. Finally, *phkResult* is a Long variable passed by reference, which receives the handle of the key opened by the function if the operation is successful. You can test the success of the open operation by looking at the return value of the *RegOpenKeyEx* function: A zero value means that the operation succeeded, and any non-zero value is an error code. This behavior is common to all the Registry API functions, so you can easily set up a function that tests the success state of any call. (See the MSDN documentation for the list of error codes.)

As I mentioned earlier, you must close any open key as soon as you don't need it any longer, which you do with the *RegCloseKey* API function. This function takes the handle of the key to be closed as its only argument, and returns 0 if the operation is successful:

```
Declare Function RegCloseKey Lib "advapi32.dll" (ByVal hKey As Long) _
    As Long
```

Frequently, the presence of a subkey is enough to store significant data in a key. For example, if the machine has a math coprocessor, Windows creates the following key:

```
HKEY_LOCAL_MACHINE\HARDWARE\DESCRIPTION\System\FloatingPointProcessor
```

so you can test the presence of the coprocessor using this routine:

```
' Assumes that all symbolic constants are correctly declared elsewhere.
Function MathProcessor() As Boolean
    Dim hKey As Long, Key As String
    Key = "HARDWARE\DESCRIPTION\System\FloatingPointProcessor"
    If RegOpenKeyEx(HKEY_LOCAL_MACHINE, Key, 0, KEY_READ, hKey) = 0 Then
```

```
        ' If the open operation succeeded, the key exists.
        MathProcessor = True
        ' Important: close the key before exiting.
        RegCloseKey hKey
    End If
End Function
```

As you might expect, the Registry API includes a function for creating new keys, but its syntax is overly complex:

```
Declare Function RegCreateKeyEx Lib "advapi32.dll" Alias "RegCreateKeyExA"_
    (ByVal hKey As Long, ByVal lpSubKey As String, ByVal Reserved As Long,_
    ByVal lpClass As Long, ByVal dwOptions As Long, _
    ByVal samDesired As Long, ByVal lpSecurityAttributes As Long, _
    phkResult As Long, lpdwDisposition As Long) As Long
```

Most of the arguments have the same names and syntax as those that I've already described for the *RegOpenKeyEx* function, and I won't describe most of the new arguments because they constitute a topic too advanced for this context. You can pass a Long variable to the *lpdwDisposition* argument, and when the function returns you can test the contents in this variable. The value REG_CREATED_NEW_KEY (1) means that the key didn't exist and has been created and opened by this function, whereas the value REG_OPENED_EXISTING_KEY (2) means that the key already existed and the function just opened it without altering the Registry in any way. To reduce the confusion, I use the following routine, which creates a key if necessary and returns True if the key already existed:

```
Function CreateRegistryKey(ByVal hKey As Long, ByVal KeyName As String) _
    As Boolean
    Dim handle As Long, disp As Long
    If RegCreateKeyEx(hKey, KeyName, 0, 0, 0, 0, 0, handle, disp) Then
        Err.Raise 1001, , "Unable to create the Registry key"
    Else
        ' Return True if the key already existed.
        If disp = REG_OPENED_EXISTING_KEY Then CreateRegistryKey = True
        ' Close the key.
        RegCloseKey handle
    End If
End Function
```

The following code snippet shows how you can use the *CreateRegistryKey* function to create a key with the name of your company under the key HKEY_CURRENT_USER\Software, which contains another key with the name of your application. This is the approach followed by most commercial applications, including all those by Microsoft and other leading software companies:

```
CreateRegistryKey HKEY_CURRENT_USER, "Software\YourCompany"
CreateRegistryKey HKEY_CURRENT_USER, "Software\YourCompany\YourApplication"
```

> **NOTE** The *CreateRegistryKey* function, like all other Registry routines provided on the companion CD, always closes a key before exiting. This approach makes them "safe," but it also imposes a slight performance penalty because each call opens and closes a key that you might have to reopen immediately afterwards, as in the preceding example. You can't always have it all.

Finally, you can delete a key from the Registry, using the *RegDeleteKey* API function:

```
Declare Function RegDeleteKey Lib "advapi32.dll" Alias "RegDeleteKeyA" _
    (ByVal hKey As Long, ByVal lpSubKey As String) As Long
```

Under Windows 95 and 98, this function deletes a key and all its subkeys, whereas under Windows NT you get an error if the key being deleted contains other keys. For this reason, you should manually delete all the subkeys first:

```
' Delete the keys created in the previous example.
RegDeleteKey HKEY_CURRENT_USER, "Software\YourCompany\YourApplication"
RegDeleteKey HKEY_CURRENT_USER, "Software\YourCompany"
```

Working with values

In many cases, a Registry key contains one or more values, so you must learn how to read these values. To do so, you need the *RegQueryValueEx* API function:

```
Declare Function RegQueryValueEx Lib "advapi32.dll" Alias _
    "RegQueryValueExA" (ByVal hKey As Long, ByVal lpValueName As String, _
    ByVal lpReserved As Long, lpType As Long, lpData As Any, _
    lpcbData As Long) As Long
```

hKey is the handle of the open key that contains the value. *lpValueName* is the name of the value you want to read. (Use an empty string for the default value.) *lpReserved* must be zero. *lpType* is the type of the key. *lpData* is a pointer to a buffer that will receive the data. *lpcbData* is a Long variable passed by reference; on entry it has to contain the size in bytes of the buffer, and on exit it contains the number of bytes actually stored in the buffer. Most Registry values you'll want to read are of type REG_DWORD (a Long value), REG_SZ (a null-terminated string), or REG_BINARY (array of bytes).

The Visual Basic environment stores some of its configuration settings as values under the following key:

```
HKEY_CURRENT_USER\Software\Microsoft\VBA\Microsoft Visual Basic
```

You can read the FontHeight value to retrieve the size of the font used for the code editor, whereas the FontFace value holds the name of the font. Because the former value is a Long number and the latter is a string, you need two different coding techniques for them. Reading a Long value is simpler because you just pass a Long variable by reference to *lpData* and pass its length in bytes (which is 4 bytes) in *lpcbData*. To retrieve a string value, on the other hand, you must prepare a buffer and pass it by value, and when the function returns you must strip the excess characters:

```
Dim KeyName As String, handle As Long
Dim FontHeight As Long, FontFace As String, FontFaceLen As Long

KeyName = "Software\Microsoft\VBA\Microsoft Visual Basic"
If RegOpenKeyEx(HKEY_CURRENT_USER, KeyName, 0, KEY_READ, handle) Then
    MsgBox "Unable to open the specified Registry key"
Else
    ' Read the "FontHeight" value.
    If RegQueryValueEx(handle, "FontHeight", 0, REG_DWORD, FontHeight, 4) _
        = 0 Then
        Print "Face Height = " & FontHeight
    End If

    ' Read the "FontFace" value.
    FontFaceLen = 128                        ' Prepare the receiving buffer.
    FontFace = Space$(FontFaceLen)
    ' Notice that FontFace is passed using ByVal.
    If RegQueryValueEx(handle, "FontFace", 0, REG_SZ, ByVal FontFace, _
        FontFaceLen) = 0 Then
        ' Trim excess characters, including the trailing Null char.
        FontFace = Left$(FontFace, FontFaceLen - 1)
        Print "Face Name = " & FontFace
    End If
    ' Close the Registry key.
    RegCloseKey handle
End If
```

Because you need to read Registry values often, I've prepared a reusable function that performs all the necessary operations and returns the value in a Variant. You can also specify a default value, which you can use if the specified key or value doesn't exist. This tactic is similar to what you do with the Visual Basic intrinsic *GetSetting* function.

```
Function GetRegistryValue(ByVal hKey As Long, ByVal KeyName As String, _
    ByVal ValueName As String, ByVal KeyType As Integer, _
    Optional DefaultValue As Variant = Empty) As Variant

    Dim handle As Long, resLong As Long
    Dim resString As String, length As Long
    Dim resBinary() As Byte
    ' Prepare the default result.
    GetRegistryValue = DefaultValue
    ' Open the key, exit if not found.
    If RegOpenKeyEx(hKey, KeyName, 0, KEY_READ, handle) Then Exit Function
```

(continued)

```
        Select Case KeyType
            Case REG_DWORD
                ' Read the value, use the default if not found.
                If RegQueryValueEx(handle, ValueName, 0, REG_DWORD, _
                    resLong, 4) = 0 Then
                    GetRegistryValue = resLong
                End If
            Case REG_SZ
                length = 1024: resString = Space$(length)
                If RegQueryValueEx(handle, ValueName, 0, REG_SZ, _
                    ByVal resString, length) = 0 Then
                    ' If value is found, trim excess characters.
                    GetRegistryValue = Left$(resString, length - 1)
                End If
            Case REG_BINARY
                length = 4096
                ReDim resBinary(length - 1) As Byte
                If RegQueryValueEx(handle, ValueName, 0, REG_BINARY, _
                    resBinary(0), length) = 0 Then
                    ReDim Preserve resBinary(length - 1) As Byte
                    GetRegistryValue = resBinary()
                End If
            Case Else
                Err.Raise 1001, , "Unsupported value type"
        End Select
        RegCloseKey handle
End Function
```

To create a new Registry value or to modify the data of an existing value, you use the *RegSetValueEx* API function:

```
Declare Function RegSetValueEx Lib "advapi32.dll" Alias "RegSetValueExA" _
    (ByVal hKey As Long, ByVal lpValueName As String, _
    ByVal Reserved As Long, ByVal dwType As Long, lpData As Any, _
    ByVal cbData As Long) As Long
```

Let's see how we can add a LastLogin value in the key HKEY_CURRENT_USER\Software\YourCompany\YourApplication, that we created in the previous section:

```
Dim handle As Long, strValue As String
' Open the key, check whether any error occurred.
If RegOpenKeyEx(HKEY_CURRENT_USER, "Software\YourCompany\YourApplication",_
    0, KEY_WRITE, handle) Then
    MsgBox "Unable to open the key."
Else
    ' We want to add a "LastLogin" value of type string.
    strValue = FormatDateTime(Now)
    ' Strings must be passed using ByVal.
    RegSetValueEx handle, "LastLogin", 0, REG_SZ, ByVal strValue, _
```

```
        Len(strValue)
    ' Don't forget to close the key.
    RegCloseKey handle
End If
```

On the companion CD, you'll find the source code of the *SetRegistryValue* function, which automatically uses the correct syntax according to the type of value you're creating. Finally, by using the *RegDeleteValue* API function, you can delete a value under a key that you opened previously:

```
Declare Function RegDeleteValue Lib "advapi32.dll" Alias "RegDeleteValueA"_
    (ByVal hKey As Long, ByVal lpValueName As String) As Long
```

Enumerating keys and values

When you're exploring the Registry, you often need to enumerate all the keys or all the values under a key. The function you use to enumerate keys is *RegEnumKey*:

```
Private Declare Function RegEnumKey Lib "advapi32.dll" _
    Alias "RegEnumKeyA" (ByVal hKey As Long, ByVal dwIndex As Long, _
    ByVal lpName As String, ByVal cbName As Long) As Long
```

You must pass the handle of an open Registry key in the *hKey* argument, and then you repeatedly call this function, passing increasing index values in *dwIndex*. The *lpName* argument must be a string buffer of at least 260 characters (the maximum length for a key name), and *lpcbName* is the length of the buffer. When you exit the routine, the buffer contains a Null-terminated string, so you have to strip all the excess characters. To simplify your job, I've prepared a function that iterates on all the subkeys of a given key and returns a String array that contains the names of all the subkeys:

```
Function EnumRegistryKeys(ByVal hKey As Long, ByVal KeyName As String) _
    As String()
    Dim handle As Long, index As Long, length As Long
    ReDim result(0 To 100) As String

    ' Open the key, exit if not found.
    If Len(Keyname) Then
        If RegOpenKeyEx(hKey, KeyName, 0, KEY_READ, handle) Then
            Exit Function
        End If
        ' Subsequent functions use hKey.
        hKey = handle
    End If

    For index = 0 To 999999
        ' Make room in the array.
        If index > UBound(result) Then
            ReDim Preserve result(index + 99) As String
```

(continued)

```
      End If
      length = 260                    ' Max length for a key name.
      result(index) = Space$(length)
      If RegEnumKey(hKey, index, result(index), length) Then Exit For
      ' Trim excess characters.
      result(index) = Left$(result(index), InStr(result(index), _
          vbNullChar) - 1)
   Next

   ' Close the key if it was actually opened.
   If handle Then RegCloseKey handle
   ' Trim unused items in the array, and return the results to the caller.
   ReDim Preserve result(index - 1) As String
   EnumRegistryKeys = result()
End Function
```

Thanks to the *EnumRegistryKey* function, it's simple to dig a lot of useful information out of the Registry. For example, see how easy it is to fill a ListBox control with the names of all the components registered on the machine under the HKEY_CLASS_ROOT key:

```
Dim keys() As String, i As Long
keys() = EnumRegistryKeys(HKEY_CLASSES_ROOT, "")
List1.Clear
For i = LBound(keys) To UBound(keys)
    List1.AddItem keys(i)
Next
```

The companion CD includes a demonstration program (shown in Figure A-7) that displays the list of installed COM components as well as their CLSIDs and the DLL or EXE file that contains each one of them. You can easily expand this first version to create your own utilities that track anomalies in the Registry. For example, you can list all the DLL and EXE files that aren't in the locations listed in the Registry. (COM raises an error when you try to instantiate such components.)

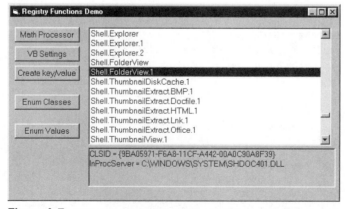

Figure A-7. *You can use Registry API routines to list all the components installed on your machine, with their CLSIDs and the locations of their executable files.*

The Windows API also exposes a function for enumerating all the values under a given open key:

```
Declare Function RegEnumValue Lib "advapi32.dll" Alias "RegEnumValueA" _
    (ByVal hKey As Long, ByVal dwIndex As Long, ByVal lpValueName As _
    String, lpcbValueName As Long, ByVal lpReserved As Long, _
    lpType As Long, lpData As Any, lpcbData As Long) As Long
```

This function returns the type of each value in the *lpType* variable and the contents of the value in *lpData*. The difficulty is that you don't know in advance what the type of the value is, and therefore you don't know the kind of variable—Long, String, or Byte array—you should pass in *lpData*. The solution to this problem is to pass a Byte array and then move the result into a Long variable using the *CopyMemory* API routine or into a String variable using the VBA *StrConv* function. On the companion CD, you'll find the complete source of the *EnumRegistryValues* routine, which encapsulates all these details and returns a two-dimensional array of Variants containing all the values' names and data. For example, you can use this routine to retrieve all the Microsoft Visual Basic configuration values:

```
Dim values() As Variant, i As Long
values() = EnumRegistryValues(HKEY_CURRENT_USER, _
    "Software\Microsoft\VBA\Microsoft Visual Basic")
For i = LBound(values, 2) To UBound(values, 2)
    ' Row 0 holds the value's name, row 1 holds its value.
    List1.AddItem values(0, i) & " = " & values(1, i)
Next
```

CALLBACK AND SUBCLASSING

As you probably remember from the "A World of Messages" section near the beginning of this appendix, Windows deals with two types of messages: control messages and notification messages. Although sending a control message is just a matter of using the *SendMessage* API function, you'll see that intercepting a notification message is much more difficult and requires that you adopt an advanced programming technique known as *window subclassing*. But to understand how this technique works, you need to know what the *AddressOf* keyword does and how you can use it to set up a callback procedure.

Callback Techniques

Callback and subclassing capabilities are relatively new to Visual Basic in that they weren't possible until version 5. What made these techniques available to Visual Basic programmers was the introduction of the new *AddressOf* keyword under Visual Basic 5. This keyword can be used as a prefix for the name of a routine defined in a BAS module, and evaluates to the 32-bit address of the first statement of that routine.

System timers

To show this keyword in action, I'll show you how you can create a timer without a Timer control. Such a timer might be useful, for example, when you want to periodically execute a piece of code located in a BAS module, and you don't want to add a form to the application just to get a pulse at regular intervals. Setting up a system timer requires only a couple of API functions:

```
Declare Function SetTimer Lib "user32" (ByVal hWnd As Long, ByVal nIDEvent_
    As Long, ByVal uElapse As Long, ByVal lpTimerFunc As Long) As Long

Declare Function KillTimer Lib "user32" (ByVal hWnd As Long, _
    ByVal nIDEvent As Long) As Long
```

For our purposes, we can ignore the first two arguments to the *SetTimer* function and just pass the *uElapse* value (which corresponds to the *Interval* property of a Timer control) and the *lpTimerFunc* value (which is the address of a routine in our Visual Basic program). This routine is known as the *callback procedure* because it's meant to be called from Windows and not from the code in our application. The *SetTimer* function returns the ID of the timer being created or 0 in case of error:

```
Dim timerID As Long
' Create a timer that sends a notification every 500 milliseconds.
timerID = SetTimer(0, 0, 500, AddressOf Timer_CBK)
```

You need the return value when it's time to destroy the timer, a step that you absolutely must perform before closing the application if you don't want the program to crash:

```
' Destroy the timer created previously.
KillTimer 0, timerID
```

Let's see now how to build the *Timer_CBK* callback procedure. You derive the number and types of the arguments that Windows sends to it from the Windows SDK documentation or from MSDN:

```
Sub Timer_CBK(ByVal hWnd As Long, ByVal uMsg As Long, _
    ByVal idEvent As Long, ByVal SysTime As Long)
    ' Just display the system time in a label control.
    Form1.lblTimer = SysTime
End Sub
```

In this implementation, you can safely ignore the first three parameters and concentrate on the last one, which receives the number of milliseconds elapsed since the system started. This particular callback routine doesn't return a value and is therefore implemented as a procedure; you'll see later that in most cases callback routines return values to the operating system and therefore are implemented as functions. As usual, you'll find on the companion CD a complete demonstration program that contains all the routines described in this section.

Windows enumeration

Interesting and useful examples of using callback techniques are provided by the *EnumWindows* and *EnumChildWindows* API functions, which enumerate the top-level windows and the child windows of a given window, respectively. The approach used by these functions is typical of most API functions that enumerate Windows objects. Instead of loading the list of windows in an array or another structure, these functions use a callback procedure in the main application for each window found. Inside the callback function, you can do what you want with such data, including loading it into an array or into a ListBox or TreeView control. The syntax for these functions is the following:

```
Declare Function EnumWindows Lib "user32" (ByVal lpEnumFunc As Long, _
    ByVal lParam As Long) As Long

Declare Function EnumChildWindows Lib "user32" (ByVal hWndParent As Long, _
    ByVal lpEnumFunc As Long, ByVal lParam As Long) As Long
```

hWndParent is the handle of the parent window. *lpEnumFunc* is the address of the callback function. And *lParam* is a parameter passed to the callback function; this value can be used when the same callback routine is used for different purposes in the application. The syntax of the callback function is the same for both *EnumWindows* and *EnumChildWindows*:

```
Function EnumWindows_CBK(ByVal hWnd As Long, ByVal lParam As Long) As Long
    ' Process the window's data here.
End Function
```

where *hWnd* is the handle of the window found, and *lParam* is the value passed as the last argument to the *EnumWindows* or *EnumChildWindows* function. This function returns 1 to ask the operating system to continue the enumeration or 0 to stop the enumeration.

It's easy to create a reusable procedure that builds on these API functions and returns an array with the handles of all the child windows of a given window:

```
' An array of Longs holding the handles of all child windows
Dim windows() As Long
' The number of elements in the array.
Dim windowsCount As Long

' Return an array of Longs holding the handles of all the child windows
' of a given window. If hWnd = 0, return the top-level windows.
Function ChildWindows(ByVal hWnd As Long) As Long()
    windowsCount = 0                      ' Reset the result array.
    If hWnd Then
        EnumChildWindows hWnd, AddressOf EnumWindows_CBK, 1
    Else
        EnumWindows AddressOf EnumWindows_CBK, 1
    End If
```

(continued)

```
    ' Trim uninitialized elements, and return to caller.
    ReDim Preserve windows(windowsCount) As Long
    ChildWindows = windows()
End Function

' The callback routine, common to both EnumWindows and EnumChildWindows
Function EnumWindows_CBK(ByVal hWnd As Long, ByVal lParam As Long) As Long
    If windowsCount = 0 Then
        ' Create the array at the first iteration.
        ReDim windows(100) As Long
    ElseIf windowsCount >= UBound(windows) Then
        ' Make room in the array if necessary.
        ReDim Preserve windows(windowsCount + 100) As Long
    End If
    ' Store the new item.
    windowsCount = windowsCount + 1
    windows(windowsCount) = hWnd
    ' Return 1 to continue the enumeration process.
    EnumWindows_CBK = 1
End Function
```

On the companion CD, you'll find the source code of an application—also shown in Figure A-8—that displays the hierarchy of all the windows that are currently open in the system. This is the code that loads the TreeView control with the window hierarchy. Thanks to the recursion technique, the code is surprisingly compact:

```
Private Sub Form_Load()
    ShowWindows TreeView1, 0, Nothing
End Sub

Sub ShowWindows(tvw As TreeView, ByVal hWnd As Long, ParentNode As Node)
    Dim winHandles() As Long
    Dim i As Long, Node As MSComctlLib.Node

    If ParentNode Is Nothing Then
        ' If no Parent node, let's add a "desktop" root node.
        Set ParentNode = tvw.Nodes.Add(, , "Desktop")
    End If
    ' Retrieve all the child windows.
    winHandles() = ChildWindows(hWnd)
    For i = 1 To UBound(winHandles)
        ' Add a node for this child window--WindowDescription is a routine
        ' (not shown here) that returns a descriptive string for the window.
        Set Node = tvw.Nodes.Add(ParentNode.Index, tvwChild, , _
            WindowDescription(winHandles(i)))
        ' Recursively call this routine to show this window's children.
        ShowWindows tvw, winHandles(i), Node
    Next
End Sub
```

Figure A-8. *A utility to explore all the open windows in the system.*

Subclassing Techniques

Now that you know what a callback procedure is, comprehending how subclassing works will be a relatively easy job.

Basic subclassing

You already know that Windows communicates with applications via messages, but you don't know yet how the mechanism actually works at a lower level. Each window is associated with a *window default procedure*, which is called any time a message is sent to the window. If this procedure were written in Visual Basic, it would look like this:

```
Function WndProc(ByVal hWnd As Long, ByVal uMsg As Long, _
    ByVal wParam As Long, ByVal lParam As Long) As Long
    ...
End Function
```

The four parameters that a window procedure receives are exactly the arguments that you (or the operating system) pass to *SendMessage* when you send a message to a given window. The purpose of the window procedure is to process all the incoming messages and react appropriately. Each class of windows—top-level windows, MDI windows, TextBox controls, ListBox controls, and so on—behave differently because their window procedures are different.

The principle of the subclassing technique is simple: You write a custom window procedure, and you ask Windows to call your window procedure instead of the standard window procedure associated with a given window. The code in your

Visual Basic application traps all the messages sent to the window before the window itself (more precisely, its default window procedure) has a chance to process them, as I explain in the following illustration:

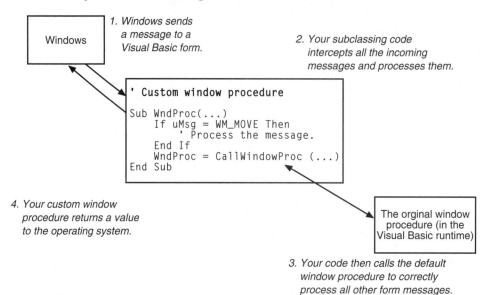

1. Windows sends a message to a Visual Basic form.

2. Your subclassing code intercepts all the incoming messages and processes them.

```
' Custom window procedure

Sub WndProc(...)
     If uMsg = WM_MOVE Then
          ' Process the message.
     End If
     WndProc = CallWindowProc (...)
End Sub
```

4. Your custom window procedure returns a value to the operating system.

The orginal window procedure (in the Visual Basic runtime)

3. Your code then calls the default window procedure to correctly process all other form messages.

To substitute the standard window procedure with your customized procedure, you must use the *SetWindowLong* API function, which stores the address of the custom routine in the internal data table that is associated with each window:

```
Const GWL_WNDPROC = -4
Declare Function SetWindowLong Lib "user32" Alias "SetWindowLongA" _
     (ByVal hWnd As Long, ByVal ndx As Long, ByVal newValue As Long) As Long
```

hWnd is the handle of the window. *ndx* is the index of the slot in the internal data table where you want to store the value. And *newValue* is the 32-bit value to be stored in the internal data table at the position pointed to by *nxd*. This function returns the value that was previously stored in that slot of the table; you must store such a value in a variable because you must definitely restore it before the application terminates or the subclassed window is closed. If you don't restore the address of the original window procedure, you're likely to get a GPF. In summary, this is the minimal code that subclasses a window:

```
Dim saveHWnd As Long      ' The handle of the subclassed window
Dim oldProcAddr As Long   ' The address of the original window procedure

Sub StartSubclassing(ByVal hWnd As Long)
     saveHWnd = hWnd
     oldProcAddr = SetWindowLong(hWnd, GWL_WNDPROC, AddressOf WndProc)
End Sub
```

```
Sub StopSubclassing()
    SetWindowLong saveHWnd, GWL_WNDPROC, oldProcAddr
End Sub

Function WndProc(ByVal hWnd As Long, ByVal uMsg As Long, _
    ByVal wParam As Long, ByVal lParam As Long) As Long
    ' Process the incoming messages here.
End Function
```

Let's focus on what the custom window procedure actually does. This procedure can't just process a few messages and forget about the others. On the contrary, it's responsible for correctly forwarding all the messages to the original window procedure; otherwise, the window wouldn't receive all the vital messages that inform it when it has to resize, close, or repaint itself. In other words, if the window procedure stops all messages from reaching the original window procedure, the application won't work as expected any longer. The API function that does the message forwarding is *CallWindowProc*:

```
Declare Function CallWindowProc Lib "user32" Alias "CallWindowProcA" _
    (ByVal lpPrevWndFunc As Long, ByVal hwnd As Long, ByVal Msg As Long, _
    ByVal wParam As Long, ByVal lParam As Long) As Long
```

lpPrevWndFunc is the address of the original window procedure—the value that we saved in the *oldProcAddr* variable—and the other arguments are those received by the custom window procedure.

Let's see a practical example of the subclassing technique. When a top-level window—a form, in Visual Basic parlance—moves, the operating system sends it a WM_MOVE message. The Visual Basic runtime eats this message without exposing it as an event to the application's code, but you can write a custom window procedure that intercepts it before Visual Basic sees it:

```
Function WndProc(ByVal hWnd As Long, ByVal uMsg As Long, _
    ByVal wParam As Long, ByVal lParam As Long) As Long
    ' Send the message to the original window procedure, and then
    ' return to Windows the return value from the original procedure.
    WndProc = CallWindowProc(oldProcAddr, hWnd, uMsg, wParam, lParam)
    ' See if this is the message we're waiting for.
    If uMsg = WM_MOVE Then
        ' The window has moved.
    End If
End Function
```

I've prepared a demonstration program that uses the code described in this section to trap a few messages related to forms, such as WM_MOVE, WM_RESIZING, and WM_APPACTIVATE. (See Figure A-9.) The last message is important because it lets you determine when an application loses and regains the input focus, something that you can't easily do in pure Visual Basic code. For example, the Windows hierarchy utility shown in Figure A-8 might subclass this message to automatically refresh its contents when the user switches to another application and then goes back to the utility.

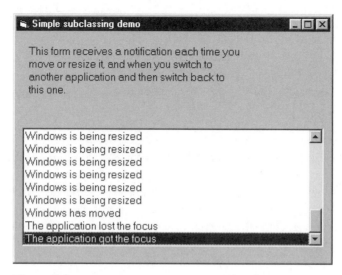

Figure A-9. *A program that demonstrates the basic concepts of window subclassing.*

You can generally process the incoming messages before or after calling the *CallWindowProc* API function. If you're interested only in knowing when a message is sent to the window, it's often preferable to trap it after the Visual Basic runtime has processed it because you can query updated form's properties. Remember, Windows expects that you return a value to it, and the best way to comply with this requirement is by using the value returned by the original window procedure. If you process a message before forwarding it to the original procedure, you can change the values in *wParam* or *lParam*, but this technique requires an in-depth knowledge of the inner workings of Windows. Any error in this phase is fatal because it prevents the Visual Basic application from working correctly.

> **CAUTION** Of all the advanced programming techniques you can employ in Visual Basic, subclassing is undoubtedly the most dangerous one. If you make a mistake in the custom window procedure, Windows won't forgive you and won't give you a chance to fix the error. For this reason, you should *always* save your code before running the program in the environment. Moreover, you should *never* stop a running program using the End button, an action which immediately stops the running program and prevents the *Unload* and *Terminate* events from executing, therefore depriving you of the opportunity to restore the original window procedure.

A class for subclassing

Although the code presented in the previous version works flawlessly, it doesn't meet the requirements of real-world applications. The reason is simple: In a complex program, you usually subclass multiple forms and controls. This practice raises a couple of interesting problems:

- You can't use simple variables to store the window's handle and the address of the original window procedure—as the previous simplified example does—but you need an array or a collection to account for multiple windows.

- The custom window procedure must reside in a BAS form, so the same procedure must serve multiple subclassed windows and you need a way to understand which window each message is bound to.

The best solution to both problems is to build a class module that manages all the subclassing chores in the program. I've prepared such a class, named MsgHook, and as usual you'll find it on the companion CD. Here's an abridged version of its source code:

```
' The MsgHook.cls class module
Event AfterMessage(ByVal hWnd As Long, ByVal uMsg As Long, _
    ByVal wParam As Long, ByVal lParam As Long, retValue As Long)


Private m_hWnd As Long          ' Handle of the window being subclassed


' Start the subclassing.
Sub StartSubclass(ByVal hWnd As Long)
    ' Terminate current subclassing if necessary.
    If m_hWnd Then StopSubclass
    ' Store argument in member variable.
    m_hWnd = hWnd
    ' Add a new item to the list of subclassed windows.
    If m_hWnd Then HookWindow Me, m_hWnd
End Sub


' Stop the subclassing.
Sub StopSubclass()
    ' Delete this item from the list of subclassed windows.
    If m_hWnd Then UnhookWindow Me
End Sub


' This procedure is called when a message is sent to this window.
' (It's Friend because it's meant to be called by the BAS module only.)
Friend Function WndProc(ByVal hWnd As Long, ByVal uMsg As Long, _
    ByVal wParam As Long, ByVal lParam As Long, _
    ByVal oldWindowProc As Long) As Long

    Dim retValue As Long, Cancel As Boolean
    ' Call original window procedure.
    retValue = CallWindowProc(oldWindowProc, hWnd, uMsg, wParam, lParam)
    ' Call the application.
    ' The application can modify the retValue argument.
    RaiseEvent AfterMessage(hWnd, uMsg, wParam, lParam, retValue)
```

(continued)

```
    ' Return the value to Windows.
    WndProc = retValue
End Function

' Stop the subclassing when the object goes out of scope.
Private Sub Class_Terminate()
    If m_hWnd Then StopSubclass
End Sub
```

As you see, the class communicates with its clients through the *AfterMessage* event, which is called immediately after the original window procedure has processed the message. From the client application's standpoint, subclassing a window has become just a matter of responding to an event, an action familiar to all Visual Basic programmers.

Now analyze the code in the BAS module in which the subclassing actually occurs. First of all, you need an array of UDTs, where you can store information about each window being subclassed:

```
' The WndProc.Bas module
Type WindowInfoUDT
    hWnd As Long            ' Handle of the window being subclassed
    oldWndProc As Long      ' Address of the original window procedure
    obj As MsgHook          ' The MsgHook object serving this window
End Type

' This array stores data on subclassed windows.
Dim WindowInfo() As WindowInfoUDT
' This is the number of elements in the array.
Dim WindowInfoCount As Long
```

The *HookWindow* and *UnhookWindow* procedures are called by the MsgHook class's *StartSubclass* and *StopSubclass* methods, respectively:

```
' Start the subclassing of a window.
Sub HookWindow(obj As MsgHook, ByVal hWnd As Long)
    ' Make room in the array if necessary.
    If WindowInfoCount = 0 Then
        ReDim WindowInfo(10) As WindowInfoUDT
    ElseIf WindowInfoCount > UBound(WindowInfo) Then
        ReDim Preserve WindowInfo(WindowInfoCount + 9) As WindowInfoUDT
    End If
    WindowInfoCount = WindowInfoCount + 1

    ' Store data in the array, and start the subclassing of this window.
    With WindowInfo(WindowInfoCount)
        .hWnd = hWnd
        Set .obj = obj
        .oldWndProc = SetWindowLong(hWnd, GWL_WNDPROC, AddressOf WndProc)
```

```
    End With
End Sub

' Stop the subclassing of the window associated with an object.
Sub UnhookWindow(obj As MsgHook)
    Dim i As Long, objPointer As Long
    For i = 1 To WindowInfoCount
        If WindowInfo(i).obj Is obj Then
            ' We've found the object that's associated with this window.
            SetWindowLong WindowInfo(i).hWnd, GWL_WNDPROC, _
                WindowInfo(i).oldWndProc
            ' Remove this element from the array.
            WindowInfo(i) = WindowInfo(WindowInfoCount)
            WindowInfoCount = WindowInfoCount - 1
            Exit For
        End If
    Next
End Sub
```

The last procedure left to be seen in the BAS module is the custom window procedure. This procedure has to search for the handle of the target window of the incoming message among those stored in the *WindowInfo* array and notify the corresponding instance of the MsgHook class that a message has arrived:

```
' The custom window procedure
Function WndProc(ByVal hWnd As Long, ByVal uMsg As Long, _
    ByVal wParam As Long, ByVal lParam As Long) As Long
    Dim i As Long, obj As MsgHook
    Const WM_DESTROY = &H2

    ' Find this handle in the array.
    For i = 1 To WindowInfoCount
        If WindowInfo(i).hWnd = hWnd Then
            ' Notify the object that a message has arrived.
            WndProc = WindowInfo(i)obj.WndProc(hWnd, uMsg, wParam, lParam,_
                WindowInfo(i).oldWndProc)
            ' If it's a WM_DESTROY message, the window is about to close,
            ' so there is no point in keeping this item in the array.
            If uMsg = WM_DESTROY Then WindowInfo(i).obj.StopSubclass
            Exit For
        End If
    Next
End Function
```

> **NOTE** The preceding code looks for the window handle in the array using a simple linear search; when the array contains only a few items, this approach is sufficiently fast and doesn't add significant overhead to the class. If you plan to subclass more than a dozen forms and controls, you should implement a more sophisticated search algorithm, such as a binary search or a hash table.

In general, a window is subclassed until the client application calls the *StopSubclass* method of the related MsgHook object or until the object itself goes out of scope. (See the code in the class's *Terminate* event procedure.) The code in the *WndProc* procedure uses an additional trick to ensure that the original window procedure is restored before the window is closed. Because it's already subclassing the window, it can trap the WM_DESTROY message, which is the last message (or at least one of the last messages) sent to a window before it closes. When this message is detected, the code immediately stops subclassing the window.

Using the MsgHook class

Using the MsgHook class is pretty simple: You assign an instance of it to a WithEvents variable, and then you invoke its *StartSubclass* method to actually start the subclassing. For example, you can trap WM_MOVE messages using this code:

```
Dim WithEvents FormHook As MsgHook

Private Sub Form_Load()
    Set FormHook = New MsgHook
    FormHook.StartSubclass Me.hWnd
End Sub

Private Sub FormHook_AfterMessage(ByVal hWnd As Long, ByVal uMsg As Long, _
    ByVal wParam As Long, ByVal lParam As Long, retValue As Long)
    Const WM_MOVE = &H3
    If uMsg = WM_MOVE Then
        lblStatus.Caption = "The window has moved."
    End If
End Sub
```

If you want to subclass other forms or controls, you have to create multiple instances of the MsgHook class—one for each window to be subclassed—and assign them to distinct WithEvents variables. And of course, you have to write the proper code in each *AfterMessage* event procedure. The complete class provided on the companion CD supports some additional features, including a *BeforeMessage* event that fires before the original window procedure processes the message and an *Enabled* property that lets you temporarily disable the subclassing for a given window. Keep in mind that the MsgHook class can subclass only windows belonging to the current application; interprocess window subclassing is beyond the current capabilities of Visual Basic and requires some C/C++ wizardry.

The MsgHook class module encapsulates most of the dangerous details of the subclassing technique. When you turn it into an ActiveX DLL component—or use the version provided on the companion CD—you can safely subclass any window created by the current application. You can even stop an interpreted program without any adverse effects because the End button doesn't prevent the *Terminate* event from firing if the class has been compiled in a separate component. The compiled version also solves most—but not all—of the problems that occur when an interpreted code enters break mode, during which the subclassing code can't respond to messages. In such situations, you usually get an application crash, but the MsgHook class will prevent it from happening. I plan to release a more complete version of this class, which I'll make available for download from my Web site at *http://www.vb2themax.com*.

More subclassing examples

Now that you have a tool that implements all the nitty-gritty details of subclassing, you might finally see how subclassing can actually help you deliver better applications. The examples I show in this section are meant to be just hints of what you can really do with this powerful technique. As usual, you'll find all the code explained in this section in a sample application provided on the companion CD. The demonstration application is also shown in Figure A-10.

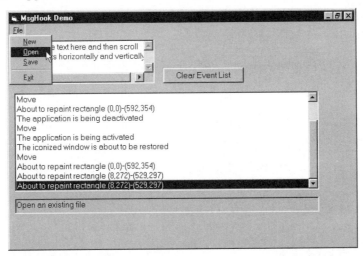

Figure A-10. *The demonstration application that shows what you can achieve with the MsgHook ActiveX DLL.*

Windows sends Visual Basic forms a lot of messages that the Visual Basic runtime doesn't expose as events. Sometimes you don't have to manipulate incoming parameters because you're subclassing the form only to find out when the message arrives. There are many examples of such messages, including WM_MOUSEACTIVATE (the form or control is being activated with the mouse), WM_TIMECHANGE (the system date and time has changed), WM_DISPLAYCHANGE (the screen resolution has changed), WM_COMPACTING (Windows is low in memory and is asking applications to release as much memory as possible), and WM_QUERYOPEN (a form is about to be restored to normal size from an icon).

Many other messages can't be dealt with so simply, though. For example, the WM_GETMINMAXINFO message is sent to a window when the user begins to move or resize it. When this message arrives, *lParam* contains the address of a MINMAXINFO structure, which in turn holds information about the region to which the form can be moved and the minimum and maximum size that the window can take. You can retrieve and modify this data, thus effectively controlling a form's size and position when the user resizes or maximizes it. (If you carefully look at Figure A-10, you'll see from the buttons in the window's caption that this form is maximized, even if it doesn't take the entire screen estate.) To move this information into a local structure, you need the *CopyMemory* API function:

```
Type POINTAPI
    X As Long
    Y As Long
End Type
Type MINMAXINFO
    ptReserved As POINTAPI
    ptMaxSize As POINTAPI
    ptMaxPosition As POINTAPI
    ptMinTrackSize As POINTAPI
    ptMaxTrackSize As POINTAPI
End Type

Private Sub FormHook_AfterMessage(ByVal hWnd As Long, ByVal uMsg As Long, _
    ByVal wParam As Long, ByVal lParam As Long, retValue As Long)
    Select Case uMsg
        Case WM_GETMINMAXINFO
            ' Windows is querying the form for its
            ' minimum and maximum size and position.
            Dim mmInfo As MINMAXINFO
            ' Read contents of structure pointed to by lParam.
            CopyMemory mmInfo, ByVal lParam, Len(mmInfo)
            With mmInfo
                ' ptMaxSize is the size of the maximized form.
                .ptMaxSize.X = 600
                .ptMaxSize.Y = 400
                ' ptMaxPosition is the position of the maximized form.
                .ptMaxPosition.X = 100
                .ptMaxPosition.Y = 100
                ' ptMinTrackSize is the minimum size of a form when
                ' resized with the mouse.
                .ptMinTrackSize.X = 300
                .ptMinTrackSize.Y = 200
                ' ptMinTrackSize is the maximum size of a form when
                ' resized with the mouse (usually equal to ptMaxSize).
                .ptMaxTrackSize.X = 600
                .ptMaxTrackSize.Y = 400
            End With
```

```
            ' Copy the data back into the original structure in memory.
            CopyMemory ByVal lParam, mmInfo, Len(mmInfo)
            ' Return 0 to say that the structure has been modified.
            retValue = 0
    End Select
End Sub
```

By subclassing the WM_MENUSELECT message, you can add a professional touch to your application. This message fires whenever the user highlights a menu item using the mouse or arrow keys, and you can employ it for displaying a short explanation of the menu item, as most commercial programs do (as shown in Figure A-10). The problem with this message is that you have to process the values stored in *wParam* and *lParam* to extract the caption of the highlighted menu item:

```
' Put this code inside a FormHook_AfterMessage event procedure.
Case WM_MENUSELECT
    ' The menu item identifier is in the low-order word of wParam.
    ' The menu handle is in lParam.
    Dim mnuId As Long, mnuCaption As String, length As Long
    mnuId = (wParam And &HFFFF&)
    ' Get the menu caption.
    mnuCaption = Space$(256)
    length = GetMenuString(lParam, mnuId, mnuCaption, Len(mnuCaption), 0)
    mnuCaption = Left$(mnuCaption, length)
    Select Case mnuCaption
        Case "&New"
            lblStatus.Caption = "Create a new file"
        Case "&Open"
            lblStatus.Caption = "Open an existing file"
        Case "&Save"
            lblStatus.Caption = "Save a file to disk"
        Case "E&xit"
            lblStatus.Caption = "Exit the program"
    End Select
```

WM_COMMAND is a multipurpose message that a form receives on many occasions—for example, when a menu command has been selected or when a control sends the form a notification message. You can trap EN_HSCROLL and EN_VSCROLL notification messages that TextBox controls send their parent forms when their edit area has been scrolled:

```
' Put this code inside a FormHook_AfterMessage event procedure.
Case WM_COMMAND
    ' If this is a notification from a control, lParam holds its handle.
    If lParam = txtEditor.hwnd Then
        ' In this case, the notification message is in the
        ' high-order word of wParam.
        Select Case (wParam \ &H10000)
            Case EN_HSCROLL
```

(continued)

```
                       ' The TextBox control has been scrolled horizontally.
                   Case EN_VSCROLL
                       ' The TextBox control has been scrolled vertically.
               End Select
           End If
```

Of course, you can subclass any control that exposes the *hWnd* property, not just forms. For example, TextBox controls receive a WM_CONTEXTMENU message when the user right-clicks on them. The default action for this message is to display the default edit pop-up menu, but you can subclass the TextBox control to suppress this action so that you might display your own pop-up menu. (Compare this technique with the trick shown in the "Pop-Up Menus" tip in Chapter 3.) To achieve this result, you need to write code in the *BeforeMessage* event procedure and you must set the procedure's *Cancel* parameter to False to ask the MsgHook class not to execute the original window procedure. (This is one of the few cases when it's safe to do so.)

```
Dim WithEvents TextBoxHook As MsgHook

Private Sub Form_Load()
    Set TextBoxHook = New MsgHook
    TextBoxHook.StartSubclass txtEditor.hWnd
End Sub

Private Sub TextBoxHook_BeforeMessage(hWnd As Long, uMsg As Long, _
    wParam As Long, lParam As Long, retValue As Long, Cancel As Boolean)
    If uMsg = WM_CONTEXTMENU Then
        ' Show a custom popup menu.
        PopupMenu mnuMyCustomPopupMenu
        ' Cancel the default processing (i.e., the default context menu).
        Cancel = True
    End If
End Sub
```

This appendix has taken you on quite a long journey through API territory. But as I told you at the beginning, these pages only scratch the surface of the immense power that Windows API functions give you, especially if you couple them with subclassing techniques. The MsgHook class on the companion CD is a great tool for exploring these features because you don't have to worry about the implementation details, and you can concentrate on the code that produces the effects you're interested in.

If you want to learn more about this subject, I suggest that you get a book, such as *Visual Basic Programmer's Guide to the Win32 API* by Dan Appleman, specifically on this topic. You should also always have the Microsoft Developer Network at hand for the official documentation of the thousands of functions that Windows exposes. Become an expert in API programming, and you'll see that there will be very little that you can't do in Visual Basic.

Index

Index

Index

FRANCESCO BALENA

Kathleen Atkins

Francesco began to study programming when it was customary to write code on punched cards. Since then, he has closely followed the evolution of hardware and software, at least when he wasn't busy playing alto sax with his jazz combo.

In recent years, he has written four books and over 150 articles for programming magazines. He is a contributing editor of *Visual Basic Programming Journal*, coauthor of *Platinum Edition Using VB5* (QUE), and founder and editor-in-chief of *Visual Basic Journal*, VBPJ's Italian licensee. He works as a trainer and consultant, speaks at several conferences for developers—including Microsoft DevDays, American and European editions of VBITS, and Italian VB Forum workshops—and also teaches on-line seminars via the Internet. (For more information, go to his *http://www.vb2themax.com* Web site.)

When not traveling, Francesco lives in Bari, Italy, with his wife, Adriana, and his son, Andrea.

The manuscript for this book was prepared using Microsoft Word 97. Pages were composed by Microsoft Press using Adobe PageMaker 6.52 for Windows, with text in Garamond and display type in Helvetica Black. Composed pages were delivered to the printer as electronic prepress files.

Cover Graphic Designer

Girvin, Inc.

Cover Illustrator

Glenn Mitsui

Interior Graphic Artist

Alton Lawson

Principal Compositor

Elizabeth Hansford

Principal Proofreader/Copy Editor

Roger LeBlanc

Indexer

Shane-Armstrong Information Systems

Visit *www.vb2themax.com*, the Web site operated by Francesco Balena, and download hundreds of Visual Basic tips, ready-to-use highly optimized routines, and many add-ins, components, and utilities.

The site also contains a comprehensive and continuously updated bug list and several technical articles that aren't available any where else. You'll also find updated code and notes complementing the book, *Programming Microsoft Visual Basic 6.0.*

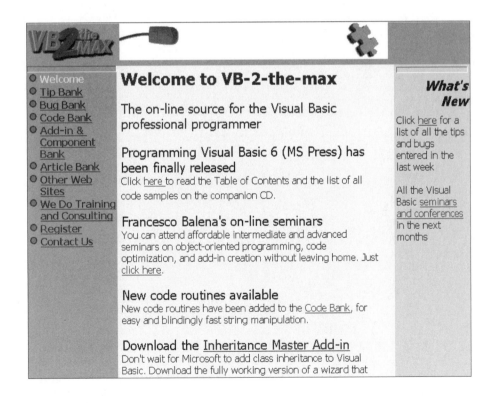

Visual Basic
design and
development
to the **extreme**

U.S.A. **$59.99**
U.K. £55.49 [V.A.T. included]
Canada $86.99
ISBN 1-57231-893-7

With the release of Visual Basic® 6.0, the Visual Basic product family has added functionality at the very highest level of the developer workspace—fully supporting the next evolution of distributed enterprise development. And for intermediate and advanced Visual Basic programmers looking to push this tool to its new limits, the experts at the renowned Mandelbrot Set (International) Limited have once again delivered the definitive, upper-strata Visual Basic reference.

Microsoft®

mspress.microsoft.com